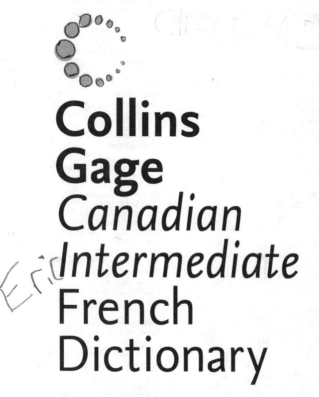

Collins
Gage
Canadian
Intermediate
French
Dictionary

Français-Anglais
English-French

Collins

THOMSON

NELSON

HarperCollins Publishers
Westerhill Road, Bishopbriggs,
Glasgow G64 2QT, Great Britain

First Edition/Première Édition 2005

Reprint 10 9 8 7 6 5 4 3 2 1

© HarperCollins Publishers 2005

Collins® and Bank of English® are registered
trademarks of HarperCollins Publishers
Limited

www.collins.co.uk

school distribution by
Nelson, a division of
Thomson Canada Limited
1120 Birchmount Road, Toronto, ON M1K 5G4
www.nelson.com

trade distribution by
HarperCollins Canada
2 Bloor Street East,
Toronto, ON M4W 1A8
www.harpercollins.ca

ISBN 0-00-639579-1

National Library of Canada
Cataloguing in Publication Data

Collins Gage Canadian Intermediate
French dictionary.

1. French language—Dictionaries—
English. 2. English language—
Dictionaries—French.
PC2640.C658 2005   443'.21
C2005-902169-1

Typeset by Thomas Callan
Supplements typeset by Wordcraft, Glasgow

Printed in Italy by Legoprint S.P.A.

Acknowledgements
We would like to thank those authors and
publishers who kindly gave permission for
copyright material to be used in the Collins
Word Web. We would also like to thank
Times Newspapers Ltd for providing
valuable data.

PROJECT MANAGEMENT
Michela Clari, Helen Forrest, David Friend

EDITORS
Annie Bourret, Art Coulbeck, Laura Jones,
Lisa Peterson, Jodi Ravn, Françoise Roy, Debbie
Sawczak, Maggie Seaton, Marie Turcotte

SERIES EDITOR, COLLINS
Lorna Knight

DIRECTOR OF REFERENCE PUBLISHING, NELSON
Joe Banel

OUR THANKS TO THE FOLLOWING FOR THEIR HELP
IN RESEARCHING THE PROJECT
Maree Airlie, Teresa Álvarez, Phyllis Gautier,
Janet Gough, Sharon Hunter, Mary James,
Cordelia Lilly, Carol MacLeod, Jill McNair,
Janet Chalmers

REVIEWED BY THE FOLLOWING EDUCATORS
Darlene Abbie
School District #53—
Okanagan Similkameen
British Columbia

Jamie Krutkevich
Présidente, L'association manitobaine des profs
de français
Seven Oaks School Division
Manitoba

Aamer Zuberi
Peel District School Board
Ontario

Collins Gage Canadian reference resources
combine the strengths of the Collins and
Gage reference lines. They contain the most
accurate and up-to-date information,
prepared in consultation with Canadian
educators for Canadian students.

Collins is one of the world's leading
reference publishers. The **Collins Word Web**
contains 125 million words of Canadian
English and grows at over 1.5 million words
per month.

Gage represents a 40-year tradition of
Canadian dictionary making. Today, Gage is
the reference division of **Thomson Nelson**,
Canada's foremost educational publisher.

CONTENTS

ABOUT THIS DICTIONARY

The *Collins Gage Canadian Intermediate French Dictionary* is specially designed to be easy to read, easy to use, and easy to understand. Here are the main features that make this dictionary ideal for anyone in the early stages of learning French:

- colour font used for entry words
- simple translations
- selection of the most common meaning(s)
- lots of example phrases and sentences
- helpful language notes

This dictionary is also special because it's Canadian. The entry words and all the examples accurately reflect how both English and French are spoken and written in Canada. We've placed a maple leaf icon 🍁 beside words and expressions that originated in Canada or are used here in a unique way. You'll also find information boxes throughout the dictionary, many of which describe a distinctive feature of Canadian French or English or of life in Canada.

On the next page you'll find a Guide to Features with brief explanations of all the important elements of this dictionary. As well, the following special sections will help you move more easily between French and English:

Develop Your Dictionary Skills (pp. 6–12)

- a how-to guide for using this dictionary, including activities and an answer key

French Grammar Guide (pp. 289–317)

- an introduction to French grammar, with basic information about each part of speech
- a special focus on verbs, including extensive verb tables for regular and irregular verbs

French in Action (pp. 319–331)

- handy examples for writing letters and e-mail; talking on the telephone; using dates and numbers; and telling the time
- a table showing how to refer to countries and their inhabitants in French

▶ Guide to Features

Guide words show the first and last word on each page.

nothing → nut

Each **entry word** is printed in blue. The **part of speech** is shown immediately after each entry word. Below the entry word is a brief **translation**, which is underlined. A **white diamond** provides an example phrase or sentence to show how the word is used. A **black diamond** shows a very common phrase or sentence, or a translation that isn't obvious. **Labels** in brackets help to narrow the meaning.

sauter VERB
to jump ◊ *Nous avons sauté par-dessus la barrière.* We jumped over the gate.
♦ **sauter à la corde** to skip (*with a rope*)

If an entry has more than one meaning, each meaning is **numbered**. **Always** look at every meaning of a word before you choose one.

la **cheminée** NOUN
1 chimney
2 fireplace

If the word can be more than one part of speech, you'll find a separate entry for each one, with a helpful cross reference.

heat NOUN
see also **heat** VERB
la chaleur

The **maple leaf icon** shows a word or expression that originated in Canada or is used in a unique way in Canada.

🍁 **chinook** NOUN
le chinook (*wind*)

If the entry word is a French noun, you can always tell what gender it is by the use of **le** or **la**, or by the MASC or FEM indicator.

market NOUN
le marché

l' **ascenseur** MASC NOUN
elevator

Assume that a plural is formed regularly unless otherwise indicated.

twin NOUN
le jumeau (*boy*)
la jumelle (*girl*)
(PL les jumeaux)
(FEM PL les jumelles)

Assume that an adjective is regular unless otherwise indicated.

envious ADJECTIVE
envieux MASC
envieuse FEM

Language notes give important information about usage.

*Be careful not to translate the French word **cité** as **city**.*

Infoboxes ❶ provide extra information, often about some aspect of Canadian life.

❶ *Le **pouding-chômeur** is a dessert consisting of a thickened mixture of brown sugar, water, and butter, sometimes mixed with maple syrup, under a layer of cake.*

The **hand** symbol tells you to turn the page to see the rest of the entry.

☞

DEVELOP YOUR DICTIONARY SKILLS

This is a **bilingual** dictionary, which means it tells you about two different languages. You may need to learn some new dictionary skills to get the most out of this book. This section tells you about those skills and gives you a chance to try them.

▶ Look at the correct side of the dictionary.

This dictionary is divided into two sides:

Français-Anglais   ➜   French words plus their meanings in English
English-French   ➜   English words plus their meanings in French

Tip: The two sides are separated by a section of blue pages that deal with French grammar.

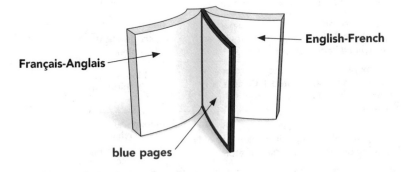

Français-Anglais

English-French

blue pages

Your turn! À ton tour!

Look at the list of words below. If you wanted to find the meaning of each of these words, which side of the dictionary would you use? In your notebook, write the word, the side of the dictionary that holds the word, and the page number on which you found its meaning.

Example
le chat   *Français-Anglais side*   *page 53*

1. l'âge
2. melon
3. le garage
4. example
5. le biscuit

▶ Use the alphabet.

The entry words in this dictionary are in alphabetical order. If you're looking up a French word that starts with D, turn to the D section in the French half of the dictionary.

Tip: Use the blue tabs at the edge of the pages to help you quickly find the right section.

Your turn! À ton tour!

In your notebook, write the page number where each of these sections begins.

Example

  D   *Français-Anglais*   *English-French*
        page 77   *page 392*

  6. C
  7. T
  8. M
  9. S
10. O

11. What are the five letters with the fewest entry words on the French-English side? On the English-French side?

Some words start with exactly the same letters, but they are still placed in alphabetical order. The words *accomplir* and *accident* (page 14) both start with *acc*. Which comes first?

> l' **accident** MASC NOUN
>   accident ◊ *un accident de la route* a
>   road accident ◊ *Elle a eu un acciden*
>   *de ski.* She had a skiing accident.
>   ◆ **par accident** by chance
>
> **accompagner** VERB
>   to accompany
>
> **accomplir** VERB
>   to carry out ◊ *Il n'a pas réussi à*
>   *accomplir cette tâche.* He didn't
>   manage to carry out this task.

As you can see, *accident* comes first because **i** comes before **o**.

Tip: In this dictionary, French entry words that are nouns always have *le*, *la*, or *les* in front. Ignore the *le*, *la*, or *les* when you are looking up words. For example, to find *le gâteau*, look in the G section, not in the L section.

7

▶ Look at the guide words.

At the top of each page of the dictionary are two words. For example:

acadien → acheter

These words are called **guide words**. The guide word on the left is the first
entry word to appear on the page. The guide word on the right is last entry
word on the page. All the entry words on that page will fall between the
two guide words alphabetically.

Tip: Looking at guide words helps you find the entry you want more
quickly.

▶ Make sure you look at the right entry.

Sometimes when you look for a word, you'll find two entries that are spelled
the same way, and each one has a different meaning. How do you know
which entry to check?

plat ADJECTIVE

> *see also* **plat** NOUN

flat
♦ **être à plat ventre** to be lying face
down
♦ **l'eau plate** still water

8

le **plat** NOUN

> see also **plat** ADJECTIVE

1 dish
2 course ◊ *le plat principal* the main
course
♦ **un plat cuisiné** a pre-cooked meal
♦ **le plat du jour** the daily special

Beside each entry word there's a label that tells you what part of speech it is. In the examples above, you can see that *plat* can be either an adjective or a noun. If you needed to know what the adjective *plat* means, you would look at the entry on the left.

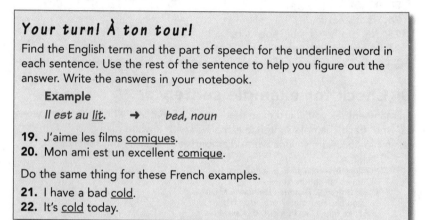

Your turn! À ton tour!

Find the English term and the part of speech for the underlined word in each sentence. Use the rest of the sentence to help you figure out the answer. Write the answers in your notebook.

Example

Il est au lit. → *bed, noun*

19. J'aime les films <u>comiques</u>.
20. Mon ami est un excellent <u>comique</u>.

Do the same thing for these French examples.

21. I have a bad <u>cold</u>.
22. It's <u>cold</u> today.

▶ Choose the appropriate meaning.

Words often have more than one meaning and can be expressed in more than one way. When you are trying to find the right word in French, be careful to choose the word that has the meaning you want. The dictionary offers you a lot of help with this.

desk NOUN
1 (*in office*)
le <u>bureau</u>
(PL les bureaux)
2 le <u>pupitre</u> (*for student*)
3 la <u>réception</u> (*in hotel*)
4 le <u>comptoir</u> (*at airport*)

Imagine you need to find the French term for the word *desk* in the following sentence:

The teacher gave me a new desk.

If you look at the entry for *desk* on page 397, you can see that the second meaning tells you that *le pupitre* is the French term for a desk for students.

▶ Check for example sentences.

In many entries you'll find example sentences that show how the entry word is used. Each example sentence is marked with a white diamond ◊. For example, there are several white diamonds at the entry for *aimer*.

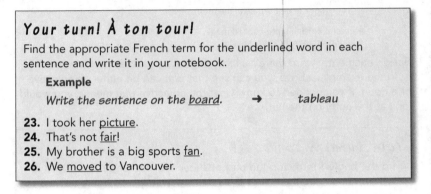

aimer VERB
1 to love ◊ *Il aime ses enfants.* He loves his children.
2 to like ◊ *Tu aimes le chocolat?* Do you like chocolate? ◊ *J'aime bien cette fille.* I like this girl. ◊ *J'aime bien jouer au tennis.* I like playing tennis. ◊ *J'aimerais aller en Grèce.* I'd like to go to Greece.

Tip: When the entry word has more than one meaning, reading the example sentences can help you choose the right one.

▶ Watch for the black diamonds.

Phrases that start with a black diamond ♦ are phrases that are very common or useful:

> le **fauteuil** NOUN
>> armchair
>> ♦ **un fauteuil roulant** a wheelchair

Sometimes the phrase has a meaning that doesn't seem to match the meaning of the entry word:

> le **dommage** NOUN
>> damage ◊ *La tempête a causé d'importants dommages.* The storm caused a lot of damage.
>> ♦ **C'est dommage.** Too bad. ◊ *C'est dommage que tu ne puisses pas venir.* Too bad you can't come.

Tip: It's important to check each black diamond carefully to make sure you understand the phrase and use it appropriately.

Your turn! À ton tour!

Look up the underlined words. Use the black diamonds to find the word or phrase that fits the context.

Example

Make fun of → *se moquer de quelqu'un*

31. make <u>money</u>
32. <u>sortir</u> avec quelqu'un
33. <u>poser</u> une question à quelqu'un
34. to be in a good <u>mood</u>

▶ Look at the accents.

Accents in French often change the sound of a letter and can change the meaning of a word. For example, *âge* and *âgé* have different meanings:

l'**âge** NOUN	means	age
âgé ADJECTIVE	means	old

Tip: When you look up a word, pay close attention to any accents to make sure you select the word that has the meaning you want.

Your turn! À ton tour!

Write each of the following French words in your notebook, with its meaning(s) beside it.

Example

sûr (adjective) → *sûr: sure, reliable, safe*

35. la branche (noun)
36. branché (adjective)
37. sale (adjective)

▶ Answers

1.	l'âge:	Français-Anglais	p. 17		
2.	melon:	English-French	p. 489		
3.	le garage:	Français-Anglais	p. 128		
4.	example:	English-French	p. 415		
5.	le biscuit:	Français-Anglais	p. 36		

6.	C:	Français-Anglais	p. 44	English-French	p. 366
7.	T:	Français-Anglais	p. 263	English-French	p. 601
8.	M:	Français-Anglais	p. 162	English-French	p. 483
9.	S:	Français-Anglais	p. 244	English-French	p. 563
10.	O:	Français-Anglais	p. 188	English-French	p. 509

11. French-English: K,W,X,Y,Z   English-French: J,Q,X,Y,Z

12. genre, geste
13. lookout, loon
14. appel, appeler
15. dodgeball, dogsled
16. céder, cèdre

17. cap, carré
18. carotte, carnaval

19. comical, adjective
20. comedian, noun
21. rhume, noun
22. froid, adjective

23. photo
24. juste
25. fan
26. déménager (or avons déménagé)

27. oublier
28. laisser tomber
29. to put on
30. to fail

31. gagner de l'argent
32. to be going out with somebody
33. to ask somebody a question
34. être de bonne humeur

35. branch
36. trendy
37. dirty

A

a VERB *see* **avoir**

> *a should not be confused with the preposition à.*

♦ **Elle a beaucoup d'amis.** She has a lot of friends.
♦ **Il a mangé des frites.** He had some fries.
♦ **Il a neigé pendant la nuit.** It snowed during the night.
♦ **il y a (1)** there is ◊ *Il y a un bon film à la télé.* There's a good film on TV.
♦ **il y a (2)** there are ◊ *Il y a beaucoup de monde.* There are lots of people.

à PREPOSITION

> *à should not be confused with the verb form a. See also au (=à+le) and aux (=à+les).*

① **at** ◊ *être à la maison* to be at home ◊ *à trois heures* at 3 o'clock
② **in** ◊ *être à Truro* to be in Truro ◊ *habiter au Portugal* to live in Portugal ◊ *habiter à la campagne* to live in the country ◊ *au printemps* in the spring ◊ *au mois de juin* in June
③ **to** ◊ *aller à Regina* to go to Regina ◊ *aller au Portugal* to go to Portugal ◊ *aller à la campagne* to go to the country ◊ *donner quelque chose à quelqu'un* to give something to somebody ◊ *Cette veste appartient à ma sœur.* This jacket belongs to my sister. ◊ *Je n'ai rien à faire.* I have nothing to do.
♦ **Ce livre est à mon père.** This book is my father's.
♦ **Cette voiture est à nous.** This car is ours.
④ **by** ◊ *à bicyclette* by bicycle ◊ *être payé à l'heure* to be paid by the hour
♦ **à pied** on foot
♦ **C'est à côté de chez moi.** It's near my house.
♦ **C'est à dix kilomètres d'ici.** It's 10 kilometres from here.
♦ **C'est à dix minutes d'ici.** It's 10 minutes from here.
♦ **cent kilomètres à l'heure** 100 kilometres an hour
♦ **À bientôt!** See you soon! ◊ *À demain!* See you tomorrow! ◊ *À samedi!* See you on Saturday! ◊ *À tout à l'heure!* See you later!

abandonner VERB
① **to abandon** ◊ *Elle a abandonné sa voiture à côté de la route.* She abandoned her car at the side of the road.
② **to quit** ◊ *J'ai décidé d'abandonner mes leçons de natation.* I've decided to quit swimming lessons.

l' **abeille** FEM NOUN
bee

abîmer VERB
to damage
♦ **s'abîmer** to get damaged

❋ l' **aboiteau** MASC NOUN (PL les **aboiteaux**)
aboiteau

> ❶ In New Brunswick and Nova Scotia, dikes were built on the Bay of Fundy to reclaim the marshland next to the sea. A gate in the dike, called an **aboiteau**, opened as the tide went out so marsh water could run into the ocean. The gate closed when the tide came in so seawater would not flow into the marsh. Modern aboiteaux use the same principle.

abolir VERB
to do away with (*law, custom*)

l' **abonnement** MASC NOUN
① season ticket
② subscription (*to magazine*)

s' **abonner** VERB
♦ **s'abonner à une revue** to take out a subscription to a magazine

l' **abord** MASC NOUN
♦ **d'abord** first ◊ *Je vais rentrer chez moi d'abord.* I'll go home first.

aboyer VERB
to bark

l' **abri** MASC NOUN
shelter
♦ **être à l'abri** to be under cover
♦ **se mettre à l'abri** to take shelter

l' **abricot** MASC NOUN
apricot

s' **abriter** VERB
to take shelter

l' **absence** FEM NOUN
absence
♦ **Il est passé pendant ton absence.** He came while you were away.

absent ADJECTIVE
absent

❋ l' **Acadie** FEM NOUN
Acadia ◊ *Mes ancêtres étaient originaires de l'Acadie.* My ancestors were from Acadia.

❀ **acadien** ADJECTIVE, NOUN (FEM SING
acadienne)
Acadian
♦ **un Acadien** an Acadian (*man*)
♦ **une Acadienne** an Acadian (*woman*)
♦ **les Acadiens** the Acadians

l' **accélérateur** MASC NOUN
accelerator

accélérer VERB
to accelerate

l' **accent** MASC NOUN
accent ◊ *Elle a l'accent de Terre-Neuve.* She has a Newfoundland accent.
♦ **un accent aigu** an acute accent
♦ **un accent grave** a grave accent
♦ **un accent circonflexe** a circumflex

accentuer VERB
to stress

accepter VERB
to accept
♦ **accepter de faire quelque chose** to agree to do something

l' **accès** MASC NOUN
access ◊ *avoir accès à quelque chose* to have access to something
♦ **être d'accès facile** to be approachable

l' **accessoire** MASC NOUN
① accessory ◊ *les accessoires de mode* fashion accessories
② prop

l' **accident** MASC NOUN
accident ◊ *un accident de la route* a road accident ◊ *Elle a eu un accident de ski.* She had a skiing accident.
♦ **par accident** by chance

accompagner VERB
to accompany

accomplir VERB
to carry out ◊ *Il n'a pas réussi à accomplir cette tâche.* He didn't manage to carry out this task.

l' **accord** MASC NOUN
agreement
♦ **être d'accord** to agree ◊ *Tu es d'accord avec moi?* Do you agree with me?
♦ **se mettre d'accord** to come to an agreement
♦ **D'accord!** OK!

l' **accordéon** MASC NOUN
accordion ◊ *Il joue de l'accordéon.* He plays the accordion.

accorder VERB
① to grant ◊ *accorder la permission* to grant permission
② to tune ◊ *accorder une guitare* to tune a guitar
③ to make agree (*grammatically*)

◊ *accorder un adjectif avec un nom* to make an adjective agree with a noun
♦ **s'accorder** to agree ◊ *Ils s'accordent pour dire que le film est ennuyant.* They agree that the movie is boring.

l' **accotement** MASC NOUN
shoulder ◊ *Elle s'est stationnée sur l'accotement.* She parked on the shoulder.

l' **accrochage** MASC NOUN
fender-bender

accrocher VERB
♦ **accrocher quelque chose à (1)** to hang something on ◊ *Il a accroché sa veste au portemanteau.* He hung his jacket on the coat rack.
♦ **accrocher quelque chose à (2)** to hitch something up to ◊ *Ils ont accroché la remorque à leur voiture.* They hitched the trailer up to their car.
♦ **s'accrocher à quelque chose** to catch on something ◊ *Sa jupe s'est accrochée à une branche.* Her skirt got caught on a branch.

s' **accroupir** VERB
to squat down

l' **accueil** MASC NOUN
welcome ◊ *un accueil chaleureux* a warm welcome.
♦ **Elle s'occupe de l'accueil des visiteurs.** She's in charge of looking after visitors.

accueillant ADJECTIVE
welcoming ◊ *Ses parents ont été très accueillants.* Her parents were very welcoming.

accueillir VERB
to welcome

accumuler VERB
to accumulate
♦ **s'accumuler** to pile up

l' **accusé** MASC NOUN
accused ◊ *L'accusé a déclaré que...* The accused stated that...

l' **accusée** FEM NOUN
accused

accuser VERB
to accuse ◊ *accuser quelqu'un de quelque chose* to accuse somebody of something

l' **achat** MASC NOUN
purchase
♦ **faire des achats** to do some shopping

acheter VERB
to buy ◊ *J'ai acheté des livres à la librairie.* I bought some books at the bookstore.
♦ **acheter quelque chose à quelqu'un (1)** to buy something for somebody

◊ *Qu'est-ce que tu lui as acheté pour son anniversaire?* What did you buy her for her birthday?
♦ **acheter quelque chose à quelqu'un (2)** to buy something from somebody ◊ *J'ai acheté des œufs au fermier.* I bought some eggs from the farmer.

l' **achigan** MASC NOUN
bass (*fish*)

l' **acide** MASC NOUN
acid

l' **acier** MASC NOUN
steel

l' **acné** FEM NOUN
acne ◊ *Elle a de l'acné.* She has acne.

acquérir VERB
to acquire

acquis VERB *see* **acquérir**

acquitter VERB
to acquit ◊ *L'accusé a été acquitté.* The accused was acquitted.

l' **acrobate** MASC/FEM NOUN
acrobat

l' **acrobatie** FEM NOUN
acrobatics

l' **acte** MASC NOUN
act
♦ **un acte de naissance** a birth certificate

l' **acteur** MASC NOUN
actor ◊ *Il est acteur.* He's an actor.
◊ *un acteur de cinéma* a film actor

actif ADJECTIVE (FEM SING **active**)
active

l' **action** FEM NOUN
action
♦ **une bonne action** a good deed

l' **Action de grâce** FEM NOUN
Thanksgiving

s' **activer** VERB
① to bustle about ◊ *Elle s'activait à préparer le repas.* She bustled about preparing the meal.
② to get moving ◊ *Allez! Active-toi!* Come on! Get moving!

l' **activité** FEM NOUN
activity

l' **actrice** FEM NOUN
actress ◊ *Elle est actrice.* She's an actress. ◊ *une actrice de cinéma* a film actress

l' **actualité** FEM NOUN
current events
♦ **un problème d'actualité** a current issue
♦ **les actualités** the news

actuel ADJECTIVE (FEM SING **actuelle**)

present ◊ *le système actuel* the present system
♦ **à l'heure actuelle** at the present time

Be careful! **actuel** does not mean **actual**.

actuellement ADVERB
at present

Be careful! **actuellement** does not mean **actually**.

l' **adaptateur** MASC NOUN
adapter

l' **adaptation** FEM NOUN
adaptation ◊ *une adaptation télévisée d'un roman* a TV adaptation of a novel

l' **addition** FEM NOUN
bill ◊ *L'addition, s'il vous plaît!* Can we have the bill, please?

additionner VERB
to add up

adhésif ADJECTIVE (FEM SING **adhésive**)
♦ **le ruban adhésif** sticky tape

adieu EXCLAMATION
farewell!

l' **adjectif** MASC NOUN
adjective

admettre VERB
① to admit ◊ *Il refuse d'admettre qu'il s'est trompé.* He won't admit that he made a mistake.
② to allow ◊ *Les chiens ne sont pas admis dans le restaurant.* Dogs are not allowed in the restaurant.

l' **administration** FEM NOUN
administration

admirable ADJECTIVE
wonderful

l' **admirateur** MASC NOUN
admirer

l' **admiratrice** FEM NOUN
admirer

admirer VERB
to admire

admis VERB *see* **admettre**

l' **adolescence** FEM NOUN
adolescence

l' **adolescent** MASC NOUN
teenager

l' **adolescente** FEM NOUN
teenager

adopter VERB
to adopt

adoptif ADJECTIVE (FEM SING **adoptive**)
① adopted ◊ *un enfant adoptif* an adopted child

☞

② adoptive ◊ *les parents adoptifs* the adoptive parents

adorable ADJECTIVE
lovely

adorer VERB
to love ◊ *Il adore le chocolat.* He loves chocolate. ◊ *J'adore jouer au tennis.* I love playing tennis.

l' **adresse** FEM NOUN
address
♦ **mon adresse électronique** my e-mail address

adresser VERB
♦ **adresser la parole à quelqu'un** to speak to someone
♦ **s'adresser à quelqu'un (1)** to speak to somebody ◊ *C'est à toi que je m'adresse.* It's you I'm speaking to.
♦ **s'adresser à quelqu'un (2)** to go and see somebody ◊ *Adressez-vous à la patronne.* Go and see the boss. ◊ *Adressez-vous au bureau de renseignements.* Ask at the information desk.
♦ **s'adresser à quelqu'un (3)** to be aimed at somebody ◊ *Ce film s'adresse surtout aux enfants.* This film is aimed mainly at children.

l' **adulte** MASC/FEM NOUN
adult

l' **adverbe** MASC NOUN
adverb

l' **adversaire** MASC/FEM NOUN
opponent

aérien ADJECTIVE (FEM SING **aérienne**)
♦ **une compagnie aérienne** an airline

l' **aérobic** MASC NOUN
aerobics ◊ *Elle fait de l'aérobic.* She does aerobics.

l' **aérogare** FEM NOUN
terminal (*airport*)

l' **aéroport** MASC NOUN
airport

l' **affaire** FEM NOUN

⸻ *see also* **les affaires** ⸻

① case ◊ *une affaire de vol* a case of theft
② business ◊ *Leur affaire marche bien.* Their business is doing well.
♦ **une bonne affaire** a real bargain
♦ **Ça fera l'affaire.** This will do nicely.
♦ **avoir affaire à quelqu'un** to deal with somebody

les **affaires** FEM NOUN

⸻ *see also* **l'affaire** ⸻

① things ◊ *Va chercher tes affaires!* Go and get your things!
② business ◊ *Les affaires marchent*

bien en ce moment. Business is good at the moment. ◊ *Mêle-toi de tes affaires.* (*informal*) Mind your own business.
♦ **une femme d'affaires** a businesswoman

l' **affection** FEM NOUN
affection

affectueux ADJECTIVE (FEM SING **affectueuse**)
affectionate

l' **affiche** FEM NOUN
poster

afficher VERB
to post (*a notice*) ◊ *Ils ont affiché les résultats dans le couloir.* They've posted the results in the hallway.
♦ **« Défense d'afficher »** "Post no bills"

affilée
♦ **d'affilée** ADVERB at a stretch ◊ *Elle a travaillé douze heures d'affilée.* She worked 12 hours at a stretch.

l' **affirmation** FEM NOUN
assertion

affirmer VERB
to claim ◊ *Il a affirmé que c'était la vérité.* He claimed it was the truth.
♦ **s'affirmer** to assert oneself ◊ *Il est trop timide, il faut qu'il s'affirme.* He's too shy, he should assert himself.

l' **affluence** FEM NOUN
♦ **les heures d'affluence** rush hour ◊ *Durant les heures d'affluence, les autobus passent toutes les sept minutes.* During rush hour, buses come every 7 minutes.

s' **affoler** VERB
to panic ◊ *Ne t'affole pas!* Don't panic!

affranchir VERB
to stamp ◊ *Elle a affranchi mon passeport.* She stamped my passport.

affreux ADJECTIVE (FEM SING **affreuse**)
awful

affronter VERB
to face ◊ *Vancouver affronte Montréal en finale.* Vancouver will face Montréal in the final.

afin de CONJUNCTION
♦ **afin de faire quelque chose** in order to do something ◊ *Je me suis levé très tôt afin d'être prêt à temps.* I got up very early in order to be ready on time.

afin que CONJUNCTION
so that

⸻ *afin que* is followed by a verb in the subjunctive. ⸻

◊ *Il m'a téléphoné afin que je sois prêt à temps.* He phoned me so that I'd be ready on time.

agacer VERB
<u>to get on somebody's nerves</u> ◊ *Tu m'agaces avec tes questions!* You're getting on my nerves with all your questions!

l' **âge** MASC NOUN
<u>age</u>
♦ **Quel âge as-tu?** How old are you?

âgé ADJECTIVE
<u>old</u> ◊ *Mon grand-père est âgé.* My grandfather's old. ◊ *Elle est âgée de dix ans.* She's 10 years old.
♦ **les personnes âgées** the elderly

l' **agence** FEM NOUN
<u>agency</u> ◊ *l'agence pour l'emploi* the employment agency
♦ **une agence de voyages** a travel agency
♦ **une agence immobilière** a real estate agency

l' **agenda** MASC NOUN
<u>agenda</u> (*daybook*) ◊ *J'ai perdu mon agenda.* I've lost my agenda.

s' **agenouiller** VERB
<u>to kneel down</u>

l' **agent** MASC NOUN
♦ **un agent d'infiltration** a secret agent
♦ **un agent de police** a police officer
♦ **un agent de la GRC** a Mountie

l' **agente** FEM NOUN
♦ **une agente d'infiltration** a secret agent
♦ **une agente de police** a police officer
♦ **une agente de bord** a flight attendant

l' **agglomération** FEM NOUN
<u>urban area</u>
♦ **l'agglomération de Toronto** Greater Toronto

aggraver VERB
<u>to make worse</u>
♦ **s'aggraver** to get worse

agir VERB
1 <u>to act</u> ◊ *Il a agi par vengeance.* He acted out of revenge.
2 <u>to take effect</u> ◊ *Ce médicament agit vite.* This medicine takes effect quickly.
♦ **Il s'agit de...** It's about... ◊ *Il s'agit du club d'art dramatique.* It's about the drama club. ◊ *De quoi s'agit-il?* What is it about?
♦ **Il s'agit de faire attention.** We must be careful.

agité ADJECTIVE
1 <u>restless</u> ◊ *Les élèves sont agités.* The students are restless.

2 <u>rough</u> ◊ *La mer est agitée.* The sea is rough.
♦ **un sommeil agité** troubled sleep

agiter VERB
<u>to shake</u> ◊ *Agitez la bouteille.* Shake the bottle.

l' **agneau** MASC NOUN (PL les **agneaux**)
<u>lamb</u>

l' **agrafe** FEM NOUN
<u>staple</u> (*for papers*)

l' **agrafeuse** FEM NOUN
<u>stapler</u>

agrandir VERB
1 <u>to enlarge</u> ◊ *J'ai fait agrandir mes photos.* I got my photos enlarged.
2 <u>to extend</u> ◊ *Ils ont agrandi leur jardin.* They've extended their garden.
♦ **s'agrandir** to expand ◊ *Leur magasin s'est agrandi.* Their store has expanded.

agréable ADJECTIVE
<u>nice</u>

agréer VERB
♦ **Veuillez agréer, Madame, l'expression de mes sentiments distingués.** Jane Ormal. Yours sincerely, Jane Ormal.

agressif ADJECTIVE (FEM SING **agressive**)
<u>aggressive</u>

l' **agressivité** FEM NOUN
<u>aggression</u>
♦ **faire preuve d'agressivité envers quelqu'un** to be aggressive towards somebody
♦ **l'agressivité au volant** road rage

agricole ADJECTIVE
<u>agricultural</u> ◊ *le matériel agricole* agricultural machinery
♦ **une exploitation agricole** a farm

l' **agriculteur** MASC NOUN
<u>farmer</u>
♦ **Il est agriculteur.** He's a farmer.

l' **agricultrice** FEM NOUN
<u>farmer</u>
♦ **Elle est agricultrice.** She's a farmer.

l' **agriculture** FEM NOUN
<u>farming</u>

ai VERB *see* **avoir**
♦ **J'ai deux chats.** I have two cats.
♦ **J'ai bien dormi.** I slept well.

l' **aide** FEM NOUN
1 <u>help</u> ◊ *J'ai besoin de ton aide.* I need your help. ◊ *appeler quelqu'un à l'aide* to call to somebody for help
♦ **À l'aide!** Help!
2 <u>aid</u> ◊ *une aide financière* financial aid
♦ **à l'aide de** using ◊ *J'ai réussi à ouvrir la boîte de conserve à l'aide d'un*

☞

couteau. I managed to open the can using a knife.

l' **aide-infirmier** MASC NOUN (PL les **aides-infirmiers**)
nurse's aid
♦ **Il est aide-infirmier.** He's a nurse's aid.

l' **aide-infirmière** FEM NOUN (PL les **aides-infirmières**)
nurse's aid ◊ *Elle est aide-infirmière.* She is a nurse's aid.

aider VERB
to help

aie VERB *see* **avoir**

aïe EXCLAMATION
Ouch!

aigre ADJECTIVE
sour

aigu ADJECTIVE (FEM SING **aiguë**)
sharp (*pain*) ◊ *J'ai ressenti une douleur aiguë dans le bas du dos.* I felt a sharp pain in my lower back.
♦ **e accent aigu** e with an acute accent

l' **aiguille** FEM NOUN
needle ◊ *une aiguille à tricoter* a knitting needle
♦ **les aiguilles d'une montre** the hands of a watch

l' **ail** MASC NOUN
garlic

l' **aile** FEM NOUN
wing

aille VERB *see* **aller**

ailleurs ADVERB
somewhere else
♦ **partout ailleurs** everywhere else
♦ **nulle part ailleurs** nowhere else
♦ **d'ailleurs** besides

aimable ADJECTIVE
kind

l' **aimant** MASC NOUN
magnet

aimer VERB
1 to love ◊ *Il aime ses enfants.* He loves his children.
2 to like ◊ *Tu aimes le chocolat?* Do you like chocolate? ◊ *J'aime bien cette fille.* I like this girl. ◊ *J'aime bien jouer au tennis.* I like playing tennis. ◊ *J'aimerais aller en Grèce.* I'd like to go to Greece.
♦ **J'aimerais mieux ne pas y aller.** I'd rather not go.

aîné ADJECTIVE

see also **aîné** NOUN

elder ◊ *mon frère aîné* my big brother

l' **aîné** MASC NOUN

see also **aîné** ADJECTIVE

oldest child ◊ *Il est l'aîné.* He's the oldest child.

l' **aînée** FEM NOUN
oldest child ◊ *Elle est l'aînée.* She's the oldest child.

ainsi ADVERB
in this way ◊ *Il faut faire ainsi.* This is the way to do it.
♦ **C'est ainsi qu'il a réussi.** That's how he succeeded.
♦ **ainsi que** as well as
♦ **et ainsi de suite** and so on

l' **air** MASC NOUN
1 air ◊ *l'air chaud* warm air
♦ **prendre l'air** to get some fresh air
2 tune ◊ *Elle a joué un air au piano.* She played a tune on the piano.
♦ **Elle a l'air fatiguée.** She looks tired.
♦ **Il a l'air d'un clown.** He looks like a clown.

l' **aire de jeux** FEM NOUN
playground

l' **aire de repos** FEM NOUN
rest area (*on highway*)

l' **aise** FEM NOUN
♦ **être à l'aise** to be at ease ◊ *Elle est à l'aise avec tout le monde.* She's at ease with everybody.
♦ **être mal à l'aise** to be ill at ease
♦ **se mettre à l'aise** to make oneself comfortable

ait VERB *see* **avoir**

ajouter VERB
to add

l' **alarme** FEM NOUN
alarm ◊ *donner l'alarme* to raise the alarm

l' **Alberta** FEM NOUN
Alberta

l' **album** MASC NOUN
album

l' **alcool** MASC NOUN
alcohol ◊ *Je ne bois pas d'alcool.* I don't drink alcohol.
♦ **les alcools forts** spirits

alcoolisé ADJECTIVE
alcoholic
♦ **une boisson non alcoolisée** a soft drink

les **alentours** MASC NOUN
♦ **dans les alentours** in the area
♦ **aux alentours d'Ottawa** in the Ottawa area
♦ **aux alentours de cinq heures** around 5 o'clock

l' **algèbre** FEM NOUN
algebra

l' **algue** FEM NOUN
  seaweed

l' **alibi** MASC NOUN
  alibi

l' **aliment** MASC NOUN
  food ◊ *Le fromage est un aliment très nutritif.* Cheese is a very nutritious food. ◊ *les aliments solides* solid food
  ♦ **les aliments naturels** health food ◊ *un magasin d'aliments naturels* a health food store

alimentaire ADJECTIVE
  ① food ◊ *un groupe alimentaire* a food group ◊ *une banque alimentaire* a food bank
  ♦ **Le guide alimentaire canadien** Canada's Food Guide
  ② eating ◊ *nos habitudes alimentaires* our eating habits

l' **alimentation** FEM NOUN
  diet ◊ *Elle a une alimentation saine.* She has a healthy diet.

l' **allée** FEM NOUN
  ① path ◊ *les allées du parc* the paths in the park
  ② drive (*in street names*)
  ♦ **les allées et venues** comings and goings

allégé ADJECTIVE
  low-fat ◊ *un yogourt allégé* a low-fat yogurt

aller VERB

  see also **aller** NOUN

  Present tense:
  je vais   nous allons
  tu vas   vous allez
  il/elle va   ils/elles vont

  Past participle:
  allé

  to go ◊ *Elle est allée à Edmonton.* She went to Edmonton. ◊ *Je dois y aller.* I've got to go. ◊ *Elle ira le voir.* She'll go and see him. ◊ *Je vais me fâcher.* I'm going to get angry.
  ♦ **s'en aller** to go away ◊ *Je m'en vais demain.* I'm leaving tomorrow.
  ♦ **aller bien à quelqu'un** to suit somebody ◊ *Cette robe te va bien.* This dress suits you.
  ♦ **Allez! Dépêche-toi!** Come on! Hurry up!
  ♦ **« Comment allez-vous? » « Je vais bien. »** "How are you?" "I'm fine."
  ♦ **« Comment ça va? » « Ça va bien. »** "How are you?" "I'm fine."
  ♦ **aller mieux** to be better (*after an illness*)

l' **aller** MASC NOUN

  see also **aller** VERB

  ① outward journey ◊ *L'aller nous a pris trois heures.* The journey there took us three hours.
  ② one-way ticket ◊ *Je voudrais un aller pour Halifax.* I'd like a one-way ticket to Halifax.
  ♦ **un aller simple** a one-way ticket
  ♦ **un aller et retour (1)** a return ticket ◊ *Je voudrais deux allers et retours pour Montréal.* I'd like two return tickets to Montréal.
  ♦ **un aller et retour (2)** a round trip ◊ *Elle a fait l'aller et retour en dix heures.* She did the round trip in ten hours.

l' **allergie** FEM NOUN
  allergy ◊ *J'ai des allergies.* I have allergies.
  ♦ **une allergie alimentaire** a food allergy

allergique ADJECTIVE
  ♦ **allergique à** allergic to ◊ *Je suis allergique aux poils de chat.* I'm allergic to cat hair.

allô EXCLAMATION
  Hello! (*on phone*) ◊ *Allô! Je voudrais parler à la directrice.* Hello! I'd like to speak to the principal.

s' **allonger** VERB
  to lie down ◊ *Il s'est allongé sur son lit.* He lay down on his bed.

✻ **allophone** ADJECTIVE

  see also **allophone** NOUN

  allophone

  ❶ *Allophone* is a word used mostly in French Canada to refer to people whose first language is neither English nor French.

✻ l' **allophone** MASC/FEM NOUN

  see also **allophone** ADJECTIVE

  allophone

allumer VERB
  ① to turn on ◊ *Tu peux allumer la lumière?* Can you turn the light on? ◊ *Allume la radio.* Switch on the radio.
  ② to light ◊ *Elle a allumé une bougie.* She lit a candle.
  ♦ **s'allumer** (*light*) to come on ◊ *La lumière s'est allumée.* The light came on.

l' **allumette** FEM NOUN
  match ◊ *une boîte d'allumettes* a box of matches

l' **allure** FEM NOUN
  ① speed ◊ *à toute allure* at top speed
  ② look ◊ *avoir une drôle d'allure* to

☞

look odd

alors ADVERB
1 then ◊ *Tu as fini? Alors je m'en vais.* Are you finished? I'm going then.
2 so ◊ *Alors je lui ai dit de partir.* So I told him to leave.
♦ **Et alors?** So what?
3 at that time ◊ *Elle habitait alors à Vancouver.* She was living in Vancouver at that time.
♦ **alors que (1)** as ◊ *Il est arrivé alors que je partais.* He arrived just as I was leaving.
♦ **alors que (2)** while ◊ *Alors que je travaillais dur, lui se reposait.* While I was working hard, he was resting.

l' **alphabet** MASC NOUN
alphabet

alphabétique ADJECTIVE
alphabetical ◊ *par ordre alphabétique* in alphabetical order

l' **aluminium** MASC NOUN
aluminum

l' **amande** FEM NOUN
almond
♦ **la pâte d'amandes** marzipan

l' **amant** MASC NOUN
lover

l' **amante** FEM NOUN
lover

amateur ADJECTIVE (FEM SING **amateur**)

see also **amateur** NOUN

amateur ◊ *Elle est pianiste amateur.* She's an amateur pianist.

*For the adjective **amateur**, the same form is used for both masculine and feminine, but for the noun, there is a feminine form **l'amatrice**.*

l' **amateur** MASC NOUN

see also **amateur** ADJECTIVE

1 amateur
♦ **en amateur** as a hobby ◊ *Il fait de la photo en amateur.* He takes photos as a hobby.
2 fan
♦ **C'est un amateur de jazz.** He's a jazz fan.

l' **amatrice** FEM NOUN
1 amateur
♦ **en amatrice** as a hobby ◊ *Elle joue du violon classique en amatrice.* She plays classical violin as a hobby.
2 fan
♦ **C'est une amatrice de sport.** She's a sports fan.

l' **ambiance** FEM NOUN
atmosphere ◊ *Je n'aime pas*

l'ambiance ici. I don't like the atmosphere here. ◊ *Il y a de l'ambiance dans ce café.* This café has a lot of atmosphere.
♦ **la musique d'ambiance** background music

ambitieux ADJECTIVE (FEM SING **ambitieuse**)
ambitious

l' **ambition** FEM NOUN
ambition ◊ *Elle a l'ambition de devenir première ministre.* Her ambition is to become Prime Minister.
♦ **Il a beaucoup d'ambition.** He's very ambitious.

l' **ambulance** FEM NOUN
ambulance

l' **ambulancier** MASC NOUN
ambulance driver

l' **ambulancière** FEM NOUN
ambulance driver

l' **âme** FEM NOUN
soul

l' **amélioration** FEM NOUN
improvement

améliorer VERB
to improve
♦ **s'améliorer** to improve ◊ *Le temps s'améliore.* The weather's improving.

l' **amende** FEM NOUN
fine ◊ *une amende de cinquante dollars* a 50 dollar fine

amener VERB
to bring ◊ *Qu'est-ce qui t'amène?* What brings you here? ◊ *Est-ce que je peux amener un ami?* Can I bring a friend?

amer ADJECTIVE (FEM SING **amère**)
bitter

l' **ami** MASC NOUN
friend
♦ **C'est son petit ami.** He's her boyfriend.

amical ADJECTIVE (MASC PL **amicaux**)
friendly

l' **amie** FEM NOUN
friend
♦ **C'est sa petite amie.** She's his girlfriend.

l' **amitié** FEM NOUN
friendship
♦ **Fais mes amitiés à tes parents.** Give my regards to your parents.
♦ **Amitiés** (*in letter*) Regards

l' **amour** MASC NOUN
love ◊ *l'amour paternel* paternal love
♦ **faire l'amour** to make love

amoureux ADJECTIVE (FEM SING **amoureuse**)
in love ◊ *être amoureux de quelqu'un*

to be in love with somebody

l' **amour-propre** MASC NOUN
self-esteem

amplement ADVERB
♦ **Nous avons amplement le temps.** We
have plenty of time.

l' **ampoule** FEM NOUN
[1] light bulb
[2] blister ◊ *J'ai une ampoule au pied.*
I have a blister on my foot.

amusant ADJECTIVE
amusing

les **amuse-gueule** MASC NOUN
snacks

amuser VERB
to amuse
♦ **s'amuser (1)** to play ◊ *Les enfants
s'amusent dehors.* The children are
playing outside.
♦ **s'amuser (2)** to enjoy oneself ◊ *On
s'est bien amusés à cette soirée.* We
really enjoyed ourselves at that party.

les **amygdales** FEM NOUN
tonsils ◊ *se faire opérer des
amygdales* to have one's tonsils
removed

l' **amygdalite** FEM NOUN
tonsilitis

l' **an** MASC NOUN
year
♦ **avoir neuf ans** to be nine years old
✻ ♦ **le jour de l'An** New Year's Day
♦ **le Nouvel An** New Year's

l' **analyse** FEM NOUN
[1] analysis
[2] test (*medical*) ◊ *une analyse de
sang* a blood test

analyser VERB
to analyse

l' **ananas** MASC NOUN
pineapple

l' **ancêtre** MASC/FEM NOUN
ancestor

l' **anchois** MASC NOUN
anchovy

ancien ADJECTIVE (FEM SING **ancienne**)
[1] former ◊ *C'est une ancienne élève.*
She's a former student.
[2] old ◊ *notre ancienne voiture* our
old car
[3] antique ◊ *un fauteuil ancien* an
antique chair

l' **ancre** FEM NOUN
anchor

l' **âne** MASC NOUN
donkey

l' **ange** MASC NOUN

angel
♦ **être aux anges** to be over the moon

anglais ADJECTIVE, NOUN
English ◊ *la grammaire anglaise*
English grammar ◊ *Est-ce que vous
parlez anglais?* Do you speak English?

l' **angle** MASC NOUN
[1] angle ◊ *un angle droit* a right angle
[2] corner ◊ *à l'angle de la rue* at the
corner of the street

✻ **anglophone** ADJECTIVE

see also **anglophone** NOUN

Anglophone ◊ *une communauté
anglophone* an Anglophone
community

✻ l' **anglophone** MASC/FEM NOUN

see also **anglophone** ADJECTIVE

Anglophone ◊ *Beaucoup
d'anglophones habitent à Montréal.* A
lot of Anglophones live in Montréal.

angoissé ADJECTIVE
anxious ◊ *Il était angoissé à l'idée
de prendre l'avion.* He was anxious
about flying.

l' **animal** MASC NOUN (PL les **animaux**)
animal

l' **animal de compagnie** MASC NOUN
pet
♦ **« les animaux de compagnie ne sont
pas acceptés »** "No pets"

l' **animalerie** FEM NOUN
pet shop

l' **animateur** MASC NOUN
[1] host ◊ *Il est animateur à la télé.*
He's a TV host.
[2] youth leader ◊ *Il est animateur au
centre sportif.* He is a youth leader at
the sports centre.

l' **animatrice** FEM NOUN
[1] host ◊ *Elle est animatrice à la télé.*
She's a TV host.
[2] youth leader ◊ *Elle est animatrice
au centre sportif.* She is a youth
leader at the sports centre.

animé ADJECTIVE
lively ◊ *Cette rue est très animée.*
This is a very lively street.
♦ **un dessin animé** a cartoon

l' **anneau** MASC NOUN (PL les **anneaux**)
ring

l' **année** FEM NOUN
year ◊ *l'année dernière* last year
◊ *l'année prochaine* next year

l' **anniversaire** MASC NOUN
[1] birthday ◊ *C'est l'anniversaire de
ma sœur.* It's my sister's birthday.
[2] anniversary ◊ *un anniversaire de
mariage* a wedding anniversary

l' **annonce** FEM NOUN
ad ◊ *J'ai lu votre annonce dans le journal.* I saw your ad in the paper.
◊ *passer une annonce* to place an ad
♦ **les petites annonces** the classified ads
♦ **une annonce publicitaire** a commercial
♦ **une annonce radiophonique** a radio ad
♦ **une annonce télévisée** a TV commercial

annoncer VERB
to announce ◊ *Ils ont annoncé leurs fiançailles.* They've announced their engagement.

l' **annuaire** MASC NOUN
1 phone book
2 yearbook

annuel ADJECTIVE (FEM SING **annuelle**)
annual

annuler VERB
to cancel

anonyme ADJECTIVE
anonymous

l' **anorexie** FEM NOUN
anorexia

l' **antenne** FEM NOUN
1 aerial
♦ **antenne parabolique** satellite dish
♦ **être à l'antenne** to be on the air
2 antenna

l' **antibiotique** MASC NOUN
antibiotic

l' **antigel** MASC NOUN
antifreeze

antimoustiques ADJECTIVE (MASC, FEM, PL)
insect repellent ◊ *une lotion antimoustiques* insect repellent lotion

✹ l' **antimoustiques** MASC NOUN
insect repellent

antipathique ADJECTIVE
unpleasant ◊ *Je le trouve plutôt antipathique.* I find him rather unpleasant.

l' **antiquaire** MASC/FEM NOUN
antique dealer ◊ *Elle est antiquaire.* She's an antique dealer.

l' **antiquité** FEM NOUN
antique ◊ *un magasin d'antiquités* an antique shop
♦ **pendant l'Antiquité** in classical times

l' **antivol** MASC NOUN
lock (*on bike*)

anxieux ADJECTIVE (FEM SING **anxieuse**)
anxious ◊ *Il est anxieux de nature.* He's a born worrier.

août MASC NOUN
August
♦ **en août** in August

apercevoir VERB
to see ◊ *J'aperçois la côte.* I can see the shore.
♦ **s'apercevoir de quelque chose** to notice something
♦ **s'apercevoir que...** to notice that...

apparaître VERB
to appear

l' **appareil** MASC NOUN
device
♦ **un appareil orthodontique** braces
♦ **les appareils ménagers** domestic appliances
♦ **un appareil photo** a camera
♦ **Qui est à l'appareil?** Who's speaking? (*on phone*)

apparemment ADVERB
apparently

l' **apparence** FEM NOUN
appearance

l' **apparition** FEM NOUN
appearance ◊ *Il n'a fait qu'une brève apparition.* He appeared only briefly.

l' **appartement** MASC NOUN
apartment

appartenir VERB
♦ **appartenir à quelqu'un** to belong to somebody

apparu VERB *see* **apparaître**

l' **appel** MASC NOUN
1 cry ◊ *un appel au secours* a cry for help
2 phone call
♦ **faire appel à quelqu'un** to appeal to somebody
♦ **formule d'appel** salutation (*in letter*)

appeler VERB
to call ◊ *Elle a appelé le médecin.* She called the doctor. ◊ *J'ai appelé mon cousin à Trois-Rivières.* I called my cousin in Trois-Rivières.
♦ **s'appeler** to be called ◊ *Comment ça s'appelle?* What is it called? ◊ *Elle s'appelle Muriel.* Her name's Muriel. ◊ *Comment tu t'appelles?* What's your name?

appétissant ADJECTIVE
appetizing

l' **appétit** MASC NOUN
appetite
♦ **Bon appétit!** Enjoy your meal!

applaudir VERB
to clap (*applaud*)

les **applaudissements** MASC NOUN
applause SING

l' **application**

application (*computer*) ◊ *lancer une application* to open an application

appliquer VERB
① to apply
② to enforce ◊ *appliquer la loi* to enforce the law
♦ **s'appliquer** to apply oneself ◊ *Elle s'est appliquée à étudier.* She applied herself to studying.

apporter VERB
to bring

appréhender VERB
to dread ◊ *J'appréhende cette réunion.* I'm dreading this meeting.

apprendre VERB
① to learn ◊ *apprendre quelque chose par cœur* to learn something by heart
♦ **apprendre à faire quelque chose** to learn to do something ◊ *J'apprends à faire la cuisine.* I'm learning to cook.
② to hear (*news*) ◊ *J'ai appris son départ.* I heard that she had left.
♦ **apprendre quelque chose à quelqu'un (1)** to teach somebody something ◊ *Ma mère m'a appris l'anglais.* My mother taught me English. ◊ *Elle lui a appris à conduire.* She taught him to drive.
♦ **apprendre quelque chose à quelqu'un (2)** to tell somebody something ◊ *Il m'a appris la nouvelle.* He told me the news.

l' **apprentissage** MASC NOUN
learning ◊ *On dit que l'apprentissage de l'arabe est très difficile.* They say learning Arabic is very difficult.

appris VERB *see* **apprendre**

l' **approbation** FEM NOUN
approval ◊ *donner son approbation* to give one's approval

approcher VERB
♦ **approcher de** to approach ◊ *Nous approchons de Fredericton.* We are approaching Fredericton.
♦ **s'approcher de** to come close to ◊ *Ne t'approche pas, j'ai la grippe!* Don't get too close to me, I've got the flu!

approprié ADJECTIVE
suitable ◊ *une réponse appropriée* a suitable answer

approuver VERB
to approve of ◊ *Je n'approuve pas ses méthodes.* I don't approve of his methods.

approximatif ADJECTIVE (FEM SING **approximative**)
① approximate ◊ *un prix approximatif* an approximate price
② rough ◊ *un calcul approximatif* a rough calculation

l' **appui** MASC NOUN
support ◊ *J'ai besoin de votre appui.* I need your support.

appuyer VERB
to lean ◊ *Elle a appuyé son vélo contre la porte.* She leaned her bike against the door.
♦ **appuyer sur** to press ◊ *Appuyez sur le bouton.* Press the button.
♦ **s'appuyer** to lean ◊ *Elle s'est appuyée contre le mur.* She leaned against the wall. ◊ *Il s'est appuyé sur la table.* He leaned on the table.

après PREPOSITION, ADVERB
① after ◊ *après le déjeuner* after lunch ◊ *après son départ* after he had left ◊ *après qu'il est parti* after he left ◊ *Nous viendrons après avoir fait la vaisselle.* We'll come after we've done the dishes.
② afterwards ◊ *aussitôt après* immediately afterwards
♦ **après coup** afterwards ◊ *J'y ai repensé après coup.* I thought about it again afterwards.
♦ **d'après** according to ◊ *D'après elle, c'est une erreur.* According to her, that's a mistake.
♦ **après tout** after all

après-demain ADVERB
the day after tomorrow

l' **après-midi** MASC OR FEM NOUN
afternoon

l' **arachide** FEM NOUN
peanut ◊ *le beurre d'arachide* peanut butter

l' **araignée** FEM NOUN
spider

l' **arbitre** MASC/FEM NOUN
① referee
② umpire

l' **arbre** MASC NOUN
tree
♦ **un arbre généalogique** a family tree

l' **arbuste** MASC NOUN
shrub

l' **arc** MASC NOUN
bow ◊ *son arc et ses flèches* his bow and arrows

l' **arc-en-ciel** MASC NOUN (PL les **arcs-en-ciel**)
rainbow

l' **architecte** MASC/FEM NOUN
architect ◊ *Elle est architecte.* She's an architect.

l' **architecture** FEM NOUN
architecture

l' **aréna** MASC NOUN

☞

arena ◊ *On construit un nouvel aréna à Timmins.* They're building a new arena in Timmins.

l' **arène** FEM NOUN
bullring
♦ **des arènes romaines** a Roman amphitheatre
♦ **l'arène politique** the political arena

l' **arête** FEM NOUN
fish bone

l' **argent** MASC NOUN
1 silver ◊ *une bague en argent* a silver ring
2 money ◊ *Je n'ai plus d'argent.* I have no more money.
♦ **l'argent de poche** allowance ◊ *Est-ce que tu reçois de l'argent de poche chaque semaine?* Do you get a weekly allowance?
♦ **l'argent liquide** cash

l' **argile** FEM NOUN
clay

l' **argot** MASC NOUN
slang

l' **arme** FEM NOUN
weapon
♦ **une arme à feu** a firearm

l' **armée** FEM NOUN
army
♦ **l'armée de l'air** the Air Force

l' **armoire** FEM NOUN
wardrobe

l' **armure** FEM NOUN
armour ◊ *un chevalier en armure* a knight in armour

arnaquer VERB (*informal*)
to con

aromatisé ADJECTIVE
flavoured

l' **arôme** MASC NOUN
1 aroma
2 flavouring (*added to food*)
♦ **arômes naturels** natural flavours

arpenter VERB
to pace up and down ◊ *Il arpentait le couloir.* He was pacing up and down the corridor.

arrache-pied
♦ **d'arrache-pied** ADVERB furiously ◊ *travailler d'arrache-pied* to work furiously

arracher VERB
1 to take out ◊ *La dentiste m'a arraché une dent.* The dentist took one of my teeth out.
2 to tear out ◊ *Arrachez la page.* Tear the page out.
3 to pull up ◊ *Il a arraché les*

mauvaises herbes. He pulled up the weeds.
♦ **arracher quelque chose à quelqu'un** to snatch something from somebody

arranger VERB
1 to arrange ◊ *arranger des fleurs dans un vase* to arrange flowers in a vase
2 to suit ◊ *Ça t'arrange de partir plus tôt?* Would it suit you to leave earlier?
♦ **s'arranger** to come to an agreement ◊ *Arrangez-vous avec le patron.* You'll have to come to an agreement with the boss.
♦ **Je vais m'arranger pour venir.** I'll organize things so that I can come.
♦ **Ça va s'arranger.** Things will work themselves out.

l' **arrestation** FEM NOUN
arrest ◊ *en état d'arrestation* under arrest

l' **arrêt** MASC NOUN
stop ◊ *un arrêt d'autobus* a bus stop
♦ **sans arrêt (1)** non-stop ◊ *Elle travaille sans arrêt.* She works non-stop.
♦ **sans arrêt (2)** continually ◊ *Ils se disputent sans arrêt.* They quarrel continually.

arrêter VERB
1 to stop
♦ **Arrête!** Stop it!
♦ **arrêter de faire quelque chose** to stop doing something
2 to switch off ◊ *Il a arrêté le moteur.* He switched the engine off.
3 to arrest ◊ *Ma voisine a été arrêtée.* My neighbour's been arrested.
♦ **s'arrêter** to stop ◊ *Il s'est arrêté devant une vitrine.* He stopped in front of a store window.
♦ **s'arrêter de faire quelque chose** to stop doing something ◊ *s'arrêter de fumer* to stop smoking

l' **arrière** MASC NOUN

see also **arrière** ADJECTIVE

back ◊ *l'arrière de la maison* the back of the house
♦ **à l'arrière** at the back
♦ **en arrière** behind ◊ *Ils sont restés en arrière.* They stayed behind.

arrière ADJECTIVE (MASC, FEM, PL)

see also **arrière** NOUN

back ◊ *le siège arrière* the back seat ◊ *les roues arrière* the rear wheels

l' **arrière-grand-mère** FEM NOUN (PL les **arrière-grands-mères**)
great-grandmother

l' **arrière-grand-père** MASC NOUN (PL les **arrière-grands-pères**) great-grandfather

l' **arrivée** FEM NOUN
arrival ◊ *l'arrivée des passagers* the passengers' arrival
♦ **ligne d'arrivée** finish line ◊ *Elle a franchi la ligne d'arrivée.* She crossed the finish line.

arriver VERB
1 to arrive ◊ *J'arrive à l'école à huit heures.* I arrive at school at 8 o'clock.
2 to happen ◊ *Qu'est-ce qui est arrivé à maman?* What happened to Mom?
♦ **arriver à faire quelque chose** to manage to do something ◊ *J'espère que je vais y arriver.* I hope I can manage it.
♦ **Il m'arrive de dormir jusqu'à midi.** I sometimes sleep till noon.

arrogant ADJECTIVE
arrogant

l' **arrondissement** MASC NOUN
district

arroser VERB
to water ◊ *Il arrose ses tomates.* He is watering his tomatoes.

l' **arrosoir** MASC NOUN
watering can

l' **art** MASC NOUN
art

l' **artère** FEM NOUN
1 artery
2 main road ◊ *les grandes artères de Calgary* the main roads of Calgary

l' **article** MASC NOUN
1 article ◊ *un article de journal* a newspaper article
2 item ◊ *les articles en promotion* items on special
♦ **un article de forum** a post (*on a listserv*)

l' **articulation** FEM NOUN
joint ◊ *l'articulation du genou* the knee joint

articuler VERB
to pronounce clearly

artificiel ADJECTIVE (FEM SING **artificielle**)
artificial ◊ *des plantes artificielles* artificial plants

l' **artisan** MASC NOUN
crafter (*self-employed*)
♦ **être artisan de quelque chose** to be the architect of something

l' **artisanat** MASC NOUN
crafts
♦ **boutique d'artisanat** craft shop

l' **artisane** FEM NOUN
crafter (*self-employed*)

l' **artiste** MASC/FEM NOUN
1 artist
2 performer

artistique ADJECTIVE
artistic

les **arts plastiques** MASC NOUN
fine arts

as VERB *see* **avoir**
[*see also* **as** NOUN]
♦ **Tu as de beaux cheveux.** You have nice hair.

l' **as** MASC NOUN
[*see also* **as** VERB]
ace ◊ *l'as de trèfle* the ace of clubs

l' **ascenseur** MASC NOUN
elevator

l' **aspect** MASC NOUN
appearance

l' **asperge** FEM NOUN
asparagus

l' **aspirateur** MASC NOUN
vacuum cleaner
♦ **passer l'aspirateur** to vacuum

l' **aspirine** FEM NOUN
aspirin

assaisonner VERB
to season

l' **assassin** MASC NOUN
murderer ◊ *Cette femme est un assassin.* This woman is a murderer.

assassiner VERB
to murder

✱ l' **Assemblée des Premières Nations** FEM NOUN
Assembly of First Nations

assembler VERB
to assemble
♦ **s'assembler** to gather ◊ *Une foule énorme s'était assemblée.* A huge crowd had gathered.

s' **asseoir** VERB
to sit down ◊ *Asseyez-vous, s'il vous plaît.* Please sit down. ◊ *Assieds-toi à côté de moi.* Sit beside me.

assez ADVERB
1 enough ◊ *Nous n'avons pas assez de temps.* We don't have enough time. ◊ *Est-ce qu'il y a assez de pain?* Is there enough bread?
♦ **J'en ai assez!** I've had enough!
2 quite ◊ *Il faisait assez beau.* The weather was quite nice.

l' **assiette** FEM NOUN
plate ◊ *une assiette à dessert* a dessert plate
♦ **une assiette de charcuterie** assorted cold cuts

assis VERB *see* **asseoir**

assis ADJECTIVE
<u>sitting</u> ◊ *Elle est assise par terre.* She's sitting on the floor.

l' **assistance** FEM NOUN
1 <u>audience</u> ◊ *Y a-t-il un médecin dans l'assistance?* Is there a doctor in the audience?
2 <u>aid</u> ◊ *l'assistance humanitaire* humanitarian aid
3 <u>assistance</u> ◊ *avec l'assistance de quelqu'un* with the assistance of somebody

l' **assistant** MASC NOUN
<u>assistant</u>

l' **assistante** FEM NOUN
<u>assistant</u>

assister VERB
♦ **assister à un accident** to witness an accident
♦ **assister à un cours** to attend a class
♦ **assister à un concert** to be at a concert

l' **association** FEM NOUN
<u>association</u>

l' **associé** MASC NOUN
<u>partner</u> (*in business*)

l' **associée** FEM NOUN
<u>partner</u> (*in business*)

associer VERB
<u>to connect</u> ◊ *J'associe l'été au camping.* I connect summer with camping.
♦ **s'associer** to go into partnership

assommer VERB
<u>to knock out</u> ◊ *Un coup fort l'a assommé.* A heavy blow knocked him out.

assorti ADJECTIVE
1 <u>matching</u> ◊ *des couleurs assorties* matching colours
2 <u>assorted</u> ◊ *des chocolats assortis* assorted chocolates
♦ **être assorti à quelque chose** to match something ◊ *Son sac à main est assorti à ses chaussures.* Her purse matches her shoes.

l' **assortiment** MASC NOUN
<u>assortment</u>

l' **assurance** FEM NOUN
1 <u>insurance</u> ◊ *une assurance maladie* medical insurance
2 <u>confidence</u> ◊ *parler avec assurance* to speak with confidence

assurer VERB
1 <u>to insure</u> ◊ *La maison est assurée.* The house is insured. ◊ *être assuré contre quelque chose* to be insured against something

2 <u>to assure</u> ◊ *Je t'assure que c'est vrai!* I assure you it's true!
♦ **s'assurer de quelque chose** to make sure of something ◊ *Il s'est assuré que la porte était fermée.* He made sure the door was shut.

l' **asthme** MASC NOUN
<u>asthma</u> ◊ *une crise d'asthme* an asthma attack

l' **astronaute** MASC/FEM NOUN
<u>astronaut</u>

l' **astronome** MASC/FEM NOUN
<u>astronomer</u>

l' **astronomie** FEM NOUN
<u>astronomy</u>

astucieux ADJECTIVE (FEM SING **astucieuse**)
<u>clever</u>

l' **atelier** MASC NOUN
1 <u>workshop</u>
2 <u>studio</u> (*artist's*)

l' **athlète** MASC/FEM NOUN
<u>athlete</u>

l' **athlétisme** MASC NOUN
<u>track and field</u> ◊ *un championnat d'athlétisme* a track and field championship

l' **atlas** MASC NOUN
<u>atlas</u>

l' **atmosphère** FEM NOUN
<u>atmosphere</u>

atomique ADJECTIVE
<u>atomic</u> ◊ *la bombe atomique* the atomic bomb

l' **atout** MASC NOUN
1 <u>asset</u> ◊ *L'atout principal de ce joueur, c'est sa vitesse.* This player's main asset is his speed.
2 <u>trump card</u> ◊ *J'avais quatre atouts dans mon jeu.* I had four trump cards in my hand.

atroce ADJECTIVE
<u>terrible</u>

attachant ADJECTIVE
<u>lovable</u>

attacher VERB
<u>to tie up</u> ◊ *Elle a attaché ses cheveux avec un élastique.* She tied her hair up with an elastic band.
♦ **s'attacher à quelqu'un** to become attached to somebody
♦ **une poêle qui n'attache pas** a non-stick frying pan

attaquer VERB
<u>to attack</u>

atteindre VERB
<u>to reach</u>

attendant

♦ **en attendant** ADVERB in the meantime

attendre VERB
to wait ◊ *attendre quelqu'un* to wait for someone ◊ *J'attends d'avoir un appartement à moi.* I'm waiting until I have an apartment of my own. ◊ *Attends qu'il ne pleuve plus.* Wait until it stops raining.
♦ **attendre un enfant** to be expecting a baby
♦ **s'attendre à** to expect ◊ *Je m'attends à ce qu'ils soient en retard.* I expect they'll be late.

> Be careful! **attendre** does not mean *to attend*.

l' **attentat** MASC NOUN
♦ **un attentat à la bombe** a terrorist bombing

l' **attente** FEM NOUN
wait ◊ *deux heures d'attente* a two-hour wait
♦ **la salle d'attente** the waiting room

attentif ADJECTIVE (FEM SING **attentive**)
attentive

l' **attention** FEM NOUN
attention ◊ *à l'attention de* to the attention of
♦ **faire attention (1)** to be careful
♦ **faire attention (2)** to pay attention ◊ *Ne fais pas attention à cette remarque-là.* Pay no attention to that remark.
♦ **Attention!** Watch out! ◊ *Attention, tu vas te faire écraser!* Watch out, you'll get run over!

attentionné ADJECTIVE
thoughtful

attentivement ADVERB
① carefully ◊ *lire attentivement* to read carefully
② closely ◊ *observer attentivement* to observe closely

atterrir VERB
to land

l' **atterrissage** MASC NOUN
landing (of plane)

attirant ADJECTIVE
attractive

attirer VERB
to attract ◊ *attirer l'attention de quelqu'un* to attract somebody's attention
♦ **s'attirer des ennuis** to get into trouble ◊ *Si tu continues, tu vas t'attirer des ennuis.* If you keep that up, you'll get yourself into trouble.

l' **attitude** FEM NOUN
attitude

l' **attraction** FEM NOUN
♦ **une attraction touristique** a tourist attraction
♦ **un parc d'attractions** an amusement park

attraper VERB
to catch

attrayant ADJECTIVE
attractive

au PREPOSITION *see* **à**

> *au is the contracted form of à + le.*

♦ **au printemps** in the spring

l' **aube** FEM NOUN
dawn ◊ *à l'aube* at dawn

l' **auberge** FEM NOUN
inn
♦ **une auberge de jeunesse** a youth hostel

aucun ADJECTIVE, PRONOUN
① no ◊ *Il n'a aucun ami.* He has no friends. ◊ *Aucun enfant ne pourrait le faire.* No child could do that.
② none ◊ *Aucun d'entre eux n'est venu.* None of them came. ◊ *Aucune de mes amies n'aime le football.* None of my female friends like football. ◊ *« Tu aimes ses films? » « Je n'en ai vu aucun. »* "Do you like his films?" "I haven't seen any of them."
♦ **sans aucun doute** without any doubt

au-delà ADVERB
♦ **au-delà de** beyond ◊ *Votre ticket n'est pas valable au-delà de cette limite.* Your ticket is not valable beyond this point.

au-dessous ADVERB
① downstairs ◊ *Ils habitent au-dessous.* They live downstairs.
② underneath
♦ **au-dessous de** under ◊ *au-dessous du pont* under the bridge ◊ *dix degrés au-dessous de zéro* ten degrees below zero

au-dessus ADVERB
① upstairs ◊ *J'habite au-dessus.* I live upstairs.
② above
♦ **au-dessus de** above ◊ *au-dessus de la table* above the table

audio ADJECTIVE (MASC, FEM, PL)
audio ◊ *des fichiers audio* audio files ◊ *le matériel audio* audio equipment
♦ **un audioclip** an audio clip

audiovisuel ADJECTIVE (FEM SING **audiovisuelle**)
audiovisual

l' **auditeur** MASC NOUN

listener (*to radio*)

l' **audition** FEM NOUN
audition

auditionner VERB
to audition

l' **auditrice** FEM NOUN
listener (*to radio*)

l' **augmentation** FEM NOUN
rise ◊ *une augmentation de prix* a
rise in prices
♦ **une augmentation de salaire** a raise

augmenter VERB
to increase

aujourd'hui ADVERB
today

auparavant ADVERB
first ◊ *Vous pouvez utiliser
l'ordinateur, mais auparavant vous
devez taper le mot de passe.* You can
use the computer but first you have
to key in the password.

auquel PRONOUN (MASC PL **auxquels**, FEM PL
auxquelles)

> *auquel is the contracted form of à +
> lequel.*

◊ *l'homme auquel j'ai parlé* the man
I spoke to

**aura, aurai, auras, aurez, aurons,
auront** VERB *see* **avoir**

l' **aurore boréale** FEM NOUN
northern lights

aussi ADVERB
1 too ◊ *« Dors bien. » « Toi aussi. »*
"Sleep well." "You too." ◊ *Elle aussi
parle espagnol.* She too speaks
Spanish.
2 also ◊ *J'aimerais aussi que tu
achètes le journal.* I'd also like you to
get the paper. ◊ *Je parle anglais et
aussi allemand.* I speak English and
also German.
♦ **aussi ... que** as ... as ◊ *aussi grand
que moi* as big as me

aussitôt ADVERB
right away ◊ *aussitôt après son
retour* right after his return
♦ **aussitôt que** as soon as ◊ *aussitôt
que tu auras fini* as soon as you're
finished

autant ADVERB
♦ **autant de (1)** so much ◊ *Je ne veux
pas autant de gâteau.* I don't want so
much cake.
♦ **autant de (2)** so many ◊ *Je n'ai
jamais vu autant de monde.* I've never
seen so many people.
♦ **autant ... que (1)** as much ... as ◊ *J'ai
autant d'argent que toi.* I've got as

much money as you have.
♦ **autant ... que (2)** as many ... as ◊ *J'ai
autant d'amis que lui.* I've got as
many friends as he has.
♦ **d'autant plus que** all the more since
◊ *Elle est d'autant plus déçue qu'ils
le lui avaient promis.* She's all the
more disappointed since they had
promised her.
♦ **d'autant moins que** even less since
◊ *C'est d'autant moins pratique
pour nous que nous devons changer
deux fois d'autobus.* It's even less
convenient for us since we have to
change buses twice.

l' **auteur** MASC NOUN
author

l' **auteure** FEM NOUN
author

l' **auto** FEM NOUN
car

l' **autobus** MASC NOUN
bus ◊ *en autobus* by bus ◊ *l'autobus
scolaire* school bus

autochtone ADJECTIVE, MASC/FEM NOUN
Aboriginal
♦ **un autochtone** an Aboriginal man
♦ **une autochtone** an Aboriginal woman
♦ **les autochtones** the Aboriginal
peoples

autocollant ADJECTIVE

> *see also* **autocollant** NOUN

self-adhesive ◊ *une étiquette
autocollante* a self-adhesive label
♦ **une enveloppe autocollante** a self-
seal envelope

l' **autocollant** MASC NOUN

> *see also* **autocollant** ADJECTIVE

sticker

l' **auto-école** FEM NOUN (PL **les auto-écoles**)
driving school

automatique ADJECTIVE
automatic

l' **automne** MASC NOUN
fall
♦ **en automne** in the fall

automobile ADJECTIVE

> *see also* **automobile** NOUN

♦ **une course automobile** a car race

l' **automobile** FEM NOUN

> *see also* **automobile** ADJECTIVE

car

l' **automobiliste** MASC/FEM NOUN
motorist

l' **autoradio** MASC NOUN
car radio

l' **autorisation** FEM NOUN
⓵ permission ◊ *Elle m'a donné l'autorisation de sortir ce soir.* She's given me permission to go out tonight.
⓶ permit ◊ *Il faut une autorisation pour camper ici.* You need a permit to camp here.

autoriser VERB
to give permission for ◊ *Il m'a autorisé à en parler.* He's given me permission to talk about it.

autoritaire ADJECTIVE
authoritarian

l' **autorité** FEM NOUN
authority

l' **autoroute** FEM NOUN
highway

l' **auto-stop** MASC NOUN
♦ **faire de l'auto-stop** to hitchhike

l' **auto-stoppeur** MASC NOUN
hitchhiker

l' **auto-stoppeuse** FEM NOUN
hitchhiker

autour ADVERB
around ◊ *autour de la maison* around the house

autre ADJECTIVE, PRONOUN
other ◊ *Je viendrai un autre jour.* I'll come some other day. ◊ *J'ai d'autres projets.* I've got other plans.
♦ **autre chose** something else
♦ **un autre** another ◊ *Tu veux un autre morceau de gâteau?* Would you like another piece of cake?
♦ **l'autre** the other ◊ *Non, pas celui-ci, l'autre.* No, not that one, the other one.
♦ **d'autres** others ◊ *Je t'en apporterai d'autres.* I'll bring you some others.
♦ **les autres** the others ◊ *Les autres sont arrivés plus tard.* The others arrived later.
♦ **ni l'un ni l'autre** neither of them
♦ **entre autres** among other things ◊ *Nous avons parlé, entre autres, de nos projets de vacances.* We talked about our holiday plans, among other things.

autrefois ADVERB
in the old days

autrement ADVERB
⓵ differently ◊ *Elle l'a fait autrement.* She did it differently.
⓶ otherwise ◊ *Je n'ai pas pu faire autrement.* I couldn't do otherwise.
♦ **autrement dit** in other words

l' **autruche** FEM NOUN
ostrich

aux PREPOSITION *see* **à**

> ***aux** is the contracted form of **à** + **les**.*

◊ *J'ai dit aux enfants d'aller jouer.* I told the children to go and play.

auxquelles PRONOUN

> ***auxquelles** is the contracted form of **à** + **lesquelles**.*

◊ *les revues auxquelles il est abonné* the magazines to which he subscribes

auxquels PRONOUN

> ***auxquels** is the contracted form of **à** + **lesquels**.*

◊ *les enfants auxquels il a parlé* the children he spoke to

avaient, avais, avait VERB *see* **avoir**
♦ **Il y avait beaucoup de monde.** There were a lot of people.

l' **avalanche** FEM NOUN
avalanche

avaler VERB
to swallow

l' **avance** FEM NOUN
♦ **être en avance** to be early
♦ **à l'avance** beforehand ◊ *réserver une place à l'avance* to book a seat beforehand
♦ **d'avance** in advance ◊ *payer d'avance* to pay in advance
♦ **l'avance rapide** fast forward

avancé ADJECTIVE
advanced ◊ *à un niveau avancé* at an advanced level
♦ **bien avancé** well under way ◊ *Les travaux sont déjà bien avancés.* The work is already well under way.

avancer VERB
⓵ to move forward ◊ *Elle avançait prudemment.* She was moving forward cautiously.
⓶ to move up (*date*) ◊ *La date de l'examen a été avancée.* The date of the exam has been moved up.
⓷ to put ahead ◊ *Il a avancé sa montre d'une heure.* He put his watch ahead an hour.
⓸ to be fast (*watch*) ◊ *Ma montre avance d'une heure.* My watch is an hour fast.
⓹ to lend ◊ *Peux-tu m'avancer dix dollars?* Can you lend me 10 dollars?

avant PREPOSITION, ADJECTIVE

> *see also* **avant** NOUN

⓵ before ◊ *avant qu'il ne pleuve* before it rains ◊ *avant de partir* before leaving
⓶ front ◊ *la roue avant* the front wheel ◊ *le siège avant* the front seat

♦ **avant tout** above all

l' **avant** MASC NOUN

see also **avant** PREPOSITION

front ◊ *l'avant de la voiture* the front of the car
♦ **à l'avant** in front
♦ **en avant** forward ◊ *Elle a fait un pas en avant.* She took a step forward.

l' **avantage** MASC NOUN
advantage

avant-dernier ADJECTIVE (FEM **avant-dernière**, MASC PL **avant-derniers**)
second-last ◊ *l'avant-dernière page* the second-last page ◊ *Ils sont arrivés avant-derniers.* They arrived second-last.

avant-hier ADVERB
the day before yesterday ◊ *Il est arrivé avant-hier.* He arrived the day before yesterday.

avec PREPOSITION
with ◊ *avec ma mère* with my mother
♦ **Et avec ça?** Anything else? (*in store*)

l' **avenir** MASC NOUN
future
♦ **à l'avenir** in future ◊ *À l'avenir, essayez d'être à l'heure.* Try to be on time in future.
♦ **dans un proche avenir** in the near future

l' **aventure** FEM NOUN
adventure

aventureux ADJECTIVE (FEM SING **aventureuse**)
adventurous

l' **aventurier** MASC NOUN
adventurer

l' **aventurière** FEM NOUN
adventurer

l' **avenue** FEM NOUN
avenue

l' **averse** FEM NOUN
shower (*of rain*)

avertir VERB
to warn
♦ **avertir quelqu'un de quelque chose** to warn somebody about something

l' **avertissement** MASC NOUN
warning

aveugle ADJECTIVE
blind

l' **avion** MASC NOUN
plane
♦ **aller en avion** to go by plane ◊ *Il est allé en Alberta en avion.* He flew to Alberta.
♦ **par avion** by airmail

l' **aviron** MASC NOUN
paddle (*canoe*) ◊ *un aviron en bois* a wooden paddle

l' **avis** MASC NOUN
[1] opinion ◊ *J'aimerais avoir ton avis.* I'd like to have your opinion.
♦ **à mon avis** in my opinion
♦ **changer d'avis** to change one's mind ◊ *J'ai changé d'avis.* I've changed my mind.
[2] notice ◊ *jusqu'à nouvel avis* until further notice

l' **avocat** MASC NOUN
[1] lawyer ◊ *Il est avocat.* He's a lawyer.
[2] avocado

l' **avocate** FEM NOUN
lawyer ◊ *Elle est avocate.* She's a lawyer.

l' **avoine** FEM NOUN
oats

avoir VERB

Present tense:	
j'ai	*nous avons*
tu as	*vous avez*
il/elle a	*ils/elles ont*
Past participle:	
eu	

[1] to have ◊ *Ils ont deux enfants.* They have two children. ◊ *Elle a les yeux bleus.* She has blue eyes. ◊ *J'ai déjà mangé.* I've already eaten. ◊ *Est-ce que tu as vu ce film?* Have you seen this film? ◊ *Je leur ai parlé hier.* I spoke to them yesterday.
♦ **On t'a bien eu!** (*informal*) You've been had!
[2] to be ◊ *Elle a trois ans.* She's three. ◊ *J'avais dix ans quand je l'ai rencontré.* I was ten when I met him.
♦ **il y a (1)** there is ◊ *Il y a quelqu'un à la porte.* There's somebody at the door.
♦ **il y a (2)** there are ◊ *Il y a des chocolats sur la table.* There are some chocolates on the table.
♦ **il y a (3)** ago ◊ *Je l'ai rencontré il y a deux ans.* I met him two years ago.
♦ **Qu'est-ce qu'il y a?** What's the matter?
♦ **Il n'y a qu'à partir plus tôt.** We'll just have to leave earlier.

l' **avortement** MASC NOUN
abortion

avouer VERB
to admit

avril MASC NOUN
April
♦ **en avril** in April

ayez, ayons VERB *see* **avoir**

B

le **babillard** NOUN
billboard
♦ **un babillard électronique** a bulletin board (*computer*)

le **baby-foot** NOUN
foosball ◊ *jouer au baby-foot* to play foosball

le **bac** NOUN = baccalauréat

le **baccalauréat** NOUN
B.A. ◊ *un baccalauréat en histoire* a B.A. in history

bâcler VERB
to botch ◊ *Je déteste le travail bâclé!* I hate work that's not done properly!

le **bagage** NOUN
luggage
♦ **faire ses bagages** to pack
♦ **les bagages à main** hand luggage
◊ *un bagage à main* a piece of hand luggage

la **bagarre** NOUN
fight ◊ *Une bagarre a éclaté dans la cour de l'école.* A fight broke out in the schoolyard.

se **bagarrer** VERB
to fight ◊ *Il s'est encore bagarré avec son frère.* He's been fighting with his brother again.

la **bague** NOUN
ring

le **baguel** NOUN
bagel ◊ *un baguel grillé* a toasted bagel

la **baguette** NOUN
① stick of French bread
② chopstick ◊ *manger avec des baguettes* to eat with chopsticks
♦ **une baguette magique** a magic wand

la **baie** NOUN
① bay
② berry

la **baie d'Hudson**
Hudson Bay

la **baignade** NOUN
♦ **« baignade interdite »** "no swimming"

se **baigner** VERB
to go swimming ◊ *Si on allait se baigner?* Shall we go swimming?

la **baignoire** NOUN
bathtub

bâiller VERB
to yawn

le **bain** NOUN
bath ◊ *prendre un bain* to take a bath ◊ *prendre un bain de soleil* to sunbathe

le **baiser** NOUN
kiss

la **baisse** NOUN
decrease ◊ *la baisse du taux de chômage* the fall in the unemployment rate
♦ **être en baisse** to be falling

baisser VERB
① to turn down ◊ *Tu peux baisser le chauffage.* You can turn down the heat.
② to fall ◊ *Le prix des lecteurs MP3 a baissé.* The price of MP3 players has fallen.
♦ **se baisser** to bend down ◊ *Elle s'est baissée pour ramasser son cahier.* She bent down to pick up her notebook.

le **bal** NOUN
dance ◊ *un bal populaire* a local dance

la **balade** NOUN (*informal*)
walk ◊ *faire une balade* to go for a walk

se **balader** VERB (*informal*)
to wander around ◊ *J'adore me balader dans les rues du Vieux-Québec.* I love to wander around the streets of old Quebec City.

le **baladeur** NOUN
personal stereo

le **balai** NOUN
broom ◊ *Je vais donner un coup de balai dans la cuisine.* I'm going to sweep the kitchen.

la **balance** NOUN
scales PL (*for weighing*)
♦ **la Balance** Libra ◊ *Elle est Balance.* She's a Libra.

se **balancer** VERB
to swing

la **balançoire** NOUN
swing

balayer VERB
① to sweep ◊ *J'ai balayé la cuisine.* I swept the kitchen.
② to sweep up ◊ *Va balayer les feuilles sur le patio.* Go and sweep up the leaves on the patio.

balbutier VERB
to stammer

le **balcon** NOUN
balcony

la **baleine** NOUN
whale

la **balle** NOUN
① ball ◊ *une balle de tennis* a tennis ball
② bullet

la **ballerine** NOUN
① ballet dancer
② ballet shoe ◊ *une paire de ballerines rouges* a pair of red ballet shoes

le **ballet** NOUN
ballet

le **ballon** NOUN
① ball ◊ *lancer le ballon* to throw the ball
♦ **un ballon de football** a football
♦ **le ballon chasseur** dodgeball
② balloon

balnéaire ADJECTIVE
♦ **une station balnéaire** a seaside resort

banal ADJECTIVE (MASC PL **banaux**)
① commonplace ◊ *La violence est devenue banale à la télévision.* Violence has become commonplace on television.
② clichéd ◊ *L'intrigue du film est très banale.* The plot of the film is very clichéd.

la **banane** NOUN
banana ◊ *La banane est un fruit.* The banana is a fruit.

le **banc** NOUN
bench
♦ **le banc de neige** snowbank

bancaire ADJECTIVE
♦ **une carte bancaire** a bank card

le **bandage** NOUN
bandage

la **bande** NOUN
① gang ◊ *une bande de voyous* a gang of thugs
② bunch ◊ *C'est une bande d'idiots!* They're a bunch of idiots!
✱ ③ boards (*hockey*) ◊ *L'autre joueuse m'a poussée dans la bande.* The other player shoved me into the boards.
♦ **une bande dessinée** a comic strip
♦ **une bande magnétique** a tape
♦ **la bande sonore** the sound track
♦ **Elle fait toujours bande à part.** She always keeps to herself.

le **bandeau** NOUN (PL les **bandeaux**)
headband

bander VERB
to bandage ◊ *L'infirmière lui a bandé la jambe.* The nurse bandaged his leg.

le **bandit** NOUN
bandit

la **banique** NOUN
bannock

la **banlieue** NOUN
suburbs ◊ *Elle habite en banlieue.* She lives in the suburbs.
♦ **les trains de banlieue** commuter trains

la **banque** NOUN
bank
♦ **la banque alimentaire** food bank

le **banquet** NOUN
banquet ◊ *le banquet annuel de l'association* the club's annual banquet

la **banquette** NOUN
seat ◊ *la banquette arrière de la voiture* the back seat of the car

le **baquet** NOUN
tub (*laundry*)

✱ le **barachois** NOUN
barachois

> ⓘ A **barachois** is a tidal pond partly obstructed by a sand bar. In the Atlantic provinces and the Gulf of St. Lawrence, people often moor small boats in barachois. Many restaurants and hotels bear names such as "Au Barachois" or "Auberge Le Barachois".

barbare ADJECTIVE
barbaric

la **barbe** NOUN
beard ◊ *Il porte la barbe.* He has a beard.
♦ **la barbe à papa** cotton candy

le **barbecue** NOUN
barbecue ◊ *être invité à un barbecue* to be invited to a barbecue ◊ *faire griller du saumon au barbecue* to barbecue salmon
♦ **du poulet grillé au barbecue** barbecued chicken

barbouiller VERB
to smear ◊ *Les murs étaient barbouillés de graffitis.* The walls were plastered with graffiti.
♦ **J'ai l'estomac barbouillé.** (*informal*) I feel queasy.

barbu ADJECTIVE
bearded ◊ *un grand barbu* a big, bearded man

le **baromètre** NOUN
barometer

le **barrage** NOUN
dam
♦ **un barrage de police** a police roadblock

la **barre** NOUN
bar (*metal*) ◊ *une barre de fer* an iron bar
♦ **la barre d'outils** toolbar (*computer*)
♦ **la barre oblique inverse** backslash

le **barreau** NOUN (PL les **barreaux**)
bar (*on window*) ◊ *Il s'est retrouvé derrière les barreaux.* He ended up behind bars.

barrer VERB
to block ◊ *Il y a un tronc d'arbre qui barre la route.* There's a tree trunk blocking the road.

la **barrette** NOUN
barrette

la **barrière** NOUN
fence

le **bas** NOUN

see also **bas** ADJECTIVE

① bottom ◊ *en bas de la page* at the bottom of the page ◊ *en bas de l'escalier* at the bottom of the stairs
② stocking ◊ *une paire de bas* a pair of stockings

bas ADJECTIVE, ADVERB (FEM SING **basse**)

see also **bas** NOUN

low ◊ *parler à voix basse* to speak in a low voice
♦ **en bas (1)** down ◊ *Ça me donne le vertige de regarder en bas.* I get dizzy if I look down.
♦ **en bas (2)** at the bottom ◊ *Son nom est tout en bas.* His name is at the bottom. ◊ *Il y a une porte en bas de l'escalier.* There's a door at the bottom of the stairs.
♦ **en bas (3)** downstairs ◊ *Elle habite en bas.* She lives downstairs.

le **Bas-Canada** NOUN
Lower Canada

la **base** NOUN
base ◊ *la base de la pyramide* the base of the pyramid
♦ **de base** basic ◊ *Le pain et le lait sont des aliments de base.* Bread and milk are basic foods.
♦ **à base de** made from ◊ *des produits de beauté à base de plantes* cosmetics made from plants
♦ **une base de données** a database

le **basket-ball** NOUN
basketball ◊ *jouer au basket-ball* to play basketball

basse ADJECTIVE *see* **bas**

la **basse-cour** NOUN (PL les **basses-cours**)
barnyard

le **bassin** NOUN
① pond ◊ *Il y a un bassin à poissons rouges dans le parc.* There's a goldfish pond in the park.
② pelvis ◊ *une fracture du bassin* a fractured pelvis

la **bassine** NOUN
washbasin

le **bas-ventre** NOUN
stomach ◊ *Elle se plaint de douleurs dans le bas-ventre.* She is complaining of pains in her stomach.

la **bataille** NOUN
battle

le **bateau** NOUN (PL les **bateaux**)
boat

le **bateau-mouche** NOUN (PL les **bateaux-mouches**)
pleasure boat

bâti ADJECTIVE
♦ **bien bâti** well-built

le **bâtiment** NOUN
building

bâtir VERB
to build

le **bâton** NOUN
stick ◊ *un coup de bâton* a blow with a stick ◊ *un bâton de hockey* a hockey stick

le **battement** NOUN
♦ **J'ai dix minutes de battement.** I've got ten minutes free.
♦ **un battement de cœur** heartbeat

la **batterie** NOUN
① battery (*car*) ◊ *La batterie est à plat.* The battery is dead.
② drums ◊ *jouer de la batterie* to play the drums
♦ **la batterie de cuisine** the pots and pans

le **batteur** NOUN
drummer

battre VERB
to beat ◊ *Quand je la vois, mon cœur bat plus vite.* When I see her, my heart beats faster.
♦ **se battre** to fight ◊ *Je me bats souvent avec mon frère.* I fight a lot with my brother.
♦ **battre les cartes** to shuffle the cards
♦ **battre les blancs en neige** beat the egg whites until stiff
♦ **battre son plein** to be in full swing ◊ *A minuit, la fête battait son plein.* At midnight, the party was in full swing.

bavard ADJECTIVE

talkative

le **bavardage** NOUN
chat

bavarder VERB
to chat

baveux ADJECTIVE (FEM SING **baveuse**)
1 runny ◊ *une omelette baveuse* a runny omelette
2 arrogant (*informal*) ◊ *Il est un peu trop baveux à mon goût.* I find him a bit too arrogant.

la **bavure** NOUN
blunder ◊ *une bavure policière* a police blunder

la **BD** NOUN (= *bande dessinée*)
comic strip ◊ *Elle adore les BD.* She loves comic strips.

béant ADJECTIVE
gaping ◊ *un trou béant* a gaping hole

beau ADJECTIVE, ADVERB (FEM SING **belle**, MASC PL **beaux**)
1 lovely ◊ *un beau cadeau* a lovely present ◊ *une belle journée* a lovely day

> *beau* changes to *bel* before a vowel and most words beginning with "h".

◊ *un bel été* a lovely summer
2 beautiful ◊ *C'est une belle femme.* She is a beautiful woman.
3 handsome ◊ *C'est un beau garçon.* He is a handsome boy.
♦ **Il fait beau aujourd'hui.** It's a nice day today.
♦ **J'ai beau essayer, je n'y arrive pas.** No matter how hard I try, I just can't do it.

beaucoup ADVERB
1 a lot ◊ *Il mange beaucoup.* He eats a lot.
2 much ◊ *Elle n'a pas beaucoup d'argent.* She doesn't have much money. ◊ *Elle est beaucoup plus grande que moi.* She is much taller than me.
♦ **beaucoup de** a lot of ◊ *Il y avait beaucoup de monde au concert.* There were a lot of people at the concert. ◊ *J'ai fait beaucoup de fautes.* I made a lot of mistakes.
♦ **J'ai eu beaucoup de chance.** I was very lucky.

le **beau-fils** NOUN (PL les **beaux-fils**)
1 son-in-law
2 stepson

le **beau-frère** NOUN (PL les **beaux-frères**)
brother-in-law

le **beau-père** NOUN (PL les **beaux-pères**)
1 father-in-law
2 stepfather

la **beauté** NOUN
beauty

les **beaux-arts** MASC NOUN
fine arts

les **beaux-parents** MASC NOUN
in-laws

le **bébé** NOUN
baby

le **bec** NOUN
1 beak
2 little kiss ◊ *un petit bec sur la joue* a little kiss on the cheek
♦ **le bec sucré** sweet tooth ◊ *Ma petite sœur a le bec sucré.* My little sister has a sweet tooth.

la **bêche** NOUN
spade

bêcher VERB
to dig ◊ *Il bêchait son jardin.* He was digging the garden.

bégayer VERB
to stammer

beige ADJECTIVE
beige

le **beigne** NOUN
doughnut

bel ADJECTIVE *see* **beau**

le **bélier** MASC NOUN
ram
♦ **le Bélier** Aries ◊ *Elle est Bélier.* She's an Aries.

belle ADJECTIVE *see* **beau**

la **belle-famille** NOUN (PL les **belles-familles**)
in-laws

la **belle-fille** NOUN (PL les **belles-filles**)
1 daughter-in-law
2 stepdaughter

la **belle-mère** NOUN (PL les **belles-mères**)
1 mother-in-law
2 stepmother

la **belle-sœur** NOUN (PL les **belles-sœurs**)
sister-in-law

la **bénédiction** NOUN
blessing

le **bénéfice** NOUN
profit ◊ *On a réalisé un bénéfice de 170 $ sur la vente de chocolats.* We made a profit of $170 on the chocolate sales.

bénévole ADJECTIVE

> see also **bénévole** NOUN

volunteer ◊ *du travail bénévole* volunteer work

le/la **bénévole** NOUN

B

see also **bénévole** ADJECTIVE
volunteer

bénir VERB
to bless

le **benjamin** NOUN

> ⓘ The youngest child in a family is sometimes called *le benjamin* or *la benjamine*.

la **béquille** NOUN
crutch ◊ *Il marche avec des béquilles.* He walks on crutches.

le **berceau** NOUN (PL les **berceaux**)
cradle

bercer VERB
to rock

la **berceuse** NOUN
lullaby

le **béret** NOUN
beret
♦ **les bérets bleus** peacekeepers

la **berge** NOUN
bank (*of river*)

la **bernache du Canada** NOUN
Canada goose

le **besoin** NOUN
need
♦ **avoir besoin de quelque chose** to need something ◊ *J'ai besoin d'argent.* I need some money. ◊ *J'ai besoin d'y réfléchir.* I need to think about it.
♦ **une famille dans le besoin** a needy family

le **bétail** NOUN
livestock

la **bête** NOUN

see also **bête** ADJECTIVE
animal

bête ADJECTIVE

see also **bête** NOUN
stupid

la **bêtise** NOUN
♦ **faire une bêtise** to do something stupid ◊ *Je crois que j'ai fait une bêtise.* I think I've done something stupid.
♦ **dire des bêtises** to talk nonsense ◊ *Tu dis des bêtises!* You're talking nonsense!

le **béton** NOUN
concrete
♦ **un alibi en béton** a cast-iron alibi

la **betterave** NOUN
beet

le **beurre** NOUN
butter ◊ *une sauce au beurre* a sauce made with butter
♦ **beurre d'arachide** peanut butter

beurrer VERB
to butter

le **biberon** NOUN
baby's bottle

la **bibliographie** NOUN
bibliography

le/la **bibliothécaire** NOUN
librarian

la **bibliothèque** NOUN
1 library ◊ *emprunter un livre à la bibliothèque* to borrow a book from the library
2 bookcase ◊ *une bibliothèque en chêne massif* a solid oak bookcase

la **bicyclette** NOUN
bicycle

le **bidon** NOUN
can ◊ *un bidon d'essence* a can of gas

le **bidonville** NOUN
shanty town

bidouiller VERB
to hack (*computer*) ◊ *Il passe des heures chaque soir à bidouiller sur son ordinateur.* He spends hours hacking on his computer every night.

le **bidouilleur** NOUN
hacker (*computer*)

la **bidouilleuse** NOUN
hacker (*computer*)

le **bien** NOUN

see also **bien** ADJECTIVE
1 good ◊ *le bien et le mal* good and evil ◊ *Elle m'a dit beaucoup de bien de toi.* She told me a lot of good things about you. ◊ *C'est pour ton bien.* It's for your own good.
♦ **faire du bien à quelqu'un** to do somebody good ◊ *Ses vacances lui ont fait beaucoup de bien.* His holiday has done him a lot of good.
2 possession ◊ *son bien le plus précieux* her most treasured possession

bien ADJECTIVE, ADVERB

see also **bien** NOUN
1 well ◊ *Elle travaille bien.* She works well. ◊ *Je me sens bien.* I feel fine. ◊ *Je ne me sens pas bien.* I don't feel well.
2 good ◊ *Ce restaurant est vraiment bien.* This restaurant is really good.
3 quite ◊ *bien assez* quite enough
♦ **Je veux bien le faire.** I'm quite willing

☞

to do it.
♦ **bien mieux** much better
♦ **J'espère bien y aller.** I very much hope to go.
④ right ◊ *Ce n'est pas bien de dire du mal des gens.* It's not right to say nasty things about people. ◊ *Il croyait bien faire.* He thought he was doing the right thing.
♦ **C'est bien fait pour lui!** It serves him right!

le **bien-être** NOUN
well-being ◊ *une sensation de bien-être* a feeling of well-being

la **bienfaisance** NOUN
charity
♦ **une œuvre de bienfaisance** a charity

bien que CONJUNCTION
although ◊ *Il fait assez chaud bien qu'il n'y ait pas de soleil.* It's quite warm although there's no sun.

bien sûr ADVERB
of course

bientôt ADVERB
soon ◊ *À bientôt!* See you soon!

le **bienvenu** NOUN
♦ **Vous êtes le bienvenu!** You are welcome! (*to visitor*) ◊ *Vous êtes tous les bienvenus!* You're all welcome!

la **bienvenue** NOUN
welcome ◊ *Bienvenue à Calgary!* Welcome to Calgary! ◊ *Vous êtes la bienvenue!* You're welcome!

le **bifteck** NOUN
steak

le **bijou** NOUN (PL les **bijoux**)
jewel

la **bijouterie** NOUN
jewellery store

le **bijoutier** NOUN
jeweller

la **bijoutière** NOUN
jeweller ◊ *Elle est bijoutière.* She's a jeweller.

le **bilan** NOUN
♦ **faire le bilan de quelque chose** to assess something ◊ *Il faut faire le bilan de la situation.* We need to assess the situation.

bilingue ADJECTIVE
bilingual

le **bilinguisme** NOUN
bilingualism

le **billard** NOUN
pool

la **bille** NOUN
marble (*toy*)

le **billet** NOUN
① ticket ◊ *un billet d'avion* a plane ticket
② bill (*paper money*) ◊ *un billet de dix dollars* a 10-dollar bill

le **billion** NOUN
trillion

la **binette** NOUN
smiley (*emoticon*)

biodégradable ADJECTIVE
biodegradable

la **biographie** NOUN
biography

la **biologie** NOUN
biology

biologique ADJECTIVE
① organic ◊ *des légumes biologiques* organic vegetables
② biological ◊ *des armes biologiques* biological weapons

la **biscotte** NOUN
toasted bread (*sold in packets*)

le **biscuit** NOUN
cookie

la **bise** NOUN
kiss ◊ *Grosses bises de Terre-Neuve.* Love and kisses from Newfoundland.
♦ **faire la bise à quelqu'un** (*informal*) to give somebody a peck on the cheek ◊ *Elle m'a fait la bise.* She gave me a peck on the cheek.

le **bison** NOUN
bison

le **bisou** NOUN (*informal*)
kiss ◊ *Viens faire un bisou à maman!* Come and give Mummy a little kiss!

bissextile ADJECTIVE
♦ **une année bissextile** a leap year

bizarre ADJECTIVE
strange

la **blague** NOUN (*informal*)
① joke ◊ *raconter une blague* to tell a joke
♦ **Sans blague!** No kidding!
② trick ◊ *Il nous a encore fait une blague!* He's played a trick on us again!

blaguer VERB (*informal*)
to joke

blâmer VERB
to blame

blanc ADJECTIVE (FEM SING **blanche**)
⎾ *see also* **blanc** NOUN ⏋
① white ◊ *un chemisier blanc* a white blouse
② blank ◊ *une page blanche* a blank page

B

le **blanc** NOUN

> see also **blanc** ADJECTIVE

white ◊ *Elle était habillée tout en blanc.* She was dressed all in white.
♦ **un blanc d'œuf** an egg white

le **Blanc** NOUN
white man

la **Blanche** NOUN
white woman

blanche ADJECTIVE see **blanc**

le **blé** NOUN
wheat
❀ ♦ **le blé d'Inde** corn

blessé ADJECTIVE

> see also **blessé** NOUN

injured

le **blessé** NOUN

> see also **blessé** ADJECTIVE

injured person ◊ *L'accident a fait trois blessés.* Three people were injured in the accident.

la **blessée** NOUN
injured person

blesser VERB
[1] to injure ◊ *Il a été blessé dans un accident de voiture.* He was injured in a car accident.
[2] to hurt ◊ *Elle a fait exprès de le blesser.* She hurt him on purpose.
♦ **se blesser** to hurt oneself ◊ *Je me suis blessé au pied.* I've hurt my foot.

la **blessure** NOUN
injury

bleu ADJECTIVE

> see also **bleu** NOUN

[1] blue ◊ *une veste bleue* a blue jacket
[2] very rare (*steak*)

le **bleu** NOUN

> see also **bleu** ADJECTIVE

[1] blue ◊ *J'aime le bleu.* I like blue.
[2] bruise ◊ *Il a un bleu au front.* He's got a bruise on his forehead.

le **bleuet** NOUN
blueberry ◊ *la tarte aux bleuets* blueberry pie

bleu marine ADJECTIVE (MASC, FEM, PL)
navy blue ◊ *des vêtements bleu marine* navy blue clothes

le **bloc** NOUN
pad ◊ *un bloc de papier à lettres* a pad of writing paper
♦ **un bloc de glace** a block of ice

le **bloc-notes** NOUN (PL les **blocs-notes**)
notepad

le **blogue** NOUN
blog

blond ADJECTIVE
blond ◊ *les cheveux blonds* blond hair
♦ **blond cendré** ash blond ◊ *Elle a les cheveux blond cendré.* She has ash blond hair.

❀ la **blonde** NOUN (*informal*)
girlfriend ◊ *Ma blonde a fait son propre site Web.* My girlfriend made her own Web site.

bloquer VERB
to block ◊ *bloquer le passage* to block the way
♦ **être bloqué dans un embouteillage** to be stuck in a traffic jam

se **blottir** VERB
to huddle ◊ *Ils étaient blottis l'un contre l'autre.* They were huddled together.

la **blouse** NOUN
blouse

le **blouson** NOUN
jacket ◊ *un blouson en cuir* a leather jacket

les **bobettes** FEM NOUN
underpants

la **bobine** NOUN
reel ◊ *une bobine de fil* a reel of thread

le **bocal** NOUN (PL les **bocaux**)
jar

le **bœuf** NOUN
[1] ox
[2] beef ◊ *un rôti de bœuf* a roast of beef

bof EXCLAMATION (*informal*)
♦ **« Le film t'a plu? » « Bof! C'était pas terrible! »** "Did you like the film?" "Well... it wasn't that great!"
♦ **« Comment ça va? » « Bof! Pas très bien. »** "How is it going?" "Oh... not too well actually."

boire VERB
to drink

le **bois** NOUN
wood
♦ **en bois** wooden ◊ *une table en bois* a wooden table

la **boisson** NOUN
drink ◊ *une boisson chaude* a hot drink ◊ *une boisson non alcoolisée* a soft drink

la **boîte** NOUN
[1] box ◊ *une boîte d'allumettes* a box of matches
♦ **une boîte aux lettres** a mailbox

☞

② can ◊ *une boîte de thon* a can of tuna
♦ **une boîte de conserve** a can (*of food*)
♦ **en boîte** canned ◊ *des petits pois en boîte* canned peas

boiter VERB
to limp

le **bol** NOUN
bowl

bombarder VERB
to bomb

la **bombe** NOUN
① bomb
② spray can ◊ *du déodorant en bombe aérosol* spray deodorant

bon ADJECTIVE, ADVERB (FEM SING **bonne**)

see also **bon** NOUN

① good ◊ *un bon restaurant* a good restaurant ◊ *Le tabac n'est pas bon pour la santé.* Smoking isn't good for you.
♦ **être bon en maths** to be good at math
♦ **sentir bon** to smell good
♦ **Bon courage!** Good luck!
♦ **Bon voyage!** Have a good trip!
♦ **Bonne fin de semaine!** Have a good weekend!
♦ **Bonne chance!** Good luck!
♦ **Bonne journée!** Have a good day!
♦ **Bonne nuit!** Good night!
♦ **Bon anniversaire!** Happy birthday!
♦ **Bonne Année!** Happy New Year!
② right ◊ *Il est arrivé au bon moment.* He arrived at the right moment. ◊ *Ce n'est pas la bonne réponse.* That's not the right answer.
♦ **de bonne heure** early
♦ **bon marché** cheap ◊ *Les fraises ne sont pas bon marché en hiver.* Strawberries aren't cheap in winter.
♦ **Ah bon?** Really? ◊ *« Je pars aux États-Unis la semaine prochaine. » « Ah bon? »* "I'm going to the States next week." "Really?"
♦ **« J'aimerais vraiment que tu viennes! » « Bon, d'accord. »** "I'd really like you to come!" "OK then, I will."
♦ **Est-ce que ce yogourt est encore bon?** Is this yogurt still OK?

le **bon** NOUN

see also **bon** ADJECTIVE

voucher ◊ *un bon d'achat* a voucher
♦ **le bon de réduction** coupon
♦ **pour de bon** for good ◊ *Cette fois, c'est pour de bon.* This time it's for good.

le **bonbon** NOUN
candy

♦ **les bonbons haricots** jelly beans

bondé ADJECTIVE
crowded

bondir VERB
to leap

le **bonheur** NOUN
happiness
♦ **porter bonheur** to bring luck

le **bonhomme** NOUN (PL les **bonshommes**)
♦ **un bonhomme de neige** a snowman

> ℹ️ Le **Bonhomme Carnaval**, a large snowman wearing a red tuque and a woven belt, symbolizes the Carnaval de Québec and can be seen at the various activities throughout its two week duration. The Carnaval is the biggest festival in the world.

bonjour EXCLAMATION
① Hello! ◊ *Donne le bonjour à tes parents de ma part.* Say hello to your parents for me.
② Good morning!
③ Good afternoon!

> *bonjour* is used in the morning and afternoon; in the evening **bonsoir** is used instead.

♦ **C'est simple comme bonjour!** It's easy as pie!

bonne ADJECTIVE *see* **bon**

le **bonnet** NOUN
hat ◊ *un bonnet de laine* a woolly hat (*women's*)
♦ **un bonnet de bain** a bathing cap

bonsoir EXCLAMATION
Good evening!

la **bonté** NOUN
kindness

le **bord** NOUN
① edge ◊ *le bord de la table* the edge of the table
② side ◊ *Jane a garé sa voiture au bord de la route.* Jane parked her car on the side of the road.
♦ **au bord de la mer** by the sea
♦ **au bord de l'eau** by the water
♦ **monter à bord** to go on board
♦ **être au bord des larmes** to be on the verge of tears

border VERB
① to line ◊ *une route bordée d'arbres* a tree-lined street
② to trim ◊ *un col bordé de dentelle* a collar trimmed with lace
③ to tuck in ◊ *Ma mère borde ma petite sœur tous les soirs.* My mother tucks in my little sister every night.

la **bordure** NOUN

border
♦ **une auberge en bordure de mer** an inn right by the sea

la **bosse** NOUN
bump ◊ *Elle a une grosse bosse au front.* She has a big bump on her forehead. ◊ *La route est pleine de bosses.* The road is very bumpy.

botanique ADJECTIVE

see also **botanique** NOUN

botanical ◊ *les jardins botaniques* the botanical gardens

la **botanique** NOUN

see also **botanique** ADJECTIVE

botany

la **botte** NOUN
1 boot ◊ *une paire de bottes* a pair of boots
♦ **les bottes de caoutchouc** rubber boots
2 bunch ◊ *une botte de radis* a bunch of radishes

le **bottin** NOUN
phone book

le **bouc** NOUN
1 goatee
2 billy goat
♦ **un bouc émissaire** a scapegoat

la **bouche** NOUN
mouth
♦ **une bouche d'égout** a maintenance hole (*in road*)
♦ **une bouche de métro** a subway entrance

la **bouchée** NOUN
mouthful

boucher VERB

see also **boucher** NOUN

to plug ◊ *boucher un trou* to plug a hole ◊ *L'évier est bouché.* The sink is clogged. ◊ *J'ai le nez bouché.* My nose is stuffed up.

le **boucher** NOUN

see also **boucher** VERB

butcher ◊ *Il est boucher.* He's a butcher.

la **bouchère** NOUN
butcher ◊ *Elle est bouchère.* She's a butcher.

la **boucherie** NOUN
butcher shop

le **bouchon** NOUN
1 top (*of plastic bottle*)
2 cork (*of wine bottle*)
3 traffic jam ◊ *Il y avait beaucoup de bouchons sur l'autoroute.* There were a lot of traffic jams on the motorway.

la **boucle** NOUN
curl (*of hair*)
♦ **une boucle d'oreille** an earring ◊ *une paire de boucles d'oreille* a pair of earrings

bouclé ADJECTIVE
curly

le **bouclier** NOUN
shield
♦ **le Bouclier canadien** the Canadian Shield

bouddhiste ADJECTIVE

see also **bouddhiste** NOUN

Buddhist

le/la **bouddhiste** NOUN

see also **bouddhiste** ADJECTIVE

Buddhist

bouder VERB
to sulk

la **boue** NOUN
mud

la **bouée** NOUN
buoy
♦ **une bouée de sauvetage** a life buoy

boueux ADJECTIVE (FEM SING **boueuse**)
muddy

la **bouffe** NOUN (*informal*)
food ◊ *La bouffe est infecte à la cafétéria.* The food in the cafeteria is revolting.

la **bouffée** NOUN
♦ **une bouffée d'air frais** a breath of fresh air

la **bouffe-minute** NOUN
fast food

bouffer VERB (*informal*)
to eat

bouger VERB
to move

la **bougie** NOUN
candle

la **bouillabaisse** NOUN
fish soup

bouillant ADJECTIVE
1 boiling ◊ *Faites cuire les pâtes à l'eau bouillante.* Cook the pasta in boiling water.
2 piping hot ◊ *La soupe est servie bouillante.* The soup should be served piping hot.

bouillir VERB
to boil ◊ *L'eau bout.* The water's boiling.
♦ **Je bous d'impatience.** I'm bursting with impatience.

la **bouilloire** NOUN

kettle

le **bouillon** NOUN
stock ◊ *du bouillon de légumes*
vegetable stock

le **boulanger** NOUN
baker ◊ *Il est boulanger.* He's a baker.

la **boulangère** NOUN
baker ◊ *Elle est boulangère.* She's a
baker.

la **boulangerie** NOUN
bakery

la **boule** NOUN
ball ◊ *une boule de cristal* a crystal
ball
♦ **une boule de neige** a snowball
❈ ♦ **la machine à boules** pinball machine

le **bouleau** NOUN
birch

bouleverser VERB
1 to move deeply ◊ *Leur histoire
déchirante m'a bouleversée.* I was
very moved by their heartbreaking
story.
2 to shatter ◊ *La mort de son ami l'a
bouleversé.* He was shattered by the
death of his friend.
3 to turn upside down ◊ *Cette
rencontre a bouleversé sa vie.* This
meeting turned her life upside down.

la **boulimie** NOUN
bulimia

le **boulot** NOUN (*informal*)
1 job ◊ *Elle a trouvé du boulot.* She
has found a job.
2 work ◊ *J'ai beaucoup de boulot en
ce moment.* I've got a lot of work to
do at the moment.

le **bouquet** NOUN
bunch of flowers ◊ *un bouquet de
roses* a bunch of roses

bourdonner VERB
to buzz

bourgeois ADJECTIVE
middle-class ◊ *un quartier bourgeois*
a posh area

le **bourgeon** NOUN
bud

bourré ADJECTIVE
♦ **bourré de** stuffed with ◊ *un
portefeuille bourré de billets* a wallet
stuffed with bills

le **bourreau** NOUN (PL les **bourreaux**)
♦ **C'est un véritable bourreau de travail.**
He's a real workaholic.

bourrer VERB
to stuff ◊ *bourrer une valise de
vêtements* to stuff clothes into a
suitcase

la **bourse** NOUN
grant
♦ **la Bourse** the Stock Exchange

bous VERB *see* **bouillir**

la **bousculade** NOUN
rush ◊ *la bousculade de dernière
minute* the last-minute rush

bousculer VERB
1 to jostle ◊ *être bousculé par la
foule* to be jostled by the crowd
2 to rush ◊ *Je n'aime pas qu'on me
bouscule.* I don't like to be rushed.

la **boussole** NOUN
compass

bout VERB *see* **bouillir**

le **bout** NOUN
1 end ◊ *Elle habite au bout de la rue.*
She lives at the end of the street. ◊ *Il
est assis en bout de table.* He is sitting
at the end of the table.
2 tip ◊ *le bout du nez* the tip of the
nose
3 little piece ◊ *un petit bout de
fromage* a little piece of cheese
♦ **un bout de papier** a scrap of paper
♦ **au bout de** after ◊ *Au bout d'un
moment, il s'est endormi.* After a
while he fell asleep.
♦ **au bout du compte** ultimately ◊ *Au
bout du compte, c'est à toi de décider.*
Ultimately, it's your decision.
♦ **Elle est à bout.** She's at the end of her
tether.

la **bouteille** NOUN
bottle ◊ *une bouteille d'eau* a bottle
of water

la **boutique** NOUN
shop ◊ *une boutique de cadeaux* a
giftshop ◊ *une boutique de souvenirs*
a souvenir shop

le **bouton** NOUN
1 button
2 pimple ◊ *J'ai un bouton sur le nez.*
I've got a pimple on my nose.
3 bud ◊ *un bouton de rose* a rosebud
♦ **un bouton d'or** a buttercup

la **boxe** NOUN
boxing

le **boxeur** NOUN
boxer

boycotter VERB
to boycott

le **bracelet** NOUN
bracelet

le **bracelet-montre** NOUN (PL les **bracelets-
montres**)
wristwatch

la **branche** NOUN

branch

branché ADJECTIVE (*informal*)
trendy ◊ *avoir un look branché* to look trendy

brancher VERB
1. to connect ◊ *Le téléphone est branché?* Is the phone connected?
2. to plug in ◊ *L'aspirateur n'est pas branché.* The vacuum cleaner isn't plugged in.

le **bras** NOUN
arm

la **brasse** NOUN
breaststroke ◊ *nager la brasse* to do the breaststroke

brave ADJECTIVE
1. nice ◊ *C'est un brave type.* He's a nice guy.
2. brave ◊ *Ta mère est une femme très brave.* Your mother is a very brave woman.

> Be careful! The meaning of the French adjective **brave** changes according to its position. Before the noun, it means "nice"; after the noun, it means "brave".

bravo EXCLAMATION
Bravo!

bref ADJECTIVE, ADVERB (FEM SING **brève**)
short ◊ *Sa lettre était brève.* Her letter was short.
♦ **en bref** in brief ◊ *l'actualité en bref* the news in brief
♦ **Bref, ça s'est bien terminé.** In short, it turned out all right in the end.
♦ **être bref et précis** to be short and to the point

la **bretelle** NOUN
strap ◊ *La bretelle de son soutien-gorge dépasse.* Her bra strap is showing.
♦ **les bretelles** suspenders ◊ *Il porte des bretelles.* He's wearing suspenders.

brève ADJECTIVE *see* **bref**

le **bricolage** NOUN
do-it-yourself ◊ *Il aime le bricolage.* He loves working on do-it-yourself projects. ◊ *un magasin de bricolage* a store selling do-it-yourself supplies

bricoler VERB
to work on do-it-yourself projects ◊ *Il aime bricoler.* He loves working on do-it-yourself projects.

brièvement ADVERB
briefly ◊ *Expliquez-moi brièvement ce qui s'est passé.* Tell me briefly what happened.

la **brigade** NOUN
squad (*of police*) ◊ *la brigade des stups* (*informal*) the drug squad

brillamment ADVERB
brilliantly ◊ *Il a réussi brillamment à son examen.* He did brilliantly in the exam.

brillant ADJECTIVE
1. brilliant ◊ *une brillante carrière* a brilliant career
2. shiny ◊ *des cheveux brillants* shiny hair

briller VERB
to shine

le **brin** NOUN
♦ **un brin d'herbe** a blade of grass
♦ **un brin de muguet** a sprig of lily of the valley

la **brindille** NOUN
twig

la **brioche** NOUN
bun

la **brique** NOUN
brick

le **briquet** NOUN
lighter

la **brise** NOUN
breeze

le **brise-glace** NOUN (PL **brise-glaces**)
ice-breaker ◊ *On utilise des brise-glaces pour naviguer dans l'Arctique.* Ice-breakers are used to navigate the Arctic.

se **briser** VERB
to break ◊ *Le vase s'est brisé en mille morceaux.* The vase broke into a thousand pieces.

la **brisure** NOUN
chocolate chip ◊ *un biscuit aux brisures de chocolat* a chocolate chip cookie

la **broche** NOUN
brooch ◊ *une broche en argent* a silver brooch
♦ **à la broche** spit-roasted ◊ *un poulet à la broche* a spit-roasted chicken

le **brochet** NOUN
pike

la **brochette** NOUN
skewer
♦ **les brochettes d'agneau** lamb kebabs

la **brocheuse** NOUN
stapler

la **brochure** NOUN
brochure

broder VERB
to embroider

la **broderie** NOUN

embroidery

la **bronchite** NOUN
bronchitis ◊ *avoir une bronchite* to have bronchitis

le **bronze** NOUN
bronze

bronzer VERB
to get a tan ◊ *Il est bien bronzé.* He's got a good tan.
♦ **se bronzer** to sunbathe

la **brosse** NOUN
brush
♦ **une brosse à cheveux** a hairbrush
♦ **une brosse à dents** a toothbrush

brosser VERB
to brush
♦ **se brosser les dents** to brush one's teeth ◊ *Je me brosse les dents tous les soirs.* I brush my teeth every night.

la **brouette** NOUN
wheelbarrow

le **brouillard** NOUN
fog ◊ *Il y a du brouillard.* It's foggy.

le **brouillon** NOUN
first draft ◊ *Ce n'est qu'un brouillon.* It's just a first draft.

les **broussailles** FEM NOUN
undergrowth SING

brouter VERB
to graze (*animals*)

broyer VERB
to crush
♦ **broyer du noir** to be down in the dumps

la **bruine** NOUN
drizzle ◊ *On prévoit de la bruine aujourd'hui.* They're forecasting drizzle today.

bruiner VERB
to drizzle

le **bruit** NOUN
1 noise ◊ *J'ai entendu un bruit.* I heard a noise. ◊ *faire du bruit* to make a noise
♦ **sans bruit** without a sound
2 rumour ◊ *Des bruits circulent à son sujet.* There are rumours going round about him.

le **bruitage** NOUN
sound effects PL

le **bruiteur** NOUN
sound effect specialist

la **bruiteuse** NOUN
sound effect specialist

brûlant ADJECTIVE
1 blazing ◊ *un soleil brûlant* a blazing sun

2 boiling hot ◊ *Elle boit son café brûlant.* She drinks her coffee boiling hot.

le **brûlé** NOUN
smell of burning ◊ *Ça sent le brûlé.* There's a smell of burning.

brûler VERB
to burn
♦ **se brûler** to burn oneself

la **brûlure** NOUN
burn
♦ **des brûlures d'estomac** heartburn

la **brume** NOUN
mist

brumeux ADJECTIVE (FEM SING **brumeuse**)
misty

brun ADJECTIVE
brown
♦ **Elle est brune.** She has dark hair.

le **brunch** NOUN
brunch ◊ *prendre le brunch* to have brunch

brusque ADJECTIVE
abrupt
♦ **d'un ton brusque** brusquely

brusquer VERB
to rush ◊ *Il ne faut pas la brusquer.* You mustn't rush her.

brut ADJECTIVE
♦ **le champagne brut** dry champagne
♦ **le pétrole brut** crude oil
♦ **son salaire brut** his gross salary

brutaliser VERB
to treat roughly ◊ *Il a été brutalisé par la police.* He was treated roughly by the police.

bruyamment ADVERB
noisily

bruyant ADJECTIVE
noisy

bu VERB *see* **boire**

✹ la **buanderie** NOUN
coin laundry

le **bûcheron** NOUN
woodcutter

le **budget** NOUN
budget

le **buffet** NOUN
1 sideboard ◊ *un buffet en chêne* an oak sideboard
2 buffet ◊ *un buffet froid* a cold buffet
♦ **un buffet à salades** a salad bar

le **buisson** NOUN
bush

la **bulle** NOUN

bubble ◊ *une bulle de savon* a soap bubble

le **bulletin** NOUN

　① bulletin

　♦ **le bulletin d'informations** the news bulletin

　② report card ◊ *Ton bulletin n'est pas fameux.* Your report card isn't very good.

　♦ **le bulletin de salaire** pay slip

　♦ **le bulletin de vote** the ballot

　♦ **le bulletin scolaire** report card

le **bureau** NOUN (PL les **bureaux**)

　① desk ◊ *Posez le dossier sur mon bureau.* Put the file on my desk.

　② office ◊ *Il vous attend dans son bureau.* He's waiting for you in his office.

　♦ **le Bureau** the desktop (*computer*)

　♦ **un bureau de change** a foreign exchange

　♦ **le bureau de poste** the post office

　♦ **le bureau de vote** the polling station

bus VERB *see* **boire**

le **bus** NOUN

　bus

le **buste** NOUN

　bust

but VERB *see* **boire**

le **but** NOUN

　① aim ◊ *Ils n'ont pas de but dans la vie.* They have no aim in life.

　♦ **Quel est le but de votre visite?** What's the reason for your visit?

　♦ **dans le but de** with the intention of ◊ *Je suis venue dans le but de vous aider.* I came to help you.

　② goal ◊ *marquer un but* to score a goal

le **butane** NOUN

　butane

le **butin** NOUN

　loot ◊ *Les cambrioleurs se sont partagé le butin.* The burglars shared the loot.

buvais, buvait VERB *see* **boire**

C

c' PRONOUN *see* **ce**

ça PRONOUN
  ① this ◊ *Est-ce que vous pouvez m'aider avec ça?* Can you help me with this?
  ② that ◊ *Est-ce que tu peux prendre ça, là-bas dans le coin?* Can you bring that from over there in the corner?
  ③ it ◊ *Ça ne fait rien.* It doesn't matter.
  ♦ **Comment ça va?** How are you?
  ♦ **Ça alors!** Well, well!
  ♦ **C'est ça.** That's right.
  ♦ **Ça y est!** That's it!

çà ADVERB
  ♦ **çà et là** here and there

la **cabane** NOUN
  hut
🦋 ♦ **la cabane à sucre** sugar shack
  ♦ **une cabane dans l'arbre** a treehouse

la **cabine** NOUN
  cabin (*on a ship*)
  ♦ **une cabine d'essayage** a fitting room
  ♦ **une cabine téléphonique** a phone box

le **cabinet** NOUN
  consulting room (*of doctor, of dentist*)
  ♦ **un cabinet d'avocats** a law firm

le **câble** NOUN
  cable
  ♦ **la télévision par câble** cable (*television*)
  ♦ **les câbles de démarrage** booster cables

cabosser VERB
  to dent

le **cacao** NOUN
  cocoa
  ♦ **le beurre de cacao** cocoa butter

cache-cache MASC NOUN

> *No article is ever used with **cache-cache**.*

  ♦ **jouer à cache-cache** to play hide-and-seek

cacher VERB
  to hide ◊ *J'ai caché les cadeaux sous le lit.* I hid the presents under the bed. ◊ *Tu me caches quelque chose!* You're hiding something!
  ♦ **se cacher** to hide ◊ *Elle s'est cachée sous la table.* She's hiding under the table.

le **cachet** NOUN
  ① tablet
  ♦ **un cachet d'aspirine** an aspirin
  ② fee (*for performer*) ◊ *Il a touché un gros cachet pour ce concert.* He got a big fee for the concert.
  ♦ **le cachet de la poste** the postmark

la **cachette** NOUN
  hiding place
  ♦ **en cachette** on the sly ◊ *Il est sorti en cachette sans réveiller ses parents.* He crept out on the sly without waking his parents.
🦋 ♦ **jouer à la cachette** to play hide-and-seek

le **cadavre** NOUN
  corpse

le **cadeau** NOUN (PL les **cadeaux**)
  present ◊ *un cadeau d'anniversaire* a birthday present
  ♦ **faire un cadeau à quelqu'un** to give somebody a present

le **cadenas** NOUN
  padlock

cadet ADJECTIVE (FEM SING **cadette**)

  | *see also* **cadet** NOUN |

  ① younger (*brother, sister*) ◊ *ma sœur cadette* my younger sister
  ② youngest (*son, daughter*) ◊ *son fils cadet* his youngest son

le **cadet** NOUN

  | *see also* **cadet** ADJECTIVE |

  youngest ◊ *C'est le cadet de la famille.* He's the youngest in the family.

la **cadette** NOUN
  youngest ◊ *C'est la cadette de la famille.* She's the youngest in the family.

le **cadre** NOUN
  ① frame ◊ *un cadre en bois* a wooden frame
  ② surroundings ◊ *L'hôtel est situé dans un très beau cadre.* The hotel is located in beautiful surroundings.
  ③ executive ◊ *un cadre supérieur* a senior executive

le **café** NOUN
  ① coffee
  ② café

la **cafétéria** NOUN
  cafeteria

la **cafetière** NOUN
  ① coffee maker

2 coffee pot

la cage NOUN
cage
♦ **la cage d'escalier** the stairwell

la cagoule NOUN
balaclava

le cahier NOUN
1 workbook
2 notebook

le caillou NOUN (PL les **cailloux**)
pebble

la caisse NOUN
1 box ◊ *une caisse à outils* a tool box
2 cash register
♦ **le ticket de caisse** the sales slip
3 checkout ◊ *J'ai dû faire la queue
à la caisse.* I had to wait in line at the
checkout.

le caissier NOUN
cashier

la caissière NOUN
cashier

cajun ADJECTIVE, NOUN (FEM SING **cajun**)
Cajun ◊ *la cuisine cajun* Cajun
cuisine
♦ **un Cajun** a Cajun (*man*)
♦ **une Cajun** a Cajun (*woman*)

le calcul NOUN
1 calculation ◊ *Je me suis trompé
dans mes calculs.* I made a mistake in
my calculations.
2 arithmetic ◊ *Je ne suis pas très
bon en calcul.* I'm not very good at
arithmetic.

la calculatrice NOUN
calculator

calculer VERB
to work out ◊ *J'ai calculé combien ça
allait coûter.* I worked out how much
it was going to cost.

la cale NOUN
wedge

le caleçon NOUN
underpants ◊ *un caleçon* a pair of
underpants (*men's*)

le calendrier NOUN
calendar

le calepin NOUN
notebook

caler VERB
to stall ◊ *La voiture a calé dans une
côte.* The car stalled on a hill.

câlin ADJECTIVE

see also **câlin** NOUN

cuddly

le câlin NOUN

see also **câlin** ADJECTIVE

cuddle ◊ *faire un câlin à quelqu'un* to
give somebody a cuddle

le calmant NOUN
tranquillizer

calme ADJECTIVE

see also **calme** NOUN

1 quiet ◊ *un endroit calme* a quiet
place
2 calm ◊ *Il est resté très calme.* He
stayed very calm.

le calme NOUN

see also **calme** ADJECTIVE

peace and quiet ◊ *J'ai besoin de
calme pour travailler.* I need peace
and quiet to work.
♦ **Du calme, s'il vous plaît!** Please stay
calm!

calmer VERB
to soothe ◊ *Cette pommade calme
les démangeaisons.* This ointment
soothes itching.
♦ **se calmer** to calm down ◊ *Calme-toi!*
Calm down!

la calorie NOUN
calorie

le/la camarade NOUN
friend
♦ **un camarade de classe** a school
friend

le cambriolage NOUN
burglary

cambrioler VERB
to burgle

le cambrioleur NOUN
burglar

la cambrioleuse NOUN
burglar

✹ **le/la camelot** NOUN
paper carrier

la camelote NOUN (*informal*)
junk ◊ *C'est vraiment de la camelote.*
It's absolute junk.

la caméra NOUN
camera (*movie, TV*)
♦ **une caméra numérique** a digital
camera

le caméscope NOUN
camcorder

le camion NOUN
truck
♦ **un camion citerne** a tanker truck

la camionnette NOUN
pickup truck

le camionneur NOUN
truck driver

la **camionneuse** NOUN
truck driver

la **camisole** NOUN
undershirt (*men's or women's*)

la **camomille** NOUN
camomile tea

le **camp** NOUN
camp ◊ *un camp d'été* a summer
camp ◊ *un camp de prisonniers* a
prison camp

la **campagne** NOUN
1 country
♦ **à la campagne** in the country ◊ *Nous
passons nos vacances à la campagne.*
We spend our holidays in the country.
2 campaign ◊ *une campagne
publicitaire* a marketing campaign

camper VERB
to camp

le **campeur** NOUN
camper

la **campeuse** NOUN
camper

le **camping** NOUN
camping ◊ *faire du camping* to go
camping
♦ **un terrain de camping** a campground
♦ **le camping sauvage** wilderness
camping

le **Canada** NOUN
Canada
♦ **au Canada (1)** in Canada
♦ **au Canada (2)** to Canada

canadien ADJECTIVE, NOUN (FEM SING
canadienne)
Canadian
♦ **un Canadien** a Canadian (*man*)
♦ **une Canadienne** a Canadian (*woman*)

canadien-anglais ADJECTIVE (FEM SING
canadienne-anglaise)
English Canadian

le **Canadien anglais** NOUN (PL les
Canadiens anglais)
English Canadian (*man*)

la **Canadienne anglaise** NOUN (PL les
Canadiennes anglaises)
English Canadian (*woman*)

canadien-français ADJECTIVE (FEM SING
canadienne-française)
French Canadian

le **Canadien français** NOUN (PL les
Canadiens français)
French Canadian (*man*)

la **Canadienne française** NOUN (PL les
Canadiennes françaises)
French Canadian (*woman*)

le **canal** NOUN (PL les **canaux**)
canal

le **canapé** NOUN
open-faced sandwich

le **canard** NOUN
duck

le **cancer** NOUN
cancer ◊ *le cancer du poumon* lung
cancer
♦ **le Cancer** Cancer ◊ *Elle est Cancer.*
She's a Cancer.

le **candidat** NOUN
1 candidate (*in exam, election*)
2 applicant (*for job*)

la **candidate** NOUN
1 candidate (*in exam, election*)
2 applicant (*for job*)

la **candidature** NOUN
♦ **poser sa candidature à un poste**
to apply for a job ◊ *Il a posé sa
candidature à des dizaines de postes.*
He has applied for dozens of jobs.

le **caneton** NOUN
duckling

la **canette** NOUN
♦ **une canette de boisson gazeuse** a can
of pop

le **caniche** NOUN
poodle

la **canicule** NOUN
heat wave

le **canif** NOUN
jackknife

la **canne** NOUN
walking stick
♦ **une canne à pêche** a fishing rod

la **canneberge** NOUN
cranberry ◊ *du jus de canneberge*
cranberry juice

la **cannelle** NOUN
cinnamon ◊ *une brioche à la cannelle*
cinnamon roll

le **canola** NOUN
canola ◊ *de l'huile de canola* canola
oil

le **canon** NOUN
cannon

le **canot** NOUN
1 canoe
2 dinghy ◊ *un canot pneumatique* a
rubber dinghy
♦ **un canot de sauvetage** a lifeboat

le **canotage** NOUN
canoeing ◊ *faire du canotage* to go
canoeing

la **cantine** NOUN
snack bar

le **caoutchouc** NOUN
rubber

♦ des bottes en caoutchouc rubber boots

le **cap** NOUN
cape (*landform*)

capable ADJECTIVE
♦ Elle est capable de marcher pendant des heures. She can walk for hours.
♦ Il est capable de changer d'avis au dernier moment. He's capable of changing his mind at the last minute.

la **cape** NOUN
cape (*garment*)

la **capitale** NOUN
capital ◊ *la capitale de la Colombie-Britannique* the capital of British Columbia

le **capot** NOUN
hood (*of car*)

le **caprice** NOUN
♦ faire des caprices to make a fuss ◊ *Il n'aime pas les enfants qui font des caprices.* He doesn't like children who make a fuss.

capricieux ADJECTIVE (FEM SING **capricieuse**)
♦ un enfant capricieux a difficult child

le **Capricorne** NOUN
Capricorn ◊ *Elle est Capricorne.* She's a Capricorn.

captivant ADJECTIVE
fascinating

la **captivité** NOUN
captivity ◊ *en captivité* in captivity

capturer VERB
to capture

la **capuche** NOUN
hood ◊ *un manteau à capuche* a coat with a hood

le **capuchon** NOUN
cap (*of pen*)

car CONJUNCTION
because ◊ *Nous sommes inquiets car ils ne sont pas encore rentrés.* We're worried because they're not back yet.

la **carabine** NOUN
rifle

le **caractère** NOUN
personality ◊ *Elle a le même caractère que son père.* She has the same personality as her father.
♦ Il a bon caractère. He's good-natured.
♦ Elle a mauvais caractère. She's bad-tempered.
♦ Il n'a pas un caractère facile. He isn't easy to get along with.

caractéristique ADJECTIVE
see also **caractéristique** NOUN
characteristic

la **caractéristique** NOUN
see also **caractéristique** ADJECTIVE
characteristic

la **carafe** NOUN
jug ◊ *une carafe d'eau* a jug of water

le **caramel** NOUN
① caramel ◊ *la crème caramel* crème caramel
② toffee

la **caravane** NOUN
RV

carbonique ADJECTIVE
♦ le gaz carbonique carbon dioxide

le **carburant** NOUN
fuel

🦡 le **carcajou** NOUN
wolverine

cardiaque ADJECTIVE
♦ une crise cardiaque a heart attack
♦ Ma tante est cardiaque. My aunt has heart trouble.

le/la **cardiologue** NOUN
heart specialist

la **caresse** NOUN
stroke ◊ *faire des caresses à un chat* to caress a cat

caresser VERB
to stroke

le **caribou** NOUN
caribou
♦ la peau de caribou caribou hide

la **caricature** NOUN
cartoon (*drawing*)

la **carie** NOUN
tooth decay ◊ *J'ai une carie.* I have a cavity.

caritatif ADJECTIVE (FEM SING **caritative**)
♦ une organisation caritative a charity

le **carnaval** NOUN
carnival

le **carnet** NOUN
① notebook
② book ◊ *un carnet d'adresses* an address book ◊ *un carnet de chèques* a cheque book ◊ *un carnet de timbres* a book of stamps

la **carotte** NOUN
carrot ◊ *les carottes râpées* grated carrots

carré ADJECTIVE
see also **carré** NOUN
square
♦ un mètre carré a square metre

le **carré** NOUN

see also **carré** ADJECTIVE
square
✹ ♦ **le carré au chocolat** brownie

le **carreau** NOUN (PL les **carreaux**)
1 check (*pattern*) ◊ *une chemise à carreaux* a checked shirt
2 tile (*floor, wall*) ◊ *Je viens de laver les carreaux de la cuisine.* I've just washed the kitchen floor.
3 pane ◊ *Elle a cassé un carreau.* She broke a windowpane.
4 diamonds (*cards*) ◊ *l'as de carreau* the ace of diamonds

le **carrefour** NOUN
intersection

le **carrelage** NOUN
tiled floor

carrément ADVERB
1 completely ◊ *C'est carrément impossible.* It's completely impossible.
2 straight out ◊ *Dis-moi carrément ce que tu penses.* Tell me straight out what you think.

la **carrière** NOUN
career
♦ **un militaire de carrière** a professional soldier

la **carrure** NOUN
build ◊ *Il a une carrure d'athlète.* He has an athletic build.

✹ le **cartable** NOUN
binder

la **carte** NOUN
1 card
♦ **une carte d'anniversaire** a birthday card
♦ **une carte postale** a postcard
♦ **une carte de vœux** a Christmas card
♦ **une carte bancaire** a bank card
♦ **une carte de crédit** a credit card
♦ **une carte de fidélité** a frequent customer card
♦ **une carte d'embarquement** a boarding card
♦ **une carte d'identité** an ID card
♦ **une carte de séjour** a residence permit
♦ **une carte téléphonique** a phonecard
♦ **un jeu de cartes (1)** a pack of cards
♦ **un jeu de cartes (2)** a card game
2 map ◊ *une carte du Manitoba* a map of Manitoba ◊ *une carte routière* a road map
♦ **manger à la carte** to eat à la carte ◊ *Nous allons manger à la carte.* We'll choose from the à la carte menu.

le **carton** NOUN
cardboard ◊ *un morceau de carton* a piece of cardboard
♦ **une boîte de carton** a cardboard box
◊ *un carton à chaussures* a shoe box

la **cartouche** NOUN
cartridge
♦ **une cartouche d'imprimante** a printer cartridge

le **cas** NOUN (PL les **cas**)
case ◊ *plusieurs cas* several cases
♦ **ne faire aucun cas de** to take no notice of
♦ **en aucun cas** under no circumstances
♦ **en tout cas** at any rate
♦ **au cas où** in case ◊ *Prends un sandwich au cas où la cantine serait fermée.* Take a sandwich in case the snack bar's closed.
♦ **en cas de** in case of ◊ *En cas d'incendie, appelez ce numéro.* In case of fire, call this number.

la **cascade** NOUN
waterfall

le **cascadeur** NOUN
stuntman

la **cascadeuse** NOUN
stuntwoman

la **case** NOUN
1 square (*in board game*)
2 box (*on form*)
♦ **la case postale** post office box

la **caserne** NOUN
barracks

le **casier** NOUN
locker

le **casque** NOUN
helmet
♦ **un casque d'écoute** a pair of headphones

la **casquette** NOUN
cap

cassant ADJECTIVE
♦ **Il m'a parlé d'un ton cassant.** He spoke to me curtly.

le **casse-croûte** NOUN (PL les **casse-croûte**)
snack

le **casse-noix** NOUN (PL les **casse-noix**)
nutcracker

casser VERB
to break ◊ *J'ai cassé un verre.* I've broken a glass.
♦ **se casser** to break (*bone*) ◊ *Il s'est cassé la jambe en faisant du ski.* He broke his leg skiing.
♦ **se casser la tête** (*informal*) to go to a lot of trouble ◊ *Je ne vais pas me casser la tête pour le dîner : je vais ouvrir une boîte de conserve.* I'm not going to go to a whole lot of trouble over dinner: I'll just open a can.

la casserole NOUN
  1 saucepan
  2 casserole ◊ *une casserole de thon* a tuna casserole

le casse-tête NOUN (PL les **casse-tête**)
  ♦ **C'est un vrai casse-tête!** It's a real headache!

la cassette NOUN
  cassette

le cassis NOUN
  black currant

la cassonade NOUN
  brown sugar

le castor NOUN
  beaver

le catalogue NOUN
  catalogue

la catastrophe NOUN
  disaster

la catégorie NOUN
  category

catégorique ADJECTIVE
  firm ◊ *un refus catégorique* a flat refusal

la cathédrale NOUN
  cathedral

catholique ADJECTIVE
  see also **catholique** NOUN
  Catholic

le/la catholique NOUN
  see also **catholique** ADJECTIVE
  Catholic

le cauchemar NOUN
  nightmare ◊ *faire un cauchemar* to have a nightmare

la cause NOUN
  cause
  ♦ **à cause de** because of ◊ *Nous n'avons pas pu sortir à cause du mauvais temps.* We couldn't go out because of the bad weather.

causer VERB
  to cause ◊ *La tempête a causé beaucoup de dégâts.* The storm caused a lot of damage.

le cavalier NOUN
  1 rider
  2 partner (*at dance*)

la cavalière NOUN
  rider

la cave NOUN
  cellar

la caverne NOUN
  cave

le CD NOUN (PL les **CD**)
  CD

le CD-ROM NOUN (PL les **CD-ROM**)
  CD-ROM

ce ADJECTIVE (MASC SING **cet**, FEM SING **cette**, PL **ces**)
  see also **ce** PRONOUN

  *ce changes to **cet** before a vowel and most words beginning with "h".*

  1 this ◊ *Tu peux prendre ce livre.* You can take this book. ◊ *cet après-midi* this afternoon ◊ *cet hiver* this winter
  ♦ **ce livre-ci** this book
  ♦ **cette voiture-ci** this car
  2 that ◊ *Je n'ai pas du tout aimé ce film.* I didn't like that movie at all.
  ♦ **ce livre-là** that book
  ♦ **cette voiture-là** that car

ce PRONOUN
  see also **ce** ADJECTIVE

  *ce changes to **c'** before the vowel in **est, était** and **étaient**.*

  it ◊ *Ce n'est pas facile.* It's not easy.
  ♦ **c'est (1)** it is ◊ *C'est vraiment trop cher.* It's really too expensive. ◊ *Ouvre, c'est moi!* Open the door, it's me!
  ♦ **c'est (2)** he is ◊ *C'est un peintre du début du siècle.* He's a painter from the turn of the century.
  ♦ **c'est (3)** she is ◊ *C'est une actrice très célèbre.* She's a very famous actress.
  ♦ **c'est (4)** this is ◊ *C'est inacceptable!* This is unacceptable!
  ♦ **c'est (5)** that is ◊ *C'est bien beau, mais...* That's all very fine, but...
  ♦ **ce sont** they are ◊ *Ce sont des amis à mes parents.* They're friends of my parents'.
  ♦ **Qui est-ce?** Who is it?
  ♦ **Qu'est-ce que c'est?** What is it?
  ♦ **ce qui** what ◊ *C'est ce qui compte.* That's what matters.
  ♦ **tout ce qui** everything that ◊ *J'ai rangé tout ce qui traînait par terre.* I've tidied up everything that was on the floor.
  ♦ **ce que** what ◊ *Je vais lui dire ce que je pense.* I'm going to tell her what I think.
  ♦ **tout ce que** everything ◊ *Tu peux avoir tout ce que tu veux.* You can have everything you want.

ceci PRONOUN
  this ◊ *Prends ceci, tu en auras besoin.* Take this, you'll need it.

céder VERB
  to give in ◊ *Elle a tellement insisté qu'il a fini par céder.* She was so adamant that he finally gave in.

♦ **céder à** to give in to ◊ *Je ne veux pas céder à ses caprices.* I'm not going to give in to his whims.

le **cédérom** NOUN
CD-ROM

la **cédille** NOUN
cedilla

le **cèdre** NOUN
cedar
♦ **le bois de cèdre** cedar (wood)

✹ le **cégep** NOUN (= *collège d'enseignement général et professionnel*)
CEGEP (*general and vocational college*)

> ❶ *In Québec, a **cégep** is an institution offering two- or three-year programs in pre-university and vocational studies.*

la **ceinture** NOUN
belt ◊ *une ceinture en cuir* a leather belt
♦ **une ceinture de sauvetage** a lifebelt
♦ **votre ceinture de sécurité** your seatbelt

cela PRONOUN
① it ◊ *Cela dépend.* It depends.
② that ◊ *Je n'aime pas cela.* I don't like that.
♦ **C'est cela.** That's right.
♦ **à part cela** apart from that

célèbre ADJECTIVE
famous

célébrer VERB
to celebrate

le **céleri** NOUN
celery
♦ **des branches de céleri** celery stalks

célibataire ADJECTIVE, NOUN
single
♦ **un célibataire** a bachelor
♦ **une célibataire** a single woman

celle PRONOUN *see* **celui**

celles PRONOUN *see* **ceux**

la **cellule** NOUN
cell

Celsius ADJECTIVE (FEM, PL **Celsius**)
Celsius ◊ *vingt degrés Celsius* 20 degrees Celsius

celui PRONOUN (FEM **celle**, MASC PL **ceux**, FEM PL **celles**)
the one ◊ *Prends celui que tu préfères.* Take the one you like best.
◊ *Je n'ai pas d'appareil photo mais je peux emprunter celui de ma sœur.* I don't have a camera but I can borrow my sister's. ◊ *Je n'ai pas de planche*

à roulettes mais je peux emprunter celle de mon frère. I don't have a skateboard but I can borrow my brother's.
♦ **celui-ci** this one
♦ **celle-ci** this one
♦ **celui-là** that one
♦ **celle-là** that one

la **cendre** NOUN
ash

le **cendrier** NOUN
ashtray

censé ADJECTIVE
♦ **être censé faire quelque chose** to be supposed to do something ◊ *Vous êtes censé arriver à l'heure.* You're supposed to get here on time.

cent NUMBER
a hundred ◊ *cent dollars* a hundred dollars

> **cent** is spelt with an **-s** when there are two or more hundreds, but not when it is followed by another number, as in "a hundred and two."

◊ *trois cents ans* 300 years ◊ *cent deux kilomètres* 102 kilometres ◊ *trois cent cinquante kilomètres* 350 kilometres ◊ *trois cent mille kilomètres* 300 000 kilometres

le **cent** NOUN
cent (*currency*)

la **centaine** NOUN
about a hundred ◊ *Il y avait une centaine de personnes dans la salle.* There were about a hundred people in the hall.
♦ **des centaines de** hundreds of ◊ *Des centaines de réfugiés se sont présentés à l'ambassade.* Hundreds of refugees came to the embassy.

le **centenaire** NOUN
centennial

centième ADJECTIVE
hundredth

le **centimètre** NOUN
centimetre

central ADJECTIVE (MASC PL **centraux**)
central

la **centrale** NOUN
power plant ◊ *une centrale nucléaire* a nuclear power plant

le **centre** NOUN
centre
♦ **un centre commercial** a shopping centre
♦ **un centre communautaire** a community centre
♦ **un centre d'appels** a call centre
✹ ♦ **le centre local de services**

communautaires (*also* **CLSC**) local community service centre (*in* Québec)
♦ **le centre de jour** drop-in centre
♦ **le centre de villégiature** resort

le **centre-ville** NOUN (PL les **centres-villes**)
town centre

cependant ADVERB
however

le **cercle** NOUN
circle ◊ *Entourez d'un cercle la bonne réponse.* Put a circle round the right answer.
♦ **un cercle vicieux** a vicious circle

le **cercueil** NOUN
coffin

les **céréales** FEM NOUN
cereal ◊ *un bol de céréales* a bowl of cereal
♦ **un pain multicéréales** a multigrain loaf

la **cérémonie** NOUN
ceremony

le **cerf** NOUN
deer

le **cerf-volant** NOUN (PL les **cerfs-volants**)
kite

la **cerise** NOUN
cherry

le **cerisier** NOUN
cherry tree

cerné ADJECTIVE
♦ **avoir les yeux cernés** to have dark circles under one's eyes ◊ *Elle avait les yeux cernés.* She had dark circles under her eyes.

cerner VERB
♦ **J'ai du mal à le cerner.** I can't figure him out.

certain ADJECTIVE
① certain ◊ *Je suis certain que je l'ai remis en place.* I'm certain that I put it back. ◊ *Ce n'est pas certain.* It's not certain.
② some ◊ *Certaines personnes n'aiment pas la crème.* Some people don't like cream.
♦ **un certain temps** quite some time ◊ *J'ai mis un certain temps à comprendre ce qu'elle disait.* It took me quite some time to understand what she was saying.

certainement ADVERB
① definitely ◊ *C'est certainement le meilleur film que j'ai vu cette année.* It's definitely the best film I've seen this year.
② of course ◊ *« Est-ce que je peux t'emprunter ton stylo? » « Mais certainement! »* "Can I borrow your pen?" "Of course!"

certains PRONOUN
① some ◊ *certains de ses amis* some of his friends ◊ *certains d'entre vous* some of you
② some people ◊ *Certains pensent que le film est meilleur que le roman.* Some people think that the film is better than the novel.

certes ADVERB
certainly ◊ *Nous nous connaissons, certes, mais nous ne sommes pas amis.* We know each other, certainly, but we are not friends.

le **certificat** NOUN
certificate
♦ **le certificat-cadeau** gift certificate

le **cerveau** NOUN (PL les **cerveaux**)
brain

la **cervelle** NOUN
brain
♦ **se creuser la cervelle** (*informal*) to rack one's brains

ces ADJECTIVE
① these ◊ *Tu peux prendre ces photos si tu veux.* You can have these photos if you like.
♦ **ces photos-ci** these photos
② those ◊ *Ces montagnes sont dangereuses en hiver.* Those mountains are dangerous in winter.
♦ **ces livres-là** those books

cesse
♦ **sans cesse** ADVERB continually
♦ **Elle me dérange sans cesse.** She keeps interrupting me.

cesser VERB
to stop ◊ *cesser de faire quelque chose* to stop doing something

le **cessez-le-feu** NOUN (PL les **cessez-le-feu**)
ceasefire

c'est-à-dire ADVERB
that is ◊ *Est-ce que tu peux venir lundi prochain, c'est-à-dire le quinze?* Can you come next Monday, that is, the 15th?

cet ADJECTIVE (FEM SING **cette**)

> *ce* changes to **cet** before a vowel and most words beginning with "h".

① this ◊ *cet après-midi* this afternoon ◊ *cet hiver* this winter ◊ *cette année* this year
♦ **cette semaine-ci** this week
② that ◊ *Est-ce que tu peux me passer cette assiette?* Could you pass me that plate?
♦ **cet homme-là** that man
♦ **cette nuit (1)** tonight ◊ *On prévoit de l'orage pour cette nuit.* A storm is

☞

forecast for tonight.
♦ **cette nuit (2)** last night ◊ *J'ai très mal dormi cette nuit.* I slept very badly last night.

ceux PRONOUN (FEM PL **celles**)
the ones ◊ *Prends ceux que tu préfères.* Take the ones you like best. ◊ *Je n'ai pas de skis mais je peux emprunter ceux de ma sœur.* I don't have any skis but I can borrow my sister's. ◊ *Je n'ai pas de jumelles mais je peux emprunter celles de mon frère.* I don't have any binoculars but I can borrow my brother's.
♦ **ceux-ci** these ones
♦ **celles-ci** these ones
♦ **ceux-là** those ones
♦ **celles-là** those ones

chacun PRONOUN
① each ◊ *Il nous a donné un cadeau à chacun.* He gave us each a present. ◊ *Nous avons chacun donné dix dollars.* We each gave 10 dollars. ◊ *Ces verres coûtent cinq dollars chacun.* These glasses cost 5 dollars each.
② everyone ◊ *Chacun fait ce qu'il veut.* Everyone does what they like.

le **chagrin** NOUN
♦ **avoir du chagrin** to be very upset ◊ *Elle a eu beaucoup de chagrin à la mort de son oncle.* She was terribly upset by the death of her uncle.

le **chahut** NOUN
bedlam ◊ *Il y avait du chahut dans la classe.* There was bedlam in the classroom.

la **chaîne** NOUN
① chain ◊ *une chaîne en or* a gold chain
② channel (on TV) ◊ *Le film passe sur quelle chaîne?* What channel is the film on?
♦ **la chaîne alimentaire** food chain
♦ **une chaîne de montagnes** a mountain range
♦ **une chaîne stéréo** an audio system
♦ **travailler à la chaîne** to work on an assembly line

la **chair** NOUN
flesh
♦ **en chair et en os** in the flesh ◊ *Je l'ai vu en chair et en os.* I saw him in the flesh.
♦ **avoir la chair de poule** to have goose pimples

la **chaise** NOUN
chair
✹ ♦ **une chaise berçante** a rocking chair
♦ **une chaise longue** a lounge chair

la **chaleur** NOUN

① heat
② warmth

chaleureux ADJECTIVE (FEM SING **chaleureuse**)
warm ◊ *un accueil chaleureux* a warm welcome

✹ la **chaloupe** NOUN
rowboat ◊ *Les enfants sont partis en chaloupe.* The kids left in the rowboat.

se **chamailler** VERB (*informal*)
to squabble ◊ *Elle se chamaille sans cesse avec son frère.* She's always squabbling with her brother.

la **chambre** NOUN
room ◊ *C'est la chambre de ma sœur.* This is my sister's room.
♦ **une chambre à coucher** a bedroom
♦ **une chambre d'amis** a spare room
♦ **une chambre à un lit** a single room
♦ **une chambre pour une personne** a single room
♦ **une chambre pour deux personnes** a double room
♦ **la Chambre des communes** House of Commons

le **chameau** NOUN (PL les **chameaux**)
camel

le **champ** NOUN
field

le **champignon** NOUN
mushroom ◊ *une omelette aux champignons* a mushroom omelette

le **champion** NOUN
champion

le **championnat** NOUN
championship ◊ *le championnat du monde* the world championship

la **championne** NOUN
champion

la **chance** NOUN
① luck
♦ **Bonne chance!** Good luck!
♦ **par chance** luckily
♦ **avoir de la chance** to be lucky ◊ *Tu as de la chance de partir au soleil!* You're lucky, going off to a sunny place!
② chance ◊ *Il n'a aucune chance.* He doesn't have a chance. ◊ *Elle a des chances de réussir.* She has a good chance of passing.

le **chandail** NOUN
sweater ◊ *un chandail de laine* a wool sweater

le **change** NOUN
exchange ◊ *le taux de change* the exchange rate

le **changement** NOUN
change ◊ *Elle n'aime pas le changement.* She doesn't like change.

changer VERB
to change ◊ *Elle n'a pas beaucoup changé.* She hasn't changed much. ◊ *J'ai changé les draps ce matin.* I changed the sheets this morning. ◊ *J'ai changé trois cents dollars.* I changed 300 dollars.
♦ **se changer** to get changed ◊ *Je vais me changer avant de sortir.* I'm going to get changed before I go out.
♦ **changer de** to change ◊ *Je change de chaussures et j'arrive!* I'll change my shoes and then I'll be ready!
♦ **changer d'avis** to change one's mind ◊ *Appelle-moi si tu changes d'avis.* Call me if you change your mind.
♦ **changer de chaîne** to change the channel

la **chanson** NOUN
song

le **chant** NOUN
singing ◊ *des cours de chant* singing lessons
♦ **un chant de Noël** a Christmas carol

le **chantage** NOUN
blackmail ◊ *faire du chantage à quelqu'un* to blackmail somebody

chanter VERB
to sing

le **chanteur** NOUN
singer

la **chanteuse** NOUN
singer

le **chantier** NOUN
building site

la **Chantilly** NOUN
whipped cream

chantonner VERB
to hum

le **chapeau** NOUN (PL les **chapeaux**)
hat

le **chapitre** NOUN
chapter

chaque ADJECTIVE
1 every ◊ *chaque année* every year
2 each ◊ *Donne un livre à chaque élève.* Give a book to each student.

le **char** NOUN
tank (*military*)

le **charabia** NOUN (*informal*)
gibberish ◊ *Je n'y comprends rien : c'est du charabia.* I don't understand any of it: it's gibberish.

la **charade** NOUN
1 riddle
2 charade ◊ *jouer aux charades* to play charades

le **charbon** NOUN
coal
♦ **le charbon de bois** charcoal
♦ **être sur des charbons ardents** to be on pins and needles

la **charcuterie** NOUN
1 deli
2 cold cuts

le **chardon** NOUN
thistle

charger VERB
to load
♦ **charger quelqu'un de faire quelque chose** to tell somebody to do something ◊ *Il m'a chargé de vous dire que la clé est sous le paillasson.* He told me to tell you that the key's under the mat.

le **chariot** NOUN
shopping cart

charmant ADJECTIVE
charming

le **charme** NOUN
charm

charmer VERB
to charm

la **charrue** NOUN
plough

la **chasse** NOUN
hunting ◊ *un chien de chasse* a hunting dog ◊ *la chasse au canard* duck hunting
♦ **tirer la chasse d'eau** to flush the toilet

le **chasse-neige** NOUN (PL les **chasse-neige**)
snowplow

chasser VERB
1 to hunt ◊ *Mon père chasse le lapin.* My father hunts rabbits.
2 to chase away ◊ *Ils ont chassé les cambrioleurs.* They chased away the robbers.
3 to get rid of ◊ *Ouvre donc la fenêtre pour chasser les odeurs de cuisine.* Open the window to get rid of the cooking smells.

le **chasseur** NOUN
hunter

la **chasseuse** NOUN
hunter

le **chat** NOUN
cat

châtain ADJECTIVE (MASC, FEM, PL)
brown ◊ *J'ai les cheveux châtain.* I've got brown hair.

le **château** NOUN (PL les **châteaux**)
1 castle
♦ **un château fort** a castle
2 palace ◊ *le château de Versailles* the palace of Versailles

le **chaton** NOUN
kitten

chatouiller VERB
to tickle

chatouilleux ADJECTIVE (FEM SING **chatouilleuse**)
① ticklish
② touchy ◊ *Il est un peu chatouilleux sur cette question.* He's a bit touchy on that issue.

la **chatte** NOUN
cat (*female*)

chaud ADJECTIVE
① warm ◊ *des vêtements chauds* warm clothes
♦ **avoir chaud** to be warm or hot ◊ *J'ai assez chaud.* I'm warm enough.
② hot ◊ *Il fait chaud aujourd'hui.* It's hot today. ◊ *un plat chaud* a hot dish ◊ *Attention, c'est chaud!* Careful, it's hot! ◊ *J'ai trop chaud!* I'm too hot!

le **chauffage** NOUN
heating ◊ *Le chauffage est en panne.* The heating isn't working. ◊ *Baisse le chauffage.* Turn down the heat.
♦ **le chauffage central** central heating

le **chauffe-eau** NOUN (PL les **chauffe-eau**)
water heater

chauffer VERB
to heat ◊ *Je vais mettre de l'eau à chauffer pour faire du thé.* I'm going to put some water on to make tea.

le **chauffeur** NOUN
driver ◊ *un chauffeur de taxi* a taxi driver

la **chauffeuse** NOUN
driver ◊ *une chauffeuse d'autobus* a bus driver

la **chaussée** NOUN
roadway ◊ *Ne fais pas de la planche à roulettes sur la chaussée.* Don't skateboard on the road.

chausser VERB
♦ **Vous chaussez du combien?** What size shoe do you take?

la **chaussette** NOUN
sock

le **chausson** NOUN
slipper
♦ **un chausson aux pommes** an apple turnover

la **chaussure** NOUN
shoe
♦ **les chaussures de ski** ski boots

chauve ADJECTIVE
bald

la **chauve-souris** NOUN (PL les **chauves-souris**)
bat (*animal*)

le/la **chef** NOUN
① head ◊ *une chef de famille monoparentale* a single parent
♦ **le chef de l'État** the Head of State
♦ **un chef d'entreprise** the director of a company
② chef ◊ *la spécialité de la chef* the chef's specialty
♦ **un chef d'orchestre** a conductor
⚹ ♦ **le chef de bande** band chief

le **chef-d'œuvre** NOUN (PL les **chefs-d'œuvre**)
masterpiece

le **chemin** NOUN
① path ◊ *Je suis descendu à la plage par un petit chemin.* I took a little path down to the beach.
② way ◊ *Quel est le chemin le plus court pour aller à l'aéroport?* What's the quickest way to the airport?
♦ **en chemin** on the way ◊ *Je mangerai mon sandwich en chemin.* I'll eat my sandwich on the way.
♦ **le chemin de fer** the railway

la **cheminée** NOUN
① chimney
② fireplace

la **chemise** NOUN
① shirt ◊ *une chemise à carreaux* a checked shirt
♦ **une chemise de nuit** a nightgown
② folder

le **chemisier** NOUN
blouse

le **chêne** NOUN
oak ◊ *une armoire en chêne* an oak wardrobe

le **chenil** NOUN
kennels

la **chenille** NOUN
caterpillar

le **chèque** NOUN
cheque
♦ **les chèques de voyage** traveller's cheques

le **chéquier** NOUN
chequebook

cher ADJECTIVE, ADVERB (FEM SING **chère**)
① dear ◊ *Chère Madame...* Dear Madam...
② expensive ◊ *C'est trop cher.* It's too expensive. ◊ *coûter cher* to be expensive

chercher VERB
① to look for ◊ *Je cherche mes clés.* I'm looking for my keys.
② to look up ◊ *chercher un mot dans le dictionnaire* to look up a word in

the dictionary
- **aller chercher (1)** to go to get ◊ *Il est allé chercher du pain pour ce midi.* He's gone to get some bread for lunch.
- **aller chercher (2)** to pick up ◊ *J'irai te chercher à la bibliothèque.* I'll pick you up at the library.

le **chercheur** NOUN
　researcher

la **chercheuse** NOUN
　researcher

　chère ADJECTIVE *see* **cher**

　chéri ADJECTIVE

　　| *see also* **chéri** NOUN |

　darling ◊ *ma petite fille chérie* my darling daughter

le **chéri** NOUN

　　| *see also* **chéri** ADJECTIVE |

　darling
- **mon chéri** darling

la **chérie** NOUN
　darling
- **ma chérie** darling

le **cheval** NOUN (PL les **chevaux**)
　horse ◊ *un cheval de course* a racehorse
- **à cheval** on horseback
- **faire du cheval** to go riding

le **chevalier** NOUN
　knight

les **chevaux** MASC NOUN *see* **cheval**

le **chevet** NOUN
- **une table de chevet** a bedside table
- **une lampe de chevet** a bedside lamp

les **cheveux** MASC NOUN
　hair SING ◊ *Elle a les cheveux courts.* She has short hair.
- **tiré par les cheveux** far-fetched ◊ *Son excuse était complètement tirée par les cheveux.* His excuse was totally far-fetched.

la **cheville** NOUN
　ankle ◊ *se fouler la cheville* to sprain one's ankle

la **chèvre** NOUN
　goat
- **le fromage de chèvre** goat cheese

le **chevreau** NOUN (PL les **chevreaux**)
　kid (*animal, leather*)

le **chevreuil** NOUN
　① deer
　② venison

chez PREPOSITION
- **chez mon ami (1)** at my friend's house
- **chez mon ami (2)** to my friend's

house
- **chez moi (1)** at my house ◊ *Je suis resté chez moi cette fin de semaine.* I stayed home this weekend.
- **chez moi (2)** to my house ◊ *Je vais rentrer chez moi.* I'm going home.
- **chez le dentiste (1)** at the dentist's ◊ *J'ai rendez-vous chez le dentiste demain matin.* I've got an appointment at the dentist's tomorrow morning.
- **chez le dentiste (2)** to the dentist's ◊ *Je vais chez le dentiste.* I'm going to the dentist's.

chic ADJECTIVE (MASC, FEM, PL)
　① smart ◊ *une tenue chic* a smart outfit
　② nice ◊ *C'est chic de sa part.* (*informal*) That was nice of her.

le **chien** NOUN
　dog
- **« Attention, chien méchant »** "Beware of dog"

la **chienne** NOUN
　bitch (*dog*)

le **chiffon** NOUN
　cloth (*cleaning, polishing*)

　chiffonner VERB
　to crease ◊ *Ma robe est toute chiffonnée.* My dress is all creased.

le **chiffre** NOUN
　figure ◊ *en chiffres ronds* in round figures
- **les chiffres romains** Roman numerals

le **chignon** NOUN
　bun (*hair*) ◊ *Elle s'est fait un chignon.* She put her hair in a bun.

la **chimie** NOUN
　chemistry ◊ *un cours de chimie* a chemistry lesson

　chimique ADJECTIVE
　chemical ◊ *une réaction chimique* a chemical reaction
- **les armes chimiques** chemical weapons
- **les produits chimiques** chemicals

🦌 le **chinook** NOUN
　chinook (*warm wind*) ◊ *Un coup de chinook peut faire fondre trente centimètres de neige en une heure.* A chinook can melt 30 centimetres of snow in one hour.

le **chiot** NOUN
　puppy

　chirurgical ADJECTIVE (MASC PL **chirurgicaux**)
- **une intervention chirurgicale** an operation

la **chirurgie** NOUN

☞

surgery
♦ **la chirurgie esthétique** plastic surgery

le **chirurgien** NOUN
surgeon

la **chirurgienne** NOUN
surgeon

le **choc** NOUN
shock ◊ *Ça m'a fait un choc de le voir comme ça.* It gave me a shock to see him in that state.
♦ **Elle est encore sous le choc.** She's still in shock.

le **chocolat** NOUN
chocolate
♦ **un chocolat chaud** a hot chocolate
♦ **le chocolat noir** dark chocolate

choisir VERB
to choose

le **choix** NOUN
1 choice
♦ **avoir le choix** to have the choice
2 selection ◊ *Il n'y a pas beaucoup de choix dans ce magasin.* There's not a very wide selection in this store.

le **chômage** NOUN
unemployment
♦ **être au chômage** to be unemployed

le **chômeur** NOUN
unemployed person ◊ *Il est chômeur.* He's unemployed.

la **chômeuse** NOUN
unemployed woman ◊ *Elle est chômeuse.* She's unemployed.

choquer VERB
to shock ◊ *Cette remarque m'a choqué.* I was shocked by that remark.

la **chorale** NOUN
choir

la **chose** NOUN
thing ◊ *J'ai fait des choses intéressantes pendant les vacances.* I did some interesting things during the holidays.
♦ **C'est peu de chose.** It's nothing really.

le **chou** NOUN (PL les **choux**)
cabbage
♦ **les choux de Bruxelles** Brussels sprouts
♦ **un chou à la crème** a cream puff

le **chouchou** NOUN (*informal*)
teacher's pet

la **chouchoute** NOUN (*informal*)
teacher's pet

la **choucroute** NOUN
sauerkraut (*with sausages and ham*)

la **chouette** NOUN

see also **chouette** ADJECTIVE

1 owl
2 dear (*to young girl*) (*informal*)
◊ *Oui, ma chouette!* Yes, my dear!

chouette ADJECTIVE (*informal*)

see also **chouette** NOUN

interesting ◊ *un jeu très chouette* a very interesting game

le **chou-fleur** NOUN (PL les **choux-fleurs**)
cauliflower

chrétien ADJECTIVE (FEM SING **chrétienne**)
Christian ◊ *Il est chrétien.* He's a Christian.

chronique ADJECTIVE
chronic ◊ *une toux chronique* a chronic cough

la **chronique** NOUN
column ◊ *Il écrit une chronique pour le journal de l'école.* He writes a column for the school newspaper.

chronologique ADJECTIVE
chronological

le **chronomètre** NOUN
stopwatch

chronométrer VERB
to time

chuchoter VERB
to whisper

chut EXCLAMATION
Shh!

la **chute** NOUN
fall
♦ **faire une chute** to fall
♦ **les chutes Niagara** Niagara Falls
♦ **une chute d'eau** a waterfall

-ci ADVERB
♦ **ce livre-ci** this book
♦ **ces bottes-ci** these boots

la **cible** NOUN
target

la **ciboulette** NOUN
chives

la **cicatrice** NOUN
scar

se **cicatriser** VERB
to heal up ◊ *Cette plaie s'est vite cicatrisée.* This wound has healed up quickly.

ci-contre ADVERB
opposite ◊ *la page ci-contre* the opposite page

ci-dessous ADVERB
below ◊ *la photo ci-dessous* the picture below

ci-dessus ADVERB
above

le **cidre** NOUN

cider

le **ciel** NOUN
    ① sky ◊ *un ciel nuageux* a cloudy sky
    ② heaven ◊ *être au ciel* to be in
    heaven

le **cierge** NOUN
    candle (*in church*)

la **cigale** NOUN
    cricket

le **cigare** NOUN
    cigar ◊ *Il ne fume plus le cigare.* He
    no longer smokes cigars.

la **cigarette** NOUN
    cigarette

ci-joint ADVERB
    enclosed ◊ *Veuillez trouver ci-joint*
    mon curriculum vitæ. Please find
    enclosed my résumé.

le **cil** NOUN
    eyelash

le **ciment** NOUN
    cement

le **cimetière** NOUN
    cemetery

le/la **cinéaste** NOUN
    filmmaker

le **cinéma** NOUN
    movie theatre

cinq NUMBER
    five ◊ *Il est cinq heures du matin.* It's
    five in the morning. ◊ *Elle a cinq ans.*
    She's five.
    ♦ **le cinq février** the fifth of February

la **cinquantaine** NOUN
    about fifty ◊ *Il y avait une*
    cinquantaine de personnes. There
    were about fifty people there.
    ♦ **Il a la cinquantaine.** He's in his fifties.

cinquante NUMBER
    fifty ◊ *Elle a cinquante ans.* She's fifty.
    ♦ **cinquante et un** fifty-one
    ♦ **cinquante-deux** fifty-two

cinquième ADJECTIVE

    | see also **cinquième** NOUN |

    fifth ◊ *au cinquième étage* on the fifth
    floor ◊ *Mon frère est en cinquième*
    année. My brother is in Grade 5.

le **cintre** NOUN
    coat hanger

le **cirage** NOUN
    shoe polish

circonflexe ADJECTIVE
    ♦ **un accent circonflexe** a circumflex

la **circonstance** NOUN
    circumstance ◊ *dans les*
    circonstances actuelles in the present

circumstances

la **circulation** NOUN
    ① traffic ◊ *Il y avait beaucoup de*
    circulation. There was a lot of traffic.
    ② circulation ◊ *Elle a des problèmes*
    de circulation. She has bad
    circulation.

circuler VERB
    to run ◊ *Il n'y a qu'un autobus sur*
    trois qui circule. Only one bus in three
    is running.

la **cire** NOUN
    wax

cirer VERB
    to polish (*shoes, floor*)
    ♦ **papier ciré** waxed paper

le **cirque** NOUN
    circus

les **ciseaux** MASC NOUN
    ♦ **une paire de ciseaux** a pair of scissors

le **citadin** NOUN
    city person

la **citation** NOUN
    quotation

la **cité** NOUN
    town ◊ *une cité industrielle* an
    industrial town

    Be careful not to translate the French
    word cité as city.

    ♦ **une cité universitaire** a university
    campus
    ♦ **la cité parlementaire** Parliament
    buildings (in Québec city)

citer VERB
    to quote

le **citoyen** NOUN
    citizen

la **citoyenne** NOUN
    citizen

la **citoyenneté** NOUN
    citizenship

le **citron** NOUN
    lemon

la **citrouille** NOUN
    pumpkin

la **civière** NOUN
    stretcher

civil ADJECTIVE
    civilian
    ♦ **en civil** in civilian clothes

la **civilisation** NOUN
    civilization

civique ADJECTIVE
    ① civic ◊ *son devoir civique* one's
    civic duty
    ② civil ◊ *les droits civiques* civil

rights
♦ **avoir le sens civique** to be public-spirited

clair ADJECTIVE, ADVERB
1 light ◊ *vert clair* light green ◊ *C'est une pièce très claire.* It's a very bright room.
2 clear (*water*)
♦ **voir clair** to see clearly
♦ **le clair de lune** moonlight

clairement ADVERB
clearly

la **clairière** NOUN
clearing

clandestin ADJECTIVE
♦ **un passager clandestin** a stowaway

la **claque** NOUN
slap

claquer VERB
1 to bang ◊ *On entend des volets qui claquent.* You can hear shutters banging.
2 to slam ◊ *Elle est partie en claquant la porte.* She left, slamming the door behind her.

la **claquette** FEM NOUN
♦ **danser la claquette** to tap-dance

la **clarinette** NOUN
clarinet

la **classe** NOUN
1 class ◊ *C'est le meilleur élève de la classe.* He's the best student in the class. ◊ *voyager en première classe* to travel first class
2 classroom

classer VERB
to arrange ◊ *Les livres sont classés par ordre alphabétique.* The books are arranged in alphabetical order.

le **classeur** NOUN
filing cabinet

classique ADJECTIVE
1 classical ◊ *de la musique classique* classical music
2 classic ◊ *un style classique* a classic style

le **clavardage** NOUN
chat (*online*)

clavarder VERB
to chat (*online*)

le **clavardoir** NOUN
chat room

le **clavier** NOUN
keyboard (*computer, typewriter*)
♦ **le clavier numérique** keypad

la **clé** NOUN
1 key ◊ *une clé de voiture* a car key
2 clef ◊ *la clé de sol* the treble clef

◊ *la clé de fa* the bass clef
♦ **une clé anglaise** a wrench

la **clef** NOUN = **clé**

le **clic** NOUN
click (*computer mouse*)

le **client** NOUN
customer

la **cliente** NOUN
customer

la **clientèle** NOUN
customers

cligner VERB
♦ **cligner des yeux** to blink

le **clignotant** NOUN
turn signal ◊ *Il a mis son clignotant gauche.* He's signalling left.

le **climat** NOUN
climate

la **climatisation** NOUN
air conditioning

climatisé ADJECTIVE
air-conditioned ◊ *L'hôtel est climatisé.* The hotel is air-conditioned.

le **clin d'œil** NOUN (PL les **clins d'œil**)
wink
♦ **en un clin d'œil** in a flash

la **clinique** NOUN
clinic

le **clipart** NOUN
clip-art

cliquer VERB
to click ◊ *cliquer sur une icône* to click on an icon

le **clochard** NOUN
tramp

la **cloche** NOUN
bell

le **clone** NOUN
clone

cloner VERB
to clone

le **clou** NOUN
nail
♦ **un clou de girofle** a clove

le/la **clown** NOUN
clown

✻ le **CLSC** NOUN (= *Centre local de services communautaires*)

> ❶ The **CLSC**, known as a **local community service centre** in English, is a public institution found in Québec communities. It provides social and health services.

le **club** NOUN

club

le **cobaye** NOUN
  guinea pig

la **cocaïne** NOUN
  cocaine

la **coccinelle** NOUN
  ladybug

cocher VERB
  to mark with a check ◊ *Cochez la bonne réponse.* Put a check beside the right answer.

le **cochon** NOUN
  pig
  ♦ **un cochon d'Inde** a guinea pig

le **coco** NOUN
  ♦ **une noix de coco** a coconut

la **cocotte** NOUN
  casserole (*pan*)

le **code** NOUN
  code
  ♦ **le code à barres** barcode
  ♦ **le code postal** the postal code

le **cœur** NOUN
  heart
  ♦ **avoir bon cœur** to be kind-hearted
  ♦ **la dame de cœur** the queen of hearts
  ♦ **avoir mal au cœur** to feel sick
  ♦ **par cœur** by heart ◊ *apprendre quelque chose par cœur* to learn something by heart

le **coffre** NOUN
  ① trunk (*of car*)
  ② chest (*furniture*)

le **coffre-fort** NOUN (PL les **coffres-forts**)
  safe

le **coffret** NOUN
  ♦ **un coffret à bijoux** a jewellery box

se **cogner** VERB
  ♦ **se cogner à quelque chose** to bump into something ◊ *Je me suis cogné à la table.* I bumped into the table. ◊ *Je me suis cogné la tête contre la porte du placard.* I bumped my head on the cupboard door.

coiffé ADJECTIVE
  ♦ **Tu es bien coiffée.** Your hair looks nice.

coiffer VERB
  ♦ **se coiffer** to do one's hair

le **coiffeur** NOUN
  hairdresser

la **coiffeuse** NOUN
  hairdresser

la **coiffure** NOUN
  hairstyle ◊ *Cette coiffure te va bien.* That hairstyle suits you.
  ♦ **un salon de coiffure** a hair salon

le **coin** NOUN
  corner
  ♦ **au coin de la rue** on the corner of the street
  ♦ **Tu habites dans le coin?** Do you live around here?
  ♦ **le dépanneur du coin** the local convenience store

coincé ADJECTIVE
  ① stuck ◊ *La clé est coincée dans la serrure.* The key is stuck in the lock.
  ② stuffy ◊ *Il est un peu coincé.* (*informal*) He's a bit stuffy.

coincer VERB
  to jam ◊ *La porte est coincée.* The door's jammed.

la **coïncidence** NOUN
  coincidence

le **col** NOUN
  ① collar
  ♦ **un col roulé** a turtleneck
  ② pass (*mountain*)

la **colère** NOUN
  anger
  ♦ **Je suis en colère.** I'm angry.
  ♦ **se mettre en colère** to get angry

la **colique** NOUN
  stomach pain

le **colis** NOUN
  parcel

collaborer VERB
  to collaborate

collant ADJECTIVE

  see also **collant** NOUN

  ① sticky
  ② clingy
  ♦ **Je la trouve un peu collante.** (*informal*) She's always hanging around me.

le **collant** NOUN

  see also **collant** ADJECTIVE

  tights ◊ *un collant en laine* woollen tights

la **collation** NOUN
  snack

la **colle** NOUN
  glue ◊ *un tube de colle* a tube of glue
  ♦ **Je n'en sais rien : tu me poses une colle.** (*informal*) I really don't know: you've got me there.

la **collecte** NOUN
  collection (*of money*) ◊ *On a fait une collecte au profit des victimes.* There was a collection for the victims.
  ♦ **une collecte de bouteilles vides** a bottle drive

la **collection** NOUN
  collection ◊ *une collection de*

timbres a stamp collection

collectionner VERB
to collect

le **collège** NOUN
college

✹ ♦ **collège communautaire** community
college

le **collégien** NOUN
student

la **collégienne** NOUN
student

le/la **collègue** NOUN
colleague

coller VERB
① to stick ◊ *Il y a de la gomme à
mâcher collée sous la chaise.* There's
a wad of chewing gum stuck under
the chair.
② to be sticky ◊ *Ce ruban ne colle
plus.* This tape is no longer sticky.
③ to press ◊ *J'ai collé mon oreille au
mur pour écouter.* I pressed my ear
against the wall to listen.

le **collier** NOUN
① necklace ◊ *un collier de perles* a
pearl necklace
② collar (*of dog, cat*)

la **colline** NOUN
hill
♦ **la Colline du Parlement** Parliament
Hill (in Ottawa)

la **collision** NOUN
crash

la **colombe** NOUN
dove

la **Colombie-Britannique** NOUN
British Columbia

la **colonie** NOUN
colony ◊ *la colonie de la Nouvelle
France* the colony of New France

la **colonne** NOUN
pillar
♦ **la colonne vertébrale** the spine

le **colorant** NOUN
① colouring
② dye

le **coma** NOUN
coma ◊ *être dans le coma* to be in a
coma

le **combat** NOUN
fighting ◊ *Les combats ont repris
ce matin.* Fighting started again this
morning.
♦ **un combat de boxe** a boxing match

le **combattant** NOUN
♦ **un ancien combattant** a war veteran

combattre VERB

to fight

combien ADVERB
① how much ◊ *Vous en voulez
combien? Un kilo?* How much do you
want? One kilo?
♦ **C'est combien?** How much is that?
◊ *Combien est-ce que ça coûte?* How
much does it cost? ◊ *Combien ça fait?*
How much does it come to?
② how many ◊ *Tu en veux combien?
Deux?* How many do you want? Two?
♦ **combien de (1)** how much ◊ *Combien
de purée de pomme de terre est-ce
que je vous sers?* How much mashed
potato shall I give you?
♦ **combien de (2)** how many ◊ *Combien
de personnes as-tu invitées?* How
many people have you invited?
♦ **combien de temps** how long
◊ *Combien de temps est-ce que tu
seras absente?* How long will you be
away?
♦ **Il y a combien de temps?** How long
ago? ◊ *Il est parti il y a combien de
temps?* How long ago did he leave?
♦ **« On est le combien aujourd'hui? »
« On est le vingt. »** "What's the date
today?" "It's the 20th."

la **combinaison** NOUN
combination ◊ *J'ai changé la
combinaison de mon antivol.* I've
changed the combination on my bike
lock.
♦ **une combinaison de plongée** a
wetsuit
♦ **une combinaison de ski** a ski suit

la **comédie** NOUN
comedy
♦ **une comédie musicale** a musical

le **comédien** NOUN
actor

la **comédienne** NOUN
actress

comestible ADJECTIVE
edible

comique ADJECTIVE
⎡ see also **comique** NOUN ⎤
comical

le/la **comique** NOUN
⎡ see also **comique** ADJECTIVE ⎤
comedian

le **comité** NOUN
committee

le **commandant** NOUN
captain (*ship, plane*)

la **commandante** NOUN
captain (*ship, plane*)

la **commande** NOUN

order ◊ *un bon de commande* an order form
♦ **être aux commandes** to be at the controls

commander VERB
① to order ◊ *J'ai commandé une robe par catalogue.* I've ordered a dress from the catalogue.
② to give orders ◊ *C'est moi qui commande ici, pas vous!* I give the orders here, not you!
♦ **Elle commande le respect.** She commands respect.

comme CONJUNCTION, ADVERB
① like ◊ *Elle est comme son père.* She's like her father. ◊ *Je voudrais un manteau comme celui de la photo.* I'd like a coat like the one in the picture.
② for ◊ *Qu'est-ce que tu veux comme dessert?* What would you like for dessert?
③ as ◊ *J'ai travaillé comme serveuse cet été.* I worked as a waitress this summer. ◊ *Faites comme bon vous semble.* Do as you like.
♦ **comme ça** like this ◊ *Ça se plie comme ça.* You fold it like this. ◊ *C'était un poisson grand comme ça.* The fish was this big.
♦ **comme il faut** properly ◊ *Mets le couvert comme il faut!* Set the table properly!
♦ **Comme tu as grandi!** How you've grown!
♦ **Regarde comme c'est beau!** Look, isn't it lovely!
♦ **comme ci comme ça** so-so ◊ *« Comment est-ce que tu as trouvé le film? » « Comme ci comme ça. »* "What did you think of the film?" "So-so."

le **commencement** NOUN
beginning

commencer VERB
to start ◊ *Les cours commencent à huit heures.* Classes start at 8 o'clock. ◊ *Il a commencé à pleuvoir.* It started raining. ◊ *J'ai commencé de réviser pour les examens.* I've started studying for the exams.

comment ADVERB
how ◊ *Comment arrives-tu à travailler dans ce bruit?* How can you possibly work with this noise?
♦ **Comment allez-vous?** How are you?
♦ **Comment dit-on « pomme » en anglais?** How do you say "pomme" in English?
♦ **Comment s'appelle-t-elle?** What's her name?
♦ **Comment?** What did you say?

le **commentaire** NOUN

comment

les **commérages** MASC NOUN
gossip SING

le **commerçant** NOUN
storekeeper

la **commerçante** NOUN
storekeeper

le **commerce** NOUN
① trade ◊ *le commerce extérieur* foreign trade
♦ **le commerce électronique** e-commerce
② business ◊ *Il fait des études de commerce.* He's studying business. ◊ *tenir un commerce* to have a business

commercial ADJECTIVE (MASC PL **commerciaux**)
♦ **un centre commercial** a shopping centre

commettre VERB
to commit ◊ *Elle a commis un crime grave.* She has committed a serious crime.

les **commissions** FEM NOUN
errands ◊ *J'ai quelques commissions à faire.* I've got some errands to run.

commode ADJECTIVE

see also **commode** NOUN

handy ◊ *Ce sac est très commode pour les voyages.* This bag is very handy for travelling.
♦ **Son père n'est pas commode.** His father is a difficult character.

la **commode** NOUN

see also **commode** ADJECTIVE

dresser

commun ADJECTIVE
shared ◊ *une salle de bain commune* a shared bathroom ◊ *Nous avons des intérêts communs.* We have interests in common.
♦ **en commun** in common ◊ *Ils n'ont rien en commun.* They have nothing in common.
♦ **les transports en commun** public transport
♦ **mettre quelque chose en commun** to share something ◊ *Nous mettons tous nos livres en commun.* We share all our books.

la **communauté** NOUN
community

la **communication** NOUN
communication
♦ **une communication scientifique** a scientific conference

communiquer VERB

to communicate

communiste ADJECTIVE
communist ◊ *le Parti communiste*
the Communist Party

compact ADJECTIVE
compact
♦ **un disque compact** a compact disc

la **compagne** NOUN
① companion
② partner (*living together*)

la **compagnie** NOUN
company ◊ *J'aime avoir de la
compagnie.* I like to have company.
◊ *Je viendrai te tenir compagnie.* I'll
come and keep you company.
♦ **une compagnie d'assurances** an
insurance company
♦ **une compagnie aérienne** an airline

le **compagnon** NOUN
① companion
② partner (*living together*)

la **comparaison** NOUN
comparison ◊ *en comparaison de* in
comparison with

comparer VERB
to compare

le **compartiment** NOUN
compartment

le **compas** NOUN
compass (*for drawing circles*)

compatible ADJECTIVE
compatible

la **compétence** NOUN
① skill ◊ *compétences de vie* life
skills
② competence

compétent ADJECTIVE
competent

compétitif ADJECTIVE (FEM SING
compétitive)
competitive

la **compétition** NOUN
competition
♦ **avoir l'esprit de compétition** to be
competitive

complet ADJECTIVE (FEM SING **complète**)

see also **complet** NOUN

① complete ◊ *les œuvres complètes
de Shakespeare* the complete works
of Shakespeare
② full ◊ *L'hôtel est complet.* The hotel
is full.
♦ **« complet »** "no vacancies"

le **complet** NOUN

see also **complet** ADJECTIVE

suit (*men's*)

complètement ADVERB

completely ◊ *J'avais complètement
oublié que tu venais.* I'd completely
forgotten that you were coming.

compléter VERB
to complete ◊ *Complétez les phrases
suivantes.* Complete the following
sentences.

complexe ADJECTIVE
complex

la **complication** NOUN
complication

le/la **complice** NOUN
accomplice

les **compliments** MASC NOUN
compliment SING
♦ **faire des compliments** to compliment
◊ *Il m'a fait des compliments sur ma
robe.* He complimented me on my
dress.

compliqué ADJECTIVE
complicated ◊ *C'est une histoire
compliquée.* It's a complicated story.

le **complot** NOUN
plot (*conspiracy*)

le **comportement** NOUN
behaviour

comporter VERB
① to consist of ◊ *Le château
comporte trois parties.* The castle
consists of three parts.
② to have (*as a part*) ◊ *Ce modèle
comporte un écran couleur.* This
model has a colour screen.
♦ **se comporter** to behave ◊ *Elle s'est
comportée de façon odieuse.* She
behaved atrociously.

composer VERB
to compose (*music, text*)
♦ **composer un numéro** to dial a
number
♦ **se composer de** to consist of
◊ *L'uniforme se compose d'une veste,
d'un pantalon et d'une cravate.* The
uniform consists of a jacket, pants,
and a tie.

le **compositeur** NOUN
composer

la **composition** NOUN
composition (*music, writing*)

la **compositrice** NOUN
composer

le **compostage** NOUN
composting

composter VERB
to compost

la **compote** NOUN
stewed fruit
♦ **la compote de prunes** stewed plums

compréhensible ADJECTIVE
understandable

compréhensif ADJECTIVE (FEM SING
compréhensive)
understanding

> Be careful! **compréhensif** does not
> mean **comprehensive**.

la **compréhension** NOUN
1 comprehension ◊ la
compréhension orale listening
comprehension
2 sympathy
♦ **Elle a fait preuve de beaucoup
de compréhension.** She was very
sympathetic.

comprendre VERB
1 to understand ◊ Je ne comprends
pas ce que vous dites. I don't
understand what you're saying.
2 to include ◊ Le forfait ne
comprend pas la location des skis.
The package doesn't include ski
rental.

compris ADJECTIVE
included ◊ Le service n'est pas
compris. Service is not included.
♦ **y compris** including ◊ Ils ont tout
vendu, y compris leur voiture. They
sold everything, including their car.
♦ **non compris** excluding ◊ vingt
dollars, frais de livraison non compris
20 dollars, excluding delivery charges
♦ **cent dollars tout compris** 100 dollars
all-inclusive

compromettre VERB
to compromise

le **compromis** NOUN
compromise ◊ Ils sont parvenus
à un compromis. They came to a
compromise.

la **comptabilité** NOUN
accounting ◊ un cours de
comptabilité a course in accounting

le/la **comptable** NOUN
accountant ◊ Elle est comptable.
She's an accountant.

comptant ADVERB
♦ **payer comptant** to pay cash

le **compte** NOUN
1 account ◊ J'ai déposé le chèque
dans mon compte. I've deposited the
cheque into my account.
2 bill ◊ le compte d'électricité
electricity bill ◊ le compte de
téléphone telephone bill
♦ **Le compte est bon.** That's the right
amount.
♦ **tenir compte de (1)** to take into
account ◊ Ils ont tenu compte de mon

expérience. They took my experience
into account.
♦ **tenir compte de (2)** to pay attention
to ◊ Il n'a pas tenu compte de mes
conseils. He paid no attention to my
advice.
♦ **travailler à son compte** to be self-
employed
♦ **en fin de compte** all things
considered ◊ Le voyage ne s'est pas
mal passé, en fin de compte. The trip
wasn't bad, all things considered.

compter VERB
to count

le **compte rendu** NOUN (PL les **comptes
rendus**)
report

le **compteur** NOUN
meter

le **comptoir** NOUN
counter ◊ au comptoir at the counter

se **concentrer** VERB
to concentrate ◊ J'ai du mal à
me concentrer. I'm having trouble
concentrating.

la **conception** NOUN
design

concernant PREPOSITION
regarding ◊ Concernant notre
nouveau projet, je voudrais ajouter
que... Regarding our new project, I
would like to add that...

concerner VERB
to concern ◊ en ce qui me concerne
as far as I'm concerned
♦ **Je ne me sens pas concerné.** I figure
it has nothing to do with me.

le **concert** NOUN
concert

le/la **concierge** NOUN
caretaker

conclure VERB
to conclude

la **conclusion** NOUN
conclusion

le **concombre** NOUN
cucumber

concorder VERB
to match (agree) ◊ Les dates
concordent. The dates match.

le **concours** NOUN
1 competition ◊ un concours de
chant a singing competition
2 contest

concret ADJECTIVE (FEM SING **concrète**)
concrete

conçu VERB
designed ◊ Ces appartements sont

très mal conçus. These apartments are very badly designed.

la **concurrence** NOUN
competition ◊ *La concurrence est vive sur ce marché.* There's a lot of competition in this market.

le **concurrent** NOUN
competitor

la **concurrente** NOUN
competitor

condamner VERB
[1] to sentence ◊ *Il a été condamné à deux ans de prison.* He was sentenced to two years in prison. ◊ *condamner à mort* to sentence to death
[2] to condemn ◊ *Le gouvernement a condamné cette décision.* The government condemned this decision.

la **condition** NOUN
condition ◊ *Je le ferai à une condition...* I'll do it, on one condition...
♦ **à condition que** provided that ◊ *Je viendrai à condition qu'elle me le demande.* I'll come provided she asks me to.
♦ **les conditions de vie** living conditions

le **conditionnel** NOUN
conditional tense

les **condoléances** FEM NOUN
sympathy SING ◊ *Veuillez accepter mes plus sincères condoléances.* Please accept my sincere sympathy.

le **condom** NOUN
condom

le **conducteur** NOUN
driver

la **conductrice** NOUN
driver

conduire VERB
to drive ◊ *Est-ce que tu sais conduire?* Can you drive? ◊ *Je te conduirai chez le docteur.* I'll drive you to the doctor's.
♦ **se conduire** to behave ◊ *Il s'est mal conduit.* He behaved badly.

la **conduite** NOUN
behaviour
♦ **la conduite en état d'ivresse** impaired driving

la **confédération** NOUN
confederation ◊ *Le Canada est une confédération.* Canada is a confederation.
🍁 ♦ **la Confédération** Confederation

la **conférence** NOUN
[1] lecture ◊ *donner une conférence* to give a lecture
[2] conference ◊ *une conférence internationale* an international conference

le **confetti** MASC NOUN
confetti

la **confiance** NOUN
[1] trust
♦ **avoir confiance en quelqu'un** to trust somebody ◊ *Je n'ai pas confiance en lui.* I don't trust him.
[2] confidence
♦ **Tu peux avoir confiance. Il sera à l'heure.** You don't need to worry. He'll be on time.
♦ **confiance en soi** self-confidence ◊ *Elle manque de confiance en elle.* She lacks self-confidence.

confiant ADJECTIVE
confident

les **confidences** FEM NOUN
♦ **faire des confidences à quelqu'un** to confide in someone ◊ *Elle me fait quelquefois des confidences.* She sometimes confides in me.

confidentiel ADJECTIVE (FEM SING **confidentielle**)
confidential

confier VERB
♦ **se confier à quelqu'un** to confide in somebody ◊ *Il s'est confié à son meilleur ami.* He confided in his best friend.

confirmer VERB
to confirm

la **confiserie** NOUN
candy store

confisquer VERB
to confiscate

la **confiture** NOUN
jam ◊ *la confiture de fraises* strawberry jam

le **conflit** NOUN
conflict

confondre VERB
to mix up ◊ *On la confond souvent avec sa sœur.* People often get her mixed up with her sister.

le **confort** NOUN
comfort
♦ **tout confort** luxurious ◊ *un appartement tout confort* a luxurious apartment

confortable ADJECTIVE
comfortable ◊ *des chaussures confortables* comfortable shoes

confus ADJECTIVE
[1] unclear ◊ *J'ai trouvé ses*

explications confuses. I thought his explanation was unclear.
② embarrassed ◊ *Il avait l'air confus.* He looked embarrassed.

la **confusion** NOUN
① confusion
② embarrassment ◊ *rougir de confusion* to blush with embarrassment

le **congé** NOUN
① holiday ◊ *une semaine de congé* a week off
♦ **en congé** on holiday ◊ *Je serai en congé la semaine prochaine.* I'll be on holiday next week.
② leave ◊ *être en congé de maladie* to be on sick leave ◊ *congé de maternité* maternity leave

le **congélateur** NOUN
freezer

congeler VERB
to freeze

la **conjonction** NOUN
conjunction

la **conjugaison** NOUN
conjugation

la **connaissance** NOUN
① knowledge ◊ *pour approfondir vos connaissances* to increase your knowledge
② acquaintance ◊ *Ce n'est pas vraiment une amie, juste une connaissance.* She's not really a friend, just an acquaintance.
♦ **perdre connaissance** to lose consciousness
♦ **faire la connaissance de quelqu'un** to meet somebody ◊ *J'ai fait la connaissance de sa mère.* I met her mother.

connaître VERB
to know ◊ *Je ne connais pas du tout cette région.* I don't know this area at all. ◊ *Je le connais de vue.* I know him by sight.
♦ **Ils se sont connus à Sudbury.** They first met in Sudbury.
♦ **s'y connaître en quelque chose** to know about something ◊ *Je ne m'y connais pas beaucoup en musique classique.* I don't know much about classical music.

se **connecter** VERB
to log on ◊ *Je me suis connecté sur Internet il y a dix minutes.* I logged onto the Internet ten minutes ago.
♦ **être connecté à un serveur** to be connected to a server

connu ADJECTIVE
well-known ◊ *C'est un acteur connu.*

He's a well-known actor.

conquérir VERB
to conquer

consacrer VERB
to devote ◊ *Il consacre beaucoup de temps à ses enfants.* He devotes a lot of time to his children. ◊ *Je suis désolé, je n'ai pas beaucoup de temps à y consacrer.* I'm afraid I can't spare much time for it.

la **conscience** NOUN
conscience ◊ *avoir mauvaise conscience* to have a guilty conscience
♦ **prendre conscience de** to become aware of ◊ *Ils ont fini par prendre conscience de la gravité de la situation.* They eventually became aware of the seriousness of the situation.

consciencieux ADJECTIVE (FEM SING **consciencieuse**)
conscientious

conscient ADJECTIVE
conscious

consécutif ADJECTIVE (FEM SING **consécutive**)
consecutive

le **conseil** NOUN
advice ◊ *Est-ce que je peux te demander conseil?* Can I ask you for some advice?
♦ **un conseil** a piece of advice
✹ ♦ **un conseil de bande** a band council
♦ **le conseil étudiant** student council
♦ **le conseil municipal** city council

conseiller VERB

see also **conseiller** NOUN

① to advise ◊ *Je te conseille de ne pas y aller.* I advise you not to go there.
② to recommend ◊ *Il m'a conseillé ce livre.* He recommended this book to me.

le **conseiller** NOUN

see also **conseiller** VERB

① councillor (*political*) ◊ *un conseiller municipal* a town councillor
② adviser
③ counsellor
♦ **un conseiller en orientation** a guidance counsellor

la **conseillère** NOUN
① councillor (*political*) ◊ *une conseillère municipale* a town councillor
② adviser
③ counsellor ◊ *une conseillère familiale* a family counsellor

♦ **une conseillère en orientation** a guidance counsellor

le **consentement** NOUN
consent ◊ *le consentement de tes parents* your parents' consent

consentir VERB
to agree ◊ *consentir à quelque chose* to agree to something

la **conséquence** NOUN
consequence
♦ **en conséquence** consequently

conséquent ADJECTIVE
① rational ◊ *un comportement conséquent* rational behaviour
② consistent ◊ *de manière conséquente* in a consistent manner
♦ **par conséquent** consequently

le **conservatoire** NOUN
school of music ◊ *Elle fait du piano au conservatoire.* She's taking piano at the school of music.

la **conserve** NOUN
can ◊ *Je vais ouvrir une conserve.* I'll open a can.
♦ **une boîte de conserve** a can
♦ **les conserves** canned food ◊ *Il n'est pas bon de manger des conserves tous les jours.* It's not healthy to eat canned food every day.
♦ **en conserve** canned ◊ *des petits pois en conserve* canned peas

conserver VERB
to keep ◊ *J'ai conservé toutes ses lettres.* I've kept all her letters.
♦ **se conserver** to keep ◊ *Ce pain se conserve plus d'une semaine.* This bread will keep for more than a week.

considérable ADJECTIVE
considerable ◊ *Il a fait des progrès considérables.* He's made considerable progress.

la **considération** NOUN
♦ **prendre quelque chose en considération** to take something into consideration

considérer VERB
to consider ◊ *Je la considère compétente.* I consider her to be competent.
♦ **considérer que** to believe that ◊ *Elle considère que la décision du directeur était juste.* She believes that the principal's decision was fair.

consistant ADJECTIVE
substantial ◊ *un petit déjeuner consistant* a substantial breakfast

Be careful! **consistant** *does not mean* **consistent**.

consister VERB
♦ **consister à** to consist of ◊ *Mon travail consiste à répondre au téléphone et à recevoir les clients.* My job consists of answering the phone and welcoming customers. ◊ *En quoi consiste votre travail?* What does your job involve?

la **console de jeu** NOUN
game console

consoler VERB
to comfort

le **consommateur** NOUN
① consumer
② customer (*in café*)

la **consommation** NOUN
consumption ◊ *la consommation d'électricité* hydro consumption

la **consommatrice** NOUN
① consumer
② customer (*in café*)

consommer VERB
to use ◊ *Ces grosses voitures consomment beaucoup d'essence.* These big cars use a lot of gas.

la **consonne** NOUN
consonant

constamment ADVERB
constantly ◊ *Elle se plaint constamment.* She's constantly complaining.

constant ADJECTIVE
constant

constater VERB
to notice

constitué ADJECTIVE
♦ **être constitué de** to consist of

constituer VERB
to make up ◊ *les dix provinces et les trois territoires qui constituent le Canada* the ten provinces and three territories that make up Canada

la **constitution** NOUN
constitution ◊ *la Constitution canadienne* the Canadian Constitution

la **construction** NOUN
building ◊ *des matériaux de construction* building materials
♦ **une maison en construction** a house being built

construire VERB
to build ◊ *Ils font construire une maison neuve.* They're having a new house built.

la **consultation** NOUN
consultation

consulter VERB
① to consult ◊ *Tu devrais consulter un médecin.* You should see a doctor.

2 to see patients ◊ *La docteure ne consulte pas le samedi.* The doctor doesn't see patients on Saturdays.

le **contact** NOUN
contact ◊ *les contacts humains* human contact
♦ **garder le contact avec quelqu'un** to keep in touch with somebody

contacter VERB
to get in touch with ◊ *Je te contacterai dès que j'aurai des nouvelles.* I'll get in touch with you as soon as I have some news.

contagieux ADJECTIVE (FEM SING **contagieuse**)
1 infectious ◊ *une maladie contagieuse* an infectious disease
2 contagious ◊ *Restez chez vous si vous êtes contagieux.* Stay at home if you're contagious.

contaminer VERB
to contaminate ◊ *de l'eau contaminée* contaminated water

le **conte** NOUN
story ◊ *un livre de contes* a storybook
♦ **un conte de fées** a fairy tale

contempler VERB
to gaze at

contemporain ADJECTIVE
contemporary
♦ **un auteur contemporain** a modern writer

le **contenant** NOUN
container ◊ *un contenant en plastique* a plastic container

contenir VERB
to contain ◊ *un portefeuille contenant de l'argent* a wallet containing money

content ADJECTIVE
glad ◊ *Je suis content que tu sois venu.* I'm glad you came.
♦ **content de** pleased with ◊ *Elle m'a dit qu'elle était contente de mon travail.* She told me she was pleased with my work.

contenter VERB
to please ◊ *Il est difficile à contenter.* He's hard to please.
♦ **Je me contente de peu.** I can make do with very little.

contesté ADJECTIVE
controversial ◊ *Cette décision est très contestée.* This is a very controversial decision.

le **conteur** NOUN
storyteller

la **conteuse** NOUN
storyteller

le **continent** NOUN
mainland

continu ADJECTIVE
continuous

continuellement ADVERB
constantly

continuer VERB
to continue ◊ *Continuez sans moi!* Go on without me! ◊ *Il ne veut pas continuer ses études.* He doesn't want to continue his studies.
♦ **continuer à faire quelque chose** to go on doing something ◊ *Ils ont continué à regarder la télé sans me dire bonjour.* They went on watching TV without saying hello to me.
♦ **continuer de faire quelque chose** to go on doing something ◊ *Elle continue de fumer malgré son asthme.* She continues to smoke despite her asthma.

contourner VERB
to go around ◊ *La route contourne la ville.* The road goes around the town.

le **contraceptif** NOUN
contraceptive

la **contraception** NOUN
contraception

la **contradiction** NOUN
contradiction
♦ **par esprit de contradiction** just to be difficult ◊ *Il a refusé de venir par esprit de contradiction.* He refused to come, just to be difficult.

le **contraire** NOUN
opposite ◊ *C'est exactement le contraire.* It's just the opposite.
♦ **au contraire** on the contrary

contrarier VERB
1 to annoy ◊ *Il avait l'air contrarié.* He looked annoyed.
2 to upset ◊ *Est-ce que tu serais contrariée si je ne venais pas?* Would you be upset if I didn't come?

le **contraste** NOUN
contrast

le **contrat** NOUN
contract

la **contravention** NOUN
parking ticket

contre PREPOSITION
1 against ◊ *Ne mets pas ton vélo contre le mur.* Don't put your bike against the wall. ◊ *Tu es pour ou contre ce projet?* Are you for or against this plan?
2 for ◊ *échanger quelque chose contre quelque chose* to trade

something for something
♦ **par contre** on the other hand

la **contrebande** NOUN
smuggling
♦ **des produits de contrebande** smuggled goods

la **contrebasse** NOUN
double bass

contrecœur
♦ **à contrecœur** ADVERB reluctantly ◊ *Elle est venue à contrecœur.* She came reluctantly.

contredire VERB
to contradict ◊ *Il ne supporte pas d'être contredit.* He can't stand being contradicted.

le **contretemps** NOUN
♦ **Désolé d'être en retard; j'ai eu un contretemps.** Sorry I'm late; I was held up.

contribuer VERB
to contribute ◊ *contribuer au succès d'un projet* to contribute to the success of a project

le **contrôle** NOUN
① control ◊ *le contrôle des passeports* passport control
② check
♦ **un contrôle d'identité** an identity check
♦ **le contrôle des billets** ticket inspection
③ test ◊ *un contrôle antidopage* a drug test

contrôler VERB
to check ◊ *Personne n'a contrôlé mon billet.* Nobody checked my ticket.

controversé ADJECTIVE
controversial

convaincre VERB
① to persuade ◊ *Il a essayé de me convaincre de rester.* He tried to persuade me to stay.
② to convince ◊ *Tu n'as pas l'air convaincu.* You don't look convinced.

convenable ADJECTIVE
decent ◊ *un hôtel convenable* a decent hotel
♦ **Ce n'est pas convenable.** It's bad manners.

convenir VERB
♦ **convenir à** to suit ◊ *Est-ce que cette date te convient?* Does this date suit you? ◊ *J'espère que cela vous conviendra.* I hope this will suit you.
♦ **convenir de** to agree on ◊ *Nous avons convenu d'une date.* We've agreed on a date.

convenu ADJECTIVE

agreed ◊ *au moment convenu* at the agreed time

la **conversation** NOUN
conversation

convivial ADJECTIVE
user-friendly ◊ *Ce logiciel est très convivial.* This program is very user-friendly.

cool ADJECTIVE (*informal*)
cool

coopératif ADJECTIVE (FEM SING **coopérative**)
co-operative ◊ *Elle s'est montrée très coopérative.* She was very co-operative.

la **coopération** NOUN
co-operation

la **coopérative** NOUN
co-op ◊ *une coopérative d'habitation* a housing co-op

coopérer VERB
to co-operate

les **coordonnées** FEM NOUN
contact information ◊ *As-tu ses coordonnées?* Do you have his contact information?

le **copain** NOUN (*informal*)
① friend ◊ *C'est un bon copain.* He's a good friend.
② boyfriend ◊ *Je l'ai vue avec son copain.* I saw her with her boyfriend.

la **copie** NOUN
copy ◊ *Ce tableau n'est qu'une copie.* This picture is only a copy.

copier VERB
to copy
♦ **copier-coller** to copy and paste

copieux ADJECTIVE (FEM SING **copieuse**)
hearty ◊ *un repas copieux* a hearty meal

la **copine** NOUN (*informal*)
① friend ◊ *Je sors avec une copine ce soir.* I'm going out with a friend tonight.
② girlfriend ◊ *Je ne savais pas qu'il avait une copine.* I didn't know he had a girlfriend.

✳ la **copropriété** NOUN
condominium

le **coq** NOUN
rooster

la **coque** NOUN
hull (*of boat*)
♦ **un œuf à la coque** a soft-boiled egg

le **coquelicot** NOUN
poppy

✳ la **coquerelle** NOUN

cockroach

le **coquillage** NOUN
shell ◊ *Nous avons ramassé des coquillages sur la plage.* We picked up some shells on the beach.

la **coquille** NOUN
shell
♦ **une coquille d'œuf** an eggshell
♦ **une coquille Saint-Jacques** a scallop

le **cor** NOUN
horn (*instrument*) ◊ *Je joue du cor.* I play the horn.

le **corbeau** NOUN (PL les **corbeaux**)
crow

la **corbeille** NOUN
basket ◊ *une corbeille de fruits* a basket of fruit
♦ **une corbeille à papier** a wastepaper basket

la **corde** NOUN
1 rope
2 string (*guitar, tennis racquet*)
♦ **une corde à linge** a clothes line
♦ **une corde élastique** a bungee cord

la **cordonnerie** NOUN
shoe repair shop

la **corne** NOUN
horn (*on animal*)

la **cornemuse** NOUN
bagpipes ◊ *jouer de la cornemuse* to play the bagpipes

le **cornet** NOUN
♦ **un cornet de crème glacée** an ice cream cone

le **cornichon** NOUN
pickle

le **corps** NOUN
body

correct ADJECTIVE
1 correct ◊ *Ce n'est pas tout à fait correct.* That's not quite correct.
2 acceptable ◊ *C'est correct de faire des erreurs quand on apprend.* It's OK to make mistakes when you're learning. ◊ *Le repas était tout à fait correct.* The meal was quite acceptable.

la **correction** NOUN
correction

la **correspondance** NOUN
1 correspondence ◊ *La secrétaire s'occupe de toute la correspondance.* The secretary takes care of all the correspondence.
2 connection (*train, plane*) ◊ *Il y a une correspondance pour Montréal à dix heures.* There's a connection for Montréal at ten o'clock.

le **correspondant** NOUN
penpal

la **correspondante** NOUN
penpal

correspondre VERB
to correspond ◊ *Écrivez le numéro qui correspond à votre réponse.* Write down the number that corresponds to your answer. ◊ *Elle correspond avec sa grand-mère en Inde.* She corresponds with her grandmother in India.

le **corridor** NOUN
hallway

corriger VERB
to mark ◊ *Vous pouvez corriger mon test?* Can you mark my test?

la **corvée** NOUN
chore ◊ *Quelle corvée!* What a drag!

costaud ADJECTIVE
well-built

le **costume** NOUN
1 suit (*man's*) ◊ *Tu devrais mettre un costume et une cravate pour l'entrevue.* You should wear a suit and tie for the interview.
2 costume (*theatre*) ◊ *Nous avons fait nous-mêmes tous les costumes pour la pièce.* We made all the costumes for the play ourselves.

la **côte** NOUN
1 coastline ◊ *La route longe la côte.* The road follows the coastline.
♦ **la côte Ouest** the West Coast
2 hill ◊ *J'ai grimpé la côte.* I went up the hill.
3 rib ◊ *Il s'est cassé une côte en tombant.* He broke a rib when he fell.
♦ **côte à côte** side by side
♦ **les côtes levées** spareribs

le **côté** NOUN
side
♦ **à côté de (1)** next to ◊ *Le café est à côté du sucre.* The coffee's next to the sugar.
♦ **à côté de (2)** next door to ◊ *Elle habite à côté de chez moi.* She lives next door to me.
♦ **de l'autre côté** on the other side ◊ *La pharmacie est de l'autre côté de la rue.* The drugstore is on the other side of the street.
♦ **De quel côté sont-ils partis?** Which way did they go?
♦ **mettre quelque chose de côté** to save something ◊ *J'ai mis de l'argent de côté.* I've saved some money.

la **côtelette** NOUN
chop ◊ *une côtelette d'agneau* a lamb chop

le **coton** NOUN
cotton ◊ *une chemise en coton* a cotton shirt
♦ **le coton hydrophile** cotton wool

le **cou** NOUN
neck

couchant ADJECTIVE
♦ **le soleil couchant** the setting sun

la **couche** NOUN
1 layer ◊ *la couche d'ozone* the ozone layer
2 coat (*of paint, varnish*)
3 diaper

couché ADJECTIVE
1 lying down ◊ *Il était couché sur le tapis.* He was lying on the carpet.
2 in bed ◊ *Il est déjà couché.* He's already in bed.

le **coucher** NOUN

> see also **coucher** VERB

♦ **un coucher de soleil** a sunset

se **coucher** VERB

> see also **coucher** NOUN

1 to go to bed ◊ *Je me suis couché tard hier soir.* I went to bed late last night.
2 to set (*sun*)

la **couchette** NOUN
crib

le **coude** NOUN
elbow
♦ **donner un coup de coude à quelqu'un** to nudge somebody

coudre VERB
1 to sew ◊ *J'aime coudre.* I like sewing.
2 to sew on ◊ *Je ne sais même pas coudre un bouton.* I can't even sew a button on.

la **couette** NOUN
duvet

les **couettes** FEM NOUN
pigtails ◊ *Quand j'étais petite, ma mère me faisait des couettes.* When I was little, my mother put my hair in pigtails.

couler VERB
1 to run ◊ *Ne laissez pas couler les robinets.* Don't leave the taps running. ◊ *J'ai le nez qui coule.* My nose is running.
2 to flow ◊ *La rivière coulait lentement.* The river was flowing slowly.
3 to leak ◊ *Mon stylo coule.* My pen's leaking.
4 to sink ◊ *Le bateau a coulé.* The boat sank.

la **couleur** NOUN
colour ◊ *De quelle couleur est leur voiture?* What colour is their car? ◊ *un film couleur* a colour film
♦ **Tu as pris des couleurs.** You've got a tan.

la **couleuvre** NOUN
garter snake

les **coulisses** FEM NOUN
wings (*in theatre*)
♦ **dans les coulisses** behind the scenes

le **couloir** NOUN
hallway

le **coup** NOUN
1 knock ◊ *donner un coup à quelque chose* to give something a knock
2 blow
♦ **Il m'a donné un coup!** He hit me!
♦ **un coup de coude** a nudge
♦ **un coup de pied** a kick
♦ **un coup de poing** a punch
3 shock ◊ *Ça m'a fait un coup de le voir comme ça!* (*informal*) It gave me a shock to see him like that!
♦ **un coup de feu** a shot
♦ **un coup de téléphone** (*informal*) a call ◊ *Je te donnerai un coup de téléphone demain.* I'll give you a call tomorrow.
♦ **donner un coup de main à quelqu'un** to give somebody a hand ◊ *Je viendrai te donner un coup de main.* I'll come and give you a hand.
♦ **un coup d'œil** a quick look ◊ *jeter un coup d'œil sur quelque chose* to take a quick look at something
♦ **attraper un coup de soleil** to get sunburned
♦ **un coup de tonnerre** a clap of thunder
♦ **après coup** afterwards ◊ *Après coup j'ai regretté de m'être mis en colère.* Afterwards I was sorry I'd got angry.
♦ **à tous les coups** (*informal*) every time ◊ *Je me trompe de rue à tous les coups.* I get the street wrong every time.
♦ **du premier coup** on the first try ◊ *Elle a été reçue au permis du premier coup.* She passed her driving test on the first try.
♦ **sur le coup** right away ◊ *Sur le coup je ne l'ai pas reconnu.* I didn't recognize him right away.

coupable ADJECTIVE

> see also **coupable** NOUN

guilty

le/la **coupable** NOUN

> see also **coupable** ADJECTIVE

culprit

la **coupe** NOUN

cup (*sport*) ◊ *la coupe du monde* the World Cup
♦ **une coupe de cheveux** a haircut
♦ **la coupe glacée** sundae

le **coupe-ongle** NOUN
  nail clippers

couper VERB
  ① to cut
  ② to turn off ◊ *couper le courant* to turn off the power
  ③ to take a shortcut ◊ *On peut couper par la forêt.* There's a shortcut through the woods.
♦ **couper l'appétit** to spoil one's appetite
♦ **se couper** to cut oneself ◊ *Je me suis coupé le doigt.* I cut my finger.
♦ **couper la parole à quelqu'un** to interrupt somebody
♦ **couper les cheveux en quatre** to split hairs

couper-coller VERB
  to cut and paste

le **coupe-vent** NOUN (PL les **coupe-vent**)
  windbreaker (*jacket*)

le **couple** NOUN
  couple

la **coupure** NOUN
  cut
♦ **une coupure de courant** a power outage

la **cour** NOUN
  ① yard ◊ *la cour de l'école* the school yard
  ② court ◊ *la cour provinciale* the provincial court

le **courage** NOUN
  courage

courageux ADJECTIVE (FEM SING **courageuse**)
  brave

couramment ADVERB
  ① fluently ◊ *Elle parle couramment japonais.* She speaks Japanese fluently.
  ② commonly ◊ *C'est une expression que l'on emploie couramment.* It's a commonly used phrase.

courant ADJECTIVE

  see also **courant** NOUN

  ① common ◊ *C'est une erreur courante.* It's a common mistake.
  ② standard ◊ *C'est un modèle courant.* It's a standard model.

le **courant** NOUN

  see also **courant** ADJECTIVE

  ① current (*of river*)
♦ **un courant d'air** a draft

  ② power ◊ *une panne de courant* a power failure
♦ **Je le ferai dans le courant de la semaine.** I'll do it some time during the week.
♦ **être au courant de quelque chose** to know about something ◊ *Je ne suis pas au courant de ses projets pour l'été.* I don't know about her plans for the summer.
♦ **mettre quelqu'un au courant de quelque chose** to tell somebody about something
♦ **Tu es au courant?** Have you heard?
♦ **se tenir au courant de quelque chose** to keep up with something ◊ *J'essaie de me tenir au courant de l'actualité.* I try to keep up with the news.

courbe ADJECTIVE
  curved ◊ *une surface courbe* a curved surface

courbé ADJECTIVE
  bent ◊ *des branches courbées sous le poids de la neige* branches bent by the weight of the snow

la **courbe** NOUN
  ① curve
  ② bend

le **coureur** NOUN
  runner
♦ **un coureur à pied** a runner
♦ **un coureur cycliste** a racing cyclist
♦ **un coureur automobile** a race car driver
✻ ♦ **coureur des bois** trapper

la **coureuse** NOUN
  runner

la **courgette** NOUN
  zucchini

courir VERB
  to run ◊ *Il a traversé la rue en courant.* He ran across the street.
♦ **courir un risque** to run a risk

la **couronne** NOUN
  crown

courons, courez VERB *see* **courir**

le **courriel** NOUN
  e-mail ◊ *Envoie-moi un courriel.* Send me an e-mail.

le **courrier** NOUN
  mail ◊ *Est-ce qu'il y avait du courrier ce matin?* Was there any mail this morning?
♦ **N'oublie pas de poster le courrier.** Don't forget to mail the letters.
♦ **le courrier électronique** e-mail

  *Be careful! The French word **courrier** does not mean **courier**.*

le **cours** NOUN

🖙

① lesson ◊ *un cours de danse* a dance lesson ◊ *des cours particuliers* private lessons
② course ◊ *un cours intensif* a crash course
③ rate ◊ *le cours du change* the exchange rate
♦ **au cours de** during ◊ *Il a été réveillé trois fois au cours de la nuit.* He was woken up three times during the night.

la **course** NOUN
① running ◊ *la course de fond* long-distance running
② race ◊ *une course hippique* a horse race
③ errand ◊ *J'ai juste une course à faire.* I've just got one errand to do.

court ADJECTIVE
short

le **court de tennis** NOUN
tennis court

couru VERB *see* **courir**

le **couscous** NOUN
couscous

le **cousin** NOUN
cousin

la **cousine** NOUN
cousin

le **coussin** NOUN
cushion

le **coût** NOUN
cost ◊ *le coût de la vie* the cost of living
♦ **réduire les coûts** to cut costs

le **couteau** NOUN (PL les **couteaux**)
knife

coûter VERB
to cost ◊ *Est-ce que ça coûte cher?* Does it cost a lot?
♦ **Combien ça coûte?** How much is it?

coûteux ADJECTIVE (FEM SING **coûteuse**)
expensive

la **coutume** NOUN
custom

la **couture** NOUN
① sewing ◊ *Je n'aime pas la couture.* I don't like sewing.
♦ **faire de la couture** to sew
② seam ◊ *La couture de mon pantalon s'est défaite.* The seam of my pants has come apart.

le **couturier** NOUN
fashion designer ◊ *un grand couturier* a top designer

la **couturière** NOUN
dressmaker

le **couvercle** NOUN
① lid (*pot, jar, box, garbage can*)
② cap (*tube, bottle, spray can*)

couvert VERB *see* **couvrir**

couvert ADJECTIVE
overcast (*sky*)
♦ **couvert de** covered with ◊ *Cet arbre est couvert de fleurs au printemps.* This tree is covered with blossoms in spring.

les **couverts** MASC NOUN
cutlery SING ◊ *Les couverts sont dans le tiroir de gauche.* The cutlery is in the left-hand drawer.

la **couverture** NOUN
① blanket
② cover ◊ *la couverture arrière du livre* the back cover of the book
♦ **une page couverture** a cover page
③ coverage ◊ *la couverture médiatique de l'évènement* media coverage of the event

le **couvre-lit** NOUN
bedspread

couvrir VERB
to cover ◊ *Le chien est revenu couvert de boue.* The dog came back covered with mud.
♦ **se couvrir (1)** to dress warmly ◊ *Couvre-toi bien : il fait très froid dehors.* Dress warmly: it's very cold outside.
♦ **se couvrir (2)** to cloud over ◊ *Le ciel se couvre.* The sky's clouding over.

le **crabe** NOUN
crab

cracher VERB
to spit

le **crachin** NOUN
drizzle

la **craie** NOUN
chalk

craindre VERB
to fear ◊ *Tu n'as rien à craindre.* You have nothing to fear.

la **crainte** NOUN
fear
♦ **de crainte de** for fear of ◊ *Il n'ose rien dire de crainte de la vexer.* He doesn't dare say anything for fear of upsetting her.

craintif ADJECTIVE (FEM SING **craintive**)
timid

la **crampe** NOUN
cramp ◊ *J'ai une crampe au mollet.* I've got a cramp in my calf.

le **cran** NOUN
hole (*in belt*)
♦ **avoir du cran** (*informal*) to have guts

le **crâne** NOUN
skull

le **crapaud** NOUN
toad

le **craquelin** NOUN
cracker

craquer VERB
1 to creak ◊ *Le plancher craque.* The floor creaks.
2 to break ◊ *Les coutures ont craqué sous l'effort.* The seams broke under the strain.
3 to have a nervous breakdown ◊ *Je vais finir par craquer!* (*informal*) I'll have a nervous breakdown at this rate!
♦ **Quand j'ai vu cette robe, j'ai craqué!** (*informal*) When I saw that dress, I couldn't resist it!

la **crasse** NOUN
filth

crasseux ADJECTIVE (FEM SING **crasseuse**)
filthy

la **cravate** NOUN
tie

le **crawl** NOUN
crawl ◊ *nager le crawl* to do the crawl

le **crayon** NOUN
pencil ◊ *un crayon de couleur* a pencil crayon
♦ **un crayon feutre** a felt pen

la **création** NOUN
creation

le **crédit** NOUN
credit

créer VERB
to create

la **crème** NOUN
cream
♦ **la crème anglaise** custard
♦ **la crème Chantilly** whipped cream
♦ **la crème fouettée** whipped cream
♦ **la crème glacée** ice cream ◊ *un cornet de crème glacée* an ice cream cone
♦ **une crème caramel** a crème caramel
♦ **une crème au chocolat** a chocolate mousse

crémeux ADJECTIVE (FEM SING **crémeuse**)
creamy

la **crêpe** NOUN
crêpe

> ⓘ A **crêpe** is like a pancake, but very thin and not as sweet. It can be eaten with syrup or other toppings -- sweet ones like fruit and whipped cream, or savoury ones like seafood or vegetables in a cream or cheese sauce. Often the crêpe is rolled up with these inside.

la **crêperie** NOUN
restaurant serving crêpes

le **crépuscule** NOUN
dusk

creuser VERB
to dig (*a hole*)
♦ **creuser l'appétit** to give an appetite
♦ **se creuser la cervelle** (*informal*) to rack one's brains

creux ADJECTIVE (FEM SING **creuse**)
hollow

la **crevaison** NOUN
flat tire

crevé ADJECTIVE
1 flat (*tire*)
2 bagged ◊ *Je suis complètement crevé!* (*informal*) I'm bagged!

crever VERB
1 to burst (*balloon*)
2 to have a flat tire (*motorist*) ◊ *J'ai crevé sur l'autoroute.* I had a flat tire on the highway.
♦ **Je crève de faim!** (*informal*) I'm starving!
♦ **Je crève de froid!** (*informal*) I'm freezing!

la **crevette** NOUN
shrimp

le **cri** NOUN
1 scream ◊ *J'ai entendu un cri.* I heard a scream. ◊ *pousser des cris de douleur* to scream with pain
2 shout ◊ *des cris de colère* angry shouts
3 call ◊ *Il sait reconnaître les cris des oiseaux.* He can identify bird calls.
♦ **C'est le dernier cri.** It's the latest style. ◊ *Ce haut est du dernier cri.* This top is the latest style.

criard ADJECTIVE
garish (*colours*)

le **cric** NOUN
jack (*for car*)

crier VERB
to shout
♦ **crier de douleur** to scream with pain

le **crime** NOUN
crime ◊ *un crime de guerre* a war crime

criminel → crottin

le **criminel** NOUN
criminal ◊ *un criminel de guerre* a war criminal

la **criminelle** NOUN
criminal

la **crinière** NOUN
mane

la **crique** NOUN
creek

le **criquet** NOUN
grasshopper

la **crise** NOUN
1 crisis
♦ **la crise économique** the recession
2 attack ◊ *une crise d'asthme* an asthma attack ◊ *une crise cardiaque* a heart attack
♦ **une crise de foie** an upset stomach
♦ **piquer une crise de nerfs** to go hysterical
♦ **avoir une crise de fou rire** to have the giggles

le **cristal** NOUN (PL les **cristaux**)
crystal ◊ *un verre en cristal* a crystal glass

le **critère** NOUN
criterion

critique ADJECTIVE

> see also **critique** NOUN

critical

le/la **critique** NOUN

> see also **la critique** and **critique** ADJECTIVE

critic ◊ *un critique de cinéma* a film critic

la **critique** NOUN

> see also **le/la critique** and **critique** ADJECTIVE

1 criticism ◊ *Elle ne supporte pas les critiques.* She can't stand being criticized.
2 review ◊ *Le film a reçu de bonnes critiques.* The film got good reviews.

critiquer VERB
to criticize

le **crochet** NOUN
1 hook
2 detour ◊ *faire un crochet* to make a detour
3 crochet ◊ *un chandail au crochet* a crocheted sweater
4 square bracket

le **crocodile** NOUN
crocodile

croire VERB
to believe ◊ *Il croit tout ce qu'on lui raconte.* He believes everything he's told.
♦ **croire que** to think that ◊ *Tu crois qu'il fera meilleur demain?* Do you think the weather will be better tomorrow?
♦ **croire à quelque chose** to believe in something
♦ **croire en Dieu** to believe in God

crois VERB see **croire**

croîs VERB see **croître**

le **croisement** NOUN
intersection ◊ *Tournez à gauche au croisement.* Turn left at the intersection.

croiser VERB
♦ **J'ai croisé ta sœur dans la rue.** I bumped into your sister in the street.
♦ **croiser les bras** to fold one's arms
♦ **croiser les jambes** to cross one's legs
♦ **se croiser** to pass each other ◊ *Nous nous croisons dans l'escalier tous les matins.* We pass each other on the stairs every morning.

la **croisière** NOUN
cruise

la **croissance** NOUN
growth

le **croissant** NOUN
croissant ◊ *un croissant au beurre* a butter croissant
♦ **le Croissant-Rouge** the Red Crescent

croit VERB see **croire**

croître VERB
to grow

la **croix** NOUN
cross
♦ **la Croix-Rouge** the Red Cross

le **croque-madame** NOUN

> ℹ A **croque-madame** is a toasted ham and cheese sandwich with a fried egg on top. The same thing without the fried egg is a **croque-monsieur**. The plural form of each is the same as the singular.

croquer VERB
to munch ◊ *croquer une pomme* to munch an apple

le **croquis** NOUN
sketch

la **crosse** NOUN
lacrosse

la **crotte** NOUN
♦ **une crotte de chien** dog dirt

le **crottin** NOUN
1 manure ◊ *du crottin de cheval* horse manure

2 small block of goat cheese

croustillant ADJECTIVE
1 crisp
♦ **un croustillant aux pommes** an apple crisp
2 crusty

la **croustille** NOUN
potato chip ◊ *un sac de croustilles* a bag of chips
♦ **des croustilles de maïs** corn chips

la **croûte** NOUN
1 crust (*of bread*)
♦ **en croûte** in pastry
2 rind (*of cheese*)
3 scab (*on skin*)

le **croûton** NOUN
1 crust (*end of loaf*)
2 crouton ◊ *des croûtons frottés d'ail* garlic croutons

croyons, croyez VERB *see* **croire**

cru VERB *see* **croire**

crû VERB *see* **croître**

la **cruauté** NOUN
cruelty

la **cruche** NOUN
jug

les **crudités** FEM NOUN
raw vegetables (*cut up as hors d'œuvre*)

cruel ADJECTIVE (FEM SING **cruelle**)
cruel

les **crustacés** MASC NOUN
shellfish

le **cube** NOUN
cube
♦ **un mètre cube** a cubic metre

la **cueillette** NOUN
picking ◊ *la cueillette des fraises* strawberry picking

cueillir VERB
to pick (*flowers, fruit*)

la **cuiller** NOUN
spoon
♦ **une cuiller à café** a teaspoon
♦ **une cuiller à soupe** a soup spoon

la **cuillère** NOUN
spoon
♦ **une cuillère à café** a teaspoon
♦ **une cuillère à soupe** a soup spoon

la **cuillerée** NOUN
spoonful

le **cuir** NOUN
leather ◊ *un sac en cuir* a leather bag
♦ **le cuir chevelu** the scalp

cuire VERB
to cook ◊ *cuire quelque chose à feu vif* to cook something on high heat
♦ **cuire quelque chose au four** to bake something
♦ **cuire quelque chose à la vapeur** to steam something
♦ **faire cuire** to cook ◊ *« Faire cuire pendant une heure »* "Cook for one hour"
♦ **bien cuit** well done
♦ **trop cuit** overdone

la **cuisine** NOUN
1 kitchen
2 cooking ◊ *la cuisine française* French cooking
♦ **faire la cuisine** to cook

cuisiné ADJECTIVE
♦ **un plat cuisiné** a ready-made meal

cuisiner VERB
to cook ◊ *J'aime beaucoup cuisiner.* I love cooking.

le **cuisinier** NOUN
cook

la **cuisinière** NOUN
1 cook
2 stove ◊ *une cuisinière à gaz* a gas stove

la **cuisse** NOUN
thigh
♦ **une cuisse de poulet** a chicken leg

la **cuisson** NOUN
cooking ◊ *« une heure de cuisson »* "cooking time: one hour"

cuit VERB *see* **cuire**

le **cuivre** NOUN
copper

le **culot** NOUN (*informal*)
nerve (*brazenness*) ◊ *Quel culot!* What nerve!

la **culotte** NOUN
underpants (*women's*)

le **cultivateur** NOUN
farmer

la **cultivatrice** NOUN
farmer

cultivé ADJECTIVE
cultured ◊ *Elle est très cultivée.* She's very cultured.

cultiver VERB
to grow ◊ *Ils cultivent la vigne.* They grow grapes.
♦ **cultiver la terre** to farm the land

la **culture** NOUN
1 culture ◊ *la culture québécoise* Québecois culture
2 education ◊ *Pour cet emploi, on demande une bonne culture générale.* For this job, a good general education is needed.

♦ **la culture physique** physical
   education
   ③ farming ◊ *les cultures intensives*
   intensive farming

le **culturisme** NOUN
   bodybuilding

le **cure-dent** NOUN (PL les **cure-dents**)
   toothpick

curieux ADJECTIVE (FEM SING **curieuse**)
   curious

la **curiosité** NOUN
   curiosity

le **curling** NOUN
   curling

le **curriculum vitæ** NOUN
   résumé

le **curseur** NOUN
   cursor

la **cuvette** NOUN
   bowl ◊ *une cuvette en plastique* a

plastic bowl

le **CV** NOUN (= *curriculum vitæ*)
   résumé

le **cybercafé** NOUN
   Internet café

cyclable ADJECTIVE
   ♦ **une piste cyclable** a bike path

le **cycle** NOUN
   cycle

le **cyclisme** NOUN
   cycling

le/la **cycliste** NOUN
   cyclist

le **cyclone** NOUN
   cyclone

le **cygne** NOUN
   swan

cynique ADJECTIVE
   cynical

D

d' PREPOSITION, ARTICLE *see* **de**

la **dactylo** NOUN
1 typist ◊ *Elle est dactylo.* She's a typist.
2 typing ◊ *Je prends des cours de dactylo.* I'm doing typing lessons.

le **daim** NOUN
suede ◊ *une veste en daim* a suede jacket

la **dame** NOUN
1 lady
2 queen (*in cards, chess*)

les **dames** FEM NOUN
checkers

le **danger** NOUN
danger
♦ **être en danger** to be in danger
♦ **« Danger de mort »** "Extremely dangerous"

dangereux ADJECTIVE (FEM SING **dangereuse**)
dangerous

✱ la **danoise** NOUN
danish (*pastry*)

dans PREPOSITION
1 in ◊ *Je suis dans la cuisine.* I'm in the kitchen. ◊ *dans deux mois* two months from now
2 into ◊ *Il est entré dans mon bureau.* He came into my office.
3 out of ◊ *On a bu dans des verres en plastique.* We drank out of plastic glasses.

la **danse** NOUN
1 dance ◊ *la danse moderne* modern dance ◊ *des danses folkloriques* folk dances
♦ **la danse classique** ballet
2 dancing ◊ *des cours de danse* dancing lessons

danser VERB
to dance

le **danseur** NOUN
dancer

la **danseuse** NOUN
dancer

la **date** NOUN
date ◊ *votre date de naissance* your date of birth ◊ *la date limite de vente* the best-before date
♦ **un ami de longue date** an old friend

dater VERB
♦ **dater de** to date from ◊ *Cette*

coutume date du moyen âge. This custom dates from the Middle Ages.

la **datte** NOUN
date (*fruit*)

le **dauphin** NOUN
dolphin

davantage ADVERB
more ◊ *Le gouvernement doit aider les pauvres davantage.* The government must help poor people more.
♦ **davantage de** more ◊ *Il faudrait davantage de stages de formation.* There should be more training courses.

le **DC** NOUN (= *disque compact*)
CD

de PREPOSITION, ARTICLE

> *See also* **du** (= **de** + **le**) *and* **des** (= **de** + **les**). **de** *changes to* **d'** *before a vowel and most words beginning with "h".*

1 of ◊ *le toit de la maison* the roof of the house ◊ *la capitale de Terre-Neuve* the capital of Newfoundland ◊ *la voiture de mes parents* my parents' car ◊ *la population de l'Alberta* the population of Alberta ◊ *deux bouteilles de vin* two bottles of wine ◊ *un litre d'essence* a litre of gas
♦ **un bébé d'un an** a one-year-old baby
♦ **un billet de cinquante dollars** a 50-dollar bill
2 from ◊ *de Prince George à Whitehorse* from Prince George to Whitehorse ◊ *Je viens de Kingston.* I come from Kingston. ◊ *une lettre de ma sœur* a letter from my sister
3 by ◊ *augmenter de dix dollars* to increase by ten dollars

> *You use* **de** *to form expressions with the meaning of* **some** *and* **any**.

♦ **Je voudrais de l'eau.** I'd like some water. ◊ *du pain et de la confiture* bread and jam
♦ **Il n'a pas de famille.** He hasn't got any family.
♦ **Il n'y a plus de biscuits.** There aren't any more cookies.

le **dé** NOUN
die (*one of a pair of dice*)
♦ **un dé à coudre** a thimble

✱ la **débâcle** NOUN
break-up (*ice*) ◊ *La débâcle*

printanière cause souvent des inondations. The spring break-up often creates floods.

déballer VERB
to unpack

✹ la **débarbouillette** NOUN
washcloth

le **débardeur** NOUN
tank top

débarquer VERB
[1] to disembark (*plane, ship*) ◊ *Nous avons dû débarquer à Halifax.* We had to disembark at Halifax.
✹ [2] to get off (*bus, train*) ◊ *débarquer de l'autobus* to get off the bus
♦ **débarquer chez quelqu'un** (*informal*) to descend on somebody ◊ *Ils ont débarqué chez nous à dix heures du soir.* They descended on us at ten o'clock at night.

le **débarras** NOUN
junk room
♦ **Bon débarras!** Good riddance!

débarrasser VERB
to clear ◊ *Tu peux débarrasser la table, s'il te plaît?* Can you clear the table please?
♦ **se débarrasser de quelque chose** to get rid of something ◊ *Je me suis débarrassé de mon vieux frigo.* I got rid of my old fridge.

le **débat** NOUN
debate

se **débattre** VERB
to struggle

débile ADJECTIVE
crazy ◊ *C'est complètement débile!* (*informal*) That's totally crazy!

débordé ADJECTIVE
♦ **être débordé** to be snowed under

déborder VERB
to overflow (*river*)
♦ **déborder d'énergie** to be full of energy

le **débouché** NOUN
job prospect ◊ *Quels débouchés y a-t-il après ces études?* What sort of job does this course qualify you for?

déboucher VERB
[1] to unblock (*sink, pipe*)
[2] to open (*bottle*)
♦ **déboucher sur** to lead into ◊ *La rue débouche sur une place.* The street leads into a square.

debout ADVERB
[1] standing up ◊ *Il a mangé ses céréales debout.* He ate his cereal standing up.
[2] upright ◊ *Mets les livres debout*

sur l'étagère. Put the books upright on the shelf.
[3] up ◊ *Tu es déjà debout?* Are you up already?
♦ **Debout!** Get up!

déboutonner VERB
to unbutton

débrancher VERB
to unplug

le **débris** NOUN
♦ **des débris de verre** bits of glass

débrouillard ADJECTIVE
resourceful

se **débrouiller** VERB
to manage ◊ *C'était difficile, mais je ne me suis pas trop mal débrouillé.* It was difficult, but I managed OK.
♦ **Débrouille-toi tout seul.** Work things out for yourself.

le **début** NOUN
beginning ◊ *au début* at the beginning
♦ **début mai** in early May

le **débutant** NOUN
beginner

la **débutante** NOUN
beginner

débuter VERB
to start ◊ *Le président a débuté comme concierge.* The president started as a janitor. ◊ *La réunion a débuté par un discours.* The meeting started with a speech.

décaféiné ADJECTIVE
decaffeinated

le **décalage horaire** NOUN
time difference (*between time zones*) ◊ *Il y a une heure de décalage horaire entre le Nouveau-Brunswick et l'Ontario.* There's an hour's time difference between New Brunswick and Ontario.

décalquer VERB
to trace

décapotable ADJECTIVE
convertible

décéder VERB
to die ◊ *Son père est décédé il y a trois ans.* Her father died three years ago.

décembre MASC NOUN
December
♦ **en décembre** in December

décemment ADVERB
decently

décent ADJECTIVE
decent

la **déception** NOUN
disappointment

décerner VERB
to award

le **décès** NOUN
death

décevant ADJECTIVE
disappointing ◊ *Ses résultats sont plutôt décevants.* His results are rather disappointing.

décevoir VERB
to disappoint

décharger VERB
to unload

se **déchausser** VERB
to take off one's shoes

les **déchets** MASC NOUN
waste SING ◊ *les déchets nucléaires* nuclear waste ◊ *les déchets toxiques* toxic waste ◊ *les déchets dangereux* hazardous waste

déchiffrer VERB
to decipher

déchirant ADJECTIVE
heart-rending

déchirer VERB
1 to tear (*clothes*)
2 to tear up ◊ *déchirer une lettre* to tear up a letter
3 to tear out ◊ *déchirer une page d'un livre* to tear a page out of a book
♦ **se déchirer un muscle** to tear a muscle

la **déchirure** NOUN
tear (*rip*)
♦ **une déchirure musculaire** a torn muscle

décidé ADJECTIVE
determined
♦ **C'est décidé.** It's decided.

décidément ADVERB
certainly ◊ *Décidément, je n'ai pas de chance aujourd'hui.* I'm certainly not having much luck today.

décider VERB
to decide
♦ **décider de faire quelque chose** to decide to do something ◊ *Ils ont décidé de passer leurs vacances en Alberta.* They decided to go to Alberta for their holiday.
♦ **se décider** to make up one's mind ◊ *Elle n'arrive pas à se décider.* She can't make up her mind.

décisif ADJECTIVE (FEM SING **décisive**)
decisive

la **décision** NOUN
decision

la **déclaration** NOUN
statement ◊ *Je n'ai aucune déclaration à faire.* I have no statement to make.
♦ **faire une déclaration de vol** to report something as stolen

déclarer VERB
to declare ◊ *déclarer la guerre à un pays* to declare war on a country
♦ **se déclarer** to break out ◊ *Un feu s'est déclaré dans le gymnase.* A fire broke out in the gymnasium.

déclencher VERB
to set off (*alarm, explosion*)
♦ **se déclencher** to go off

le **déclic** NOUN
click

décoiffé ADJECTIVE
♦ **Elle était toute décoiffée.** Her hair was in a real mess.

le **décollage** NOUN
takeoff (*of plane*)

décoller VERB
1 to remove (*sticker*) ◊ *décoller une étiquette* to remove a label
♦ **se décoller** to come unstuck
2 to take off ◊ *L'avion a décollé avec dix minutes de retard.* The plane took off ten minutes late.

décolleté ADJECTIVE
see also **décolleté** NOUN
low-cut

le **décolleté** NOUN
see also **décolleté** ADJECTIVE
♦ **un décolleté plongeant** a plunging neckline

se **décolorer** VERB
to fade ◊ *Ce T-shirt s'est décoloré au lavage.* This T-shirt faded in the wash.
♦ **se faire décolorer les cheveux** to get one's hair bleached

les **décombres** MASC NOUN
rubble SING

se **décommander** VERB
to back out ◊ *Il devait venir mais il s'est décommandé à la dernière minute.* He was supposed to come, but he backed out at the last minute.

déconcerté ADJECTIVE
disconcerted

décongeler VERB
to thaw

se **déconnecter** VERB
to log out

déconseiller VERB
♦ **déconseiller à quelqu'un de faire quelque chose** to advise somebody

☞

not to do something ◊ *Je lui ai déconseillé d'y aller.* I advised her not to go.
♦ **C'est déconseillé.** It's not recommended.

décontenancé ADJECTIVE
disconcerted

décontracté ADJECTIVE
relaxed
♦ **des vêtements décontractés** casual clothes

se **décontracter** VERB
to relax ◊ *Il est allé faire du jogging pour se décontracter.* He went jogging to relax.

le **décor** NOUN
① décor
② scenery ◊ *un décor de montagnes* mountain scenery
③ set (for movie, play) ◊ *un décor de cinéma* the set of a film ◊ *un superbe décor de théâtre* a superb stage set
♦ **faire partie du décor** to be part of the furniture

le **décorateur** NOUN
interior decorator

la **décoration** NOUN
decoration

la **décoratrice** NOUN
interior decorator

décorer VERB
to decorate

décortiquer VERB
to shell
♦ **des crevettes décortiquées** peeled shrimp

découdre VERB
♦ **se découdre** to come unstitched

découper VERB
to cut out ◊ *J'ai découpé cet article dans le journal.* I cut this article out of the paper.

décourageant ADJECTIVE
discouraging

décourager VERB
to discourage
♦ **se décourager** to get discouraged ◊ *Ne te décourage pas!* Don't give up!

décousu ADJECTIVE
unstitched ◊ *L'ourlet est décousu.* The hem's come unstitched.

le **découvert** NOUN
overdraft

la **découverte** NOUN
discovery

découvrir VERB
to discover

décriminaliser VERB
to decriminalize

décrire VERB
to describe

décrocher VERB
① to take down ◊ *Tu peux m'aider à décrocher les rideaux?* Can you help me take down the curtains?
② to pick up the phone ◊ *Il a décroché et a composé le numéro.* He picked up the phone and dialled the number.
③ to drop out (school) ◊ *Il a décroché avant de terminer son secondaire cinq.* He dropped out before finishing Grade 12.
♦ **décrocher le téléphone** to take the phone off the hook

le **décrocheur** NOUN
dropout

la **décrocheuse** NOUN
dropout

déçu VERB
disappointed

dédaigneux ADJECTIVE (FEM SING **dédaigneuse**)
disdainful ◊ *d'un air dédaigneux* disdainfully

le **dédain** NOUN
disdain ◊ *avec dédain* with disdain

dedans ADVERB
inside ◊ *C'est une jolie boîte : qu'est-ce qu'il y a dedans?* That's a nice box: what's in it?
♦ **là-dedans (1)** in there ◊ *J'ai trouvé les clés là-dedans.* I found the keys in there.
♦ **là-dedans (2)** in that ◊ *Il y a du vrai là-dedans.* There's some truth in that.

dédicacé ADJECTIVE
♦ **un exemplaire dédicacé** a signed copy

dédier VERB
to dedicate

déduire VERB
to deduct ◊ *Tu as déduit les vingt dollars que je te devais?* Did you deduct the twenty dollars I owed you?
♦ **déduire que** to deduce that ◊ *J'en déduis qu'elle m'a menti.* That means she must have been lying.

la **déesse** NOUN
goddess

défaire VERB
to undo
♦ **défaire sa valise** to unpack
♦ **se défaire** to come undone

la **défaite** NOUN
defeat

le **défaut** NOUN
fault

défavorable ADJECTIVE
unfavourable

défavorisé ADJECTIVE
underprivileged

défectueux ADJECTIVE (FEM SING **défectueuse**)
faulty

défendre VERB
1 to forbid
♦ **défendre à quelqu'un de faire quelque chose** to forbid somebody to do something ◊ *Sa mère lui a défendu de le revoir.* Her mother forbade her to see him again.
2 to defend ◊ *défendre ses idées* to defend one's ideas ◊ *défendre quelqu'un* to defend somebody

défendu ADJECTIVE
forbidden ◊ *C'est défendu.* It's not allowed.

la **défense** NOUN
1 defence ◊ *prendre la défense de quelqu'un* to take somebody's side
♦ **« défense de fumer »** "no smoking"
2 tusk (*of elephant*)

le **défi** NOUN
challenge
♦ **d'un air de défi** defiantly
♦ **sur un ton de défi** defiantly

défier VERB
1 to challenge ◊ *Je te défie de trouver un meilleur exemple.* I challenge you to find a better example.
2 to dare ◊ *Il m'a défié d'aller à l'école en pyjama.* He dared me to go to school in my pyjamas.

défigurer VERB
to disfigure

le **défilé** NOUN
1 parade
♦ **un défilé de mode** a fashion show
2 march

défiler VERB
to march

définir VERB
to define

définitif ADJECTIVE (FEM SING **définitive**)
final
♦ **en définitive** in the end ◊ *En définitive, ils ont décidé de rester.* In the end, they decided to stay.

définitivement ADVERB
for good ◊ *Elle s'est définitivement installée en Nouvelle-Écosse en 1980.* She moved to Nova Scotia for good in 1980.

déformer VERB
to stretch ◊ *Ne tire pas sur ton chandail, tu vas le déformer.* Don't pull down on your sweater, you'll stretch it.
♦ **se déformer** to stretch ◊ *Ce T-shirt s'est déformé au lavage.* This T-shirt got stretched in the wash.

se **défouler** VERB
to unwind (*relax*) ◊ *Je fais de l'aérobic pour me défouler.* I do aerobics to unwind.

dégagé ADJECTIVE
♦ **d'un air dégagé** casually
♦ **sur un ton dégagé** casually

dégager VERB
1 to free ◊ *Ils ont mis une heure à dégager les victimes.* They took an hour to free the victims.
2 to clear ◊ *des gouttes qui dégagent le nez* drops to clear your nose
♦ **Ça se dégage.** It's clearing up. (*weather*)

se **dégarnir** VERB
to go bald

les **dégâts** MASC NOUN
damage

le **dégel** NOUN
thaw

dégeler VERB
to thaw ◊ *faire dégeler un poulet congelé* to thaw out a frozen chicken

dégivrer VERB
1 to defrost
2 to de-ice

dégonfler VERB
to let the air out of ◊ *Quelqu'un a dégonflé mes pneus.* Somebody let the air out of my tires.
♦ **se dégonfler** (*informal*) to chicken out

dégouliner VERB
to trickle

dégourdi ADJECTIVE
smart ◊ *Il est assez dégourdi.* He's on the ball.

dégourdir VERB
♦ **se dégourdir les jambes** to stretch one's legs

le **dégoût** NOUN
disgust ◊ *une expression de dégoût* a disgusted expression
♦ **avec dégoût** disgustedly

dégoûtant ADJECTIVE
disgusting

dégoûté ADJECTIVE
disgusted
♦ **être dégoûté de tout** to be sick of

D

☞

everything

dégoûter VERB
to <u>disgust</u> ◊ *Ce genre de comportement me dégoûte.* That kind of behaviour makes me sick.
♦ **dégoûter quelqu'un de quelque chose** to put somebody off something ◊ *Ça m'a dégoûté de la viande.* That put me off meat.

se **dégrader** VERB
to <u>deteriorate</u>

le **degré** NOUN
<u>degree</u>
♦ **dix degrés Celsius** 10°C

dégringoler VERB
1 <u>to rush down</u> ◊ *Il a dégringolé l'escalier.* He rushed down the stairs.
2 <u>to collapse</u> ◊ *Elle a fait dégringoler la pile de livres.* She knocked over the stack of books.

dégueulasse ADJECTIVE (*rude*)
<u>disgusting</u>

le **déguisement** NOUN
<u>disguise</u>

déguiser VERB
♦ **se déguiser en quelque chose** to dress up as something ◊ *Elle s'est déguisée en vampire.* She dressed up as a vampire.

déguster VERB
1 <u>to taste</u> (*sample*)
2 <u>to enjoy</u>

dehors ADVERB
<u>outside</u> ◊ *Je t'attends dehors.* I'll wait for you outside.
♦ **jeter quelqu'un dehors** to throw somebody out
♦ **en dehors de** apart from ◊ *En dehors de lui, tout le monde était content.* Apart from him, everybody was happy.

déjà ADVERB
1 <u>already</u> ◊ *J'ai déjà fini.* I'm already finished.
2 <u>before</u> ◊ *Tu es déjà venu au Canada?* Have you been to Canada before?

déjeuner VERB
see also **déjeuner** NOUN
✹ to have breakfast

le **déjeuner** NOUN
see also **déjeuner** VERB
✹ breakfast

🛈 *In Canada, Belgium, Switzerland, and some areas of France, **le déjeuner** is the morning meal. Elsewhere in the francophone world, it refers to the noon meal.*

le **délai** NOUN
1 <u>extension</u> ◊ *J'ai demandé un délai d'une semaine.* I asked for a week's extension.
2 <u>time limit</u> ◊ *être dans les délais* to be within the time limit

*Be careful! **délai** does not mean **delay**.*

délasser VERB
to <u>relax</u> ◊ *La lecture délasse.* Reading is relaxing.
♦ **se délasser** to relax ◊ *J'ai pris un bain pour me délasser.* I had a bath to relax.

délavé ADJECTIVE
<u>faded</u> ◊ *un jean délavé* a pair of faded jeans

le **délégué** NOUN
<u>representative</u> ◊ *les délégués de classe* the class representatives

la **déléguée** NOUN
<u>representative</u>

déléguer VERB
to <u>delegate</u>

délibéré ADJECTIVE
<u>deliberate</u>

délicat ADJECTIVE
1 <u>delicate</u> ◊ *avoir la peau délicate* to have delicate skin
2 <u>tricky</u> ◊ *une situation délicate* a tricky situation
3 <u>tactful</u> ◊ *Il est toujours très délicat.* He's always very tactful.
4 <u>thoughtful</u> ◊ *C'est une attention délicate de sa part.* That was a kind thought on her part.

délicatement ADVERB
1 <u>gently</u>
2 <u>tactfully</u>

le **délice** NOUN
<u>delight</u> ◊ *Vivre ici est un vrai délice.* Living here is a real delight. ◊ *Ce gâteau est un vrai délice.* This cake is a real treat.

délicieux ADJECTIVE (FEM SING **délicieuse**)
<u>delicious</u>

la **délinquance** NOUN
<u>crime</u> ◊ *de nouvelles mesures pour combattre la délinquance juvénile* new measures to fight juvenile delinquency

le **délinquant** NOUN

criminal

la **délinquante** NOUN
criminal

délirer VERB
♦ **Mais tu délires!** (*informal*) You're crazy!

délivrer VERB
to set free (*prisoner*)

le **deltaplane** NOUN
hang-glider
♦ **faire du deltaplane** to go hang-gliding

demain ADVERB
tomorrow
♦ **À demain!** See you tomorrow!

la **demande** NOUN
request
♦ **une demande en mariage** an offer of marriage
♦ **faire une demande d'emploi** to apply for a job
♦ **« demandes d'emploi »** "employment wanted"

demandé ADJECTIVE
♦ **très demandé** very much in demand

demander VERB
1 to ask for ◊ *J'ai demandé la permission.* I've asked for permission. ◊ *On a demandé notre chemin à un chauffeur de taxi.* We asked a taxi driver the way. ◊ *Je lui ai demandé de m'aider.* I asked him to help me.
2 to require ◊ *un travail qui demande beaucoup de temps* a job that requires a lot of time
♦ **se demander** to wonder ◊ *Je me demande à quelle heure elle va venir.* I wonder what time she'll be coming.

Be careful! ***demander*** *does not mean to demand.*

le **demandeur d'emploi** NOUN
job applicant

la **demandeuse d'emploi** NOUN
job applicant

la **démangeaison** NOUN
itching

démanger VERB
to itch ◊ *Ça me démange.* It itches.

le **démaquillant** NOUN
make-up remover

démaquiller VERB
♦ **se démaquiller** to remove one's make-up

la **démarche** NOUN
1 way of walking ◊ *une drôle de démarche* a funny way of walking
2 step ◊ *faire les démarches nécessaires* to take the necessary steps

démarrer VERB
1 to start (*car*)
2 to boot up

démêler VERB
to untangle

le **déménagement** NOUN
move (*house*) ◊ *C'était le jour de notre déménagement.* It was the day we moved.
♦ **un camion de déménagement** a moving van

déménager VERB
to move (*house*)

dément ADJECTIVE
crazy

démentiel ADJECTIVE (FEM SING **démentielle**)
insane

demeurer VERB
to live

demi ADJECTIVE, ADVERB
half ◊ *Il a trois ans et demi.* He's three and a half.
♦ **Il est trois heures et demie.** It's half past three.
♦ **Il est midi et demi.** It's half past twelve.
♦ **à demi endormi** half-asleep

le **demi-cercle** NOUN
semicircle

la **demi-douzaine** NOUN
half-dozen ◊ *une demi-douzaine d'œufs* half a dozen eggs

la **demie** NOUN
half-hour ◊ *L'autobus passe à la demie.* The bus comes by on the half-hour.

la **demi-finale** NOUN
semifinal

le **demi-frère** NOUN
half-brother

la **demi-heure** NOUN
half an hour ◊ *dans une demi-heure* in half an hour ◊ *toutes les demi-heures* every half-hour

le **demi-litre** NOUN
half litre ◊ *un demi-litre de lait* half a litre of milk

la **demi-sœur** NOUN
half-sister

la **démission** NOUN
resignation
♦ **donner sa démission** to hand in one's resignation

démissionner VERB
to resign

le **demi-tarif** NOUN

☞

1 half-price ◊ *un billet à demi-tarif* a half-price ticket
2 half-fare ◊ *voyager à demi-tarif* to travel half-fare

le **demi-tour** NOUN
♦ **faire demi-tour** to turn back ◊ *La nuit commence à tomber; il est temps de faire demi-tour.* It's getting dark; it's time we turned back.

la **démocratie** NOUN
democracy

démocratique ADJECTIVE
democratic

démodé ADJECTIVE
old-fashioned

la **demoiselle** NOUN
young lady
♦ **une demoiselle d'honneur** a bridesmaid

démolir VERB
to demolish

le **démon** NOUN
devil

démonter VERB
1 to take down (*tent*)
2 to take apart (*machine*)

démontrer VERB
to show

déneiger VERB
to clear of snow ◊ *déneiger l'entrée* to shovel the driveway ◊ *déneiger les rues* to plow the streets

✹ la **déneigeuse** NOUN
1 snowplow
2 snowblower

✹ le **denim** NOUN
denim ◊ *une veste en denim* a denim jacket

dénoncer VERB
to denounce
♦ **se dénoncer** to give oneself up ◊ *Elle s'est dénoncée à la police.* She gave herself up to the police.

le **dénouement** NOUN
outcome

la **dent** NOUN
tooth ◊ *une dent de lait* a baby tooth ◊ *une dent de sagesse* a wisdom tooth

dentaire ADJECTIVE
dental

la **dentelle** NOUN
lace ◊ *un chemisier en dentelle* a lacy blouse

le **dentier** NOUN
denture

le **dentifrice** NOUN
toothpaste

le/la **dentiste** NOUN
dentist

le **déodorant** NOUN
deodorant

le **dépannage** NOUN
♦ **un service de dépannage** roadside assistance

dépanner VERB
1 to fix ◊ *Elle a dépanné la voiture en cinq minutes.* She fixed the car in five minutes.
2 to help out ◊ *Il m'a prêté dix dollars pour me dépanner.* (*informal*) He lent me 10 dollars to help me out.

✹ le **dépanneur** NOUN
convenience store

la **dépanneuse** NOUN
tow truck

le **départ** NOUN
departure ◊ *Le départ est à onze heures.* The departure is at 11.
♦ **Je lui téléphonerai la veille de son départ.** I'll phone him the day before he leaves.

le **département** NOUN
department ◊ *le département d'anglais à l'université* the English department at the university
✹ ◊ *le département des articles ménagers* the appliances department (*in store*)

dépasser VERB
1 to pass ◊ *Nous avons dépassé Windsor.* We've passed Windsor. ◊ *Il y a une voiture qui essaie de nous dépasser.* There's a car trying to overtake us.
2 to exceed (*sum, limit*)

dépaysé ADJECTIVE
disoriented

se **dépêcher** VERB
to hurry ◊ *Dépêche-toi!* Hurry up!

dépendre VERB
♦ **dépendre de** to depend on ◊ *Ça dépend du temps.* It depends on the weather.
♦ **dépendre de quelqu'un** to be dependent on somebody
♦ **Ça dépend.** It depends.

dépenser VERB
to spend (*money*)

dépensier ADJECTIVE (FEM SING **dépensière**)
♦ **Il est dépensier.** He's a big spender.
♦ **Elle n'est pas dépensière.** She's not exactly extravagant.

dépilatoire ADJECTIVE
♦ **une crème dépilatoire** a depilatory cream

le **dépit** NOUN
- ♦ **en dépit de** in spite of ◊ *Il y est allé en dépit de mes conseils.* He went in spite of my advice.

déplacé ADJECTIVE
  uncalled-for ◊ *C'était une remarque déplacée.* That remark was uncalled-for.

le **déplacement** NOUN
  trip ◊ *Ça vaut le déplacement.* It's worth the trip.

déplacer VERB
  ① to move ◊ *Tu peux m'aider à déplacer la table?* Can you help me move the table?
  ② to put off ◊ *déplacer un rendez-vous* to put off an appointment
- ♦ **se déplacer (1)** to travel around ◊ *Elle se déplace beaucoup pour son travail.* She travels around a lot for her work.
- ♦ **se déplacer (2)** to get around ◊ *Elle a du mal à se déplacer.* She has difficulty getting around.
- ♦ **se déplacer une vertèbre** to slip a disc

déplaire VERB
- ♦ **Cela me déplaît.** I dislike this.

déplaisant ADJECTIVE
  unpleasant

le **dépliant** NOUN
  brochure ◊ *un dépliant touristique* a tourist brochure
- ♦ **un dépliant publicitaire** a flyer

déplier VERB
  to unfold

déposer VERB
  ① to leave ◊ *J'ai déposé mon manteau dans le vestiaire.* I left my coat in the cloakroom.
  ② to put down ◊ *Déposez le paquet sur la table.* Put the parcel down on the table.
  ③ to deposit ◊ *J'ai déposé cent dollars dans mon compte.* I deposited 100 dollars into my account.
- ♦ **déposer quelqu'un** to drop somebody off

le **dépotoir** NOUN
  dump

dépourvu ADJECTIVE
  destitute ◊ *des gens dépourvus* destitute people
- ♦ **être dépourvu de quelque chose** to lack something ◊ *Elle n'est pas dépourvue de talent.* She has no lack of talent.
- ♦ **prendre quelqu'un au dépourvu** to take somebody by surprise ◊ *Sa question m'a pris au dépourvu.* His question took me by surprise.

la **dépression** NOUN
  depression
- ♦ **faire de la dépression** to be suffering from depression
- ♦ **faire une dépression** to have a nervous breakdown

déprimant ADJECTIVE
  depressing

déprimer VERB
  to get depressed ◊ *Il déprime tout le temps.* He gets depressed all the time.
- ♦ **Ce genre de temps me déprime.** This kind of weather makes me depressed.

depuis PREPOSITION, ADVERB
  ① since ◊ *Elle habite Saskatoon depuis 1993.* She's been living in Saskatoon since 1993. ◊ *Je ne lui ai pas parlé depuis.* I haven't spoken to her since.
- ♦ **depuis que** since ◊ *Il a plu tous les jours depuis qu'elle est arrivée.* It's rained every day since she arrived.
  ② for ◊ *Il habite St. Catharines depuis cinq ans.* He's been living in St. Catharines for five years.
- ♦ **Depuis combien de temps?** How long? ◊ *Depuis combien de temps est-ce que vous la connaissez?* How long have you known her?
- ♦ **Depuis quand?** How long? ◊ *Depuis quand est-ce que vous le connaissez?* How long have you known him?

le **député** NOUN
  Member of Parliament
- ✹ ♦ **un député à l'Assemblée législative** a Member of the Legislative Assembly
- ✹ ♦ **un député à l'Assemblée nationale** a Member of the National Assembly
- ✹ ♦ **un député provincial** a Member of Provincial Parliament

la **députée** NOUN
  Member of Parliament
- ✹ ♦ **une députée à l'Assemblée législative** a Member of the Legislative Assembly
- ✹ ♦ **une députée à l'Assemblée nationale** a Member of the National Assembly
- ✹ ♦ **une députée provinciale** a Member of Provincial Parliament

déraciner VERB
  to uproot

le **dérangement** NOUN
- ♦ **en dérangement** out of order ◊ *Le téléphone est en dérangement.* The phone's out of order.

☞

ⓘ *Le Grand Dérangement*, or *Great Deportation*, refers to the mass expulsion of Acadians by the British military between 1755 and 1762. The exiles were scattered throughout the Maritimes and several American colonies, including Louisiana.

déranger VERB
1️⃣ to bother ◊ *Excusez-moi de vous déranger.* I'm sorry to bother you.
♦ **Ne vous dérangez pas, je vais répondre au téléphone.** You stay there, I'll answer the phone.
2️⃣ to disorganize ◊ *Ne dérange pas mes livres, s'il te plaît.* Don't disorganize my books, please.

déraper VERB
to skid

le/la **dermatologue** NOUN
dermatologist ◊ *Elle est dermatologue.* She's a dermatologist.

dernier ADJECTIVE (FEM SING **dernière**)
1️⃣ last ◊ *Il est arrivé dernier.* He arrived last. ◊ *la dernière fois* the last time
2️⃣ latest ◊ *leur dernier film* their latest film
♦ **en dernier** last ◊ *Ajoutez le lait en dernier.* Put the milk in last.

dernièrement ADVERB
recently

dérouler VERB
1️⃣ to unroll
2️⃣ to unwind
♦ **se dérouler** to take place ◊ *L'action se déroule dans les années vingt.* The action takes place in the 1920s.
♦ **Tout s'est déroulé comme prévu.** Everything went as planned.

derrière ADVERB, PREPOSITION

see also **derrière** NOUN

behind

le **derrière** NOUN

see also **derrière** ADVERB

1️⃣ back ◊ *la porte de derrière* the back door
2️⃣ backside ◊ *un coup de pied dans le derrière* a kick in the backside

💥 le **DES** NOUN (= *diplôme d'études secondaires*)
secondary school diploma

des ARTICLE

des is the contracted form of *de* + *les*.

1️⃣ some ◊ *Tu veux des croustilles?* Would you like some chips?

des is sometimes not translated.

◊ *J'ai des cousins en France.* I have cousins in France. ◊ *pendant des mois* for months
2️⃣ any ◊ *Tu as des frères?* Do you have any brothers? ◊ *la fin des vacances* the end of the holidays ◊ *la voiture des Durand* the Durands' car
♦ **Ils arrivent des États-Unis.** They're arriving from the United States.

dès PREPOSITION
as early as ◊ *dès le mois de novembre* from November
♦ **dès le début** right from the start
♦ **Elle vous appellera dès son retour.** She'll call you as soon as she gets back.
♦ **dès que** as soon as ◊ *Il m'a reconnu dès qu'il m'a vu.* He recognized me as soon as he saw me.

désabusé ADJECTIVE
disillusioned

le **désaccord** NOUN
disagreement

désagréable ADJECTIVE
unpleasant

désaltérer VERB
♦ **L'eau gazeuse désaltère bien.** Sparkling water is very thirst-quenching.
♦ **se désaltérer** to quench one's thirst ◊ *Nous sommes allés dans un café pour nous désaltérer.* We went into a café to have a drink.

désapprobateur ADJECTIVE (FEM SING **désapprobatrice**)
disapproving ◊ *un regard désapprobateur* a disapproving look

le **désastre** NOUN
disaster

le **désavantage** NOUN
disadvantage

désavantager VERB
♦ **désavantager quelqu'un** to put somebody at a disadvantage ◊ *Cette nouvelle loi va désavantager les femmes.* The new law will put women at a disadvantage.

descendre VERB
1️⃣ to go down ◊ *Je suis tombé en descendant l'escalier.* I fell as I was going down the stairs.
2️⃣ to come down ◊ *Attends en bas; je descends!* Wait downstairs; I'm coming down!
3️⃣ to get down ◊ *Vous pouvez descendre ma valise, s'il vous plaît?* Can you get my suitcase down, please?

④ to get off ◊ *Nous descendons à la prochaine station.* We're getting off at the next station.

la **descente** NOUN
way down ◊ *Je t'attendrai au bas de la descente.* I'll wait for you at the bottom of the hill.
♦ **une descente de police** a police raid

la **description** NOUN
description

déséquilibré ADJECTIVE
unbalanced

déséquilibrer VERB
♦ **déséquilibrer quelqu'un** to throw somebody off balance ◊ *Le coup de poing l'a déséquilibré.* The punch threw him off balance.

désert ADJECTIVE

see also **désert** NOUN

deserted ◊ *Le dimanche, l'école est déserte.* On Sundays, the school is deserted.
♦ **une île déserte** a desert island

le **désert** NOUN

see also **désert** ADJECTIVE

desert

déserter VERB
to desert

désertique ADJECTIVE
desert ◊ *une région désertique* a desert region

désespéré ADJECTIVE
desperate

désespérer VERB
to despair ◊ *Il ne faut pas désespérer.* Don't despair.

le **désespoir** NOUN
despair

déshabiller VERB
to undress
♦ **se déshabiller** to get undressed

déshériter VERB
to disinherit
♦ **les déshérités** the underprivileged

déshydraté ADJECTIVE
dehydrated

désigner VERB
to choose ◊ *On l'a désignée pour remettre le prix.* She was chosen to present the prize.
♦ **désigner quelque chose du doigt** to point at something

le **désinfectant** NOUN
disinfectant

désinfecter VERB
to disinfect

désintéressé ADJECTIVE
① unselfish ◊ *un acte désintéressé* an unselfish action
② impartial ◊ *un conseil désintéressé* impartial advice

désintéresser VERB
♦ **se désintéresser de quelque chose** to lose interest in something

le **désir** NOUN
① wish ◊ *Vos désirs sont des ordres.* Your wish is my command.
② will ◊ *le désir de réussir* the will to succeed
③ desire ◊ *Ses yeux brillaient de désir.* Her eyes were shining with desire.

désirer VERB
to want ◊ *Vous désirez?* (*in store*) What would you like?

désobéir VERB
♦ **désobéir à quelqu'un** to disobey somebody

désobéissant ADJECTIVE
disobedient

désobligeant ADJECTIVE
unpleasant ◊ *faire une remarque désobligeante* to make an unpleasant remark

le **désodorisant** NOUN
air freshener

désolé ADJECTIVE
sorry ◊ *Je suis vraiment désolé.* I'm very sorry.
♦ **Désolé!** Sorry!

désopilant ADJECTIVE
hilarious

désordonné ADJECTIVE
untidy

le **désordre** NOUN
messiness
♦ **Quel désordre!** What a mess!
♦ **en désordre** messy ◊ *Sa chambre est toujours en désordre.* His bedroom is always messy.

désorganisé ADJECTIVE
disorganized

désormais ADVERB
from now on ◊ *Désormais, je travaillerai plus fort.* From now on I'll work harder.

desquelles PRONOUN

desquelles *is the contracted form of de + **lesquelles**.*

◊ *des négociations au cours desquelles les patrons ont fait des concessions* negotiations during which the employers made concessions

desquels PRONOUN

> ***desquels** is the contracted form of **de** + **lesquels**.*

◊ *les lacs au bord desquels nous avons campé* the lakes on the banks of which we camped

dessécher VERB
to dry out ◊ *Le soleil dessèche la peau.* The sun dries your skin out.

desserrer VERB
to loosen

le **dessert** NOUN
dessert ◊ *Qu'est-ce que vous désirez comme dessert?* What would you like for dessert?

le **dessin** NOUN
drawing ◊ *C'est un dessin de ma petite sœur.* It's a drawing my little sister did.
♦ **un dessin animé** a cartoon (*film*)
♦ **un dessin humoristique** a cartoon (*drawing*)

dessiner VERB
to draw

dessous ADVERB

> *see also* **dessous** NOUN

underneath
♦ **en dessous** underneath ◊ *Soulève le pot de fleurs; la clé est en dessous.* Lift the flowerpot; the key's underneath.
♦ **par-dessous** underneath ◊ *Le grillage ne sert à rien; les lapins passent par-dessous.* The fence is useless; the rabbits get in underneath.
♦ **là-dessous** under there ◊ *Elle s'est cachée là-dessous.* She hid under there.
♦ **ci-dessous** below ◊ *Complétez les phrases ci-dessous.* Complete the sentences below.
♦ **au-dessous de** below ◊ *au-dessous de la moyenne* below average

le **dessous** NOUN

> *see also* **dessous** ADVERB

underneath
♦ **les voisins du dessous** the downstairs neighbours
♦ **les dessous** underwear ◊ *des dessous en soie* silk underwear

dessus ADVERB

> *see also* **dessus** NOUN

on top ◊ *un gâteau avec des bougies dessus* a cake with candles on top
♦ **par-dessus** over ◊ *Nous avons sauté par-dessus la barrière.* We jumped over the gate.
♦ **au-dessus** above ◊ *la taille au-dessus*

the size above ◊ *au-dessus du lit* above the bed
♦ **là-dessus (1)** on there ◊ *Tu peux écrire là-dessus.* You can write on there.
♦ **là-dessus (2)** with that ◊ *« Je démissionne! » Là-dessus, il est parti.* "I resign!" With that, he left.
♦ **ci-dessus** above ◊ *l'exemple ci-dessus* the example above

le **dessus** NOUN

> *see also* **dessus** ADVERB

top
♦ **les voisins du dessus** the upstairs neighbours
♦ **avoir le dessus** to have the upper hand

le/la **destinataire** NOUN
addressee

la **destination** NOUN
destination
♦ **les passagers à destination de Calgary** passengers travelling to Calgary

destiné ADJECTIVE
intended for ◊ *Ce livre est destiné aux enfants.* This book is intended for children.
♦ **Elle était destinée à faire ce métier.** She was destined to go into that job.

la **destruction** NOUN
destruction

le **détachant** NOUN
stain remover

détacher VERB
to undo
♦ **se détacher de quelque chose** to come off something ◊ *La poignée de la porte s'est détachée.* The doorknob came off. ◊ *Un wagon s'est détaché du reste du train.* One car broke away from the rest of the train.

le **détail** NOUN
detail
♦ **en détail** in detail

le/la **détective** NOUN
detective ◊ *un détective privé* a private detective

déteindre VERB
to fade (*in wash*)

détendre VERB
to relax ◊ *La lecture, ça me détend.* I find reading relaxing.
♦ **se détendre** to relax ◊ *prendre un bain pour se détendre* to take a bath in order to relax

la **détente** NOUN
relaxation

le **détenu** NOUN

prisoner

la **détenue** NOUN
prisoner

se **détériorer** VERB
to deteriorate

déterminé ADJECTIVE
1 determined ◊ *C'est un homme déterminé.* He's a determined man.
2 specific ◊ *un but déterminé* a specific aim

détestable ADJECTIVE
horrible

détester VERB
to hate

la **détonation** NOUN
bang ◊ *J'ai entendu une détonation.* I heard a bang.

le **détour** NOUN
detour
♦ **Ça vaut le détour.** It's worth the trip.
♦ **sans détour** to someone's face ◊ *Elle me l'a dit sans détour.* She said it right to my face.

le **détournement** NOUN
♦ **un détournement d'avion** a hijacking

détrempé ADJECTIVE
waterlogged

les **détritus** MASC NOUN
litter SING

détruire VERB
to destroy

la **dette** NOUN
debt

le **deuil** NOUN
♦ **être en deuil** to be in mourning

deux NUMBER
two ◊ *Il était deux heures.* It was two o'clock. ◊ *Elle a deux ans.* She's two.
♦ **deux fois** twice
♦ **le deux-points** colon
♦ **tous les deux** both ◊ *Nous y sommes allées toutes les deux.* We both went.
♦ **le deux février** the second of February

deuxième ADJECTIVE
second ◊ *au deuxième étage* on the second floor

deuxièmement ADVERB
secondly

devais, devait, devaient VERB *see* **devoir**

dévaliser VERB
to rob

devant ADVERB, PREPOSITION

see also **devant** NOUN

1 in front ◊ *Il marchait devant.* He was walking in front.

2 in front of ◊ *Il était assis devant moi.* He was sitting in front of me.
♦ **passer devant** to go past ◊ *Nous sommes passés devant chez toi.* We went past your house.

le **devant** NOUN

see also **devant** ADVERB

front ◊ *le devant de la maison* the front of the house
♦ **les pattes de devant** the front legs

le **développement** NOUN
development
♦ **les pays en voie de développement** developing countries

développer VERB
to develop ◊ *donner un film à développer* to take a film to be developed
♦ **se développer** to develop

devenir VERB
to become

devez VERB *see* **devoir**

deviez VERB *see* **devoir**

deviner VERB
to guess

la **devinette** NOUN
riddle ◊ *poser une devinette à quelqu'un* to ask somebody a riddle

devions VERB *see* **devoir**

dévisager VERB
♦ **dévisager quelqu'un** to stare at somebody

la **devise** NOUN
currency ◊ *les devises étrangères* foreign currency

dévisser VERB
to unscrew

dévoiler VERB
to unveil

devoir VERB

see also **devoir** NOUN

Present tense:
je dois	nous devons
tu dois	vous devez
il/elle doit	ils/elles doivent

Past participle:
dû

1 to have to ◊ *Je dois partir.* I've got to go.
2 must ◊ *Tu dois être fatigué.* You must be tired.
3 to be due to ◊ *Le nouveau centre commercial doit ouvrir en mai.* The new shopping centre is due to open in May.
♦ **devoir quelque chose à quelqu'un**

to owe somebody something
◊ *Combien est-ce que je vous dois?*
How much do I owe you?

le **devoir** NOUN

see also **devoir** VERB

☐ exercise
♦ **les devoirs** homework
☐ duty ◊ *Aller voter fait partie des devoirs du citoyen.* Voting is part of one's duty as a citizen.

devons VERB see **devoir**

dévorer VERB
to devour

dévoué ADJECTIVE
devoted

devra, devrai, devras, devrez, devrons, devront VERB see **devoir**

le **diabète** NOUN
diabetes

diabétique ADJECTIVE
diabetic ◊ *Je suis diabétique.* I'm diabetic.

le **diable** NOUN
devil

diagonal ADJECTIVE (MASC PL **diagonaux**)
diagonal

la **diagonale** NOUN
diagonal
♦ **en diagonale** diagonally

le **diagramme** NOUN
diagram

le **dialecte** NOUN
dialect

le **dialogue** NOUN
dialogue

le **diamant** NOUN
diamond

le **diamètre** NOUN
diameter

la **diapo** NOUN (*informal*)
slide
♦ **un film diapo** a slide film

la **diapositive** NOUN
slide ◊ *projeter des diapositives* to show some slides

la **diarrhée** NOUN
diarrhoea ◊ *avoir la diarrhée* to have diarrhoea

le **dictateur** NOUN
dictator

la **dictatrice** NOUN
dictator

la **dictature** NOUN
dictatorship

la **dictée** NOUN
dictation

dicter VERB
to dictate

le **dictionnaire** NOUN
dictionary

le/la **diététiste** NOUN
dietitian

le **dieu** NOUN (PL les **dieux**)
god ◊ *Dieu* God ◊ *Mon Dieu!* Oh my God!

le **différé** NOUN
♦ **une émission en différé** a recording

la **différence** NOUN
difference
♦ **la différence d'âge** the age difference
♦ **à la différence de** unlike ◊ *À la différence de certains élèves, j'aime étudier.* Unlike some students, I like to study.

différent ADJECTIVE
☐ different ◊ *pour des raisons différentes* for different reasons
☐ various ◊ *pour différentes raisons* for various reasons
♦ **différent de** different from ◊ *Son point de vue est différent du mien.* Her point of view is different from mine.

difficile ADJECTIVE
difficult ◊ *C'est difficile à comprendre.* It's difficult to understand.

difficilement ADVERB
♦ **faire quelque chose difficilement** to have trouble doing something ◊ *Ma grand-mère se déplace difficilement.* My grandmother has trouble getting around.
♦ **Je pouvais difficilement refuser.** It was difficult for me to refuse.

la **difficulté** NOUN
difficulty ◊ *avec difficulté* with difficulty
♦ **être en difficulté** to be in difficulties

digérer VERB
to digest

digne ADJECTIVE
♦ **digne de** worthy of ◊ *digne de confiance* trustworthy

la **dignité** NOUN
dignity

le **dilemme** NOUN
dilemma ◊ *être devant un dilemme* to be faced with a dilemma

diluer VERB
to dilute

le **dimanche** NOUN
☐ Sunday ◊ *Aujourd'hui, on est*

dimanche. It's Sunday today.
② on Sunday ◊ *Dimanche, nous allons déjeuner chez mes grands-parents.* On Sunday we're having lunch at my grandparents'.
♦ **le dimanche** on Sundays ◊ *Le dimanche, je fais la grasse matinée.* I sleep in on Sundays.
♦ **tous les dimanches** every Sunday
♦ **dimanche dernier** last Sunday
♦ **dimanche prochain** next Sunday

la **dimension** NOUN
① size ◊ *avoir la même dimension* to be the same size
② measurement ◊ *Quelles sont les dimensions de cette pièce?* What are the measurements of this room?
③ scope ◊ *la dimension du projet* the scope of the project

diminuer VERB
to decrease ◊ *Est-ce que tu peux diminuer le son?* Could you turn down the sound?

la **diminution** NOUN
① reduction
② decrease

la **dinde** NOUN
turkey ◊ *la dinde de Noël* the Christmas turkey

le **dindon** NOUN
turkey

> *le dindon* refers to a live turkey, whereas *la dinde* refers most often to the meat; *la dinde* can, however, refer to the live female bird as well.

le **dîner** NOUN
| see also **dîner** VERB |

🐾 lunch

> ℹ In Canada, Belgium, Switzerland, and some areas of France, *le dîner* is the noon meal. Elsewhere in the francophone world, it refers to the evening meal.

dîner VERB
| see also **dîner** NOUN |

🐾 to have lunch

dingue ADJECTIVE (*informal*)
crazy

diplomate ADJECTIVE
| see also **diplomate** NOUN |
diplomatic

le/la **diplomate** NOUN
| see also **diplomate** ADJECTIVE |
diplomat

la **diplomatie** NOUN
diplomacy

le **diplôme** NOUN
diploma

dire VERB
① to say ◊ *Il a dit qu'il ne viendrait pas.* He said he wouldn't come.
♦ **on dit que...** they say that... ◊ *On dit que la nourriture est excellente là-bas.* They say that the food is excellent there.
② to tell
♦ **dire quelque chose à quelqu'un** to tell somebody something ◊ *Elle m'a dit la vérité.* She told me the truth. ◊ *Elle nous a dit de regarder cette émission.* She told us to watch this program.
♦ **On dirait qu'il va pleuvoir.** It looks as if it's going to rain.
♦ **se dire quelque chose** ◊ *Quand je l'ai vu, je me suis dit qu'il avait vieilli.* When I saw him, I thought to myself that he'd aged.
♦ **Est-ce que ça se dit?** Can you say that?
♦ **Ça ne me dit rien.** That doesn't appeal to me.

direct ADJECTIVE
direct
♦ **en direct** live ◊ *une émission en direct* a live broadcast

directement ADVERB
straight ◊ *Elle est rentrée directement chez elle.* She went straight home.

le **directeur** NOUN
① principal ◊ *Il est directeur.* He's a principal.
② manager ◊ *Il est directeur du personnel.* He's a personnel manager.

la **direction** NOUN
① management ◊ *la direction et les ouvriers* management and labour
② direction ◊ *dans toutes les directions* in all directions

la **directrice** NOUN
① principal ◊ *Elle est directrice.* She's a principal.
② manager ◊ *Elle est directrice commerciale.* She's a sales manager.

dirent VERB *see* **dire**

le **dirigeant** NOUN
leader

la **dirigeante** NOUN
leader

diriger VERB
to manage ◊ *Il dirige une petite entreprise.* He manages a small company.
♦ **se diriger vers** to head for ◊ *Il se dirigeait vers la gare.* He was heading for the station.

dis VERB *see* **dire**
♦ **Dis-moi la vérité!** Tell me the truth!
♦ **dis donc** hey ◊ *Elle a drôlement changé, dis donc!* Hey, she's really changed! ◊ *Dis donc, tu te souviens de cette chanson?* Hey, do you remember this song?

disaient, disais, disait VERB *see* **dire**

le **discours** NOUN
speech

discret ADJECTIVE (FEM SING **discrète**)
discreet

la **discrimination** NOUN
discrimination ◊ *la discrimination raciale* racial discrimination ◊ *la discrimination sexuelle* sex discrimination

la **discussion** NOUN
discussion

discutable ADJECTIVE
debatable

discuter VERB
[1] to talk ◊ *Nous avons discuté pendant des heures.* We talked for hours.
[2] to argue ◊ *C'est ce que j'ai décidé, alors ne discutez pas!* That's what I've decided, so don't argue!

disent, disiez, disions VERB *see* **dire**

disons VERB *see* **dire**
let's say ◊ *C'est à, disons, une demi-heure à pied.* It's half an hour's walk, say.

disparaître VERB
to disappear
♦ **faire disparaître quelque chose (1)** to make something disappear ◊ *Il a fait disparaître le lapin dans son chapeau.* He made the rabbit disappear in his hat.
♦ **faire disparaître quelque chose (2)** to get rid of something ◊ *Ils ont fait disparaître tous les documents compromettants.* They got rid of all the incriminating documents.

la **disparition** NOUN
disappearance
♦ **une espèce en voie de disparition** an endangered species

disparu ADJECTIVE
♦ **être porté disparu** to be reported missing

✵ **dispendieux** ADJECTIVE (FEM SING **dispendieuse**)
expensive

dispensé ADJECTIVE
♦ **être dispensé de quelque chose** to be excused from something ◊ *Elle est dispensée de gymnastique.* She's excused from gym.

disperser VERB
to break up ◊ *La police a dispersé les manifestants.* The police broke up the demonstrators.
♦ **se disperser** to break up ◊ *Une fois l'ambulance partie, la foule s'est dispersée.* Once the ambulance had left, the crowd broke up.

disponible ADJECTIVE
[1] available ◊ *Il y a encore des billets disponibles pour le concert.* Tickets are still available for the concert. ◊ *Ce livre est disponible en librairie.* This book is available in bookstores.
[2] free ◊ *Elle est toujours disponible le vendredi après-midi.* She's always free on Friday afternoons.

disposé ADJECTIVE
♦ **être disposé à faire quelque chose** to be willing to do something ◊ *Il était disposé à m'aider.* He was willing to help me.

disposer VERB
♦ **disposer de quelque chose** to have access to something ◊ *Je dispose d'un ordinateur.* I have access to a computer.

la **disposition** NOUN
♦ **prendre ses dispositions** to make arrangements ◊ *Est-ce que vous avez pris vos dispositions pour partir en voyage?* Have you made arrangements for your trip?
♦ **avoir quelque chose à sa disposition** to have something at one's disposal ◊ *J'ai un graveur de DC à ma disposition pour la semaine.* I have a CD burner at my disposal for the week.
♦ **Je suis à votre disposition.** I am at your service.
♦ **Je tiens ces livres à votre disposition.** The books are at your disposal.

la **dispute** NOUN
argument

se **disputer** VERB
to argue

le **disque** NOUN
record
♦ **un disque compact** a compact disc
♦ **le disque dur** hard disk

la **disquette** NOUN
floppy disk

disséminé ADJECTIVE
scattered

disséquer VERB
to dissect

la **dissertation** NOUN

essay

dissimuler VERB
to conceal

se **dissiper** VERB
to lift ◊ *Le brouillard va se dissiper dans l'après-midi.* The fog will lift during the afternoon.

le **dissolvant** NOUN
1. solvent
2. nail polish remover

dissoudre VERB
to dissolve
♦ **se dissoudre** to dissolve

dissuader VERB
♦ **dissuader quelqu'un de faire quelque chose** to dissuade somebody from doing something ◊ *Elle m'a dissuadé d'aller voir ce film.* She dissuaded me from going to see the movie.

la **distance** NOUN
distance

distingué ADJECTIVE
distinguished

distinguer VERB
to distinguish

la **distraction** NOUN
entertainment ◊ *Il lit beaucoup : c'est sa seule distraction.* He reads a lot: it's his only form of entertainment.

distraire VERB
♦ **Va voir un film, ça te distraira.** Go see a movie, it'll take your mind off things.

distrait ADJECTIVE
absent-minded

distribuer VERB
1. to give out ◊ *Distribue les livres, s'il te plaît.* Give out the books, please.
2. to deal (*cards*)

✷ la **distributrice** NOUN
vending machine

dit VERB *see* **dire**

dit ADJECTIVE
known as ◊ *Toronto, dite Hogtown* Toronto, known as Hogtown

dites VERB *see* **dire**
♦ **Dites-moi ce que vous pensez.** Tell me what you think.
♦ **dites donc** hey ◊ *Dites donc, vous, là-bas!* Hey, you there!

le **divan** NOUN
sofa
♦ **le divan-lit** sofa bed

divers ADJECTIVE
diverse
♦ **pour diverses raisons** for various reasons

se **divertir** VERB
to enjoy oneself

divertissant ADJECTIVE
entertaining

les **divertissements** MASC NOUN
entertainment ◊ *Le centre touristique offre des sports de plein air, des soirées vidéo et d'autres divertissements.* The resort offers outdoor sports, video nights, and other entertainment.

divin ADJECTIVE
divine

diviser VERB
to divide ◊ *Quatre divisé par deux égalent deux.* 4 divided by 2 equals 2.

le **divorcé** NOUN
divorcee

la **divorcée** NOUN
divorcee

divorcer VERB
to get divorced

dix NUMBER
ten ◊ *Elle a dix ans.* She's ten. ◊ *à dix heures* at ten o'clock
♦ **le dix février** the tenth of February

dix-huit NUMBER ◊ *Il a dix-huit ans.* He's eighteen. ◊ *à dix-huit heures* at 6 p.m.

dixième ADJECTIVE
tenth ◊ *au dixième étage* on the tenth floor

dix-neuf NUMBER ◊ *Elle a dix-neuf ans.* She's nineteen. ◊ *à dix-neuf heures* at 7 p.m.

dix-sept NUMBER ◊ *Il a dix-sept ans.* He's seventeen. ◊ *à dix-sept heures* at 5 p.m.

la **dizaine** NOUN
about ten ◊ *une dizaine de jours* about ten days

le **do** NOUN
1. C ◊ *en do majeur* in C major
2. do ◊ *do, ré, mi...* do, re, mi...

le **docteur** NOUN
doctor

la **docteure** NOUN
doctor

le **document** NOUN
document

le **documentaire** NOUN
documentary

la **documentation** NOUN
documentation

documenter VERB
♦ **se documenter sur quelque chose** to

dodu → dossier

gather information on something

dodu ADJECTIVE
plump

le **doigt** NOUN
finger
♦ **les doigts de pied** the toes

dois, doit, doivent VERB *see* **devoir**

le **domaine** NOUN
① estate ◊ *Il possède un immense domaine en Colombie-Britannique.* He owns a huge estate in British Columbia.
② field ◊ *La chimie n'est pas son domaine.* Chemistry's not his field.

domestique ADJECTIVE
domestic
♦ **les animaux domestiques** pets

le **domicile** NOUN
place of residence
♦ **à domicile** at home ◊ *Il travaille à domicile.* He works at home.

dominer VERB
to dominate
♦ **se dominer** to control oneself

les **dominos** MASC NOUN
dominoes ◊ *jouer aux dominos* to play dominoes

le **dommage** NOUN
damage ◊ *La tempête a causé d'importants dommages.* The storm caused a lot of damage.
♦ **C'est dommage.** Too bad. ◊ *C'est dommage que tu ne puisses pas venir.* Too bad you can't come.

dompter VERB
to tame

le **dompteur** NOUN
animal tamer

la **dompteuse** NOUN
animal tamer

le **don** NOUN
① donation
② gift ◊ *avoir un don pour quelque chose* to have a gift for something
♦ **Elle a le don de mettre les gens à l'aise.** She's got the knack of putting people at ease.

donc CONJUNCTION
so

le **donjon** NOUN
keep (*of castle*)

les **données** FEM NOUN
data

donner VERB
① to give
♦ **donner quelque chose à quelqu'un** to give somebody something ◊ *Elle m'a donné son adresse.* She gave me her address.
♦ **Ça m'a donné faim.** That made me feel hungry.
② to give away ◊ *« Tu as toujours ta veste en daim? » « Non, je l'ai donnée. »* "Do you still have your suede jacket?" "No, I gave it away."
♦ **donner sur quelque chose** to overlook something ◊ *une fenêtre qui donne sur la mer* a window overlooking the sea

dont PRONOUN
① of which ◊ *deux livres, dont l'un est en anglais* two books, one of which is in English ◊ *le prix dont il est si fier* the prize he's so proud of
② of whom ◊ *dix blessés, dont deux grièvement* ten people injured, two of them seriously ◊ *la fille dont je t'ai parlé* the girl I told you about

doré ADJECTIVE

see also **doré** NOUN

golden ◊ *une étoile dorée* a golden star
✹ ♦ **le pain doré** French toast

✹ le **doré** NOUN

see also **doré** ADJECTIVE

walleye (*fish*)

dorénavant ADVERB
from now on ◊ *Dorénavant, tu feras attention.* From now on, you'll be careful.

dorloter VERB
to pamper

dormir VERB
① to sleep ◊ *Tu as bien dormi?* Did you sleep well?
② to be asleep ◊ *Ne faites pas de bruit, il dort.* Don't make any noise, he's asleep.

le **dortoir** NOUN
dormitory

le **dos** NOUN
back ◊ *dos à dos* back to back
♦ **faire quelque chose dans le dos de quelqu'un** to do something behind somebody's back ◊ *Elle me critique dans mon dos.* She criticizes me behind my back.
♦ **de dos** from behind
♦ **nager le dos crawlé** to swim the backstroke
♦ **« voir au dos »** "see other side"

la **dose** NOUN
dose ◊ *Ne pas dépasser la dose prescrite.* Do not exceed the stated dose.

le **dossier** NOUN
① file ◊ *une pile de dossiers* a stack

of files
② <u>record</u> ◊ *un bon dossier scolaire* a good academic record
③ <u>folder</u> (*computer*)
④ <u>feature</u> (*in magazine*)
⑤ <u>back</u> (*of chair*)

la **douane** NOUN
<u>customs</u>

le **douanier** NOUN
<u>customs officer</u>

la **douanière** NOUN
<u>customs officer</u>

double ADJECTIVE

| see also **double** NOUN |

<u>double</u>
♦ **à double interligne** double-spaced
♦ **le double échec** cross-checking
◊ *faire double échec à un adversaire* to cross-check an opponent

le **double** NOUN

| see also **double** ADJECTIVE |

♦ **le double** twice as much ◊ *Il gagne le double.* He earns twice as much. ◊ *le double du prix normal* twice the normal price
♦ **en double** in duplicate ◊ *Garde cette photo, je l'ai en double.* Keep this photo, I've got a copy of it.
♦ **le double messieurs** the men's doubles (*tennis*)

double-cliquer VERB
<u>to double-click</u> ◊ *double-cliquer sur une icône* to double-click on an icon

doubler VERB
① <u>to double</u> ◊ *Le prix a doublé en dix ans.* The price has doubled in 10 years.
② <u>to pass</u> (*in car*) ◊ *Il est dangereux de doubler sur cette route.* It's dangerous to pass on this road.
♦ **un film doublé** a dubbed film

douce ADJECTIVE *see* **doux**

doucement ADVERB
① <u>gently</u> ◊ *Elle a frappé doucement à la porte.* She knocked gently at the door.
② <u>slowly</u> ◊ *Roulez doucement!* Drive slowly! ◊ *Je ne comprends pas; parle plus doucement.* I don't understand; speak more slowly.

la **douceur** NOUN
① <u>softness</u> ◊ *Cette crème maintient la douceur de votre peau.* This cream keeps your skin soft.
② <u>gentleness</u> ◊ *parler avec douceur* to speak gently
♦ **L'avion a atterri en douceur.** The plane made a smooth landing.

la **douche** NOUN

<u>shower</u>
♦ **les douches** the shower room
♦ **prendre une douche** to have a shower

se **doucher** VERB
<u>to take a shower</u>

doué ADJECTIVE
<u>talented</u>
♦ **être doué en quelque chose** to be good at something ◊ *Elle est douée en maths.* She's good at math.

douillet ADJECTIVE (FEM SING **douillette**)
① <u>cozy</u> ◊ *un chandail douillet* a cozy sweater
② <u>soft</u> ◊ *Je ne supporte pas la douleur; je suis très douillette.* I can't stand pain; I'm a real softie.

❉ la **douillette** NOUN
<u>comforter</u>

la **douleur** NOUN
<u>pain</u>

douloureux ADJECTIVE (FEM SING **douloureuse**)
<u>painful</u>

le **doute** NOUN
<u>doubt</u>
♦ **sans doute** probably

douter VERB
<u>to doubt</u>
♦ **douter de quelque chose** to doubt something ◊ *Je doute de sa sincérité.* I have my doubts about his sincerity.
♦ **se douter de quelque chose** to suspect something ◊ *Je ne me doutais de rien.* I didn't suspect anything.
♦ **Je m'en doutais.** I thought as much.

douteux ADJECTIVE (FEM SING **douteuse**)
① <u>dubious</u> ◊ *une plaisanterie d'un goût douteux* a joke in dubious taste
② <u>suspicious-looking</u> ◊ *un individu douteux* a suspicious-looking person

doux ADJECTIVE (FEM SING **douce**, MASC PL **doux**)
① <u>soft</u> ◊ *un tissu doux* soft fabric
◊ *les drogues douces* soft drugs
② <u>sweet</u> ◊ *du cidre doux* sweet cider
③ <u>mild</u> ◊ *Il fait doux aujourd'hui.* It's mild out today.
④ <u>gentle</u> ◊ *C'est quelqu'un de très doux.* He's a very gentle person.
♦ **en douce** on the quiet ◊ *Elle m'a donné cinq dollars en douce.* She slipped me 5 dollars on the quiet.

la **douzaine** NOUN
<u>dozen</u> ◊ *une douzaine d'œufs* a dozen eggs
♦ **une douzaine de personnes** about twelve people

douze NUMBER

☞

twelve ◊ *Il a douze ans.* He's twelve.
♦ **le douze février** the twelfth of February

douzième ADJECTIVE
twelfth ◊ *au douzième étage* on the twelfth floor

dramatique ADJECTIVE
tragic ◊ *une situation dramatique* a tragic situation
♦ **l'art dramatique** drama

le **drame** NOUN
drama (*incident*)
♦ **Ça n'est pas un drame si tu ne viens pas.** It's not the end of the world if you don't come.

le **drap** NOUN
sheet (*for bed*)

le **drapeau** NOUN (PL les **drapeaux**)
flag ◊ *le drapeau canadien* the Canadian flag

dressé ADJECTIVE
trained ◊ *un chien bien dressé* a well-trained dog

dresser VERB
1 to draw up ◊ *dresser une liste* to draw up a list
2 to train ◊ *dresser un chien* to train a dog
♦ **dresser l'oreille** to perk up one's ears ◊ *Quand elle a dit ça, il a dressé l'oreille.* When she said that, he perked up his ears.

la **drogue** NOUN
drug ◊ *le problème de la drogue* the drug problem ◊ *la lutte contre la drogue* the war against drugs
♦ **les drogues douces** soft drugs
♦ **les drogues dures** hard drugs

le **drogué** NOUN
drug addict

la **droguée** NOUN
drug addict

droguer VERB
♦ **droguer quelqu'un** to drug somebody
♦ **se droguer** to take drugs

droit ADJECTIVE, ADVERB

see also **droit** NOUN

1 right ◊ *le bras droit* the right arm ◊ *le côté droit* the right-hand side
2 straight ◊ *une ligne droite* a straight line ◊ *Tiens-toi droite!* Stand up straight!
♦ **tout droit** straight ahead

le **droit** NOUN

see also **droit** ADJECTIVE

1 right ◊ *les droits de la personne* human rights
♦ **avoir le droit de faire quelque chose**

to be allowed to do something ◊ *On n'a pas le droit de fumer à l'école.* We're not allowed to smoke at school.
2 law (*profession*) ◊ *faire son droit* to study law ◊ *un étudiant en droit* a law student ◊ *pratiquer le droit* to practise law

la **droite** NOUN

see also **droit** ADJECTIVE

right ◊ *sur votre droite* on your right
♦ **à droite (1)** on the right ◊ *la troisième rue à droite* the third street on the right
♦ **à droite (2)** to the right ◊ *à droite de la fenêtre* to the right of the window ◊ *Tournez à droite.* Turn right.
♦ **la voie de droite** the right-hand lane
♦ **la droite** the right (*in politics*) ◊ *Il est très à droite.* He's very right-wing.
♦ **une droite** (*math*) a straight line

droitier ADJECTIVE (FEM SING **droitière**)
right-handed ◊ *Elle est droitière.* She's right-handed.

drôle ADJECTIVE
funny ◊ *Ça n'est pas drôle.* It's not funny.
♦ **un drôle de temps** funny weather

du ARTICLE

*du is the contracted form of **de** + **le**.*

1 some ◊ *Tu veux du fromage?* Would you like some cheese?
2 any ◊ *Tu as du chocolat?* Do you have any chocolate? ◊ *la porte du garage* the door of the garage ◊ *le bureau du directeur* the principal's office

dû VERB see **devoir**

see also **dû** ADJECTIVE

♦ **Nous avons dû nous arrêter.** We had to stop.

dû ADJECTIVE (FEM **due**, MASC PL **dus**)

see also **dû** VERB

♦ **dû à** due to ◊ *un retard dû au mauvais temps* a delay due to bad weather

la **dualité** NOUN
duality ◊ *la dualité linguistique du Canada* Canada's linguistic duality

dupe ADJECTIVE
♦ **Elle me ment mais je ne suis pas dupe.** She lies to me but I'm not taken in.

le **duplex** NOUN (PL les **duplex**)
duplex

dur ADJECTIVE, ADVERB
hard ◊ *travailler dur* to work hard ◊ *être dur avec quelqu'un* to be hard on somebody

durant PREPOSITION

⒈ during ◊ *durant la nuit* during the night

⒉ for ◊ *durant des années* for years
◊ *des mois durant* for months

la **durée** NOUN

length (*time*) ◊ *Quelle est la durée des études d'ingénieur?* How long does it take to train as an engineer?

♦ **pour une durée de deux semaines** for a period of two weeks

♦ **de courte durée** short ◊ *un séjour de courte durée* a short stay

♦ **de longue durée** long ◊ *une absence de longue durée* a long absence

durement ADVERB

harshly

durer VERB

to last

la **dureté** NOUN

harshness ◊ *traiter quelqu'un avec dureté* to treat somebody harshly

le **DVD** NOUN

DVD

D

dynamique ADJECTIVE

dynamic

dyslexique ADJECTIVE

dyslexic

E

l' **eau** FEM NOUN (PL les **eaux**)
  water
  ♦ **l'eau minérale** mineral water
  ♦ **l'eau plate** still water
  ♦ **tomber à l'eau** to fall through ◊ *Nos projets sont tombés à l'eau.* Our plans have fallen through.

ébahi ADJECTIVE
  amazed

éblouir VERB
  to dazzle

ébouillanter VERB
  to scald

l' **écaille** FEM NOUN
  scale (*of fish*)

s' **écailler** VERB
  to peel (*paint*)

l' **écart** MASC NOUN
  gap
  ♦ **à l'écart de** away from ◊ *Ils se sont assis à l'écart des autres.* They sat down away from the others.

écarté ADJECTIVE
  remote
  ♦ **les bras écartés** arms outstretched
  ♦ **les jambes écartées** legs apart

écarter VERB
  to spread apart
  ♦ **écarter les bras** to open one's arms wide
  ♦ **s'écarter** to move ◊ *Ils se sont écartés pour la laisser passer.* They moved to let her pass.

l' **échafaudage** MASC NOUN
  scaffolding

l' **échalote** FEM NOUN
  shallot

l' **échange** MASC NOUN
  exchange ◊ *en échange de* in exchange for
  ♦ **un échange étudiant** a student exchange

échanger VERB
  to trade ◊ *Je t'échange cette carte de hockey contre celle-là.* I'll trade you this hockey card for that one.

l' **échantillon** MASC NOUN
  sample

échapper VERB
  ♦ **échapper à** to escape from ◊ *Le prisonnier a réussi à échapper à la police.* The prisoner managed to escape from the police.

  ♦ **s'échapper** to escape ◊ *Il s'est échappé de prison.* He escaped from prison.
  ♦ **l'échapper belle** to have a narrow escape ◊ *Nous l'avons échappé belle.* We had a narrow escape.

l' **écharde** FEM NOUN
  splinter

s' **échauffer** VERB
  to warm up (*before exercise*) ◊ *Les joueurs se sont échauffés avant le match.* The players warmed up before the game.

l' **échec** MASC NOUN
  failure
  ♦ **subir un échec** to suffer a setback
  ♦ **voué à l'échec** bound to fail

les **échecs** MASC NOUN
  chess SING ◊ *jouer aux échecs* to play chess

l' **échelle** FEM NOUN
  [1] ladder
  [2] scale (*of map*)

l' **écho** MASC NOUN
  echo

échouer VERB
  ♦ **échouer à un examen** to fail an exam

éclabousser VERB
  to splash

l' **éclair** MASC NOUN
  flash of lightning
  ♦ **un éclair au chocolat** a chocolate éclair
  ♦ **à la vitesse de l'éclair** with lightning speed
  ♦ **un éclair de génie** a brainwave

l' **éclairage** MASC NOUN
  lighting

l' **éclaircie** FEM NOUN
  sunny period

éclairer VERB
  ♦ **Cette lampe éclaire bien.** This lamp gives good light.

l' **éclat** MASC NOUN
  [1] fragment (*of glass*) ◊ *Le vase a volé en éclats.* The vase smashed into pieces.
  [2] brightness (*of sun, colour*)
  ♦ **des éclats de rire** roars of laughter

éclatant ADJECTIVE
  brilliant ◊ *un jaune éclatant* a brilliant yellow ◊ *une lumière éclatante* a brilliant light

éclater VERB

① to burst (*tire, balloon*)
♦ **éclater de rire** to burst out laughing
♦ **éclater en sanglots** to burst into tears
② to break out ◊ *La Seconde Guerre mondiale a éclaté en 1939.* The Second World War broke out in 1939.

l' **éclipse** FEM NOUN
eclipse

écœurant ADJECTIVE
sickening

écœurer VERB
♦ **Tous ces mensonges m'écœurent.** All these lies make me sick.

l' **école** FEM NOUN
school ◊ *aller à l'école* to go to school
◊ *une école privée* a private school
◊ *une école publique* a public school

l' **écolier** MASC NOUN
schoolboy

l' **écolière** FEM NOUN
schoolgirl

l' **écologie** FEM NOUN
ecology

écologique ADJECTIVE
ecological ◊ *un détergent écologique* an environmentally-friendly detergent

éconergétique ADJECTIVE
energy-efficient

l' **économie** FEM NOUN
① economy ◊ *l'économie du Canada* the Canadian economy
② economics ◊ *un cours d'économie* an economics class

les **économies** FEM NOUN
savings
♦ **faire des économies** to save up
◊ *Je fais des économies pour partir en vacances.* I'm saving up for my holidays.

économique ADJECTIVE
① economic ◊ *une crise économique* an economic crisis
② economical ◊ *Il est plus économique d'acheter une grande boîte de détergent.* It's more economical to buy a big box of detergent. ◊ *Cette petite voiture est économique.* This little car is cheap to run.

économiser VERB
to save

l' **économiseur d'écran** MASC NOUN
screen saver

l' **écorce** FEM NOUN
① bark (*of tree*)
♦ **l'écorce de bouleau** birch bark
② peel (*of orange, lemon*)

s' **écorcher** VERB
♦ **Je me suis écorché le genou.** I've grazed my knee.

l' **écosystème** MASC NOUN
ecosystem

s' **écouler** VERB
① to flow out (*water*)
② to pass ◊ *Le temps s'écoule trop vite.* Time passes too quickly.

écouter VERB
to listen to ◊ *J'aime écouter de la musique.* I like listening to music.
♦ **Écoute-moi!** Listen!

l' **écouteur** MASC NOUN
earpiece (*of phone*)

l' **écran** MASC NOUN
screen
♦ **le petit écran** television
♦ **l'écran solaire** sunblock

écraser VERB
① to crush ◊ *Écrasez une gousse d'ail.* Crush a clove of garlic.
② to run over ◊ *Regarde bien avant de traverser, sinon tu vas te faire écraser.* Look carefully before you cross or you'll get run over.
♦ **s'écraser** to crash ◊ *L'avion s'est écrasé dans le désert.* The plane crashed in the desert.

écrémé ADJECTIVE
♦ **le lait écrémé** skim milk

l' **écrevisse** FEM NOUN
crayfish

écrire VERB
to write ◊ *Nous nous écrivons régulièrement.* We write to each other regularly.
♦ **Ça s'écrit comment?** How do you spell that?

l' **écrit** MASC NOUN
piece of writing ◊ *les écrits de Gabrielle Roy* the writings of Gabrielle Roy
♦ **par écrit** in writing

l' **écriture** FEM NOUN
writing ◊ *J'ai du mal à lire son écriture.* I can't read her writing.

l' **écrivain** MASC NOUN
writer ◊ *Il est écrivain.* He's a writer.

l' **écrivaine** FEM NOUN
writer ◊ *Elle est écrivaine.* She's a writer.

l' **écrou** MASC NOUN
nut (*metal*)

s' **écrouler** VERB
to collapse

écru ADJECTIVE
off-white

E

l' **écureuil** MASC NOUN
squirrel

l' **écurie** FEM NOUN
stable

éditer VERB
① to publish ◊ *On vient d'éditer un nouveau dictionnaire.* A new dictionary has just been published.
② to edit (*computer file*)

l' **éditeur** MASC NOUN
publisher

l' **édition** FEM NOUN
① edition ◊ *une édition de poche* a paperback edition
② publishing ◊ *Elle travaille dans l'édition.* She works in publishing.

l' **éducateur** MASC NOUN
teacher (*of people with special needs*)

éducatif ADJECTIVE (FEM SING **éducative**)
educational ◊ *un jeu éducatif* an educational game

l' **éducation** FEM NOUN
① education
♦ **le cours d'éducation civique** Civics course ◊ *l'éducation physique* physical education ◊ *Il n'a pas beaucoup d'éducation.* He's not very well educated.
② upbringing ◊ *Elle a reçu une éducation très stricte.* She had a very strict upbringing.

l' **éducatrice** FEM NOUN
teacher (*of people with special needs*)

éduquer VERB
to educate

effacer VERB
to erase

effarant ADJECTIVE
amazing ◊ *Il a mangé une quantité effarante de pain.* He ate an amazing amount of bread.

effectivement ADVERB
indeed ◊ *Il est effectivement plus rapide de passer par là.* It is indeed quicker to go this way. ◊ *Oui, effectivement.* Yes, indeed.

*Be careful! **effectivement** does not mean **effectively**.*

effectuer VERB
① to make ◊ *Ils ont effectué de nombreux changements.* They have made a lot of changes.
② to do ◊ *On vient d'effectuer des travaux dans le bâtiment.* They have just done some work in the building.

l' **effet** MASC NOUN
effect
♦ **faire de l'effet** to take effect ◊ *Ce médicament fait rapidement de l'effet.* This medicine takes effect quickly.
♦ **Ça m'a fait un drôle d'effet de le revoir.** It gave me a strange feeling to see him again.
♦ **en effet** yes indeed ◊ *« Je ne me sens pas très bien. » « En effet, tu as l'air pâle. »* "I don't feel very well." "Yes, you do look pale."

efficace ADJECTIVE
① efficient ◊ *C'est une travailleuse efficace.* She's an efficient worker.
② effective ◊ *un médicament efficace* an effective medicine

s' **effondrer** VERB
to collapse

s' **efforcer** VERB
♦ **s'efforcer de faire quelque chose** to try hard to do something ◊ *Il s'efforce d'être aimable avec la clientèle.* He tries hard to be polite to the customers.

l' **effort** MASC NOUN
effort ◊ *faire un effort* to make an effort

effrayant ADJECTIVE
frightening

effrayer VERB
to frighten

effronté ADJECTIVE
mouthy ◊ *Cet enfant est vraiment effronté.* That kid is really mouthy.

effroyable ADJECTIVE
horrifying

égal ADJECTIVE (MASC PL **égaux**)
equal ◊ *une quantité égale de farine et de sucre* equal quantities of flour and sugar
♦ **Ça m'est égal. (1)** I have no preference. ◊ *« Tu préfères du riz ou des pâtes ? » « Ça m'est égal. »* "Would you rather have rice or pasta?" "Either is fine with me."
♦ **Ça m'est égal. (2)** I don't care. ◊ *Fais ce que tu veux, ça m'est égal.* Do what you like, I don't care.

également ADVERB
also

égaler VERB
to equal

l' **égalité** FEM NOUN
equality
♦ **être à égalité** to be tied ◊ *Maintenant les deux joueurs sont à égalité.* The two players are now tied.

l' **égard** MASC NOUN
♦ **à cet égard** in this respect

égarer VERB
to mislay ◊ *J'ai égaré mes clés.* I've

mislaid my keys.
♦ **s'égarer** to get lost ◊ *Ils se sont égarés dans la forêt.* They got lost in the forest.

l' **église** FEM NOUN
church ◊ *aller à l'église* to go to church

l' **égoïsme** MASC NOUN
selfishness

égoïste ADJECTIVE
selfish

l' **égout** MASC NOUN
sewer

l' **égratignure** FEM NOUN
scratch

eh EXCLAMATION
hey!
♦ **eh bien** well

l' **élan** MASC NOUN
♦ **prendre de l'élan** to gather speed

s' **élancer** VERB
to rush ◊ *Il s'est élancé vers moi.* He rushed towards me.

élargir VERB
1 to widen
2 to expand
♦ **élargir ses horizons** to broaden one's horizons

l' **élastique** MASC NOUN
rubber band

l' **électeur** MASC NOUN
voter

l' **élection** FEM NOUN
election ◊ *une élection provinciale* a provincial election

l' **électrice** FEM NOUN
voter (*woman*)

l' **électricien** MASC NOUN
electrician

l' **électricienne** FEM NOUN
electrician

l' **électricité** FEM NOUN
1 electricity
✹ 2 hydro ◊ *une facture d'électricité* a hydro bill
♦ **allumer l'électricité** to turn on the light
♦ **éteindre l'électricité** to turn off the light

électrique ADJECTIVE
electric ◊ *le courant électrique* electric current

l' **électronique** FEM NOUN
electronics

élégant ADJECTIVE
elegant

élémentaire ADJECTIVE
elementary

l' **éléphant** MASC NOUN
elephant

l' **élevage** MASC NOUN
cattle farming ◊ *faire de l'élevage* to raise cattle
♦ **un élevage de porcs** a pig farm
♦ **un élevage de poulets** a chicken farm
♦ **le saumon d'élevage** farmed salmon

élevé ADJECTIVE
high ◊ *Le prix est trop élevé.* The price is too high.
♦ **être bien élevé** to be well brought up
♦ **être mal élevé** to be not very well brought up

l' **élève** MASC/FEM NOUN
student (*elementary school*)

élever VERB
1 to bring up ◊ *Il a été élevé par sa grand-mère.* He was brought up by his grandmother.
2 to breed ◊ *Son oncle élève des chevaux.* Her uncle breeds horses.
♦ **élever la voix** to raise one's voice
♦ **s'élever à** to come to ◊ *À combien s'élèvent les dégâts?* How much does the damage come to?

l' **éleveur** MASC NOUN
1 breeder (*dogs, horses*)
2 farmer (*cattle, pigs, chickens*)

éliminatoire ADJECTIVE
♦ **une note éliminatoire** a failing mark
♦ **une épreuve éliminatoire** a qualifying round (*sport*)

les **éliminatoires** FEM NOUN
playoffs ◊ *regarder les éliminatoires de hockey à la télévision* to watch the hockey playoffs on TV

éliminer VERB
to eliminate

élire VERB
to elect

elle PRONOUN
1 she ◊ *Elle est institutrice.* She is a primary school teacher.
2 her ◊ *Vous pouvez avoir confiance en elle.* You can trust her.
3 it ◊ *Prends cette chaise : elle est plus confortable.* Take this chair: it's more comfortable.

elle is also used for emphasis.

◊ *Elle, elle est toujours en retard!* Oh, SHE's always late!
♦ **elle-même** herself ◊ *Elle l'a choisi elle-même.* She chose it herself.

elles PRONOUN
they ◊ *« Où sont les filles? » « Elles*

☞

sont allées au cinéma. » "Where are the girls?" "They've gone to the movies."

♦ **elles-mêmes** themselves

élogieux ADJECTIVE (FEM SING **élogieuse**)
<u>complimentary</u> ◊ *Ton professeur a été très élogieux à propos de ton travail.* Your teacher was very complimentary about your work.

éloigné ADJECTIVE
<u>distant</u>

s' **éloigner** VERB
<u>to go far away</u> ◊ *Ne vous éloignez pas : le dîner est bientôt prêt!* Don't go far away: dinner will soon be ready!

♦ **Vous vous éloignez du sujet.** You are getting off the point.

l' **emballage** MASC NOUN
♦ **le papier d'emballage** wrapping paper

emballer VERB
<u>to wrap</u>
♦ **s'emballer** (*informal*) to get excited ◊ *Elle s'est emballée pour ce projet.* She got really excited about this plan.

l' **embarquement** MASC NOUN
<u>boarding</u> ◊ *« embarquement immédiat »* "now boarding" ◊ *L'embarquement des passagers n'a pas encore été annoncé.* Passenger boarding has not been announced yet.

l' **embarras** MASC NOUN
<u>embarrassment</u> ◊ *Votre question me met dans l'embarras.* Your question is an awkward one.
♦ **Vous n'avez que l'embarras du choix.** The only problem is choosing.

embarrassant ADJECTIVE
<u>embarrassing</u>

embarrasser VERB
<u>to embarrass</u> ◊ *Cela m'embarrasse de vous demander encore un service.* I'm embarrassed to ask another favour from you.

embaucher VERB
<u>to hire</u> ◊ *L'entreprise vient d'embaucher cinquante ouvriers.* The firm has just hired fifty workers.

embêtant ADJECTIVE
<u>annoying</u>

l' **embêtement** MASC NOUN
<u>trouble</u> ◊ *J'ai eu un embêtement : la voiture est tombée en panne.* I had some trouble: the car broke down.

embêter VERB
<u>to bother</u> ◊ *Tu m'embêtes avec tes questions.* You're bothering me with

your questions.

l' **embouteillage** MASC NOUN
<u>traffic jam</u>

embrasser VERB
<u>to kiss</u> ◊ *Elle m'a embrassé.* She kissed me. ◊ *Ils se sont embrassés.* They kissed.

s' **embrouiller** VERB
<u>to get confused</u> ◊ *Il s'embrouille dans ses explications.* He gets confused when he explains things.

émerveiller VERB
<u>to amaze</u>

l' **émeute** FEM NOUN
<u>riot</u>

émigrer VERB
<u>to emigrate</u>

l' **émission** FEM NOUN
[1] <u>show</u> (*radio, TV*) ◊ *une émission de télévision* a TV show
[2] <u>emission</u> ◊ *les émissions de gaz toxique* toxic gas emissions

emmêler VERB
[1] <u>to tangle up</u> ◊ *Mes cheveux sont tout emmêlés.* My hair is all tangled up.
[2] <u>to confuse</u> ◊ *Elle emmêle tout.* She confuses everything.
♦ **s'emmêler** to get tangled up ◊ *Sa ligne de pêche s'est emmêlée dans la mienne.* His fishing line got tangled up with mine.

emménager VERB
<u>to move in</u> ◊ *Nous venons d'emménager dans une nouvelle maison.* We've just moved into a new house.

emmener VERB
<u>to take</u> ◊ *Ils m'ont emmené au cinéma pour mon anniversaire.* They took me to the movies for my birthday.

émotif ADJECTIVE (FEM SING **émotive**)
<u>emotional</u> ◊ *Il est très émotif.* He's very emotional.

l' **émotion** FEM NOUN
<u>emotion</u>

émotionnel ADJECTIVE (FEM SING **émotionnelle**)
<u>emotional</u> ◊ *un choc émotionnel* an emotional shock

émouvoir VERB
<u>to move</u> ◊ *Ta lettre l'a beaucoup émue.* She was deeply moved by your letter.

s' **emparer** VERB
♦ **s'emparer de** to grab ◊ *Elle s'est emparée de ma valise.* She grabbed

my suitcase.

l' **empêchement** MASC NOUN
♦ **Nous avons eu un empêchement de dernière minute.** We were held up at the last minute.

empêcher VERB
to prevent ◊ *Le café le soir m'empêche de dormir.* Coffee at night keeps me awake.
♦ **Il n'a pas pu s'empêcher de rire.** He couldn't help laughing.

empiler VERB
to pile up

empirer VERB
to worsen ◊ *La situation a encore empiré.* The situation got even worse.

l' **emplacement** MASC NOUN
site ◊ *Un panneau indique l'ancien emplacement du château.* A sign shows the former site of the castle.
♦ **un emplacement de camping** a campsite

l' **emploi** MASC NOUN
1 job ◊ *trouver un emploi* to find a job
2 use ◊ *prêt à l'emploi* ready for use
♦ **un emploi du temps** a timetable
♦ **le mode d'emploi** directions for use

l' **employé** MASC NOUN
employee
♦ **un employé de bureau** an office worker

l' **employée** FEM NOUN
employee
♦ **une employée de banque** a bank clerk

employer VERB
1 to use ◊ *Quelle méthode employez-vous?* What method do you use?
2 to employ ◊ *L'entreprise emploie dix ingénieurs.* The firm employs ten engineers.

l' **employeur** MASC NOUN
employer

empoisonner VERB
to poison

emporter VERB
to take ◊ *N'emportez que le strict nécessaire.* Take only the bare minimum.
♦ **mets à emporter** takeout food
♦ **s'emporter** to lose one's temper ◊ *Je m'emporte facilement.* I'm quick to lose my temper.

l' **empreinte** FEM NOUN
♦ **une empreinte digitale** a fingerprint

s' **empresser** VERB
♦ **s'empresser de faire quelque chose** to be quick to do something ◊ *Ils se*

sont empressés de nous annoncer la nouvelle. They were quick to tell us the news.

emprisonner VERB
to imprison

l' **emprunt** MASC NOUN
loan

emprunter VERB
to borrow
♦ **emprunter quelque chose à quelqu'un** to borrow something from somebody ◊ *Je peux t'emprunter dix dollars?* Can I borrow ten dollars from you?

ému ADJECTIVE
touched ◊ *J'ai été très ému par sa gentillesse.* I was very touched by her kindness.

en PREPOSITION, PRONOUN
1 in ◊ *Il habite en Terre-Neuve.* He lives in Newfoundland. ◊ *La mariée est en blanc.* The bride is in white. ◊ *Je le verrai en mai.* I'll see him in May.
2 to ◊ *Je vais en Saskatchewan cet été.* I'm going to Saskatchewan this summer.
3 by ◊ *C'est plus rapide en voiture.* It's faster by car. ◊ *On peut apprendre beaucoup en lisant.* You can learn a lot by reading.
4 made of ◊ *C'est en verre.* It's made of glass. ◊ *un collier en argent* a silver necklace
5 while ◊ *Il s'est coupé le doigt en ouvrant une boîte de conserve.* He cut his finger while opening a tin.
♦ **Elle est sortie en courant.** She ran out.

When **en** is used with **avoir** and **il y a**, it is not translated in English.

◊ *« Est-ce que tu as un dictionnaire? » « Oui, j'en ai un. »* "Have you got a dictionary?" "Yes, I've got one."
◊ *« Combien d'élèves y a-t-il dans ta classe? » « Il y en a trente. »* "How many pupils are there in your class?" "There are 30."

en is also used with verbs and expressions normally followed by **de** to avoid repeating the same word.

◊ *Si tu as un problème, tu peux m'en parler.* If you have a problem, you can talk to me about it. ◊ *Est-ce que tu peux me rendre ce livre? J'en ai besoin.* Can you give me back that book? I need it. ◊ *Il a un beau jardin et il en est très fier.* He's got a beautiful garden and is very proud of it.
♦ **J'en ai assez.** I've had enough.

encaisser VERB
to cash (cheque)

enceinte ADJECTIVE
pregnant ◊ Elle est enceinte de six mois. She's 6 months pregnant.

encercler VERB
to circle ◊ Encerclez la bonne réponse. Circle the right answer.

enchanté ADJECTIVE
delighted ◊ Ma mère est enchantée de sa nouvelle voiture. My mother's delighted with her new car.
♦ **Enchanté!** Pleased to meet you!

encombrant ADJECTIVE
bulky

encombrer VERB
to clutter

encore ADVERB
1 again ◊ Il m'a encore demandé de l'argent. He asked me for money again.
2 more ◊ Mange encore un peu. Have some more to eat.
3 still ◊ Il est encore au travail. He's still at work. ◊ Il reste encore deux morceaux de gâteau. There are two pieces of cake left.
4 even ◊ C'est encore mieux. That's even better.
♦ **encore une fois** once again
♦ **pas encore** not yet ◊ Je n'ai pas encore fini. I'm not finished yet.

encourageant ADJECTIVE
encouraging

encourager VERB
to encourage

l' **encre** FEM NOUN
ink

l' **encyclopédie** FEM NOUN
encyclopedia

endommager VERB
to damage

endormi ADJECTIVE
asleep

endormir VERB
1 to put to sleep ◊ Il a endormi le bébé en lui chantant une berceuse. He put the baby to sleep by singing a lullaby. ◊ Son long discours m'a endormi. Her long speech put me to sleep.
2 to put under (with anesthetic) ◊ On l'a endormie pour son opération. They put her under for the operation.
♦ **s'endormir** to go to sleep

l' **endroit** MASC NOUN
place ◊ C'est un endroit très tranquille. It's a very quiet place.

♦ **à l'endroit (1)** right side out ◊ Remets ton T-shirt à l'endroit. Put your T-shirt on again right side out.
♦ **à l'endroit (2)** the right way up ◊ Ce tableau est de travers. Il faut le remettre à l'endroit. This picture is sideways. It must be put the right way up.

endurant ADJECTIVE
tough (person)

endurcir VERB
to toughen up ◊ Ces exercices servent à vous endurcir. These exercises are to toughen you up.
♦ **s'endurcir** to become hardened

endurer VERB
to endure

l' **énergie** FEM NOUN
1 energy ◊ Je n'ai pas beaucoup d'énergie ce matin. I don't have much energy this morning.
2 power ◊ l'énergie nucléaire nuclear power
♦ **avec énergie** vigorously ◊ Il a protesté avec énergie. He protested vigorously.

énergique ADJECTIVE
energetic
♦ **des mesures énergiques** strong measures

énerver VERB
♦ **Il m'énerve!** He gets on my nerves!
♦ **Ce bruit m'énerve.** This noise gets on my nerves.
♦ **s'énerver** to get worked up
♦ **Ne t'énerve pas!** Take it easy!

l' **enfance** FEM NOUN
childhood
♦ **Je la connais depuis l'enfance.** I've known her since I was a child.

l' **enfant** MASC/FEM NOUN
child

l' **enfer** MASC NOUN
hell

enfermer VERB
1 to lock (in a place) ◊ garder son sac à main enfermé dans son tiroir to keep one's purse locked in a drawer
2 to shut in ◊ Ne restons pas enfermés par ce beau temps. Let's not stay inside in this lovely weather.
♦ **Il s'est enfermé dans sa chambre.** He shut himself up in his bedroom.

enfiler VERB
1 to put on ◊ J'ai rapidement enfilé un chandail avant de sortir. I quickly put on a sweater before going out.
2 to thread ◊ J'ai du mal à enfiler cette aiguille. I am having a hard time threading this needle.

enfin ADVERB
finally ◊ *J'ai enfin réussi à la joindre.* I have finally managed to contact her.

enfler VERB
to swell

enfoncer VERB
♦ **Elle marchait, les mains enfoncées dans les poches.** She was walking with her hands thrust into her pockets.
♦ **s'enfoncer** to sink ◊ *Les roues de la voiture s'enfonçaient dans la boue.* The wheels of the car were sinking into the mud.

s' **enfuir** VERB
to run off

l' **engagement** MASC NOUN
commitment

engager VERB
to hire

s' **engager** VERB
to commit oneself ◊ *Le premier ministre s'est engagé à combattre le chômage.* The Prime Minister has committed himself to fighting unemployment.
♦ **Elle a décidé de ne pas s'engager dans l'armée.** She decided not to join the army.

l' **engin** MASC NOUN
device

> *Be careful! The French word engin does not mean engine.*

l' **engouement** MASC NOUN
fad

engueuler VERB (*informal*)
♦ **engueuler quelqu'un** to tell somebody off ◊ *Tu vas te faire engueuler!* You're going to get told off!

l' **énigme** FEM NOUN
riddle

s' **enivrer** VERB
to get drunk

l' **enjambée** FEM NOUN
stride ◊ *monter l'escalier en trois enjambées* to go up the stairs in three strides

enjamber VERB
① to climb over (*by swinging one leg over at a time*) ◊ *enjamber une barrière* to climb over a fence
② to step over ◊ *enjamber un fossé* to step over a ditch
③ to straddle

l' **enlèvement** MASC NOUN
kidnapping

enlever VERB
① to take off ◊ *Enlève donc ton manteau!* Take off your coat!
② to kidnap ◊ *Un groupe terroriste a enlevé la femme du ministre.* A terrorist group has kidnapped the minister's wife.

enneigé ADJECTIVE
snow-covered ◊ *Les routes sont encore enneigées.* The roads are still covered with snow.

l' **ennemi** MASC NOUN
enemy

l' **ennemie** FEM NOUN
enemy

l' **ennui** MASC NOUN
① boredom ◊ *C'est à mourir d'ennui.* It's enough to bore you to death.
② problem ◊ *avoir des ennuis* to have problems

ennuyer VERB
① to inconvenience ◊ *J'espère que cela ne vous ennuie pas trop.* I hope it doesn't inconvenience you too much.
② to bother ◊ *Arrête de m'ennuyer avec tes questions.* Stop bothering me with your questions.
♦ **s'ennuyer** to be bored

ennuyeux ADJECTIVE (FEM SING **ennuyeuse**)
① boring
② inconvenient ◊ *Tu ne peux pas venir plus tôt? C'est bien ennuyeux.* You can't come any earlier? That's rather inconvenient.

énorme ADJECTIVE
huge

énormément ADVERB
♦ **Il a énormément maigri.** He's gotten terribly thin.
♦ **Il y a énormément de neige.** There's an enormous amount of snow.

l' **enquête** FEM NOUN
① investigation ◊ *La police a ouvert une enquête.* The police have launched an investigation.
② survey ◊ *une enquête parmi les étudiants a montré que...* a survey of students has shown that...

enquêter VERB
to investigate ◊ *La police enquête actuellement sur le crime.* The police are currently investigating the crime.

enrageant ADJECTIVE
infuriating

enrager VERB
to be furious ◊ *J'enrage de n'avoir pas eu le droit de vous accompagner.* I'm furious that I wasn't allowed to go with you.

E

l' **enregistrement** MASC NOUN
recording
♦ **l'enregistrement des bagages**
baggage check-in

enregistrer VERB
1 to record ◊ *Ils viennent d'enregistrer un nouvel album.* They've just recorded a new album. ◊ *J'ai enregistré l'émission sur vidéocassette.* I taped the TV show.
2 to check (*baggage*) ◊ *Vous pouvez enregistrer plusieurs valises.* You can check more than one suitcase.

s' **enrhumer** VERB
to catch a cold ◊ *Elle s'est enrhumée.* She caught a cold.

s' **enrichir** VERB
to get rich

enrouler VERB
to wind ◊ *Enroulez le fil autour de la bobine.* Wind the thread around the bobbin.

l' **enseignant** MASC NOUN
teacher

l' **enseignante** FEM NOUN
teacher

l' **enseignement** MASC NOUN
1 education ◊ *les réformes de l'enseignement* reforms in education
2 teaching ◊ *l'enseignement des langues étrangères* the teaching of foreign languages

enseigner VERB
to teach ◊ *Mon père enseigne les maths dans une école secondaire.* My father teaches math in a secondary school.

ensemble ADVERB

see also **ensemble** NOUN

together ◊ *tous ensemble* all together

l' **ensemble** MASC NOUN

see also **ensemble** ADVERB

1 outfit ◊ *Elle portait un ensemble vert.* She was wearing a green outfit.
2 set ◊ *un ensemble de couteaux* a set of knives
♦ **l'ensemble de** the whole of ◊ *L'ensemble du personnel est en grève.* The whole staff is on strike.
♦ **aller ensemble** to go together ◊ *Le tapis et les meubles ne vont pas ensemble.* The carpet and furniture don't go together.
♦ **dans l'ensemble** on the whole

ensoleillé ADJECTIVE
sunny

ensuite ADVERB

then ◊ *Nous sommes allés au cinéma et ensuite au restaurant.* We went to a movie and then to a restaurant.

entamer VERB
to start ◊ *Qui a entamé le gâteau?* Who started on the cake? ◊ *entamer des négociations* to begin negotiations

entasser VERB
to cram ◊ *J'ai tout entassé dans un tiroir.* I crammed everything into a drawer.
♦ **Ils se sont tous entassés dans ma voiture.** They all crammed into my car.

entendre VERB
1 to hear ◊ *Je ne t'entends pas.* I can't hear you.
♦ **J'ai entendu dire qu'il est dangereux de nager ici.** I've heard that it's dangerous to swim here.
2 to mean ◊ *Qu'est-ce que tu entends par là?* What do you mean by that?
♦ **s'entendre** to get along ◊ *Il s'entend bien avec sa sœur.* He gets along well with his sister.

entendu ADJECTIVE
♦ **C'est entendu!** Agreed! ◊ *Je passerai te prendre à sept heures, c'est entendu.* That's agreed then, I'll pick you up at 7 o'clock.
♦ **bien entendu** of course ◊ *Il est bien entendu que je n'en parlerai à personne.* I won't tell anybody about it, of course.

l' **enterrement** MASC NOUN
funeral (*with burial*)
♦ **avoir une mine d'enterrement** to look gloomy

enterrer VERB
to bury

entêté ADJECTIVE
stubborn

s' **entêter** VERB
to persist ◊ *Il s'entête à refuser de voir le médecin.* He persists in refusing to go to the doctor.

l' **enthousiasme** MASC NOUN
enthusiasm

s' **enthousiasmer** VERB
to get enthusiastic ◊ *Elle s'enthousiasme facilement.* She gets very enthusiastic about things.

entier ADJECTIVE (FEM SING **entière**)
whole ◊ *Il a mangé une quiche entière.* He ate a whole quiche. ◊ *Je n'ai pas lu le livre en entier.* I haven't read the whole book.
♦ **le lait entier** whole milk

entièrement ADVERB
completely

l' **entorse** FEM NOUN
sprain ◊ *Elle s'est fait une entorse à la cheville.* She sprained her ankle.

entourer VERB
to surround ◊ *Le jardin est entouré d'un mur de pierres.* The garden is surrounded by a stone wall.

l' **entracte** MASC NOUN
intermission

l' **entraînement** MASC NOUN
training

entraîner VERB
1 to lead ◊ *Il se laisse facilement entraîner par les autres.* He's easily led.
2 to coach ◊ *Il entraîne l'équipe de soccer depuis cinq ans.* He's been training the soccer team for five years.
3 to involve ◊ *Un mariage entraîne beaucoup de dépenses.* A wedding involves a lot of expense.
♦ **s'entraîner** to train ◊ *Elle s'entraîne au hockey tous les samedis matins.* She has hockey practice every Saturday morning.

l' **entraîneur** MASC NOUN
coach

l' **entraîneure** FEM NOUN
coach

entre PREPOSITION
between ◊ *Il est assis entre son père et sa tante.* He's sitting between his father and his aunt.
♦ **entre eux** among themselves
♦ **l'un d'entre eux** one of them

l' **entrée** FEM NOUN
1 entrance
2 driveway
3 appetizer (*of meal*) ◊ *Qu'est ce que vous prenez comme entrée?* What would you like for an appetizer?

> *Be careful! The French word entrée does not mean entree.*

♦ **la touche Entrée** the Enter key

l' **entreposage** MASC NOUN
storage

entreprendre VERB
to start (*a process*) ◊ *Elle a entrepris des travaux de rénovation.* She has started renovations.

l' **entrepreneur** MASC NOUN
small business owner

l' **entrepreneure** FEM NOUN
small business owner

l' **entreprise** FEM NOUN
business (*company*)

entrer VERB
1 to come in ◊ *Entrez donc!* Come on in!
2 to go in ◊ *Ils sont tous entrés dans la maison.* They all went into the house.
♦ **entrer à l'hôpital** to go into the hospital
♦ **entrer des données** to enter data ◊ *J'ai entré toutes les adresses de mes amis sur mon ordinateur.* I've entered the addresses of all my friends into my computer.

entre-temps ADVERB
meanwhile

l' **entretien** MASC NOUN
1 maintenance ◊ *un contrat d'entretien* a maintenance contract
2 conversation ◊ *un entretien téléphonique* a telephone conversation

l' **entrevue** FEM NOUN
1 interview ◊ *une entrevue avec le ministre* an interview with the minister
2 job interview ◊ *mon frère a passé une entrevue pour travailler dans un restaurant.* My brother had a job interview to work in a restaurant.

entrouvert ADJECTIVE
half open ◊ *La porte était entrouverte.* The door was half open.

envahir VERB
to invade

l' **envahissement** MASC NOUN
invasion

l' **enveloppe** FEM NOUN
envelope

envelopper VERB
to wrap

envers PREPOSITION

> see also **envers** NOUN

towards ◊ *Il est très respectueux envers elle.* He's very respectful towards her. ◊ *son attitude envers moi* his attitude to me

l' **envers** MASC NOUN

> see also **envers** PREPOSITION

♦ **à l'envers (1)** inside out ◊ *Je dois repasser ce chemisier à l'envers.* I have to iron this blouse inside out.
♦ **à l'envers (2)** messy ◊ *Ta chambre est à l'envers.* Your room is messy.

l' **envie** FEM NOUN
♦ **avoir envie de faire quelque chose** to feel like doing something ◊ *J'avais envie de pleurer.* I felt like crying.

☞

♦ **Ce gâteau me fait envie.** I wouldn't mind some of that cake.

envier VERB
to envy

environ ADVERB
about ◊ *C'est à soixante kilomètres environ.* It's about 60 kilometres away.

l' **environnement** MASC NOUN
environment

l' **environnementaliste** MASC/FEM NOUN
environmentalist

les **environs** MASC NOUN
area SING ◊ *les environs d'Ottawa* the Ottawa area ◊ *Il y a beaucoup de choses intéressantes à voir dans les environs.* There are a lot of interesting things to see in the area.
♦ **aux environs de dix-neuf heures** around 7 p.m.

envisager VERB
to consider ◊ *Est-ce que vous envisagez de changer d'école?* Are you considering changing schools?

s' **envoler** VERB
① to fly away ◊ *Le papillon s'est envolé.* The butterfly flew away.
② to blow away ◊ *Toutes mes notes de cours se sont envolées.* All my class notes blew away.

envoyer VERB
to send ◊ *Ma tante m'a envoyé une carte pour mon anniversaire.* My aunt sent me a card for my birthday.
♦ **envoyer quelqu'un chercher quelque chose** to send somebody to get something ◊ *Sa mère l'a envoyé chercher du pain.* His mother sent him to get some bread.
♦ **envoyer un courriel à quelqu'un** to send somebody an e-mail

épais ADJECTIVE (FEM SING **épaisse**)
thick

l' **épaisseur** FEM NOUN
thickness

épargner VERB
to save (*money, energy*)

épatant ADJECTIVE (*informal*)
great ◊ *C'est un type épatant.* He's a great guy.

l' **épaulard** MASC NOUN
killer whale

l' **épaule** FEM NOUN
shoulder

l' **épée** FEM NOUN
sword

épeler VERB
to spell ◊ *Est-ce que vous pouvez épeler votre nom s'il vous plaît?* Could you spell your name please?

l' **épice** FEM NOUN
spice

épicé ADJECTIVE
spicy ◊ *Ce n'est pas assez épicé pour moi : je trouve ça trop fade.* It's not spicy enough for me: I think it's too bland.

l' **épicerie** FEM NOUN
grocery store
❀ ♦ **faire l'épicerie** to go grocery shopping

l' **épi de maïs** MASC NOUN
corn on the cob

l' **épidémie** FEM NOUN
epidemic

les **épinards** MASC NOUN
spinach SING

l' **épine** FEM NOUN
thorn

❀ l' **épinette** FEM NOUN
spruce

❀ ♦ **la bière d'épinette** rootbeer

l' **épingle** FEM NOUN
pin
♦ **une épingle de sûreté** a safety pin

l' **épisode** MASC NOUN
episode

éplucher VERB
to peel

❀ l' **épluchette** FEM NOUN

> In French Canada, **l'épluchette** is an end-of-summer celebration where people gather to eat corn on the cob.

l' **éponge** FEM NOUN
sponge

l' **époque** FEM NOUN
time ◊ *à cette époque de l'année* at this time of year
♦ **à l'époque** at that time ◊ *À l'époque, beaucoup de gens n'avaient pas l'eau courante.* At that time a lot of people didn't have running water.

l' **épouse** FEM NOUN
wife

épouser VERB
to marry

épouvantable ADJECTIVE
terrible

l' **épouvante** FEM NOUN
terror
♦ **un film d'épouvante** a horror film

épouvanter VERB
to terrify

l' **époux** MASC NOUN
husband
♦ **les nouveaux époux** the newlyweds

l' **épreuve** FEM NOUN
  [1] test ◊ *une épreuve orale* an oral test ◊ *une épreuve écrite* a written test
  [2] event (*sports*)

éprouver VERB
  to feel ◊ *Qu'est-ce que vous avez éprouvé à ce moment-là?* What did you feel at that moment?

épuisé ADJECTIVE
  exhausted

épuiser VERB
  to wear out ◊ *Ce travail m'a complètement épuisé.* This job has completely worn me out.
  ♦ **s'épuiser** to wear oneself out ◊ *Il s'épuise à garder un jardin impeccable.* He wears himself out keeping his garden immaculate.

l' **équateur** MASC NOUN
  equator

l' **équation** FEM NOUN
  equation

l' **équerre** FEM NOUN
  set square

l' **équilibre** MASC NOUN
  balance ◊ *J'ai failli perdre l'équilibre.* I nearly lost my balance.

équilibré ADJECTIVE
  well-balanced

l' **équipage** MASC NOUN
  crew

l' **équipe** FEM NOUN
  team

équipé ADJECTIVE
  ♦ **bien équipé** well-equipped

l' **équipement** MASC NOUN
  equipment

les **équipements** MASC NOUN
  facilities ◊ *les équipements sportifs* sports facilities

l' **équitation** FEM NOUN
  riding ◊ *faire de l'équitation* to go riding

l' **équivalent** MASC NOUN
  equivalent

l' **érable** MASC NOUN
  maple
  ♦ **le sirop d'érable** maple syrup

❋ l' **érablière** FEM NOUN
  sugar bush ◊ *Nous irons à une partie de sucre à l'érablière.* We're going to a sugaring-off party in the sugar bush.

l' **erreur** FEM NOUN
  mistake
  ♦ **faire erreur** to be mistaken

es VERB *see* **être**

♦ **Tu es très gentille.** You're very kind.

l' **escabeau** MASC NOUN (PL les **escabeaux**)
  stepladder

l' **escalade** FEM NOUN
  rock climbing ◊ *faire de l'escalade* to go rock climbing

escalader VERB
  to climb

l' **escale** FEM NOUN
  ♦ **faire escale** to stop off

l' **escalier** MASC NOUN
  stairs ◊ *un escalier roulant* an escalator

l' **escargot** MASC NOUN
  snail

l' **escarpement** MASC NOUN
  escarpment ◊ *l'escarpement de Niagara* the Niagara escarpment

l' **esclavage** MASC NOUN
  slavery

l' **esclave** MASC/FEM NOUN
  slave

l' **escrime** FEM NOUN
  fencing

l' **escroc** MASC NOUN
  crook ◊ *Cette femme est un escroc.* That woman is a crook.

l' **espace** MASC NOUN
  space
  ♦ **espace de travail** workspace

s' **espacer** VERB
  to become less frequent ◊ *Ses visites se sont peu à peu espacées.* His visits became less and less frequent.

l' **espadrille** FEM NOUN
❋ running shoe

l' **espèce** FEM NOUN
  [1] sort ◊ *Elle portait une espèce de cape en velours.* She was wearing a sort of velvet cloak.
  [2] species ◊ *une espèce en voie de disparition* an endangered species

les **espèces** FEM NOUN
  cash SING ◊ *payer en espèces* to pay cash

espérer VERB
  to hope
  ♦ **J'espère bien.** I hope so. ◊ *« Tu penses avoir réussi? » « Oui, j'espère bien. »* "Do you think you passed?" "Yes, I hope so."

espiègle ADJECTIVE
  mischievous

l' **espion** MASC NOUN
  spy

l' **espionnage** MASC NOUN
spying
♦ **un roman d'espionnage** a spy novel

l' **espionne** FEM NOUN
spy

l' **espoir** MASC NOUN
hope

l' **esprit** MASC NOUN
mind ◊ *Ça ne m'est pas venu à l'esprit.* It didn't cross my mind.
♦ **avoir de l'esprit** to be witty ◊ *Il a beaucoup d'esprit.* He's very witty.

l' **essai** MASC NOUN
attempt ◊ *Ce n'est pas mal pour un coup d'essai.* It's not bad for a first attempt.
♦ **prendre quelqu'un à l'essai** to hire somebody for a trial period

essayer VERB
[1] to try ◊ *Essaie de rentrer de bonne heure.* Try to come home early.
[2] to try on ◊ *Essaie ce chandail : il devrait bien t'aller.* Try this sweater on: it ought to look good on you.

l' **essence** FEM NOUN
gas (*for car*)

essentiel ADJECTIVE (FEM SING **essentielle**)
essential
♦ **Tu es là : c'est l'essentiel.** You're here: that's the main thing.

s' **essouffler** VERB
to get out of breath

l' **essuie-glace** MASC NOUN
windshield wiper

essuyer VERB
to wipe
♦ **essuyer la vaisselle** to dry the dishes
♦ **essuyer un échec** to suffer a setback
♦ **s'essuyer** to dry oneself ◊ *Vous pouvez vous essuyer les mains avec cette serviette.* You can dry your hands on this towel.

est VERB *see* **être**

> *see also* **est** ADJECTIVE, NOUN

♦ **Elle est merveilleuse.** She's marvellous.

est ADJECTIVE

> *see also* **est** VERB, NOUN

[1] east ◊ *la côte est du Canada* the east coast of Canada
[2] eastern ◊ *dans la partie est du pays* in the eastern part of the country

l' **est** MASC NOUN

> *see also* **est** VERB, ADJECTIVE

east ◊ *Je vis dans l'est.* I live in the East.
♦ **vers l'est** eastward
♦ **à l'est de Rainy River** east of Rainy

River
♦ **l'Europe de l'Est** Eastern Europe
♦ **le vent d'est** the east wind

est-ce que ADVERB
♦ **Est-ce que c'est cher?** Is it expensive?
♦ **Quand est-ce qu'il part?** When is he leaving?

l' **esthéticienne** FEM NOUN
beautician

l' **estimation** FEM NOUN
estimate ◊ *Nous avons demandé une estimation avant de faire réparer la voiture.* We asked for an estimate before getting the car repaired.

l' **estime** FEM NOUN
♦ **J'ai beaucoup d'estime pour elle.** I have a lot of respect for her.

estimer VERB
♦ **estimer quelqu'un** to have great respect for somebody ◊ *Mon père les estime beaucoup.* My father has a lot of respect for them.
♦ **estimer que** to be of the opinion that ◊ *J'estime que c'est de sa faute.* My opinion is that it's her fault.

l' **estomac** MASC NOUN
stomach

l' **estrade** FEM NOUN
platform ◊ *La ministre a prononcé son discours sur l'estrade.* The minister gave her speech from the platform.

et CONJUNCTION
and

établir VERB
to establish
♦ **s'établir à son compte** to set up a business

l' **établissement** MASC NOUN
establishment
♦ **un établissement scolaire** a school

l' **étage** MASC NOUN
floor ◊ *au premier étage* on the first floor
♦ **à l'étage** upstairs

l' **étagère** FEM NOUN
shelf

étaient VERB *see* **être**

étais, était VERB *see* **être**
♦ **Il était très jeune.** He was very young.

l' **étalage** MASC NOUN
display

étaler VERB
to spread out ◊ *Il a étalé la carte sur la table.* He spread the map out on the table.

étanche ADJECTIVE
[1] watertight ◊ *Le toit n'est pas*

E

étanche. The roof isn't watertight.
② waterproof (*watch*)

l' **étang** MASC NOUN▸
pond

étant VERB *see* **être**
♦ *Mes revenus étant limités...* My
income being limited...

l' **étape** FEM NOUN
stage ◊ *une étape importante de la
vie* an important stage in life
♦ **faire étape** to stop off

l' **État** MASC NOUN
state (*nation*) ◊ *un chef d'État* a head
of state

l' **état** MASC NOUN
① state ◊ *dans votre état de santé* in
your state of health ◊ *le chef d'État*
the head of state
② condition ◊ *en bon état* in good
condition ◊ *en mauvais état* in poor
condition
♦ **remettre quelque chose en état** to
repair something
♦ **un état d'âme** a frame of mind
♦ **être dans tous ses états** to be beside
oneself with anxiety

été VERB *see* **être**

boxed{*see also* **été** NOUN}

♦ *Elle a été licenciée.* She's been laid
off.

l' **été** MASC NOUN

boxed{*see also* **été** VERB}

underline{summer}
♦ **en été** in the summer
✱ ♦ **l'été indien** Indian summer

éteindre VERB
① to turn off (*light, TV*) ◊ *N'oubliez
pas d'éteindre la lumière en sortant.*
Don't forget to turn off the light when
you leave.
② to shut down (*computer*) ◊ *Quitte
l'application avant d'éteindre
l'ordinateur.* Exit the application
before shutting down the computer.
③ to put out (*cigarette*)

étendre VERB
to spread ◊ *Il a étendu une nappe
propre sur la table.* He spread a clean
cloth on the table.
♦ **étendre le linge** to hang out the wash
♦ **s'étendre** to lie down ◊ *Je vais
m'étendre cinq minutes.* I'm going to
lie down for five minutes.

l' **éternité** FEM NOUN
♦ *J'ai attendu une éternité chez le
médecin.* I waited for ages at the
doctor's.

éternuer VERB
to sneeze

êtes VERB *see* **être**
♦ **Vous êtes en retard.** You're late.

étiez VERB *see* **être**

étinceler VERB
to sparkle

étions VERB *see* **être**

l' **étiquette** FEM NOUN
label ◊ *L'étiquette du pot de confiture
s'est décollée.* The label has come off
the jam jar.

s' **étirer** VERB
to stretch ◊ *Elle s'est étirée
paresseusement.* She stretched lazily.

l' **étoile** FEM NOUN
star
♦ **une étoile de mer** a starfish
♦ **une étoile filante** a shooting star
♦ **dormir à la belle étoile** to sleep under
the stars
♦ **le match des étoiles** the all-star game

étonnant ADJECTIVE
amazing

étonner VERB
to surprise ◊ *Cela m'étonnerait de
le voir ici.* I'd be surprised to see him
here.

étouffer VERB
♦ **On étouffe ici; ouvre donc les
fenêtres.** It's stifling in here; open the
windows.
♦ **étouffer un cri** to muffle a cry
♦ **étouffer un incendie** to put out a fire
♦ **s'étouffer** to choke ◊ *Ne mange pas
si vite : tu vas t'étouffer!* Don't eat so
fast: you'll choke!

l' **étourderie** FEM NOUN
absent-mindedness
♦ **une erreur d'étourderie** a careless
error

étourdi ADJECTIVE
scatterbrained

l' **étourdissement** MASC NOUN
♦ **avoir des étourdissements** to feel
dizzy

étrange ADJECTIVE
strange

étranger ADJECTIVE (FEM SING **étrangère**)

boxed{*see also* **étranger** NOUN}

foreign ◊ *un pays étranger* a foreign
country
♦ **une personne étrangère** a stranger

l' **étranger** MASC NOUN

boxed{*see also* **étranger** ADJECTIVE}

① foreigner
② stranger
♦ **à l'étranger** abroad

l' **étrangère** FEM NOUN

① foreigner
② stranger

étrangler VERB
to strangle
♦ **s'étrangler** to choke ◊ *s'étrangler avec quelque chose* to choke on something

l' **être** MASC NOUN

> see also **être** VERB

♦ **un être humain** a human being

être VERB

> see also **être** NOUN

Present tense:

je suis	nous sommes
tu es	vous êtes
il/elle est	ils/elles sont

Past participle:
été

① to be ◊ *Je suis heureux.* I'm happy. ◊ *Mon père est journaliste.* My father's a journalist. ◊ *Il est dix heures.* It's 10 o'clock.
② to have ◊ *Il n'est pas encore arrivé.* He hasn't arrived yet.

étroit ADJECTIVE
narrow
♦ **être à l'étroit** to be cramped ◊ *Nous sommes un peu à l'étroit dans cet appartement.* We're a bit cramped in this apartment.

l' **étude** FEM NOUN
study ◊ *une étude de cas* a case study
♦ **faire des études** to be studying ◊ *Elle fait des études de droit.* She's studying law.

l' **étudiant** MASC NOUN
student (*college and university*)

l' **étudiante** FEM NOUN
student (*college and university*)

étudier VERB
to study ◊ *étudier pour un examen* to study for an exam ◊ *étudier une question sous toutes ses coutures* to study a question from every angle

l' **étui** MASC NOUN
case ◊ *un étui à lunettes* a glasses case

eu VERB *see* **avoir**
♦ **J'ai eu une bonne note.** I got a good mark.

euh EXCLAMATION
uh ◊ *Euh...je ne m'en souviens pas.* Uh...I can't remember.

l' **euro** MASC NOUN
euro (*currency*)

eux PRONOUN
them ◊ *Je pense souvent à eux.* I often think of them.

> *eux is also used for emphasis.*

◊ *Elle a accepté l'invitation, mais eux ont refusé.* She accepted the invitation, but THEY refused.

évacuer VERB
to evacuate

s' **évader** VERB
to escape

s' **évanouir** VERB
to faint

s' **évaporer** VERB
to evaporate

évasif ADJECTIVE (FEM SING **évasive**)
evasive

l' **évasion** FEM NOUN
escape ◊ *Ils ont préparé leur évasion pendant des mois.* They spent months planning their escape.

éveillé ADJECTIVE
① awake ◊ *Elle est restée éveillée toute la nuit.* She stayed awake all night.
② bright ◊ *C'est un enfant très éveillé.* He's very bright.

s' **éveiller** VERB
to awaken

l' **événement** MASC NOUN
event

l' **éventail** MASC NOUN
fan (*handheld*)
♦ **un large éventail de prix** a wide range of prices

l' **éventualité** FEM NOUN
♦ **dans l'éventualité d'un retard** in the event of a delay

éventuel ADJECTIVE (FEM SING **éventuelle**)
possible ◊ *une solution éventuelle* a possible solution ◊ *les conséquences éventuelles* the possible consequences

> *Be careful! éventuel does not mean eventual.*

éventuellement ADVERB
possibly ◊ *Nous pourrions éventuellement avoir besoin de vous.* It's possible we may need you.

> *Be careful! éventuellement does not mean eventually.*

évidemment ADVERB
① obviously ◊ *Les tomates sont évidemment chères en cette saison.* Tomatoes are obviously expensive at this time of year.

② of course ◊ « *Est-ce que je peux utiliser ton téléphone?* » « *Évidemment, tu n'as pas besoin de demander.* » "Can I use your phone?" "Of course, you don't need to ask."

l' **évidence** FEM NOUN
   ♦ **C'est une évidence.** It's quite obvious.
   ♦ **de toute évidence** obviously ◊ *De toute évidence, elle ne veut pas nous voir.* Obviously she doesn't want to see us.
   ♦ **être en évidence** to be clearly visible ◊ *La lettre était en évidence sur la table.* The letter was clearly visible on the table.
   ♦ **mettre en évidence** to reveal

évident ADJECTIVE
   obvious

l' **évier** MASC NOUN
   sink

éviter VERB
   to avoid

évolué ADJECTIVE
   advanced ◊ *une technologie très évoluée* very advanced technology

évoluer VERB
   to progress ◊ *La chirurgie esthétique a beaucoup évolué.* Plastic surgery has progressed a great deal.
   ♦ **Il a beaucoup évolué.** He has come a long way.

l' **évolution** FEM NOUN
   ① development ◊ *une évolution rapide* rapid development
   ② evolution ◊ *la théorie de l'évolution* the theory of evolution

évoquer VERB
   to mention ◊ *Elle a évoqué divers problèmes dans son discours.* She mentioned various problems in her speech.

exact ADJECTIVE
   ① right ◊ *Avez-vous l'heure exacte?* Have you got the right time? ◊ « *Tu es en secondaire trois, n'est-ce pas?* » « *C'est exact.* » "You're in grade nine, right?" "Right."
   ② exact ◊ *le prix exact, taxes comprises* the exact price including tax

exactement ADVERB
   exactly ◊ *C'est exactement ce que je cherchais.* That's exactly what I was looking for.

ex æquo ADJECTIVE
   ♦ **Ils sont arrivés ex æquo.** They finished neck and neck.

exagérer VERB
   ① to exaggerate ◊ *Vous exagérez!*

You're exaggerating!
   ② to go too far ◊ *Ça fait trois fois que tu arrives en retard : tu exagères!* That's three times you've been late: you've gone too far!

l' **examen** MASC NOUN
   exam ◊ *Nous allons passer l'examen d'anglais vendredi matin.* We're doing our English exam on Friday morning. ◊ *un examen de français* a French exam
   ♦ **un examen médical** a medical

examiner VERB
   to examine

exaspérant ADJECTIVE
   infuriating

exaspérer VERB
   to infuriate

l' **excédent** MASC NOUN
   ♦ **l' excédent de bagages** excess baggage

excéder VERB
   to exceed ◊ *excéder la limite de vitesse* to exceed the speed limit
   ♦ **excéder quelqu'un** to drive somebody crazy ◊ *Les cris des enfants l'excédaient.* The noise of the children was driving her crazy.

excellent ADJECTIVE
   excellent

excentrique ADJECTIVE
   eccentric

excepté PREPOSITION
   except ◊ *Toutes les chaussures excepté les sandales sont en solde.* All the shoes except sandals are reduced.

l' **exception** FEM NOUN
   exception
   ♦ **à l'exception de** except

exceptionnel ADJECTIVE (FEM SING **exceptionnelle**)
   exceptional

l' **excès** MASC NOUN
   ♦ **faire des excès** to overindulge ◊ *On fait souvent des excès aux environs de l'Action de grâce.* People often overindulge around Thanksgiving.
   ♦ **les excès de vitesse** speeding

excessif ADJECTIVE (FEM SING **excessive**)
   excessive

excitant ADJECTIVE
   | see also **excitant** NOUN |
   exciting

l' **excitant** MASC NOUN
   | see also **excitant** ADJECTIVE |
   stimulant ◊ *Le thé et le café sont*

☞

des excitants. Tea and coffee are stimulants.

l' **excitation** FEM NOUN
excitement

exciter VERB
to excite ◊ *Il était tout excité à l'idée de revoir ses cousins.* He was all excited about seeing his cousins again.
♦ **s'exciter** (*informal*) to get excited ◊ *Ne t'excite pas trop vite : ça ne va peut-être pas marcher!* Don't get excited too soon: it may not work!

l' **exclamation** FEM NOUN
exclamation

exclu ADJECTIVE
excluded ◊ *Elle se sentait exclue du groupe.* She felt excluded from the group.
♦ **Il n'est pas exclu que...** It's not impossible that...

exclusif ADJECTIVE (FEM SING **exclusive**)
exclusive

l' **excursion** FEM NOUN
1 trip ◊ *faire une excursion* to go on a trip
2 hike ◊ *une excursion dans la montagne* a hike in the hills

l' **excuse** FEM NOUN
1 excuse ◊ *Tu trouves toujours une bonne excuse pour ne pas faire la vaisselle.* You always find a good excuse for not doing the dishes.
2 apology ◊ *présenter ses excuses* to offer one's apologies
♦ **un mot d'excuse** a note (*of explanation*) ◊ *Vous devez apporter un mot d'excuse signé par vos parents.* You have to bring a note signed by your parents.

excuser VERB
to excuse ◊ *Son retard a été excusé.* His lateness was excused.
♦ **Excusez-moi. (1)** Sorry! ◊ *Excusez-moi, je ne vous avais pas vu.* Sorry, I didn't see you.
♦ **Excusez-moi. (2)** Excuse me. ◊ *Excusez-moi, est-ce que vous avez l'heure?* Excuse me, have you got the time?
♦ **s'excuser** to apologize ◊ *Elle s'est excusée de son retard.* She apologized for being late.

exécuter VERB
1 to execute ◊ *Le prisonnier a été exécuté à l'aube.* The prisoner was executed at dawn.
2 to perform ◊ *La pianiste va maintenant exécuter une valse de Chopin.* The pianist will now perform a waltz by Chopin.

l' **exemplaire** MASC NOUN
copy

l' **exemple** MASC NOUN
example ◊ *donner l'exemple* to set an example
♦ **par exemple** for example

s' **exercer** VERB
to practise ◊ *Pour jouer bien, tu devras t'exercer davantage.* To play well, you'll have to practise more. ◊ *s'exercer à parler français* to practise speaking French

l' **exercice** MASC NOUN
exercise
♦ **un exercice d'incendie** a fire drill

exhiber VERB
to show off ◊ *Il aime bien exhiber ses décorations.* He likes showing off his medals.
♦ **s'exhiber** to expose oneself

exigeant ADJECTIVE
1 hard to please ◊ *Elle est vraiment exigeante.* She's really hard to please.
2 demanding ◊ *un cours très exigeant* a very demanding course

exiger VERB
1 to demand ◊ *Le propriétaire exige d'être payé immédiatement.* The landlord is demanding to be paid immediately.
2 to require ◊ *Ce travail exige beaucoup de patience.* This job requires a lot of patience.

l' **exil** MASC NOUN
exile

exister VERB
to exist ◊ *Ça n'existe pas.* It doesn't exist. ◊ *Ce manteau existe également en rose.* This coat is also available in pink.

exotique ADJECTIVE
exotic ◊ *une plante exotique* an exotic plant ◊ *un yogourt aux fruits exotiques* a tropical fruit yogurt

expédier VERB
to send ◊ *expédier un colis* to send a parcel

l' **expéditeur** MASC NOUN
sender

l' **expédition** FEM NOUN
expedition

l' **expéditrice** FEM NOUN
sender

l' **expérience** FEM NOUN
1 experience ◊ *Elle a plusieurs années d'expérience.* She's got several years of experience.
2 experiment ◊ *une expérience de chimie* a chemistry experiment

expérimenter VERB
to test ◊ *Ces produits de beauté n'ont pas été expérimentés sur des animaux.* These cosmetics have not been tested on animals.

l' **expert** MASC NOUN
expert

l' **experte** FEM NOUN
expert

expirer VERB
1 to expire (*document, passport*)
2 to run out (*time allowed*)
3 to breathe out (*person*)

l' **explication** FEM NOUN
explanation

expliquer VERB
to explain ◊ *Elle m'a expliqué comment faire.* She explained to me how to do it.
♦ **s'expliquer** to explain oneself

l' **exploit** MASC NOUN
achievement

l' **exploitation** FEM NOUN
exploitation ◊ *Cet organisme lutte contre l'exploitation des femmes.* This organization fights against the exploitation of women.
♦ **une exploitation agricole** a farm

exploiter VERB
to exploit ◊ *Il s'est fait exploiter par le patron du restaurant.* He was exploited by the owner of the restaurant.

explorer VERB
to explore

exploser VERB
to explode ◊ *La bombe a explosé en pleine rue.* The bomb exploded in the middle of the street.

l' **explosif** MASC NOUN
explosive

l' **explosion** FEM NOUN
explosion

l' **exportation** FEM NOUN
export

exporter VERB
to export

l' **exposé** MASC NOUN
presentation ◊ *un exposé sur l'environnement* a presentation on the environment
♦ **un exposé écrit** an essay

exposer VERB
1 to show ◊ *Il expose ses peintures dans une galerie d'art.* He shows his paintings in a private art gallery.
2 to expose ◊ *N'exposez pas le film à la lumière.* Do not expose the film to light.
3 to lay out (*explain*) ◊ *Elle nous a exposé les raisons de son départ.* She laid out the reasons for her departure.
♦ **s'exposer au soleil** to stay out in the sun ◊ *Ne vous exposez pas trop longtemps au soleil.* Don't stay out in the sun too long.

l' **exposition** FEM NOUN
exhibition ◊ *une exposition de peinture* an exhibition of paintings

exprès ADVERB
1 on purpose ◊ *Je suis sûr qu'il l'a fait exprès.* I'm sure he did it on purpose.
2 specially ◊ *J'ai fait ce gâteau exprès pour toi.* I made this cake specially for you.

l' **express** MASC NOUN
express (*bus, train*) ◊ *Elle a décidé de prendre l'express de dix heures.* She decided to catch the express at 10 o'clock.

l' **expression** FEM NOUN
1 expression
2 phrase

exprimer VERB
to express
♦ **s'exprimer** to express oneself ◊ *Il s'exprime très bien pour un enfant de huit ans.* For a child of 8, he expresses himself very well.

exquis ADJECTIVE
exquisite

extérieur ADJECTIVE
see also **extérieur** NOUN
outside

l' **extérieur** MASC NOUN
see also **extérieur** ADJECTIVE
outside
♦ **à l'extérieur** outside ◊ *Prenons le déjeuner à l'extérieur.* Let's eat lunch outside.

l' **extincteur** MASC NOUN
fire extinguisher

extra ADJECTIVE (MASC, FEM, PL)
excellent ◊ *Ce fromage est extra!* This cheese is excellent!

extraire VERB
to extract

l' **extrait** MASC NOUN
extract

extraordinaire ADJECTIVE
extraordinary

l' **extra-terrestre** MASC/FEM NOUN
alien

extravagant ADJECTIVE

E

extravagant

extrême ADJECTIVE

> see also **extrême** NOUN

extreme ◊ *l'extrême droite et l'extrême gauche* the far right and the far left

l' **extrême** MASC NOUN

> see also **extrême** ADJECTIVE

extreme

♦ **pousser les choses à l'extrême** to go to extremes

extrêmement ADVERB
extremely

l' **Extrême-Orient** MASC NOUN
the Far East

l' **extrémité** FEM NOUN
end ◊ *La gare est à l'autre extrémité de la ville.* The station is at the other end of the town.

F

le **fa** NOUN
F (*music*)

la **fabrication** NOUN
manufacture

fabriquer VERB
to make ◊ *fabriqué au Canada* made
in Canada

la **face** NOUN
♦ **face à face** face to face
♦ **en face de** opposite ◊ *L'autobus
s'arrête en face de chez moi.* The bus
stops opposite my house.
♦ **faire face à quelque chose** to face
something
♦ **perdre la face** to lose face
♦ **« Pile ou face? » « Face. »** "Heads or
tails?" "Heads."

fâché ADJECTIVE
angry
♦ **être fâché contre quelqu'un** to be
angry with somebody ◊ *Elle est
fâchée contre moi.* She's angry with
me.
♦ **être fâché avec quelqu'un** to be on
bad terms with somebody ◊ *Elle est
fâchée avec sa sœur.* She's on bad
terms with her sister.

se **fâcher** VERB
♦ **se fâcher contre quelqu'un** to lose
one's temper with somebody
♦ **se fâcher avec quelqu'un** to fall out
with somebody ◊ *Il s'est fâché avec
son frère.* He had a fight with his
brother.

facile ADJECTIVE
easy
♦ **facile à faire** easy to do

facilement ADVERB
easily

la **facilité** NOUN
♦ **un logiciel d'une grande facilité
d'utilisation** a very user-friendly piece
of software
♦ **Il a de la facilité en langues.** He has a
gift for languages.
*Be careful! **facilité** does not mean
facility.*

la **façon** NOUN
way ◊ *De quelle façon?* In what way?
♦ **de toute façon** anyway

le **facteur** NOUN
letter carrier

la **factrice** NOUN
letter carrier

la **facture** NOUN
bill ◊ *une facture de gaz* a gas bill

facultatif ADJECTIVE (FEM SING **facultative**)
optional

la **faculté** NOUN
faculty
♦ **avoir une grande faculté de
concentration** to have great powers
of concentration

fade ADJECTIVE
tasteless ◊ *La soupe est un peu fade.*
The soup is a bit tasteless.

faible ADJECTIVE
weak ◊ *Je me sens encore faible.* I
still feel a bit weak.
♦ **Il est faible en maths.** He's not very
good at math.

la **faiblesse** NOUN
weakness

faillir VERB
♦ **J'ai failli tomber.** I nearly fell down.

la **faillite** NOUN
bankruptcy
♦ **une entreprise en faillite** a bankrupt
business
♦ **faire faillite** to go bankrupt

la **faim** NOUN
hunger
♦ **avoir faim** to be hungry

fainéant ADJECTIVE
lazy

faire VERB

Present tense:	
je fais	nous faisons
tu fais	vous faites
il/elle fait	ils/elles font
Past participle:	
fait	

⒈ to make ◊ *Je vais faire un gâteau
pour ce soir.* I'm going to make a cake
for tonight. ◊ *Ils font trop de bruit.*
They're making too much noise. ◊ *Je
voudrais me faire de nouveaux amis.*
I'd like to make new friends.
⒉ to do ◊ *Qu'est-ce que tu fais?* What
are you doing? ◊ *Elle fait de l'italien.*
She's doing Italian. ◊ *Qui veut faire la
vaisselle?* Who'll do the dishes?
⒊ to be ◊ *Qu'est-ce qu'il fait chaud!*
Is it ever hot! ◊ *Espérons qu'il fera
beau demain.* Let's hope it'll be nice
weather tomorrow.
♦ **Ça ne fait rien.** It doesn't matter.

☞

♦ **Ça fait cinquante-trois dollars en tout.** That makes fify-three dollars in all.

♦ **Ça fait trois ans qu'elle habite à Peterborough.** She's lived in Peterborough for three years.

♦ **faire tomber** to knock over ◊ *Le chat a fait tomber le vase.* The cat knocked over the vase.

♦ **faire faire quelque chose** to get something done ◊ *Je dois faire réparer ma voiture.* I've got to get my car repaired.

♦ **Je vais me faire couper les cheveux.** I'm going to get my hair cut.

♦ **Ne t'en fais pas!** Don't worry!

♦ **se faire des idées** to imagine things

fais, faisaient, faisais, faisait, faisiez, faisions, faisons, fait VERB *see* **faire**

le **fait** NOUN
<u>fact</u> ◊ *Le fait que...* The fact that...

♦ **un fait divers** a news item

♦ **au fait** by the way ◊ *Au fait, tu as aimé le film d'hier?* By the way, did you enjoy the movie yesterday?

♦ **en fait** actually ◊ *En fait, je n'ai pas beaucoup de temps.* I haven't got much time actually.

♦ **aller au fait** to get to the point

faites VERB *see* **faire**

la **falaise** NOUN
<u>cliff</u>

falloir VERB *see* **faut, faudra, faudrait**

famé ADJECTIVE
♦ **un quartier mal famé** a rough area

fameux ADJECTIVE (FEM SING **fameuse**)
<u>famous</u> ◊ *La Colombie-Britannique est fameuse pour ses montagnes.* British Columbia is famous for its mountains.

♦ **Ce n'est pas fameux.** It's not great.

familial ADJECTIVE (MASC PL **familiaux**)
<u>family</u> ◊ *une atmosphère familiale* a family atmosphere

♦ **les allocations familiales** child benefit

familier ADJECTIVE (FEM SING **familière**)
<u>familiar</u>

la **famille** NOUN
[1] <u>family</u> ◊ *une famille nombreuse* a big family ◊ *Nous fêtons les anniversaires en famille.* We have family birthday celebrations.

♦ **une famille monoparentale** a single-parent family

♦ **une famille nucléaire** a nuclear family

♦ **une famille reconstituée** a blended family

[2] <u>relatives</u> ◊ *J'ai de la famille à Windsor.* I've got relatives in Windsor.

la **famine** NOUN
<u>famine</u>

fanatique ADJECTIVE
| *see also* **fanatique** NOUN |
<u>fanatical</u>

le/la **fanatique** NOUN
| *see also* **fanatique** ADJECTIVE |
<u>fanatic</u>

la **fanfare** NOUN
<u>brass band</u>

le **fanion** NOUN
<u>pennant</u>

la **fantaisie** NOUN
[1] <u>imagination</u> ◊ *un roman plein de fantaisie* a novel full of imagination
[2] <u>whim</u> ◊ *Ils lui passent toutes ses fantaisies.* They give in to all his whims.

♦ **des bijoux de fantaisie** costume jewellery

fantastique ADJECTIVE
<u>fantastic</u>

le **fantôme** NOUN
<u>ghost</u>

le **faon** NOUN
<u>fawn</u>

la **farce** NOUN
[1] <u>stuffing</u> (*for chicken, turkey*)
[2] <u>practical joke</u> ◊ *Elle aime faire des farces.* She likes to play practical jokes.

farci ADJECTIVE
<u>stuffed</u> ◊ *des poivrons verts farcis* stuffed green peppers

la **farine** NOUN
<u>flour</u>

fascinant ADJECTIVE
<u>fascinating</u>

fasciner VERB
<u>to fascinate</u>

le **fascisme** NOUN
<u>fascism</u>

fasse, fassent, fasses, fassiez, fassions VERB *see* **faire**

♦ **Pourvu qu'il fasse beau demain!** Let's hope it'll be nice out tomorrow!

fatal ADJECTIVE
<u>fatal</u>

♦ **C'était fatal.** It was bound to happen.

la **fatalité** NOUN
<u>fate</u>

> *Be careful!* **fatalité** *does not mean* **fatality***.*

fatigant ADJECTIVE
<u>tiring</u>

la **fatigue** NOUN
<u>tiredness</u>

fatigué ADJECTIVE
  tired

se **fatiguer** VERB
  to get tired

fauché ADJECTIVE (*informal*)
  hard up

le **faucon** NOUN
  hawk

faudra VERB

> *faudra is the future tense of falloir.*

♦ **Il faudra qu'on soit plus rapide.** We'll have to be quicker.

faudrait VERB

> *faudrait is the conditional tense of falloir.*

♦ **Il faudrait qu'on fasse attention.** We ought to be careful.

se **faufiler** VERB
♦ **Il s'est faufilé à travers la foule.** He made his way through the crowd.

la **faune** NOUN
  wildlife

faunique ADJECTIVE
✻ ♦ **une réserve faunique** a wildlife reserve

fausse ADJECTIVE *see* **faux**

faut VERB

> *faut is the present tense of falloir.*

♦ **Il faut faire attention.** You have to be careful.
♦ **Nous n'avons pas le choix, il faut y aller.** We have no choice, we've got to go.
♦ **Il faut que je parte.** I have to go.
♦ **Il faut du courage pour faire ce métier.** It takes courage to do that job.
♦ **Il me faut de l'argent.** I need money.
♦ **s'il le faut** if need be

la **faute** NOUN
  ① mistake ◊ *faire une faute* to make a mistake
  ② fault ◊ *Ce n'est pas de ma faute.* It's not my fault.
♦ **sans faute** without fail ◊ *Je t'appellerai sans faute.* I'll phone you without fail.

le **fauteuil** NOUN
  armchair
♦ **un fauteuil roulant** a wheelchair

faux ADJECTIVE, ADVERB (FEM SING **fausse**)
  see also **faux** NOUN
  ① untrue ◊ *C'est entièrement faux.* It's totally untrue.
  ② forged ◊ *un faux passeport* a forged passport
♦ **faire un faux pas** to trip

♦ **Elle chante faux.** She sings out of tune.
♦ **un faux ami** a false friend

le **faux** NOUN
  see also **faux** ADJECTIVE
  fake ◊ *Ce tableau est un faux.* This painting is a fake.

la **faveur** NOUN
  favour

favori ADJECTIVE (FEM SING **favorite**)
  favourite

favoriser VERB
  to favour ◊ *Ce système d'examen favorise ceux qui ont de la mémoire.* This exam system favours people with good memories.

fédéral ADJECTIVE
  federal ◊ *le gouvernement fédéral* the federal government

la **fée** NOUN
  fairy

les **félicitations** FEM NOUN
  congratulations

féliciter VERB
  to congratulate

la **femelle** NOUN
  female (*animal*)

féminin ADJECTIVE
  ① female ◊ *les personnages féminins du roman* the female characters in the novel
  ② feminine ◊ *Elle est très féminine.* She's very feminine.
  ③ women's ◊ *Elle joue dans l'équipe féminine du Canada.* She plays in the Canadian women's team.

féministe ADJECTIVE
  feminist

la **femme** NOUN
  ① woman
  ② wife ◊ *la femme du directeur* the principal's wife
♦ **une femme au foyer** a housewife
♦ **une femme d'affaires** a businesswoman
♦ **une femme d'État** a stateswoman
♦ **une femme de tête** a strong-minded intelligent woman

se **fendre** VERB
  to crack

la **fenêtre** NOUN
  window

la **fente** NOUN
  slot

le **fer** NOUN
  iron
♦ **un fer à cheval** a horseshoe

F

♦ **un fer à friser** a curling iron
♦ **un fer à repasser** an iron

fera, ferai, feras, ferez VERB *see* **faire**

férié ADJECTIVE
♦ **un jour férié** a public holiday

feriez, ferions VERB *see* **faire**

ferme ADJECTIVE

> *see also* **ferme** NOUN

firm ◊ *Il s'est montré très ferme à mon égard.* He was very firm with me.

la **ferme** NOUN

> *see also* **ferme** ADJECTIVE

farm

fermé ADJECTIVE
① closed ◊ *La pharmacie est fermée.* The drugstore is closed.
② off ◊ *Est-ce que le gaz est fermé?* Is the gas off?

fermer VERB
① to close ◊ *N'oublie pas de fermer la fenêtre.* Don't forget to close the window.
② to turn off ◊ *As-tu bien fermé le robinet?* Did you turn the tap off?
♦ **fermer à clef** to lock ◊ *N'oublie pas de fermer la porte à clef!* Don't forget to lock the door!

la **fermeture** NOUN
♦ **les heures de fermeture** closing times

la **fermeture éclair** MC NOUN (PL les **fermetures éclair**)
zipper

le **fermier** NOUN
farmer

la **fermière** NOUN
① farmer (*woman*)
② farmer's wife

féroce ADJECTIVE
fierce

ferons, feront VERB *see* **faire**

les **fesses** FEM NOUN
buttocks

le **festival** NOUN
festival

la **fête** NOUN
① party ◊ *On organise une petite fête pour son départ.* We're having a little farewell party for him.
♦ **faire la fête** to party
🌺 ② birthday ◊ *C'est sa fête aujourd'hui.* It's his birthday today.
♦ **une fête foraine** a funfair
♦ **la fête du Canada** Canada Day
🌺 ♦ **la fête de Dollard** Dollard Day
♦ **la fête du Travail** Labour Day
♦ **la fête de la Reine** Victoria Day

♦ **les fêtes de fin d'année** the festive season

> ℹ️ In Québec, **la fête de Dollard** is the same day as Victoria Day. It commemorates the death of Adam Dollard des Ormeaux and his 16 companions in 1660 in a hopeless battle to avert an Iroquois siege of Ville Marie (now Montréal). In 2002, this holiday was officially replaced by **la Journée nationale des patriotes**.

fêter VERB
to celebrate

le **feu** NOUN (PL les **feux**)
① fire ◊ *prendre feu* to catch fire ◊ *faire du feu* to make a fire
♦ **Au feu!** Fire!
♦ **un feu de camp** a campfire
♦ **un feu de joie** a bonfire
② traffic light ◊ *un feu rouge* a red light ◊ *le feu vert* the green light ◊ *Tournez à gauche aux feux.* Turn left at the lights.
♦ **Avez-vous du feu?** Have you got a light?
③ heat ◊ *...mijoter à feu doux* ...simmer over low heat
♦ **un feu d'artifice** a firework display
🌺 ♦ **un feu sauvage** a cold sore

le **feuillage** NOUN
leaves

la **feuille** NOUN
① leaf ◊ *des feuilles mortes* fallen leaves
🌺 ♦ **la feuille d'érable** the maple leaf (*to mean "Canada"*)
② sheet ◊ *une feuille de papier* a sheet of paper
♦ **la feuille de présence** attendance sheet
♦ **une feuille de calcul** a spreadsheet (*file*)

feuilleté ADJECTIVE
♦ **de la pâte feuilletée** flaky pastry

feuilleter VERB
to leaf through

le **feuilleton** NOUN
serial

le **feutre** NOUN
felt
♦ **un stylo-feutre** a felt pen

la **fève** NOUN
bean ◊ *les fèves vertes* green beans ◊ *les fèves jaunes* wax beans
🌺 ♦ **les fèves au lard** baked beans ◊ *Il aime ajouter de la mélasse à ses fèves au lard.* He likes to add molasses to his baked beans.

février MASC NOUN

February
♦ **en février** in February

fiable ADJECTIVE
reliable

les **fiançailles** FEM NOUN
engagement SING
♦ **rompre ses fiançailles** to break off one's engagement

fiancé ADJECTIVE
♦ **être fiancé à quelqu'un** to be engaged to somebody

se **fiancer** VERB
to get engaged

la **ficelle** NOUN
1 string ◊ *Passe-moi un bout de ficelle.* Give me a piece of string.
2 thin baguette (*bread*)

la **fiche** NOUN
form ◊ *Remplissez cette fiche s'il vous plaît.* Fill in this form, please.

se **ficher** VERB (*informal*)
♦ **Je m'en fiche!** I don't care!
♦ **Fiche-moi la paix!** Leave me alone!
♦ **Quoi, tu n'as fait que ça? Tu te fiches de moi?** You've only done that much? You can't be serious!

le **fichier** NOUN
file
♦ **un fichier joint** an attachment (*e-mail*)

fichu ADJECTIVE (*informal*)
♦ **Ce parapluie est fichu.** This umbrella's busted.

fidèle ADJECTIVE
faithful

fier ADJECTIVE (FEM SING **fière**)
proud

la **fierté** NOUN
pride

la **fièvre** NOUN
fever ◊ *J'ai de la fièvre.* I have a temperature. ◊ *Elle a trente-neuf de fièvre.* She has a temperature of 39°C.

fiévreux ADJECTIVE (FEM SING **fiévreuse**)
feverish

la **figue** NOUN
fig

la **figure** NOUN
1 face ◊ *Il a reçu le ballon en pleine figure.* The ball hit him smack in the face.
2 figure (*illustration*) ◊ *Voir figure 2.1, page 32.* See figure 2.1, page 32.

le **fil** NOUN
1 thread ◊ *le fil à coudre* sewing thread
2 cord ◊ *une souris sans fil* a cordless mouse
♦ **le fil de fer** wire

la **file** NOUN
line (*of people, objects*)
♦ **une file d'attente** a lineup ◊ *se mettre à la file* to go stand in line
♦ **à la file** one after the other

filer VERB
to speed along ◊ *Les voitures filent sur l'autoroute.* The cars are speeding along the highway.
♦ **File dans ta chambre!** Off to your room with you!

le **filet** NOUN
net

la **fille** NOUN
1 girl ◊ *C'est une école de filles.* It's a girls' school.
2 daughter ◊ *C'est leur fille aînée.* She's their oldest daughter.

la **fillette** NOUN
little girl

le **film** NOUN
1 movie
♦ **un film policier** a thriller
♦ **un film d'aventures** an action movie
♦ **un film d'épouvante** a horror movie
2 film ◊ *Avec une caméra numérique, on n'a pas besoin de film.* With a digital camera, you don't need film.

le **fils** NOUN
son

la **fin** NOUN

see also **fin** ADJECTIVE

end ◊ *Elle n'a pas regardé la fin du film.* She didn't watch the end of the film.
♦ **« Fin »** "The End"
♦ **À la fin, il a réussi à se décider.** In the end he managed to make up his mind.
♦ **Elle sera en vacances fin juin.** She'll be on holiday at the end of June.
♦ **en fin de journée** at the end of the day
♦ **en fin de compte** ultimately
♦ **sans fin** endless

fin ADJECTIVE

see also **fin** NOUN

1 fine
♦ **des fines herbes** mixed herbs
2 nice (*informal*) ◊ *Elle est vraiment fine!* She is so nice!

la **finale** NOUN
final (*sports*) ◊ *les quarts de finale* the quarter finals

finalement ADVERB
1 at last ◊ *Nous sommes finalement arrivés.* At last we arrived.
2 after all ◊ *Finalement, tu avais raison.* You were right after all.

F

✻ la **fin de semaine** NOUN
weekend ◊ *Nous avons passé la fin de semaine au chalet.* We spent the weekend at the cottage.

fini ADJECTIVE
finished

finir VERB
to finish ◊ *Le cours finit à onze heures.* The class finishes at 11 o'clock. ◊ *Je viens de finir ce livre.* I've just finished this book.
♦ **Elle a fini par se décider.** She made up her mind in the end.

✻ le **finissant** NOUN
graduating student
♦ **le bal des finissants** graduation party

✻ la **finissante** NOUN
graduating student

la **firme** NOUN
firm

fis VERB *see* **faire**

la **fissure** NOUN
crack

fit VERB *see* **faire**

fixe ADJECTIVE
① steady ◊ *Il n'a pas d'emploi fixe.* He doesn't have a steady job.
② set ◊ *Elle mange toujours à heures fixes.* She always eats at set times.
♦ **un menu à prix fixe** a set menu
♦ **une idée fixe** an obsession

fixer VERB
① to hold in place ◊ *Les volets sont fixés avec des crochets.* The shutters are held in place with hooks.
② to set (*time*) ◊ *Nous avons fixé une heure pour nous retrouver.* We set a time to meet.
③ to stare at ◊ *Ne fixe pas les gens comme ça!* Don't stare at people like that!

le **flacon** NOUN
bottle ◊ *un flacon de parfum* a bottle of perfume

flambé ADJECTIVE
♦ **des bananes flambées** flambéed bananas

la **flamme** NOUN
flame
♦ **en flammes** on fire

le **flan** NOUN
baked custard

flâner VERB
to stroll

la **flaque** NOUN
puddle (*of water*)

le **flash** NOUN (PL les **flashes**)
flash (*of camera*)

flatter VERB
to flatter

la **flèche** NOUN
arrow

les **fléchettes** FEM NOUN
darts ◊ *jouer aux fléchettes* to play darts

le **flétan** NOUN
halibut

la **fleur** NOUN
flower

la **fleur de lis** NOUN
fleur-de-lis

> ⓘ The **fleur-de-lis** is the provincial emblem of Québec and is on the provincial flag. It is a legacy of New France, as it was also the emblem for French royalty.

✻ le **fleurdelisé** NOUN
the Québec flag

fleuri ADJECTIVE
① full of flowers ◊ *Son jardin était très fleuri.* Her garden was full of flowers.
② flowery ◊ *un papier peint fleuri* flowery wallpaper

fleurir VERB
to flower ◊ *Cette plante fleurit en automne.* This plant flowers in the fall.

le/la **fleuriste** NOUN
florist

le **fleuve** NOUN
river

flirter VERB
to flirt

le **flocon** NOUN
flake

flotter VERB
to float

flou ADJECTIVE
blurry

le **fluorure** NOUN
♦ **le dentifrice au fluorure** fluoride toothpaste

la **flûte** NOUN
flute ◊ *Je joue de la flûte.* I play the flute.
♦ **une flûte à bec** a recorder

la **foi** NOUN
faith

le **foie** NOUN
liver
♦ **une crise de foie** a stomach upset

le **foin** NOUN

hay
♦ **un rhume des foins** hay fever

la **foire** NOUN
fair
♦ **la foire du livre** book fair

la **fois** NOUN
time ◊ *la première fois* the first time
◊ *à chaque fois* each time ◊ *À chaque
fois que je vais à la bibliothèque,
j'oublie ma carte.* Every time I go to
the library, I forget my card. ◊ *deux
fois deux font quatre* 2 times 2 is 4
♦ **une fois** once
♦ **deux fois** twice ◊ *deux fois plus de
gens* twice as many people ◊ *Je vais
nager deux fois par semaine.* I go
swimming twice a week.
♦ **une fois que** once ◊ *Tu te sentiras
mieux une fois que tu auras mangé.*
You'll feel better once you've had
something to eat.
♦ **à la fois** at once ◊ *Je ne peux pas
faire deux choses à la fois.* I can't do
two things at once.

la **folie** NOUN
madness ◊ *C'est de la folie pure!* It's
absolute madness!
♦ **faire une folie** to be extravagant

folklorique ADJECTIVE
folk ◊ *de la musique folklorique* folk
music

folle ADJECTIVE *see* **fou**

foncé ADJECTIVE
dark ◊ *bleu foncé* dark blue

foncer VERB (*informal*)
♦ **Je vais foncer à la boulangerie.** I'm
just going to whip over to the bakery.

la **fonction** NOUN
function
♦ **une voiture de fonction** a company
car

le/la **fonctionnaire** NOUN
civil servant

fonctionner VERB
to work

le **fond** NOUN
⓵ bottom ◊ *Mon porte-monnaie est
au fond de mon sac.* My wallet is at
the bottom of my purse.
⓶ end ◊ *Les toilettes sont au fond du
couloir.* The washrooms are at the end
of the hall.
♦ **dans le fond** all things considered
◊ *Dans le fond, ce n'est pas si grave.*
All things considered, it's not that
bad.

fonder VERB
to found ◊ *Charles Camsell a fondé
la Société géographique royale du*
Canada. Charles Camsell founded
the Royal Geographical Society of
Canada.

fondre VERB
to melt ◊ *La tablette de chocolat a
fondu dans ma poche.* The bar of
chocolate melted in my pocket.
♦ **fondre en larmes** to burst into tears

fondu ADJECTIVE
♦ **du beurre fondu** melted butter

font VERB *see* **faire**

la **fontaine** NOUN
fountain

le **foot** NOUN (*informal*)
football

le **football** NOUN
football ◊ *jouer au football* to play
football

la **force** NOUN
strength ◊ *Je n'ai pas beaucoup
de force dans les bras.* I haven't got
much strength in my arms.
♦ **à force de** by ◊ *Il a grossi à force de
manger autant.* He got fat by eating
so much.
♦ **de force** by force ◊ *Ils lui ont enlevé
son pistolet de force.* They took the
gun from her by force.
♦ **les forces armées** the armed forces

forcé ADJECTIVE
forced ◊ *un sourire forcé* a forced
smile
♦ **C'est forcé.** (*informal*) It's inevitable.

forcément ADVERB
♦ **Ça devait forcément arriver.** That was
bound to happen.
♦ **pas forcément** not necessarily

la **foresterie** NOUN
forestry ◊ *Elle veut étudier en
foresterie.* She wants to study
forestry.

la **forêt** NOUN
forest

le **forfait** NOUN
package deal
♦ **C'est compris dans le forfait.** It's
included in the package.

la **formalité** NOUN
formality ◊ *Ce n'est qu'une simple
formalité.* It's just a formality.

le **format** NOUN
size

le **formatage** NOUN
formatting

formater VERB
to format ◊ *formater un document* to
format a document

la **formation** NOUN

☞

training ◊ *la formation*
professionnelle vocational training
♦ **Il a une formation d'ingénieur.** He is a
trained engineer.

la **forme** NOUN
shape
♦ **être en forme** to be in good shape
♦ **Je ne suis pas en forme aujourd'hui.**
I'm not feeling too good today.
♦ **Tu as l'air en forme.** You're looking
well.

formellement ADVERB
strictly ◊ *Il est formellement interdit*
de fumer dans les couloirs. It is
strictly forbidden to smoke in the
corridors.

former VERB
to form

formidable ADJECTIVE
great

le **formulaire** NOUN
form (*to fill out*)

fort ADJECTIVE, ADVERB
① strong ◊ *Le café est trop fort.* The
coffee's too strong.
② good ◊ *Elle est très forte en*
espagnol. She's very good at Spanish.
③ loud ◊ *Est-ce que vous pouvez*
parler plus fort? Can you speak
louder?
④ hard ◊ *frapper fort* to hit hard
◊ *travailler fort* to work hard

la **fortune** NOUN
fortune
♦ **de fortune** makeshift ◊ *Nous avons*
traversé la rivière sur un radeau de
fortune. We crossed the river on a
makeshift raft.

le **forum de discussion** NOUN
discussion group (*Internet*)

le **fossé** NOUN
ditch

fou ADJECTIVE (FEM SING **folle**)
mad
♦ **Il y a un monde fou sur la plage!**
(*informal*) There are tons of people on
the beach!
♦ **attraper le fou rire** to get the giggles

la **foudre** NOUN
lightning ◊ *Il a été frappé par la*
foudre. He was struck by lightning.

foudroyant ADJECTIVE
instant ◊ *un succès foudroyant* an
instant hit

le **fouet** NOUN
whisk

fouetter VERB
to whip ◊ *la crème à fouetter*
whipping cream

la **fougère** NOUN
fern

fouiller VERB
to rummage

le **fouillis** NOUN
mess ◊ *Sa chambre est un vrai*
fouillis. Her bedroom is a mess.

le **foulard** NOUN
scarf ◊ *un foulard en soie* a silk scarf

la **foule** NOUN
crowd
♦ **une foule de** tons of ◊ *J'ai une foule*
de choses à faire en fin de semaine.
I have tons of things to do this
weekend.

se **fouler** VERB
♦ **se fouler la cheville** to sprain one's
ankle

la **foulure** NOUN
sprain

le **four** NOUN
oven ◊ *un four à micro-ondes* a
microwave oven
♦ **un four à céramique** a kiln

la **fourchette** NOUN
fork

la **fourmi** NOUN
ant
♦ **avoir des fourmis dans les jambes** to
have pins and needles

le **fourneau** NOUN (PL les **fourneaux**)
stove

fourni ADJECTIVE
thick (*beard, hair*)

fournir VERB
to supply

le **fournisseur** NOUN
supplier
♦ **un fournisseur de services Internet** an
Internet service provider

les **fournitures** FEM NOUN
♦ **les fournitures scolaires** school
supplies

fourré ADJECTIVE
filled ◊ *un gâteau fourré à la*
confiture a cake with a jam filling

fourrer VERB (*informal*)
to put ◊ *Où as-tu fourré mon sac?*
Where have you put my bag?

le **fourre-tout** NOUN (PL les **fourre-tout**)
tote bag

la **fourrure** NOUN
fur ◊ *un manteau de fourrure* a fur
coat

le **foyer** NOUN
home ◊ *dans la plupart des foyers*
canadiens-français in most French-

Canadian homes
♦ **un foyer de jeunes** a youth club

la **fracture** NOUN
fracture

fragile ADJECTIVE
fragile ◊ *Attention, c'est fragile!* Be careful, it's fragile!

fraîche ADJECTIVE *see* **frais**

la **fraîcheur** NOUN
1 cool ◊ *la fraîcheur du soir* the cool of the evening
2 freshness ◊ *Je ne suis pas sûre de la fraîcheur de ce poisson.* I'm not sure about the freshness of this fish.

frais ADJECTIVE (FEM SING **fraîche**)

see also **frais** NOUN

1 fresh ◊ *des œufs frais* fresh eggs ◊ *Cette salade n'est pas très fraîche.* This lettuce isn't very fresh.
2 chilly ◊ *Il fait un peu frais ce soir.* It's a bit chilly this evening.
3 cold ◊ *des boissons fraîches* cold drinks
♦ **« servir frais »** "serve chilled"
♦ **garder au frais** to store in a cool place

les **frais** MASC NOUN

see also **frais** ADJECTIVE

expenses

la **fraise** NOUN
strawberry ◊ *une fraise des bois* a wild strawberry

la **framboise** NOUN
raspberry

franc ADJECTIVE (FEM SING **franche**)
frank

français ADJECTIVE, NOUN
French ◊ *la grammaire française* French grammar ◊ *Il parle français couramment.* He speaks French fluently.

franche ADJECTIVE *see* **franc**

franchement ADVERB
1 frankly ◊ *Elle m'a parlé franchement.* She spoke to me frankly.
2 really ◊ *C'est franchement mauvais.* It's really bad.

franchir VERB
to get over ◊ *franchir une clôture* to get over a fence ◊ *Un sourire franchit toutes les barrières linguistiques.* A smile crosses all language barriers.

la **franchise** NOUN
frankness

francophone ADJECTIVE

see also **francophone** NOUN

French-speaking

le/la **francophone** NOUN

see also **francophone** ADJECTIVE

Francophone ◊ *C'est un francophone.* He's a Francophone.

la **francophonie** NOUN
the Francophone world

ⓘ *La francophonie* refers to the more than 50 French-speaking countries and regions of the world collectively.

la **frange** NOUN
1 fringe
2 bangs PL

la **frangipane** NOUN
almond cream

frapper VERB
to strike ◊ *Il n'a jamais frappée ses enfants.* He has never struck his children. ◊ *Son air fatigué m'a frappé.* I was struck by how tired she looked.

fredonner VERB
to hum

le **frein** NOUN
brake
♦ **le frein à main** handbrake

freiner VERB
to brake

frêle ADJECTIVE
frail

le **frelon** NOUN
hornet

frémir VERB
shudder ◊ *Cette idée me fait frémir.* The idea makes me shudder.

fréquemment ADVERB
frequently

fréquent ADJECTIVE
frequent

fréquenté ADJECTIVE
busy ◊ *une rue très fréquentée* a very busy street

fréquenter VERB
1 to see (*person*) ◊ *Je ne le fréquente pas beaucoup.* I don't see him often.
2 to go to (*place*) ◊ *Tu fréquentes les ventes-débarras?* Do you go to garage sales?

le **frère** NOUN
brother

le **friand** NOUN
sausage roll

les **friandises** FEM NOUN
sweets

le **fric** NOUN (*informal*)

F

cash

✷ le **frigidaire** NOUN
refrigerator

le **frigo** NOUN (*informal*)
fridge

frileux ADJECTIVE (FEM SING **frileuse**)
♦ **être frileux** to feel the cold ◊ *Je suis très frileuse.* I really feel the cold.

fripé ADJECTIVE
crumpled

frire VERB
♦ **faire frire** to fry ◊ *Faites frire les boulettes de viande dans de l'huile très chaude.* Fry the meatballs in very hot oil.

frisé ADJECTIVE
curly ◊ *Elle est très frisée.* She has very curly hair.

le **frisson** NOUN
shiver

frissonner VERB
to shiver

frit ADJECTIVE
fried ◊ *du poisson frit* fried fish

les **frites** FEM NOUN
fries
♦ **poisson et frites** fish and chips

la **friture** NOUN
1 fried food ◊ *On lui a conseillé d'éviter les fritures.* He's been advised to avoid fried food.
2 fried fish ◊ *Nous allons faire une friture ce soir.* We're going to have fried fish tonight.
3 static ◊ *Il y a de la friture sur la ligne.* There's static on the line.

froid ADJECTIVE

see also **froid** NOUN

cold ◊ *Ça me laisse froid.* It leaves me cold. ◊ *de la viande froide* cold meat

le **froid** NOUN

see also **froid** ADJECTIVE

cold
♦ **Il fait froid.** It's cold.
♦ **avoir froid** to be cold ◊ *Est-ce que tu as froid?* Are you cold?

se **froisser** VERB
1 to crease ◊ *Ce tissu se froisse très facilement.* This material creases very easily.
2 to take offence ◊ *Il se froisse très facilement.* He's very quick to take offence.
♦ **se froisser un muscle** to strain a muscle

frôler VERB

1 to brush against ◊ *Le chat m'a frôlé au passage.* The cat brushed against me as it went past.
2 to narrowly avoid ◊ *Nous avons frôlé la catastrophe.* We narrowly avoided disaster.

le **fromage** NOUN
cheese
♦ **le fromage à la crème** cream cheese
♦ **le fromage en grains** cheese curds

la **fromagerie** NOUN
cheese shop

le **froment** NOUN
wheat

froncer VERB
♦ **froncer les sourcils** to frown

le **front** NOUN
forehead

la **frontière** NOUN
border

frotter VERB
to rub ◊ *se frotter les yeux* to rub one's eyes
♦ **frotter une allumette** to strike a match

le **fruit** NOUN
fruit
♦ **un fruit** a piece of fruit ◊ *Est-ce que vous voulez manger un fruit?* Would you like some fruit?
♦ **les fruits de mer** seafood

fruité ADJECTIVE
fruity

frustrer VERB
to frustrate

la **fugue** NOUN
♦ **faire une fugue** to run away

fuir VERB
1 to flee ◊ *fuir devant un danger* to flee from danger
2 to leak ◊ *Le robinet fuit.* The tap is leaking.

la **fuite** NOUN
1 leak ◊ *Il y a une fuite de gaz.* There is a gas leak.
2 flight (*escape*)
♦ **être en fuite** to be on the run

fumé ADJECTIVE
smoked ◊ *du saumon fumé* smoked salmon

la **fumée** NOUN
smoke

fumer VERB
to smoke

le **fumeur** NOUN
smoker

la **fumeuse** NOUN
smoker

les **funérailles** FEM NOUN
> <u>funeral</u> ◊ *Les funérailles auront lieu demain.* The funeral is tomorrow.

fur
- ♦ **au fur et à mesure** ADVERB as you go along ◊ *Je vérifie mon travail au fur et à mesure.* I check my work as I go along.
- ♦ **au fur et à mesure que** as ◊ *Je réponds à mon courrier au fur et à mesure que je le reçois.* I answer my mail as I receive it.

le **furet** NOUN
> <u>ferret</u>

la **fureur** NOUN
> <u>fury</u>
- ♦ **faire fureur** to be all the rage ◊ *Ce genre de sac à dos fait fureur actuellement.* This sort of backpack is all the rage at the moment.

furieux ADJECTIVE (FEM SING **furieuse**)
> <u>furious</u>

le **furoncle** NOUN
> <u>boil</u> (*on skin*)

fus VERB *see* **être**

la **fusée** NOUN
> <u>rocket</u>

le **fusil** NOUN
> <u>gun</u>

fut VERB *see* **être**

futé ADJECTIVE
> <u>crafty</u>

le **futur** NOUN
> <u>future</u>

futuriste ADJECTIVE
> <u>futuristic</u>

F

G

gâcher VERB
to waste ◊ *Je n'aime pas gâcher la nourriture.* I don't like to waste food.

le **gâchis** NOUN
mess ◊ *Le chien a fait un beau gâchis sur le tapis.* The dog made a real mess on the carpet.

la **gaffe** NOUN
♦ **faire une gaffe** to do something stupid

✹ la **gageure** NOUN
challenge ◊ *J'ai fait la gageure d'apprendre l'espagnol.* I took the challenge of learning Spanish.
◊ *Réussir ce projet tient de la gageure.* To succeed in this project will be a challenge.

le **gagnant** NOUN
winner

la **gagnante** NOUN
winner

gagner VERB
to win ◊ *Qui a gagné?* Who won?
♦ **gagner du temps** to gain time
♦ **Il gagne bien sa vie.** He makes a good living.

gai ADJECTIVE
cheerful ◊ *Elle est très gaie.* She's very cheerful.

la **gaieté** NOUN
cheerfulness

la **galerie** NOUN
gallery ◊ *une galerie d'art* an art gallery
♦ **une galerie marchande** a shopping arcade

le **galet** NOUN
pebble

la **galette** NOUN
round flat cake ◊ *une galette de blé noir* a buckwheat pancake

✹ la **galvaude** NOUN

> ❶ *La galvaude* is a kind of *poutine*. It consists of French fries topped with bits of chicken, green peas, cheese curds, and gravy.

le **gamin** NOUN (*informal*)
kid

la **gamine** NOUN (*informal*)
kid

la **gamme** NOUN
scale (*in music*) ◊ *Je dois faire des gammes tous les soirs.* I have to do my scales every night.
♦ **une gamme de produits** a range of products
♦ **haut de gamme** top-of-the-line

gammée ADJECTIVE
♦ **la croix gammée** the swastika

le **gant** NOUN
glove ◊ *des gants en laine* woollen gloves

le **garage** NOUN
garage

le/la **garagiste** NOUN
① garage owner
② mechanic

la **garantie** NOUN
guarantee

garantir VERB
to guarantee

le **garçon** NOUN
boy
♦ **un vieux garçon** a bachelor

le/la **garde** NOUN

> *see also* **la garde**

♦ **un garde de sécurité** a security guard
♦ **un garde du corps** a bodyguard
♦ **un garde forestier** a ranger

la **garde** NOUN

> *see also* **le/la garde**

① guarding ◊ *Elle est chargée de la garde des prisonniers.* She's responsible for guarding the prisoners.
② guard ◊ *la relève de la garde* the changing of the guard
♦ **être de garde** to be on duty ◊ *Mon père est de garde ce soir.* My father is on duty tonight.
♦ **la garde des enfants** child custody (*in divorce*) ◊ *Le père a eu la garde des enfants.* Child custody was given to the father.
♦ **mettre en garde** to warn ◊ *Elle m'a mis en garde contre les voleurs à la tire.* She warned me about pickpockets.

le **garde-côte** NOUN (PL les **garde-côtes**)
coast guard (*boat*)

garder VERB
① to keep ◊ *Tu as gardé toutes ses lettres?* Did you keep all his letters?
② to look after ◊ *Je garde mon petit cousin samedi après-midi.* I'm looking

after my little cousin on Saturday
afternoon.

③ to guard ◊ *Ils ont pris un gros
chien pour garder la maison.* They got
a big dog to guard the house.
♦ **garder le lit** to stay in bed
♦ **se garder** to keep ◊ *Ces crêpes se
gardent bien.* These pancakes keep
well.

la **garderie** NOUN
daycare

la **garde-robe** NOUN
① wardrobe (*clothes*) ◊ *Elle a une
garde-robe bien fournie.* She's got an
extensive wardrobe.
② closet ◊ *Son garde-robe est bourré
de vêtements de sport.* His closet is
filled with sportswear.

> In Canadian French, when **garde-
> robe** is used to mean **closet**, it can be
> either masculine or feminine.

le **gardien** NOUN
♦ **un gardien de but** a goalkeeper
♦ **un gardien de la paix** a peacekeeper
♦ **un gardien d'enfants** a babysitter
♦ **un gardien de prison** a prison guard

la **gardienne** NOUN
♦ **une gardienne de but** a goalkeeper
♦ **une gardienne de la paix** a
peacekeeper
♦ **une gardienne d'enfants** a babysitter
♦ **une gardienne de prison** a prison
guard

la **gare** NOUN

> *see also* **gare** EXCLAMATION

station ◊ *la gare d'autobus* the bus
station

gare EXCLAMATION

> *see also* **gare** NOUN

♦ **Gare aux serpents!** Watch out for
snakes!

garer VERB
to park
♦ **se garer** to park ◊ *Où t'es-tu garé?*
Where are you parked?

garni ADJECTIVE
♦ **un plat garni** a dish served with
something on the side (*vegetables,
fries, rice, etc.*)
❋ ♦ **une pizza garnie** a pizza with
everything on it

le **gars** NOUN (*informal*)
guy

le **gaspillage** NOUN
waste ◊ *Quel gaspillage!* What a
waste!

gaspiller VERB
to waste ◊ *Je n'aime pas gaspiller*

de la nourriture. I don't like to waste
food.

le **gâteau** NOUN (PL les **gâteaux**)
cake
❋ ♦ **le gâteau des anges** angel food cake

gâter VERB
to spoil ◊ *Il aime gâter ses petits
enfants.* He likes to spoil his
grandchildren.
♦ **se gâter (1)** to go bad ◊ *Ces bananes
se gâtent.* These bananas are going
bad.
♦ **se gâter (2)** to change for the worse
◊ *Le temps va se gâter.* The weather's
going to change for the worse.

gauche ADJECTIVE

> *see also* **gauche** NOUN

left ◊ *le bras gauche* the left arm ◊ *le
côté gauche* the left-hand side

la **gauche** NOUN

> *see also* **gauche** ADJECTIVE

left ◊ *sur votre gauche* on your left
♦ **à gauche (1)** on the left ◊ *la deuxième
rue à gauche* the second street on
the left
♦ **à gauche (2)** to the left ◊ *à gauche de
l'armoire* to the left of the cupboard
◊ *Tournez à gauche.* Turn left.
♦ **la voie de gauche** the left-hand lane
♦ **la gauche** the left (*in politics*) ◊ *Elle
est de gauche.* She's left-wing.

gaucher ADJECTIVE (FEM SING **gauchère**)
left-handed

la **gaufre** NOUN
waffle

la **gaufrette** NOUN
wafer

le **gaz** NOUN
gas

gazeux ADJECTIVE (FEM SING **gazeuse**)
♦ **une boisson gazeuse** a soft drink
♦ **de l'eau gazeuse** sparkling water

le **gazon** NOUN
lawn

le **geai bleu** NOUN
blue jay

le **géant** NOUN
giant

le **gel** NOUN
① frost
❋ ② freeze-up ◊ *Nous devons aller
fermer le chalet avant la saison du
gel.* We have to go close the cottage
before freeze-up.

la **gelée** NOUN
jelly

geler VERB

G

to freeze ◊ *Il a gelé cette nuit.* There was a frost last night.

la **gélule** NOUN
capsule (*containing medicine*)

les **Gémeaux** MASC NOUN
Gemini ◊ *Je suis Gémeaux.* I'm a Gemini.

gémir VERB
to moan

gênant ADJECTIVE
embarrassing ◊ *des questions gênantes* embarrassing questions ◊ *un silence gênant* an awkward silence

la **gencive** NOUN
gum (*in mouth*)

la **Gendarmerie royale du Canada** NOUN
Royal Canadian Mounted Police

le **gendre** NOUN
son-in-law

gêné ADJECTIVE
embarrassed

gêner VERB
1 to bother ◊ *Je ne voudrais pas vous gêner.* I don't want to bother you.
2 to embarrass ◊ *Son regard la gênait.* The way he was looking at her made her feel embarrassed.
✱ 3 to make nervous ◊ *Faire un exposé oral me gêne.* Giving oral presentations makes me nervous.

général ADJECTIVE (MASC PL **généraux**)
general
♦ **en général** usually

généralement ADVERB
generally

le/la **généraliste** NOUN
family doctor

la **génération** NOUN
generation

généreux ADJECTIVE (FEM SING **généreuse**)
generous

la **générosité** NOUN
generosity

la **génétique** NOUN
genetics

génétiquement ADVERB
genetically ◊ *génétiquement modifié* genetically-modified ◊ *les aliments génétiquement modifiés* GM foods ◊ *un organisme génétiquement modifié* a genetically-modified organism

génial ADJECTIVE (MASC PL **géniaux**)
(*informal*)
great ◊ *Le film d'hier soir était génial.*

The film last night was great.

le **genou** NOUN (PL les **genoux**)
knee ◊ *Je me suis cogné le genou contre la table.* I banged my knee on the table.
♦ **à genoux** on one's knees
♦ **se mettre à genoux** to kneel down

le **genre** NOUN
kind ◊ *C'est un genre de gâteau.* It's a kind of cake.

les **gens** MASC NOUN
people

gentil ADJECTIVE (FEM SING **gentille**)
1 nice ◊ *Nos voisins sont très gentils.* Our neighbours are very nice.
2 kind ◊ *C'était très gentil de votre part.* It was very kind of you.

la **gentillesse** NOUN
kindness ◊ *Je l'ai remerciée de sa gentillesse.* I thanked her for her kindness. ◊ *C'est un homme d'une grande gentillesse.* He is a very nice man.

gentiment ADVERB
1 nicely ◊ *Demande-le lui gentiment.* Ask him nicely.
2 kindly ◊ *Ils nous ont gentiment proposé de rester dîner.* They kindly invited us to stay for dinner.

la **géographie** NOUN
geography

la **géométrie** NOUN
geometry

le **gérant** NOUN
manager (*bank, store*)

la **gérante** NOUN
manager (*bank, store*)

gercé ADJECTIVE
chapped ◊ *les lèvres gercées* chapped lips

gérer VERB
to manage ◊ *Qui gère cette entreprise?* Who's managing this outfit?

germain ADJECTIVE
♦ **un cousin germain** a first cousin

le **geste** NOUN
gesture ◊ *s'exprimer par des gestes* to express oneself using one's hands ◊ *un geste de bonne volonté* a gesture of goodwill
♦ **Ne faites pas un geste!** Don't move!

la **gestion** NOUN
management

la **gifle** NOUN
slap on the face

gifler VERB
to slap on the face

gigantesque ADJECTIVE
gigantic

le **gigaoctet** NOUN
gigabyte ◊ *un disque dur de cent vingt gigaoctets* a 120-gigabyte hard disk

le **gilet** NOUN
cardigan ◊ *un gilet tricoté à la main* a hand-knitted cardigan
♦ **un gilet de sauvetage** a life jacket

le **gingembre** NOUN
ginger

la **girafe** NOUN
giraffe

le **gîte** NOUN
♦ **un gîte du passant** a bed-and-breakfast

la **glace** NOUN
ice ◊ *L'étang est recouvert de glace.* The pond is covered with ice.
♦ **la glace noire** black ice (*roads*)
♦ **rompre la glace** to break the ice

glacé ADJECTIVE
1 icy ◊ *Il soufflait un vent glacé.* An icy wind was blowing.
2 iced ◊ *un thé glacé* an iced tea
♦ **la crème glacée** ice cream

glacial ADJECTIVE (MASC PL **glaciaux**)
icy

le **glaçon** NOUN
1 ice cube
2 icicle

la **glissade** NOUN
ice slide ◊ *L'hiver, la ville construit une glissade dans le parc.* In winter the city builds an ice slide in the park.

glissant ADJECTIVE
slippery

le **glissement de terrain** NOUN
landslide

glisser VERB
1 to slip ◊ *J'ai glissé sur une peau de banane.* I slipped on a banana skin.
2 to be slippery ◊ *Attention, ça glisse!* Watch out, it's slippery!
3 to slide ◊ *descendre la colline en glissant* to slide down the hill
4 to glide ◊ *glisser sur la neige* to glide over the snow
♦ **glisser-déposer** drag and drop

global ADJECTIVE (MASC PL **globaux**)
total ◊ *la somme globale* the total amount

la **gloire** NOUN
glory

le **glucide** NOUN
carbohydrate ◊ *Les pâtes contiennent beaucoup de glucides.*

Pasta is high in carbohydrates.

le **goéland** NOUN
seagull

le **golf** NOUN
golf ◊ *Elle joue au golf.* She plays golf.

le **golfe** NOUN
gulf ◊ *le golfe du Saint-Laurent* the Gulf of St. Lawrence

la **gomme** NOUN
eraser (*for pencil*)

la **gomme à mâcher** NOUN
chewing gum ◊ *de la gomme à mâcher à saveur de cannelle* cinnamon-flavoured chewing gum

gommer VERB
to erase (*pencil*)

gonflé ADJECTIVE
1 swollen ◊ *Elle a les pieds gonflés.* Her feet are swollen.
2 inflated ◊ *Le ballon de soccer était mal gonflé.* The soccer ball wasn't properly inflated.

gonfler VERB
1 to blow up ◊ *gonfler un ballon* to blow up a balloon
2 to pump up ◊ *Tu devrais gonfler ton pneu arrière.* You should pump up your back tire.

la **gorge** NOUN
1 throat ◊ *J'ai mal à la gorge.* I've got a sore throat.
2 gorge ◊ *la gorge Elora* the Elora Gorge

la **gorgée** NOUN
sip ◊ *une gorgée d'eau* a sip of water

le **gorille** NOUN
gorilla

le **goudron** NOUN
tar

le **gouffre** NOUN
chasm
♦ **Cette voiture est un vrai gouffre!** This car is a money pit!

gourmand ADJECTIVE
greedy

la **gourmandise** NOUN
greed

le **gourou** NOUN
guru

la **gousse** NOUN
♦ **une gousse d'ail** a clove of garlic

le **goût** NOUN
taste ◊ *Ça n'a pas de goût.* It has no taste. ◊ *Elle a très bon goût.* She has very good taste.
♦ **avoir le goût de** to feel like (*doing*

G

something) ◊ *J'ai le goût d'aller au cinéma.* I feel like going to the movies.
♦ **de bon goût** in good taste
♦ **de mauvais goût** in bad taste ◊ *Sa blague était de mauvais goût.* His joke was in bad taste.

goûter VERB
to taste ◊ *Goûte donc ce fromage : tu verras comme il est bon!* Have a taste of this cheese: you'll see how good it is!

la **goutte** NOUN
drop
♦ **C'est la goutte d'eau qui a fait déborder le vase!** That was the last straw!
♦ **C'est une goutte d'eau dans l'océan.** It's a drop in the bucket.

le **gouvernement** NOUN
government

gouverner VERB
to govern

✹ le **gouverneur général** NOUN
Governor General

✹ la **gouverneure générale** NOUN
Governor General

la **grâce** NOUN
♦ **grâce à** thanks to ◊ *Je suis arrivé à l'heure grâce à toi.* I arrived on time thanks to you.

gracieux ADJECTIVE (FEM SING **gracieuse**)
graceful

les **gradins** MASC NOUN
1 stands (*indoor*)
2 bleachers (*outdoor*)

graduel ADJECTIVE (FEM SING **graduelle**)
gradual

le **grain** NOUN
grain ◊ *un grain de sable* a grain of sand
♦ **un grain de café** a coffee bean
♦ **un grain de poivre** a peppercorn
♦ **un grain de raisin** a grape

la **graine** NOUN
seed

la **graisse** NOUN
fat

la **grammaire** NOUN
grammar

le **gramme** NOUN
gram

grand ADJECTIVE, ADVERB
1 tall ◊ *Il est grand pour son âge.* He's tall for his age.
2 big ◊ *une grande valise* a big suitcase ◊ *ma grande sœur* my big sister

♦ **une grande personne** a grown-up
3 long ◊ *un grand voyage* a long journey
4 great ◊ *C'est un grand ami à moi.* He's a great friend of mine.
♦ **un grand magasin** a department store
♦ **au grand air** out in the open air ◊ *Ça te fera beaucoup de bien d'être au grand air.* It'll be very good for you to be out in the open air.
♦ **grand ouvert** wide open
5 important ◊ *Le centenaire de la ville a été un grand événement.* The city's 100th anniversary was an important event. ◊ *Je porte cette chemise durant les grandes occasions.* I wear this shirt on important occasions.

grand-chose NOUN
♦ **pas grand-chose** not much ◊ *Je n'ai pas acheté grand-chose au marché.* I didn't buy much at the market. ◊ *Voici un petit cadeau : ce n'est pas grand-chose.* Here's a little present: it's nothing much.

la **grandeur** NOUN
size

grandir VERB
to grow ◊ *Elle a beaucoup grandi.* She's grown a lot.

la **grand-mère** NOUN (PL les **grands-mères**)
grandmother

grand-peine
♦ **à grand-peine** ADVERB with great difficulty

le **grand-père** NOUN (PL les **grands-pères**)
grandfather

✹ les **Grands Lacs** MASC NOUN
Great Lakes

les **grands-parents** MASC NOUN
grandparents

la **grange** NOUN
barn

le **graphique** NOUN
1 graph ◊ *un graphique à barres* a bar graph
2 chart ◊ *un graphique circulaire* a pie chart

la **grappe** NOUN
♦ **une grappe de raisin** a bunch of grapes

gras ADJECTIVE (FEM SING **grasse**)
1 fatty (*food*) ◊ *Évitez les aliments gras.* Avoid fatty foods.
2 greasy ◊ *des cheveux gras* greasy hair
3 oily ◊ *une peau grasse* oily skin
♦ **faire la grasse matinée** to sleep in
4 bold (*type*) ◊ *Mets le titre en*

caractères gras. Put the title in bold type.

le **gratte-ciel** NOUN (PL les **gratte-ciel**)
skyscraper

gratter VERB
1 to scratch ◊ *Ne gratte pas tes piqûres de moustiques.* Don't scratch your mosquito bites.
2 to be itchy ◊ *C'est épouvantable comme ça gratte!* It's terribly itchy!

gratuit ADJECTIVE
free ◊ *entrée gratuite* entrance free ◊ *J'ai deux places gratuites pour le concert.* I've got two complimentary tickets for the concert.

grave ADJECTIVE
1 serious ◊ *une maladie grave* a serious illness ◊ *Elle avait l'air grave.* She was looking serious.
2 deep ◊ *Il a une voix grave.* He's got a deep voice.
♦ **Ce n'est pas grave.** It doesn't matter. ◊ *« J'ai oublié ma clé. » « Ce n'est pas grave, j'ai la mienne. »* "I forgot my key." "It doesn't matter, I've got mine."

gravement ADVERB
seriously ◊ *Il a été gravement blessé.* He was seriously injured.

graver VERB
1 to burn (*CDs*)
2 to engrave ◊ *Son nom était gravé sur la bague.* Her name was engraved on the ring.

le **graveur** NOUN
♦ **un graveur de DC** a CD burner

la **grêle** NOUN
hail

grêler VERB
♦ **Il grêle.** It's hailing.

grelotter VERB
to shiver

la **grenade** NOUN
1 pomegranate
2 grenade

le **grenier** NOUN
attic

la **grenouille** NOUN
frog

la **grève** NOUN
1 strike
♦ **en grève** on strike ◊ *Ils sont en grève depuis dix jours.* They have been on strike for ten days.
♦ **être en grève** to be on strike
♦ **se mettre en grève** to go on strike
♦ **un piquet de grève** a picket line
2 shore ◊ *Nous nous sommes promenés le long de la grève.* We

went for a walk along the shore.

le/la **gréviste** NOUN
striker

grièvement ADVERB
♦ **grièvement blessé** seriously injured

la **griffe** NOUN
1 claw ◊ *Le chat m'a donné un coup de griffe.* The cat scratched me.
2 label ◊ *la griffe d'un grand couturier* the label of a top designer

griffer VERB
to scratch ◊ *Le chat m'a griffé.* The cat scratched me.

grignoter VERB
to nibble

la **grillade** NOUN
grilled food ◊ *une grillade de légumes* grilled vegetables

la **grille** NOUN
1 fence (*chain-link*) ◊ *L'usine est entourée d'une haute grille.* The factory is surrounded by a high fence.
2 gate (*metal*) ◊ *la grille du jardin* the garden gate

le **grille-pain** NOUN (PL les **grille-pain**)
toaster

griller VERB
1 to toast
♦ **du pain grillé** toast
2 to grill ◊ *des saucisses grillées* grilled sausages

la **grimace** NOUN
♦ **faire des grimaces** to make faces

grimper VERB
to climb

grincer VERB
to creak

grincheux ADJECTIVE (FEM SING **grincheuse**)
grumpy

la **grippe** NOUN
flu
♦ **avoir la grippe** to have the flu ◊ *J'ai eu une mauvaise grippe l'hiver dernier.* I had a bad attack of the flu last winter.

grippé ADJECTIVE
♦ **être grippé** to have the flu

gris ADJECTIVE
grey

le **grizzly** NOUN
grizzly bear

grogner VERB
to growl ◊ *Le chien a grogné quand je me suis approché de lui.* The dog growled when I went near it.

gronder VERB
1 to rumble ◊ *J'entends le tonnerre*

G

gronder au loin. I hear thunder rumbling in the distance.
2 to roar (*animal*)
♦ **se faire gronder** to get told off ◊ *Tu vas te faire gronder par ton père!* You're going to get bawled out by your father!

gros ADJECTIVE (FEM SING **grosse**)
1 big ◊ *une grosse pomme* a big apple
2 fat
♦ **le gros plan** close-up ◊ *Voici un gros plan de mon petit ami.* Here's a close-up of my boyfriend.

la **groseille** NOUN
♦ **la groseille rouge** redcurrant
♦ **la groseille à maquereau** gooseberry

la **grossesse** NOUN
pregnancy

grossier ADJECTIVE (FEM SING **grossière**)
rude ◊ *Ne sois pas si grossier!* Don't be so rude!
♦ **une erreur grossière** a serious mistake

grossir VERB
to put on weight ◊ *Il a beaucoup grossi.* He's put on a lot of weight.

grosso modo ADVERB
roughly ◊ *Dis-moi grosso modo ce que tu en penses.* Give me a rough idea what you think of it.

la **grotte** NOUN
cave

le **groupe** NOUN
group ◊ *votre groupe sanguin* your blood group

grouper VERB
to group ◊ *On nous a groupés dans différentes classes selon notre niveau.* We were grouped in different classes according to our level.
♦ **se grouper** to gather ◊ *Nous nous sommes groupés autour du feu.* We gathered round the fire.

❋ le **gruau** NOUN
porridge

la **guêpe** NOUN
wasp

guérir VERB
to recover ◊ *Elle est maintenant complètement guérie.* She's now completely recovered.

la **guérison** NOUN
recovery

♦ **la guérison spirituelle** spiritual healing

la **guerre** NOUN
war ◊ *en guerre* at war ◊ *une guerre civile* a civil war ◊ *la Deuxième Guerre mondiale* the Second World War

guetter VERB
to watch for ◊ *Elle guette l'arrivée du facteur tous les matins.* She watches for the letter carrier every morning.

la **gueule** NOUN
mouth (*rude when used for people*) ◊ *Le chat a ramené une souris dans sa gueule.* The cat brought a mouse in its mouth.

gueuler VERB (*informal*)
to bawl

le **guichet** NOUN
counter (*in bank, airport*)
♦ **le guichet automatique** bank machine

le **guide** NOUN
guide

guider VERB
to guide

le **guidon** NOUN
handlebars

les **guillemets** MASC NOUN
quotation marks ◊ *entre guillemets* in quotes

> In French, be careful to use angled quotation marks and leave a space between the text and each mark, e.g. **« Fin »** for "The End".

la **guimauve** NOUN
marshmallow
♦ **à la guimauve** sappy (*sentimental*) ◊ *C'est vraiment un film à la guimauve.* This is a really sappy movie.

la **guirlande** NOUN
♦ **des guirlandes** tinsel
♦ **des guirlandes en papier** paper chains

la **guitare** NOUN
guitar ◊ *Sais-tu jouer de la guitare?* Can you play the guitar?

le **gymnase** NOUN
gym ◊ *L'école a un nouveau gymnase.* The school has a new gym.

la **gymnastique** NOUN
gymnastics ◊ *faire de la gymnastique* to do gymnastics

H

habile ADJECTIVE
<u>skilful</u> ◊ *Elle est très habile de ses mains.* She's very skilled with her hands.

habillé ADJECTIVE
1 <u>dressed</u> ◊ *Il n'est pas encore habillé.* He's not dressed yet.
2 <u>smart</u> ◊ *Cette robe fait très habillé.* This dress looks very smart.

s' **habiller** VERB
1 <u>to get dressed</u> ◊ *Je me suis rapidement habillé.* I got dressed quickly.
2 <u>to dress up</u> ◊ *Est-ce qu'il faut s'habiller pour la réception?* Do you have to dress up to go to the party?

l' **habitant** MASC NOUN
<u>inhabitant</u> ◊ *Les habitants du quartier sont contre ce projet.* The local people are against this plan.

l' **habitante** FEM NOUN
<u>inhabitant</u>

l' **habitat** MASC NOUN
<u>habitat</u> ◊ *l'habitat naturel du castor* the natural habitat of the beaver ◊ *un habitat menacé* a threatened habitat
♦ **la conservation de l'habitat** habitat conservation

habiter VERB
<u>to live</u> ◊ *Il habite à Kitimat.* He lives in Kitimat.

les **habits** MASC NOUN
<u>clothes</u>

> *Be sure to make the liaison in the phrase les habits.*

l' **habitude** FEM NOUN
<u>habit</u> ◊ *une mauvaise habitude* a bad habit
♦ **avoir l'habitude de quelque chose** to be used to something ◊ *Elle a l'habitude des enfants.* She's used to children. ◊ *Je n'ai pas l'habitude de parler en public.* I'm not used to speaking in public.
♦ **d'habitude** usually
♦ **comme d'habitude** as usual

habituel ADJECTIVE (FEM SING **habituelle**)
<u>usual</u>

s' **habituer** VERB
♦ **s'habituer à quelque chose** to get used to something ◊ *Il faudra que tu t'habitues à te lever tôt.* You'll have to get used to getting up early.

la **hache** NOUN
<u>axe</u>
✻ ♦ **mettre la hache dans les frais** to cut expenses drastically

hacher VERB
<u>to grind</u> (*meat*)
♦ **du bœuf haché** ground beef

la **haie** NOUN
<u>hedge</u>

la **haine** NOUN
<u>hatred</u>

haïr VERB
<u>to hate</u> ◊ *Je hais les piqûres de moustique.* I hate mosquito bites.

l' **haleine** FEM NOUN
<u>breath</u> ◊ *avoir mauvaise haleine* to have bad breath ◊ *être hors d'haleine* to be out of breath

le **hall** NOUN
<u>lobby</u> (*hotel*)
♦ **le hall d'exposition** exhibition hall

la **halte** NOUN
<u>stop</u> ◊ *faire halte* to make a stop
♦ **Halte!** Stop!
♦ **une halte routière** a rest stop

l' **haltérophilie** FEM NOUN
<u>weightlifting</u>

le **hamburger** NOUN
<u>hamburger</u>

l' **hameçon** MASC NOUN
<u>fish hook</u>

le **hamster** NOUN
<u>hamster</u>

la **hanche** NOUN
<u>hip</u>

le **handball** NOUN
<u>handball</u> ◊ *jouer au handball* to play handball

le **handicapé** NOUN
<u>disabled man</u>

la **handicapée** NOUN
<u>disabled woman</u>

le **harcèlement** NOUN
<u>harassment</u> ◊ *le harcèlement sexuel* sexual harassment

le **hareng** NOUN
<u>herring</u>

le **harfang** NOUN
<u>snowy owl</u>

le **haricot** NOUN
<u>bean</u>

☞

harpon → heure

♦ **les haricots au lard** baked beans
♦ **les haricots verts** green beans

le **harpon** NOUN
  harpoon

le **hasard** NOUN
  coincidence ◊ *C'était un pur hasard.*
  It was pure coincidence.
  ♦ **au hasard** at random ◊ *Choisis un numéro au hasard.* Choose a number at random.
  ♦ **par hasard** by chance ◊ *Je l'ai rencontrée tout à fait par hasard au supermarché.* I ran into her completely by chance at the supermarket.
  ♦ **à tout hasard (1)** just in case ◊ *Prends un parapluie à tout hasard.* Take an umbrella just in case.
  ♦ **à tout hasard (2)** on the off chance ◊ *Je ne sais pas s'il est chez lui, mais je vais l'appeler à tout hasard.* I don't know if he's at home, but I'll phone on the off chance.

la **hâte** NOUN
  ♦ **à la hâte** hurriedly ◊ *Elle s'est habillée à la hâte.* She got dressed hurriedly.
  ♦ **J'ai hâte de te voir.** I can't wait to see you.

la **hausse** NOUN
  ① increase ◊ *la hausse des prix* price increase
  ② rise ◊ *On annonce une légère hausse de température.* They're forecasting a slight rise in temperature.

hausser VERB
  ♦ **hausser les épaules** to shrug one's shoulders

haut ADJECTIVE, ADVERB
  | see also **haut** NOUN |
  ① high ◊ *une haute montagne* a high mountain
  ② aloud ◊ *penser tout haut* to think aloud

le **haut** NOUN
  | see also **haut** ADJECTIVE |
  top
  ♦ **un mur de trois mètres de haut** a wall 3 metres high
  ♦ **en haut (1)** upstairs ◊ *La salle de bain est en haut.* The bathroom is upstairs.
  ♦ **en haut (2)** at the top ◊ *Le nid est tout en haut de l'arbre.* The nest is right at the top of the tree.

❉ le **Haut-Canada** NOUN
  Upper Canada

la **hauteur** NOUN
  height

le **haut-parleur** NOUN (PL les **haut-parleurs**)
  speaker (*stereo, computer*)

l' **hebdomadaire** MASC NOUN
  weekly (*magazine*)

l' **hébergement** MASC NOUN
  accommodation

héberger VERB
  to put up (*guest*) ◊ *Mon cousin a dit qu'il nous hébergerait.* My cousin said he would put us up.

hein? EXCLAMATION
  eh?
❉ ♦ **C'était tout un match, hein?** That was quite a game, eh?
❉ ♦ **Tu as pris le dernier morceau de tarte, hein?** You took the last piece of pie, eh?
  ♦ **Hein? Qu'est-ce que tu dis?** Eh? What did you say?

hélas ADVERB
  unfortunately ◊ *Hélas, il ne restait plus de billets.* Unfortunately there were no tickets left.

l' **hélicoptère** MASC NOUN
  helicopter

l' **herbe** FEM NOUN
  grass
  ♦ **les fines herbes** herbs
❉ ♦ **l'herbe à poux** ragweed
❉ ♦ **l'herbe à puce** poison ivy

hériter VERB
  to inherit

hermétique ADJECTIVE
  airtight

l' **héroïne** FEM NOUN
  heroine ◊ *l'héroïne du roman* the heroine of the novel

le **héros** NOUN
  hero

l' **hésitation** FEM NOUN
  hesitation

hésiter VERB
  to hesitate ◊ *Il n'a pas hésité à nous aider.* He didn't hesitate to help us. ◊ *J'ai hésité entre le chandail vert et la chemise jaune.* I couldn't decide between the green pullover and the yellow shirt. ◊ « *Est-ce que tu viens ce soir?* » « *J'hésite...* » "Are you coming tonight?" "I'm not sure..."
  ♦ **sans hésiter** without hesitating

l' **heure** FEM NOUN
  ① hour ◊ *Le trajet dure six heures.* The trip takes six hours.
  ② time ◊ *Vous avez l'heure?* Have you got the time?
  ♦ **Quelle heure est-il?** What time is it?
  ♦ **À quelle heure?** What time? ◊ *À quelle heure arrivons-nous?* What

time do we arrive?
♦ **deux heures du matin** 2 o'clock in the morning
♦ **être à l'heure** to be on time
♦ **l'heure avancée** daylight-saving time
♦ **l'heure normale** standard time

heureusement ADVERB
luckily ◊ *Heureusement qu'elle n'a pas été blessée.* Luckily she wasn't hurt.

heureux ADJECTIVE (FEM SING **heureuse**)
happy

heurter VERB
to hit ◊ *Je me suis heurté la tête contre la porte.* I hit my head on the door.

hiberner VERB
to hibernate

le **hibou** NOUN (PL les **hiboux**)
owl

hier ADVERB
yesterday
♦ **avant-hier** the day before yesterday

hindou AJECTIVE

see also **hindou** NOUN

Hindu

l' **hindou** MASC NOUN

see also **hindou** ADJECTIVE

Hindu

l' **hindoue** FEM NOUN
Hindu

l' **hippopotame** MASC NOUN
hippopotamus

l' **histoire** FEM NOUN
1 history ◊ *un cours d'histoire* a history lesson
2 story ◊ *Ce roman raconte l'histoire de deux enfants.* This novel tells the story of two children.
♦ **Ne fais pas d'histoires!** Don't make a fuss!
♦ **une histoire à succès** a success story

historique ADJECTIVE
1 historic ◊ *un monument historique* a historic monument
2 historical ◊ *un musée historique* a historical museum

l' **hiver** MASC NOUN
winter
♦ **en hiver** in winter

le **hockey** NOUN
hockey ◊ *une joueuse de hockey* a hockey player ◊ *un bâton de hockey* a hockey stick
♦ **le hockey sur glace** ice hockey

le **homard** NOUN
lobster

l' **hommage** MASC NOUN
tribute

l' **homme** MASC NOUN
man
♦ **un homme d'affaires** a businessman

homosexuel ADJECTIVE (FEM SING **homosexuelle**)
homosexual

honnête ADJECTIVE
honest
♦ **bien honnête** decent (*person*)

l' **honnêteté** FEM NOUN
honesty

l' **honneur** MASC NOUN
honour ◊ *en l'honneur de nos grands-parents* in honour of our grandparents

la **honte** NOUN
shame ◊ *avoir honte de quelque chose* to be ashamed of something

l' **hôpital** MASC NOUN (PL les **hôpitaux**)
hospital

le **hoquet** NOUN
♦ **avoir le hoquet** to have hiccups

l' **horaire** MASC NOUN
1 timetable
2 schedule
♦ **l' horaire d'autobus** the bus schedule

l' **horizon** MASC NOUN
horizon

horizontal ADJECTIVE (MASC PL **horizontaux**)
horizontal

l' **horloge** FEM NOUN
clock

l' **horreur** FEM NOUN
horror ◊ *un film d'horreur* a horror movie
♦ **avoir horreur de** to hate ◊ *J'ai horreur du chou.* I hate cabbage.

horrible ADJECTIVE
horrible

hors PREPOSITION
♦ **hors de** out of ◊ *Elle est hors de danger maintenant.* She's out of danger now.
♦ **hors taxes** duty-free

le **hors-d'œuvre** NOUN (PL les **hors-d'œuvre**)
appetizer

hospitalier ADJECTIVE (FEM SING **hospitalière**)
hospitable ◊ *Ils sont très hospitaliers.* They're very hospitable.
♦ **les services hospitaliers** hospital services

l' **hospitalité** FEM NOUN

H

☞

hospitality

hostile ADJECTIVE
hostile

le **hot-dog** NOUN
hot dog ◊ *des hot-dogs relish-moutarde* hot dogs with relish and mustard

l' **hôte** MASC/FEM NOUN
1 host ◊ *N'oubliez pas de remercier vos hôtes.* Don't forget to thank your hosts.
2 guest ◊ *des hôtes payants* paying guests

l' **hôtel** MASC NOUN
hotel
♦ **l'hôtel de ville** the town hall

l' **hôtesse** FEM NOUN
hostess

la **housse** NOUN
cover ◊ *une housse de couette* a quilt cover ◊ *une housse de siège* a seat cover

le **houx** NOUN
holly

le **huard** NOUN
1 loon
2 loonie

l' **huile** FEM NOUN
oil
♦ **l'huile solaire** suntan oil

huit NUMBER
eight ◊ *Il est huit heures du matin.* It's eight in the morning. ◊ *Il a huit ans.* He's eight.
♦ **le huit février** the eighth of February
♦ **dans huit jours** in a week's time

la **huitaine** NOUN
♦ **une huitaine de jours** about a week ◊ *Nous serons de retour dans une huitaine de jours.* We'll be back in about a week.

huitième ADJECTIVE
eighth ◊ *au huitième étage* on the eighth floor

l' **huître** FEM NOUN
oyster

humain ADJECTIVE

see also **humain** NOUN

human

l' **humain** MASC NOUN

see also **humain** ADJECTIVE

human being

l' **humeur** FEM NOUN
mood ◊ *Il est de bonne humeur.* He's in a good mood. ◊ *Elle était de mauvaise humeur.* She was in a bad mood.

humide ADJECTIVE
1 damp ◊ *L'herbe est humide.* The grass is damp. ◊ *un climat humide* a damp climate
2 moist
3 humid

l' **humidex** NOUN
humidex

humilier VERB
to humiliate

humoristique ADJECTIVE
humorous
♦ **des dessins humoristiques** cartoons

l' **humour** MASC NOUN
humour ◊ *Il n'a pas beaucoup d'humour.* He doesn't have much sense of humour.

hurler VERB
to howl

la **hutte** NOUN
hut

hydratant ADJECTIVE
♦ **une crème hydratante** a moisturizing cream

l' **hygiène** FEM NOUN
hygiene

hygiénique ADJECTIVE
hygienic
♦ **une serviette hygiénique** a sanitary napkin
♦ **le papier hygiénique** toilet paper

l' **hymne** MASC NOUN
♦ **l'hymne national** the national anthem ◊ *Notre hymne national est Ô Canada.* Our national anthem is O Canada.

l' **hyperlien** MASC NOUN
hyperlink

hypermétrope ADJECTIVE
long-sighted

l' **hypothèse** FEM NOUN
hypothesis

I

l' **iceberg** MASC NOUN
iceberg
♦ **la pointe de l'iceberg** the tip of the iceberg

ici ADVERB
here ◊ *Les assiettes sont ici.* The plates are here.
♦ **La mer monte parfois jusqu'ici.** The tide sometimes comes in as far as this.
♦ **jusqu'ici** so far

l' **icône** FEM NOUN
icon

idéal ADJECTIVE (MASC PL **idéaux**)
ideal ◊ *C'est l'endroit idéal pour faire un pique-nique.* It's an ideal place to have a picnic.

l' **idée** FEM NOUN
idea ◊ *C'est une bonne idée.* It's a good idea.

identifier VERB
to identify ◊ *La police a identifié le voleur.* The police have identified the thief.

identique ADJECTIVE
identical ◊ *Ils ont obtenu des résultats identiques.* They obtained identical results.

l' **identité** FEM NOUN
identity
♦ **une pièce d'identité** a piece of identification ◊ *Avez-vous une pièce d'identité?* Do you have any identification?

idiot ADJECTIVE
1 stupid ◊ *une plaisanterie idiote* a stupid joke
2 silly ◊ *Ne sois pas idiot!* Don't be silly!

l' **iglou** MASC NOUN
igloo

ignoble ADJECTIVE
horrible ◊ *Il a été ignoble avec elle.* He was horrible to her.

ignorant ADJECTIVE
ignorant

ignorer VERB
1 not to know ◊ *J'ignore son nom.* I don't know his name.
2 to ignore ◊ *Il m'a complètement ignoré.* He completely ignored me.

il PRONOUN
1 he ◊ *Il est parti ce matin de bonne heure.* He left early this morning.

2 it ◊ *Méfie-toi de ce chien : il mord.* Be careful of that dog: it bites. ◊ *Il pleut.* It's raining.

l' **île** FEM NOUN
island
♦ **l'île du Cap-Breton** Cape Breton Island
♦ **l'île de Vancouver** Vancouver Island

illégal ADJECTIVE (MASC PL **illégaux**)
illegal

illimité ADJECTIVE
unlimited

illisible ADJECTIVE
illegible ◊ *une écriture illisible* illegible handwriting

illuminer VERB
to floodlight ◊ *Les chutes sont illuminées tous les soirs pendant l'été.* The falls are floodlit every night in the summer.

l' **illusion** FEM NOUN
illusion
♦ **Tu te fais des illusions!** Don't kid yourself!

l' **illustration** FEM NOUN
illustration

illustré ADJECTIVE

| *see also* **illustré** NOUN |

illustrated

l' **illustré** MASC NOUN

| *see also* **illustré** ADJECTIVE |

comic

illustrer VERB
to illustrate ◊ *Vous pouvez illustrer votre rédaction avec des exemples.* You may illustrate your essay with examples.

ils PRONOUN
they ◊ *Ils nous ont appelés hier soir.* They phoned us last night.

l' **image** FEM NOUN
picture ◊ *Les films donnent une fausse image de l'Amérique.* Movies give a false picture of America.

l' **imagination** FEM NOUN
imagination ◊ *Elle a beaucoup d'imagination.* She has a vivid imagination.

imaginer VERB
to imagine

l' **imam** MASC NOUN
imam

l' **imbécile** MASC/FEM NOUN
idiot

l' **imitation** FEM NOUN
imitation

imiter VERB
to imitate

l' **immatriculation** FEM NOUN
♦ **une plaque d'immatriculation** a licence plate (of car)

l' **immédiat** MASC NOUN
♦ **dans l'immédiat** for the moment ◊ Je n'ai pas besoin de ce livre dans l'immédiat. I don't need this book for the moment.

immédiatement ADVERB
immediately

immense ADJECTIVE
1 huge ◊ une immense fortune a huge fortune
2 tremendous ◊ un immense soulagement a tremendous relief

l' **immeuble** MASC NOUN
building ◊ un immeuble résidentiel an apartment building ◊ un immeuble de bureaux an office building

l' **immigration** FEM NOUN
immigration

l' **immigré** MASC NOUN
immigrant

l' **immigrée** FEM NOUN
immigrant

immobile ADJECTIVE
motionless

immobilier ADJECTIVE (FEM SING **immobilière**)

see also **immobilier** NOUN

♦ **une agence immobilière** a real estate agency

l' **immobilier** MASC NOUN

see also **immobilier** ADJECTIVE

real estate

immobiliser VERB
to immobilize

immunisé ADJECTIVE
immunized

l' **impact** MASC NOUN
impact

impair ADJECTIVE
odd ◊ un nombre impair an odd number

impardonnable ADJECTIVE
unforgivable

l' **impasse** FEM NOUN
dead end

l' **impatience** FEM NOUN

impatience

impatient ADJECTIVE
impatient

impeccable ADJECTIVE
1 immaculate ◊ Sa cuisine est toujours impeccable. Her kitchen is always immaculate.
2 perfect ◊ Il a fait un travail impeccable. He's done a perfect job. ◊ C'est impeccable! That's perfect!

l' **impératif** MASC NOUN
imperative

l' **imperméable** MASC NOUN
raincoat

impertinent ADJECTIVE
mouthy ◊ Ne sois pas impertinent! Don't be mouthy!

impitoyable ADJECTIVE
merciless

impliquer VERB
to mean ◊ Si tu vas à l'université, ça implique que tu vas devoir nous quitter. If you go to university, that means you'll have to leave us.
♦ **être impliqué dans** to be involved in ◊ Il est impliqué dans un scandale financier. He's involved in a financial scandal.

impoli ADJECTIVE
rude

l' **importance** FEM NOUN
importance ◊ C'est sans importance. It doesn't matter.

important ADJECTIVE
1 important ◊ un rôle important an important role
2 considerable ◊ une somme importante a considerable sum

l' **importation** FEM NOUN
import ◊ Les importations de pétrole ont baissé. Oil imports have fallen.

importer VERB

see also **n'importe**

1 to import (goods)
2 to matter ◊ Peu importe. It doesn't matter.

imposant ADJECTIVE
imposing

imposer VERB
to impose
♦ **imposer quelque chose à quelqu'un** to make somebody do something

impossible ADJECTIVE

see also **impossible** NOUN

impossible

l' **impossible** MASC NOUN

see also **impossible** ADJECTIVE

♦ **Nous ferons l'impossible pour finir à temps.** We'll do our utmost to finish on time.

l' **imposteur** MASC NOUN
fake ◊ *Cette femme est un imposteur.* This woman is a fake.

l' **impôt** MASC NOUN
tax

♦ **une déclaration d'impôts** an income tax return

imprécis ADJECTIVE
imprecise

l' **impression** FEM NOUN
impression ◊ *Il a fait bonne impression à ma mère.* He made a good impression on my mother.

impressionnant ADJECTIVE
impressive

impressionner VERB
to impress

imprévisible ADJECTIVE
unpredictable

imprévu ADJECTIVE
unexpected

l' **imprimante** FEM NOUN
printer (*for computer*)

imprimé ADJECTIVE
printed ◊ *un tissu imprimé* a printed fabric ◊ *C'est imprimé en grandes lettres.* It's printed in large letters.

imprimer VERB
to print

l' **improvisation** FEM NOUN
improv (*theatre*) ◊ *Nous avons fondé une ligue d'improvisation à l'école.* We started an improv club at our school.

improviser VERB
to improvise

improviste ADVERB

♦ **arriver à l'improviste** to arrive unexpectedly

l' **imprudence** FEM NOUN
carelessness

♦ **Ne fais pas d'imprudences!** Don't do anything stupid!

imprudent ADJECTIVE
1 unwise ◊ *Il serait imprudent de prendre la voiture aujourd'hui.* It would be unwise to take the car today.
2 careless ◊ *un conducteur imprudent* a careless driver

impuissant ADJECTIVE
helpless ◊ *Elle se sentait complètement impuissante.* She felt completely helpless.

impulsif ADJECTIVE (FEM SING **impulsive**)
impulsive

inabordable ADJECTIVE
unaffordable ◊ *des prix inabordables* unaffordable prices

inaccessible ADJECTIVE
inaccessible ◊ *Cette plage est inaccessible par la route.* This beach is inaccessible by road.

inachevé ADJECTIVE
unfinished

inadmissible ADJECTIVE
unacceptable ◊ *Ce type de comportement est inadmissible!* This sort of behaviour is unacceptable!

inanimé ADJECTIVE
unconscious ◊ *On l'a retrouvé inanimé sur la route.* He was found unconscious on the road.

inaperçu ADJECTIVE

♦ **passer inaperçu** to go unnoticed

inattendu ADJECTIVE
unexpected

l' **inattention** FEM NOUN

♦ **une faute d'inattention** a careless mistake

inaugurer VERB
to open (*an exhibition*)

incapable ADJECTIVE
incapable ◊ *être incapable de faire quelque chose* to be incapable of doing something

incassable ADJECTIVE
unbreakable

l' **incendie** MASC NOUN
fire ◊ *un incendie de forêt* a forest fire

incertain ADJECTIVE
1 uncertain ◊ *Son avenir est encore incertain.* Her future is still uncertain.
2 unsettled ◊ *Le temps est incertain.* The weather is unsettled.

inciter VERB

♦ **inciter quelqu'un à faire quelque chose** to encourage somebody to do something ◊ *J'ai incité mes parents à partir en voyage.* I encouraged my parents to go on a trip.

inclure VERB
to enclose ◊ *Veuillez inclure une enveloppe timbrée libellée à votre adresse.* Please enclose a stamped self-addressed envelope.

♦ **Les piles sont incluses.** Batteries are included.

incohérent ADJECTIVE
incoherent

incolore ADJECTIVE
colourless

incompétent ADJECTIVE
incompetent

incompris ADJECTIVE
misunderstood

l' **inconnu** MASC NOUN
stranger ◊ *Ne parle pas à des inconnus.* Don't speak to strangers.
♦ **l'inconnu** the unknown ◊ *la peur de l'inconnu* the fear of the unknown

l' **inconnue** FEM NOUN
stranger

inconsciemment ADVERB
unconsciously

inconscient ADJECTIVE
unconscious ◊ *Il est resté inconscient quelques minutes.* He was unconscious for several minutes.

incontestable ADJECTIVE
indisputable

incontournable ADJECTIVE
essential ◊ *Ce livre est incontournable.* This book is essential reading.

l' **inconvénient** MASC NOUN
disadvantage
♦ **si vous n'y voyez pas d'inconvénient** if you have no objection

incorrect ADJECTIVE
1 incorrect ◊ *une réponse incorrecte* an incorrect answer
2 rude ◊ *Il a été incorrect avec la voisine.* He was rude to the woman next door.

incroyable ADJECTIVE
incredible

inculper VERB
♦ **inculper de** to charge with ◊ *Elle a été inculpée de fraude.* She was charged with fraud.

indécis ADJECTIVE
1 indecisive ◊ *Il est constamment indécis.* He's always indecisive.
2 undecided ◊ *Je suis encore indécis.* I'm still undecided.

indéfiniment ADVERB
indefinitely

indélicat ADJECTIVE
tactless

indemne ADJECTIVE
unharmed ◊ *Elle s'en est sortie indemne.* She escaped unharmed.

indemniser VERB
to compensate ◊ *Les victimes demandent maintenant à être indemnisées.* The victims are now demanding compensation.

indépendamment ADVERB
independently
♦ **indépendamment de** irrespective of ◊ *Les allocations familiales devraient être versées indépendamment des revenus.* The child tax credit should be given irrespective of income.

l' **indépendance** FEM NOUN
independence

indépendant ADJECTIVE
independent

l' **index** MASC NOUN
1 index finger
2 index (*in book*)

indicatif ADJECTIVE (FEM SING **indicative**)
see also **indicatif** NOUN
♦ **à titre indicatif** for your information

l' **indicatif** MASC NOUN
see also **indicatif** ADJECTIVE
1 indicative (*of verb*)
2 theme song (*of TV show*)
♦ **l'indicatif régional** area code

les **indications** FEM NOUN
instructions ◊ *Il suffit de suivre les indications.* You just have to follow the instructions.

l' **indice** MASC NOUN
clue ◊ *La police cherche des indices.* The police are looking for clues.

l' **indifférence** FEM NOUN
indifference

indifférent ADJECTIVE
indifferent

indigène ADJECTIVE
native ◊ *les peuples indigènes du Canada* the native peoples of Canada ◊ *Cette espèce n'est pas indigène au Canada.* This species is not native to Canada.

indigeste ADJECTIVE
indigestible

l' **indigestion** FEM NOUN
indigestion

indigne ADJECTIVE
unworthy

indigner VERB
to outrage ◊ *Ses propos ont indigné toute l'équipe.* Her remarks outraged the whole team.
♦ **s'indigner de quelque chose** to be outraged by something

indiqué ADJECTIVE
advisable ◊ *Ce n'est pas très indiqué.* It's not really advisable.

indiquer VERB
to point out ◊ *Il m'a indiqué la mairie.* He pointed out the town hall

to me.

indirect ADJECTIVE
indirect

indiscipliné ADJECTIVE
unruly

indiscret ADJECTIVE (FEM SING **indiscrète**)
indiscreet

indispensable ADJECTIVE
indispensable

l' **individu** MASC NOUN
individual

individuel ADJECTIVE (FEM SING
individuelle)
individual ◊ *servi en portions
individuelles* served in individual
portions
♦ **Vous aurez une chambre individuelle.**
You'll have a room to yourself.

indolore ADJECTIVE
painless

indulgent ADJECTIVE
indulgent
♦ **Elle est trop indulgente avec son fils.**
She's not firm enough with her son.

l' **industrie** FEM NOUN
industry

industriel ADJECTIVE (FEM SING **industrielle**)
industrial

inédit ADJECTIVE
unpublished

inefficace ADJECTIVE
1 ineffective (*treatment*)
2 inefficient ◊ *un service de
transports publics inefficace* an
inefficient public transit system

inégal ADJECTIVE (MASC PL **inégaux**)
1 unequal ◊ *un combat inégal* an
unequal struggle
2 uneven ◊ *La qualité est inégale.*
The quality is uneven.

inévitable ADJECTIVE
unavoidable
♦ **C'était inévitable!** That was bound to
happen!

inexact ADJECTIVE
inaccurate

infaillible ADJECTIVE
foolproof

l' **infarctus** MASC NOUN
coronary

infatigable ADJECTIVE
tireless ◊ *Il est infatigable.* He's a
tireless worker.

infect ADJECTIVE
revolting (*meal*)

s' **infecter** VERB

to get infected ◊ *La plaie s'est
infectée.* The wound has become
infected.

l' **infection** FEM NOUN
infection

inférieur ADJECTIVE
lower ◊ *les membres inférieurs* the
lower limbs ◊ *C'est moins cher, mais
de qualité inférieure.* It's cheaper but
of lower quality.

infernal ADJECTIVE (MASC PL **infernaux**)
terrible ◊ *Ils faisaient un bruit
infernal.* They were making a terrible
noise.

l' **infini** MASC NOUN
infinite
♦ **à l'infini** indefinitely ◊ *On pourrait en
parler à l'infini.* We could discuss this
indefinitely.

l' **infinitif** MASC NOUN
infinitive

l' **infirmerie** FEM NOUN
sick room ◊ *Elle est à l'infirmerie.*
She's in the sick room.

l' **infirmier** MASC NOUN
nurse

l' **infirmière** FEM NOUN
nurse

inflammable ADJECTIVE
flammable

l' **influence** FEM NOUN
influence

influencer VERB
to influence

l' **infopublicité** FEM NOUN
infomercial (*TV, radio*)

l' **informaticien** MASC NOUN
computer scientist

l' **informaticienne** FEM NOUN
computer scientist

l' **information** FEM NOUN
information ◊ *Je voudrais de
l'information sur la Saskatchewan, s'il
vous plaît.* I'd like some information
about Saskatchewan, please.
♦ **une information** a piece of
information
♦ **les informations** the news (*TV, radio*)

l' **informatique** FEM NOUN
computer technology

informer VERB
to inform
♦ **s'informer** to find out ◊ *Je ne connais
pas les heures de fermeture, mais je
vais m'informer.* I don't know when
they close, but I'm going to find out.

infuser VERB

I

☞

to steep (*tea*)

l' **infusion** FEM NOUN
herbal tea

l' **ingénieur** MASC NOUN
engineer

l' **ingénieure** FEM NOUN
engineer

ingénieux ADJECTIVE (FEM SING **ingénieuse**)
clever ◊ *Quelle solution ingénieuse!*
What a clever solution!

ingrat ADJECTIVE
ungrateful

l' **ingrédient** MASC NOUN
ingredient

inhabituel ADJECTIVE (FEM SING
inhabituelle)
unusual

inhumain ADJECTIVE
inhuman

ininflammable ADJECTIVE
nonflammable

initial ADJECTIVE (MASC PL **initiaux**)
initial

l' **initiale** FEM NOUN
initial

l' **initiation** FEM NOUN
introduction ◊ *un stage d'initiation
à la planche à voile* an introductory
course in windsurfing

l' **initiative** FEM NOUN
initiative ◊ *avoir de l'initiative* to
have initiative

injecter VERB
to inject

l' **injection** FEM NOUN
injection

l' **injure** FEM NOUN
1 insult ◊ *Il a pris ça comme une
injure.* He took it as an insult.
2 abuse ◊ *lancer des injures à
quelqu'un* to hurl abuse at somebody

injurier VERB
to insult

injurieux ADJECTIVE (FEM SING **injurieuse**)
abusive (*language*)

injuste ADJECTIVE
unfair

innocent ADJECTIVE
innocent

innombrable ADJECTIVE
countless

innover VERB
to break new ground

inoccupé ADJECTIVE
empty ◊ *un appartement inoccupé* an

empty apartment

inoffensif ADJECTIVE (FEM SING **inoffensive**)
harmless

l' **inondation** FEM NOUN
flood

inoubliable ADJECTIVE
unforgettable

inoxydable ADJECTIVE
♦ *l'acier inoxydable* stainless steel

inquiet ADJECTIVE (FEM SING **inquiète**)
worried

inquiétant ADJECTIVE
worrying

inquiéter VERB
to worry ◊ *La santé de ma grand-
mère inquiète mes parents.* My
grandmother's health worries my
parents.
♦ *s'inquiéter* to worry (*be worried*) ◊ *Ne
t'inquiète pas!* Don't worry!

l' **inquiétude** FEM NOUN
anxiety

insatisfait ADJECTIVE
dissatisfied

l' **inscription** FEM NOUN
registration (*for school, course*)

s' **inscrire** VERB
♦ *s'inscrire à (1)* to join ◊ *Je me suis
inscrit au club de tennis.* I've joined
the tennis club.
♦ *s'inscrire à (2)* to register ◊ *N'attends
pas trop pour t'inscrire à des cours
de natation.* Don't leave it too long to
register for swimming lessons.

l' **insecte** MASC NOUN
insect

insensible ADJECTIVE
insensitive ◊ *Il la trouve insensible.*
He thinks she's insensitive.

insérer VERB
insert ◊ *Insère le CD dans le lecteur.*
Insert the CD in the drive. ◊ *Tu
devrais insérer un paragraphe ici
pour expliquer.* You should insert
a paragraph here, explaining your
point.

l' **insigne** MASC NOUN
badge

insignifiant ADJECTIVE
insignificant

insister VERB
to insist
♦ *N'insiste pas!* Don't keep harping
on it!

l' **insolation** FEM NOUN
sunstroke

insolent ADJECTIVE

cheeky

insouciant ADJECTIVE
carefree

insoutenable ADJECTIVE
unbearable ◊ *une douleur
insoutenable* an unbearable pain

inspecter VERB
to inspect

l' **inspecteur** MASC NOUN
inspector

l' **inspection** FEM NOUN
inspection

l' **inspectrice** FEM NOUN
inspector

inspirer VERB
1 to inspire
♦ **s'inspirer de** to take one's inspiration
from ◊ *Le peintre s'est inspiré
d'un poème.* The painter took his
inspiration from a poem.
2 to breathe in ◊ *Inspirez! Expirez!*
Breathe in! Breathe out!

instable ADJECTIVE
1 wobbly (*piece of furniture*)
2 unstable (*person*)

les **installations** FEM NOUN
facilities ◊ *Cet appartement est
pourvu de toutes les installations
modernes.* This apartment has all
modern facilities.

installer VERB
to install ◊ *installer un logiciel* to
install a computer program ◊ *installer
des étagères* to put up some shelves
♦ **s'installer** to settle in ◊ *Nous nous
sommes installés dans notre nouvel
appartement.* We've settled into our
new apartment.
♦ **Installez-vous, je vous en prie.** Have a
seat, please.

l' **instant** MASC NOUN
moment ◊ *dans un instant* in a
moment ◊ *Le dîner sera prêt dans
un instant.* Dinner will be ready in
a moment. ◊ *pour l'instant* for the
moment

instantané ADJECTIVE
instant ◊ *du café instantané* instant
coffee

l' **instinct** MASC NOUN
instinct

l' **institut** MASC NOUN
institute

l' **institution** FEM NOUN
institution

l' **instruction** FEM NOUN
1 instruction ◊ *J'ai suivi ses
instructions.* I followed her

instructions.
2 education ◊ *Il n'a pas beaucoup
d'instruction.* He's not very well-
educated.

s' **instruire** VERB
to educate oneself

instruit ADJECTIVE
educated

l' **instrument** MASC NOUN
instrument ◊ *un instrument de
musique* a musical instrument

insuffisant ADJECTIVE
insufficient
♦ **« travail insuffisant »** (*on report card*)
"must make more effort"

l' **insuline** FEM NOUN
insulin

insultant ADJECTIVE
insulting ◊ *Il s'est montré insultant
avec elle.* He was insulting towards
her.

l' **insulte** FEM NOUN
insult

insulter VERB
to insult

insupportable ADJECTIVE
unbearable

intact ADJECTIVE
intact

intégral ADJECTIVE (MASC PL **intégraux**)
♦ **le texte intégral** unabridged version
♦ **un remboursement intégral** a full
refund

l' **intelligence** FEM NOUN
intelligence

intelligent ADJECTIVE
intelligent

intense ADJECTIVE
intense

intensif ADJECTIVE (FEM SING **intensive**)
intensive
♦ **un cours intensif** a crash course

l' **intention** FEM NOUN
intention
♦ **avoir l'intention de faire quelque
chose** to intend to do something
◊ *J'ai l'intention de lui en parler.* I
intend to speak to her about it.

l' **interdiction** FEM NOUN
♦ **« interdiction de stationner »** "no
parking"
♦ **« interdiction de fumer »** "no
smoking"

interdire VERB
to forbid ◊ *Ses parents lui ont
interdit de sortir.* His parents have
forbidden him to go out.

interdit ADJECTIVE
⊡ forbidden ◊ *Il est interdit de fumer dans les couloirs.* Smoking in the halls is forbidden.
② off-limits ◊ *Cette salle est interdite aux élèves.* This room is off-limits for students.

intéressant ADJECTIVE
interesting ◊ *un livre intéressant* an interesting book
♦ **On lui a fait une offre intéressante.** They made her an attractive offer.
♦ **On trouve des CD à des prix très intéressants dans ce magasin.** You can get CDs really cheap in this store.

intéresser VERB
to interest ◊ *Est-ce que cela t'intéresse?* Does that interest you?
♦ **s'intéresser à** to be interested in ◊ *Est-ce que vous vous intéressez à la politique?* Are you interested in politics?

l' **intérêt** MASC NOUN
interest
♦ **avoir intérêt à faire quelque chose** had better do something ◊ *Tu as intérêt à te dépêcher si tu veux prendre le prochain autobus.* You'd better hurry up if you want to catch the next bus.

l' **intérieur** MASC NOUN
inside ◊ *Il fait plus frais à l'intérieur de la maison.* It's cooler inside the house.

l' **interligne** MASC NOUN
♦ **à double interligne** double-spaced

l' **interlocuteur** MASC NOUN
♦ **son interlocuteur** the man he's speaking to

l' **interlocutrice** FEM NOUN
♦ **son interlocutrice** the woman he's speaking to

l' **intermédiaire** MASC NOUN
intermediary
♦ **par l'intermédiaire de** through ◊ *Je l'ai rencontrée par l'intermédiaire de sa sœur.* I met her through her sister.

international ADJECTIVE (MASC PL **internationaux**)
international

l' **internaute** MASC/FEM NOUN
Internet user

l' **Internet** MASC NOUN
Internet ◊ *sur Internet* on the Internet

l' **interphone** MASC NOUN
intercom

l' **interprète** MASC/FEM NOUN
interpreter

interpréter VERB

to interpret

interrogatif ADJECTIVE (FEM SING **interrogative**)
interrogative

l' **interrogation** FEM NOUN
⊡ question
② test ◊ *une interrogation écrite* a written test

l' **interrogatoire** MASC NOUN
questioning
♦ **C'est un interrogatoire ou quoi?** What are you doing, cross-examining me?

interroger VERB
to question

interrompre VERB
to interrupt

l' **interrupteur** MASC NOUN
switch

l' **interruption** FEM NOUN
interruption
♦ **sans interruption** without stopping ◊ *Il a parlé pendant deux heures sans interruption.* He spoke for two hours without stopping.

l' **interurbain** MASC NOUN
long-distance call ◊ *faire un interurbain* to make a long-distance call

l' **intervalle** MASC NOUN
interval
♦ **dans l'intervalle** in the meantime

intervenir VERB
⊡ to intervene
② to take action ◊ *La police est intervenue.* The police took action.

l' **intervention** FEM NOUN
intervention ◊ *une intervention militaire* a military intervention
♦ **une intervention chirurgicale** a surgical operation
♦ **une intervention d'urgence** emergency response

l' **interview** FEM NOUN
interview (*on radio, TV*)

l' **intestin** MASC NOUN
intestine

intime ADJECTIVE
intimate
♦ **un journal intime** a diary

intimider VERB
to intimidate

l' **intimité** FEM NOUN
♦ **dans l'intimité** in private ◊ *Dans l'intimité, il est moins guindé.* He's less formal in private.
♦ **Le mariage a eu lieu dans l'intimité.** The wedding ceremony was private.

intitulé ADJECTIVE

entitled ◊ *un article intitulé « Les jeunes du Canada »* an article entitled "Canada's Youth"

intolérable ADJECTIVE
intolerable

l' **intolérance** FEM NOUN
intolerance ◊ *une intolérance aux antibiotiques* an antibiotics intolerance ◊ *une attitude d'intolérance envers les autres* an attitude of intolerance towards others

l' **intoxication** FEM NOUN
♦ **une intoxication alimentaire** food poisoning

l' **Intranet** MASC NOUN
intranet

intransigeant ADJECTIVE
uncompromising

l' **intrigue** FEM NOUN
plot (*of book, film*)

l' **introduction** FEM NOUN
introduction

introduire VERB
to introduce

l' **intuition** FEM NOUN
intuition

inuit ADJECTIVE, NOUN
Inuit
♦ **un Inuit** an Inuk (*man*)
♦ **une Inuite** an Inuk (*woman*)
♦ **les Inuits** the Inuit

inusable ADJECTIVE
durable

inutile ADJECTIVE
useless

l' **invalide** MASC/FEM NOUN
disabled person

l' **invasion** FEM NOUN
invasion

inventer VERB
1 to invent
2 to make up ◊ *inventer une excuse* to make up an excuse

l' **inventeur** MASC NOUN
inventor

l' **invention** FEM NOUN
invention

l' **inventrice** FEM NOUN
inventor

inverse ADJECTIVE

see also **inverse** NOUN

♦ **dans l'ordre inverse** in reverse order
♦ **en sens inverse** in the opposite direction

l' **inverse** MASC NOUN

see also **inverse** ADJECTIVE

reverse
♦ **Tu t'es trompé, c'est l'inverse.** You've got it wrong, it's the other way round.

l' **investissement** MASC NOUN
investment

invisible ADJECTIVE
invisible

l' **invitation** FEM NOUN
invitation

l' **invité** MASC NOUN
guest

l' **invitée** FEM NOUN
guest

inviter VERB
to invite

involontaire ADJECTIVE
unintentional ◊ *C'était tout à fait involontaire.* It was quite unintentional.

invraisemblable ADJECTIVE
unlikely ◊ *une histoire invraisemblable* an unlikely story

ira, irai, iraient, irais VERB *see* **aller**
♦ **J'irai demain au supermarché.** I'll go to the supermarket tomorrow.

iras, irez VERB *see* **aller**

l' **ironie** FEM NOUN
irony

ironique ADJECTIVE
ironic

irons, iront VERB *see* **aller**
♦ **Nous irons à la plage cet après-midi.** We'll go to the beach this afternoon.

irrationnel ADJECTIVE (FEM SING **irrationnelle**)
irrational

irréel ADJECTIVE (FEM SING **irréelle**)
unreal

irrégulier ADJECTIVE (FEM SING **irrégulière**)
irregular

irrésistible ADJECTIVE
irresistible

irritable ADJECTIVE
irritable

irriter VERB
to irritate

islamique ADJECTIVE
Islamic

isolé ADJECTIVE
isolated ◊ *une ferme isolée* an isolated farm

l' **issue** FEM NOUN
♦ **une voie sans issue** a dead end
♦ **l'issue de secours** emergency exit

l' **italique** FEM NOUN
italics ◊ *mettre un mot en italique* to
put a word in italics

l' **itinéraire** MASC NOUN
route

l' **itinérance** FEM NOUN
homelessness ◊ *Le problème de
l'itinérance doit être résolu.* The
issue of homelessness needs to be
resolved.

l' **itinérant** MASC NOUN

homeless man

l' **itinérante** FEM NOUN
homeless woman

ivre ADJECTIVE
drunk

l' **ivresse** FEM NOUN
drunkenness
♦ **l'ivresse au volant** drunk driving

l' **ivrogne** MASC/FEM NOUN
drunk

J

j' PRONOUN *see* **je**

la **jalousie** NOUN
jealousy

jaloux ADJECTIVE (FEM SING **jalouse**)
jealous

jamais ADVERB
1 never ◊ *« Tu vas souvent au cinéma? » « Non, jamais. »* "Do you go to the movies often?" "No, never." ◊ *Il n'écoute jamais la radio.* He never listens to the radio.
2 ever

> *When you use a superlative with **jamais** meaning **ever**, remember to put the verb in the subjunctive.*

◊ *C'est la plus belle chose que j'aie jamais vue.* It's the most beautiful thing I've ever seen.

la **jambe** NOUN
leg

※ la **jambette** NOUN
♦ **donner une jambette à quelqu'un** to trip somebody up

le **jambon** NOUN
ham

janvier MASC NOUN
January
♦ **en janvier** in January

japper VERB
to bark ◊ *Le chien des voisins jappe constamment.* The neighbours' dog is constantly barking.

le **jardin** NOUN
garden ◊ *un jardin potager* a vegetable garden

le **jardinage** NOUN
gardening

le **jardinier** NOUN
gardener

la **jardinière** NOUN
1 gardener
2 flowerpot

jaser VERB
※ to chat ◊ *Ton père jase avec le voisin.* Your father is chatting with the neighbour.
♦ **faire jaser** to make people talk (*gossip*) ◊ *Cela va faire jaser tout le quartier.* That'll set the whole neighbourhood gossiping.

jaune ADJECTIVE

> *see also* **jaune** NOUN

yellow

le **jaune** NOUN

> *see also* **jaune** ADJECTIVE

yellow
♦ **un jaune d'œuf** an egg yolk

jaunir VERB
to turn yellow

Javel NOUN
♦ **l'eau de Javel** bleach

le **jazz** NOUN
jazz

J.-C. ABBREVIATION (= *Jésus-Christ*)
♦ **44 avant J.-C.** 44 BCE
♦ **115 après J.-C.** 115 CE

je PRONOUN

> *je changes to **j'** before a vowel and most words beginning with "h".*

I ◊ *Je t'appellerai ce soir.* I'll phone you this evening. ◊ *J'arrive!* I'm coming! ◊ *J'hésite.* I'm not sure.

les **jeans** MASC NOUN
jeans

le **jet** NOUN
jet (*of water*)
♦ **un jet d'eau** a fountain

jetable ADJECTIVE
disposable

la **jetée** NOUN
pier

jeter VERB
1 to throw ◊ *Elle a jeté son sac sur le lit.* She threw her bag onto the bed.
2 to throw away ◊ *Ils ne jettent jamais rien.* They never throw anything away.
♦ **jeter un coup d'œil sur** to have a look at

le **jeton** NOUN
counter (*in board game*)

le **jeu** NOUN (PL les **jeux**)
game ◊ *J'aime les jeux d'adresse.* I like games of skill.
♦ **un jeu d'arcade** a video game
♦ **un jeu de cartes (1)** a pack of cards
♦ **un jeu de cartes (2)** a card game
♦ **un jeu de hasard** a game of chance
♦ **un jeu de mots** a pun
♦ **un jeu électronique** an electronic game
♦ **un jeu interactif** an interactive game
♦ **les Jeux Olympiques** the Olympic games

☞

♦ **le jeu de rôle (1)** role-play ◊ *Nous avons fait un jeu de rôle sur les restaurants dans le cours de français.* In French class we did a role-play about going to a restaurant. ◊ *Le jeu de rôle est une bonne stratégie d'apprentissage.* Role-play is a good learning strategy.
♦ **le jeu de rôle (2)** role-playing game (*computer*)
♦ **un jeu de société (1)** a board game
♦ **un jeu de société (2)** a party game
♦ **les jeux vidéo** video games
♦ **en jeu** at stake ◊ *Des vies humaines sont en jeu.* Human lives are at stake.
♦ **hors jeu** (*sports*) offside

le **jeudi** NOUN
⚀ Thursday ◊ *Aujourd'hui, nous sommes jeudi.* It's Thursday today.
② on Thursday ◊ *Il arrivera jeudi matin.* He's arriving on Thursday morning.
♦ **le jeudi** on Thursdays ◊ *Le musée est fermé le jeudi.* The museum is closed on Thursdays.
♦ **tous les jeudis** every Thursday
♦ **jeudi dernier** last Thursday
♦ **jeudi prochain** next Thursday

jeun
♦ **à jeun** ADVERB on an empty stomach ◊ *Mange quelque chose. Il est difficile d'étudier à jeun!* Eat something. It's hard to study on an empty stomach!

jeune ADJECTIVE

see also **jeune** NOUN

young ◊ *un jeune homme* a young man ◊ *une jeune femme* a young woman
♦ **une jeune fille** a girl

le/la **jeune** NOUN

see also **jeune** ADJECTIVE

young person ◊ *un concours pour les jeunes* a contest for young people

la **jeunesse** NOUN
youth

✹ la **job** NOUN (*informal*)
job

la **joie** NOUN
joy

joindre VERB
⚀ to put together ◊ *On va joindre les deux tables.* We're going to put the two tables together.
② to contact ◊ *Vous pouvez le joindre chez lui.* You can contact him at home.

joint ADJECTIVE
♦ **une pièce jointe** an enclosure (*in letter*)

joli ADJECTIVE
pretty

le **jonc** NOUN
cattail

la **jonquille** NOUN
daffodil

la **joue** NOUN
cheek

jouer VERB
⚀ to play ◊ *Il est allé jouer avec les petits voisins.* He's gone to play with the children next door.
♦ **jouer de** to play (*instrument*) ◊ *Il joue de la guitare et du piano.* He plays the guitar and the piano.
♦ **jouer à** to play (*sport, game*) ◊ *Elle joue au hockey.* She plays hockey. ◊ *jouer aux cartes* to play cards
② to act ◊ *Je trouve qu'il joue très bien dans ce film.* I think his acting is very good in this film.
♦ **On joue Hamlet au Théâtre de la Ville.** Hamlet is on at the Théâtre de la Ville.

le **jouet** NOUN
toy

le **joueur** NOUN
player
♦ **être mauvais joueur** to be a bad loser

la **joueuse** NOUN
player

le **jour** NOUN
day ◊ *J'ai passé trois jours chez mes cousins.* I stayed with my cousins for three days.
♦ **Il fait jour.** It's light out.
♦ **mettre quelque chose à jour** to update something
♦ **le jour de l'An** New Year's Day
♦ **un jour de congé** a day off
✹ ♦ **le jour de la marmotte** Groundhog Day
♦ **un jour férié** a public holiday
♦ **dans quinze jours** in two weeks
♦ **de nos jours** nowadays

le **journal** NOUN (PL les **journaux**)
⚀ newspaper
♦ **le journal télévisé** the news on TV
② diary ◊ *Elle tient un journal depuis l'âge de douze ans.* She has been keeping a diary since she was 12.
③ journal

journalier ADJECTIVE (FEM SING **journalière**)
daily

le **journalisme** NOUN
journalism

le/la **journaliste** NOUN
journalist ◊ *Elle est journaliste.* She's a journalist.

la **journée** NOUN

day

> **❶** *In Québec,* **la Journée nationale des patriotes** *is a holiday that falls on the same day as Victoria Day. It has replaced* **la fête de Dollard.**

joyeux ADJECTIVE (FEM SING **joyeuse**)
　happy
　♦ **Joyeux anniversaire!** Happy birthday!
　♦ **Joyeux Noël!** Merry Christmas!

le **judo** NOUN
　judo

le/la **juge** NOUN
　judge

juger VERB
　to judge

juif ADJECTIVE (FEM SING **juive**)
　Jewish ◊ *la cuisine juive* Jewish cooking
　♦ **un juif** a Jew (*man*)
　♦ **une juive** a Jew (*woman*)

juillet MASC NOUN
　July
　♦ **en juillet** in July

juin MASC NOUN
　June
　♦ **en juin** in June

le **jumeau** NOUN (PL les **jumeaux**)
　twin

jumeler VERB
　to twin ◊ *Thunder Bay est jumelée avec Siderno en Italie.* Thunder Bay is twinned with Siderno, Italy.

la **jumelle** NOUN
　twin

les **jumelles** FEM NOUN
　binoculars

la **jument** NOUN
　mare

la **jungle** NOUN
　jungle

la **jupe** NOUN
　skirt

jurer VERB
　to swear ◊ *Je jure que c'est vrai!* I swear it's true!

juridique ADJECTIVE
　legal (*to do with law*)

le **jury** NOUN
　jury

le **jus** NOUN
　juice
　♦ **un jus de fruit** a fruit juice

jusqu'à PREPOSITION
　① as far as ◊ *Nous avons marché jusqu'au village.* We walked as far as the village.
　② until ◊ *Il fait généralement chaud jusqu'à la mi-août.* It's usually hot until mid-August.
　♦ **jusqu'à ce que** until ◊ *Tu peux rester ici jusqu'à ce qu'il cesse de pleuvoir.* You can stay here until it stops raining.
　♦ **jusqu'à présent** so far

jusque PREPOSITION
　as far as ◊ *Je l'ai raccompagnée jusque chez elle.* I went with her as far as her house. ◊ *Jusqu'ici nous n'avons pas eu de problèmes.* Up to now we've had no problems. ◊ *Jusqu'où es-tu allé?* How far did you go?

juste ADJECTIVE, ADVERB
　① fair ◊ *Elle est sévère, mais juste.* She's strict but fair.
　② tight ◊ *Ce veston est un peu juste.* This jacket is a bit tight.
　♦ **juste assez** just enough
　♦ **chanter juste** to sing in tune

justement ADVERB
　just ◊ *C'est justement pour cela qu'il est parti!* That's just the reason he left!

la **justesse** NOUN
　♦ **de justesse** just barely ◊ *Il a eu son permis de justesse.* He just barely passed his driving test.

la **justice** NOUN
　justice

justifier VERB
　to justify

juteux ADJECTIVE (FEM SING **juteuse**)
　juicy

juvénile ADJECTIVE
　youthful

J

K

kaki ADJECTIVE
khaki

le **kangourou** NOUN
kangaroo

le **karaté** NOUN
karate

le **kayak** NOUN
kayak ◊ *Ils ont fait une expédition de kayak aux îles de la Reine-Charlotte.* They went on a kayak trip to the Queen Charlotte Islands.
♦ **faire du kayak** to go kayaking

le/la **kayakiste** NOUN
kayaker

✹ **kétaine** ADJECTIVE
tacky ◊ *un bijou kétaine* a tacky piece of jewellery ◊ *des meubles kétaines* tacky furniture

le **ketchup** NOUN
ketchup

kidnapper VERB
to kidnap

le **kidnappeur** NOUN
kidnapper

la **kidnappeuse** NOUN
kidnapper

le **kilo** NOUN
kilo

le **kilogramme** NOUN
kilogram

le **kilomètre** NOUN
kilometre

le **kiosque** NOUN
kiosk
♦ **un kiosque à journaux** a newsstand

le **kit** NOUN
♦ **en kit** ready to assemble ◊ *Nous avons acheté une étagère en kit.* We bought a bookshelf that you put together yourself.

> *Be careful!* **le kit** *does not always mean* **kit**.

le **klaxon** NOUN
horn (*of car*)

klaxonner VERB
to blow the horn

km ABBREVIATION (= *kilomètre*)
♦ **km/h** kph (= kilometres per hour)

L

l' ARTICLE, PRONOUN *see* **la, le**

la ARTICLE, PRONOUN

see also **la** NOUN

la changes to l' before a vowel and most words beginning with "h".

① the ◊ *la maison* the house
◊ *l'actrice* the actress ◊ *l'herbe* the grass
② her ◊ *Je la connais depuis longtemps.* I've known her for a long time. ◊ *C'est une femme intelligente : je l'admire beaucoup.* She's an intelligent woman: I admire her very much.
③ it ◊ *C'est une bonne émission : je la regarde tous les jours.* It's a good program: I watch it every day.
④ one's
♦ **se mordre la langue** to bite one's tongue ◊ *Je me suis mordu la langue.* I bit my tongue.
♦ **deux dollars la douzaine** two dollars a dozen

le la NOUN

see also **la** ARTICLE

① A ◊ *en la bémol* in A flat
② la ◊ *sol, la, si, do* so, la, ti, do

là ADVERB

① there ◊ *Ton livre est là, sur la table.* Your book's there, on the table.
② here ◊ *Elle n'est pas là.* She isn't here.
♦ **C'est là que... (1)** That's where...
◊ *C'est là que je suis né.* That's where I was born.
♦ **C'est là que... (2)** That's when...
◊ *C'est là que j'ai réalisé que je m'étais trompé.* That's when I realized I had made a mistake.

là-bas ADVERB
over there

le laboratoire NOUN
laboratory

labourer VERB
to plough (*fields, soil*)

le Labrador NOUN
Labrador

le labyrinthe NOUN
maze

le lac NOUN
lake

lacer VERB
to do up (*shoes*)

le lacet NOUN
lace
♦ **des chaussures à lacets** lace-up shoes

lâche ADJECTIVE

see also **lâche** NOUN

① loose ◊ *Le nœud est trop lâche.* The knot's too loose.
② cowardly
♦ **Il est lâche.** He's a coward.

le lâche NOUN

see also **lâche** ADJECTIVE

coward

lâcher VERB
① to let go of ◊ *Elle n'a pas lâché ma main de tout le film.* She didn't let go of my hand through the whole movie.
② to drop ◊ *Il a été tellement surpris qu'il a lâché son verre.* He was so surprised that he dropped his glass.
③ to fail ◊ *Les freins ont lâché.* The brakes failed.

la lâcheté NOUN
cowardice

lacrymogène ADJECTIVE
♦ **le gaz lacrymogène** tear gas

la lacune NOUN
gap

là-dedans ADVERB
in there ◊ *Qu'est-ce qu'il y a là-dedans?* What's in there?

là-dessous ADVERB
① under there ◊ *Mon carnet d'adresses est quelque part là-dessous.* My address book is under there somewhere.
② behind it ◊ *Il y a quelque chose de louche là-dessous.* There's something fishy behind it.

là-dessus ADVERB
on there

là-haut ADVERB
up there

laid ADJECTIVE
ugly

la laideur NOUN
ugliness

la laine NOUN
wool ◊ *un chandail en laine* a wool sweater
♦ **la laine polaire** fleece (*fabric*) ◊ *une veste en laine polaire* a fleece vest

laïque ADJECTIVE

☞

♦ **une école laïque** a state school

la **laisse** NOUN
leash ◊ *Tenez votre chien en laisse.*
Keep your dog on a leash.

laisser VERB
1 to leave ◊ *J'ai laissé mon
parapluie à la maison.* I've left my
umbrella at home.
2 to let ◊ *Laisse-le parler.* Let him
speak.
♦ **Elle se laisse aller.** She's letting
herself go.
♦ **laisser entendre** to imply ◊ *Elle a
laissé entendre qu'elle ne venait pas.*
She implied that she wasn't coming.
♦ **laisser tomber quelqu'un** to break up
with somebody ◊ *Il a laissé tomber
sa copine.* He broke up with his
girlfriend.

le **laisser-aller** NOUN
carelessness

le **lait** NOUN
milk
♦ **un lait fouetté** a milk shake
♦ **du lait concentré** condensed milk

laitier ADJECTIVE (FEM SING **laitière**)
dairy ◊ *une vache laitière* a dairy cow
♦ **les produits laitiers** dairy products

la **laitue** NOUN
lettuce

les **lambeaux** MASC NOUN
♦ **en lambeaux** tattered

la **lame** NOUN
blade ◊ *une lame de rasoir* a razor
blade

la **lamelle** NOUN
thin strip

lamentable ADJECTIVE
appalling

se **lamenter** VERB
to moan

le **lampadaire** NOUN
1 floor lamp
2 street light

la **lampe** NOUN
lamp
♦ **une lampe de poche** a flashlight

la **lance** NOUN
spear

le **lancement** NOUN
launch

lancer VERB

> see also **lancer** NOUN

1 to throw ◊ *Lance-moi le ballon!*
Throw me the ball!
2 to launch ◊ *Ils viennent de lancer
un nouveau modèle.* They've just
launched a new model.
♦ **se lancer** to embark on ◊ *Il s'est
lancé là-dedans sans bien réfléchir.*
He embarked on it without thinking it
through.

le **lancer** NOUN

> see also **lancer** VERB

♦ **le lancer de poids** the shot put
🏒 ♦ **le lancer frappé** slapshot

le **lanceur** NOUN
pitcher (*baseball*)

la **lanceuse** NOUN
pitcher (*baseball*)

lancinant ADJECTIVE
♦ **une douleur lancinante** a shooting
pain

le **langage** NOUN
language (*other than a specific
language*) ◊ *l'origine du langage*
the origin of language ◊ *le langage
corporel* body language ◊ *Surveille
ton langage!* Watch your language!

la **langouste** NOUN
crayfish

la **langue** NOUN
1 tongue ◊ *Un petit garçon m'a tiré
la langue.* A little boy stuck out his
tongue at me.
♦ **sa langue maternelle** her mother
tongue
2 language ◊ *une langue étrangère*
a foreign language ◊ *une langue
vivante* a modern language ◊ *les
langues officielles du Canada* the
official languages of Canada
♦ **la langue non sexiste** inclusive
language

la **lanière** NOUN
strap

la **lanterne** NOUN
lantern

le **lapin** NOUN
rabbit

le **laps** NOUN
♦ **un laps de temps** a space of time

la **laque** NOUN
hair spray

laquelle PRONOUN (PL **lesquelles**)
1 which ◊ *Laquelle de ces photos
préfères-tu?* Which of these photos do
you prefer? ◊ *À laquelle de tes sœurs
ressembles-tu?* Which of your sisters
do you look like?
2 whom ◊ *la personne à laquelle
vous faites référence* the person to
whom you are referring

> *laquelle* is often not translated in
> English.

◊ *la personne à laquelle je pense* the person I'm thinking of

le **lard** NOUN
   fatty pork

large ADJECTIVE, ADVERB

   ⎡ *see also* **large** NOUN ⎤

   wide
♦ **voir large** to allow a bit extra
   ◊ *Achète un autre pain : il vaut mieux voir large.* Buy another loaf of bread: it's better to have a bit extra.

le **large** NOUN

   ⎡ *see also* **large** ADJECTIVE ⎤

♦ **cinq mètres de large** 5 m wide
♦ **le large** the open sea
♦ **au large de** off the coast of ◊ *Le bateau est actuellement au large du Labrador.* The boat is off the coast of Labrador at the moment.

largement ADVERB
♦ **Vous avez largement le temps.** You have plenty of time.
♦ **C'est largement suffisant.** That's plenty.

la **largeur** NOUN
   width

la **larme** NOUN
   tear ◊ *être en larmes* to be in tears

la **laryngite** NOUN
   laryngitis

la **lasagne** NOUN
   lasagna

le **laser** NOUN
   laser
♦ **une imprimante laser** a laser printer

lasser VERB
♦ **se lasser de** to get tired of ◊ *Il s'est lassé de la tapisserie à fleurs du salon.* He got tired of the flowery wallpaper in the living room.

les **Laurentides** FEM NOUN
   the Laurentians ◊ *Nous avons fait du camping dans les Laurentides.* We went camping in the Laurentians.

lavable ADJECTIVE
   washable

le **lavabo** NOUN
   sink (*bathroom*)

le **lavage** NOUN
   wash ◊ *Ce chandail a rétréci au lavage.* This sweater shrank in the wash. ◊ *Avez-vous quelque chose à mettre au lavage?* Do you have anything to put in the wash?
♦ **faire le lavage** to do laundry
♦ **le lavage de cerveau** brainwashing

☀ le **lave-auto** NOUN (PL les **lave-autos**)
   car wash

laver VERB
   to wash
♦ **se laver** to wash ◊ *se laver les mains* to wash one's hands

la **lavette** NOUN
   dishcloth

la **laveuse** NOUN
   washing machine

le **lave-vaisselle** NOUN (PL les **lave-vaisselle**)
   dishwasher

le **lavoir** NOUN
   coin laundry

le ARTICLE, PRONOUN

   ⎡ *le* changes to *l'* before a vowel and most words beginning with "h". ⎤

   ⎡1⎤ the ◊ *le livre* the book ◊ *l'arbre* the tree ◊ *l'hélicoptère* the helicopter
   ⎡2⎤ him ◊ *C'est un vieil ami : je le connais depuis plus de vingt ans.* He's an old friend: I've known him for over 20 years.
   ⎡3⎤ it ◊ *Où est mon stylo? Je ne le trouve plus.* Where's my pen? I can't find it. ◊ *« Où est le fromage? » « Je l'ai mis au frigo. »* "Where's the cheese?" "I put it in the fridge."
   ⎡4⎤ one's
♦ **se laver le visage** to wash one's face ◊ *Évitez de vous laver le visage avec du savon.* Avoid washing your face with soap.
♦ **trois dollars le kilo** 3 dollars a kilo
♦ **Il est arrivé le douze mai.** He arrived on 12 May.

lécher VERB
   to lick

la **leçon** NOUN
   lesson

le **lecteur** NOUN
   ⎡1⎤ reader
   ⎡2⎤ (disk) drive (*computer*) ◊ *Insérer la disquette dans le lecteur A.* Insert the disk in drive A.
♦ **un lecteur de cassettes** a cassette player
♦ **un lecteur de CD** a CD player
♦ **un lecteur de DVD** a DVD player
♦ **un lecteur de MP3** an MP3 player

la **lectrice** NOUN
   reader

la **lecture** NOUN
   reading

   ⎡ Be careful! The French word **lecture** does not mean **lecture**. ⎤

légal ADJECTIVE (MASC PL **légaux**)
   legal

L

légende → lever

la **légende** NOUN
1. legend
2. key (of map)
3. caption (of picture)

léger ADJECTIVE (FEM SING **légère**)
1. light
2. slight ◊ un léger retard a slight delay
♦ **à la légère** thoughtlessly ◊ Elle a agi à la légère. She acted thoughtlessly.

légèrement ADVERB
1. lightly ◊ Habille-toi légèrement : il va faire chaud. Wear light clothes: it's going to be hot.
2. slightly ◊ Il est légèrement plus grand que sa sœur. He's slightly taller than his sister.

le **légume** NOUN
vegetable

le **lendemain** NOUN
next day ◊ le lendemain de son arrivée the day after she arrived
♦ **le lendemain matin** the next morning
♦ **le lendemain de Noël** Boxing Day

lent ADJECTIVE
slow

lentement ADVERB
slowly

la **lenteur** NOUN
slowness

la **lentille** NOUN
lentil ◊ un rôti de porc aux lentilles roast pork with lentils
♦ **des lentilles cornéennes** contact lenses

le **léopard** NOUN
leopard

lequel PRONOUN (FEM SING **laquelle**, MASC PL **lesquels**, FEM PL **lesquelles**)
1. which ◊ Lequel de ces deux films as-tu préféré? Which of these two movies did you prefer?
2. whom ◊ l'homme avec lequel elle a été vue pour la dernière fois the man with whom she was last seen

lequel is often not translated in English.

◊ le garçon avec lequel elle est sortie the boy she went out with

les ARTICLE, PRONOUN
1. the ◊ les arbres the trees
2. them ◊ Elle les a invités à dîner. She invited them to dinner.
3. one's
♦ **se brosser les dents** to brush one's teeth ◊ Elle s'est brossé les dents. She brushed her teeth.

la **lesbienne** NOUN

lesbian

lesquels PRONOUN (FEM **lesquelles**)
1. which ◊ Lesquelles de ces photos préfères-tu? Which of these photos do you prefer?
2. whom ◊ les personnes avec lesquelles il joue au hockey the people with whom he plays hockey

lesquels is often not translated in English.

◊ les gens chez lesquels nous avons dîné the people we had dinner with

la **lessive** NOUN
wash (laundry)
♦ **faire la lessive** to do the washing

leste ADJECTIVE
nimble

la **lettre** NOUN
letter ◊ écrire une lettre to write a lettre

leur ADJECTIVE, PRONOUN
1. their ◊ leur ami their friend
2. them ◊ Je leur ai dit la vérité. I told them the truth.
♦ **le leur** theirs ◊ mon camion et le leur my truck and theirs ◊ Ma voiture est rouge, la leur est bleue. My car's red, theirs is blue.

leurs ADJECTIVE, PRONOUN
their ◊ leurs amis their friends
♦ **les leurs** theirs ◊ tes livres et les leurs your books and theirs

levé ADJECTIVE
♦ **être levé** to be up ◊ Est-ce qu'elles sont levées? Are they up?

la **levée** NOUN
collection (of mail) ◊ Prochaine levée : 17 heures Next collection: 5 p.m.
❋ ♦ **la levée de fonds** fund-raising

lever VERB

see also **lever** NOUN

to raise ◊ Levez la main si vous connaissez la réponse. Raise your hand if you know the answer.
❋ ♦ **lever le nez sur quelque chose** to turn something down ◊ Ils ont levé le nez sur notre offre. They turned down our offer.
♦ **lever les yeux** to look up
♦ **se lever (1)** to get up ◊ Elle se lève tous les jours à six heures. She gets up at 6 o'clock every day. ◊ Lève-toi! Get up!
♦ **se lever (2)** to rise ◊ Le soleil se lève plus tard en hiver. The sun rises later in winter.
♦ **se lever (3)** to stand up ◊ Levez-vous! Stand up!

le **lever** NOUN

> see also **lever** VERB

♦ **le lever du soleil** sunrise

le **levier** NOUN
   lever

la **lèvre** NOUN
   lip

la **levure** NOUN
   yeast
♦ **la levure chimique** baking powder

le **lexique** NOUN
   word list

le **lézard** NOUN
   lizard

la **liaison** NOUN

   ① affair ◊ *Ils ont eu une liaison dans leur jeunesse.* They had an affair when they were younger.
   ② liaison (*in pronunciation*) ◊ *Il faut faire la liaison dans l'expression « les amis ».* You have to make a liaison in the phrase "les amis".

la **libellule** NOUN
   dragonfly

libérer VERB
   to free ◊ *Les otages ont été libérés hier soir.* The hostages were freed last night.
♦ **se libérer** to find time ◊ *J'essaierai de me libérer cet après-midi.* I'll try to find time this afternoon.

la **liberté** NOUN
   freedom ◊ *la liberté d'expression* freedom of speech
♦ **mettre en liberté** to release ◊ *Il a été mis en liberté au bout d'un an de prison.* He was released after a year in prison.
♦ **en liberté surveillée** on probation

le/la **libraire** NOUN
   bookseller

la **librairie** NOUN
   bookstore

> *Be careful!* **librairie** *does not mean* **library***.*

libre ADJECTIVE
   ① free ◊ *Tu es libre de faire ce que tu veux.* You are free to do as you wish. ◊ *Est-ce que cette place est libre?* Is this seat free?
♦ **Avez-vous une chambre de libre?** Have you got a free room?
   ② clear ◊ *La route est libre : vous pouvez traverser.* The road is clear: you can cross.

le **libre-échange** NOUN
   free trade ◊ *un accord de libre-échange* a free-trade agreement

le **libre-service** NOUN (PL les **libres-services**)
   self-serve ◊ *Cette station-service est un libre-service.* This gas station is a self-serve.

la **licence** NOUN
   licence ◊ *une licence d'exportation* an export licence ◊ *la licence de logiciel* software licence

le **licenciement** NOUN
   layoff

licencier VERB
   to lay off ◊ *Ils viennent de licencier sept employés.* They've just laid off 7 employees.

le **liège** NOUN
   cork ◊ *des sous-verres en liège* cork coasters
♦ **un bouchon en liège** a cork (*for bottle*)

le **lien** NOUN
   ① connection ◊ *Il n'y a aucun lien entre ces deux événements.* There's no connection between these two events.
♦ **un lien de parenté** a family tie
   ② link (*in computing*)

lier VERB
♦ **lier conversation avec quelqu'un** to get into conversation with somebody
♦ **se lier avec quelqu'un** to make friends with somebody ◊ *Je ne me lie pas facilement.* I don't make friends easily.

le **lierre** NOUN
   ivy

le **lieu** NOUN (PL les **lieux**)
   place ◊ *votre lieu de travail* your place of work
♦ **avoir lieu** to take place ◊ *La cérémonie a eu lieu dans la salle des fêtes.* The ceremony took place in the community hall.
♦ **au lieu de** instead of ◊ *J'aimerais une pomme au lieu de la crème glacée.* I'd like an apple instead of ice cream.

✱ le **lieutenant-gouverneur** NOUN
   lieutenant-governor

✱ la **lieutenante-gouverneure** NOUN
   lieutenant-governor

le **lièvre** NOUN
   hare

la **ligne** NOUN
   ① line ◊ *La ligne est occupée.* The line is busy. ◊ *des lignes d'autobus* bus lines ◊ *les lignes électriques* power lines
♦ **en ligne** (*computing*) online
♦ **la ligne d'écoute téléphonique**

L

☞

helpline
② figure ◊ *C'est mauvais pour la ligne.* It's bad for your figure.

ligoter VERB
to tie up

la **ligue** NOUN
league

le **lilas** NOUN
lilac

la **limace** NOUN
slug

la **lime** NOUN
♦ **une lime à ongles** a nail file

la **limitation** NOUN
♦ **la limitation de vitesse** the speed limit

la **limite** NOUN
① boundary (*of property, sports field*)
② limit ◊ *Est-ce qu'il y a une limite d'âge?* Is there an age limit?
♦ **À la limite, on pourrait prendre l'autobus.** At a pinch we could go by bus.
♦ **la date limite** the deadline
♦ **la date limite d'utilisation** the best-before date

limiter VERB
to limit ◊ *Le nombre de billets est limité à deux par personne.* The number of tickets is limited to two per person.

la **limonade** NOUN
lemonade

le **lin** NOUN
linen ◊ *un veston en lin* a linen jacket

le **linge** NOUN
① linen ◊ *le linge sale* dirty linen ◊ *le linge de maison* household linens
② washing ◊ *laver le linge* to do the washing
✳ ♦ **le linge à vaisselle** tea towel

le **lion** NOUN
lion
♦ **le Lion** Leo ◊ *Il est Lion.* He is a Leo.

la **lionne** NOUN
lioness

la **liqueur** NOUN
pop (*beverage*)

liquide ADJECTIVE

see also **liquide** NOUN

liquid

le **liquide** NOUN

see also **liquide** ADJECTIVE

liquid
♦ **payer quelque chose en liquide** to pay cash for something

lire VERB

to read ◊ *Tu as lu des contes de Roch Carrier?* Have you read any stories by Roch Carrier?

lis, lisent, lisez VERB *see* **lire**
♦ **Je lis beaucoup.** I read a lot.

lisible ADJECTIVE
legible

lisse ADJECTIVE
smooth

la **liste** NOUN
list
♦ **faire la liste de** to make a list of ◊ *J'ai fait la liste de tout ce dont j'ai besoin.* I've made a list of all the things I need.

lit VERB *see* **lire**

le **lit** NOUN
bed ◊ *un grand lit* a double bed
◊ *aller au lit* to go to bed
♦ **faire son lit** to make one's bed ◊ *Je n'ai pas eu le temps de faire mon lit ce matin.* I didn't have time to make my bed this morning.
♦ **un lit de camp** a cot
♦ **un lit d'enfant** a crib

la **literie** NOUN
bedding

la **litière** NOUN
① litter (*for cat*)
② bedding (*of caged pet*)

le **litre** NOUN
litre

littéraire ADJECTIVE
literary
♦ **une œuvre littéraire** a work of literature

la **littérature** NOUN
literature

le **littoral** NOUN (PL les **littoraux**)
coast

la **livraison** NOUN
delivery

le **livre** NOUN

see also **la livre**

book
♦ **un livre de poche** a paperback

la **livre** NOUN

see also **le livre**

pound

> ❶ The **pound** is a nonmetric unit of mass equal to 454 g.

◊ *une livre de beurre* a pound of butter

livrer VERB
to deliver

le **livret** NOUN
  booklet

le **livreur** NOUN
  delivery person

la **livreuse** NOUN
  delivery person

local ADJECTIVE (MASC PL **locaux**)
  see also **local** NOUN
  local

le **local** NOUN (PL les **locaux**)
  see also **local** ADJECTIVE
  venue ◊ *Nous cherchons un local
  pour les répétitions.* We are looking
  for a venue to rehearse in.

le/la **locataire** NOUN
  tenant

la **location** NOUN
  ♦ **location de voitures** car rental
  ♦ **location de skis** ski rental

  *Be careful! The French word location
  does not mean location.*

locaux ADJECTIVE, NOUN see **local**

la **locomotive** NOUN
  locomotive

la **loge** NOUN
  dressing room

le **logement** NOUN
  ① housing
  ② accommodation

loger VERB
  to stay ◊ *Elle loge chez sa cousine.*
  She's staying with her cousin.
  ♦ **trouver à se loger** to find somewhere
  to live ◊ *Ils ont eu du mal à trouver
  à se loger.* They had difficulty finding
  somewhere to live.

le **logiciel** NOUN
  program (computer) ◊ *un logiciel de
  traitement de texte* a word-processing
  program
  ♦ **un logiciel antivirus** a piece of
  antivirus software
  ♦ **le coût des logiciels pour les écoles**
  the cost of software for schools

logique ADJECTIVE
  see also **logique** NOUN
  logical

la **logique** NOUN
  see also **logique** ADJECTIVE
  logic

la **loi** NOUN
  law

loin ADVERB
  ① far ◊ *Le restaurant n'est pas très
  loin d'ici.* The restaurant is not very

far from here.
  ② far off ◊ *La semaine de relâche
  n'est plus tellement loin.* March break
  isn't far off now.
  ③ a long time ago ◊ *Les vacances
  paraissent déjà tellement loin!* The
  holidays already seem such a long
  time ago!
  ♦ **au loin** in the distance ◊ *On aperçoit
  la mer au loin.* You can see the ocean
  in the distance.
  ♦ **de loin (1)** from a long way away
  ◊ *On voit l'église de loin.* You can see
  the church from a long way away.
  ♦ **de loin (2)** by far ◊ *C'est de loin
  l'élève le plus brillant.* He is by far the
  brightest student.
  ♦ **C'est plus loin que le cinéma.** It's past
  the movie theatre.

lointain ADJECTIVE
  see also **lointain** NOUN
  distant ◊ *un pays lointain* a distant
  country ◊ *C'est un parent lointain de
  ma mère.* He's a distant relation of my
  mother.

le **lointain** NOUN
  see also **lointain** ADJECTIVE
  ♦ **dans le lointain** in the distance

le **loir** NOUN
  ♦ **dormir comme un loir** to sleep like
  a log

les **loisirs** MASC NOUN
  ① free time SING ◊ *Qu'est-ce que vous
  faites pendant vos loisirs?* What do
  you do in your free time?
  ② hobby ◊ *Le ski et l'équitation sont
  des loisirs coûteux.* Skiing and riding
  are expensive hobbies.

long ADJECTIVE (FEM SING **longue**)
  see also **long** NOUN
  long
  ❋ ♦ **à l'année longue** all year round

le **long** NOUN
  see also **long** ADJECTIVE
  ♦ **un bateau de trois mètres de long** a
  boat 3 m long
  ♦ **tout le long de** all along ◊ *Il y a des
  sentiers de randonnée tout le long
  de la côte.* There are hiking trails all
  along the coast.
  ♦ **marcher de long en large** to walk up
  and down

longer VERB
  ♦ **La route longe la forêt.** The road runs
  along the edge of the forest.
  ♦ **Nous avons longé la rivière Rideau à
  pied.** We walked along the Rideau.

longtemps ADVERB
  a long time ◊ *J'ai attendu longtemps*
  ☞

chez le dentiste. I waited a long time
at the dentist's.
♦ **pendant longtemps** for a long time
◊ *On a cru pendant longtemps que
la Terre était plate.* For a long time
people thought the Earth was flat.
♦ **mettre longtemps à faire quelque
chose** to take a long time to do
something ◊ *Il a mis longtemps à
répondre à ma lettre.* He took a long
time to answer my letter.

longue ADJECTIVE *see* **long**

la **longue** NOUN
♦ **à la longue (1)** in the end ◊ *Elle a
fini par convaincre tout le monde
à la longue.* In the end she won
everybody over.
♦ **à la longue (2)** over the long term ◊ *À
la longue, la malbouffe est mauvaise
pour la santé.* Over the long term,
junk food is bad for your health.

longuement ADVERB
at length ◊ *Il m'a longuement parlé
de ses projets d'avenir.* He talked to
me at length about his future plans.

la **longueur** NOUN
length
♦ **à longueur de journée** all day long
◊ *Elle mâche de la gomme à longueur
de journée.* She chews gum all day
long.
♦ **dans le sens de la longueur**
lengthwise

les **loques** FEM NOUN
♦ **être en loques** to be torn to shreds
◊ *Sa chemise était en loques.* His shirt
was torn to shreds.

lors de PREPOSITION
during ◊ *Je l'ai rencontrée lors de
ma visite à Prince George.* I met her
during my stay in Prince George.

lorsque CONJUNCTION
when ◊ *J'allais composer ton
numéro lorsque tu as appelé.* I was
about to dial your number when you
called.

le **lot** NOUN
prize (*in draw*)
♦ **le gros lot** the jackpot

la **loterie** NOUN
① lottery ◊ *une loterie nationale* a
national lottery
② raffle ◊ *J'ai gagné ce baladeur
dans une loterie.* I won this personal
CD player in a raffle.

la **lotion** NOUN
lotion ◊ *une bouteille de lotion
solaire* a bottle of suntan lotion
♦ **une lotion après-rasage** an aftershave
♦ **une lotion démaquillante** facial

cleanser

le **loto** NOUN
lottery
♦ **un loto sportif** a sports pool

louche ADJECTIVE

see also **louche** NOUN

fishy ◊ *une histoire louche* a fishy
story

la **louche** NOUN

see also **louche** ADJECTIVE

ladle

loucher VERB
to squint

louer VERB
① to rent out ◊ *Ils louent des
chambres à des étudiants.* They rent
out rooms to students.
♦ **« à louer »** "for rent"
② to rent ◊ *Ma sœur loue un petit
appartement au centre-ville.* My sister
rents a little apartment in the centre
of town. ◊ *Nous allons louer une
voiture pour le week-end.* We're going
to rent a car for the weekend.
③ to praise ◊ *Les journaux ont
loué le courage des pompiers.* The
newspapers praised the courage of
the firefighters.

le **loup** NOUN
wolf

la **loupe** NOUN
magnifying glass

lourd ADJECTIVE
① heavy ◊ *Mon sac à dos est très
lourd.* My backpack is very heavy.
② muggy (*weather*) ◊ *Le temps est
lourd aujourd'hui.* It's muggy out
today.

la **loutre** NOUN
otter

le **louveteau** NOUN
wolf cub

loyal ADJECTIVE (MASC PL **loyaux**)
loyal

la **loyauté** NOUN
loyalty

le **loyer** NOUN
rent

lu VERB *see* **lire**

la **lucarne** NOUN
skylight

la **luge** NOUN
sled

lugubre ADJECTIVE
gloomy

lui PRONOUN

① him ◊ *Il a été très content du cadeau que je lui ai offert.* He was very pleased with the present I gave him. ◊ *C'est bien lui!* It's definitely him! ◊ *J'ai pensé à lui toute la journée.* I thought about him all day long.

② to him ◊ *Mon père est d'accord : je lui ai parlé ce matin.* My father said yes: I spoke to him this morning.

③ her ◊ *Elle a été très contente du cadeau que je lui ai offert.* She was very pleased with the present I gave her.

④ to her ◊ *Ma mère est d'accord : je lui ai parlé ce matin.* My mother said yes: I spoke to her this morning.

⑤ it ◊ *« Qu'est-ce que tu donnes à ton chat? » « Je lui donne de la nourriture sèche. »* "What do you give your cat?" "I give it dry food."

lui is also used for emphasis.

◊ *Lui, il est toujours en retard!* Oh him, he's always late!

♦ **lui-même** himself ◊ *Il a construit ce bateau lui-même.* He built this boat himself.

la **lumière** NOUN
light
♦ **la lumière du jour** daylight

lumineux ADJECTIVE (FEM SING **lumineuse**)
♦ **une enseigne lumineuse** a neon sign

lunatique ADJECTIVE
① absent-minded ◊ *Ma sœur est très lunatique.* My sister is very absent-minded.
② temperamental ◊ *Il est plutôt lunatique.* He's rather temperamental.

✵ le **lunch** NOUN
lunch (*midday meal*)
◊ *Habituellement, j'apporte mon lunch à l'école.* I usually bring my lunch to school.

ℹ In Canada, **le lunch** is the noon meal. In France, it refers to a light meal consisting of a cold buffet.

le **lundi** NOUN
① Monday ◊ *Aujourd'hui, nous sommes lundi.* It's Monday today.
② on Monday ◊ *Ils sont arrivés lundi.* They arrived on Monday.
♦ **le lundi** on Mondays ◊ *Le lundi, je vais à la piscine.* I go swimming on Mondays.
♦ **tous les lundis** every Monday
♦ **lundi dernier** last Monday
♦ **lundi prochain** next Monday
♦ **le lundi de Pâques** Easter Monday

la **lune** NOUN
moon
♦ **la lune de miel** honeymoon
♦ **être dans la lune** to daydream ◊ *Elle ne t'entend pas; elle est dans la lune.* She doesn't hear you; she's daydreaming.

les **lunettes** FEM NOUN
glasses
♦ **des lunettes de soleil** sunglasses
♦ **des lunettes de natation** swimming goggles

la **lutte** NOUN
① fight ◊ *la lutte contre le racisme* the fight against racism
② wrestling ◊ *une épreuve de lutte* a wrestling bout

lutter VERB
to fight

le **luxe** NOUN
luxury
♦ **de luxe** luxury ◊ *un hôtel de luxe* a luxury hotel

luxueux ADJECTIVE (FEM SING **luxueuse**)
luxurious

le **lynx** NOUN
lynx

L

M

M. ABBREVIATION (= *Monsieur*)
Mr ◊ *M. Bernard* Mr Bernard

m' PRONOUN *see* **me**

ma ADJECTIVE
my ◊ *ma mère* my mother ◊ *ma montre* my watch

✽ le **macaron** NOUN
button (*with slogan, image*) ◊ *Elle portait un macaron qui disait : « J'aime le français! »* She was wearing a button that said, "I like French!"

les **macaronis** MASC NOUN
macaroni SING

la **macédoine** NOUN
♦ **la macédoine de fruits** fruit salad
♦ **la macédoine de légumes** mixed vegetables

mâcher VERB
to chew

le **machin** NOUN (*informal*)
thingy ◊ *Passe-moi le machin pour râper les carottes.* Pass me the thingy for grating carrots. ◊ *Qu'est-ce que c'est que ce vieux machin?* What's this old thing?

machinalement ADVERB
♦ **Elle a regardé sa montre machinalement.** She looked at her watch without thinking.

la **machine** NOUN
machine
♦ **une machine à laver** a washing machine
♦ **une machine à écrire** a typewriter
♦ **une machine à coudre** a sewing machine
✽ ♦ **une machine à boules** a pinball machine

le **machiste** NOUN
male chauvinist

la **mâchoire** NOUN
jaw

mâchonner VERB
to chew

Madame FEM NOUN (PL **Mesdames**)
1 Mrs ◊ *Madame Legall* Mrs Legall
2 lady ◊ *Occupez-vous de Madame.* Could you look after this lady?
3 Madam ◊ *Madame,...* Dear Madam,... (*in letter*)
♦ **Madame! Vous avez oublié votre parapluie!** Ma'am, you forgot your umbrella!

Mademoiselle FEM NOUN (PL **Mesdemoiselles**)
Miss ◊ *Mademoiselle Martin* Miss Martin

> ⓘ **Mademoiselle** is rarely used for single women any more, except in reference to a girl. It is better to use **Madame**, the French equivalent of **Ms**, in person or in a letter.

✽ **maganer** VERB (*informal*)
to wreck ◊ *La pluie a magané la récolte de fraises.* The rain wrecked the strawberry crop. ◊ *J'ai magané mon baladeur MP3.* I wrecked my portable MP3 player.

le **magasin** NOUN
store ◊ *Les magasins ouvrent à huit heures.* The stores open at 8 o'clock.
♦ **faire les magasins** to go shopping

✽ le **magasinage** NOUN
shopping ◊ *J'ai du magasinage à faire.* I have some shopping to do.
♦ **faire du magasinage** to go shopping

✽ **magasiner** VERB
to shop

✽ le **magasineur** NOUN
shopper

✽ la **magasineuse** NOUN
shopper

le **magazine** NOUN
magazine

le **magicien** NOUN
magician

la **magicienne** NOUN
magician

la **magie** NOUN
magic ◊ *un tour de magie* a magic trick

magique ADJECTIVE
magic ◊ *une baguette magique* a magic wand

magnétique ADJECTIVE
magnetic

le **magnétophone** NOUN
tape recorder
♦ **un magnétophone à cassettes** a cassette recorder

le **magnétoscope** NOUN
VCR

magnifique ADJECTIVE
superb

mai MASC NOUN
May
♦ **en mai** in May

maigre ADJECTIVE
1 skinny ◊ *Mon père me trouve trop maigre.* My father says I'm too skinny.
2 lean (*meat*)
3 low-fat (*cheese, yogurt*)

maigrir VERB
to lose weight ◊ *Il fait un régime pour essayer de maigrir.* He's on a diet to try to lose weight. ◊ *Elle a maigri de deux kilos en un mois.* She's lost 2 kilos in a month.

le **maillot de bain** NOUN
swimsuit

la **main** NOUN
hand ◊ *Donne-moi la main!* Give me your hand!
♦ **serrer la main à quelqu'un** to shake hands with somebody
♦ **se serrer la main** to shake hands ◊ *Les deux présidents se sont serré la main.* The two presidents shook hands.
♦ **sous la main** handy ◊ *Est-ce que tu as son adresse sous la main?* Have you got his address handy?

la **main-d'œuvre** NOUN
workforce ◊ *la main-d'œuvre canadienne* the Canadian workforce ◊ *la main-d'œuvre de l'usine* the factory workers
♦ **les frais de main-d'œuvre** labour costs

maintenant ADVERB
1 now ◊ *Qu'est-ce que tu veux faire maintenant?* What do you want to do now? ◊ *C'est maintenant ou jamais.* It's now or never.
2 nowadays ◊ *Maintenant la plupart des gens font leurs courses au supermarché.* Nowadays most people do their shopping at the supermarket.

maintenir VERB
to maintain ◊ *Il maintient qu'il n'était pas là le jour du crime.* He maintains he wasn't there on the day of the crime.
♦ **se maintenir** to hold ◊ *Espérons que le beau temps va se maintenir pour la fin de semaine!* Let's hope the good weather will hold over the weekend!

le **maintien de la paix** NOUN
peacekeeping ◊ *les opérations du maintien de la paix au Rwanda* peacekeeping operations in Rwanda

le/la **maire** NOUN
mayor

la **mairie** NOUN
town hall

mais CONJUNCTION
but ◊ *C'est cher mais de très bonne qualité.* It's expensive, but very good quality.

le **maïs** NOUN
corn
♦ **du maïs soufflé** popcorn

la **maison** NOUN

see also **maison** ADJECTIVE

house ◊ *Ils habitent dans la maison qui est au bout de la rue.* They live in the house at the end of the street.
♦ **une maison de jeunes** a youth club
♦ **une maison de transition** a halfway house
♦ **des maisons jumelées** semi-detached houses
♦ **des maisons en rangée** townhouses
♦ **à la maison (1)** at home ◊ *Je serai à la maison cet après-midi.* I'll be at home this afternoon.
♦ **à la maison (2)** home ◊ *Elle est rentrée à la maison.* She's gone home.

maison ADJECTIVE (MASC, FEM, PL)

see also **maison** NOUN

homemade ◊ *Je préfère les tartes maison à celles qui sont achetées.* I prefer homemade pies to store-bought ones.

le/la **maître** NOUN
1 teacher (*in primary school*)
2 master (*of dog*)
♦ **un maître d'hôtel** a head waiter (*in restaurant*)
♦ **un maître nageur** a lifeguard
♦ **une maître nageuse** a lifeguard

la **maîtresse** NOUN
teacher (*in primary school*)
♦ **la maîtresse de la maison** the lady of the house

la **maîtrise** NOUN
master's degree ◊ *Elle a une maîtrise d'anglais.* She's got a master's degree in English.
♦ **la maîtrise de soi** self-control

maîtriser VERB
♦ **se maîtriser** to control oneself ◊ *Il se met facilement en colère et a du mal à se maîtriser.* He loses his temper easily and finds it hard to control himself.

majestueux ADJECTIVE (FEM SING **majestueuse**)
majestic

majeur ADJECTIVE
♦ **être majeur** to be of age ◊ *Tu feras ce que tu voudras quand tu seras*

M

majeure. You can do what you like once you're of age. ◊ *Elle sera majeure en août.* She comes of age in August.
♦ **la majeure partie** most ◊ *la majeure partie de mon salaire* most of my salary

la **majorité** NOUN
majority ◊ *dans la majorité des cas* in the majority of cases
♦ **la majorité et l'opposition** the government and the opposition

la **majuscule** NOUN
upper-case letter ◊ *un M majuscule* an upper-case M

mal ADVERB, ADJECTIVE (MASC, FEM, PL)

see also **mal** NOUN

1 badly ◊ *Ce travail a été mal fait.* The work was badly done. ◊ *Il a mal compris.* He misunderstood.
2 wrong ◊ *C'est mal de mentir.* It's wrong to tell lies.
♦ **aller mal** to be ill ◊ *Son grand-père va très mal.* Her grandfather is very ill.
♦ **pas mal** quite good ◊ *Je te trouve pas mal sur cette photo.* I think you look quite good in this photo.

le **mal** NOUN (PL les **maux**)

see also **mal** ADVERB

1 ache ◊ *J'ai mal à la tête.* I have a headache. ◊ *J'ai mal aux dents.* I have a toothache. ◊ *J'ai mal au dos.* My back hurts. ◊ *Est-ce que vous avez mal à la gorge?* Do you have a sore throat?
♦ **le mal des transports** motion sickness
♦ **Ça fait mal.** It hurts.
♦ **Où est-ce que tu as mal?** Where does it hurt?
♦ **faire mal à quelqu'un** to hurt somebody ◊ *Attention, tu me fais mal!* Be careful, you're hurting me!
♦ **se faire mal** to hurt oneself ◊ *Je me suis fait mal au bras.* I hurt my arm.
♦ **se donner du mal pour faire quelque chose** to go to a lot of trouble to do something ◊ *Il s'est donné beaucoup de mal pour que cette soirée soit réussie.* He went to a lot of trouble to make the party a success.
♦ **avoir le mal de mer** to be seasick
♦ **avoir le mal du pays** to be homesick
♦ **avoir mal au cœur** to feel nauseous
2 evil ◊ *le bien et le mal* good and evil
♦ **dire du mal de quelqu'un** to speak ill of somebody

malade ADJECTIVE

see also **malade** NOUN

ill
♦ **tomber malade** to fall ill

le/la **malade** NOUN

see also **malade** ADJECTIVE

patient

la **maladie** NOUN
1 illness
2 disease
♦ **la maladie de la vache folle** mad cow disease

maladif ADJECTIVE (FEM SING **maladive**)
sickly ◊ *C'est un enfant maladif.* He's a sickly child.

la **maladresse** NOUN
clumsiness

maladroit ADJECTIVE
clumsy

le **malaise** NOUN
♦ **avoir un malaise** to feel faint ◊ *Elle a eu un malaise après le déjeuner.* She felt faint after lunch.
♦ **Son arrivée a créé un malaise parmi les invités.** Her arrival made the guests uncomfortable.

la **malbouffe** NOUN
junk food ◊ *Mes parents sont contre la malbouffe.* My parents are against junk food. ◊ *La malbouffe est devenue un problème dans notre société.* Junk food has become a problem in our society.

la **malchance** NOUN
bad luck

mâle ADJECTIVE
male

la **malédiction** NOUN
curse

mal en point ADJECTIVE (MASC, FEM, PL)
♦ **Il avait l'air mal en point quand je l'ai vu hier soir.** He didn't look too good when I saw him last night.

le **malentendu** NOUN
misunderstanding

le **malfaiteur** NOUN
criminal

la **malfaitrice** NOUN
criminal

mal famé ADJECTIVE (FEM **mal famée**, MASC PL **mal famés**)
♦ **un quartier mal famé** a rough neighbourhood

malgré PREPOSITION
in spite of ◊ *Il est toujours généreux malgré ses problèmes d'argent.* He's always generous in spite of his financial problems.
♦ **malgré tout** anyway (*nevertheless*) ◊ *Il faisait mauvais mais nous sommes sortis malgré tout.* The weather was bad but we went out

anyway.

le malheur NOUN

tragedy ◊ *Elle a eu beaucoup de malheurs dans sa vie.* She's had a lot of tragedy in her life.

♦ **faire un malheur** (*informal*) to be a smash hit ◊ *Leur dernier album a fait un malheur.* Their latest album was a smash hit.

malheureusement ADVERB
unfortunately

malheureux ADJECTIVE (FEM SING **malheureuse**)

miserable ◊ *Qu'est-ce que tu as? Tu as l'air malheureux.* What's wrong with you? You look miserable.

malhonnête ADJECTIVE
dishonest

la malice NOUN

mischief ◊ *Son regard était plein de malice.* Her eyes were full of mischief.

malicieux ADJECTIVE (FEM SING **malicieuse**)
mischievous

> *Be careful!* **malicieux** *does not mean* **malicious**.

malin ADJECTIVE (FEM SING **maligne**)
1 crafty

♦ **C'est malin!** (*informal*) That's clever! ◊ *Ah c'est malin! Nous voilà enfermés à cause de toi!* You've gone and locked us in!
2 malignant ◊ *une tumeur maligne* a malignant tumor

malodorant ADJECTIVE
smelly

malpropre ADJECTIVE
dirty

malsain ADJECTIVE
unhealthy

maltraiter VERB

to abuse ◊ *Il maltraite son chien.* He abuses his dog. ◊ *des enfants maltraités* abused children

malveillant ADJECTIVE
malicious ◊ *des rumeurs malveillantes* malicious rumours

la maman NOUN
mom

le mammifère NOUN
mammal

la manche NOUN

see also **le manche**

1 sleeve (*of clothes*)
2 round (*of game*) ◊ *Ils ont gagné la première manche du match.* They won the first round of the match.

> *The word* **manche** *can be translated as* **set**, **inning**, **heat**, *or* **round**, *depending on what kind of sport or game is being played.*

le manche NOUN

see also **la manche**

handle (*of pot, pan*)

la manchette NOUN
headline

♦ **faire la manchette** to make headlines

la mandarine NOUN
mandarin orange

le manège NOUN
amusement park ride

♦ **Nous avons deviné son manège.** We've seen through his game.

la manette NOUN
1 lever
2 joystick

mangeable ADJECTIVE
edible ◊ *C'est à peine mangeable!* It's practically inedible!

manger VERB
to eat

la mangue NOUN
mango

maniaque ADJECTIVE
fussy

la manie NOUN
1 obsession

♦ **avoir la manie de** to be obsessive about ◊ *Il a la manie du rangement.* He's obsessive about tidying up.
2 habit ◊ *J'essaie de respecter ses petites manies.* I try to go along with her little ways.

manier VERB
to handle

la manière NOUN

see also **les manières**

NOUN
way

♦ **de manière à** so as to ◊ *Nous sommes partis tôt de manière à éviter la circulation.* We left early so as to avoid the traffic.

♦ **de toute manière** in any case ◊ *Je n'aurais pas pu venir de toute manière.* I couldn't have come in any case.

les manières

see also **la manière**

FEM NOUN
1 manners ◊ *apprendre les bonnes manières* to learn good manners
2 fuss ◊ *Ne fais pas de manières : mange ta soupe!* Don't make a fuss:

M

☞

eat your soup!

le **manifestant** NOUN
demonstrator

la **manifestante** NOUN
demonstrator

la **manifestation** NOUN
demonstration ◊ *une manifestation pour la paix* a peace demonstration

manifester VERB
to demonstrate

manipuler VERB
① to handle ◊ *Ce vase doit être manipulé avec soin.* This vase must be handled with care.
② to manipulate ◊ *Tous les partis essaient de manipuler l'opinion publique.* All the parties are trying to manipulate public opinion.
③ to rig ◊ *L'élection a été manipulée.* The election was rigged.

le **Manitoba** NOUN
Manitoba

le **mannequin** NOUN
model ◊ *Elle est mannequin.* She's a model.

manœuvrer VERB
to manœuvre

le **manque** NOUN
① lack ◊ *Le manque de sommeil peut provoquer toutes sortes de troubles.* Lack of sleep can cause all sorts of problems.
② withdrawal ◊ *un drogué en état de manque* a drug addict suffering withdrawal symptoms

manqué ADJECTIVE
♦ **un garçon manqué** a tomboy

manquer VERB
to miss ◊ *Tu n'as rien manqué : le film n'était pas très bon.* You didn't miss anything: the movie wasn't very good. ◊ *Il manque des pages à ce livre.* There are some pages missing from this book.
♦ **Mes parents me manquent.** I miss my parents.
♦ **Ma sœur me manque.** I miss my sister.
♦ **Il manque encore dix dollars.** We are still 10 dollars short.
♦ **manquer de** to lack ◊ *La quiche manque de sel.* The quiche doesn't have enough salt. ◊ *Je trouve qu'il a manqué de tact.* I don't think he was very tactful.
♦ **Il a manqué se tuer.** He nearly got killed.

le **manteau** NOUN (PL les **manteaux**)
coat

manuel ADJECTIVE (FEM SING **manuelle**)
see also **manuel** NOUN
manual

le **manuel** NOUN
see also **manuel** ADJECTIVE
① textbook
② handbook

le **maquereau** NOUN (PL les **maquereaux**)
mackerel

la **maquette** NOUN
model ◊ *une maquette de bateau* a model boat

le **maquillage** NOUN
make-up

se **maquiller** VERB
to put on one's make-up ◊ *Je vais me maquiller en vitesse.* I'll just quickly put on my make-up.

✹ **marabout** ADJECTIVE (FEM SING **marabout**)
grumpy ◊ *Elles sont marabouts ce matin.* They're grumpy this morning.

le **marais** NOUN
marsh

le **marbre** NOUN
marble ◊ *une statue en marbre* a marble statue

le **marchand** NOUN
① storekeeper
② merchant

la **marchande** NOUN
① storekeeper
♦ **une marchande de fruits et de légumes** a fruit and vegetable seller
② merchant

marchander VERB
to haggle

la **marchandise** NOUN
goods

la **marche** NOUN
① step ◊ *Fais attention à la marche!* Mind the step!
② walking ◊ *La marche me fait du bien.* Walking does me good.
♦ **être en état de marche** to be in working order ◊ *Cette voiture est en parfait état de marche.* This car is in perfect running order.
♦ **Ne montez jamais dans un train en marche.** Never try to get into a moving train.
♦ **mettre en marche** to start ◊ *Comment est-ce qu'on met la machine à laver en marche?* How do you start the washing machine?
♦ **la marche arrière** reverse gear
♦ **faire marche arrière** to back up (*vehicle*)
③ march ◊ *une marche militaire* a

military march

le **marché** NOUN
> market
> ♦ **un marché aux puces** a flea market
> ♦ **le marché noir** the black market
> ♦ **un marché de producteurs** a farmers' market
> ♦ **le marché du travail** the labour market

marcher VERB
> ① to walk ◊ *Elle marche cinq kilomètres par jour.* She walks 5 kilometres every day.
> ② to run ◊ *Le métro marche normalement aujourd'hui.* The subway is running normally today.
> ③ to work ◊ *Est-ce que l'ascenseur marche?* Is the elevator working?
> ④ to go well ◊ *Est-ce que les affaires marchent actuellement?* Is business going well right now?
> ♦ **Alors les études, ça marche?** (*informal*) How are you doing at school?
> ♦ **faire marcher quelqu'un** to pull somebody's leg ◊ *Il essaie de te faire marcher.* He's pulling your leg.

❊ la **marchette** NOUN
> walker (*for babies, elderly*)

le **marcheur** NOUN
> walker

la **marcheuse** NOUN
> walker

le **mardi** NOUN
> ① Tuesday ◊ *Aujourd'hui, nous sommes mardi.* It's Tuesday today.
> ② on Tuesday ◊ *Ils reviennent mardi.* They're coming back on Tuesday.
> ♦ **le mardi** on Tuesdays ◊ *Le mardi, j'ai mes cours de piano.* I have piano lessons on Tuesdays.
> ♦ **tous les mardis** every Tuesday
> ♦ **mardi dernier** last Tuesday
> ♦ **mardi prochain** next Tuesday

la **mare** NOUN
> pond

le **marécage** NOUN
> marsh

la **marée** NOUN
> tide ◊ *la marée haute* high tide ◊ *la marée basse* low tide ◊ *La marée monte.* The tide is coming in. ◊ *La marée descend.* The tide is going out.
> ♦ **une marée noire** an oil slick

la **margarine** NOUN
> margarine

la **marge** NOUN
> margin

le **mari** NOUN

husband ◊ *son mari* her husband

le **mariage** NOUN
> ① marriage
> ② wedding ◊ *un mariage civil* a civil ceremony ◊ *un mariage religieux* a church wedding

marié ADJECTIVE
> see also **marié** NOUN
> married

le **marié** NOUN
> see also **marié** ADJECTIVE
> bridegroom
> ♦ **les mariés** the bride and groom

la **mariée** NOUN
> bride

se **marier** VERB
> to marry ◊ *Elle s'est mariée avec un ami d'enfance.* She married a childhood friend.

marin ADJECTIVE
> see also **marin** NOUN
> sea ◊ *l'air marin* the sea air

le **marin** NOUN
> see also **marin** ADJECTIVE
> sailor

la **marinade** NOUN
> marinade
❊ ♦ **les marinades** pickles

marine ADJECTIVE (MASC, FEM, PL)
> see also **marine** NOUN
> ♦ **bleu marine** navy-blue ◊ *un chandail bleu marine* a navy-blue sweater

la **marine** NOUN
> see also **marine** ADJECTIVE
> navy ◊ *la marine canadienne* the Canadian navy

❊ le **maringouin** NOUN
> mosquito ◊ *une piqûre de maringouin* a mosquito bite

la **marionnette** NOUN
> puppet

maritime ADJECTIVE
> maritime ◊ *les provinces maritimes* the Maritime provinces
❊ ♦ **les Maritimes** the Maritimes
> ♦ **un chantier maritime** a shipyard

la **marmelade** NOUN
> ♦ **la marmelade de pommes** applesauce
> ♦ **la marmelade d'oranges** marmalade

la **marmite** NOUN
> large cooking pot

marmonner VERB
> to mumble

la **marmotte** NOUN
> groundhog

☞

M

♦ **le jour de la marmotte** Groundhog Day

la **maroquinerie** NOUN
leather goods store

marquant ADJECTIVE
significant ◊ *un événement marquant* a significant event

la **marque** NOUN
1 mark ◊ *des marques de doigts* fingermarks
2 make ◊ *De quelle marque est ta voiture?* What make is your car?
3 brand ◊ *une grande marque de beurre d'arachide* a well-known brand of peanut butter
♦ **l'image de marque** the public image ◊ *La ministre tient à son image de marque.* The minister cares about her public image.
♦ **une marque déposée** a registered trademark
♦ **A vos marques! prêts! partez!** Ready, set, go!

marquer VERB
1 to mark ◊ *Peux-tu marquer sur la carte où se trouve le village?* Can you mark where the village is on the map?
2 to score ◊ *L'équipe canadienne a marqué dix points.* The Canadian team scored ten points.
3 to have a lasting effect on ◊ *La guerre a marqué ces enfants.* War has had a lasting effect on these kids. ◊ *Cette peintre a marqué son époque.* This painter had a lasting effect on her time.

marrant ADJECTIVE (*informal*)
funny

marre ADVERB (*informal*)
♦ **en avoir marre de quelque chose** to be fed up with something ◊ *J'en ai marre de faire la vaisselle.* I'm fed up with doing the dishes.

le **marron** NOUN

see also **marron** ADJECTIVE

chestnut ◊ *les marrons grillés* roasted chestnuts

marron ADJECTIVE (MASC, FEM, PL)

see also **marron** NOUN

brown ◊ *des chaussures marron* brown shoes

le **marronnier** NOUN
chestnut tree

mars MASC NOUN
March
♦ **en mars** in March

le **marteau** NOUN (PL les **marteaux**)
hammer

martyriser VERB
to batter ◊ *des enfants martyrisés* battered children

la **mascotte** NOUN
mascot ◊ *La mascotte de notre équipe est le carcajou.* Our team's mascot is a wolverine.

masculin ADJECTIVE
1 men's ◊ *la mode masculine* men's fashion
2 masculine ◊ *« Chat » est un nom masculin.* "Chat" is a masculine noun. ◊ *Elle a une allure assez masculine.* She looks rather masculine.

le **masque** NOUN
mask

le **massacre** NOUN
massacre

massacrer VERB
to massacre

le **massage** NOUN
massage

la **masse** NOUN
1 mass (*volume, weight*) ◊ *la masse musculaire* muscular mass
2 majority ◊ *la grande masse des jeunes* the vast majority of young people
♦ **produire en masse** to mass-produce ◊ *Ces jouets sont produits en masse en Chine.* These toys are mass-produced in China.
♦ **venir en masse** to come en masse ◊ *Les gens sont venus en masse pour accueillir Nelson Mandela.* People came en masse to welcome Nelson Mandela.

masser VERB
to massage
♦ **se masser** to gather ◊ *Les manifestants se sont massés devant l'ambassade.* The demonstrators gathered in front of the embassy.

massif ADJECTIVE (FEM SING **massive**)
1 solid (*gold, silver, wood*) ◊ *un bracelet en or massif* a solid gold bracelet
2 massive ◊ *une dose massive d'antibiotiques* a massive dose of antibiotics
3 mass ◊ *des départs massifs* a mass exodus

mat ADJECTIVE
matte ◊ *blanc mat* matte white ◊ *Je voudrais mes photos en fini mat.* I would like my photos matte.
♦ **être mat** to be checkmated (*chess*)

le **match** NOUN
game ◊ *un match de hockey* a hockey game

♦ **faire match nul** to be tied

le **matelas** NOUN
mattress ◊ *un matelas gonflable* an air mattress

le **matelot** NOUN
sailor

les **matériaux** MASC NOUN
materials

le **matériel** NOUN
① equipment ◊ *du matériel de laboratoire* laboratory equipment
② hardware (*computer*) ◊ *C'est un problème de matériel ou de logiciel?* Is the problem with the hardware or the software?
③ gear ◊ *Il a pris tout son matériel de pêche avec lui.* He took all his fishing gear with him.

maternel ADJECTIVE (FEM SING **maternelle**)
motherly ◊ *Elle est très maternelle.* She's very motherly.
♦ **ma grand-mère maternelle** my mother's mother
♦ **mon oncle maternel** my mother's brother

la **maternelle** NOUN
kindergarten

la **maternité** NOUN
♦ **le congé de maternité** maternity leave ◊ *Notre professeur de musique est en congé de maternité.* Our music teacher is on maternity leave.

les **mathématiques** FEM NOUN
mathematics

les **maths** FEM NOUN (*informal*)
math SING

la **matière** NOUN
subject ◊ *Ma matière préférée, c'est le français.* My favourite subject is French.
♦ **sans matières grasses** fat-free
♦ **les matières premières** raw materials

le **matin** NOUN
morning ◊ *à trois heures du matin* at 3 o'clock in the morning
♦ **du matin au soir** from morning till night
♦ **de bon matin** early in the morning

matinal ADJECTIVE (MASC PL **matinaux**)
morning ◊ *Je fais mes étirements matinaux avant de déjeuner.* I do my morning stretches before breakfast.
♦ **être matinal** to be up early ◊ *Tu es bien matinal aujourd'hui!* You're up early today!

la **matinée** NOUN
morning ◊ *Je t'appellerai demain dans la matinée.* I'll call you sometime tomorrow morning.

◊ *en début de matinée* early in the morning

le **matou** NOUN
tomcat

maudire VERB
to curse

maudit ADJECTIVE (*informal*)
darned ◊ *Où est passé ce maudit parapluie?* Where's that darned umbrella got to?

maussade ADJECTIVE
sulky

mauvais ADJECTIVE, ADVERB
① bad ◊ *une mauvaise note* a bad mark ◊ *Tu arrives au mauvais moment.* You've come at a bad time.
♦ **Il fait mauvais.** The weather's bad.
♦ **être mauvais en** to be bad at ◊ *Je suis mauvais en orthographe.* I'm bad at spelling.
② poor ◊ *de mauvaise qualité* of poor quality ◊ *Il est en mauvaise santé.* His health is poor.
♦ **Tu as mauvaise mine.** You don't look well.
③ wrong ◊ *Vous avez fait le mauvais numéro.* You've dialled the wrong number.
♦ **des mauvaises herbes** weeds
♦ **sentir mauvais** to smell

les **maux** MASC NOUN (SING **le mal**)
♦ **des maux de dents** toothache SING
♦ **des maux de ventre** stomachache SING
♦ **des maux de tête** headache SING

maximal ADJECTIVE (MASC PL **maximaux**)
maximum

le **maximum** NOUN
maximum
♦ **au maximum (1)** as much as one can ◊ *Remplis le seau au maximum.* Fill the pail as full as you can.
♦ **au maximum (2)** at the very most ◊ *Ça va vous coûter deux cents dollars au maximum.* It'll cost you 200 dollars at the very most.

la **mayonnaise** NOUN
mayonnaise

le **mazout** NOUN
oil (*for furnace*)

me PRONOUN

> **me** changes to **m'** before a vowel and most words beginning with "h".

① me ◊ *Elle me téléphone tous les jours.* She phones me every day. ◊ *Il m'attend depuis une heure.* He's been waiting for me for an hour.
② to me ◊ *Il me parle en français.* He talks to me in French. ◊ *Elle m'a expliqué la situation.* She explained

M

☞

the situation to me.
③ myself ◊ *Je vais me préparer quelque chose à manger.* I'm going to make myself something to eat.

With reflexive verbs, me is often not translated.

◊ *Je me lève à sept heures tous les matins.* I get up at 7 every morning.

le **mécanicien** NOUN
mechanic

la **mécanicienne** NOUN
mechanic

la **mécanique** NOUN
① mechanics
② mechanism (*of watch, clock*)

le **mécanisme** NOUN
mechanism

méchamment ADVERB
nastily ◊ *Elle lui a répondu méchamment.* She answered her nastily.

la **méchanceté** NOUN
meanness

méchant ADJECTIVE
nasty ◊ *C'est un homme méchant.* He's a nasty man.
♦ **Ne sois pas méchant avec ton petit frère.** Don't be mean to your little brother.
♦ **« Attention, chien méchant »** "Beware of the dog"

la **mèche** NOUN
lock (*of hair*)

mécontent ADJECTIVE
♦ **mécontent de** unhappy with ◊ *Elle est mécontente de sa coupe de cheveux.* She's unhappy with her haircut.

le **mécontentement** NOUN
displeasure ◊ *Il a exprimé son mécontentement.* He expressed his displeasure.

la **médaille** NOUN
medal

le/la **médecin** NOUN
doctor ◊ *aller chez le médecin* to go to the doctor

la **médecine** NOUN
medicine (*subject*) ◊ *Elle étudie la médecine.* She's studying medicine.

les **médias** MASC NOUN
media

médical ADJECTIVE (MASC PL **médicaux**)
medical ◊ *la recherche médicale* medical research
♦ **passer une visite médicale** to have a medical

le **médicament** NOUN
medicine (*drug*)

médiéval ADJECTIVE (MASC PL **médiévaux**)
medieval

médiocre ADJECTIVE
poor ◊ *des notes médiocres* poor marks

la **méduse** NOUN
jellyfish

la **méfiance** NOUN
mistrust

méfiant ADJECTIVE
mistrustful

se **méfier** VERB
♦ **se méfier de quelqu'un** to distrust somebody ◊ *Si j'étais toi, je me méfierais de lui.* I wouldn't trust him if I were you.

le **mégaoctet** NOUN
megabyte

la **mégarde** NOUN
♦ **par mégarde** by mistake ◊ *J'ai emporté ton livre par mégarde.* I took your book by mistake.

meilleur ADJECTIVE, ADVERB, NOUN
better ◊ *Ce serait meilleur avec du fromage râpé.* It would be better with grated cheese. ◊ *Il paraît que le film est meilleur que le livre.* They say that the film is better than the book.
♦ **le meilleur** the best ◊ *C'est elle qui est la meilleure en sport.* She's the best at sports. ◊ *Je préfère garder le meilleur pour la fin.* I like to keep the best for last.
♦ **le meilleur des deux** the better of the two
♦ **meilleur marché** cheaper ◊ *Les vêtements sont meilleur marché dans ce magasin.* Clothes are cheaper in this store.

mélancolique ADJECTIVE
gloomy

le **mélange** NOUN
mixture

mélanger VERB
① to mix ◊ *Mélangez le tout.* Mix everything together.
② to muddle up ◊ *Tu mélanges tout!* You're muddling everything up!

le **mélangeur** NOUN
blender

la **mêlée** NOUN
scuffle

mêler VERB
♦ **se mêler** to mix ◊ *Elle ne cherche pas à se mêler aux autres.* She doesn't try to mix with the others.

♦ **Mêle-toi de tes affaires!** (*informal*)
Mind your own business!

la **mélodie** NOUN
melody

le **melon** NOUN
melon

🌺 ♦ **le melon d'eau** watermelon

le **membre** NOUN
① limb
② member ◊ *un membre de la famille* a member of the family
◊ *les pays membres de l'OTAN* the member countries of NATO

même ADJECTIVE, ADVERB, PRONOUN
① same ◊ *J'ai le même manteau.*
I've got the same coat. ◊ *Tiens, c'est curieux, j'ai le même!* That's strange, I've got the same one!
♦ **en même temps** at the same time
♦ **moi-même** myself ◊ *Je l'ai fait moi-même.* I did it myself.
♦ **toi-même** yourself ◊ *Est-ce que tu vas faire les travaux toi-même?* Are you going to do the work yourself?
♦ **eux-mêmes** themselves
② even ◊ *Il n'a même pas pleuré.* He didn't even cry.

la **mémoire** NOUN
memory

la **menace** NOUN
threat

menacer VERB
to threaten

le **ménage** NOUN
housework ◊ *faire le ménage* to do the housework
♦ **une femme de ménage** a cleaning woman

ménager ADJECTIVE (FEM SING **ménagère**)
♦ **les travaux ménagers** housework

le **mendiant** NOUN
beggar

la **mendiante** NOUN
beggar

mendier VERB
to beg

mener VERB
to lead ◊ *Cette rue mène directement au parc.* This street leads straight to the park.
♦ **Cela ne vous mènera à rien!** That will get you nowhere!

les **menottes** FEM NOUN
handcuffs

le **mensonge** NOUN
lie

mensuel ADJECTIVE (FEM SING **mensuelle**)
monthly

les **mensurations** FEM NOUN
measurements

le **menteur** NOUN
liar

la **menteuse** NOUN
liar

la **menthe** NOUN
mint

mentionner VERB
to mention

mentir VERB
to lie ◊ *Tu mens!* You're lying!

le **menton** NOUN
chin

menu ADJECTIVE, ADVERB

  see also **menu** NOUN

① slim ◊ *Elle est menue.* She's slim.
② very fine ◊ *Les oignons doivent être coupés menu.* The onions have to be cut up very fine.

le **menu** NOUN

  see also **menu** ADJECTIVE

menu ◊ *le menu du jour* today's menu ◊ *le menu d'aide* the help menu

la **menuiserie** NOUN
woodwork

le **menuisier** NOUN
carpenter

la **menuisière** NOUN
carpenter

le **mépris** NOUN
contempt ◊ *Il nous a traités avec mépris.* He treated us with contempt.

méprisant ADJECTIVE
contemptuous

mépriser VERB
to despise

la **mer** NOUN
① sea ◊ *en mer* at sea
♦ **au bord de la mer** at the seaside
② tide ◊ *La mer est basse.* The tide is out. ◊ *La mer sera haute à sept heures.* It'll be high tide at 7 o'clock.

merci EXCLAMATION
thank you ◊ *Merci de m'avoir raccompagné.* Thank you for taking me home.
♦ **merci beaucoup** thank you very much

le **mercredi** NOUN
① Wednesday ◊ *Aujourd'hui, nous sommes mercredi.* It's Wednesday today.
② on Wednesday ◊ *Nous comptons partir mercredi.* We plan to leave on Wednesday.
♦ **le mercredi** on Wednesdays ◊ *Le*

M

☞

musée est fermé le mercredi. The
museum is shut on Wednesdays.
♦ **tous les mercredis** every Wednesday
♦ **mercredi dernier** last Wednesday
♦ **mercredi prochain** next Wednesday

la **mère** NOUN
mother
♦ **la fête des Mères** Mother's Day

méridional ADJECTIVE (MASC PL
méridionaux)
southern ◊ *la partie méridionale du
Québec* the southern part of Québec

la **meringue** NOUN
meringue

mériter VERB
to deserve
🐾 ♦ **se mériter** to win ◊ *Vous pourriez
vous mériter un voyage pour deux
aux chutes Niagara!* You could win a
trip for two to Niagara Falls!

le **merle** NOUN
blackbird

la **merveille** NOUN
♦ **Cet ordinateur est une vraie
merveille!** This computer's really
wonderful!
♦ **à merveille** wonderfully ◊ *Elle joue
du violon à merveille.* She plays the
violin wonderfully.
♦ **les sept merveilles du monde** the
seven wonders of the world

merveilleux ADJECTIVE (FEM SING
merveilleuse)
extraordinary ◊ *Elle a un don
merveilleux pour l'écriture.* She has
an extraordinary gift for writing.

> *Be careful!* **merveilleux** *does not
> mean* **marvellous**.

mes ADJECTIVE
my ◊ *mes parents* my parents

Mesdames FEM NOUN
ladies ◊ *Bonjour, Mesdames.* Good
morning, ladies.

Mesdemoiselles FEM NOUN
ladies ◊ *Bonjour, Mesdemoiselles.*
Good morning, ladies.

mesquin ADJECTIVE
mean

le **message** NOUN
message

la **messagerie** NOUN
♦ **une messagerie vocale** voice mail
♦ **la messagerie électronique** e-mail
♦ **la messagerie instantanée** instant
messaging

la **messe** NOUN
mass ◊ *aller à la messe* to go to mass

Messieurs MASC NOUN
gentlemen ◊ *Que puis-je faire pour
vous, Messieurs?* What can I do for
you, gentlemen?
♦ **Messieurs,...** Dear Sirs,... (*in letter*)

la **mesure** NOUN
① measurement ◊ *J'ai pris les
mesures de la fenêtre.* I took the
measurements of the window.
♦ **sur mesure** tailor-made ◊ *un costume
sur mesure* a tailor-made suit
② measure ◊ *L'école a pris des
mesures pour lutter contre le
vandalisme.* The school has taken
measures to combat vandalism.
♦ **au fur et à mesure** as one goes along
◊ *Quand je cuisine, je préfère faire
la vaisselle au fur et à mesure.* When
I'm cooking, I prefer to wash up as I
go along.
♦ **être en mesure de faire quelque
chose** to be in a position to do
something ◊ *Nous ne sommes pas
en mesure de vous renseigner.* We
are not in a position to give you any
information.

mesurer VERB
to measure ◊ *Mesurez la longueur
et la largeur.* Measure the length and
the width.
♦ **Il mesure un mètre quatre-vingts.**
He's 1 m 80 tall.

met VERB *see* **mettre**

le **métal** NOUN (PL les **métaux**)
metal

métallique ADJECTIVE
metallic

la **météo** NOUN
weather forecast ◊ *Qu'est-ce que
dit la météo pour cet après-midi?*
What's the weather forecast for this
afternoon?

la **méthode** NOUN
method ◊ *des méthodes
d'enseignement modernes* modern
teaching methods
♦ **une méthode de guitare** a teach-
yourself-guitar book

le **métier** NOUN
job ◊ *Tu aimerais faire quel métier
plus tard?* What job would you like to
do when you're older?

métis ADJECTIVE, NOUN (FEM SING **métisse**)
Métis ◊ *Les communautés métisses
datent de 1690.* Métis communities
date back to 1690.
♦ **un Métis** a Métis (*man*)
♦ **une Métisse** a Métis (*woman*)

le **mètre** NOUN
metre

♦ **un mètre à ruban** a tape measure

le **métro** NOUN
    subway ◊ *prendre le métro* to take
    the subway

mets VERB *see* **mettre**

le **metteur en scène** NOUN (PL les **metteurs en scène**)
    ① producer (*of play*)
    ② director (*of film*)

la **metteure en scène** NOUN (PL les **metteures en scène**)
    ① producer (*of play*)
    ② director (*of film*)

mettre VERB

Present tense:	
je mets	nous mettons
tu mets	vous mettez
il/elle met	ils/elles mettent

Past participle:
mis

    ① to put ◊ *Où est-ce que tu as mis les clés?* Where did you put the keys?
    ② to put on ◊ *Je mets mon manteau et j'arrive.* I'll put on my coat and then I'll be ready. ◊ *Il fait froid. Je vais mettre le chauffage.* It's cold. I'm going to put the heating on.
    ③ to wear ◊ *Elle ne met pas souvent de jupe.* She doesn't often wear a skirt. ◊ *Je n'ai rien à me mettre!* I've got nothing to wear!
    ④ to take ◊ *Combien de temps as-tu mis pour aller à Chapleau?* How long did it take you to get to Chapleau? ◊ *Il met des heures à se préparer.* He takes hours to get ready.
♦ **mettre à pied** to lay off
♦ **mettre quelqu'un en échec** to bodycheck somebody
♦ **mettre en marche** to start ◊ *Comment met-on la machine à laver en marche?* How do you start the washing machine?
♦ **mettre les points sur les i** to spell something out (*make clear*)
♦ **Vous pouvez vous mettre là.** You can sit there.
♦ **se mettre au lit** to get into bed
♦ **se mettre en maillot de bain** to put on one's swimsuit
♦ **se mettre à** to start ◊ *Il s'est mis à la peinture à cinquante ans.* He started painting when he was 50. ◊ *Il est temps de se mettre au travail.* It's time to start work. ◊ *Elle s'est mise à pleurer.* She started crying.

le **meuble** NOUN
    piece of furniture ◊ *Je me suis cogné contre un meuble.* I bumped into a piece of furniture. ◊ *Ce*

magasin vend de beaux meubles. This store sells nice furniture.

le **meublé** NOUN
    furnished apartment

meubler VERB
    to furnish

le **meurtre** NOUN
    murder

le **meurtrier** NOUN
    murderer

la **meurtrière** NOUN
    murderess

le **mi** NOUN
    ① E ◊ *mi bémol* E flat
    ② mi ◊ *do, ré, mi...* do, re, mi...

mi- PREFIX
    ① half- ◊ *mi-clos* half-shut
    ② mid- ◊ *à la mi-janvier* in mid-January

miauler VERB
    to meow

mi-chemin
♦ **à mi-chemin** ADVERB halfway

le **micro** NOUN
    microphone

le **microbe** NOUN
    germ

le **micro-ondes** NOUN
    microwave oven

le **microscope** NOUN
    microscope

le **midi** NOUN
    ① noon ◊ *à midi* at noon
♦ **midi et demi** 12:30
    ② lunchtime ◊ *On a bien mangé à midi.* We had a good meal at lunchtime.

la **mie** NOUN
    breadcrumbs

le **miel** NOUN
    honey

mien PRONOUN
♦ **le mien** mine ◊ *Ce vélo-là, c'est le mien.* That bike is mine.

mienne PRONOUN
♦ **la mienne** mine ◊ *Cette valise-là, c'est la mienne.* That suitcase is mine.

miennes PRONOUN
♦ **les miennes** mine ◊ *Heureusement que tu as tes clés : j'ai oublié les miennes.* It's lucky you've got your keys: I forgot mine.

miens PRONOUN
♦ **les miens** mine ◊ *Ces CD-là, ce sont les miens.* Those CDs are mine.

la **miette** NOUN

M

☞

crumb (of bread, cake)

mieux ADVERB, ADJECTIVE, NOUN
better ◊ Je la connais mieux que son frère. I know her better than her brother. ◊ Elle va mieux. She's better. ◊ Les cheveux courts lui vont mieux. She looks better with short hair.
♦ **Il vaut mieux que tu appelles ta mère.** You'd better phone your mother.
♦ **le mieux** the best ◊ C'est la région que je connais le mieux. It's the area I know best.
♦ **faire de son mieux** to do one's best ◊ Essaie de faire de ton mieux. Try to do your best.
♦ **de mieux en mieux** better and better
♦ **au mieux** at best

mignon ADJECTIVE (FEM SING **mignonne**)
cute ◊ Qu'est-ce qu'il est mignon! Isn't he cute!

la **migraine** NOUN
migraine ◊ J'ai la migraine. I have a migraine.

mijoter VERB
to simmer

le **milieu** NOUN (PL les **milieux**)
[1] middle
♦ **au milieu de** in the middle of ◊ Place le vase au milieu de la table. Put the vase in the middle of the table.
♦ **au beau milieu de** in the middle of ◊ Quelqu'un a sonné à la porte au beau milieu de la nuit. Somebody rang the doorbell in the middle of the night.
[2] background ◊ le milieu familial the family background ◊ Il vient d'un milieu modeste. He comes from a modest background.
[3] environment ◊ le milieu marin the marine environment

militaire ADJECTIVE

see also **militaire** NOUN

military ◊ faire son service militaire to do one's military service

le/la **militaire** NOUN

see also **militaire** ADJECTIVE

serviceman
servicewoman
♦ **Son père est militaire.** Her father is in the armed forces.
♦ **un militaire de carrière** a professional soldier

mille NUMBER
a thousand ◊ mille dollars a thousand dollars ◊ deux mille personnes two thousand people

le **millefeuille** NOUN

ⓘ A **millefeuille** is a rectangular dessert consisting of several layers of flaky puff pastry with a mixture of fruit jelly and cream between them.

le **millénaire** NOUN
millennium ◊ le troisième millénaire the third millennium

le **millénium** NOUN
millennium

le **milliard** NOUN
billion ◊ cinq milliards de dollars five billion dollars

le/la **milliardaire** NOUN
billionaire

le **millier** NOUN
thousand ◊ des milliers de personnes thousands of people
♦ **par milliers** by the thousand

le **milligramme** NOUN
milligram

le **millimètre** NOUN
millimetre

le **million** NOUN
million ◊ deux millions de personnes two million people

le/la **millionnaire** NOUN
millionaire

le/la **mime** NOUN
mime artist

mimer VERB
to mimic

mince ADJECTIVE
[1] thin ◊ une mince tranche de jambon a thin slice of ham
[2] slim ◊ Il est grand et mince. He's tall and slim.

la **minceur** NOUN
[1] thinness ◊ la minceur des murs the thinness of the walls
[2] slimness (of person)

la **mine** NOUN
[1] expression (facial)
♦ **avoir bonne mine** to look well
♦ **Il a mauvaise mine.** He doesn't look well.
♦ **avoir une mine fatiguée** to look tired
[2] appearance ◊ Il ne faut pas juger les gens d'après leur mine. You shouldn't judge people by their appearance.
[3] lead (of pencil)
[4] mine ◊ une mine de charbon a coal mine
♦ **faire mine de faire quelque chose** to pretend to do something ◊ Elle a fait mine de le croire. She pretended to believe him.

♦ **mine de rien** somehow or other
◊ *Elle a réussi mine de rien à y entrer.*
Somehow or other she got in.

minéral ADJECTIVE (MASC PL **minéraux**)
mineral ◊ *l'eau minérale* mineral
water

mineur ADJECTIVE

| see also **mineur** NOUN |

minor

le **mineur** NOUN

| see also **mineur** ADJECTIVE |

① minor (*underage boy*)
♦ **les mineurs** minors ◊ *Il est illégal de
vendre des cigarettes aux mineurs.*
It's illegal to sell cigarettes to minors.
② miner ◊ *Mon grand-père était
mineur.* My grandfather was a miner.

la **mineure** NOUN
minor (*underage girl*)

la **minijupe** NOUN
miniskirt

minimal ADJECTIVE (MASC PL **minimaux**)
minimum

le **minimum** NOUN
minimum ◊ *Elle en fait le minimum.*
She does the absolute minimum.
♦ **au minimum** at the very least

le **ministère** NOUN
ministry ◊ *le ministère de
l'Environnement* the Ministry of the
Environment

le/la **ministre** NOUN
minister ◊ *la ministre de la Santé* the
Minister of Health

la **minorité** NOUN
minority

le **minuit** NOUN
midnight ◊ *à minuit et quart* at a
quarter past midnight

minuscule ADJECTIVE

| see also **minuscule** NOUN |

tiny

la **minuscule** NOUN

| see also **minuscule** ADJECTIVE |

lower-case letter

la **minute** NOUN
minute
♦ **à la minute** just this minute ◊ *Je
viens de l'appeler à la minute.* I just
called him this minute.

minutieux ADJECTIVE (FEM SING
minutieuse)
meticulous
♦ **C'est un travail minutieux.** It's a fiddly
job.

le **miracle** NOUN

miracle

le **miroir** NOUN
mirror

mis VERB *see* **mettre**

mis ADJECTIVE
♦ **bien mis** well-dressed ◊ *Elle est
toujours bien mise.* She's always well-
dressed.

la **mise** NOUN
♦ **être de mise** to be appropriate ◊ *Ces
paroles blessantes ne sont pas de
mise.* These hurtful remarks are not
appropriate.
♦ **une mise à jour** an update
♦ **la mise à pied** layoff
♦ **la mise au jeu** face-off (*hockey*)
♦ **la mise en page** layout (*document*)

miser VERB (*informal*)
to count on ◊ *On ne peut pas miser
là-dessus.* We can't count on it.

misérable ADJECTIVE
① destitute ◊ *une famille misérable* a
destitute family
♦ **d'aspect misérable** shabby-looking
② pitiful ◊ *des conditions de vie
misérable* pitiful living conditions

la **misère** NOUN
extreme poverty
♦ **un salaire de misère** starvation wages

le/la **missionnaire** NOUN
missionary

🌸 la **mitaine** NOUN
mitten

🌸 ♦ **la mitaine à four** oven mitt

la **mi-temps** NOUN
① half (*of game*) ◊ *la première mi-
temps* the first half ◊ *la deuxième
mi-temps* the second half
② half-time ◊ *Je lui parlerai à la mi-
temps.* I'll speak to her at half-time.
♦ **travailler à mi-temps** to work part-
time

miteux ADJECTIVE (FEM SING **miteuse**)
① shabby ◊ *un imperméable miteux*
a shabby raincoat
② pathetic

mixte ADJECTIVE
♦ **un mariage mixte** a mixed marriage
♦ **une peau mixte** combination skin

Mlle ABBREVIATION (PL **Mlles**) (=
Mademoiselle)
Miss ◊ *Mlle Renoir* Miss Renoir

> ⓘ **Mlle** is rarely used for single
> women any more, except in reference
> to a girl. It is better to use **Mme**, the
> French equivalent of **Ms**, in person or
> in a letter.

Mme ABBREVIATION (PL **Mmes**) (= *Madame*)
Mrs ◊ *Mme Leroy* Mrs Leroy

le **mobile** NOUN
motive ◊ *Quel était le mobile du crime?* What was the motive for the crime?

le **mobilier** NOUN
furniture

le **mocassin** NOUN
moccasin

moche ADJECTIVE (*informal*)
awful ◊ *Cette couleur est vraiment moche.* That colour is really awful.
♦ **Il a la grippe. C'est moche pour lui.** He's got the flu. That's a drag for him.

la **mode** NOUN

| see also **le mode** |

fashion ◊ *être à la mode* to be fashionable

le **mode** NOUN

| see also **la mode** |

♦ **le mode d'emploi** directions for use
♦ **le mode de vie** the way of life

le **modèle** NOUN
① model ◊ *Le nouveau modèle sort en septembre.* The new model is coming out in September.
② style (*of clothes*) ◊ *Est-ce que vous avez le même modèle en plus grand?* Have you got the same style in a bigger size?

modéré ADJECTIVE
moderate

moderne ADJECTIVE
modern

moderniser VERB
to modernize

modeste ADJECTIVE
modest ◊ *Ne sois pas si modeste!* Don't be so modest!

la **modestie** NOUN
modesty

moelleux ADJECTIVE (FEM SING **moelleuse**)
soft ◊ *un coussin moelleux* a soft cushion

les **mœurs** FEM NOUN
social attitudes
♦ **l'évolution des mœurs** changing attitudes

moi PRONOUN
me ◊ *Coucou, c'est moi!* Hello, it's me!
♦ **Moi, je pense que tu as tort.** I personally think you're wrong.
♦ **à moi** mine ◊ *Ce livre n'est pas à moi.* This book isn't mine. ◊ *un ami à moi* a friend of mine

moi-même PRONOUN
myself ◊ *J'ai tricoté ce chandail moi-même.* I knitted this sweater myself.

moindre ADJECTIVE
♦ **le moindre** the slightest ◊ *Il ne fait pas le moindre effort.* He doesn't make the slightest effort. ◊ *Je n'en ai pas la moindre idée.* I haven't the slightest idea.

le **moine** NOUN
monk

le **moineau** NOUN (PL les **moineaux**)
sparrow

moins ADVERB, PREPOSITION
① less ◊ *Ça coûte moins de deux cents dollars.* It costs less than 200 dollars.
② fewer ◊ *Il y a moins de gens aujourd'hui.* There are fewer people today.
♦ **Il est cinq heures moins dix.** It's 10 to 5.
③ minus ◊ *quatre moins trois* 4 minus 3 ◊ *Il a fait moins cinq la nuit dernière.* It was minus 5 last night.
♦ **le moins** the least ◊ *C'est le modèle le moins cher.* It's the least expensive model. ◊ *Ce sont les plages qui sont les moins polluées.* These are the least polluted beaches. ◊ *C'est l'album que j'aime le moins.* This is the album I like least.
♦ **de moins en moins** less and less ◊ *Elle vient nous voir de moins en moins.* She comes to see us less and less often.
♦ **Tu as trois ans de moins que moi.** You're three years younger than me.
♦ **au moins** at least ◊ *Ne te plains pas : au moins il ne pleut pas!* Don't complain: at least it's not raining!
♦ **à moins que** unless

à moins que is followed by a verb in the subjunctive.

◊ *Je te retrouverai à dix heures à moins que le train n'ait du retard.* I'll meet you at 10 o'clock unless the train is late.

le **mois** NOUN
month

le **moisi** NOUN
mould ◊ *Il y a du moisi sur le fromage.* There is mould on the cheese.
♦ **Ça sent le moisi.** It smells musty.

moisir VERB
to go mouldy ◊ *Le pain a moisi.* The bread has gone mouldy.

la **moisson** NOUN
harvest

moite ADJECTIVE
   sweaty ◊ *J'ai toujours les mains moites.* My hands are always sweaty.

la **moitié** NOUN
   half ◊ *Il a mangé la moitié du gâteau à lui seul.* He ate half the cake all by himself.
   ♦ **la moitié du temps** half the time
   ♦ **à la moitié de** halfway through ◊ *Elle est partie à la moitié du film.* She left halfway through the movie.
   ♦ **à moitié** half ◊ *Ton verre est encore à moitié plein.* Your glass is still half-full. ◊ *Ce manteau était à moitié prix.* This coat was half-price.
   ♦ **partager moitié moitié** to split fifty-fifty ◊ *On partage moitié moitié, d'accord?* We'll split it fifty-fifty, OK?

la **molaire** NOUN
   back tooth

molle ADJECTIVE
   lethargic ◊ *Je la trouve un peu molle.* I find her a bit lethargic. *see* **mou**

le **mollet** NOUN

   | *see also* **mollet** ADJECTIVE |

   calf (*of leg*)

mollet ADJECTIVE

   | *see also* **mollet** NOUN |

   ♦ **un œuf mollet** a soft-boiled egg

le **moment** NOUN
   moment
   ♦ **en ce moment** at the moment ◊ *Nous avons beaucoup de travail en ce moment.* We have a lot of work at the moment.
   ♦ **pour le moment** for the moment ◊ *Nous restons ici pour le moment.* We're staying here for the moment.
   ♦ **au moment où** just as ◊ *Il est arrivé au moment où j'allais partir.* He turned up just as I was leaving.
   ♦ **à ce moment-là (1)** at that point ◊ *À ce moment-là, on a vu arriver la police.* At that point, we saw the police coming.
   ♦ **à ce moment-là (2)** in that case ◊ *À ce moment-là, je devrai partir plus tôt.* In that case I'll have to leave earlier.
   ♦ **à tout moment (1)** at any moment ◊ *Elle peut arriver à tout moment.* She could arrive at any moment.
   ♦ **à tout moment (2)** constantly ◊ *Il nous dérange à tout moment pour des riens.* He's constantly bothering us about nothing.
   ♦ **sur le moment** at the time ◊ *Sur le moment je n'ai rien dit.* At the time I didn't say anything.
   ♦ **par moments** at times ◊ *Elle se sent seule par moments.* She feels lonely at times.

momentané ADJECTIVE
   momentary

la **momie** NOUN
   mummy (*Egyptian*)

mon ADJECTIVE (FEM SING **ma**, PL **mes**)
   my ◊ *mon frère* my brother ◊ *mon ami* my friend

la **monarchie** NOUN
   monarchy

le **monastère** NOUN
   monastery

le **monde** NOUN
   ① world ◊ *faire le tour du monde* to go around the world
   ② people ◊ *Il y avait beaucoup de monde au concert.* There were a lot of people at the concert. ◊ *peu de monde* not many people
   ♦ **Il y a du monde.** There are a lot of people.

mondial ADJECTIVE (MASC PL **mondiaux**)
   ① world ◊ *la population mondiale* the world population
   ② world-wide ◊ *une crise mondiale* a world-wide crisis

le **moniteur** NOUN
   ① instructor ◊ *un moniteur de voile* a sailing instructor
   ② monitor ◊ *le moniteur de mon ordinateur* my computer monitor

la **monitrice** NOUN
   instructor ◊ *une monitrice de ski* a ski instructor

la **monnaie** NOUN
   ♦ **une pièce de monnaie** a coin
   ♦ **avoir de la monnaie** to have change ◊ *Est-ce que tu as de la monnaie?* Do you have any change? ◊ *Est-ce que vous avez la monnaie de dix dollars?* Do you have change for 10 dollars?
   ♦ **rendre la monnaie à quelqu'un** to give somebody their change

monopoliser VERB
   to monopolize ◊ *monopoliser la conversation* to monopolize the conversation ◊ *Tu monopolises le téléphone!* You're monopolizing the phone!

monotone ADJECTIVE
   monotonous

Monsieur MASC NOUN (PL **Messieurs**)
   ① Mr ◊ *Monsieur Dupont* Mr Dupont
   ② man ◊ *Il y a un monsieur qui veut te voir.* There's a man to see you.
   ③ Sir ◊ *Monsieur,...* Dear Sir,... (*in letter*) ◊ *Monsieur! Vous avez oublié votre parapluie!* Sir! You forgot your umbrella!

le **monstre** NOUN

M

☞

see also **monstre** ADJECTIVE

monster

monstre ADJECTIVE

see also **monstre** NOUN

♦ **Nous avons un travail monstre.** We have a terrific amount of work.

le **mont** NOUN
mount
♦ **le mont Logan** Mount Logan

la **montagne** NOUN
mountain ◊ *de hautes montagnes* high mountains ◊ *Nous passons nos vacances à la montagne.* We spend our holidays in the mountains.
♦ **les montagnes russes** roller coaster
♦ **se faire une montagne de quelque chose** to blow something out of proportion ◊ *Ils s'en font une montagne.* They're blowing it out of proportion.
♦ **Tu te fais une montagne d'un petit incident de rien.** You're making a mountain out of a molehill.

montagneux ADJECTIVE (FEM SING **montagneuse**)
mountainous ◊ *une région montagneuse* a mountainous area

montant ADJECTIVE
[1] rising ◊ *la marée montante* the rising tide ◊ *une étoile montante* a rising star
[2] high ◊ *un manteau à col montant* a high-necked coat

monter VERB
[1] to go up ◊ *Elle a du mal à monter les escaliers.* She has difficulty going up stairs. ◊ *Les prix ont encore monté.* Prices have gone up again.
[2] to assemble ◊ *Est-ce que ces étagères sont difficiles à monter?* Are these shelves difficult to assemble?
♦ **monter dans** to board ◊ *Il est temps de monter dans l'avion.* It's time to board the plane.
♦ **monter sur** to climb on ◊ *Tu vas devoir monter sur une chaise pour changer l'ampoule.* You'll have to climb on a chair to change the light bulb.
♦ **monter à cheval** to ride
♦ **se monter à** to amount to (*total*) ◊ *Ses achats se montaient à quinze dollars.* His purchases amounted to 15 dollars.
♦ **se monter la tête** to get worked up ◊ *Elle s'est montée la tête pour rien.* She got worked up over nothing.

la **montre** NOUN
watch

montrer VERB

to show ◊ *Est-ce que vous pouvez me montrer le musée sur le plan?* Can you show me the museum on the map?

la **monture** NOUN
frames (*of glasses*)

le **monument** NOUN
monument

se **moquer** VERB
♦ **se moquer de (1)** to make fun of ◊ *Ils se sont moqués de mes chaussures jaunes.* They made fun of my yellow shoes.
♦ **se moquer de (2)** (*informal*) not to care about ◊ *Il se moque complètement de la mode.* He couldn't care less about fashion.

la **moquette** NOUN
broadloom

moqueur ADJECTIVE (FEM SING **moqueuse**)
mocking

moral ADJECTIVE (MASC PL **moraux**)

see also **moral** NOUN

moral ◊ *une obligation morale* a moral obligation

le **moral** NOUN

see also **moral** ADJECTIVE

♦ **Elle a le moral.** She's in good spirits.
♦ **J'ai le moral à zéro.** I'm feeling really down.

la **morale** NOUN
[1] moral ◊ *La morale de cette histoire est...* The moral of the story is...
♦ **faire la morale à quelqu'un** to lecture somebody
[2] morality ◊ *la morale traditionelle* traditional morality

le **morceau** NOUN (PL les **morceaux**)
piece ◊ *un morceau de pain* a piece of bread

mordiller VERB
to nibble ◊ *Ne mordille pas ton crayon.* Don't nibble on your pencil.

mordre VERB
to bite

mordu ADJECTIVE
♦ **Il est mordu de jazz.** (*informal*) He's crazy about jazz.

morne ADJECTIVE
[1] drab ◊ *un décor morne* a drab décor
[2] gloomy (*person, weather*) ◊ *Pourquoi as-tu l'air tellement morne?* Why are you looking so gloomy? ◊ *un temps morne* gloomy weather

le **morse** NOUN
walrus

la **morsure** NOUN
　bite

la **mort** NOUN

> see also **mort** ADJECTIVE

　death

mort ADJECTIVE

> see also **mort** NOUN

　dead ◊ *Nous avons trouvé un oiseau mort.* We found a dead bird. ◊ *Anne Hébert, écrivaine canadienne, est morte en 2000.* Canadian writer Anne Hébert died in 2000.
♦ **Il était mort de peur.** He was scared to death.
♦ **Je suis morte de fatigue.** I'm dead tired.

mortel ADJECTIVE (FEM SING **mortelle**)
　① deadly ◊ *un poison mortel* a deadly poison ◊ *Ces réunions de famille sont mortelles!* (*informal*) These family gatherings are deadly!
　② fatal ◊ *une chute mortelle* a fatal fall

la **morue** NOUN
　cod

la **mosquée** NOUN
　mosque

le **mot** NOUN
　① word ◊ *mot à mot* word for word
♦ **des mots croisés** a crossword
♦ **le mot de passe** the password
　② note ◊ *Je vais lui écrire un mot pour lui dire qu'on arrive.* I'll write her a note to say we're coming.

le **motard** NOUN
　motorcyclist

la **motarde** NOUN
　motorcyclist

le **mot-clé** NOUN
　keyword ◊ *Entrez le mot-clé dans le moteur de recherche.* Enter the keyword in the search engine.

le **moteur** NOUN
　engine
♦ **un bateau à moteur** a motor boat
♦ **un moteur de recherche** a search engine

le **motif** NOUN
　pattern ◊ *des rideaux avec un motif d'oiseaux* curtains with a bird pattern
♦ **sans motif** for no reason ◊ *Il s'est fâché sans motif.* He got angry for no reason.

motivé ADJECTIVE
　motivated

la **moto** NOUN
　motorbike
♦ **la moto tout-terrain** trail bike

le/la **motocycliste** NOUN
　motorcyclist

✴ la **motoneige** NOUN
　snowmobile

✴ le/la **motoneigiste** NOUN
　snowmobiler

mou ADJECTIVE (FEM SING **molle**)
　① soft ◊ *Mon matelas est trop mou.* My mattress is too soft.
　② lethargic ◊ *Je le trouve un peu mou.* I find him a bit lethargic.
　③ limp ◊ *devenir mou* to go limp

la **mouche** NOUN
　fly (*insect*)
✴ ♦ **la mouche noire** black fly
♦ **prendre la mouche** to get bent out of shape

se **moucher** VERB
　to blow one's nose

le **mouchoir** NOUN
　handkerchief
♦ **un mouchoir en papier** a tissue

moudre VERB
　to grind

la **moue** NOUN
　pout
♦ **faire la moue** to pout

la **mouette** NOUN
　seagull

✴ la **moufette** NOUN
　skunk

mouillé ADJECTIVE
　wet

mouiller VERB
　to get wet ◊ *J'ai mouillé les manches de mon chandail.* I got the sleeves of my sweater wet.
♦ **se mouiller** to get wet ◊ *Attention, tu vas te mouiller!* Careful, you'll get wet!

moulant ADJECTIVE
　slinky ◊ *une robe moulante* a slinky dress

la **moule** NOUN

> see also **le moule**

　mussel

le **moule** NOUN

> see also **la moule**

♦ **un moule à gâteaux** a cake tin

le **moulin** NOUN
　mill

moulu VERB *see* **moudre**

mourir VERB
　to die
♦ **mourir de faim** to starve ◊ *Des centaines de personnes sont mortes*

M

☞

de faim. Hundreds of people starved to death.
♦ **Je meurs de faim!** I'm starving!
♦ **mourir de froid** to die of exposure
♦ **Je meurs de froid!** I'm freezing!
♦ **mourir d'envie de faire quelque chose** to be dying to do something ◊ *Je meurs d'envie d'aller me baigner.* I'm dying to go for a swim.

la **mousse** NOUN
    ① moss ◊ *un rocher recouvert de mousse* a rock covered with moss
    ② froth (*on soft drink*)
    ③ lather (*of soap, shampoo*)
    ④ mousse ◊ *une mousse au chocolat* a chocolate mousse ◊ *une mousse au saumon* a salmon mousse
    ♦ **la mousse à raser** shaving foam

la **moustache** NOUN
    moustache
    ♦ **les moustaches** whiskers

le/la **moustiquaire** NOUN
    ① screen (*on window*)
    ② mosquito net

> In Canada, **moustiquaire** is often masculine. It is usually feminine in other French-speaking countries.

le **moustique** NOUN
    mosquito

la **moutarde** NOUN
    mustard

le **mouton** NOUN
    ① sheep ◊ *une peau de mouton* a sheepskin
    ② mutton ◊ *un gigot de mouton* a leg of mutton

le **mouvement** NOUN
    movement

mouvementé ADJECTIVE
    eventful ◊ *une époque mouvementée de l'histoire du Canada* an eventful period in Canada's history

moyen ADJECTIVE (FEM SING **moyenne**)

    | see also **moyen** NOUN |

    ① average ◊ *Je suis plutôt moyenne en langues.* I'm just average at languages.
    ② medium ◊ *Elle est de taille moyenne.* She's of medium height.
    ♦ **le Moyen Âge** the Middle Ages
    ♦ **le Moyen Orient** the Middle East

le **moyen** NOUN

    | see also **moyen** ADJECTIVE |

    way ◊ *Quel est le meilleur moyen de le convaincre?* What's the best way to convince him?
    ♦ **Je n'en ai pas les moyens.** I can't afford it.

♦ **Ils n'ont pas les moyens de s'acheter une voiture.** They can't afford to buy a car.
♦ **un moyen de transport** a means of transport
♦ **par tous les moyens** by every possible means

la **moyenne** NOUN
    ♦ **avoir la moyenne** to get a passing grade ◊ *J'espère avoir la moyenne en maths.* I hope to get a passing grade in math.
    ♦ **en moyenne** on average
    ♦ **la moyenne d'âge** the average age

muet ADJECTIVE (FEM SING **muette**)
    mute
    ♦ **un film muet** a silent film

multiculturel ADJECTIVE (FEM SING **multiculturelle**)
    multicultural

multiple ADJECTIVE
    numerous ◊ *en de multiples occasions* on numerous occasions

multiplier VERB
    to multiply

municipal ADJECTIVE (MASC PL **municipaux**)
    ♦ **une élection municipale** a municipal election
    ♦ **les règlements municipaux** city by-laws
    ♦ **la bibliothèque municipale** the public library

la **municipalité** NOUN
    town council

munir VERB
    ♦ **munir quelqu'un de** to equip someone with
    ♦ **se munir de** to equip oneself with

les **munitions** FEM NOUN
    ammunition SING

le **mur** NOUN
    wall

mûr ADJECTIVE
    ① ripe (*fruit*)
    ② mature (*person*)

la **mûre** NOUN
    blackberry

mûrir VERB
    ① to ripen ◊ *Les fraises ont mis du temps à mûrir.* The strawberries took a while to ripen.
    ② to make mature ◊ *Cette expérience l'a beaucoup mûrie.* That experience has made her much more mature.

murmurer VERB
    to whisper ◊ *Il m'a murmuré à l'oreille qu'il allait partir.* He whispered in my ear that he was

going to go.

la **muscade** NOUN
nutmeg

le **muscle** NOUN
muscle

musclé ADJECTIVE
muscular

le **museau** NOUN (PL les **museaux**)
muzzle

le **musée** NOUN
museum

musical ADJECTIVE (MASC PL **musicaux**)
musical
♦ **avoir l'oreille musicale** to be musical

le **music-hall** NOUN (PL **les music-halls**)
variety ◊ *une chanteuse de music-hall* a variety singer

le **musicien** NOUN
musician ◊ *Il est musicien de jazz.* He's a jazz musician.

la **musicienne** NOUN
musician ◊ *Elle est musicienne de rue.* She's a street musician.

la **musique** NOUN
music

musulman ADJECTIVE, NOUN
Muslim
♦ **un musulman** a Muslim (*man*)
♦ **une musulmane** a Muslim (*woman*)

la **mutation** NOUN
transfer (*job*) ◊ *Il a demandé sa mutation à Winnipeg.* He asked for a transfer to Winnipeg.

✸ la **mye** NOUN
clam ◊ *une chaudrée de myes* clam chowder

myope ADJECTIVE
short-sighted

le **mystère** NOUN
mystery

mystérieux ADJECTIVE (FEM SING **mystérieuse**)
mysterious

le **mythe** NOUN
myth

M

N

n' PRONOUN *see* ne

la **nage** NOUN
- ♦ **traverser une rivière à la nage** to swim across a river
- ♦ **être en nage** to be sweating profusely

la **nageoire** NOUN
fin

nager VERB
to swim

le **nageur** NOUN
swimmer

la **nageuse** NOUN
swimmer

naïf ADJECTIVE (FEM SING **naïve**)
naïve

le **nain** NOUN
dwarf

la **naine** NOUN
dwarf

la **naissance** NOUN
birth
- ♦ **votre date de naissance** your date of birth
- ♦ **de naissance** from birth ◊ *Il est sourd de naissance.* He was born deaf.

naître VERB
to be born
- ♦ **Il est né en 1982.** He was born in 1982.

la **nappe** NOUN
tablecloth

le **napperon** NOUN
placemat

la **narine** NOUN
nostril

natal ADJECTIVE (MASC PL **natals**)
native ◊ *mon pays natal* my native country

la **natation** NOUN
swimming ◊ *La natation est mon sport favori.* Swimming is my favourite sport.
- ♦ **faire de la natation** to go swimming

la **nation** NOUN
nation ◊ *les Nations unies* the United Nations

national ADJECTIVE (MASC PL **nationaux**)
national
- ♦ **la fête nationale espagnole** the national day of Spain

la **nationalité** NOUN
nationality

la **nature** NOUN

see also **nature** ADJECTIVE

nature

nature ADJECTIVE (PL **nature**)

see also **nature** NOUN

plain ◊ *un yogourt nature* a plain yogurt ◊ *des framboises nature* plain strawberries

naturel ADJECTIVE (FEM SING **naturelle**)
natural

naturellement ADVERB
of course ◊ *« Vous viendrez à notre fête? » « Naturellement! »* "Are you coming to our party?" "Of course!" ◊ *Naturellement, elle est encore en retard.* Of course, she's late again.

le **naufrage** NOUN
shipwreck

la **nausée** NOUN
nausea
- ♦ **avoir la nausée** to feel nauseous
- ♦ **Cela m'a donné la nausée.** It made me nauseous.

nautique ADJECTIVE
- ♦ **la sécurité nautique** water safety
- ♦ **les sports nautiques** water sports
- ♦ **le ski nautique** water-skiing
- ♦ **une carte nautique** a nautical chart

le **navet** NOUN
turnip

la **navette** NOUN
shuttle ◊ *la navette entre l'hôtel et l'aéroport* the shuttle between the hotel and the airport
- ♦ **faire la navette** to commute ◊ *Je fais la navette entre Guelph et Burlington.* I commute between Guelph and Burlington.

le **navetteur** NOUN
commuter

la **navetteuse** NOUN
commuter

le **navigateur** NOUN
browser (*on computer*) ◊ *un navigateur Web* Web browser

la **navigation** NOUN
[1] boat traffic ◊ *Il y a beaucoup de navigation sur les Grands Lacs.* There is considerable boat traffic on the Great Lakes.
- ♦ **La navigation est interdite ici.** Boating is not allowed here.
[2] navigation ◊ *Les récifs rendent*

la navigation difficile. Reefs make navigation difficult.

♦ **un système de navigation par écluses** a canal and locks system

naviguer VERB
1 to sail
2 to surf (*Internet*) ◊ *naviguer sur Internet* to surf the Net

le **navire** NOUN
ship

ne ADVERB

> *ne is combined with words such as **pas**, **personne**, **plus**, and **jamais** to form negative phrases.*

◊ *Je ne peux pas venir.* I can't come. ◊ *Ils ne regardent jamais la télé.* They never watch TV. ◊ *Je ne connais personne ici.* I don't know anyone here.

> *ne changes to **n'** before a vowel and most words beginning with "h".*

◊ *Je n'ai pas d'argent.* I don't have any money. ◊ *Il n'habite plus à Labrador City.* He doesn't live in Labrador City any more.

> *ne is sometimes not translated.*

◊ *C'est plus loin que je ne le croyais.* It's further than I thought.

né VERB *see* **naître**
born ◊ *Elle est née en 1980.* She was born in 1980.

néanmoins ADVERB
nevertheless

nécessaire ADJECTIVE
necessary ◊ *Il est nécessaire de réserver.* It's necessary to make reservations.

négatif ADJECTIVE (FEM SING **négative**)

> *see also* **négatif** NOUN

negative

le **négatif** NOUN

> *see also* **négatif** ADJECTIVE

negative (*of photo*)

négligé ADJECTIVE
scruffy ◊ *une tenue négligée* scruffy clothes

négliger VERB
to neglect ◊ *Ces derniers temps il a négligé son travail.* He's been neglecting his work recently.

négocier VERB
to negotiate

la **neige** NOUN
snow
✹ ♦ **la neige fondante** slush
♦ **un bonhomme de neige** a snowman

neiger VERB
to snow

le **nénuphar** NOUN
water lily

le **néon** NOUN
neon ◊ *une lampe au néon* a neon light ◊ *La cuisine est éclairée au néon.* The kitchen has a neon light.

le **nerf** NOUN
nerve
♦ **taper sur les nerfs de quelqu'un** to get on somebody's nerves ◊ *Il me tape sur les nerfs.* He's getting on my nerves.

nerveux ADJECTIVE (FEM SING **nerveuse**)
nervous

la **nervosité** NOUN
nervousness

n'est-ce pas ADVERB

> *n'est-ce pas is used to check that something is true.*

◊ *Nous sommes le douze aujourd'hui, n'est-ce pas?* It's the 12th today, isn't it? ◊ *Ils sont venus l'an dernier, n'est-ce pas?* They came last year, didn't they? ◊ *Elle aura dix-huit ans en octobre, n'est-ce pas?* She'll be 18 in October, won't she?

net ADJECTIVE, ADVERB (FEM SING **nette**)
1 clear ◊ *L'image n'est pas nette.* The picture isn't very clear.
2 net ◊ *Poids net : 500 g.* Net weight: 500 g.
3 flatly ◊ *Il a refusé net de nous aider.* He flatly refused to help us.
♦ **s'arrêter net** to stop dead

nettement ADVERB
much ◊ *Ce magasin est nettement plus cher.* This store is much more expensive.

le **nettoyage** NOUN
cleaning
♦ **le nettoyage à sec** dry cleaning

nettoyer VERB
to clean

✹ le **nettoyeur** NOUN
dry-cleaner ◊ *Je vais porter ce manteau chez le nettoyeur.* I'm going to take this coat to the dry-cleaner's.

neuf NUMBER

> *see also* **neuf** ADJECTIVE

nine ◊ *Elle a neuf ans.* She's nine. ◊ *Il est neuf heures du matin.* It's nine in the morning.
♦ **le neuf février** the ninth of February

neuf ADJECTIVE (FEM SING **neuve**)

> *see also* **neuf** NUMBER

N

☞

new ◊ *des chaussures neuves* new shoes

neutre ADJECTIVE
neutral

neuve ADJECTIVE *see* **neuf**

neuvième ADJECTIVE
ninth ◊ *au neuvième étage* on the ninth floor

le **neveu** NOUN (PL les **neveux**)
nephew

le **nez** NOUN
nose
♦ **se trouver nez à nez avec quelqu'un** to come face to face with somebody
♦ **C'était juste sous mon nez.** It was right under my nose.
♦ **mettre le nez dehors** to go outside
♦ **ne pas voir plus loin que le bout de son nez** to lack foresight

ni CONJUNCTION
♦ **ni...ni...** neither...nor... ◊ *Je n'aime ni les lentilles ni les épinards.* I like neither lentils nor spinach. ◊ *Elles ne sont venues ni l'une ni l'autre.* Neither of them came.

❋ **niaiser** VERB (*informal*)
① to kid (*someone*) ◊ *Arrête de nous niaiser, avec tes histoires incroyables.* Stop kidding us with your unbelievable stories.
② to fool around (*waste time*) ◊ *Au bout du compte, on a niaisé tout l'après-midi.* We ended up just fooling around the whole afternoon.

❋ la **niaiserie** NOUN (*informal*)
nonsense ◊ *Elle t'a raconté des niaiseries.* What she told you was nonsense. ◊ *Tu dis des niaiseries!* You're talking nonsense!
♦ **faire des niaiseries** to get into trouble ◊ *Il faut surveiller ce petit garçon, sinon il fait des niaiseries.* This little boy needs to be supervised, otherwise he gets into trouble.

❋ **niaiseux** ADJECTIVE (FEM **niaiseuse**) (*informal*)
stupid ◊ *J'ai trouvé ce film complètement niaiseux.* I thought that movie was utterly stupid. ◊ *Ne sois pas niaiseuse, fais tes devoirs.* Don't be stupid; do your homework.

la **niche** NOUN
kennel

le **nid** NOUN
nest

la **nièce** NOUN
niece

nier VERB
to deny

n'importe ADVERB
♦ **n'importe quel** any ◊ *N'importe quel stylo fera l'affaire.* Any pen will do.
♦ **n'importe qui** anybody ◊ *N'ouvre pas la porte à n'importe qui.* Don't open the door to just anybody.
♦ **n'importe quoi** anything ◊ *Je ferais n'importe quoi pour lui.* I'd do anything for him.
♦ **Tu dis n'importe quoi.** You're talking nonsense.
♦ **n'importe où** anywhere ◊ *On trouve ces fleurs n'importe où.* You can find these flowers anywhere.
♦ **Ne laisse pas tes affaires n'importe où.** Don't leave your things lying everywhere.
♦ **n'importe quand** any time ◊ *Tu peux venir n'importe quand.* You can come any time.
♦ **n'importe comment** any old way ◊ *Ces livres sont rangés n'importe comment.* These books have been put away any old way.

le **NIP** ABBREVIATION (= *le numéro d'identification personnel*)
PIN number

le **niveau** NOUN (PL les **niveaux**)
level ◊ *le niveau de l'eau* the water level ◊ *Ces deux enfants n'ont pas le même niveau.* These two children aren't at the same level.
♦ **le niveau de vie** the standard of living

noble ADJECTIVE
noble

la **noblesse** NOUN
nobility

la **noce** NOUN
wedding
♦ **un repas de noce** a wedding reception
♦ **leurs noces d'or** their golden wedding anniversary

nocif ADJECTIVE (FEM SING **nocive**)
harmful ◊ *une substance nocive* a harmful substance

le **Noël** NOUN
Christmas
♦ **Joyeux Noël!** Merry Christmas!

le **nœud** NOUN
① knot ◊ *Il a fait un nœud à la corde.* He tied a knot in the rope.
② bow ◊ *La petite fille avait un nœud dans les cheveux.* The little girl had a bow in her hair.
♦ **un nœud papillon** a bow tie
❋ ♦ **frapper un nœud** to hit a snag (*problem*)

noir ADJECTIVE
see also **noir** NOUN

① <u>black</u> ◊ *Elle porte une robe noire.* She's wearing a black dress. ◊ *Il est noir.* He's black.
② <u>dark</u> ◊ *Il fait noir dehors.* It's dark outside.

le **noir** NOUN

> | see also **noir** ADJECTIVE |

<u>dark</u> ◊ *J'ai peur du noir.* I'm afraid of the dark.
♦ **le travail au noir** moonlighting

le **Noir** NOUN
<u>black</u> (*man*)
♦ **les Noirs** black people

✷ la **noirceur** NOUN
<u>darkness</u> ◊ *Nous avons perdu notre chemin dans la noirceur.* We lost our way in the darkness.

la **Noire** NOUN
<u>black</u> (*woman*)

la **noisette** NOUN
<u>hazelnut</u>

la **noix** NOUN (PL les **noix**)
<u>walnut</u>
♦ **une noix de coco** a coconut
♦ **les noix de cajou** cashews
♦ **une noix de beurre** a dab of butter

✷ **nolisé** ADJECTIVE
<u>charter</u> ◊ *le vol nolisé* charter flight

le **nom** NOUN
① <u>name</u> ◊ *votre nom* your name
♦ **mon nom de famille** my surname
♦ **son nom de jeune fille** her maiden name
② <u>noun</u> (*in grammar*) ◊ *un nom commun* a common noun ◊ *un nom propre* a proper noun
♦ **le nom d'utilisateur** login ID

le **nombre** NOUN
<u>number</u> ◊ *Treize est un nombre impair.* Thirteen is an odd number. ◊ *un grand nombre d'amis* a large number of friends

nombreux ADJECTIVE (FEM SING **nombreuse**)
① <u>many</u> ◊ *Il a gagné de nombreux matchs.* He's won many games.
② <u>large</u> ◊ *une famille nombreuse* a large family
♦ **être plus nombreux que** to outnumber
♦ **peu nombreux** few ◊ *Nous étions peu nombreux à la réunion.* There were few of us at the meeting.

le **nombril** NOUN
<u>navel</u>

nommer VERB
① <u>to name</u> ◊ *Elle n'a voulu nommer personne.* She didn't want to name anybody.

② <u>to appoint</u> ◊ *Elle a été nommée directrice.* She was appointed director.

non ADVERB
<u>no</u> ◊ *« Tu as vu mon frère ? » « Non. »* "Have you seen my brother?" "No."
♦ **non seulement** not only ◊ *Il est non seulement intelligent, mais aussi très gentil.* Not only is he intelligent, he's also very nice.
♦ **moi non plus** Neither do I. ◊ *« Je n'aime pas les hamburgers. » « Moi non plus. »* "I don't like hamburgers." "Neither do I." ◊ *Elle n'y est pas allée et moi non plus.* She didn't go and neither did I.

non alcoolisé ADJECTIVE
<u>non-alcoholic</u> ◊ *les boissons non alcoolisées* non-alcoholic drinks

le **non-fumeur** NOUN
<u>non-smoker</u> ◊ *Je suis un non-fumeur.* I'm a non-smoker.
♦ **la section non-fumeurs** the non-smoking section

la **non-fumeuse** NOUN
<u>non-smoker</u> ◊ *Ma sœur est une non-fumeuse.* My sister is a non-smoker.

le **nord** NOUN

> | see also **nord** ADJECTIVE |

<u>north</u> ◊ *Ils vivent dans le nord de l'île.* They live in the north of the island.
♦ **vers le nord** northwards
♦ **au nord de Jonquière** north of Jonquière
♦ **l'Amérique du Nord** North America
♦ **le vent du nord** the north wind

nord ADJECTIVE

> | see also **nord** NOUN |

① <u>north</u> ◊ *la face nord de la montagne* the north face of the mountain
♦ **le pôle Nord** the North Pole
② <u>northern</u> ◊ *Nous avons visité la partie nord de la province.* We visited the northern part of the province.

le **nord-est** NOUN
<u>northeast</u> ◊ *les régions du nord-est* northeastern regions

le **nord-ouest** NOUN
<u>northwest</u>
♦ **le Passage du Nord-Ouest** The Northwest Passage

normal ADJECTIVE (MASC PL **normaux**)
① <u>normal</u> ◊ *un bébé normal* a normal baby
② <u>natural</u> ◊ *C'est tout à fait normal.* It's perfectly natural.
♦ **Vous trouvez que c'est normal?** Does

☞

that seem right to you?

normalement ADVERB

normally ◊ *Les aéroports fonctionnent tous normalement.* The airports are all operating normally.

♦ **Normalement, elle doit arriver à huit heures.** She's supposed to arrive at 8 o'clock.

♦ **« Tu es libre en fin de semaine? » « Oui, normalement. »** "Are you free this weekend?" "Yes, I should be."

nos ADJECTIVE

our ◊ *Où sont nos affaires?* Where's our stuff?

le/la **notaire** NOUN

lawyer ◊ *Sa mère est notaire.* His mother's a lawyer.

la **note** NOUN

① note ◊ *J'ai pris des notes pendant la classe.* I took notes in class. ◊ *Il a joué quelques notes au piano.* He played a few notes on the piano.

② mark ◊ *Elle a de bonnes notes en maths.* She gets good marks in math.

noter VERB

to make a note of ◊ *Tu as noté leur adresse?* Did you make a note of their address?

les **notions** FEM NOUN

basics ◊ *Il faut avoir des notions d'anglais.* You have to have some basic English. ◊ *Elle a des notions de traitement de texte.* She knows the basics of word processing.

notoire ADJECTIVE

notorious ◊ *un criminel notoire* a notorious criminal

notre ADJECTIVE (PL **nos**)

our ◊ *Voici notre maison.* Here's our house.

nôtre PRONOUN

♦ **le nôtre** ours ◊ *« À qui est ce chien? » « C'est le nôtre. »* "Whose dog is this?" "It's ours." ◊ *Leur voiture est rouge; la nôtre est bleue.* Their car is red; ours is blue.

nôtres PRONOUN

♦ **les nôtres** ours ◊ *Ces places-là sont les nôtres.* Those seats are ours.

nouer VERB

to tie

les **nouilles** FEM NOUN

noodles

le **nounours** NOUN

teddy bear

nourrir VERB

to feed

la **nourriture** NOUN

food

♦ **la nourriture pour animaux de compagnie** pet food

♦ **une nourriture saine** a healthy diet

nous PRONOUN

① we ◊ *Nous avons deux enfants.* We have two children.

② us ◊ *Viens avec nous.* Come with us.

♦ **nous-mêmes** ourselves

nouveau ADJECTIVE (FEM SING **nouvelle**, MASC PL **nouveaux**)

see also **nouveau** NOUN

new ◊ *Il me faut un nouveau pantalon.* I need some new pants. ◊ *Ils ont une nouvelle voiture.* They've a new car.

> ***nouveau** changes to **nouvel** before a vowel and most words beginning with "h".*

◊ *le nouvel élève dans ma classe* The new boy in my class

♦ **le Nouvel An** New Year's

♦ **le nouvel âge** New Age ◊ *la musique nouvel âge* New Age music

le **nouveau** NOUN (PL les **nouveaux**)

see also **nouveau** ADJECTIVE

new person ◊ *Il y a plusieurs nouveaux dans la classe.* There are several new people in the class.

♦ **de nouveau** again ◊ *Il pleut de nouveau.* It's raining again.

le **Nouveau-Brunswick** NOUN

New Brunswick

le **nouveau-né** NOUN (MASC PL les **nouveau-nés**, FEM SING la **nouveau-née**, FEM PL les **nouveau-nées**)

newborn

la **nouveauté** NOUN

novelty

nouvel ADJECTIVE see **nouveau**

nouvelle ADJECTIVE

see also **nouvelle** NOUN

see **nouveau**

la **nouvelle** NOUN

see also **nouvelle** ADJECTIVE

① news (*single item*) ◊ *Tu connais la nouvelle? Ma grand-mère a gagné à la loto.* Have you heard the news? My grandmother won the lottery. ◊ *C'est une bonne nouvelle.* That's good news.

② short story ◊ *une nouvelle de Janet Lunn* a short story by Janet Lunn

♦ **les nouvelles** the news ◊ *J'ai écouté les nouvelles à la radio.* I listened to the news on the radio.

♦ **avoir des nouvelles de quelqu'un** to hear from somebody ◊ *Je n'ai pas eu de nouvelles de lui.* I haven't heard from him.

la **Nouvelle-Écosse** NOUN
    Nova Scotia

novembre MASC NOUN
    November
♦ **en novembre** in November

le **noyau** NOUN (PL les **noyaux**)
    stone (*of fruit*) ◊ *un noyau d'abricot* an apricot stone

se **noyer** VERB
    to drown ◊ *Il s'est noyé dans la rivière.* He drowned in the river.

nu ADJECTIVE
    ⬚1 naked ◊ *Ils se sont baignés nus.* They went swimming naked. ◊ *tout nus* stark naked
    ⬚2 bare ◊ *Elle avait les bras nus.* Her arms were bare. ◊ *Les murs étaient nus.* The walls were bare.

le **nuage** NOUN
    cloud
♦ **être dans les nuages** to daydream

nuageux ADJECTIVE (FEM SING **nuageuse**)
    cloudy

nucléaire ADJECTIVE
    nuclear ◊ *l'énergie nucléaire* nuclear power ◊ *la famille nucléaire* the nuclear family

le/la **nudiste** NOUN
    nudist

la **nuit** NOUN
    ⬚1 night ◊ *Ils ont fait du bruit toute la nuit.* They were noisy all night.
    ⬚2 at night ◊ *se promener la nuit* to go for a walk at night
♦ **Il fait nuit.** It's dark out.
♦ **cette nuit** tonight ◊ *Il va rentrer cette nuit.* He'll be back tonight.
♦ **Bonne nuit!** Good night!
♦ **de nuit (1)** by night ◊ *voyager de nuit* to travel by night
♦ **de nuit (2)** nights ◊ *Il travaille de nuit.* He works nights.
♦ **une nuit blanche** a sleepless night

◊ *J'ai encore passé une nuit blanche.* I had yet another sleepless night.

nul ADJECTIVE (FEM SING **nulle**)
    no good (*informal*)
♦ **être nul** to be no good ◊ *Je suis nul en éducation physique.* I'm no good at phys ed. ◊ *Ce film est nul.* This movie's no good.
♦ **un match nul** a tie (*sports*) ◊ *Ils ont fait match nul.* It was a tie.
♦ **nulle part** nowhere ◊ *Je ne le vois nulle part.* I can't see it anywhere.

numérique ADJECTIVE
    digital ◊ *un appareil photo numérique* a digital camera

le **numéro** NOUN
    number ◊ *J'habite au numéro trois.* I live at number 3.
♦ **mon numéro de téléphone** my phone number
♦ **le numéro de compte** the account number
♦ **le numéro d'identification personnel** PIN number
♦ **le numéro confidentiel** unlisted number

le **Nunavut** NOUN
    Nunavut

nu-pieds ADJECTIVE, ADVERB
    barefoot ◊ *Il se promenait nu-pieds.* He was walking barefoot.

la **nuque** NOUN
    nape of the neck

le **nutriment** NOUN
    nutrient

nutritif ADJECTIVE (FEM SING **nutritive**)
    ⬚1 nutritious ◊ *une collation nutritive* a nutritious snack
    ⬚2 nutritional ◊ *La malbouffe n'a presque aucune valeur nutritive.* Junk food has almost no nutritional value.

la **nutrition** NOUN
    nutrition

le/la **nutritionniste** NOUN
    nutritionist

le **nylon** NOUN
    nylon

N

o

obéir VERB
to obey
♦ **obéir à quelqu'un** to obey somebody ◊ *Elle refuse d'obéir à ses parents.* She refuses to obey her parents.

obéissant ADJECTIVE
obedient

l' **objet** MASC NOUN
object
♦ **les objets de valeur** valuables
♦ **les objets perdus** the lost-and-found

obligatoire ADJECTIVE
compulsory

obliger VERB
♦ **obliger quelqu'un à faire quelque chose** to force somebody to do something
♦ **Je suis bien obligé d'accepter.** I can't really refuse.

obscur ADJECTIVE
dark

l' **obscurité** FEM NOUN
darkness ◊ *dans l'obscurité* in the dark

obséder VERB
to obsess ◊ *Il est obsédé par le travail.* He's obsessed by work.

l' **observation** FEM NOUN
comment ◊ *J'ai une ou deux observations à faire.* I've got one or two comments to make.

observer VERB
⚀ to watch ◊ *Nous observions les canards sur le lac.* We watched the ducks on the lake.
⚁ to observe (*respect, keep*) ◊ *Ils observent le règlement.* They observe the rules. ◊ *observer une minute de silence pour le Jour du Souvenir* to observe a minute of silence on Remembrance Day

l' **obstacle** MASC NOUN
obstacle ◊ *surmonter un obstacle* to overcome an obstacle
♦ **une course d'obstacles** an obstacle race

obstiné ADJECTIVE
stubborn

obtenir VERB
⚀ to get ◊ *Ils ont obtenu cinquante pour cent des voix.* They got 50% of the votes.
⚁ to achieve ◊ *Nous avons obtenu de bons résultats.* We achieved good results.

l' **occasion** FEM NOUN
⚀ opportunity ◊ *C'est une occasion à ne pas manquer.* It's an opportunity not to be missed.
⚁ occasion ◊ *à l'occasion de sa fête* on the occasion of his birthday ◊ *à plusieurs occasions* on several occasions
⚂ bargain ◊ *Cet ordinateur est une bonne occasion.* This computer's a real bargain.
♦ **d'occasion** second-hand ◊ *une voiture d'occasion* a second-hand car

l' **Occident** MASC NOUN
West (*western world*)
♦ **en Occident** in the West

occidental ADJECTIVE (MASC PL **occidentaux**)
western
♦ **les pays occidentaux** the West

l' **occupation** FEM NOUN
occupation (*by troops*) ◊ *la France sous l'Occupation* France during the Occupation

occupé ADJECTIVE
⚀ busy ◊ *Le directeur est très occupé.* The director's very busy. ◊ *La ligne est occupée.* The line is busy.
⚁ taken ◊ *Est-ce que cette place est occupée?* Is this seat taken?
⚂ occupied ◊ *Les toilettes sont occupées.* The washroom is occupied.

occuper VERB
to occupy ◊ *Les enfants ne sont pas faciles à occuper quand il pleut.* Children aren't easy to keep occupied when it rains.
♦ **s'occuper de quelque chose (1)** to be in charge of something ◊ *Elle s'occupe d'un club de sport.* She's in charge of a sports club.
♦ **s'occuper de quelque chose (2)** to deal with something ◊ *Je vais m'occuper de ce problème tout de suite.* I'm going to deal with this problem right away.

l' **océan** MASC NOUN
ocean ◊ *l'océan Indien* the Indian Ocean

octobre MASC NOUN
October
♦ **en octobre** in October

l' **odeur** FEM NOUN
smell ◊ *Il y a une drôle d'odeur ici.*

There's a funny smell here.

l' **œil** MASC NOUN (PL les **yeux**)
eye ◊ *J'ai quelque chose dans l'œil.*
I've got something in my eye.
♦ **à l'œil nu** with the naked eye
♦ **un coup d'œil** a glance ◊ *Pourrais-tu jeter un coup d'œil sur ce que j'ai écrit, s'il te plaît?* Could you have a glance at what I've written, please?

l' **œillet** MASC NOUN
carnation

l' **œuf** MASC NOUN
egg
♦ **un œuf à la coque** a soft-boiled egg
♦ **un œuf dur** a hard-boiled egg
♦ **un œuf au plat** a fried egg
✱ ♦ **un œuf au miroir** an egg fried sunny side up
✱ ♦ **un œuf tourné** an egg fried over easy
♦ **les œufs brouillés** scrambled eggs
♦ **un œuf de Pâques** an Easter egg

l' **œuvre** FEM NOUN
work ◊ *les œuvres complètes de Shakespeare* the complete works of Shakespeare
♦ **une œuvre d'art** a work of art

✱ **œuvrer** VERB
to work ◊ *Elle œuvre auprès des jeunes sans-abri.* She works with homeless youth. ◊ *Toute sa vie, il a œuvré pour la cause de la paix.* He has worked all his life for peace.

offenser VERB
to offend ◊ *Est-ce que ma plaisanterie t'a offensé?* Did my joke offend you?
♦ **s'offenser de quelque chose** to be offended by something

offert VERB *see* **offrir**

l' **office** MASC NOUN
office (*government agency*)
♦ **un office du tourisme** a tourist office

> **ⓘ** *Created in 1977, the Office québécois de la langue française has the general mission to promote French and enforce the application of the Charter of French language in Québec. It offers numerous free French language resources, especially on the Web.*

officiel ADJECTIVE (FEM SING **officielle**)
official

l' **offre** FEM NOUN
offer ◊ *une offre spéciale* a special offer
♦ **« offres d'emploi »** "Employment Opportunities"

offrir VERB

♦ **offrir quelque chose (1)** to offer something ◊ *On lui a offert un poste de secrétaire.* They offered him a secretarial post. ◊ *Elle m'a offert à boire.* She offered me a drink.
♦ **offrir quelque chose (2)** to present something ◊ *Il lui a offert des roses.* He presented her with roses.
♦ **s'offrir quelque chose** to treat oneself to something ◊ *Je me suis offert un sous-marin de 12 pouces.* I treated myself to a twelve-inch sub.

l' **oie** FEM NOUN
goose

l' **oignon** MASC NOUN
onion

l' **oiseau** MASC NOUN (PL les **oiseaux**)
bird

l' **olive** FEM NOUN
olive ◊ *l'huile d'olive* olive oil

olympique ADJECTIVE
♦ **les Jeux olympiques** the Olympic Games

l' **ombre** FEM NOUN
① shade ◊ *Je vais me mettre à l'ombre.* I'm going to sit in the shade.
② shadow
♦ **l'ombre à paupières** eye shadow

l' **omnipraticien** MASC NOUN
general practitioner ◊ *Il est omnipraticien.* He's a general practitioner.

l' **omnipraticienne** FEM NOUN
general practitioner ◊ *Elle est omnipraticienne.* She's a general practitioner.

on PRONOUN
① we ◊ *On va à la plage demain.* We're going to the beach tomorrow. ◊ *On a pensé que ça te ferait plaisir.* We thought you'd be pleased.
② someone ◊ *On m'a volé mon sac à main.* Someone has stolen my purse.
♦ **On m'a dit d'attendre.** I was told to wait.
♦ **On vous demande au téléphone.** There's a phone call for you.
③ you ◊ *On peut visiter le château en été.* You can visit the castle in the summer. ◊ *D'ici on peut voir la tour CN.* From here you can see the CN Tower.

l' **oncle** MASC NOUN
uncle

l' **onde** FEM NOUN
wave (*on radio*) ◊ *sur les ondes courtes* on shortwave

l' **ongle** MASC NOUN
nail

O

☞

♦ **se couper les ongles** to cut one's nails ◊ *Elle s'est coupé les ongles.* She cut her nails.

ont VERB *see* **avoir**
♦ **Ils ont beaucoup d'argent.** They have lots of money.
♦ **Elles ont passé de bonnes vacances.** They had a good holiday.

l' **Ontario** MASC NOUN
Ontario

l' **ONU** FEM NOUN (= *Organisation des Nations unies*)
UN (= United Nations)

onze NUMBER
eleven ◊ *Il a onze ans.* He's eleven. ◊ *à onze heures* at eleven o'clock
♦ **le onze février** the eleventh of February

onzième ADJECTIVE
eleventh ◊ *au onzième étage* on the eleventh floor

l' **opéra** MASC NOUN
opera

l' **opération** FEM NOUN
operation

opérer VERB
to operate on ◊ *Elle a été opérée de l'appendicite.* She was operated on for appendicitis.
♦ **se faire opérer** to have an operation ◊ *Il s'est fait opérer.* He had an operation.

l' **opinion** FEM NOUN
opinion

opposé ADJECTIVE

| *see also* **opposé** NOUN |

opposite ◊ *Elle est partie dans la direction opposée.* She went off in the opposite direction.
♦ **être opposé à quelque chose** to be opposed to something

l' **opposé** MASC NOUN

| *see also* **opposé** ADJECTIVE |

the opposite

opposer VERB
♦ **opposer quelqu'un à quelqu'un** to pit somebody against somebody ◊ *Ce match oppose Edmonton à Toronto.* This match pits Edmonton against Toronto.
♦ **s'opposer** to conflict ◊ *Ces deux points de vue s'opposent.* These two points of view conflict.
♦ **s'opposer à quelque chose** to oppose something ◊ *Son père s'oppose à son mariage.* Her father's against her marriage.

l' **opposition** FEM NOUN

opposition
♦ **par opposition à** as opposed to ◊ *la littérature contemporaine par opposition à la littérature classique* modern literature, as opposed to classics

l' **opticien** MASC NOUN
optician ◊ *Il est opticien.* He's an optician.

l' **opticienne** FEM NOUN
optician ◊ *Elle est opticienne.* She's an optician.

optimiste ADJECTIVE
optimistic

l' **option** FEM NOUN
option
♦ **une matière à option** an optional subject

l' **or** MASC NOUN

| *see also* **or** CONJUNCTION |

gold ◊ *un bracelet en or* a gold bracelet

or CONJUNCTION

| *see also* **or** NOUN |

and yet ◊ *Il était sûr de gagner, or il a perdu.* He was sure he would win, and yet he lost.

l' **orage** MASC NOUN
thunderstorm

orageux ADJECTIVE (FEM SING **orageuse**)
stormy

oral ADJECTIVE (MASC PL **oraux**)
oral
♦ **une présentation orale** an oral presentation
♦ **une épreuve orale** an oral test
♦ **à prendre par voie orale** to be taken orally

l' **orange** FEM NOUN

| *see also* **orange** ADJECTIVE |

orange (*fruit*)

orange ADJECTIVE (MASC, FEM, PL)

| *see also* **orange** NOUN |

orange (*in colour*) ◊ *des fleurs orange* orange flowers

l' **orchestre** MASC NOUN
1 orchestra ◊ *un orchestre symphonique* a symphony orchestra
2 band ◊ *un orchestre de jazz* a jazz band

ordinaire ADJECTIVE

| *see also* **ordinaire** NOUN |

ordinary ◊ *des gens ordinaires* ordinary people

l' **ordinaire** MASC NOUN

| *see also* **ordinaire** ADJECTIVE |

♦ **sortir de l'ordinaire** to be out of the ordinary

l' **ordinateur** MASC NOUN
computer
♦ **un ordinateur portatif** a laptop

l' **ordonnance** FEM NOUN
prescription

ordonné ADJECTIVE
tidy

ordonner VERB
to order ◊ *La prof nous a ordonné de nous taire.* The teacher ordered us to stop talking. ◊ *On a ordonné aux grévistes de retourner au travail.* The strikers were ordered to go back to work.

l' **ordre** MASC NOUN
order ◊ *en ordre alphabétique* in alphabetical order
♦ **dans l'ordre** in order ◊ *dans le bon ordre* in the right order
♦ **mettre en ordre** to tidy up
♦ **jusqu'à nouvel ordre** until further notice
♦ **l'ordre publique** law and order

les **ordures** FEM NOUN
garbage SING

l' **oreille** FEM NOUN
ear
♦ **avoir de l'oreille** to have a good ear (*for music*)
♦ **écouter de toutes ses oreilles** to be all ears
♦ **Je n'écoutais que d'une oreille.** I was only half listening.
♦ **Les oreilles ont dû lui siffler.** Her ears must have been burning.

l' **oreiller** MASC NOUN
pillow

les **oreillons** MASC NOUN
mumps

l' **organe** MASC NOUN
organ (*in body*)

l' **organisateur** MASC NOUN
organizer
♦ **l'organisateur graphique** graphic organizer

l' **organisation** FEM NOUN
organization

l' **organisatrice** FEM NOUN
organizer

organiser VERB
to organize
♦ **s'organiser** to get organized ◊ *Elle ne sait pas s'organiser.* She can't get organized.

l' **organisme** MASC NOUN
body (*organization*)

l' **orgue** MASC NOUN
organ ◊ *Il joue de l'orgue.* He plays the organ.

orgueilleux ADJECTIVE (FEM SING **orgueilleuse**)
proud

l' **Orient** MASC NOUN
East (*eastern world*)
♦ **en Orient** in the East

oriental ADJECTIVE (MASC PL **orientaux**)
① oriental ◊ *un palais oriental* an oriental palace
② eastern ◊ *la frontière orientale de la Saskatchewan* the eastern border of Saskatchewan

l' **orientation** FEM NOUN
orientation
♦ **avoir le sens de l'orientation** to have a good sense of direction
♦ **l'orientation professionnelle** career counselling

originaire ADJECTIVE
♦ **Elle est originaire de Halifax.** She's from Halifax.

original ADJECTIVE (MASC PL **originaux**)
see also **original** NOUN.
original ◊ *un film en version originale* a film in the original language

l' **original** MASC NOUN (PL les **originaux**)
see also **original** ADJECTIVE
original ◊ *L'original est au Musée des beaux-arts de l'Ontario.* The original is in the Art Gallery of Ontario.
♦ **un vieil original** an old eccentric

l' **origine** FEM NOUN
origin
♦ **à l'origine** originally

✹ l' **orignal** MASC NOUN
moose

l' **orphelin** MASC NOUN
orphan

l' **orpheline** FEM NOUN
orphan

l' **orteil** MASC NOUN
toe ◊ *mon gros orteil* my big toe

l' **orthographe** FEM NOUN
spelling

l' **os** MASC NOUN
bone

oser VERB
to dare
♦ **oser faire quelque chose** to dare to do something

l' **otage** MASC NOUN
hostage

ôter VERB

O

☞

1 to take off ◊ *Elle a ôté son manteau.* She took off her coat.
2 to take away

ou CONJUNCTION
or
♦ **ou...ou...** either...or... ◊ *Je prendrai ou du lait ou du jus.* I'll have either milk or juice.
♦ **ou bien** or else ◊ *On pourrait aller au cinéma ou bien rentrer directement.* We could go to a movie or else go straight home.

où PRONOUN, ADVERB
1 where ◊ *Où est ton frère?* Where's your brother? ◊ *Où allez-vous?* Where are you going? ◊ *Je sais où il est.* I know where he is. ◊ *C'est la maison où je suis né.* That's the house where I was born. ◊ *la ville d'où je viens* the town I come from
2 that ◊ *Le jour où il est parti, tout le monde a pleuré.* The day that he left, everyone cried.
♦ **Par où allons-nous passer?** Which way are we going to go?

l' **ouate** FEM NOUN
cotton wool

oublier VERB
1 to forget ◊ *N'oublie pas de fermer la porte.* Don't forget to shut the door.
2 to leave (*behind*) ◊ *J'ai oublié mon sac à dos dans l'autobus.* I left my backpack on the bus.

l' **ouest** MASC NOUN

see also **ouest** ADJECTIVE

west ◊ *Elle vit dans l'ouest du Québec.* She lives in the western part of Québec.
♦ **à l'ouest de Saint-Boniface** west of St. Boniface
♦ **vers l'ouest** westwards
♦ **les provinces de l'Ouest** the Western provinces
♦ **le vent d'ouest** the west wind

ouest ADJECTIVE (MASC, FEM, PL)

see also **ouest** NOUN

1 west ◊ *la côte ouest du Canada* the west coast of Canada
2 western ◊ *la partie ouest du pays* the western part of the country

ouf EXCLAMATION
phew!

oui ADVERB
yes

l' **ouragan** MASC NOUN

hurricane

l' **ourlet** MASC NOUN
seam

l' **ours** MASC NOUN
bear
♦ **un ours en peluche** a teddy bear

l' **ourson** MASC NOUN
bear cub

l' **outarde** FEM NOUN
Canada goose

l' **outil** MASC NOUN
tool

outré ADJECTIVE
outraged ◊ *Il a été outré de son insolence.* He was outraged at her lack of respect.

ouvert VERB see **ouvrir**

ouvert ADJECTIVE
1 open ◊ *Le magasin est ouvert.* The store is open.
2 on ◊ *Tu as laissé le robinet ouvert.* You left the tap on.
♦ **avoir l'esprit ouvert** to be open-minded

l' **ouverture** FEM NOUN
opening ◊ *les heures d'ouverture* hours of operation

l' **ouvre-boîte** MASC NOUN
can opener

l' **ouvre-bouteille** MASC NOUN (PL **les ouvre-bouteilles**)
bottle-opener

l' **ouvrier** MASC NOUN
worker ◊ *Mon père est ouvrier dans une usine.* My dad is a factory worker.

l' **ouvrière** FEM NOUN
worker

ouvrir VERB
to open ◊ *Ouvrez!* Open up! ◊ *Elle a ouvert la porte.* She opened the door.
♦ **s'ouvrir** to open ◊ *La porte s'est ouverte.* The door opened.

ovale ADJECTIVE
oval

l' **ovni** MASC NOUN (= *objet volant non identifié*)
UFO

l' **oxygène** MASC NOUN
oxygen

l' **ozone** MASC NOUN
ozone ◊ *la couche d'ozone* the ozone layer

P

la **pacane** NOUN
pecan ◊ *la tarte aux pacanes* pecan pie

le/la **pacifiste** NOUN
pacifist

la **pagaie** NOUN
paddle (*chiefly kayak*)

la **pagaille** NOUN
mess SING ◊ *Quelle pagaille!* What a mess!

la **page** NOUN
page ◊ *Tournez la page.* Turn the page.
♦ **la page d'accueil** the home page

la **paie** NOUN
wages

le **paiement** NOUN
payment

le **paillasson** NOUN
doormat

la **paille** NOUN
straw

le **pain** NOUN
① bread ◊ *un morceau de pain* a piece of bread ◊ *une tranche de pain* a slice of bread
② loaf ◊ *J'ai acheté un pain.* I bought a loaf of bread.
♦ **le pain de blé entier** whole grain bread
♦ **le pain d'épice** gingerbread
♦ **le pain aux raisins** raisin bread
♦ **le pain doré** French toast

pair ADJECTIVE
even ◊ *un nombre pair* an even number

la **paire** NOUN
pair ◊ *une paire de chaussures* a pair of shoes

paisible ADJECTIVE
peaceful ◊ *un village paisible* a peaceful village

la **paix** NOUN
peace
♦ **faire la paix (1)** to make peace ◊ *Les deux pays ont fait la paix.* The two countries have made peace with each other.
♦ **faire la paix (2)** to make up (*after quarrel*) ◊ *Elle a fait la paix avec son frère.* She made up with her brother.
♦ **avoir la paix** to have peace and quiet ◊ *J'aimerais bien avoir la paix.* I'd like to have a bit of peace and quiet.

♦ **Fiche-lui la paix!** (*informal*) Leave him alone!

le **palais** NOUN
① palace ◊ *le palais Montcalm* Montcalm Palace
♦ **le palais de justice** court house
♦ **le palais de congrès** convention centre
♦ **le palais des expositions** exhibition hall
♦ **le palais des sports** sports complex
② palate (*in mouth*)

pâle ADJECTIVE
pale ◊ *bleu pâle* pale blue

la **pâleur** NOUN
paleness

le **palier** NOUN
landing (*on stairway*) ◊ *Elle m'attendait sur le palier.* She was waiting for me on the landing.

pâlir VERB
to go pale

la **palme** NOUN
flipper (*on animal*)

palmé ADJECTIVE
webbed ◊ *Les canards ont les pieds palmés.* Ducks have webbed feet.

le **palmier** NOUN
palm tree

la **palourde** NOUN
clam

palpitant ADJECTIVE
thrilling ◊ *un roman palpitant* a thrilling novel

le **pamplemousse** NOUN
grapefruit

pancanadien ADJECTIVE (FEM SING **pancanadienne**)
Canada-wide ◊ *une campagne pancanadienne contre le tabac* a Canada-wide campaign against tobacco

la **pancarte** NOUN
sign ◊ *Il y a une pancarte dans la vitrine.* There's a sign in the window.

pané ADJECTIVE
breaded ◊ *du poisson pané* breaded fish

le **panier** NOUN
basket

la **panique** NOUN
panic

paniquer VERB
to panic

la **panne** NOUN
breakdown
◆ **être en panne** to have broken down
◊ *L'ascenseur est en panne.* The
elevator's not working.
◆ **tomber en panne** to break down
◊ *Nous sommes tombés en panne
sur l'autoroute.* We broke down on
the highway. ◊ *Nous sommes tombés
en panne d'essence.* We've run out
of gas.
◆ **une panne de courant** a power cut

le **panneau** NOUN (PL les **panneaux**)
sign ◊ *Ce panneau dit que la maison
est à vendre.* This sign says that the
house is for sale.
◆ **panneau d'affichage** billboard

le **panorama** NOUN
panorama

le **pansement** NOUN
1 bandage
2 bandaid

le **pantalon** NOUN
pants PL ◊ *Son pantalon est trop
court.* His pants are too short.
◆ **un pantalon de ski** a pair of ski pants

la **panthère** NOUN
panther

la **pantoufle** NOUN
slipper

le **paon** NOUN
peacock

le **papa** NOUN
dad

le **pape** NOUN
pope

la **papeterie** NOUN
stationery

le **papier** NOUN
paper ◊ *une feuille de papier* a sheet
of paper
◆ **Vos papiers, s'il vous plaît.** Your
papers, please.
◆ **les papiers d'identité** identification
(*documents*)
◆ **le papier à lettres** writing paper
◆ **le papier hygiénique** toilet paper
◆ **le papier peint** wallpaper

le **papillon** NOUN
butterfly

la **pâquerette** NOUN
daisy

Pâques MASC NOUN
Easter ◊ *Je viendrai te voir à Pâques.*
I'll come and see you at Easter.

le **paquet** NOUN

1 pack ◊ *Je voudrais un paquet de
gomme à mâcher.* I'd like a pack of
gum.
2 parcel ◊ *Sa mère lui a envoyé un
paquet.* His mother sent him a parcel.
◆ **un paquet de** a ton of (*informal*)
◊ *J'ai un paquet de choses à faire.*
I've got a ton of things to do. ◊ *Il est
tombé un paquet de neige.* A ton of
snow has fallen.

le **paquet-cadeau** NOUN (PL les **paquets-
cadeaux**)
gift-wrapped parcel ◊ *La vendeuse
m'a fait un paquet-cadeau.* The
salesperson gift-wrapped it for me.

par PREPOSITION
1 by ◊ *La lettre a été écrite par son
fils.* The letter was written by his son.
◆ **deux par deux** two by two ◊ *Les
élèves sont entrés deux par deux.* The
pupils went in two by two.
2 with ◊ *Son nom commence par un
H.* His name begins with H.
3 out of ◊ *Elle regardait par la
fenêtre.* She was looking out of the
window. ◊ *par habitude* out of habit
4 via ◊ *Nous sommes passés par
Windsor pour aller aux États-Unis.* We
went via Windsor to the US.
5 through ◊ *Il faut passer par la
douane avant de prendre l'avion.* You
have to go through customs before
boarding the plane.
6 per ◊ *Prenez trois cachets par
jour.* Take three tablets per day. ◊ *Le
voyage coûte deux mille dollars par
personne.* The trip costs two thousand
dollars per person.
◆ **par ici (1)** this way ◊ *Il faut passer par
ici pour y arriver.* You have to go this
way to get there.
◆ **par ici (2)** around here ◊ *Il y a
beaucoup de touristes par ici.* There
are lots of tourists around here.
◆ **par-ci, par-là** here and there

le **parachute** NOUN
parachute

le/la **parachutiste** NOUN
parachutist

le **paradis** NOUN
heaven

les **parages** MASC NOUN
◆ **dans les parages** in the area ◊ *Il n'y
a pas d'hôtel dans les parages.* There
are no hotels in the area.

le **paragraphe** NOUN
paragraph

paraître VERB
1 to seem ◊ *Ça paraît incroyable.* It
seems unbelievable.
2 to look ◊ *Elle paraît plus jeune que*

son frère. She looks younger than her brother.

♦ **il paraît que** it seems that ◊ *Il paraît que c'est la faute de la direction.* It seems that it's the fault of the management.

parallèle ADJECTIVE

see also **le parallèle** and **la parallèle**

parallel ◊ *les barres parallèles* parallel bars

le **parallèle** NOUN

see also **parallèle** ADJECTIVE and **la parallèle**

parallel ◊ *Il a fait un parallèle entre ces deux événements.* He drew a parallel between the two events.

la **parallèle** NOUN

see also **parallèle** ADJECTIVE and **le parallèle**

parallel line

paralysé ADJECTIVE
paralysed

le **parapluie** NOUN
umbrella

parascolaire ADJECTIVE
extracurricular ◊ *L'école offre plusieurs activités parascolaires.* The school offers several extracurricular activities.

le **parasol** NOUN
parasol

le **parc** NOUN
① park ◊ *Le dimanche, elle va se promener au parc.* On Sundays she goes for a walk in the park.
♦ **un parc d'attractions** an amusement park
② grounds ◊ *Le château est situé au milieu d'un grand parc.* The castle is surrounded by extensive grounds.
♦ **le parc industriel** industrial park

parce que CONJUNCTION
because ◊ *Il n'est pas venu parce qu'il n'avait pas de voiture.* He didn't come because he didn't have a car.

le **parcomètre** NOUN
parking meter

parcourir VERB
① to cover ◊ *Elle a parcouru cinquante kilomètres à vélo.* She covered 50 kilometres on her bike.
② to glance through ◊ *J'ai parcouru le journal d'aujourd'hui.* I glanced through today's newspaper.

le **parcours** NOUN
journey

par-dessous ADVERB
underneath ◊ *Il portait un chandail*

et une chemise par-dessous. He was wearing a sweater with a shirt underneath.

le **pardessus** NOUN
overcoat

par-dessus ADVERB, PREPOSITION
① on top ◊ *Elle porte un chemisier et un chandail rouge par-dessus.* She's wearing a blouse with a red sweater on top.
② over ◊ *Elle a sauté par-dessus le mur.* She jumped over the wall.
♦ **en avoir par-dessus la tête** to have had enough ◊ *J'en ai par-dessus la tête de tous ces problèmes.* I've had enough of all these problems.

le **pardon** NOUN

see also **pardon** EXCLAMATION

forgiveness

pardon EXCLAMATION

see also **pardon** NOUN

① sorry! ◊ *Oh, pardon! J'espère que je ne vous ai pas fait mal.* Oh, sorry! I hope I didn't hurt you.
♦ **demander pardon à quelqu'un** to apologize to somebody ◊ *Il leur a demandé pardon.* He apologized to them.
♦ **Je vous demande pardon.** I'm sorry.
② excuse me! ◊ *Pardon, madame! Pouvez-vous me dire où se trouve le bureau de poste?* Excuse me! Could you tell me where the post office is?
③ pardon? ◊ *Pardon? Je n'ai pas compris ce que vous avez dit.* Pardon? I didn't understand what you said.

pardonner VERB
to forgive ◊ *Nous lui avons pardonné de nous avoir menti.* We forgave him for lying to us.

le **pare-brise** NOUN (PL les **pare-brise**)
windshield

le **pare-chocs** NOUN
bumper

pareil ADJECTIVE (FEM SING **pareille**)
① the same ◊ *Ces deux photos ne sont pas pareilles.* These two photos aren't the same.
② like that ◊ *J'aime bien sa montre. J'en veux une pareille.* I like her watch. I want one like that.
③ such ◊ *Je refuse d'écouter des bêtises pareilles.* I won't listen to such nonsense.
♦ **sans pareil** unequalled ◊ *un talent sans pareil* unequalled talent

la **parenthèse** NOUN
bracket ◊ *entre parenthèses* in brackets

P

les **parents** MASC NOUN
  1 parents (*mother and father*)
  2 relatives ◊ *parents et amis* friends and relatives

la **paresse** NOUN
  laziness

paresseux ADJECTIVE (FEM SING **paresseuse**)
  lazy

parfait ADJECTIVE
  perfect

parfaitement ADVERB
  perfectly ◊ *Il parle parfaitement l'arabe.* He speaks perfect Arabic.

parfois ADVERB
  sometimes

le **parfum** NOUN
  1 perfume
  2 flavour ◊ *« Je voudrais une crème glacée. » « Quel parfum veux-tu? »* "I'd like an ice cream." "What flavour would you like?"

parfumé ADJECTIVE
  1 fragrant ◊ *une rose très parfumée* a very fragrant rose
  2 flavoured ◊ *des biscuits parfumés au café* coffee-flavoured cookies

le **pari** NOUN
  bet

parier VERB
  to bet

le **parlement** NOUN
  parliament
  ♦ **le Parlement du Canada** the Canadian Parliament

parlementaire ADJECTIVE
  parliamentary ◊ *un débat parlementaire* a parliamentary debate
  ♦ **la Colline parlementaire** Parliament Hill

parler VERB
  1 to speak ◊ *Vous parlez français?* Do you speak French?
  2 to talk ◊ *Nous étions en train de parler quand la directrice est entrée.* We were talking when the principal came in.
  ♦ **parler de quelque chose à quelqu'un** to tell somebody about something ◊ *Il m'a parlé de son nouveau vélo.* He told me about his new bike.

parmi PREPOSITION
  among ◊ *Ils étaient parmi les meilleurs de la classe.* They were among the best in the class.

la **paroi** NOUN
  wall
  ♦ **une paroi rocheuse** a rock face

la **paroisse** NOUN

parish

la **parole** NOUN
  1 speech ◊ *l'usage de la parole* the power of speech
  2 word ◊ *Il m'a donné sa parole.* He gave me his word. ◊ *Elle a tenu parole.* She kept her word.
  ♦ **les paroles** lyrics ◊ *J'aime les paroles de cette chanson.* I like the lyrics of this song.

le **parquet** NOUN
  floor (*wooden*)

parrainer VERB
  to sponsor ◊ *Cette entreprise parraine notre équipe de hockey.* This company is sponsoring our hockey team.

pars VERB *see* **partir**

la **part** NOUN
  1 share ◊ *Vous n'avez pas eu votre part.* You haven't had your share.
  2 piece ◊ *une part de gâteau* a piece of cake
  ♦ **prendre part à quelque chose** to take part in something ◊ *Elle va prendre part à la réunion.* She's going to take part in the meeting.
  ♦ **de la part de (1)** on behalf of ◊ *Je dois vous remercier de la part de mon frère.* I must thank you on behalf of my brother.
  ♦ **de la part de (2)** from ◊ *C'est un cadeau pour toi, de la part de ma sœur.* It's a present for you, from my sister.
  ♦ **à part** except ◊ *Ils sont tous venus à part lui.* They all came except him.

partager VERB
  1 to share ◊ *Ils partagent un appartement.* They share a flat.
  2 to divide ◊ *Nous avons partagé le gâteau en quatre.* We divided the cake into four.

le/la **partenaire** NOUN
  partner

le **parti** NOUN
  party ◊ *le Parti vert* the Green Party

le **participant** NOUN
  participant

la **participante** NOUN
  participant

la **participation** NOUN
  participation

le **participe** NOUN
  participle
  ♦ **le participe passé** the past participle
  ♦ **le participe présent** the present participle

participer VERB

♦ **participer à quelque chose (1)** to take part in something ◊ *Mon frère va participer à la course.* My brother is going to take part in the race.

♦ **participer à quelque chose (2)** to contribute to something ◊ *Je voudrais participer aux frais.* I would like to contribute to the cost.

la **particularité** NOUN
   characteristic

particulier ADJECTIVE (FEM SING **particulière**)
   ① private ◊ *une maison particulière* a private house
   ② distinctive ◊ *Ce fromage a un arôme particulier.* This cheese has a distinctive flavour.
   ③ particular ◊ *Dans ce cas particulier, la procédure est différente.* In this particular case, the procedure is different.

♦ **en particulier (1)** particularly ◊ *J'aime les fruits, en particulier les fraises.* I like fruit, particularly strawberries.

♦ **en particulier (2)** in private ◊ *Est-ce que je peux vous parler en particulier?* Can I speak to you in private?

particulièrement ADVERB
   particularly

la **partie** NOUN
   ① part ◊ *Une partie du groupe restera à la ferme.* Part of the group will stay at the farm.
   ② game ◊ *Nous avons fait une partie de badminton.* We played a game of badminton. ◊ *une partie de cartes* a game of cards

♦ **en partie** partly ◊ *Cela explique en partie le problème.* That partly explains the problem.

♦ **en grande partie** largely ◊ *Son histoire est en grande partie vraie.* Her story is largely true.

♦ **faire partie de** to be part of ◊ *Ce tableau fait partie de la collection familiale.* This picture is part of the family collection.

partiel ADJECTIVE (FEM SING **partielle**)
   partial

partir VERB
   to go ◊ *Je t'ai téléphoné mais tu étais déjà parti.* I phoned you but you were already gone.

♦ **partir en vacances** to go on holiday

♦ **partir de** to leave ◊ *Il est parti de Regina à sept heures.* He left Regina at 7.

♦ **à partir de** from ◊ *Je serai chez moi à partir de huit heures.* I'll be at home from eight o'clock onwards.

la **partition** NOUN

score (*in music*) ◊ *une partition de piano* a piano score

partout ADVERB
   everywhere

🐾 le **party** NOUN
   party ◊ *un party d'Halloween* a Halloween party

paru VERB *see* **paraître**

la **parution** NOUN
   publication ◊ *la parution de son nouveau livre* the publication of her new book

♦ **Ce roman a eu beaucoup de succès dès sa parution.** This novel was a hit from the moment it came out.

parvenir VERB

♦ **parvenir à faire quelque chose** to manage to do something ◊ *Elle est finalement parvenue à ouvrir la porte.* She finally managed to open the door.

♦ **faire parvenir quelque chose à quelqu'un** to send something to somebody ◊ *Je vous ferai parvenir le colis avant lundi.* I'll send you the parcel before Monday.

pas ADVERB

   | *see also* **pas** NOUN |

♦ **ne...pas** not ◊ *Il ne pleut pas.* It's not raining. ◊ *Elle n'est pas venue.* She didn't come. ◊ *Ils n'ont pas de voiture.* They don't have a car.

♦ **Vous viendrez à notre soirée, n'est-ce pas?** You're coming to our party, aren't you?

♦ **C'est lui qui a gagné, n'est-ce pas?** He won, didn't he?

♦ **pas moi** not me ◊ *Elle veut aller au cinéma, pas moi.* She wants to go to a movie, but I don't.

♦ **pas du tout** not at all ◊ *Je n'aime pas du tout ça.* I don't like that at all.

♦ **pas mal** not bad ◊ *Ce n'est pas mal pour un début.* That's not bad for a first attempt. ◊ *« Comment allez-vous? » « Pas mal. »* "How are you?" "Not bad."

♦ **pas mal de** quite a lot of ◊ *Il y avait pas mal de monde au concert.* There were quite a lot of people at the concert.

le **pas** NOUN

   | *see also* **pas** ADVERB |

   ① pace ◊ *Il marchait d'un pas rapide.* He walked at a fast pace.
   ② step ◊ *Faites trois pas en avant.* Take three steps forward. ◊ *un pas en arrière* a step backwards
   ③ footstep ◊ *J'entends des pas dans l'escalier.* I can hear footsteps on the

P

☞

stairs.

♦ **au pas** at a walk ◊ *Le cheval est parti au pas.* The horse set off at a walk.

♦ **faire les cent pas** to pace up and down ◊ *Il faisait les cent pas dans le corridor.* He was pacing up and down the corridor.

le **passage** NOUN

passage ◊ *J'ai traduit un passage de ce livre.* I translated a passage from this book.

♦ **J'ai été éclaboussé au passage de la voiture.** I was splashed by a passing car.

♦ **de passage** passing through ◊ *Nous sommes de passage à Cornwall.* We're just passing through Cornwall.

♦ **un passage à niveau** a railway crossing

♦ **un passage à piétons** a pedestrian crossing

♦ **un passage souterrain** an underground walkway

passager ADJECTIVE (FEM SING **passagère**)

see also **passager** NOUN

temporary

le **passager** NOUN

see also **passager** ADJECTIVE

passenger

♦ **un passager clandestin** a stowaway

la **passagère** NOUN
passenger

le **passant** NOUN
passer-by

la **passante** NOUN
passer-by

passé ADJECTIVE

see also **passé** NOUN

① last ◊ *Je l'ai vue la semaine passée.* I saw her last week.
② past ◊ *Il est minuit passé.* It's past midnight.

le **passé** NOUN

see also **passé** ADJECTIVE

① past ◊ *dans le passé* in the past
② past tense ◊ *Mettez ce verbe au passé.* Put this verb into the past tense.

♦ **le passé composé** the perfect tense

le **passeport** NOUN
passport

passer VERB

① to cross ◊ *Nous avons passé la frontière ontarienne.* We crossed the Ontario border.
② to go through ◊ *Il faut passer la douane en sortant.* You have to go through customs on the way out.

③ to take ◊ *Mon frère a passé ses examens la semaine dernière.* My brother took his exams last week.

> Be careful! **passer un examen** does not mean **to pass an exam**.

④ to spend ◊ *Elle a passé la journée à ne rien faire.* She spent the day doing nothing. ◊ *Ils passent toujours leurs vacances au Québec.* They always spend their holidays in Quebec.
⑤ to pass ◊ *Passe-moi le sel, s'il te plaît.* Pass me the salt, please.
⑥ to show ◊ *On passe un nouveau film d'animation au cinéma cette semaine.* They're showing a new animated film at the movie theatre this week.
⑦ to drop by ◊ *Je passerai chez vous ce soir.* I'll drop by this evening.

♦ **passer à la radio** to be on the radio ◊ *Mon père passe à la radio demain soir.* My father's going to be on the radio tomorrow night.

♦ **passer à la télévision** to be on TV ◊ *Mon film préféré passe à la télé ce soir.* My favourite movie is on TV tonight.

♦ **Ne quittez pas, je vous passe la gérante.** Hold on please, I'm putting you through to the manager.

♦ **passer par** to go through ◊ *Ils sont passés par Brandon pour aller à Winnipeg.* They went through Brandon to get to Winnipeg.

♦ **en passant** in passing ◊ *Je lui ai dit en passant que j'allais me marier.* I told her in passing that I was getting married.

♦ **laisser passer** to let through ◊ *Il m'a laissé passer.* He let me through.

♦ **se passer (1)** to take place ◊ *Cette histoire se passe au Moyen Âge.* This story takes place in the Middle Ages.

♦ **se passer (2)** to go ◊ *Comment s'est passé le match?* How did the game go?

♦ **se passer (3)** to happen ◊ *Que s'est-il passé? Un accident?* What happened? Was there an accident?

♦ **Qu'est-ce qui se passe? Pourquoi est-ce que tu pleures?** What's the matter? Why are you crying?

♦ **se passer de** to do without ◊ *Je me passerai de confiture ce matin.* I'll do without jam this morning.

la **passerelle** NOUN
① footbridge (*over river*)
② gangway (*onto plane, boat*)

le **passe-temps** NOUN
pastime

passif ADJECTIVE (FEM SING **passive**)

see also **passif** NOUN

passive

le **passif** NOUN

see also **passif** ADJECTIVE

passive ◊ *Mettez ce verbe au passif.* Put this verb into the passive.

la **passion** NOUN
passion

passionnant ADJECTIVE
fascinating

passionné ADJECTIVE
avid ◊ *Il est un lecteur passionné.* He's an avid reader.
♦ **Elle est passionnée de voile.** She's a sailing fanatic.

passionner VERB
♦ **Son travail le passionne.** He's passionate about his work.
♦ **se passionner pour quelque chose** to have a passion for something ◊ *Elle se passionne pour la photographie.* She has a passion for photography.

la **passoire** NOUN
strainer

la **pastèque** NOUN
watermelon

la **pastille** NOUN
cough drop

la **patate** NOUN (*informal*)
potato
✹ ♦ **les patates pilées** mashed potatoes
♦ **une patate douce** a sweet potato

la **pâte** NOUN
① pastry
② dough
③ cake batter
♦ **la pâte à crêpes** pancake batter
♦ **la pâte à modeler** Plasticine ᴹᶜ
♦ **la pâte d'amandes** marzipan
♦ **la pâte dentifrice** toothpaste

le **pâté** NOUN
pâté ◊ *Nous avons mangé du pâté en entrée.* We had pâté as an appetizer.
✹ ♦ **le pâté chinois** shepherd's pie
♦ **un pâté de maisons** a block (*of houses*)

✹ la **patente** NOUN
thing (*imprecise*) ◊ *Pourrais-tu me passer la patente en arrière de la chaise, là?* Could you pass me that thing behind the chair?
♦ **les patentes** stuff ◊ *Ma mère a laissé tes patentes sur la table.* My mom left your stuff on the table. ◊ *J'ai plein de patentes à faire en fin de semaine.* I have a ton of stuff to do this weekend.

paternel ADJECTIVE (FEM SING **paternelle**)
♦ **ma grand-mère paternelle** my

grandmother on my father's side
♦ **mon oncle paternel** my uncle on my father's side

les **pâtes** FEM NOUN
pasta SING

la **patience** NOUN
patience

patient ADJECTIVE

see also **patient** NOUN

patient

le **patient** NOUN

see also **patient** ADJECTIVE

patient

la **patiente** NOUN
patient

patienter VERB
to wait ◊ *Veuillez patienter un instant, s'il vous plaît.* Please wait a moment.

le **patin** NOUN
① skate ◊ *Il a enfilé ses patins.* He put his skates on.
② skating ◊ *Ils font du patin tous les mercredis.* They go skating every Wednesday.
✹ ♦ **accrocher ses patins** to retire
✹ ♦ **être vite sur ses patins** to act very fast
♦ **les patins à glace** ice skates
♦ **les patins à roues alignées** inline skates
♦ **les patins à roulettes** roller skates

le **patinage** NOUN
skating
♦ **le patinage artistique** figure skating
♦ **le patinage de vitesse** speed skating

patiner VERB
to skate

le **patineur** NOUN
skater

la **patineuse** NOUN
skater

la **patinoire** NOUN
skating rink

la **pâtisserie** NOUN
cake shop
♦ **faire de la pâtisserie** to bake ◊ *J'adore faire de la pâtisserie.* I love baking.
♦ **les pâtisseries** cakes

la **patrie** NOUN
homeland

le **patron** NOUN
① boss
② pattern (*for dressmaking*)

la **patronne** NOUN
boss

P

☞

♦ **Elle est patronne de café.** She runs
a café.

la **patrouille** NOUN
patrol

la **patte** NOUN
⒈ paw (of dog, cat)
⒉ leg (of bird, animal)

la **paupière** NOUN
eyelid

la **pause** NOUN
⒈ break ◊ *Ils font une pause.* They're
having a break. ◊ *une pause de midi*
a lunch break
⒉ pause ◊ *Il y a eu une pause dans
la conversation.* There was a pause in
the conversation.

pauvre ADJECTIVE
poor ◊ *Sa famille est pauvre.* Her
family is poor. ◊ *Pauvre lui! Il n'a
pas eu de chance!* Poor him! He was
unlucky!

> *Be careful! The meaning of **pauvre**
> changes according to its position.
> After the noun, it means **not rich**;
> before the noun, it means **pitiable**.*

la **pauvreté** NOUN
poverty

pavé ADJECTIVE
cobbled ◊ *Les rues étaient pavées.*
The streets were cobbled.

le **pavé numérique** NOUN
keypad

payant ADJECTIVE
⒈ paying ◊ *Ce sont des hôtes
payants.* They're paying guests.
⒉ profitable
♦ **C'est une profession payante.** It's a
highly-paid profession.
♦ **C'est payant.** You have to pay.
◊ *L'entrée de la foire est payante.* You
have to pay to get into the fair.

la **paye** NOUN
wages

payer VERB
⒈ to pay for ◊ *Combien as-tu payé
ta planche à roulettes?* How much did
you pay for your skateboard?
♦ **J'ai payé ce T-shirt vingt dollars.** I
paid 20 dollars for this T-shirt.
⒉ to pay ◊ *Elle a été payée
aujourd'hui.* She got paid today.
◊ *Son métier paye bien.* His job pays
well. ◊ *Elle est mal payée.* She is
underpaid.
♦ **faire payer quelque chose à quelqu'un**
to charge somebody for something
◊ *Il me l'a fait payer dix dollars.* He
charged me 10 dollars for it.
♦ **payer quelque chose à quelqu'un** to

buy somebody something ◊ *Allez, je
vous paye un café.* Come on, I'll buy
you a coffee.

le **pays** NOUN
country

le **paysage** NOUN
landscape

le **paysan** NOUN
farmer

la **paysanne** NOUN
farmer

le **PC** NOUN
PC (= personal computer) ◊ *Il a tapé
le rapport sur son PC.* He typed the
report on his PC.

le **péage** NOUN
toll ◊ *Nous avons payé cinq dollars
de péage.* We paid a toll of 5 dollars.

la **peau** NOUN (PL les **peaux**)
skin ◊ *Tu as la peau douce.* You have
soft skin.

la **pêche** NOUN
⒈ peach
⒉ fishing
♦ **aller à la pêche** to go fishing
♦ **la pêche à la ligne** rod fishing
♦ **la pêche sous la glace** ice fishing

le **péché** NOUN
sin

pêcher VERB
⒈ to fish for ◊ *Ils sont partis pêcher
la truite.* They've gone fishing for
trout.
⒉ to catch ◊ *On a pêché deux
saumons.* We caught two salmon.

le **pêcheur** NOUN
fisherman ◊ *Son père est pêcheur.*
Her father's a fisherman.

la **pêcheuse** NOUN
fisherman (woman) ◊ *Elle est
pêcheuse.* She's a fisherman.

pédagogique ADJECTIVE
educational

la **pédale** NOUN
pedal

pédestre ADJECTIVE
♦ **une randonnée pédestre** a hike

le **peigne** NOUN
comb

peigner VERB
to comb ◊ *Elle peigne le bébé.* She's
combing the baby's hair.
♦ **se peigner** to comb one's hair ◊ *Il
faut que je me peigne.* I must comb
my hair.

le **peignoir** NOUN
dressing gown

♦ **un peignoir de bain** a bathrobe

peindre VERB
to paint

la **peine** NOUN
trouble
♦ **avoir de la peine à faire quelque chose** to have a hard time doing something ◊ *J'ai eu beaucoup de peine à la convaincre.* I had a really hard time convincing her.
♦ **se donner de la peine** to go to a lot of trouble ◊ *Il s'est donné beaucoup de peine pour obtenir ces renseignements.* He went to a lot of trouble to get this information.
♦ **prendre la peine de faire quelque chose** to go to the trouble of doing something ◊ *Il a pris la peine de me rapporter ma valise.* He went to the trouble of returning my suitcase to me.
♦ **faire de la peine à quelqu'un** to upset somebody ◊ *Ça me fait de la peine de te voir pleurer.* It upsets me to see you crying.
♦ **ce n'est pas la peine** there's no point ◊ *Ce n'est pas la peine de téléphoner.* There's no point in phoning.
♦ **à peine (1)** hardly ◊ *J'ai à peine eu le temps de me changer.* I hardly had time to get changed.
♦ **à peine (2)** only just ◊ *Elle vient à peine de se lever.* She only just got up.

le/la **peintre** NOUN
painter

la **peinture** NOUN
① painting ◊ *On expose des peintures d'Emily Carr au musée.* There's an exhibition of Emily Carr's paintings at the museum.
② paint ◊ *J'ai acheté de la peinture verte.* I bought some green paint.
♦ **« peinture fraîche »** "wet paint"

pêle-mêle ADVERB
higgledy-piggledy

peler VERB
to peel

la **pelle** NOUN
① shovel ◊ *une pelle à neige* a snow shovel
② spade

la **pellicule de plastique** NOUN
plastic wrap

les **pellicules** FEM NOUN
dandruff SING

la **pelote** NOUN
ball ◊ *une pelote de laine* a ball of wool

la **pelouse** NOUN
lawn

la **peluche** NOUN
♦ **un animal en peluche** a stuffed animal

✱ le **pemmican** NOUN
pemmican

le **penchant** NOUN
♦ **avoir un penchant pour quelque chose** to have a liking for something

pencher VERB
to tilt ◊ *Ce tableau penche vers la droite.* The picture is tilted to the right.
♦ **se pencher (1)** to lean over ◊ *Elle s'est penchée sur la table.* She leaned over the table.
♦ **se pencher (2)** to bend down ◊ *Il s'est penché pour ramasser sa casquette.* He bent down to pick up his cap.
♦ **se pencher (3)** to lean out ◊ *Ne te penche pas par la fenêtre.* Don't lean out of the window.

pendant PREPOSITION
during ◊ *Ça s'est passé pendant l'été.* It happened during the summer.
♦ **pendant que** while ◊ *Il a téléphoné pendant que sa sœur prenait son bain.* He phoned while his sister was having a bath.

le **pendentif** NOUN
pendant

pendre VERB
to hang ◊ *Il a pendu son manteau dans la garde-robe.* He hung his coat in the closet.

la **pendule** NOUN
clock

pénétrer VERB
① to enter ◊ *Ils ont pénétré dans la maison en passant par le jardin.* They entered the house through the garden.
② to penetrate ◊ *Le soleil ne pénètre pas ce feuillage dense.* The sun cannot penetrate this thick foliage.

pénible ADJECTIVE
difficult ◊ *une tâche pénible* a difficult task
♦ **Il est vraiment pénible.** He's a real pain.

péniblement ADVERB
with difficulty

le **pénis** NOUN
penis

la **pénombre** NOUN
half-light

la **pensée** NOUN
thought ◊ *Il était perdu dans ses pensées.* He was lost in thought.

P

penser VERB
to think ◊ *Je pense qu'elle a eu raison de partir.* I think she was right to leave.
♦ **penser à quelque chose** to think about something ◊ *Je pense à mes vacances.* I'm thinking about my holidays. ◊ *Pensez-y.* Think about it.
♦ **faire penser quelqu'un à quelque chose** to remind someone of something ◊ *Cette photo me fait penser à notre voyage.* This photo reminds me of our trip.
♦ **faire penser quelqu'un à faire quelque chose** to remind someone to do something ◊ *Fais-moi penser à téléphoner à mes parents.* Remind me to phone my parents.
♦ **penser faire quelque chose** to be planning to do something ◊ *Ils pensent partir en Colombie-Britannique en juillet.* They're planning to go to British Columbia in July.

la **pension** NOUN
pension ◊ *Ma grand-mère reçoit sa pension tous les mois.* My grandmother gets her pension every month.

le **pensionnat** NOUN
boarding school

la **pente** NOUN
slope ◊ *une pente raide* a steep slop
♦ **en pente** sloping ◊ *Le toit de cette maison est en pente.* This house has a sloping roof.

le **pépin** NOUN
seed (*in fruit*) ◊ *Cette orange est pleine de pépins.* This orange is full of seeds.

perçant ADJECTIVE
1 sharp ◊ *Il a une vue perçante.* He has very sharp eyes.
2 piercing ◊ *un cri perçant* a piercing cry

percer VERB
to pierce ◊ *Elle s'est fait percer les oreilles.* She got her ears pierced.

percuter VERB
to smash into

le **perdant** NOUN
loser

la **perdante** NOUN
loser

perdre VERB
to lose ◊ *Il a perdu ses clés.* He lost his keys.
♦ **J'ai perdu mon chemin.** I've lost my way.
♦ **perdre un match** to lose a game

♦ **perdre du temps** to waste time ◊ *J'ai perdu beaucoup de temps ce matin.* I've wasted a lot of time this morning. ◊ *Nous avons perdu notre temps à cette réunion.* That meeting was a waste of time.
♦ **se perdre** to get lost ◊ *Je me suis perdu en route.* I got lost on the way here.

perdu VERB *see* **perdre**

le **père** NOUN
father

perfectionné ADJECTIVE
sophisticated

perfectionner VERB
to improve ◊ *Elle a besoin de perfectionner son anglais.* She needs to improve her English.

le **pergélisol** NOUN
permafrost

périmé ADJECTIVE
out-of-date ◊ *Mon passeport est périmé.* My passport is out of date.
♦ **Ces yogourts sont périmés.** These yogurts are past their best-before date.

la **période** NOUN
period

périodiquement ADVERB
periodically

périphérique ADJECTIVE
outlying ◊ *un quartier périphérique* an outlying district

la **perle** NOUN
pearl

la **permanence** NOUN
♦ **assurer une permanence** to offer a basic service ◊ *Ma banque assure une permanence le samedi matin.* My bank offers a basic service on Saturday mornings.
♦ **être de permanence** to be on duty ◊ *Elle ne peut pas venir, elle est de permanence ce soir.* She can't come, she's on duty tonight.
♦ **en permanence** permanently ◊ *Il se plaint en permanence.* He's always complaining.

permanent ADJECTIVE
1 permanent ◊ *Il a un poste permanent.* He has a permanent job.
2 continuous ◊ *J'en ai assez de tes critiques permanentes.* I've had enough of your constant criticism.

la **permanente** NOUN
perm

permettre VERB
to allow
♦ **permettre à quelqu'un de faire**

quelque chose to allow somebody to do something ◊ *Ses parents lui permettent de sortir le soir.* His parents allow him to go out at night.

le **permis** NOUN
permit ◊ *Il vous faut un permis pour camper ici.* You need a permit to camp here.
♦ **le permis de conduire** driver's licence
♦ **un permis de pêche** a fishing licence
♦ **un permis de travail** a work permit

la **permission** NOUN
permission ◊ *Qui t'a donné la permission d'entrer?* Who gave you permission to come in?
♦ **avoir la permission de faire quelque chose** to have permission to do something ◊ *J'ai la permission d'utiliser son baladeur.* I've got his permission to use his personal stereo.
♦ **être en permission** to be on leave (*from the army*)

perpétuel ADJECTIVE (FEM SING **perpétuelle**)
perpetual

perplexe ADJECTIVE
puzzled ◊ *Ma question l'a laissé perplexe.* She was puzzled by my question.

le **perroquet** NOUN
parrot

la **perruche** NOUN
budgie

la **perruque** NOUN
wig

le **persil** NOUN
parsley

le **personnage** NOUN
① figure ◊ *des personnages historiques* historical figures
② character ◊ *le personnage principal du film* the main character in the film

la **personnalité** NOUN
① personality ◊ *Il a une personnalité forte.* He has a strong personality.
② prominent figure ◊ *Il y avait beaucoup de personnalités politiques à ce dîner.* There were lots of prominent political figures at the dinner.

la **personne** NOUN

see also **personne** PRONOUN

person ◊ *Il y avait une trentaine de personnes dans la pièce.* There were about 30 people in the room. ◊ *une personne âgée* an elderly person
♦ **en personne** in person

personne PRONOUN

see also **personne** NOUN

① nobody ◊ *Il n'y a personne à la maison.* There's nobody at home. ◊ *Personne n'est venu me chercher.* Nobody came to fetch me.
② anybody ◊ *Elle ne veut voir personne.* She doesn't want to see anybody.

personnel ADJECTIVE (FEM SING **personnelle**)

see also **personnel** NOUN

personal

le **personnel** NOUN

see also **personnel** ADJECTIVE

staff ◊ *Il nous faut plus de personnel.* We need more staff.
♦ **le service du personnel** the personnel department

personnellement ADVERB
personally ◊ *Personnellement, je ne suis pas d'accord.* Personally, I don't agree.

persuader VERB
to persuade
♦ **persuader quelqu'un de faire quelque chose** to persuade somebody to do something ◊ *Elle m'a persuadé de l'accompagner au cinéma.* She persuaded me to go to the movie theatre with her.

la **perte** NOUN
① loss ◊ *la perte de poids* weight loss ◊ *Ça fait huit victoires et deux pertes pour notre équipe.* That's 8 wins and 2 losses for our team.
② waste ◊ *Cette réunion a été une perte de temps.* That meeting was a waste of time.

perturber VERB
to disrupt ◊ *Le bruit dans le couloir perturbait la classe.* The noise in the hallway was disrupting the class.

le **pèse-personne** NOUN
bathroom scales PL

peser VERB
to weigh ◊ *Il pèse cinquante kilos.* He weighs 50 kilos.
♦ **peser lourd** to be heavy ◊ *Cette valise pèse lourd.* This suitcase is heavy.

pessimiste ADJECTIVE
pessimistic

le **pétale** NOUN
petal

le **pétard** NOUN
firecracker

pétillant ADJECTIVE
sparkling

petit ADJECTIVE

P

☞

1 small ◊ *Nous habitons une petite ville.* We live in a small town.
2 little ◊ *Elle a une jolie petite maison.* She has a nice little house.
♦ **petit à petit** bit by bit
♦ **un petit ami** a boyfriend
♦ **une petite amie** a girlfriend
♦ **un petit pain** a bread roll
♦ **des petits pois** peas
♦ **les petits** young (of *animal*) ◊ *la lionne et ses petits* the lioness and her young

la **petite-fille** NOUN (PL les **petites-filles**)
granddaughter

le **petit-fils** NOUN (PL les **petits-fils**)
grandson

les **petits-enfants** MASC NOUN
grandchildren

le **pétoncle** NOUN
scallop

le **pétrole** NOUN
oil ◊ *un puits de pétrole* an oil well

peu ADVERB, NOUN
not much ◊ *J'ai peu mangé à midi.* I didn't eat much for lunch. ◊ *Il voyage peu.* He doesn't travel much.
♦ **un peu** a bit ◊ *Elle est un peu timide.* She's a bit shy. ◊ *un peu de gâteau* a bit of cake
♦ **un petit peu** a little bit ◊ *un petit peu de crème* a little bit of cream
♦ **peu de (1)** not many ◊ *Il y a peu de bons films au cinéma.* There aren't many good movies playing at the theatre. ◊ *Elle a peu d'amis.* She doesn't have many friends.
♦ **peu de (2)** not much ◊ *Il a peu d'espoir de réussir.* He doesn't have much hope of succeeding. ◊ *Il lui reste peu d'argent.* He doesn't have much money left.
♦ **à peu près (1)** more or less ◊ *J'ai à peu près fini.* I've more or less finished.
♦ **à peu près (2)** about ◊ *Le voyage prend à peu près deux heures.* The journey takes about two hours.
♦ **peu à peu** little by little
♦ **peu avant** shortly before
♦ **peu après** shortly afterwards
♦ **de peu** just (by a narrow margin) ◊ *Elle a manqué son train de peu.* She just missed her train.

le **peuple** NOUN
people ◊ *le peuple canadien* the Canadian people

la **peur** NOUN
fear
♦ **avoir peur de** to be afraid of ◊ *Je n'ai pas peur du noir.* I'm not afraid of the dark.

♦ **avoir peur de faire quelque chose** to be afraid to do something ◊ *Elle a peur d'y aller toute seule.* She's afraid to go on her own.
♦ **faire peur à quelqu'un** to scare somebody ◊ *Cet homme-là me fait peur.* That man scares me.

peureux ADJECTIVE (FEM SING **peureuse**)
fearful

peut VERB *see* **pouvoir**
♦ **Il ne peut pas venir.** He can't come.

peut-être ADVERB
maybe ◊ *Je l'ai peut-être oublié à la maison.* Maybe I left it at home.
♦ **peut-être que** it could be that ◊ *Peut-être qu'elles n'ont pas pu téléphoner.* It could be that they weren't able to phone.

peuvent, peux VERB *see* **pouvoir**
♦ **Je ne peux pas le faire.** I can't do it.

p. ex. ABBREVIATION (= *par exemple*)
e.g.

le **phare** NOUN
1 lighthouse ◊ *On voit le phare depuis le pont du bateau.* You can see the lighthouse from the ship's deck.
2 headlight ◊ *Il a laissé les phares de sa voiture allumés.* He left his headlights on.

la **pharmacie** NOUN
drugstore

le **pharmacien** NOUN
pharmacist

la **pharmacienne** NOUN
pharmacist

le **phénomène** NOUN
phenomenon

la **philosophie** NOUN
philosophy

le **phoque** NOUN
seal (*animal*)

la **photo** NOUN
photo ◊ *Elle a fait développer ses photos.* She got her photos developed.
♦ **en photo** in pictures ◊ *Je n'ai vu les montagnes qu'en photo.* I've only ever seen the mountains in pictures.
♦ **prendre quelqu'un en photo** to take a picture of somebody ◊ *Maman nous a pris en photo.* Mom took a picture of us.
♦ **une photo d'identité** a passport photo

la **photocopie** NOUN
photocopy

photocopier VERB
to photocopy

la **photocopieuse** NOUN

photocopier

le/la **photographe** NOUN
photographer

la **photographie** NOUN
1 photography
2 photograph

photographier VERB
to photograph

la **phrase** NOUN
sentence

physique ADJECTIVE

see also **physique** NOUN

physical

le **physique** NOUN

see also **la physique** and **physique** ADJECTIVE

♦ **Il a un physique agréable.** He's quite good-looking.

la **physique** NOUN

see also **le physique** and **physique** ADJECTIVE

physics ◊ *Il est professeur de physique.* He's a physics teacher.

le/la **pianiste** NOUN
pianist ◊ *Elle est pianiste.* She's a pianist.

le **piano** NOUN
piano

le **pic** NOUN
peak ◊ *les pics enneigés des Rocheuses* the snowy peaks of the Rockies
♦ **à pic (1)** straight down ◊ *La falaise tombe à pic dans la mer.* The cliff drops straight down into the sea.
♦ **à pic (2)** just at the right time ◊ *Tu es arrivé à pic.* You arrived just at the right time.

❋ le **pic-bois** NOUN
woodpecker

la **pièce** NOUN
1 room ◊ *Mon lit est au centre de la pièce.* My bed is in the middle of the room.
2 play ◊ *On joue une pièce de Robert Lepage au théâtre.* There's a play by Robert Lepage on at the theatre.
3 part ◊ *Il faut changer une pièce du moteur.* There's an engine part that needs changing.
4 coin ◊ *des pièces de un dollar* some one-dollar coins
♦ **cinquante dollars pièce** 50 dollars each ◊ *J'ai acheté ces T-shirts dix dollars pièce.* I bought these T-shirts for ten dollars each.
♦ **un maillot une pièce** a one-piece swimsuit

♦ **un maillot deux-pièces** a two-piece swimsuit
♦ **Avez-vous une pièce d'identité?** Do you have any identification?
♦ **une pièce jointe** an e-mail attachment

le **pied** NOUN
foot ◊ *J'ai mal aux pieds.* My feet are hurting.
♦ **à pied** on foot
♦ **avoir pied** to be able to touch bottom ◊ *Elle n'aime pas nager là où elle n'a pas pied.* She doesn't like swimming where she can't touch bottom.
❋ ♦ **avoir les deux pieds dans la même bottine** to be clumsy
♦ **des pieds à la tête** from head to foot
♦ **le pied d'athlète** athlete's foot
♦ **le pied de page** footer (*in document*)

le **piège** NOUN
trap
♦ **prendre quelqu'un au piège** to trap somebody

piéger VERB
to trap
♦ **un colis piégé** a parcel bomb
♦ **une voiture piégée** a car bomb

la **pierre** NOUN
stone
♦ **une pierre précieuse** a precious stone
♦ **faire d'une pierre deux coups** to kill two birds with one stone

le **piéton** NOUN
pedestrian

la **piétonne** NOUN
pedestrian

piétonnier ADJECTIVE (FEM SING **piétonnière**)
♦ **une rue piétonnière** a traffic-free street
♦ **un quartier piétonnier** a pedestrian zone

la **pieuvre** NOUN
octopus

le **pigeon** NOUN
pigeon

piger VERB (*informal*)
to understand

la **pile** NOUN

see also **pile** ADVERB

1 pile ◊ *Il y a une pile de disques sur la table.* There's a pile of records on the table.
2 battery ◊ *La pile de ma montre est usée.* The battery in my watch is dead.

pile ADVERB

see also **pile** NOUN

♦ **à deux heures pile** at two on the dot
♦ **jouer à pile ou face** to flip a coin

P

☞

♦ **Pile ou face?** Heads or tails?

le/la **pilote** NOUN
pilot
♦ **un pilote de course** a race car driver
♦ **un pilote de ligne** an airline pilot

piloter VERB
to fly (a plane)

la **pilule** NOUN
pill
♦ **prendre la pilule** to be on the Pill

le **piment** NOUN
chili pepper

le **pin** NOUN
pine

la **pince** NOUN
① pliers PL (tool)
② pincer (of crab)
♦ **une pince à épiler** tweezers
♦ **une pince à linge** a clothespin

le **pinceau** NOUN (PL les **pinceaux**)
paintbrush

la **pincée** NOUN
♦ **une pincée de sel** a pinch of salt

pincer VERB
to pinch ◊ Il m'a pincé le bras. He pinched my arm.

le **pingouin** NOUN
penguin

le **ping-pong** NOUN
table tennis ◊ jouer au ping-pong to play table tennis

le **pion** NOUN
① pawn (chess)
② piece (in checkers)

le **pionnier** NOUN
pioneer

la **pionnière** NOUN
pioneer

la **pipe** NOUN
pipe (for smoking)

piquant ADJECTIVE
① prickly
② spicy

le **pique** NOUN
spades PL ◊ l'as de pique the ace of spades

le **pique-nique** NOUN
picnic

piquer VERB
① to bite ◊ Nous avons été piqués par les maringouins. We were bitten by mosquitoes.
② to burn ◊ Cette sauce me pique la langue. This sauce is burning my tongue.
③ to steal ◊ On m'a piqué mon porte-monnaie. (informal) My wallet was stolen.
♦ **se piquer** to prick oneself ◊ Il s'est piqué avec une aiguille. He pricked himself with a needle.

le **piquet** NOUN
① stake ◊ Le chien est attaché à un piquet. The dog is tied to a stake.
② peg ◊ Il nous manque un des piquets de la tente. One of our tent pegs is missing.
♦ **le piquet de grève** the picket line

la **piqûre** NOUN
① injection ◊ Le médecin m'a fait une piqûre. The doctor gave me an injection.
② bite ◊ une piqûre de maringouin a mosquito bite
③ sting ◊ une piqûre d'abeille a bee sting

le/la **pirate** NOUN
pirate
♦ **un pirate informatique** a hacker

pire ADJECTIVE, NOUN
worse ◊ C'est encore pire qu'avant. It's even worse than before.
♦ **le pire** the worst ◊ C'est la pire journée que j'aie jamais passée. That's the worst day I've ever had. ◊ Ce gamin est le pire de la bande. That boy is the worst in the group.
♦ **le pire de** the worst of ◊ Le pire de tout, c'est qu'on s'ennuie tout le temps. The worst of it is that we're always bored.

la **piscine** NOUN
swimming pool

la **pistache** NOUN
pistachio ◊ une crème glacée à la pistache a pistachio ice cream

la **piste** NOUN
① trail ◊ La police est sur la piste du criminel. The police are on the criminal's trail.
② runway ◊ L'avion s'est posé sur la piste. The plane landed on the runway.
③ ski run ◊ La skieuse a descendu la piste. The skier came down the ski run.
♦ **la piste de danse** the dance floor
♦ **une piste cyclable** a bike path

le **pistolet** NOUN
pistol

la **pitié** NOUN
pity
♦ **Elle me fait pitié.** I feel sorry for her.
♦ **avoir pitié de quelqu'un** to feel sorry for somebody

✹ **pitonner** VERB
① to zap (TV)

2 to key in (*computer*)

pittoresque ADJECTIVE
picturesque

la **pizza** NOUN
pizza

le **placard** NOUN
cupboard

la **place** NOUN
1 place ◊ *Elle a eu la troisième place au concours.* She got third place in the competition. ◊ *remettre quelque chose en place* to put something back in its place
2 square ◊ *la place du marché* the market square
3 room (*space*) ◊ *Il ne reste plus de place pour se garer.* There's no more room to park. ◊ *Ça prend de la place.* It takes up a lot of room.
4 seat ◊ *Toutes les places ont été vendues.* All the seats have been sold.
♦ sur place on the spot
♦ à la place instead ◊ *Il ne reste plus de tarte; désirez-vous quelque chose d'autre à la place?* There's no pie left; would you like something else instead?
♦ à la place de instead of

placer VERB
1 to seat ◊ *Nous étions placés près de la porte.* We were seated near the door.
2 to invest ◊ *Il a placé ses économies à la Bourse.* He invested his money on the Stock Exchange.

le **plafond** NOUN
ceiling

la **plage** NOUN
beach

le **plagiat** NOUN
plagiarism

la **plaie** NOUN
wound

plaindre VERB
♦ plaindre quelqu'un to feel sorry for somebody ◊ *Je te plains.* I feel sorry for you.
♦ se plaindre to complain ◊ *Il n'arrête pas de se plaindre.* He never stops complaining.
♦ se plaindre à quelqu'un to complain to somebody ◊ *Ils se sont plaints à la gérente.* They complained to the manager.
♦ se plaindre de quelque chose to complain about something ◊ *Elle s'est plainte du bruit.* She complained about the noise.

la **plaine** NOUN
plain (*level area*)

la **plainte** NOUN
complaint
♦ porter plainte to lodge a complaint

plaire VERB
♦ Ce cadeau me plaît beaucoup. I like this present a lot.
♦ Ce film plaît beaucoup aux jeunes. The film is very popular with young people.
♦ Ça t'a plu d'aller en Nouvelle-Écosse? Did you enjoy going to Nova Scotia?
♦ Elle lui plaît. He likes her.
♦ s'il te plaît please
♦ s'il vous plaît please

plaisanter VERB
to joke

la **plaisanterie** NOUN
joke

le **plaisir** NOUN
pleasure
♦ faire plaisir à quelqu'un to please somebody ◊ *J'y suis allé pour lui faire plaisir.* I went there to please her. ◊ *Ce cadeau me fait très plaisir.* I'm very happy with this present.

plaît VERB *see* **plaire**

le **plan** NOUN
1 plan
2 map ◊ *un plan du centre commercial* a map of the mall
♦ un plan de la ville a street map
♦ au premier plan in the foreground

la **planche** NOUN
plank
♦ une planche à neige a snowboard
♦ une planche à repasser an ironing board
♦ une planche à roulettes a skateboard
♦ une planche à voile a sailboard
♦ une planche de surf a surfboard

le **plancher** NOUN
floor

le/la **planchiste** NOUN
boarder (*skateboarder, snowboarder*)

planer VERB
to glide ◊ *Un oiseau planait dans l'air.* A bird glided through the air.

la **planète** NOUN
planet

la **plante** NOUN
plant

planter VERB
1 to plant ◊ *Mon père a planté des tomates.* My dad planted some tomatoes.
2 to hammer in ◊ *Elle a planté un clou dans le mur.* She hammered a nail into the wall.
3 to pitch ◊ *Les filles ont planté leur*

P

☞

tente au bord du lac. The girls pitched their tent beside the lake.

④ to crash (*computer*) ◊ *Mon ordinateur a encore planté.* My computer crashed again.

♦ **Ne reste pas planté là!** Don't just stand there!
♦ **se planter** (*informal*) to fail ◊ *Je me suis planté en maths.* I failed math.

la **plaque** NOUN
(metal) plate
♦ **une plaque de verglas** a patch of ice

plaqué ADJECTIVE
♦ **plaqué or** gold-plated
♦ **plaqué argent** silver-plated

le **plastique** NOUN
plastic

plat ADJECTIVE

see also **plat** NOUN

flat
♦ **être à plat ventre** to be lying face down
♦ **l'eau plate** still water

le **plat** NOUN

see also **plat** ADJECTIVE

① dish
② course ◊ *le plat principal* the main course
♦ **un plat cuisiné** a pre-cooked meal
♦ **le plat du jour** the daily special

le **plateau** NOUN (PL les **plateaux**)
① tray
♦ **un plateau de fromages** a selection of cheeses
② plateau

le **platine** NOUN

see also **la platine**

platinum

la **platine** NOUN

see also **le platine**

turntable (*of record player*)
♦ **une platine laser** a CD player

le **plâtre** NOUN
plaster ◊ *une statue en plâtre* a plaster statue
♦ **avoir un bras dans le plâtre** to have one's arm in a cast

plein ADJECTIVE

see also **plein** NOUN

full
♦ **à plein temps** full-time ◊ *Elle travaille à plein temps.* She works full-time.
♦ **plein de** (*informal*) lots of ◊ *un gâteau avec plein de crème* a cake with lots of cream
♦ **Il y a plein de gens dans la rue.** The street is full of people.
♦ **en plein air** in the open air

♦ **en pleine nuit** in the middle of the night
♦ **en plein jour** in broad daylight

le **plein** NOUN

see also **plein** ADJECTIVE

♦ **faire le plein** to fill it up (*gas*) ◊ *Faites le plein, s'il vous plaît.* Fill it up, please.

pleurer VERB
to cry

pleut VERB see **pleuvoir**

pleuvoir VERB
to rain ◊ *Il pleut.* It's raining.
♦ **pleuvoir à boire debout** to rain cats and dogs

le **pli** NOUN
① fold
② pleat ◊ *une jupe à plis* a pleated skirt
③ crease ◊ *Il y a un pli sur la manche de ta chemise.* There's a crease in the sleeve of your shirt.

pliant ADJECTIVE
folding ◊ *un lit pliant* a folding bed

plier VERB
① to fold ◊ *plier une serviette* to fold a towel
② to bend ◊ *Il a plié le bras.* He bent his arm.

le **plomb** NOUN
lead ◊ *un tuyau en plomb* a lead pipe
♦ **l'essence sans plomb** unleaded gas

le **plombier** NOUN
plumber
♦ **Il est plombier.** He's a plumber.

la **plombière** NOUN
plumber
♦ **Elle est plombière.** She's a plumber.

la **plongée** NOUN
diving ◊ *faire de la plongée* to go diving

le **plongeoir** NOUN
diving board

le **plongeon** NOUN
dive

plonger VERB
to dive ◊ *Il a plongé dans la piscine.* He dived into the swimming pool.
♦ **J'ai plongé ma main dans l'eau.** I plunged my hand into the water.
♦ **être plongé dans son travail** to be absorbed in one's work
♦ **se plonger dans un livre** to get absorbed in a book

plu VERB see **plaire, pleuvoir**

la **pluie** NOUN
rain ◊ *sous la pluie* in the rain

la **plume** NOUN
> feather ◊ *une plume d'oiseau* a bird's feather
♦ **un stylo à plume** a fountain pen

plupart
♦ **la plupart** PRONOUN most (of them)
> ◊ *La plupart ont moins de quinze ans.* Most of them are under 15.
♦ **la plupart de** most of ◊ *La plupart de mes amis sont allés au concert.* Most of my friends went to the concert.
> ◊ *La plupart des élèves ont fait les devoirs.* Most of the students did the homework.
♦ **la plupart des** most ◊ *La plupart des gens ont déjà vu ce film.* Most people have already seen this film.
♦ **la plupart du temps** most of the time

le **pluriel** NOUN
> plural
♦ **au pluriel** in the plural

plus ADVERB, PREPOSITION
♦ **ne...plus** not...anymore ◊ *Il ne travaille plus ici.* He doesn't work here anymore.
♦ **Je n'ai plus de pain.** I have no more bread.
♦ **plus...que** more...than ◊ *Il est plus extraverti que son frère.* He's more outgoing than his brother. ◊ *Elle travaille plus que moi.* She works more than me. ◊ *Elle est plus grande que moi.* She's bigger than me.
♦ **C'est le plus grand de la famille.** He's the tallest in his family.
♦ **plus...plus...** the more...the more... ◊ *Plus elle gagne d'argent, plus elle en veut.* The more money she earns, the more she wants.
♦ **plus de (1)** more ◊ *Il nous faut plus de pain.* We need more bread.
♦ **plus de (2)** more than ◊ *Il y avait plus de dix personnes.* There were more than 10 people.
♦ **de plus** more ◊ *Il nous faut un joueur de plus.* We need one more player. ◊ *Le voyage a pris trois heures de plus que prévu.* The journey took 3 more hours than planned.
♦ **en plus** more ◊ *J'ai apporté quelques couvertures en plus.* I brought a few more blankets.
♦ **de plus en plus** more and more ◊ *Il y a de plus en plus de touristes par ici.* There are getting to be more and more tourists around here. ◊ *Il fait de plus en plus chaud.* It's getting hotter and hotter out.
♦ **un peu plus difficile** a bit more difficult ◊ *Il fait un peu plus froid qu'hier.* It's a bit colder than yesterday.
♦ **plus ou moins** more or less

♦ **Quatre plus deux égalent six.** 4 plus 2 is 6.

plusieurs PRONOUN
> several ◊ *Elle a acheté plusieurs chemises.* She bought several shirts. ◊ *Il y en a plusieurs.* There are several of them.

le **plus-que-parfait** NOUN
> pluperfect

plutôt ADVERB
> ① quite ◊ *Elle est plutôt forte.* She's quite strong.
> ② rather ◊ *La nourriture ici est plutôt chère.* The food here is rather expensive
> ③ instead ◊ *Demande-leur plutôt de venir avec toi.* Ask them to come with you instead.
♦ **plutôt que** rather than ◊ *Je prendrai la salade plutôt que les frites avec ça.* I'll have the salad rather than the fries with that.

pluvieux ADJECTIVE (FEM SING **pluvieuse**)
> rainy

le **pneu** NOUN
> tire

la **pneumonie** NOUN
> pneumonia

la **poche** NOUN
> pocket
♦ **l'argent de poche** pocket money
♦ **un livre de poche** a paperback
♦ **un ordinateur de poche** a handheld computer

la **poêle** NOUN
> frying pan
♦ **une poêle à frire** a frying pan

le **poème** NOUN
> poem

la **poésie** NOUN
> ① poetry
> ② poem

le/la **poète** NOUN
> poet

le **poids** NOUN
> weight ◊ *vendre quelque chose au poids* to sell something by weight
♦ **prendre du poids** to put on weight ◊ *Il a pris du poids.* He's put on weight.
♦ **perdre du poids** to lose weight ◊ *Il a perdu du poids.* He's lost weight.
♦ **un poids lourd** a truck

la **poignée** NOUN
> ① handful ◊ *une poignée de riz* a handful of rice
> ② handle ◊ *la poignée de la porte* the door handle
♦ **une poignée de main** a handshake

le **poignet** NOUN

P

☞

① <u>wrist</u> ◊ *Je me suis fait mal au poignet.* I hurt my wrist.
② <u>cuff</u> (*of shirt*)

le **poil** NOUN
① <u>hair</u> ◊ *Il y a des poils de chat partout sur la moquette.* There are cat hairs all over the carpet.
② <u>fur</u> ◊ *Ton chien a un beau poil.* Your dog has beautiful fur.
♦ **à poil** (*informal*) stark naked

poilu ADJECTIVE
<u>hairy</u>

poinçonner VERB
<u>to punch</u> ◊ *Le contrôleur a poinçonné les billets.* The conductor punched the tickets.

le **poing** NOUN
<u>fist</u>
♦ **un coup de poing** a punch

le **point** NOUN
① <u>point</u> ◊ *Je ne suis pas d'accord sur ce point.* I don't agree with this point. ◊ *Son point faible, c'est qu'elle est un peu paresseuse.* Her weak point is that she's a bit lazy.
♦ **le point de départ** the starting line (*in a race*)
♦ **point de vue** point of view
② <u>period</u> (*punctuation*)
③ <u>dot</u> ◊ *metter un point sur un « i »* to dot an "i"
♦ **être sur le point de faire quelque chose** to be just about to do something ◊ *J'étais sur le point de te téléphoner.* I was just about to phone you.
♦ **mettre au point** to finalize
♦ **Ce n'est pas encore au point.** It's not finalized yet.
♦ **à point** medium ◊ *« Comment voulez-vous votre steak? » « À point. »* "How would you like your steak?" "Medium."
♦ **un point d'exclamation** an exclamation mark
♦ **un point d'interrogation** a question mark
♦ **un point noir** a blackhead

le **pointage** NOUN
<u>score</u> (*sports*)

la **pointe** NOUN
<u>point</u> ◊ *la pointe d'un couteau* the point of a knife
♦ **être à la pointe du progrès** to be in the forefront of progress
♦ **sur la pointe des pieds** on tiptoe
♦ **les heures de pointe** peak hours

le **pointillé** NOUN
<u>dotted line</u>

pointilleux ADJECTIVE (FEM SING **pointilleuse**)
<u>picky</u> ◊ *Notre prof est pointilleuse sur la grammaire.* Our teacher is picky about grammar.

pointu ADJECTIVE
<u>pointed</u> ◊ *un chapeau pointu* a pointed hat

la **pointure** NOUN
<u>size</u> (*of shoes*) ◊ *Quelle est votre pointure?* What size shoes do you take?

le **point-virgule** NOUN (PL **points-virgules**)
<u>semicolon</u>

la **poire** NOUN
<u>pear</u>

le **poireau** NOUN (PL les **poireaux**)
<u>leek</u> ◊ *la soupe aux poireaux* leek soup

le **pois** NOUN
<u>pea</u>
♦ **les petits pois** peas
♦ **les pois chiches** chickpeas
♦ **à pois** polka-dotted ◊ *une robe à pois* a polka-dotted dress

le **poison** NOUN
<u>poison</u>

le **poisson** NOUN
<u>fish</u> ◊ *Je n'aime pas le poisson.* I don't like fish. ◊ *Elle a attrapé deux poissons.* She caught two fish.
♦ **les Poissons** Pisces ◊ *Elle est Poissons.* She's a Pisces.
♦ **Poisson d'avril!** April fool!
♦ **un poisson rouge** a goldfish

la **poitrine** NOUN
① <u>chest</u> ◊ *J'ai mal à la poitrine.* I'm having chest pains.
② <u>bust</u> ◊ *Quel est votre tour de poitrine?* What's your bust size?
③ <u>breast</u> ◊ *une poitrine de poulet* a chicken breast

le **poivre** NOUN
<u>pepper</u> (*spice*)

le **poivron** NOUN
<u>pepper</u> (*vegetable*)

le **pôle** NOUN
<u>pole</u>
♦ **le pôle Nord** the North Pole
♦ **le pôle Sud** the South Pole

poli ADJECTIVE
<u>polite</u>

la **police** NOUN
<u>police</u> ◊ *La police recherche le voleur.* The police are looking for the thief.
♦ **la police de caractères** font
♦ **une police d'assurance** an insurance policy

policier ADJECTIVE (FEM SING **policière**)

see also **policier** NOUN

♦ **un roman policier** a detective novel

le **policier** NOUN

see also **policier** ADJECTIVE

police officer ◊ *Il est policier.* He's a
police officer.

la **policière** NOUN

see also **policier** ADJECTIVE

police officer ◊ *Elle est policière.*
She's a police officer.

la **politesse** NOUN
politeness

la **politique** NOUN

see also **politique** ADJECTIVE

① politics ◊ *La politique ne
l'intéresse pas du tout.* He's not at all
interested in politics.
♦ **pratiquer la politique de l'autruche** to
bury one's head in the sand
② policy ◊ *la politique sociale du
gouvernement* the government's
social policy

politique ADJECTIVE

see also **politique** NOUN

political ◊ *une question politique* a
political issue

politiquement correct ADJECTIVE
politically correct

polluer VERB
to pollute ◊ *Les lacs ont été pollués.*
The lakes have been polluted.

le **pollupostage** NOUN
spam

le **polluriel** NOUN
spam message

la **pollution** NOUN
pollution

❈ la **polyvalente** NOUN

> ⓘ *In Québec,* **la polyvalente** *is
> a high school that provides both
> academic and vocational programs.*

la **pommade** NOUN
ointment

la **pomme** NOUN
apple
♦ **les pommes de terre** potatoes

la **pompe** NOUN
pump
♦ **une pompe à essence** a gas pump

le **pompier** NOUN
firefighter

la **pompière** NOUN
firefighter

ponctuel ADJECTIVE (FEM SING **ponctuelle**)

① punctual ◊ *Elle est toujours
très ponctuelle.* She's always very
punctual.
② occasional
♦ **On a rencontré quelques problèmes
ponctuels.** We've had the occasional
problem.

pondre VERB
to lay (*eggs*)

le **poney** NOUN
pony

le **pont** NOUN
① bridge
② deck (*of ship*)

pop ADJECTIVE
pop (*music*) ◊ *des groupes pop* pop
bands

populaire ADJECTIVE
① popular ◊ *Ce chanteur est très
populaire au Québec.* This singer's
very popular in Québec.
② working-class ◊ *un quartier
populaire de la ville* a working-class
area of town

la **population** NOUN
population
♦ **la population active** the workforce

le **porc** NOUN
① pig ◊ *Ils élèvent des porcs.* They
breed pigs.
② pork ◊ *du rôti de porc* roast pork

la **porcelaine** NOUN
china ◊ *une tasse en porcelaine* a
china cup

le **porc-épic** NOUN (PL les **porcs-épics**)
porcupine

le **port** NOUN
① harbour
② port

❈ le **portage** NOUN
portage ◊ *Cette rivière comporte huit
portages.* This river has 8 portages.
♦ **faire du portage** to portage

❈ **portager** VERB
to portage

le **portail** NOUN
portal (*Web*)

portatif ADJECTIVE (FEM SING **portative**)
portable

la **porte** NOUN
① door ◊ *Ferme la porte, s'il te plaît.*
Close the door, please.
♦ **la porte d'entrée** the front door
② gate ◊ *Vol 432 à destination de
Calgary : porte numéro trois.* Flight
432 to Calgary: gate 3.
♦ **mettre quelqu'un à la porte** to fire
somebody

P

le **porte-bagages** NOUN
    luggage rack
    ♦ **le porte-bagages de toit** roof rack

le **porte-clés** NOUN
    keychain

la **portée** NOUN
    ♦ **à portée de la main** within arm's reach
    ♦ **hors de portée** out of reach

le **portefeuille** NOUN
    wallet

le **portemanteau** NOUN (PL les **portemanteaux**)
    coat rack

le **porte-monnaie** NOUN (PL les **porte-monnaie**)
    wallet

le/la **porte-parole** NOUN (PL les **porte-parole**)
    spokesperson ◊ *Elle est la porte-parole de notre conseil étudiant.* She's the spokesperson for our student council.

porter VERB
    ① to carry ◊ *Il portait une valise.* He was carrying a suitcase.
    ② to wear ◊ *Elle porte une robe bleue.* She's wearing a blue dress.
    ♦ **se porter bien** to be well
    ♦ **se porter mal** to be unwell

le **porteur** NOUN
    porter

la **portion** NOUN
    portion

le **portrait** NOUN
    portrait

poser VERB
    ① to put down ◊ *J'ai posé la cafetière sur la table.* I put the coffee pot down on the table.
    ② to pose ◊ *Cela pose un problème.* That poses a problem.
    ♦ **poser une question à quelqu'un** to ask somebody a question
    ♦ **poser des rideaux** to put up curtains
    ♦ **poser sa candidature** to apply for a job
    ♦ **se poser** to land ◊ *L'avion s'est posé à huit heures.* The plane landed at 8 o'clock.

positif ADJECTIVE (FEM SING **positive**)
    positive

la **position** NOUN
    position

posséder VERB
    to own ◊ *Ils possèdent une jolie maison.* They own a lovely home.

la **possibilité** NOUN
    possibility

possible ADJECTIVE
    possible ◊ *Nous leur avons dit que ce n'était pas possible.* We told them it wasn't possible.
    ♦ **le plus de gens possible** as many people as possible
    ♦ **le plus tôt possible** as early as possible
    ♦ **le moins d'argent possible** as little money as possible
    ♦ **Il travaille le moins possible.** He works as little as possible.
    ♦ **dès que possible** as soon as possible
    ♦ **faire son possible** to do all one can ◊ *Je ferai tout mon possible.* I'll do all I can.

la **poste** NOUN
    │ see also **le poste** │
    mail ◊ *Je vais l'envoyer par la poste.* I'm going to send it by mail.
    ♦ **le bureau de poste** the post office
    ♦ **mettre une lettre à la poste** to mail a letter

le **poste** NOUN
    │ see also **la poste** │
    ① job ◊ *Elle a trouvé un poste de professeure.* She has found a teaching job.
    ② extension (*phone*) ◊ *Pouvez-vous me passer le poste de M. Salzedo?* Can you put me through to Mr Salzedo's extension?
    ③ set ◊ *un poste de radio* a radio set
    ♦ **le poste de péage** tollbooth
    ♦ **un poste de police** a police station

poster VERB
    │ see also **poster** NOUN │
    to mail ◊ *Je vais poster ce colis.* I'm going to mail this parcel.

le **poster** NOUN
    │ see also **poster** VERB │
    poster

le **pot** NOUN
    jar ◊ *J'ai fait trois pots de confiture.* I've made three jars of jam.
    ♦ **un pot de fleurs** a flowerpot

potable ADJECTIVE
    ♦ **eau potable** drinking water
    ♦ **« eau non potable »** "not drinking water"

le **pot-de-vin** NOUN (PL les **pots-de-vin**)
    bribe

le **poteau** NOUN (PL les **poteaux**)
    post ◊ *Elle s'est appuyée contre un poteau.* She leaned against a post.
    ♦ **un poteau indicateur** a signpost

potentiel ADJECTIVE (FEM SING **potentielle**)
    potential

la **poterie** NOUN

⓵ pottery ◊ *Nous avons fait de la poterie à l'école.* We did pottery at school.

⓶ piece of pottery ◊ *J'ai acheté deux poteries.* I bought two pieces of pottery.

✳ le **potlatch** NOUN
potlatch

le **pou** NOUN (PL les **poux**)
louse

la **poubelle** NOUN
garbage can

le **pouce** NOUN

⓵ thumb ◊ *Je me suis coincé le pouce dans la porte.* I trapped my thumb in the door.

♦ **donner un coup de pouce à quelqu'un** to help out someone
✳ ♦ **faire du pouce** to hitchhike

⓶ inch

> **ⓘ** An **inch** is a nonmetric unit of length equal to about 2.5 cm.

✳ le **pouding-chômeur** NOUN

> **ⓘ** Le **pouding-chômeur** is a dessert consisting of a thickened mixture of brown sugar, water, and butter, sometimes mixed with maple syrup, under a layer of cake.

la **poudre** NOUN

⓵ powder

⓶ face powder

♦ **le lait en poudre** powdered milk
♦ **le café en poudre** instant coffee

✳ la **poudrerie** NOUN
blizzard ◊ *Les écoles sont fermées à cause de la poudrerie.* The schools are closed because of the blizzard.

le **poulain** NOUN
foal

la **poule** NOUN
hen

le **poulet** NOUN
chicken ◊ *J'adore le poulet.* I love chicken. ◊ *un poulet rôti* a roast chicken

le **pouls** NOUN
pulse ◊ *Il m'a pris le pouls.* He took my pulse.

le **poumon** NOUN
lung

la **poupée** NOUN
doll

pour PREPOSITION
for ◊ *C'est un cadeau pour toi.* It's a present for you. ◊ *Qu'est-ce que tu veux pour ton déjeuner?* What would you like for breakfast?

♦ **pour faire quelque chose** in order to do something ◊ *Je lui ai téléphoné pour l'inviter.* I phoned him in order to invite him.

♦ **Pour aller à Kamloops, s'il vous plaît?** Which way is it to Kamloops, please?

♦ **pour que** so that

> *pour que* is followed by a verb in the subjunctive.

◊ *Je lui ai prêté mon chandail pour qu'elle n'ait pas froid.* I lent her my sweater so that she wouldn't be cold.

♦ **pour cent** per cent

le **pourboire** NOUN
tip ◊ *Elle a donné un pourboire au garçon.* She gave the waiter a tip.

le **pourcentage** NOUN
percentage

pourquoi ADVERB, CONJUNCTION
why ◊ *Pourquoi est-ce qu'il ne vient pas avec nous?* Why isn't he coming with us? ◊ *Elle ne m'a pas dit pourquoi.* She didn't tell me why.

pourra, pourrai, pourras, pourrez VERB
see **pouvoir**

pourri ADJECTIVE
rotten

pourrir VERB
to go bad ◊ *Ces poires ont pourri.* These pears have gone bad.

pourrons, pourront VERB *see* **pouvoir**

la **poursuite** NOUN
chase

♦ **se lancer à la poursuite de quelqu'un** to chase after somebody

poursuivre VERB
to carry on with ◊ *Ils ont poursuivi leur travail.* They carried on with their work.

♦ **se poursuivre** to go on ◊ *Le concert s'est poursuivi très tard.* The concert went on very late.

pourtant ADVERB
however ◊ *Il a raté son examen. Pourtant, il n'est pas bête.* He failed his exam. However, he's not stupid.

♦ **C'est pourtant facile!** But it's easy!

pourvu ADJECTIVE

> *pourvu que* is followed by a verb in the subjunctive.

♦ **pourvu que... (1)** let's hope that... ◊ *Pourvu qu'il ne pleuve pas!* Let's hope it doesn't rain!

♦ **pourvu que... (2)** as long as... (on condition that) ◊ *Tu peux y aller, pourvu que tu fasses tes devoirs*

P

☞

avant le souper. You can go, as long as you do your homework before supper.

pousser VERB
1 to push ◊ *Elle a pu pousser la voiture.* She was able to push the car.
2 to grow ◊ *Mes cheveux poussent vite.* My hair grows quickly.
♦ **pousser un cri** to give a cry
♦ **se pousser** to move over ◊ *Pousse-toi, je ne vois rien.* Move over, I can't see a thing.

la **poussette** NOUN
stroller

la **poussière** NOUN
dust ◊ *La table est couverte de poussière.* The table's covered with dust.

poussiéreux ADJECTIVE (FEM SING **poussiéreuse**)
dusty

le **poussin** NOUN
chick

✻ la **poutine** NOUN

> **ⓘ** *La poutine*, a Québécois fast food staple, consists of French fries topped with cheese curds and gravy. In one famous version (**la poutine italienne**), the gravy is replaced with a meat spaghetti sauce. **La poutine râpée** is a traditional Acadian dish consisting of dumplings made of grated potato, salted and filled with pork.

le **pouvoir** NOUN

> *see also* **pouvoir** VERB

power ◊ *Le premier ministre a beaucoup de pouvoir.* The prime minister has a lot of power.

pouvoir VERB

> *see also* **pouvoir** NOUN

Present tense:
je peux	nous pouvons
tu peux	vous pouvez
il/elle peut	ils/elles peuvent

Past participle:
pu

can ◊ *Je peux lui téléphoner si tu veux.* I can phone her if you want.
◊ *Puis-je venir vous voir samedi?* May I come and see you on Saturday?
◊ *Je ne pourrai pas venir samedi.* I can't come on Saturday. ◊ *J'ai fait tout ce que j'ai pu.* I did all I could.
♦ **Je n'en peux plus.** I'm exhausted.
♦ **Il se peut que...** It's possible that...

> *il se peut que* is followed by a verb in the subjunctive.

◊ *Il se peut qu'elle ait déménagé.* It's possible that she's moved. ◊ *Il se peut que j'y aille.* I might go.

la **prairie** NOUN
prairie
♦ **les provinces des Prairies** the Prairie provinces

la **pratique** NOUN

> *see also* **pratique** ADJECTIVE

practice ◊ *Je manque de pratique.* I'm out of practice.

pratique ADJECTIVE

> *see also* **pratique** NOUN

practical ◊ *Ce sac à main est très pratique.* This purse is very practical.

pratiquement ADVERB
practically ◊ *J'ai pratiquement fini.* I've practically finished.

pratiquer VERB
to practise ◊ *Je dois pratiquer mon anglais.* I need to practise my English.
♦ **Pratiquez-vous un sport?** Do you play any sports?

le **pré** NOUN
meadow

la **précaution** NOUN
precaution ◊ *prendre ses précautions* to take precautions
♦ **par précaution** as a precaution ◊ *Il a pris une assurance par précaution.* He took out insurance as a precaution.
♦ **avec précaution** cautiously
♦ **« à manipuler avec précaution »** "handle with care"

précédemment ADVERB
previously

précédent ADJECTIVE
previous

précieux ADJECTIVE (FEM SING **précieuse**)
precious
♦ **une pierre précieuse** a precious stone
♦ **de précieux conseils** invaluable advice

le **précipice** NOUN
ravine ◊ *Leur voiture est tombée dans un précipice.* Their car fell into a ravine.

précipitamment ADVERB
hurriedly ◊ *Elle est partie précipitamment.* She left hurriedly.

la **précipitation** NOUN
haste ◊ *Il a agi avec précipitation.* He acted hastily.

se **précipiter** VERB
to rush

précis ADJECTIVE
precise
♦ **à huit heures précises** at exactly eight o'clock

précisément ADVERB
precisely

préciser VERB
1 to be more specific about ◊ *Pouvez-vous préciser ce que vous voulez dire?* Can you be more specific about what you're trying to say?
2 to specify ◊ *Pouvez-vous préciser les raisons de ce changement?* Can you specify the reasons for this change?

la **précision** NOUN
1 precision
2 detail ◊ *Peux-tu me donner quelques précisions?* Can you give me some details?

prédire VERB
1 to predict ◊ *Les climatologues n'ont pas prédit ce tsunami.* Climatologists did not predict this tsunami.
2 to foretell ◊ *Personne ne peut prédire l'avenir.* No one can foretell the future.

préférable ADJECTIVE
preferable

préféré ADJECTIVE
favourite

la **préférence** NOUN
preference ◊ *Je n'ai pas de préférence.* I have no preference.
♦ **de préférence** preferably

préférer VERB
to prefer ◊ *Je préfère la cuisine de mon père.* I prefer my dad's cooking. ◊ *Je préfère manger à la cafétéria.* I prefer to eat in the cafeteria.
♦ **Je préférerais du thé.** I'd rather have tea.
♦ **préférer quelque chose à quelque chose** to prefer something to something ◊ *Je préfère celui-ci à celui-là.* I prefer this one to that one.

préhistorique ADJECTIVE
prehistoric

le **préjugé** NOUN
prejudice ◊ *avoir des préjugés contre quelqu'un* to be prejudiced against somebody

la **prématernelle** NOUN
junior kindergarten

premier ADJECTIVE (FEM SING **première**)
see also **première** NOUN
first ◊ *au premier étage* on the first floor ◊ *C'est notre premier jour de vacances.* It's the first day of our holidays. ◊ *C'est la première fois que je viens ici.* It's the first time I've been here. ◊ *le premier mai* the first of May ◊ *Elle est arrivée première.* She came first.
♦ **le premier ministre (1)** the prime minister
♦ **le premier ministre (2)** the premier (*of province*)

la **première** NOUN
see also **premier** ADJECTIVE
1 first class ◊ *Nous avons voyagé en première.* We travelled first class.
2 first gear ◊ *Passe en première pour prendre ce virage.* Change into first to go around this bend.

premièrement ADVERB
firstly

✱ les **Premières Nations** FEM NOUN
First Nations ◊ *l'Assemblée des Premières Nations* the Assembly of First Nations

prendre VERB
to take ◊ *Prends tes affaires et viens avec moi.* Take your things and come with me.
♦ **prendre quelque chose à quelqu'un** to take something from somebody ◊ *Elle m'a pris mon stylo!* She took my pen!
♦ **Nous avons pris le vol de huit heures.** We took the eight o'clock flight.
♦ **Je prends toujours l'autobus pour aller à l'école.** I always go to school by bus
♦ **passer prendre** to pick up ◊ *Nous devons passer prendre sa sœur.* We have to pick up his sister.
♦ **prendre à gauche** to turn left ◊ *Prenez à gauche en arrivant à la prochaine intersection.* Turn left at the next intersection.
♦ **Il se prend pour un génie.** He thinks he's a genius.
♦ **s'en prendre à quelqu'un** to take it out on somebody (*verbally*) ◊ *Il s'en est pris à moi.* He took it out on me.
♦ **s'y prendre** to go about it ◊ *Tu t'y prends mal!* You're goting about it the wrong way!
♦ **prendre une décision** to make a decision

le **prénom** NOUN
first name ◊ *Quel est votre prénom?* What's your first name?

préoccupé ADJECTIVE
worried

la **préparation** NOUN
preparation

P

préparer VERB

⓵ to prepare ◊ *Il prépare le dîner.* He's preparing dinner.

⓶ to make ◊ *Je vais préparer le café.* I'm going to make the coffee.

⓷ to prepare for ◊ *Ma sœur prépare son examen d'économie.* My sister's preparing for her economics exam.

♦ **se préparer** to get ready ◊ *Ils se préparent à partir.* They're getting ready to go.

la **préposition** NOUN
preposition

près ADVERB

♦ **tout près** nearby ◊ *J'habite tout près.* I live nearby.

♦ **près de (1)** near (to) ◊ *Est-ce que c'est près d'ici?* Is it near here?

♦ **près de (2)** next to ◊ *Assieds-toi près de moi.* Sit down next to me.

♦ **près de (3)** nearly ◊ *Il y avait près de cinq cents spectateurs.* There were nearly 500 spectators.

♦ **de près** closely ◊ *Elle a regardé la photo de près.* She looked closely at the photo.

♦ **à peu de chose près** more or less

✿ la **prescription** NOUN
prescription (*medical*)

la **présence** NOUN

⓵ presence ◊ *Sa présence est rassurante.* Her presence is reassuring.

⓶ attendance ◊ *La présence aux cours est obligatoire.* Attendance at classes is compulsory.

présent ADJECTIVE

see also **présent** NOUN

present

le **présent** NOUN

see also **présent** ADJECTIVE

present tense

♦ **à présent** now

la **présentation** NOUN
presentation

♦ **faire les présentations** to do the introductions

présenter VERB

to present ◊ *Il a présenté son rapport à la classe.* He presented his report to the class.

♦ **présenter quelqu'un à quelqu'un** to introduce somebody to somebody ◊ *Il m'a présenté à sa sœur.* He introduced me to his sister.

♦ **Marc, je te présente Anaïs.** Marc, this is Anaïs.

♦ **se présenter (1)** to introduce oneself ◊ *Elle s'est présentée à ses collègues.* She introduced herself to her colleagues.

♦ **se présenter (2)** to arise ◊ *Si l'occasion se présente, nous irons au Yukon.* If the chance arises, we'll go to the Yukon.

♦ **se présenter (3)** to stand ◊ *Elle se présente encore aux élections.* She's standing for election again.

le **préservatif** NOUN
condom

préserver VERB
to protect ◊ *préserver du froid* to protect from the cold

le **président** NOUN

⓵ president ◊ *le président des États-Unis* the president of the United States

⓶ chair (*person*) ◊ *le président du conseil d'administration* the chair of the board of directors

la **présidente** NOUN

⓵ president

⓶ chair (*person*) ◊ *Elle est présidente du conseil d'administration.* She's the chair of the board of directors.

présider VERB

⓵ to chair ◊ *Elle a présidé la réunion.* She chaired the meeting.

⓶ to be the guest of honour ◊ *Il présidait à table.* He was the guest of honour at the table.

presque ADVERB

nearly ◊ *Il est presque six heures.* It's nearly 6 o'clock. ◊ *Nous sommes presque arrivés.* We're nearly there.

♦ **presque rien** hardly anything ◊ *Elle n'a presque rien mangé.* She's hardly eaten anything.

♦ **presque pas** hardly at all ◊ *Il ne dort presque pas.* He hardly sleeps at all.

♦ **presque pas de** hardly any ◊ *Il n'y a presque pas de place.* There's hardly any room.

la **presqu'île** NOUN
peninsula

la **presse** NOUN
press ◊ *les représentants de la presse* representatives of the press

pressé ADJECTIVE

⓵ in a hurry ◊ *Je ne peux pas rester, je suis pressé.* I can't stay, I'm in a hurry.

⓶ urgent ◊ *Ce n'est pas très pressé.* It's not very urgent.

presser VERB

⓵ to squeeze ◊ *presser un citron* to squeeze a lemon

⓶ to be urgent ◊ *Est-ce que ça presse?* Is it urgent?

♦ **se presser** to hurry up ◊ *Allez, presse-*

toi, on va être en retard! Come on, hurry up, we're going to be late!
♦ **Rien ne presse.** There's no hurry.

la **pression** NOUN
pressure
♦ **faire pression sur quelqu'un** to put pressure on somebody
♦ **la pression des pairs** peer pressure

prêt ADJECTIVE

see also **prêt** NOUN

ready ◊ *Le déjeuner est prêt.* Breakfast is ready. ◊ *Tu es prête?* Are you ready?

le **prêt** NOUN

see also **prêt** ADJECTIVE

loan

le **prêt-à-porter** NOUN
off-the-rack clothing

prétendre VERB
to claim ◊ *Il prétend qu'on lui a volé son sac à dos.* He claims his knapsack was stolen. ◊ *Elle prétend ne pas le connaître.* She claims she doesn't know him.

Be careful! **prétendre** does not mean **to pretend.**

prétendu ADJECTIVE
so-called ◊ *un prétendu expert* a so-called expert

prétentieux ADJECTIVE (FEM SING **prétentieuse**)
pretentious

prêter VERB
♦ **prêter quelque chose à quelqu'un** to lend something to someone ◊ *Elle m'a prêté sa calculatrice.* She lent me her calculator.
♦ **prêter attention à quelque chose** to pay attention to something

le **prétexte** NOUN
excuse ◊ *Il avait un prétexte pour ne pas venir.* He had an excuse for not coming.
♦ **sous aucun prétexte** under no circumstances ◊ *Il ne faut la déranger sous aucun prétexte.* She is not to be disturbed under any circumstances.

prétexter VERB
to give as an excuse ◊ *Elle a prétexté une réunion.* She gave a meeting as her excuse. ◊ *Il a prétexté qu'il avait un rendez-vous.* He gave the excuse that he had an appointment.

le **prêtre** NOUN
priest

la **preuve** NOUN
① evidence ◊ *Il y a des preuves*

contre lui. There's evidence against him.
② proof ◊ *Vous n'avez aucune preuve.* You have no proof.
♦ **faire preuve de courage** to show courage
♦ **faire ses preuves** to prove oneself ◊ *Pour être embauché ici, il faut faire ses preuves.* To be employed here, you need to prove yourself.

prévenir VERB
♦ **prévenir quelqu'un** to warn somebody ◊ *Je te préviens, elle est de mauvaise humeur.* I'm warning you, she's in a bad mood.

la **prévention** NOUN
prevention
♦ **des mesures de prévention** preventive measures
♦ **la prévention des incendies** fire prevention
♦ **la prévention routière** road safety

la **prévision** NOUN
♦ **les prévisions météorologiques** the weather forecast
♦ **en prévision de quelque chose** in anticipation of something

prévoir VERB
① to plan ◊ *Nous prévoyons un pique-nique pour dimanche.* We're planning to have a picnic on Sunday.
♦ **Le départ est prévu pour dix heures.** The departure's scheduled for 10 o'clock.
② to allow ◊ *J'ai prévu assez à manger pour quatre.* I allowed enough food for four.
③ to foresee ◊ *J'avais prévu ce problème dès le début.* I had foreseen this problem from the start.
♦ **Je prévois qu'il me faudra une heure de plus.** I figure it'll take me another hour.

prier VERB
to pray ◊ *Les Grecs de l'Antiquité priaient Dionysos.* The Ancient Greeks prayed to Dionysos.
♦ **prier quelqu'un de faire quelque chose** to ask somebody to do something ◊ *Elle l'a prié de sortir.* She asked him to leave.
♦ **je vous en prie (1)** please do ◊ *« Je peux m'asseoir? » « Je vous en prie. »* "May I sit down?" "Please do."
♦ **je vous en prie (2)** please ◊ *Je vous en prie, ne me laissez pas seule.* Please, don't leave me alone.
♦ **je vous en prie (3)** don't mention it ◊ *« Merci pour votre aide. » « Je vous en prie. »* "Thanks for your help." "Don't mention it."

la **prière** NOUN

P

☞

prayer ◊ *faire ses prières* to say one's prayers
♦ **« prière de ne pas fumer »** "no smoking please"

le **primaire** NOUN
elementary school ◊ *Ses enfants sont encore au primaire.* His children are still in elementary school.
♦ **une école primaire** an elementary school

la **prime** NOUN
① bonus ◊ *Il a eu une prime de son employeur.* He got a bonus from his employer.
② free gift ◊ *J'ai eu ce stylo en prime avec l'agenda.* I got this pen as a free gift with the diary.
③ premium ◊ *une prime d'assurance* an insurance premium

le **prince** NOUN
prince ◊ *le prince de Galles* the Prince of Wales

la **princesse** NOUN
princess ◊ *la princesse de Galles* the Princess of Wales

principal ADJECTIVE (MASC PL **principaux**)
see also **principal** NOUN
main ◊ *le rôle principal* the main role

le **principal** NOUN (PL les **principaux**)
see also **principal** ADJECTIVE
main thing ◊ *Personne n'a été blessé; c'est le principal.* Nobody was injured; that's the main thing.

le **principe** NOUN
principle
♦ **pour le principe** on principle
♦ **en principe (1)** as a rule ◊ *Elle prend son lunch en principe à midi et demi.* As a rule she has lunch at 12.30.
♦ **en principe (2)** in theory ◊ *En principe le travail doit être assez facile.* In theory, the work should be fairly easy.

le **printemps** NOUN
spring
♦ **au printemps** in spring

la **priorité** NOUN
① priority ◊ *C'est à faire en priorité.* This needs to be a priority.
② right of way ◊ *Tu n'as pas la priorité.* You don't have the right of way.

pris VERB *see* **prendre**

pris ADJECTIVE
① taken ◊ *Est-ce que cette place est prise?* Is this seat taken?
② busy ◊ *Je serai très pris la semaine prochaine.* I'll be very busy next week.
♦ **être pris de panique** to be panic-stricken

la **prise** NOUN
① plug
② socket
♦ **une prise de courant** an electrical outlet
♦ **une prise de sang** a blood test

la **prison** NOUN
prison ◊ *aller en prison* to go to prison ◊ *être en prison* to be in prison

prisonnier ADJECTIVE
see also **prisonnier** NOUN
captive

le **prisonnier** NOUN
see also **prisonnier** ADJECTIVE
prisoner

la **prisonnière** NOUN
prisoner

privé ADJECTIVE
private ◊ *la propriété privée* private property ◊ *ma vie privée* my private life
♦ **en privé** in private

priver VERB
♦ **priver quelqu'un de quelque chose** to deprive somebody of something ◊ *Le prisonnier a été privé de nourriture.* The prisoner was deprived of food.
♦ **Tu seras privé de dessert!** You won't get any dessert!

le **prix** NOUN
① price ◊ *Je n'arrive pas à lire le prix de ce livre.* I can't see the price of this book.
② prize ◊ *Elle a eu le prix de la meilleure actrice.* She got the prize for best actress.
♦ **hors de prix** exorbitantly priced ◊ *Les repas sont hors de prix ici!* Meal prices here are exorbitant!
♦ **à aucun prix** not at any price ◊ *Je n'irai là-bas à aucun prix.* I'm not going there, not at any price.
♦ **à tout prix** at all costs ◊ *Je veux à tout prix voir ce film.* I want to see this movie at all costs.

probable ADJECTIVE
likely ◊ *Il est probable qu'elle viendra.* It's likely she'll come.
♦ **C'est peu probable.** That's unlikely.

probablement ADVERB
probably

le **problème** NOUN
problem

le **procédé** NOUN
process

le **procès** NOUN
trial ◊ *Le procès du meurtrier commence mardi.* The murder trial

starts on Tuesday.

♦ **Il est en procès avec son employeur.** He's involved in a lawsuit with his employer.

prochain ADJECTIVE

next ◊ *Nous descendons au prochain arrêt.* We're getting off at the next stop.

♦ **la prochaine fois** next time
♦ **la semaine prochaine** next week
♦ **À la prochaine!** See you!

prochainement ADVERB

soon

proche ADJECTIVE

① near ◊ *Les magasins les plus proches étaient à trois kilomètres.* The nearest stores were 3 kilometres away. ◊ *dans un proche avenir* in the near future

② close ◊ *un ami proche* a close friend

♦ **proche de** near ◊ *La cathédrale est proche du château.* The cathedral is near the castle.

les **proches** MASC NOUN

close relatives

proclamer VERB

to proclaim

procurer VERB

♦ **procurer quelque chose à quelqu'un** to get something for somebody ◊ *C'est elle qui m'a procuré ce travail.* She got me this job.

♦ **se procurer quelque chose** to get something ◊ *Je me suis procuré leur dernier catalogue.* I got their latest catalogue.

le **producteur** NOUN

producer

la **production** NOUN

production

la **productrice** NOUN

producer

produire VERB

to produce

♦ **se produire** to take place ◊ *Ces changements se sont produits l'an dernier.* The changes took place last year.

le **produit** NOUN

product ◊ *les produits de beauté* beauty products

le/la **prof** NOUN (*informal*)

teacher ◊ *Elle est prof de maths.* She's a math teacher.

le **professeur** NOUN

① teacher ◊ *Il est professeur d'histoire.* He's a history teacher.
② professor

la **professeure** NOUN

① teacher ◊ *Elle est professeure de physique.* She's a physics teacher.
② professor ◊ *Elle est professeure agrégée.* She's a full professor.

la **profession** NOUN

profession ◊ *Quelle est votre profession?* What's your profession?

professionnel ADJECTIVE (FEM SING **professionnelle**)

professional

le **profil** NOUN

① profile (*of person*) ◊ *de profil* in profile
② contours (*of object*)

le **profit** NOUN

profit ◊ *La société a fait des profits importants.* The company made significant profits.

♦ **tirer profit de quelque chose** to profit from something

♦ **au profit de** in aid of ◊ *un spectacle au profit d'un organisme de charité local* a show in aid of a local charity

profiter VERB

♦ **profiter de quelque chose** to take advantage of something ◊ *Profitez du beau temps pour aller faire du vélo.* Take advantage of the good weather to go biking.

♦ **Profitez-en bien!** Make the most of it!

profond ADJECTIVE

deep

♦ **peu profond** shallow

la **profondeur** NOUN

depth

le **programme** NOUN

① program ◊ *le programme du festival* the festival program
② curriculum ◊ *le programme de maths* the math curriculum
③ program ◊ *un programme informatique* a computer program

programmer VERB

to program ◊ *Mon ordinateur n'est pas programmé pour ça.* My computer isn't programmed to do that.

♦ **être programmé** to be showing ◊ *Ce film est programmé dimanche soir.* That movie is showing Sunday night.

le **programmeur** NOUN

programmer ◊ *Il est programmeur.* He's a programmer.

la **programmeuse** NOUN

programmer ◊ *Elle est programmeuse.* She's a programmer.

le **progrès** NOUN

progress ◊ *faire des progrès* to make

P

☞

progress

progresser VERB
to progress

progressif ADJECTIVE (FEM SING
progressive)
progressive

le **projecteur** NOUN
① projector ◊ *un vieux projecteur de diapositives* an old slide projector
② spotlight ◊ *sous les projecteurs* in the spotlight

le **projet** NOUN
plan ◊ *des projets de vacances* holiday plans
♦ **le projet de construction** building plans ◊ *le projet de construction d'un musée* the building plans for a museum
♦ **un projet de loi** a bill (*in parliament*)

projeter VERB
① to plan ◊ *Ils projettent d'acheter une maison.* They're planning to buy a house.
② to cast ◊ *L'arbre projetait une ombre sur le mur.* The tree cast a shadow on the wall.
♦ **Elle a été projetée hors de la voiture.** She was thrown out of the car.

la **prolongation** NOUN
overtime (*sports*)

prolonger VERB
① to prolong ◊ *Ne prolonge pas tes souffrances; va chez le médecin!* Don't prolong the agony; go to the doctor!
② to extend ◊ *Je vais prolonger mon abonnement.* I'm going to extend my subscription.
♦ **se prolonger** to go on ◊ *La réunion s'est prolongée tard.* The meeting went on late.

la **promenade** NOUN
walk ◊ *Il y a de belles promenades par ici.* There are some nice walks around here.
♦ **faire une promenade** to go for a walk
♦ **faire une promenade en voiture** to go for a drive
♦ **faire une promenade à vélo** to go for a bike ride

promener VERB
to take for a walk ◊ *Il promène son chien tous les jours.* He takes his dog for a walk every day.
♦ **se promener** to go for a walk ◊ *Elle est partie se promener.* She has gone for a walk.

la **promesse** NOUN
promise ◊ *faire une promesse* to make a promise ◊ *tenir sa promesse*

to keep one's promise

promettre VERB
to promise ◊ *On m'a promis un billet gratuit.* They promised me a free ticket. ◊ *Elle m'a promis de me téléphoner.* She promised to phone me.

la **promotion** NOUN
promotion ◊ *Il espère avoir bientôt une promotion.* He's hoping to get promotion soon.
♦ **être en promotion** to be on special ◊ *Les côtelettes de porc sont en promotion.* Pork chops are on special.

le **pronom** NOUN
pronoun

prononcer VERB
① to pronounce ◊ *Ce mot est difficile à prononcer.* That word is difficult to pronounce.
② to deliver ◊ *prononcer un discours* to deliver a speech
♦ **se prononcer** to be pronounced ◊ *Le « e » final ne se prononce pas.* The final "e" isn't pronounced.

la **prononciation** NOUN
pronunciation

la **propagande** NOUN
propaganda

se **propager** VERB
to spread ◊ *Le feu s'est propagé rapidement.* The fire spread quickly.

la **proportion** NOUN
proportion

le **propos** NOUN
♦ **à propos** by the way ◊ *À propos, quand est-ce que tu viens?* By the way, when are you coming?
♦ **à propos de quelque chose** about something ◊ *C'est à propos de la soirée de vendredi.* It's about the party on Friday.

proposer VERB
♦ **proposer quelque chose à quelqu'un (1)** to suggest something to somebody ◊ *Nous lui avons proposé une promenade en bateau.* We suggested a boat ride to him.
♦ **proposer quelque chose à quelqu'un (2)** to offer somebody something ◊ *Ils m'ont proposé des chocolats.* They offered me some chocolates.

la **proposition** NOUN
offer ◊ *J'accepte ta proposition avec plaisir.* I accept your offer with pleasure.

propre ADJECTIVE
① clean ◊ *Ce mouchoir n'est pas propre.* This handkerchief isn't clean.

♦ **recopier quelque chose au propre** to make a clean copy of something
2️⃣ own ◊ *Elle l'a fabriqué de ses propres mains.* She made it with her own hands.

♦ **propre à** characteristic of ◊ *C'est une coutume propre à la Gaspésie.* It's a custom you find in the Gaspé region.

proprement ADVERB
properly ◊ *Mange proprement!* Eat properly!

♦ **le village proprement dit** the village itself

♦ **à proprement parler** strictly speaking

la **propreté** NOUN
cleanliness

le/la **propriétaire** NOUN
1️⃣ owner
2️⃣ landlord
landlady

la **propriété** NOUN
property ◊ *la propriété privée* private property

le **prospectus** NOUN
brochure

prospère ADJECTIVE
prosperous

protecteur ADJECTIVE (FEM SING **protectrice**)
1️⃣ protective ◊ *un vernis protecteur* a protective varnish
2️⃣ patronizing ◊ *un ton protecteur* a patronizing tone

la **protection** NOUN
protection

protéger VERB
to protect

la **protéine** NOUN
protein

protestant ADJECTIVE (FEM SING **protestante**)
Protestant ◊ *une église protestante* a Protestant church

la **protestation** NOUN
protest

protester VERB
to protest ◊ *Ils protestent contre leurs mauvaises conditions de travail.* They're protesting their poor working conditions.

prouver VERB
to prove

la **provenance** NOUN
origin

♦ **un avion en provenance de Winnipeg** a plane arriving from Winnipeg

provenir VERB
♦ **provenir de (1)** to come from ◊ *Ces pêches proviennent de la région du Niagara.* These peaches come from the Niagara region.

♦ **provenir de (2)** to be the result of ◊ *Cela provient d'un manque d'organisation.* This is the result of a lack of organization.

le **proverbe** NOUN
proverb

la **province** NOUN
province

provincial ADJECTIVE (MASC PL **provinciaux**)
provincial ◊ *le gouvernement provincial* the provincial government

la **provision** NOUN
supply ◊ *une provision de pommes de terre* a supply of potatoes

les **provisions** FEM NOUN
food ◊ *Nous n'avons plus beaucoup de provisions.* We don't have much food left.

♦ **faire les provisions** to go grocery shopping

provisoire ADJECTIVE
temporary ◊ *un emploi provisoire* a temporary job

provoquer VERB
1️⃣ to provoke ◊ *Il l'a provoquée en la traitant d'imbécile.* He provoked her by calling her stupid.
2️⃣ to cause ◊ *Cet accident a provoqué la mort de quarante personnes.* The accident caused the death of 40 people.

la **proximité** NOUN
proximity

♦ **à proximité** nearby ◊ *Elle habite à proximité.* She lives nearby.

prudemment ADVERB
1️⃣ carefully ◊ *Conduisez prudemment!* Drive carefully!
2️⃣ wisely ◊ *Prudemment, il a fait des économies.* He wisely saved some money.
3️⃣ cautiously ◊ *Le gouvernement a réagi prudemment.* The government reacted cautiously.

la **prudence** NOUN
caution

♦ **avec prudence** carefully ◊ *Ils ont conduit avec prudence.* They drove carefully.

prudent ADJECTIVE
1️⃣ careful ◊ *Soyez prudents!* Be careful!
2️⃣ wise ◊ *Laisse ton passeport à la maison, c'est plus prudent.* It would be wiser to leave your passport at home.

la **prune** NOUN

P

☞

plum

le **pruneau** NOUN (PL les **pruneaux**)
prune

le/la **psychiatre** NOUN
psychiatrist

la **psychologie** NOUN
psychology

psychologique ADJECTIVE
psychological

le/la **psychologue** NOUN
psychologist

pu VERB see **pouvoir**
♦ **Je n'ai pas pu venir.** I couldn't come.

la **pub** NOUN (informal)
[1] advertising ◊ C'est de l'excellente pub. That's excellent advertising.
[2] ad ◊ des pub percutantes powerful ads

public ADJECTIVE (FEM SING **publique**)

see also **public** NOUN

public ◊ le transport public public transport ◊ une école publique a public school

le **public** NOUN

see also **public** ADJECTIVE

[1] public ◊ Ce parc est ouvert au public. This park is open to the public.
[2] audience ◊ Le public a applaudi le chanteur. The audience applauded the singer.
♦ **en public** in public ◊ Je déteste parler en public. I hate speaking in public.

publicitaire ADJECTIVE
♦ **une agence publicitaire** an advertising agency
♦ **une campagne publicitaire** a publicity campaign

la **publicité** NOUN
[1] advertising ◊ Elle travaille dans la publicité. She works in advertising.
[2] ad ◊ Il y a trop de publicités dans ce journal. There are too many ads in this newspaper.
♦ **faire de la publicité pour quelque chose** to publicize something

publier VERB
to publish ◊ Il vient de publier son nouveau roman. He has just published his new novel.

publique ADJECTIVE see **public**

la **puce** NOUN
[1] flea ◊ Ce chien a des puces. This dog has fleas.
♦ **un marché aux puces** a flea market
[2] chip ◊ une puce électronique a microchip
♦ **une carte à puce** a smart card

puer VERB
to stink ◊ Ça pue le tabac ici! It stinks of tobacco here!

puis VERB

see also **puis** ADVERB

see **pouvoir**
♦ **Puis-je venir vous voir samedi?** May I come and see you on Saturday?

puis ADVERB

see also **puis** VERB

then ◊ Faites dorer le poulet, puis ajoutez la sauce au miel et à l'ail. Fry the chicken till golden, then add the honey garlic sauce.

puisque CONJUNCTION
since ◊ Puisque c'est si cher, nous irons manger ailleurs. Since it's so expensive, we'll eat elsewhere.

la **puissance** NOUN
power ◊ la puissance de l'imagination the power of imagination ◊ Ce pays est une puissance nucléaire. This country is a nuclear power.

puissant ADJECTIVE
powerful

le **puits** NOUN
well ◊ Il a un puits dans son jardin. He has a well in his garden.
♦ **un puits de pétrole** an oil well

le **pulvérisateur** NOUN
spray ◊ un pulvérisateur de parfum a perfume spray

pulvériser VERB
[1] to pulverize ◊ L'explosion a pulvérisé le bâtiment. The explosion pulverized the building.
[2] to spray ◊ Elle ne pulvérise jamais d'insecticide sur ses plantes. She never sprays insecticide on her plants.

la **punaise** NOUN
thumbtack

punir VERB
to punish ◊ Il a été puni pour avoir menti. He was punished for lying.

la **punition** NOUN
[1] punishment
[2] penalty (sports)
♦ **le banc de punition** the penalty box

le **pupitre** NOUN
desk (for student)

pur ADJECTIVE
pure ◊ L'eau de cette source est très pure. The water from this spring is very pure.
♦ **c'est de la folie pure** it's sheer madness

la **purée** NOUN
  purée
  ♦ **la purée de pommes de terre** mashed potatoes

le **puzzle** NOUN
  jigsaw puzzle

le **pyjama** NOUN
  pyjamas PL

la **pyramide** NOUN
  pyramid

P

Q

le **QI** NOUN (= *quotient intellectuel*)
IQ

le **quai** NOUN
1 dock
♦ **Le navire est à quai.** The ship has docked.
2 platform ◊ *Le train partira du quai numéro quatre.* The train will leave from platform 4.

qualifié ADJECTIVE
qualified

qualifier VERB
♦ **se qualifier** to qualify ◊ *Il s'est qualifié pour la demi-finale.* He has qualified for the semifinal.

la **qualité** NOUN
quality ◊ *Ces outils sont de très bonne qualité.* These are very good quality tools.

quand CONJUNCTION, ADVERB
when ◊ *Quand est-ce que tu pars en vacances?* When are you going on vacation? ◊ *Quand je serai riche, j'achèterai une belle maison.* When I'm rich, I'll buy a nice house.
♦ **quand même** anyway ◊ *Je ne voulais pas finir mes devoirs, mais je les ai faits quand même.* I didn't want to finish my homework, but I did it anyway.

quant à PREPOSITION
regarding ◊ *Quant au problème de chauffage...* Regarding the heating problem... ◊ *Quant à moi, je n'arriverai qu'à dix heures.* As for me, I won't be arriving till 10 o'clock.

la **quantité** NOUN
amount
♦ **des quantités de** a great deal of

la **quarantaine** NOUN
about forty ◊ *une quarantaine de personnes* about forty people
♦ **Elle a la quarantaine.** She's in her forties.

quarante NUMBER
forty ◊ *Elle a quarante ans.* She's forty.
♦ **quarante et un** forty-one
♦ **quarante-deux** forty-two

le **quart** NOUN
quarter
♦ **le quart de** a quarter of ◊ *Il a mangé le quart du gâteau.* He ate a quarter of the cake.
♦ **trois quarts** three quarters

♦ **un quart d'heure** a quarter of an hour
♦ **deux heures et quart** a quarter after two
♦ **dix heures moins le quart** a quarter to ten

le **quartier** NOUN
area (of town) ◊ *un quartier tranquille* a quiet area
♦ **un cinéma de quartier** a local movie theatre

le **quartz** NOUN
♦ **une montre à quartz** a quartz watch

quasi ADVERB
nearly ◊ *La quasi-totalité des récoltes a été détruite.* Nearly all of the crop was destroyed.

quasiment ADVERB
nearly ◊ *Le film est quasiment fini.* The movie's nearly over.
♦ **quasiment jamais** hardly ever ◊ *Ils ne vont quasiment jamais au cinéma.* They hardly ever go to the movies.

quatorze NUMBER
fourteen ◊ *Mon frère a quatorze ans.* My brother's fourteen. ◊ *à quatorze heures* at 2 p.m.
♦ **le quatorze février** the fourteenth of February

quatre NUMBER
four ◊ *Il est quatre heures du matin.* It's four in the morning. ◊ *Elle a quatre ans.* She's four.
♦ **le quatre février** the fourth of February

quatre-vingts NUMBER
eighty

> ***quatre-vingts** is spelled with an -s when it is followed by a noun, but not when it is followed by another number.*

◊ *quatre-vingts élèves* eighty students ◊ *Elle a quatre-vingt-deux ans.* She's eighty-two.
♦ **quatre-vingt-dix** ninety
♦ **quatre-vingt-onze** ninety-one
♦ **quatre-vingt-quinze** ninety-five
♦ **quatre-vingt-dix-huit** ninety-eight

quatrième ADJECTIVE
fourth ◊ *au quatrième étage* on the fourth floor ◊ *Il est en quatrième année.* He's in Grade 4.

que CONJUNCTION, PRONOUN, ADVERB
1 that ◊ *Il sait que tu es là.* He knows that you're here.

que is sometimes not translated.

◊ *la dame que j'ai rencontrée hier*
the lady I met yesterday ◊ *Le gâteau
qu'elle a fait est délicieux.* The cake
she made is delicious.
♦ **Je veux que tu viennes.** I want you
to come.
② <u>what</u> ◊ *Que fais-tu?* What are you
doing? ◊ *Que vas-tu lui dire?* What
are you going to tell her?
♦ **Qu'est-ce que...?** What...? ◊ *Qu'est-
ce que tu fais?* What are you doing?
◊ *Qu'est-ce que c'est?* What's that?
♦ **plus...que** more...than ◊ *C'est plus
difficile que je ne le pensais.* It's more
difficult than I thought. ◊ *Il est plus
grand que moi.* He's bigger than me.
♦ **aussi...que** as...as ◊ *Elle est aussi
intelligente que toi.* She's as smart as
you are. ◊ *Le train est aussi cher que
l'avion.* The train is as expensive as
the plane.
♦ **ne...que** only ◊ *Il ne boit que de l'eau.*
He only drinks water. ◊ *Je ne l'ai vu
qu'une fois.* I've only seen him once.
♦ **Que tu es bête!** You're so silly!

le **Québec** NOUN
  <u>Québec</u>

québécois ADJECTIVE, NOUN
  <u>Québec</u> ◊ *la culture québécoise*
  Québec culture
♦ **un Québécois** a Quebecker (*man*)
♦ **une Québécoise** a Quebecker
(*woman*)

quel ADJECTIVE (FEM SING **quelle**)
  ① <u>what</u> ◊ *Quelle est ta couleur
  préférée?* What's your favourite
  colour?
  ② <u>which</u> ◊ *Quel groupe préfères-tu?*
  Which band do you like best?
  ③ <u>who</u> ◊ *Quel est ton chanteur
  préféré?* Who's your favourite singer?
  ◊ *Quelle heure est-il?* What time is
  it? ◊ *Quelle bonne surprise!* What a
  surprise!
♦ **quel que soit (1)** whatever ◊ *quel que
soit votre avis* whatever your opinion
♦ **quel que soit (2)** whoever ◊ *quel que
soit le coupable* whoever is the guilty
one

quelle ADJECTIVE *see* **quel**

quelque ADJECTIVE, ADVERB
  ① <u>some</u> ◊ *Il a quelques amis à
  Victoria.* He has some friends in
  Victoria. ◊ *J'ai acheté quelques
  disques.* I bought some records.
  ② <u>a few</u> ◊ *Il reste quelques pointes
  de pizza.* There are a few pizza slices
  left.
  ③ <u>few</u> ◊ *Ils ont fini les quelques
  sandwichs qui restaient.* They finished

the few sandwiches that were left.
♦ **quelque chose (1)** something ◊ *J'ai
quelque chose pour toi.* I've got
something for you. ◊ *Je voudrais
quelque chose de moins cher.* I'd like
something cheaper.
♦ **quelque chose (2)** anything ◊ *Avez-
vous quelque chose à déclarer?* Have
you got anything to declare? ◊ *Tu as
pensé à quelque chose d'autre?* Did
you think of anything else?
♦ **quelque part (1)** somewhere ◊ *J'ai
oublié mes lunettes quelque part.* I've
left my glasses somewhere.
♦ **quelque part (2)** anywhere ◊ *Vous
allez quelque part en fin de semaine?*
Are you going anywhere this
weekend?

quelquefois ADVERB
  <u>sometimes</u>

quelques-uns PRONOUN (FEM **quelques-
unes**)
  <u>some</u> ◊ *As-tu vu ses films? J'en ai
  vu quelques-uns.* Have you seen her
  films? I've seen some of them.

quelqu'un PRONOUN
  ① <u>somebody</u> ◊ *Quelqu'un t'a
  appelé.* Somebody phoned you.
  ◊ *Il y a quelqu'un à la porte.* There's
  somebody at the door.
  ② <u>anybody</u> ◊ *Est-ce que quelqu'un a
  vu mon parapluie?* Has anybody seen
  my umbrella? ◊ *Il y a quelqu'un?* Is
  there anybody there?

✹ la **quenouille** NOUN
  <u>cattail</u>

qu'est-ce que *see* **que**

qu'est-ce qui *see* **qui**

la **question** NOUN
  ① <u>question</u> ◊ *Je t'ai posé une
  question.* I asked you a question.
  ② <u>matter</u> ◊ *Ils se sont disputés pour
  des questions d'argent.* They argued
  over money matters.
  ③ <u>issue</u> ◊ *une importante question
  politique* an important political issue
♦ **Il n'en est pas question.** There's
no question about it. ◊ *Il n'est pas
question que je paye.* There's no
question of me paying.
♦ **De quoi est-il question?** What's it
about?
♦ **Il est question de l'organisation du
concert.** It's about organizing the
concert.
♦ **hors de question** out of the question
◊ *Il est hors de question que nous
restions ici.* It's out of the question
that we stay here.

le **questionnaire** NOUN
  <u>questionnaire</u>

Q

questionner VERB
to question

✹ **quétaine** ADJECTIVE
tacky ◊ *des meubles quétaines* tacky furniture ◊ *un bijou quétaine* a tacky piece of jewellery

la **queue** NOUN
[1] tail ◊ *Le chien a agité la queue.* The dog wagged its tail.
♦ **faire la queue** to line up
♦ **une queue de cheval** a ponytail
[2] rear ◊ *en queue du train* at the rear of the train
[3] bottom ◊ *en queue de liste* at the bottom of the list
[4] stem (*of fruit, leaf*) ◊ *la queue d'une cerise* a cherry stem

qui PRONOUN
[1] who ◊ *Qui a téléphoné?* Who phoned?
[2] whom ◊ *C'est la personne à qui j'ai parlé hier.* It's the person to whom I spoke yesterday.
[3] that ◊ *Donne-moi le manteau qui est sur la chaise.* Give me the jacket that's on the chair.
♦ **Qui est-ce qui...?** Who...? ◊ *Qui est-ce qui t'emmène au spectacle?* Who's taking you to the show?
♦ **Qui est-ce que...?** Whom...? ◊ *Qui est-ce que tu as vu à cette soirée?* Whom did you see at the party?
♦ **Qu'est-ce qui...?** What...? ◊ *Qu'est-ce qui est sur la table?* What's on the table? ◊ *Qu'est-ce qui te prend?* What's the matter with you?
♦ **À qui est ce sac à dos?** Whose knapsack is this?
♦ **À qui parlais-tu?** Who were you talking to?

la **quille** NOUN
bowling pin
♦ **jouer aux quilles** to go bowling

la **quincaillerie** NOUN
hardware store

la **quinzaine** NOUN
about fifteen ◊ *Il y avait une quinzaine de personnes.* There were about fifteen people there.

♦ **une quinzaine de jours** two weeks

quinze NUMBER
fifteen ◊ *Elle a quinze ans.* She's fifteen. ◊ *à quinze heures* at 3 p.m.
♦ **le quinze février** the fifteenth of February
♦ **dans quinze jours** two weeks from now

quitter VERB
to leave ◊ *J'ai quitté la maison à huit heures.* I left the house at 8 o'clock.
♦ **se quitter** to part ◊ *Les deux amis se sont quittés devant le café.* The two friends parted in front of the café.
♦ **Ne quittez pas.** (*on telephone*) Hold the line. ◊ *Ne quittez pas, je vous passe la directrice.* Hold on please, I'll put you through to the director.

quoi PRONOUN
what? ◊ *À quoi penses-tu?* What are you thinking about? ◊ *C'est quoi, ce truc?* What's this thing?
♦ **Quoi de neuf?** What's new?
♦ **As-tu de quoi écrire?** Have you got anything to write with?
♦ **Quoi qu'il arrive.** Whatever happens.
♦ **Il n'y a pas de quoi.** Don't mention it.
♦ **Il n'y a pas de quoi s'énerver.** There's no reason to get worked up.
♦ **En quoi puis-je vous aider?** How may I help you?

quoique CONJUNCTION
even though ◊ *Il va l'acheter quoique ce soit cher.* He's going to buy it even though it's expensive.

quotidien ADJECTIVE (FEM SING **quotidienne**)

see also **quotidien** NOUN

daily ◊ *Il est parti faire sa promenade quotidienne.* He's gone for his daily walk.
♦ **la vie quotidienne** everyday life

le **quotidien** NOUN

see also **quotidien** ADJECTIVE

daily paper ◊ *Le Globe and Mail est un quotidien. The Globe and Mail* is a daily paper.

R

le **rabais** NOUN
reduction (*in price*) ◊ *25 pour cent de rabais* 25 percent off
♦ **au rabais** at a discount

le **rabbin** NOUN
rabbi

raccompagner VERB
to take home ◊ *Peux-tu me raccompagner?* Can you take me home?

le **raccourci** NOUN
shortcut (*also computer*)

raccrocher VERB
to hang up (*telephone*)

la **race** NOUN
1 race ◊ *la race humaine* the human race
2 breed ◊ *De quelle race est ton chat?* What breed is your cat?

racheter VERB
1 to buy another ◊ *J'ai racheté un portefeuille.* I bought another wallet. ◊ *racheter du lait* to buy more milk
2 to buy ◊ *Il m'a racheté mon vélo.* He bought my bike from me.

la **racine** NOUN
root

✱ la **racinette** NOUN
root beer

le **racisme** NOUN
racism

raciste ADJECTIVE
racist

raconter VERB
to tell ◊ *Raconte-moi ce qui s'est passé.* Tell me what happened. ◊ *Raconte-moi une histoire.* Tell me a story.
♦ **Qu'est-ce que tu racontes?** What are you talking about?

le **radar** NOUN
radar

le **radiateur** NOUN
radiator
♦ **un radiateur électrique** an electric heater

la **radio** NOUN
1 radio ◊ *à la radio* on the radio
2 X-ray
♦ **passer une radio** to have an X-ray ◊ *Elle a passé une radio des poumons.* She had a chest X-ray.

le **radio-réveil** NOUN (PL les **radios-réveils**)

clock radio

le **radis** NOUN
radish

raffoler VERB
♦ **raffoler de** to be crazy about ◊ *Elle raffole de la tarte aux pommes.* She really loves apple pie.

rafraîchir VERB
to cool down
♦ **se rafraîchir (1)** to get cooler ◊ *Le temps se rafraîchit.* The weather's getting cooler.
♦ **se rafraîchir (2)** to freshen up ◊ *Il a pris une douche pour se rafraîchir.* He had a shower to freshen up.

rafraîchissant ADJECTIVE
refreshing

la **rage** NOUN
rabies
♦ **une rage de dents** a raging toothache
♦ **la rage au volant** road rage

le **ragoût** NOUN
stew

raide ADJECTIVE
1 steep ◊ *Cette pente est raide.* This is a steep slope.
2 straight ◊ *Elle a les cheveux raides.* She has straight hair.
3 stiff ◊ *Son bras est encore raide.* His arm's still stiff.

la **raie** NOUN
1 parting (*in hair*)
2 ray (*fish*)

le **rail** NOUN
rail ◊ *par rail* by rail

le **raisin** NOUN
grapes ◊ *le raisin blanc* green grapes ◊ *J'ai mangé du raisin.* I ate some grapes.
♦ **un grain de raisin** a grape
♦ **des raisins secs** raisins

la **raison** NOUN
reason ◊ *sans raison* for no reason ◊ *Raison de plus pour y aller.* All the more reason for going.
♦ **Ce n'est pas une raison.** That's no excuse.
♦ **avoir raison** to be right ◊ *Tu as raison.* You're right.
♦ **en raison de** because of ◊ *en raison d'une grève* because of a strike

raisonnable ADJECTIVE
sensible ◊ *Elle est très raisonnable pour son âge.* She's very sensible for

☞

her age.

le **raisonnement** NOUN
reasoning ◊ *J'ai du mal à suivre son raisonnement.* I have a hard time following his reasoning.

rajouter VERB
to add (*more*) ◊ *Ne rajoute pas de sel, j'en ai déjà mis.* Don't add more salt, I already put some in.
♦ **en rajouter** to exaggerate ◊ *Elle en rajoute toujours.* She always exaggerates.

ralentir VERB
to slow down

le **ramassage** NOUN
♦ **le ramassage scolaire** the school bus service

ramasser VERB
1 to pick up ◊ *Il a ramassé son crayon.* He picked up his pencil.
2 to collect ◊ *Il a ramassé les copies.* He collected the exam papers.

la **rame** NOUN
1 oar (*of boat*)
2 subway train

le **rameau** NOUN (PL les **rameaux**)
branch

ramener VERB
1 to bring back ◊ *Je t'ai ramené un souvenir de Jonquière.* I brought you back a souvenir from Jonquière.
2 to take home ◊ *Peux-tu me ramener à la maison?* Will you take me home?

ramer VERB
to row ◊ *C'est ma sœur qui ramait.* My sister was rowing.

la **rampe** NOUN
banister

ramper VERB
to crawl

la **rancune** NOUN
♦ **garder rancune à quelqu'un** to hold a grudge against somebody
♦ **Sans rancune!** No hard feelings!

rancunier ADJECTIVE (FEM SING **rancunière**)
♦ **Elle est un peu rancunière.** She tends to hold grudges.

la **randonnée** NOUN
♦ **une randonnée à vélo** a bike ride
♦ **une randonnée pédestre** a hike
♦ **faire de la randonnée** to go hiking

le **randonneur** NOUN
hiker

la **randonneuse** NOUN
hiker

le **rang** NOUN
row (*line*) ◊ *au premier rang* in the front row ◊ *se mettre en rangs* to form rows

la **rangée** NOUN
row (*line*) ◊ *une rangée de chaises* a row of chairs

ranger VERB
1 to put away ◊ *J'ai rangé tes affaires.* I put your things away.
2 to tidy up ◊ *Va ranger ta chambre.* Go and tidy up your room.

le **rap** NOUN
rap ◊ *un chanteur de rap* a rap singer

la **râpe à fromage** NOUN
cheese grater

râper VERB
to grate ◊ *le fromage râpé* grated cheese

rapide ADJECTIVE

see also **rapide** NOUN

1 fast ◊ *Cette voiture est très rapide.* This is a very fast car.
2 quick ◊ *J'ai jeté un coup d'œil rapide sur ton travail.* I had a quick glance at your work.

le **rapide** NOUN

see also **rapide** ADJECTIVE

rapids PL ◊ *Ils ont descendu les rapides en canot.* They went down the rapids in a canoe. ◊ *Ce rapide est très difficile à naviguer.* This set of rapids is very difficult to navigate.

rapidement ADVERB
quickly

le **rappel** NOUN
1 booster (*vaccination*)
2 curtain call

rappeler VERB
to call back ◊ *Je te rappelle dans cinq minutes.* I'll call you back in 5 minutes.
♦ **rappeler quelque chose à quelqu'un** to remind somebody of something ◊ *Cette odeur me rappelle mon enfance.* This smell reminds me of my childhood.
♦ **rappeler à quelqu'un de faire quelque chose** to remind somebody to do something ◊ *Rappelle-moi d'acheter des billets.* Remind me to get tickets.
♦ **se rappeler** to remember ◊ *Il s'est rappelé qu'il avait une course à faire.* He remembered he had an errand to run.

le **rapport** NOUN

see also **les rapports**

1 report ◊ *Elle a écrit un rapport.* She wrote a report.
2 connection ◊ *Je ne vois pas le*

rapport. I can't see the connection.
♦ **par rapport à** in comparison with

rapporter VERB
to bring back ◊ *Je leur ai rapporté un cadeau.* I brought them back a present.

le **rapporteur** NOUN
tattletale

la **rapporteuse** NOUN
tattletale

les **rapports** MASC NOUN

see also **le rapport**

relations ◊ *Leurs rapports avec leurs voisins se sont améliorés.* Their relations with their neighbours have improved.
♦ **les rapports sexuels** sexual intercourse

rapprocher VERB
1 to bring together ◊ *Cet accident a rapproché les deux frères.* The accident brought the two brothers together.
2 to bring closer ◊ *Elle a rapproché le fauteuil de la télé.* She brought the armchair closer to the TV.
♦ **se rapprocher** to come closer
◊ *Rapproche-toi, tu verras mieux.* Come closer, you'll see better.

la **raquette** NOUN
1 racquet (*tennis*)
2 paddle (*table tennis*)

rare ADJECTIVE
rare ◊ *une plante rare* a rare plant

rarement ADVERB
rarely

ras ADJECTIVE, ADVERB
short ◊ *un chien à poil ras* a short-haired dog
♦ **à ras bords** to the brim ◊ *Elle a rempli son verre à ras bords.* She filled her glass to the brim.
♦ **un chandail ras du cou** a crew-neck sweater

raser VERB
to shave off ◊ *Mon père a rasé sa barbe.* My dad has shaved off his beard.
♦ **se raser** to shave

le **rasoir** NOUN
razor

rassembler VERB
to gather together ◊ *Il a rassemblé les enfants dans la cour.* He gathered the children together in the playground.
♦ **se rassembler** to gather ◊ *Les passagers se sont rassemblés près de l'autobus.* The passengers gathered near the bus.

rassurer VERB
to reassure
♦ **Je suis rassuré.** I don't need to worry any more.
♦ **se rassurer** to be reassured
◊ *Rassure-toi!* Don't worry!

le **rat** NOUN
rat

raté ADJECTIVE
unsuccessful
♦ **Le gâteau est raté.** The cake didn't turn out.

le **râteau** NOUN (PL les **râteaux**)
rake

rater VERB
1 to miss ◊ *Elle a raté son train.* She missed her train.
2 to fail ◊ *J'ai raté mon examen de maths.* I failed my math exam. ◊ *Elle a raté sa pizza.* Her pizza didn't turn out right.

le **raton laveur** NOUN
raccoon

rattacher VERB
to tie again ◊ *rattacher ses lacets* to tie one's laces

le **rattrapage** NOUN
catching up ◊ *À cause de mon absence, j'ai beaucoup de rattrapage scolaire.* I have a lot of catching up to do at school because I was away.
♦ **le cours de rattrapage** remedial class

rattraper VERB
1 to recapture ◊ *La police a rattrapé le voleur.* The police recaptured the thief.
2 to catch up with ◊ *Je vais la rattraper.* I'll catch up with her. ◊ *Je dois rattraper mon retard à l'école.* I have to catch up at school.
3 to make up for ◊ *Il faut rattraper le temps perdu.* We must make up for lost time. ◊ *J'ai des heures à rattraper.* I have some hours to make up.
♦ **se rattraper** to make up for it ◊ *Je n'ai pas le temps de sortir, mais je me rattraperai après les examens.* I don't have time to go out, but I'll make up for it after the exams.

la **rature** NOUN
correction ◊ *un texte sans ratures* a text with no corrections

ravi ADJECTIVE
♦ **être ravi** to be delighted ◊ *Ils étaient ravis de nous voir.* They were delighted to see us. ◊ *Je suis ravi que vous puissiez venir.* I'm delighted that you can come.

R

se **raviser** VERB
> to change your mind ◊ *Il allait accepter, mais il s'est ravisé.* He was going to accept, but he changed his mind.

ravissant ADJECTIVE
> lovely

rayé ADJECTIVE
> striped ◊ *une chemise rayée* a striped shirt

rayer VERB
> 1 to scratch ◊ *Il a rayé la peinture de sa voiture.* He scratched the paint on his car.
> 2 to cross off ◊ *Son nom a été rayé de la liste.* Her name has been crossed off the list.

le **rayon** NOUN
> 1 ray ◊ *un rayon de soleil* a ray of sunshine
> 2 radius ◊ *le rayon d'un cercle* the radius of a circle
> 3 shelf ◊ *les rayons d'une bibliothèque* the shelves of a bookcase
> 4 department ◊ *le rayon des chaussures* the shoe department
> ♦ **les rayons X** X-rays

la **rayure** NOUN
> stripe

le **ré** NOUN
> 1 D ◊ *en ré majeur* in D major
> 2 re ◊ *do, ré, mi...* do, re, mi...

la **réaction** NOUN
> reaction

réagir VERB
> to react

le **réalisateur** NOUN
> director (*of film*) ◊ *Atom Egoyan est réalisateur.* Atom Egoyan is a film director.

la **réalisation** NOUN
> 1 achievement ◊ *Elle compte de nombreuses réalisations à son actif.* She has several achievements to her credit.
> 2 fulfillment ◊ *la réalisation d'un grand rêve* the fulfillment of a great dream

> Be careful! **la réalisation** does not mean **realization**.

la **réalisatrice** NOUN
> director (*of film*) ◊ *Patricia Rozema est réalisatrice.* Patricia Rozema is a film director.

réaliser VERB
> 1 to carry out ◊ *Ils ont réalisé leur projet.* They carried out their plan.

> 2 to fulfill ◊ *Il a réalisé son rêve.* He has fulfilled his dream.
> 3 to realize ◊ *Réalises-tu ce que tu dis?* Do you realize what you're saying?
> 4 to make ◊ *réaliser un film* to make a movie
> ♦ **se réaliser** to come true ◊ *Mon rêve s'est réalisé.* My dream has come true.

réaliste ADJECTIVE
> realistic

la **réalité** NOUN
> reality
> ♦ **en réalité** in fact

le/la **rebelle** NOUN
> rebel

rebondir VERB
> to bounce

le **rebord** NOUN
> edge ◊ *le rebord du lavabo* the edge of the sink
> ♦ **le rebord de la fenêtre** the window ledge

récemment ADVERB
> recently

récent ADJECTIVE
> recent

le **récepteur** NOUN
> receiver

la **réception** NOUN
> reception (*in office*)

le/la **réceptionniste** NOUN
> receptionist ◊ *Il est réceptionniste.* He's a receptionist.

la **recette** NOUN
> recipe

recevoir VERB
> 1 to receive ◊ *J'ai reçu une lettre.* I received a letter.
> 2 to see ◊ *Elle a déjà reçu trois clients.* She's already seen three clients.
> 3 to have over ◊ *Je reçois des amis à dîner.* I'm having friends over for dinner.

le **rechange** NOUN
> ♦ **de rechange** spare (*battery, bulb*) ◊ *des vêtements de rechange* a change of clothes

la **recharge** NOUN
> refill

le **réchaud** NOUN
> stove (*portable*)

réchauffer VERB
> 1 to reheat ◊ *Je vais réchauffer les légumes.* I'll reheat the vegetables.
> 2 to warm up ◊ *Un bon chocolat chaud va te réchauffer.* A nice cup of

hot chocolate will warm you up.
♦ **se réchauffer** to warm oneself ◊ *Je vais me réchauffer près du feu.* I'm going to warm up by the fire.

la **recherche** NOUN
research ◊ *Je voudrais faire de la recherche.* I'd like to do some research.
♦ **être à la recherche de quelque chose** to be looking for something ◊ *Je suis à la recherche d'un emploi.* I'm looking for a job.
♦ **les recherches** search ◊ *La police a interrompu les recherches.* The police called off the search.

recherché ADJECTIVE
① much sought-after (*book, painting, speaker*)
② wanted (*criminal*)

rechercher VERB
to look for ◊ *La police recherche l'assassin.* The police are looking for the killer.

la **rechute** NOUN
relapse

le **récipient** NOUN
container

le **récit** NOUN
story

réciter VERB
to recite

la **réclamation** NOUN
complaint ◊ *J'ai une réclamation à faire.* I want to make a complaint.
♦ **les réclamations** the complaints department

réclamer VERB
① to demand ◊ *Nous réclamons la semaine de trente heures.* We demand a 30-hour week.
② to complain ◊ *Elles sont toujours en train de réclamer.* They're always complaining about something.

reçois VERB *see* **recevoir**

la **récolte** NOUN
harvest

récolter VERB
① to harvest ◊ *Ils ont récolté le blé.* They harvested the wheat.
② to collect ◊ *Ils ont récolté deux cents dollars.* They collected 200 dollars.
③ to get ◊ *Elle a récolté une amende.* (*informal*) She got a fine.

le **recommandé** NOUN
♦ **en recommandé** by registered mail ◊ *Je voudrais envoyer ce paquet en recommandé.* I'd like to register this parcel.

recommander VERB

to recommend ◊ *Je vous recommande ce restaurant.* I recommend this restaurant.

recommencer VERB
① to start again ◊ *Il a recommencé à pleuvoir.* It's started raining again.
② to do again ◊ *S'il n'est pas puni, il va recommencer.* If he's not punished, he'll do it again.

la **récompense** NOUN
reward

récompenser VERB
to reward ◊ *Il m'a récompensée de mes efforts.* He rewarded me for my efforts.

réconcilier VERB
♦ **se réconcilier avec quelqu'un** to make up with somebody ◊ *Il s'est réconcilié avec sa sœur.* He has made up with his sister.

reconnaissant ADJECTIVE
grateful

reconnaître VERB
① to recognize ◊ *Je ne l'ai pas reconnu.* I didn't recognize him.
② to admit ◊ *Je reconnais que j'ai eu tort.* I admit I was wrong.

reconstruire VERB
to rebuild

le **record** NOUN
record ◊ *battre un record* to break a record

recouvrir VERB
to cover ◊ *La neige recouvre le sol.* Snow covers the ground.

la **récréation** NOUN
recess ◊ *Les élèves sont en récréation.* The students are having recess.
♦ **la cour de récréation** the playground (*of school*)

le **rectangle** NOUN
rectangle

rectangulaire ADJECTIVE
rectangular

rectifier VERB
to correct

la **rectitude politique** NOUN
political correctness

le **reçu** NOUN
see also **reçu** VERB
receipt

reçu VERB *see* **recevoir**
see also **reçu** NOUN
♦ **J'ai reçu un colis ce matin.** I received a parcel this morning.

reculer VERB
① to step back ◊ *Il a reculé pour la*

R

☞

laisser entrer. He stepped back to let her in.
2 to back up (*vehicle*) ◊ *J'ai reculé pour laisser passer le camion.* I backed up to let the truck past.
3 to postpone ◊ *Ils ont reculé la date du spectacle.* They postponed the show.

reculons
♦ **à reculons** ADVERB backwards ◊ *Elle est entrée à reculons.* She came in backwards.

récupérer VERB
1 to get back ◊ *Je vais essayer de récupérer mon argent.* I'm going to try to get my money back.
2 to recover ◊ *J'ai besoin de récupérer.* I need to recover.
3 to retrieve (*data, files*)

recycler VERB
to recycle
♦ **se recycler** to retrain ◊ *Il a décidé de se recycler en informatique.* He decided to retrain as a computer programmer.

la **rédaction** NOUN
1 writing ◊ *Voici des exercices pour améliorer vos aptitudes en rédaction.* Here are some exercises to improve your writing skills.
2 essay ◊ *Il faut remettre la rédaction sur notre future carrière demain.* We have to hand in the essay on our future career tomorrow.

redemander VERB
1 to ask again for ◊ *Je vais lui redemander son adresse.* I'll ask her for her address again.
2 to ask for more ◊ *Je vais redemander des carottes.* I'm going to ask for more carrots.

redémarrer VERB
1 to reboot ◊ *J'ai redémarré l'ordinateur.* I rebooted the computer.
2 to start up again ◊ *La voiture a redémarré.* The car started up again.

redescendre VERB
to go back down ◊ *Il est redescendu au premier étage.* He went back down to the first floor. ◊ *Elle a redescendu l'escalier.* She went back down the stairs.

la **rediffusion** NOUN
rerun
♦ **en rediffusion** ◊ *Le téléjournal sera en rediffusion à onze heures.* The news will be rebroadcast at 11.

redoubler VERB
to repeat a year ◊ *Il a raté son examen et doit redoubler.* He failed his exam and will have to repeat the

year.

la **réduction** NOUN
1 reduction ◊ *une réduction du nombre des touristes* a reduction in the number of tourists
2 discount ◊ *une réduction de vingt dollars* a 20 dollar discount

réduire VERB
to cut ◊ *Ils ont réduit leurs prix.* They've cut their prices. ◊ *Elle a réduit de moitié ses dépenses.* She has cut her spending by half.
♦ **Réduire, réutiliser, recycler.** Reduce, reuse, recycle.

réel ADJECTIVE (FEM SING **réelle**)
real

réellement ADVERB
really

refaire VERB
1 to do again ◊ *Je dois refaire ce rapport.* I've got to do this report again.
2 to take up again ◊ *Je voudrais refaire du ski.* I'd like to take up skiing again.

la **référence** NOUN
reference
♦ **faire référence à quelque chose** to refer to something
♦ **Ce n'est pas une référence!** That's no recommendation!

réfléchi ADJECTIVE
reflexive (*verb*)
♦ **C'est tout réfléchi.** My mind's made up.

réfléchir VERB
to think ◊ *Il est en train de réfléchir.* He's thinking.
♦ **réfléchir à quelque chose** to think about something ◊ *Je vais réfléchir à ta proposition.* I'll think about your suggestion.

le **reflet** NOUN
reflection ◊ *les reflets du soleil sur la mer* the reflection of the sun on the sea

refléter VERB
to reflect

le **réflexe** NOUN
reflex ◊ *avoir de bons réflexes* to have good reflexes

la **réflexion** NOUN
1 thought ◊ *Elle est en pleine réflexion.* She's deep in thought.
2 remark ◊ *faire des réflexions désagréables* to make nasty remarks
♦ **réflexion faite** on reflection

le **refrain** NOUN
chorus (*of song*)

le **réfrigérateur** NOUN
refrigerator

refroidir VERB
to cool ◊ *Laissez le gâteau refroidir.* Leave the cake to cool.
♦ **se refroidir** to get colder ◊ *Le temps se refroidit.* It's getting colder out.

le **refroidissement éolien** NOUN
wind chill ◊ *Le facteur de refroidissement éolien est de moins dix degrés aujourd'hui.* The wind chill factor is -10 today.

se **réfugier** VERB
to take shelter ◊ *Je me suis réfugié sous un arbre.* I took shelter under a tree.

le **refus** NOUN
refusal
♦ **Ce n'est pas de refus.** I wouldn't say no. ◊ *« Voulez-vous du thé glacé? » « Ce n'est pas de refus. »* "Would you like some iced tea?" "I wouldn't say no."

refuser VERB
to refuse ◊ *Il a refusé de payer sa part.* He refused to pay his share. ◊ *On lui a refusé la permission.* She was refused permission.
♦ **Je refuse qu'on me parle ainsi!** I won't let anybody talk to me like that!

se **régaler** VERB
♦ **Merci beaucoup : je me suis régalé!** Thank you very much: it was absolutely delicious!

le **regard** NOUN
look ◊ *Il nous a jeté un regard méfiant.* He gave us a mistrustful look. ◊ *On voyait à son regard qu'elle était contrariée.* You could tell from the look in her eyes that she was upset.
♦ **Tous les regards se sont tournés vers lui.** All eyes turned towards him.

regarder VERB
① to look at ◊ *Il regardait ses photos de vacances.* He was looking at his vacation photos. ◊ *Regarde! J'ai presque fini.* Look! I'm almost finished.
② to watch ◊ *Je regarde la télévision.* I'm watching television. ◊ *Regarde où tu mets les pieds!* Watch where you put your feet!
③ to concern ◊ *Ça ne nous regarde pas.* It doesn't concern us.
♦ **ne pas regarder à la dépense** to spare no expense

le **régime** NOUN
① régime (*of a country*)
② diet ◊ *un régime sans sel* a salt-free diet ◊ *se mettre au régime* to go on a diet ◊ *suivre un régime* to be on a diet
♦ **un régime de bananes** a bunch of bananas

la **région** NOUN
region
✹ ♦ **la région des Barrens** the Barrens

régional ADJECTIVE (MASC PL **régionaux**)
regional

le **registre** NOUN
register (*record book*) ◊ *Veuillez signer le registre.* Please sign the register.

la **règle** NOUN
① ruler ◊ *Elle a souligné son nom avec une règle.* She underlined her name with a ruler.
② rule ◊ *C'est la règle.* That's the rule. ◊ *en règle générale* as a general rule
♦ **être en règle** to be in order ◊ *Est-ce que tout est en règle pour votre voyage?* Is everything in order for your trip?
♦ **les règles** period (*menstruation*)

le **règlement** NOUN
rules ◊ *Le règlement est affiché à l'entrée.* The rules are posted by the entrance.

régler VERB
① to adjust ◊ *Il faut que je règle mon rétroviseur.* I have to adjust my rearview mirror.
② to set ◊ *J'ai réglé le thermostat à vingt degrés.* I've set the thermostat to 20 degrees.
③ to solve ◊ *Le problème est réglé.* The problem is solved.
④ to settle (*pay up*) ◊ *Elle a réglé sa facture.* She settled her bill.

la **réglisse** NOUN
licorice

le **règne** NOUN
reign ◊ *sous le règne de Henri IV* in the reign of Henry IV

régner VERB
to reign

le **regret** NOUN
regret
♦ **à regret** reluctantly

regretter VERB
① to regret ◊ *Elle regrette ce qu'elle a dit.* She regrets what she said.
♦ **Je regrette.** I'm sorry. ◊ *Je regrette, je ne peux pas vous aider.* I'm sorry, I can't help you.
② to miss ◊ *Je regrette mon ancienne école.* I miss my old school.

regrouper VERB

R

☞

to group together ◊ *Nous avons regroupé les enfants selon leur âge.* We grouped the children together according to age.
♦ **se regrouper** to join together ◊ *Les agriculteurs se sont regroupés pour constituer un syndicat.* The farmers joined together to form a union.

régulier ADJECTIVE (FEM SING **régulière**)
⊡ regular ◊ *des livraisons régulières* regular deliveries ◊ *des autobus réguliers* a regular bus service
⊡ steady ◊ *à un rythme régulier* at a steady rate
⊡ scheduled ◊ *des vols réguliers pour Whitehorse* scheduled flights to Whitehorse

régulièrement ADVERB
regularly

le **rein** NOUN
kidney
♦ **les reins** back (*of body*) ◊ *J'ai mal aux reins.* My back hurts.

la **reine** NOUN
queen

rejoindre VERB
to go back to ◊ *J'ai rejoint mes amis.* I went back to my friends.
♦ **Je te rejoins au café.** I'll see you at the café.
♦ **se rejoindre** to meet up ◊ *Elles se sont rejointes une heure après.* They met up an hour later.

relâcher VERB
to release (*prisoner, animal*)
♦ **se relâcher** to get slack ◊ *Il se relâche dans son travail.* He's slacking off in his work.

le **relais** NOUN
relay race ◊ *le relais quatre fois cent mètres* the 4 x 100 metre relay
♦ **prendre le relais** to take over
♦ **le relais routier** truck stop

la **relation** NOUN
relationship
♦ **les relations entre le Canada et les États-Unis** Canada-US relations
♦ **les relations publiques** public relations

se **relaxer** VERB
to relax

se **relayer** VERB
♦ **se relayer pour faire quelque chose** to take turns doing something

le **relevé** NOUN
♦ **un relevé de compte** a bank statement

relever VERB
⊡ to find ◊ *J'ai relevé six erreurs*

dans ton devoir. I found six mistakes in your homework.
⊡ to react to ◊ *Je n'ai pas relevé sa réflexion.* I didn't react to his remark.
♦ **relever la tête** to look up
♦ **se relever** to get up ◊ *Il est tombé mais s'est relevé aussitôt.* He fell, but got up immediately.

la **religieuse** NOUN
nun

religieux ADJECTIVE (FEM **religieuse**)
religious

la **religion** NOUN
religion

relire VERB
⊡ to read over ◊ *Elle a relu son examen avant de le rendre.* She read her exam paper over before handing it in.
⊡ to read again ◊ *Je voudrais relire ce roman.* I'd like to read this novel again.

remarquable ADJECTIVE
remarkable

la **remarque** NOUN
⊡ remark ◊ *une remarque désagréable* a nasty remark
⊡ comment ◊ *Avez-vous des remarques à faire?* Do you have any comments?

remarquer VERB
to notice ◊ *J'ai remarqué qu'elle avait l'air triste.* I noticed she was looking sad.
♦ **faire remarquer quelque chose à quelqu'un** to point something out to somebody ◊ *Je lui ai fait remarquer que c'était un peu cher.* I pointed out to him that it was a bit expensive.
♦ **Remarquez, elle n'est pas si bête que ça.** Mind you, she's not as stupid as all that.
♦ **se remarquer** to be noticeable ◊ *Il ne s'est pas rasé ce matin. Ça se remarque.* It's obvious he didn't shave this morning.
♦ **se faire remarquer** to call attention to oneself

le **remboursement** NOUN
refund

rembourser VERB
⊡ to pay back ◊ *Il m'a remboursé l'argent qu'il me devait.* He paid me back the money he owed me.
⊡ to refund ◊ *Le vol a été annulé et on m'a remboursé mon billet.* The flight was cancelled and they refunded my ticket.

le **remède** NOUN
⊡ medicine

② cure

remercier VERB

to thank ◊ *Je te remercie pour ton cadeau.* Thank you for your present.

♦ **remercier quelqu'un d'avoir fait quelque chose** to thank somebody for doing something ◊ *Je vous remercie de m'avoir invité.* Thank you for inviting me.

remettre VERB

① to put back on ◊ *Elle a remis son chandail.* She put her sweater back on.

② to put back ◊ *Il a remis son manteau dans le garde-robe.* He put his coat back in the closet.

③ to put off ◊ *J'ai dû remettre mon rendez-vous.* I had to put off my appointment.

♦ **se remettre** to recover (*from illness*) ◊ *Ma tante s'est bien remise de son opération.* My aunt has fully recovered from her operation.

✹ ♦ **« Satisfaction garantie ou argent remis »** "Satisfaction guaranteed or your money back"

le **remonte-pente** NOUN

ski lift

remonter VERB

① to go back up ◊ *Il est remonté à sa chambre.* He's gone back up to his room.

② to go up ◊ *Ils ont remonté la pente.* They went up the hill.

③ to comfort ◊ *Cette nouvelle m'a un peu remontée.* The news comforted me a bit.

♦ **remonter le moral à quelqu'un** to lift somebody's spirits

le **remords** NOUN

♦ **avoir des remords** to feel remorse

la **remorque** NOUN

trailer (*of car*)

les **remparts** MASC NOUN

city walls

le **remplaçant** NOUN

supply teacher

la **remplaçante** NOUN

supply teacher

remplacer VERB

to replace ◊ *Il faut remplacer cette ampoule.* We need to replace this bulb. ◊ *Il remplace le prof de maths.* He's replacing the math teacher.

♦ **remplacer par** to replace with

rempli ADJECTIVE

full ◊ *une journée bien remplie* a very full day

♦ **rempli de** full of ◊ *La salle était remplie de monde.* The room was full

of people.

remplir VERB

① to fill up ◊ *Elle a rempli son verre d'eau.* She filled her glass with water.

② to fill out ◊ *Tu as rempli ton formulaire?* Have you filled out your form?

♦ **se remplir** to fill up ◊ *La salle s'est remplie de monde.* The room filled up with people.

le **remue-méninges** NOUN (PL les **remue-méninges**)

brainstorming ◊ *une séance de remue-méninges* a brainstorming session

remuer VERB

① to move ◊ *Elle a remué le bras.* She moved her arm.

② to stir ◊ *Remuez la sauce pendant deux minutes.* Stir the sauce for two minutes.

le **renard** NOUN

fox

le **renardeau** NOUN (PL les **renardeaux**)

fox cub

la **rencontre** NOUN

♦ **faire la rencontre de quelqu'un** to meet somebody ◊ *J'ai fait la rencontre de personnes intéressantes ce soir.* I met some interesting people this evening.

♦ **aller à la rencontre de quelqu'un** to go and meet somebody ◊ *Je viendrai à ta rencontre.* I'll come and meet you.

rencontrer VERB

to meet

♦ **se rencontrer** to meet ◊ *Ils se sont rencontrés il y a deux ans.* They met two years ago.

le **rendez-vous** NOUN

① appointment ◊ *J'ai rendez-vous chez le coiffeur.* I've got an appointment at the hairdresser's. ◊ *prendre rendez-vous avec quelqu'un* to make an appointment with somebody

② date ◊ *« Tu sors ce soir? » « Oui, j'ai un rendez-vous. »* "Are you going out tonight?" "Yes, I've got a date."

♦ **donner rendez-vous à quelqu'un** to arrange to meet somebody

rendre VERB

① to give back ◊ *J'ai rendu ses disques à ta sœur.* I've given your sister her records back.

② to take back ◊ *J'ai rendu mes livres à la bibliothèque.* I've taken my books back to the library.

♦ **rendre quelqu'un célèbre** to make somebody famous

♦ **se rendre** to give oneself up ◊ *Le*

R

☞

voleur s'est rendu à la police. The robber gave himself up to the police.
♦ **se rendre compte de quelque chose** to realize something

le **renfermé** NOUN
♦ **sentir le renfermé** to smell stuffy

renifler VERB
to sniff

le **renne** NOUN
reindeer

renommé ADJECTIVE
renowned ◊ *La baie de Fundy est renommée pour ses marées.* The Bay of Fundy is renowned for its tides.

renoncer VERB
♦ **renoncer à** to give up ◊ *Ils ont renoncé à leur projet.* They've given up their plan.
♦ **renoncer à faire quelque chose** to give up the idea of doing something

renouvelable ADJECTIVE
renewable
♦ **les ressources non renouvelables** non-renewable resources

renouveler VERB
to renew (passport, contract)
♦ **se renouveler** to happen again ◊ *J'espère que ça ne se renouvellera pas.* I hope that won't happen again.

le **renseignement** NOUN
piece of information ◊ *Il me manque un renseignement.* There's one piece of information I still need.
♦ **les renseignements (1)** information ◊ *Il m'a donné des renseignements.* He gave me some information.
♦ **les renseignements (2)** information desk

renseigner VERB
♦ **renseigner quelqu'un sur quelque chose** to give somebody information about something
♦ **se renseigner** to inquire ◊ *Nous nous sommes renseignés sur l'horaire.* We inquired about the schedule.

rentable ADJECTIVE
profitable

la **rentrée** NOUN
♦ **la rentrée (des classes)** the start of the new school year
♦ **la vente de la rentrée** back-to-school sale

rentrer VERB
1 to come in ◊ *Rentre, tu vas prendre froid.* Come in, you'll catch cold.
2 to go in ◊ *Elle est rentrée dans le magasin.* She went into the store.
3 to get home ◊ *Je suis rentré à*

sept heures hier soir. I got home at 7 o'clock last night.
4 to bring in ◊ *As-tu rentré ton vélo?* Did you bring your bike in?
♦ **rentrer dans** to crash into ◊ *Sa voiture est rentrée dans un arbre.* He crashed into a tree.
♦ **rentrer dans l'ordre** to get back to normal

la **renverse** NOUN
♦ **tomber à la renverse** to fall backwards

renverser VERB
1 to knock over ◊ *J'ai renversé mon verre.* I knocked over my glass.
2 to run over ◊ *Elle a été renversée par une voiture.* She was run over by a car.
3 to spill ◊ *Il a renversé de l'eau partout.* He has spilled water everywhere.
♦ **se renverser** to fall over (glass, vase)

renvoyer VERB
1 to send back ◊ *Il a renvoyé les documents.* He sent back the documents.
2 to fire ◊ *On a renvoyé deux employés.* Two employees have been fired.

répandu ADJECTIVE
widespread ◊ *C'est une croyance très répandue.* It's a very widespread belief.
♦ **du jus répandu sur la table** juice spilled on the table
♦ **des papiers répandus sur le sol** papers scattered over the floor

le **réparateur** NOUN
repairman

la **réparation** NOUN
repair

la **réparatrice** NOUN
repairwoman

réparer VERB
to repair

repartir VERB
to set off again ◊ *Il s'est arrêté pour manger avant de repartir.* He stopped to eat before setting off again. ◊ *Il était là tout à l'heure, mais il est reparti.* He was here a moment ago, but he's gone again.
♦ **repartir à zéro** to start from scratch again

le **repas** NOUN
meal
♦ **le repas de midi** lunch
♦ **le repas du soir** supper

le **repassage** NOUN
ironing ◊ *Je déteste le repassage.* I hate ironing.

repasser VERB
  1 to come back ◊ *Je repasserai demain.* I'll come back tomorrow.
  2 to go back ◊ *Je dois repasser au magasin.* I've got to go back to the store.
  3 to iron ◊ *J'ai repassé ma chemise.* I ironed my shirt.
  4 to resit ◊ *Elle doit repasser son examen.* She has to rewrite her exam.

repérer VERB
  to spot ◊ *J'ai repéré deux fautes.* I spotted two mistakes.
  ♦ **se repérer** to find one's way around ◊ *J'ai du mal à me repérer de nuit.* I have a hard time finding my way at night.

le **répertoire** NOUN
  directory

répéter VERB
  1 to repeat ◊ *Elle répète toujours la même chose.* She keeps repeating the same thing.
  2 to rehearse ◊ *Les acteurs répètent une scène.* The actors are rehearsing a scene.
  ♦ **se répéter** to happen again ◊ *J'espère que cela ne se répétera pas!* I hope this won't happen again!

la **répétition** NOUN
  1 repetition ◊ *Il y a beaucoup de répétitions dans ce texte.* There's a lot of repetition in this text.
  ♦ **des grèves à répétition** repeated strikes
  2 rehearsal ◊ *Ils ont une répétition cet après-midi.* They have a rehearsal this afternoon.
  ♦ **la répétition générale** the dress rehearsal

le **répondeur** NOUN
  answering machine

répondre VERB
  to answer ◊ *répondre à quelqu'un* to answer somebody

la **réponse** NOUN
  answer ◊ *C'est la bonne réponse.* That's the right answer.

le **reportage** NOUN
  1 report ◊ *J'ai vu ce reportage aux informations.* I saw that report on the news.
  2 story ◊ *J'ai lu ce reportage dans La Gazette.* I read that story in the *Gazette*.

le **repos** NOUN
  rest

reposer VERB
  to put back down ◊ *Elle a reposé son verre sur la table.* She put her glass back down on the table.
  ♦ **se reposer** to rest ◊ *Tu pourras te reposer demain.* You'll be able to rest tomorrow.
  ♦ **se reposer sur quelqu'un** to rely on somebody

repousser VERB
  1 to grow again ◊ *Ses cheveux ont repoussé.* Her hair has grown again.
  2 to postpone ◊ *Le voyage est repoussé.* The trip's been postponed.

reprendre VERB
  1 to take back ◊ *Il a repris son livre.* He took back his book.
  2 to go back to ◊ *Elle a repris le travail.* She went back to work.
  3 to start again ◊ *La réunion reprendra à deux heures.* The meeting will start again at 2 o'clock.
  ♦ **reprendre du pain** to take more bread
  ♦ **reprendre la route** to set off again
  ♦ **reprendre son souffle** to catch one's breath

le **représentant** NOUN
  rep ◊ *Il est représentant chez une grande maison d'édition.* He's a rep for a major publisher.

la **représentante** NOUN
  rep ◊ *Elle est représentante pour une grande société d'informatique.* She's a sales rep for a big software company.

la **représentation** NOUN
  performance ◊ *la dernière représentation d'une pièce* the final performance of a play

représenter VERB
  1 to show ◊ *Le tableau représente un enfant et un chat.* The picture shows a child with a cat.
  2 to represent
  ♦ **se représenter** to come up again ◊ *Cette occasion ne se représentera pas.* This opportunity won't come up again.

la **reprise** NOUN
  1 rerun ◊ *La série* Le Canada : une histoire populaire *est en reprise ce soir à la télé.* There is a rerun of the series *Canada: A People's History* on TV tonight.
  2 recovery ◊ *la reprise économique* economic recovery
  ♦ **à plusieurs reprises** repeatedly

le **reproche** NOUN
  ♦ **faire des reproches à quelqu'un** to reproach somebody

reprocher VERB
  ♦ **reprocher quelque chose à quelqu'un** to reproach somebody for something ◊ *Il m'a reproché mon retard.* He

R

☞

reproached me for being late.
♦ **Qu'est-ce que tu lui reproches?** What have you got against her?

la **reproduction** NOUN
reproduction

reproduire VERB
to reproduce
♦ **se reproduire** to happen again ◊ *Je te promets que ça ne se reproduira pas!* I promise it won't happen again!

la **république** NOUN
republic ◊ *Le Canada n'est pas une république, c'est une confédération.* Canada is not a republic, it's a confederation.

répugnant ADJECTIVE
repulsive

la **réputation** NOUN
reputation

le **requin** NOUN
shark

le **réseau** NOUN (PL les **réseaux**)
network

✹ le **réseautage** NOUN
networking ◊ *de bonnes techniques de réseautage* good networking techniques ◊ *Il est spécialiste du réseautage.* He's a networking specialist.

la **réservation** NOUN
reservation ◊ *J'ai fait des réservations pour un groupe de six personnes.* I made reservations for a group of six.

la **réserve** NOUN
supply ◊ *une réserve énorme d'énergie* an enormous supply of energy
♦ **avoir quelque chose en réserve** to have something in stock
♦ **mettre quelque chose en réserve** to put something aside
✹ ♦ **la réserve indienne** First Nations reserve

réserver VERB
1 to reserve ◊ *Cette table est réservée.* This table is reserved.
2 to book ◊ *Nous avons réservé une chambre.* We've booked a room.

le **réservoir** NOUN
gas tank

la **résidence** NOUN
residence ◊ *une résidence pour personnes âgées* a seniors' residence
♦ **en résidence surveillée** under house arrest
♦ **le lieu de résidence** place of residence
♦ **une résidence secondaire** a second home

résistant ADJECTIVE
1 durable ◊ *Ce tissu est résistant.* This fabric is durable.
2 tough (*strong*) ◊ *Il faut être résistant pour faire ce travail.* You have to be tough to do this work. ◊ *Elle est rarement malade; elle est très résistante.* She's hardly ever sick; she's very tough.

résister VERB
to resist

résolu ADJECTIVE
♦ **Le problème est résolu.** The problem's solved.

résoudre VERB
to solve

le **respect** NOUN
respect
♦ **manquer de respect** to be disrespectful

respecter VERB
to respect

la **respiration** NOUN
breathing

respirer VERB
to breathe

la **responsabilité** NOUN
responsibility

responsable ADJECTIVE

| see also **responsable** NOUN |

responsible ◊ *être responsable de quelque chose* to be responsible for something

le/la **responsable** NOUN

| see also **responsable** ADJECTIVE |

1 person in charge ◊ *Je voudrais parler au responsable.* I'd like to speak to the person in charge.
2 person responsible ◊ *Il faut punir les responsables.* Those responsible must be punished.

ressembler VERB
♦ **ressembler à (1)** to look like ◊ *Elle ne ressemble pas à sa sœur.* She doesn't look like her sister.
♦ **ressembler à (2)** to be like ◊ *Ça ressemble à un conte de fées.* It's like a fairy tale.
♦ **se ressembler (1)** to look alike ◊ *Les deux frères ne se ressemblent pas.* The two brothers don't look alike.
♦ **se ressembler (2)** to be very similar ◊ *Ces deux jeux vidéo se ressemblent.* These two video games are quite similar.

le **ressort** NOUN
spring (*metal*) ◊ *Le ressort est cassé.* The spring is broken.

ressortir VERB
to go out again

le **restaurant** NOUN
restaurant

le **restauroute** NOUN
roadside restaurant ◊ *Nous avons mangé au restauroute.* We ate at the roadside restaurant.

le **reste** NOUN
rest
♦ **un reste de poulet** some leftover chicken
♦ **les restes** the leftovers

rester VERB
① to stay ◊ *Je reste à la maison en fin de semaine.* I'm staying home this weekend.
② to be left ◊ *Il reste du pain.* There's some bread left. ◊ *Il me reste assez de temps.* I still have enough time.
♦ **Il ne me reste plus qu'à...** I just have to... ◊ *Il ne me reste plus qu'à ranger mes affaires.* I just have to put my things away.
♦ **Restons-en là.** Let's leave it at that.

le **résultat** NOUN
result ◊ *le résultat des examens* the exam results

le **résumé** NOUN
summary

> *Be careful!* **le résumé** *does not mean the same as* **résumé** *in English.*

résumer VERB
to summarize

> *Be careful!* **résumer** *does not mean* **to resume***.*

se **rétablir** VERB
to get well

le **retard** NOUN
delay ◊ *un retard de livraison* a delay in delivery
♦ **avoir du retard** to be late
♦ **être en retard de deux heures** to be two hours late
♦ **prendre du retard** to be delayed

retarder VERB
① to be slow ◊ *Ma montre retarde.* My watch is slow.
② to put back ◊ *Je dois retarder l'horloge d'une heure.* I have to put the clock back an hour.
♦ **être retardé** to be delayed ◊ *J'ai été retardé par un coup de téléphone.* I was held up by a phone call.

retenir VERB
① to remember ◊ *Tu as retenu leur adresse?* Do you remember their address?

② to book ◊ *J'ai retenu une chambre à l'hôtel.* I've booked a room at the hotel.
♦ **retenir son souffle** to hold one's breath

retenu ADJECTIVE
① reserved ◊ *Cette place est retenue.* This seat is reserved.
② held up ◊ *J'ai été retenu par un coup de téléphone.* I was held up by a phone call.

la **retenue** NOUN
detention ◊ *Il est en retenue.* He has a detention.

retirer VERB
① to withdraw ◊ *Elle a retiré de l'argent.* She withdrew some money.
② to take off ◊ *Il a retiré son chandail.* He took off his sweater.

le **retour** NOUN
return
♦ **être de retour** to be back ◊ *Je serai de retour la semaine prochaine.* I'll be back next week.

retourner VERB
① to go back ◊ *Est-ce que tu es retourné à Whitehorse?* Have you been back to Whitehorse?
② to turn over ◊ *Elle a retourné la crêpe.* She flipped the pancake over. ◊ *Il a retourné la poubelle.* He turned the garbage can upside down.
♦ **se retourner (1)** to turn around ◊ *Elle s'est retournée.* She turned around.
♦ **se retourner (2)** to turn over ◊ *La voiture s'est retournée.* The car turned over.

la **retraite** NOUN
♦ **être à la retraite** to be retired
♦ **prendre sa retraite** to retire

retraité ADJECTIVE

> see also **retraité** NOUN

retired ◊ *Mon oncle est maintenant retraité.* My uncle is now retired.

le **retraité** NOUN

> see also **retraité** ADJECTIVE

retiree

la **retraitée** NOUN
retiree

rétrécir VERB
to shrink ◊ *Mon chandail a rétréci au lavage.* My sweater shrank in the wash.
♦ **se rétrécir** to get narrower ◊ *La rue se rétrécit.* The street gets narrower.

retrouver VERB
① to find (*something lost*) ◊ *J'ai retrouvé mon portefeuille.* I found my wallet.

R

2 **to meet up with** ◊ *Je te retrouve au café à trois heures.* I'll meet you at the coffee shop at 3 o'clock.
♦ **se retrouver (1)** to meet up ◊ *Ils se sont retrouvés devant le cinéma.* They met up in front of the movie theatre.
♦ **se retrouver (2)** to find one's way around ◊ *Je n'arrive pas à me retrouver.* I can't find my way around.

le **rétroviseur** NOUN
rearview mirror

la **réunion** NOUN
meeting

se **réunir** VERB
to meet ◊ *Ils se sont réunis à cinq heures.* They met at 5 o'clock.

réussi ADJECTIVE
successful ◊ *une soirée très réussie* a very successful party
♦ **être réussi** to be a success ◊ *Le repas était très réussi.* The meal was a hit.

réussir VERB
to be successful ◊ *Tous ses enfants ont très bien réussi.* All her children are very successful.
♦ **réussir à faire quelque chose** to succeed in doing something
♦ **réussir à un examen** to pass an exam

la **réussite** NOUN
success

réutiliser VERB
to reuse ◊ *Les trois R sont « réduire, réutiliser et recycler ».* The 3 Rs are "reduce, reuse, recycle".

la **revanche** NOUN
1 revenge
2 return game
♦ **prendre sa revanche** to get even ◊ *Il a pris sa revanche en refusant de lui prêter son vélo.* He got even by refusing to lend her his bike.
♦ **en revanche** on the other hand ◊ *C'est cher mais en revanche c'est de la bonne qualité.* It's expensive but on the other hand it's good quality.

le **rêve** NOUN
dream
♦ **des vacances de rêve** a dream vacation

le **réveil** NOUN
alarm clock
♦ **mettre le réveil à huit heures** to set the alarm for eight o'clock

le **réveille-matin** NOUN (PL les **réveille-matin**)
alarm clock

réveiller VERB
to wake up ◊ *réveiller quelqu'un* to wake somebody up

♦ **se réveiller** to wake up

le **réveillon** NOUN
♦ **le réveillon du Jour de l'An** New Year's Eve celebrations
♦ **le réveillon de Noël** Christmas Eve celebrations

réveillonner VERB
1 to celebrate New Year's Eve
2 to celebrate Christmas Eve

revenir VERB
to come back ◊ *Reviens vite!* Come back soon! ◊ *Son nom m'est revenu cinq minutes après.* His name came back to me five minutes later.
♦ **Ça revient au même.** It comes to the same thing.
♦ **Ça revient cher.** It costs a lot.
♦ **Je n'en reviens pas!** I can't get over it!
♦ **revenir sur ses pas** to retrace one's steps

le **revenu** NOUN
income

rêver VERB
to dream
♦ **rêver de quelque chose** to dream of something ◊ *J'ai rêvé de mes vacances cette nuit.* I dreamed about my holidays last night.

le **réverbère** NOUN
streetlight

le **revers** NOUN
1 backhand ◊ *Tu as un excellent revers.* You have an excellent backhand.
2 lapel (*of jacket*)
♦ **le revers de la médaille** the other side of the coin

revient VERB *see* **revenir**

réviser VERB
1 to study ◊ *Je dois réviser mon français.* I have to study my French.
2 to review ◊ *La prof a révisé l'unité avec nous.* The teacher reviewed the unit with us.
3 to revise ◊ *l'édition révisée* the revised edition
4 to service ◊ *Je dois faire réviser ma voiture.* I must get my car serviced.

la **révision** NOUN
1 studying ◊ *Malgré deux heures de révision, il a raté l'examen.* Despite two hours of studying, he failed the exam.
2 review ◊ *une révision complète* a thorough review

revoir VERB
1 to see again ◊ *Je l'ai revue hier soir.* I saw her again last night.

② to study ◊ *Il est en train de revoir sa géographie.* He's studying his geography.
♦ **au revoir** goodbye

la **révolution** NOUN
revolution ◊ *la révolution tranquille* the Quiet Revolution

> **ⓘ *La révolution tranquille***
> is the name given to the rapid political, social, and economic modernization of Québec in the 1960s. The government took on a more prominent role in all spheres of power, quickly displacing the Roman Catholic Church.

la **revue** NOUN
magazine

le **rez-de-chaussée** NOUN (PL les **rez-de-chaussée**)
ground floor ◊ *au rez-de-chaussée* on the ground floor

le **rhinocéros** NOUN
rhinoceros

la **rhubarbe** NOUN
rhubarb

le **rhume** NOUN
cold ◊ *J'ai attrapé un rhume.* I've caught a cold.
♦ **un rhume de cerveau** a head cold
♦ **le rhume des foins** hay fever

ri VERB *see* **rire**
♦ **Nous avons bien ri.** We had a good laugh.

riche ADJECTIVE
rich ◊ *Sa famille est très riche.* His family's very rich. ◊ *riche en vitamines* rich in vitamins

le **rideau** NOUN (PL les **rideaux**)
curtain ◊ *tirer les rideaux* to draw the curtains
✿ ♦ **grimper dans les rideaux** to climb the walls ◊ *Cela la fait grimper dans les rideaux quand je suis en retard.* It drives her up the wall when I'm late.

ridicule ADJECTIVE
ridiculous ◊ *Je trouve ça complètement ridicule.* I think that's absolutely ridiculous.

rien PRONOUN

> *see also* **rien** NOUN

① nothing ◊ *« Qu'est-ce que tu as acheté? » « Rien. »* "What have you bought?" "Nothing." ◊ *Il a fait tout ce travail pour rien.* He did all this work for nothing.
♦ **Ça n'a rien à voir.** It has nothing to do with it.
♦ **rien d'intéressant** nothing interesting

♦ **rien d'autre** nothing else
♦ **rien du tout** nothing at all
② anything ◊ *Il n'a rien dit.* He didn't say anything.
♦ **rien que (1)** just ◊ *rien que pour lui faire plaisir* just to please her ◊ *Rien que la voiture coûte soixante mille dollars.* The car alone costs sixty thousand dollars.
♦ **rien que (2)** nothing but ◊ *rien que la vérité* nothing but the truth
♦ **De rien!** You're welcome! ◊ *« Merci beaucoup! » « De rien! »* "Thank you very much!" "You're welcome!"

le **rien** NOUN

> *see also* **rien** PRONOUN

♦ **pour un rien** at the slightest thing ◊ *Elle se met en colère pour un rien.* She loses her temper over the slightest thing.
♦ **en un rien de temps** in no time at all

rigoler VERB (*informal*)
① to laugh ◊ *Elle a rigolé durant tout le film.* She laughed all the way through the movie.
② to have fun ◊ *On a bien rigolé hier soir.* We had a lot of fun last night.
③ to be joking ◊ *Ne te fâche pas, je rigolais.* Don't get upset, I was only joking.
♦ **pour rigoler** for a laugh

rigolo ADJECTIVE (FEM SING **rigolote**) (*informal*)
funny

rincer VERB
to rinse

rire VERB

> *see also* **rire** NOUN

to laugh ◊ *Ce film m'a vraiment fait rire.* That movie really made me laugh. ◊ *Nous avons bien ri.* We had a good laugh.
♦ **pour rire** for a laugh
♦ **Oups, c'était juste pour rire.** Oops, that was just a joke.

le **rire** NOUN

> *see also* **rire** VERB

laughter ◊ *Il a un rire bruyant.* He has a loud laugh.

le **risque** NOUN
① risk ◊ *prendre des risques* to take risks ◊ *à tes risques et périls* at your own risk
② danger ◊ *Il n'y a pas de risque qu'il l'apprenne.* There's no danger of him finding out.

risqué ADJECTIVE
risky

risquer VERB

R

☞

to risk
♦ **Ça ne risque rien.** It's quite safe.
♦ **Elle risque de se tuer.** She could get herself killed.
♦ **C'est ce qui risque de se passer.** That's what might well happen.

le **rivage** NOUN
shore

la **rivière** NOUN
river

le **riz** NOUN
rice

la **robe** NOUN
dress
♦ **une robe de soirée** an evening gown
♦ **une robe de mariée** a wedding dress
♦ **une robe de chambre** a dressing gown

le **robinet** NOUN
tap

le **robot** NOUN
robot
♦ **le robot culinaire** food processor

la **roche** NOUN
rock (*stone*)

le **rocher** NOUN
rock

le **rock** NOUN
rock (*music*) ◊ *un chanteur de rock* a rock singer

rôder VERB
to lurk

les **rognons** MASC NOUN
kidneys (*in cooking*)

le **roi** NOUN
king

le **rôle** NOUN
role

romain ADJECTIVE
Roman ◊ *des ruines romaines* Roman ruins

le **roman** NOUN
novel
♦ **un roman policier** a detective novel
♦ **un roman d'espionnage** a spy novel

le **romancier** NOUN
novelist

la **romancière** NOUN
novelist

romantique ADJECTIVE
romantic

rompre VERB
1 to split up ◊ *Mon frère et sa petite amie ont rompu.* My brother and his girlfriend have split up.
2 to break off ◊ *Ils ont rompu leurs fiançailles.* They've broken off their engagement.

♦ **rompre la glace** to break the ice

les **ronces** FEM NOUN
thornbushes

ronchonner VERB (*informal*)
to gripe

rond ADJECTIVE

see also **rond** NOUN

1 round ◊ *La Terre est ronde.* The earth is round.
♦ **ouvrir des yeux ronds** to stare in amazement
2 chubby ◊ *Il a les joues rondes.* He has chubby cheeks.

le **rond** NOUN

see also **rond** ADJECTIVE

circle ◊ *Elle a dessiné un rond sur le sable.* She drew a circle in the sand.
♦ **en rond** in a circle ◊ *Ils se sont assis en rond.* They sat down in a circle.
♦ **tourner en rond** to go around in circles

la **rondelle** NOUN
1 puck
2 slice (*of something round*) ◊ *une rondelle de citron* a slice of lemon

ronfler VERB
to snore

ronronner VERB
to purr

le **rosbif** NOUN
roast beef

la **rose** NOUN

see also **rose** ADJECTIVE

rose

rose ADJECTIVE

see also **rose** NOUN

pink

le **rosier** NOUN
rosebush

le **rôti** NOUN
roast meat
♦ **un rôti de bœuf** a roast of beef

rôtir VERB
to roast ◊ *faire rôtir quelque chose* to roast something

la **roue** NOUN
wheel ◊ *les roues arrière d'une voiture* the rear wheels of a vehicle

rouge ADJECTIVE

see also **rouge** NOUN

red
♦ **brûler un feu rouge** to go through a red light ◊ *Il a brûlé un feu rouge.* He went through a red light.

le **rouge** NOUN

see also **rouge** ADJECTIVE

red ◊ *Le rouge est ma couleur préférée.* Red is my favourite colour.
♦ **passer au rouge** to change to red ◊ *Le feu est passé au rouge.* The light changed to red.
♦ **le rouge à lèvres** lipstick

la **rougeole** NOUN
　measles

rougir VERB
　[1] to blush ◊ *Il a rougi en me voyant.* He blushed when he saw me.
　[2] to turn red ◊ *Elle a rougi de colère.* She turned red with anger.

la **rouille** NOUN
　rust

rouillé ADJECTIVE
　rusty

rouiller VERB
　to rust

roulant ADJECTIVE
♦ **un fauteuil roulant** a wheelchair
♦ **une table roulante** a serving cart
♦ **un tapis roulant (1)** a treadmill
♦ **un tapis roulant (2)** a moving sidewalk

le **rouleau** NOUN (PL les **rouleaux**)
　roll ◊ *un rouleau de tapisserie* a roll of wallpaper
♦ **un rouleau du printemps** a spring roll
♦ **un rouleau à pâtisserie** a rolling pin

rouler VERB
　[1] to go ◊ *Le train roulait à 250 km/h.* The train was going at 250 km an hour.
　[2] to drive ◊ *Il a roulé sans s'arrêter.* He drove without stopping.
　[3] to roll ◊ *Elle a roulé le ballon vers moi.* She rolled the ball towards me.
　[4] to roll up ◊ *Il a roulé le tapis.* He rolled up the carpet.
　[5] to con ◊ *Ils se sont fait rouler.* (*informal*) They were conned.

rousse ADJECTIVE *see* **roux**

la **rousse** NOUN
　redhead

la **route** NOUN
　[1] road ◊ *au bord de la route* at the roadside
　[2] way ◊ *Je ne connais pas la route.* I don't know the way.
♦ **Il y a trois heures de route.** It's a 3-hour journey.
♦ **en route** on the way ◊ *Ils se sont arrêtés en route.* They stopped on the way.
♦ **mettre en route** to start up ◊ *Elle a mis le moteur en route.* She started up the engine.
♦ **se mettre en route** to set off ◊ *Nous nous sommes mis en route à cinq heures.* We set off at 5 o'clock.

le **routier** NOUN
　truck driver ◊ *Mon père est routier.* My father's a truck driver.

la **routière** NOUN
　truck driver

la **routine** NOUN
　routine

roux ADJECTIVE (FEM SING **rousse**)
　see also **roux** NOUN
　[1] red ◊ *Il a les cheveux roux.* He has red hair.
　[2] red-haired ◊ *la petite fille rousse* the little red-haired girl

le **roux** NOUN
　see also **roux** ADJECTIVE
　redhead

royal ADJECTIVE (MASC PL **royaux**)
　royal

le **royaume** NOUN
　kingdom

le **ruban** NOUN
　ribbon
♦ **le ruban adhésif** adhesive tape

le **ruban-cache** NOUN
　masking tape

la **rubéole** NOUN
　German measles

la **ruche** NOUN
　hive

la **rue** NOUN
　street

la **ruelle** NOUN
　alley

rugueux ADJECTIVE (FEM SING **rugueuse**)
　rough

la **ruine** NOUN
　ruin ◊ *les ruines de la cathédrale* the ruins of the cathedral

ruiner VERB
　to ruin

le **ruisseau** NOUN (PL les **ruisseaux**)
　stream

la **rumeur** NOUN
　rumour

la **rupture** NOUN
　break-up

la **ruse** NOUN
　trickery ◊ *une ruse* a trick

rusé ADJECTIVE
　cunning

le **rythme** NOUN
　[1] rhythm ◊ *J'aime le rythme de cette musique.* I like the beat of this music.
　[2] pace ◊ *Elle marche à un bon rythme.* She walks at a good pace.

R

S

s' PRONOUN *see* **se**

sa ADJECTIVE
 1 his ◊ *Il est allé voir sa grand-mère.*
 He's gone to see his grandmother.
 2 her ◊ *Elle a embrassé sa mère.* She
 kissed her mother.

le **sable** NOUN
 sand
 ♦ **les sables bitumineux** tar sands
 ♦ **des sables mouvants** quicksand

le **sablé** NOUN
 shortbread cookie

le **sabot** NOUN
 1 clog
 2 hoof (*of horse*)

le **sac** NOUN
 bag
 ♦ **un sac de voyage** a travel bag
 ♦ **un sac de couchage** a sleeping bag
 ♦ **un sac à main** a purse
 ♦ **un sac à dos** a knapsack
 ♦ **un sac gonflable** an airbag
 ♦ **voyager avec son sac au dos** to go
 backpacking

le **sachet** NOUN
 packet (*of sugar, coffee*)
 ♦ **du potage en sachet** instant soup

la **sacoche** NOUN
 1 bag (*for mail, newspapers*)
 2 pannier (*bicycle*)
 ♦ **une sacoche de bicyclette** a seat pack
 (*for bike*)

le **sacre** NOUN
 swearword

 sacré ADJECTIVE
 sacred

 sacrer VERB
 to swear

 sage ADJECTIVE
 1 good (*well-behaved*) ◊ *Sois sage.*
 Be good.
 2 wise (*sensible*) ◊ *Il serait plus sage
 d'attendre.* It would be wiser to wait.

la **sagesse** NOUN
 wisdom ◊ *Il a eu la sagesse de ne
 pas y aller.* He wisely didn't go.
 ♦ **une dent de sagesse** a wisdom tooth

le **Sagittaire** NOUN
 Sagittarius ◊ *Il est Sagittaire.* He's a
 Sagittarius.

 saignant ADJECTIVE
 rare (*meat*)

 saigner VERB
 to bleed
 ♦ **saigner du nez** to have a nosebleed

 sain ADJECTIVE
 healthy
 ♦ **sain et sauf** safe and sound

 saint ADJECTIVE
 | *see also* **saint** NOUN |
 holy
 ♦ **la Saint-Jean-Baptiste** Saint-Jean-
 Baptiste Day

 > **ℹ** *la Saint-Jean-Baptiste* is
 > celebrated on June 24 throughout
 > French Canada. It combines a
 > celebration of the summer solstice
 > and of Saint Jean-Baptiste, the patron
 > saint of French Canadians by official
 > proclamation in 1908.

le **saint** NOUN
 | *see also* **saint** ADJECTIVE |
 saint

la **sainte** NOUN
 saint

 sais VERB *see* **savoir**
 ♦ **Je ne sais pas.** I don't know.

 saisir VERB
 to take hold of
 ♦ **saisir l'occasion de faire quelque
 chose** to seize the opportunity to do
 something

la **saison** NOUN
 season ◊ *Ce n'est pas la saison
 des fraises.* Strawberries are out of
 season.
 ♦ **la belle saison** summer

 sait VERB *see* **savoir**
 ♦ **Il sait que...** He knows that...
 ♦ **On ne sait jamais!** You never know!

la **salade** NOUN
 1 lettuce
 2 salad ◊ *une salade composée* a
 mixed salad ◊ *une salade de fruits*
 a fruit salad ◊ *une salade César* a
 Caesar salad
 ♦ **la salade de chou** cole slaw

le **saladier** NOUN
 salad bowl

le **salaire** NOUN
 salary

le **salami** NOUN
 salami

 sale ADJECTIVE

dirty

salé ADJECTIVE

salty ◊ *La soupe est trop salée.* The soup is too salty.

saler VERB

to put salt in ◊ *J'ai oublié de saler la soupe.* I forgot to put salt in the soup.

la **saleté** NOUN

dirt ◊ *J'ai horreur de la saleté.* I hate dirt. ◊ *Il y a une saleté sur ta chemise.* There's some dirt on your shirt.

salir VERB

♦ **salir quelque chose** to get something dirty

♦ **se salir** to get oneself dirty ◊ *Mets un tablier, sinon tu vas te salir.* Put on an apron or you'll get yourself dirty.

la **salle** NOUN

① room

② audience ◊ *Toute la salle l'a applaudi.* The whole audience applauded him.

③ ward (*in hospital*) ◊ *Elle est à la salle douze.* She's in Ward 12.

♦ **la salle à manger** the dining room

※ ♦ **la salle de lavage** the laundry room

♦ **la salle de bains** the bathroom

♦ **la salle d'attente** the waiting room

♦ **une salle de classe** a classroom

♦ **une salle de concert** a concert hall

le **salon** NOUN

※ living room

♦ **le salon des professeurs** staff room (*in school*)

※ ♦ **le salon funéraire** funeral parlour

♦ **un salon de coiffure** a hair salon

♦ **un salon de beauté** a beauty salon

la **salopette** NOUN

overalls

saluer VERB

♦ **saluer quelqu'un (1)** to say hello to somebody ◊ *Je l'ai croisé dans la rue et il m'a salué.* I met him in the street and he said hello.

♦ **saluer quelqu'un (2)** to say goodbye to somebody ◊ *Elle nous a salués et elle est partie.* She said goodbye and left.

salut EXCLAMATION (*informal*)

Hi!

la **salutation** NOUN

greeting

le **samedi** NOUN

① Saturday ◊ *Aujourd'hui, nous sommes samedi.* It's Saturday today.

② on Saturday ◊ *Nous sommes allés au cinéma samedi.* We went to the movies on Saturday.

♦ **le samedi** on Saturdays ◊ *Le magasin ferme à dix-huit heures le samedi.* The store closes at 6 p.m. on Saturdays.

♦ **tous les samedis** every Saturday

♦ **samedi dernier** last Saturday

♦ **samedi prochain** next Saturday

la **sandale** NOUN

sandal

le **sandwich** NOUN

sandwich

※ ♦ **un sandwich au smoked meat** a smoked meat sandwich

le **sang** NOUN

blood

♦ **en sang** covered with blood

le **sang-froid** NOUN

♦ **garder son sang-froid** to keep calm

♦ **perdre son sang-froid** to lose one's cool

♦ **faire quelque chose de sang-froid** to do something in cold blood

la **sangle** NOUN

strap (*on sandal, backpack*)

le **sanglot** NOUN

♦ **éclater en sanglots** to burst into tears

sans PREPOSITION

without ◊ *Elle est venue sans son frère.* She came without her brother.

♦ **un haut sans manches** a sleeveless top

le/la **sans-abri** NOUN (PL les **sans-abri**)

homeless person ◊ *les sans-abri* the homeless

sans-gêne ADJECTIVE

inconsiderate

la **santé** NOUN

health ◊ *en bonne santé* in good health

le **sapin** NOUN

fir tree

♦ **un sapin de Noël** a Christmas tree

la **sardine** NOUN

sardine

la **Saskatchewan** NOUN

Saskatchewan

le **satellite** NOUN

satellite ◊ *la télévision par satellite* satellite TV

satisfaire VERB

to satisfy

satisfaisant ADJECTIVE

satisfactory

satisfait ADJECTIVE

satisfied ◊ *être satisfait de quelque chose* to be satisfied with something

la **sauce** NOUN

① sauce

② gravy

la **saucisse** NOUN

S

☞

sausage

le **saucisson** NOUN
sausage (*eaten sliced, cold*)

sauf PREPOSITION
except ◊ *Tout le monde est venu sauf elle.* Everyone came except her.
♦ **sauf si** unless ◊ *On ira se promener, sauf s'il fait mauvais.* We'll go for a walk, unless the weather's bad.
♦ **sauf que** except that ◊ *Tout s'est bien passé, sauf que nous sommes arrivés en retard.* Everything went OK, except that we arrived late.

le **saule à chaton** NOUN
pussy willow

le **saumon** NOUN
salmon
♦ **le saumon atlantique** Atlantic salmon
♦ **le saumon quinnat** Chinook salmon
♦ **le saumon rouge** Sockeye salmon

le **saut** NOUN
jump
♦ **le saut en longueur** the long jump
♦ **le saut en hauteur** the high jump
♦ **le saut à la perche** the pole vault
♦ **le saut à l'élastique** bungee jumping
♦ **un saut périlleux** a somersault

sauter VERB
to jump ◊ *Nous avons sauté par-dessus la barrière.* We jumped over the gate.
♦ **sauter à la corde** to skip (*with a rope*)
♦ **faire sauter quelque chose** to blow something up ◊ *On a fait sauter le poste de police la nuit dernière.* The police station was blown up last night.
♦ **faire sauter** (*food*) to stir-fry ◊ *J'ai fait sauter les légumes.* I stir-fried the vegetables.

la **sauterelle** NOUN
grasshopper

sauvage ADJECTIVE
① wild ◊ *les animaux sauvages* wild animals ◊ *le camping sauvage* wilderness camping
♦ **une région sauvage** a wilderness area
② shy ◊ *Il est sauvage.* He's shy.

sauvegarder VERB
to save (*file on computer*)

sauver VERB
to save
♦ **se sauver (1)** to run away ◊ *Elle s'est sauvée à toutes jambes.* She ran away as fast as she could.
♦ **se sauver (2)** (*informal*) to be off ◊ *Allez, je me sauve!* Right, I'm off.

le **sauvetage** NOUN
rescue

le **sauveteur** NOUN
① rescuer
② lifeguard

la **sauveteure** NOUN
① rescuer
② lifeguard

savais, savait VERB see **savoir**
♦ **Je ne savais pas qu'il devait venir.** I didn't know he was going to come.

savent VERB see **savoir**
♦ **Ils ne savent pas ce qu'ils veulent.** They don't know what they want.

la **saveur** NOUN
flavour

savez VERB see **savoir**
♦ **Est-ce que vous savez où elle habite?** Do you know where she lives?

savoir VERB
to know ◊ *Je ne sais pas où elle est allée.* I don't know where she's gone. ◊ *Nous ne savons pas s'il est bien arrivé.* We don't know if he's arrived safely. ◊ *Savais-tu que Winnipeg était la capitale du Manitoba?* Did you know Winnipeg was the capital of Manitoba? ◊ *Il ne sait pas ce qu'il va faire ce week-end.* He doesn't know what he's going to do this weekend.
♦ **Tu sais nager?** Can you swim?

le **savon** NOUN
① soap
② bar of soap

savons VERB see **savoir**

savoureux ADJECTIVE (FEM SING **savoureuse**) tasty

le **saxophone** NOUN
sax

le/la **saxophoniste** NOUN
sax player

le **scandale** NOUN
scandal
♦ **faire scandale** to cause a scandal ◊ *Ce film a fait scandale.* The film caused a scandal.

scandaleux ADJECTIVE (FEM SING **scandaleuse**)
outrageous

le **scarabée** NOUN
beetle

la **scène** NOUN
① scene ◊ *une scène d'amour* a love scene ◊ *la scène du crime* the scene of the crime ◊ *Il m'a fait une scène.* He made a scene.
♦ **une scène de ménage** a domestic quarrel
② stage ◊ *Elle fait ses débuts sur la scène.* It is her stage debut.

♦ **les arts de la scène** performing arts

sceptique ADJECTIVE
sceptical

le **schéma** NOUN
diagram

schématique ADJECTIVE
oversimplified ◊ *Cette interprétation est un peu trop schématique.* This interpretation is a bit oversimplified.

la **scie** NOUN
saw

la **science** NOUN
science
♦ **Elle est forte en sciences.** She is good at science.
♦ **les sciences physiques** the physical sciences
♦ **les sciences naturelles** the natural sciences
♦ **les sciences économiques** economics
♦ **les sciences politiques** political science ◊ *Il a un diplôme de sciences politiques.* He has a degree in political science.

la **science-fiction** NOUN
science fiction

scientifique ADJECTIVE

see also **scientifique** NOUN

scientific

le/la **scientifique** NOUN

see also **scientifique** ADJECTIVE

scientist

scier VERB
to saw

scolaire ADJECTIVE
school ◊ *l'année scolaire* the school year ◊ *les vacances scolaires* the school holidays ◊ *le transport scolaire* school transportation
♦ **l'abandon scolaire** dropping out of school

le **Scorpion** NOUN
Scorpio ◊ *Elle est Scorpion.* She's a Scorpio.

le **scrupule** NOUN
scruple

sculpter VERB
to sculpt

le **sculpteur** NOUN
sculptor

la **sculpteure** NOUN
sculptor

la **sculpture** NOUN
sculpture

se PRONOUN

se forms part of reflexive constructions.

1 himself ◊ *Il se regarde dans le miroir.* He's looking at himself in the mirror.
2 herself ◊ *Elle se regarde dans le miroir.* She's looking at herself in the mirror.
3 itself ◊ *Le chien s'est fait mal.* The dog hurt itself.
4 oneself ◊ *se regarder dans un miroir* to look at oneself in a mirror
5 themselves ◊ *Ils se sont regardés dans le miroir.* They looked at themselves in the mirror.

se changes to s' before a vowel and most words beginning with "h".

◊ *Elle s'admire dans sa nouvelle robe.* She's admiring herself in her new dress.
6 each other ◊ *Ils s'aiment.* They love each other.

la **séance** NOUN
session ◊ *une séance de physiothérapie* a physiotherapy session

le **seau** NOUN (PL les **seaux**)
bucket

sec ADJECTIVE (FEM SING **sèche**)
1 dry ◊ *un shampooing pour les cheveux secs* shampoo for dry hair ◊ *Mes mitaines sont sèches.* My mitts are dry.
2 dried ◊ *des figues sèches* dried figs

le **séchage** NOUN
drying ◊ *Voulez-vous un séchage à la brosse?* Would you like a blow-dry? ◊ *Le séchage à la machine n'est pas recommandé pour ce chandail.* Machine drying is not recommended for this sweater.

le **sèche-cheveux** NOUN (PL les **sèche-cheveux**)
hair dryer

sécher VERB
to dry
♦ **Faire sécher à plat.** Lay flat to dry.
♦ **sécher à la brosse** to blow-dry
♦ **se sécher** to dry oneself ◊ *Sèche-toi avec cette serviette.* Dry yourself with this towel.

la **sécheresse** NOUN
drought ◊ *une terrible sécheresse* a terrible drought

✹ la **sécheuse** NOUN
dryer

le **séchoir** NOUN
dryer

S

second ADJECTIVE
second ◊ *Il est arrivé second.* He came second.

secondaire ADJECTIVE

see also **secondaire** NOUN

secondary ◊ *l'école secondaire* secondary school
♦ **des effets secondaires** side effects

❋ le **secondaire** NOUN

see also **secondaire** ADJECTIVE

high school (*level*) ◊ *les enseignants et les élèves du secondaire* high school teachers and students ◊ *Elle est en secondaire cinq.* She's in Grade 12.

> ❶ *Québec high schools have five grades:* **le secondaire un, deux, trois, quatre** *and* **cinq,** *corresponding to Grades 8 to 12. Grades are written in Roman numerals: you say* **le secondaire trois,** *but write* **le secondaire III.**

la **seconde** NOUN
second ◊ *Attends une seconde!* Wait a second!

secouer VERB
to shake ◊ *secouer la tête* to shake one's head ◊ *L'accident l'a beaucoup secouée.* The accident has really shaken her.

secourir VERB
to rescue

le **secourisme** NOUN
first aid ◊ *J'ai un brevet de secourisme.* I have a first aid certificate.

le **secours** NOUN
help ◊ *Elle est allée chercher du secours.* She went to get help. ◊ *Au secours!* Help!
♦ **les premiers secours** first aid
♦ **une sortie de secours** an emergency exit
♦ **le pneu de secours** the spare tire

le **secret** NOUN

see also **secret** ADJECTIVE

secret

secret ADJECTIVE (FEM SING **secrète**)

see also **secret** NOUN

secret

le/la **secrétaire** NOUN
secretary

le **secrétariat** NOUN
secretary's office

le **secteur** NOUN
sector ◊ *le secteur public* the public

sector ◊ *le secteur privé* the private sector

la **section** NOUN
section (*of school*)

❋ **sécuritaire** ADJECTIVE
safe ◊ *un milieu de travail sécuritaire* a safe working environment

la **sécurité** NOUN
① safety
♦ **être en sécurité** to be safe ◊ *On ne se sent pas en sécurité dans ce quartier.* You don't feel safe in this neighbourhood.
♦ **la sécurité routière** road safety
♦ **une ceinture de sécurité** a seatbelt
② security ◊ *par mesure de sécurité* as a security measure
♦ **la sécurité de l'emploi** job security

séduisant ADJECTIVE
attractive

le **seigle** NOUN
rye ◊ *un pain de seigle* a loaf of rye bread

le **Seigneur** NOUN
the Lord (*God*)

le **sein** NOUN
breast
♦ **au sein de** within ◊ *le statut des autochtones au sein du Canada* the status of Aboriginals within Canada

seize NUMBER
sixteen ◊ *Elle a seize ans.* She's sixteen. ◊ *à seize heures* at 4 p.m.
♦ **le seize février** the sixteenth of February

seizième ADJECTIVE
sixteenth

le **séjour** NOUN
stay ◊ *J'ai fait un séjour d'une semaine en Alberta.* I stayed in Alberta for a week.

le **sel** NOUN
salt

sélectionner VERB
to select

la **selle** NOUN
saddle

selon PREPOSITION
according to ◊ *selon lui* according to him ◊ *selon mon humeur* according to what mood I'm in ◊ *Ils sont répartis selon leur âge.* They're divided up according to age.

la **semaine** NOUN
week
♦ **en semaine** on weekdays
♦ **la semaine de relâche** March Break
♦ **la fin de semaine** the weekend

semblable ADJECTIVE
similar

le **semblant** NOUN
♦ **faire semblant de faire quelque chose**
to pretend to do something ◊ *Elle fait*
semblant de dormir. She's pretending
to be asleep.

sembler VERB
to seem ◊ *Le temps semble*
s'améliorer. The weather seems to be
improving. ◊ *Il me semble inutile de*
s'en inquiéter. It seems pointless to
me to worry about it.

la **semelle** NOUN
① sole
② insole

le **Sénat** NOUN
Senate

le **sens** NOUN
① sense ◊ *avoir le sens de l'humour*
to have a sense of humour ◊ *Je n'ai*
pas le sens de l'orientation. I have
no sense of direction. ◊ *avoir le sens*
du rythme to have a sense of rhythm
◊ *Ça n'a pas de sens.* It doesn't make
sense.
♦ **le bon sens** common sense
❋ ♦ **sans bon sens** unreasonably ◊ *Elle*
conduit vite sans bons sens. She
drives unreasonably fast.
② direction ◊ *Tu tournes la poignée*
dans le mauvais sens. You're turning
the handle in the wrong direction.
♦ **sens dessus dessous** upside down
♦ **un sens interdit** a one-way street
◊ *J'ai failli prendre un sens interdit.*
I nearly went the wrong way down a
one-way street.
♦ **un sens unique** a one-way street

la **sensation** NOUN
feeling

sensationnel ADJECTIVE (FEM SING
sensationnelle)
sensational

sensé ADJECTIVE
sensible

sensible ADJECTIVE
① sensitive ◊ *Elle est très sensible.*
She's very sensitive. ◊ *Ce film est*
déconseillé aux personnes sensibles.
This film contains scenes which some
viewers may find disturbing.
② noticeable ◊ *une amélioration*
sensible a noticeable improvement

*Be careful! The French word **sensible***
*does not mean **sensible**.*

sensiblement ADVERB
① noticeably ◊ *Elle a sensiblement*
progressé. She has noticeably

progressed.
② approximately ◊ *Elles sont*
sensiblement de la même taille. They
are approximately the same height.

la **sentence** NOUN
sentence (*judgement*)

le **sentier** NOUN
path

le **sentiment** NOUN
feeling

sentimental ADJECTIVE (MASC PL
sentimentaux)
sentimental

sentir VERB
① to smell ◊ *Ça sent bon.* That smells
good. ◊ *Ça sent mauvais.* It smells
bad.
② to smell of ◊ *Ça sent les frites ici.* It
smells like fries in here.
③ to taste ◊ *Tu sens l'ail dans le rôti?*
Can you taste the garlic in the roast?
④ to feel ◊ *« Ça t'a fait mal? » « Non,*
je n'ai rien senti. » "Did it hurt?" "No,
I didn't feel a thing." ◊ *Je ne me sens*
pas bien. I don't feel well.
♦ **Il ne peut pas la sentir.** (*informal*) He
can't stand her.

la **séparation** NOUN
separation

le **séparatisme** NOUN
separatism

séparé ADJECTIVE
separated ◊ *Mes parents sont*
séparés. My parents are separated.

séparément ADVERB
separately

séparer VERB
to separate ◊ *Séparez le blanc du*
jaune. Separate the yolk from the
white.
♦ **se séparer** to separate ◊ *Mes parents*
se sont séparés l'année dernière. My
parents separated last year.

sept NUMBER
seven ◊ *Il est arrivé à sept heures.*
He arrived at seven o'clock. ◊ *Il a sept*
ans. He's seven.
♦ **le sept février** the seventh of February
❋ ♦ **ouvert sept jours sur sept** open 7
days a week

septembre MASC NOUN
September
♦ **en septembre** in September

septième ADJECTIVE
seventh ◊ *au septième étage* on the
seventh floor

sera, serai, seras, serez VERB *see* **être**
♦ **Je serai de retour à dix heures.** I'll be
back at 10 o'clock.

S

la **série** NOUN
series

sérieusement ADVERB
seriously

sérieux ADJECTIVE (FEM SING **sérieuse**)

see also **sérieux** NOUN

[1] serious ◊ « Il plaisantait? » « Non, il était sérieux. » "Was he joking?" "No, he was serious."
[2] responsible ◊ C'est une employée très sérieuse. She's a very responsible employee.

le **sérieux** NOUN

see also **sérieux** ADJECTIVE

♦ **garder son sérieux** to keep a straight face ◊ J'ai eu du mal à garder mon sérieux. I had trouble keeping a straight face.
♦ **prendre quelque chose au sérieux** to take something seriously
♦ **prendre quelqu'un au sérieux** to take somebody seriously
♦ **Il manque un peu de sérieux.** He's not very responsible.

la **seringue** NOUN
syringe

séronégatif ADJECTIVE (FEM SING **séronégative**)
HIV-negative

serons, seront VERB see **être**

séropositif ADJECTIVE (FEM SING **séropositive**)
HIV-positive

le **serpent** NOUN
snake

la **serre** NOUN
greenhouse
♦ **l'effet de serre** the greenhouse effect

serré ADJECTIVE
[1] tight ◊ Mon pantalon est trop serré. My pants are too tight.
[2] close (competition) ◊ Ça a été un match serré. It was a close game.

serrer VERB
♦ **Ce pantalon me serre trop.** These pants are too tight for me.
♦ **serrer la main à quelqu'un** to shake hands with somebody
♦ **se serrer** to make yourself compact ◊ Serrez-vous un peu pour que je puisse m'asseoir. Squeeze over a bit so I can sit down.
♦ **serrer quelqu'un dans ses bras** to hug somebody

la **serrure** NOUN
lock

sers, sert VERB see **servir**

le **serveur** NOUN

[1] waiter (in café)
[2] server (computer)

la **serveuse** NOUN
waitress

serviable ADJECTIVE
helpful

le **service** NOUN
[1] service (in restaurant) ◊ Le service est compris. Service is included.
♦ **être de service** to be on duty
♦ **hors service** out of order
♦ **faire le service** to serve (at table) ◊ Tu peux faire le service s'il te plaît? Could you serve, please?
♦ **le service d'assistance téléphonique** directory assistance
[2] favour ◊ rendre service à quelqu'un to do somebody a favour ◊ Est-ce que je peux te demander un service? Can I ask you a favour?
[3] serve (sports) ◊ Il a un bon service. He has a good serve.
♦ **un service commémoratif** a memorial service
♦ **le service militaire** military service
♦ **les services sociaux** social services
♦ **les services secrets** the secret service

la **serviette** NOUN
[1] towel ◊ une serviette de bain a bath towel
♦ **une serviette hygiénique** a sanitary napkin
[2] serviette (napkin)
[3] briefcase

servir VERB
to serve ◊ Est-ce qu'on vous a servi? Have you been served?
♦ **À toi de servir.** (tennis) It's your serve.
♦ **se servir** to help oneself ◊ Servez-vous. Help yourself.
♦ **se servir de** to use ◊ Te sers-tu souvent de ton vélo? Do you use your bike a lot?
♦ **servir à quelqu'un** to be of use to somebody ◊ Ça m'a beaucoup servi. It was very useful.
♦ **À quoi ça sert?** What's it for?
♦ **Ça ne sert à rien.** It's no use. ◊ Ça ne sert à rien d'insister. It's no use insisting.

ses ADJECTIVE
[1] his ◊ Il est parti voir ses grands-parents. He's gone to see his grandparents.
[2] her ◊ Elle a oublié ses livres. She forgot her books.
[3] its ◊ la ville et ses alentours the town and its surroundings

le **seuil** NOUN
doorstep

seul ADJECTIVE, ADVERB

① alone ◊ *vivre seul* to live alone
② by oneself ◊ *Elle est venue seule.*
She came by herself.
♦ **faire quelque chose tout seul** to do
something by oneself ◊ *Elle a fait ça
toute seule?* Did she do it by herself?
♦ **se sentir seul** to feel lonely
♦ **un seul livre** one book only ◊ *Vous
avez droit à un seul livre.* You're
entitled to one book only.
♦ **Il reste une seule nectarine.** There's
only one nectarine left.
♦ **le seul livre que...** the only book that...
◊ *C'est le seul Troon Harrison que
je n'aie pas lu.* That's the only Troon
Harrison I haven't read.
♦ **le seul** the only one ◊ *C'est le seul
que je ne connaisse pas.* He's the only
one I don't know.

seulement ADVERB
  only
♦ **non seulement...mais** not only...but
◊ *Non seulement il a plu, mais en
plus il a fait froid.* Not only did it rain,
but it was cold as well.

sévère ADJECTIVE
  strict ◊ *Mon prof de maths est très
sévère.* My math teacher is very strict.

le **sexe** NOUN
  sex

sexuel ADJECTIVE (FEM SING **sexuelle**)
  sexual ◊ *l'éducation sexuelle* sex
education ◊ *l'orientation sexuelle*
sexual orientation

le **shampooing** NOUN
  shampoo
♦ **se faire un shampooing** to wash one's
hair

le **short** NOUN
  shorts ◊ *Il était en short.* He was
wearing shorts.

le **si** NOUN

  | see also **si** CONJUNCTION |

  ① B ◊ *en si bémol* in B flat
  ② ti ◊ *la, si, do* la, ti, do

si CONJUNCTION, ADVERB

  | see also **si** NOUN |

  ① if ◊ *si tu veux* if you like ◊ *Je me
demande si elle va venir.* I wonder if
she'll come. ◊ *si seulement* if only
  ② so ◊ *Elle est si gentille.* She's
so kind. ◊ *Tout s'est passé si vite.*
Everything happened so fast.

le **sida** NOUN
  AIDS ◊ *Il a le sida.* He has AIDS.

le **siècle** NOUN
  century ◊ *le vingtième siècle* the
twentieth century

le **siège** NOUN
  seat (*in vehicle*)
♦ **un siège pliant** a folding chair
♦ **le siège social** head office

sien PRONOUN
♦ **le sien (1)** his ◊ *« Est-ce que c'est
le vélo de ton frère? » « Oui, c'est le
sien. »* "Is this your brother's bike?"
"Yes, it's his."
♦ **le sien (2)** hers ◊ *« Est-ce que c'est
le vélo de ta sœur? » « Oui, c'est le
sien. »* "Is this your sister's bike?"
"Yes, it's hers."

sienne PRONOUN
♦ **la sienne (1)** his ◊ *« Est-ce que c'est
la montre de ton père? » « Oui, c'est
la sienne. »* "Is this your father's
watch?" "Yes, it's his."
♦ **la sienne (2)** hers ◊ *« Est-ce que c'est
la montre de ta mère? » « Oui, c'est
la sienne. »* "Is this your mother's
watch?" "Yes, it's hers."

siennes PRONOUN
♦ **les siennes (1)** his ◊ *« Est-ce que ce
sont les bottes de ton frère? » « Oui,
ce sont les siennes. »* "Are these your
brother's boots?" "Yes, they're his."
♦ **les siennes (2)** hers ◊ *« Est-ce que ce
sont les lunettes de ta tante? » « Oui,
ce sont les siennes. »* "Are these your
aunt's glasses?" "Yes, they're hers."

siens PRONOUN
♦ **les siens (1)** his ◊ *« Est-ce que ce sont
les sandwichs de ton frère? » « Oui,
ce sont les siens. »* "Are these your
brother's sandwiches?" "Yes, they're
his."
♦ **les siens (2)** hers ◊ *« Est-ce que ce
sont les sandwichs de ta sœur? »
« Oui, ce sont les siens. »* "Are these
your sister's sandwiches?" "Yes,
they're hers."

la **sieste** NOUN
  nap ◊ *faire la sieste* to have a nap

siffler VERB
  to whistle

le **sifflet** NOUN
  whistle

🐾 le **siffleux** NOUN
  marmot

le **sigle** NOUN
  acronym

le **signal** NOUN (PL les **signaux**)
  signal

la **signature** NOUN
  signature

le **signe** NOUN
  sign
♦ **faire un signe de la main** to wave
♦ **faire signe à quelqu'un d'entrer** to

S

☞

motion to somebody to come in
♦ **les signes du zodiaque** the signs of
the zodiac

signer VERB
to sign

le **signet** NOUN
bookmark
♦ **mettre un signet à un site Web** to
bookmark a website

la **signification** NOUN
meaning

signifier VERB
to mean ◊ *Que signifie ce mot?* What
does this word mean?

le **silence** NOUN
silence
♦ **Silence!** Be quiet!

silencieux ADJECTIVE (FEM SING **silencieuse**)
1 silent ◊ *Elle est restée silencieuse.*
She remained silent.
2 quiet ◊ *C'est très silencieux ici.* It's
very quiet here.

la **silhouette** NOUN
figure ◊ *J'ai vu une silhouette dans le
brouillard.* I saw a figure in the mist.

similaire ADJECTIVE
similar

le **simple** NOUN

see also **simple** ADJECTIVE

singles (*tennis*) ◊ *le simple messieurs*
the men's singles ◊ *le simple dames*
the women's singles

simple ADJECTIVE

see also **simple** NOUN

simple

simplement ADVERB
simply ◊ *C'est tout simplement
inadmissible.* It's simply
unacceptable.

simuler VERB
to simulate

simultané ADJECTIVE
simultaneous

sincère ADJECTIVE
sincere

sincèrement ADVERB
sincerely

la **sincérité** NOUN
sincerity

le **singe** NOUN
monkey

le **singulier** NOUN
singular ◊ *au féminin singulier* in the
feminine singular

sinistre ADJECTIVE
sinister

sinon CONJUNCTION
otherwise ◊ *Dépêche-toi, sinon je
pars sans toi.* Hurry up, otherwise I'll
leave without you.

la **sinusite** NOUN
sinusitis ◊ *avoir de la sinusite* to
have sinusitis

la **sirène** NOUN
mermaid
♦ **la sirène d'alarme** the fire alarm

le **sirop** NOUN
syrup
♦ **le sirop contre la toux** cough syrup
✹ ♦ **le sirop d'érable** maple syrup

le **site** NOUN
setting ◊ *un site très sauvage*
a wilderness setting ◊ *un site
d'enfouissement* a landfill site
♦ **un site pittoresque** a scenic attraction
♦ **un site touristique** a tourist attraction
♦ **un site archéologique** an
archaeological site
♦ **un site Web** a website

sitôt ADVERB
♦ **sitôt dit, sitôt fait** no sooner said than
done
♦ **pas de sitôt** not for a long time ◊ *On
ne le reverra pas de sitôt.* We won't
see him again for a long time.

la **situation** NOUN
1 situation
♦ **la situation de famille** marital status
2 job ◊ *Il a une belle situation.* He's
got a good job.
♦ **la situation économique** economic
conditions

se **situer** VERB
to be situated ◊ *Sudbury se situe
à l'ouest de North Bay.* Sudbury is
situated to the west of North Bay.
♦ **bien situé** well situated

six NUMBER
six ◊ *Elle est rentrée à six heures.*
She got back at six o'clock. ◊ *Il a six
ans.* He's six.
♦ **le six février** the sixth of February

sixième ADJECTIVE
sixth ◊ *au sixième étage* on the sixth
floor

le **ski** NOUN
1 ski ◊ *J'ai loué des skis.* I rented
skis.
2 skiing ◊ *J'adore le ski.* I love skiing.
◊ *faire du ski* to go skiing
♦ **le ski de fond** cross-country skiing
♦ **le ski nautique** water-skiing
♦ **le ski alpin** downhill skiing
♦ **le ski de randonnée** cross-country
skiing

skier VERB

to ski

le **skieur** NOUN
skier

la **skieuse** NOUN
skier

✹ la **sloche** NOUN
slush

snob ADJECTIVE (FEM SING **snob**)
snobbish

le **snorkel** NOUN
snorkel
♦ **faire du snorkel** to go snorkelling

sobre ADJECTIVE
① sober
② plain ◊ *C'est une veste très sobre.*
It's a very plain jacket.

sociable ADJECTIVE
sociable

social ADJECTIVE (MASC PL **sociaux**)
social

le/la **socialiste** NOUN
socialist

la **société** NOUN
① society
✹ ♦ **la société distincte** distinct society
② company ◊ *une société financière*
a finance company

la **sociologie** NOUN
sociology

la **sœur** NOUN
sister
♦ **une bonne sœur** (*informal*) a nun

soi PRONOUN
oneself ◊ *avoir confiance en soi* to
have confidence in oneself
♦ **rester chez soi** to stay at home
♦ **Ça va de soi.** It goes without saying.

soi-disant ADVERB, ADJECTIVE
supposedly ◊ *Il était soi-disant parti
à Moncton.* He had supposedly left for
Moncton.
♦ **un soi-disant poète** a so-called poet

la **soie** NOUN
silk

la **soif** NOUN
thirst
♦ **avoir soif** to be thirsty

soigner VERB
to look after (*ill person, animal*)
◊ *Soigne-toi bien en fin de semaine!*
Take care of yourself this weekend!

soigneux ADJECTIVE (FEM SING **soigneuse**)
careful ◊ *Tu devrais être plus
soigneux avec tes livres.* You should
be more careful with your books.

soi-même PRONOUN
oneself ◊ *Il vaut mieux le faire soi-*

même. It's better to do it oneself.

le **soin** NOUN
care
♦ **prendre soin de quelque chose** to
take care of something ◊ *Prends bien
soin de ce livre.* Take good care of this
book.

les **soins** MASC NOUN
treatment SING
♦ **les premiers soins** first aid

le **soir** NOUN
evening ◊ *ce soir* this evening
♦ **à sept heures du soir** at 7 p.m.
♦ **demain soir** tomorrow night
♦ **hier soir** last night

la **soirée** NOUN
evening ◊ *en tenue de soirée* in
evening dress

sois VERB *see* **être**
♦ **Sois tranquille!** Be quiet!

soit CONJUNCTION
♦ **soit..., soit... (1)** either...or... ◊ *soit
lundi, soit mardi* either Monday or
Tuesday
♦ **soit..., soit... (2)** whether...or...
◊ *Je les ferai, mes devoirs, soit
aujourd'hui, soit demain.* I'll do my
homework eventually, whether today
or tomorrow.

la **soixantaine** NOUN
about sixty ◊ *une soixantaine de
personnes* about sixty people
♦ **Elle a la soixantaine.** She's in her
sixties.

soixante NUMBER
sixty ◊ *Il a soixante ans.* He's sixty.
◊ *soixante et un* sixty-one ◊ *soixante-
deux* sixty-two
♦ **soixante et onze** seventy-one
♦ **soixante-quinze** seventy-five

soixante-dix NUMBER
seventy ◊ *Il a soixante-dix ans.* He's
seventy.

le **sol** NOUN
① floor ◊ *un sol carrelé* a tiled floor
♦ **à même le sol** on the floor
② soil ◊ *sur le sol canadien* on
Canadian soil
③ G ◊ *sol dièse* G sharp
④ so ◊ *do, ré, mi, fa, sol...* do, re, mi,
fa, so...

solaire ADJECTIVE
solar ◊ *le système solaire* the solar
system
♦ **la crème solaire** sun cream

le **soldat** NOUN
soldier

la **soldate** NOUN
soldier

S

le **solde** NOUN
- ♦ **être en solde** to be on sale ◊ *Les chemisiers sont en solde.* The blouses are on sale.
- ♦ **les soldes** the sales ◊ *les soldes de janvier* the January sales

soldé ADJECTIVE
- ♦ **être soldé** to be on sale ◊ *un article soldé à dix dollars* an item on sale for 10 dollars

la **sole** NOUN
sole (*fish*)

le **soleil** NOUN
sun ◊ *au soleil* in the sun
- ♦ **Il fait soleil.** It's sunny out.
- ♦ **le coup de soleil** sunburn
- ♦ **le coucher de soleil** sunset

le **solfège** NOUN
musical theory ◊ *Elle joue du violon sans connaître le solfège.* She plays the violin but she can't read music.

solidaire ADJECTIVE
- ♦ **être solidaire de quelqu'un** to back somebody up

solide ADJECTIVE
1. strong (*person*)
2. solid (*object*)

solitaire ADJECTIVE

see also **solitaire** NOUN

solitary

le/la **solitaire** NOUN

see also **solitaire** ADJECTIVE

loner

la **solitude** NOUN
loneliness

la **solution** NOUN
solution
- ♦ **une solution de facilité** an easy way out

sombre ADJECTIVE
dark

le **sommaire** NOUN
summary

la **somme** NOUN

see also **le somme**

sum

le **somme** NOUN

see also **la somme**

nap ◊ *faire un somme* to take a nap

le **sommeil** NOUN
sleep
- ♦ **avoir sommeil** to be sleepy

sommes VERB see **être**
- ♦ **Nous sommes en vacances.** We're on vacation.

le **sommet** NOUN
summit

le **somnifère** NOUN
sleeping pill

somptueux ADJECTIVE (FEM SING **somptueuse**)
sumptuous

son ADJECTIVE (FEM SING **sa**, PL **ses**)

see also **son** NOUN

1. his ◊ *son père* his father ◊ *Il a perdu son portefeuille.* He lost his wallet.
2. her ◊ *son père* her father ◊ *Elle a perdu son manteau.* She lost her coat.

le **son** NOUN

see also **son** ADJECTIVE

1. sound ◊ *Le son n'est pas très bon.* The sound is not very good. ◊ *baisser le son* to turn down the sound
2. bran
- ♦ **le pain de son** bran bread

le **sondage** NOUN
survey
- ♦ **un sondage d'opinion** an opinion poll

sonder VERB
to poll ◊ *Nous avons sondé l'opinion des élèves pour savoir quelle station de radio est la plus populaire.* We polled the students to find out which radio station was most popular.

sonner VERB
to ring ◊ *On a sonné.* Somebody rang the doorbell. ◊ *Le téléphone a sonné.* The phone rang.

la **sonnerie** NOUN
bell (*electric*) ◊ *La sonnerie du téléphone l'a réveillée.* She was woken by the phone ringing.

la **sonnette** NOUN
bell ◊ *la sonnette d'alarme* the alarm bell

sont VERB see **être**
- ♦ **Ils sont en vacances.** They're on holiday.

sophistiqué ADJECTIVE
sophisticated

le **sorcier** NOUN
wizard

la **sorcière** NOUN
witch

le **sort** NOUN
1. spell ◊ *jeter un sort à quelqu'un* to cast a spell on somebody
- ♦ **un mauvais sort** a curse
- ♦ **jeter un sort à quelque chose** to put a jinx on something
2. fate ◊ *abandonner quelqu'un à son triste sort* to leave somebody to their fate

♦ **tirer au sort** to draw lots

la **sorte** NOUN

sort ◊ *C'est une sorte de gâteau.*
It's a sort of cake. ◊ *toutes sortes de
choses* all sorts of things

la **sortie** NOUN

way out ◊ *Où est la sortie?* Where's
the way out?

♦ **la sortie de secours** the emergency
exit

♦ **une sortie éducative** a field trip

sortir VERB

① to go out ◊ *Elle est sortie sans rien
dire.* She went out without saying a
word. ◊ *Il est sorti acheter un journal.*
He's gone out to buy a newspaper.
◊ *J'aime sortir.* I like going out.
② to come out ◊ *Elle sort de l'hôpital
demain.* She's coming out of the
hospital tomorrow. ◊ *Je l'ai rencontré
en sortant de la pharmacie.* I met him
coming out of the drugstore. ◊ *Ce
modèle vient juste de sortir.* This
model has just come out.
③ to take out ◊ *Elle a sorti son
porte-monnaie de son sac.* She took
her wallet out of her purse. ◊ *Je vais
sortir la voiture du garage.* I'll get the
car out of the garage.

♦ **sortir avec quelqu'un** to be going out
with somebody ◊ *Tu sors avec lui?*
Are you going out with him?

♦ **s'en sortir** to manage ◊ *Ne t'en fais
pas, tu t'en sortiras.* Don't worry,
you'll manage OK.

la **sottise** NOUN

♦ **Ne fais pas de sottises.** Don't do
anything silly.

♦ **Ne dis pas de sottises.** Don't talk
nonsense.

le **sou** NOUN

cent (*informal*) ◊ *Les tranches de
pizza ne coûtent que quatre-vingt-
neuf sous aujourd'hui.* Pizza slices are
only 89 cents today.

♦ **Je n'ai pas un sou sur moi.** I haven't
got a penny on me.

♦ **être près de ses sous** (*informal*) to be
tight-fisted

le **souci** NOUN

worry

♦ **se faire du souci** to worry

soucieux ADJECTIVE (FEM SING **soucieuse**)
worried ◊ *Tu as l'air soucieux.* You
look worried.

la **soucoupe** NOUN

saucer

♦ **une soucoupe volante** a flying saucer

soudain ADJECTIVE, ADVERB

① sudden ◊ *une douleur soudaine* a
sudden pain
② suddenly ◊ *Soudain, il s'est fâché.*
Suddenly he got angry.

le **souffle** NOUN

breath

♦ **à bout de souffle** out of breath

le **soufflé** NOUN

soufflé ◊ *un soufflé au fromage* a
cheese soufflé

souffler VERB

① to blow ◊ *Le vent soufflait fort.* The
wind was blowing hard.
② to blow out ◊ *Souffle les bougies!*
Blow out the candles!

la **souffleuse** NOUN

snowblower ◊ *Mon père a passé la
souffleuse pour déneiger l'entrée.* My
father used the snowblower to clear
the driveway.

la **souffrance** NOUN

suffering

souffrant ADJECTIVE

unwell

souffrir VERB

to be in pain ◊ *Elle souffre
beaucoup.* She's in a lot of pain.

le **souhait** NOUN

wish ◊ *faire un souhait* to make a
wish ◊ *Tous nos souhaits de réussite.*
All our best wishes for your success.
◊ *les souhaits de bonne année* New
Year's wishes

♦ **« Atchoum! » « À tes souhaits! »**
"Atchoo!" "Bless you!"

souhaiter VERB

to wish ◊ *Je souhaite aller à
l'université.* I wish to go to university.
◊ *Nous vous souhaitons une bonne
année.* We wish you a happy New
Year.

soûl ADJECTIVE (*informal*)
drunk

soulager VERB

to relieve

soulever VERB

① to lift ◊ *Je n'arrive pas à soulever
cette valise.* I can't lift this suitcase.
② to raise ◊ *Il faudra soulever la
question lors de la réunion.* We'll have
to raise the matter at the meeting.

♦ **soulever un bon point** to make a
good point

le **soulier** NOUN

shoe

souligner VERB

to underline

le **soupçon** NOUN

suspicion

S

♦ **un soupçon de** a dash of ◊ *Ajoutez un soupçon de crème.* Add a dash of cream.

soupçonner VERB
to suspect

la **soupe** NOUN
soup ◊ *la soupe au poulet et aux nouilles* chicken noodle soup

✱ le **souper** NOUN

see also **souper** VERB

supper ◊ *Qu'est-ce qu'il y a pour souper?* What's for supper?

✱ **souper** VERB

see also **souper** NOUN

to have supper

le **soupir** NOUN
sigh

soupirer VERB
to sigh

souple ADJECTIVE
flexible

la **source** NOUN
spring ◊ *l'eau de source* spring water

le **sourcil** NOUN
eyebrow

sourd ADJECTIVE
deaf

souriant ADJECTIVE
cheerful

le **sourire** NOUN

see also **sourire** VERB

smile
♦ **avoir le sourire fendu jusqu'aux oreilles** to grin from ear to ear

sourire VERB

see also **sourire** NOUN

to smile ◊ *sourire à quelqu'un* to smile at somebody

la **souris** NOUN
mouse (*also computer*)

sournois ADJECTIVE
sly

sous PREPOSITION
under
♦ **sous terre** underground
♦ **sous la pluie** in the rain

sous-entendu ADJECTIVE

see also **sous-entendu** NOUN

implied

le **sous-entendu** NOUN

see also **sous-entendu** ADJECTIVE

insinuation

sous-marin ADJECTIVE

see also **sous-marin** NOUN

underwater

le **sous-marin** NOUN

see also **sous-marin** ADJECTIVE

1 submarine ◊ *un sous-marin nucléaire* a nuclear submarine
2 sub (*sandwich*) ◊ *un sous-marin bacon, laitue et tomates* a BLT sub

le **sous-produit** NOUN
by-product

le **sous-sol** NOUN
basement

le **sous-titre** NOUN
subtitle

sous-titré ADJECTIVE
with subtitles

la **soustraction** NOUN
subtraction

soustraire VERB
to subtract

les **sous-vêtements** MASC NOUN
underwear SING

soutenir VERB
to support ◊ *Il m'a toujours soutenu.* He's always supported me.
♦ **soutenir que** to maintain that ◊ *Elle soutenait que c'était impossible.* She maintained that it was impossible.
♦ **soutenir l'allure** to keep up ◊ *Elle marchait trop vite et je n'arrivais pas à soutenir l'allure.* She was walking too fast and I couldn't keep up.

souterrain ADJECTIVE

see also **souterrain** NOUN

underground

le **souterrain** NOUN

see also **souterrain** ADJECTIVE

underground passage

le **soutien** NOUN
support

le **soutien-gorge** NOUN (PL les **soutiens-gorge**)
bra

le **souvenir** NOUN

see also **se souvenir** VERB

1 memory ◊ *garder un bon souvenir de quelque chose* to have happy memories of something
2 souvenir
♦ **Garde ce livre en souvenir de moi.** Keep this book to remember me by.
♦ **le jour du Souvenir** Remembrance Day

se **souvenir** VERB

see also **souvenir** NOUN

♦ **se souvenir de quelque chose** to remember something ◊ *Je ne me souviens pas de son adresse.* I can't remember his address.

♦ **se souvenir que** to remember that ◊ *Je me souviens qu'il neigeait.* I remember it was snowing.

souvent ADVERB
often

la **souveraineté** NOUN
sovereignty ◊ *Êtes-vous en faveur de la souveraineté du Québec?* Are you in favour of Québec sovereignty?

le/la **souverainiste** NOUN
sovereigntist

le **soya** NOUN
soya
♦ **des germes de soya** bean sprouts
♦ **du lait de soya** soy milk

soyez, soyons VERB *see* **être**

spacieux ADJECTIVE (FEM SING **spacieuse**)
spacious

les **spaghettis** MASC NOUN
spaghetti SING

spécial ADJECTIVE (MASC PL **spéciaux**)
[1] special ◊ *« Qu'est-ce que tu fais en fin de semaine? » « Rien de spécial. »* "What are you doing this weekend?" "Nothing special."
♦ **les effets spéciaux** special effects
[2] peculiar ◊ *Elle a des goûts un peu spéciaux.* She has rather peculiar tastes.

spécialement ADVERB
[1] specially ◊ *Il est venu spécialement pour te parler.* He came specially to speak to you.
[2] particularly ◊ *Ce n'est pas spécialement difficile.* It's not particularly difficult.

se **spécialiser** VERB
♦ **se spécialiser dans quelque chose** to specialize in something ◊ *Je vais me spécialiser dans biologie marine.* I'm going to specialize in marine biology.

le/la **spécialiste** NOUN
specialist

la **spécialité** NOUN
specialty

spécifier VERB
to specify

le **spectacle** NOUN
show

spectaculaire ADJECTIVE
spectacular

le **spectateur** NOUN
[1] member of the audience
[2] spectator

la **spectatrice** NOUN
[1] member of the audience
[2] spectator

le **spermophile** NOUN
gopher

spirituel ADJECTIVE (FEM SING **spirituelle**)
[1] spiritual
[2] witty

splendide ADJECTIVE
magnificent

spontané ADJECTIVE
spontaneous

le **sport** NOUN

| *see also* **sport** ADJECTIVE |

sport ◊ *faire du sport* to do sports
♦ **les sports d'hiver** winter sports
♦ **le sport extrême** extreme sport

sport ADJECTIVE (MASC, FEM, PL)

| *see also* **sport** NOUN |

casual ◊ *une veste sport* a casual jacket

sportif ADJECTIVE (FEM SING **sportive**)

| *see also* **sportif** NOUN |

[1] athletic ◊ *Elle est très sportive.* She's very athletic.
[2] sports ◊ *un club sportif* a sports club

le **sportif** NOUN

| *see also* **sportif** ADJECTIVE |

sportsman

la **sportive** NOUN
sportswoman

le **squelette** NOUN
skeleton

le **SRAS** NOUN = **syndrome respiratoire aigu sévère**
SARS

stable ADJECTIVE
stable
♦ **un emploi stable** a steady job

le **stade** NOUN
stadium

le **stage** NOUN
[1] training course ◊ *faire un stage de formation professionnelle* to take a vocational training course
[2] co-op placement ◊ *Il a fait un stage dans une bibliothèque.* He did a co-op placement in a library.
♦ **faire un stage en entreprise** to do a work placement

Be careful! The French word stage does not mean stage.

le/la **stagiaire** NOUN
trainee

S

le **stampede** NOUN
♦ **le Stampede de Calgary** Calgary Stampede

le **stand** NOUN
1. booth (*at exhibition*)
2. stall (*at fair*)

le/la **standardiste** NOUN
operator

la **station** NOUN
♦ **une station de métro** a subway station
♦ **une station de taxis** a taxi stand
♦ **une station de ski** a ski resort

le **stationnement** NOUN
1. parking
2. parking lot
♦ **« stationnement interdit »** "no parking"

stationner VERB
to park ◊ *J'ai stationné la voiture dans la rue.* I parked the car on the street.

> *Use **se stationner** if there is no object after the verb.*

♦ **se stationner** to park ◊ *Elle s'est stationnée dans la rue.* She's parked on the street.

la **station-service** NOUN (PL les **stations-service**)
service station

la **statistique** NOUN
1. statistic ◊ *Voici des statistiques sur les exportations canadiennes.* Here are some statistics on Canadian exports.
2. statistics (*the science*)

le **steak** NOUN
steak
♦ **un steak haché** a hamburger patty
♦ **le steak haché** hamburger meat ◊ *J'ai acheté du steak haché.* I bought some hamburger meat.

stérile ADJECTIVE
sterile

stimulant ADJECTIVE
stimulating

stimuler VERB
to stimulate

stopper VERB
to stop

le **store** NOUN
blind (*on window*) ◊ *un store horizontal* horizontal blinds ◊ *Toutes les fenêtres ont des stores verticaux.* All the windows have vertical blinds.

la **stratégie** NOUN
strategy

stratégique ADJECTIVE
strategic

stressant ADJECTIVE
stressful

stressé ADJECTIVE
stressed out

strict ADJECTIVE
1. strict (*person*) ◊ *Mon prof de français est très strict.* My French teacher's very strict.
2. plain (*clothes*) ◊ *une tenue très stricte* a very plain outfit
♦ **le strict minimum** the bare minimum

la **strophe** NOUN
stanza

studieux ADJECTIVE (FEM SING **studieuse**)
studious

le **studio** NOUN
1. studio apartment
2. studio ◊ *un studio de télévision* a television studio ◊ *un studio de peintre* a painter's studio

stupéfait ADJECTIVE
astonished

les **stupéfiants** MASC NOUN
narcotics

stupéfier VERB
to astonish ◊ *Sa réponse m'a stupéfié.* I was astonished by his answer.

stupide ADJECTIVE
stupid

le **style** NOUN
style

le/la **styliste** NOUN
designer

le **stylo** NOUN
pen
♦ **un stylo plume** a fountain pen
♦ **un stylo à bille** a ballpoint pen
♦ **un stylo-feutre** a felt pen

su VERB *see* **savoir**
♦ **Si j'avais su...** If I'd known...

subir VERB
to suffer (*defeat*)
♦ **subir une opération** to have an operation

subit ADJECTIVE
sudden

subitement ADVERB
suddenly

subjectif ADJECTIVE (FEM SING **subjective**)
subjective

le **subjonctif** NOUN
subjunctive

substituer VERB

to substitute ◊ *substituer un mot à un autre* to substitute one word for another

subtil ADJECTIVE
subtle

la **subvention** NOUN
subsidy

subventionner VERB
to subsidize

le **succès** NOUN
success ◊ *avoir du succès* to be successful

le **successeur** NOUN
successor

la **successeure** NOUN
successor

la **succursale** NOUN
branch (*of company*)

sucer VERB
to suck

✲ le **suçon** NOUN
lollipop

le **sucre** NOUN
sugar ◊ *« Combien de sucre dans votre café? » « Deux sucres, s'il vous plaît. »* "How many sugars do you take in your coffee?" "Two, please."
♦ **le sucre brun** brown sugar
♦ **le sucre d'érable** maple sugar
♦ **du sucre en cubes** sugar cubes
♦ **un sucre d'orge** a barley sugar
♦ **du sucre à glacer** icing sugar

sucré ADJECTIVE
1️⃣ sweet ◊ *Ce gâteau est un peu trop sucré.* This cake is a bit too sweet.
2️⃣ sweetened ◊ *du lait concentré sucré* sweetened condensed milk

sucrer VERB
to add sugar ◊ *J'ai sucré mon café.* I added sugar to my coffee.
♦ **se sucrer le bec** to eat sweets ◊ *Elle adore se sucrer le bec.* She loves sweets.

les **sucreries** FEM NOUN
sweets

le **sucrier** NOUN
sugar bowl

le **sud** NOUN

see also **sud** ADJECTIVE

south ◊ *Ils vivent dans le sud de la Colombie-Britannique.* They live in the south of British Columbia.
♦ **vers le sud** southwards
♦ **au sud d'Edmonton** south of Edmonton
♦ **l'Amérique du Sud** South America
♦ **le vent du sud** the south wind

sud ADJECTIVE

see also **sud** NOUN

1️⃣ south ◊ *la côte sud de Terre-Neuve* the south coast of Newfoundland
♦ **le pôle sud** the South Pole
2️⃣ southern ◊ *Nous avons visité la partie sud du pays.* We visited the southern part of the country.

le **sud-est** NOUN
southeast ◊ *au sud-est* in the southeast

le **sud-ouest** NOUN
southwest ◊ *au sud-ouest* in the southwest

suer VERB
to sweat

la **sueur** NOUN
sweat
♦ **en sueur** sweating

suffire VERB
to be enough ◊ *Tiens, voilà dix dollars. Ça te suffit?* Here's 10 dollars. Is that enough for you?
♦ **Ça suffit!** That's enough!

suffisamment ADVERB
enough ◊ *Ça n'est pas suffisamment grand.* It's not big enough. ◊ *Il n'y a pas suffisamment de chaises.* There aren't enough chairs.

suffisant ADJECTIVE
1️⃣ good enough ◊ *Ça n'est pas une raison suffisante.* That's not a good enough reason.
2️⃣ smug ◊ *Il est un peu trop suffisant.* He's a bit too smug.

suffoquer VERB
to suffocate

suggérer VERB
to suggest

se **suicider** VERB
to commit suicide

suis VERB see **être** see **suivre**
♦ **Je suis rapide.** I'm fast.
♦ **Suis-moi.** Follow me.

✲ le **suisse** NOUN
chipmunk

la **suite** NOUN
1️⃣ rest ◊ *Je vous raconterai la suite de l'histoire demain.* I'll tell you the rest of the story tomorrow.
2️⃣ sequel (*to book, film*)
♦ **tout de suite** right away ◊ *J'y vais tout de suite.* I'll go right away.
♦ **de suite** in a row ◊ *Il a commis la même erreur trois fois de suite.* He made the same mistake three times in a row.
♦ **par la suite** later ◊ *Elle s'est avérée par la suite qu'elle était coupable.* She

S

later turned out to be guilty.

suivant ADJECTIVE
following ◊ *le jour suivant* the following day ◊ *l'exercice suivant* the following exercise
♦ **Au suivant!** Next!

suivre VERB
① to follow ◊ *Il m'a suivie jusque chez moi.* He followed me home. ◊ *Vous me suivez ou est-ce que je parle trop vite?* Are you following me, or am I talking too fast?
② to take (*course*) ◊ *Elle suit un cours d'anglais au collège.* She's taking an English course at college.
③ to keep up ◊ *Il n'arrive pas à suivre en maths.* He can't keep up in math. ◊ *J'aime suivre l'actualité.* I like to keep up with the news.
♦ « à suivre » "to be continued"
♦ **suivre un régime** to be on a diet

sujet ADJECTIVE (FEM SING **sujette**)

see also **sujet** NOUN

♦ **être sujet à** to be prone to ◊ *Il est sujet au vertige.* He suffers from fear of heights.

le **sujet** NOUN

see also **sujet** ADJECTIVE

subject
♦ **au sujet de** about ◊ *« C'est à quel sujet? » « C'est au sujet de l'annonce parue dans le* Globe and Mail *d'aujourd'hui. »* "What's it about?" "It's about the advertisement in today's *Globe and Mail.*"
♦ **un sujet de conversation** a topic of conversation
♦ **un sujet d'examen** an examination question
♦ **un sujet de plaisanterie** something to joke about

super MASC, FEM, PL ADJECTIVE
great ◊ *C'est super que tu puisses venir avec nous!* It's great that you can come with us!

superficiel ADJECTIVE (FEM SING **superficielle**)
superficial

superflu ADJECTIVE
superfluous

supérieur ADJECTIVE
① upper ◊ *la lèvre supérieure* the upper lip
② superior ◊ *qualité supérieure* superior quality ◊ *Ne me parle pas sur ce ton supérieur.* Don't talk to me in that superior tone of voice.
♦ **supérieur à** greater than ◊ *Choisissez un nombre supérieur à cent.* Choose a number greater than 100.

le **supermarché** NOUN
supermarket

superposé ADJECTIVE
♦ **des lits superposés** bunk beds

superstitieux ADJECTIVE (FEM SING **superstitieuse**)
superstitious

le **suppléant** NOUN
substitute teacher

la **suppléante** NOUN
substitute teacher

le **supplément** NOUN
♦ **payer un supplément** to pay an additional charge
♦ **Le toit ouvrant est en supplément.** The sunroof is extra.
♦ **un supplément de travail** extra work

supplémentaire ADJECTIVE
additional ◊ *Voici quelques exercices supplémentaires.* Here are some additional exercises.
♦ **faire des heures supplémentaires** to do overtime

le **supplice** NOUN
torture ◊ *C'était un supplice.* It was torture.

supplier VERB
♦ **supplier quelqu'un de faire quelque chose** to beg somebody to do something ◊ *Je t'en supplie!* I'm begging you!

supportable ADJECTIVE
bearable

supporter VERB
to stand (*tolerate*) ◊ *Je ne supporte pas l'hypocrisie.* I can't stand hypocrisy. ◊ *Elle ne supporte pas qu'on la critique.* She can't stand being criticized. ◊ *Je ne peux pas la supporter.* I can't stand her. ◊ *Je supporte mal la chaleur.* I can't stand hot weather.

Be careful! **supporter** *does not mean* ***to support.***

supposer VERB
to suppose

supprimer VERB
① to cut ◊ *Deux mille emplois ont été supprimés.* Two thousand jobs have been cut.
② to cancel ◊ *L'autobus de Nelson a été supprimé.* The bus to Nelson has been cancelled.
③ to get rid of ◊ *Ils ont supprimé les témoins de l'enlèvement.* They got rid of the witnesses to the kidnapping.
④ to delete ◊ *Elle a supprimé quelques vieux fichiers.* She deleted

some old files.

suprême ADJECTIVE
supreme ◊ *la Cour suprême* the
Supreme Court

sur PREPOSITION
1 on ◊ *Pose-le sur la table.* Put it on
the table. ◊ *Vous verrez l'hôpital sur
votre droite.* You'll see the hospital
on your right. ◊ *une conférence sur
l'écologie* a lecture on ecology
2 in ◊ *une personne sur dix* 1 person
in 10
3 out of ◊ *J'ai eu neuf sur dix en
maths.* I got 9 out of 10 in math.
4 by ◊ *quatre mètres sur deux* 4
metres by 2

sûr ADJECTIVE
1 sure ◊ *Tu es sûr?* Are you sure?
♦ **sûr et certain** absolutely certain
2 reliable ◊ *C'est quelqu'un de très
sûr.* He's a very reliable person.
3 safe ◊ *Ce quartier n'est pas très sûr
la nuit.* This neighbourhood isn't very
safe at night.
♦ **sûr de soi** self-confident ◊ *Elle est
très sûre d'elle.* She's very self-
confident.

la surdose NOUN
overdose

sûrement ADVERB
certainly ◊ *Sûrement pas!* Certainly
not! ◊ *Il est sûrement déjà parti.* He's
sure to have already left.

la sûreté NOUN
♦ **mettre quelque chose en sûreté** to
put something in a safe place

le surf NOUN
surfing
♦ **le surf des neiges** snow surfing

la surface NOUN
surface
♦ **les grandes surfaces** the
supermarkets

la surfaceuse NOUN
Zamboni™

surfer VERB
to go surfing
♦ **surfer sur Internet** to surf the Net

surgelé ADJECTIVE
frozen ◊ *des frites surgelées* frozen
fries

les surgelés MASC NOUN
frozen foods SING

surhumain ADJECTIVE
superhuman

le surintendant NOUN
superintendent ◊ *Son père est
surintendant de police.* Her father is a
police superintendent.

la surintendante NOUN
superintendent ◊ *Sa mère est
surintendante scolaire.* His mother is
a school superintendent.

sur-le-champ ADVERB
immediately

le surlendemain NOUN
♦ **le surlendemain de son arrivée** two
days after she arrived
♦ **le surlendemain dans la matinée** two
days later, in the morning

se surmener VERB
to work too hard ◊ *Ne te surmène
pas trop pendant la fin de semaine.*
Don't work too hard over the
weekend.

surmonter VERB
to overcome ◊ *Il nous reste de
nombreux obstacles à surmonter.*
We still have many obstacles to
overcome.

surnaturel ADJECTIVE (FEM SING
surnaturelle)
supernatural

le surnom NOUN
nickname

surnommer NOUN
to nickname ◊ *On l'a surnommé « la
bolle des maths ».* We nicknamed him
"the math whiz".

surpeuplé ADJECTIVE
overpopulated

surprenant ADJECTIVE
surprising

surprendre VERB
to surprise ◊ *Ça me surprendrait
beaucoup qu'elle arrive à l'heure.* I'd
be very surprised if she arrived on
time.
♦ **surprendre quelqu'un en train de faire
quelque chose** to catch somebody
doing something ◊ *Je l'ai surpris en
train de fouiller dans mon casier.* I
caught him rummaging in my locker.

surpris ADJECTIVE
surprised ◊ *Elle était surprise de me
voir.* She was surprised to see me.

la surprise NOUN
surprise ◊ *faire une surprise à
quelqu'un* to give somebody a
surprise

sursauter VERB
to jump ◊ *J'ai sursauté en entendant
mon nom.* I jumped when I heard my
name.

surtout ADVERB
1 especially ◊ *Il est assez timide,
surtout avec les filles.* He's rather shy,
especially with girls.

S

2 above all ◊ *Ce manteau est bon marché, pratique et, surtout, paraît bien.* This coat is reasonably priced, practical, and above all great-looking. ◊ *Surtout, ne répète pas ce que je t'ai dit!* Whatever you do, don't repeat what I told you!

surveiller VERB
1 to keep an eye on ◊ *Tu peux surveiller mes bagages?* Can you keep an eye on my luggage?
2 to keep a watch on ◊ *La police a surveillé la maison pendant une semaine.* The police kept the house under surveillance for a week.
3 to supervise ◊ *Nous sommes toujours surveillés pendant la récréation.* We're always supervised during recess.
♦ **surveiller sa ligne** to watch one's figure

le **survêtement** NOUN
track suit ◊ *un haut de survêtement* a track top ◊ *un pantalon de survêtement* track pants

la **survie** NOUN
survival

le **survivant** NOUN
survivor

la **survivante** NOUN
survivor

survivre VERB
to survive ◊ *survivre à un accident* to survive an accident

survoler VERB
to fly over

sus ADVERB
♦ **en sus** in addition

susceptible ADJECTIVE
touchy

suspect ADJECTIVE
suspicious ◊ *dans des circonstances suspectes* under suspicious circumstances

suspecter VERB
to suspect

le **suspense** NOUN
suspense
♦ **un film à suspense** a thriller

la **suture** NOUN
♦ **un point de suture** a stitch

svelte ADJECTIVE
slender

SVP ABBREVIATION (= *s'il vous plaît*)
please

la **syllabe** NOUN
syllable

le **symbole** NOUN
symbol

symbolique ADJECTIVE
symbolic

symboliser VERB
to symbolize

symétrique ADJECTIVE
symmetrical

la **sympathie** NOUN
♦ **J'ai beaucoup de sympathie pour lui.** I like him a lot.

sympathique ADJECTIVE
nice ◊ *Ce sont des gens très sympathiques.* They're very nice people.

> *Be careful!* **sympathique** *does not mean* **sympathetic**.

sympathiser VERB
to get along well ◊ *Nous avons immédiatement sympathisé avec nos voisins.* We hit it off with our neighbours right away.

> *Be careful!* **sympathiser** *does not mean* **sympathize**.

le **symptôme** NOUN
symptom

la **synagogue** NOUN
synagogue

le **syndicat** NOUN
trade union

le **syndrome** NOUN
syndrome
✹ ♦ **le syndrome de Down** Down syndrome
♦ **le syndrome respiratoire aigu sévère** Severe Acute Respiratory Syndrome

synonyme ADJECTIVE
see also **synonyme** NOUN
synonymous ◊ *être synonyme de* to be synonymous with

le **synonyme** NOUN
see also **synonyme** ADJECTIVE
synonym

synthétique ADJECTIVE
synthetic

✹ **syntoniser** VERB
to tune (radio) ◊ *J'ai syntonisé la radio sur Radio-Canada.* I tuned the radio to CBC.

systématique ADJECTIVE
systematic

le **système** NOUN
system
♦ **le système d'exploitation** DOS (disk operating system)

T

t' PRONOUN *see* **te**

ta ADJECTIVE
<u>your</u> ◊ *J'ai vu ta sœur hier.* I saw your sister yesterday.

le **tabac** NOUN
① <u>tobacco</u> ◊ *Le tabac est originaire d'Amérique.* Tobacco is native to America.
② <u>smoking</u> ◊ *Le tabac est mauvais pour la santé.* Smoking is bad for you.

la **table** NOUN
<u>table</u>
♦ **mettre la table** to set the table
♦ **se mettre à table** to sit down to eat
♦ **À table!** Dinner's ready!
♦ **une table de jeu** card table
♦ **une table de nuit** a night table
♦ **table des matières** table of contents

le **tableau** NOUN (PL les **tableaux**)
① <u>painting</u> ◊ *un tableau de Monet* a painting by Monet
♦ **le tableau d'affichage** the notice board
♦ **le tableau noir** the chalkboard
② <u>chart</u>

la **tablette** NOUN
♦ **une tablette de chocolat** a bar of chocolate

le **tableur** NOUN
<u>spreadsheet</u>

le **tablier** NOUN
<u>apron</u>

le **tabloïd** NOUN
<u>tabloid</u>

le **tabouret** NOUN
<u>stool</u>

la **tache** NOUN
<u>mark</u> (*stain*)
♦ **des taches de rousseur** freckles

la **tâche** NOUN
<u>task</u>

tacher VERB
<u>to leave a stain</u>

tâcher VERB
♦ **tâcher de faire quelque chose** to try to do something ◊ *Tâche d'être à l'heure!* Try to be on time!

la **tactique** NOUN
<u>tactics</u>
♦ **changer de tactique** to try something different

la **taie** NOUN
♦ **une taie d'oreiller** a pillowcase

la **taille** NOUN
① <u>waist</u> ◊ *avoir la taille fine* to have a slim waist
② <u>height</u> ◊ *Ils sont de la même taille.* They are the same height.
③ <u>size</u> ◊ *Avez-vous ma taille?* Have you got my size?

le **taille-crayon** NOUN
<u>pencil sharpener</u>

le **tailleur** NOUN
① <u>tailor</u>
② <u>suit</u> (*women's*)
♦ **Il est assis en tailleur.** He's sitting cross-legged.

se **taire** VERB
<u>to stop talking</u>
♦ **Taisez-vous!** Be quiet!

le **talent** NOUN
<u>talent</u> ◊ *Elle a le talent de mettre les gens à l'aise.* She has a talent for putting people at ease.
♦ **avoir du talent** to have talent

talentueux ADJECTIVE (FEM SING **talentueuse**)
<u>talented</u>

la **talle** NOUN
<u>patch of shrubs or berries</u> ◊ *une talle de bleuets* a patch of blueberries

le **talon** NOUN
<u>heel</u>
♦ **les talons hauts** high heels

le **tambour** NOUN
<u>drum</u>

le **tampon** NOUN
<u>pad</u> ◊ *un tampon à récurer* a scouring pad
♦ **un tampon hygiénique** a tampon

tandis que CONJUNCTION
<u>while</u> ◊ *Elle a toujours de bonnes notes, tandis que les miennes sont mauvaises.* She always gets good marks, while mine are poor.

tant ADVERB
<u>so much</u> ◊ *Je l'aime tant!* I love him so much!
♦ **tant de (1)** so much ◊ *tant de nourriture* so much food
♦ **tant de (2)** so many ◊ *tant de livres* so many books
♦ **tant pis (1)** never mind
♦ **tant pis (2)** too bad
♦ **tant que (1)** until ◊ *Tu ne sortiras pas tant que tu n'auras pas fini tes devoirs.* You're not going out until

☞

you've finished your homework.

♦ **tant que (2)** while ◊ *Profites-en tant que tu peux.* Make the most of it while you can.

♦ **tant mieux** so much the better

♦ **tant pis** never mind

la **tante** NOUN
aunt

tantôt ADVERB
sometimes ◊ *Nous venons tantôt à pied, tantôt en autobus.* Sometimes we walk, sometimes we come by bus.

le **tapage** NOUN
① racket ◊ *Ils ont fait du tapage toute la nuit.* They made a racket all night long.
② fuss ◊ *On a fait beaucoup de tapage autour de cette affaire.* There was a lot of fuss about that business.

taper VERB
① to beat down ◊ *Le soleil tape.* The sun's really beating down.
♦ **taper quelqu'un** to hit somebody ◊ *Maman, elle m'a tapé dessus!* Mom, she hit me!
♦ **taper sur quelque chose** to bang on something
♦ **taper des pieds** to stamp one's feet
♦ **taper des mains** to clap one's hands
② to type ◊ *Tapez votre mot de passe.* Type your password.

le **tapis** NOUN
carpet
♦ **le tapis roulant (1)** the moving sidewalk
♦ **le tapis roulant (2)** the conveyor belt (*in factory*)
♦ **un tapis de souris** a mouse pad

tapisser VERB
to paper

la **tapisserie** NOUN
① wallpaper ◊ *Tu aimes la tapisserie de ma chambre?* Do you like the wallpaper in my bedroom?
② tapestry

tapoter VERB
① to pat ◊ *Elle lui a tapoté l'épaule affectueusement.* She patted his shoulder affectionately.
② to tap ◊ *Il tapotait impatiemment sur la table.* He was tapping impatiently on the table.

taquiner VERB
to tease

tard ADVERB
late ◊ *Il est tard.* It's late.
♦ **plus tard** later on
♦ **au plus tard** at the latest

tardif ADJECTIVE (FEM SING **tardive**)
late ◊ *un petit lunch tardif* a late

breakfast

le **tarif** NOUN
♦ **payer plein tarif** to pay full price
♦ **payer le tarif étudiant** to pay the student rate
♦ **le tarif horaire** hourly rate

la **tarte** NOUN
pie
♦ **tarte au sucre** sugar pie

la **tartelette** NOUN
tart ◊ *une tartelette aux raisins secs* butter tart

la **tartine** NOUN
slice of bread ◊ *une tartine de confiture* a slice of bread and jam

tartiner VERB
to spread
♦ **le fromage à tartiner** cheese spread

le **tas** NOUN
heap ◊ *un tas de sable* a heap of sand
♦ **un tas de** (*informal*) a ton of ◊ *J'ai lu un tas de livres pendant les vacances.* I read a ton of books on the holidays.

la **tasse** NOUN
cup

le **taureau** NOUN (PL les **taureaux**)
bull
♦ **le Taureau** Taurus ◊ *Ils sont tous les deux Taureau.* They are both Tauruses.

le **taux** NOUN
rate ◊ *le taux de change* the exchange rate

la **taxe** NOUN
tax

le **taxi** NOUN
taxi
♦ **la station de taxi** taxi stand

te PRONOUN

> *te* changes to *t'* before a vowel and most words beginning with "h".

① you ◊ *Je te vois.* I can see you.
◊ *Elle t'a vu?* Did she see you?
② to you ◊ *Est-ce qu'il te parle en français?* Does he talk to you in French? ◊ *Elle t'a parlé?* Did she speak to you?
③ yourself ◊ *Tu vas te rendre malade.* You'll make yourself sick.

> With reflexive verbs, *te* is often not translated.

◊ *Comment tu t'appelles?* What's your name?

le **technicien** NOUN
technician

la **technicienne** NOUN
technician

technique ADJECTIVE
see also **technique** NOUN
technical

la **technique** NOUN
see also **technique** ADJECTIVE
technique

la **techno** NOUN
techno music

la **technologie** NOUN
technology

teindre VERB
to dye
♦ **se teindre les cheveux** to dye one's hair

le **teint** NOUN
complexion ◊ *avoir le teint clair* to have a clear complexion

la **teinte** NOUN
shade (*colour*)

teinté ADJECTIVE
tinted ◊ *des lunettes teintées* tinted glasses

tel ADJECTIVE (FEM SING **telle**)
♦ **Il a un tel enthousiasme!** He's got such enthusiasm!
♦ **rien de tel** nothing like ◊ *Il n'y a rien de tel qu'une bonne nuit de sommeil.* There's nothing like a good night's sleep.
♦ **J'ai tout laissé tel quel.** I left everything as it was.
♦ **tel que** such as

la **télé** NOUN
TV ◊ *à la télé* on TV

le **téléavertisseur** NOUN
pager

la **télécarte** NOUN
phonecard

le **téléchargement** NOUN
download/downloading
♦ **un téléchargement vers le serveur** an upload

télécharger VERB
to download
♦ **télécharger vers le serveur** to upload

la **télécommande** NOUN
remote control

la **téléconférence** NOUN
video conference

la **télécopie** NOUN
fax

télécopier VERB
to fax

le **télécopieur** NOUN
fax machine

le **téléphérique** NOUN
cable car

le **téléphone** NOUN
telephone ◊ *Elle est au téléphone.* She's on the phone.
♦ **un téléphone cellulaire** cellphone

téléphoner VERB
to phone ◊ *Je vais lui téléphoner.* I'll phone her. ◊ *Je peux téléphoner?* Can I make a phone call?

téléphonique ADJECTIVE
♦ **une carte téléphonique prépayée** a prepaid phone card
♦ **un appel téléphonique** a phone call

le/la **téléphoniste** NOUN
operator (*telephone*)

le **téléroman** NOUN
soap opera

le **télésiège** NOUN
chairlift

le **téléski** NOUN
ski lift

le **téléspectateur** NOUN
viewer (*TV*)

la **téléspectatrice** NOUN
viewer (*TV*)

le **téléviseur** NOUN
television set

la **télévision** NOUN
television ◊ *à la télévision* on television
♦ **la télévision à haute définition** HDTV (high-definition TV)
♦ **la télévision numérique** digital TV

telle ADJECTIVE
♦ **Je n'ai jamais eu une telle peur.** I've never been so scared.
♦ **telle que** such as

tellement ADVERB
① so ◊ *Il est tellement gentil.* He's so nice. ◊ *Il travaille tellement.* He works so hard.
② so much ◊ *J'ai tellement mangé que...* I ate so much that...
③ so many ◊ *Il y avait tellement de monde.* There were so many people.

telles ADJECTIVE
such ◊ *Je n'ai jamais entendu de telles niaiseries!* I've never heard such nonsense!

tels ADJECTIVE
such ◊ *Nous n'avons pas de tels orages chez nous.* We don't have such storms back home.

le **témoignage** NOUN
testimony

témoigner VERB
to testify

T

le/la **témoin** NOUN
> witness

la **température** NOUN
> temperature ◊ *avoir de la température* to have a temperature

la **tempête** NOUN
> storm

le **temple** NOUN
> ① church (*Protestant*)
> ② temple (*Hindu, Sikh, Buddhist*)

temporaire ADJECTIVE
> temporary

le **temps** NOUN
> ① weather ◊ *Quel temps fait-il?* What's the weather like?
> ② time ◊ *Je n'ai pas le temps.* I don't have time. ◊ *Prends ton temps.* Take your time. ◊ *Il est temps de partir.* It's time to go.
> ♦ **juste à temps** just in time
> ♦ **de temps en temps** from time to time
> ♦ **en même temps** at the same time
> ♦ **à temps** in time ◊ *Nous sommes arrivés à temps pour le match.* We arrived in time for the game.
> ♦ **à plein temps** full time ◊ *Elle travaille à plein temps.* She works full time.
> ♦ **à temps complet** full time
> ♦ **à temps partiel** part time ◊ *le travail à temps partiel* part-time work
> ♦ **dans le temps** at one time ◊ *Dans le temps, on pouvait circuler en vélo sans danger.* At one time, it was safe to go around by bike.
> ③ tense (*of verb*)

tenais, tenait VERB *see* **tenir**

la **tendance** NOUN
> ♦ **avoir tendance à faire quelque chose** to tend to do something ◊ *Elle a tendance à exagérer.* She tends to exaggerate.

tendre ADJECTIVE

> *see also* **tendre** VERB

> tender

tendre VERB

> *see also* **tendre** ADJECTIVE

> to stretch out ◊ *Ils ont tendu une corde entre deux arbres.* They stretched a rope between two trees.
> ♦ **tendre quelque chose à quelqu'un** to hold something out to somebody ◊ *Il lui a tendu les clés.* He held out the keys to her.
> ♦ **tendre la main** to hold out one's hand
> ♦ **tendre le bras** to reach out
> ♦ **tendre un piège à quelqu'un** to set a trap for someone

la **tendresse** NOUN
> tenderness

tendu ADJECTIVE
> tense ◊ *Il était très tendu aujourd'hui.* He was very tense today.

tenir VERB
> to hold ◊ *Tu peux tenir la lampe de poche, s'il te plaît?* Can you hold the flashlight, please? ◊ *Elle tenait un enfant par la main.* She was holding a child by the hand.
> ♦ **Tenez votre chien en laisse.** Keep your dog on the leash.
> ♦ **tenir à quelqu'un** to be attached to somebody ◊ *Il tient beaucoup à elle.* He's very attached to her.
> ♦ **tenir à faire quelque chose** to be determined to do something ◊ *Il tient à y aller.* He's determined to go.
> ♦ **tenir de quelqu'un** to take after somebody ◊ *Il tient de son père.* He takes after his father.
> ♦ **Tiens, voilà un stylo.** Here's a pen.
> ♦ **Tiens, c'est ta sœur là-bas!** Look, that's your sister over there!
> ♦ **Tiens?** Really?
> ♦ **se tenir (1)** to stand ◊ *Elle se tenait près de la porte.* She was standing by the door.
> ♦ **se tenir (2)** to be held ◊ *Le festival va se tenir au centre communautaire.* The festival will be held at the community centre.
> ♦ **se tenir droit (1)** to stand up straight ◊ *Tiens-toi droit!* Stand up straight!
> ♦ **se tenir droit (2)** to sit up straight ◊ *Arrête de manger le nez dans ton assiette, tiens-toi droit.* Don't slouch while you're eating, sit up straight.
> ♦ **se tenir mal** to have bad posture
> ♦ **Tiens-toi bien!** Behave yourself!

le **tennis** NOUN
> ① tennis ◊ *Elle joue au tennis.* She plays tennis.
> ♦ **le tennis de table** table tennis
> ② tennis court ◊ *Il est au tennis.* He's at the tennis court.

tentant ADJECTIVE
> tempting

la **tentation** NOUN
> temptation

la **tentative** NOUN
> attempt

la **tente** NOUN
> tent

tenter VERB
> to tempt ◊ *J'ai été tenté de tout abandonner.* I was tempted to give up. ◊ *Ça ne me tente vraiment pas d'aller à la piscine.* I don't really feel like going to the swimming pool.
> ♦ **tenter de faire quelque chose** to try to do something ◊ *Il a tenté plusieurs*

fois de s'évader. He tried several times to escape.

tenu VERB *see* **tenir**

la **tenue** NOUN
  clothes

le **terme** NOUN
  ♦ **à court terme** short-term
  ♦ **à long terme** long-term

la **terminaison** NOUN
  ending (*on a word*) ◊ *une terminaison féminine* a feminine ending

terminer VERB
  to finish
  ♦ **se terminer** to end ◊ *Les vacances se terminent demain.* The holidays end tomorrow.

le **terrain** NOUN
  land ◊ *Elle veut acheter un terrain en Ontario.* She wants to buy some land in Ontario.
  ♦ **un terrain de camping** a campground
  ♦ **un terrain de football** a football field
  ♦ **un terrain de golf** a golf course
  ♦ **un terrain de jeu** a playground

la **terrasse** NOUN
  terrace
  ♦ **Si on s'asseyait à la terrasse?** Shall we sit outside? (*at café*)

la **terre** NOUN
  earth
  ♦ **la Terre** the Earth
  ♦ **Elle s'est assise par terre.** She sat on the floor.
  ♦ **Il est tombé par terre.** He fell down.
  ♦ **la terre cuite** terracotta ◊ *un pot en terre cuite* a terracotta pot
  ♦ **la terre glaise** clay

Terre-Neuve FEM NOUN
  Newfoundland ◊ *un voyage à Terre-Neuve* a trip to Newfoundland ◊ *La capitale de Terre-Neuve est St. John's.* The capital of Newfoundland is St. John's.

la **terreur** NOUN
  terror ◊ *un régime de terreur* a reign of terror

terrible ADJECTIVE
  terrible ◊ *Quelque chose de terrible est arrivé.* Something terrible has happened.

le **territoire** NOUN
  territory

les **Territoires du Nord-Ouest** MASC NOUN
  Northwest Territories ◊ *J'habite aux Territoires du Nord-Ouest.* I live in the Northwest Territories.

terrorisé ADJECTIVE
  terrified

le **terrorisme** NOUN
  terrorism

le/la **terroriste** NOUN
  terrorist

tes ADJECTIVE
  your ◊ *J'aime bien tes chaussures de course.* I like your running shoes.

le **test** NOUN
  test

le **testament** NOUN
  will ◊ *Il est mort sans testament.* He died without leaving a will.

tester VERB
  to test

le **tétanos** NOUN
  tetanus

le **têtard** NOUN
  tadpole

la **tête** NOUN
  head ◊ *de la tête aux pieds* from head to foot
  ♦ **se laver la tête** to wash one's hair
  ♦ **la tête la première** headfirst
  ♦ **tenir tête à quelqu'un** to stand up to somebody
  ♦ **en avoir par-dessus la tête** to be fed up
  ♦ **avoir la tête sur les épaules** to be level-headed
  ♦ **avoir mal à la tête** to have a headache
  ♦ **prendre la tête** to take the lead

têtu ADJECTIVE
  stubborn ◊ *Elle est trop têtue pour changer d'opinion.* She is too stubborn to change her opinion.

le **texte** NOUN
  text

le **thé** NOUN
  tea ◊ *Je vous offre un thé?* Would you like a cup of tea?

le **théâtre** NOUN
  theatre
  ♦ **faire du théâtre** to act ◊ *Est-ce que tu as déjà fait du théâtre?* Have you ever acted?

la **théière** NOUN
  teapot

le **thème** NOUN
  subject ◊ *Quel est le thème de l'émission?* What's the program about?

la **théorie** NOUN
  theory

le **thermomètre** NOUN
  thermometer

le **thon** NOUN
  tuna
  ♦ **la salade de thon** tuna salad

T

le **tibia** NOUN
> 1 shinbone ◊ *une fracture du tibia* a broken shinbone
> 2 shin ◊ *Elle m'a donné un coup de pied dans le tibia.* She kicked me in the shin.

le **tic** NOUN
> nervous twitch

le **ticket** NOUN
> ticket ◊ *un ticket de métro* a subway ticket
> ♦ **le ticket de caisse** the cash register receipt

tiède ADJECTIVE
> 1 warm (*water, air*)
> 2 lukewarm (*food, drink*)

tien PRONOUN
> ♦ **le tien** yours ◊ *J'ai oublié mon stylo. Tu peux me prêter le tien?* I forgot my pen. Can you lend me yours?

tienne PRONOUN
> ♦ **la tienne** yours ◊ *Ce n'est pas ma raquette, c'est la tienne.* It's not my racquet, it's yours.

tiennes PRONOUN
> ♦ **les tiennes** yours ◊ *J'ai pris mes lunettes de soleil, mais j'ai oublié les tiennes.* I brought my sunglasses, but I forgot yours.

tiens PRONOUN
> ♦ **les tiens** yours ◊ *Je ne trouve pas mes feutres. Je peux utiliser les tiens?* I can't find my markers. Can I use yours?

tiens, tient VERB *see* **tenir**

le **tiers** NOUN
> third ◊ *Un tiers de la classe était pour.* A third of the class were in favour.

la **tige** NOUN
> stem

le **tigre** NOUN
> tiger

le **timbre** NOUN
> stamp

timide ADJECTIVE
> shy

timidement ADVERB
> shyly

la **timidité** NOUN
> shyness

le **tirage** NOUN
> ♦ **par tirage au sort** by drawing lots
> ◊ *Les prix seront attribués par tirage au sort.* The prizes will be awarded by drawing lots.

la **tire** NOUN
> taffy

> ♦ **la tire d'érable** maple taffy

le **tire-bouchon** NOUN
> corkscrew

tirer VERB
> 1 to pull ◊ *Elle a tiré un mouchoir de son sac à main.* She pulled a handkerchief out of her purse. ◊ *Il m'a tiré les cheveux.* He pulled my hair. ◊ *« Tirer »* "Pull"
> 2 to draw ◊ *tirer les rideaux* to draw the curtains ◊ *tirer un trait* to draw a line ◊ *tirer des conclusions* to draw conclusions
> ♦ **tirer au sort** to draw lots
> 3 to fire ◊ *Il a tiré plusieurs coups de feu.* He fired several shots. ◊ *Elle a tiré sur les policiers.* She fired at the police.

le **tiret** NOUN
> dash (*hyphen*)

le **tiroir** NOUN
> drawer

la **tisane** NOUN
> herbal tea

tisser VERB
> to weave

le **tissu** NOUN
> material

le **titre** NOUN
> title
> ♦ **les gros titres** the headlines

tituber VERB
> to stagger

le **toast** NOUN
> piece of toast

toi PRONOUN
> you ◊ *« Ça va? » « Oui, et toi? »* "How are you?" "Fine, and you?" ◊ *J'ai faim, pas toi?* I'm hungry, aren't you?
> ♦ **Assieds-toi.** Sit down.
> ♦ **C'est à toi de jouer.** It's your turn to play.
> ♦ **Est-ce que ce stylo est à toi?** Is this pen yours?

la **toile** NOUN
> ♦ **un pantalon de toile** cotton pants
> ♦ **un sac de toile** a canvas bag
> ♦ **une toile d'araignée** a spiderweb

la **toilette** NOUN
> ♦ **faire sa toilette** to wash oneself
> ♦ **une toilette élégante** an elegant outfit

les **toilettes** FEM NOUN
> washroom SING
> ♦ **les toilettes extérieures** outhouse

toi-même PRONOUN
> yourself ◊ *Tu as fait ça toi-même?* Did you do it yourself?

le **toit** NOUN

roof
♦ **un toit ouvrant** a sunroof

tolérant ADJECTIVE
tolerant

tolérer VERB
to tolerate

la **tomate** NOUN
tomato
♦ **être rouge comme une tomate** to be beet red

la **tombe** NOUN
grave

le **tombeau** NOUN (PL les **tombeaux**)
tomb

la **tombée** NOUN
♦ **à la tombée de la nuit** at nightfall

tomber VERB
to fall ◊ *Attention, tu vas tomber!* Be careful, you'll fall!
♦ **laisser tomber (1)** to drop ◊ *Elle a laissé tomber son stylo.* She dropped her pen.
♦ **laisser tomber (2)** to give up ◊ *Elle a laissé tomber le piano.* She quit piano.
♦ **laisser tomber (3)** to let down ◊ *Il ne laisse jamais tomber ses amis.* He never lets his friends down.
♦ **tomber sur quelqu'un** to bump into someone ◊ *Je suis tombé sur lui en sortant du restaurant.* I bumped into him coming out of the restaurant.
♦ **Ça tombe bien.** That's lucky.
♦ **Il tombe de sommeil.** He's asleep on his feet.

ton ADJECTIVE (FEM SING **ta**, PL **tes**)

see also **ton** NOUN

your ◊ *C'est ton stylo?* Is this your pen?

le **ton** NOUN

see also **ton** ADJECTIVE

① tone of voice ◊ *Ne me parle pas sur ce ton.* Don't speak to me in that tone of voice.
② colour ◊ *J'adore les tons pastel.* I love pastel colours.

la **tonalité** NOUN
dial tone

la **tondeuse** NOUN
lawnmower

tondre VERB
to mow

tonique ADJECTIVE
energizing

la **tonne** NOUN
tonne

le **tonneau** NOUN (PL les **tonneaux**)
barrel

le **tonnerre** NOUN
thunder

le **tonus** NOUN
♦ **avoir du tonus** to be energetic

le **torchon** NOUN
tea towel

tordre VERB
♦ **se tordre la cheville** to twist one's ankle

tordu ADJECTIVE
① bent ◊ *Ce clou est un peu tordu.* This nail's a bit bent.
② crazy ◊ *une histoire complètement tordue* a crazy story

la **tornade** NOUN
tornado

le **torrent** NOUN
mountain stream

le **torse** NOUN
chest ◊ *Il était torse nu.* He was barechested.

le **tort** NOUN
♦ **avoir tort** to be wrong
♦ **donner tort à quelqu'un** to lay the blame on somebody

le **torticolis** NOUN
stiff neck ◊ *J'ai le torticolis.* I've got a stiff neck.

la **tortue** NOUN
tortoise

la **torture** NOUN
torture

torturer VERB
to torture

tôt ADVERB
early
♦ **au plus tôt** at the earliest
♦ **tôt ou tard** sooner or later

total ADJECTIVE (MASC PL **totaux**)

see also **total** NOUN

total

le **total** NOUN (PL les **totaux**)

see also **total** ADJECTIVE

total ◊ *faire le total* to add up the total
♦ **au total** in total

totalement ADVERB
totally

totaliser NOUN
to add up ◊ *Totalise ces chiffres.* Add up these numbers.

la **totalité** NOUN
♦ **la totalité des profs** all the teachers
♦ **la totalité du personnel** the entire staff

T

touchant ADJECTIVE
touching

toucher VERB
① to touch ◊ *Ne touche pas à mes livres!* Don't touch my books!
♦ **Nos deux jardins se touchent.** Our gardens are next to each other.
② to feel ◊ *Ce chandail a l'air doux. Je peux toucher?* That sweater looks soft. Can I feel it?
③ to hit ◊ *La rondelle l'a touché en pleine poitrine.* The puck hit him right in the chest.
④ to affect ◊ *Ces nouvelles réformes ne nous touchent pas.* The new reforms don't affect us.
⑤ to receive ◊ *Elle a touché une grosse somme d'argent.* She received a large sum of money.

toujours ADVERB
① always ◊ *Il est toujours très gentil.* He's always very nice.
♦ **pour toujours** forever
② still ◊ *Quand on est revenus, maman était toujours là.* When we got back Mom was still there.

la **toundra** NOUN
tundra

le **toupet** NOUN (*informal*)
♦ **avoir du toupet** to have a nerve

la **tour** NOUN

| see also **le tour** |

① tower ◊ *la Tour CN* the CN Tower
② high-rise
♦ **une tour à bureaux** an office tower
♦ **une tour d'habitation** an apartment high-rise

le **tour** NOUN

| see also **la tour** |

turn ◊ *C'est ton tour de jouer.* It's your turn to play.
♦ **faire un tour** to go for a walk ◊ *Allons faire un tour dans le parc.* Let's go for a walk in the park.
♦ **faire un tour en voiture** to go for a drive
♦ **faire un tour à vélo** to go for a ride ◊ *Tu veux aller faire un tour à vélo?* Do you want to go for a bike ride?
♦ **faire le tour du monde** to travel around the world
♦ **à tour de rôle** alternately
♦ **un tour de magie** magic trick ◊ *faire des tours de magie* to do magic tricks
♦ **le tour du chapeau** (*sports*) hat trick

le **tourbillon** NOUN
whirlpool

le **tourisme** NOUN
tourism

le/la **touriste** NOUN
tourist

touristique ADJECTIVE
tourist

se **tourmenter** VERB
to fret ◊ *Ne te tourmente pas, ça s'arrangera.* Don't fret about it, it'll be all right.

le **tournant** NOUN
① bend ◊ *Il y a beaucoup de tournants dangereux sur cette route.* There are a lot of dangerous bends in this road.
② turning point ◊ *Ça a été un tournant dans sa vie.* It was a turning point in his life.

la **tournée** NOUN
① round ◊ *Le facteur commence sa tournée à sept heures du matin.* The letter carrier starts his round at 7 o'clock in the morning.
② tour ◊ *Elle est en tournée aux T.N.-O.* She's on tour in the NWT.

tourner VERB
① to turn ◊ *Tournez à droite au prochain feu.* Turn right at the next lights. ◊ *Tourne-toi un peu plus vers moi, et souris!* Turn towards me a bit more, and smile!
② to go sour ◊ *Le lait a tourné.* The milk has gone sour.
♦ **mal tourner** to go wrong ◊ *Ça a mal tourné.* It all went wrong.
♦ **tourner le dos à quelqu'un** to have one's back to somebody
♦ **tourner un film** to shoot a movie

le **tournesol** NOUN
sunflower

le **tournevis** NOUN
screwdriver

le **tournoi** NOUN
tournament

la **tourtière** NOUN

> ❶ In Canada, *la tourtière* is a pie made with various combinations of ground meat (beef, lamb, veal, and primarily pork) and served at Christmastime. The *tourtière du Lac-Saint-Jean* is a variation using cubed game, chicken, pork, potatoes, and onions, baked for several hours.

tous ADJECTIVE, PRONOUN *see* **tout**

tousser VERB
to cough

tout ADJECTIVE, ADVERB, PRONOUN (MASC PL **tous**, FEM PL **toutes**)
① all ◊ *tout le lait* all the milk ◊ *toute la nuit* all night ◊ *tous les livres* all

the books ◊ *toutes les filles* all the girls ◊ *toute la journée* all day ◊ *tout le temps* all the time ◊ *C'est tout.* That's all. ◊ *Je les connais tous.* I know them all. ◊ *Nous y sommes toutes allées.* We all went. ◊ *Ça fait combien en tout?* How much is that all together?
♦ **Elle est toute seule.** She's all alone.
♦ **pas du tout** not at all
♦ **tout de même** all the same
   ② every ◊ *tous les jours* every day ◊ *tous les deux jours* every two days
♦ **tout le monde** everybody
♦ **tous les deux** both ◊ *Nous y sommes allés tous les deux.* We both went.
♦ **tous les trois** all three ◊ *Je les ai invités tous les trois.* I invited all three of them.
   ③ everything ◊ *Il a tout organisé.* He organized everything.
   ④ very ◊ *J'habite tout près.* I live very close by.
♦ **tout en haut** right at the top
♦ **tout droit** straight ahead
♦ **tout d'abord** first of all
♦ **tout à coup** suddenly
♦ **tout à fait** absolutely
   ⑤ quite
♦ **tout à l'heure (1)** just now ◊ *Je l'ai vu tout à l'heure.* I saw him just now.
♦ **tout à l'heure (2)** in a moment ◊ *Je finirai ça tout à l'heure.* I'll finish it in a moment.
♦ **À tout à l'heure!** See you later!
♦ **tout de suite** right away
♦ **Nous avons fait notre travail tout en chantant.** We sang as we worked.

tout-aller ADJECTIVE
   casual ◊ *des chaussures tout-aller* casual shoes ◊ *un manteau tout-aller* casual coat

toutefois ADVERB
   however

toutes ADJECTIVE, PRONOUN *see* **tout**

la **toux** NOUN
   cough

le/la **toxicomane** NOUN
   drug addict

la **toxicomanie** NOUN
   drug addiction

toxique ADJECTIVE
   toxic
   ♦ **les déchets toxiques** toxic waste

la **TPS** NOUN
   GST ◊ *Est-ce qu'il faut payer la TPS sur les livres?* Do you have to pay GST on books?

le **trac** NOUN
   ♦ **avoir le trac** to be feeling nervous

tracasser VERB
   to worry ◊ *La santé de ma mère me tracasse.* My mom's health worries me.
♦ **se tracasser** to worry ◊ *Arrête de te tracasser pour rien!* Stop worrying about nothing!

la **trace** NOUN
   ① trace ◊ *Le voleur n'a pas laissé de traces.* The thief left no traces.
   ② mark ◊ *des traces de doigts* finger marks
   ♦ **des traces de pas** footprints

tracer VERB
   to draw ◊ *tracer un trait* to draw a line

le **tracteur** NOUN
   tractor

la **tradition** NOUN
   tradition

traditionnel ADJECTIVE (FEM SING **traditionnelle**)
   traditional

le **traducteur** NOUN
   translator

la **traduction** NOUN
   translation

la **traductrice** NOUN
   translator

traduire VERB
   to translate

le **trafic** NOUN
   traffic ◊ *le trafic aérien* air traffic
   ♦ **le trafic de drogue** drug trafficking

le **trafiquant** NOUN
   ♦ **un trafiquant de drogue** a drug trafficker

tragique ADJECTIVE
   tragic

trahir VERB
   to betray

la **trahison** NOUN
   betrayal

le **train** NOUN
   train
   ♦ **un train électrique** a train set
   ♦ **Elle est en train de manger.** She's eating.
   ♦ **le train de banlieue** commuter train

le **traîneau** NOUN (PL les **traîneaux**)
   sled

traîner VERB
   ① to wander around ◊ *J'ai vu des jeunes qui traînaient en ville.* I saw some young people wandering around town.
   ② to dawdle ◊ *Dépêche-toi, ne traîne pas!* Hurry up, don't dawdle!

T

☞

③ to drag on ◊ *La réunion a traîné jusqu'à midi.* The meeting dragged on till 12 o'clock.
♦ **traîner des pieds** to drag one's feet
♦ **laisser traîner qch** to leave sth lying around ◊ *Ne laisse pas traîner tes affaires.* Don't leave your things lying around.

✹ la **traîne sauvage** NOUN
toboggan
♦ **faire de la traîne sauvage** to go tobogganing

le **train-train** NOUN
daily routine

traire VERB
to milk

le **trait** NOUN
① line ◊ *Tracez un trait.* Draw a line.
② feature ◊ *avoir les traits réguliers* to have regular features
③ characteristic ◊ *un de tes plus beaux traits* one of the nicest things about you
♦ **un trait de personnalité** personality trait
♦ **boire quelque chose d'un trait** to drink something down in one gulp
♦ **un trait d'union** a hyphen

le **traité** NOUN
treaty

le **traitement** NOUN
treatment
♦ **le traitement de texte** word processing
♦ **le traitement de données** data processing

traiter VERB
to treat ◊ *Elle le traite bien.* She treats him well.
♦ **Il m'a traité d'imbécile.** He called me an idiot.
♦ **traiter de** to be about ◊ *Cet article traite des sans-abri.* This article is about the homeless.

le **traiteur** NOUN
caterer

le **trajet** NOUN
① journey ◊ *Ils n'ont pas arrêté de parler pendant tout le trajet.* They talked for the whole journey. ◊ *J'ai une heure de trajet pour aller au travail.* My journey to work takes an hour.
② route ◊ *C'est le trajet le plus court.* It's the shortest route.

le **tramway** NOUN
streetcar

tranchant ADJECTIVE
sharp (*knife*)

la **tranche** NOUN
slice

tranquille ADJECTIVE
quiet ◊ *Cette rue est très tranquille.* This is a very quiet street.
♦ **Sois tranquille, il ne va rien lui arriver.** Don't worry, nothing will happen to him.
♦ **Tiens-toi tranquille!** Be quiet!
♦ **Laisse-moi tranquille.** Leave me alone.
♦ **Laisse ça tranquille.** Leave it alone.

tranquillement ADVERB
quietly ◊ *Nous étions tranquillement installés dans le salon.* We were just sitting quietly in the living room.
♦ **Je peux travailler tranquillement cinq minutes?** Can I have five minutes to work in peace?

la **tranquillité** NOUN
peace and quiet

la **Transcanadienne** NOUN
Trans-Canada Highway

transférer VERB
to transfer

transformer VERB
① to transform ◊ *Son séjour en Saskatchewan l'a transformé.* His stay in Saskatchewan has transformed him.
② to convert ◊ *Ils ont transformé la grange en garage.* They've converted the barn into a garage.
♦ **se transformer en** to turn into ◊ *La chenille se transforme en papillon.* The caterpillar turns into a butterfly.

la **transfusion** NOUN
♦ **une transfusion sanguine** a blood transfusion

transiger VERB
to compromise

transmettre VERB
to broadcast ◊ *On a transmis le discours du premier ministre à la radio.* They broadcast the prime minister's speech on the radio.
♦ **transmettre quelque chose à quelqu'un** to pass something on to somebody

le **transparent** NOUN
transparency ◊ *Mets le transparent dans le rétroprojecteur.* Put the transparency on the overhead projector.

transpercer VERB
to go through ◊ *La pluie a transpercé mes vêtements.* The rain went through my clothes.

la **transpiration** NOUN

perspiration

transpirer VERB
to perspire

le **transport** NOUN
transport
♦ **les transports en commun** public transport

transporter VERB
① to carry ◊ *Le train transportait des marchandises.* The train was carrying freight.
② to move ◊ *Je ne sais pas comment je vais transporter mes affaires.* I don't know how I'm going to move my stuff.

traumatiser VERB
to traumatize

le **travail** NOUN (PL les **travaux**)
① work ◊ *J'ai beaucoup de travail.* I've got a lot of work.
② job ◊ *Il a un travail intéressant.* He's got an interesting job.
♦ **Il est sans travail depuis un an.** He has been out of work for a year.
♦ **le travail au noir** moonlighting

travailler VERB
to work

travailleur ADJECTIVE (FEM SING **travailleuse**)

see also **travailleur** NOUN

hard-working

le **travailleur** NOUN

see also **travailleur** ADJECTIVE

worker

la **travailleuse** NOUN
worker

les **travaillistes** MASC NOUN
the Labour Party SING

les **travaux** MASC NOUN
① work SING ◊ *des travaux de construction* building work
② roadworks ◊ *Il y a beaucoup de bruit à cause des travaux dans la rue.* There's a lot of noise from the roadworks.
♦ **être en travaux** to be undergoing alterations
♦ **les travaux dirigés** supervised practical work
♦ **les travaux manuels** handicrafts
♦ **les travaux ménagers** housework
♦ **les travaux pratiques** practical work

le **travers** NOUN
♦ **en travers de** across ◊ *Il y avait un arbre en travers de la route.* There was a tree lying across the road.
♦ **de travers** crooked ◊ *Son chapeau était de travers.* His hat was crooked.

♦ **comprendre de travers** to misunderstand ◊ *Elle comprend toujours tout de travers.* She always gets the wrong idea.
♦ **J'ai avalé de travers.** Something went down the wrong way.
♦ **à travers** through ◊ *Cette vitre est tellement sale qu'on ne voit rien à travers.* This window is so dirty you can't see anything through it.

la **traversée** NOUN
crossing

traverser VERB
① to cross ◊ *Traversez la rue.* Cross the street.
② to go through ◊ *Nous avons traversé l'Alberta pour aller en Colombie-Britannique.* We went through Alberta on the way to British Columbia. ◊ *La pluie a traversé mon manteau.* The rain went through my coat.

le **traversier** NOUN
ferry

trébucher VERB
to stumble (*trip*)

le **trèfle** NOUN
① clover
② clubs (*at cards*) ◊ *le roi de trèfle* the king of clubs

treize NUMBER
thirteen ◊ *Il a treize ans.* He's thirteen.
◊ *à treize heures* at 1 p.m.
♦ **le treize février** the thirteenth of February

treizième ADJECTIVE
thirteenth

le **tremblement de terre** NOUN
earthquake

trembler VERB
to tremble ◊ *trembler de peur* to tremble with fear
♦ **trembler de froid** to shiver

trempé ADJECTIVE
soaking wet
♦ **trempé jusqu'aux os** soaked to the skin

tremper VERB
to soak
♦ **tremper sa main dans l'eau** to dip one's hand in the water

la **trempette** NOUN
dip ◊ *une trempette à l'ail* a garlic dip

le **tremplin** NOUN
① diving board
② ski jump

la **trentaine** NOUN
about thirty ◊ *une trentaine de personnes* about thirty people

T

☞

♦ **Il a la trentaine.** He's in his thirties.

trente NUMBER
thirty ◊ *Elle a trente ans.* She's thirty.
♦ **le trente janvier** the thirtieth of January
♦ **trente et un** thirty-one
♦ **trente-deux** thirty-two

trentième ADJECTIVE
thirtieth

très ADVERB
very

le **trésor** NOUN
treasure

la **tresse** NOUN
braid
♦ **les tresses rasta** dreadlocks

tresser VERB
to braid

le **triangle** NOUN
triangle

le **tribunal** NOUN (PL les **tribunaux**)
court

la **tribune téléphonique** NOUN
hotline (*phone-in show*)

tricher VERB
to cheat

le **tricot** NOUN
knitting ◊ *Ma grand-mère aime faire du tricot.* My grandmother enjoys knitting.

tricoter VERB
to knit

trier VERB
to sort out ◊ *Je vais trier mes papiers avant de partir en vacances.* I'm going to sort out my papers before I go on holiday.

le **trimestre** NOUN
term

le **triomphe** NOUN
triumph

triompher VERB
to triumph

le **triple** NOUN
♦ **Ça m'a coûté le triple.** It cost me three times as much.
♦ **Il gagne le triple de mon salaire.** He earns three times my salary.

les **triplées** FEM NOUN
triplets

tripler VERB
to treble

les **triplés** MASC NOUN
triplets

triste ADJECTIVE
sad

la **tristesse** NOUN
sadness

le **trognon** NOUN
core ◊ *un trognon de pomme* an apple core

trois NUMBER
three ◊ *à trois heures du matin* at three in the morning ◊ *Elle a trois ans.* She's three. ◊ *trois fois* three times
♦ **le trois février** the third of February

troisième ADJECTIVE
third ◊ *au troisième étage* on the third floor

les **trois-quarts** MASC NOUN
three-quarters ◊ *les trois-quarts de la classe* three-quarters of the class

le **trombone** NOUN
① trombone ◊ *Il joue du trombone.* He plays the trombone.
② paper clip

la **trompe** NOUN
trunk ◊ *la trompe d'un éléphant* an elephant's trunk

tromper VERB
to deceive
♦ **se tromper** to make a mistake ◊ *Tout le monde peut se tromper.* Anyone can make a mistake.
♦ **se tromper de jour** to get the wrong day
♦ **Vous vous êtes trompé de numéro.** You've got the wrong number.

la **trompette** NOUN
trumpet ◊ *Elle joue de la trompette.* She plays the trumpet.
♦ **Elle a le nez en trompette.** She has a turned-up nose.

le **tronc** NOUN
trunk ◊ *un tronc d'arbre* a tree trunk

trop ADVERB
① too ◊ *Il conduit trop vite.* He drives too fast.
② too much ◊ *J'ai trop mangé.* I've eaten too much.
♦ **trop de (1)** too much ◊ *J'ai acheté trop de pain.* I bought too much bread. ◊ *trois dollars de trop* 3 dollars too much
♦ **trop de (2)** too many ◊ *Nous avons apporté trop de vêtements.* We brought too many clothes.
♦ **trois personnes de trop** 3 people too many

le **tropique** NOUN
tropic

le **trottoir** NOUN
sidewalk

le **trou** NOUN

hole
♦ **J'ai eu un trou de mémoire.** My mind went blank.
♦ **le trou noir** black hole

trouble ADJECTIVE, ADVERB
cloudy ◊ *L'eau est trouble.* The water's cloudy.

le **trouble** NOUN
♦ **une période de troubles politiques** a period of political instability
♦ **le trouble alimentaire** eating disorder

trouer VERB
to make a hole in

la **trouille** NOUN
♦ **avoir la trouille** (*informal*) to be scared to death

la **troupe** NOUN
troop
♦ **une troupe de théâtre** a theatre company

le **troupeau** NOUN (PL les **troupeaux**)
♦ **un troupeau de moutons** a flock of sheep
♦ **un troupeau de vaches** a herd of cows

la **trousse** NOUN
kit ◊ *une trousse de secours* a first-aid kit
♦ **une trousse de maquillage** a make-up bag

trouver VERB
① to find ◊ *Je ne trouve pas mes lunettes.* I can't find my glasses.
② to think ◊ *Je trouve que c'est bête.* I think it's stupid.
♦ **se trouver** to be ◊ *Où se trouve le bureau de poste?* Where is the post office? ◊ *Hull se trouve au Québec.* Hull is in Québec.
♦ **se trouver mal** to pass out

le **truc** NOUN (*informal*)
① thing ◊ *un truc en plastique* a plastic thing
② trick ◊ *Je vais te montrer un truc qui réussit à tous les coups.* I'll show you a trick that never fails.

la **truite** NOUN
trout

le **T-shirt** NOUN
T-shirt

tu PRONOUN
you ◊ *Est-ce que tu as un animal*

domestique? Have you got a pet?

le **tuba** NOUN
① tuba ◊ *Je joue du tuba.* I play the tuba.
② snorkel

le **tube** NOUN
tube ◊ *un tube de dentifrice* a tube of toothpaste
♦ **un tube de rouge à lèvres** a lipstick

tuer VERB
to kill
♦ **se tuer** to get killed ◊ *Elle s'est tuée dans un accident de voiture.* She got killed in a car accident.

la **tuile** NOUN
tile

la **tunique** NOUN
tunic

le **tunnel** NOUN
tunnel ◊ *Empruntez le tunnel qui passe sous le fleuve Fraser.* Take the tunnel under the Fraser River.

turbulent ADJECTIVE
boisterous

tutoyer VERB
♦ **tutoyer quelqu'un** to address somebody as "tu"

> ❶ *tutoyer quelqu'un* means to use *tu* when speaking to someone, rather than *vous*. Use *tu* only when talking to one person and when that person is someone of your own age or whom you know well; use *vous* to everyone else. If in doubt use *vous*.

♦ **On se tutoie?** Shall we use "tu" to each other?

le **tuyau** NOUN (PL les **tuyaux**)
pipe
♦ **un tuyau d'arrosage** a hose

le **tympan** NOUN
eardrum

le **type** NOUN
type (*kind*) ◊ *Il y a plusieurs types de vélo de montagne.* There are many types of mountain bike.

typique ADJECTIVE
typical

le **tyran** NOUN
tyrant ◊ *C'est un vrai tyran.* He's a real tyrant.

T

U

un ARTICLE, PRONOUN, ADJECTIVE

⒈ a ◊ *un garçon* a boy
an ◊ *un œuf* an egg
⒉ one ◊ *l'un des meilleurs* one of the best ◊ *un citron et deux oranges* one lemon and two oranges ◊ *« Combien de timbres? » « Un. »* "How many stamps?" "One." ◊ *Elle a un an.* She's one year old.

♦ **l'un..., l'autre...** one..., the other...
◊ *L'un est grand, l'autre est petit.* One is tall, the other is short.

♦ **les uns..., les autres...** some..., others... ◊ *Les uns marchaient, les autres couraient.* Some were walking, others were running.

♦ **l'un ou l'autre** either of them
◊ *Prends l'un ou l'autre, ça m'est égal.* Take either of them, I don't mind.

♦ **un par un** one by one ◊ *Ils entraient un par un.* They went in one by one.

unanime ADJECTIVE
unanimous

l' **unanimité** FEM NOUN
♦ **à l'unanimité** unanimously

une ARTICLE, PRONOUN, ADJECTIVE

⒈ a ◊ *une fille* a girl
an ◊ *une pomme* an apple
⒉ one ◊ *une pomme et deux bananes* one apple and two bananas ◊ *« Combien de cartes postales? » « Une. »* "How many postcards?" "One." ◊ *à une heure du matin* at one in the morning ◊ *l'une des meilleures* one of the best

♦ **l'une..., l'autre...** one..., the other...
◊ *L'une est grande, l'autre est petite.* One is tall, the other is short.

♦ **les unes..., les autres...** some..., others... ◊ *Les unes marchaient, les autres couraient.* Some were walking, others were running.

♦ **l'une ou l'autre** either of them
◊ *Prends l'une ou l'autre, ça m'est égal.* Take either of them, I don't mind.

♦ **une par une** one by one ◊ *Elles entraient une par une.* They went in one by one.

uni ADJECTIVE

⒈ plain ◊ *un tissu uni* a plain fabric
⒉ close-knit ◊ *une famille unie* a close-knit family

l' **unifolié** MASC NOUN
the Canadian flag

l' **uniforme** MASC NOUN
uniform

unilingue ADJECTIVE
unilingual

l' **union** FEM NOUN
union

unique ADJECTIVE
unique ◊ *Tout individu a des empreintes uniques.* Everyone's fingerprints are unique. ◊ *C'est une occasion unique.* It's a unique opportunity.

♦ **Il est fils unique.** He's an only child.

♦ **Elle est fille unique.** She's an only child.

uniquement ADVERB
only

l' **unité** FEM NOUN

⒈ unity ◊ *l'unité nationale* national unity

⒉ unit ◊ *une unité de mesure* a unit of measurement

l' **univers** MASC NOUN
universe

universitaire ADJECTIVE
university ◊ *un diplôme universitaire* a university degree ◊ *le campus universitaire* university campus

♦ **faire des études universitaires** to study at university

l' **université** FEM NOUN
university ◊ *aller à l'université* to go to university

l' **urgence** FEM NOUN

♦ **C'est une urgence.** It's urgent.

♦ **Il n'y a pas urgence.** It's not urgent.

♦ **le service des urgences** the emergency department

♦ **Il a été transporté d'urgence à l'hôpital.** He was rushed to hospital.

♦ **Téléphonez d'urgence.** Phone as soon as possible.

urgent ADJECTIVE
urgent

l' **urine** FEM NOUN
urine

l' **usage** MASC NOUN
use ◊ *à usage interne* for internal use ◊ *à usage externe* for external use only

♦ **hors d'usage** out of service ◊ *Cet appareil est hors d'usage.* That machine's out of service.

usagé ADJECTIVE

⒈ old ◊ *un manteau usagé* an old coat

2 used ◊ *une seringue usagée* a used syringe

l' **usager** MASC NOUN
user ◊ *les usagers de la route* road users

l' **usagère** FEM NOUN
user ◊ *une usagère des transports publics* a public transit user

usé ADJECTIVE
worn ◊ *Mes jeans sont un peu usés.* My jeans are a bit worn.

s' **user** VERB
to wear out ◊ *Mes pantoufles se sont usées en quinze jours.* My slippers wore out in two weeks.

l' **usine** FEM NOUN
factory ◊ *une usine de meubles* a furniture factory

l' **ustensile** MASC NOUN
♦ **un ustensile de cuisine** a kitchen utensil
🌙 ♦ **les ustensiles** cutlery

usuel ADJECTIVE (FEM SING **usuelle**)
everyday ◊ *la langue usuelle* everyday language

utile ADJECTIVE
useful

l' **utilisateur** MASC NOUN
user (*technology*) ◊ *un utilisateur d'Internet* an Internet user

l' **utilisation** FEM NOUN
use ◊ *L'utilisation des calculatrices est interdite.* It is forbidden to use calculators.

l' **utilisatrice** FEM NOUN
user (*technology*) ◊ *une utilisatrice d'Internet* an Internet user

utiliser VERB
to use

l' **utilité** FEM NOUN
use (*usefulness*) ◊ *Cet objet n'est pas d'une grande utilité.* This object isn't much use.

U

V

va VERB *see* **aller**

les **vacances** FEM NOUN
　① vacation ◊ *aller en vacances* to go on vacation ◊ *être en vacances* to be on vacation
　② holidays ◊ *les vacances de Noël* the Christmas holidays ◊ *les vacances de Pâques* the Easter holidays ◊ *les vacances d'été* the summer holidays

le **vacarme** NOUN
　racket ◊ *Qu'est-ce que c'est que ce vacarme?* What's all this racket?

le **vaccin** NOUN
　vaccination

la **vaccination** NOUN
　vaccination ◊ *La vaccination est obligatoire.* Vaccination is compulsory.

vacciner VERB
　to vaccinate ◊ *se faire vacciner contre la rubéole* to be vaccinated against German measles

la **vache** NOUN
　| *see also* **vache** ADJECTIVE |
　cow

vache ADJECTIVE (*informal*)
　| *see also* **vache** NOUN |
　mean ◊ *C'est vraiment vache, ce qu'il a dit.* What he said was really mean.

✴ la **vadrouille** NOUN
　mop ◊ *J'ai passé la vadrouille sur le plancher.* I mopped the floor.

le **vagabond** NOUN
　transient

la **vagabonde** NOUN
　transient

le **vagin** NOUN
　vagina

la **vague** NOUN
　| *see also* **vague** ADJECTIVE |
　wave (*in sea*)
　♦ *une vague de chaleur* a heat wave

vague ADJECTIVE
　| *see also* **vague** NOUN |
　vague ◊ *J'ai un vague souvenir d'elle.* I vaguely remember her.

vain ADJECTIVE
　♦ *en vain* in vain

vaincre VERB
　① to defeat ◊ *L'armée a été vaincue.* The army was defeated.

　② to overcome ◊ *Il a réussi à vaincre sa timidité.* He managed to overcome his shyness.

le **vainqueur** NOUN
　winner

vais VERB *see* **aller**
　♦ *Je vais écrire à mes cousins.* I'm going to write to my cousins.

le **vaisseau** NOUN (PL les **vaisseaux**)
　♦ *un vaisseau spatial* a spaceship
　♦ *un vaisseau sanguin* a blood vessel

la **vaisselle** NOUN
　dishes ◊ *Je vais faire la vaisselle.* I'll do the dishes. ◊ *Peux-tu ranger la vaisselle s'il te plaît?* Can you put the dishes away please?

valable ADJECTIVE
　valid ◊ *Ce billet d'avion est valable un an.* This plane ticket is valid for one year.

le **valentin** NOUN
　valentine (*person*) ◊ *Seras-tu mon valentin?* Will you be my valentine?

la **valentine** NOUN
　valentine (*person*) ◊ *Seras-tu ma valentine?* Will you be my valentine?

le **valet** NOUN
　jack (*in card games*) ◊ *le valet de carreau* the jack of diamonds

la **valeur** NOUN
　value ◊ *sans valeur* of no value
　♦ *des objets de valeur* valuables ◊ *Ne laissez pas d'objets de valeur dans votre chambre.* Don't leave any valuables in your room.

valider VERB
　to stamp ◊ *Vous devez faire valider votre billet avant votre départ.* You must get your ticket stamped before you leave.

la **valise** NOUN
　suitcase
　♦ *faire sa valise* to pack

la **vallée** NOUN
　valley
　♦ *la vallée du Bas-Fraser* the Lower Mainland

valoir VERB
　to be worth ◊ *Ça vaut combien?* How much is it worth? ◊ *Cette voiture vaut très cher.* This car's worth a lot of money.
　♦ *Ça vaut mieux.* That would be better.

◊ *Il vaut mieux ne rien dire.* It would be better to say nothing.
♦ **valoir la peine** to be worth it ◊ *Ça vaudrait la peine d'essayer.* It would be worth a try.

le/la **vampire** NOUN
vampire

le/la **vandale** NOUN
vandal

vandaliser VERB
to vandalize

le **vandalisme** NOUN
vandalism

la **vanille** NOUN
vanilla ◊ *une crème glacée à la vanille* a vanilla ice cream

la **vanité** NOUN
vanity

vaniteux ADJECTIVE (FEM SING **vaniteuse**)
conceited

se **vanter** VERB
to brag

la **vapeur** NOUN
steam ◊ *des légumes cuits à la vapeur* steamed vegetables

variable ADJECTIVE
changeable (*weather*)

la **varicelle** NOUN
chickenpox ◊ *Elle a la varicelle.* She has chickenpox.

varié ADJECTIVE
varied ◊ *Son travail est très varié.* His job is very varied.

varier VERB
to vary
♦ **Le menu varie tous les jours.** The menu changes every day.

la **variété** NOUN
variety ◊ *Il n'y a pas beaucoup de variété.* There isn't much variety.
♦ **une émission de variétés** a variety show (*television*)

vas VERB *see* **aller**

le **vase** NOUN
| *see also* **la vase** |
vase

la **vase** NOUN
| *see also* **le vase** |
mud

vaste ADJECTIVE
vast

vaudrait, vaut VERB *see* **valoir**

le **vautour** NOUN
vulture

le **veau** NOUN (PL les **veaux**)

① calf (*animal*)
② veal (*meat*)

vécu VERB *see* **vivre**
♦ **Elle a vécu à Laval pendant dix ans.** She lived in Laval for ten years.

la **vedette** NOUN
① star ◊ *une vedette de cinéma* a movie star
② motorboat

végétal ADJECTIVE (MASC PL **végétaux**)
vegetable ◊ *l'huile végétale* vegetable oil

végétalien ADJECTIVE (FEM SING **végétalienne**)
vegan

végétarien ADJECTIVE (FEM SING **végétarienne**)
vegetarian ◊ *Je suis végétarien.* I'm a vegetarian.

la **végétation** NOUN
vegetation

le **véhicule** NOUN
vehicle ◊ *le véhicule utilitaire sport* sport utility vehicle

la **veille** NOUN
the day before ◊ *la veille de son départ* the day before he left ◊ *la veille au soir* the previous evening
♦ **la veille de Noël** Christmas Eve
♦ **la veille du jour de l'An** New Year's Eve
♦ **la mode Veille** standby mode (*computing*)

veiller VERB
to stay up
♦ **veiller sur quelqu'un** to watch over somebody

la **veine** NOUN
vein
♦ **avoir de la veine** (*informal*) to be lucky

le/la **véliplanchiste** NOUN
windsurfer

le **vélo** NOUN
bike ◊ *faire du vélo* to go biking
♦ **un vélo de montagne** a mountain bike
♦ **un vélo d'exercice** an exercise bike

le **vélomoteur** NOUN
moped

le **velours** NOUN
velvet ◊ *une robe en velours* a velvet dress
♦ **le velours côtelé** corduroy ◊ *un pantalon en velours côtelé* corduroy pants

le **vendeur** NOUN
salesperson (*in store*)

la **vendeuse** NOUN
  salesperson (*in store*)

vendre VERB
  to sell
  ♦ **vendre quelque chose à quelqu'un** to sell somebody something ◊ *Elle m'a vendu son vélo.* She sold me her bike.
  ♦ **« à vendre »** "for sale"

le **vendredi** NOUN
  ① Friday ◊ *Aujourd'hui, nous sommes vendredi.* It's Friday today.
  ② on Friday ◊ *Il est venu vendredi.* He came on Friday.
  ♦ **le vendredi** on Fridays ◊ *Je joue au hockey le vendredi.* I play hockey on Fridays.
  ♦ **tous les vendredis** every Friday
  ♦ **vendredi dernier** last Friday
  ♦ **vendredi prochain** next Friday
  ♦ **le Vendredi saint** Good Friday

vénéneux ADJECTIVE (FEM SING **vénéneuse**)
  poisonous (*plant*) ◊ *un champignon vénéneux* a poisonous mushroom

la **vengeance** NOUN
  revenge

se **venger** VERB
  to get revenge

venimeux ADJECTIVE (FEM SING **venimeuse**)
  poisonous (*animal*) ◊ *un serpent venimeux* a poisonous snake

le **venin** NOUN
  poison

venir VERB
  to come ◊ *Il viendra demain.* He'll come tomorrow. ◊ *Elle est venue nous voir.* She came to see us.
  ♦ **venir de** to have just ◊ *Je viens de la voir.* I've just seen her. ◊ *Je viens de lui téléphoner.* I've just phoned her.
  ♦ **faire venir quelqu'un** to send for somebody ◊ *faire venir le plombier* to send for the plumber

le **vent** NOUN
  wind ◊ *Il y a du vent.* It's windy.

la **vente** NOUN
  sale
  ♦ **en vente** on sale ◊ *Ce modèle est en vente dans les grands magasins.* This model is on sale in department stores.
  ♦ **la vente par téléphone** telemarketing
  ♦ **une vente aux enchères** an auction
  ✵ ♦ **une vente de garage** a garage sale

le **ventilateur** NOUN
  fan (*for cooling*)

le **ventre** NOUN
  stomach ◊ *avoir mal au ventre* to have a stomachache

venu VERB *see* **venir**

le **ver** NOUN
  worm
  ♦ **un ver de terre** an earthworm

le **verbe** NOUN
  verb

le **verbomoteur** NOUN
  talkative person

la **verbomotrice** NOUN
  talkative person ◊ *Cette politicienne est plutôt verbomotrice.* This politician is quite a talkative person.

le **verger** NOUN
  orchard

verglacé ADJECTIVE
  icy ◊ *La route était verglacée.* The road was icy.

le **verglas** NOUN
  black ice
  ♦ **la tempête de verglas** ice storm

véridique ADJECTIVE
  truthful

la **vérification** NOUN
  check ◊ *une vérification d'identité* an identity check

vérifier VERB
  to check

véritable ADJECTIVE
  real ◊ *C'était un véritable cauchemar.* It was a real nightmare.
  ♦ **en cuir véritable** made of real leather

la **vérité** NOUN
  truth ◊ *dire la vérité* to tell the truth

verni ADJECTIVE
  varnished

vernir VERB
  to varnish

le **vernis** NOUN
  varnish
  ♦ **le vernis à ongles** nail polish

verra, verrai, verras VERB *see* **voir**
  ♦ **on verra...** we'll see...

le **verre** NOUN
  ① glass ◊ *un bibelot en verre* a glass ornament ◊ *un verre d'eau* a glass of water
  ② lens (*of spectacles*) ◊ *des verres de contact* contact lenses

verrez, verrons, verront VERB *see* **voir**

le **verrou** NOUN
  bolt (*on door*)

verrouiller VERB
  to bolt ◊ *N'oublie pas de verrouiller la porte du garage.* Don't forget to bolt the garage door.

la **verrue** NOUN
  wart

le **vers** NOUN

> see also **vers** PREPOSITION

line (*of poetry*) ◊ *au troisième vers* in the third line

vers PREPOSITION

> see also **vers** NOUN

1 towards ◊ *Il allait vers l'école.* He was going towards the school.
2 at about ◊ *Nous sommes rentrés chez nous vers cinq heures.* We went home at about 5 o'clock.

verse
♦ **à verse** ADVERB ◊ *Il pleut à verse.* It's pouring rain.

le **Verseau** NOUN

Aquarius ◊ *Il est Verseau.* He's an Aquarius.

le **versement** NOUN

instalment ◊ *en cinq versements* in 5 instalments

verser VERB

to pour ◊ *Est-ce que tu peux me verser un verre d'eau?* Could you pour me a glass of water?

la **version** NOUN

1 version
2 translation (*from the foreign language*)
♦ **un film en version originale** a film in the original language

le **verso** NOUN

back (*of sheet of paper*)
♦ **voir au verso** see other side

vert ADJECTIVE

green

la **vertèbre** NOUN

vertebra

vertical ADJECTIVE (MASC PL **verticaux**)

vertical

le **vertige** NOUN

fear of heights ◊ *avoir le vertige* to be afraid of heights

la **veste** NOUN

1 jacket
2 vest (*sleeveless*) ◊ *une veste en polaire* a polar fleece vest

le **vestiaire** NOUN

1 cloakroom (*in theatre, museum*)
2 changing room (*at school, sports complex*)

le **vestibule** NOUN

hall

le **vêtement** NOUN

article of clothing
♦ **les vêtements** clothes

le/la **vétérinaire** NOUN

vet ◊ *Elle est vétérinaire.* She's a vet.

le **veuf** NOUN

widower ◊ *Il est veuf.* He's a widower.

veuille, veuillez, veuillons, veulent, veut VERB see **vouloir**
♦ **Veuillez fermer la porte en sortant.** Please shut the door when you go out.

la **veuve** NOUN

widow ◊ *Elle est veuve.* She's a widow.

veux VERB see **vouloir**

vexer VERB
♦ **vexer quelqu'un** to hurt somebody's feelings
♦ **se vexer** to be offended

la **viande** NOUN

meat
♦ **la viande hachée** hamburger meat

vibrer VERB

to vibrate

le **vice** NOUN

vise

la **victime** NOUN

victim

la **victoire** NOUN

victory

🐝 les **vidanges** FEM NOUN

garbage ◊ *As-tu mis les vidanges dehors?* Did you put the garbage out?
🐝 ♦ **le camion de vidanges** garbage truck
🐝 ♦ **le sac de vidanges** garbage bag

vide ADJECTIVE

> see also **vide** NOUN

empty

le **vide** NOUN

> see also **vide** ADJECTIVE

vacuum ◊ *emballé sous vide* vacuum-packed
♦ **avoir peur du vide** to be afraid of heights

la **vidéo** NOUN

> see also **vidéo** ADJECTIVE

video

vidéo ADJECTIVE (MASC, FEM, PL)

> see also **vidéo** NOUN

video ◊ *des jeux vidéo* video games ◊ *une caméra vidéo* a video camera

la **vidéocassette** NOUN

videocassette

le **vidéoclip** NOUN

music video

le **vidéoclub** NOUN

video rental store

la **vidéoconférence** NOUN

V

☞

videoconference

vider VERB
to empty

la **vie** NOUN
life
♦ **être en vie** to be alive

vieil ADJECTIVE *see* **vieux**

le **vieillard** NOUN
old man

vieille ADJECTIVE

see also **vieille** NOUN

see **vieux**

la **vieille** NOUN

see also **vieille** ADJECTIVE

old woman
♦ **Eh bien, ma vieille...** (*informal*) Well, my dear...

la **vieillesse** NOUN
old age

vieillir VERB
to age ◊ *Il a beaucoup vieilli depuis la dernière fois que je l'ai vu.* He's aged a lot since I last saw him.

viendrai, vienne, viens VERB *see* **venir**
♦ **Je viendrai dès que possible.** I'll come as soon as possible.
♦ **Je voudrais que tu viennes.** I'd like you to come.
♦ **Viens ici!** Come here!

la **Vierge** NOUN

see also **vierge** ADJECTIVE

Virgo ◊ *Elle est Vierge.* She's a Virgo.

vierge ADJECTIVE

see also **Vierge** NOUN

1 virgin ◊ *Il est vierge.* He's a virgin.
2 blank ◊ *une cassette vierge* a blank cassette

vieux ADJECTIVE (FEM SING **vieille**)

see also **vieux** NOUN

old ◊ *un vieux livre* an old book ◊ *une vieille dame* an old lady

*vieux changes to **vieil** before a vowel and most words beginning with "h."*

◊ *un vieil arbre* an old tree ◊ *Il fait plus vieux que son âge.* He looks older than he is.

le **vieux** NOUN

see also **vieux** ADJECTIVE

old man ◊ *Eh bien, mon vieux...* (*informal*) Well, old friend...

vieux jeu ADJECTIVE (MASC, FEM, PL)
old-fashioned ◊ *Elle est un peu vieux jeu.* She's a bit old-fashioned.

vif ADJECTIVE (FEM SING **vive**)

1 sharp (*mentally*) ◊ *Elle est très vive.* She's very sharp.
♦ **avoir l'esprit vif** to be quick-witted
2 crisp ◊ *L'air est plus vif à la campagne qu'en ville.* The air is crisper in the country than in the city.
3 bright (*colour*) ◊ *un bleu vif* a bright blue

la **vigne** NOUN
vine

le **vignoble** NOUN
vineyard

vilain ADJECTIVE
naughty ◊ *C'est très vilain de dire des mensonges.* It's very naughty to tell lies.

le **village** NOUN
village

le **villageois** NOUN
villager

la **villageoise** NOUN
villager

la **ville** NOUN
town ◊ *Je vais en ville.* I'm going into town.
♦ **une grande ville** a city

le **vinaigre** NOUN
vinegar

la **vinaigrette** NOUN
salad dressing

vingt NUMBER
twenty ◊ *Elle a vingt ans.* She's twenty. ◊ *à vingt heures* at 8 p.m.
♦ **le vingt février** the twentieth of February
♦ **vingt et un** twenty-one
♦ **vingt-deux** twenty-two

la **vingtaine** NOUN
about twenty ◊ *une vingtaine de personnes* about twenty people
♦ **Il a une vingtaine d'années.** He's about twenty.

vingtième ADJECTIVE
twentieth

le **viol** NOUN
rape

violemment ADVERB
violently

la **violence** NOUN
violence
♦ **la violence familiale** family violence

violent ADJECTIVE
violent

violer VERB
to rape

violet ADJECTIVE (FEM SING **violette**)
purple

le **violon** NOUN
　violin ◊ *Je joue du violon.* I play the violin.

le **violoncelle** NOUN
　cello ◊ *Elle joue du violoncelle.* She plays the cello.

le/la **violoniste** NOUN
　violinist

la **vipère** NOUN
　viper

le **virage** NOUN
　bend ◊ *une route pleine de virages dangereux* a road full of dangerous turns

la **virgule** NOUN
　① comma
　② decimal point ◊ *trois virgule cinq* three point five

le **virus** NOUN
　virus (*also computing*)

vis VERB *see* **vivre**
　　see also **vis** NOUN

la **vis** NOUN
　　see also **vis** VERB
　screw

le **visa** NOUN
　visa

le **visage** NOUN
　face ◊ *Elle a le visage rond.* She's got a round face.

vis-à-vis de PREPOSITION (*informal*)
　with regard to ◊ *Ce n'est pas très juste vis-à-vis de lui.* It's not very fair to him.

viser VERB
　to aim at ◊ *Il faut viser la cible.* You have to aim at the target.

la **visibilité** NOUN
　visibility

visible ADJECTIVE
　visible

la **visière** NOUN
　visor (*of cap*)

la **visite** NOUN
　visit
　♦ **rendre visite à quelqu'un** to visit somebody ◊ *Je vais rendre visite à mon grand-père.* I'm going to visit my grandfather.
　♦ **avoir de la visite** to have visitors ◊ *Nous avons de la visite aujourd'hui.* We have visitors today.
　♦ **une visite guidée** a guided tour
　♦ **une visite médicale** a medical examination

visiter VERB
　to visit

le **visiteur** NOUN
　visitor

la **visiteuse** NOUN
　visitor

※ le **visou** NOUN
　aim (*skill at aiming*) ◊ *Ça prend du visou pour jouer au billard.* You have to have good aim to play pool.

vit VERB *see* **vivre**
　♦ **Il vit chez ses parents.** He lives with his parents.

vital ADJECTIVE (MASC PL **vitaux**)
　vital ◊ *C'est une question vitale.* It's of vital importance.
　♦ **les signes vitaux** vital signs

la **vitamine** NOUN
　vitamin

vite ADVERB
　① quick ◊ *Vite, ils arrivent!* Quick, they're coming! ◊ *« Je peux aller dire au revoir à ma mère? » « Oui, mais fais ça vite! »* "Can I go and say goodbye to my mom?" "Yes, but be quick!" ◊ *Prenons la voiture, ça va aller plus vite.* Let's take the car, it'll be quicker.
　♦ **Le temps passe vite.** Time flies.
　② fast ◊ *Elle roule trop vite.* She drives too fast.
　③ soon ◊ *Il va vite oublier.* He'll soon forget.

la **vitesse** NOUN
　① speed ◊ *à toute vitesse* at top speed ◊ *Nous sommes rentrés à toute vitesse.* We rushed back home.
　② gear ◊ *en première vitesse* in first gear

le **vitrail** NOUN (PL les **vitraux**)
　stained-glass window

la **vitre** NOUN
　window ◊ *Il a cassé une vitre.* He broke a window.

la **vitrine** NOUN
　store window

vivant ADJECTIVE
　① living ◊ *les êtres vivants* living creatures ◊ *les expériences sur les animaux vivants* experiments on live animals
　② lively ◊ *Elle est très vivante.* She's very lively.

vive ADJECTIVE (MASC SING **vif**)
　　see also **vive** EXCLAMATION
　① sharp (*mentally*) ◊ *Elle est très vive.* She's very sharp.
　② bright (*colour*) ◊ *Lavez les couleurs vives à l'eau froide.* Wash bright colours in cold water.
　♦ **à vive allure** at a brisk pace

V

☞

♦ **de vive voix** in person ◊ *Je te le dirai de vive voix.* I'll tell you about it when I see you.

vive EXCLAMATION

see also **vive** ADJECTIVE

♦ **Vive la reine!** Long live the queen!

vivement ADVERB
1 quickly ◊ *Elle a réagi vivement.* She reacted quickly.
2 brightly ◊ *des tissus vivement colorés* brightly coloured fabrics

vivre VERB
to live ◊ *J'aimerais vivre à l'étranger.* I'd like to live abroad. ◊ *Et ta grand-mère? Elle vit encore en bonne santé?* What about your grandmother? Is she still in good health?

le **vocabulaire** NOUN
vocabulary

la **vocation** NOUN
vocation

le **vœu** NOUN (PL les **vœux**)
wish ◊ *faire un vœu* to make a wish ◊ *Meilleurs vœux de bonne année!* Best wishes for the New Year!

la **vogue** NOUN
fashion ◊ *C'est très en vogue en ce moment.* It's very fashionable at the moment.

voici PREPOSITION
1 this is ◊ *Voici mon frère et voilà ma sœur.* This is my brother and that's my sister.
2 here is ◊ *Tu as perdu ton stylo? Tiens, en voici un autre.* Have you lost your pen? Here's another one.
♦ **Le voici!** Here he is! ◊ *Tu veux tes clés? Tiens, les voici!* You want your keys? Here you are!

la **voie** NOUN
lane ◊ *une route à trois voies* a 3-lane road
♦ **par voie buccale** orally ◊ *à prendre par voie buccale* to be taken orally
♦ **la voie ferrée** the railway track
♦ **la voie maritime du Saint-Laurent** the Saint Lawrence Seaway

voilà PREPOSITION
1 there is ◊ *Tiens! Voilà ton frère.* Look! There's your brother. ◊ *Tu as perdu ton stylo? Tiens, en voilà un autre.* Have you lost your pen? There's another one.
♦ **Les voilà!** There they are!
2 that is ◊ *Voilà ma sœur.* That's my sister.
♦ **Et voilà!** That's it!

le **voile** NOUN

see also **la voile**

veil ◊ *un voile de mariée* a wedding veil
♦ **un voile blanc** a whiteout

la **voile** NOUN

see also **le voile**

1 sail
2 sailing ◊ *faire de la voile* to go sailing
♦ **un bateau à voiles** a sailboat

le **voilier** NOUN
sailboat

voir VERB

Present tense:	
je vois	nous voyons
tu vois	vous voyez
il/elle voit	ils/elles voient

Past participle:
vu

to see ◊ *Venez me voir quand vous serez à Edmonton.* Come and see me when you're in Edmonton. ◊ *Je ne vois pas pourquoi il a fait ça.* I can't see why he did that.
♦ **faire voir quelque chose à quelqu'un** to show somebody something ◊ *Il m'a fait voir sa collection de timbres.* He showed me his stamp collection.
♦ **se voir** to be obvious ◊ *Est-ce que cette tache se voit?* Does that stain show? ◊ *« Ça fait des années qu'elle n'a pas joué au soccer » « Oui, ça se voit! »* "She hasn't played soccer for years" "Yes, you can tell!"
♦ **avoir quelque chose à voir avec** to have something to do with ◊ *Ça n'a rien à voir avec lui, c'est entre toi et moi.* It's nothing to do with him, it's between you and me.

le **voisin** NOUN
neighbour

le **voisinage** NOUN
♦ **dans le voisinage** in the neighbourhood

la **voisine** NOUN
neighbour

la **voiture** NOUN
car ◊ *une voiture de sport* a sports car

la **voix** NOUN (PL les **voix**)
1 voice ◊ *à voix basse* in a low voice
♦ **à haute voix** aloud
2 vote ◊ *Il a obtenu cinquante pour cent des voix.* He got 50% of the votes.

le **vol** NOUN
1 flight
♦ **à vol d'oiseau** as the crow flies
2 theft ◊ *un vol à main armée* an

armed robbery

la **volaille** NOUN
poultry

le **volant** NOUN
1 steering wheel
2 birdie (*badminton*)

le **volcan** NOUN
volcano

la **volée** NOUN
volley (*in tennis*)
♦ **rattraper une balle à la volée** to catch
a ball in mid-air

voler VERB
1 to fly ◊ *J'aimerais savoir voler.* I'd
like to be able to fly.
2 to steal ◊ *On a volé mon appareil
photo.* My camera's been stolen.
♦ **voler quelque chose à quelqu'un** to
steal something from somebody ◊ *Ça
n'est pas son stylo, il me l'a volé.*
That's not his pen, he stole it from
me.
♦ **voler quelqu'un** to rob somebody

le **volet** NOUN
shutter

le **voleur** NOUN
thief
♦ **Au voleur !** Stop thief!

la **voleuse** NOUN
thief

le **volley-ball** NOUN
volleyball ◊ *jouer au volley-ball* to
play volleyball

le/la **volontaire** NOUN
volunteer

la **volonté** NOUN
willpower ◊ *Elle a beaucoup de
volonté.* She has a lot of willpower.
♦ **la bonne volonté** goodwill
♦ **la mauvaise volonté** lack of goodwill

volontiers ADVERB
gladly ◊ *Je l'aiderais volontiers si elle
me le demandait.* I'd gladly help her if
she asked me.

le **volume** NOUN
volume ◊ *un dictionnaire en deux
volumes* a two-volume dictionary

volumineux ADJECTIVE (FEM SING
volumineuse)
bulky

vomir VERB
to vomit ◊ *Il a vomi toute la nuit.* He
was vomiting all night.

vont VERB *see* **aller**

vos ADJECTIVE
your ◊ *Rangez vos jouets, les
enfants!* Children, put your toys
away! ◊ *Merci pour vos fleurs.* Thanks

for your flowers.

le **vote** NOUN
vote

voter VERB
to vote

votre ADJECTIVE (PL **vos**)
your ◊ *C'est votre manteau?* Is this
your coat?

vôtre PRONOUN
♦ **le vôtre** yours ◊ *J'aime bien notre
prof de maths, mais la vôtre est plus
patiente.* I like our math teacher, but
yours is more patient. ◊ *À qui est ce
foulard? C'est le vôtre?* Whose scarf is
this? Is it yours?

vôtres PRONOUN
♦ **les vôtres** yours ◊ *J'ai oublié mes
lunettes de soleil. Vous avez apporté
les vôtres?* I forgot my sunglasses.
Did you bring yours?

**voudra, voudrai, voudrais, voudras,
voudrez, voudrons, voudront** VERB
see **vouloir**
♦ **Je voudrais...** I'd like... ◊ *Je voudrais
deux litres de lait, s'il vous plaît.* I'd
like two litres of milk, please.

vouloir VERB

Present tense:	
je veux	*nous voulons*
tu veux	*vous voulez*
il/elle veut	*ils/elles veulent*
Past participle:	
voulu	

to want ◊ *Elle veut un vélo pour
sa fête.* She wants a bike for her
birthday. ◊ *Je ne veux pas de dessert.*
I don't want any dessert. ◊ *Il ne
veut pas venir.* He doesn't want to
come. ◊ *« On va au cinéma? » « Si tu
veux. »* "Shall we go to the movies?"
"If you like."
♦ **Je veux bien.** I'll be happy to. ◊ *Je
veux bien le faire à ta place si ça
t'arrange.* I don't mind doing it for
you if you prefer.
♦ **sans le vouloir** without meaning to
◊ *Je l'ai vexé sans le vouloir.* I upset
him without meaning to.
♦ **en vouloir à quelqu'un** to be angry at
somebody ◊ *Il m'en veut de ne pas
l'avoir invité à ma fête.* He's angry at
me for not inviting him to my birthday
party.
♦ **vouloir dire** to mean ◊ *Qu'est-ce que
ça veut dire?* What does that mean?

voulu VERB *see* **vouloir**

vous PRONOUN
1 you ◊ *Vous aimez la pizza?* Do you
like pizza?

V

② to you ◊ *Je vous écrirai bientôt.* I'll
write to you soon.
③ yourself ◊ *Vous vous êtes fait mal?*
Have you hurt yourself?
♦ **vous-même** yourself ◊ *Vous l'avez
fait vous-même?* Did you do it
yourself?

vouvoyer VERB
♦ **vouvoyer quelqu'un** to address
somebody as "vous"

> ⓘ *vouvoyer quelqu'un* means to
> use *vous* when speaking to someone,
> rather than *tu*. Use *tu* only when
> talking to one person and when that
> person is someone of your own age
> or whom you know well; use *vous* to
> everyone else. If in doubt use *vous*.

♦ **Est-ce que je dois vouvoyer ta sœur?**
Should I use "vous" to your sister?

le **voyage** NOUN
journey ◊ *Avez-vous fait bon voyage?*
Did you have a good journey?
♦ **Bon voyage!** Have a good trip!

voyager VERB
to travel

le **voyageur** NOUN
passenger

> ⓘ A *voyageur* was also a man
> employed by a fur company as a
> guide or to transport goods to and
> from remote stations in the North
> West, mostly by boat.

♣ la **voyageuse** NOUN
passenger

voyaient, voyais, voyait VERB *see* **voir**

la **voyelle** NOUN
vowel

voyez, voyiez, voyions VERB *see* **voir**

voyons VERB *see* **voir**
① let's see ◊ *Voyons ce qu'on peut
faire.* Let's see what we can do.
② come on ◊ *Voyons, sois
raisonnable!* Come on, be
reasonable!

le/la **voyou** NOUN
thug

vrac
♦ **en vrac** ADVERB loose ◊ *du thé en vrac*
loose tea ◊ *des épices en vrac* loose
spices

vrai ADJECTIVE
true ◊ *une histoire vraie* a true story
◊ *C'est vrai?* Is that true?
♦ **à vrai dire** to tell the truth

vraiment ADVERB
really

vraisemblable ADJECTIVE
likely ◊ *C'est peu vraisemblable.*
That's not very likely. ◊ *Il va falloir
trouver une excuse vraisemblable.*
We'll have to find a convincing
excuse.

VU PREPOSITION
given ◊ *vu la situation* given the
circumstances
♣ ♦ **vu que** in view of the fact that ◊ *vu
qu'il est toujours en retard* in view of
the fact that he's always late

la **vue** NOUN
① eyesight ◊ *J'ai une mauvaise vue.*
I've got bad eyesight.
② view ◊ *Il y a une belle vue d'ici.*
There's a lovely view from here.
♦ **à vue d'œil** visibly ◊ *Elle grandit à
vue d'œil.* Every time you see her,
she's taller.

vulgaire ADJECTIVE
vulgar ◊ *Ne dit pas ça, c'est très
vulgaire.* Don't say that, it's very
vulgar.

W

le **wagon** NOUN
railway car

le **wagon-lit** NOUN (PL les **wagons-lits**)
sleeping car (*on train*)

le **wagon-restaurant** NOUN (PL les **wagons-restaurants**)
dining car

le **wapiti** NOUN
elk

le **Web** NOUN
Web
♦ **naviguer sur le Web** to browse the

Web

le/la **webmestre** NOUN
webmaster

la **webographie** NOUN
webography

le **webzine** NOUN
webzine

le **western** NOUN
western (*film*)

le **wok** NOUN
wok

X

xénophobe ADJECTIVE
prejudiced against foreigners

la **xénophobie** NOUN
prejudice against foreigners

le **xylophone** NOUN

xylophone ◊ *Elle joue du xylophone.*

She plays the xylophone.

Y

y PRONOUN
there ◊ *Nous y sommes allés l'été dernier.* We went there last summer. ◊ *Regarde dans le tiroir : je pense que les clés y sont.* Look in the drawer: I think the keys are in there.

> **y** replaces phrases with **à** in constructions like the ones below:

♦ **« Je pensais à l'examen. » « Mais arrête d'y penser! »** "I was thinking about the exam." "Well, stop thinking about it!"
♦ **« Je ne m'attendais pas à ça. » « Moi, je m'y attendais. »** "I wasn't expecting that." "I was expecting it."

les **yeux** MASC NOUN (SING **œil**)

eyes ◊ *Elle a les yeux bleus.* She has blue eyes.
♦ **regarder quelqu'un dans les yeux** to look someone in the eye

le **yoga** NOUN
yoga

le **yogourt** NOUN
yogurt ◊ *un yogourt nature* a plain yogurt ◊ *un yogourt aux bleuets* a blueberry yogurt

youpi EXCLAMATION
Yippee!

le **yoyo** NOUN (PL les **yoyo**)
yo-yo

le **Yukon** NOUN
Yukon

Z

zapper VERB
to channel hop

✹ la **zappette** NOUN
remote control (*for TV*)

✹ le **zappeur** NOUN
remote control (*for TV*)

le **zèbre** NOUN
zebra

le **zéro** NOUN
zero
♦ **Ils ont gagné trois à zéro.** They won three-nothing.

zézayer VERB
to lisp ◊ *Il zézaie.* He's got a lisp.

✹ **zigonner** VERB
to fiddle ◊ *Comme la serrure était*

gelée, j'ai zigonné avec la clef. Since the lock was frozen, I tried fiddling with the key.

le **zigzag** NOUN
♦ **faire des zigzags** to zigzag

la **zone** NOUN
zone
♦ **la zone de but** crease (*sports*)
♦ **une zone piétonne** a pedestrian zone

le **zoo** NOUN
zoo

zoologique ADJECTIVE
zoological ◊ *un jardin zoologique* zoological gardens

zut EXCLAMATION
Oh heck!

FRENCH GRAMMAR GUIDE

▶ Parts of speech

Articles

● Articles (**les articles**) are small words placed in front of nouns to identify the gender of a noun (masculine or feminine).

● Articles also tell whether a noun is singular or plural.

● The definite articles are: **le** (masculine); **la** (feminine); **l'** (masculine and feminine in front of a vowel or a silent *h*); **les** (plural). They indicate a specific thing or person and mean **the**.

● The indefinite articles are: **un** (masculine); **une** (feminine); **des** (plural). They mean **a, an,** or **some**.

● To determine the gender of the noun using this dictionary, look at the article that precedes the noun (**le, la, l', un, une**). If the noun starts with a vowel or silent *h*, the article will be **l'**, and the gender will be indicated by FEM or MASC after the noun.

Nouns

● A noun (**un nom**) names a person, place, thing, or idea.

> C'est mon **père**.   Il a beaucoup de **patience**.
> J'habite à **St. John**.   Elle a une **voiture**.

● Nouns are either masculine or feminine, singular or plural.

Pronouns

● A pronoun (**un pronom**) is a word that replaces a noun. It must be masculine or feminine, singular or plural, depending on the noun it replaces.

● The subject pronoun (**le pronom sujet**) indicates the person or thing doing the action.

● The subject pronouns are **je, tu, il, elle, on, nous, vous, ils, elles**.

Note: The subject pronouns **il(s)** and **elle(s)** can indicate both people and things.

● French uses two pronouns to express **you**.

  ● To address a friend, a family member, or someone younger, use **tu**.

    Tu veux jouer au hockey, Pierre?

- To address an older person or a stranger, it is better to use **vous**.

    Qu'est-ce que **vous** choisissez, madame?

- To address more than one person, always use **vous**.

    Salut, Jean et Jacques! Jouez-**vous** au hockey?
    Qu'est-ce que **vous** choisissez, mesdames?

- French uses the pronoun **on** when the subject of the sentence is general (**they, people, you, one**). **On** is always singular and works just like **il** or **elle**.

On dit que c'est un bon film.	→	**They** say it's a very good movie.
On doit faire attention aux feux rouges.	→	**You** must pay attention to red lights.

Adjectives

- An adjective (**un adjectif**) is a word that describes a noun.

- An adjective must be feminine or masculine, and singular or plural, depending on the noun it modifies.

    - For most adjectives, add an **e** to the masculine form for the feminine. Add an **s** to create the plural.
    - If an adjective ends with an **s** or **x** in the masculine singular, it remains the same in the plural.
    - If an adjective ends with an **e** in the masculine, it remains the same in the feminine.
    - An adjective that ends in **é** in the masculine adds an e in the feminine.

Les adjectifs réguliers

MASC SING	FEM SING	MASC PLUR	FEM PLUR
petit	petite	petits	petites
gris	grise	gris	grises
rouge	rouge	rouges	rouges
fatigué	fatiguée	fatigués	fatiguées

Note: Only the **masculine singular** form of regular adjectives is shown in the dictionary.

- The following table shows how to form some common adjectives in French that don't follow the pattern shown above.

Les adjectifs iréguliers

MASC SING	FEM SING	MASC PLUR	FEM PLUR
sportif	sportive	sportifs	sportives
blanc	blanche	blancs	blanches
heureux	heureuse	heureux	heureuses
jaloux	jalouse	jaloux	jalouses
doux	douce	doux	douces
gentil	gentille	gentils	gentilles
canadien	canadienne	canadiens	canadiennes
long	longue	longs	longues

Note: If the **feminine** or **plural** form of an adjective does not follow the above rules, the irregular form is also given.

- The adjectives **beau, nouveau,** and **vieux** have special forms when they are found in front of a masculine singular noun that starts with a vowel or a silent *h*. See the following table for examples.

MASC SING	MASC SING (before a vowel)	FEM SING	MASC PLUR	FEM PLUR
beau	bel	belle	beaux	belles
nouveau	nouvel	nouvelle	nouveaux	nouvelles
vieux	vieil	vieille	vieux	vieilles

- In French, most adjectives are placed after the noun. But the following adjectives are placed before the noun.

beau/belle	jeune	nouveau/nouvelle
bon/bonne	joli/jolie	petit/petite
grand/grande	long/longue	vieux/vieille
gros/grosse	mauvais/mauvaise	

Adverbs

- An adverb (**un adverbe**) is a word that describes a verb or an adjective. To form most adverbs, add **ment** to the feminine form of the adjective.

MASC	FEM	+ ment
seul	seule	seulement

- Adjectives ending in **i, u, ai,** or **é** are formed from the masculine form.

     vrai   ➔   vraiment

- Some adverbs (the ones that tell when something happens or describe how much) do not follow the pattern above.

jamais	souvent	beaucoup
rarement	toujours	très
quelquefois	assez	trop

Prepositions

- A preposition (**une préposition**) is a word that shows a relationship between a noun or pronoun and another word in the sentence. Some examples are **to, beside, with, in, of, behind, under, on**. Prepositions are followed by a noun or a pronoun.

     dans   Les poissons rouges sont **dans** le bocal.
     avec   Le petit garçon joue **avec** lui.

Negation

- The word **not** is expressed in French with two words: **ne** and **pas**. Place **ne** before the verb and **pas** after: **ne** + verb + **pas**.

     Je suis canadien. Je **ne** suis **pas** américain.
     J'aime les bananes. Je **n**'aime **pas** les ananas.
     Je veux chanter. Je **ne** veux **pas** jouer d'un instrument.

Verbs

- A verb (**un verbe**) is a word that expresses an action or a state of being. The verb is central to almost every statement you will make.

- Most French verbs are **regular**. Once you have learned the basic pattern, you will be able to use any verb in the category.

- Some French verbs are **irregular**. They do not fall into an established pattern and must be learned separately.

- The next section, French Verb Tables, tells you how to form both regular and irregular verbs.

▶ How to Form French Verbs

Verb tenses

- The tense of a verb tells when something happens. In the verb tables that follow (pages 298–314), you'll find out how to form six different tenses of several verbs:

  - **le présent**: to describe an action that is happening as you speak or that happens regularly

  - **le futur proche**: to talk about things that are going to happen very soon

  - **l'imparfait**: to describe things in the past and to talk about things that happened often

  - **le passé composé**: to talk about things that happened once in the past

  - **le futur simple**: to describe things that will take place in the future

  - **le conditionnel**: to talk about things that would result in certain circumstances

- At the top of each table you will find **l'infinitif, l'impératif,** and **le participe passé**.

Note: Remember that English verb forms such as **am, is, does,** and **has** do not appear in the dictionary because they are forms of the verbs **to be, to do,** and **to have**. You must look up the basic (infinitive) form of the verb, that is, **be, do,** or **have,** and then use the appropriate form of the French verb you find there.

- There are three groups of regular verbs:
  1. **-er** verbs, formed like **aimer** on page 298
  2. **-ir** verbs (a), formed like **finir** on page 299
     -ir verbs (b), formed like **partir** on page 300
  3. **-re** verbs, formed like **attendre** on page 301

- Each verb tense is made up of the stem (**le radical**) to which the endings (**les terminaisons**) are added.

Regular Verbs

Le présent

To find the stem for *le présent*

VERB	FORMATION	STEM
-er aimer	remove **-er** from l'infinitif	aim
-ir (a) finir	Singular: remove **-ir** from l'infinitif Plural: replace **-ir** by **-iss**	fin finiss
-ir (b) partir	Singular: remove last three letters of l'infinitif Plural: remove **-ir** from l'infinitif	par part
-re attendre	remove **-re** from l'infinitif	attend

To form *le présent* using the stem and the endings

VERB	STEM	ENDINGS	LE PRÉSENT
-er aimer	aim	**e, es, e** **ons, ez, ent**	j'aim**e**, tu aim**es**, il aim**e** nous aim**ons**, vous aim**ez**, ils aim**ent**
-ir (a) finir	fin (singular) finiss (plural)	**is, is, it** **ons, ez, ent**	je fin**is**, tu fin**is**, il fin**it** nous finiss**ons**, vous finiss**ez**, ils finiss**ent**
-ir (b) partir	par (singular) part (plural)	**s, s, t** **ons, ez, ent**	je par**s**, tu par**s**, il par**t** nous part**ons**, vous part**ez**, ils part**ent**
-re attendre	attend	**s, s, —** **ons, ez, ent**	j'attend**s**, tu attend**s**, il attend nous attend**ons**, vous attend**ez**, ils attend**ent**

Le passé composé

● **Le passé composé** is composed of two parts, the auxiliary verb and the past participle (**le participe passé**).

To form *le participe passé*

VERB	FORMATION	LE PARTICIPE PASSÉ
-er aimer	replace the last two letters of l'infinitif with **é**	aim**é**
-ir (a) and **-ir** (b) finir partir	replace the last two letters of l'infinitif with **i**	fin**i** part**i**
-re verbs attendre	replace the last two letters of l'infinitif with **u**	attend**u**

To form *le passé composé*

VERB	AUXILIARY VERB	LE PASSÉ COMPOSÉ
-er aimer	avoir	j'ai aimé
-ir (a) finir	avoir	j'ai fini
-ir (b) partir	être	je suis parti(e)
-re attendre	avoir	j'ai attendu

● There are two auxiliary verbs used to form **le passé composé**: **avoir** and **être**. Most verbs use **avoir**.

● Learn the list of verbs that use **être** to form **le passé composé**:

aller	entrer	partir	revenir
arriver	monter	rentrer	sortir
descendre	mourir	rester	tomber
devenir	naître	retourner	venir

Note: Refer to the table above (**To form** *le participe passé*) to find out how to form **le participe passé** of these verbs, except for those that have an irregular **participe passé** (see below).

● The following verbs have irregular **participes passés**:

devenir	➜ devenu	naître	➜ né	venir	➜ venu
mourir	➜ mort	revenir	➜ revenu		

- When verbs using **être** are written in **le passé composé**, **le participe passé** is treated as an adjective and takes the same form as its subject, for example, **ils sont allés**. Remember that **je, tu,** and **nous** can be either masculine or feminine: **je suis allé** if a male is writing, **je suis allée** if a female is writing. **Vous** can have any of four forms:

    - **vous êtes allé**: (one person, masculine)
    - **vous êtes allée**: (one person, feminine)
    - **vous êtes allés**: (more than one person, masculine)
    - **vous êtes allées**: (more than one person, feminine)

L'imparfait

- To form **l'imparfait**, use the **nous** form of **le présent** as the stem, and remove the final **ons**.

- Add the appropriate endings: **ais, ais, ait, ions, iez, aient**.

Le futur simple and le conditionnel

- **L'infinitif** is the stem for both. Remove the final **e** from **l'infinitif** of **-re** verbs.

- Add the appropriate endings to the stem.

    - For **le future simple**: **ai, as, a, ons, ez, ont**
    - For **le conditionnel**: **ais, ais, ait, ions, iez, aient**

Irregular verbs

- Many of the most commonly used verbs in French are irregular, that is, they do not follow a pattern and must be learned individually.

    - Some of the most important irregular verbs have individual verb tables in the pages that follow.
    - See pages 315–317 for the Irregular Verb Forms table.
    - Some irregular verb forms are included as separate entries in the dictionary.

FRENCH VERB TABLES

▶ aimer

to like or to love

IMPÉRATIF

aime
aimons
aimez

PARTICIPE PASSÉ

aimé

EXEMPLES

Tu **aimes** le chocolat? Do you like chocolate?
Je t'**aime**. I love you.
J'**aimerais** aller en Grèce. I'd like to go to Greece.

PRÉSENT

j'	aim**e**
tu	aim**es**
il	aim**e**
nous	aim**ons**
vous	aim**ez**
ils	aim**ent**

PASSÉ COMPOSÉ

j'	ai aimé
tu	as aimé
il	a aimé
nous	avons aimé
vous	avez aimé
ils	ont aimé

FUTUR SIMPLE

j'	aimerai
tu	aimeras
il	aimera
nous	aimerons
vous	aimerez
ils	aimeront

FUTUR PROCHE

je	vais aimer
tu	vas aimer
il	va aimer
nous	allons aimer
vous	allez aimer
ils	vont aimer

IMPARFAIT

j'	aimais
tu	aimais
il	aimait
nous	aimions
vous	aimiez
ils	aimaient

CONDITIONNEL

j'	aimerais
tu	aimerais
il	aimerait
nous	aimerions
vous	aimeriez
ils	aimeraient

FRENCH VERB TABLES

▶ finir

to finish

EXEMPLES

Finis *ta soupe!* Finish your soup!
*J'**ai fini!*** I've finished!
*Je **finirai** mes devoirs demain.* I'll
finish my homework tomorrow.

IMPÉRATIF

finis
finissons
finissez

PARTICIPE PASSÉ

fini

PRÉSENT

je	fin**is**
tu	fin**is**
il	fin**it**
nous	finiss**ons**
vous	finiss**ent**
ils	finiss**ent**

PASSÉ COMPOSÉ

j'	ai fini
tu	as fini
il	a fini
nous	avons fini
vous	avez fini
ils	ont fini

FUTUR SIMPLE

je	finirai
tu	finiras
il	finira
nous	finirons
vous	finirez
ils	finiront

FUTUR PROCHE

je	vais finir
tu	vas finir
il	va finir
nous	allons finir
vous	allez finir
ils	vont finir

IMPARFAIT

je	finissais
tu	finissais
il	finissait
nous	finissions
vous	finissiez
ils	finissaient

CONDITIONNEL

je	finirais
tu	finirais
il	finirait
nous	finirions
vous	finiriez
ils	finiraient

FRENCH VERB TABLES

▶ partir

* also **dormir, mentir, sentir servir, sortir**

to leave

IMPÉRATIF

pars
partons
partez

EXEMPLES

*Elle **part** pour Paris.* She's leaving for Paris.
*Nous **sommes partis** en vacances.* We left on vacation.
*Je **partirai** bientôt.* I'll leave soon.

PARTICIPE PASSÉ

attendu

PRÉSENT

je	par**s**
tu	par**s**
il	par**t**
nous	par**tons**
vous	par**tez**
ils	par**tent**

PASSÉ COMPOSÉ

je	suis parti/partie
tu	es parti/partie
il	est parti/elle est partie
nous	sommes partis/parties
vous	êtes parti/partie/partis/parties
ils	sont partis/elles sont parties

FUTUR SIMPLE

je	partirai
tu	partiras
il	partira
nous	partirons
vous	partirez
ils	partiront

FUTUR PROCHE

je	vais partir
tu	vas partir
il	va partir
nous	allons partir
vous	allez partir
ils	vont partir

IMPARFAIT

je	partais
tu	partais
il	partait
nous	partions
vous	partiez
ils	partaient

CONDITIONNEL

je	partirais
tu	partirais
il	partirait
nous	partirions
vous	partiriez
ils	partiraient

FRENCH VERB TABLES

▶ attendre

to wait for

IMPÉRATIF

attends
attendons
attendez

EXEMPLES

Attends-*moi!* Wait for me!
Tu **attends** *depuis longtemps?* Have you been waiting long?
*Je l'***ai attendu** *à la poste.* I waited for him at the post office.

PARTICIPE PASSÉ

attendu

PRÉSENT

j'	attend**s**
tu	attend**s**
il	attend
nous	attend**ons**
vous	attend**ez**
ils	attend**ent**

PASSÉ COMPOSÉ

j'	ai attendu
tu	as attendu
il	a attendu
nous	avons attendu
vous	avez attendu
ils	ont attendu

FUTUR SIMPLE

j'	attendrai
tu	attendras
il	attendra
nous	attendrons
vous	attendrez
ils	attendront

FUTUR PROCHE

je	vais attendre
tu	vas attendres
il	va attendre
nous	allons attendre
vous	allez attendre
ils	vont attendre

IMPARFAIT

j'	attendais
tu	attendais
il	attendait
nous	attendions
vous	attendiez
ils	attendaient

CONDITIONNEL

j'	attendrais
tu	attendrais
il	attendrait
nous	attendrions
vous	attendriez
ils	attendraient

FRENCH VERB TABLES

▶ se lever

to get up

EXEMPLES

*Je **me lève** chaque matin à sept heures.*
  I get up at seven o'clock every morning.
*Il doit **se lever** tôt le matin.* He has
  to get up early in the morning.
*Tu **t'es levée** de bonne heure, Corinne?*
  You got up early, Corinne?

IMPÉRATIF

lève-toi
levons-nous
levez-vous

PARTICIPE PASSÉ

levé

PRÉSENT

je	me lève
tu	te lèves
il	se lève
nous	nous levons
vous	vous levez
ils	se lèvent

PASSÉ COMPOSÉ

je	me suis levé/levée
tu	t'es levé/levée
il	s'est levé/elle s'est levée
nous	nous sommes levés/levées
vous	vous êtes levé/levée/levés/ levées
ils	se sont levés/elles se sont levées

FUTUR SIMPLE

je	me lèverai
tu	te lèveras
il	se lèvera
nous	nous lèverons
vous	vous lèverez
ils	se lèveront

FUTUR PROCHE

je	vais me lever
tu	vas te lever
il	va se lever
nous	allons nous lever
vous	allez vous lever
ils	vont se lever

IMPARFAIT

je	me levais
tu	te levais
il	se levait
nous	nous levions
vous	vous leviez
ils	se levaient

CONDITIONNEL

je	me lèverais
tu	te lèverais
il	se lèverait
nous	nous lèverions
vous	vous lèveriez
ils	se lèveraient

FRENCH VERB TABLES

▶ avoir

to have

IMPÉRATIF

aie
ayons
ayez

EXEMPLES

Il **a** les yeux bleus. He's got blue eyes.
Quel âge **as**-tu? How old are you?
Il **a eu** un accident. He's had an accident.
J'**avais** faim. I was hungry.

PARTICIPE PASSÉ

eu

PRÉSENT

j'	ai
tu	as
il	a
nous	avons
vous	avez
ils	ont

PASSÉ COMPOSÉ

j'	ai eu
tu	as eu
il	a eu
nous	avons eu
vous	avez eu
ils	ont eu

FUTUR SIMPLE

j'	aurai
tu	auras
il	aura
nous	aurons
vous	aurez
ils	auront

FUTUR PROCHE

je	vais avoir
tu	vas avoir
il	va avoir
nous	allons avoir
vous	allez avoir
ils	vont avoir

IMPARFAIT

j'	avais
tu	avais
il	avait
nous	avions
vous	aviez
ils	avaient

CONDITIONNEL

j'	aurais
tu	aurais
il	aurait
nous	aurions
vous	auriez
ils	auraient

FRENCH VERB TABLES

▶ être

to be

EXEMPLES

Mon père **est** *professeur.* My father's
a teacher.
Quelle heure **est***-il? Il* **est** *10 heures.*
What time is it? It's 10 o'clock.
Ils **vont être** *à la maison ce soir.*
They'll be home tonight.

IMPÉRATIF

sois
soyons
soyez

PARTICIPE PASSÉ

été

PRÉSENT

je	suis
tu	es
il	est
nous	sommes
vous	êtes
ils	sont

PASSÉ COMPOSÉ

j'	ai été
tu	as été
il	a été
nous	avons été
vous	avez été
ils	ont été

FUTUR SIMPLE

je	serai
tu	seras
il	sera
nous	serons
vous	serez
ils	seront

FUTUR PROCHE

je	vais être
tu	vas être
il	va être
nous	allons être
vous	allez être
ils	vont être

IMPARFAIT

j'	étais
tu	étais
il	était
nous	étions
vous	étiez
ils	étaient

CONDITIONNEL

je	serais
tu	serais
il	serait
nous	serions
vous	seriez
ils	seraient

FRENCH VERB TABLES

▶ aller

to go

IMPÉRATIF

va
allons
allez

EXEMPLES

*Vous **allez** au cinéma?* Are you going
to the cinema?
*Je **suis allé** à Londres.* I went to
London.
***Est**-elle déjà **allée** chez elle?*
Has she already gone home?

PARTICIPE PASSÉ

allé

PRÉSENT

je	vais
tu	vas
il	va
nous	allons
vous	allez
ils	vont

PASSÉ COMPOSÉ

je	suis allé
tu	es allé
il	est allé
nous	sommes allés
vous	êtes allés
ils	sont allés

FUTUR SIMPLE

j'	irai
tu	iras
il	ira
nous	irons
vous	irez
ils	iront

FUTUR PROCHE

je	vais aller
tu	vas aller
il	va aller
nous	allons aller
vous	allez aller
ils	vont aller

IMPARFAIT

j'	allais
tu	allais
il	allait
nous	allions
vous	alliez
ils	allaient

CONDITIONNEL

j'	irais
tu	irais
il	irait
nous	irions
vous	iriez
ils	iraient

FRENCH VERB TABLES

▶ devoir

to have to

EXEMPLES

*Je **dois** aller faire les courses ce matin.*
  I have to do the shopping this morning.
*Il **a dû** faire ses devoirs hier soir.* He had
  to do his homework last night.
*Il **devait** prendre le train pour aller
  travailler.* He had to go to work by train.

IMPÉRATIF

dois
devons
devez

PARTICIPE PASSÉ

dû

PRÉSENT

je	dois
tu	dois
il	doit
nous	devons
vous	devez
ils	doivent

PASSÉ COMPOSÉ

j'	ai dû
tu	as dû
il	a dû
nous	avons dû
vous	avez dû
ils	ont dû

FUTUR SIMPLE

je	devrai
tu	devras
il	devra
nous	devrons
vous	devrez
ils	devront

FUTUR PROCHE

je	vais devoir
tu	vas devoir
il	va devoir
nous	allons devoir
vous	allez devoir
ils	vont devoir

IMPARFAIT

je	devais
tu	devais
il	devait
nous	devions
vous	deviez
ils	devaient

CONDITIONNEL

je	devrais
tu	devrais
il	devrait
nous	devrions
vous	devriez
ils	devraient

FRENCH VERB TABLES

▶ dire

to say

IMPÉRATIF

dis
disons
dites

EXEMPLES

*Je **dis** toujours la vérité.* I always tell the truth.
*Elle nous **a dit** bonjour.* She said good morning to us.
***Dites** bonjour, tout le monde!* Say hello, everybody!

PARTICIPE PASSÉ

dit

PRÉSENT

je	dis
tu	dis
il	dit
nous	disons
vous	dites
ils	disent

PASSÉ COMPOSÉ

j'	ai dit
tu	as dit
il	a dit
nous	avons dit
vous	avez dit
ils	ont dit

FUTUR SIMPLE

je	dirai
tu	diras
il	dira
nous	dirons
vous	direz
ils	diront

FUTUR PROCHE

je	vais dire
tu	vas dire
il	va dire
nous	allons dire
vous	allez dire
ils	vont dire

IMPARFAIT

je	disais
tu	disais
il	disait
nous	disions
vous	disiez
ils	disaient

CONDITIONNEL

je	dirais
tu	dirais
il	dirait
nous	dirions
vous	diriez
ils	diraient

FRENCH VERB TABLES

▶ faire

to do, to make

EXEMPLES

*Qu'est-ce que tu **fais**?* What are
  you doing?
*Qu'est-ce qu'il **a fait**?* What has he
  done? *or* What did he do?
*J'**ai fait** un gâteau.* I made a cake.

IMPÉRATIF

fais
faisons
faites

PARTICIPE PASSÉ

fait

PRÉSENT

je	fais
tu	fais
il	fait
nous	faisons
vous	faites
ils	font

PASSÉ COMPOSÉ

j'	ai fait
tu	as fait
il	a fait
nous	avons fait
vous	avez fait
ils	ont fait

FUTUR SIMPLE

je	ferai
tu	feras
il	fera
nous	ferons
vous	ferez
ils	feront

FUTUR PROCHE

je	vais faire
tu	vas faire
il	va faire
nous	allons faire
vous	allez faire
ils	vont faire

IMPARFAIT

je	faisais
tu	faisais
il	faisait
nous	faisions
vous	faisiez
ils	faisaient

CONDITIONNEL

je	ferais
tu	ferais
il	ferait
nous	ferions
vous	feriez
ils	feraient

FRENCH VERB TABLES

▶ mettre

to put

IMPÉRATIF

mets
mettons
mettez

PARTICIPE PASSÉ

mis

EXEMPLES

Mets *ton manteau!* Put your coat on!
*Où est-ce que tu **as mis** les clés?*
  Where did you put the keys?
*J'**ai mis** le livre sur la table.* I put
  the book on the table.

PRÉSENT

je	mets
tu	mets
il	met
nous	mettons
vous	mettez
ils	mettent

PASSÉ COMPOSÉ

j'	ai mis
tu	as mis
il	a mis
nous	avons mis
vous	avez mis
ils	ont mis

FUTUR SIMPLE

je	mettrai
tu	mettras
il	mettra
nous	mettrons
vous	mettrez
ils	mettront

FUTUR PROCHE

je	vais mettre
tu	vas mettre
il	va mettre
nous	allons mettre
vous	allez mettre
ils	vont mettre

IMPARFAIT

je	mettais
tu	mettais
il	mettait
nous	mettions
vous	mettiez
ils	mettaient

CONDITIONNEL

je	mettrais
tu	mettrais
il	mettrait
nous	mettrions
vous	mettriez
ils	mettraient

FRENCH VERB TABLES

▶ pouvoir

can

EXEMPLES

Je **peux** t'aider, si tu veux. I can help
   you if you like.
J'ai fait tout ce que j'**ai pu**. I did all I could.
Je ne **pourrai** pas venir samedi. I won't
   be able to come on Saturday.

IMPÉRATIF

the imperative of **pouvoir**
is not used

PARTICIPE PASSÉ

pu

PRÉSENT

je	peux
tu	peux
il	peut
nous	pouvons
vous	pouvez
ils	peuvent

PASSÉ COMPOSÉ

j'	ai pu
tu	as pu
il	a pu
nous	avons pu
vous	avez pu
ils	ont pu

FUTUR SIMPLE

je	pourrai
tu	pourras
il	pourra
nous	pourrons
vous	pourrez
ils	pourront

FUTUR PROCHE

je	vais pouvoir
tu	vas pouvoir
il	va pouvoir
nous	allons pouvoir
vous	allez pouvoir
ils	vont pouvoir

IMPARFAIT

je	pouvais
tu	pouvais
il	pouvait
nous	pouvions
vous	pouviez
ils	pouvaient

CONDITIONNEL

je	pourrais
tu	pourrais
il	pourrait
nous	pourrions
vous	pourriez
ils	pourraient

FRENCH VERB TABLES

▶ prendre

*also **apprendre, comprendre**

to take

IMPÉRATIF

prends
prenons
prenez

EXEMPLES

*Nous **prenons** le café après le souper.*
  We have coffee after supper.
*Il **a pris** mon livre.* He took my book.
***Prends** ces clés.* Take these keys.

PARTICIPE PASSÉ

pris

PRÉSENT

je	prends
tu	prends
il	prend
nous	prenons
vous	prenez
ils	prennent

PASSÉ COMPOSÉ

j'	ai pris
tu	as pris
il	a pris
nous	avons pris
vous	avez pris
ils	ont pris

FUTUR SIMPLE

je	prendrai
tu	prendras
il	prendra
nous	prendrons
vous	prendrez
ils	prendront

FUTUR PROCHE

je	vais prendre
tu	vas prendre
il	va prendre
nous	allons prendre
vous	allez prendre
ils	vont prendre

IMPARFAIT

je	prenais
tu	prenais
il	prenait
nous	prenions
vous	preniez
ils	prenaient

CONDITIONNEL

je	prendrais
tu	prendrais
il	prendrait
nous	prendrions
vous	prendriez
ils	prendraient

FRENCH VERB TABLES

▶ venir

to come

viens
venons
venez

EXEMPLES

Ils **viennent** *nous voir ce soir.*
  They're coming to see us tonight.
Viens *avec moi.* Come with me.
Elles **est venue** *toute seule.* She
  came alone.

PARTICIPE PASSÉ

venu

PRÉSENT

je	viens
tu	viens
il	vient
nous	venons
vous	venez
ils	viennent

PASSÉ COMPOSÉ

je	suis venu/venue
tu	es venu/venue
il	est venu/elle est venue
nous	sommes venus/venues
vous	êtes venu/venue/venus/ venues
ils	sont venus/elles sont venues

FUTUR SIMPLE

je	viendrai
tu	viendras
il	viendra
nous	viendrons
vous	viendrez
ils	viendront

FUTUR PROCHE

je	vais venir
tu	vas venir
il	va venir
nous	allons venir
vous	allez venir
ils	vont venir

IMPARFAIT

je	venais
tu	venais
il	venait
nous	venions
vous	veniez
ils	venaient

CONDITIONNEL

je	viendrais
tu	viendrais
il	viendrait
nous	viendrions
vous	viendriez
ils	viendraient

FRENCH VERB TABLES

▶ voir

to see

IMPÉRATIF

vois
voyons
voyez

EXEMPLES

*Venez me **voir** quand vous serez à Paris.*
 Come and see me when you're in Paris.
*Je ne **vois** rien sans mes lunettes.*
 I can't see anything without my glasses.
*Est-ce que tu l'**as vu**?* Did you see
 him? *or* Have you seen him?

PARTICIPE PASSÉ

vu

PRÉSENT

je	vois
tu	vois
il	voit
nous	voyons
vous	voyez
ils	voient

PASSÉ COMPOSÉ

j'	ai vu
tu	as vu
il	a vu
nous	avons vu
vous	avez vu
ils	ont vu

FUTUR SIMPLE

je	verrai
tu	verras
il	verra
nous	verrons
vous	verrez
ils	verront

FUTUR PROCHE

je	vais voir
tu	vas voir
il	va voir
nous	allons voir
vous	allez voir
ils	vont voir

IMPARFAIT

je	voyais
tu	voyais
il	voyait
nous	voyions
vous	voyiez
ils	voyaient

CONDITIONNEL

je	verrais
tu	verrais
il	verrait
nous	verrions
vous	verriez
ils	verraient

FRENCH VERB TABLES

▶ vouloir

to want

EXEMPLES

*Elle **veut** un vélo pour Noël.*
  She wants a bike for Christmas.
*Ils **voulaient** aller au cinéma.*
  They wanted to go to the cinema.
*Tu **voudrais** une tasse de thé?*
  Would you like a cup of tea?

IMPÉRATIF

veuille
veuillons
veuillez

PARTICIPE PASSÉ

voulu

PRÉSENT

je	veux
tu	veux
il	veut
nous	voulons
vous	voulez
ils	veulent

PASSÉ COMPOSÉ

j'	ai voulu
tu	as voulu
il	a voulu
nous	avons voulu
vous	avez voulu
ils	ont voulu

FUTUR SIMPLE

je	voudrai
tu	voudras
il	voudra
nous	voudrons
vous	voudrez
ils	voudront

FUTUR PROCHE

je	vais vouloir
tu	vas vouloir
il	va vouloir
nous	allons vouloir
vous	allez vouloir
ils	vont vouloir

IMPARFAIT

je	voulais
tu	voulais
il	voulait
nous	voulions
vous	vouliez
ils	voulaient

CONDITIONNEL

je	voudrais
tu	voudrais
il	voudrait
nous	voudrions
vous	voudriez
ils	voudraient

IRREGULAR VERB FORMS

The following list is a summary of the main forms of other irregular verbs that you are likely to encounter. For **le présent,** all **je** and **nous** forms are shown. The **il, vous,** and **ils** forms are also included wherever the part of the verb that goes with them follows an unusual pattern. For all other tenses, only the **je** form is given.

INFINITIF	PRÉSENT	PASSÉ COMPOSÉ	IMPARFAIT	FUTUR	FUTUR PROCHE
acheter	j'achète nous achetons ils achètent	j'ai acheté	j'achetais	j'achèterai	je vais acheter
appeler	j'appelle il appelle nous appelons	j'ai appelé	j'appelais	j'appellerai	je vais appeler
apprendre	j'apprends nous apprenons vous apprenez ils apprennent	j'ai appris	j'apprenais	j'apprendrai	je vais apprendre
s'asseoir	je m'assieds nous nous asseyons vous vous asseyez ils s'asseyent	je me suis assis	je m'asseyais	je m'assiérai	je vais m'asseoir
battre	je bats il bat nous battons	j'ai battu	je battais	je battrai	je vais battre
boire	je bois nous buvons ils boivent	j'ai bu	je buvais	je boirai	je vais boire
bouillir	je bous nous bouillons	j'ai bouilli	je bouillais	je bouillirai	je vais bouillir
conclure	je conclus nous concluons	j'ai conclu	je concluais	je conclurai	je vais conclure
conduire	je conduis nous conduisons	j'ai conduit	je conduisais	je conduirai	je vais conduire
connaître	je connais il connaît nous connaissons	j'ai connu	je connaissais	je connaîtrai	je vais connaître
coudre	je couds nous cousons vous couse ils cousent	j'ai cousu	je cousais	je coudrai	je vais coudre
courir	je cours nous courons	j'ai couru	je courais	je courrai	je vais courir
couvrir	je couvre nous couvrons	j'ai couvert	je couvrais	je couvrirai	je vais couvrir
craindre	je crains nous craignons	j'ai craint	je craignais	je craindrai	je vais craindre
créer	je crée nous créons	j'ai créé	je créais	je créerai	je vais créer
croire	je crois nous croyons ils croient	j'ai cru	je croyais	je croirai	je vais croire

INFINITIF	PRÉSENT	PASSÉ COMPOSÉ	IMPARFAIT	FUTUR	FUTUR PROCHE
croître	je croîs nous croissons	j'ai crû	je croissais	je croîtrai	je vais croître
cueillir	je cueille nous cueillons	j'ai cueilli	je cueillais	je cueillerai	je vais cueillir
cuire	je cuis nous cuisons ils cuisent	j'au cuit	je cuisais	je cuirai	je vais cuire
dormir	je dors nous dormons	j'ai dormi	je dormais	je dormirai	je vais dormir
écrire	j'écris nous écrivons	j'ai écrit	j'écrivais	j'écrirai	je vais écrire
falloir	il faut	il a fallu	il fallait	il faudra	il va falloir
fuir	je fuis nous fuyons ils fuient	j'ai fui	je fuyais	je fuirai	je vais fuir
haïr	je hais nous haïssons ils haïssent	j'ai haï	je haïssais	je haïrai	je vais haïr
jeter	je jette nous jetons ils jettent	j'ai jeté	je jetais	je jetterai	je vais jeter
joindre	je joins nous joignons	j'ai joint	je joignais	je joindrai	je vais joindre
lever	je lève nous levons ils lèvent	j'ai levé	je levais	je lèverai	je vais lever
lire	je lis nous lisons	j'ai lu	je lisais	je lirai	je vais lire
manger	je mange nous mangeons	j'ai mangé	je mangeais	je mangerai	je vais manger
mentir	je mens nous mentons	j'ai menti	je mentais	je mentirai	je va mentir
mourir	je meurs nous mourons ils meurent	je suis mort je suis morte	je mourais	je mourrai	je vais mourir
naître	je nais il naît nous naissons	je suis né je suis née	je naissais	je naîtrai	je vais naître
offrir	j'offre nous offrons	j'ai offert	j'offrais	j'offrirai	je vais offrir
paraître	je parais il paraît nous paraissons	j'ai paru	je paraissais	je paraîtrai	je vais paraître
partir	je pars nous partons	je suis parti je suis partie	je partais	je partirai	je vais partir
plaire	je plais il plaît nous plaisons	j'ai plu	je plaisais	je plairai	je vais plaire
pleuvoir	il pleut	il a plu	il pleuvait	il pleuvra	il va pleuvoir
prendre	je prends nous prenons ils prennent	j'ai pris	je prenais	je prendrai	je vais prendre
recevoir	je reçois il reçoit ils reçoivent	j'ai reçu	je recevais	je recevrai	je vais recevoir

INFINITIF	PRÉSENT	PASSÉ COMPOSÉ	IMPARFAIT	FUTUR	FUTUR PROCHE
rire	je ris nous rions	j'ai ri	je riais	je rirai	je vais rire
savoir	je sais nous savons ils savent	j'ai su	je savais	je saurai	je vais savoir
servir	je sers nous servons	j'ai servi	je servais	je servirai	je vais servir
sortir	je sors nous sortons	je suis sorti je suis sortie	je sortais	je sortirai	je vais sortir
souffrir	je souffre nous souffrons	j'ai souffert	je souffrais	je souffrirai	je vais souffrir
suffire	je suffis nous suffisons	j'ai suffi	je suffisais	je suffirai	je vais suffire
suivre	je suis nous suivons	j'ai suivi	je suivais	je suivrai	je vais suivre
se taire	je me tais nous nous taisons	je me suis tu	je me taisais	je me tairai	je vais me taire
tenir	je tiens nous tenons ils tiennent	j'ai tenu	je tenais	je tiendrai	je vais tenir
vaincre	je vaincs il vainc nous vainquons	j'ai vaincu	je vainquais	je vaincrai	je vais vaincre
valoir	je vaux il vaut nous valons	j'ai valu	je valais	je vaudrai	je vais valoir
venir	je viens nous venons ils viennent	je suis venu je suis venue	je venais	je viendrai	je vais venir
vivre	je vis nous vivons	j'ai vécu	je vivais	je vivrai	je vais vivre

FRENCH IN ACTION

CORRESPONDENCE

▶ PERSONAL LETTER

Address of sender

Place & Date

Nathalie Leduc
18, rue des Cèdres
Chibougamau (Québec) G8P 1G1
Gervais, le 8 juin 2005

Chère grand-maman, cher grand-papa,

Merci beaucoup pour les disques compacts que vous m'avez envoyés. Vous avez vraiment bien choisi car ce sont mes deux chanteurs préférés : je n'arrête pas de les écouter!

Rien de nouveau ici. Je passe presque tout mon temps à étudier pour les examens de fin d'année. Je suis pas mal certaine que je vais les réussir, mais l'examen de mathématiques est toujours difficile pour moi, car c'est la matière que j'aime le moins.

Maman m'a dit que vous partiez pour le Yukon la semaine prochaine. Je vous souhaite de très bonnes vacances, et pas trop de maringouins.

Grosses bises

Nathalie

Or:
Affectueusement

STARTING A PERSONAL LETTER

Merci pour ta lettre.
Ça m'a fait plaisir d'avoir de tes nouvelles.
Je suis désolé de ne pas t'avoir écrit plus tôt.

Thank you for your letter.
It was lovely to hear from you.
I'm sorry I didn't write sooner.

ENDING A PERSONAL LETTER

Donne de tes nouvelles!
Embrasse Sophie pour moi.
Paul te fait ses amitiés.

Keep in touch!
Give my love to Sophie.
Paul sends his best wishes.

CORRESPONDENCE

▶ BUSINESS LETTER

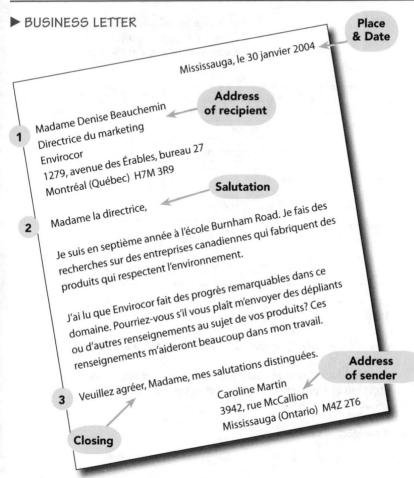

Place & Date

Mississauga, le 30 janvier 2004

Address of recipient

1
Madame Denise Beauchemin
Directrice du marketing
Envirocor
1279, avenue des Érables, bureau 27
Montréal (Québec) H7M 3R9

Salutation

2
Madame la directrice,

Je suis en septième année à l'école Burnham Road. Je fais des recherches sur des entreprises canadiennes qui fabriquent des produits qui respectent l'environnement.

J'ai lu que Envirocor fait des progrès remarquables dans ce domaine. Pourriez-vous s'il vous plaît m'envoyer des dépliants ou d'autres renseignements au sujet de vos produits? Ces renseignements m'aideront beaucoup dans mon travail.

Address of sender

3
Veuillez agréer, Madame, mes salutations distinguées.

Caroline Martin
3942, rue McCallion
Mississauga (Ontario) M4Z 2T6

Closing

1
- Start with the name of the individual.
- Follow with that person's position in the company.
- Do not use a comma at the end of each line.

2
- Do not use *cher* or *chère* in a business letter.
- Do not include the person's name after *Monsieur* or *Madame*.
- If you don't know the person's title, *Monsieur* or *Madame* is sufficient.

3
- Other possible closings include
  Veuillez recevoir, Madame, mes plus cordiales salutations.
  Veuillez agréer, Madame, mes sincères salutations.

CORRESPONDENCE

▶ E-MAIL

To give your email address to
someone in French, say:
Julie a commercial a b c point c a

	Nouveau message
A :	julie@abc.ca
De :	patrick@onemo.net
Objet :	spectacle
Cc :	antoine@blt.com
Copie cachée :	
	Fichier joint Envoyer

Salut!

Je viens d'acheter le nouvel album de Rockstar. Il est génial!

J'ai trois billets gratuits pour leur spectacle à Montréal samedi prochain et j'espère que vous pourrez venir avec moi tous les deux!

À bientôt!

Nouveau message	New message
A	To
De	From
Objet	Subject
Cc	cc
Copie cachée	bcc
Fichier joint	Attachment
Envoyer	Send

TELEPHONE

▶ WHEN YOU DIAL A NUMBER

– Bonjour! J'aimerais parler à Valérie.
– Hello! Could I speak to Valérie, please?

– Pourriez-vous lui demander de me rappeler, s'il vous plaît?
– Would you ask him/her to call me back, please?

– Je rappellerai dans une demi-heure.
– I'll call back in half an hour.

▶ ANSWERING THE TELEPHONE

– Bonjour! C'est Marc à l'appareil.   – Hello! It's Marc speaking.

– C'est moi.   – Speaking.

– Qui est à l'appareil?   – Who's speaking?

▶ WHEN THE SWITCHBOARD ANSWERS

– C'est de la part de qui?   – Who shall I say is calling?

– Je vous le/la passe.   – I'm putting you through.

– Ne quittez pas.   – Please hold.

– Voulez-vous laisser un message?   – Would you like to leave a message?

▶ DIFFICULTIES

– Je n'arrive pas à le/la/les rejoindre.
– I can't get through.

– La ligne est occupée.
– The line is busy.

– Je suis désolé, j'ai dû faire un faux numéro.
– I'm sorry, I dialled the wrong number.

– La ligne est très mauvaise.
– This is a very bad line.

– Leur téléphone est en dérangement.
– Their phone is out of order.

NUMBERS

▶ CARDINAL NUMBERS

0	**zéro**	14	**quatorze**	71	**soixante et onze**
1	**un, une**	15	**quinze**	72	**soixante-douze**
2	**deux**	16	**seize**	80	**quatre-vingts**
3	**trois**	17	**dix-sept**	81	**quatre-vingt-un(e)**
4	**quatre**	18	**dix-huit**	90	**quatre-vingt-dix**
5	**cinq**	19	**dix-neuf**	91	**quatre-vingt-onze**
6	**six**	20	**vingt**	100	**cent**
7	**sept**	21	**vingt et un(e)**		
8	**huit**	22	**vingt-deux**		
9	**neuf**	30	**trente**		
10	**dix**	40	**quarante**		
11	**onze**	50	**cinquante**		
12	**douze**	60	**soixante**		
13	**treize**	70	**soixante-dix**		

101	**cent un(e)**	2,000	**deux mille**
300	**trois cents**	1,000,000	**un million**
301	**trois cent un(e)**		
1,000	**mille**		

▶ BIG NUMBERS

There are two systems for dealing with larger numbers: the Systéme international and the American system (used in the United States and in English Canada). The following chart shows the main differences.

Systéme international		American system
un million	1 000 000	one million
un milliard	1 000 000 000	one billion
un billion	1 000 000 000 000	one trillion
un trillion	1 000 000 000 000 000 000	one quintillion

NUMBERS

▶ FRACTIONS, DECIMALS, PERCENT

1/2	**un demi**
1/3	**un tiers**
2/3	**deux tiers**
1/4	**un quart**
1/5	**un cinquième**
0.5	**zéro virgule cinq (0,5)**
3.4	**trois virgule quatre (3,4)**
10%	**dix pour cent (10 %)**
100%	**cent pour cent (100 %)**

▶ ORDINAL NUMBERS

Use ordinal numbers for ranking people or things.

1st	**premier (1er), première (1re)**	14th	**quatorzième (14e)**
2nd	**deuxième (2e)**	15th	**quinzième (15e)**
3rd	**troisième (3e)**	16th	**seizième (16e)**
4th	**quatrième (4e)**	17th	**dix-septième (17e)**
5th	**cinquième (5e)**	18th	**dix-huitième (18e)**
6th	**sixième (6e)**	19th	**dix-neuvième (19e)**
7th	**septième (7e)**	20th	**vingtième (20e)**
8th	**huitième (8e)**	21st	**vingt et unième (21e)**
9th	**neuvième (9e)**	22nd	**vingt-deuxième (22e)**
10th	**dixième (10e)**	30th	**trentième (30e)**
11th	**onzième (11e)**	100th	**centième (100e)**
12th	**douzième (12e)**	101st	**cent unième (101e)**
13th	**treizième (13e)**	1000th	**millième (1000e)**

Use cardinal numbers for naming all days of the month except for the first day of the month. For the first, use the ordinal number.

Mon anniversaire est le dix-sept octobre.
C'est le premier mai.

DATE

▶ DAYS OF THE WEEK

Monday	**lundi**
Tuesday	**mardi**
Wednesday	**mercredi**
Thursday	**jeudi**
Friday	**vendredi**
Saturday	**samedi**
Sunday	**dimanche**

Next + day of week
Mardi prochain, nous allons au musée.
Next Tuesday we are going to the museum.

Last + day of week
Mercredi dernier, elle est allée au restaurant.
Last Wednesday she went to a restaurant.

▶ MONTHS OF THE YEAR

January	**janvier**
February	**février**
March	**mars**
April	**avril**
May	**mai**
June	**juin**
July	**juillet**
August	**août**
September	**septembre**
October	**octobre**
November	**novembre**
December	**décembre**

▶ RELIGIOUS FESTIVALS

Baisakhi	**Vaisakhi**
Christmas	**Noël**
Diwali	**Diwali**
Easter	**Pâques**
Eid	**Eid**
Good Friday	**Vendredi saint**
Hanukkah	**Hanoukka**
Holi	**Holi**
Passover	**la Pâque juive**
Ramadan	**Ramadan**
Wesak	**Wesak**
Yom Kippur	**Yom Kippour**

TIME

Quelle heure est-il? What time is it?
Il est... It's...

À quelle heure? At what time?

une heure

une heure dix

une heure et quart

une heure et demie

deux heures moins vingt

deux heures moins le quart

à minuit

à midi

à une heure (de l'après-midi)

à huit heures (du soir)

French times are often given using the twenty-four hour clock.

à 11 h 15
or
onze heures quinze

à 20 h 45
or
vingt heures quarante-cinq

COUNTRIES

In the table below, the first column is the English name of the country and the second column is the French name of the country. The last two columns are the French words for the nationality, as a noun. The corresponding adjective is the same, but is **not** capitalized:

Canadian (ADJECTIVE) = **canadien** MASC, **canadienne** FEM

Country names marked with an F have French as an official or administrative language.

Using prepositions with countries

- MASC country name: *in Canada, to Canada* = **au Canada**
                          from Canada, of Canada = **du Canada**

- FEM country name: *in China, to China* = **en Chine**
                          from China, of China = **de la Chine**

- PL country name: *in the Bahamas, to the Bahamas* = **aux Bahamas**
                          from the Bahamas, of the Bahamas = **des Bahamas**

- remember that both **du** and **de la** become **de l'** before a vowel or silent *h*, and **au** becomes **à l'**: **à l'Afghanistan, de l'Angleterre**

Country	French name	Nationality – MASC	Nationality – FEM
Afghanistan	l'Afghanistan MASC	Afghan	Afghane
Albania	l'Albanie FEM	Albanais	Albanaise
Algeria	F l'Algérie FEM	Algérien	Algérienne
Angola	l'Angola MASC	Angolais	Angolaise
Argentina	l'Argentine FEM	Argentin	Argentine
Armenia	l'Arménie FEM	Arménien	Arménienne
Australia	l'Australie FEM	Australien	Australienne
Austria	l'Autriche FEM	Autrichien	Autrichienne
Azerbaijan	l'Azerbaïdjan MASC	Azerbaïdjanais	Azerbaïdjanaise
Bahamas	les Bahamas FEM	Bahamien	Bahamienne
Bangladesh	le Bangladesh	Bangladais	Bangladaise
Barbados	la Barbade	Barbadien	Barbadienne
Belarus	la Biélorussie	Biélorusse	Biélorusse
Belgium	F la Belgique	Belge	Belge
Belize	le Bélize	Bélizien	Bélizienne
Benin	F le Bénin	Béninois	Béninoise
Burkina Faso	F le Burkina Faso	Burkinabé	Burkinabée
Bolivia	la Bolivie	Bolivien	Bolivienne
Bosnia-Herzegovina	la Bosnie-Herzégovnie	Bosniaque	Bosniaque
Brazil	le Brésil	Brésilien	Brésilienne

Country	French name	Nationality – MASC	Nationality – FEM
Bulgaria	la Bulgarie	Bulgare	Bulgare
Cambodia	le Cambodge	Cambodgien	Cambodgienne
Cameroon	F le Cameroun	Camerounais	Camerounaise
Canada	F le Canada	Canadien	Canadienne
Chile	le Chili	Chilien	Chilienne
China	la Chine	Chinois	Chinoise
Colombia	la Colombie	Colombien	Colombienne
Congo	F le Congo	Congolais	Congolaise
Costa Rica	le Costa Rica	Costaricain	Costaricaine
Croatia	la Croatie	Croate	Croate
Cuba	Cuba* FEM	Cubain	Cubaine
Czech Republic	la République tchèque	Tchèque	Tchèque
Denmark	le Danemark	Danois	Danoise
Ecuador	l'Équateur MASC	Équatorien	Équatorienne
Egypt	l'Égypte FEM	Égyptien	Égyptienne
El Salvador	le Salvador	Salvadorien	Salvadorienne
England	l'Angleterre FEM	Anglais	Anglaise
Estonia	l'Estonie FEM	Estonien	Estonienne
Ethiopia	l'Éthiopie FEM	Éthiopien	Éthiopienne
Finland	la Finlande	Finnois	Finnoise
France	F la France	Français	Française
Gabon	F le Gabon	Gabonais	Gabonaise
Gambia	la Gambie	Gambien	Gambienne
Germany	l'Allemagne FEM	Allemand	Allemande
Ghana	le Ghana	Ghanéen	Ghanéenne
Greece	la Grèce	Grec	Grecque
Guatemala	le Guatemala	Guatémaltèque	Guatémaltèque
Guinea	F la Guinée	Guinéen	Guinéenne
Guyana	F la Guyane	Guyanais	Guyanaise
Haiti	F Haïti* MASC	Haïtien	Haïtienne
Holland	la Hollande	Hollandais	Hollandaise
Honduras	le Honduras	Hondurien	Hondurienne
Hungary	la Hongrie	Hongrois	Hongroise
Iceland	l'Islande FEM	Islandais	Islandaise
India	l'Inde FEM	Indien	Indienne
Indonesia	l'Indonésie FEM	Indonésien	Indonésienne
Iran	l'Iran MASC	Iranien	Iranienne
Iraq	l'Iraq MASC	Iraquien	Iraquienne
Ireland	l'Irlande FEM	Irlandais	Irlandaise

Country	French name	Nationality – MASC	Nationality – FEM
Israel	Israël* MASC	Israélien	Israélienne
Italy	l'Italie FEM	Italien	Italienne
Ivory Coast	F la Côte d'Ivoire	Ivoirien	Ivoirienne
Jamaica	la Jamaïque	Jamaïquain	Jamaïquaine
Japan	le Japon	Japonais	Japonaise
Kazakhstan	le Kazakhstan	Kazakh	Kazakhe
Kenya	le Kenya	Kényan	Kényane
Korea, North	la Corée du Nord	Nord-Coréen	Nord-Coréenne
Korea, South	la Corée du Sud	Sud-Coréen	Sud-Coréenne
Kuwait	le Koweït	Koweïtien	Koweïtienne
Laos	le Laos	Laotien	Laotienne
Latvia	la Lettonie	Letton	Lettone
Lebanon	le Liban	Libanais	Libanaise
Libya	la Libye	Libyen	Libyenne
Lithuania	la Lituanie	Lituanien	Lituanienne
Luxemburg	F le Luxembourg	Luxembourgeois	Luxembourgeoise
Madagascar	F Madagascar* MASC	Malgache	Malgache
Malaysia	la Malaisie	Malais	Malaise
Mali	F le Mali	Malien	Malienne
Mauritius	F Maurice* FEM	Mauricien	Mauricienne
Mauritania	F la Mauritanie	Mauritanien	Mauritanienne
Mexico	le Mexique	Mexicain	Mexicaine
Morocco	F le Maroc	Marocain	Marocaine
Mozambique	le Mozambique	Mozambicain	Mozambicaine
Namibia	la Namibie	Namibien	Namibienne
New Zealand	la Nouvelle-Zélande	Néo-Zélandais	Néo-Zélandaise
Nicaragua	le Nicaragua	Nicaraguayen	Nicaraguayenne
Niger	F le Niger	Nigérien	Nigérienne
Nigeria	le Nigeria	Nigérian	Nigériane
Norway	la Norvège	Norvégien	Norvégienne
Pakistan	le Pakistan	Pakistanais	Pakistanaise
Panama	le Panama	Panaméen	Panaméenne
Paraguay	le Paraguay	Paraguayen	Paraguayenne
Peru	le Pérou	Péruvien	Péruvienne
Philippines	les Philippines FEM	Philippin	Philippine
Poland	la Pologne	Polonais	Polonaise
Portugal	le Portugal	Portugais	Portugaise
Romania	la Roumanie	Roumain	Roumaine
Russia	la Russie	Russe	Russe

Country	French name	Nationality – MASC	Nationality – FEM
Rwanda	F le Rwanda	Rwandais	Rwandaise
Saudi Arabia	l'Arabie Saoudite FEM	Saoudien	Saoudienne
Scotland	l'Écosse FEM	Écossais	Écossaise
Senegal	F le Sénégal	Sénégalais	Sénégalaise
Serbia	la Serbie	Serbe	Serbe
Singapore	Singapour*	Singapourien	Singapourienne
Slovakia	la Slovaquie	Slovaque	Slovaque
Somalia	la Somalie	Somalien	Somalienne
South Africa	l'Afrique du Sud FEM	Sud-Africain	Sud-Africaine
Spain	l'Espagne FEM	Espagnol	Espagnole
Sri Lanka	le Sri Lanka	Sri-Lankais	Sri-Lankaise
Sudan	le Soudan	Soudanais	Soudanaise
Sweden	la Suède	Suédois	Suédoise
Switzerland	F la Suisse	Suisse	Suisse
Syria	la Syrie	Syrien	Syrienne
Taiwan	Taïwan*	Taïwanais	Taïwanaise
Tajikistan	le Tadjikistan	Tadjik	Tadjike
Tanzania	la Tanzanie	Tanzanien	Tanzanienne
Thailand	la Thaïlande	Thaïlandais	Thaïlandaise
Tunisia	F la Tunisie	Tunisien	Tunisienne
Turkey	la Turquie	Turc	Turque
Uganda	l'Ouganda MASC	Ougandais	Ougandaise
Ukraine	l'Ukraine FEM	Ukrainien	Ukrainienne
United Arab Emirates	les Émirats arabes unis MASC	Émirien	Émirienne
United Kingdom	le Royaume-Uni	Britannique	Britannique
United States	les États-Unis MASC	Américain	Américaine
Uruguay	l'Uruguay MASC	Uruguayen	Uruguayenne
Uzbekistan	l'Ouzbékistan MASC	Ouzbek	Ouzbek
Venezuela	le Venezuela	Vénézuélien	Vénézuélienne
Vietnam	le Vietnam	Vietnamien	Vietnamienne
Zaïre	F le Zaïre	Zaïrois	Zaïroise
Zambia	la Zambie	Zambien	Zambienne
Zimbabwe	le Zimbabwe	Zimbabwéen	Zimbabwéenne

*There is no article with **Cuba**, **Haïti**, **Israël**, **Maurice**, **Madagascar**, **Singapour** or **Taïwan.**

For **Cuba**, **Maurice**, **Madagascar**, **Singapour** or **Taïwan**, use **à** for *in* or *to*, and **de** for *of* or *from*.

For **Haïti** or **Israël**, use **en** for *in* or *to*, and **d'** for *of* or *from*.

A

a ARTICLE

> *Use* **un** *for masculine nouns,* **une** *for feminine nouns.*

un MASC ◊ *a book* un livre ◊ *a year ago* il y a un an
une FEM ◊ *an apple* une pomme ◊ *a car* une auto

> *You do not translate* **a** *when you want to describe somebody's job in French.*

◊ *He's a butcher.* Il est boucher.
◊ *She's a doctor.* Elle est médecin.
♦ **once a week** une fois par semaine
♦ **10 km an hour** dix kilomètres à l'heure
♦ **3 dollars a kilo** trois dollars le kilo
♦ **a hundred times** cent fois

to **abandon** VERB
abandonner

abbreviation NOUN
l' abréviation FEM

ability NOUN
♦ **to have the ability to do something** être capable de faire quelque chose

able ADJECTIVE
♦ **to be able to do something** être capable de faire quelque chose

❋ **aboiteau** NOUN
l' aboiteau MASC
(PL les aboiteaux) ◊ *Aboiteaus open as the tide comes in and close as it goes out.* Les aboiteaux ouvrent à marée montante et ferment à marée descendante.

to **abolish** VERB
abolir

❋ **Aboriginal** ADJECTIVE
autochtone ◊ *Aboriginal languages* les langues autochtones ◊ *Aboriginal rights* les droits des autochtones ◊ *the Aboriginal peoples of Canada* les autochtones du Canada

abortion NOUN
l' avortement MASC

about PREPOSITION, ADVERB
[1] à propos de (*concerning*) ◊ *I'm phoning you about tomorrow's meeting.* Je vous appelle à propos de la réunion de demain.
[2] environ (*approximately*) ◊ *It takes about 10 hours.* Ça prend dix heures environ.
♦ **about a hundred pages** une centaine de pages

♦ **at about 11 o'clock** vers onze heures
[3] dans (*around*) ◊ *to walk around town* se promener dans la ville
[4] sur ◊ *a book about Manitoba* un livre sur Manitoba
♦ **to be about to do something** être sur le point de faire quelque chose ◊ *I was about to go out.* J'étais sur le point de sortir.
♦ **to talk about something** parler de quelque chose
♦ **What's it about?** De quoi s'agit-il?
♦ **How about going to the movies?** Et si nous allions au cinéma?

above PREPOSITION, ADVERB
[1] au-dessus de (*higher than*) ◊ *He put his hands above his head.* Il a mis ses mains au-dessus de sa tête.
♦ **the floor above** l'étage du dessus
♦ **mentioned above** mentionné ci-dessus
♦ **above all** par-dessus tout
[2] plus de (*more than*) ◊ *above 40 degrees* plus de quarante degrés

abroad ADVERB
à l'étranger ◊ *to go abroad* partir à l'étranger

abrupt ADJECTIVE
brusque ◊ *He was a bit abrupt with me.* Il s'est montré un peu brusque avec moi.

absence NOUN
l' absence FEM

absent ADJECTIVE
absent

absent-minded ADJECTIVE
distrait ◊ *She's a bit absent-minded.* Elle est un peu distraite.

absolutely ADVERB
[1] tout à fait (*completely*) ◊ *You're absolutely right.* Tu as tout à fait raison.
[2] absolument ◊ *"Do you think it's a good idea?" "Absolutely!"* « Tu trouves que c'est une bonne idée? » « Absolument! »

absorbed ADJECTIVE
♦ **to be absorbed in something** être absorbé par quelque chose
♦ **to be absorbed in a book** être plongé dans un livre

absurd ADJECTIVE
absurde ◊ *That's absurd!* C'est absurde!

abuse NOUN

☞

see also **abuse** VERB

l' <u>abus</u> MASC (*misuse*)
♦ **to shout abuse at somebody** insulter quelqu'un
♦ **the issue of child abuse** la question des enfants maltraités
♦ **the problem of drug abuse** le problème de la drogue

to **abuse** VERB

see also **abuse** NOUN

① <u>maltraiter</u> ◊ *abused children* les enfants maltraités
♦ **to be abused** être maltraité (*child, woman*)
② <u>injurier</u> (*insult*)
♦ **to abuse drugs** se droguer
③ <u>abuser de</u> ◊ *to abuse a privilege* abuser d'un privilège

abusive ADJECTIVE
<u>insultant</u> (*insulting*) ◊ *abusive behaviour* un comportement insultant
♦ **When I refused, he became abusive.** Quand j'ai refusé, il s'est mis à m'injurier.
♦ **children with abusive parents** les enfants maltraités par leurs parents

academic ADJECTIVE
<u>scolaire</u> ◊ *the academic year* l'année scolaire

academy NOUN
le <u>collège</u> ◊ *a military academy* un collège militaire

🌂 **Acadia** NOUN
l' <u>Acadie</u> FEM ◊ *My ancestors were from Acadia.* Mes ancêtres étaient originaires de l'Acadie.

> 🛈 **Acadia** *was the part of New France that stretched from south of the St. Lawrence eastward to the sea. It took in the area now covered by part of Québec and the Maritimes, as well as part of what is now the US, and was disputed by the French and British for many years. Many descendants of the original Acadians, who were deported by the British in the mid-1700s, still consider this their homeland.*

🌂 **Acadian** ADJECTIVE
<u>acadien</u> MASC
<u>acadienne</u> FEM ◊ *the Acadian flag* le drapeau acadien ◊ *Acadian poutine* la poutine acadienne

🌂 **Acadian** NOUN
l' <u>Acadien</u> MASC
l' <u>Acadienne</u> FEM ◊ *He's an Acadian.* C'est un Acadien. ◊ *She's an Acadian.* C'est une Acadienne.

to **accelerate** VERB
<u>accélérer</u>

accelerator NOUN
l' <u>accélérateur</u> MASC

accent NOUN
l' <u>accent</u> MASC ◊ *She's got a French accent.* Elle a l'accent français.

to **accept** VERB
<u>accepter</u>

acceptable ADJECTIVE
<u>acceptable</u>

access NOUN
① l' <u>accès</u> MASC ◊ *He has access to confidential information.* Il a accès à des renseignements confidentiels.
② le <u>droit de visite</u> ◊ *Her ex-husband has access to the children.* Son ex-mari a le droit de visite.

accessible ADJECTIVE
<u>accessible</u>

accessory NOUN
l' <u>accessoire</u> MASC ◊ *fashion accessories* les accessoires de mode

accident NOUN
l' <u>accident</u> MASC ◊ *to have an accident* avoir un accident
♦ **by accident (1)** (*by mistake*) accidentellement ◊ *I hit her with my elbow by accident.* Je l'ai heurtée accidentellement du coude.
♦ **by accident (2)** (*by chance*) par hasard ◊ *She met him by accident.* Elle l'a rencontré par hasard.

accidental ADJECTIVE
<u>accidentel</u> MASC
<u>accidentelle</u> FEM

to **accommodate** VERB
<u>recevoir</u> ◊ *The hotel can accommodate 50 people.* L'hôtel peut recevoir cinquante personnes.

accommodation NOUN
le <u>logement</u>

to **accompany** VERB
<u>accompagner</u>

accord NOUN
♦ **of one's own accord** de son plein gré ◊ *She left of her own accord.* Elle est partie de son plein gré.

accordingly ADVERB
<u>en conséquence</u>

according to PREPOSITION
<u>selon</u> ◊ *according to him* selon lui

accordion NOUN
l' <u>accordéon</u> MASC

account NOUN
① le <u>compte</u> ◊ *a bank account* un compte en banque
♦ **to do the accounts** tenir la

comptabilité

2 (*report*)

le compte rendu

(PL les comptes rendus) ◊ *He gave a detailed account of what happened.* Il a donné un compte rendu détaillé des événements.

♦ **to take something into account** tenir compte de quelque chose

♦ **on account of** à cause de ◊ *We couldn't go out on account of the bad weather.* Nous n'avons pas pu sortir à cause du mauvais temps.

to **account for** VERB

expliquer ◊ *If she was ill, that would account for her poor results.* Si elle était malade, cela expliquerait ses résultats médiocres.

accountable ADJECTIVE

♦ **to be accountable to someone for something** être responsable de quelque chose devant quelqu'un

accountancy NOUN

la comptabilité

accountant NOUN

le/la comptable ◊ *She's an accountant.* Elle est comptable.

accuracy NOUN

l' exactitude FEM

accurate ADJECTIVE

précis ◊ *accurate information* des renseignements précis MASC

accurately ADVERB

avec précision

accusation NOUN

l' accusation FEM

to **accuse** VERB

♦ **to accuse somebody of something** accuser quelqu'un de quelque chose ◊ *Her parents accused her of being lazy.* Ses parents l'ont accusée d'être paresseuse.

ace NOUN

l' as MASC ◊ *the ace of hearts* l'as de cœur

ache NOUN

see also **ache** VERB

la douleur

to **ache** VERB

see also **ache** NOUN

♦ **My leg aches.** J'ai mal à la jambe.

to **achieve** VERB

1 atteindre (*an aim*)

2 remporter (*victory*)

achievement NOUN

l' exploit MASC ◊ *That was quite an achievement.* C'était un véritable exploit.

acid NOUN

l' acide MASC

acid rain NOUN

les pluies acides FEM PL

acne NOUN

l' acné FEM

acre NOUN

le demi-hectare

> **ℹ** In France, land is measured in hectares. One acre is about 0.4 hectares.

acrobat NOUN

l' acrobate MASC/FEM ◊ *He's an acrobat.* Il est acrobate.

acrobatics NOUN

l' acrobatie FEM

across PREPOSITION, ADVERB

de l'autre côté de ◊ *the house across the road* la maison de l'autre côté de la rue

♦ **to walk across the road** traverser la rue

♦ **to run across the road** traverser la rue en courant

♦ **across from** (*opposite*) en face de ◊ *He sat down across from us.* Il s'est assis en face de nous.

to **act** VERB

see also **act** NOUN

1 jouer (*in play, film*) ◊ *He acts really well.* Il joue vraiment bien. ◊ *She's acting the part of Juliet.* Elle joue le rôle de Juliette.

2 agir (*take action*) ◊ *The police acted quickly.* La police a agi rapidement.

♦ **She acts as his interpreter.** Elle lui sert d'interprète.

♦ **to act like an idiot** se comporter comme un imbécile

act NOUN

see also **act** VERB

l' acte MASC (*in play*) ◊ *in the first act* au premier acte

action NOUN

l' action FEM ◊ *The film was full of action.* Il y avait beaucoup d'action dans le film.

♦ **to take firm action against** prendre des mesures énergiques contre

active ADJECTIVE

actif MASC

active FEM ◊ *He's very active.* Il est très actif.

♦ **an active volcano** un volcan en activité

activity NOUN

l' <u>activité</u> FEM ◊ *outdoor activities* les activités de plein air

actor NOUN
l' <u>acteur</u> MASC

actress NOUN
l' <u>actrice</u> FEM

actual ADJECTIVE
<u>réel</u> MASC
<u>réelle</u> FEM ◊ *The film is based on actual events.* Le film repose sur des faits réels.
♦ **What's the actual amount?** Quel est le montant exact?

> *Be careful not to translate **actual** by* ***actuel***.

actually ADVERB
[1] <u>vraiment</u> (*really*) ◊ *Did it actually happen?* Est-ce que c'est vraiment arrivé?
[2] <u>en fait</u> (*in fact*) ◊ *Actually, I don't know her at all.* En fait, je ne la connais pas du tout.

> *Be careful not to translate **actually** by* ***actuellement***.

acupuncture NOUN
l' <u>acuponcture</u> FEM

ad NOUN
[1] l' <u>annonce</u> FEM (*in paper*)
[2] la <u>pub</u> (*on TV, radio*)

AD ABBREVIATION
<u>ap. J.-C.</u> (= après Jésus-Christ) ◊ *in 800 AD* en huit cents après Jésus-Christ

to **adapt** VERB
<u>adapter</u> ◊ *Her novel was adapted for television.* Son roman a été adapté pour la télévision.
♦ **to adapt to something** (*get used to*) s'adapter à quelque chose ◊ *He adapted to his new school very quickly.* Il s'est adapté très vite à sa nouvelle école.

adaptation NOUN
l' <u>adaptation</u> FEM ◊ *a TV adaptation of a novel* une adaptation télévisée d'un roman

adapter NOUN
l' <u>adaptateur</u> MASC

to **add** VERB
<u>ajouter</u> ◊ *Add two eggs to the mixture.* Ajoutez deux œufs au mélange.
♦ **to add up** additionner ◊ *Add up the figures.* Additionnez les chiffres.

addict NOUN
(*drug addict*)
le <u>drogué</u>
la <u>droguée</u>

♦ **She's a football addict.** C'est une mordue de football.

addicted ADJECTIVE
♦ **to be addicted to** (*drug*) s'adonner à
♦ **He's addicted to soap operas.** C'est un mordu des téléromans.
♦ **I'm addicted to chocolate.** Je ne peux résister au chocolat.

addition NOUN
♦ **in addition** en plus ◊ *He's broken his leg and, in addition, he's caught a cold.* Il s'est cassé la jambe et en plus, il a attrapé un rhume.
♦ **in addition to** en plus de ◊ *In addition to the price of the cassette, there's a charge for postage.* En plus du prix de la cassette, il y a des frais de port.

address NOUN
l' <u>adresse</u> FEM ◊ *What's your address?* Quelle est votre adresse?

adjective NOUN
l' <u>adjectif</u> MASC

to **adjust** VERB
<u>régler</u> ◊ *You can adjust the height of the chair.* Tu peux régler la hauteur de la chaise.
♦ **to adjust to something** (*get used to*) s'adapter à quelque chose ◊ *He adjusted to his new school very quickly.* Il s'est adapté très vite à sa nouvelle école.

adjustable ADJECTIVE
<u>réglable</u>

administration NOUN
l' <u>administration</u> FEM

to **admire** VERB
<u>admirer</u>

admission NOUN
l' <u>entrée</u> FEM ◊ *"free admission"* « entrée gratuite »

to **admit** VERB
[1] <u>admettre</u> (*agree*) ◊ *I must admit that...* Je dois admettre que...
[2] <u>reconnaître</u> (*confess*) ◊ *She admitted that she'd done it.* Elle a reconnu qu'elle l'avait fait.

admittance NOUN
♦ **"no admittance"** « accès interdit »

adolescence NOUN
l' <u>adolescence</u> FEM

adolescent NOUN
l' <u>adolescent</u> MASC
l' <u>adolescente</u> FEM

to **adopt** VERB
<u>adopter</u> ◊ *I was adopted.* J'ai été adopté.

adopted ADJECTIVE
<u>adoptif</u> MASC

adoptive FEM ◊ *an adopted son* un fils adoptif

adoption NOUN
l' adoption FEM

to **adore** VERB
adorer

adult NOUN
l' adulte MASC/FEM
♦ **adult education** l'éducation des adultes MASC

to **advance** VERB

see also **advance** NOUN

1 avancer (*move forward*) ◊ *The troops are advancing.* Les troupes avancent.
2 progresser (*progress*)
◊ *Technology has advanced a lot.* La technologie a beaucoup progressé.

advance NOUN

see also **advance** VERB

♦ **in advance** à l'avance ◊ *They bought the tickets in advance.* Ils ont acheté les billets à l'avance.

advanced ADJECTIVE
avancé

advantage NOUN
l' avantage MASC ◊ *Going to university has many advantages.* Aller à l'université présente de nombreux avantages.
♦ **to take advantage of something** profiter de quelque chose ◊ *He took advantage of the good weather to go for a walk.* Il a profité du beau temps pour faire une promenade.
♦ **to take advantage of somebody** exploiter quelqu'un ◊ *The company was taking advantage of its employees.* La société exploitait ses employés.

adventure NOUN
l' aventure FEM

adventurer NOUN
l' aventurier MASC
l' aventurière FEM

adventurous ADJECTIVE
aventureux FEM SING

adverb NOUN
l' adverbe MASC

to **advertise** VERB
faire de la publicité pour ◊ *They're advertising the new model.* Ils font de la publicité pour leur nouveau modèle.
♦ **Jobs are advertised in the paper.** Le journal publie des annonces d'emplois.

advertisement NOUN

1 la publicité (*on TV*)
2 l' annonce FEM (*in newspaper*)

advertising NOUN
la publicité

advice NOUN
les conseils MASC PL ◊ *to give somebody advice* donner des conseils à quelqu'un
♦ **a piece of advice** un conseil ◊ *She gave me a good piece of advice.* Elle m'a donné un bon conseil.

to **advise** VERB
conseiller ◊ *They advised me to wait.* Il m'ont conseillé d'attendre. ◊ *I advise you not to go there.* Je te conseille de ne pas y aller.

aerial NOUN
l' antenne FEM

aerobics PL NOUN
l' aérobic FEM SING ◊ *I'm going to aerobics tonight.* Je vais au cours d'aérobic ce soir.

affair NOUN
1 l' aventure FEM (*romantic*) ◊ *to have an affair with somebody* avoir une aventure avec quelqu'un
2 l' affaire FEM (*event*)

to **affect** VERB
1 concerner ◊ *It affects all of us.* Cela nous concerne tous.
2 avoir des conséquences pour ◊ *If you smoke, it will affect the people around you.* Si tu fumes, cela aura des conséquences pour les gens autour de toi.
3 décourager ◊ *We mustn't let it affect us.* Nous ne devons pas nous laisser décourager par cela.

*Be careful not to translate **affect** by the French verb **affecter**.*

affectionate ADJECTIVE
affectueux FEM SING

to **afford** VERB
avoir les moyens d'acheter ◊ *I can't afford a new pair of jeans.* Je n'ai pas les moyens d'acheter un nouveau jean.
♦ **We can't afford to go on a holiday.** Nous n'avons pas les moyens de partir en vacances.

afraid ADJECTIVE
♦ **to be afraid of something** avoir peur de quelque chose ◊ *I'm afraid of spiders.* J'ai peur des araignées.
♦ **I'm afraid I can't come.** Je crains de ne pouvoir venir.
♦ **I'm afraid so.** Hélas oui.
♦ **I'm afraid not.** Hélas non.

after PREPOSITION, ADVERB, CONJUNCTION

après ◊ *after dinner* après le dîner
◊ *He ran after me.* Il a couru après
moi. ◊ *soon after* peu après
♦ **after I've had a rest** après m'être
reposé
♦ **after having asked** après avoir
demandé
♦ **after all** après tout

afternoon NOUN
l' après-midi MASC/FEM ◊ *3 o'clock in
the afternoon* trois heures de l'après-
midi ◊ *this afternoon* cet après-midi
◊ *on Saturday afternoon* samedi
après-midi

afterwards ADVERB
après ◊ *She left not long afterwards.*
Elle est partie peu de temps après.

again ADVERB
[1] encore une fois (*one more time*)
◊ *Can you tell me again?* Tu peux me
le dire encore une fois?
[2] de nouveau (*once more*) ◊ *They're
friends again.* Ils sont de nouveau
amis.
♦ **not... again** ne... plus ◊ *I won't go
there again.* Je n'y retournerai plus.
♦ **Do it again!** Refais-le!
♦ **again and again** à plusieurs reprises

against PREPOSITION
contre ◊ *He leaned against the wall.*
Il s'est appuyé contre le mur. ◊ *I'm
against nuclear testing.* Je suis contre
les essais nucléaires.

age NOUN
l' âge MASC ◊ *at the age of 16* à l'âge
de seize ans ◊ *an age limit* une limite
d'âge
♦ **I haven't been to the movies in ages.**
Ça fait une éternité que je ne suis pas
allé au cinéma.

aged ADJECTIVE
♦ **aged 10** âgé de dix ans
♦ **their aged parents** leurs parents âgés

agency NOUN
l' agence FEM ◊ *a travel agency* une
agence de voyages ◊ *a real estate
agency* une agence immobilière

agenda NOUN
[1] l' ordre du jour MASC ◊ *on the
agenda* à l'ordre du jour ◊ *the agenda
for today's meeting* l'ordre du jour de
la réunion d'aujourd'hui
[2] l' agenda MASC (*daybook*) ◊ *I wrote
it in my agenda.* Je l'ai écrit dans mon
agenda.

agent NOUN
l' agent MASC
l' agente FEM
♦ **a real estate agent** un agent
immobilier

♦ **She's a travel agent.** Elle est agente
de voyage.

aggressive ADJECTIVE
agressif FEM SING

ago ADVERB
♦ **two days ago** il y a deux jours
♦ **two years ago** il y a deux ans
♦ **not long ago** il y a pas longtemps
♦ **How long ago did it happen?** Il y a
combien de temps que c'est arrivé?

agony NOUN
♦ **to be in agony** souffrir le martyre ◊ *I
was in agony.* Je souffrais le martyre.

to **agree** VERB
♦ **to agree with** être d'accord avec ◊ *I
agree with her.* Je suis d'accord avec
elle.
♦ **to agree to do something** accepter de
faire quelque chose ◊ *He agreed to
go and pick her up.* Il a accepté d'aller
la chercher.
♦ **to agree that...** admettre que... ◊ *I
agree that it's difficult.* J'admets que
c'est difficile.
♦ **Garlic doesn't agree with me.** Je ne
supporte pas l'ail.

agreed ADJECTIVE
convenu ◊ *at the agreed time* au
moment convenu

agreement NOUN
l' accord MASC
♦ **to be in agreement** être d'accord
◊ *Everybody was in agreement with
me.* Tout le monde était d'accord avec
moi.

agricultural ADJECTIVE
agricole

agriculture NOUN
l' agriculture FEM

ahead ADVERB
devant ◊ *She looked straight ahead.*
Elle regardait droit devant elle.
♦ **ahead of time** en avance
♦ **to plan ahead** organiser à l'avance
♦ **Our team is 5 points ahead.** Notre
équipe a cinq points d'avance.
♦ **Go ahead!** Allez-y!

aid NOUN
♦ **in aid of charity** au profit
d'associations caritatives

AIDS NOUN
le sida

to **aim** VERB
| see also **aim** NOUN |
[1] pointer ◊ *He aimed his flashlight
at me.* Il a pointé sa lampe de poche
sur moi.
[2] viser ◊ *Aim at the target.* Vise la
cible.

③ avoir l'intention de ◊ *We aim to leave at 5 o'clock.* Nous avons l'intention de partir à cinq heures.
♦ **The film is aimed at children.** Le film est destiné aux enfants.

aim NOUN

see also **aim** VERB

l' objectif MASC ◊ *The aim of the festival is to raise money.* L'objectif du festival est de collecter des fonds.
♦ **My aim is bad.** Je vise mal.

air NOUN
l' air MASC ◊ *to get some fresh air* prendre l'air
♦ **by air** en avion ◊ *I prefer to travel by air.* Je préfère voyager en avion.

air bag NOUN
le sac gonflable

air-conditioned ADJECTIVE
climatisé

air conditioning NOUN
la climatisation

Air Force NOUN
l' armée de l'air FEM

airline NOUN
la compagnie aérienne

airmail NOUN
♦ **by airmail** par avion

airplane NOUN
l' avion MASC

airport NOUN
l' aéroport MASC

aisle NOUN
① l' allée FEM (*theatre, supermarket*)
② le couloir (*airplane*)

alarm NOUN
l' alarme FEM (*warning*)
♦ **a fire alarm** un avertisseur d'incendie

alarm clock NOUN
le réveil

Alberta
l' Alberta FEM

album NOUN
l' album MASC

alcohol NOUN
l' alcool MASC

alcoholic NOUN

see also **alcoholic** ADJECTIVE

l' alcoolique MASC/FEM ◊ *a clinic for alcoholics* une clinique pour les alcooliques

alcoholic ADJECTIVE

see also **alcoholic** NOUN

alcoolisé ◊ *alcoholic drinks* des boissons alcoolisées

alert ADJECTIVE
① (*bright*)
vif MASC
vive FEM ◊ *a very alert baby* un bébé très vif
② vigilant (*paying attention*) ◊ *We must stay alert.* Nous devons rester vigilants.

alibi NOUN
l' alibi MASC

alien NOUN
l' extra-terrestre MASC/FEM (*from outer space*)

alike ADVERB
♦ **to look alike** se ressembler ◊ *The two sisters look alike.* Les deux sœurs se ressemblent.

alive ADJECTIVE
vivant

all ADJECTIVE, PRONOUN, ADVERB
tout
(MASC PL tous) ◊ *all the time* tout le temps ◊ *I ate all of it.* J'ai tout mangé. ◊ *all day* toute la journée ◊ *all the books* tous les livres ◊ *all the girls* toutes les filles
♦ **All of us went.** Nous y sommes tous allés.
♦ **after all** après tout ◊ *After all, nobody can make us go.* Après tout, personne ne peut nous obliger à y aller.
♦ **all alone** tout seul ◊ *She's all alone.* Elle est toute seule.
♦ **not at all** pas du tout ◊ *I'm not tired at all.* Je ne suis pas du tout fatigué.
♦ **The score is 5 all.** Le score est de cinq partout.

allergic ADJECTIVE
allergique
♦ **to be allergic to something** être allergique à quelque chose ◊ *I'm allergic to cat hair.* Je suis allergique aux poils de chat.

allergy NOUN
l' allergie FEM ◊ *I have allergies.* J'ai des allergies.
♦ **a food allergy** une allergie alimentaire

alley NOUN
la ruelle

✳ **allophone** ADJECTIVE

see also **allophone** NOUN
allophone MASC/FEM

✳ **allophone** NOUN

see also **allophone** ADJECTIVE
l' allophone MASC/FEM ◊ *Allophones speak neither French nor English as their first language.* La langue maternelle des allophones n'est ni le français ni l'anglais.

to **allow** VERB
- ♦ **to be allowed to do something** être autorisé à faire quelque chose ◊ *He's not allowed to go out at night.* Il n'est pas autorisé à sortir le soir.
- ♦ **to allow somebody to do something** permettre à quelqu'un de faire quelque chose ◊ *His mom allowed him to go out.* Sa mère lui a permis de sortir.

allowance NOUN
l' argent de poche MASC ◊ *Do you get a weekly allowance?* Est-ce que tu reçois de l'argent de poche chaque semaine?

all right ADVERB
1 bien (*okay*) ◊ *Everything turned out all right.* Tout s'est bien terminé.
- ♦ **Are you all right?** Ça va?
2 pas mal (*not bad*) ◊ *The film was all right.* Le film n'était pas mal.
3 d'accord (*when agreeing*) ◊ *"We'll talk about it later." "All right."* « On en reparlera plus tard. » « D'accord. »
- ♦ **Is that all right with you?** Tu es d'accord?

almond NOUN
l' amande FEM

almost ADVERB
presque ◊ *I'm almost finished.* J'ai presque fini.

alone ADJECTIVE, ADVERB
seul ◊ *He lives alone.* Il habite seul.
- ♦ **to leave somebody alone** laisser quelqu'un tranquille ◊ *Leave me alone!* Laisse-moi tranquille!
- ♦ **to leave something alone** ne pas toucher à quelque chose ◊ *Leave my things alone!* Ne touche pas à mes affaires!

along PREPOSITION, ADVERB
le long de ◊ *I was walking along the beach.* Je me promenais le long de la plage.
- ♦ **all along** depuis le début ◊ *He was lying to me all along.* Il m'a menti depuis le début.

aloud ADVERB
à haute voix ◊ *He read the poem aloud.* Il a lu le poème à haute voix.

alphabet NOUN
l' alphabet MASC

alphabetical ADJECTIVE
alphabétique ◊ *in alphabetical order* en ordre alphabétique

already ADVERB
déjà ◊ *She had already gone.* Elle était déjà partie.

also ADVERB
aussi

altar NOUN
l' autel MASC

to **alter** VERB
changer

alternate ADJECTIVE
- ♦ **on alternate days** tous les deux jours

alternative NOUN

> see also **alternative** ADJECTIVE

le choix ◊ *You have no alternative.* Tu n'a pas le choix.
- ♦ **Fruit is a healthy alternative to chocolate.** Les fruits sont plus sains que le chocolat.
- ♦ **There are several alternatives.** Il y a plusieurs possibilités.

alternative ADJECTIVE

> see also **alternative** NOUN

autre ◊ *They made alternative plans.* Ils ont pris d'autres dispositions.
- ♦ **an alternative solution** une solution de rechange
- ♦ **alternative medicine** la médecine douce

alternatively ADVERB
- ♦ **Alternatively, we could just stay at home.** On pourrait aussi rester à la maison.

although CONJUNCTION
bien que

> **bien que** has to be followed by a verb in the subjunctive.

◊ *Although she was tired, she stayed up late.* Bien qu'elle soit fatiguée, elle s'est couchée tard.

altogether ADVERB
1 en tout (*in total*) ◊ *You owe me $20 altogether.* Tu me dois vingt dollars en tout.
2 tout à fait (*completely*) ◊ *I'm not altogether happy with your work.* Je ne suis pas tout à fait satisfait de votre travail.

aluminum NOUN
l' aluminium MASC

always ADVERB
toujours ◊ *He's always grumbling.* Il est toujours en train de ronchonner.

am VERB *see* **be**

a.m. ABBREVIATION
du matin ◊ *at 4 a.m.* à quatre heures du matin

amateur NOUN
l' amateur MASC
- ♦ **amateur sports** le sport amateur

amazed ADJECTIVE
stupéfait ◊ *their amazed parents* leurs parents stupéfaits ◊ *I was*

A

amazed that I managed to do it.
J'étais stupéfait d'avoir réussi.

amazing ADJECTIVE
 ① stupéfiant (*surprising*) ◊ *That's amazing news!* C'est une nouvelle stupéfiante!
 ② (*excellent*)
 exceptionnel MASC
 exceptionnelle FEM ◊ *My dad's an amazing cook.* Mon père est un cuisinier exceptionnel.

ambassador NOUN
 l' ambassadeur MASC
 l' ambassadrice FEM

ambition NOUN
 l' ambition FEM

ambitious ADJECTIVE
 ambitieux MASC
 ambitieuse FEM ◊ *She's very ambitious.* Elle est très ambitieuse.

ambulance NOUN
 l' ambulance FEM

amenities PL NOUN
 les aménagements MASC
 ♦ **The hotel has very good amenities.** L'hôtel est très bien aménagé.

among PREPOSITION
 parmi ◊ *There were six children among them.* Il y avait six enfants parmi eux.
 ♦ **We were among friends.** Nous étions entre amis.
 ♦ **among other things** entre autres

amount NOUN
 ① la somme ◊ *a large amount of money* une grosse somme d'argent
 ② la quantité
 ♦ **a huge amount of rice** une énorme quantité de riz

amp NOUN
 ① l' ampère MASC (*of electricity*)
 ② l' amplificateur MASC (*amplifier*)

amplifier NOUN
 l' amplificateur MASC (*for hi-fi*)

to **amuse** VERB
 amuser ◊ *She was not amused by their rude jokes.* Leurs blagues grossières ne l'ont pas amusée.

amusement arcade NOUN
 la salle de jeux électroniques

an ARTICLE *see* **a**

analysis NOUN
 l' analyse FEM

to **analyze** VERB
 analyser

ancestor NOUN
 l' ancêtre MASC/FEM

anchor NOUN

l' ancre FEM

ancient ADJECTIVE
 ① antique (*civilization*) ◊ *ancient Greece* la Grèce antique
 ② (*custom, building*)
 ancien MASC
 ancienne FEM ◊ *an ancient monument* un monument ancien

and CONJUNCTION
 et ◊ *you and me* toi et moi ◊ *2 and 2 are 4* deux et deux font quatre
 ♦ **Please try and come!** Essaie de venir!
 ♦ **He talked and talked.** Il n'a pas arrêté de parler.
 ♦ **better and better** de mieux en mieux

angel NOUN
 l' ange MASC

anger NOUN
 la colère

angle NOUN
 l' angle MASC

✱ **Anglophone** NOUN
 | *see also* **Anglophone** ADJECTIVE |
 l' anglophone MASC/FEM ◊ *A lot of Anglophones live in Montréal.* Beaucoup d'anglophones habitent à Montréal.

✱ **Anglophone** ADJECTIVE
 | *see also* **Anglophone** NOUN |
 anglophone ◊ *an Anglophone community* une communauté anglophone

angry ADJECTIVE
 en colère ◊ *Dad looks very angry.* Papa a l'air très en colère.
 ♦ **to be angry with somebody** être furieux contre quelqu'un ◊ *Mom's really angry with you.* Maman est vraiment furieuse contre toi.
 ♦ **to get angry** se fâcher

animal NOUN
 l' animal MASC
 (PL les animaux)

animation NOUN
 ① le film d'animation ◊ *We went to see the new 3D animation.* Nous sommes allés voir le nouveau film d'animation 3D.
 ② l' animation FEM ◊ *She's studying animation.* Elle étudie l'animation.
 ♦ **computer animation** l'animatique FEM

ankle NOUN
 la cheville

anniversary NOUN
 l' anniversaire MASC ◊ *a wedding anniversary* un anniversaire de mariage

to **announce** VERB

☞

annoncer

announcement NOUN
l' annonce FEM

to **annoy** VERB
agacer ◊ *He's really annoying me.* Il m'agace vraiment.
♦ **to get annoyed** se fâcher ◊ *Don't get so annoyed!* Ne vous fâchez pas!

annoying ADJECTIVE
agaçant ◊ *It's really annoying.* C'est vraiment agaçant.

annual ADJECTIVE
annuel MASC
annuelle FEM ◊ *an annual meeting* une réunion annuelle

anorexia NOUN
l' anorexie FEM

another ADJECTIVE
un autre
une autre ◊ *Would you like another piece of cake?* Tu veux un autre morceau de gâteau? ◊ *Have you got another skirt?* Tu as une autre jupe?

to **answer** VERB

see also **answer** NOUN

répondre à ◊ *Can you answer my question?* Peux-tu répondre à ma question? ◊ *to answer the phone* répondre au téléphone
♦ **to answer the door** aller ouvrir ◊ *Can you answer the door please?* Tu peux aller ouvrir s'il te plaît?

answer NOUN

see also **answer** VERB

1 la réponse (*to question*)
2 la solution (*to problem*)

answering machine NOUN
le répondeur

ant NOUN
la fourmi

to **antagonize** VERB
contrarier ◊ *He didn't want to antagonize her.* Il ne voulait pas la contrarier.

Antarctic NOUN
l' Antarctique FEM

anthem NOUN
♦ **the national anthem** l'hymne national MASC ◊ *Our national anthem is "O Canada".* Notre hymne national est « Ô Canada ».

antibiotic NOUN
l' antibiotique MASC

antifreeze NOUN
l' antigel MASC

antique NOUN
l' antiquité FEM

♦ **an antique dealer** un marchand d'antiquités

antique shop NOUN
le magasin d'antiquités

antivirus software NOUN
le logiciel antivirus ◊ *to download free antivirus software* télécharger un logiciel antivirus gratuit

antlers PL NOUN
les bois MASC ◊ *The moose sheds its antlers every year.* Les bois de l'orignal tombent chaque année.

anxious ADJECTIVE
anxieux FEM SING ◊ *He's a little anxious about the test.* Il est un peu anxieux à propos du test.
♦ **to be anxious to do something** avoir hâte de faire quelque chose

any ADJECTIVE, PRONOUN, ADVERB

Use du, de la or des to translate any according to the gender of the French noun that follows it. du and de la become de l' when they're followed by a noun starting with a vowel.

1 du ◊ *Do you want any bread?* Tu veux du pain?
de la ◊ *Is there any ice cream?* Est-ce qu'il y a de la crème glacée?
de l' ◊ *Have you got any mineral water?* Avez-vous de l'eau minérale?
des ◊ *Do you have any CDs?* Avez-vous des DC?

If you want to say you don't have any of something, use de whatever the gender of the following noun is. de becomes d' when it comes before a noun starting with a vowel.

2 de ◊ *I don't have any books.* Je n'ai pas de livres.
d' ◊ *I don't have any money.* Je n'ai pas d'argent.

Use en where there is no noun after any.

3 en ◊ *Sorry, I don't have any.* Désolé, je n'en ai pas.
♦ **any more (1)** (*additional*) encore de ◊ *Would you like any more coffee?* Est-ce que tu veux encore du café?
♦ **any more (2)** (*no longer*) ne... plus ◊ *I don't see her any more.* Je ne la vois plus.

anybody PRONOUN
1 quelqu'un (*in question*) ◊ *Does anybody have a pen?* Est-ce que quelqu'un a un stylo?
2 n'importe qui (*no matter who*) ◊ *Anybody can learn to swim.* N'importe qui peut apprendre à nager.

*Use **ne... personne** in a negative sentence. **ne** comes before the verb, **personne** after it.*

③ ne... personne ◊ *I can't see anybody.* Je ne vois personne.

anyone PRONOUN

① quelqu'un (*in question*) ◊ *Has anyone got a pen?* Est-ce que quelqu'un a un stylo?
② n'importe qui (*no matter who*) ◊ *Anyone can learn to swim.* N'importe qui peut apprendre à nager.

*Use **ne... personne** in a negative sentence. **ne** comes before the verb, **personne** after it.*

③ ne... personne ◊ *I can't see anyone.* Je ne vois personne.

anything PRONOUN

① quelque chose (*in question*) ◊ *Would you like anything to eat?* Tu veux manger quelque chose?
② n'importe quoi (*no matter what*) ◊ *Anything could happen.* Il pourrait arriver n'importe quoi.

*Use **ne... rien** in a negative sentence. **ne** comes before the verb, **rien** after it.*

③ ne... rien ◊ *I can't hear anything.* Je n'entends rien.

anyway ADVERB

de toute façon ◊ *He doesn't want to go out, and anyway he's not allowed.* Il ne veut pas sortir et de toute façon il n'y est pas autorisé.

anywhere ADVERB

① quelque part (*in question*) ◊ *Have you seen my coat anywhere?* Est-ce que tu as vu mon manteau quelque part?
② n'importe où ◊ *You can buy stamps almost anywhere.* On peut acheter des timbres presque n'importe où.

*Use **ne... nulle part** in a negative sentence. **ne** comes before the verb, **nulle part** after it.*

③ ne... nulle part ◊ *I can't find it anywhere.* Je ne le trouve nulle part.

apart ADVERB

♦ **The two towns are 10 kilometres apart.** Les deux villes sont à dix kilomètres l'une de l'autre.
♦ **apart from** à part ◊ *Apart from that, everything's fine.* À part ça, tout va bien.

apartment NOUN

l' appartement MASC

to **apologize** VERB

s'excuser ◊ *He apologized for being late.* Il s'est excusé de son retard.
♦ **I apologize!** Je m'excuse.

apology NOUN

les excuses FEM PL

apostrophe NOUN

l' apostrophe FEM

apparatus NOUN

① le matériel (*in lab*)
② les agrès MASC PL (*in gym*)

apparent ADJECTIVE

apparent

apparently ADVERB

apparemment

to **appeal** VERB

> *see also* **appeal** NOUN

lancer un appel ◊ *They appealed for help.* Ils ont lancé un appel au secours.
♦ **Greece doesn't appeal to me.** Ça ne me tente pas d'aller en Grèce.
♦ **Does that appeal to you?** Ça te tente?

appeal NOUN

> *see also* **appeal** VERB

l' appel MASC ◊ *They have launched an appeal.* Ils ont lancé un appel.

to **appear** VERB

① apparaître (*come into view*) ◊ *The bus appeared around the corner.* L'autobus est apparu au coin de la rue.
♦ **to appear on TV** passer à la télé
② paraître (*seem*) ◊ *She appeared to be asleep.* Elle paraissait dormir.

appearance NOUN

l' apparence FEM (*looks*) ◊ *He takes great care over his appearance.* Il prend grand soin de son apparence.

appendicitis NOUN

l' appendicite FEM

appetite NOUN

l' appétit MASC

to **applaud** VERB

applaudir

applause NOUN

les applaudissements MASC PL

apple NOUN

la pomme
♦ **an apple tree** un pommier

applicant NOUN

le candidat
la candidate ◊ *There were a hundred applicants for the job.* Il y avait cent candidats pour ce poste.

application NOUN

l' application FEM (*computer*) ◊ *to*

☞

open an application lancer une application
♦ **a job application** une demande d'emploi

application form NOUN
1 le dossier de candidature (*for job*)
2 la demande d'admission (*college or university*)

to **apply** VERB
♦ **to apply for a job** poser sa candidature à un poste
♦ **to apply to** (*be relevant*) s'appliquer à ◊ *This rule doesn't apply to us.* Ce règlement ne s'applique pas à nous.

appointment NOUN
le rendez-vous ◊ *I have a dental appointment.* J'ai rendez-vous chez le dentiste.

to **appreciate** VERB
être reconnaissant de ◊ *I really appreciate your help.* Je vous suis extrêmement reconnaissant de votre aide.

apprentice NOUN
l' apprenti MASC
l' apprentie FEM

to **approach** VERB
1 s'approcher de (*get nearer to*) ◊ *She approached the house.* Elle s'est approchée de la maison.
2 aborder (*tackle*) ◊ *to approach a problem* aborder un problème

appropriate ADJECTIVE
approprié ◊ *That dress isn't very appropriate for an interview.* Cette robe n'est pas très appropriée pour une entrevue.

approval NOUN
l' approbation FEM

to **approve** VERB
♦ **to approve of** approuver ◊ *I don't approve of your choice.* Je n'approuve pas ton choix.
♦ **They didn't approve of his girlfriend.** Sa copine ne leur a pas plu.

approximate ADJECTIVE
approximatif MASC
approximative FEM

apricot NOUN
l' abricot MASC

April NOUN
avril MASC
♦ **in April** en avril
♦ **April Fool's Day** le premier avril

apron NOUN
le tablier

Aquarius NOUN
le Verseau ◊ *I'm Aquarius.* Je suis Verseau.

Arabic NOUN
l' arabe MASC

arch NOUN
l' arc MASC

archaeologist NOUN
l' archéologue MASC/FEM ◊ *He's an archaeologist.* Il est archéologue.

archaeology NOUN
l' archéologie FEM

architect NOUN
l' architecte MASC/FEM ◊ *She's an architect.* Elle est architecte.

architecture NOUN
l' architecture FEM

Arctic NOUN
l' Arctique MASC

are VERB *see* **be**

area NOUN
1 la région ◊ *I live in the Kingston area.* J'habite dans la région de Kingston.
2 le quartier ◊ *This is my favourite area of Montréal.* C'est le quartier de Montréal que je préfère.
3 la superficie ◊ *The field has an area of 1500 m².* Le champ a une superficie de mille cinq cent mètres carrés.

area code NOUN
l' indicatif régional MASC

arena NOUN
l' aréna MASC ◊ *They're building a new arena in Timmins.* On construit un nouvel aréna à Timmins.

to **argue** VERB
se disputer ◊ *They never stop arguing.* Ils n'arrêtent pas de se disputer.

argument NOUN
♦ **to have an argument** se disputer ◊ *They had an argument.* Ils se sont disputés.

Aries NOUN
le Bélier ◊ *I'm Aries.* Je suis Bélier.

arm NOUN
le bras

armchair NOUN
le fauteuil

armour NOUN
l' armure FEM

army NOUN
l' armée FEM

around PREPOSITION, ADVERB
1 autour de ◊ *She wore a scarf around her neck.* Elle portait une écharpe autour du cou.
2 environ (*approximately*) ◊ *It costs*

around $100. Cela coûte environ cent dollars.

③ <u>vers</u> (*date, time*) ◊ *Let's meet at around 8 p.m.* Retrouvons-nous vers vingt heures.

♦ **around here (1)** (*nearby*) près d'ici ◊ *Is there a drugstore around here?* Est-ce qu'il y a une pharmacie près d'ici?

♦ **around here (2)** (*in this area*) dans les parages ◊ *He lives around here.* Il habite dans les parages.

to **arrange** VERB

♦ **to arrange to do something** prévoir de faire quelque chose ◊ *They arranged to go out together on Friday.* Ils ont prévu de sortir ensemble vendredi.

♦ **to arrange a meeting** convenir d'un rendez-vous ◊ *Can we arrange a meeting?* Pouvons-nous convenir d'un rendez-vous?

♦ **to arrange a party** organiser une fête

arrangement NOUN

l' <u>arrangement</u> MASC (*plan*)

♦ **They made arrangements to go out on Friday night.** Ils ont organisé une sortie vendredi soir.

to **arrest** VERB

see also **arrest** NOUN

<u>arrêter</u> ◊ *The police have arrested 5 people.* La police a arrêté cinq personnes.

arrest NOUN

see also **arrest** VERB

l' <u>arrestation</u> FEM ◊ *You're under arrest!* Vous êtes en état d'arrestation!

arrival NOUN

l' <u>arrivée</u> FEM

♦ **to welcome the new arrivals** accueillir les nouveaux venus

to **arrive** VERB

<u>arriver</u> ◊ *I arrived at 5 o'clock.* Je suis arrivé à cinq heures.

arrogant ADJECTIVE

<u>arrogant</u>

arrow NOUN

la <u>flèche</u>

art NOUN

l' <u>art</u> MASC

artery NOUN

l' <u>artère</u> FEM

art gallery NOUN

la <u>galerie d'art</u>

article NOUN

l' <u>article</u> MASC ◊ *a newspaper article* un article de journal

artificial ADJECTIVE

artificiel MASC
<u>artificielle</u> FEM

artist NOUN

l' <u>artiste</u> MASC/FEM ◊ *She's an artist.* C'est une artiste.

artistic ADJECTIVE

<u>artistique</u>

as CONJUNCTION, ADVERB

① <u>au moment où</u> (*while*) ◊ *He came in as I was leaving.* Il est arrivé au moment où je partais.

② <u>puisque</u> (*since*) ◊ *As it's a holiday, you can sleep in.* Tu peux faire la grasse matinée, puisque c'est un jour de congé.

♦ **as... as** aussi... que ◊ *I'm as tall as he is.* Je suis aussi grand que lui.

♦ **twice as... as** deux fois plus... que ◊ *Her coat cost twice as much as mine.* Son manteau a coûté deux fois plus cher que le mien.

♦ **as much... as** autant... que ◊ *I don't have as much money as you.* Je n'ai pas autant d'argent que toi.

♦ **as soon as possible** dès que possible ◊ *I'll do it as soon as possible.* Je le ferai dès que possible.

♦ **as of tomorrow** à partir de demain ◊ *As of tomorrow, the store will stay open until 10 p.m.* À partir de demain, le magasin restera ouvert jusqu'à vingt-deux heures.

♦ **as though** comme si ◊ *She acted as though she hadn't seen me.* Elle a fait comme si elle ne m'avait pas vu.

♦ **as if** comme si

♦ **He works as a waiter.** Il travaille comme serveur.

ASAP ABBREVIATION (= *as soon as possible*)

<u>dès que possible</u>

ashamed ADJECTIVE

♦ **to be ashamed** avoir honte ◊ *I was ashamed of my rude behaviour.* J'avais honte d'avoir été si impoli.

ashtray NOUN

le <u>cendrier</u>

to **ask** VERB

① <u>demander</u> (*inquire, request*) ◊ *"Are you finished?" she asked.* « Tu as fini? » a-t-elle demandé.

♦ **to ask somebody something** demander quelque chose à quelqu'un ◊ *He asked her how old she was.* Il lui a demandé quel âge elle avait.

♦ **to ask for something** demander quelque chose ◊ *He asked for a cup of tea.* Il a demandé une tasse de thé.

♦ **to ask somebody to do something** demander à quelqu'un de faire quelque chose ◊ *She asked him to do*

☞

the shopping. Elle lui a demandé de faire les courses.
♦ **to ask about something** se renseigner sur quelque chose ◊ *I asked about tourist attractions.* Je me suis renseigné sur les attractions touristiques.
♦ **to ask somebody a question** poser une question à quelqu'un
② inviter ◊ *Have you asked him to the party?* Est-ce que tu l'as invité à la fête?
♦ **He asked her out.** (*on a date*) Il lui a demandé de sortir avec lui.

asleep ADJECTIVE
♦ **to be asleep** dormir ◊ *She's asleep.* Elle dort.
♦ **to fall asleep** s'endormir ◊ *I fell asleep in front of the TV.* Je me suis endormi devant la télé.

asparagus NOUN
les asperges FEM PL

aspect NOUN
l' aspect MASC

aspirin NOUN
l' aspirine FEM

to **assemble** VERB
① assembler ◊ *You have to assemble the bookshelf yourself.* Tu dois assembler l'étagère toi-même.
② se réunir ◊ *The students assembled in the gym.* Les élèves se sont réunis dans le gymnase.

assembly NOUN
la réunion d'école (*school*) ◊ *The winner was announced in the assembly on Friday.* Le nom du gagnant a été annoncé durant la réunion d'école vendredi.

✹ **Assembly of First Nations** NOUN
l' Assemblée des Premières Nations FEM

asset NOUN
l' atout MASC ◊ *Her experience will be an asset to the firm.* Son expérience sera un atout pour l'entreprise.

assignment NOUN
le devoir (*in school*)

assistance NOUN
l' aide FEM

> Be careful not to translate **assistance** by *l'assistance*.

assistant NOUN
① (*in store*)
le vendeur
la vendeuse
② (*helper*)
l' assistant MASC
l' assistante FEM

association NOUN
l' association FEM

assorted ADJECTIVE
assorti ◊ *assorted chocolates* des chocolats assortis

assortment NOUN
l' assortiment MASC

to **assume** VERB
supposer ◊ *I assume you won't be coming.* Je suppose que tu ne viendras pas.

to **assure** VERB
assurer ◊ *He assured me he was coming.* Il m'a assuré qu'il viendrait.

asthma NOUN
l' asthme MASC ◊ *I have asthma.* J'ai de l'asthme.

to **astonish** VERB
étonner

astonishing ADJECTIVE
étonnant

astrology NOUN
l' astrologie FEM

astronaut NOUN
l' astronaute MASC/FEM

astronomer NOUN
l' astronome MASC/FEM

astronomy NOUN
l' astronomie FEM

asylum seeker NOUN
① le demandeur d'asile
② la demandeuse d'asile

at PREPOSITION

> *à + **le** becomes **au**, à + **les** becomes **aux**.*

à ◊ *at 4 o'clock* à quatre heures
◊ *at Christmas* à Noël ◊ *at 50 km/h* à cinquante km/h ◊ *at home* à la maison ◊ *two at a time* deux à la fois
◊ *at school* à l'école
au ◊ *at the office* au bureau
aux ◊ *at the races* aux courses
♦ **at night** la nuit

ate VERB *see* **eat**

athlete NOUN
l' athlète MASC/FEM
♦ **athlete's foot** pied d'athlète

athletic ADJECTIVE
athlétique

Atlantic Provinces PL NOUN
les provinces atlantiques FEM

atlas NOUN
l' atlas MASC

atmosphere NOUN
① l' atmosphère FEM
② l' ambiance FEM ◊ *J'aime*

l'ambiance de ce café. I like the atmosphere in this café.

atom NOUN
l' <u>atome</u> MASC

atomic ADJECTIVE
<u>atomique</u>

to **attach** VERB
<u>fixer</u> ◊ *He attached a rope to the car.* Il a fixé une corde à la voiture.
♦ **Please find attached...** Veuillez trouver ci-joint...

attached ADJECTIVE
♦ **to be attached to** être attaché à ◊ *He's very attached to his family.* Il est très attaché à sa famille.

attachment NOUN
la <u>pièce jointe</u> (*email*)

to **attack** VERB

> see also **attack** NOUN

<u>attaquer</u> ◊ *The dog attacked her.* Le chien l'a attaquée.

attack NOUN

> see also **attack** VERB

l' <u>attaque</u> FEM

attempt NOUN

> see also **attempt** VERB

la <u>tentative</u> ◊ *She gave up after several attempts.* Elle y a renoncé après plusieurs tentatives.

to **attempt** VERB

> see also **attempt** NOUN

♦ **to attempt to do something** essayer de faire quelque chose ◊ *I attempted to write a song.* J'ai essayé d'écrire une chanson.

to **attend** VERB
<u>assister à</u> ◊ *to attend a meeting* assister à une réunion

> *Be careful not to translate* **to attend** *by* **attendre**.

attendance NOUN
♦ **to take attendance** prendre les présences

attention NOUN
l' <u>attention</u> FEM
♦ **to pay attention to** faire attention à ◊ *He didn't pay attention to what I was saying.* Il ne faisait pas attention à ce que je disais.

attic NOUN
le <u>grenier</u>

attitude NOUN
l' <u>attitude</u> FEM (*way of thinking*) ◊ *I really don't like your attitude!* Je n'aime pas du tout ton attitude!

to **attract** VERB
<u>attirer</u> ◊ *Niagara Falls attracts lots of tourists.* Les chutes Niagara attirent de nombreux touristes.

attraction NOUN
l' <u>attraction</u> FEM ◊ *a tourist attraction* une attraction touristique

attractive ADJECTIVE
<u>séduisant</u> ◊ *She's very attractive.* Elle est très séduisante.

auction NOUN
la <u>vente aux enchères</u>

audience NOUN
les <u>spectateurs</u> MASC PL (*in theatre*)

audio ADJECTIVE
<u>audio</u> MASC, FEM, PL ◊ *audio files* des fichiers audio ◊ *an audio clip* un audioclip ◊ *audio equipment* le matériel audio

audition NOUN

> see also **audition** VERB

l' <u>audition</u> FEM

to **audition** VERB

> see also **audition** NOUN

<u>auditionner</u>

August NOUN
<u>août</u> MASC
♦ **in August** en août

aunt, aunty NOUN
la <u>tante</u> ◊ *my aunt* ma tante

author NOUN
l' <u>auteur</u> MASC
l' <u>auteure</u> FEM

autobiography NOUN
l' <u>autobiographie</u> FEM

autograph NOUN
l' <u>autographe</u> MASC

automatic ADJECTIVE
<u>automatique</u> ◊ *an automatic door* une porte automatique

autumn NOUN
l' <u>automne</u> MASC
♦ **in autumn** en automne

available ADJECTIVE
<u>disponible</u> ◊ *Free brochures are available on request.* Des brochures gratuites sont disponibles sur demande. ◊ *Is he available today?* Est-ce qu'il est disponible aujourd'hui?

avalanche NOUN
l' <u>avalanche</u> FEM

avenue NOUN
l' <u>avenue</u> FEM

average NOUN

> see also **average** ADJECTIVE

☞

la moyenne ◊ *on average* en
moyenne

average ADJECTIVE

> *see also* **average** NOUN

moyen MASC
moyenne FEM ◊ *the average price* le
prix moyen

avocado NOUN
l' avocat MASC

to **avoid** VERB
éviter ◊ *We avoid him when he's in a
bad mood.* Nous l'évitons lorsqu'il est
de mauvaise humeur.

♦ **to avoid doing something** éviter de
faire quelque chose ◊ *Avoid going
out on your own at night.* Évite de
sortir seul le soir.

awake ADJECTIVE

♦ **to be awake** être réveillé ◊ *Is she
awake?* Elle est réveillée?

♦ **He was still awake.** Il ne dormait pas
encore.

award NOUN
le prix ◊ *She won an award.* Elle a
remporté un prix. ◊ *the award for the
best actor* le prix du meilleur acteur

aware ADJECTIVE

♦ **to be aware of something** être
conscient de quelque chose

away ADJECTIVE, ADVERB
absent (*not here*) ◊ *She's away today.*
Elle est absente aujourd'hui.

♦ **He's away for a week.** Il est parti pour
une semaine.

♦ **The town's 2 kilometres away.** La ville
est à deux kilomètres d'ici.

♦ **The coast is 2 hours away by car.** La
côte est à deux heures de route.

♦ **Go away!** Va-t'en!

♦ **to put something away** ranger
quelque chose ◊ *He put the dishes
away in the cupboard.* Il a rangé la
vaisselle dans le placard.

away game NOUN
le match à l'extérieur
(PL les matchs à l'extérieur)

awful ADJECTIVE
affreux MASC
affreuse FEM ◊ *That's awful!* C'est
affreux!

♦ **an awful lot of...** énormément de...

awkward ADJECTIVE
1 délicat (*difficult to deal with*) ◊ *an
awkward situation* une situation
délicate
2 gênant (*embarrassing*) ◊ *an
awkward question* une question
gênante

♦ **It's a bit awkward for me to come
today.** Ce n'est pas très pratique pour
moi de venir aujourd'hui.

axe NOUN
la hache

B

BA NOUN
le baccalauréat
♦ **a BA in French** un baccalauréat en français

baby NOUN
le bébé

to **babysit** VERB
garder des enfants

babysitter NOUN
le gardien d'enfants
la gardienne d'enfants

babysitting NOUN
la garde d'enfants

bachelor NOUN
le célibataire ◊ *He's a bachelor.* Il est célibataire.

back NOUN

see also **back** ADJECTIVE, VERB

[1] le dos (*of person, horse, book*)
[2] l' arrière MASC (*of car, house*) ◊ *in the back* à l'arrière
[3] le verso (*of page*) ◊ *on the back* au verso
[4] le fond (*of room, garden*) ◊ *at the back* au fond

back ADJECTIVE, ADVERB

see also **back** NOUN, VERB

arrière MASC, FEM, PL ◊ *the back seat* le siège arrière ◊ *the back wheel of my bike* la roue arrière de mon vélo
♦ **the back door** la porte de derrière
♦ **to get back** rentrer ◊ *What time did you get back?* À quelle heure est-ce que tu es rentré?
♦ **We went there by bus and walked back.** Nous y sommes allés en autobus et nous sommes rentrés à pied.
♦ **She's not back yet.** Elle n'est pas encore rentrée.
♦ **to call somebody back** rappeler quelqu'un ◊ *I'll call back later.* Je rappellerai plus tard.

to **back** VERB

see also **back** NOUN, ADJECTIVE

soutenir (*support*) ◊ *I'm backing the other candidate.* Je soutiens l'autre candidat.
♦ **to back out** se désister ◊ *They promised to help and then backed out.* Ils avaient promis de nous aider et ils se sont désistés.
♦ **to back somebody up** soutenir quelqu'un

backache NOUN
le mal au dos ◊ *to have backache* avoir mal au dos

to **backfire** VERB
avoir l'effet inverse ◊ *Her tactics could backfire on her.* Sa stratégie pourrait avoir l'effet inverse.

background NOUN
[1] l' arrière-plan MASC (*of picture*) ◊ *a house in the background* une maison à l'arrière-plan
♦ **background noise** les bruits de fond MASC PL
[2] le milieu
(PL les milieux) ◊ *his family background* son milieu familial

backhand NOUN
le revers

backing NOUN
le soutien (*support*)

backpack NOUN
le sac à dos

backpacker NOUN
[1] (*globetrotter*)
le routard
la routarde
[2] (*hiker*)
le randonneur
la randonneuse

backpacking NOUN
♦ **to go backpacking** voyager sac au dos

back pain NOUN
le mal au dos ◊ *to have back pain* avoir mal au dos

backside NOUN
le derrière

backslash NOUN
la barre oblique inverse

backstroke NOUN
le dos crawlé

backup NOUN
le soutien (*support*)
♦ **a backup file** une sauvegarde

backwards ADVERB
en arrière ◊ *to take a step backwards* faire un pas en arrière
♦ **to fall backwards** tomber à la renverse

backyard NOUN
la cour

bacon NOUN
[1] le bacon (*British type*) ◊ *bacon and*

☞

eggs des œufs au bacon
2 le <u>lard</u> (*French type*)

bad ADJECTIVE
1 <u>mauvais</u> ◊ *a bad film* un mauvais film ◊ *the bad weather* le mauvais temps ◊ *to be in a bad mood* être de mauvaise humeur
♦ **to be bad at something** être mauvais en quelque chose ◊ *I'm really bad at math.* Je suis vraiment mauvais en maths.
2 <u>grave</u> (*serious*) ◊ *a bad accident* un accident grave
3 <u>vilain</u> (*naughty*) ◊ *bad words* vilains mots
♦ **to go bad** (*food*) se gâter
♦ **I feel bad about it.** Ça m'ennuie.
♦ **not bad** pas mal ◊ *That's not bad at all.* Ce n'est pas mal du tout.

badge NOUN
le <u>badge</u>

badly ADVERB
<u>mal</u> ◊ *badly paid* mal payé
♦ **badly wounded** grièvement blessé
♦ **He badly needs a rest.** Il a sérieusement besoin de se reposer.

badminton NOUN
le <u>badminton</u> ◊ *to play badminton* jouer au badminton

bad-tempered ADJECTIVE
♦ **to be bad-tempered (1)** (*by nature*) avoir mauvais caractère ◊ *She's a really bad-tempered person.* Elle a vraiment mauvais caractère.
♦ **to be bad-tempered (2)** (*temporarily*) être de mauvaise humeur ◊ *He was really bad-tempered yesterday.* Il était vraiment de mauvaise humeur hier.

Baffin Island NOUN
l' <u>île de Baffin</u> FEM

baffled ADJECTIVE
<u>déconcerté</u>

bag NOUN
le <u>sac</u>

bagel NOUN
le <u>baguel</u> ◊ *a toasted bagel* un baguel grillé

baggage NOUN
les <u>bagages</u> MASC PL

baggy ADJECTIVE
<u>ample</u>

bagpipes PL NOUN
la <u>cornemuse</u> SING ◊ *She plays the bagpipes.* Elle joue de la cornemuse.

to **bake** VERB
♦ **to bake a cake** faire un gâteau

baked ADJECTIVE
<u>cuit au four</u> ◊ *baked potatoes* les pommes de terre cuites au four FEM

♦ **baked beans** les haricots au lard MASC

baker NOUN
le <u>boulanger</u>
la <u>boulangère</u> ◊ *She's a baker.* Elle est boulangère.

bakery NOUN
la <u>boulangerie</u>

baking ADJECTIVE
♦ **It's baking in here!** Il fait une chaleur torride ici!

balance NOUN
l' <u>équilibre</u> MASC ◊ *to lose one's balance* perdre l'équilibre

balanced ADJECTIVE
<u>équilibré</u>

balcony NOUN
le <u>balcon</u>

bald ADJECTIVE
<u>chauve</u>

ball NOUN
1 la <u>balle</u> (*tennis, golf, baseball*)
2 le <u>ballon</u> (*football, soccer*)

ballet NOUN
le <u>ballet</u> ◊ *We went to a ballet.* Nous sommes allés voir un ballet.
♦ **ballet lessons** les cours de danse classique

ballet dancer NOUN
le <u>danseur classique</u>
la <u>danseuse classique</u>

ballet shoes PL NOUN
les <u>chaussons de danse</u> MASC PL

balloon NOUN
le <u>ballon</u> (*for parties*)
♦ **a hot-air balloon** une montgolfière

ballpoint pen NOUN
le <u>stylo à bille</u>

ban NOUN
| see also **ban** VERB |
l' <u>interdiction</u> FEM
♦ **a ban on video games** une interdiction de jeux vidéo

to **ban** VERB
| see also **ban** NOUN |
<u>interdire</u>

banana NOUN
la <u>banane</u> ◊ *a banana peel* une peau de banane

band NOUN
1 le <u>groupe</u> (*rock band*)
2 la <u>fanfare</u> (*brass band*)
❀ 3 la <u>bande</u> (*First Nations*)
❀ ♦ **a band chief** un chef de bande

bandage NOUN
| see also **bandage** VERB |
le <u>bandage</u>

B

to **bandage** VERB

> see also **bandage** NOUN

mettre un bandage à ◊ *The nurse bandaged my arm.* L'infirmière m'a mis un bandage au bras.

bandaid NOUN
le pansement adhésif

✹ **band council** NOUN
le conseil de bande

bandit NOUN
le bandit

bang NOUN

> see also **bang** VERB

① la détonation ◊ *I heard a loud bang.* J'ai entendu une forte détonation.
② le coup ◊ *a bang on the head* un coup sur la tête
♦ **Bang!** Pan!

to **bang** VERB

> see also **bang** NOUN

se cogner (*part of body*) ◊ *I banged my head.* Je me suis cogné la tête.
♦ **to bang the door** claquer la porte
♦ **to bang on the door** cogner à la porte

bangs PL NOUN
la frange SING ◊ *short bangs* une frange courte

bank NOUN
① la banque (*financial*)
② le bord (*of river, lake*)

bank account NOUN
le compte en banque

banker NOUN
le banquier

banned ADJECTIVE
interdit

bannock NOUN
la banique

banquet NOUN
le banquet ◊ *the graduation banquet* le banquet des finissants

bar NOUN
la barre (*metal*)
♦ **a chocolate bar** une tablette de chocolat
♦ **a bar of soap** une savonnette

barbaric ADJECTIVE
barbare

barbecue NOUN

> see also **barbecue** VERB

le barbecue
♦ **barbecue sauce** la sauce barbecue

to **barbecue** VERB

> see also **barbecue** NOUN

griller au barbecue ◊ *to barbecue chicken* griller du poulet au barbecue
♦ **barbecued pork chops** des côtelettes de porc grillées au barbecue

barber NOUN
le coiffeur pour hommes

bare ADJECTIVE
nu

barefoot ADJECTIVE, ADVERB
nu-pieds MASC, FEM, PL ◊ *The children go around barefoot.* Les enfants se promènent nu-pieds.
♦ **to be barefoot** avoir les pieds nus ◊ *She was barefoot.* Elle avait les pieds nus.

barely ADVERB
à peine ◊ *I could barely hear what they were saying.* J'entendais à peine ce qu'ils disaient.

bargain NOUN
l'affaire FEM ◊ *It was a bargain!* C'était une affaire!

bark NOUN

> see also **bark** VERB

l'écorce FEM (*tree*)

to **bark** VERB

> see also **bark** NOUN

aboyer

barn NOUN
la grange

barrel NOUN
le tonneau
(PL les tonneaux)

✹ **Barrens** PL NOUN
la région des Barrens

barrier NOUN
la barrière

base NOUN
la base

baseball NOUN
le baseball
♦ **a baseball cap** une casquette de baseball

based ADJECTIVE
♦ **based on** fondé sur

basement NOUN
le sous-sol

basic ADJECTIVE
① de base ◊ *It's a basic model.* C'est un modèle de base.
② rudimentaire ◊ *The accommodation is pretty basic.* Le logement est plutôt rudimentaire.

basically ADVERB
tout simplement ◊ *Basically, I just don't like him.* Tout simplement, je ne l'aime pas.

basics PL NOUN
les <u>rudiments</u> MASC PL

basin NOUN
le <u>lavabo</u> (*washbasin*)

basis NOUN
♦ **on a daily basis** quotidiennement
♦ **on a regular basis** régulièrement

basket NOUN
le <u>panier</u>

basketball NOUN
le <u>basket</u>

bass NOUN
⊡ la <u>basse</u> (*guitar, singer*) ◊ *She plays the bass.* Elle joue de la basse. ◊ *He's a bass.* Il est basse.
♦ **a bass guitar** une guitare basse
♦ **a double bass** une contrebasse
⊡ les <u>graves</u> MASC PL (*on stereo*)
⊡ l' <u>achigan</u> (*fish*)

bass drum NOUN
la <u>grosse caisse</u>

bassoon NOUN
le <u>basson</u> ◊ *I play the bassoon.* Je joue du basson.

bat NOUN
⊡ la <u>batte</u> (*for baseball*)
♦ **Who's up to bat?** Qui est à la batte?
⊡ la <u>raquette</u> (*for table tennis*)
⊡ (*animal*)
la <u>chauve-souris</u>
(PL les chauves-souris)

bath NOUN
⊡ le <u>bain</u> ◊ *to have a bath* prendre un bain
♦ **a hot bath** un bain chaud
⊡ la <u>baignoire</u> (*bathtub*) ◊ *There's a spider in the bath.* Il y a une araignée dans la baignoire.

to **bathe** VERB
se <u>baigner</u>

bathing suit NOUN
le <u>maillot de bain</u>

bathroom NOUN
la <u>salle de bains</u>

batter NOUN
⊡ la <u>pâte</u> ◊ *cake batter* la pâte à gâteau
⊡ le <u>batteur</u> (*baseball*)

battery NOUN
⊡ la <u>pile</u> (*for flashlight, toy*)
⊡ la <u>batterie</u> (*of car*)

battle NOUN
la <u>bataille</u> ◊ *the Battle of the Plains of Abraham* la bataille des Plaines d'Abraham
♦ **It was a battle, but we succeeded in the end.** Il a fallu se battre, mais on a fini par y arriver.

bay NOUN
la <u>baie</u>

bazaar NOUN
le <u>bazar</u> ◊ *Our school holds a bazaar every spring.* Notre école tient un bazar tous les printemps.

BC ABBREVIATION (= *before Christ*)
<u>av. J.-C.</u> (= avant Jésus-Christ) ◊ *in 200 BC* en deux cents avant Jésus-Christ

BCE ABBREVIATION (= *before the Common Era*)
<u>av. J.-C.</u> (= avant Jésus-Christ) ◊ *in 200 BCE* en deux cents avant Jésus-Christ

to **be** VERB
<u>être</u> ◊ *I'm tired.* Je suis fatigué. ◊ *You're late.* Tu es en retard. ◊ *She's English.* Elle est anglaise. ◊ *Iqaluit is in Nunavut.* Iqaluit est au Nunavut. ◊ *It's 4 o'clock.* Il est quatre heures. ◊ *We are all happy.* Nous sommes tous heureux. ◊ *They are in Moncton at the moment.* Ils sont à Moncton en ce moment. ◊ *I've been ill.* J'ai été malade.
♦ **It's the 28th of October today.** Nous sommes le vingt-huit octobre.
♦ **Have you been to Greece before?** Est-ce que tu es déjà allé en Grèce?
♦ **I've never been to Chicoutimi.** Je ne suis jamais allé à Chicoutimi.
♦ **to be killed** être tué

When you are saying what somebody's occupation is, you leave out the "a" in French.

◊ *She's a doctor.* Elle est médecin.
◊ *He's a student.* Il est étudiant.

With certain adjectives, such as "cold", "hot", "hungry" and "thirsty", use avoir instead of être.

♦ **I'm cold.** J'ai froid.
♦ **I'm hungry.** J'ai faim.

When saying how old somebody is, use avoir not être.

♦ **I'm fourteen.** J'ai quatorze ans.
♦ **How old are you?** Quel âge as-tu?

When referring to the weather, use faire.

♦ **It's cold.** Il fait froid.
♦ **It's too hot.** Il fait trop chaud.
♦ **It's a nice day.** Il fait beau.

beach NOUN
la <u>plage</u>

bead NOUN
la <u>perle</u>

beak NOUN
le <u>bec</u>

beam NOUN

[1] le rayon (of light)
[2] la poutre (wooden)

beans NOUN
[1] les haricots MASC PL
[2] les haricots au lard MASC PL (baked beans) ◊ I had beans on toast. J'ai mangé des haricots au lard sur du pain grillé.
♦ **green beans** les haricots verts MASC
♦ **kidney beans** les haricots rouges MASC

bear NOUN

| see also **bear** VERB |

l' ours MASC
♦ **a bear cub** un ourson

to **bear** VERB

| see also **bear** NOUN |

supporter
♦ **I can't bear it!** C'est insupportable!
♦ **to bear up** tenir le coup
♦ **Bear up!** Tiens bon!

beard NOUN
la barbe
♦ **He has a beard.** Il est barbu.
♦ **a man with a beard** un barbu

bearded ADJECTIVE
barbu

beat NOUN

| see also **beat** VERB |

le rythme

to **beat** VERB

| see also **beat** NOUN |

battre ◊ We beat them 3-0. On les a battus trois à zéro.

beautiful ADJECTIVE
beau MASC
belle FEM
(MASC PL beaux) ◊ a beautiful smile un beau sourire

*The form **beau** changes to **bel** before a vowel and most words beginning with h.*

◊ a beautiful afternoon un bel après-midi

beautifully ADVERB
admirablement

beauty NOUN
la beauté

beaver NOUN
le castor

became VERB see **become**

because CONJUNCTION
parce que ◊ I did it because... Je l'ai fait parce que...
♦ **because of** à cause de ◊ because of the weather à cause du temps

to **become** VERB

devenir ◊ She became a famous writer. Elle est devenue un grand écrivain.

bed NOUN
le lit ◊ in bed au lit
♦ **to go to bed** aller se coucher

bed and breakfast NOUN
la chambre d'hôte ◊ We stayed in a bed and breakfast. Nous avons logé dans une chambre d'hôte.
♦ **How much is it for bed and breakfast?** C'est combien pour la chambre et le petit déjeuner?

bedding NOUN
la literie

bedroom NOUN
la chambre

bedspread NOUN
le dessus-de-lit
(PL les dessus-de-lit)

bedtime NOUN
♦ **Ten o'clock is my usual bedtime.** Je me couche généralement à dix heures.
♦ **Bedtime!** Au lit!

bee NOUN
l' abeille FEM

beef NOUN
le bœuf
♦ **roast beef (1)** le rosbif (served rare)
♦ **roast beef (2)** le rôti de bœuf (served well done)

been VERB see **be**

beep NOUN
le bip ◊ Leave your message after the beep. Laissez votre message après le bip.

beet NOUN
la betterave rouge

beetle NOUN
le scarabée

before PREPOSITION, CONJUNCTION, ADVERB
[1] avant ◊ before Tuesday avant mardi
[2] avant de ◊ before going avant de partir ◊ Before opening the box, read the instructions. Avant d'ouvrir la boîte, lisez le mode d'emploi. ◊ I'll phone before I leave. J'appellerai avant de partir.
[3] déjà (already) ◊ I've seen this film before. J'ai déjà vu ce film. ◊ Have you been to Alberta before? Vous êtes déjà venu en Alberta?
♦ **the day before** la veille
♦ **the week before** la semaine précédente

beforehand ADVERB
à l'avance

to **beg** VERB
  ① mendier (*for money*)
  ② supplier ◊ *I beg you to stop.* Je te
  supplie d'arrêter.

began VERB *see* **begin**

beggar NOUN
  le mendiant
  la mendiante

to **begin** VERB
  commencer
  ♦ **to begin doing something**
  commencer à faire quelque chose

beginner NOUN
  le débutant
  la débutante ◊ *I'm just a beginner.* Je
  ne suis qu'un débutant.

beginning NOUN
  le début ◊ *in the beginning* au début

begun VERB *see* **begin**

behalf NOUN
  ♦ **on behalf of somebody** pour
  quelqu'un

to **behave** VERB
  se comporter ◊ *He behaved like an
  idiot.* Il s'est comporté comme un
  idiot. ◊ *She behaved very badly.* Elle
  s'est très mal comportée.
  ♦ **to behave oneself** être sage ◊ *Did the
  children behave themselves?* Est-ce
  que les enfants ont été sages?
  ♦ **Behave!** Sois sage!

behaviour NOUN
  le comportement

behind PREPOSITION, ADVERB

  > *see also* **behind** NOUN

  derrière ◊ *behind the television*
  derrière la télévision
  ♦ **to be behind** (*late*) avoir du retard
  ◊ *I'm behind with my homework.* J'ai
  du retard dans mes devoirs.

behind NOUN

  > *see also* **behind** PREPOSITION, ADVERB

  le derrière

beige ADJECTIVE
  beige

to **believe** VERB
  croire ◊ *I don't believe you.* Je ne te
  crois pas.
  ♦ **to believe in something** croire à
  quelque chose ◊ *Do you believe in
  ghosts?* Tu crois aux fantômes?
  ♦ **to believe in God** croire en Dieu

bell NOUN
  ① la sonnette (*doorbell*)
  ♦ **to ring the bell** sonner à la porte
  ② la cloche (*in church*)
  ③ la sonnerie (*in school*)
  ④ la clochette ◊ *Our cat has a bell*

around its neck. Notre chat a une
clochette sur son collier.

belly NOUN
  le ventre

to **belong** VERB
  ♦ **to belong to somebody** être à
  quelqu'un ◊ *Who does it belong to?*
  C'est à qui? ◊ *That belongs to me.*
  C'est à moi.
  ♦ **Do you belong to any clubs?** Est-ce
  que tu es membre d'un club?
  ♦ **Where does this belong?** Où est-ce
  que ça va?

belongings PL NOUN
  les affaires FEM PL

below PREPOSITION, ADVERB
  ① au-dessous de ◊ *below sea level*
  au-dessous du niveau de la mer
  ② en dessous ◊ *on the floor below* à
  l'étage en dessous
  ♦ **10 degrees below freezing** moins dix

belt NOUN
  la ceinture

bench NOUN
  ① le banc (*seat*)
  ② l' établi MASC (*workbench*)

bend NOUN

  > *see also* **bend** VERB

  ① le virage (*in road*)
  ② le coude (*in river*)

to **bend** VERB

  > *see also* **bend** NOUN

  ① courber (*one's back*)
  ② plier (*leg, arm*) ◊ *I can't bend my
  arm.* Je n'arrive pas à plier le bras.
  ♦ **"do not bend"** « ne pas plier »
  ③ tourner (*road*) ◊ *The road bends
  to the right.* La route tourne vers la
  droite.
  ④ tordre (*object*) ◊ *You've bent it.* Tu
  l'as tordu.
  ⑤ se tordre ◊ *It bends easily.* Ça se
  tord facilement.
  ♦ **to bend down** se baisser
  ♦ **to bend over** se pencher

beneath PREPOSITION
  sous

benefit NOUN

  > *see also* **benefit** VERB

  l' avantage MASC (*advantage*)
  ♦ **unemployment benefit** les allocations
  de chômage

to **benefit** VERB

  > *see also* **benefit** NOUN

  ♦ **He'll benefit from the change.** Le
  changement lui fera du bien.

bent VERB *see* **bend**

bent ADJECTIVE
tordu ◊ *a bent fork* une fourchette tordue

beret NOUN
le béret

berry NOUN
la baie

berserk ADJECTIVE
♦ **to go berserk** devenir fou furieux ◊ *She went berserk.* Elle est devenue folle furieuse.

beside PREPOSITION
à côté de ◊ *beside the television* à côté de la télévision
♦ **He was beside himself.** Il était hors de lui.
♦ **That's beside the point.** Cela n'a rien à voir.

besides ADVERB
en plus ◊ *Besides, it's too expensive.* En plus, c'est trop cher.

best ADJECTIVE, ADVERB
① meilleur ◊ *He's the best player on the team.* Il est le meilleur joueur de l'équipe. ◊ *She's the best at math.* Elle est la meilleure en maths.
② le mieux ◊ *She sings best.* C'est elle qui chante le mieux. ◊ *That's the best I can do.* Je ne peux pas faire mieux.
♦ **to do one's best** faire de son mieux ◊ *It's not perfect, but I did my best.* Ça n'est pas parfait, mais j'ai fait de mon mieux.
♦ **to make the best of it** s'en contenter ◊ *We'll have to make the best of it.* Il va falloir nous en contenter.

best man NOUN
le garçon d'honneur

bet NOUN
⎡ see also **bet** VERB ⎤
le pari ◊ *to make a bet* faire un pari

to **bet** VERB
⎡ see also **bet** NOUN ⎤
parier ◊ *I bet you he won't come.* Je te parie qu'il ne viendra pas. ◊ *I bet she forgot.* Je parie qu'elle a oublié.

to **betray** VERB
trahir

betrayal NOUN
la trahison

better ADJECTIVE, ADVERB
① meilleur ◊ *This one's better than that one.* Celui-ci est meilleur que celui-là. ◊ *a better way to do it* une meilleure façon de le faire
② mieux ◊ *That's better!* C'est mieux comme ça. ◊ *This pen writes better.*

Ce stylo-ci écrit mieux.
♦ **better still** encore mieux ◊ *Go and see her tomorrow, or better still, go today.* Va la voir demain, ou encore mieux, vas-y aujourd'hui.
♦ **to get better (1)** (*improve*) s'améliorer ◊ *I hope the weather gets better soon.* J'espère que le temps va s'améliorer bientôt. ◊ *My French is getting better.* Mon français s'améliore.
♦ **to get better (2)** (*from illness*) se remettre ◊ *I hope you get better soon.* J'espère que tu vas vite te remettre.
♦ **to feel better** se sentir mieux ◊ *Are you feeling better now?* Tu te sens mieux maintenant?
♦ **You'd better do it right away.** Vous feriez mieux de le faire immédiatement.
♦ **I'd better go home.** Je ferais mieux de rentrer.

between PREPOSITION
entre ◊ *Moose Jaw is between Swift Current and Regina.* Moose Jaw est entre Swift Current et Regina. ◊ *between 15 and 20 minutes* entre quinze et vingt minutes

beware VERB
se méfier ◊ *Beware of strangers.* Méfie-toi des inconnus.
♦ **"Beware of dog"** « Attention, chien méchant »

bewildered ADJECTIVE
♦ **He looked bewildered.** Il avait l'air perplexe.

beyond PREPOSITION
au-delà de ◊ *There was a lake beyond the mountain.* Il y avait un lac au-delà de la montagne.
♦ **beyond belief** incroyable
♦ **beyond repair** irréparable

biased ADJECTIVE
partial

bibliography NOUN
la bibliographie

bicycle NOUN
le vélo

big ADJECTIVE
① grand ◊ *a big house* une grande maison ◊ *her big sister* sa grande sœur
♦ **He's a big guy.** C'est un grand gaillard.
② (*car, animal, book, package*) gros MASC
grosse FEM ◊ *a big car* une grosse voiture

bike NOUN
le vélo ◊ *by bike* en vélo

bikini NOUN

☞

le <u>bikini</u>

bilingual ADJECTIVE
<u>bilingue</u>

bilingualism NOUN
le <u>bilinguisme</u>

bill NOUN
[1] l' <u>addition</u> FEM (*in restaurant*) ◊ *Can we have the bill, please?* L'addition, s'il vous plaît.
[2] la <u>facture</u> (*for gas, electricity*)
[3] le <u>billet</u> ◊ *a five-dollar bill* un billet de cinq dólares

billion NOUN
le <u>milliard</u> ◊ *two billion people* deux milliards de gens

binder NOUN
la <u>reliure</u>

bingo NOUN
le <u>bingo</u>

binoculars PL NOUN
les <u>jumelles</u> FEM PL
♦ **a pair of binoculars** des jumelles

biochemistry NOUN
la <u>biochimie</u>

biodegradable ADJECTIVE
<u>biodégradable</u>

biography NOUN
la <u>biographie</u>

biology NOUN
la <u>biologie</u>

birch NOUN
le <u>bouleau</u>
(PL les bouleaux)
♦ **birch bark** l'écorce de bouleau FEM

bird NOUN
l' <u>oiseau</u> MASC
(PL les oiseaux)

birth NOUN
la <u>naissance</u> ◊ *date of birth* la date de naissance

birth certificate NOUN
l' <u>acte de naissance</u> MASC

birth control NOUN
la <u>contraception</u>

birthday NOUN
l' <u>anniversaire</u> MASC ◊ *When's your birthday?* Quelle est la date de ton anniversaire?
♦ **a birthday cake** un gâteau d'anniversaire
♦ **a birthday card** une carte d'anniversaire
♦ **I'm going to have a birthday party.** Je vais faire une fête pour mon anniversaire.

bison NOUN
le <u>bison</u>

bit VERB *see* **bite**

bit NOUN
♦ **a bit** un peu ◊ *I'm a bit tired.* Je suis un peu fatigué. ◊ *a bit too hot* un peu trop chaud ◊ *Stay a bit longer.* Reste un peu plus longtemps. ◊ *"Do you play soccer?" "A bit."* « Tu joues au soccer? » « Un peu. »
♦ **a bit of** un peu de ◊ *a bit of music* un peu de musique
♦ **It's a bit of a nuisance.** C'est ennuyeux.
♦ **bit by bit** petit à petit

to **bite** VERB

> *see also* **bite** NOUN

[1] <u>mordre</u> (*person, dog*)
[2] <u>piquer</u> (*insect*) ◊ *I got bitten by mosquitoes.* Je me suis fait piquer par des moustiques.
♦ **to bite one's nails** se ronger les ongles

bite NOUN

> *see also* **bite** VERB

[1] la <u>piqûre</u> (*insect bite*)
[2] la <u>morsure</u> (*animal bite*)
♦ **to have a bite to eat** manger un morceau

bitten VERB *see* **bite**

bitter ADJECTIVE
[1] <u>amer</u> MASC
<u>amère</u> FEM
[2] (*weather, wind*)
<u>glacial</u>
(MASC PL glaciaux) ◊ *It's bitter out today.* Il fait un froid glacial aujourd'hui.

bizarre ADJECTIVE
<u>bizarre</u> ◊ *a bizarre dream* un rêve bizarre

black ADJECTIVE
<u>noir</u> ◊ *a black jacket* une veste noire ◊ *She's black.* Elle est noire.

blackberry NOUN
la <u>mûre</u>

black currant NOUN
le <u>cassis</u>

black fly NOUN
la <u>mouche noire</u>

black hole NOUN
le <u>trou noir</u>

blackmail NOUN

> *see also* **blackmail** VERB

le <u>chantage</u> ◊ *That's blackmail!* C'est du chantage!

to **blackmail** VERB

> *see also* **blackmail** NOUN

♦ **to blackmail somebody** faire chanter

English ~ French

quelqu'un ◊ *He blackmailed them.* Il les a fait chanter.

blackout NOUN
la <u>panne d'électricité</u> (*power cut*)

blade NOUN
la <u>lame</u>

to **blame** VERB
♦ **Don't blame me!** Ça n'est pas ma faute!
♦ **I blame the police.** À mon avis, c'est la faute de la police.
♦ **He blamed it on my sister.** Il a dit que c'était la faute de ma sœur.

blank ADJECTIVE

see also **blank** NOUN

1 (*paper*)
<u>blanc</u> MASC
<u>blanche</u> FEM
2 <u>vierge</u> (*cassette, video, page*)
♦ **My mind went blank.** J'ai eu un trou.

blank NOUN

see also **blank** ADJECTIVE

le <u>blanc</u> ◊ *Fill in the blanks.* Remplissez les blancs.

blank cheque NOUN
le <u>chèque en blanc</u>

blanket NOUN
la <u>couverture</u>

blast NOUN
♦ **a bomb blast** une explosion

blatant ADJECTIVE
<u>flagrant</u>

blaze NOUN
l' <u>incendie</u> MASC

blazer NOUN
le <u>blazer</u>

bleach NOUN
l' <u>eau de Javel</u> FEM

to **bleach** VERB
<u>décolorer</u> ◊ *She bleached her hair.* Elle a décoloré ses cheveux.
♦ **bleached jeans** jeans délavés

bleachers PL NOUN
les <u>gradins</u> MASC PL ◊ *a seat in the bleachers* un siège dans les gradins

bleak ADJECTIVE
<u>désolé</u> (*place*)
♦ **The future looks bleak.** L'avenir semble peu prometteur.

to **bleed** VERB
<u>saigner</u> ◊ *My nose is bleeding.* Je saigne du nez.

blender NOUN
le <u>mélangeur</u>

to **bless** VERB
<u>bénir</u> (*religiously*)

♦ **Bless you!** (*after sneezing*) À tes souhaits!

blew VERB *see* **blow**

blind ADJECTIVE

see also **blind** NOUN

<u>aveugle</u>

blind NOUN

see also **blind** ADJECTIVE

le <u>store</u> (*for window*)

blindfold NOUN

see also **blindfold** VERB

le <u>bandeau</u>
(PL les bandeaux)

to **blindfold** VERB

see also **blindfold** NOUN

♦ **to blindfold somebody** bander les yeux à quelqu'un

to **blink** VERB
<u>cligner des yeux</u>

bliss NOUN
♦ **It was bliss!** C'était merveilleux!

blister NOUN
l' <u>ampoule</u> FEM

blizzard NOUN
la <u>tempête de neige</u>

blob NOUN
la <u>goutte</u> ◊ *a blob of glue* une goutte de colle

block NOUN

see also **block** VERB

1 la <u>bille</u> (*wood*)
2 le <u>bloc</u> (*stone*)
♦ **They live on our block.** Ils habitent notre quartier.
♦ **It's two blocks away.** C'est à deux coins de rue.
♦ **to go around the block** faire le tour du pâté de maisons

to **block** VERB

see also **block** NOUN

<u>bloquer</u>

blockage NOUN
l' <u>obstruction</u> FEM

blog NOUN
le <u>blogue</u>

blond ADJECTIVE
<u>blond</u> ◊ *She has blond hair.* Elle a les cheveux blonds.

blood NOUN
le <u>sang</u>

blood pressure NOUN
♦ **to have high blood pressure** faire de la tension

blood test NOUN

☞

la prise de sang

blouse NOUN
le chemisier

blow NOUN

see also **blow** VERB

le coup

to **blow** VERB

see also **blow** NOUN

souffler (*wind, person*)
♦ **to blow one's nose** se moucher
♦ **to blow a whistle** siffler
♦ **to blow out a candle** éteindre une bougie
♦ **to blow up (1)** faire sauter ◊ *They blew up the old bridge and built a new one.* Ils ont fait sauter le vieux pont et en ont bâti un nouveau.
♦ **to blow up (2)** gonfler ◊ *to blow up a balloon* gonfler un ballon
♦ **The house blew up.** La maison a sauté.

blow-dry NOUN

see also **blow-dry** VERB

le séchage à la brosse
♦ **A cut and blow-dry, please.** Une coupe et un séchage à la brosse, s'il vous plaît.

to **blow-dry** VERB

see also **blow-dry** NOUN

sécher à la brosse ◊ *I blow-dry my hair.* Je me sèche les cheveux à la brosse.

blown VERB *see* **blow**

blue ADJECTIVE
bleu ◊ *a blue dress* une robe bleue
♦ **It came out of the blue.** C'était complètement inattendu.

blueberry NOUN
le bleuet ◊ *blueberry pie* la tarte aux bleuets

blue jay NOUN
le geai bleu

blues PL NOUN
le blues SING ◊ *I like blues (music).* J'aime le blues.
♦ **to have the blues** avoir le cafard

to **bluff** VERB

see also **bluff** NOUN

bluffer

bluff NOUN

see also **bluff** VERB

le bluff ◊ *It's just a bluff.* C'est du bluff.

blunder NOUN
la gaffe

blunt ADJECTIVE

① brusque (*person*)
② émoussé (*knife*)

blurry ADJECTIVE
flou

to **blush** VERB
rougir

board NOUN
① la planche (*wooden*)
② la planche à roulettes (*skateboard*)
③ la planche à neige (*snowboard*)
④ (*chalkboard*)
le tableau
(PL les tableaux) ◊ *on the board* au tableau
⑤ (*notice board*)
le panneau
(PL les panneaux)
⑥ (*for board games*)
le jeu
(PL les jeux)
⑦ l' échiquier MASC (*for chess*)
♦ **on board** à bord

boarder NOUN
l' interne MASC/FEM

board game NOUN
le jeu de société
(PL les jeux de société)

boarding NOUN
① la planche à roulettes
(*skateboarding*) ◊ *He loves boarding.* Il adore la planche à roulettes.
② la planche à neige (*snowboarding*)
◊ *She's great at boarding.* Elle est formidable à la planche à neige.
◊ *Want to go boarding?* Si on faisait de la planche à neige?

boarding card NOUN
la carte d'embarquement

boarding school NOUN
le pensionnat
♦ **I go to boarding school.** Je suis pensionnaire.

boards PL NOUN
la bande SING (*hockey*) ◊ *The other player shoved me into the boards.* L'autre joueur m'a poussé dans la bande.

boat NOUN
le bateau
(PL les bateaux)

body NOUN
le corps

bodybuilding NOUN
le culturisme

to **bodycheck** VERB
mettre en échec ◊ *You bodychecked him.* Tu l'as mis en échec.

bodyguard NOUN
le garde du corps

B

bog NOUN
   la tourbière (*marsh*)

boil NOUN
   ⎜ *see also* **boil** VERB ⎜
   le furoncle

to **boil** VERB
   ⎜ *see also* **boil** NOUN ⎜
   ① faire bouillir ◊ *to boil some water*
   faire bouillir de l'eau
   ♦ **to boil an egg** faire cuire un œuf
   ② bouillir ◊ *The water's boiling.* L'eau
   bout. ◊ *The water's boiled.* L'eau a
   bouilli.
   ♦ **to boil over** déborder

boiled ADJECTIVE
   ① à l'eau ◊ *boiled potatoes* des
   pommes de terre à l'eau
   ② bouilli ◊ *boiled water* eau bouillie
   ♦ **a boiled egg** un œuf à la coque

boiling ADJECTIVE
   ♦ **It's boiling in here!** Il fait une chaleur
   torride ici!
   ♦ **boiling hot** torride ◊ *a boiling hot day*
   une journée torride

bolt NOUN
   ① le verrou (*on door*)
   ② le boulon (*with nut*)

bomb NOUN
   ⎜ *see also* **bomb** VERB ⎜
   la bombe

to **bomb** VERB
   ⎜ *see also* **bomb** NOUN ⎜
   bombarder

bomber NOUN
   le bombardier

bombing NOUN
   l' attentat à la bombe MASC

bond NOUN
   le lien

bone NOUN
   ① l' os MASC (*of human, animal*)
   ② l' arête FEM (*of fish*)

bone dry ADJECTIVE
   complètement sec MASC
   complètement sèche FEM

bonfire NOUN
   le feu de joie
   (PL les feux de joie)

bonus NOUN
   ① la prime (*extra payment*)
   ② le plus (*added advantage*)

book NOUN
   ⎜ *see also* **book** VERB ⎜
   le livre

to **book** VERB

   ⎜ *see also* **book** NOUN ⎜
   réserver ◊ *We haven't booked.* Nous
   n'avons pas réservé.

bookcase NOUN
   la bibliothèque

booklet NOUN
   la brochure

bookmark NOUN
   ⎜ *see also* **bookmark** VERB ⎜
   le signet (*also computing*)

to **bookmark** VERB
   ⎜ *see also* **bookmark** NOUN ⎜
   mettre un signet à ◊ *I'm going to*
   bookmark this Web site. Je mets un
   signet à ce site Web.

bookshelf NOUN
   l' étagère à livres FEM

bookstore NOUN
   la librairie

to **boost** VERB
   stimuler ◊ *to boost the economy*
   stimuler l'économie
   ♦ **The win boosted the team's morale.**
   La victoire a remonté le moral de
   l'équipe.

boot NOUN
   ① la botte (*fashion boot*)
   ② la chaussure de marche (*for*
   hiking)

to **boot up** VERB
   démarrer

border NOUN
   la frontière

bore VERB *see* **bear**

bored ADJECTIVE
   ♦ **to be bored** s'ennuyer ◊ *I was bored.*
   Je m'ennuyais.
   ♦ **to get bored** s'ennuyer

boredom NOUN
   l' ennui MASC

boring ADJECTIVE
   ennuyeux MASC
   ennuyeuse FEM

born ADJECTIVE
   ♦ **to be born** naître ◊ *I was born in*
   1994. Je suis né en mille neuf cent
   quatre-vingt-quatorze.

to **borrow** VERB
   emprunter ◊ *Can I borrow your pen?*
   Je peux emprunter ton stylo?
   ♦ **to borrow something from somebody**
   emprunter quelque chose à quelqu'un
   ◊ *I borrowed some money from a*
   friend. J'ai emprunté de l'argent à
   un ami.

boss NOUN

☞

le <u>patron</u>
la <u>patronne</u>

to **boss around** VERB
♦ **to boss somebody around** donner des ordres à quelqu'un

bossy ADJECTIVE
<u>autoritaire</u>

both ADJECTIVE, PRONOUN
<u>tous les deux</u> MASC PL
<u>toutes les deux</u> FEM PL ◊ *We both went.* Nous y sommes allés tous les deux. ◊ *Emma and Jane both went.* Emma et Jane y sont allées toutes les deux. ◊ *Both of your answers are wrong.* Vos réponses sont toutes les deux mauvaises. ◊ *Both of them have left.* Ils sont partis tous les deux. ◊ *Both of us went.* Nous y sommes allés tous les deux. ◊ *Both Maggie and John are against it.* Maggie et John sont tous les deux contre.
♦ **He speaks both German and Italian.** Il parle allemand et italien.

to **bother** VERB
① tracasser (*worry*) ◊ *What's bothering you?* Qu'est-ce qui te tracasse?
② déranger (*disturb*) ◊ *I'm sorry to bother you.* Je suis désolé de vous déranger.
♦ **no bother** aucun problème
♦ **Don't bother!** Ça n'est pas la peine!
♦ **to bother to do something** prendre la peine de faire quelque chose ◊ *He didn't bother to tell me about it.* Il n'a pas pris la peine de m'en parler.

bottle NOUN
la <u>bouteille</u>

bottle-opener NOUN
l' <u>ouvre-bouteille</u> MASC

bottom NOUN
see also **bottom** ADJECTIVE
① le <u>fond</u> (*of container, bag, sea*)
② le <u>bas</u> (*of page, list*)

bottom ADJECTIVE
see also **bottom** NOUN
<u>inférieur</u> ◊ *the bottom shelf* l'étagère inférieure
♦ **the bottom sheet** le drap de dessous

bought VERB *see* **buy**

to **bounce** VERB
<u>rebondir</u>

bouncer NOUN
le <u>videur</u>

bound ADJECTIVE
♦ **He's bound to win.** Il va sûrement gagner.

boundary NOUN

la <u>frontière</u>

bounds PL NOUN
♦ **out of bounds (1)** interdit ◊ *The creek is out of bounds for students.* Le ruisseau est interdit aux élèves.
♦ **out of bounds (2)** à l'extérieur du terrain ◊ *The ball landed out of bounds.* Le ballon est tombé à l'extérieur du terrain.

bow NOUN
see also **bow** VERB
① le <u>nœud</u> (*knot*) ◊ *to tie a bow* faire un nœud
② l' <u>arc</u> MASC ◊ *a bow and arrows* un arc et des flèches

to **bow** VERB
see also **bow** NOUN
<u>faire une révérence</u>

bowl NOUN
see also **bowl** VERB
le <u>bol</u> (*for soup, cereal*)

bowling NOUN
le <u>jeu de quilles</u>
♦ **to go bowling** jouer aux quilles
♦ **a bowling alley** une salle de quilles

bow tie NOUN
le <u>nœud papillon</u>

box NOUN
la <u>boîte</u> ◊ *a box of matches* une boîte d'allumettes
♦ **a cardboard box** un carton

boxer NOUN
le <u>boxeur</u>

boxer shorts PL NOUN
le <u>caleçon</u> SING ◊ *a pair of boxer shorts* un caleçon

boxing NOUN
la <u>boxe</u>

Boxing Day NOUN
le <u>lendemain de Noël</u> ◊ *on Boxing Day* le lendemain de Noël

boy NOUN
le <u>garçon</u>

to **boycott** VERB
<u>boycotter</u>

boyfriend NOUN
le <u>copain</u> ◊ *Do you have a boyfriend?* Est-ce que tu as un copain?

bra NOUN
le <u>soutien-gorge</u>
(PL les soutiens-gorge)

brace NOUN
l' <u>appareil orthopédique</u> MASC ◊ *He wears a leg brace.* Il porte un appareil orthopédique pour sa jambe.

bracelet NOUN

le <u>bracelet</u>

braces NOUN
l' <u>appareil orthodontique</u> MASC (*on teeth*) ◊ *She wears braces.* Elle a un appareil orthodontique.

brackets PL NOUN
♦ **in brackets** entre parenthèses

to **brag** VERB
se <u>vanter</u> ◊ *Stop bragging!* Arrête de te vanter!
♦ **to brag about something** se vanter de quelque chose

braid NOUN

see also **braid** VERB

la <u>tresse</u> (*hair*)

to **braid** VERB

see also **braid** NOUN

<u>tresser</u> ◊ *to braid one's hair* se tresser les cheveux

brain NOUN
le <u>cerveau</u>
(PL les cerveaux)

to **brainstorm** VERB
<u>faire un remue-méninges</u>
♦ **a brainstorming session** une session de remue-méninges

brainteaser NOUN
le <u>casse-tête</u>

brake NOUN

see also **brake** VERB

le <u>frein</u>

to **brake** VERB

see also **brake** NOUN

<u>freiner</u>

branch NOUN
① la <u>branche</u> (*of tree*)
② la <u>succursale</u> (*of bank*)

brand NOUN
la <u>marque</u> ◊ *a well-known brand of cereal* une marque de céréales bien connue

brand name NOUN
la <u>marque</u>

brand-new ADJECTIVE
<u>tout neuf</u> MASC
<u>toute neuve</u> FEM

brass NOUN
le <u>cuivre</u>
♦ **the brass section** les cuivres

brass band NOUN
la <u>fanfare</u>

brave ADJECTIVE
<u>courageux</u> MASC
<u>courageuse</u> FEM

bread NOUN

le <u>pain</u> ◊ *brown bread* le pain de blé entier ◊ *white bread* le pain blanc
♦ **bread and butter** les tartines de pain beurrées FEM

break NOUN

see also **break** VERB

① la <u>pause</u> (*rest*) ◊ *to take a break* faire une pause
② la <u>récréation</u> (*at school*) ◊ *during morning break* pendant la récréation du matin
♦ **the Christmas break** les vacances de Noël
♦ **Give me a break!** Laisse-moi tranquille!
♦ **to give somebody a break** donner sa chance à quelqu'un

to **break** VERB

see also **break** NOUN

① <u>casser</u> ◊ *Careful, you'll break something!* Attention, tu vas casser quelque chose!
② <u>se casser</u> (*get broken*) ◊ *Careful, it'll break!* Attention, ça va se casser!
♦ **to break one's leg** se casser la jambe. ◊ *I broke my leg.* Je me suis cassé la jambe.
♦ **She broke her arm.** Elle s'est cassé le bras.
♦ **to break a promise** rompre une promesse
♦ **to break a record** battre un record
♦ **to break the law** violer la loi

to **break down** VERB
<u>tomber en panne</u> ◊ *The car broke down.* La voiture est tombée en panne.

to **break in** VERB
<u>entrer par effraction</u>

to **break off** VERB
① <u>casser</u> ◊ *He broke off a piece of chocolate.* Il a cassé un bout de chocolat.
② <u>se casser</u> ◊ *The branch broke off.* La branche s'est cassée.
♦ **She broke off the engagement.** Elle a rompu ses fiançailles.

to **break out** VERB
① <u>se déclarer</u> (*fire*)
② <u>éclater</u> (*war*)
③ <u>s'évader</u> (*prisoner*)
♦ **to break out in a rash** être couvert de boutons

to **break up** VERB
① <u>se séparer</u> (*couple*)
♦ **He broke up with his girlfriend.** Il a rompu avec sa petite amie.
② <u>se disperser</u> (*crowd*)
③ <u>se terminer</u> (*meeting, party*)
④ <u>répartir</u> (*divide*) ◊ *Break up into*

B

☞

groups. Répartissez-vous en groupes.
♦ **to break up a fight** mettre fin à une
bagarre

breakdown NOUN
　① la panne (*in vehicle*) ◊ *to have a*
breakdown tomber en panne
　② la dépression (*mental*) ◊ *to have a*
breakdown faire une dépression

breakfast NOUN
　le déjeuner ◊ *What would you like*
for breakfast? Qu'est-ce vous voulez
pour le déjeuner?

break-in NOUN
　le cambriolage

to **break open** VERB
　forcer (*door, cupboard*)

break-up NOUN
　① la rupture (*friendship*)
✷　② la débâcle (*ice*) ◊ *After spring*
break-up you often get floods. Après
la débâcle printanière, on a souvent
des inondations.

breast NOUN
　le sein (*of woman*)
♦ **chicken breast** la poitrine de poulet

breath NOUN
　l' haleine FEM ◊ *to have bad breath*
avoir mauvaise haleine
♦ **to be out of breath** être essoufflé
♦ **to catch one's breath** reprendre son
souffle

to **breathe** VERB
　respirer

to **breathe in** VERB
　inspirer

to **breathe out** VERB
　expirer

to **breed** VERB
　se reproduire (*reproduce*)
♦ **to breed dogs** faire de l'élevage de
chiens

breed NOUN
　la race

breeze NOUN
　la brise

to **bribe** VERB
　soudoyer

brick NOUN
　la brique
♦ **a brick wall** un mur en brique

bricklayer NOUN
　le maçon

bride NOUN
　la mariée

bridegroom NOUN
　le marié

bridesmaid NOUN

la demoiselle d'honneur

bridge NOUN
　① le pont ◊ *a suspension bridge* un
pont suspendu
　② le bridge ◊ *to play bridge* jouer au
bridge

brief ADJECTIVE
　bref MASC
　brève FEM

briefcase NOUN
　la serviette

briefly ADVERB
　brièvement

briefs PL NOUN
　① la culotte (*women's*)
　② le caleçon (*men's*)

bright ADJECTIVE
　① (*colour, light*)
　vif MASC
　vive FEM ◊ *a bright colour* une couleur
vive
♦ **bright blue** bleu vif ◊ *a bright blue*
car une voiture bleu vif
　② intelligent ◊ *He's very bright.* Il est
très intelligent.

brilliant ADJECTIVE
　① brillant (*clever*) ◊ *a brilliant*
scientist un savant brillant
　② éclatant (*colour, light*)

to **bring** VERB
　① apporter ◊ *Bring warm clothes.*
Apportez des vêtements chauds.
　◊ *Could you bring me my mitts?* Tu
peux m'apporter mes mitaines?
　② amener (*person*) ◊ *Can I bring a*
friend? Est-ce que je peux amener
un ami?

to **bring about** VERB
　provoquer ◊ *The war brought about*
a change in people's attitudes. La
guerre a provoqué un changement
dans l'attitude des gens.

to **bring back** VERB
　rapporter

to **bring up** VERB
　① mentionner ◊ *You've brought up*
an interesting point. Tu as mentionné
un fait intéressant.
　② élever ◊ *She brought up the*
children on her own. Elle a élevé les
enfants toute seule.

British Columbia NOUN
　la Colombie-Britannique

broad ADJECTIVE
　large (*wide*)
♦ **in broad daylight** en plein jour

broadcast NOUN

　| *see also* **broadcast** VERB |

l' émission FEM

to **broadcast** VERB

see also **broadcast** NOUN

diffuser ◊ *The interview was broadcast all over the world.* L'entrevue a été diffusée dans le monde entier.
♦ **to broadcast live** retransmettre en direct

broad-minded ADJECTIVE
large d'esprit

broccoli NOUN
le brocoli

brochure NOUN
la brochure

to **broil** VERB
faire griller
♦ **broiled fish** le poisson grillé

broke VERB *see* **break**

broke ADJECTIVE
♦ **to be broke** (*without money*) être fauché

broken ADJECTIVE
cassé ◊ *It's broken.* C'est cassé. ◊ *a broken leg* une jambe cassée ◊ *She's got a broken arm.* Elle a le bras cassé.

bronchitis NOUN
la bronchite

bronze NOUN
le bronze ◊ *the bronze medal* la médaille de bronze

brooch NOUN
la broche

broom NOUN
le balai

brother NOUN
le frère ◊ *my brother* mon frère ◊ *my big brother* mon grand frère

brother-in-law NOUN
le beau-frère
(PL les beaux-frères)

brought VERB *see* **bring**

brown ADJECTIVE
1 (*clothes*)
marron MASC, FEM, PL
2 brun (*hair*)
3 bronzé (*tanned*)
♦ **brown bread** le pain de blé entier
♦ **brown sugar** la cassonade

brownie NOUN
le carré au chocolat

to **browse** VERB
1 naviguer sur Internet
♦ **Browse button** bouton Naviguer
2 feuilleter (*magazine, book*)
3 regarder (*store*)

browser NOUN
le navigateur (*for internet*)

bruise NOUN
le bleu

brunch NOUN
le brunch ◊ *to have brunch* prendre le brunch

brush NOUN

see also **brush** VERB

1 la brosse
2 (*paintbrush*)
le pinceau
(PL les pinceaux)

to **brush** VERB

see also **brush** NOUN

brosser
♦ **to brush one's hair** se brosser les cheveux ◊ *I brushed my hair.* Je me suis brossé les cheveux.
♦ **to brush one's teeth** se brosser les dents ◊ *I brush my teeth every night.* Je me brosse les dents tous les soirs.

Brussels sprout NOUN
le chou de Bruxelles
(PL les choux)

brutal ADJECTIVE
brutal
(MASC PL brutaux)

BSc NOUN (= *Bachelor of Science*)
le baccalauréat ès sciences
♦ **a BSc in biology** un baccalauréat en biologie

bubble NOUN
la bulle

bubble bath NOUN
le bain moussant

bubble gum NOUN
la gomme à mâcher

bucket NOUN
le seau
(PL les seaux)

buckle NOUN
la boucle (*on belt, watch, shoe*)

Buddhist ADJECTIVE

see also **Buddhist** NOUN

bouddhiste

Buddhist NOUN

see also **Buddhist** ADJECTIVE

le/la bouddhiste

buddy NOUN
le copain
la copine

budget NOUN
le budget

budgie NOUN
la perruche

buffet NOUN
le buffet

bug NOUN
1 l' insecte MASC (*insect*)
2 le microbe (*infection*) ◊ *There's a bug going round.* Il y a un microbe qui traîne.
3 le bogue (*in computer*)

bugged ADJECTIVE
sur écoute ◊ *The room was bugged.* La pièce était sur écoute.

to **build** VERB
construire ◊ *We're building a garage.* Nous construisons un garage.
♦ to **build up** (*increase*) s'accumuler

builder NOUN
1 l' entrepreneur MASC (*owner of firm*)
2 le maçon (*worker*)

building NOUN
le bâtiment

built VERB *see* **build**

bulb NOUN
l' ampoule FEM (*electric*)

bulimia NOUN
la boulimie

bull NOUN
le taureau
(PL les taureaux)

bullet NOUN
la balle

bulletin board NOUN
le tableau d'affichage

bully NOUN

see also **bully** VERB

l' intimidateur MASC ◊ *He's a bully.* C'est un intimidateur. ◊ *She's a bully.* Elle fait de l'intimidation.

to **bully** VERB

see also **bully** NOUN

intimider

bullying NOUN
l' intimidation FEM ◊ *a workshop about bullying* un atelier sur l'intimidation ◊ *The school has a policy on bullying.* L'école a adopté une politique sur l'intimidation.

bum NOUN
le derrière (*bottom*)

bump NOUN

see also **bump** VERB

la bosse (*lump*)

to **bump** VERB

see also **bump** NOUN

♦ to **bump into something** rentrer dans quelque chose ◊ *We bumped into her car.* Nous sommes rentrés dans sa voiture.
♦ to **bump into somebody (1)** (*literally*) rentrer dans quelqu'un ◊ *He stopped suddenly and I bumped into him.* Il s'est arrêté subitement et je lui suis rentré dedans.
♦ to **bump into somebody (2)** (*meet by chance*) rencontrer par hasard ◊ *I bumped into your sister in the supermarket.* J'ai rencontré ta sœur par hasard au supermarché.

bumper NOUN
le pare-chocs
(PL les pare-chocs)

bumpy ADJECTIVE
cahoteux MASC
cahoteuse FEM

bun NOUN
le petit pain

bunch NOUN
♦ a **bunch of flowers** un bouquet de fleurs
♦ a **bunch of grapes** une grappe de raisin
♦ a **bunch of keys** un trousseau de clés
♦ A **bunch of students are going.** Un groupe d'élèves y vont.

bungalow NOUN
le bungalow

bungee cord NOUN
la corde élastique

bungee jumping NOUN
le saut à l'élastique

bunk NOUN
la couchette
♦ **bunk beds** les lits superposés

buoy NOUN
la bouée (*swimming*)

burger NOUN
le hamburger

burglar NOUN
le cambrioleur
la cambrioleuse

to **burglarize** VERB
cambrioler

burglary NOUN
le cambriolage

burn NOUN

see also **burn** VERB

1 la brûlure
2 le coup de soleil (*sunburn*)

to **burn** VERB

see also **burn** NOUN

1 brûler
2 faire brûler (*food*) ◊ *I burned the cake.* J'ai fait brûler le gâteau.

♦ **to burn oneself** se brûler ◊ *I burned myself on the oven door.* Je me suis brûlé sur la porte du four.
♦ **I've burned my hand.** Je me suis brûlé la main.
♦ **to burn down** brûler ◊ *The factory burned down.* L'usine a brûlé.
③ graver (*CD*)

to **burst** VERB
éclater ◊ *The balloon burst.* Le ballon a éclaté.
♦ **to burst a balloon** faire éclater un ballon
♦ **to burst out laughing** éclater de rire
♦ **to burst into flames** prendre feu
♦ **to burst into tears** fondre en larmes

to **bury** VERB
enterrer

bus NOUN
l' autobus MASC ◊ *a bus stop* un arrêt d'autobus
♦ **the school bus** l'autobus scolaire
♦ **a bus station** une gare routière
♦ **a bus ticket** un ticket d'autobus

bush NOUN
① le buisson (*shrub*)
② les bois MASC PL (*forest*)
♦ **a sugar bush** une érablière

business NOUN
① l' entreprise FEM (*firm*) ◊ *He's got his own business.* Il a sa propre entreprise.
② les affaires FEM PL (*commerce*) ◊ *She's away on business.* Elle est en voyage d'affaires.
♦ **a business trip** un voyage d'affaires
♦ **It's none of my business.** Ça ne me regarde pas.

businessman NOUN
l' homme d'affaires MASC

businesswoman NOUN
la femme d'affaires

bust NOUN
la poitrine (*chest*)

busy ADJECTIVE
① occupé (*person, phone line*)
② chargé (*day, schedule*)
③ très fréquenté (*store, street*)

busy signal NOUN
la tonalité « occupé »

but CONJUNCTION
mais ◊ *I'd like to come, but I'm busy.* J'aimerais venir mais je suis occupé.

butcher NOUN
le boucher ◊ *He's a butcher.* Il est boucher.

butcher shop NOUN
la boucherie

butter NOUN
le beurre

butterfly NOUN
le papillon

buttocks PL NOUN
les fesses FEM PL

button NOUN
le bouton

to **buy** VERB

$\boxed{\text{see also } \textbf{buy} \text{ NOUN}}$

acheter ◊ *She bought me an ice cream.* Elle m'a acheté une crème glacée. ◊ *I bought her an ice cream.* Je lui ai acheté une crème glacée.
♦ **to buy something from somebody** acheter quelque chose à quelqu'un ◊ *I bought a watch from him.* Je lui ai acheté une montre.

buy NOUN

$\boxed{\text{see also } \textbf{buy} \text{ VERB}}$

♦ **It was a good buy.** C'était une bonne affaire.

to **buzz** VERB
① bourdonner (*insect*)
② appeler par interphone (*intercom*)

buzzer NOUN
la sonnerie

by PREPOSITION
① par ◊ *The thieves were caught by the police.* Les voleurs ont été arrêtés par la police.
② de ◊ *a painting by Emily Carr* un tableau d'Emily Carr ◊ *a book by Kenneth Oppel* un livre de Kenneth Oppel
③ en ◊ *by car* en voiture ◊ *by train* en train ◊ *by bus* en autobus
④ à côté de (*close to*) ◊ *"Where's the bank?" "It's by the post office."* « Où est la banque? » « Elle est à côté de la poste. »
⑤ avant (*not later than*) ◊ *We have to be there by 4 o'clock.* Nous devons y être avant quatre heures.
♦ **by the time...** quand... ◊ *By the time I got there it was too late.* Quand je suis arrivé il était déjà trop tard. ◊ *It'll be ready by the time you get back.* Ça sera prêt quand vous reviendrez.
♦ **That's fine by me.** Ça me va.
♦ **all by himself** tout seul
♦ **all by herself** toute seule
♦ **I did it all by myself.** Je l'ai fait tout seul.
♦ **by the way** au fait

bye EXCLAMATION
salut!

by-product NOUN
le sous-produit

C

cab NOUN
le taxi

cabbage NOUN
le chou
(PL les choux)

cabin NOUN
le chalet (*cottage*)
♦ **a log cabin** un chalet en bois rond

cabinet NOUN
♦ **a medicine cabinet** une armoire de salle de bain

cable NOUN
le câble

cable car NOUN
le téléphérique

cable television NOUN
la télévision par câble

cactus NOUN
le cactus

café NOUN
le café

cafeteria NOUN
la cafétéria

cage NOUN
la cage

Cajun ADJECTIVE

see also **Cajun** NOUN

cajun MASC, FEM, PL ◊ *Cajun cuisine* la cuisine cajun

Cajun NOUN

see also **Cajun** ADJECTIVE

le/la Cajun

cake NOUN
le gâteau
(PL les gâteaux)

to **calculate** VERB
calculer

calculation NOUN
le calcul

calculator NOUN
la calculatrice

calendar NOUN
le calendrier

calf NOUN
1 (*of cow*)
le veau
(PL les veaux)
2 le mollet (*of leg*)

call NOUN

see also **call** VERB

l' appel MASC (*by phone*) ◊ *Thanks for your call.* Merci de votre appel.
♦ **a phone call** un coup de téléphone
♦ **to be on call** (*doctor*) être de permanence ◊ *She's on call this evening.* Elle est de permanence ce soir.

to **call** VERB

see also **call** NOUN

appeler ◊ *I'll tell him you called.* Je lui dirai que vous avez appelé. ◊ *This is the number to call.* C'est le numéro à appeler. ◊ *We called the police.* Nous avons appelé la police. ◊ *Everyone calls her Marie.* Tout le monde l'appelle Marie.
♦ **to be called** s'appeler ◊ *The game is called Drago.* Le jeu s'appelle Drago. ◊ *What's this dish called?* Comment s'appelle ce plat?
♦ **to call somebody names** insulter quelqu'un
♦ **He called me an idiot.** Il m'a traité d'imbécile.

to **call back** VERB
rappeler (*phone again*) ◊ *I'll call back at 6 o'clock.* Je rappellerai à six heures.

to **call for** VERB
passer prendre (*pick up*) ◊ *I'll call for you at 2:30.* Je passerai te prendre à deux heures et demie.
♦ **This calls for a celebration!** Il faut fêter ça!

to **call off** VERB
annuler ◊ *The game was called off.* Le match a été annulé.

calm ADJECTIVE
calme

to **calm down** VERB
se calmer ◊ *Calm down!* Calme-toi!

calorie NOUN
la calorie

calves PL NOUN *see* **calf**

camcorder NOUN
le caméscope

came VERB *see* **come**

camel NOUN
le chameau
(PL les chameaux)

camera NOUN
1 (*for photos*)
l' appareil photo MASC

(PL les appareils photo)
② la caméra (*movie, TV*)

cameraman NOUN
① le cadreur
② la cadreuse

to **camp** VERB

> *see also* **camp** NOUN

camper

camp NOUN

> *see also* **camp** VERB

le camp
♦ **a camp stove** un réchaud de camping
♦ **to break camp** lever le camp
♦ **to set up camp** installer son camp
◊ *We set up camp by the river.* Nous avons installé notre camp à côté de la rivière.

campaign NOUN
la campagne

camper NOUN
① (*person*)
le campeur
la campeuse
② la caravane (*van*)

campfire NOUN
le feu de camp

campground NOUN
le terrain de camping

camping NOUN
le camping
♦ **to go camping** faire du camping ◊ *We went camping in the Yukon.* Nous avons fait du camping au Yukon.

campsite NOUN
l' emplacement (de camping) MASC

campus NOUN
le campus

can NOUN

> *see also* **can** VERB

① la boîte (*food*) ◊ *a can of corn* une boîte de maïs
② la canette (*drink*) ◊ *a can of pop* une canette de boisson gazeuse

can VERB

> *see also* **can** NOUN

① pouvoir (*be able to, be allowed to*)
◊ *I can't come.* Je ne peux pas venir.
◊ *Can I help you?* Est-ce que je peux vous aider? ◊ *Can I use your phone?* Est-ce que je peux me servir de votre téléphone? ◊ *You could rent a bike.* Tu pourrais louer un vélo. ◊ *I couldn't sleep because of the noise.* Je ne pouvais pas dormir à cause du bruit.

> *can* is sometimes not translated.

◊ *I can't hear you.* Je ne t'entends pas. ◊ *I can't remember.* Je ne m'en

souviens pas. ◊ *Can you speak French?* Parlez-vous français?
② savoir (*know how to*) ◊ *I can swim.* Je sais nager. ◊ *He can't drive.* Il ne sait pas conduire.
♦ **That can't be true!** Ce n'est pas possible!
♦ **You could be right.** Vous avez peut-être raison.

Canada NOUN
le Canada
♦ **in Canada** au Canada
♦ **to Canada** au Canada

🦫 **Canada Day** NOUN
la Fête du Canada

Canada goose NOUN
l' outarde FEM

Canadian ADJECTIVE

> *see also* **Canadian** NOUN

canadien MASC
canadienne FEM

Canadian NOUN

> *see also* **Canadian** ADJECTIVE

le Canadien
la Canadienne

Canadian Shield NOUN
le Bouclier canadien

canal NOUN
le canal
(PL les canaux)

canary NOUN
le canari

to **cancel** VERB
annuler ◊ *The game was cancelled.* Le match a été annulé.

cancellation NOUN
l' annulation FEM

cancer NOUN
① le cancer ◊ *She's got cancer.* Elle a le cancer.
② le Cancer ◊ *I'm a Cancer.* Je suis Cancer.

candidate NOUN
le candidat
la candidate

candle NOUN
la bougie

candy NOUN
les bonbons MASC PL
♦ **a candy** un bonbon

canned ADJECTIVE
en conserve (*food*)

cannot VERB *see* **can**

canoe NOUN
le canot

canoeing NOUN

le canotage
♦ **to go canoeing** faire du canotage
◊ *We went canoeing.* Nous avons fait du canotage.

🌟 **canola** NOUN
le canola ◊ *canola oil* l'huile de canola FEM

can opener NOUN
l' ouvre-boîte MASC

can't VERB *see* **can**

canvas NOUN
la toile

cap NOUN
1 la casquette (*hat*)
2 le bouchon (*of bottle, tube*)

capable ADJECTIVE
capable

capital NOUN
1 la capitale ◊ *Toronto is the capital of Ontario.* Toronto est la capitale de l'Ontario.
2 la majuscule (*letter*) ◊ *Write your address in capitals.* Écris ton adresse en majuscules.

capital punishment NOUN
la peine capitale

Capricorn NOUN
le Capricorne ◊ *I'm a Capricorn.* Je suis Capricorne.

to **capsize** VERB
1 chavirer ◊ *The boat capsized.* Le bateau a chaviré.
2 faire chavirer ◊ *Careful, you'll capsize the boat.* Attention, tu vas faire chavirer le bateau.

captain NOUN
le capitaine ◊ *She's captain of the hockey team.* Elle est capitaine de l'équipe de hockey.

caption NOUN
la légende

to **capture** VERB
capturer

car NOUN
la voiture
♦ **to go by car** aller en voiture ◊ *We went by car.* Nous y sommes allés en voiture.
♦ **a car accident** un accident de voiture

caramel NOUN
le caramel

carbohydrate NOUN
le glucide ◊ *Pasta is high in carbohydrates.* Les pâtes contiennent beaucoup de glucides.

card NOUN
la carte
♦ **a card game** un jeu de cartes

cardboard NOUN
le carton

cardigan NOUN
le cardigan

care NOUN
see also **care** VERB
le soin ◊ *with care* avec soin
♦ **to take care of** s'occuper de ◊ *I take care of the children on Saturdays.* Le samedi, je m'occupe des enfants.
♦ **Take care! (1)** (*Be careful!*) Fais attention!
♦ **Take care! (2)** (*Look after yourself!*) Prends bien soin de toi!

to **care** VERB
see also **care** NOUN
♦ **to care about** se soucier de ◊ *They don't care about their image.* Ils se soucient peu de leur image.
♦ **I don't care!** Ça m'est égal! ◊ *He doesn't care.* Ça lui est égal.
♦ **to care for somebody** (*patients, elderly people*) s'occuper de quelqu'un

career NOUN
la carrière
♦ **Career day** la journée d'orientation
♦ **Career Studies** (*course*) Choix de carrières

careful ADJECTIVE
♦ **Be careful!** Fais attention!

carefully ADVERB
1 soigneusement ◊ *He carefully avoided talking about it.* Il évitait soigneusement d'en parler.
2 prudemment (*safely*) ◊ *Drive carefully!* Conduisez prudemment!
♦ **Think carefully!** Réfléchis bien!

caregiver NOUN
1 (*for children*)
le gardien
la gardienne
2 (*for sick person*)
le soignant
la soignante

careless ADJECTIVE
1 peu soigné (*work*)
♦ **a careless mistake** une faute d'inattention
2 (*person*)
peu soigneux MASC
peu soigneuse FEM ◊ *She's very careless.* Elle est bien peu soigneuse.
3 imprudent ◊ *a careless driver* un conducteur imprudent

caribou NOUN
le caribou
♦ **caribou hide** la peau de caribou

caring ADJECTIVE

♦ **She's a very caring teacher.** C'est un professeur qui se préoccupe du bien-être de ses élèves.
♦ **She has very caring parents.** Ses parents sont très affectueux.

carnation NOUN
l' œillet MASC

carnival NOUN
le carnaval

carol NOUN
♦ **a Christmas carol** une cantique de Noël

carpenter NOUN
le menuisier
la menuisière ◊ *He's a carpenter.* Il est menuisier.

carpentry NOUN
la menuiserie

carpet NOUN
1 le tapis ◊ *a Persian carpet* un tapis persan
2 la moquette (*broadloom*)

car rental NOUN
la location de voitures

carrot NOUN
la carotte

to **carry** VERB
1 porter ◊ *I'll carry your bag.* Je vais porter ton sac.
2 transporter ◊ *a plane carrying 100 passengers* un avion transportant cent passagers

to **carry on** VERB
1 soutenir ◊ *How can you carry on a conversation with all this noise?* Comment peut-on soutenir une conversation avec tout ce bruit?
2 continuer ◊ *Carry on!* Continue! ◊ *She carried on with her life as before.* Elle a continué sa vie comme auparavant.

to **carry out** VERB
exécuter (*orders*)

cart NOUN
la charrette

carton NOUN
le carton (*milk, cream*)

cartoon NOUN
1 le dessin animé (*film*)
2 la caricature (*in newspaper*)

cartridge NOUN
la cartouche
♦ **printer cartridge** une cartouche d'imprimante

to **carve** VERB
1 sculpter ◊ *He carved a little boat out of wood.* Il a sculpté un petit bateau en bois.

2 graver ◊ *We carved our initials into the bench.* Nous avons gravé nos initiales sur le banc.

car wash NOUN
le lave-auto
(PL les lave-autos)

case NOUN
1 l' étui MASC ◊ *a violin case* un étui de violon
2 le cas
(PL les cas) ◊ *in some cases* dans certains cas
♦ **in that case** dans ce cas ◊ *"I don't want it." "In that case, I'll take it."* « Je n'en veux pas. » « Dans ce cas, je le prends. »
♦ **in case** au cas où ◊ *in case it rains* au cas où il pleuvrait
♦ **just in case** à tout hasard ◊ *Take some money, just in case.* Prends de l'argent à tout hasard.

cash NOUN
l' argent MASC ◊ *I'm a bit short of cash.* Je suis un peu à court d'argent.
♦ **in cash** en liquide ◊ *$200 in cash* deux cent dollars en liquide
♦ **to pay cash** payer comptant
♦ **a cash card** une carte de retrait
♦ **the cash desk** la caisse
♦ **a cash dispenser** un guichet automatique
♦ **a cash register** une caisse

cashew NOUN
la noix de cajou

cashier NOUN
le caissier
la caissière

cashmere NOUN
le cachemire ◊ *a cashmere sweater* un chandail en cachemire

casino NOUN
le casino

casserole NOUN
la casserole ◊ *a tuna casserole* une casserole de thon
♦ **a casserole dish** une cocotte

cassette NOUN
la cassette
♦ **a cassette player** un lecteur de cassettes
♦ **a cassette recorder** un magnétophone

cast NOUN
1 les acteurs MASC PL ◊ *After the play, we met the cast.* Après la représentation, nous avons rencontré les acteurs.
2 le plâtre (*for broken bone*)

castle NOUN
le château
(PL les châteaux)

casual ADJECTIVE
  [1] décontracté ◊ *casual clothes* les vêtements décontractés
  [2] désinvolte ◊ *a casual attitude* une attitude désinvolte
  [3] en passant ◊ *It was just a casual remark.* C'était juste une remarque en passant.

casually ADVERB
  ♦ **to dress casually** s'habiller de façon décontractée

cat NOUN
  le chat
  la chatte

catalogue NOUN
  le catalogue

catastrophe NOUN
  la catastrophe

to **catch** VERB
  [1] attraper ◊ *to catch a thief* attraper un voleur ◊ *My cat catches birds.* Mon chat attrape des oiseaux.
  ♦ **to catch somebody doing something** attraper quelqu'un en train de faire quelque chose ◊ *if they catch you cheating* s'ils t'attrapent en train de tricher
  ♦ **to catch a cold** attraper un rhume
  [2] prendre (*bus, train*) ◊ *We caught the last bus.* On a pris le dernier autobus.
  [3] saisir (*hear*) ◊ *I didn't catch his name.* Je n'ai pas saisi son nom.
  ♦ **to catch up** rattraper son retard ◊ *I have to catch up: I was away last week.* Je dois rattraper mon retard : j'étais absent la semaine dernière.
  ♦ **to catch up with somebody** rattraper quelqu'un
  ♦ **to get caught up in something** être pris dans quelque chose

category NOUN
  la catégorie

cathedral NOUN
  la cathédrale

Catholic ADJECTIVE

  | *see also* **Catholic** NOUN |

  catholique

Catholic NOUN

  | *see also* **Catholic** ADJECTIVE |

  le/la catholique ◊ *I'm a Catholic.* Je suis catholique.

cattle PL NOUN
  le bétail SING

caught VERB *see* **catch**

cauliflower NOUN
  le chou-fleur
  (PL les choux-fleurs)

cause NOUN

  | *see also* **cause** VERB |

  la cause

to **cause** VERB

  | *see also* **cause** NOUN |

  provoquer ◊ *to cause an accident* provoquer un accident

caution INTERJECTION
  Attention!

cautious ADJECTIVE
  prudent

cautiously ADVERB
  avec précaution ◊ *She cautiously opened the door.* Elle a ouvert la porte avec précaution.
  ♦ **He reacted cautiously.** Il a réagi prudemment.

cave NOUN
  la grotte

cavity NOUN
  la carie (*in tooth*) ◊ *I have cavities.* J'ai des caries.

CCTV (= *closed-circuit television*) NOUN
  la télévision en circuit fermé

CD NOUN
  le DC (*abbreviation for disque compact*)
  (PL les DC)

CD burner NOUN
  le graveur de DC

CD player NOUN
  le lecteur de DC

CD-ROM NOUN
  le CD-ROM
  (PL les CD-ROM)

  CD-ROM can also be written cédérom (PL cédéroms) in French.

CE ABBREVIATION (= *Common Era*)
  ap. J.-C. (= après Jésus-Christ) ◊ *in 800 CE* en huit cents après Jésus-Christ

ceasefire NOUN
  le cessez-le-feu
  (PL les cessez-le-feu)

cedar NOUN
  le cèdre

ceiling NOUN
  le plafond

to **celebrate** VERB
  fêter

celebrity NOUN
  la célébrité

celery NOUN
  le céleri

cell NOUN

la <u>cellule</u>

cellar NOUN
la <u>cave</u>

cello NOUN
le <u>violoncelle</u> ◊ *I play the cello.* Je joue du violoncelle.

cellphone NOUN
la <u>téléphone cellulaire</u>

Celsius ADJECTIVE
<u>Celsius</u> ◊ *20 degrees Celsius* vingt degrés Celsius

cement NOUN
le <u>ciment</u>

cemetery NOUN
le <u>cimetière</u>

cent NOUN
le <u>cent</u> ◊ *twenty cents* vingt cents

centennial NOUN
le <u>centenaire</u>

centimetre NOUN
le <u>centimètre</u>

central ADJECTIVE
<u>central</u>
(MASC PL centraux)

central heating NOUN
le <u>chauffage central</u>

centre NOUN
le <u>centre</u> ◊ *a sports centre* un centre sportif

century NOUN
le <u>siècle</u> ◊ *the 20th century* le vingtième siècle ◊ *the 21st century* le vingt et unième siècle

cereal NOUN
les <u>céréales</u> FEM PL ◊ *I have cereal for breakfast.* Je prends des céréales au petit déjeuner.

ceremony NOUN
la <u>cérémonie</u>

certain ADJECTIVE
<u>certain</u> ◊ *a certain person* une certaine personne ◊ *I'm absolutely certain it was him.* Je suis absolument certain que c'était lui.
♦ **I don't know for certain.** Je n'en suis pas certain.
♦ **to make certain** s'assurer ◊ *I made certain the door was locked.* Je me suis assuré que la porte était fermée à clé.

certainly ADVERB
<u>vraiment</u> ◊ *I certainly expected something better.* Je m'attendais vraiment à quelque chose de mieux.
♦ **Certainly not!** Certainement pas!
♦ **"So it was a surprise?" "It certainly was!"** « C'était donc une surprise? » « Ça oui alors! »

certificate NOUN
le <u>certificat</u>

CFCs PL NOUN
les <u>CFC</u> MASC

chain NOUN
la <u>chaîne</u>

chair NOUN
[1] la <u>chaise</u> ◊ *a table and 4 chairs* une table et quatre chaises
[2] le <u>fauteuil</u> (*armchair*)

chairlift NOUN
le <u>télésiège</u>

chairperson NOUN
le <u>président</u>
la <u>présidente</u>

chalet NOUN
le <u>chalet</u>

chalk NOUN
la <u>craie</u>

chalkboard NOUN
le <u>tableau</u>

challenge NOUN

see also **challenge** VERB

le <u>défi</u>

to **challenge** VERB

see also **challenge** NOUN

[1] <u>défier</u> ◊ *to challenge authority* défier l'autorité
♦ **She challenged me to a race.** Elle m'a proposé de faire la course avec elle.
[2] <u>contester</u> ◊ *to challenge somebody's opinion* contester l'avis de quelqu'un

challenging ADJECTIVE
<u>stimulant</u> ◊ *a challenging job* un travail stimulant

champion NOUN
le <u>champion</u>
la <u>championne</u>

championship NOUN
le <u>championnat</u>

chance NOUN
[1] la <u>chance</u> ◊ *Do you think I've got a chance?* Tu crois que j'ai une chance? ◊ *Their chances of winning are very good.* Ils ont de fortes chances de gagner.
♦ **Not a chance!** Pas question!
[2] l' <u>occasion</u> FEM ◊ *I'd like to have a chance to travel.* J'aimerais avoir l'occasion de voyager.
♦ **I'll write when I get the chance.** J'écrirai quand j'aurai un moment.
♦ **by chance** par hasard ◊ *We met by chance.* Nous nous sommes rencontrés par hasard.
♦ **to take a chance** prendre un risque ◊ *I'm taking no chances!* Je ne veux

C

prendre aucun risque!

to **change** VERB

see also **change** NOUN

1 changer ◊ *The town has changed a lot.* La ville a beaucoup changé. ◊ *I'd like to change $50.* Je voudrais changer cinquante dollars.

Use **changer de** when you change one thing for another.

2 changer de ◊ *You have to change planes in Edmonton.* Il faut changer d'avion à Edmonton. ◊ *I'm going to change my shoes.* Je vais changer de chaussures. ◊ *He wants to change his job.* Il veut changer d'emploi.

♦ **to change one's mind** changer d'avis ◊ *I've changed my mind.* J'ai changé d'avis.

♦ **to change gears** changer de vitesse

3 se changer ◊ *She's changing to go out.* Elle est en train de se changer pour sortir.

♦ **to get changed** se changer ◊ *I'm going to get changed.* Je vais me changer.

4 échanger (*exchange*) ◊ *Can I change this sweater? It's too small.* Est-ce que je peux échanger ce chandail? Il est trop petit.

change NOUN

see also **change** VERB

1 le changement ◊ *There's been a change of plan.* Il y a eu un changement de programme.
2 la monnaie (*money*) ◊ *I haven't got any change.* Je n'ai pas de monnaie.

♦ **a change of clothes** des vêtements de rechange

♦ **for a change** pour changer ◊ *Let's play tennis for a change.* Si on jouait au tennis pour changer?

changeable ADJECTIVE
variable

change room NOUN
1 le salon d'essayage (*in store*)
2 le vestiaire (*for sport*)

channel NOUN
la chaîne (*TV*) ◊ *There's hockey on the other channel.* Il y a du hockey sur l'autre chaîne.

chaos NOUN
le chaos

chapel NOUN
la chapelle (*part of church*)

chapped ADJECTIVE
gercé ◊ *I have chapped lips.* J'ai les lèvres gercées.

chapter NOUN
le chapitre

character NOUN
1 le caractère ◊ *Give me some idea of his character.* Décris-moi un peu son caractère.

♦ **She's quite a character.** C'est un drôle de numéro.
2 le personnage (*in play, film*) ◊ *The character played by Donald Sutherland...* Le personnage joué par Donald Sutherland...

characteristic NOUN
la caractéristique

charcoal NOUN
le charbon de bois

charge NOUN

see also **charge** VERB

les frais MASC PL ◊ *Is there a charge for delivery?* Est-ce qu'il y a des frais de livraison?

♦ **an extra charge** un supplément
♦ **free of charge** gratuit
♦ **to reverse the charges** appeler à frais virés ◊ *I'd like to reverse the charges.* Je voudrais appeler à frais virés.
♦ **to be in charge** être responsable ◊ *She was in charge of the group.* Elle était responsable du groupe.

to **charge** VERB

see also **charge** NOUN

1 prendre (*money*) ◊ *How much did she charge you?* Combien est-ce qu'elle vous a demandé? ◊ *They charge $10 an hour.* Ils demandent dix dollars de l'heure.
2 inculper (*with crime*) ◊ *The police have charged him with fraud.* La police l'a inculpé de fraude.

charity NOUN
l' association caritative FEM ◊ *They gave the money to charity.* Ils ont donné l'argent à une association caritative.

charm NOUN
le charme ◊ *He's got a lot of charm.* Il a beaucoup de charme.

charming ADJECTIVE
charmant

chart NOUN
le tableau
(PL les tableaux) ◊ *The chart shows the increase in unemployment.* Le tableau indique la progression du chômage.

♦ **the charts** le palmarès ◊ *This album is number one in the charts.* Cet album est numéro un au palmarès.

to **chase** VERB

see also **chase** NOUN

pourchasser

C

chase NOUN

see also **chase** VERB

la poursuite ◊ *a car chase* une poursuite en voiture

chat NOUN

see also **chat** VERB

[1] le bavardage ◊ *Enough chat; let's get to work.* Assez de bavardage; mettons-nous au travail.
[2] le clavardage (*online*)
♦ **to have a chat** bavarder

to **chat** VERB

see also **chat** NOUN

[1] bavarder
[2] clavarder (*online*)

chat room NOUN
le clavardoir

chauvinist NOUN
♦ **a male chauvinist** un machiste

cheap ADJECTIVE
bon marché MASC, FEM, PL ◊ *a cheap T-shirt* un T-shirt bon marché

cheaper ADJECTIVE
moins cher MASC
moins chère FEM ◊ *It's cheaper by bus.* C'est moins cher en autobus.

to **cheat** VERB
tricher ◊ *You're cheating!* Tu triches!

cheater NOUN
le tricheur
la tricheuse

check NOUN

see also **check** VERB

[1] le contrôle ◊ *a security check* un contrôle de sécurité
[2] la coche (*mark*)
[3] le carreau (*square in pattern*)

to **check** VERB

see also **check** NOUN

vérifier ◊ *I'll check the time of the flight.* Je vais vérifier l'heure du vol. ◊ *Could you check the oil, please?* Pourriez-vous vérifier le niveau d'huile, s'il vous plaît?
♦ **to check in (1)** (*at airport*) se présenter à l'enregistrement ◊ *What time do I have to check in?* À quelle heure est-ce que je dois me présenter à l'enregistrement?
♦ **to check in (2)** (*in hotel*) se présenter à la réception
♦ **to check on** jeter un coup d'œil sur ◊ *Check on the baby.* Jette un coup d'œil sur le bébé.
♦ **to check out** (*from hotel*) régler sa note

checked ADJECTIVE
à carreaux (*fabric*)

checkers NOUN
les dames FEM PL ◊ *to play checkers* jouer aux dames

check-in NOUN
l' enregistrement MASC

checkout NOUN
la caisse

checkup NOUN
l' examen de santé MASC

cheek NOUN
la joue ◊ *He kissed her on the cheek.* Il l'a embrassée sur la joue.

cheer NOUN

see also **cheer** VERB

les hourras MASC PL
♦ **to give a cheer** pousser des hourras
♦ **Cheers! (1)** (*good health*) À la vôtre!
♦ **Cheers (2)** (*goodbye*) Salut

to **cheer** VERB

see also **cheer** NOUN

applaudir
♦ **to cheer somebody up** remonter le moral à quelqu'un ◊ *I was trying to cheer them up.* J'essayais de leur remonter le moral.
♦ **Cheer up!** Ne te laisse pas abattre!

cheerful ADJECTIVE
gai

cheese NOUN
le fromage
♦ **cheese curds** du fromage en grains

chef NOUN
le chef

chemical ADJECTIVE
chimique ◊ *a chemical reaction* une réaction chimique ◊ *chemical weapons* les armes chimiques FEM PL

chemical NOUN
le produit chimique

chemist NOUN
le/la chimiste

chemistry NOUN
la chimie ◊ *the chemistry lab* le laboratoire de chimie

cheque NOUN
le chèque ◊ *to write a cheque* faire un chèque ◊ *to pay by cheque* payer par chèque

cherry NOUN
la cerise
♦ **a cherry tree** un cerisier

chess NOUN
les échecs MASC PL ◊ *to play chess* jouer aux échecs

chessboard NOUN

l' échiquier MASC

chest NOUN
la <u>poitrine</u> (*of person*) ◊ *his chest measurement* son tour de poitrine
♦ **a chest of drawers** une commode

chestnut NOUN
le <u>marron</u> ◊ *roasted chestnuts* les marrons grillés

to **chew** VERB
<u>mâcher</u>

chewing gum NOUN
le <u>gomme à mâcher</u>

chick NOUN
le <u>poussin</u> ◊ *a hen and her chicks* une poule et ses poussins

chicken NOUN
[1] le <u>poulet</u> (*meat*)
[2] la <u>poule</u> (*live bird*) ◊ *to raise chickens* élever des poules

chicken pox NOUN
la <u>varicelle</u>

chick peas PL NOUN
les <u>pois chiches</u> MASC

chief NOUN

see also **chief** ADJECTIVE

le <u>chef</u> ◊ *the chief of security* le chef de la sécurité
🐾 ♦ **band chief** un chef de bande

chief ADJECTIVE

see also **chief** NOUN

<u>principal</u> ◊ *Canada's chief exports* les articles d'exportation principaux du Canada

child NOUN
l' <u>enfant</u> MASC/FEM ◊ *all the children* tous les enfants

childish ADJECTIVE
<u>puéril</u>

children PL NOUN *see* **child**

chili NOUN
[1] le <u>piment</u> (*pepper*)
[2] le <u>chili</u> (*dish*)

to **chill** VERB
<u>mettre au frais</u> ◊ *Put the wine in the fridge to chill.* Mets le vin au frais dans le réfrigérateur.

chilly ADJECTIVE
<u>froid</u>

chimney NOUN
la <u>cheminée</u>

chin NOUN
le <u>menton</u>

china NOUN
la <u>porcelaine</u> ◊ *a china plate* une assiette en porcelaine

🐾 **chinook** NOUN
le <u>chinook</u> (*wind*)

chip NOUN
[1] la <u>croustille</u> (*potato chip*) ◊ *a bag of chips* un sac de croustilles
[2] la <u>frite</u> (*fry*) ◊ *fish and chips* poisson et frites
[3] la <u>brisure</u> (*chocolate*)
[4] la <u>puce</u> (*in computer*)
♦ **This plate has a chip in it.** Cette assiette est ébréchée.

chipmunk NOUN
🐾 le <u>suisse</u>

chives PL NOUN
la <u>ciboulette</u> SING

chocolate NOUN
le <u>chocolat</u> ◊ *a chocolate cake* un gâteau au chocolat
♦ **hot chocolate** le chocolat chaud

chocolate chip NOUN
la <u>brisure de chocolat</u>
♦ **a chocolate chip cookie** un biscuit aux brisures de chocolat

choice NOUN
le <u>choix</u> ◊ *I had no choice.* Je n'avais pas le choix.

choir NOUN
la <u>chorale</u> ◊ *I sing in the school choir.* Je chante dans la chorale de l'école.

to **choke** VERB
<u>s'étrangler</u>
♦ **He choked on a fishbone.** Il s'est étranglé avec une arête de poisson.

to **choose** VERB
<u>choisir</u> ◊ *It's difficult to choose.* C'est difficile de choisir. ◊ *I chose to stay home.* J'ai décidé de rester chez moi.

to **chop** VERB

see also **chop** NOUN

[1] <u>émincer</u> ◊ *Chop the onions.* Émincez les oignons.
[2] <u>couper</u> (*wood*)
♦ **to chop down a tree** abattre un arbre

chop NOUN

see also **chop** VERB

la <u>côtelette</u> ◊ *a pork chop* une côtelette de porc

chopsticks PL NOUN
les <u>baguettes</u> FEM PL

chose, chosen VERB *see* **choose**

Christian NOUN

see also **Christian** ADJECTIVE

le <u>chrétien</u>
la <u>chrétienne</u>

Christian ADJECTIVE

see also **Christian** NOUN

C

chrétien MASC
chrétienne FEM

Christmas NOUN
Noël MASC ◊ *Merry Christmas!* Joyeux Noël!
♦ **Christmas Day** le jour de Noël
♦ **Christmas Eve** la veille de Noël

chronic ADJECTIVE
chronique ◊ *a chronic cough* une toux chronique

chunk NOUN
le gros morceau
(PL les gros morceaux) ◊ *Cut the meat into chunks.* Coupez la viande en gros morceaux.

church NOUN
l' église FEM

cider NOUN
le cidre

cigarette NOUN
la cigarette

cinema NOUN
le cinéma

cinnamon NOUN
la cannelle

circle NOUN

| see also **circle** VERB |

le cercle ◊ *to stand in a circle* faire cercle ◊ *to draw a circle* tracer un cercle ◊ *to go around in circles* tourner en rond

to **circle** VERB

| see also **circle** NOUN |

encercler ◊ *Circle the correct answer.* Encerclez la bonne réponse.

circular ADJECTIVE
circulaire

circulation NOUN
1 la circulation (*of blood*)
2 le tirage (*of newspaper*)

circumflex NOUN
l' accent circonflexe MASC

circumstances PL NOUN
les circonstances FEM PL

circus NOUN
le cirque

citizen NOUN
le citoyen
la citoyenne ◊ *a Canadian citizen* un citoyen canadien

citizenship NOUN
la citoyenneté

city NOUN
la ville
♦ **the city centre** le centre-ville ◊ *It's in the city centre.* C'est au centre-ville.

city hall NOUN
l' hôtel de ville MASC

civilization NOUN
la civilisation

civil servant NOUN
le/la fonctionnaire

civil war NOUN
la guerre civile

to **claim** VERB

| see also **claim** NOUN |

1 prétendre ◊ *He claims to have found the money.* Il prétend avoir trouvé l'argent.
2 réclamer ◊ *No one has claimed this jacket.* Personne n'a réclamé cette veste.

claim NOUN

| see also **claim** VERB |

la demande d'indemnité (*on insurance policy*) ◊ *to make a claim* faire une demande d'indemnité

clam NOUN
la palourde

to **clap** VERB
applaudir (*applaud*)
♦ **to clap one's hands** frapper dans ses mains ◊ *I've trained my dog to sit when I clap my hands.* J'ai dressé mon chien à s'asseoir quand je frappe dans mes mains.

clarinet NOUN
la clarinette ◊ *I play the clarinet.* Je joue de la clarinette.

to **clash** VERB
1 jurer (*colours*) ◊ *These two colours clash.* Ces deux couleurs jurent.
2 tomber en même temps (*events*) ◊ *The concert clashes with my party.* Le concert tombe en même temps que ma soirée.

clasp NOUN
le fermoir (*of necklace*)

class NOUN
1 la classe (*group*) ◊ *We're in the same class.* Nous sommes dans la même classe.
2 le cours (*lesson*) ◊ *I go to dancing classes.* Je vais à des cours de danse.

classic ADJECTIVE

| see also **classic** NOUN |

classique ◊ *a classic example* un cas classique

classic NOUN

| see also **classic** ADJECTIVE |

le classique (*book, film*)

classical ADJECTIVE
classique ◊ *I like classical music.*

☞

J'aime la musique classique.

classmate NOUN
le/la camarade de classe

classroom NOUN
la classe

claw NOUN
1. la griffe (of cat, dog)
2. la serre (of bird)
3. la pince (of crab, lobster)

clay NOUN
l' argile FEM

clean ADJECTIVE

see also **clean** VERB

propre ◊ a clean shirt une chemise propre

to **clean** VERB

see also **clean** ADJECTIVE

nettoyer

cleaner NOUN
(of building)
le préposé au ménage
la préposée au ménage

cleaners NOUN
la teinturerie

clear ADJECTIVE

see also **clear** VERB

1. clair ◊ a clear explanation une explication claire ◊ It's clear you don't believe me. Il est clair que tu ne me crois pas.
2. transparent ◊ clear plastic du plastique transparent
3. net (distinct) ◊ clear handwriting une écriture nette
4. libre (road, way) ◊ The road's clear now. La route est libre maintenant.

to **clear** VERB

see also **clear** ADJECTIVE

1. dégager ◊ The police are clearing the road after the accident. La police dégage la route après l'accident.
2. se dissiper (fog, mist) ◊ The mist cleared. La brume s'est dissipée.
♦ **to clear the table** débarrasser la table ◊ I'll clear the table. Je vais débarrasser la table.
♦ **to clear up** résoudre ◊ We've cleared up the problem. Nous avons résolu le problème.
♦ **I think it's going to clear up.** (weather) Je pense que le temps va se lever.

clearing NOUN
la clairière ◊ a clearing in the forest une clairière dans la forêt

clearly ADVERB
1. clairement ◊ She explained it very clearly. Elle l'a expliqué très clairement.
2. nettement ◊ The Labrador coast was clearly visible. On distinguait nettement la côte du Labrador.
3. distinctement ◊ to speak clearly parler distinctement

clementine NOUN
la clémentine

clever ADJECTIVE
astucieux MASC
astucieuse FEM ◊ a clever system un système astucieux
♦ **What a clever idea!** Quelle bonne idée!

click NOUN

see also **click** VERB

le petit bruit sec (of door, camera)

to **click** VERB

see also **click** NOUN

cliquer (with mouse)
♦ **to click on an icon** cliquer sur une icône
♦ **The lid clicked shut.** Le couvercle s'est fermé avec un petit bruit sec.

client NOUN
le client
la cliente

cliff NOUN
la falaise

climate NOUN
le climat

to **climb** VERB
1. escalader ◊ We're going to climb the Niagara Escarpment. Nous allons escalader l'escarpement du Niagara.
2. monter (stairs)
3. grimper dans (tree)

clinic NOUN
la clinique

clip NOUN

see also **clip** VERB

1. la barrette (for hair)
2. le court extrait (film) ◊ some clips from his latest film quelques courts extraits de son dernier film

to **clip** VERB

see also **clip** NOUN

1. attacher ◊ Clip these pages together. Attache ces pages.
2. couper ◊ She clipped my bangs. Elle m'a coupé la frange.
♦ **to clip an article out of the newspaper** découper un article dans le journal

clip-art NOUN
le clipart

clippers PL NOUN
♦ **nail clippers** le coupe-ongle SING
(PL les coupe-ongles)

cloakroom NOUN
le vestiaire (*for coats*)

clock NOUN
① l' horloge FEM ◊ *the church clock*
l'horloge de l'église
② la pendule (*smaller*)
♦ **an alarm clock** un réveil
♦ **a clock-radio** un radio-réveil

clockwork NOUN
♦ **Everything went like clockwork.** Tout
a marché comme sur des roulettes.

to **clog** VERB
boucher ◊ *The drain is clogged.*
L'égout est bouché.

clone NOUN

see also **clone** VERB

le clone (*animal, plant*)

to **clone** VERB

see also **clone** NOUN

cloner ◊ *a cloned sheep* un mouton
cloné

close ADJECTIVE, ADVERB

see also **close** VERB

① près (*near*) ◊ *The mall is very
close.* Le centre commercial est tout
près.
♦ **close to** près de ◊ *The youth hostel
is close to the station.* L'auberge de
jeunesse est près de la gare.
♦ **Come closer.** Rapproche-toi.
♦ **to look at something close up**
regarder quelque chose de près
② proche (*in relationship*) ◊ *We're
just inviting close relations.* Nous
n'invitons que les parents proches.
◊ *She's a close friend of mine.* C'est
une amie proche. ◊ *I'm very close
to my brother.* Je suis très proche de
mon frère.
③ très serré (*contest*) ◊ *It's going to
be very close.* Ça va être très serré.

to **close** VERB

see also **close** ADJECTIVE

① fermer ◊ *What time does the pool
close?* La piscine ferme à quelle
heure? ◊ *The stores close at 5.30.*
Les magasins ferment à cinq heures
et demie. ◊ *Please close the door.*
Fermez la porte, s'il vous plaît.
② se fermer ◊ *The doors close
automatically.* Les portes se ferment
automatiquement.

closed ADJECTIVE
fermé ◊ *The bank's closed.* La
banque est fermée.

closely ADVERB
de près (*look, examine*)

closet NOUN
🌸 le garde-robe ◊ *She hung her coat in
the closet.* Elle a pendu son manteau
dans le garde-robe.

close-up NOUN
le gros plan ◊ *Here's a close-up of
my boyfriend.* Voici un gros plan de
mon petit ami.

cloth NOUN
le tissu (*material*)
♦ **a cloth** un chiffon ◊ *Wipe it with
a damp cloth.* Nettoyez-le avec un
chiffon humide.

clothes PL NOUN
les vêtements MASC PL ◊ *new clothes*
des vêtements neufs
♦ **a clothes line** un fil à linge
♦ **a clothes peg** une pince à linge

cloud NOUN
le nuage

cloudy ADJECTIVE
nuageux MASC
nuageuse FEM

clove NOUN
♦ **a clove of garlic** une gousse d'ail

clown NOUN
le/la clown

club NOUN
le club ◊ *a golf club* (*society and for
playing golf*) un club de golf
♦ **the youth club** le club de jeunes
♦ **clubs** (*in cards*) le trèfle ◊ *the ace of
clubs* l'as de trèfle

clue NOUN
l' indice MASC ◊ *an important clue* un
indice important
♦ **I haven't a clue.** Je n'en ai pas la
moindre idée.

clumsy ADJECTIVE
maladroit

clutch NOUN
la pédale d'embrayage (*of car*)

clutter NOUN

see also **clutter** VERB

le désordre ◊ *There's too much
clutter in here.* Il y a trop de désordre
ici.

to **clutter** VERB

see also **clutter** NOUN

encombrer ◊ *Don't clutter up the
hallway.* N'encombrez pas le couloir.
◊ *a desk cluttered with papers and
books* un bureau encombré de
papiers et de livres

coach NOUN

☞

l' entraîneur MASC
🏒 l' entraîneuse FEM ◊ *the hockey coach* l'entraîneur de l'équipe de hockey

coal NOUN
le charbon
♦ **a coal mine** une mine de charbon
♦ **a coal miner** un mineur

coarse ADJECTIVE
1 (*surface, fabric*)
rugueux MASC
rugueuse FEM ◊ *The bag was made of coarse cloth.* Le sac était fait d'un tissu rugueux.
2 (*vulgar*)
grossier MASC
grossière FEM ◊ *coarse language* un langage grossier

coast NOUN
la côte ◊ *It's on the west coast of Canada.* C'est sur la côte ouest du Canada.

coast guard NOUN
le garde-côte (*boat*)
(PL les garde-côtes)

coat NOUN
le manteau
(PL les manteaux) ◊ *a warm coat* un manteau chaud
♦ **a coat of paint** une couche de peinture

coat hanger NOUN
le cintre

cobweb NOUN
la toile d'araignée

cocoa NOUN
le cacao ◊ *a cup of cocoa* une tasse de cacao

coconut NOUN
la noix de coco

cod NOUN
la morue

code NOUN
le code

coffee NOUN
le café
♦ **A cup of coffee, please.** Un café, s'il vous plaît.

coffeepot NOUN
la cafetière

coffee table NOUN
la table basse

coffin NOUN
le cercueil

coin NOUN
la pièce de monnaie

coincidence NOUN
la coïncidence

colander NOUN
la passoire

cold ADJECTIVE

see also **cold** NOUN

froid ◊ *The water's cold.* L'eau est froide.
♦ **cold cuts** l'assiette anglaise
♦ **It's cold today.** Il fait froid aujourd'hui.
♦ **to be cold** (*person*) avoir froid ◊ *I'm cold.* J'ai froid. ◊ *Are you cold?* Est-ce que tu as froid?

cold NOUN

see also **cold** ADJECTIVE

1 le froid ◊ *I can't stand the cold.* Je ne supporte pas le froid.
2 le rhume ◊ *to catch a cold* attraper un rhume
♦ **to have a cold** avoir un rhume ◊ *I've got a bad cold.* J'ai un gros rhume.
♦ **a cold sore** un bouton de fièvre

coleslaw NOUN
la salade de chou

to **collapse** VERB
s'effondrer ◊ *He collapsed.* Il s'est effondré.

collar NOUN
1 le col (*of coat, shirt*)
2 le collier (*for animal*)

collarbone NOUN
la clavicule ◊ *I broke my collarbone.* Je me suis cassé la clavicule.

colleague NOUN
le/la collègue

to **collect** VERB

see also **collect** ADVERB

1 ramasser ◊ *The teacher collected the homework.* Le professeur a ramassé les travaux.
2 faire collection de ◊ *I collect stamps.* Je fais collection de timbres.
3 faire une collecte ◊ *They're collecting for charity.* Ils font une collecte pour une association caritative.

collect ADVERB

see also **collect** VERB

♦ **to call collect** téléphoner à frais virés

collect call NOUN
l' appel à frais virés MASC

collection NOUN
1 la collection ◊ *my CD collection* ma collection de DC
2 la collecte ◊ *a collection for charity* une collecte pour une association caritative

collector NOUN
le collectionneur

la collectionneuse

college NOUN
le collège ◊ *a technical college* un collège d'enseignement technique

to **collide** VERB
entrer en collision

collision NOUN
la collision

colon NOUN
le deux-points (*punctuation mark*) (PL les deux-points)

colony NOUN
la colonie ◊ *the colony of New France* la colonie de la Nouvelle France

colour NOUN
la couleur ◊ *What colour is it?* C'est de quelle couleur?
♦ **a colour printer** une imprimante couleur
♦ **a colour scheme** une combinaison de couleurs

colourful ADJECTIVE
aux couleurs vives ◊ *a colourful skirt* une jupe aux couleurs vives

colouring NOUN
le colorant (*for food*)

column NOUN
① la colonne ◊ *to format text in columns* disposer un texte en colonnes
② la chronique ◊ *He writes a column for the school newspaper.* Il écrit une chronique pour le journal de l'école.

coma NOUN
le coma ◊ *to be in a coma* être dans le coma

comb NOUN
| see also **comb** VERB |
le peigne

to **comb** VERB
| see also **comb** NOUN |
♦ **to comb one's hair** se peigner ◊ *You haven't combed your hair.* Tu ne t'es pas peigné.

combination NOUN
la combinaison

to **combine** VERB
① allier ◊ *The film combines humour with suspense.* Le film allie l'humour au suspense.
② concilier ◊ *It's difficult to combine a career with family.* Il est difficile de concilier carrière et vie de famille.

to **come** VERB
① venir ◊ *Can I come too?* Est-ce que je peux venir aussi? ◊ *Some friends came to see us.* Quelques amis sont venus nous voir. ◊ *I'll come with you.* Je viens avec toi.
② arriver (*arrive*) ◊ *I'm coming!* J'arrive! ◊ *They came late.* Ils sont arrivés en retard. ◊ *The letter came this morning.* La lettre est arrivée ce matin.
♦ **to come back** revenir ◊ *Come back!* Reviens!
♦ **to come down (1)** (*person, elevator*) descendre
♦ **to come down (2)** (*prices*) baisser
♦ **to come from** venir de ◊ *Where do you come from?* Tu viens d'où?
♦ **to come in** entrer ◊ *Come in!* Entrez!
♦ **Come on!** Allez!
♦ **to come out** sortir ◊ *when we came out of the movie theatre* quand nous sommes sortis du cinéma ◊ *It's just come out on video.* Ça vient de sortir en vidéo.
♦ **None of my photos came out.** Mes photos n'ont rien donné.
♦ **to come around** reprendre connaissance (*after faint, operation*)
♦ **to come up** monter ◊ *Come up here!* Monte!
♦ **to come up to somebody (1)** s'approcher de quelqu'un ◊ *She came up to me and kissed me.* Elle s'est approchée de moi et m'a embrassé.
♦ **to come up to somebody (2)** (*to speak to them*) aborder quelqu'un ◊ *A man came up to me and said...* Un homme m'a abordé et m'a dit...

comedian NOUN
le/la comique

comedy NOUN
la comédie

to **comfort** VERB
consoler ◊ *He tried to comfort her.* Il a essayé de la consoler.

comfortable ADJECTIVE
① confortable (*bed, chair*)
② à l'aise (*person*) ◊ *I'm very comfortable, thanks.* Je suis parfaitement à l'aise, merci.

comic NOUN
l' illustré MASC (*magazine*)

comic strip NOUN
la bande dessinée

coming ADJECTIVE
prochain ◊ *in the coming months* au cours des prochains mois ◊ *this coming Thursday* jeudi prochain

comma NOUN
la virgule

command NOUN
| see also **command** VERB |

☞

l' <u>ordre</u> MASC
♦ **a good command of English** une bonne maîtrise de l'anglais

to **command** VERB

see also **command** NOUN

<u>ordonner</u> ◊ *He commanded us to leave.* Il nous a ordonné de partir.
♦ **She commands respect.** Elle commande le respect.

comment NOUN

see also **comment** VERB

le <u>commentaire</u> ◊ *He made no comment.* Il n'a fait aucun commentaire.
♦ **No comment!** Je n'ai rien à dire!

to **comment** VERB

see also **comment** NOUN

♦ **to comment on something** faire des commentaires sur quelque chose

commentary NOUN
le <u>reportage en direct</u> (*on TV, radio*)

commentator NOUN
le <u>commentateur sportif</u>
la <u>commentatrice sportive</u>

commercial NOUN
l' <u>annonce publicitaire</u> FEM

commission NOUN
la <u>commission</u> ◊ *Salesmen work on commission.* Les représentants travaillent à la commission.

to **commit** VERB
♦ **to commit a crime** commettre un crime
♦ **to commit oneself** s'engager ◊ *I don't want to commit myself.* Je ne veux pas m'engager.
♦ **to commit suicide** se suicider ◊ *She committed suicide.* Elle s'est suicidée.

committee NOUN
le <u>comité</u>

common ADJECTIVE

see also **common** NOUN

<u>courant</u> ◊ *a common expression* une expression courante
♦ **in common** en commun ◊ *We have a lot in common.* Nous avons beaucoup de choses en commun.

Commons PL NOUN
♦ **the House of Commons** la Chambre des communes

common sense NOUN
le <u>bon sens</u> ◊ *Use your common sense!* Sers-toi de ton bon sens!

to **communicate** VERB
<u>communiquer</u>

communication NOUN
la <u>communication</u>

communism NOUN
le <u>communisme</u>

communist NOUN

see also **communist** ADJECTIVE

le/la <u>communiste</u>

communist ADJECTIVE

see also **communist** NOUN

<u>communiste</u>

community NOUN
la <u>communauté</u>

community centre NOUN
le <u>centre communautaire</u>

✹ **community college** NOUN
le <u>collège communautaire</u>

to **commute** VERB
<u>faire la navette</u> ◊ *She commutes between Kitchener and Toronto.* Elle fait la navette entre Kitchener et Toronto.

commuter NOUN
le <u>navetteur</u>
la <u>navetteuse</u>
♦ **a commuter train** un train de banlieue

compact disc NOUN
le <u>disque compact</u>
♦ **a compact disc player** un lecteur de DC

companion NOUN
le <u>compagnon</u>
la <u>compagne</u>

company NOUN
[1] la <u>société</u> ◊ *She works for a big company.* Elle travaille pour une grosse société.
[2] la <u>compagnie</u> ◊ *an insurance company* une compagnie d'assurance ◊ *a theatre company* une compagnie théâtrale
♦ **to keep somebody company** tenir compagnie à quelqu'un ◊ *I'll keep you company.* Je vais te tenir compagnie.

comparatively ADVERB
<u>relativement</u>

to **compare** VERB
<u>comparer</u> ◊ *People always compare him with his brother.* On le compare toujours à son frère.
♦ **compared with** en comparaison de ◊ *Victoria is small compared with Vancouver.* Victoria est une petite ville en comparaison de Vancouver.

comparison NOUN
la <u>comparaison</u>

compartment NOUN
le <u>compartiment</u>

compass NOUN

1 la <u>boussole</u> (*for directions*)
2 le <u>compas</u> (*math instrument*)

compatible ADJECTIVE
<u>compatible</u>

compelling ADJECTIVE
<u>fascinant</u> (*gripping*) ◊ *It's a compelling film.* C'est un film fascinant.

compensation NOUN
l' <u>indemnité</u> FEM ◊ *They got $2000 compensation.* Ils ont reçu une indemnité de deux mille dollars.

to **compete** VERB
<u>participer</u> ◊ *I'm competing in the marathon.* Je participe au marathon.
♦ **to compete with someone** (*sports*) concourir avec quelqu'un
♦ **to compete with someone** (*general*) rivaliser avec quelqu'un
♦ **to compete for something** se disputer quelque chose ◊ *There are 50 students competing for 6 places.* Ils sont cinquante élèves à se disputer six places.

competent ADJECTIVE
<u>compétent</u>

competition NOUN
le <u>concours</u> ◊ *a singing competition* un concours de chant

competitive ADJECTIVE
<u>compétitif</u> MASC
<u>compétitive</u> FEM ◊ *a very competitive price* un prix très compétitif
♦ **to be competitive** avoir l'esprit de compétition (*person*) ◊ *He's a very competitive person.* Il a vraiment l'esprit de compétition.

competitor NOUN
le <u>concurrent</u>
la <u>concurrente</u>

to **complain** VERB
<u>se plaindre</u> ◊ *I'm going to complain to the manager.* Je vais me plaindre à la directrice. ◊ *We complained about the noise.* Nous nous sommes plaints du bruit.

complaint NOUN
la <u>plainte</u> ◊ *There were lots of complaints about the food.* Il y a eu beaucoup de plaintes à propos de la nourriture.

complete ADJECTIVE
<u>complet</u> MASC
<u>complète</u> FEM

completely ADVERB
<u>complètement</u>

complex ADJECTIVE
<u>complexe</u>

complexion NOUN
le <u>teint</u>

complicated ADJECTIVE
<u>compliqué</u>

compliment NOUN
see also **compliment** VERB
le <u>compliment</u>

to **compliment** VERB
see also **compliment** NOUN
<u>complimenter</u> ◊ *They complimented me on my French.* Ils m'ont complimenté sur mon français.

complimentary ADJECTIVE
1 (*flattering*)
<u>élogieux</u> MASC
<u>élogieuse</u> FEM ◊ *He was very complimentary about my poem.* Il a été très élogieux à propos de mon poème.
2 <u>gratuit</u> (*free*)
♦ **I have two complimentary tickets for tonight.** J'ai deux places gratuites pour ce soir.

composer NOUN
le <u>compositeur</u>
la <u>compositrice</u>

compost NOUN
le <u>compost</u>
♦ **a compost heap** un tas de compost

comprehension NOUN
la <u>compréhension</u>

comprehensive ADJECTIVE
<u>complet</u> MASC
<u>complète</u> FEM ◊ *a comprehensive guide* un guide complet

Be careful not to translate
comprehensive *by* ***compréhensif***.

compromise NOUN
see also **compromise** VERB
le <u>compromis</u> ◊ *We reached a compromise.* Nous sommes parvenus à un compromis.

to **compromise** VERB
see also **compromise** NOUN
♦ **Let's compromise.** Essayons de trouver un compromis.

compulsory ADJECTIVE
<u>obligatoire</u>

computer NOUN
l' <u>ordinateur</u> MASC

computer game NOUN
le <u>jeu électronique</u>
(PL les jeux électroniques)

computer programmer NOUN
le <u>programmeur</u>
la <u>programmeuse</u> ◊ *She's a computer programmer.* Elle est

programmeuse.

computer room NOUN
la salle d'informatique

computer science NOUN
l' informatique FEM

computing NOUN
l' informatique FEM

to **concentrate** VERB
se concentrer ◊ *I couldn't concentrate.* Je n'arrivais pas à me concentrer.

concentration NOUN
la concentration

concern NOUN
l' inquiétude FEM (*worry*) ◊ *They expressed concern about the school's image.* Ils ont exprimé leur inquiétude concernant l'image de l'école.
♦ **That's none of your concern.** Ce n'est pas ton affaire.

concerned ADJECTIVE
♦ **to be concerned** s'inquiéter ◊ *His mother is concerned about him.* Sa mère s'inquiète à son sujet.
♦ **as far as I'm concerned** en ce qui me concerne

concerning PREPOSITION
concernant

concert NOUN
le concert

conclusion NOUN
la conclusion ◊ *Your essay should have an introduction and a conclusion.* Votre dissertation devrait avoir une introduction et une conclusion.
♦ **I came to the conclusion that...** J'ai conclu que...
♦ **in conclusion** en conclusion

concrete NOUN
le béton

to **condemn** VERB
condamner ◊ *The government has condemned the decision.* Le gouvernement a condamné cette décision.

condition NOUN
1 la condition ◊ *I'll do it, on one condition...* Je veux bien le faire, à une condition...
2 l' état MASC ◊ *in bad condition* en mauvais état ◊ *in good condition* en bon état

conditional NOUN
le conditionnel

conditioner NOUN
le revitalisant (*for hair*)

condom NOUN
le condom

condominium NOUN
✹ la copropriété ◊ *We live in a condominium.* Nous habitons dans une copropriété.

to **conduct** VERB
diriger (*orchestra*)

conductor NOUN
le chef d'orchestre

cone NOUN
le cornet ◊ *an ice cream cone* un cornet de crème glacée

✹ **Confederation** NOUN
la Confédération ◊ *fifty years after Confederation* cinquante ans après la Confédération

conference NOUN
la conférence

to **confess** VERB
avouer ◊ *He finally confessed.* Il a fini par avouer. ◊ *He confessed to the crime.* Il a avoué avoir commis le crime.

confession NOUN
la confession

confetti NOUN
les confettis MASC PL

confidence NOUN
1 la confiance ◊ *I have confidence in you.* J'ai confiance en toi.
2 l' assurance FEM ◊ *She lacks confidence.* Elle manque d'assurance.

confident ADJECTIVE
sûr ◊ *I'm confident everything will be okay.* Je suis sûr que tout ira bien.
♦ **She's seems quite confident.** Elle a l'air sûre d'elle.

confidential ADJECTIVE
confidentiel MASC
confidentielle FEM

to **confirm** VERB
confirmer (*booking*)

confirmation NOUN
la confirmation

conflict NOUN
le conflit

to **confuse** VERB
♦ **to confuse somebody** embrouiller les idées de quelqu'un ◊ *Don't confuse me!* Ne m'embrouille pas les idées!

confused ADJECTIVE
désorienté

confusing ADJECTIVE
déroutant ◊ *It was confusing at first.* C'était déroutant au début.
♦ **The traffic signs are confusing.** Les panneaux de signalisation ne sont

pas clairs.

confusion NOUN
la confusion

to **congratulate** VERB
féliciter ◊ *My friends congratulated me on passing the test.* Mes amis m'ont félicité d'avoir réussi à l'examen.

congratulations PL NOUN
les félicitations FEM PL
◊ *Congratulations on your new job!* Félicitations pour votre nouveau poste!

conjunction NOUN
la conjonction

to **connect** VERB
[1] brancher (*plug in*) ◊ *You have to connect the printer.* Tu dois brancher l'imprimante.
[2] connecter ◊ *to be connected to the Internet* être connecté à l'Internet
[3] associer ◊ *I connect summer with camping.* J'associe l'été au camping.

connection NOUN
[1] le rapport ◊ *There's no connection between the two events.* Il n'y a aucun rapport entre les deux événements.
[2] le contact (*electrical*) ◊ *There's a loose connection.* Il y a un mauvais contact.
[3] la correspondance (*of trains, planes, buses*) ◊ *We missed our connection.* Nous avons raté la correspondance.

to **conquer** VERB
conquérir

conscience NOUN
la conscience

conscientious ADJECTIVE
consciencieux MASC
consciencieuse FEM

conscious ADJECTIVE
conscient

consciousness NOUN
la connaissance
♦ **to lose consciousness** perdre connaissance ◊ *I lost consciousness.* J'ai perdu connaissance.

consequence NOUN
la conséquence ◊ *What are the consequences for the environment?* Quelles sont les conséquences pour l'environnement?
♦ **as a consequence** en conséquence
♦ **to suffer the consequences** accepter les conséquences

consequently ADVERB
par conséquent

conservation NOUN
la protection

conservative ADJECTIVE
see also **conservative** NOUN
conservateur MASC
conservatrice FEM

to **consider** VERB
[1] considérer ◊ *He considers it a waste of time.* Il considère que c'est une perte de temps.
[2] envisager ◊ *We considered cancelling our holiday.* Nous avons envisagé d'annuler nos vacances.
♦ **I'm considering the idea.** J'y songe.

considerate ADJECTIVE
délicat

considering PREPOSITION
[1] étant donné ◊ *Considering we were there for a month...* Étant donné que nous étions là pour un mois...
[2] tout compte fait ◊ *I got a good mark, considering.* J'ai eu une bonne note, tout compte fait.

to **consist** VERB
♦ **to consist of** être composé de ◊ *The band consists of three guitarists and a drummer.* Le groupe est composé de trois guitaristes et une batteuse.

consonant NOUN
la consonne

constant ADJECTIVE
constant

constantly ADVERB
constamment

constitution NOUN
la constitution ◊ *the Canadian constitution* la Constitution canadienne

to **construct** VERB
construire

construction NOUN
la construction

to **consult** VERB
consulter

consumer NOUN
le consommateur
la consommatrice

contact NOUN
see also **contact** VERB
le contact ◊ *I'm in contact with her.* Je suis en contact avec elle.

to **contact** VERB
see also **contact** NOUN
joindre ◊ *Where can we contact you?* Où pouvons-nous vous joindre?

contact lenses PL NOUN

les verres de contact MASC PL

contagious ADJECTIVE
contagieux MASC
contagieuse FEM ◊ *It's not contagious.*
Ce n'est pas contagieux.

to **contain** VERB
contenir

container NOUN
le contenant ◊ *a plastic container* un
contenant en plastique

contaminated ADJECTIVE
contaminé ◊ *contaminated water* de
l'eau contaminée

contempt NOUN
le mépris

contents PL NOUN
1 le contenu SING (*of container*)
2 la table des matières FEM (*of book*)

contest NOUN
le concours

contestant NOUN
le concurrent
la concurrente

context NOUN
le contexte

continent NOUN
le continent ◊ *How many continents
are there?* Combien y a-t-il de
continents?

continental breakfast NOUN
❋ le déjeuner continental

to **continue** VERB
1 continuer ◊ *She continued talking.*
Elle a continué à parler.
2 reprendre (*after interruption*)
◊ *We continued working after lunch.*
Nous avons repris le travail après le
déjeuner.

continuous ADJECTIVE
continu

contraceptive NOUN
le contraceptif

contract NOUN
le contrat

to **contradict** VERB
contredire

contrary NOUN
♦ **on the contrary** au contraire

contrast NOUN
le contraste

to **contribute** VERB
1 contribuer (*to success,
achievement*) ◊ *The treaty will
contribute to world peace.* Le traité va
contribuer à la paix dans le monde.
2 participer (*share in*) ◊ *They didn't
contribute to the discussion.* Ils n'ont

pas participé à la discussion.
3 donner (*give*) ◊ *She contributed
$10.* Elle a donné dix dollars.

contribution NOUN
la contribution

control NOUN
| see also **control** VERB |
le contrôle
♦ **to lose control** (*of vehicle*) perdre le
contrôle ◊ *He lost control of the car.* Il
a perdu le contrôle de son véhicule.
♦ **the controls** les commandes FEM (*of
machine*)
♦ **to be in control** être maître de la
situation
♦ **to keep control** (*of people*) se faire
obéir ◊ *He can't keep control of the
class.* Il n'arrive pas à se faire obéir de
sa classe.
♦ **out of control** (*child, class*) déchaîné

to **control** VERB
| see also **control** NOUN |
1 diriger (*country, organization*)
2 se faire obéir de ◊ *She can't
control the class.* Elle n'arrive pas à se
faire obéir de sa classe.
3 maîtriser ◊ *I couldn't control
the horse.* Je ne suis pas arrivé à
maîtriser le cheval.
4 régler (*temperature, speed*)
♦ **to control oneself** se contrôler

controversial ADJECTIVE
controversé ◊ *a controversial book*
un livre controversé

convenience store NOUN
❋ le dépanneur

convenient ADJECTIVE
♦ **The hotel is in a convenient location.**
L'hôtel est bien situé.
♦ **It's not a convenient time for me.**
C'est une heure qui ne m'arrange pas.
♦ **Would Monday be convenient
for you?** Est-ce que lundi vous
conviendrait?

conventional ADJECTIVE
conventionnel MASC
conventionnelle FEM

conversation NOUN
la conversation ◊ *a French
conversation class* un cours de
conversation française

to **convert** VERB
transformer ◊ *We've converted the
loft into a spare room.* Nous avons
transformé le grenier en chambre
d'amis.

to **convict** VERB
reconnaître coupable ◊ *She was
convicted of the crime.* Elle a été

reconnue coupable du crime.

to **convince** VERB
persuader ◊ *I'm not convinced.* Je n'en suis pas persuadé.

to **cook** VERB

see also **cook** NOUN

1 faire la cuisine ◊ *I can't cook.* Je ne sais pas faire la cuisine.
2 préparer ◊ *He's cooking supper.* Il est en train de préparer le souper.
3 faire cuire ◊ *Cook the pasta for 10 minutes.* Faites cuire les pâtes pendant dix minutes.
♦ **to be cooked** être cuit ◊ *When the potatoes are cooked...* Lorsque les pommes de terre sont cuites...

cook NOUN

see also **cook** VERB

le cuisinier
la cuisinière ◊ *Matthew's an excellent cook.* Matthew est un excellent cuisinier.

cookbook NOUN
le livre de cuisine

cookie NOUN
le biscuit

cooking NOUN
la cuisine ◊ *I like cooking.* J'aime bien faire la cuisine.

cool ADJECTIVE
1 frais MASC
fraîche FEM ◊ *a cool place* un endroit frais
2 cool (*trendy, OK*) ◊ *Your website is cool!* Ton site Web est super!
3 génial (*excellent*) ◊ *You're coming along? Cool!* Tu viens aussi? C'est génial!
♦ **to stay cool** (*keep calm*) garder son calme ◊ *She stayed cool.* Elle a gardé son calme.
♦ **keep cool!** du calme!

co-operation NOUN
la coopération

co-operative ADJECTIVE
coopératif MASC
coopérative FEM ◊ *She was very co-operative.* Elle s'est montrée très coopérative.

cop NOUN
le flic (*informal*)

to **cope** VERB
se débrouiller ◊ *It was hard, but we coped.* C'était dur, mais nous nous sommes débrouillés.
♦ **to cope with** faire face à ◊ *She has a lot of problems to cope with.* Elle doit faire face à de nombreux problèmes.

copper NOUN
le cuivre ◊ *a copper bracelet* un bracelet en cuivre

copy NOUN

see also **copy** VERB

1 la copie (*of letter, document*)
2 l' exemplaire MASC (*of book*)

to **copy** VERB

see also **copy** NOUN

copier ◊ *The teacher accused him of copying.* Le professeur l'a accusé d'avoir copié.
♦ **to copy and paste** copier-coller

cord NOUN
le fil ◊ *The cord isn't long enough.* Le fil n'est pas assez long.

cordless ADJECTIVE
sans fil ◊ *a cordless mouse* une souris sans fil

core NOUN
le trognon (*of fruit*) ◊ *an apple core* un trognon de pomme

cork NOUN
le bouchon (*of bottle*)

corkscrew NOUN
le tire-bouchon

corn NOUN
le maïs
♦ **corn on the cob** l'épi de maïs MASC

corner NOUN
le coin ◊ *in a corner of the room* dans un coin de la pièce
♦ **the shop on the corner** la boutique au coin de la rue
♦ **He lives just around the corner.** Il habite tout près d'ici.

corn starch NOUN
l' amidon de maïs MASC

corporal punishment NOUN
le châtiment corporel

corpse NOUN
le cadavre

correct ADJECTIVE

see also **correct** VERB

exact ◊ *That's correct.* C'est exact.
♦ **the correct choice** le bon choix
♦ **the correct answer** la bonne réponse

to **correct** VERB

see also **correct** ADJECTIVE

corriger

correction NOUN
la correction

correctly ADVERB
correctement

to **correspond** VERB
correspondre (*match, agree*) ◊ *Write*

down the letter that corresponds to the correct answer. Écris la lettre qui correspond à la bonne réponse.
♦ **She corresponds with her aunt in India.** Elle correspond avec sa tante en Inde.

corridor NOUN
le couloir

corruption NOUN
la corruption

cosmetics PL NOUN
les produits de beauté MASC PL

cosmetic surgery NOUN
la chirurgie esthétique

to **cost** VERB

> see also **cost** NOUN

coûter ◊ *The meal costs a hundred dollars.* Le repas coûte cent dollars. ◊ *How much does it cost?* Combien est-ce que ça coûte? ◊ *It costs too much.* Ça coûte trop cher.

cost NOUN

> see also **cost** VERB

le coût
♦ **the cost of living** le coût de la vie
♦ **at all costs** à tout prix
♦ **to cut costs** réduire les coûts

costume NOUN
le costume

cot NOUN
le lit de camp

cottage NOUN
le chalet

cottage cheese NOUN
le fromage cottage

cotton NOUN
le coton ◊ *a cotton shirt* une chemise en coton
♦ **a cotton ball** une boule de coton
♦ **cotton candy** la barbe à papa

couch NOUN
le canapé

to **cough** VERB

> see also **cough** NOUN

tousser

cough NOUN

> see also **cough** VERB

la toux ◊ *a bad cough* une mauvaise toux
♦ **I've got a cough.** Je tousse.
♦ **a cough drop** une pastille

could VERB *see* **can**

❀ **coulee** NOUN
la ravine ◊ *The coulee is usually dry in summer.* La ravine est normalement sans eau en été.

council NOUN
le conseil
♦ **He's on the city council.** Il fait partie du conseil municipal.
♦ **She's on the student council.** Elle fait partie du conseil étudiant.

councillor NOUN
le conseiller municipal
la conseillère municipale

counsellor NOUN
① le conseiller
la conseillère
♦ **a guidance counsellor** une conseillère en orientation
② (*camp*)
l' animateur MASC
l' animatrice FEM

to **count** VERB
compter
♦ **to count on** compter sur ◊ *You can count on me.* Tu peux compter sur moi.

counter NOUN
① le comptoir (*in store*)
② le guichet (*in post office, bank*)
③ le jeton (*in game*)

counterfeit ADJECTIVE
faux MASC
fausse FEM ◊ *a counterfeit bill* un faux billet ◊ *counterfeit money* la fausse monnaie

country NOUN
① le pays ◊ *the border between the two countries* la frontière entre les deux pays
② la campagne ◊ *I live in the country.* J'habite à la campagne.
♦ **country music** la musique country
♦ **a country road** une route de campagne

countryside NOUN
la campagne

county NOUN
le comté

couple NOUN
le couple ◊ *the couple who live next door* le couple qui habite à côté
♦ **a couple** deux ◊ *a couple of hours* deux heures
♦ **Could you wait a couple of minutes?** Pourriez-vous attendre quelques minutes?

coupon NOUN
le bon de réduction ◊ *I have a coupon for 10% off.* J'ai un bon de réduction de dix pour cent.

courage NOUN
le courage

courageous ADJECTIVE

courageux MASC
courageuse FEM

courier NOUN
les **messageries** FEM PL ◊ *They sent it by courier.* Ils l'ont envoyé par messageries.

> *Be careful not to translate* **courier** *by the French word* **courrier**.

course NOUN
[1] le **cours** ◊ *a French course* un cours de français ◊ *to take a course* suivre un cours
[2] le **plat** ◊ *the main course* le plat principal
♦ **the first course** l'entrée FEM
[3] le **terrain** ◊ *a golf course* un terrain de golf
♦ **of course** bien sûr ◊ *"Do you understand?" "Of course I do!"* « Tu comprends? » « Bien sûr que oui! »

court NOUN
[1] (*of law*)
le **tribunal**
(PL les **tribunaux**) ◊ *He was in court last week.* Il est passé devant le tribunal la semaine dernière.
[2] le **court** (*tennis*) ◊ *There are tennis and squash courts.* Il y a des courts de tennis et de squash.

courtyard NOUN
la **cour**

cousin NOUN
le **cousin**
la **cousine**

cover NOUN

> *see also* **cover** VERB

[1] la **couverture** (*book cover, blanket*)
[2] la **housse** (*duvet, computer*)
♦ **a cover page** une page couverture
♦ **blow someone's cover** démasquer quelqu'un

to **cover** VERB

> *see also* **cover** NOUN

[1] **couvrir** ◊ *My face was covered with mosquito bites.* J'avais le visage couvert de piqûres de moustique.
[2] **prendre en charge** ◊ *Our insurance didn't cover it.* Notre assurance ne l'a pas pris en charge.
♦ **to cover up a scandal** étouffer un scandale

coverage NOUN
la **couverture** ◊ *media coverage* la couverture médiatique

cow NOUN
la **vache**

coward NOUN
le/la **lâche** ◊ *She's a coward.* Elle est lâche.

cowardly ADJECTIVE
lâche

cowhand NOUN
le **vacher**
la **vachère**

coyote NOUN
le **coyote**

cozy ADJECTIVE
douillet MASC
douillette FEM

crab NOUN
le **crabe**

crack NOUN

> *see also* **crack** VERB

[1] la **fissure** (*in wall*)
[2] la **fêlure** (*in cup, window*)
♦ **I'll have a crack at it.** Je vais tenter le coup.

to **crack** VERB

> *see also* **crack** NOUN

casser (*nut, egg*)
♦ **to crack a joke** sortir une blague

to **crack down on** VERB
être ferme avec ◊ *The police are cracking down on motorists who drive too fast.* La police va être ferme avec les automobilistes qui roulent trop vite.

cracked ADJECTIVE
fêlé (*cup, window*)

cracker NOUN
le **craquelin** (*biscuit*)

cradle NOUN
le **berceau**
(PL les **berceaux**)

crafter NOUN
[1] l' **artisan** MASC
[2] l' **artisane** FEM

crafts NOUN
l' **artisanat** MASC ◊ *to do crafts* faire de l'artisanat
♦ **a craft shop** une boutique d'artisanat

to **cram** VERB
[1] **entasser** ◊ *We crammed our stuff into the trunk.* Nous avons entassé nos affaires dans le coffre.
[2] **préparer un examen**

crammed ADJECTIVE
♦ **crammed with** bourré de ◊ *Her pack was crammed with books.* Son sac à dos était bourré de livres.

cranberry NOUN
la **canneberge** ◊ *turkey with cranberry sauce* de la dinde aux canneberges

crane NOUN

la <u>grue</u> (*machine*)

to **crash** VERB

see also **crash** NOUN

① <u>entrer en collision</u> ◊ *The two cars crashed.* Les deux autos sont entrées en collision.
♦ **to crash into something** rentrer dans quelque chose
♦ **The dishes crashed to the floor.** La vaisselle s'est fracassée sur le plancher.
♦ **The plane crashed.** L'avion s'est écrasé.
② <u>se planter</u> (*computer*) ◊ *My computer crashed.* Mon ordinateur s'est planté.

crash NOUN

see also **crash** VERB

① la <u>collision</u> (*of car*)
② l' <u>accident</u> MASC (*of plane*)
③ le <u>fracas</u> (*sound*)
♦ **a computer crash** un plantage d'ordinateur
♦ **a crash helmet** un casque
♦ **a crash course** un cours intensif

to **crawl** VERB

see also **crawl** NOUN

<u>marcher à quatre pattes</u> (*baby*)
♦ **A spider crawled across the floor.** Une araignée avançait le long du plancher.

crawl NOUN

see also **crawl** VERB

le <u>crawl</u> ◊ *to do the crawl* nager le crawl

crazy ADJECTIVE
<u>fou</u> MASC
<u>folle</u> FEM

cream NOUN
la <u>crème</u> ◊ *strawberries and cream* les fraises à la crème
♦ **cream cheese** le fromage à la crème
♦ **a cream puff** un chou à la crème

crease NOUN
① le <u>pli</u>
※ ② la <u>zone de but</u> (*hockey*)

creased ADJECTIVE <u>froissé</u>

to **create** VERB
<u>créer</u>

creation NOUN
la <u>création</u>

creative ADJECTIVE
<u>créatif</u> MASC
<u>créative</u> FEM

creature NOUN
la <u>créature</u>

credit NOUN

le <u>crédit</u> ◊ *on credit* à crédit

credit card NOUN
la <u>carte de crédit</u>

creek NOUN
le <u>ruisseau</u>

creeps PL NOUN
♦ **It gives me the creeps.** Ça me donne la chair de poule.

to **creep up** VERB
<u>s'approcher à pas de loup</u>
♦ **to creep up on somebody** s'approcher de quelqu'un à pas de loup

crept VERB *see* **creep up**

crew NOUN
① l' <u>équipage</u> MASC (*of ship, plane*)
② l' <u>équipe</u> FEM ◊ *a film crew* une équipe de tournage

crib NOUN
le <u>lit d'enfant</u>

cricket NOUN
le <u>grillon</u>

crime NOUN
① le <u>crime</u> ◊ *Murder is a crime.* Le meurtre est un crime.
② la <u>criminalité</u> (*lawlessness*)
♦ **to reduce crime** réduire la criminalité

criminal NOUN

see also **criminal** ADJECTIVE

le <u>criminel</u>
la <u>criminelle</u>

criminal ADJECTIVE

see also **criminal** NOUN

<u>criminel</u> MASC
<u>criminelle</u> FEM ◊ *It's criminal!* C'est criminel!
♦ **It's a criminal offence.** C'est un crime puni par la loi.
♦ **to have a criminal record** avoir un casier judiciaire

crisis NOUN
la <u>crise</u>

crisp ADJECTIVE
<u>croustillant</u> (*food*)

criterion NOUN
le <u>critère</u>

critic NOUN
le/la <u>critique</u>

critical ADJECTIVE
<u>critique</u>
♦ **a critical remark** une critique

criticism NOUN
la <u>critique</u>

to **criticize** VERB
<u>critiquer</u>

to **crochet** VERB
<u>faire du crochet</u>

crocodile NOUN
le crocodile

crook NOUN
l' escroc MASC (*criminal*) ◊ *That woman is a crook.* Cette femme est un escroc.

crooked ADJECTIVE
1 tordu (*bent*) ◊ *a crooked line* une ligne tordue
2 de travers (*on an angle*) ◊ *Your tie's crooked.* Ta cravate est de travers.

crop NOUN
1 la récolte ◊ *a good crop of apples* une bonne récolte de pommes
2 la culture ◊ *Wheat is one of Canada's main crops.* Le blé est l'une des cultures les plus importantes du Canada.

cross NOUN

see also **cross** VERB

la croix

to **cross** VERB

see also **cross** NOUN

traverser (*street, bridge*)
♦ **to cross out** barrer
♦ **to cross over** traverser

⚹ to **cross-check** VERB
faire double échec à ◊ *He cross-checked his opponent.* Il a fait double échec à son adversaire.

⚹ **cross-checking** NOUN
le double échec ◊ *a penalty for cross-checking* une punition pour double-échec

cross-country NOUN
le cross (*race*)
♦ **cross-country skiing** le ski de fond

crossroads NOUN
le carrefour

crosswalk NOUN
le passage à piétons

crossword NOUN
les mots croisés MASC PL ◊ *I like doing crosswords.* J'aime faire les mots croisés.

to **crouch down** VERB
s'accroupir

crow NOUN
le corbeau
(PL les corbeaux)

crowd NOUN
la foule
♦ **the crowd** (*spectators*) les spectateurs

crowded ADJECTIVE
bondé

crown NOUN
la couronne

crude ADJECTIVE
(*vulgar*)
grossier MASC
grossière FEM

cruel ADJECTIVE
cruel MASC
cruelle FEM

cruise NOUN
la croisière ◊ *to go on a cruise* faire une croisière

crumb NOUN
la miette

crunchy ADJECTIVE
1 croustillant (*cookie*)
2 croquant (*carrot, apple*)

to **crush** VERB
écraser

crust NOUN
la croûte

crutch NOUN
la béquille

cry NOUN

see also **cry** VERB

le cri ◊ *He gave a cry of surprise.* Il a poussé un cri de surprise.
♦ **Go on, have a good cry!** Vas-y, pleure un bon coup!

to **cry** VERB

see also **cry** NOUN

pleurer ◊ *The baby's crying.* Le bébé pleure.

crystal NOUN
le cristal
(PL les cristaux)

cub NOUN
1 l' ourson MASC (*bear*)
2 (*wolf*)
le louveteau
(PL les louveteaux)
3 (*lion*)
le lionceau
(PL les lionceaux)
4 (*fox*)
le renardeau
(PL les renardeaux)

cube NOUN
le cube

cubic ADJECTIVE
♦ **a cubic metre** un mètre cube

cucumber NOUN
le concombre

cuddly ADJECTIVE
câlin

cue NOUN
1 le signal
2 la queue de billard (*for snooker, pool*)

culprit NOUN
le/la coupable

culture NOUN
la culture

cup NOUN
① la tasse ◊ *a china cup* une tasse en porcelaine
♦ **a cup of coffee** un café
② la coupe (*trophy*)

cupboard NOUN
le placard

to **cure** VERB
see also **cure** NOUN
guérir

cure NOUN
see also **cure** VERB
le remède

curious ADJECTIVE
curieux MASC
curieuse FEM

curl NOUN
see also **curl** VERB
la boucle (*in hair*)

to **curl** VERB
see also **curl** NOUN
① boucler ◊ *to curl one's hair* boucler ses cheveux
② jouer au curling (*sport*)

curling NOUN
le curling ◊ *a curling league* une ligue de curling

curling iron NOUN
le fer à friser

curly ADJECTIVE
① bouclé (*loosely curled*)
② frisé (*tightly curled*)

currency NOUN
la devise ◊ *foreign currency* les devises étrangères

current NOUN
see also **current** ADJECTIVE
le courant ◊ *The current is very strong.* Le courant est très fort.

current ADJECTIVE
see also **current** NOUN
actuel MASC
actuelle FEM
♦ **current events** l'actualité

curriculum NOUN
le programme d'études

curry NOUN
le curry

curse NOUN
la malédiction (*spell*)

cursor NOUN
le curseur

curtain NOUN
le rideau
(PL les rideaux)
♦ **to draw the curtains** tirer les rideaux

curved ADJECTIVE
courbe ◊ *a curved surface* une surface courbe
♦ **a curved line** une courbe

cushion NOUN
le coussin

custard NOUN
la crème anglaise

custody NOUN
la garde (*of child*)

custom NOUN
la coutume ◊ *It's an old custom.* C'est une ancienne coutume.

customer NOUN
le client
la cliente

customs PL NOUN
la douane SING

customs officer NOUN
le douanier
la douanière

cut NOUN
see also **cut** VERB
① la coupure ◊ *He's got a cut on his forehead.* Il a une coupure au front.
② la coupe ◊ *a cut and blow-dry* une coupe et un séchage à la brosse
③ la réduction (*in price, spending*)

to **cut** VERB
see also **cut** NOUN
① couper ◊ *I'll cut some bread.* Je vais couper du pain.
♦ **to cut oneself** se couper ◊ *I cut my foot on a piece of glass.* Je me suis coupé au pied avec un morceau de verre.
♦ **to cut and paste** couper-coller
② réduire (*price, spending*)
♦ **to cut down** abattre (*tree*)
♦ **to cut off** couper ◊ *The power was cut off.* L'électricité a été coupée.
♦ **to cut up** hacher (*vegetables, meat*)

cutback NOUN
la réduction ◊ *staff cutbacks* des réductions de personnel

cute ADJECTIVE
mignon MASC
mignonne FEM

cutlery NOUN
les couverts MASC PL

cybercafé NOUN

le cybercafé

cycle NOUN
le cycle
♦ **a vicious cycle** un cycle infernal

cycling NOUN
le cyclisme

cyclist NOUN
le/la cycliste

cylinder NOUN
le cylindre

cynical ADJECTIVE
cynique

C

D

dad NOUN
1 le <u>père</u> ◊ *my dad* mon père ◊ *his dad* son père
2 le <u>papa</u>

> *Use **papa** only when you are talking to your father or using it as his name; otherwise use **père**.*

♦ **Dad!** Papa! ◊ *I'll ask Dad.* Je vais demander à papa.

daffodil NOUN
la <u>jonquille</u>

daily ADJECTIVE, ADVERB
1 <u>quotidien</u> MASC
<u>quotidienne</u> FEM ◊ *It's part of my daily routine.* Ça fait partie de mes occupations quotidiennes.
2 <u>tous les jours</u> ◊ *The pool is open daily from 9 a.m. to 6 p.m.* La piscine est ouverte tous les jours de neuf heures à dix-huit heures.

dairy products PL NOUN
les <u>produits laitiers</u> MASC PL

daisy NOUN
la <u>pâquerette</u>

dam NOUN
le <u>barrage</u>

damage NOUN

> *see also* **damage** VERB

les <u>dégâts</u> MASC PL ◊ *The storm did a lot of damage.* La tempête a fait beaucoup de dégâts.

to **damage** VERB

> *see also* **damage** NOUN

<u>endommager</u>

damp ADJECTIVE
<u>humide</u>

dance NOUN

> *see also* **dance** VERB

1 la <u>danse</u> ◊ *The last dance was a waltz.* La dernière danse était une valse.
2 le <u>bal</u> ◊ *Are you going to the dance tonight?* Tu vas au bal ce soir?

to **dance** VERB

> *see also* **dance** NOUN

<u>danser</u>
♦ **to go dancing** aller danser ◊ *Let's go dancing!* Si on allait danser?

dancer NOUN
le <u>danseur</u>
la <u>danseuse</u>

dandruff NOUN
les <u>pellicules</u> FEM PL

danger NOUN
le <u>danger</u>
♦ **in danger** en danger ◊ *His life is in danger.* Sa vie est en danger.
♦ **to be in danger of** risquer de ◊ *We were in danger of missing the plane.* Nous risquions de rater l'avion.

dangerous ADJECTIVE
<u>dangereux</u> MASC
<u>dangereuse</u> FEM

danish NOUN
la <u>danoise</u> (*pastry*)

to **dare** VERB
<u>oser</u>
♦ **to dare to do something** oser faire quelque chose ◊ *I didn't dare tell my parents.* Je n'ai pas osé le dire à mes parents.
♦ **to dare someone to do something** défier quelqu'un de faire quelque chose

daring ADJECTIVE
<u>audacieux</u> MASC
<u>audacieuse</u> FEM

dark ADJECTIVE

> *see also* **dark** NOUN

1 <u>sombre</u> (*room*) ◊ *It's dark.* (*inside*) Il fait sombre.
♦ **It's dark outside.** Il fait nuit dehors.
♦ **It's getting dark.** La nuit tombe.
2 <u>foncé</u> (*colour*) ◊ *She's got dark hair.* Elle a les cheveux foncés. ◊ *a dark green sweater* un chandail vert foncé

dark NOUN

> *see also* **dark** ADJECTIVE

le <u>noir</u> ◊ *I'm afraid of the dark.* J'ai peur du noir.
♦ **after dark** après la tombée de la nuit

darkness NOUN
l' <u>obscurité</u> FEM ◊ *The room was in darkness.* La chambre était dans l'obscurité.

darling NOUN
le <u>chéri</u>
la <u>chérie</u> ◊ *Thank you, darling!* Merci, chéri!

dart NOUN
la <u>fléchette</u> ◊ *to play darts* jouer aux fléchettes

to **dash** VERB

see also **dash** NOUN

se précipiter ◊ *Everyone dashed to the window to look.* Tout le monde s'est précipité vers la fenêtre pour regarder.

dash NOUN

see also **dash** VERB

le tiret (*punctuation mark*)

data PL NOUN
les données FEM PL

database NOUN
la base de données (*on computer*)

date NOUN

see also **date** VERB

① la date ◊ *my date of birth* ma date de naissance
♦ **to have a date with somebody** sortir avec quelqu'un ◊ *She's got a date with her boyfriend tonight.* Elle sort avec son petit ami ce soir.
♦ **out of date (1)** (*passport*) périmé
♦ **out of date (2)** (*technology*) dépassé
♦ **out of date (3)** (*clothes*) démodé
② la datte (*fruit*)

to **date** VERB

see also **date** NOUN

sortir ensemble ◊ *They're dating.* Ils sortent ensemble. ◊ *He's dating my sister.* Il sort avec ma sœur.

daughter NOUN
la fille

daughter-in-law NOUN
la belle-fille
(PL les belles-filles)

dawn NOUN
l' aube FEM ◊ *at dawn* à l'aube

day NOUN

> Use **jour** to refer to the whole 24-hour period. **journée** only refers to the time when you are awake.

① le jour ◊ *We stayed in St. John's for three days.* Nous sommes restés trois jours à St. John's.
♦ **every day** tous les jours
② la journée ◊ *during the day* dans la journée ◊ *I stayed at home all day.* Je suis resté à la maison toute la journée.
♦ **the day before** la veille ◊ *the day before my birthday* la veille de mon anniversaire
♦ **the day after** le lendemain
♦ **the day after tomorrow** après-demain ◊ *We're leaving the day after tomorrow.* Nous partons après-demain.
♦ **the day before yesterday** avant-hier ◊ *He arrived the day before*

yesterday. Il est arrivé avant-hier.

daycare NOUN
✻ la garderie (*place*)

daylight-saving time NOUN
l' heure avancée FEM

dead ADJECTIVE, ADVERB
① mort ◊ *He was already dead when the doctor came.* Il était déjà mort quand le docteur est arrivé.
♦ **She was shot dead.** Elle a été abattue.
② absolument (*totally*) ◊ *You're dead right!* Tu as absolument raison!

dead end NOUN
l' impasse FEM

deadline NOUN
la date limite ◊ *The deadline for entries is May 2nd.* La date limite d'inscription est le deux mai.

deaf ADJECTIVE
sourd

deafening ADJECTIVE
assourdissant

deal NOUN

see also **deal** VERB

le marché
♦ **It's a deal!** Marché conclu!
♦ **to make a deal with someone** conclure un marché avec quelqu'un
♦ **a great deal** beaucoup ◊ *a great deal of money* beaucoup d'argent

to **deal** VERB

see also **deal** NOUN

donner (*cards*) ◊ *It's your turn to deal.* C'est à toi de donner.
♦ **to deal with something** s'occuper de quelque chose ◊ *She promised to deal with it immediately.* Elle a promis de s'en occuper immédiatement.

dealer NOUN
le marchand
la marchande

dealt VERB *see* **deal**

dear ADJECTIVE
cher MASC
chère FEM ◊ *Dear Mrs Duval* Chère Madame Duval
♦ **Dear Sir/Madam** (*in a circular*) Madame, Monsieur

death NOUN
la mort ◊ *after his death* après sa mort
♦ **I was bored to death.** Je me suis ennuyé à mourir.

debate NOUN

see also **debate** VERB

le débat

to **debate** VERB

☞

see also **debate** NOUN

débattre

debt NOUN
la <u>dette</u> ◊ *He's got a lot of debts.* Il a beaucoup de dettes.
♦ **to be in debt** avoir des dettes

decade NOUN
la <u>décennie</u>

decaffeinated ADJECTIVE
<u>décaféiné</u>

to **decay** VERB

see also **decay** NOUN

1 <u>pourrir</u> (*vegetation, wood*)
2 <u>se carier</u> (*teeth*)
3 <u>se délabrer</u> (*building*) ◊ *a decaying mansion* un manoir qui se délabre

decay NOUN

see also **decay** VERB

la <u>carie</u> (*tooth*)

to **deceive** VERB
<u>tromper</u>

December NOUN
<u>décembre</u> MASC
♦ **in December** en décembre

decent ADJECTIVE
<u>convenable</u> ◊ *a decent education* une éducation convenable
♦ **He's a decent person.** Il est bien honnête.

to **decide** VERB
1 <u>décider</u> ◊ *I decided to write to her.* J'ai décidé de lui écrire. ◊ *I decided not to go.* J'ai décidé de ne pas y aller.
2 <u>se décider</u> ◊ *I can't decide.* Je n'arrive pas à me décider. ◊ *Haven't you decided yet?* Tu ne t'es pas encore décidé?
♦ **to decide on something** (*together*) se mettre d'accord sur quelque chose ◊ *They haven't decided on a name yet.* Ils ne se sont pas encore mis d'accord sur un nom.

decimal ADJECTIVE
<u>décimal</u> ◊ *the decimal system* le système décimal

to **decipher** VERB
<u>déchiffrer</u> ◊ *I can't decipher his handwriting.* Je ne déchiffre pas son écriture.

decision NOUN
la <u>décision</u>
♦ **to make a decision** prendre une décision

decisive ADJECTIVE
<u>décidé</u> (*person*)

deck NOUN

1 la <u>terrasse</u> (*on house*)
2 le <u>pont</u> (*of ship*)
♦ **on deck** sur le pont
3 (*of cards*)
le <u>jeu</u>
(PL les jeux)

to **declare** VERB
<u>déclarer</u>

to **decorate** VERB
1 <u>décorer</u> ◊ *I decorated the cake with chocolate sprinkles.* J'ai décoré le gâteau avec du chocolat granulé.
2 <u>peindre</u> (*paint*)
3 <u>tapisser</u> (*wallpaper*)

decrease NOUN

see also **decrease** VERB

la <u>diminution</u> ◊ *a decrease in the number of unemployed people* une diminution du nombre de chômeurs

to **decrease** VERB

see also **decrease** NOUN

<u>diminuer</u>

to **decriminalize** VERB
<u>décriminaliser</u>

dedicated ADJECTIVE
<u>dévoué</u> ◊ *a very dedicated teacher* un professeur très dévoué
♦ **dedicated to (1)** consacré à ◊ *a museum dedicated to First Nations history* un musée consacré à l'histoire des autochtones
♦ **dedicated to (2)** dédicacé à ◊ *The book is dedicated "to Emma, with love from Mike".* Le livre est dédicacé « à Emma, avec tout mon amour, Mike ».

dedication NOUN
1 le <u>dévouement</u> (*commitment*)
2 la <u>dédicace</u> (*in book, on radio*)

to **deduct** VERB
<u>déduire</u>

deep ADJECTIVE
1 <u>profond</u> (*water, hole, cut*) ◊ *Is it deep?* Est-ce que c'est profond?
♦ **How deep is the lake?** Quelle est la profondeur du lac?
♦ **a hole 4 metres deep** un trou de quatre mètres de profondeur
2 (*snow*)
<u>épais</u> MASC
<u>épaisse</u> FEM ◊ *The snow was really deep.* Il y avait une épaisse couche de neige.
♦ **He's got a deep voice.** Il a la voix grave.
♦ **to take a deep breath** respirer à fond

deeply ADVERB
<u>profondément</u>

deer NOUN

le chevreuil

defeat NOUN

see also **defeat** VERB

la défaite

to **defeat** VERB

see also **defeat** NOUN

battre

defect NOUN
le défaut

defence NOUN
la défense

to **defend** VERB
défendre

to **define** VERB
définir

definite ADJECTIVE
[1] précis ◊ *I don't have any definite plans.* Je n'ai pas de projets précis.
[2] net MASC
nette FEM ◊ *It's a definite improvement.* Cela constitue une nette amélioration.
[3] sûr ◊ *Perhaps we'll go to the Northwest Territories, but it's not definite.* Nous irons peut-être aux Territoires du Nord-Ouest, mais ce n'est pas sûr.
♦ **She was definite about it.** Elle a été catégorique.

definitely ADVERB
vraiment ◊ *He's definitely the best player.* C'est vraiment lui le meilleur joueur.
♦ **"She's the best player." "Definitely!"** « C'est la meilleure joueuse. » « Certainement! »
♦ **I definitely think they'll come.** Je suis sûr qu'ils vont venir.

definition NOUN
la définition

degree NOUN
[1] le degré ◊ *a temperature of 30 degrees* une température de trente degrés
[2] le baccalauréat ◊ *a degree in music* un baccalauréat en musique

dehydrated ADJECTIVE
déshydraté

to **delay** VERB

see also **delay** NOUN

[1] retarder ◊ *We decided to delay our departure.* Nous avons décidé de retarder notre départ.
[2] tarder ◊ *Don't delay!* Ne tarde pas!
♦ **to be delayed** être retardé ◊ *Our flight was delayed.* Notre vol a été retardé.

delay NOUN

see also **delay** VERB

le retard ◊ *There will be delays on most flights.* Il y aura des retards sur la plupart des vols.

Be careful not to translate **delay** by **délai**.

to **delete** VERB
[1] effacer (*on computer, tape*)
[2] rayer (*cross out*)

deli NOUN
la charcuterie

deliberate ADJECTIVE
délibéré

deliberately ADVERB
exprès ◊ *She did it deliberately.* Elle l'a fait exprès.

delicate ADJECTIVE
délicat

delicious ADJECTIVE
délicieux MASC
délicieuse FEM

delight NOUN
♦ **to her delight** à sa plus grande joie

delighted ADJECTIVE
ravi ◊ *He'll be delighted to see you.* Il sera ravi de vous voir.

delightful ADJECTIVE
(*meal, evening*)
délicieux MASC
délicieuse FEM

to **deliver** VERB
[1] livrer ◊ *I deliver newspapers.* Je livre les journaux.
[2] distribuer (*mail*)

delivery NOUN
la livraison

to **demand** VERB

see also **demand** NOUN

exiger

Be careful not to translate **to demand** by **demander**.

demand NOUN

see also **demand** VERB

la demande (*for product*)

demanding ADJECTIVE
exigeant ◊ *She's a very demanding teacher.* C'est une professeure très exigeante.
♦ **It's a very demanding job.** C'est un travail très astreignant.

demo NOUN
[1] le modèle de démonstration (*product*)
[2] la version démo (*software*)
[3] le CD de démonstration

☞

(*recording*)

democracy NOUN
la <u>démocratie</u>

democratic ADJECTIVE
<u>démocratique</u>

to **demolish** VERB
<u>démolir</u>

to **demonstrate** VERB
1 <u>faire une démonstration de</u>
(*show*) ◊ *She demonstrated
the technique.* Elle a fait une
démonstration de la technique.
2 <u>manifester</u> (*protest*)
♦ **to demonstrate against something**
manifester contre quelque chose

demonstration NOUN
1 la <u>démonstration</u> (*of method,
technique*)
2 la <u>manifestation</u> (*protest*)

demonstrator NOUN (*protester*)
le <u>manifestant</u>
la <u>manifestante</u>

denim NOUN
❋ le <u>denim</u> (*fabric*) ◊ *a denim jacket*
une veste en denim

dense ADJECTIVE
1 <u>dense</u> (*crowd, fog*)
2 (*smoke*)
<u>épais</u> MASC
<u>épaisse</u> FEM

dent NOUN
see also **dent** VERB
la <u>bosse</u>

to **dent** VERB
see also **dent** NOUN
<u>cabosser</u>

dental ADJECTIVE
<u>dentaire</u>
♦ **dental floss** le fil dentaire

dentist NOUN
le/la <u>dentiste</u> ◊ *He is a dentist.* Il est
dentiste.

to **deny** VERB
<u>nier</u> ◊ *She denied everything.* Elle a
tout nié.

deodorant NOUN
le <u>déodorant</u>

to **depart** VERB
<u>partir</u>

department NOUN
le <u>département</u> ◊ *the English
department* le département d'anglais
◊ *the shoe department*
❋ le département des chaussures

department store NOUN
le <u>grand magasin</u>

departure NOUN
le <u>départ</u>

departure lounge NOUN
la <u>salle d'embarquement</u>

to **depend** VERB
♦ **to depend on** dépendre de ◊ *The
price depends on the quality.* Le prix
dépend de la qualité.
♦ **depending on the weather** selon le
temps
♦ **It depends.** Ça dépend.

to **deport** VERB
<u>expulser</u>

> ❶ *Le Grand Dérangement*, or
> *Great Deportation*, refers to the
> mass expulsion of Acadians by the
> British military between 1755 and
> 1762. The exiles were scattered
> throughout the Maritimes and
> several American colonies, including
> Louisiana.

deposit NOUN
see also **deposit** VERB
1 le <u>dépôt</u> (*bank*) ◊ *a deposit of 30
dollars* un dépôt de trente dollars
2 la <u>caution</u> (*when renting
something*) ◊ *You get the deposit
back when you return the bike.* On
vous remboursera la caution quand
vous ramènerez le vélo.
♦ **to put down a deposit** (*as
prepayment*) verser un acompte
3 la <u>consigne</u> (*on bottle*)

to **deposit** VERB
see also **deposit** NOUN
<u>déposer</u> ◊ *I deposited 100 dollars
into my account.* J'ai déposé cent
dollars dans mon compte.

depressed ADJECTIVE
<u>déprimé</u> ◊ *I'm feeling depressed.* Je
suis déprimé.

depressing ADJECTIVE
<u>déprimant</u>

depth NOUN
la <u>profondeur</u>

to **descend** VERB
<u>descendre</u>

to **describe** VERB
<u>décrire</u>

description NOUN
la <u>description</u>

desert NOUN
le <u>désert</u>

desert island NOUN
l' <u>île déserte</u> FEM

to **deserve** VERB

mé

riter

design NOUN

see also **design** VERB

① la conception ◊ *It's a completely new design.* C'est une conception entièrement nouvelle.
② le motif ◊ *a geometric design* un motif géométrique
♦ **fashion design** le stylisme

to **design** VERB

see also **design** NOUN

dessiner (*clothes, furniture*)
♦ **designed for young people** conçu pour les jeunes

designer NOUN
le/la styliste (*of clothes*)
♦ **designer clothes** les vêtements griffés

desire NOUN

see also **desire** VERB

le désir

to **desire** VERB

see also **desire** NOUN

désirer

desk NOUN
① (*in office*)
le bureau
(PL les bureaux)
② le pupitre (*for student*)
③ la réception (*in hotel*)
④ le comptoir (*at airport*)

desktop NOUN
le bureau (*on computer*) ◊ *Save the file to the desktop.* Enregistre le fichier sur le bureau.

despair NOUN
le désespoir
♦ **I was in despair**. J'étais désespéré.

desperate ADJECTIVE
désespéré ◊ *a desperate situation* une situation désespérée
♦ **to get desperate** désespérer ◊ *I was getting desperate.* Je commençais à désespérer.

desperately ADVERB
① terriblement ◊ *We're desperately worried.* Nous sommes terriblement inquiets.
② désespérément ◊ *He was desperately trying to persuade her.* Il essayait désespérément de la persuader.

to **despise** VERB
mépriser

despite PREPOSITION
malgré

dessert NOUN
le dessert ◊ *for dessert* comme dessert

destination NOUN
la destination

destitute ADJECTIVE
dépourvu ◊ *a destitute family* une famille dépourvue

to **destroy** VERB
détruire

destruction NOUN
la destruction

detail NOUN
le détail ◊ *in detail* en détail

detailed ADJECTIVE
détaillé

detective NOUN
l' enquêteur MASC
l' enquêteuse FEM
♦ **a private detective** un détective privé
♦ **a detective story** un roman policier

detention NOUN
♦ **to get a detention** être en retenue

detergent NOUN
le détergent

to **deteriorate** VERB
se détériorer

determined ADJECTIVE
déterminé
♦ **to be determined to do something** être déterminé à faire quelque chose ◊ *She's determined to succeed.* Elle est déterminée à réussir.

detour NOUN
le détour

devastated ADJECTIVE
anéanti ◊ *I was devastated.* J'étais anéanti.

devastating ADJECTIVE
① accablant (*upsetting*)
② (*flood, storm*)
dévastateur MASC
dévastatrice FEM

to **develop** VERB
① développer ◊ *to get a film developed* faire développer un film
② se développer ◊ *Girls develop faster than boys.* Les filles se développent plus vite que les garçons.
♦ **to develop into** se transformer en ◊ *The argument developed into a fight.* La dispute s'est transformée en bagarre.
♦ **a developing country** un pays en voie de développement

development NOUN
le développement ◊ *the latest developments* les derniers développements

device NOUN
l' appareil MASC PL

devil NOUN
le diable
♦ **Poor devil!** Pauvre diable!

to **devise** VERB
concevoir ◊ *We devised a plan.* Nous avons conçu un plan.

devoted ADJECTIVE
dévoué ◊ *He's completely devoted to her.* Il lui est très dévoué.

diabetes NOUN
le diabète

diabetic NOUN
le/la diabétique ◊ *I'm a diabetic.* Je suis diabétique.

diagonal ADJECTIVE
diagonal
(MASC PL diagonaux)

diagram NOUN
le diagramme

to **dial** VERB
composer (*number*)

dialogue NOUN
le dialogue

dial tone NOUN
la tonalité

diamond NOUN
le diamant ◊ *a diamond ring* une bague en diamant
♦ **diamonds** (*cards*) le carreau SING

diaper NOUN
la couche

diarrhea NOUN
la diarrhée

diary NOUN
le journal
(PL les journaux) ◊ *I keep a diary.* Je tiens un journal.

dice PL NOUN
les dés

dictation NOUN
la dictée

dictator NOUN
le dictateur
la dictatrice

dictionary NOUN
le dictionnaire

did VERB *see* **do**

to **die** VERB
mourir ◊ *He died last year.* Il est mort l'année dernière.
♦ **to be dying to do something** mourir d'envie de faire quelque chose ◊ *I'm dying to see you.* Je meurs d'envie de te voir.

diesel NOUN
🐝 ① le carburant diesel (*fuel*) ◊ *30 litres of diesel* trente litres de carburant diesel
② la voiture diesel (*car*) ◊ *Our car is a diesel.* Nous avons une voiture diesel.

diet NOUN
see also **diet** VERB
① l' alimentation FEM ◊ *a healthy diet* une alimentation saine
② le régime (*weight loss*) ◊ *I'm on a diet.* Je suis au régime.

to **diet** VERB
see also **diet** NOUN
faire un régime ◊ *I've been dieting for two months.* Je fais un régime depuis deux mois.

dietitian NOUN
le/la diététiste ◊ *He's a dietitian.* Il est diététiste.

difference NOUN
la différence ◊ *There's not much difference in age between us.* Il n'y a pas une grande différence d'âge entre nous.
♦ **It makes no difference.** Ça revient au même.

different ADJECTIVE
différent ◊ *We are very different.* Nous sommes très différents.
◊ *Victoria is different from Vancouver.* Victoria est différent de Vancouver.

difficult ADJECTIVE
difficile ◊ *It's difficult to choose.* C'est difficile de choisir.

difficulty NOUN
la difficulté ◊ *without difficulty* sans difficulté
♦ **to have difficulty doing something** avoir du mal à faire quelque chose

to **dig** VERB
① creuser (*hole*)
② bêcher (*garden*)
♦ **to dig something up** déterrer quelque chose

digestion NOUN
la digestion

digital ADJECTIVE
numérique ◊ *a digital camera* un appareil photo numérique ◊ *a digital recording* un enregistrement audionumérique
♦ **a digital watch** une montre à affichage numérique

dim ADJECTIVE
faible (*light*)

dime NOUN

la pièce de dix cents
♦ **They're a dime a dozen.** Il y en a à la pelle.

dimension NOUN
la dimension

to **diminish** VERB
diminuer

diner NOUN
le petit restaurant

dinghy NOUN
♦ **a rubber dinghy** un canot pneumatique

dining room NOUN
la salle à manger

dinner NOUN
❋ 1 le dîner (*at midday*)
❋ 2 le souper (*evening*)

> ℹ *In Canada, Belgium, Switzerland, and some areas of France,* **le dîner** *is the noon meal. In Canada,* **le souper** *is the evening meal. Elsewhere in the francophone world,* **le dîner** *refers to the evening meal and* **le souper** *happens late in the evening, usually after a show.*

dinnertime NOUN
❋ 1 l' heure du dîner FEM (*midday*)
2 l' heure du déjeuner FEM (*midday*)
❋ 3 l' heure du souper FEM (*evening*)
4 l' heure du dîner FEM (*evening*)

dinosaur NOUN
le dinosaure

dip NOUN

> see also **dip** VERB

la baisse (*decrease*) ◊ *a dip in prices* une baisse de prix
♦ **to go for a dip** aller se baigner

to **dip** VERB

> see also **dip** NOUN

tremper ◊ *She dipped a cookie into her coffee.* Elle a trempé un biscuit dans son café.

diploma NOUN
le diplôme ◊ *a high school diploma* un diplôme en études secondaires

diplomat NOUN
le/la diplomate

diplomatic ADJECTIVE
diplomatique

direct ADJECTIVE, ADVERB

> see also **direct** VERB

direct ◊ *the most direct route* le chemin le plus direct ◊ *You can fly direct from Hamilton to Ottawa.* Il y a un vol direct de Hamilton à Ottawa.

to **direct** VERB

> see also **direct** ADJECTIVE

1 réaliser (*film, program*)
2 mettre en scène (*play, show*)

direction NOUN
la direction ◊ *We're going in the wrong direction.* Nous allons dans la mauvaise direction.
♦ **to ask somebody for directions** demander son chemin à quelqu'un

directly ADVERB
directement
♦ **directly across from** juste en face de
♦ **to be directly related** avoir un rapport direct

director NOUN
1 (*of company*)
le directeur
la directrice
2 le metteur en scène
(PL les metteurs en scène)
la metteuse en scène
(PL les metteures en scène) (*of play*)
3 (*of film, programme*)
le réalisateur
la réalisatrice

directory NOUN
1 l' annuaire MASC (*phone book*)
2 le répertoire (*computing*)

dirt NOUN
la saleté

dirt bike NOUN
la moto tout-terrain
(PL les motos tout-terrains)

dirty ADJECTIVE
sale
♦ **to get dirty** se salir
♦ **to get something dirty** salir quelque chose

disabled ADJECTIVE
handicapé

disadvantage NOUN
le désavantage

to **disagree** VERB
♦ **We always disagree.** Nous ne sommes jamais d'accord.
♦ **I disagree!** Je ne suis pas d'accord!
♦ **He disagrees with me.** Il n'est pas d'accord avec moi.

disagreement NOUN
le désaccord

to **disappear** VERB
disparaître

disappearance NOUN
la disparition

disappointed ADJECTIVE
déçu

disappointing ADJECTIVE

D

décevant

disappointment NOUN
la déception

disaster NOUN
le désastre

disastrous ADJECTIVE
désastreux MASC
désastreuse FEM

disc NOUN
le disque

discipline NOUN
la discipline

disc jockey NOUN
le disc-jockey

to **disconnect** VERB
① débrancher (*unplug*)
② se déconnecter (*log off*)
③ couper (*telephone, water supply*)

discount NOUN
la réduction ◊ *a discount for students* une réduction pour les étudiants

to **discourage** VERB
décourager
♦ **to get discouraged** se décourager
◊ *Don't get discouraged!* Ne te décourage pas!

to **discover** VERB
découvrir

discrimination NOUN
la discrimination ◊ *racial discrimination* la discrimination raciale

to **discuss** VERB
① discuter ◊ *This trip has been discussed at length with my parents.* Ce voyage a été longuement discuté avec mes parents.
② discuter de ◊ *We discussed the problem of pollution.* Nous avons discuté du problème de la pollution. ◊ *We discussed it.* Nous en avons discuté.

discussion NOUN
la discussion

disease NOUN
la maladie

disgraceful ADJECTIVE
scandaleux MASC
scandaleuse FEM

to **disguise** VERB
déguiser ◊ *He was disguised as a policeman.* Il était déguisé en policier.

disgusted ADJECTIVE
dégoûté ◊ *I was absolutely disgusted.* J'étais complètement dégoûté.

disgusting ADJECTIVE

① dégoûtant (*food, smell*) ◊ *It looks disgusting.* Ça a l'air dégoûtant.
② honteux (*disgraceful*) ◊ *That's disgusting!* C'est honteux!

dish NOUN
le plat ◊ *a china dish* un plat en porcelaine ◊ *a vegetarian dish* un plat végétarien
♦ **to do the dishes** faire la vaisselle
◊ *She never does the dishes.* Elle ne fait jamais la vaisselle.

dishcloth NOUN
la lavette

dish detergent NOUN
le savon à vaisselle

dishonest ADJECTIVE
malhonnête

dishtowel NOUN
le linge à vaisselle

dishwasher NOUN
le lave-vaisselle
(PL les lave-vaisselle)

disinfectant NOUN
le désinfectant

disk NOUN
le disque
♦ **a floppy disk** une disquette
♦ **the hard disk** le disque dur

diskette NOUN
la disquette

to **dislike** VERB
see also **dislike** NOUN
ne pas aimer ◊ *I really dislike cabbage.* Je n'aime vraiment pas le chou.

dislike NOUN
see also **dislike** VERB
♦ **my likes and dislikes** ce que j'aime et ce que je n'aime pas

dismal ADJECTIVE
lugubre

to **dismiss** VERB
renvoyer (*employee*)

to **disobey** VERB
désobéir ◊ *to disobey one's parents* désobéir à ses parents
♦ **to disobey a rule** violer une règle

disorganized ADJECTIVE
désorganisé

disoriented ADJECTIVE
dépaysé

display NOUN
see also **display** VERB
l' étalage MASC ◊ *There was a lovely display of fruit in the window.* Il y avait un superbe étalage de fruits en

vitrine.
♦ **to be on display** être exposé ◊ *Her best paintings were on display.* Ses meilleurs tableaux étaient exposés.

to **display** VERB

see also **display** NOUN

① montrer ◊ *She proudly displayed her medal.* Elle a montré sa médaille avec fierté.
② exposer (*in store window*)

disposable ADJECTIVE
jetable

to **disqualify** VERB
disqualifier
♦ **to be disqualified** être disqualifié ◊ *He was disqualified.* Il a été disqualifié.

disrespectful ADJECTIVE ◊ *to be disrespectful towards someone* manquer de respect envers quelqu'un

to **disrupt** VERB
perturber ◊ *Protesters disrupted the meeting.* Des manifestants ont perturbé la réunion. ◊ *Bus service is being disrupted by the strike.* Les horaires d'autobus sont perturbés par la grève.

dissatisfied ADJECTIVE
♦ **We were dissatisfied with the service.** Nous n'étions pas satisfaits du service.

to **dissolve** VERB
dissoudre

distance NOUN
la distance ◊ *a distance of 40 kilometres* une distance de quarante kilomètres
♦ **It's within walking distance.** On peut y aller à pied.
♦ **in the distance** au loin

distant ADJECTIVE
lointain ◊ *in the distant future* dans un avenir lointain

distinction NOUN
la distinction ◊ *to make a distinction between...* faire la distinction entre...

distinctive ADJECTIVE
distinctif MASC
distinctive FEM

✱ **distinct society** NOUN
la société distincte ◊ *Quebec considers itself a distinct society within Canada.* Le Québec se considère comme une société distincte au sein du Canada.

to **distract** VERB
distraire

to **distribute** VERB
distribuer

district NOUN
① le quartier (*of town*)
② la région (*of country*)

to **disturb** VERB
déranger ◊ *I'm sorry to disturb you.* Je suis désolé de vous déranger.

ditch NOUN

see also **ditch** VERB

le fossé

to **ditch** VERB

see also **ditch** NOUN

plaquer (*informal*) ◊ *Let's ditch that idea.* Laissons tomber cette idée.

dive NOUN

see also **dive** VERB

le plongeon

to **dive** VERB

see also **dive** NOUN

plonger

diver NOUN
le plongeur
la plongeuse

to **divide** VERB
① diviser ◊ *Divide the chocolate bar in half.* Divisez la barre de chocolat en deux. ◊ *12 divided by 3 is 4.* Douze divisé par trois égalent quatre.
② se diviser ◊ *We divided into two groups.* Nous nous sommes divisés en deux groupes.

diving NOUN
la plongée
♦ **a diving board** un tremplin

division NOUN
la division

divorce NOUN
le divorce

divorced ADJECTIVE
divorcé ◊ *My parents are divorced.* Mes parents sont divorcés.

dizzy ADJECTIVE
♦ **to feel dizzy** avoir la tête qui tourne ◊ *I feel dizzy.* J'ai la tête qui tourne.

DJ NOUN
le/la disc-jockey

to **do** VERB
① faire ◊ *What are you doing this evening?* Qu'est-ce que tu fais ce soir? ◊ *I do a lot of biking.* Je fais beaucoup de vélo. ◊ *I haven't done my homework.* Je n'ai pas fait mes devoirs. ◊ *She did it by herself.* Elle l'a fait toute seule. ◊ *I'll do my best.* Je ferai de mon mieux.
♦ **to do well (1)** marcher bien ◊ *The*

☞

firm is doing well. L'entreprise marche bien. ◊ *She's doing well at school.* Ses études marchent bien.

♦ **to do well (2)** être sur la bonne voie ◊ *The patient is doing well.* La malade est sur la bonne voie.
② aller (*be enough*) ◊ *It's not very good, but it'll do.* Ce n'est pas très bon, mais ça ira.

♦ **That'll do, thanks**. Ça ira, merci.

> In English **do** is used to make questions. In French questions are made either with **est-ce que** or by reversing the order of verb and subject.

◊ *Do you like French food?* Est-ce que vous aimez la cuisine française? ◊ *Where does he live?* Où est-ce qu'il habite? ◊ *Do you speak English?* Parlez-vous anglais?

> Use **ne...pas** in negative sentences for **don't**.

◊ *I don't understand.* Je ne comprends pas. ◊ *Why didn't you come?* Pourquoi n'êtes-vous pas venus?

> **do** is not translated when it is used in place of another verb.

◊ *"I hate math." "So do I."* « Je déteste les maths. » « Moi aussi. » ◊ *"I didn't like the film." "Neither did I."* « Je n'ai pas aimé le film. » « Moi non plus. » ◊ *"Do you like horses?" "No I don't."* « Est-ce que tu aimes les chevaux? » « Non. »

> Use **n'est-ce pas** to check information.

◊ *You go swimming on Fridays, don't you?* Tu fais de la natation le vendredi, n'est-ce pas?

♦ **to do away with (1)** (*law, practice*) abolir
♦ **to do away with (2)** (*kill*) tuer
♦ **to do up (1)** (*shoes*) lacer ◊ *Do up your shoes!* Lace tes chaussures!
♦ **to do up (2)** (*shirt, cardigan*) boutonner
♦ **to do up one's fly** fermer sa braguette
♦ **to do without** se passer de ◊ *I couldn't do without my computer.* Je ne pourrais pas me passer de mon ordinateur.
♦ **That has nothing to do with it**. Cela n'a rien à voir.

dock NOUN
le dock (*for ships*)

doctor NOUN
le/la médecin ◊ *She's a doctor.* Elle est médecin.

document NOUN
le document

documentary NOUN
le documentaire

to **dodge** VERB
échapper à (*attacker*)

dodgeball NOUN
* le ballon chasseur

does VERB *see* **do**

doesn't = **does not**

dog NOUN
(*female*)
le chien
la chienne

dogsled NOUN
le traîneau à chiens ◊ *by dogsled* en traîneau à chiens.

to **dole out** VERB
distribuer

doll NOUN
la poupée

dollar NOUN
le dollar

dolphin NOUN
le dauphin

domestic ADJECTIVE
♦ **a domestic flight** un vol intérieur
♦ **domestic violence** la violence familiale

dominoes PL NOUN
♦ **to have a game of dominoes** jouer une partie de dominos

to **donate** VERB
donner

done VERB *see* **do**

donkey NOUN
l' âne MASC

donor NOUN
① (*to charity*)
le donateur
la donatrice
② (*of blood, organ for transplant*)
le donneur
la donneuse

don't = **do not**

door NOUN
① la porte ◊ *the first door on the right* la première porte à droite
② la portière (*of car, bus*)

doorbell NOUN
la sonnette
♦ **to ring the doorbell** sonner
♦ **Suddenly the doorbell rang**. Soudain, on a sonné.

doorman NOUN
le portier

doorstep NOUN
le pas de la porte

dormitory NOUN
le dortoir

dose NOUN
la dose

dot NOUN
le point (on letter "i", in e-mail address)
♦ **on the dot** à l'heure pile ◊ He arrived at 9 o'clock on the dot. Il est arrivé à neuf heures pile.

to **double** VERB

> see also **double** ADJECTIVE

doubler ◊ The number of overweight children has doubled. Le nombre d'enfants obèses a doublé.

double ADJECTIVE, ADVERB

> see also **double** VERB

double ◊ a double helping une double portion
♦ **to cost double** coûter le double ◊ First-class tickets cost double. Les billets de première classe coûtent le double.
♦ **a double bed** un grand lit
♦ **a double room** une chambre pour deux personnes

double bass NOUN
la contrebasse ◊ I play the double bass. Je joue de la contrebasse.

to **double-click** VERB
double-cliquer ◊ to double-click on an icon double-cliquer sur une icône

doubles PL NOUN
le double SING (in tennis) ◊ to play mixed doubles jouer en double mixte

double-spaced ADJECTIVE
à double interligne

doubt NOUN

> see also **doubt** VERB

le doute ◊ I have my doubts. J'ai des doutes.

to **doubt** VERB

> see also **doubt** NOUN

douter de
♦ **I doubt it.** J'en doute.
♦ **to doubt that** douter que

> **douter que** has to be followed by a verb in the subjunctive.

◊ I doubt he'll agree. Je doute qu'il soit d'accord.

doubtful ADJECTIVE
♦ **to be doubtful about doing something** hésiter à faire quelque chose ◊ I'm doubtful about going by myself. J'hésite à y aller tout seul.
♦ **It's doubtful.** Ce n'est pas sûr.
♦ **You sound doubtful.** Tu n'as pas l'air

sûr.

dough NOUN
la pâte

doughnut NOUN
le beigne ◊ a jam doughnut un beigne à la confiture

down ADVERB, ADJECTIVE, PREPOSITION
1 en bas (below) ◊ Her office is down on the first floor. Son bureau est en bas, au premier étage. ◊ It's down there. C'est là-bas.
2 à terre (to the ground) ◊ He threw down his racquet. Il a jeté sa raquette à terre.
♦ **They live just down the road.** Ils habitent tout à côté.
♦ **to come down** descendre ◊ Come down here. Descends.
♦ **to go down** descendre ◊ The rabbit went down the hole. Le lapin est descendu dans le terrier.
♦ **to sit down** s'asseoir ◊ Please sit down. Asseyez-vous, s'il vous plaît.
♦ **to feel down** se sentir déprimé ◊ I'm feeling a bit down. Je me sens un peu déprimée.
♦ **The computer's down.** L'ordinateur est en panne.

downhill skiing NOUN
le ski alpin

to **download** VERB
télécharger ◊ to download a file télécharger un fichier

downpour NOUN
la pluie torrentielle ◊ a sudden downpour une pluie soudaine et torrentielle

downstairs ADVERB, ADJECTIVE
1 au rez-de-chaussée ◊ The bathroom's downstairs. La salle de bain est au rez-de-chaussée.
2 du rez-de-chaussée ◊ the downstairs bathroom la salle de bain du rez-de-chaussée
♦ **the people downstairs** les voisins du dessous

downtown ADVERB
dans le centre-ville

to **doze** VERB
sommeiller
♦ **to doze off** s'assoupir

dozen NOUN
la douzaine ◊ two dozen deux douzaines ◊ a dozen eggs une douzaine d'œufs
♦ **I've told you that dozens of times.** Je t'ai dit ça des dizaines de fois.

drab ADJECTIVE
1 morne
2 terne (clothes)

D

draft NOUN
le courant d'air

to **drag** VERB

see also **drag** NOUN

traîner (*thing, person*)

drag NOUN

see also **drag** VERB

♦ **It's a real drag!** Quelle corvée!
(*informal*)

dragon NOUN
le dragon

dragonfly NOUN
la libellule

drain NOUN

see also **drain** VERB

l' égout MASC ◊ *The drains are
blocked.* Les égouts sont bouchés.

to **drain** VERB

see also **drain** NOUN

égoutter (*vegetables, pasta*)

drainboard NOUN
l' égouttoir MASC

drainpipe NOUN
le tuyau d'écoulement

drama NOUN
l' art dramatique MASC ◊ *Drama is my
favourite subject.* L'art dramatique est
ma matière préférée.
♦ **drama school** l'école d'art dramatique
◊ *I'd like to go to drama school.*
J'aimerais entrer dans une école d'art
dramatique.
♦ **Greek drama** le théâtre grec

dramatic ADJECTIVE
[1] spectaculaire ◊ *It was really
dramatic!* C'était vraiment
spectaculaire! ◊ *a dramatic
improvement* une amélioration
spectaculaire
[2] théâtral ◊ *a dramatic entrance* une
entrée théâtrale

drank VERB see **drink**

drapes PL NOUN
les rideaux MASC PL

drastic ADJECTIVE
(*change*)
radical
(MASC PL radicaux)
♦ **to take drastic action** prendre des
mesures énergiques

to **draw** VERB

see also **draw** NOUN

dessiner ◊ *She's good at drawing.*
Elle dessine bien.
♦ **to draw a picture** faire un dessin
♦ **to draw a picture of somebody** faire

le portrait de quelqu'un
♦ **to draw a line** tirer un trait
♦ **to draw the curtains** tirer les rideaux
♦ **to draw lots** tirer au sort

draw NOUN

see also **draw** VERB

[1] le match nul (*sport*) ◊ *The game
ended in a draw.* La partie s'est
soldée par un match nul.
[2] le tirage au sort (*in lottery*) ◊ *The
draw takes place on Saturday.* Le
tirage au sort a lieu samedi.

drawback NOUN
l' inconvénient MASC

drawer NOUN
le tiroir

drawing NOUN
le dessin

drawn VERB see **draw**

dreadful ADJECTIVE
[1] terrible ◊ *a dreadful mistake* une
terrible erreur
[2] affreux MASC
affreuse FEM ◊ *The weather was
dreadful.* Il a fait un temps affreux.

dreadlocks PL NOUN
les tresses rasta FEM

to **dream** VERB

see also **dream** NOUN

rêver ◊ *I dreamed I was in Nunavut.*
J'ai rêvé que j'étais au Nunavut.

dream NOUN

see also **dream** VERB

le rêve ◊ *It was just a dream.* Ce
n'était qu'un rêve.
♦ **a bad dream** un cauchemar

to **drench** VERB
♦ **to get drenched** se faire tremper
◊ *We got drenched.* Nous nous
sommes fait tremper.

dress NOUN

see also **dress** VERB

[1] la robe
[2] tenue ◊ *in traditional dress* en
tenue traditionnelle
♦ **a dress rehearsal** une répétition
générale

to **dress** VERB

see also **dress** NOUN

s'habiller ◊ *I got up, dressed, and
went downstairs.* Je me suis levé, je
me suis habillé et je suis descendu.
♦ **to dress somebody** habiller quelqu'un
◊ *She dressed the children.* Elle a
habillé les enfants.
♦ **to get dressed** s'habiller ◊ *I got
dressed quickly.* Je me suis habillé

rapidement.
♦ **to dress up** se déguiser ◊ *I dressed up as a ghost.* Je me suis déguisé en fantôme.

dressed ADJECTIVE
habillé ◊ *I'm not dressed yet.* Je ne suis pas encore habillé.
♦ **He was dressed in a green sweater and jeans.** Il portait un chandail vert et un jean.

dresser NOUN
la commode (*furniture*)

dressing gown NOUN
la robe de chambre

drew VERB *see* **draw**

dried VERB *see* **dry**

drift NOUN
| *see also* **drift** VERB |
♦ **a snow drift** une congère

to **drift** VERB
| *see also* **drift** NOUN |
[1] aller à la dérive (*boat*)
[2] s'amonceler (*snow*)

drill NOUN
| *see also* **drill** VERB |
la perceuse

to **drill** VERB
| *see also* **drill** NOUN |
percer ◊ *to drill a hole* percer un trou

drink NOUN
| *see also* **drink** VERB |
la boisson ◊ *a cold drink* une boisson fraîche ◊ *a hot drink* une boisson chaude
♦ **Would you like a drink?** Voulez-vous quelque chose à boire?

to **drink** VERB
| *see also* **drink** NOUN |
boire ◊ *What would you like to drink?* Qu'est-ce que vous voulez boire? ◊ *She drank three cups of tea.* Elle a bu trois tasses de thé.
♦ **Don't drink and drive.** Pas d'alcool au volant.
♦ **I don't drink.** Je ne bois pas d'alcool.

drinking water NOUN
l' eau potable FEM

to **drip** VERB
goutter (*tap*)
♦ **dripping wet** complètement trempé

drive NOUN
| *see also* **drive** VERB |
le tour en voiture
♦ **to go for a drive** aller faire un tour en voiture ◊ *We went for a drive in the country.* Nous sommes allés faire un tour à la campagne.
♦ **We've got a long drive tomorrow.** Nous avons une longue route à faire demain.

to **drive** VERB
| *see also* **drive** NOUN |
[1] conduire (*a car*) ◊ *He's learning to drive.* Il apprend à conduire. ◊ *Can you drive?* Tu sais conduire?
[2] aller en voiture (*go by car*) ◊ *"Did you fly?" "No, we drove."* « Vous êtes partis en avion? » « Non, nous y sommes allés en voiture. »
[3] emmener en voiture ◊ *My mother drives me to school.* Ma mère m'emmène à l'école en voiture.
♦ **to drive somebody home** raccompagner quelqu'un ◊ *He offered to drive me home.* Il m'a proposé de me raccompagner.
♦ **to drive somebody crazy** rendre quelqu'un fou ◊ *He drives me crazy.* Il me rend folle.

driver NOUN
[1] le conducteur
la conductrice ◊ *She's an excellent driver.* C'est une excellente conductrice.
[2] le chauffeur (*of taxi, bus*) ◊ *He's a bus driver.* Il est chauffeur d'autobus.

driver's licence NOUN
le permis de conduire

driveway NOUN
l' entrée FEM

driving lesson NOUN
la leçon de conduite

driving school NOUN
l' auto-école FEM

driving test NOUN
♦ **to take one's driving test** passer son examen de conduite automobile ◊ *He's taking his driving test tomorrow.* Il passe son examen de conduite automobile demain.
♦ **She's just passed her driving test.** Elle vient d'avoir son permis.

to **drizzle** VERB
bruiner

drop NOUN
| *see also* **drop** VERB |
[1] la goutte ◊ *a drop of water* une goutte d'eau
[2] la baisse (*decrease*) ◊ *a drop in temperature* une baisse de température

to **drop** VERB
| *see also* **drop** NOUN |
[1] laisser tomber ◊ *I dropped the*

glass and it broke. J'ai laissé tomber le verre et il s'est cassé. ◊ *I'm going to drop chemistry.* Je vais laisser tomber la chimie.
♦ **to drop out of school**
🟌 décrocher ◊ *He dropped out before finishing Grade 12.* Il a décroché avant de terminer son secondaire cinq.
② déposer ◊ *Could you drop me at the station?* Pouvez-vous me déposer à la gare?

drop-in centre NOUN
le centre de jour

dropout
🟌 le décrocheur
🟌 la décrocheuse

drought NOUN
la sécheresse

drove VERB *see* **drive**

to **drown** VERB
se noyer ◊ *A boy drowned here yesterday.* Un jeune garçon s'est noyé ici hier.

drug NOUN
① le médicament (*medicine*) ◊ *They need food and drugs.* Ils ont besoin de nourriture et de médicaments.
② la drogue (*illegal*) ◊ *hard drugs* les drogues dures ◊ *soft drugs* les drogues douces
♦ **to take drugs** se droguer
♦ **a drug addict** un drogué ◊ *She's a drug addict.* C'est une droguée.

drugstore NOUN
la pharmacie

drum NOUN
le tambour ◊ *an African drum* un tambour africain
♦ **a set of drums** une batterie
♦ **drums** la batterie SING ◊ *I play drums.* Je joue de la batterie.

drummer NOUN
(*in rock group*)
le batteur
la batteuse

drunk ADJECTIVE

| *see also* **drunk** NOUN |

ivre ◊ *He was drunk.* Il était ivre.
♦ **drunk driving** la conduite en état d'ivresse

drunk NOUN

| *see also* **drunk** ADJECTIVE |

l' ivrogne MASC/FEM

dry ADJECTIVE

| *see also* **dry** VERB |

① sec MASC
sèche FEM ◊ *The paint isn't dry yet.* La peinture n'est pas encore sèche.

② sans pluie (*weather*) ◊ *a long dry period* une longue période sans pluie

to **dry** VERB

| *see also* **dry** ADJECTIVE |

① sécher ◊ *The wash will dry quickly in the sun.* Le linge va sécher vite au soleil. ◊ *some dried flowers* des fleurs séchées
♦ **to dry one's hair** se sécher les cheveux ◊ *I haven't dried my hair yet.* Je ne me suis pas encore séché les cheveux.
② faire sécher (*clothes*) ◊ *There's nowhere to dry clothes here.* Il n'y a pas d'endroit où faire sécher les vêtements ici.
♦ **to dry the dishes** essuyer la vaisselle

dry cleaners NOUN
🟌 le nettoyeur

dryer NOUN
🟌 ① la sécheuse (*machine*)
② le séchoir (*rack*)
♦ **a hair dryer** un sèche-cheveux

dubbed ADJECTIVE
doublé ◊ *The film was dubbed into French.* Le film était doublé en français.

dubious ADJECTIVE
① réticent ◊ *My parents were a bit dubious about it.* Mes parents étaient un peu réticents à ce sujet.
② douteux ◊ *a dubious reputation* une réputation douteuse

duck NOUN
le canard

duckling NOUN
le caneton

due ADJECTIVE, ADVERB
♦ **The essay is due on Friday.** La rédaction doit être rendue vendredi.
♦ **The plane's due in half an hour.** L'avion doit arriver dans une demi-heure.
♦ **When's the baby due?** Le bébé est prévu pour quand?
♦ **due to (1)** à cause de ◊ *The trip was cancelled due to bad weather.* Le voyage a été annulé à cause du mauvais temps.
♦ **due to (2)** dû à ◊ *The fire was due to an electrical problem.* L'incendie est dû à un problème électrique.
♦ **to be due to do something** devoir faire quelque chose ◊ *He's due to arrive tomorrow.* Il doit arriver demain.

dug VERB *see* **dig**

dull ADJECTIVE
① ennuyeux MASC
ennuyeuse FEM ◊ *He's nice, but a bit*

dull. Il est sympathique, mais un peu
ennuyeux.
② maussade (*weather, day*)

dumb ADJECTIVE
bête ◊ *That was a really dumb thing I
did!* C'était vraiment bête de ma part!

dump NOUN

see also **dump** VERB

le dépotoir
♦ **It's a real dump!** C'est un endroit
miteux!

to **dump** VERB

see also **dump** NOUN

déposer ◊ *"no dumping"* « défense
de déposer des ordures » ◊ *Just
dump your things on the sofa.* Tu
peux déposer tes affaires sur le sofa.

duplex NOUN
le duplex
(PL les duplex)

duration NOUN
la durée

during PREPOSITION
pendant ◊ *during the day* pendant la
journée

dusk NOUN
le crépuscule ◊ *at dusk* au crépuscule

dust NOUN

see also **dust** VERB

la poussière

to **dust** VERB

see also **dust** NOUN

épousseter ◊ *I dusted the shelves.*
J'ai épousseté les étagères.

dusty ADJECTIVE
poussiéreux MASC
poussiéreuse FEM

duty NOUN
le devoir ◊ *It was her duty to tell the
police.* C'était son devoir de prévenir
la police.
♦ **to be on duty (1)** (*policeman*) être de
service
♦ **to be on duty (2)** (*doctor, nurse*) être
de garde

duty-free ADJECTIVE
hors taxes FEM+PL
♦ **the duty-free shop** la boutique hors
taxes

duvet NOUN
la couette

DVD NOUN
le DVD
(PL les DVD) ◊ *I've got that movie on
DVD.* J'ai ce film en DVD.

DVD player NOUN
le lecteur de DVD

dwarf NOUN
le nain
la naine

to **dye** VERB
teindre ◊ *to dye one's hair* se teindre
les cheveux ◊ *I dyed my T-shirt green.*
J'ai teint mon T-shirt en vert.

dying VERB *see* **die**

dynamic ADJECTIVE
dynamique

dyslexia NOUN
la dyslexie

D

E

each ADJECTIVE, PRONOUN

1 chaque ◊ *each day* chaque jour ◊ *Each house in our street has its own garden.* Chaque maison dans notre rue a son propre jardin.

2 chacun MASC

chacune FEM ◊ *The girls each have their own bedroom.* Les filles ont chacune leur chambre. ◊ *They have 10 points each.* Ils ont dix points chacun. ◊ *The plates cost $5 each.* Les assiettes coûtent cinq dollars chacune. ◊ *He gave each of us $10.* Il nous a donné dix dollars à chacun.

*Use a reflexive verb to translate **each other**.*

♦ **They hate each other.** Ils se détestent.
♦ **We wrote to each other.** Nous nous sommes écrit.
♦ **They don't know each other.** Ils ne se connaissent pas.

eager ADJECTIVE
♦ **to be eager to do something** être impatient de faire quelque chose

eagle NOUN
l' aigle MASC

ear NOUN
l' oreille FEM
♦ **to perk up one's ears** dresser les oreilles

earache NOUN
♦ **to have earache** avoir mal aux oreilles

earlier ADVERB

1 tout à l'heure ◊ *I saw him earlier.* Je l'ai vu tout à l'heure.

2 plus tôt (*in the day*) ◊ *I ought to get up earlier.* Je devrais me lever plus tôt.

♦ **earlier than** avant

early ADVERB, ADJECTIVE

1 tôt (*early in the day*) ◊ *I have to get up early.* Je dois me lever tôt.

♦ **to have an early night** se coucher tôt

2 d'avance (*ahead of time*) ◊ *I came early to get a good seat.* Je suis venu d'avance pour avoir une bonne place.

to **earn** VERB
gagner ◊ *She earns $4 an hour for babysitting.* Elle gagne quatre dollars de l'heure quand elle garde des enfants.

earnings PL NOUN
le salaire SING

earring NOUN

la boucle d'oreille

earth NOUN
la terre

earthquake NOUN
le tremblement de terre

easily ADVERB
facilement

east ADJECTIVE, ADVERB

see also **east** NOUN

1 est MASC, FEM, PL ◊ *the east coast* la côte est

♦ **an east wind** un vent d'est
♦ **east of** à l'est de ◊ *It's east of Red Deer.* C'est à l'est de Red Deer.

2 vers l'est ◊ *We were travelling east.* Nous allions vers l'est.

east NOUN

see also **east** ADJECTIVE

l' est MASC ◊ *in the east* dans l'est

eastbound ADJECTIVE
♦ **The car was eastbound on the highway.** La voiture se trouvait sur l'autoroute en direction de l'est.
♦ **Eastbound traffic is moving very slowly.** La circulation vers l'est avance très lentement.

Easter NOUN
Pâques FEM ◊ *at Easter* à Pâques ◊ *We went to my grandparents' for Easter.* Nous sommes allés chez mes grands-parents à Pâques.

eastern ADJECTIVE
♦ **the eastern part of the island** la partie est de l'île
♦ **Eastern Europe** l'Europe de l'Est

easy ADJECTIVE
facile

easy chair NOUN
le fauteuil

easy-going ADJECTIVE
facile à vivre
(PL faciles à vivre) ◊ *She's very easy-going.* Elle est très facile à vivre.

to **eat** VERB
manger
♦ **Would you like something to eat?** Est-ce que tu veux manger quelque chose?

eccentric ADJECTIVE
excentrique

echo NOUN

see also **echo** VERB

l' écho MASC

to **echo** VERB

> see also **echo** NOUN

retentir ◊ *Their shouts echoed across the lake.* Leurs cris ont retenti jusqu'au bout du lac.

eclipse NOUN
l' éclipse FEM ◊ *a partial eclipse* une éclipse partielle

eco-friendly ADJECTIVE
respectueux de l'environnement MASC
respectueuse de l'environnement FEM

ecological ADJECTIVE
écologique

ecology NOUN
l' écologie FEM

e-commerce NOUN
le commerce électronique

economic ADJECTIVE
économique ◊ *economic conditions* les conditions économiques

economical ADJECTIVE
1 économe (*person*)
2 économique (*purchase, car*)

economics NOUN
l' économie FEM ◊ *He's studying economics.* Il étudie les sciences économiques.

to **economize** VERB
faire des économies ◊ *to economize on something* faire des économies sur quelque chose

economy NOUN
l' économie FEM

ecosystem NOUN
l' écosystème MASC

eczema NOUN
l' eczéma MASC

edge NOUN
1 le bord
♦ **on edge** tendu
2 l' avantage (*advantage*) MASC

edgy ADJECTIVE
tendu

edible ADJECTIVE
comestible

to **edit** VERB
éditer (*text*) ◊ *I have to edit my web page.* Je dois éditer ma page Web.

editor NOUN
(*of newspaper*)
le rédacteur en chef
la rédactrice en chef

educated ADJECTIVE

cultivé

education NOUN
1 l' éducation FEM ◊ *There should be more investment in education.* On devrait investir plus dans l'éducation.
2 l' enseignement MASC (*teaching*) ◊ *She works in education.* Elle travaille dans l'enseignement.

educational ADJECTIVE
(*experience, toy*)
éducatif MASC
éducative FEM ◊ *It was very educational.* C'était très éducatif.

effect NOUN
l' effet MASC ◊ *special effects* les effets spéciaux

effective ADJECTIVE
efficace

effectively ADVERB
efficacement

> Be careful not to translate **effectively** by **effectivement**.

efficient ADJECTIVE
efficace

effort NOUN
l' effort MASC

e.g. ABBREVIATION
p. ex. (= par exemple)

egg NOUN
l' œuf MASC ◊ *a hard-boiled egg* un œuf dur ◊ *a soft-boiled egg* un œuf à la coque ◊ *a fried egg* un œuf sur le plat
♦ **scrambled eggs** les œufs brouillés

eh INTERJECTION
hein ◊ *C'était tout un match, hein?* That was quite a match, eh?

eight NUMBER
huit ◊ *She's eight.* Elle a huit ans.

eighteen NUMBER
dix-huit ◊ *He's eighteen.* Il a dix-huit ans.

eighteenth ADJECTIVE
dix-huitième ◊ *your eighteenth birthday* ton dix-huitième anniversaire ◊ *the eighteenth floor* le dix-huitième étage
♦ **the eighteenth of August** le dix-huit août

eighth ADJECTIVE
huitième ◊ *the eighth floor* le huitième étage
♦ **the eighth of August** le huit août

eighty NUMBER
quatre-vingts

either ADVERB, CONJUNCTION, PRONOUN
non plus ◊ *I don't like milk, and I*

☞

don't like eggs either. Je n'aime pas le lait, et je n'aime pas les œufs non plus. ◊ *"I've never been to Spain." "I haven't either."* « Je ne suis jamais allé en Espagne. » « Moi non plus. »
♦ **either...or** soit...soit ◊ *You can have either ice cream or yogurt.* Tu peux prendre soit une crème glacée soit un yogourt.
♦ **either of them** l'un ou l'autre ◊ *Take either of them.* Prends l'un ou l'autre.
♦ **I don't like either of them.** Je n'aime ni l'un ni l'autre.

elastic NOUN
l' <u>élastique</u> MASC

elbow NOUN
le <u>coude</u>

elder ADJECTIVE
<u>aîné</u> ◊ *my elder sister* ma sœur aînée

elderly ADJECTIVE
<u>âgé</u>
♦ **the elderly** les personnes âgées

eldest ADJECTIVE
<u>aîné</u> ◊ *my eldest sister* ma sœur aînée ◊ *He's the eldest.* C'est l'aîné.

to **elect** VERB
<u>élire</u>

election NOUN
l' <u>élection</u> FEM

electric ADJECTIVE
<u>électrique</u> ◊ *an electric guitar* une guitare électrique
♦ **an electric blanket** une couverture chauffante

electrical ADJECTIVE
<u>électrique</u>
♦ **an electrical engineer** un ingénieur électricien

electrician NOUN
l' <u>électricien</u> MASC
l' <u>électricienne</u> FEM ◊ *He's an electrician.* Il est électricien.

electricity NOUN
l' <u>électricité</u> FEM

electronic ADJECTIVE
<u>électronique</u>

electronics NOUN
l' <u>électronique</u> FEM ◊ *My hobby is electronics.* Ma passion, c'est l'électronique.

elegant ADJECTIVE
<u>élégant</u>

elementary school NOUN
l' <u>école primaire</u> FEM

elephant NOUN
l' <u>éléphant</u> MASC

elevator NOUN
l' <u>ascenseur</u> MASC

eleven NUMBER
<u>onze</u> ◊ *She's eleven.* Elle a onze ans.

eleventh ADJECTIVE
<u>onzième</u> ◊ *the eleventh floor* le onzième étage ◊ *the eleventh of August* le onze août

else ADVERB
<u>d'autre</u> ◊ *somebody else* quelqu'un d'autre ◊ *nobody else* personne d'autre ◊ *nothing else* rien d'autre
♦ **something else** autre chose
♦ **anything else** autre chose ◊ *Would you like anything else?* Désirez-vous autre chose?
♦ **I don't want anything else.** Je ne veux rien d'autre.
♦ **somewhere else** ailleurs
♦ **anywhere else** n'importe où ailleurs
♦ **or else (1)** (*otherwise*) sinon ◊ *Study well or else you'll fail.* Étudie bien, sinon tu vas échouer.
♦ **or else (2)** (*alternatively*) ou bien ◊ *You can call me, or else I can drop by your place after school.* Tu peux me téléphoner, ou bien je peux passer chez toi après l'école.

e-mail NOUN
> see also **e-mail** VERB

le <u>courriel</u>
♦ **e-mail address** l'adresse de courriel FEM ◊ *My e-mail address is...* Mon adresse de courriel, c'est...

to **e-mail** VERB
> see also **e-mail** NOUN

♦ **to e-mail somebody** envoyer un courriel à quelqu'un

embarrassed ADJECTIVE
<u>gêné</u> ◊ *I was really embarrassed.* J'étais vraiment gêné.

embarrassing ADJECTIVE
<u>gênant</u> ◊ *It was so embarrassing.* C'était tellement gênant.

emergency NOUN
l' <u>urgence</u> FEM ◊ *This is an emergency!* C'est une urgence!
♦ **in an emergency** en cas d'urgence
♦ **an emergency exit** une sortie de secours
♦ **an emergency landing** un atterrissage forcé
♦ **the emergency services** les services d'urgence

to **emigrate** VERB
<u>émigrer</u>

emission control NOUN
la <u>lutte contre les émissions</u>

emotion NOUN
l' <u>émotion</u> FEM

emotional ADJECTIVE

⓵ (*person*)
<u>émotif</u> MASC
<u>émotive</u> FEM
⓶ plein d'émotion ◊ *an emotional farewell* un adieu plein d'émotion
⓷ <u>émotionnel</u> ◊ *an emotional shock* un choc émotionnel
♦ **an emotional issue** une question qui soulève les passions
♦ **to be on an emotional roller coaster** être pris dans un tourbillon d'émotions
♦ **to become emotional** être ému

> Be careful not to confuse **émotif** *(having or showing strong emotions)* with **émotionnel** *(to do with the emotions).*

to **emphasize** VERB
♦ **to emphasize something** insister sur quelque chose
♦ **to emphasize that...** souligner que...

empire NOUN
l' <u>empire</u> MASC

to **employ** VERB
<u>employer</u> ◊ *The factory employs 600 people.* L'usine emploie six cents personnes.

employee NOUN
l' <u>employé</u> MASC
l' <u>employée</u> FEM

employer NOUN
l' <u>employeur</u> MASC
l' <u>employeuse</u> FEM

employment NOUN
l' <u>emploi</u> MASC

empty ADJECTIVE

> see also **empty** VERB

<u>vide</u>

to **empty** VERB

> see also **empty** ADJECTIVE

<u>vider</u>
♦ **to empty something out** vider quelque chose

to **encourage** VERB
<u>encourager</u>
♦ **to encourage somebody to do something** encourager quelqu'un à faire quelque chose

encouragement NOUN
l' <u>encouragement</u> MASC

encouraging ADJECTIVE
<u>encourageant</u>

encyclopedia NOUN
l' <u>encyclopédie</u> FEM

end NOUN

> see also **end** VERB

⓵ la <u>fin</u> ◊ *the end of the movie* la fin

du film ◊ *the end of the holidays* la fin des vacances
♦ **in the end** en fin de compte ◊ *In the end I decided to stay home.* En fin de compte, j'ai décidé de rester à la maison.
♦ **It turned out all right in the end.** Ça s'est bien terminé.
⓶ le <u>bout</u> ◊ *at the end of the street* au bout de la rue ◊ *at the other end of the table* à l'autre bout de la table
♦ **for hours on end** des heures entières

to **end** VERB

> see also **end** NOUN

<u>finir</u> ◊ *What time does the movie end?* À quelle heure est-ce que le film finit?
♦ **to end up doing something** finir par faire quelque chose ◊ *I ended up walking home.* J'ai fini par rentrer chez moi à pied.

ending NOUN
la <u>fin</u> ◊ *It was an exciting movie, especially the ending.* C'était un film passionnant, surtout la fin.

endless ADJECTIVE
<u>interminable</u> ◊ *The journey seemed endless.* Le voyage a paru interminable.

enemy NOUN
l' <u>ennemi</u> MASC
l' <u>ennemie</u> FEM

energetic ADJECTIVE
<u>énergique</u> (*person*)

energy NOUN
l' <u>énergie</u> FEM

energy-efficient ADJECTIVE
<u>éconergétique</u>

to **enforce** VERB
<u>faire respecter</u> ◊ *to enforce a rule* faire respecter un règlement

engaged ADJECTIVE
<u>fiancé</u> ◊ *She's engaged to my cousin.* Elle est fiancée à mon cousin.
♦ **to get engaged** se fiancer

engagement NOUN
les <u>fiançailles</u> FEM PL ◊ *an engagement ring* une bague de fiançailles ◊ *to break off one's engagement* rompre ses fiançailles

engine NOUN
le <u>moteur</u>

> Be careful not to translate **engine** by the French word **engin**.

engineer NOUN
l' <u>ingénieur</u> MASC
l' <u>ingénieure</u> FEM ◊ *She's an engineer.* Elle est ingénieure.

E

engineering NOUN
l' <u>ingénierie</u> FEM

English ADJECTIVE

see also **English** NOUN

anglais ◊ *English grammar* la grammaire anglaise

English NOUN

see also **English** ADJECTIVE

l' <u>anglais</u> MASC ◊ *Do you speak English?* Est-ce que vous parlez anglais?

English-Canadian ADJECTIVE

see also **English-Canadian** NOUN

<u>canadien-anglais</u> MASC
<u>canadiennne-anglaise</u> FEM ◊ *an English-Canadian family* une famille canadienne-anglaise

English-Canadian NOUN

see also **English-Canadian** ADJECTIVE

le <u>Canadien anglais</u>
la <u>Canadiennne anglaise</u> ◊ *She married an English-Canadian.* Elle a épousé un Canadien anglais.

engrossed ADJECTIVE
<u>absorbé</u> ◊ *She was so engrossed by her book that she didn't hear me.* Elle était si absorbée par son livre qu'elle ne m'a pas entendu.

to **enjoy** VERB
[1] <u>aimer</u> ◊ *Did you enjoy the film?* Est-ce que vous avez aimé le film?
♦ **to enjoy oneself** s'amuser ◊ *I really enjoyed myself.* Je me suis vraiment bien amusé. ◊ *Did you enjoy yourselves at the party?* Est-ce que vous vous êtes bien amusés à la fête?
[2] <u>jouir de</u> (*benefit from*) ◊ *My grandfather still enjoys good health.* Mon grand-père jouit encore d'une bonne santé.

enjoyable ADJECTIVE
<u>agréable</u>

to **enlarge** VERB
<u>agrandir</u> ◊ *to enlarge an image* agrandir une image

enormous ADJECTIVE
<u>énorme</u>

enough PRONOUN, ADJECTIVE
<u>assez de</u> ◊ *enough time* assez de temps ◊ *I didn't have enough money.* Je n'avais pas assez d'argent. ◊ *Do you have enough?* Tu en as assez? ◊ *I've had enough!* J'en ai assez!
♦ **big enough** suffisamment grand
♦ **warm enough** suffisamment chaud
♦ **That's enough.** Ça suffit.

to **enter** VERB
<u>entrer</u> ◊ *She entered the room.* Elle est entrée dans la salle. ◊ *to enter text in a file* entrer du texte dans un fichier
♦ **to enter a competition** s'inscrire à une compétition
♦ **the Enter key** la touche Entrée

to **entertain** VERB
<u>recevoir</u> (*guests*)

entertainer NOUN
l' <u>artiste de variétés</u> MASC/FEM

entertaining ADJECTIVE
<u>divertissant</u>

entertainment NOUN
le <u>divertissement</u> ◊ *The resort offers outdoor sports, video nights, and other entertainment.* Le centre de villégiature offre des sports de plein air, des soirées vidéo et d'autres divertissements.

enthusiasm NOUN
l' <u>enthousiasme</u> MASC

enthusiastic ADJECTIVE
<u>enthousiaste</u>

entire ADJECTIVE
<u>entier</u> MASC
<u>entière</u> FEM ◊ *the entire world* le monde entier

entirely ADVERB
<u>entièrement</u>

entrance NOUN
l' <u>entrée</u> FEM
♦ **an entrance exam** un examen d'admission
♦ **entrance fee** le prix d'entrée

entry NOUN
l' <u>entrée</u> FEM
♦ **"no entry" (1)** (*on door*) « défense d'entrer »
♦ **"no entry" (2)** (*on road sign*) « sens interdit »
♦ **an entry form** une feuille d'inscription

envelope NOUN
l' <u>enveloppe</u> FEM

envious ADJECTIVE
<u>envieux</u> MASC
<u>envieuse</u> FEM

environment NOUN
l' <u>environnement</u> MASC

environmental ADJECTIVE
<u>écologique</u>

environmentalist NOUN
l' <u>environnementaliste</u> MASC/FEM

environment-friendly ADJECTIVE
<u>écologique</u>

envy NOUN

see also **envy** VERB

l' <u>envie</u> FEM

to **envy** VERB

> see also **envy** NOUN

envier ◊ *I don't envy you!* Je ne t'envie pas!

epidemic NOUN
l' épidémie FEM ◊ *a flu epidemic* une épidémie de grippe

epilepsy NOUN
l' épilepsie FEM

episode NOUN
l' épisode MASC (*ofTV series, story*)

equal ADJECTIVE

> see also **equal** VERB

égal
(MASC PL égaux)

to **equal** VERB

> see also **equal** ADJECTIVE

égaler

equality NOUN
l' égalité FEM

equator NOUN
l' équateur MASC

equipment NOUN
l' équipement MASC ◊ *fishing equipment* l'équipement de pêche ◊ *skiing equipment* l'équipement de ski

equipped ADJECTIVE
♦ **equipped with** équipé de
♦ **to be well equipped** être bien équipé

equivalent NOUN
l' équivalent MASC
♦ **equivalent to** équivalent à

to **erase** VERB
effacer

eraser NOUN
la gomme

errand NOUN
la course ◊ *I have to run a few errands for my mother.* J'ai quelques courses à faire pour ma mère.

error NOUN
l' erreur FEM

escalator NOUN
l' escalier roulant MASC

escape NOUN

> see also **escape** VERB

l' évasion FEM (*from prison*)

to **escape** VERB

> see also **escape** NOUN

s'échapper ◊ *A lion has escaped.* Un lion s'est échappé.
♦ **to escape from prison** s'évader de prison

escarpment NOUN
l' escarpement MASC ◊ *the Niagara escarpment* l'escarpement de Niagara

especially ADVERB
surtout ◊ *It's very hot there, especially in the summer.* Il fait très chaud là-bas, surtout en été.

essay NOUN
la dissertation ◊ *a history essay* une dissertation d'histoire

essential ADJECTIVE
essentiel MASC
essentielle FEM ◊ *It's essential to bring warm clothes.* Il est essentiel d'apporter des vêtements chauds.

estate NOUN
la propriété

to **estimate** VERB

> see also **estimate** NOUN

estimer ◊ *They estimated it would take three weeks.* Ils ont estimé que cela prendrait trois semaines.

estimate NOUN

> see also **estimate** VERB

l' estimation FEM ◊ *We asked for an estimate before getting the car repaired.* Nous avons demandé une estimation avant de faire réparer la voiture.

etc. ABBREVIATION (= *et cetera*)
etc.

ethnic ADJECTIVE
ethnique ◊ *an ethnic minority* une minorité ethnique

euro NOUN
l' euro MASC ◊ *50 euros* 50 euros

to **evacuate** VERB
évacuer

to **evaporate** VERB
s'évaporer
♦ **evaporated milk** le lait condensé

eve NOUN
♦ **Christmas Eve** la veille de Noël
♦ **New Year's Eve**
* la veille du Jour de l'An

even ADVERB

> see also **even** ADJECTIVE

même ◊ *I like all animals, even snakes.* J'aime tous les animaux, même les serpents.
♦ **even if** même si ◊ *I'd never do that, even if you asked me to.* Je ne ferais jamais ça, même si tu me le demandais.
♦ **not even** même pas ◊ *He never stops working, not even on the weekend.* Il n'arrête jamais de travailler, même pas la fin de semaine.
♦ **even though** bien que

bien que has to be followed by a verb in the subjunctive.

◊ *She never has any money, even though her parents are quite rich.* Elle n'a jamais d'argent, bien que ses parents soient assez riches.

♦ **even more** encore plus ◊ *I liked the book even more than the movie.* J'ai encore plus aimé le livre que le film.

even ADJECTIVE

see also **even** ADVERB

1 **régulier** MASC
régulière FEM ◊ *an even layer of snow* une couche régulière de neige

2 **plat** ◊ *an even surface* une surface plate

♦ **an even number** un nombre pair

♦ **to get even with somebody** prendre sa revanche sur quelqu'un ◊ *He wanted to get even with her.* Il voulait prendre sa revanche sur elle.

♦ **The score is even.** On est à égalité.

evening NOUN

le **soir** ◊ *in the evening* le soir
◊ *yesterday evening* hier soir
◊ *tomorrow evening* demain soir

♦ **all evening** toute la soirée

♦ **Good evening!** Bonsoir!

event NOUN

l' **événement** MASC

♦ **a sporting event** une épreuve sportive

eventful ADJECTIVE
mouvementé

eventually ADVERB
finalement

Be careful not to translate **eventually** by **éventuellement**.

ever ADVERB

♦ **Have you ever been to Prince Edward Island?** Est-ce que tu es déjà allé à l'Île-du-Prince-Édouard?

♦ **more than ever** plus que jamais
◊ *happier than ever* plus heureux que jamais

♦ **Have you ever seen her?** Vous l'avez déjà vue?

♦ **I haven't ever done that.** Je ne l'ai jamais fait.

♦ **the best I've ever seen** le meilleur que j'aie jamais vu

♦ **for the first time ever** pour la première fois

♦ **ever since** depuis que ◊ *ever since I met him* depuis que je l'ai rencontré

♦ **ever since then** depuis ce moment-là

every ADJECTIVE

chaque ◊ *every student* chaque élève

♦ **every time** chaque fois ◊ *Every time I*

see him he's depressed. Chaque fois que je le vois, il est déprimé.

♦ **every day** tous les jours

♦ **every week** toutes les semaines

♦ **every now and then** de temps en temps

♦ **every other Friday** un vendredi sur deux

♦ **every three days** tous les trois jours

everybody PRONOUN

tout le monde ◊ *Everybody had a good time.* Tout le monde s'est bien amusé. ◊ *Everybody makes mistakes.* Tout le monde peut se tromper.

everyday ADJECTIVE

1 **de tous les jours** (ordinary)
◊ *everyday clothes* les vêtements de tous les jours

2 (daily)
quotidien MASC
quotidienne FEM ◊ *everyday activities* les activités quotidiennes

♦ **an everyday situation** une situation courante

everyone PRONOUN

tout le monde ◊ *Everyone opened their presents.* Tout le monde a ouvert ses cadeaux. ◊ *Everyone should have a hobby.* Tout le monde devrait avoir un passe-temps.

everything PRONOUN

tout ◊ *You've thought of everything!* Tu as pensé à tout!

♦ **Have you remembered everything?** Est-ce que tu n'as rien oublié?

♦ **Money isn't everything.** L'argent ne fait pas le bonheur.

everywhere ADVERB

partout ◊ *I looked everywhere, but I couldn't find it.* J'ai regardé partout, mais je n'ai pas pu le trouver. ◊ *There were policemen everywhere.* Il y avait des policiers partout.

evil ADJECTIVE

see also **evil** NOUN

mauvais

evil NOUN

see also **evil** ADJECTIVE

le **mal**
(PL les maux)

ex- PREFIX

ex- ◊ *his ex-wife* son ex-femme

exact ADJECTIVE

exact

exactly ADVERB

exactement ◊ *exactly the same* exactement le même ◊ *not exactly.* pas exactement.

♦ **It's exactly 10 o'clock.** Il est dix heures

précises.

to **exaggerate** VERB
exagérer

exaggeration NOUN
l' exagération FEM

exam NOUN
l' examen MASC ◊ *a French exam*
un examen de français ◊ *the exam
results* les résultats des examens MASC

examination NOUN
l' examen MASC

to **examine** VERB
examiner ◊ *He examined her
passport.* Il a examiné son passeport.
◊ *The doctor examined him.* Le
docteur l'a examiné.

example NOUN
l' exemple MASC
♦ **for example** par exemple

excellent ADJECTIVE
excellent ◊ *Her results were
excellent.* Elle a eu d'excellents
résultats.
♦ **You can come? Excellent!** Tu peux
venir? C'est super!

except PREPOSITION
sauf ◊ *everyone except me* tout le
monde sauf moi
♦ **except for** sauf
♦ **except that** sauf que ◊ *The weather
was great, except that it was a bit
cold.* Il a fait un temps superbe, sauf
qu'il a fait un peu froid.

exception NOUN
l' exception FEM
♦ **to make an exception** faire une
exception

exceptional ADJECTIVE
exceptionnel MASC
exceptionnelle FEM

to **exchange** VERB
échanger ◊ *I exchanged the book for
a video.* J'ai échangé le livre contre
une vidéo.

exchange rate NOUN
le taux de change

excited ADJECTIVE
excité

exciting ADJECTIVE
passionnant

exclamation mark NOUN
le point d'exclamation

excuse NOUN
see also **excuse** VERB
l' excuse FEM

to **excuse** VERB
see also **excuse** NOUN

① excuser ◊ *Your lateness is
excused.* Ton retard a été excusé.
◊ *She excused him from class.* Elle lui
a permis de s'absenter de la classe.
② dispenser ◊ *He was excused from
writing the exam.* On l'a dispensé de
passer l'examen.
♦ **Excuse me!** Pardon!
♦ **to excuse oneself** s'excuser

to **execute** VERB
exécuter

execution NOUN
l' exécution FEM

executive NOUN
le cadre (*in business*) ◊ *He's an
executive.* Il est cadre.

exercise NOUN
l' exercice MASC
♦ **an exercise bike** un vélo
d'appartement
♦ **an exercise book** un cahier

exhausted ADJECTIVE
épuisé

exhaust fumes PL NOUN
les gaz d'échappement MASC PL

exhaust pipe NOUN
le tuyau d'échappement

exhibition NOUN
l' exposition FEM

to **exist** VERB
exister

exit NOUN
see also **exit** VERB
la sortie

to **exit** VERB
see also **exit** NOUN
① sortir ◊ *Exit via the rear door.*
Sortez par la porte arrière.
② descendre (*from vehicle*)

exotic ADJECTIVE
exotique

to **expand** VERB
① élargir (*increase*) ◊ *to expand one's
knowledge* élargir ses connaissances
② développer (*develop*) ◊ *to expand
an idea* développer une idée

to **expect** VERB
① attendre ◊ *I'm expecting her
for dinner.* Je l'attends pour dîner.
◊ *She's expecting a baby.* Elle attend
un enfant.
② s'attendre à ◊ *I was expecting the
worst.* Je m'attendais au pire.
③ supposer ◊ *I expect it's a mistake.*
Je suppose qu'il s'agit d'une erreur.

expedition NOUN
l' expédition FEM

E

to **expel** VERB
♦ **to get expelled** (*from school*) se faire renvoyer

expenses PL NOUN
les frais MASC PL

expensive ADJECTIVE
[1] cher MASC
chère FEM
✹ [2] dispendieux MASC dispendieuse FEM

experience NOUN
l' expérience FEM

experienced ADJECTIVE
expérimenté

experiment NOUN
l' expérience FEM

expert NOUN
le spécialiste
la spécialiste ◊ *She's a computer expert.* C'est une spécialiste en informatique.
♦ **He's an expert cook.** Il cuisine très bien.

to **expire** VERB
expirer

to **explain** VERB
expliquer

explanation NOUN
l' explication FEM

to **explode** VERB
exploser

to **exploit** VERB
exploiter

exploitation NOUN
l' exploitation FEM

to **explore** VERB
[1] explorer (*place*)
[2] étudier (*issue, possibilities*)

explorer NOUN
l' explorateur MASC
l' exploratrice FEM

explosion NOUN
l' explosion FEM

explosive ADJECTIVE

| see also **explosive** NOUN |

explosif MASC
explosive FEM

explosive NOUN

| see also **explosive** ADJECTIVE |

l' explosif MASC

to **expose** VERB
[1] découvrir
[2] exposer (*to sun, radiation*)

to **express** VERB
exprimer
♦ **to express oneself** s'exprimer ◊ *It's not easy to express oneself in a foreign language.* Ce n'est pas facile de s'exprimer dans une langue étrangère.

expression NOUN
l' expression FEM ◊ *It's an English expression.* C'est une expression anglaise.

expressway NOUN
l' autoroute urbaine FEM

extension NOUN
[1] l' annexe FEM (*of building*)
[2] le poste (*telephone*)
♦ **Extension 3137, please.** Poste trente et un trente-sept, s'il vous plaît.

extensive ADJECTIVE
[1] vaste (*knowledge, range*) ◊ *an extensive property* une vaste propriété ◊ *extensive knowledge of Canadian history* une vaste connaissance de l'histoire canadienne
[2] considérable (*damage, alterations*) ◊ *The earthquake caused extensive damage.* Le tremblement de terre a causé des dommages considérables.
[3] approfondi ◊ *extensive research* des recherches approfondies
♦ **extensive surgery** plusieurs interventions chirurgicales

extensively ADVERB
♦ **He has travelled extensively in Europe.** Il a beaucoup voyagé en Europe.
♦ **The building was extensively renovated last year.** Le bâtiment a été entièrement rénové l'année dernière.

extent NOUN
♦ **to some extent** dans une certaine mesure
♦ **to the extent that** au point que

exterior ADJECTIVE
extérieur

extinct ADJECTIVE
♦ **to become extinct** disparaître
♦ **to be extinct** avoir disparu ◊ *The species is almost extinct.* Cette espèce a presque disparu.

extinguisher NOUN
l' extincteur MASC (*fire extinguisher*)

extra ADJECTIVE, ADVERB
supplémentaire ◊ *an extra blanket* une couverture supplémentaire
♦ **to pay extra** payer un supplément
♦ **Breakfast is extra.** Il y a un supplément pour le petit déjeuner.
♦ **Do you have an extra pen?** As-tu un stylo à me passer?
♦ **It costs extra.** Il y a un supplément.

extracurricular ADJECTIVE
parascolaire

extraordinary ADJECTIVE
extraordinaire

extravagant ADJECTIVE
1 (*person*)
dépensier MASC
dépensière FEM
2 (*gift, wedding*)
somptueux MASC
somptueuse FEM

extreme ADJECTIVE
extrême

extremist NOUN
l' extrémiste MASC/FEM

eye NOUN
l' œil MASC
(PL les yeux) ◊ *I have green eyes.* J'ai
les yeux verts.
♦ **to keep an eye on something**
surveiller quelque chose

eyebrow NOUN
le sourcil

eyelash NOUN
le cil

eyelid NOUN
la paupière

eyeliner NOUN
le ligneur

eye shadow NOUN
le fard à paupières

eyesight NOUN
la vue ◊ *poor eyesight* une vue faible

E

F

fabric NOUN
le <u>tissu</u>

fabulous ADJECTIVE
<u>formidable</u> ◊ *The show was fabulous.* Le spectacle était formidable.

face NOUN

see also **face** VERB

1 le <u>visage</u> (*of person*)
2 le <u>cadran</u> (*of clock*)
3 la <u>paroi</u> (*of cliff*)
♦ **on the face of it** à première vue
♦ **in the face of these difficulties** face à ces difficultés
♦ **face to face** face à face
♦ **to someone's face** sans détour ◊ *She said it right to my face.* Elle me l'a dit sans détour.

to **face** VERB

see also **face** NOUN

<u>faire face à</u> (*place, problem*)
♦ **to face up to something** faire face à quelque chose ◊ *You must face up to your responsibilities.* Vous devez faire face à vos responsabilités.

facecloth NOUN
⚹ la <u>débarbouillette</u>

⚹ **face-off** NOUN
la <u>mise au jeu</u>

facilities PL NOUN
l' <u>équipement</u> MASC SING ◊ *This school has excellent facilities.* Cette école dispose d'excellents équipements.
♦ **toilet facilities** les toilettes FEM

fact NOUN
le <u>fait</u>
♦ **in fact** en fait

factory NOUN
l' <u>usine</u> FEM

fad NOUN
l' <u>engouement</u> MASC

to **fade** VERB
1 <u>passer</u> (*colour*) ◊ *The colour has faded in the sun.* La couleur a passé au soleil.
♦ **My jeans have faded.** Mon jean est délavé.
2 <u>baisser</u> ◊ *The light was fading fast.* La lumière baissait rapidement.
3 <u>diminuer</u> ◊ *The noise gradually faded.* Le bruit a diminué peu à peu.

to **fail** VERB

see also **fail** NOUN

1 <u>rater</u> ◊ *I failed the history exam.* J'ai raté l'examen d'histoire.
2 <u>échouer</u> ◊ *In our class, no one failed.* Dans notre classe, personne n'a échoué. ◊ *Our efforts failed.* Nos efforts ont échoué.
3 <u>lâcher</u> ◊ *My brakes failed.* Mes freins ont lâché.
4 <u>tomber en panne</u> ◊ *The engine failed.* Le moteur est tombé en panne.
5 <u>faiblir</u> ◊ *His eyesight is failing.* Sa vue faiblit.
♦ **to fail to do something** ne pas faire quelque chose ◊ *She failed to return her library books.* Elle n'a pas rendu ses livres à la bibliothèque.

fail NOUN

see also **fail** VERB

♦ **without fail** sans faute

failure NOUN
1 l' <u>échec</u> MASC ◊ *feelings of failure* un sentiment d'échec SING
2 le <u>raté</u>
la <u>ratée</u> ◊ *You are not a failure.* Tu n'es pas un raté.
3 la <u>défaillance</u> ◊ *a mechanical failure* une défaillance mécanique

faint ADJECTIVE

see also **faint** VERB

<u>faible</u> ◊ *His voice was very faint.* Sa voix était très faible.
♦ **to feel faint** se trouver mal

to **faint** VERB

see also **faint** ADJECTIVE

<u>s'évanouir</u> ◊ *All of a sudden she fainted.* Tout à coup elle s'est évanouie.

fair ADJECTIVE

see also **fair** NOUN

1 <u>juste</u> ◊ *That's not fair.* Ce n'est pas juste.
2 <u>clair</u> (*skin*) ◊ *people with fair skin* les gens qui ont la peau claire
3 (*weather*)
<u>beau</u> MASC
<u>belle</u> FEM ◊ *The weather was fair.* Il faisait beau.
4 (*good enough*)
<u>assez bon</u> MASC
<u>assez bonne</u> FEM ◊ *I have a fair chance of winning.* J'ai d'assez bonnes chances de gagner.
5 <u>considérable</u> (*sizeable*) ◊ *That's a fair distance.* Ça représente une

distance considérable.

fair NOUN

> see also **fair** ADJECTIVE

la <u>foire</u> ◊ *They went to the fair.* Ils sont allés à la foire.
♦ **a trade fair** une foire commerciale
♦ **a book fair** une foire du livre

fairground NOUN
le <u>champ de foire</u>

fairly ADVERB
[1] <u>équitablement</u> ◊ *The cake was divided fairly.* Le gâteau a été partagé équitablement.
[2] <u>assez</u> (*quite*) ◊ *That's fairly good.* C'est assez bien.

fairness NOUN
la <u>justice</u>

fairy NOUN
la <u>fée</u>

fairy tale NOUN
le <u>conte de fées</u>
(PL les contes de fées)

faith NOUN
[1] la <u>foi</u> ◊ *the Catholic faith* la foi catholique
[2] la <u>confiance</u> ◊ *People have lost faith in the government.* Les gens ont perdu confiance dans le gouvernement.

faithful ADJECTIVE
<u>fidèle</u>

faithfully ADVERB
♦ **Yours faithfully...** (*in letter*) Veuillez agréer mes salutations distinguées...

fake NOUN

> see also **fake** ADJECTIVE, VERB

le <u>faux</u> ◊ *The painting was a fake.* Le tableau était un faux.

fake ADJECTIVE

> see also **fake** NOUN, VERB

<u>faux</u> MASC
<u>fausse</u> FEM ◊ *She wore fake fur.* Elle portait une fausse fourrure.

to **fake** VERB

> see also **fake** ADJECTIVE, NOUN

[1] <u>imiter</u> (*signature*)
[2] <u>truquer</u> (*photo, event*)
♦ **He faked a headache.** Il a fait semblant d'avoir mal à la tête.
♦ **She's faking it.** Elle fait semblant.

fall NOUN

> see also **fall** VERB

[1] la <u>chute</u> ◊ *a fall of snow* une chute de neige ◊ *She had a nasty fall.* Elle a fait une mauvaise chute.
♦ **the Niagara Falls** les chutes du Niagara

[2] l' <u>automne</u> MASC
🍁 ♦ **fall fair** la foire d'automne

to **fall** VERB

> see also **fall** NOUN

[1] <u>tomber</u> ◊ *He tripped and fell.* Il a trébuché et il est tombé.
[2] <u>baisser</u> ◊ *Prices are falling.* Les prix baissent.
♦ **to fall apart** tomber en morceaux
♦ **Their marriage is falling apart.** Leur mariage s'effond.
♦ **to fall behind** rester en arrière
♦ **to fall down (1)** (*person*) tomber ◊ *She's fallen down.* Elle est tombée.
♦ **to fall down (2)** (*building*) s'écrouler ◊ *The house is slowly falling down.* La maison est en train de s'écrouler.
♦ **to fall for (1)** se laisser prendre à ◊ *They fell for it.* Ils s'y sont laissé prendre.
♦ **to fall for (2)** tomber amoureux de ◊ *She's falling for him.* Elle est en train de tomber amoureuse de lui.
♦ **to fall off** tomber de ◊ *The book fell off the shelf.* Le livre est tombé de l'étagère.
♦ **to fall through** tomber à l'eau ◊ *Our plans have fallen through.* Nos projets sont tombés à l'eau.

fallen VERB *see* **fall**

false ADJECTIVE
<u>faux</u> MASC
<u>fausse</u> FEM
♦ **a false alarm** une fausse alerte
♦ **false teeth** le dentier

fame NOUN
la <u>renommée</u>

familiar ADJECTIVE
<u>familier</u> MASC
<u>familière</u> FEM ◊ *a familiar face* un visage familier
♦ **to be familiar with something** bien connaître quelque chose ◊ *I'm familiar with his work.* Je connais bien ses œuvres.

family NOUN
la <u>famille</u>
♦ **the Cooke family** la famille Cooke

famine NOUN
la <u>famine</u>

famous ADJECTIVE
<u>célèbre</u>

fan NOUN
[1] l' <u>éventail</u> MASC (*handheld*)
[2] le <u>ventilateur</u> (*electric*)
[3] le/la <u>fan</u> ◊ *I'm a fan of Jann Arden.* Je suis une fan de Jann Arden.
◊ *hockey fans* les fans de hockey

fanatic NOUN
le/la <u>fanatique</u>

F

fancy ADJECTIVE
élaboré

fantastic ADJECTIVE
fantastique

far ADJECTIVE, ADVERB
loin ◊ *Is it far?* Est-ce que c'est loin?
♦ **far from** loin de ◊ *It's not far from London.* Ce n'est pas loin de London. ◊ *It's far from easy.* C'est loin d'être facile.
♦ **How far is it?** C'est à quelle distance?
♦ **How far is it to Hull?** Combien y a-t-il jusqu'à Hull?
♦ **How far are you?** (*with a task*) Où en êtes-vous?
♦ **at the far end** à l'autre bout ◊ *at the far end of the room* à l'autre bout de la pièce
♦ **far better** beaucoup mieux
♦ **as far as I know** pour autant que je sache

fare NOUN
1 le prix du billet (*trains, buses*)
2 le prix de la course (*taxi*)
♦ **half fare** le demi-tarif
♦ **full fare** le plein tarif

Far East NOUN
l' Extrême-Orient MASC
♦ **in the Far East** en Extrême-Orient

far-fetched ADJECTIVE
tiré par les cheveux

farm NOUN
la ferme

farmer NOUN
1 l' agriculteur MASC
l' agricultrice FEM ◊ *He's a farmer.* Il est agriculteur.
2 le fermier
la fermière

farmhouse NOUN
la ferme

farming NOUN
l' agriculture FEM
♦ **dairy farming** l'industrie laitière

fascinating ADJECTIVE
fascinant

fashion NOUN
la mode ◊ *a fashion show* un défilé de mode
♦ **in fashion** à la mode

fashionable ADJECTIVE
à la mode ◊ *She wears very fashionable clothes.* Elle porte des vêtements très à la mode. ◊ *a fashionable restaurant* un restaurant à la mode

fast ADJECTIVE, ADVERB
1 vite ◊ *He can run fast.* Il sait courir vite.
2 rapide ◊ *a fast car* une voiture rapide
♦ **fast food** la bouffe-minute
♦ **fast forward** l'avance rapide FEM
♦ **That clock's fast.** Cette pendule avance.
♦ **She's fast asleep.** Elle est profondément endormie.

fat ADJECTIVE

see also **fat** NOUN

gros MASC
grosse FEM

fat NOUN

see also **fat** ADJECTIVE

1 le gras (*on meat, in food*) ◊ *It's very high in fat.* C'est très gras. ◊ *to cut down on fat* couper le gras
2 la matière grasse (*for cooking*)
♦ **body fat** le tissu adipeux

fatal ADJECTIVE
1 (*causing death*)
mortel MASC
mortelle FEM ◊ *a fatal accident* un accident mortel
2 fatal (*disastrous*) ◊ *He made a fatal mistake.* Il a fait une erreur fatale.

father NOUN
le père ◊ *my father* mon père

father-in-law NOUN
le beau-père
(PL les beaux-pères)

fault NOUN
1 la faute (*mistake*) ◊ *It's my fault.* C'est de ma faute.
2 le défaut (*defect*) ◊ *in spite of all her faults* malgré tous ses défauts
♦ **a mechanical fault** une défaillance mécanique

faulty ADJECTIVE
défectueux MASC
défectueuse FEM ◊ *This machine is faulty.* Cette machine est défectueuse.

favour NOUN
le service
♦ **to do somebody a favour** rendre service à quelqu'un ◊ *Could you do me a favour?* Tu peux me rendre service?
♦ **to be in favour of something** être pour quelque chose ◊ *I'm in favour of nuclear disarmament.* Je suis pour le désarmement nucléaire.

favourite ADJECTIVE

see also **favourite** NOUN

favori MASC
favorite FEM ◊ *Blue is my favourite colour.* Le bleu est ma couleur favorite.

favourite NOUN

see also **favourite** ADJECTIVE

1️⃣ le favori
2️⃣ la favorite ◊ *The Canadian is the favourite to win gold in speed skating.* La Canadienne est la favorite pour gagner l'or en patinage de vitesse. ◊ *The next song is my favourite.* La prochaine chanson est ma favorite.

fawn NOUN
le faon

fax NOUN

see also **fax** VERB

1️⃣ la télécopie (*document*)
♦ **to send somebody a fax** envoyer une télécopie à quelqu'un
2️⃣ le télécopieur (*machine*)

to **fax** VERB

see also **fax** NOUN

télécopier ◊ *Can you fax me your document?* Peux-tu me télécopier ton document?

fear NOUN

see also **fear** VERB

la peur

to **fear** VERB

see also **fear** NOUN

craindre ◊ *You have nothing to fear.* Vous n'avez rien à craindre.

feather NOUN
la plume

feature NOUN
la caractéristique (*of person, object*) ◊ *an important feature* une caractéristique essentielle
♦ **a feature film** un long métrage

February NOUN
février MASC
♦ **in February** en février

fed VERB *see* **feed**

federal ADJECTIVE
fédéral ◊ *the federal government* le gouvernement fédéral

fed up ADJECTIVE
♦ **to be fed up with something** en avoir marre de quelque chose ◊ *I'm fed up with waiting for him.* J'en ai marre de l'attendre.

to **feed** VERB
donner à manger à ◊ *Have you fed the cat?* Est-ce que tu as donné à manger au chat?
♦ **She worked hard to feed her family.** Elle travaillait dur pour nourrir sa famille.

feedback NOUN
la rétroaction ◊ *I need your feedback on my story.* J'ai besoin de ta rétroaction sur ma composition.

to **feel** VERB
1️⃣ se sentir ◊ *I don't feel well.* Je ne me sens pas bien. ◊ *I feel a bit lonely.* Je me sens un peu seul.
2️⃣ sentir ◊ *I didn't feel much pain.* Je n'ai presque rien senti.
3️⃣ toucher ◊ *The doctor felt my forehead.* Le docteur m'a touché le front.
♦ **I was feeling hungry.** J'avais faim.
♦ **I was feeling cold, so I went inside.** J'avais froid, alors je suis rentré.
♦ **I feel like...** (*want*) J'ai envie de... ◊ *Do you feel like an ice cream?* Tu as envie d'une crème glacée?

feeling NOUN
1️⃣ la sensation (*physical*) ◊ *a burning feeling* une sensation de brûlure
2️⃣ le sentiment (*emotional*) ◊ *a feeling of satisfaction* un sentiment de satisfaction

feet PL NOUN *see* **foot**

fell VERB *see* **fall**

felt VERB *see* **feel**

felt pen NOUN
le stylo-feutre

female ADJECTIVE

see also **female** NOUN

1️⃣ femelle ◊ *a female animal* un animal femelle
2️⃣ féminin ◊ *the female sex* le sexe féminin

female NOUN

see also **female** ADJECTIVE

la femelle (*animal*)

feminine ADJECTIVE
féminin

feminist NOUN
le/la féministe

fence NOUN
la barrière

fern NOUN
la fougère

ferret NOUN
le furet

ferry NOUN
le traversier

fertile ADJECTIVE
fertile

fertilizer NOUN
l' engrais MASC

festival NOUN
le festival ◊ *a jazz festival* un festival de jazz

to **fetch** VERB

F

fever → file

[1] aller chercher ◊ *Fetch the bucket.*
Va chercher le seau.
[2] se vendre (*sell for*) ◊ *His painting
fetched $5000.* Son tableau s'est
vendu cinq mille dollars.

fever NOUN
la fièvre (*temperature*)

few ADJECTIVE, PRONOUN
peu de (*not many*) ◊ *few books* peu
de livres
♦ **a few (1)** quelques ◊ *a few hours*
quelques heures
♦ **a few (2)** quelques-uns ◊ *"How
many apples do you want?" "A few."*
« Tu veux combien de pommes ? »
« Quelques-unes. »
♦ **quite a few people** pas mal de monde

fewer ADJECTIVE
moins de ◊ *There are fewer people
than there were yesterday.* Il y a
moins de monde qu'hier. ◊ *There
are fewer students in this class.* Il y a
moins d'élèves dans cette classe.

fiancé NOUN
le fiancé

fiancée NOUN
la fiancée

fiction NOUN
les romans MASC PL (*novels*)

field NOUN
[1] le champ (*in countryside*) ◊ *a field
of wheat* un champ de blé
[2] le terrain (*for sport*) ◊ *a soccer field*
un terrain de soccer
[3] le domaine (*subject*) ◊ *He's an
expert in his field.* C'est un expert
dans son domaine.
♦ **a field trip** une sortie éducative

fierce ADJECTIVE
[1] féroce ◊ *The dog looked very
fierce.* Le chien avait l'air très féroce.
[2] violent ◊ *The wind was very fierce.*
Le vent était très violent. ◊ *a fierce
attack* une attaque violente

fifteen NUMBER
quinze ◊ *I'm fifteen.* J'ai quinze ans.

fifteenth ADJECTIVE
quinzième ◊ *the fifteenth floor* le
quinzième étage
♦ **the fifteenth of August** le quinze août

fifth ADJECTIVE
cinquième ◊ *the fifth floor* le
cinquième étage
♦ **the fifth of August** le cinq août

fifty NUMBER
cinquante ◊ *She's fifty.* Elle a
cinquante ans.

fifty-fifty ADJECTIVE, ADVERB
moitié-moitié ◊ *They split the prize
money fifty-fifty.* Ils ont partagé
l'argent du prix moitié-moitié.
♦ **a fifty-fifty chance** une chance sur
deux

fight NOUN
 see also **fight** VERB
[1] la bagarre ◊ *There was a fight in
the hallway.* Il y a eu une bagarre
dans le couloir.
[2] la lutte ◊ *the fight against cancer* la
lutte contre le cancer

to **fight** VERB
 see also **fight** NOUN
[1] se battre ◊ *They were fighting.* Ils
se battaient.
[2] lutter contre ◊ *The doctors tried to
fight the disease.* Les médecins ont
essayé de lutter contre la maladie.
◊ *He fought against the urge to
smoke.* Il a lutté contre son envie de
fumer.

fighting NOUN
les bagarres FEM PL ◊ *Fighting broke
out in the schoolyard.* Des bagarres
ont éclaté dans la cour de l'école.

figure NOUN
[1] le chiffre (*number*) ◊ *Can you give
me the exact figures?* Pouvez-vous
me donner les chiffres exacts ?
[2] la silhouette (*outline of person*) ◊ *I
saw the figure of a man on the bridge.*
J'ai vu la silhouette d'un homme sur
le pont.
♦ **I have to watch my figure.** Je dois
faire attention à ma ligne.
[3] le personnage (*personality*)
◊ *She's an important political figure.*
C'est un personnage politique
important.

to **figure out** VERB
[1] calculer ◊ *I'll try to figure out how
much it'll cost.* Je vais essayer de
calculer combien ça va coûter.
[2] voir ◊ *I couldn't figure out what it
meant.* Je n'arrivais pas à voir ce que
ça voulait dire.
[3] cerner ◊ *I can't figure him out at
all.* Je n'arrive pas du tout à le cerner.

figure skating NOUN
le patinage artistique

file NOUN
 see also **file** VERB
[1] le dossier (*document*) ◊ *Have we
got a file on the suspect?* Est-ce que
nous avons un dossier sur le suspect ?
[2] le fichier (*on computer*)
[3] la lime (*for nails, metal*)
♦ **a file folder** une chemise

to file VERB

> see also **file** NOUN

[1] classer (*papers*)
[2] limer (*nails, metal*) ◊ *to file one's nails* se limer les ongles

to fill VERB

remplir ◊ *She filled the glass with water.* Elle a rempli le verre d'eau.
♦ **to fill in** boucher ◊ *He filled the hole in with soil.* Il a bouché le trou avec de la terre.
♦ **to fill in for somebody** remplacer quelqu'un
♦ **to fill out** remplir ◊ *Can you fill out this form, please?* Est-ce que vous pouvez remplir ce formulaire, s'il vous plaît?
♦ **to fill up** remplir ◊ *She filled the cup up to the brim.* Elle a rempli la tasse à ras bords.
♦ **Fill it up, please.** (*at gas station*) Le plein, s'il vous plaît.

film NOUN
le film

filmmaker NOUN
le/la cinéaste

filthy ADJECTIVE
crasseux MASC
crasseuse FEM

final ADJECTIVE

> see also **final** NOUN

[1] (*last*)
dernier MASC
dernière FEM ◊ *our final farewells* nos derniers adieux
[2] (*definite*)
définitif MASC
définitive FEM ◊ *a final decision* une décision définitive
♦ **I'm not going and that's final.** Je n'y vais pas, un point c'est tout.

final NOUN

> see also **final** ADJECTIVE

la finale ◊ *She's playing in the final.* Elle va disputer la finale.

finally ADVERB
[1] enfin (*lastly*) ◊ *Finally, I would like to say...* Enfin, je voudrais dire...
[2] finalement (*eventually*) ◊ *They finally decided to leave on Saturday instead of Friday.* Ils ont finalement décidé de partir samedi au lieu de vendredi.

to find VERB
[1] trouver ◊ *I can't find the exit.* Je ne trouve pas la sortie.
[2] retrouver (*something lost*) ◊ *Did you find your pen?* Est-ce que tu as retrouvé ton crayon?

♦ **to find something out** découvrir quelque chose ◊ *I'm determined to find out the truth.* Je suis décidé à découvrir la vérité.
♦ **to find out about (1)** (*make enquiries*) se renseigner sur ◊ *Try to find out about the price.* Essaye de te renseigner sur le prix.
♦ **to find out about (2)** (*by chance*) apprendre ◊ *I found out about their secret plan.* J'ai appris leur projet secret.

fine ADJECTIVE, ADVERB

> see also **fine** NOUN

[1] excellent (*very good*) ◊ *He's a fine musician.* C'est un excellent musicien.
♦ **to be fine** aller bien ◊ *"How are you?" "I'm fine."* « Comment ça va? » « Ça va bien. »
♦ **I feel fine.** Je me sens bien.
♦ **The weather is fine today.** Il fait beau aujourd'hui.
[2] fin (*not coarse*) ◊ *She has very fine hair.* Elle a les cheveux très fins.

fine NOUN

> see also **fine** ADJECTIVE

[1] l' amende FEM ◊ *She got a $50 fine.* Elle a eu une amende de cinquante dollars.
[2] la contravention (*for traffic offence*) ◊ *I got a fine for driving through a red light.* J'ai eu une contravention pour avoir grillé un feu rouge.

finger NOUN
le doigt
♦ **my little finger** mon petit doigt

fingernail NOUN
l' ongle MASC

fingerprint NOUN
l' empreinte digitale FEM

finish NOUN

> see also **finish** VERB

l' arrivée FEM (*of race*) ◊ *We saw the finish of the marathon.* Nous avons vu l'arrivée du marathon.
♦ **the finish line** la ligne d'arrivée
♦ **a fight to the finish** un combat sans merci
♦ **from start to finish** du début à la fin

to finish VERB

> see also **finish** NOUN

[1] finir ◊ *I've finished!* J'ai fini!
♦ **to finish doing something** finir de faire quelque chose
[2] terminer ◊ *I've finished the book.* J'ai terminé ce livre. ◊ *The film has finished.* Le film est terminé.

fir NOUN

F

☞

le sapin
♦ **Douglas fir** le douglas vert

fire NOUN

> see also **fire** VERB

1 le feu
(PL les feux) ◊ *He made a fire to warm himself.* Il a fait du feu pour se réchauffer.
♦ **to be on fire** être en feu
2 l' incendie MASC (*accidental*) ◊ *The house was destroyed by fire.* La maison a été détruite par un incendie.
♦ **the fire department** les pompiers MASC PL
♦ **a fire alarm** un avertisseur d'incendie
♦ **a fire drill** un exercice d'incendie
♦ **a fire engine** un camion d'incendie
♦ **a fire escape** un escalier de secours
♦ **a fire extinguisher** un extincteur
♦ **a fire hydrant**
🗷 une borne-fontaine
(PL les bornes-fontaines)
♦ **a fire station** un poste de pompiers

to **fire** VERB

> see also **fire** NOUN

tirer (*shoot*) ◊ *She fired twice.* Elle a tiré deux fois.
♦ **to fire at somebody** tirer sur quelqu'un ◊ *The terrorist fired at the crowd.* Le terroriste a tiré sur la foule.
♦ **to fire a gun** tirer un coup de feu
♦ **to fire somebody** mettre quelqu'un à la porte ◊ *He was fired from his job.* Il a été mis à la porte.

firefighter NOUN
le pompier
la pompière ◊ *She's a firefighter.* Elle est pompière.

fireplace NOUN
la cheminée

fireworks PL NOUN
le feu d'artifice SING ◊ *Are you going to see the fireworks?* Est-ce que tu vas voir le feu d'artifice?

firm ADJECTIVE

> see also **firm** NOUN

ferme ◊ *to be firm with somebody* se montrer ferme avec quelqu'un

firm NOUN

> see also **firm** ADJECTIVE

l' entreprise FEM ◊ *She works for a large firm in Kitchener.* Elle travaille pour une grande entreprise à Kitchener.

first ADJECTIVE, ADVERB

> see also **first** NOUN

1 premier MASC
première FEM ◊ *the first of September*

le premier septembre ◊ *the first time* la première fois
♦ **to come first** (*in exam, race*) arriver premier ◊ *Who came first?* Qui est arrivé premier?
2 d'abord ◊ *I want to get a job, but first I have to finish school.* Je veux trouver du travail, mais d'abord je dois finir mes études.
♦ **first of all** tout d'abord

first NOUN

> see also **first** ADJECTIVE

le premier
la première ◊ *She was the first to arrive.* Elle est arrivée la première.
♦ **at first** au début

first aid NOUN
les premiers soins MASC PL
♦ **a first aid kit** une trousse de premiers soins

first-class ADJECTIVE
1 de première classe ◊ *He has booked a first-class ticket.* Il a réservé un billet de première classe.
2 excellent ◊ *a first-class meal* un excellent repas

firstly ADVERB
premièrement ◊ *Firstly, let's see what the book is about.* Premièrement, voyons de quoi parle ce livre.

🗷 **First Ministers** PL NOUN
les premiers ministres MASC ◊ *a First Ministers' conference* une conférence des premiers ministres

🗷 **First Nations** PL NOUN
les Premières Nations FEM
◊ *the Assembly of First Nations* l'Assemblée des Premières Nations

fish NOUN

> see also **fish** VERB

le poisson ◊ *I caught three fish.* J'ai pêché trois poissons. ◊ *I don't like fish.* Je n'aime pas le poisson.
♦ **fish bone** l'arête FEM
♦ **fish sticks** les bâtonnets de poisson MASC PL

to **fish** VERB

> see also **fish** NOUN

pêcher ◊ *to fish for trout* pêcher la truite
♦ **to go fishing** aller à la pêche ◊ *We went fishing in the Miramichi River.* Nous sommes allés à la pêche sur la rivière Miramichi.

fisherman NOUN
le pêcheur
la pêcheuse ◊ *She's a fisherman.* Elle est pêcheuse.

fishing NOUN
la pêche ◊ *My hobby is fishing.* La pêche est mon passe-temps favori.

fishing boat NOUN
le bateau de pêche

fishing rod NOUN
la canne à pêche

fishing tackle NOUN
le matériel de pêche

fist NOUN
le poing

to **fit** VERB

> see also **fit** ADJECTIVE, NOUN

① être la bonne taille (*be the right size*) ◊ *Does it fit?* Est-ce que c'est la bonne taille?

In French you usually specify whether something is too big, small, tight etc.

♦ **These pants don't fit me. (1)** (*too big*) Ce pantalon est trop grand pour moi.
♦ **These pants don't fit me. (2)** (*too small*) Ce pantalon est trop petit pour moi.
② correspondre (*match*) ◊ *That story doesn't fit with what he told us.* Cette histoire ne correspond pas à ce qu'il nous a dit.
③ adapter ◊ *She fitted a plug to the hair dryer.* Elle a adapté une prise au sèche-cheveux.
♦ **to fit in** s'adapter ◊ *She fits in well at her new school.* Elle s'est bien adaptée à sa nouvelle école.

fit ADJECTIVE

> see also **fit** VERB, NOUN

en forme (*in condition*) ◊ *He felt relaxed and fit after his holiday.* Il se sentait détendu et en forme après ses vacances.

fit NOUN

> see also **fit** ADJECTIVE, VERB

♦ **to have a fit** (*be upset*) piquer une crise de nerfs ◊ *My mom will have a fit when she sees the carpet!* Ma mère va piquer une crise de nerfs quand elle va voir la moquette!
♦ **a fit of coughing** une quinte de toux
♦ **to be in fits of laughter** se tordre de rire

fitting room NOUN
la cabine d'essayage

five NUMBER
cinq ◊ *He's five.* Il a cinq ans.

to **fix** VERB
① réparer (*mend*) ◊ *Can you fix my bike?* Est-ce que tu peux réparer mon vélo?
② préparer ◊ *He fixed us a snack.* Il nous a préparé une collation.

fixed ADJECTIVE
fixe ◊ *at a fixed time* à une heure fixe ◊ *at a fixed price* à un prix fixe ◊ *a fixed-price menu* un menu à prix fixe
♦ **My parents have very fixed ideas.** Mes parents ont des idées très arrêtées.

flabby ADJECTIVE
flasque

flag NOUN
le drapeau
(PL les drapeaux)

flame NOUN
la flamme

to **flap** VERB
① battre de (*wings*) ◊ *The bird flapped its wings.* L'oiseau battait des ailes.
② claquer (*noisily*) ◊ *The flags were flapping in the wnd.* Les drapeaux claquaient dans le vent.

flash NOUN

> see also **flash** VERB

le flash
(PL les flashes) ◊ *Has your camera got a flash?* Est-ce que ton appareil photo a un flash?
♦ **a flash of lightning** un éclair
♦ **in a flash** en un clin d'œil

to **flash** VERB

> see also **flash** NOUN

① clignoter ◊ *The police car's blue light was flashing.* Le gyrophare de la voiture de police clignotait.
② projeter ◊ *They flashed a light in his face.* Ils lui ont projeté la lumière d'une lampe de poche en plein visage.
♦ **She flashed her headlights.** Elle a fait un appel de phares.

flashlight NOUN
la lampe de poche

flat ADJECTIVE, ADVERB
① plat ◊ *a flat roof* un toit plat ◊ *flat shoes* des chaussures plates
② crevé (*tire*) ◊ *I've got a flat tire.* J'ai un pneu crevé.
③ faux (*music*) ◊ *We went flat in that last song.* Nous avons chanté faux dans cette dernière chanson.
♦ **B flat** si bémol

to **flatter** VERB
flatter

flavour NOUN
① le goût (*taste*) ◊ *It has a very strong flavour.* Ça a un goût très fort.
② la saveur (*variety*) ◊ *Which flavour of ice cream would you like?* Quelle

saveur de crème glacée est-ce que tu
veux?

flavouring NOUN
l' arôme MASC

flea NOUN
la puce
♦ **a flea market** un marché aux puces

flew VERB *see* **fly**

flexible ADJECTIVE
flexible ◊ *flexible working hours* les
horaires flexibles

to **flicker** VERB
trembloter ◊ *The light flickered.* La
lumière a tremblé.

flight NOUN
le vol ◊ *What time is the flight to
Sault Ste. Marie?* À quelle heure est le
vol pour Sault Ste. Marie?
♦ **a flight of stairs** un escalier

flight attendant NOUN
l' agent de bord MASC
l' agente de bord FEM

to **flip** VERB
♦ **to flip a coin** tirer à pile ou face
♦ **to flip through a book** feuilleter un
livre
♦ **Flip the card over.** Retourne la carte.

flippers NOUN
1 les palmes FEM PL (*for people*)
2 les nageoires FEM PL (*on animals*)

to **float** VERB
flotter ◊ *A leaf was floating on the
water.* Une feuille flottait sur l'eau.

flock NOUN
♦ **a flock of sheep** un troupeau de
moutons
♦ **a flock of birds** un vol d'oiseaux

flood NOUN

> *see also* **flood** VERB

1 l' inondation FEM ◊ *The rain
has caused many floods.* La
pluie a provoqué de nombreuses
inondations.
2 le flot ◊ *He received a flood of
letters.* Il a reçu un flot de lettres.

to **flood** VERB

> *see also* **flood** NOUN

1 déborder ◊ *The river has flooded.*
La rivière a débordé.
2 inonder ◊ *The river has flooded
the village.* La rivière a inondé le
village.

flooding NOUN
les inondations FEM PL

floor NOUN
1 le plancher ◊ *a hardwood floor* un
plancher de bois franc

♦ **on the floor** par terre
2 l' étage MASC (*storey*) ◊ *the fourth
floor* le quatrième étage
♦ **the ground floor**
🕷 le premier étage
♦ **on the third floor** au troisième étage

flop NOUN
le fiasco ◊ *The movie was a flop.* Le
film a été un fiasco.

floppy disk NOUN
la disquette

florist NOUN
le/la fleuriste

flour NOUN
la farine

to **flow** VERB
1 couler (*river*)
2 s'écouler (*flow out*) ◊ *Water was
flowing from the pipe.* De l'eau
s'écoulait du tuyau.

flower NOUN
la fleur

flown VERB *see* **fly**

flu NOUN
la grippe ◊ *She has the flu.* Elle a la
grippe.

fluent ADJECTIVE
♦ **She speaks fluent French.** Elle parle
couramment le français.

flung VERB *see* **fling**

to **flush** VERB
♦ **to flush the toilet** tirer la chasse

flute NOUN
la flûte ◊ *I play the flute.* Je joue de
la flûte.

fly NOUN

> *see also* **fly** VERB

1 la mouche (*insect*)
2 la braguette (*on pants*)
3 le double toit (*on tent*)

to **fly** VERB

> *see also* **fly** NOUN

1 voler ◊ *The plane flies at a speed
of 400 km per hour.* L'avion vole à
quatre cents kilomètres à l'heure.
2 aller en avion (*passenger*)
◊ *He flew from Goose Bay to
Charlottetown.* Il est allé de Goose Bay
à Charlottetown en avion.
♦ **to fly away** s'envoler ◊ *The bird flew
away.* L'oiseau s'est envolé.

foal NOUN
le poulain

focus NOUN

> *see also* **focus** VERB

♦ **to be out of focus** être flou ◊ *The*

house is out of focus in this photo. La maison est floue sur cette photo.

to **focus** VERB

see also **focus** NOUN

mettre au point ◊ *Try to focus the binoculars.* Essaye de mettre les jumelles au point.
♦ **to focus on something (1)** (*with lens*) régler la mise au point sur quelque chose ◊ *The photographer focused on the bird.* La photographe a réglé la mise au point sur l'oiseau.
♦ **to focus on something (2)** (*concentrate*) se concentrer sur quelque chose ◊ *Let's focus on the plot of the play.* Concentrons-nous sur l'intrigue de la pièce.

fog NOUN
le brouillard

foggy ADJECTIVE
♦ **It's foggy.** Il y a du brouillard.
♦ **a foggy day** un jour de brouillard

foil NOUN (*kitchen foil*)
le papier d'aluminium ◊ *She wrapped the meat in foil.* Elle a enveloppé la viande dans du papier d'aluminium.

fold NOUN

see also **fold** VERB

le pli

to **fold** VERB

see also **fold** NOUN

plier ◊ *He folded the newspaper in half.* Il a plié le journal en deux.
♦ **to fold something up** plier quelque chose
♦ **to fold one's arms** croiser ses bras ◊ *She folded her arms.* Elle a croisé les bras.

folder NOUN
① la chemise ◊ *She kept all her letters in a folder.* Elle gardait toutes ses lettres dans une chemise.
② le dossier (*computer*)

folding ADJECTIVE
♦ **a folding chair** une chaise pliante
♦ **a folding bed** un lit pliant

to **follow** VERB
suivre ◊ *She followed him.* Elle l'a suivi. ◊ *You go first and I'll follow.* Va devant, je te suis.

following ADJECTIVE
suivant ◊ *the following day* le jour suivant

fond ADJECTIVE
♦ **to be fond of somebody** aimer beaucoup quelqu'un ◊ *I'm very fond of him.* Je l'aime beaucoup.

font NOUN
la police de caractères

food NOUN
la nourriture
♦ **We need to buy some food.** Nous devons acheter à manger.
♦ **cat food** la nourriture pour chat
♦ **dog food** la nourriture pour chien
♦ **a food bank** une banque alimentaire
♦ **the food chain** la chaîne alimentaire
♦ **food poisoning** l'intoxication alimentaire FEM

food processor NOUN
le robot

fool NOUN

see also **fool** VERB

l' idiot MASC
l' idiote FEM

to **fool** VERB

see also **fool** NOUN

① plaisanter (*tease*) ◊ *I'm only fooling.* Je ne fais que plaisanter.
② duper (*trick*) ◊ *You can't fool me.* Tu ne me duperas pas.
♦ **to fool around (1)** (*waste time*) perdre son temps ◊ *Stop fooling around and get to work.* Arrêtez de perdre votre temps et mettez-vous au travail.
♦ **to fool around (2)** (*do silly things*) faire des bêtises
♦ **to fool around (3)** (*with something*) toucher à ◊ *Don't fool around with drugs.* Ne touche pas à la drogue.

foolproof ADJECTIVE
infaillible

foosball NOUN
le baby-foot

foot NOUN
① le pied (*of person*) ◊ *My feet are aching.* J'ai mal aux pieds.
② la patte (*of animal*) ◊ *The dog's foot was injured.* Le chien était blessé à la patte.
♦ **on foot** à pied
③ le pied (*12 inches*)
♦ **My dad is 6 feet tall.** Mon père mesure un mètre quatre-vingt.

ⓘ A **foot** is a nonmetric unit of length equal to about 30 cm.

football NOUN
① le football (*game*) ◊ *I like playing football.* J'aime jouer au football.
② le ballon (*ball*) ◊ *I threw the football over the fence.* J'ai envoyé le ballon par dessus la clôture.

footer NOUN
le pied de page (*word processing*)

footprint NOUN

☞

la trace de pas ◊ *He saw some footprints in the snow.* Il a vu des traces de pas sur la neige.

footstep NOUN
le pas ◊ *I can hear footsteps on the stairs.* J'entends des pas dans l'escalier.

for PREPOSITION

There are several ways of translating for. Scan the examples to find one that is similar to what you want to say.

1 pour ◊ *a present for me* un cadeau pour moi ◊ *the bus for Sherbrooke* l'autobus pour Sherbrooke ◊ *He works for the government.* Il travaille pour le gouvernement. ◊ *I'll do it for you.* Je vais le faire pour toi. ◊ *Can you do it for tomorrow?* Est-ce que vous pouvez le faire pour demain? ◊ *Are you for or against the idea?* Êtes-vous pour ou contre cette idée? ◊ *The Bay of Fundy is famous for its high tides.* La baie de Fundy est célèbre pour la hauteur de ses marées.

When referring to periods of time, use pendant for the future and completed actions in the past, and depuis (with the French verb in the present tense) for something that started in the past and is still going on.

2 pendant ◊ *He worked in France for two years.* Il a travaillé en France pendant deux ans. ◊ *She will be away for a month.* Elle sera absente pendant un mois.
3 depuis ◊ *I've been learning French for two years.* J'apprends le français depuis deux ans. ◊ *She's been away for a month.* Elle est absente depuis un mois.

You do not translate for after sell or buy.

◊ *I sold it for 50 dollars.* Je l'ai vendu cinquante dollars. ◊ *He paid five dollars for his ticket.* Il a payé son billet cinq dollars.
♦ **What's the French for "lion"?** Comment dit-on "lion" en français?
♦ **It's time for lunch.** C'est l'heure du déjeuner.
♦ **What for?** Pour quoi faire? ◊ *"Give me some money!" "What for?"* « Donne-moi de l'argent! » « Pour quoi faire? »
♦ **What's it for?** Ça sert à quoi?
♦ **for sale** à vendre ◊ *Their house is for sale.* Leur maison est à vendre.

to **forbid** VERB
défendre
♦ **to forbid somebody to do something** défendre à quelqu'un de faire quelque chose ◊ *I forbid you to go out tonight!* Je te défends de sortir ce soir.

forbidden ADJECTIVE
défendu ◊ *Smoking is strictly forbidden.* Il est strictement défendu de fumer.

force NOUN

see also **force** VERB

la force ◊ *the force of the explosion* la force de l'explosion
♦ **in force** en vigueur ◊ *No-smoking rules are now in force.* Un règlement qui interdit de fumer est maintenant en vigueur.

to **force** VERB

see also **force** NOUN

forcer ◊ *They forced her to open the safe.* Ils l'ont obligée à ouvrir le coffre-fort.

forecast NOUN
♦ **the weather forecast** la météo

foreground NOUN
le premier plan ◊ *in the foreground* au premier plan

forehead NOUN
le front

foreign ADJECTIVE
étranger MASC
étrangère FEM

to **foresee** VERB
prévoir ◊ *She had foreseen the problem.* Elle avait prévu ce problème.

forest NOUN
la forêt

forestry NOUN
la foresterie ◊ *He wants to study forestry.* Il veut étudier en foresterie.

forever ADVERB
1 pour toujours ◊ *He's gone forever.* Il est parti pour toujours.
2 toujours (*always*) ◊ *You're forever complaining.* Tu es toujours en train de te plaindre.

forgave VERB see **forgive**

to **forge** VERB
contrefaire ◊ *She tried to forge his signature.* Elle a essayé de contrefaire sa signature.

forged ADJECTIVE
faux MASC
fausse FEM ◊ *forged banknotes* des faux billets

to **forget** VERB
oublier ◊ *I've forgotten his name.*
J'ai oublié son nom. ◊ *I'm sorry, I
completely forgot!* Je suis désolé, j'ai
complètement oublié!

to **forgive** VERB
♦ **to forgive somebody** pardonner
à quelqu'un ◊ *I forgive you.* Je te
pardonne.
♦ **to forgive somebody for doing
something** pardonner à quelqu'un
d'avoir fait quelque chose ◊ *He
forgave her for forgetting his birthday.*
Il lui a pardonné d'avoir oublié son
anniversaire.

forgot, forgotten VERB *see* **forget**

fork NOUN
① la fourchette (*for eating*)
② la fourche (*for gardening*)
③ la bifurcation (*in road*)

form NOUN
① le formulaire (*paper*) ◊ *to fill in a
form* remplir un formulaire
② la forme (*type*) ◊ *I'm against
hunting in any form.* Je suis contre la
chasse sous toutes ses formes.
♦ **in top form** en pleine forme

formal ADJECTIVE
① (*occasion*)
officiel MASC
officielle FEM ◊ *a formal dinner* un
dîner officiel
② guindé (*person*)
③ soutenu (*language*) ◊ *In English,
"residence" is a formal term.* En
anglais, "residence" est un terme
soutenu.
♦ **formal clothes** une tenue habillée
♦ **She has no formal education.** Elle n'a
pas fait beaucoup d'études.

to **format** VERB
formater ◊ *to format a document*
formater un document

formatting NOUN
le formatage

former ADJECTIVE
ancien MASC
ancienne FEM ◊ *a former student*
un ancien élève ◊ *the former Prime
Minister* l'ancien Premier ministre

formerly ADVERB
autrefois

fort NOUN
le fort

forth ADVERB
♦ **to go back and forth** aller et venir
♦ **and so forth** et ainsi de suite

fortunate ADJECTIVE
♦ **to be fortunate** avoir de la chance

◊ *He was extremely fortunate to
survive.* Il a eu énormément de
chance de survivre.
♦ **It's fortunate that I remembered the
map.** C'est une chance que j'aie pris
la carte.

fortunately ADVERB
heureusement ◊ *Fortunately, it didn't
rain.* Heureusement, il n'a pas plu.

fortune NOUN
la fortune ◊ *She earns a fortune!* Elle
gagne une fortune!
♦ **to tell somebody's fortune** dire la
bonne aventure à quelqu'un

forty NUMBER
quarante ◊ *He's forty.* Il a quarante
ans.

forward ADVERB

　see also **forward** VERB

♦ **to move forward** avancer

to **forward** VERB

　see also **forward** ADVERB

faire suivre ◊ *He forwarded all my
letters.* Il a fait suivre toutes mes
lettres.

forward slash NOUN
la barre oblique

to **foster** VERB
♦ **She has fostered more than fifteen
children.** Plus de quinze enfants ont
été placés chez elle.

foster child NOUN
l' enfant placé en foyer nourricier
MASC
l' enfant placée en foyer nourricier
FEM

fought VERB *see* **fight**

foul ADJECTIVE

　see also **foul** NOUN

infect ◊ *The weather was foul.* Le
temps était infect. ◊ *What a foul
smell!* Quelle odeur infecte!

foul NOUN

　see also **foul** ADJECTIVE

la faute ◊ *Their goalie committed a
foul.* Leur gardienne de but a fait une
faute.

found VERB *see* **find**

to **found** VERB
fonder ◊ *John Graves Simcoe
founded the town of York.* John
Graves Simcoe a fondé la ville de
York.

foundations PL NOUN
les fondations FEM PL

fountain NOUN

☞

la <u>fontaine</u>

four NUMBER
<u>quatre</u> ◊ *She's four.* Elle a quatre ans.

fourteen NUMBER
<u>quatorze</u> ◊ *I'm fourteen.* J'ai quatorze ans.

fourteenth ADJECTIVE
<u>quatorzième</u> ◊ *the fourteenth floor* le quatorzième étage
♦ **the fourteenth of August** le quatorze août

fourth ADJECTIVE
<u>quatrième</u> ◊ *the fourth floor* le quatrième étage

fox NOUN
le <u>renard</u>
♦ **a fox cub** un renardeau

fragile ADJECTIVE
<u>fragile</u>

frame NOUN
le <u>cadre</u> (*for picture*)
♦ **glasses frames** la monture de lunettes

Francophone ADJECTIVE

> *see also* **Francophone** NOUN

<u>francophone</u> ◊ *a Francophone community* une communauté francophone

Francophone NOUN

> *see also* **Francophone** ADJECTIVE

le/la <u>francophone</u> ◊ *She's a Francophone.* C'est une francophone.

frankly ADVERB
<u>franchement</u> ◊ *He spoke to me frankly.* Il m'a parlé franchement.

frantic ADJECTIVE
♦ **I was going frantic.** J'étais dans tous mes états.
♦ **to be frantic with worry** être folle d'inquiétude
♦ **a frantic attempt** un essai désespéré

fraud NOUN
① la <u>fraude</u> (*crime*) ◊ *He was jailed for fraud.* On l'a mis en prison pour fraude.
② l' <u>imposteur</u> MASC (*person*) ◊ *He's not a real doctor, he's a fraud.* Ce n'est pas un vrai médecin, c'est un imposteur.

freckles PL NOUN
les <u>taches de rousseur</u> FEM

free ADJECTIVE

> *see also* **free** VERB

① <u>gratuit</u> (*free of charge*) ◊ *a free brochure* une brochure gratuite
② <u>libre</u> (*not busy, not taken*) ◊ *Is this seat free?* Est-ce que cette place est libre? ◊ *Are you free after school?* Tu

es libre après l'école?

to **free** VERB

> *see also* **free** ADJECTIVE

<u>libérer</u>

freedom NOUN
la <u>liberté</u>

free trade NOUN
le <u>libre-échange</u>

freeware NOUN
le <u>gratuiciel</u>

to **freeze** VERB
① <u>geler</u> ◊ *The water had frozen.* L'eau avait gelé.
② <u>congeler</u> (*food*) ◊ *We froze the rest of the raspberries.* Nous avons congelé le reste des framboises.
③ <u>se figer</u> (*stop moving*)
♦ **Freeze!** Pas un geste!

freezer NOUN
le <u>congélateur</u>

freeze-up NOUN
la <u>saison du gel</u> ◊ *We have to go close the cottage before freeze-up.* Nous devons aller fermer le chalet avant la saison du gel.

freezing ADJECTIVE
♦ **It's freezing!** Il fait un froid de canard! (*informal*)
♦ **I'm freezing!** Je suis gelé! (*informal*)
♦ **3 degrees below freezing** moins trois

freight NOUN
la <u>cargaison</u> (*goods*)
♦ **a freight train** un train de marchandises

French ADJECTIVE

> *see also* **French** NOUN

<u>français</u> ◊ *a French song* une chanson en français

French NOUN

> *see also* **French** ADJECTIVE

le <u>français</u> (*language*) ◊ *Do you speak French?* Est-ce que tu parles français?
♦ **the French** (*people*) les Français

French-Canadian ADJECTIVE

> *see also* **French-Canadian** NOUN

<u>canadien-français</u> MASC
<u>canadienne-française</u> FEM ◊ *a French-Canadian family* une famille canadienne-française

French-Canadian NOUN

> *see also* **French-Canadian** ADJECTIVE

le <u>Canadien français</u>
la <u>Canadienne française</u> ◊ *She married a French-Canadian.* Elle a épousé un Canadien français.

French fries PL NOUN
les frites FEM PL

French horn NOUN
le cor (d'harmonie) ◊ *I play the French horn.* Je joue du cor.

French stick NOUN
la baguette

French toast NOUN
✱ le pain doré

French windows PL NOUN
la porte-fenêtre SING
(PL les portes-fenêtres)

frequent ADJECTIVE
fréquent ◊ *frequent showers* des averses fréquentes
♦ **There are frequent buses to the town centre.** Il y a beaucoup d'autobus pour le centre-ville.
♦ **He's a frequent visitor here.** C'est un habitué ici.

fresh ADJECTIVE
frais MASC
fraîche FEM
♦ **I need some fresh air.** J'ai besoin de prendre l'air.

to **fret** VERB
se tracasser ◊ *He was fretting about his exams.* Il se tracassait au sujet de ses examens.

Friday NOUN
le vendredi ◊ *on Friday* vendredi ◊ *on Fridays* le vendredi ◊ *every Friday* tous les vendredis ◊ *last Friday* vendredi dernier ◊ *next Friday* vendredi prochain

fridge NOUN
le frigo

fried ADJECTIVE
frit ◊ *fried mushrooms* des champignons frits
♦ **a fried egg** un œuf sur le plat

friend NOUN
l' ami MASC
l' amie FEM

friendly ADJECTIVE
① gentil MASC
gentille FEM ◊ *She's really friendly.* Elle est vraiment gentille.
② accueillant ◊ *Kitchener is a very friendly city.* Kitchener est une ville très accueillante.

friendship NOUN
l' amitié FEM

fries PL NOUN
les frites FEM PL

fright NOUN
la peur ◊ *I got a terrible fright!* Ça m'a fait une peur terrible!

to **frighten** VERB
faire peur à ◊ *Horror films frighten him.* Les films d'horreur lui font peur.

frightening ADJECTIVE
effrayant

fringe NOUN
la frange (*on rug, clothing*)

Frisbee™ NOUN
le Frisbee MC ◊ *to play Frisbee* jouer au Frisbee

fro ADVERB
♦ **to go to and fro** aller et venir

frog NOUN
la grenouille

from PREPOSITION
de ◊ *Where do you come from?* D'où venez-vous? ◊ *I come from Cape Breton Island.* Je viens de l'île du Cap-Breton. ◊ *a letter from my sister* une lettre de ma sœur ◊ *The hotel is one kilometre from the beach.* L'hôtel est à un kilomètre de la plage.
♦ **from ... to ...** de ... à ... ◊ *He drove from Lethbridge to Swift Current.* Il a conduit de Lethbridge à Swift Current. ◊ *from 1 o'clock to 2* d'une heure à deux heures ◊ *The price was reduced from $10 to $5.* Ils ont réduit le prix de dix dollars à cinq.
♦ **from ... onwards** à partir de... ◊ *We'll be at home from 7 o'clock onwards.* Nous serons chez nous à partir de sept heures.

front NOUN
> see also **front** ADJECTIVE

① le devant ◊ *the front of the house* le devant de la maison
♦ **in front** devant ◊ *a house with a car in front* une maison avec une voiture devant ◊ *the car in front* la voiture devant
♦ **in front of** devant ◊ *in front of the house* devant la maison ◊ *the car in front of us* la voiture devant nous
♦ **in the front** (*of car*) à l'avant ◊ *I was sitting in the front.* J'étais assis à l'avant.
♦ **at the front of the class** à l'avant de la classe
② le ventre (*of body*) ◊ *to lie on one's front* se coucher sur le ventre

front ADJECTIVE
> see also **front** NOUN

① de devant ◊ *the front row* la rangée de devant
② avant ◊ *the front seats of the car* les sièges avant de la voiture
♦ **the front door** la porte d'entrée

frontier NOUN

☞

la frontière

frost NOUN
le gel

frosting NOUN
le glaçage

frosty ADJECTIVE
♦ **It's frosty today.** Il gèle aujourd'hui.

to **frown** VERB
froncer les sourcils ◊ *He frowned.* Il a froncé les sourcils.

froze VERB *see* **freeze**

frozen ADJECTIVE

see also **freeze**

[1] gelé ◊ *the frozen pond* l'étang gelé
[2] congelé (*food*) ◊ *frozen vegetables* des légumes congelés

fruit NOUN
le fruit
♦ **fruit juice** le jus de fruits
♦ **a fruit salad** une salade de fruits

frustrated ADJECTIVE
frustré

to **fry** VERB
faire frire ◊ *Fry the onions for 5 minutes.* Faites frire les oignons pendant cinq minutes.

frying pan NOUN
la poêle

fudge NOUN
le fudge

fuel NOUN
le carburant (*for car, plane*) ◊ *to run out of fuel* avoir une panne de carburant

fuel-efficient ADJECTIVE
économique

to **fulfill** VERB
réaliser ◊ *He fulfilled his dream to visit China.* Il a réalisé son rêve de visiter la Chine.

full ADJECTIVE, ADVERB
[1] plein ◊ *The tank's full.* Le réservoir est plein.
[2] complet MASC
complète FEM ◊ *She asked for full information on the job.* Elle a demandé des renseignements complets sur le poste.
♦ **your full name** vos nom et prénoms ◊ *My full name is Ian John Marr.* Je m'appelle Ian John Marr.
♦ **I'm full.** (*after meal*) J'ai bien mangé.
♦ **at full speed** à toute vitesse ◊ *She drove at full speed.* Elle conduisait à toute vitesse.
♦ **There was a full moon.** C'était la pleine lune.
♦ **a full house** (*for performance*) une

salle comble

full-time ADJECTIVE, ADVERB
à plein temps ◊ *She has a full-time job.* Elle a un travail à plein temps.
◊ *She works full-time.* Elle travaille à plein temps.

fully ADVERB
complètement ◊ *He hasn't fully recovered from his illness.* Il n'est pas complètement remis de sa maladie.

fumes PL NOUN
les fumées FEM PL ◊ *The factory gave out dangerous fumes.* L'usine rejetait des fumées dangereuses.
♦ **exhaust fumes** les gaz d'échappement

fun ADJECTIVE

see also **fun** NOUN

amusant ◊ *This is a fun book.* Ce livre est très amusant.
♦ **She's a fun person.** On s'amuse bien avec elle.

fun NOUN

see also **fun** ADJECTIVE

♦ **to have fun** s'amuser ◊ *We had a lot of fun playing in the snow.* Nous nous sommes bien amusés à jouer dans la neige.
♦ **for fun** pour rire ◊ *He entered the competition just for fun.* Il a participé à la compétition juste pour rire.
♦ **to make fun of somebody** se moquer de quelqu'un ◊ *They made fun of her.* Ils se sont moqués d'elle.
♦ **It's fun!** C'est amusant!
♦ **Have fun!** Amuse-toi bien!

funds PL NOUN
les fonds MASC ◊ *to raise funds* collecter des fonds

funeral NOUN
les funérailles FEM PL
♦ **funeral home**
🐾 le salon funéraire

funny ADJECTIVE
[1] drôle (*amusing*) ◊ *It was really funny.* C'était vraiment drôle.
[2] bizarre (*strange*) ◊ *There's something funny about him.* Il est un peu bizarre.
♦ **to taste funny** avoir un drôle de goût

fur NOUN
[1] la fourrure ◊ *a fur coat* un manteau de fourrure
[2] le poil ◊ *the dog's fur* le poil du chien

furious ADJECTIVE
furieux MASC
furieuse FEM ◊ *Dad was furious with me.* Papa était furieux contre moi.

furniture NOUN
les <u>meubles</u> MASC PL ◊ *a piece of furniture* un meuble
♦ **to be part of the furniture** faire parti du décor

further ADVERB, ADJECTIVE
<u>plus loin</u> ◊ *Moncton is further from Halifax than Truro is.* Moncton est plus loin de Halifax que Truro.
♦ **How much further is it?** C'est encore loin?

fuse NOUN
le <u>fusible</u> ◊ *The fuse has blown.* Le fusible a sauté.

fuss NOUN
l' <u>agitation</u> FEM ◊ *What's all the fuss about?* Qu'est-ce que c'est que toute cette agitation?
♦ **to make a fuss** faire des histoires

◊ *He's always making a fuss about nothing.* Il fait toujours des histoires pour rien.

fussy ADJECTIVE
<u>difficile</u> ◊ *She is very fussy about her food.* Elle est très difficile sur la nourriture.

future NOUN
1 l' <u>avenir</u> MASC ◊ *What are your plans for the future?* Quels sont vos projets pour l'avenir?
♦ **in future** à l'avenir ◊ *Be more careful in future.* Sois plus prudent à l'avenir.
2 le <u>futur</u> (*in grammar*) ◊ *Put this sentence into the future.* Mettez cette phrase au futur.

futuristic ADJECTIVE
<u>futuriste</u>

F

G

gadget NOUN
le gadget ◊ *electronic gadgets* les gadgets électroniques

to **gain** VERB
gagner
♦ **to gain weight** prendre du poids
♦ **to gain speed** prendre de la vitesse

gallery NOUN
le musée ◊ *an art gallery* un musée d'art

to **gallop** VERB
galoper

to **gamble** VERB
jouer ◊ *He gambled $100 at the casino.* Il a joué cent dollars au casino.

gambler NOUN
le joueur
la joueuse

game NOUN
1 le jeu
(PL les jeux) ◊ *The children were playing a game.* Les enfants jouaient à un jeu.
2 le match ◊ *a game of football* un match de football
♦ **a game of cards** une partie de cartes

gang NOUN
la bande

gangster NOUN
le gangster

gap NOUN
1 le trou ◊ *There's a gap in the hedge.* Il y a un trou dans la haie.
2 l' intervalle MASC ◊ *a gap of four years* un intervalle de quatre ans

garage NOUN
le garage
♦ **a garage sale** une vente-débarras

garbage NOUN
les ordures FEM PL
♦ **garbage can** la poubelle

garden NOUN
le jardin

gardener NOUN
le jardinier
la jardinière ◊ *He's a gardener.* Il est jardinier.

gardening NOUN
le jardinage ◊ *She loves gardening.* Elle aime le jardinage.

garlic NOUN
l' ail MASC

garment NOUN
le vêtement

gas NOUN
1 le gaz
♦ **a gas stove** une cuisinière à gaz
♦ **a gas leak** une fuite de gaz
2 l' essence FEM (*gasoline*)
♦ **to be out of gas** avoir une panne d'essence

gasoline NOUN
l' essence FEM

gas station NOUN
la station-service

gate NOUN
1 la grille (*of garden*)
2 la barrière (*of field*)
3 la porte (*at airport*)

to **gather** VERB
1 se rassembler (*assemble*) ◊ *People gathered on Parliament Hill.* Les gens se sont rassemblés sur la Colline du Parlement.
2 ramasser (*things*) ◊ *to gather wood for a fire* ramasser du bois à brûler ◊ *He gathered up his things and left.* Il a ramassé ses affaires et est parti.
♦ **I gather she isn't coming.** Je crois comprendre qu'elle ne viendra pas.
♦ **to gather dust** prendre la poussière
♦ **to gather speed** prendre de la vitesse ◊ *The train gathered speed.* Le train a pris de la vitesse.

gave VERB *see* **give**

gay ADJECTIVE
homosexuel MASC
homosexuelle FEM

to **gaze** VERB
♦ **to gaze at something** fixer quelque chose du regard ◊ *He gazed at her.* Il l'a fixée du regard.

gear NOUN
1 la vitesse (*car, bike*) ◊ *in first gear* en première vitesse ◊ *to change gear* changer de vitesse
2 le matériel ◊ *camping gear* le matériel de camping

gearshift NOUN
le levier de vitesse

geese PL NOUN *see* **goose**

gel NOUN
le gel
♦ **hair gel** le gel pour les cheveux

gem NOUN

la pierre précieuse

Gemini NOUN
les Gémeaux MASC PL ◊ *I'm a Gemini.*
Je suis Gémeaux.

gender NOUN
1 le sexe (*of person*)
2 le genre (*of noun*)

gene NOUN
le gène

general ADJECTIVE
général
(MASC PL généraux)
♦ **in general** en général

general election NOUN
l' élection générale FEM

general knowledge NOUN
les connaissances générales FEM PL

generally ADVERB
généralement ◊ *I generally go
shopping on Saturday.* Généralement,
je fais mon magasinage le samedi.

generation NOUN
la génération ◊ *the younger
generation* la nouvelle génération

generator NOUN
le générateur

generous ADJECTIVE
généreux MASC
généreuse FEM ◊ *That's very
generous of you.* C'est très généreux
de votre part.

genetic ADJECTIVE
génétique

genetically-modified ADJECTIVE
génétiquement modifié

genetics NOUN
la génétique

genius NOUN
le génie ◊ *She's a genius!* C'est un
génie!

gentle ADJECTIVE
doux MASC
douce FEM

gentleman NOUN
le monsieur
(PL les messieurs) ◊ *Good morning,
gentlemen.* Bonjour messieurs.

gently ADVERB
doucement

genuine ADJECTIVE
1 véritable (*real*) ◊ *These are
genuine diamonds.* Ce sont de
véritables diamants.
2 sincère (*sincere*) ◊ *She's a very
genuine person.* C'est quelqu'un de
très sincère.

geography NOUN

la géographie

gerbil NOUN
la gerbille

germ NOUN
le microbe

gesture NOUN

> see also **gesture** VERB

le geste

to **gesture** VERB

> see also **gesture** NOUN

♦ **She gestured towards the door.** Elle a
désigné la porte d'un geste.
♦ **He gestured to us to stand up.** Il nous
a fait signe de nous lever.

to **get** VERB

> *There are several ways of translating
> **get**. Scan the examples to find one
> that is similar to what you want to
> say.*

1 avoir (*have, receive*) ◊ *I got lots
of presents.* J'ai eu beaucoup de
cadeaux. ◊ *He got first prize.* Il a eu
le premier prix. ◊ *She got good exam
results.* Elle a eu de bons résultats
aux examens. ◊ *How many have you
got?* Combien en avez-vous?
2 aller chercher (*fetch*) ◊ *Quick, get
help!* Allez vite chercher de l'aide!
3 attraper (*catch*) ◊ *They've got the
thief.* Ils ont attrapé le voleur.
4 prendre (*train, bus*) ◊ *I'm getting
the bus into town.* Je prends
l'autobus pour aller en ville.
5 comprendre (*understand*) ◊ *I don't
get it.* Je ne comprends pas.
6 aller (*go*) ◊ *How do you get to the
library?* Comment est-ce qu'on va à la
bibliothèque?
7 arriver (*arrive*) ◊ *He should get
here soon.* Il devrait arriver bientôt.
8 devenir (*become*) ◊ *to get old*
devenir vieux
♦ **to get along with somebody**
s'entendre avec quelqu'un ◊ *He
doesn't get along with his parents.*
Il ne s'entend pas avec ses parents.
◊ *We got along really well.* Nous
nous sommes très bien entendus.
♦ **to get at (1)** (*reach*) atteindre
♦ **to get at (2)** (*touch*) toucher à
♦ **to get away with something** faire
quelque chose impunément ◊ *He
got away with skipping class.* Il a fait
l'école buissonnière impunément.
♦ **to get something done** faire
quelque chose ◊ *to get one's hair cut*
se faire couper les cheveux
♦ **to get something for somebody**
trouver quelque chose pour
quelqu'un ◊ *The librarian got the*

G

☞

book for me. Le bibliothécaire m'a trouvé le livre.

♦ **to have got to do something** devoir faire quelque chose ◊ *I've got to tell him.* Je dois le lui dire.

♦ **to get away** s'échapper ◊ *One of the burglars got away.* L'un des cambrioleurs s'est échappé.

♦ **to get back (1)** rentrer ◊ *What time did you get back?* Tu es rentrée à quelle heure?

♦ **to get back (2)** récupérer ◊ *He got his money back.* Il a récupéré son argent.

♦ **to get in** rentrer ◊ *What time did you get in last night?* Tu es rentré à quelle heure hier soir?

♦ **to get into** monter dans ◊ *She got into the car.* Elle est montée dans la voiture.

♦ **to get off** descendre de (*vehicle, bike*) ◊ *I got off the train.* Je suis descendue du train.

♦ **to get on (1)** (*vehicle*) monter dans ◊ *She got on the bus.* Elle est montée dans l'autobus.

♦ **to get on (2)** (*bike*) enfourcher ◊ *He got on his bike.* Il a enfourché son vélo.

♦ **to get out** sortir ◊ *She got out of the car.* Elle est sortie de la voiture. ◊ *Get out!* Sortez!

♦ **to get something out** sortir quelque chose ◊ *She got the map out.* Elle a sorti la carte.

♦ **to get over (1)** se remettre ◊ *It took her a long time to get over the illness.* Il lui a fallu longtemps pour se remettre de sa maladie.

♦ **to get over (2)** surmonter ◊ *He managed to get over the problem.* Il a réussi à résoudre le problème.

♦ **to get through to someone** réussir à communiquer avec quelqu'un ◊ *I tried to phone her but couldn't get through.* J'ai essayé de lui téléphoner, mais je n'ai pas réussi à la joindre.

♦ **to get together** se retrouver ◊ *Could we get together this evening?* Pourrait-on se retrouver ce soir?

♦ **to get up** se lever ◊ *What time do you get up?* Tu te lèves à quelle heure?

ghost NOUN
le <u>fantôme</u>

giant ADJECTIVE

> see also **giant** NOUN

<u>énorme</u> ◊ *They ate a giant meal.* Ils ont mangé un énorme repas.

giant NOUN

> see also **giant** ADJECTIVE

le <u>géant</u>
la <u>géante</u>

gift NOUN
1 (*present*)
le <u>cadeau</u>
(PL les cadeaux)

♦ **a gift certificate** un chèque-cadeau
2 le <u>don</u> (*talent*)

♦ **to have a gift for something** être doué pour quelque chose ◊ *My brother has a gift for painting.* Mon frère est doué pour la peinture.

gifted ADJECTIVE
<u>doué</u> ◊ *She is a gifted dancer.* Elle est douée pour la danse.

gift shop NOUN
la <u>boutique de cadeaux</u>

gigabyte NOUN
le <u>gigaoctet</u>

gigantic ADJECTIVE
<u>gigantesque</u>

to **giggle** VERB
<u>avoir le fou rire</u> ◊ *Every time I look at her, she giggles.* Chaque fois que je la regarde, elle a le fou rire.

ginger NOUN
le <u>gingembre</u> ◊ *Add a teaspoon of ginger.* Ajoutez une cuillère à café de gingembre.

giraffe NOUN
la <u>girafe</u>

girl NOUN
1 la <u>fille</u> ◊ *They have a girl and two boys.* Ils ont une fille et deux garçons.
2 la <u>petite fille</u> (*young*) ◊ *a five-year-old girl* une petite fille de cinq ans
3 la <u>jeune fille</u> (*older*) ◊ *a sixteen-year-old girl* une jeune fille de seize ans ◊ *a Canadian girl* une jeune Canadienne

girlfriend NOUN
1 la <u>copine</u> (*romantic*) ◊ *His girlfriend's name is Justine.* Sa copine s'appelle Justine.
2 l' <u>amie</u> FEM (*friend*) ◊ *She often went out with her girlfriends.* Elle sortait souvent avec ses amies.

to **give** VERB
<u>donner</u>

♦ **to give something to somebody** donner quelque chose à quelqu'un ◊ *He gave me $10.* Il m'a donné dix dollars.

♦ **to give something back to somebody** rendre quelque chose à quelqu'un ◊ *I gave the book back to her.* Je lui ai rendu le livre.

♦ **to give something out** distribuer quelque chose ◊ *The teacher gave out the books.* Le professeur a distribué les livres.

♦ **to give in** céder ◊ *Her Mom gave in*

and let her go out. Sa mère a cédé et l'a laissée sortir.
♦ **to give out** distribuer ◊ *He gave out the exam papers.* Il a distribué les feuilles d'examen.
♦ **to give up** laisser tomber ◊ *I couldn't do it, so I gave up.* Je n'arrivais pas à le faire, alors j'ai laissé tomber.
♦ **to give up doing something** arrêter de faire quelque chose ◊ *She gave up smoking.* Elle a arrêté de fumer.
♦ **to give oneself up** se rendre ◊ *The thief gave himself up.* Le voleur s'est rendu.
♦ **to give way** s'effondrer ◊ *The floor gave way under our feet.* Le plancher s'est effondré sous nos pieds.

glacier NOUN
le glacier

glad ADJECTIVE
content ◊ *She's glad she did it.* Elle est contente de l'avoir fait.

glamorous ADJECTIVE
[1] glamour (*person*) ◊ *She's very glamorous.* Elle est très glamour.
[2] (*job*)
prestigieux MASC
prestigieuse FEM
♦ **to have a glamorous lifestyle** vivre comme une star

to **glance** VERB

see also **glance** NOUN

♦ **to glance at something** jeter un coup d'œil à quelque chose ◊ *She glanced at her watch.* Elle a jeté un coup d'œil à sa montre.

glance NOUN

see also **glance** VERB

le coup d'œil ◊ *at first glance* au premier coup d'œil

to **glare** VERB
♦ **to glare at somebody** lancer un regard furieux à quelqu'un ◊ *He glared at me.* Il m'a lancé un regard furieux.

glaring ADJECTIVE
♦ **a glaring mistake** une erreur qui saute aux yeux

glass NOUN
le verre ◊ *a glass of milk* un verre de lait

glasses PL NOUN
les lunettes FEM ◊ *My dad wears glasses.* Mon père porte des lunettes.

to **glide** VERB
[1] glisser ◊ *The sled glided across the snow.* Le traîneau glissait sur la neige.
[2] planer ◊ *A bird glided through the air.* Un oiseau planait dans l'air.

glider NOUN
le planeur

gliding NOUN
le vol à voile ◊ *My hobby is gliding.* Je fais du vol à voile.

global ADJECTIVE
mondial
(MASC PL mondiaux)
♦ **on a global scale** à l'échelle mondiale

global warming NOUN
le réchauffement de la planète

globe NOUN
le globe

gloomy ADJECTIVE
[1] morose ◊ *She's been feeling very gloomy recently.* Elle se sent très morose ces derniers temps.
[2] lugubre ◊ *They live in a small gloomy apartment.* Ils habitent un petit appartement lugubre.

glorious ADJECTIVE
magnifique

glove NOUN
le gant

glove compartment NOUN
la boîte à gants

glue NOUN

see also **glue** VERB

la colle

to **glue** VERB

see also **glue** NOUN

coller

GM ADJECTIVE (= *genetically modified*)
génétiquement modifié ◊ *GM foods* les aliments génétiquement modifiés MASC

GMO ABBREVIATION (= *genetially-modified organism*)
l' OGM MASC (= l'organisme génétiquement modifié)

to **go** VERB
[1] aller ◊ *I'm going to the movies tonight.* Je vais au cinéma ce soir.
[2] partir (*leave*) ◊ *"Where's your friend?" "He's gone."* « Où est ton ami ? » « Il est parti. »
[3] s'en aller (*go away*) ◊ *I'm going now.* Je m'en vais.
[4] marcher (*vehicle*) ◊ *My car won't go.* Ma voiture ne marche pas.
♦ **a hamburger to go** un hamburger à emporter
♦ **how to go about something** comment s'y prendre pour faire quelque chose ◊ *I don't know how to go about it.* Je ne sais pas m'y prendre.
♦ **to go home** rentrer à la maison ◊ *I go*

home at about 4 o'clock. Je rentre à la maison vers quatre heures.

♦ **to go for a walk** aller se promener ◊ *Shall we go for a walk?* Si on allait se promener?

♦ **to go through with something** mettre quelque chose à exécution

♦ **to let go of something** lâcher quelque chose

♦ **How did it go?** Comment est-ce que ça s'est passé?

♦ **I'm going to do it tomorrow.** Je vais le faire demain.

♦ **It's going to be difficult.** Ça va être difficile.

to **go after** VERB
  suivre ◊ *Quick, go after them!* Vite, suivez-les!

to **go ahead** VERB
  ♦ **The play will go ahead as planned.** La pièce aura bien lieu comme prévu.
  ♦ **Let's go ahead with your plan.** Mettons votre projet à exécution.
  ♦ **Go ahead!** Vas-y!

to **go around** VERB
  ① tourner (*turn*) ◊ *Do the wheels really go around?* Est-ce que les roues tournent vraiment?
  ② tourner autour de ◊ *The earth goes around the sun.* La terre tourne autour du soleil.
  ♦ **to go around a corner** prendre un tournant
  ♦ **to go around the shops** faire les boutiques
  ♦ **There's a bug going around.** Il y a un microbe qui circule.

to **go away** VERB
  s'en aller ◊ *Go away!* Allez-vous-en!

to **go back** VERB

> *Use **rentrer** only when you are entering a building, usually your home; otherwise use **retourner**.*

  ① retourner ◊ *We went back to the same place.* Nous sommes retournés au même endroit.
  ② rentrer ◊ *"Is she still here?" "No, she's gone back home."* « Est-ce qu'elle est encore là? » « Non, elle est rentrée chez elle. »

to **go by** VERB
  passer ◊ *Two police officers went by.* Deux policiers sont passés.

to **go down** VERB
  ① descendre (*person*) ◊ *to go down the stairs* descendre l'escalier
  ② baisser (*decrease*) ◊ *The price of computers has gone down.* Le prix des ordinateurs a baissé.
  ③ se dégonfler (*deflate*) ◊ *My airbed*

kept going down. Mon matelas gonflant se dégonflait constamment.

to **go for** VERB
  attaquer (*attack*) ◊ *Suddenly the dog went for me.* Soudain, le chien m'a attaqué.
  ♦ **Go for it!** (*go on!*) Vas-y, fonce!

to **go in** VERB
  entrer ◊ *She knocked on the door and went in.* Elle a frappé à la porte et elle est entrée.

to **go off** VERB
  ① exploser (*bomb*) ◊ *The bomb went off.* La bombe a explosé.
  ② se déclencher (*alarm, gun*) ◊ *The fire alarm went off.* L'avertisseur d'incendie s'est déclenché.
  ③ sonner (*alarm clock*) ◊ *My alarm clock goes off at seven every morning.* Mon réveil sonne à sept heures tous les matins.
  ④ surir (*food*) ◊ *The milk's gone off.* Le lait a suri.
  ⑤ partir (*go away*) ◊ *He went off in a huff.* Il est parti de mauvaise humeur.

to **go on** VERB
  ① se passer (*happen*) ◊ *What's going on?* Qu'est-ce qui se passe?
  ② continuer (*carry on*) ◊ *The concert went on until 11 o'clock at night.* Le concert a continué jusqu'à onze heures du soir.
  ③ passer ◊ *Go on to the next question.* Passe à la prochaine question.
  ♦ **to go on doing something** continuer à faire quelque chose ◊ *She went on reading.* Elle a continué à lire.
  ♦ **Go on!** Allez! ◊ *Go on, tell me what the problem is!* Allez, dis-moi quel est le problème!

to **go out** VERB
  ① sortir (*person*) ◊ *Are you going out tonight?* Tu sors ce soir?
  ♦ **to go out with somebody** sortir avec quelqu'un ◊ *Are you going out with him?* Est-ce que tu sors avec lui?
  ② s'éteindre (*light, fire, candle*) ◊ *Suddenly the lights went out.* Soudain, les lumières se sont éteintes.

to **go past** VERB
  ♦ **to go past something** passer devant quelque chose ◊ *He went past the store.* Il est passé devant le magasin.

to **go through** VERB
  traverser ◊ *We went through Manitoba to get to Saskatchewan.* Nous avons traversé Manitoba pour aller à Saskatchewan.

to **go up** VERB

1 monter (*person*) ◊ *to go up the stairs* monter l'escalier
2 augmenter (*increase*) ◊ *The price has gone up.* Le prix a augmenté.
♦ **to go up in flames** s'embraser ◊ *The whole factory went up in flames.* L'usine toute entière s'est embrasée.

to **go with** VERB
aller avec ◊ *Does this blouse go with that skirt?* Est-ce que ce chemisier va avec cette jupe?

goal NOUN
le but ◊ *to score a goal* marquer un but ◊ *His goal is to become the world champion.* Son but est de devenir champion du monde.

goalkeeper NOUN
le gardien de but
la gardienne de but

goat NOUN
la chèvre
♦ **goat cheese** le fromage de chèvre

god NOUN
le dieu
(PL les dieux) ◊ *I believe in God.* Je crois en Dieu.

goddess NOUN
la déesse

goggles PL NOUN
1 les lunettes de protection FEM (*of welder, mechanic etc*)
2 les lunettes de natation FEM (*of swimmer*)

gold NOUN
l' or MASC ◊ *They found some gold.* Ils ont trouvé de l'or. ◊ *a gold necklace* un collier en or

goldfish NOUN
le poisson rouge ◊ *I've got five goldfish.* J'ai cinq poissons rouges.

gold-plated ADJECTIVE
plaqué or MASC
plaquée or FEM

golf NOUN
le golf ◊ *My mom plays golf.* Ma mère joue au golf.
♦ **a golf club** un club de golf
♦ **a golf course** un terrain de golf

gone VERB *see* **go**

good ADJECTIVE
1 bon MASC
bonne FEM ◊ *It's a very good movie.* C'est un très bon film. ◊ *Vegetables are good for you.* Les légumes sont bons pour la santé.
♦ **to be good at something** être bon en quelque chose ◊ *Jane's very good at soccer.* Jane est très bonne en soccer.
2 (*kind*)

gentil MASC
gentille FEM ◊ *They were very good to me.* Ils ont été très gentils avec moi. ◊ *That's very good of you.* C'est très gentil de votre part.
3 sage (*not naughty*) ◊ *Be good!* Sois sage!
♦ **for good** pour de bon ◊ *One day he left for good.* Un jour il est parti pour de bon.
♦ **Good morning!** Bonjour!
♦ **Good afternoon!** Bonjour!
♦ **Good evening!** Bonsoir!
♦ **Good night!** Bonne nuit!
♦ **It's no good complaining.** Cela ne sert à rien de se plaindre.

goodbye EXCLAMATION
au revoir!

Good Friday NOUN
le Vendredi saint

good-looking ADJECTIVE
beau MASC
(ALSO bel)
belle FEM
(MASC PL beaux) ◊ *He's very good-looking.* Il est très beau.

> The form **beau** changes to **bel** before a vowel and most words beginning with h.

◊ *Who's your good-looking friend?* Qui est ton bel ami?

good-natured ADJECTIVE
facile à vivre (*person*)

goods PL NOUN
les marchandises FEM (*in store*)

goose NOUN
l' oie FEM

gooseberry NOUN
la groseille à maquereau

gopher NOUN
le spermophile

gorgeous ADJECTIVE
1 superbe ◊ *She's gorgeous!* Elle est superbe!
2 splendide ◊ *The weather was gorgeous.* Il a fait un temps splendide.

gorilla NOUN
le gorille

gospel NOUN
le gospel (*music*)

gossip NOUN

> see also **gossip** VERB

1 les cancans MASC PL (*rumours*)
◊ *Tell me the gossip!* Raconte-moi les cancans!
2 la commère (*woman*) ◊ *She's such a gossip!* C'est une vraie commère!

☞

G

③ le <u>bavard</u> (*man*) ◊ *What a gossip!* Quel bavard!

to **gossip** VERB

> *see also* **gossip** NOUN

① <u>bavarder</u> (*chat*) ◊ *They were always gossiping.* Ils étaient tout le temps en train de bavarder.
② <u>faire des commérages</u> (*about somebody*) ◊ *They gossiped about him.* Elles faisaient des commérages à son sujet.

got VERB *see* **get**

gotten VERB *see* **get**

government NOUN
le <u>gouvernement</u>

✹ **Governor General** NOUN
le <u>gouverneur général</u>
la <u>gouverneure générale</u>

GP NOUN (= *General Practitioner*)
l' <u>omnipraticien</u> MASC
l' <u>omnipraticienne</u> FEM

to **grab** VERB
<u>saisir</u>

graceful ADJECTIVE
<u>élégant</u>

grade NOUN
la <u>note</u> (*at school*) ◊ *I got good grades this year.* J'ai eu de bonnes notes cette année.

grade school NOUN
l' <u>école élémentaire</u> FEM

gradual ADJECTIVE
<u>progressif</u> MASC
<u>progressive</u> FEM

gradually ADVERB
<u>peu à peu</u> ◊ *We gradually got used to it.* Nous nous y sommes habitués peu à peu.

graduate NOUN

> *see also* **graduate** VERB

① (*from university*)
le <u>diplômé</u>
la <u>diplômée</u>
② (*from high school*)
le <u>finissant</u>
la <u>finissante</u>

to **graduate** VERB

> *see also* **graduate** NOUN

① <u>obtenir son diplôme</u> (*from high school*)
② <u>obtenir son baccalauréat</u> (*from university*)

graduation party NOUN
✹ le <u>bal des finissants</u>

graffiti PL NOUN
les <u>graffiti</u> MASC

grain NOUN
① le <u>grain</u> (*of salt, sand*)
② les <u>céréales</u> FEM PL ◊ *wheat and other grains* le blé et d'autres céréales ◊ *Grains are essential to a healthy diet.* Les céréales sont essentielles pour une alimentation saine.

gram NOUN
le <u>gramme</u>

grammar NOUN
la <u>grammaire</u>

grammatical ADJECTIVE
<u>grammatical</u>
(MASC PL **grammaticaux**)

grand ADJECTIVE
<u>somptueux</u> MASC
<u>somptueuse</u> FEM ◊ *She lives in a very grand house.* Elle habite une maison somptueuse.
♦ **a grand piano** un piano à queue

grandchild NOUN
le <u>petit-fils</u>
la <u>petite-fille</u>
♦ **my grandchildren** mes petits-enfants MASC

granddaughter NOUN
la <u>petite-fille</u>
(PL les petites-filles)

grandfather NOUN
le <u>grand-père</u>
(PL les grands-pères) ◊ *my grandfather* mon grand-père

grandmother NOUN
la <u>grand-mère</u>
(PL les grands-mères) ◊ *my grandmother* ma grand-mère

grandparents PL NOUN
les <u>grands-parents</u> MASC PL ◊ *my grandparents* mes grands-parents

grandson NOUN
le <u>petit-fils</u>
(PL les petits-fils)

to **grant** VERB
① <u>accorder</u> (*give*) ◊ *to grant political asylum* accorder l'asile politique
② <u>accepter</u> (*say yes to*) ◊ *They granted our request.* Ils ont accepté notre requête.

grape NOUN
le <u>grain de raisin</u> (*single grape*)
♦ **grapes** le raisin ◊ *a bunch of grapes* une grappe de raisin ◊ *I ate some grapes.* J'ai mangé du raisin.
♦ **grape-flavoured** à saveur de raisin

grapefruit NOUN
le <u>pamplemousse</u>

graph NOUN
le <u>graphique</u>

graphic organizer NOUN
l' <u>organisateur graphique</u> MASC

graphics PL NOUN
les <u>images de synthèse</u> FEM PL ◊ *I designed the graphics and she wrote the text.* J'ai conçu les images de synthèse et elle a écrit le texte.
♦ **He works in computer graphics.** Il fait de l'infographie.

to **grasp** VERB
<u>saisir</u>

grass NOUN
l' <u>herbe</u> FEM ◊ *The grass is long.* L'herbe est haute.
♦ **to cut the grass** tondre le gazon

grasshopper NOUN
la <u>sauterelle</u>

to **grate** VERB
<u>râper</u> ◊ *to grate some cheese* râper du fromage

grateful ADJECTIVE
<u>reconnaissant</u> ◊ *We are grateful for your help.* Nous sommes reconnaissants de votre aide.

grater NOUN
la <u>râpe</u> ◊ *a cheese grater* une râpe à fromage

grave NOUN
la <u>tombe</u>

gravel NOUN
le <u>gravier</u>

graveyard NOUN
le <u>cimetière</u>

gravy NOUN
la <u>sauce</u>

grease NOUN
[1] la <u>graisse</u> (*cooking*)
[2] le <u>lubrifiant</u> (*engine*)

greasy ADJECTIVE
<u>gras</u> MASC
<u>grasse</u> FEM ◊ *I have greasy hair.* J'ai les cheveux gras. ◊ *The food was very greasy.* La nourriture était très grasse.

great ADJECTIVE
[1] <u>génial</u>
(MASC PL géniaux) ◊ *That's great!* C'est génial!
[2] <u>grand</u> ◊ *a great event* un grand événement
♦ **Greater Vancouver** l'agglomération de Vancouver

great-grandfather NOUN
l' <u>arrière-grand-père</u> MASC
(PL les arrière-grands-pères)

great-grandmother NOUN
l' <u>arrière-grand-mère</u> FEM
(PL les arrière-grands-mères)

Great Lakes NOUN
les <u>Grands Lacs</u> MASC PL

greedy ADJECTIVE
[1] <u>gourmand</u> (*for food*) ◊ *"I want some more cake." "Don't be so greedy!"* « Je veux encore du gâteau. » « Ne sois pas si gourmand! »
[2] <u>avide</u> (*for money*)

green ADJECTIVE

see also **green** NOUN

[1] <u>vert</u> ◊ *a green car* une voiture verte ◊ *a green light* un feu vert ◊ *a green salad* une salade verte
[2] <u>écologiste</u> (*movement, candidate*) ◊ *the Green Party* le parti écologiste

green NOUN

see also **green** ADJECTIVE

le <u>vert</u> ◊ *a dark green* un vert foncé
♦ **greens** (*vegetables*) les légumes verts

greenhouse NOUN
la <u>serre</u>
♦ **the greenhouse effect** l'effet de serre MASC

to **greet** VERB
<u>accueillir</u> ◊ *He greeted me with a kiss.* Il m'a accueillie en me donnant un baiser.

greeting NOUN
♦ **Greetings from Bangor!** Bonjour de Bangor!
♦ **"Season's greetings"** "Meilleurs vœux pour les fêtes de fin d'année"

greeting card NOUN
la <u>carte de vœux</u>

grew VERB *see* **grow**

grey ADJECTIVE
<u>gris</u> ◊ *She has grey hair.* Elle a les cheveux gris.
♦ **He's going grey.** Il grisonne.

grey-haired ADJECTIVE
<u>grisonnant</u>

grief NOUN
le <u>chagrin</u>

grill NOUN

see also **grill** VERB

le <u>gril</u> (*for food*)
♦ **a mixed grill** les grillades FEM PL

to **grill** VERB

see also **grill** NOUN

♦ **to grill something** faire griller quelque chose
♦ **grilled chicken** du poulet grillé

grim ADJECTIVE
<u>sinistre</u>

to **grin** VERB

G

☞

| see also **grin** NOUN |

sourire ◊ *He grinned at me.* Il m'a
souri.

grin NOUN

| see also **grin** VERB |

le large sourire

to **grind** VERB
moudre (*coffee, pepper*)

to **grip** VERB
saisir

gripping ADJECTIVE
palpitant (*exciting*)

grizzly bear NOUN
le grizzly

to **groan** VERB

| see also **groan** NOUN |

gémir ◊ *She groaned with pain.* Elle
a gémi sous l'effet de la douleur.

groan NOUN

| see also **groan** VERB |

le gémissement (*of pain*)

groceries PL NOUN
l' épicerie FEM ◊ *Would you put the
groceries in the cupboard, please?*
Pourrais-tu ranger l'épicerie dans
l'armoire, s'il te plaît?

grocery store NOUN
l' épicerie FEM

groom NOUN
le marié (*bridegroom*) ◊ *the groom
and his best man* le marié et son
témoin

to **grope** VERB
♦ **to grope for something** chercher
quelque chose à tâtons ◊ *She groped
for the light switch.* Elle a cherché à
tâtons l'interrupteur.

gross ADJECTIVE
dégoûtant (*revolting*) ◊ *It was really
gross!* C'était vraiment dégoûtant!

grossly ADVERB
largement ◊ *They're grossly
underpaid.* Ils sont largement sous-
payés.

ground NOUN

| see also **ground** VERB |

1 le sol (*earth*) ◊ *The ground's wet.*
Le sol est mouillé.
2 la raison (*reason*) ◊ *We have
grounds for complaint.* Nous avons
des raisons de nous plaindre.
♦ **on the ground** par terre ◊ *We sat on
the ground.* Nous nous sommes assis
par terre.

ground VERB *see* **grind**

| see also **ground** NOUN |

♦ **ground coffee** le café moulu

ground floor NOUN
※ le premier étage
♦ **on the ground floor** au rez-de-
chaussée

groundhog NOUN
la marmotte commune
◊ *Groundhog Day* le jour de la
marmotte

group NOUN
le groupe
♦ **a group home** un foyer de groupe

to **grow** VERB
1 pousser (*plant*) ◊ *Grass grows
quickly.* L'herbe pousse vite.
2 grandir (*person, animal*) ◊ *How
you've grown!* Comme tu as grandi!
3 augmenter (*increase*) ◊ *The
number of unemployed people has
grown.* Le nombre de chômeurs a
augmenté.
4 faire pousser (*cultivate*) ◊ *My
mom grows tomatoes.* Ma mère fait
pousser des tomates.
♦ **to grow a beard** se laisser pousser
la barbe
♦ **to grow up** grandir ◊ *Oh, grow up!*
Ne fais pas l'enfant!
♦ **She's grown out of her jacket.** Sa
veste est devenue trop petite pour
elle.

to **growl** VERB
grogner

grown VERB *see* **grow**

growth NOUN
la croissance ◊ *economic growth* la
croissance économique

grudge NOUN
la rancune
♦ **to bear a grudge against somebody**
garder rancune à quelqu'un

gruesome ADJECTIVE
horrible

grumpy ADJECTIVE
※ 1 marabout MASC, FEM ◊ *They're
grumpy this morning.* Elles sont
marabouts ce matin.
2 grognon MASC
grognonne FEM

GST NOUN
la TPS (= taxe sur les produits et
services)

guarantee NOUN

| see also **guarantee** VERB |

la garantie
♦ **a five-year guarantee** une garantie de
cinq ans

to **guarantee** VERB

see also **guarantee** NOUN

garantir ◊ *I can't guarantee he'll come.* Je ne peux pas garantir qu'il viendra.

to **guard** VERB

see also **guard** NOUN

garder ◊ *They guarded the prisoner.* Ils gardaient le prisonnier.
♦ **to guard against something** protéger contre quelque chose

guard NOUN

see also **guard** VERB

le garde (*person*)
♦ **to catch somebody off guard** prendre quelqu'un au dépourvu
♦ **a guard dog** un chien de garde

guardian NOUN (*legal*)
le tuteur
la tuteur ◊ *The form must be signed by your parent or guardian.* La feuille doit être signée par ton parent ou tuteur.
♦ **the guardians of freedom** les gardiens de la liberté

to **guess** VERB

see also **guess** NOUN

deviner ◊ *Can you guess what it is?* Devine ce que c'est!
♦ **to guess wrong** se tromper ◊ *She guessed wrong.* Elle s'est trompée.

guess NOUN

see also **guess** VERB

la supposition ◊ *It's just a guess.* C'est une simple supposition.
♦ **Take a guess!** Devine!

guest NOUN
[1] l' invité MASC
l' invitée FEM ◊ *We have guests staying with us.* Nous avons des invités.
[2] (*of hotel*)
le client
la cliente

guide NOUN

see also **guide** VERB

le guide (*book, person*) ◊ *We bought a guide to Paris.* Nous avons acheté un guide sur Paris. ◊ *The guide showed us around the museum.* Le guide nous a fait visiter le musée.

to **guide** VERB

see also **guide** NOUN

guider ◊ *She guided us through the caves.* Elle nous a guidés à travers les cavernes. ◊ *The guide showed us round the museum.* Le guide nous a fait visiter le musée.

guidebook NOUN
le guide

guide dog NOUN
le chien d'aveugle

guideline NOUN
la directive ◊ *Here are some guidelines for your research projects.* Voici quelques directives générales pour vos projets de recherche.
♦ **a rough guideline** une indication générale

guilty ADJECTIVE
coupable ◊ *to feel guilty* se sentir coupable ◊ *She was found guilty.* Elle a été reconnue coupable.

guinea pig NOUN
le cobaye

guitar NOUN
la guitare ◊ *I play the guitar.* Je joue de la guitare.

gullible ADJECTIVE
crédule

gum NOUN
la gomme à mâcher
♦ **gums** (*in mouth*) les gencives FEM

gun NOUN
[1] le pistolet (*small*)
[2] le fusil (*rifle*)

guru NOUN
le gourou

gust NOUN
♦ **a gust of wind** une rafale de vent

guy NOUN
le type ◊ *Who's that guy?* C'est qui ce type? ◊ *He's a nice guy.* C'est un type sympa.

gym NOUN
[1] le gymnase ◊ *She goes to the gym every day.* Elle va tous les jours au gymnase.
[2] l' éducation physique FEM

gymnast NOUN
le/la gymnaste ◊ *She's a gymnast.* Elle est gymnaste.

gymnastics NOUN
la gymnastique ◊ *to do gymnastics* faire de la gymnastique

G

H

habit NOUN
l' habitude FEM ◊ *a bad habit* une mauvaise habitude

to **hack** VERB
♦ **to hack into a system** s'introduire dans un système

hacker NOUN
le/la pirate informatique

had VERB *see* **have**

hadn't = **had not**

hail NOUN
| *see also* **hail** VERB |
la grêle

to **hail** VERB
| *see also* **hail** NOUN |
grêler ◊ *It's hailing.* Il grêle.

hair NOUN
1 les cheveux MASC PL ◊ *She has long hair.* Elle a les cheveux longs. ◊ *He has black hair.* Il a les cheveux noirs. ◊ *He's losing his hair.* Il perd ses cheveux.
♦ **to brush one's hair** se brosser les cheveux ◊ *I'm brushing my hair.* Je me brosse les cheveux.
♦ **to wash one's hair** se laver les cheveux ◊ *I need to wash my hair.* Il faut que je me lave les cheveux.
♦ **to have one's hair cut** se faire couper les cheveux ◊ *I've just had my hair cut.* Je viens de me faire couper les cheveux.
♦ **a hair (1)** (*from head*) un cheveu
♦ **a hair (2)** (*from body*) un poil
2 le pelage (*fur of animal*)

hairbrush NOUN
la brosse à cheveux

hair clip NOUN
la pince à cheveux

haircut NOUN
la coupe de cheveux
♦ **to have a haircut** se faire couper les cheveux ◊ *I've just had a haircut.* Je viens de me faire couper les cheveux.

hairdresser NOUN
le coiffeur
la coiffeuse ◊ *She's a hairdresser.* Elle est coiffeuse. ◊ *at the hairdresser's* chez le coiffeur

hair gel NOUN
le gel pour les cheveux

hair spray NOUN
la laque

hairstyle NOUN
la coiffure

hairy ADJECTIVE
poilu ◊ *hairy legs* les jambes poilues

half NOUN
| *see also* **half** ADJECTIVE |
la moitié ◊ *half of the cake* la moitié du gâteau
♦ **two and a half** deux et demi
♦ **half an hour** une demi-heure
♦ **half past ten** dix heures et demie
♦ **half a kilo** cinq cents grammes
♦ **to cut something in half** couper quelque chose en deux

half ADJECTIVE, ADVERB
| *see also* **half** NOUN |
1 demi ◊ *a half chicken* un demi-poulet
2 à moitié ◊ *He was half asleep.* Il était à moitié endormi.

half-brother NOUN
le demi-frère

half-hour NOUN
la demi-heure

half-price ADJECTIVE, ADVERB
♦ **at half-price** à moitié prix

half-sister NOUN
la demi-sœur

half-time NOUN
la mi-temps ◊ *The score at half-time was 6-4.* Le pointage à la mi-temps était 6-4.

halfway ADVERB
1 à mi-chemin ◊ *halfway between Sudbury and Kenora* à mi-chemin entre Sudbury et Kenora
♦ **a halfway house** une maison de transition
2 à la moitié ◊ *halfway through the chapter* à la moitié du chapitre

hall NOUN
1 le couloir (*hallway*)
2 la salle (*large room*) ◊ *the community hall* la salle communautaire

Halloween NOUN
l' Halloween FEM

hallway NOUN
le vestibule

ham NOUN
le jambon
♦ **a ham sandwich** un sandwich au jambon

hamburger NOUN
⒈ le hamburger
⒉ le bœuf haché (*meat*)

hammer NOUN
le marteau
(PL les marteaux)

hamster NOUN
le hamster

hand NOUN

see also **hand** VERB

⒈ la main (*of person*)
♦ **by hand** à la main
♦ **to give somebody a hand (1)** (*help*)
donner un coup de main à quelqu'un
◊ *Can you give me a hand?* Tu peux
me donner un coup de main?
♦ **to give somebody a hand (2)**
(*applaud*) applaudir quelqu'un
♦ **on the one hand..., on the other
hand...** d'une part..., d'autre part...
⒉ l' aiguille FEM (*of clock*)

to **hand** VERB

see also **hand** NOUN

passer ◊ *He handed me the book.* Il
m'a passé le livre.
♦ **to hand something in** rendre quelque
chose ◊ *She handed her exam paper
in.* Elle a rendu sa copie d'examen.
♦ **to hand something out** distribuer
quelque chose ◊ *The teacher handed
out the books.* Le professeur a
distribué les livres.
♦ **to hand something over** remettre
quelque chose ◊ *She handed the keys
over to me.* Elle m'a remis les clés.

handball NOUN
le handball (*game*)
♦ **to play handball** jouer au handball

handbook NOUN
le manuel

handcuffs PL NOUN
les menottes FEM

handful NOUN
la poignée ◊ *a handful of popcorn*
une poignée de maïs soufflé

handheld ADJECTIVE
de poche ◊ *a handheld computer* un
ordinateur de poche

handkerchief NOUN
le mouchoir

handle NOUN

see also **handle** VERB

⒈ la poignée (*of door*)
⒉ l' anse FEM (*of cup*)
⒊ le manche (*of knife*)
⒋ la queue (*of saucepan*)

to **handle** VERB

see also **handle** NOUN

⒈ manœuvrer (*use, control*) ◊ *to
handle a canoe* manœuvrer un canot
⒉ toucher à (*touch*) ◊ *Don't handle
the fruit.* Ne touchez pas aux fruits.
♦ **He handled it well.** Il s'en est bien
tiré.
♦ **The teacher handled the travel
arrangements.** La professeure s'est
occupée de l'organisation du voyage.
♦ **She knows how to handle children.**
Elle sait bien s'y prendre avec les
enfants.

handlebars PL NOUN
le guidon SING

handmade ADJECTIVE
fait à la main

hands-free ADJECTIVE
mains libres MASC, FEM, PL ◊ *a hands-
free phone* un téléphone mains libres

handsome ADJECTIVE
beau MASC
belle FEM ◊ *He's handsome.* Il est
beau.

*The form **beau** changes to **bel** before
a vowel and most words beginning
with h.*

◊ *a handsome man* un bel homme

handwriting NOUN
l' écriture FEM

handy ADJECTIVE
⒈ pratique ◊ *This knife's very handy.*
Ce couteau est très pratique.
⒉ sous la main ◊ *Have you got a pen
handy?* Est-ce que tu as un stylo sous
la main?

to **hang** VERB
⒈ accrocher ◊ *I hung the painting
on the wall.* J'ai accroché le tableau
au mur.
⒉ pendre ◊ *They hanged the
criminal.* Ils ont pendu le criminel.
♦ **to hang around** traîner ◊ *Let's go
hang around in the park for a while.*
Si on allait traîner dans le parc
quelque temps?
♦ **to hang in** ne pas lâcher ◊ *Hang in
there, you're almost done!* Ne lâche
pas, tu as presque fini!
♦ **to hang on** patienter ◊ *Hang on a
minute please.* Patientez une minute
s'il vous plaît.
♦ **to hang up (1)** (*clothes*) accrocher
◊ *Hang your jacket up on the
hook.* Accrochez votre manteau au
portemanteau.
♦ **to hang up (2)** (*phone*) raccrocher ◊ *I
tried to phone her but she hung up on
me.* J'ai essayé de l'appeler, mais elle
m'a raccroché au nez.

H

hanger NOUN
le <u>cintre</u> (*coat hanger*)

hang-gliding NOUN
le <u>deltaplane</u>
♦ **to go hang-gliding** faire du deltaplane

to **happen** VERB
<u>se passer</u> ◊ *What happened?* Qu'est-ce qui s'est passé?
♦ **as it happens** justement ◊ *As it happens, I don't want to go.* Justement, je ne veux pas y aller.
♦ **I happened to find 5 dollars lying in the street.** Il m'est arrivé de trouver cinq dollars dans la rue.
♦ **Do you happen to know this neighbour?** Connaîtrais-tu ce voisin, par hasard?

happily ADVERB
1 <u>joyeusement</u> ◊ *"Don't worry!" he said happily.* « Ne te fais pas de souci! » dit-il joyeusement.
2 <u>heureusement</u> (*fortunately*) ◊ *Happily, everything went well.* Heureusement, tout s'est bien passé.

happiness NOUN
le <u>bonheur</u>

happy ADJECTIVE
<u>heureux</u> MASC
<u>heureuse</u> FEM ◊ *She looks happy.* Elle a l'air heureuse.
♦ **I'm very happy with your work.** Je suis très satisfait de ton travail.
♦ **Happy birthday!**
✹ Bonne fête!

harassment NOUN
le <u>harcèlement</u> ◊ *sexual harassment* le harcèlement sexuel

harbour NOUN
le <u>port</u>

hard ADJECTIVE, ADVERB
1 <u>dur</u> ◊ *This cheese is very hard.* Ce fromage est très dur. ◊ *He worked very hard.* Il a travaillé très dur.
2 <u>difficile</u> ◊ *This question is too hard for me.* Cette question est trop difficile pour moi.
♦ **hard copy** la copie papier
♦ **to be hard of hearing** être dur d'oreille

hard-boiled ADJECTIVE
<u>dur</u>

hard disk NOUN
le <u>disque dur</u> (*of computer*)

hardly ADVERB
♦ **I've hardly got any money.** Je n'ai presque pas d'argent.
♦ **I hardly know you.** Je te connais à peine.
♦ **hardly ever** presque jamais

hardware NOUN
1 le <u>matériel</u> (*computing*)
2 la <u>quincaillerie</u> (*bolts, hinges*)
♦ **a hardware store** une quincaillerie

hare NOUN
le <u>lièvre</u>

to **harm** VERB
♦ **to harm somebody** faire du mal à quelqu'un ◊ *I didn't mean to harm you.* Je ne voulais pas te faire de mal.
♦ **to harm something** nuire à quelque chose ◊ *Chemicals harm the environment.* Les produits chimiques nuisent à l'environnement.

harmful ADJECTIVE
<u>nuisible</u> ◊ *harmful chemicals* des produits chimiques nuisibles

harmless ADJECTIVE
<u>inoffensif</u> MASC
<u>inoffensive</u> FEM ◊ *Most spiders are harmless.* La plupart des araignées sont inoffensives.

harpoon NOUN
le <u>harpon</u>

harsh ADJECTIVE
<u>dur</u>

has VERB *see* **have**

hasn't = **has not**

hassle NOUN
♦ **It's such a hassle.** C'est toute une affaire.
♦ **It isn't worth the hassle.** Ça n'en vaut pas la peine.

hat NOUN
le <u>chapeau</u>
(PL les chapeaux)

to **hate** VERB
<u>détester</u> ◊ *I hate math.* Je déteste les maths.

hatred NOUN
la <u>haine</u>

hat trick NOUN
le <u>tour de chapeau</u>

haunted ADJECTIVE
<u>hanté</u>
♦ **a haunted house** une maison hantée

to **have** VERB
1 <u>avoir</u> ◊ *Do you have a sister?* Tu as une sœur? ◊ *He has blue eyes.* Il a les yeux bleus. ◊ *I have a cold.* J'ai un rhume. ◊ *He's done it, hasn't he?* Il l'a fait, non? ◊ *"Have you got any money?" "No, I haven't!"* « Est-ce que tu as de l'argent? » « Non, je n'en ai pas! »

*The perfect tense of some verbs is formed with **être**.*

[2] être ◊ *They have arrived.* Ils sont arrivés. ◊ *Has she gone?* Est-ce qu'elle est partie?
[3] prendre ◊ *He had his breakfast.* Il a pris son petit déjeuner. ◊ *to have a shower* prendre une douche
♦ **to have to do something** devoir faire quelque chose ◊ *She has to do it.* Elle doit le faire.
♦ **to have a party** faire une fête
♦ **to have one's hair cut** se faire couper les cheveux
♦ **I've had it!** J'en ai assez!

haven't = have not

hawk NOUN
le faucon

hay NOUN
le foin

hay fever NOUN
le rhume des foins ◊ *Do you get hay fever?* Est-ce que vous êtes sujet au rhume des foins?

hazardous waste NOUN
les déchets dangereux MASC PL

hazelnut NOUN
la noisette

he PRONOUN
il ◊ *He loves dogs.* Il aime les chiens.

head NOUN

> see also **head** VERB

[1] la tête (*of person*) ◊ *All the praise went to her head.* Tous les compliments lui sont montés à la tête. ◊ *I bumped my head.* Je me suis cogné la tête.
[2] le chef (*leader*) ◊ *a head of state* un chef d'État ◊ *She's the head of the organization.* Elle est la chef de l'organisation.
♦ **from head to toe** de la tête aux pieds
♦ **head first** la tête la première
♦ **Get it into your head that...** Mets-toi dans la tête que...
♦ **to be head over heels in love with someone** être follement amoureux de quelqu'un
♦ **to have a head for figures** être doué pour les chiffres
♦ **"Heads or tails?" "Heads."** « Pile ou face? » « Face. »

to **head** VERB

> see also **head** NOUN

♦ **to head for something** se diriger vers quelque chose ◊ *They headed for the church.* Ils se sont dirigés vers l'église.
♦ **Who's heading up the project?** Qui est à la tête du projet?

headache NOUN

♦ **I've got a headache.** J'ai mal à la tête.

headlight NOUN
le phare

headline NOUN
le titre

headphones PL NOUN
les écouteurs MASC

headquarters PL NOUN
le siège SING (*of organization*)

to **heal** VERB
[1] guérir (*person*) ◊ *He was healed.* Il a été guéri.
[2] cicatriser ◊ *The wound soon healed.* La blessure a vite cicatrisé.

health NOUN
la santé
♦ **health care** les soins de santé MASC PL ◊ *the Canadian health care system* le système de soins canadien

healthy ADJECTIVE
[1] en bonne santé (*person*) ◊ *She's a healthy person.* Elle est en bonne santé.
[2] sain (*climate, food*) ◊ *a healthy diet* une alimentation saine

heap NOUN
le tas ◊ *a heap of snow* un tas de neige

to **hear** VERB
[1] entendre ◊ *He heard the dog bark.* Il a entendu le chien aboyer. ◊ *She can't hear very well.* Elle entend mal. ◊ *I heard that she was ill.* J'ai entendu dire qu'elle était malade.
♦ **to hear about something** entendre parler de quelque chose
[2] apprendre (*news*) ◊ *Did you hear the good news?* Est-ce que tu as appris la bonne nouvelle?
♦ **to hear from somebody** avoir des nouvelles de quelqu'un ◊ *I haven't heard from him recently.* Je n'ai pas eu de ses nouvelles récemment.

heart NOUN
le cœur
♦ **in his heart of hearts** au fond de lui-même
♦ **to break someone's heart** briser le cœur de quelqu'un
♦ **to learn something by heart** apprendre quelque chose par cœur
♦ **the ace of hearts** l'as de cœur
♦ **with all my heart** de tout mon cœur

heart attack NOUN
la crise cardiaque

heartbroken ADJECTIVE
♦ **to be heartbroken** avoir le cœur brisé

heat NOUN

H

☞

see also **heat** VERB

la chaleur

to **heat** VERB

see also **heat** NOUN

faire chauffer ◊ *Heat gently for 5 minutes.* Faire chauffer à feu doux pendant cinq minutes.
♦ **to heat up (1)** (*cooked food*) faire réchauffer ◊ *He heated the soup up.* Il a fait réchauffer la soupe.
♦ **to heat up (2)** (*water, oven*) chauffer ◊ *The water is heating up.* L'eau chauffe.

heater NOUN
la chaufferette (*car, office*)

heating NOUN
le chauffage

heaven NOUN
le paradis

heavily ADVERB
lourdement ◊ *The car was heavily loaded.* La voiture était lourdement chargée.
♦ **heavily armed** fortement armé
♦ **heavily made up** très maquillé
♦ **She's heavily into jazz.** Elle est une mordue de jazz.

heavy ADJECTIVE
[1] lourd ◊ *This bag is very heavy.* Ce sac est très lourd.
♦ **heavy rain** une grosse averse
[2] chargé (*busy*) ◊ *I've got a very heavy week ahead.* Je vais avoir une semaine très chargée.
[3] dense ◊ *heavy traffic* une circulation dense
[4] gros ◊ *a heavy sigh* un gros soupir ◊ *to do the heavy work* faire le gros travail

he'd = he would, he had

hedge NOUN
la haie

heel NOUN
le talon

height NOUN
[1] la taille (*of person*)
[2] la hauteur (*of object*)
[3] l' altitude FEM (*of mountain*)
♦ **fear of heights** le vertige

held VERB *see* **hold**

helicopter NOUN
l' hélicoptère MASC

hell NOUN
l' enfer MASC

he'll = he will, he shall

hello EXCLAMATION
[1] bonjour!

[2] allô (*on phone*)

helmet NOUN
le casque

to **help** VERB

see also **help** NOUN

aider ◊ *Can you help me?* Est-ce que vous pouvez m'aider?
♦ **Help!** Au secours!
♦ **Help yourself!** Servez-vous!
♦ **He can't help it.** Il n'y peut rien.

help NOUN

see also **help** VERB

l' aide FEM ◊ *Do you need any help?* Vous avez besoin d'aide?

helpful ADJECTIVE
serviable ◊ *She was very helpful.* Elle a été très serviable.

helpline NOUN
la ligne d'écoute téléphonique

hen NOUN
la poule

her ADJECTIVE

see also **her** PRONOUN

son MASC ◊ *her father* son père
sa FEM ◊ *her mother* sa mère
ses PL ◊ *her parents* ses parents

sa becomes *son* before a vowel sound.

♦ **her friend (1)** (*male*) son ami
♦ **her friend (2)** (*female*) son amie

Do not use *son/sa/ses* with parts of the body.

◊ *She's going to wash her hair.* Elle va se laver les cheveux. ◊ *She's brushing her teeth.* Elle se brosse les dents. ◊ *She hurt her foot.* Elle s'est fait mal au pied.

her PRONOUN

see also **her** ADJECTIVE

la becomes *l'* before a vowel sound.

[1] la ◊ *I can see her.* Je la vois. ◊ *Look at her!* Regarde-la!
l' ◊ *I saw her.* Je l'ai vue.

Use *lui* when *her* means *to her*.

[2] lui ◊ *I gave her a book.* Je lui ai donné un livre. ◊ *I told her the truth.* Je lui ai dit la vérité.

Use *elle* after prepositions.

[3] elle ◊ *I'm going with her.* Je vais avec elle. ◊ *He sat next to her.* Il s'est assis à côté d'elle.

elle is also used in comparisons.

◊ *I'm older than her.* Je suis plus âgé qu'elle.

herb NOUN
l' herbe
♦ **herbs** les fines herbes FEM ◊ *What herbs do you use in this sauce?* Quelles fines herbes utilise-t-on pour cette sauce?

here ADVERB
ici ◊ *I live here.* J'habite ici.
♦ **here is...** voici... ◊ *Here's Mom.* Voici maman. ◊ *Here he is!* Le voici!
♦ **here are...** voici... ◊ *Here are the books.* Voici les livres.

heritage NOUN
le patrimoine
✹ ♦ **Heritage Day** la fête du Patrimoine

hero NOUN
le héros ◊ *He's a real hero!* C'est un véritable héros!

heroine NOUN
l' héroïne FEM ◊ *the heroine of the novel* l'héroïne du roman

hers PRONOUN
le sien + MASC NOUN ◊ *"Is this her coat?" "No, hers is black."* « C'est son manteau? » « Non, le sien est noir. »
la sienne + FEM NOUN ◊ *"Is this her car?" "No, hers is white."* « C'est sa voiture? » « Non, la sienne est blanche. »
les siens + MASC PL NOUN ◊ *my parents and hers* mes parents et les siens
les siennes + FEM PL NOUN ◊ *my reasons and hers* mes raisons et les siennes
♦ **Is this hers?** C'est à elle? ◊ *This book is hers.* Ce livre est à elle. ◊ *"Whose is this?" "It's hers."* « C'est à qui? » « À elle. »

herself PRONOUN
① se ◊ *She's hurt herself.* Elle s'est blessée.
② elle (*after preposition*) ◊ *She talked mainly about herself.* Elle a surtout parlé d'elle.
③ elle-même ◊ *She did it herself.* Elle l'a fait elle-même.
♦ **by herself** toute seule ◊ *She doesn't like travelling by herself.* Elle n'aime pas voyager toute seule.

he's = he is, he has

to **hesitate** VERB
hésiter

heterosexual ADJECTIVE
hétérosexuel MASC
hétérosexuelle FEM

hi EXCLAMATION
salut!

to **hibernate** VERB
hiberner

hiccups PL NOUN

♦ **to have hiccups** avoir le hoquet

to **hide** VERB
se cacher ◊ *He hid behind a bush.* Il s'est caché derrière un buisson.
♦ **to hide something** cacher quelque chose ◊ *We hid the present.* Nous avons caché le cadeau.

hide-and-seek NOUN
♦ **to play hide-and-seek**
✹ jouer à la cachette

hideous ADJECTIVE
hideux MASC
hideuse FEM

high ADJECTIVE, ADVERB
① haut ◊ *It's too high.* C'est trop haut.
♦ **How high is the wall?** Quelle est la hauteur du mur?
♦ **The wall is 2 metres high.** Le mur fait deux mètres de haut.
② élevé ◊ *a high price* un prix élevé ◊ *a high temperature* une température élevée
♦ **at high speed** à grande vitesse
♦ **It's very high in fat.** C'est très gras.
♦ **She's got a very high voice.** Elle a la voix très aiguë.

higher education NOUN
l' enseignement supérieur MASC

high heels PL NOUN
les chaussures à talons hauts FEM

high jump NOUN
le saut en hauteur (*sport*)

highlight NOUN
see also **highlight** VERB
le clou ◊ *the highlight of the evening* le clou de la soirée

to **highlight** VERB
see also **highlight** NOUN
① souligner (*emphasize*)
② surligner (*with highlighter pen*)

highlighter NOUN
le surligneur

high-rise NOUN
la tour ◊ *I live in a high-rise.* Je demeure dans une tour d'habitation.

high school NOUN
l' école secondaire FEM

✹ **highsticking** NOUN
le bâton élevé MASC ◊ *to get a penalty for highsticking* recevoir une punition pour bâton élevé

highway NOUN
l' autoroute FEM

to **hijack** VERB
détourner

hijacker NOUN
le/la pirate de l'air

hike NOUN
la randonnée pédestre

hiking NOUN
♦ **to go hiking** faire une randonnée pédestre
♦ **hiking boots** les chaussures de randonnée pédestre FEM

hilarious ADJECTIVE
hilarant ◊ *It was hilarious!* C'était hilarant!

hill NOUN
la colline ◊ *She walked up the hill.* Elle a gravi la colline.

him PRONOUN

> *le becomes l' before a vowel sound.*

① le ◊ *I can see him.* Je le vois.
◊ *Look at him!* Regarde-le!
l' ◊ *I saw him.* Je l'ai vu.

> *Use lui when him means to him, and after prepositions.*

② lui ◊ *I gave him a book.* Je lui ai donné un livre. ◊ *I told him the truth.* Je lui ai dit la vérité. ◊ *I'm going with him.* Je vais avec lui. ◊ *She sat next to him.* Elle s'est assise à côté de lui.

> *lui is also used in comparisons.*

◊ *I'm older than him.* Je suis plus âgé que lui.

himself PRONOUN
① se ◊ *He hurt himself.* Il s'est blessé.
② lui ◊ *He talked mainly about himself.* Il a surtout parlé de lui.
③ lui-même ◊ *He did it himself.* Il l'a fait lui-même.
♦ **by himself** tout seul ◊ *He was travelling by himself.* Il voyageait tout seul.

Hindu ADJECTIVE

> see also **Hindu** NOUN

hindou ◊ *a Hindu temple* un temple hindou

Hindu NOUN

> see also **Hindu** ADJECTIVE

l' hindou MASC
l' hindoue FEM

hint NOUN

> see also **hint** VERB

l' allusion FEM

to **hint** VERB

> see also **hint** NOUN

laisser entendre ◊ *He hinted that he was getting me a present.* Il m'a laissé entendre qu'il allait me donner un cadeau.
♦ **What are you hinting at?** Qu'est-ce que vous voulez dire par là ?

hip NOUN
la hanche

hippie NOUN
le/la hippie

hippo NOUN
l' hippopotame MASC

to **hire** VERB
engager ◊ *They hired a receptionist.* Ils ont engagé une réceptionniste.

his ADJECTIVE

> see also **his** PRONOUN

son MASC ◊ *his father* son père
sa FEM SING ◊ *his mother* sa mère
ses PL ◊ *his parents* ses parents

> *sa becomes son before a vowel sound.*

♦ **his friend (1)** (*male*) son ami
♦ **his friend (2)** (*female*) son amie

> *Do not use son/sa/ses with parts of the body.*

◊ *He's going to wash his hair.* Il va se laver les cheveux. ◊ *He's brushing his teeth.* Il se brosse les dents. ◊ *He hurt his foot.* Il s'est fait mal au pied.

his PRONOUN

> see also **his** ADJECTIVE

le sien + MASC NOUN ◊ *"Is this his coat?" "No, his is black."* « C'est son manteau ? » « Non, le sien est noir. »
la sienne + FEM NOUN ◊ *"Is this his car?" "No, his is white."* « C'est sa voiture ? » « Non, la sienne est blanche. »
les siens + MASC PL NOUN ◊ *my parents and his* mes parents et les siens
les siennes + FEM PL NOUN ◊ *my reasons and his* mes raisons et les siennes
♦ **Is this his?** C'est à lui? ◊ *This book is his.* Ce livre est à lui. ◊ *"Whose is this?" "It's his."* « C'est à qui ? » « À lui. »

history NOUN
l' histoire FEM

to **hit** VERB

> see also **hit** NOUN

① frapper ◊ *She hit the ball on the first try.* Elle a frappé la balle du premier coup.
② renverser ◊ *He was hit by a car.* Il a été renversé par une voiture.
③ toucher ◊ *The arrow hit the target.* La flèche a touché la cible.
♦ **I hit my head on the table.** Je me suis cogné la tête contre la table.
♦ **It suddenly hit me that...** Je me suis soudain rendu compte que...
♦ **to hit it off with somebody** bien s'entendre avec quelqu'un ◊ *She hit*

it off with his parents. Elle s'est bien entendue avec ses parents.

hit NOUN

see also **hit** VERB

① le tube (*song*) ◊ *the band's latest hit* le dernier tube de la bande
② le succès (*success*) ◊ *The film was a huge hit.* Le film a eu un immense succès.

hitch NOUN
le contretemps ◊ *There's been a slight hitch.* Il y a eu un léger contretemps.

to **hitchhike** VERB
✷ ① faire du pouce ◊ *She hitchhiked into town* Elle a fait du pouce jusqu'en ville.
② faire de l'auto-stop ◊ *They hitchhiked to Summerside.* Ils ont fait de l'auto-stop jusqu'à Summerside.

hitchhiker NOUN
l' auto-stoppeur MASC
l' auto-stoppeuse FEM

hitchhiking NOUN
l' auto-stop MASC ◊ *Hitchhiking can be dangerous.* Il peut être dangereux de faire de l'auto-stop.

HIV-negative ADJECTIVE
séronégatif MASC
séronégative FEM

HIV-positive ADJECTIVE
séropositif MASC
séropositive FEM

hobby NOUN
le passe-temps favori ◊ *What are your hobbies?* Quels sont tes passe-temps favoris?

hockey NOUN
le hockey ◊ *I play hockey.* Je joue au hockey.
♦ **a hockey stick** un bâton de hockey

hold NOUN

see also **hold** VERB

♦ **on hold** (*on phone*) en attente
♦ **to get hold of someone** (*reach*) contacter quelqu'un
♦ **to get hold of something** (*obtain*) trouver quelque chose ◊ *Where did you get hold of that book?* Où as-tu trouvé ce livre?

to **hold** VERB

see also **hold** NOUN

① tenir (*hold on to*) ◊ *He held the baby.* Il tenait le bébé.
② contenir (*contain*) ◊ *This bottle holds one litre.* Cette bouteille contient un litre.
♦ **to hold a meeting** avoir une réunion

♦ **Hold the line!** (*on telephone*) Ne quittez pas!
♦ **Hold it!** (*wait*) Attends!
♦ **to hold one's breath** retenir son souffle.

to **hold back** VERB
① retenir (*tears*)
② se retenir ◊ *I wanted to say something but I held back.* J'ai voulu dire quelque chose, mais je me suis retenu.

to **hold on** VERB
① tenir bon (*keep hold*) ◊ *The cliff was slippery but she managed to hold on.* La falaise était glissante, mais elle est parvenue à tenir bon.
♦ **to hold on to something** se cramponner à quelque chose ◊ *He held on to the chair.* Il se cramponnait à la chaise.
② attendre (*wait*) ◊ *Hold on, I'm coming!* Attends, je viens!
♦ **Hold on!** (*on telephone*) Ne quittez pas!

to **hold up** VERB
♦ **to hold somebody up** (*delay*) retenir quelqu'un ◊ *I was held up at the office.* J'ai été retenu au bureau.
♦ **to hold up a bank** (*rob*) cambrioler une banque (*informal*)

holdup NOUN
① le vol à main armée (*at bank*)
② le retard (*delay*)
③ le bouchon (*traffic jam*)

hole NOUN
le trou

holiday NOUN
① les vacances FEM PL ◊ *Did you have a good holiday?* Tu as passé de bonnes vacances? ◊ *our holidays in Newfoundland* nos vacances à Terre-Neuve
♦ **on holiday** en vacances ◊ *to go on holiday* partir en vacances ◊ *We are on holiday.* Nous sommes en vacances.
♦ **the school holidays** les vacances scolaires
② le jour férié (*public holiday*) ◊ *Next Wednesday is a holiday.* Mercredi prochain est un jour férié.
③ le jour de congé (*day off*) ◊ *He took a day's holiday.* Il a pris un jour de congé.
♦ **a holiday resort** un centre villégiature

hollow ADJECTIVE
creux MASC
creuse FEM

holly NOUN
le houx ◊ *a sprig of holly* un brin de houx

holy ADJECTIVE
saint

home NOUN

> *see also* **home** ADVERB

la maison
♦ **at home** à la maison
♦ **Make yourself at home.** Faites comme chez vous.

home ADVERB

> *see also* **home** NOUN

à la maison ◊ *I'll be home at 5 o'clock.* Je serai à la maison à cinq heures.
♦ **to get home** rentrer ◊ *What time did she get home?* Elle est rentrée à quelle heure?

home game NOUN
le match à domicile

homeland NOUN
la patrie

homeless ADJECTIVE
itinérant ◊ *a shelter for homeless youth* un refuge pour les jeunes itinérants
♦ **a homeless man** un itinérant
♦ **a homeless woman** une itinérante

homelessness NOUN
l' itinérance FEM

home page NOUN
la page d'accueil

homesick ADJECTIVE
♦ **to be homesick** avoir le mal du pays

homework NOUN
les devoirs MASC PL ◊ *Have you done your homework?* Est-ce que tu as fait tes devoirs? ◊ *my geography homework* mes devoirs de géographie

homosexual ADJECTIVE

> *see also* **homosexual** NOUN

homosexuel MASC
homosexuelle FEM

homosexual NOUN

> *see also* **homosexual** ADJECTIVE

l' homosexuel MASC
l' homosexuelle FEM

honest ADJECTIVE
1 honnête (*trustworthy*) ◊ *She's a very honest person.* Elle est très honnête.
2 (*sincere*)
franc MASC
franche FEM ◊ *He was very honest with her.* Il a été très franc avec elle.

honestly ADVERB
franchement ◊ *I honestly don't know.* Franchement, je n'en sais rien.

honesty NOUN
l' honnêteté FEM

honey NOUN
le miel

honeymoon NOUN
la lune de miel

honour NOUN
l' honneur MASC ◊ *in honour of our grandparents* en l'honneur de nos grands-parents
♦ **the honour roll** le tableau d'honneur

hood NOUN
1 le capuchon (*on coat*)
2 le capot (*of car*)

hook NOUN
le crochet ◊ *He hung the painting on the hook.* Il a suspendu le tableau au crochet.
♦ **to take the phone off the hook** décrocher le téléphone
♦ **a fish-hook** un hameçon

to **hope** VERB

> *see also* **hope** NOUN

espérer ◊ *I hope he comes.* J'espère qu'il va venir. ◊ *I'm hoping for good results.* J'espère avoir de bons résultats.
♦ **I hope so.** Je l'espère.
♦ **I hope not.** J'espère que non.

hope NOUN

> *see also* **hope** VERB

l' espoir MASC
♦ **to give up hope** perdre espoir ◊ *Don't give up hope!* Ne perds pas espoir!

hopeful ADJECTIVE
1 plein d'espoir ◊ *I'm hopeful.* Je suis plein d'espoir.
♦ **She's hopeful of winning.** Elle a bon espoir de gagner.
2 (*situation*)
prometteur MASC
prometteuse FEM ◊ *The prospects look hopeful.* Les perspectives semblent prometteuses.

hopefully ADVERB
avec un peu de chance ◊ *Hopefully he'll make it in time.* Avec un peu de chance, il arrivera à temps.

hopeless ADJECTIVE
1 désespéré ◊ *The situation is hopeless.* La situation est désespérée.
2 nul MASC
nulle FEM ◊ *I'm hopeless at math.* Je suis nul en maths.
♦ **It's hopeless, I can't do it!** C'est désespérant, je n'arrive pas à le faire!

horizon NOUN
l' horizon MASC

horizontal ADJECTIVE
horizontal
(MASC PL horizontaux)

horn NOUN
① le klaxon (*of car*) ◊ *He blew his horn.* Il a klaxonné.
② le cor ◊ *I play the horn.* Je joue du cor.
③ la corne (*of animal*)

horoscope NOUN
l' horoscope MASC

horrible ADJECTIVE
horrible ◊ *What a horrible dress!* Quelle robe horrible!

horrifying ADJECTIVE
effrayant

horror NOUN
l' horreur FEM ◊ *a horror movie* un film d'horreur

horse NOUN
le cheval
(PL les chevaux)

horse-racing NOUN
les courses de chevaux FEM PL

horseshoe NOUN
le fer à cheval

hose NOUN
le tuyau
(PL les tuyaux) ◊ *a garden hose* un tuyau d'arrosage

hospital NOUN
l' hôpital MASC
(PL les hôpitaux) ◊ *Take me to the hospital!* Emmenez-moi à l'hôpital!
◊ *in the hospital* à l'hôpital

hospitality NOUN
l' hospitalité FEM

host NOUN
l' hôte MASC
l' hôtesse FEM

hostage NOUN
l' otage MASC
♦ **to take somebody hostage** prendre quelqu'un en otage

hostel NOUN
le refuge (*for refugees, homeless people*)
♦ **a youth hostel** une auberge de jeunesse

hostile ADJECTIVE
hostile

hot ADJECTIVE
① chaud (*warm*) ◊ *a hot bath* un bain chaud ◊ *a hot country* un pays chaud

*When you are talking about a person being hot, you use **avoir chaud**.*
◊ *I'm hot.* J'ai chaud. ◊ *I'm too hot.*

J'ai trop chaud.

*When you mean that the weather is hot, you use **faire chaud**.*
◊ *It's hot.* Il fait chaud. ◊ *It's very hot today.* Il fait très chaud aujourd'hui.
② épicé (*spicy*) ◊ *a very hot curry* un curry très épicé

hot dog NOUN
le hot-dog

hotel NOUN
l' hôtel MASC ◊ *We stayed in a hotel.* Nous avons logé à l'hôtel.

hotline NOUN
① le service d'assistance téléphonique (*for info, advice*)
② la ligne d'écoute téléphonique (*for help in crisis*)
③ la ligne ouverte (*for phone-in show*)

hour NOUN
l' heure FEM ◊ *He always takes hours to get ready.* Il passe toujours des heures à se préparer.
♦ **a quarter of an hour** un quart d'heure
♦ **half an hour** une demi-heure
♦ **two and a half hours** deux heures et demie

hourly ADJECTIVE, ADVERB
toutes les heures ◊ *There are hourly buses.* Il y a des autobus toutes les heures.
♦ **to be paid hourly** être payé à l'heure

house NOUN
la maison
♦ **at his house** chez lui
♦ **We stayed at their house.** Nous sommes restés chez eux.
✹ ♦ **House of Assembly** (*Nfld*) la Chambre d'assemblée
♦ **House of Commons** la Chambre des communes

housework NOUN
le ménage
♦ **to do the housework** faire le ménage

how ADVERB
comment ◊ *How are you?* Comment allez-vous?
♦ **How many?** Combien?
♦ **How many...?** Combien de...? ◊ *How many students are there in the class?* Combien d'élèves y a-t-il dans la classe?
♦ **How much?** Combien?
♦ **How much...?** Combien de...? ◊ *How much sugar do you want?* Combien de sucre voulez-vous?
♦ **How old are you?** Quel âge as-tu?
♦ **How far is it to Rimouski?** Combien y a-t-il de kilomètres d'ici à Rimouski?
♦ **How long have you been here?**

H

☞

Depuis combien de temps êtes-vous là?
♦ **How do you say "apple" in French?** Comment dit-on « apple » en français?

however CONJUNCTION
pourtant ◊ *This, however, isn't true.* Pourtant, ce n'est pas vrai.

to **howl** VERB
hurler

HTML NOUN
le langage HTML ◊ *an HTML document* un document en langage HTML

Hudson Bay NOUN
la baie d'Hudson

to **hug** VERB

see also **hug** NOUN

serrer dans ses bras ◊ *He hugged her.* Il l'a serrée dans ses bras.

hug NOUN

see also **hug** VERB

♦ **to give somebody a hug** serrer quelqu'un dans ses bras ◊ *She gave them a hug.* Elle les a serrés dans ses bras.

huge ADJECTIVE
immense

to **hum** VERB
fredonner

human ADJECTIVE
humain ◊ *the human body* le corps humain
♦ **human rights** les droits de la personne ◊ *a human rights issue* une question relative aux droits de la personne
♦ **human resources** (*available people*) les ressources humaines ◊ *We have both the human resources and the funds to carry out this project.* Nous avons les ressources humaines et financières pour réaliser ce projet.

human being NOUN
l' être humain MASC

humankind NOUN
l' humanité FEM

humble ADJECTIVE
humble

❄ **humidex** NOUN
l' humidex MASC

humour NOUN
l' humour MASC
♦ **to have a sense of humour** avoir le sens de l'humour

hundred NUMBER
♦ **a hundred** cent ◊ *a hundred dollars*

cent dollars
♦ **five hundred** cinq cents
♦ **five hundred and one** cinq cent un
♦ **hundreds of people** des centaines de personnes

hung VERB *see* **hang**

hunger NOUN
la faim

hungry ADJECTIVE
♦ **to be hungry** avoir faim ◊ *I'm hungry.* J'ai faim.

to **hunt** VERB
① chasser (*animal*)
♦ **to go hunting** aller à la chasse
② pourchasser (*criminal*) ◊ *The police are hunting the criminal.* La police pourchasse le criminel.
♦ **to hunt for something** (*search*) chercher quelque chose partout ◊ *I hunted everywhere for that book.* J'ai cherché ce livre partout.

hunting NOUN
la chasse

hurdle NOUN
l' obstacle MASC

hurricane NOUN
l' ouragan MASC

to **hurry** VERB

see also **hurry** NOUN

se dépêcher ◊ *She hurried back home.* Elle s'est dépêchée de rentrer chez elle.
♦ **Hurry up!** Dépêche-toi!

hurry NOUN

see also **hurry** VERB

♦ **to be in a hurry** être pressé
♦ **to do something in a hurry** faire quelque chose en vitesse
♦ **There's no hurry.** Rien ne presse.

to **hurt** VERB

see also **hurt** ADJECTIVE

♦ **to hurt somebody (1)** (*physically*) faire mal à quelqu'un ◊ *You're hurting me!* Tu me fais mal!
♦ **to hurt somebody (2)** (*emotionally*) blesser quelqu'un ◊ *His remarks really hurt me.* Ses remarques m'ont vraiment blessé.
♦ **to hurt oneself** se faire mal ◊ *I fell and hurt myself.* Je me suis fait mal en tombant.
♦ **That hurts.** Ça fait mal. ◊ *It hurts to have a tooth out.* Ça fait mal de se faire arracher une dent.
♦ **My leg hurts.** J'ai mal à la jambe.

hurt ADJECTIVE

see also **hurt** VERB

blessé ◊ *Were you badly hurt?* Est-ce

que tu as été grièvement blessé?
◊ *He was hurt in the leg.* Il a été
blessé à la jambe. ◊ *I was hurt by
what she said.* J'ai été blessé par ce
qu'elle a dit.
♦ **Luckily, nobody got hurt.**
Heureusement, il n'y a pas eu de
blessés.

husband NOUN
le <u>mari</u>

hut NOUN

la <u>hutte</u>

✸ **hydro** NOUN
l' <u>électricité</u> FEM ◊ *Hydro costs a lot.*
L'électricité coûte cher.

hyperlink NOUN
l' <u>hyperlien</u> MASC

hyphen NOUN
le <u>trait d'union</u>

hypothesis NOUN
l' <u>hypothèse</u> FEM

H

I

I PRONOUN
1. je ◊ *I speak French.* Je parle français.

> *je changes to j' before a vowel and most words beginning with "h".*

◊ *I love cats.* J'aime les chats.
2. moi ◊ *my sister and I* ma sœur et moi

ice NOUN
1. la glace ◊ *There was ice on the lake.* Il y avait de la glace sur le lac.
2. le verglas (*on road*)
♦ **to break the ice** rompre la glace

iceberg NOUN
l' iceberg MASC
♦ **the tip of the iceberg** la pointe de l'iceberg

icebreaker NOUN
le brise-glace
(PL les brise-glaces) ◊ *Icebreakers are used to navigate the Arctic.* On utilise des brise-glaces pour naviguer dans l'Arctique.

ice cream NOUN
la crème glacée ◊ *vanilla ice cream* la crème glacée à la vanille

ice cube NOUN
le glaçon

ice fishing NOUN
la pêche sous la glace ◊ *to go ice fishing* faire de la pêche sous la glace

ice hockey NOUN
le hockey sur glace

ice rink NOUN
la patinoire

ice skating NOUN
le patinage sur glace
♦ **to go ice skating** faire du patin à glace

ice slide NOUN
la glissade ◊ *In winter the city builds an ice slide in the park.* L'hiver, la ville construit une glissade dans le parc.

ice storm NOUN
la tempête de verglas

icicle NOUN
le glaçon

icing NOUN
le glaçage (*on cake*)
♦ **icing sugar** le sucre glace

icon NOUN
l' icône FEM

icy ADJECTIVE
glacial
(MASC PL glaciaux) ◊ *There was an icy wind.* Il y avait un vent glacial.
♦ **The roads are icy.** Il y a du verglas sur les routes.

I'd = I had, I would

ID card NOUN
la carte d'identité

idea NOUN
l' idée FEM ◊ *Good idea!* Bonne idée!

ideal ADJECTIVE
idéal
(MASC PL idéaux)

identical ADJECTIVE
identique

identification NOUN
l' identification FEM

to **identify** VERB
identifier

i.e. ABBREVIATION
c.-à-d. (= c'est-à-dire)

if CONJUNCTION
si ◊ *You can have it if you like.* Tu peux le prendre si tu veux.

> *si changes to s' before il and ils.*

◊ *Do you know if he's there?* Savez-vous s'il est là?
♦ **if only** si seulement ◊ *If only I had more money!* Si seulement j'avais plus d'argent!
♦ **if not** sinon ◊ *Are you coming? If not, I'll go with my brother.* Est-ce que tu viens? Sinon, j'irai avec mon frère.

igloo NOUN
l' iglou MASC

ignorant ADJECTIVE
ignorant

to **ignore** VERB
♦ **to ignore something** ne tenir aucun compte de quelque chose ◊ *She ignored my advice.* Elle n'a tenu aucun compte de mes conseils.
♦ **to ignore somebody** ignorer quelqu'un ◊ *She saw me, but she ignored me.* Elle m'a vu, mais elle m'a ignoré.
♦ **Just ignore him!** Ne fais pas attention à lui!

ill ADJECTIVE
malade (*sick*)

I'll = I will

illegal ADJECTIVE
illégal
(MASC PL illégaux)

illegible ADJECTIVE
illisible

illness NOUN
la maladie

illusion NOUN
l' illusion FEM

illustration NOUN
l' illustration FEM

image NOUN
l' image FEM ◊ *The company has changed its image.* La société a changé d'image.

imagination NOUN
l' imagination FEM

to **imagine** VERB
imaginer ◊ *You can imagine how I felt!* Tu peux imaginer ce que j'ai ressenti! ◊ *"Is he angry?" "I imagine so."* « Est-ce qu'il est en colère? » « J'imagine que oui. »

imam NOUN
l' imam MASC

to **imitate** VERB
imiter

imitation NOUN
l' imitation FEM

immediate ADJECTIVE
immédiat ◊ *her immediate family* sa famille immédiate

immediately ADVERB
immédiatement ◊ *I'll do it immediately.* Je vais le faire immédiatement.

immigrant NOUN
l' immigré MASC
l' immigrée FEM

immigration NOUN
l' immigration FEM

immoral ADJECTIVE
immoral
(MASC PL immoraux)

impartial ADJECTIVE
impartial
(MASC PL impartiaux)

impatience NOUN
l' impatience FEM

impatient ADJECTIVE
impatient
♦ **to get impatient** s'impatienter ◊ *People are getting impatient.* Les gens commencent à s'impatienter.

impatiently ADVERB
avec impatience ◊ *We waited impatiently.* Nous avons attendu avec impatience.

impersonal ADJECTIVE
impersonnel MASC
impersonnelle FEM

to **imply** VERB
laisser entendre ◊ *She implied that she wasn't coming.* Elle a laissé entendre qu'elle ne venait pas.

importance NOUN
l' importance FEM

important ADJECTIVE
important

impossible ADJECTIVE
impossible

to **impress** VERB
impressionner ◊ *She's trying to impress you.* Elle essaie de t'impressionner.

impressed ADJECTIVE
impressionné ◊ *I'm very impressed!* Je suis très impressionné!

impression NOUN
l' impression FEM ◊ *I was under the impression that...* J'avais l'impression que...

impressive ADJECTIVE
impressionnant

improv NOUN
l' improvisation FEM ◊ *We started an improv club in our school.* Nous avons fondé une ligue d'improvisation à l'école.

to **improve** VERB
1 améliorer *(make better)* ◊ *They have improved the service.* Ils ont amélioré le service.
2 s'améliorer *(get better)* ◊ *The weather is improving.* Le temps s'améliore. ◊ *My French has improved.* Mon français s'est amélioré.

improvement NOUN
1 l' amélioration FEM *(of condition)* ◊ *It's a great improvement.* C'est une nette amélioration.
2 le progrès *(of learner)* ◊ *There's been an improvement in your French.* Tu as fait des progrès en français.

to **improvise** VERB
improviser

in PREPOSITION, ADVERB

*There are several ways of translating **in**. Scan the examples to find one that is similar to what you want to say. For other expressions with **in**, see the verbs **go**, **come**, **get**, **give** etc.*

1 dans ◊ *in the house* dans la maison ◊ *in my backpack* dans

☞

mon sac à dos ◊ *I'll see you in three weeks.* Je te verrai dans trois semaines.

② à ◊ *in the country* à la campagne ◊ *in school* à l'école ◊ *in hospital* à l'hôpital ◊ *in Steinbach* à Steinbach ◊ *in spring* au printemps ◊ *in the sun* au soleil ◊ *in the shade* à l'ombre ◊ *in a loud voice* à voix haute ◊ *the boy in the blue shirt* le garçon à la chemise bleue ◊ *It was written in pencil.* C'était écrit au crayon. ◊ *in the month of May* au mois de mai

③ en ◊ *in French* en français ◊ *in summer* en été ◊ *in May* en mai ◊ *in 1996* en dix-neuf cent quatre-vingt seize ◊ *I did it in 3 hours.* Je l'ai fait en trois heures. ◊ *in town* en ville ◊ *in prison* en prison ◊ *in tears* en larmes ◊ *in good condition* en bon état

> *When **in** refers to a country which is feminine, use **en**; when the country is masculine, use **au**; when the country is plural, use **aux**.*

◊ *in France* en France ◊ *in Portugal* au Portugal ◊ *in the United States* aux États-Unis

④ de ◊ *the best team in the world* la meilleure équipe du monde ◊ *the tallest person in the family* le plus grand de la famille ◊ *at 4 o'clock in the afternoon* à quatre heures de l'après-midi ◊ *at 6 in the morning* à six heures du matin

♦ **In the afternoon I work at the store.** L'après-midi, je travaille au magasin.
♦ **You look good in that dress.** Tu es jolie avec cette robe.
♦ **in time** à temps ◊ *We arrived in time for dinner.* Nous sommes arrivés à temps pour le dîner.
♦ **in here** ici ◊ *It's hot in here.* Il fait chaud ici.
♦ **in the rain** sous la pluie
♦ **in the sixties** durant les années soixante
♦ **one person in ten** une personne sur dix
♦ **to be in** (*at home, work*) être là ◊ *She wasn't in.* Elle n'était pas là.
♦ **to ask somebody in** inviter quelqu'un à entrer

inaccurate ADJECTIVE
inexact

inadequate ADJECTIVE
inadéquat (*measures, resources*)
♦ **I felt completely inadequate.** Je ne me sentais absolument pas à la hauteur.

incentive NOUN
♦ **There is no incentive to work.** Il n'y a rien qui incite à travailler.

inch NOUN
le pouce

> ⓘ *An inch is a nonmetric unit equal to about 2.5 cm.*

♦ **6 inches** quinze centimètres

incident NOUN
l' incident MASC

inclined ADJECTIVE
♦ **to be inclined to do something** avoir tendance à faire quelque chose ◊ *He's inclined to arrive late.* Il a tendance à arriver en retard.

to **include** VERB
comprendre ◊ *Service is not included.* Le service n'est pas compris.

including PREPOSITION
compris ◊ *It will be 200 dollars, including tax.* Ça coûtera deux cents dollars, taxes comprises.

inclusive ADJECTIVE
compris ◊ *The inclusive price is 200 dollars.* Ça coûte deux cents dollars tout compris.
♦ **pages 9 to 12 inclusive** de la page neuf à la page douze inclusivement
♦ **inclusive language** la langue non sexiste

income NOUN
le revenu

income tax NOUN
l' impôt sur le revenu MASC

incompetent ADJECTIVE
incompétent

incomplete ADJECTIVE
incomplet MASC
incomplète FEM

inconsistent ADJECTIVE
① changeant (*behaviour*)
② inégal (*work, quality*)
③ contradictoire (*statements*)
♦ **Her actions are inconsistent with what she says.** Ses actes ne concordent pas avec ce qu'elle dit.

inconvenience NOUN
♦ **I don't want to cause any inconvenience.** Je ne veux pas vous déranger.

inconvenient ADJECTIVE
inopportun ◊ *at an inconvenient time* à un moment inopportun
♦ **That's very inconvenient for me.** Ça ne m'arrange pas du tout.

incorrect ADJECTIVE
incorrect

increase NOUN

see also **increase** VERB

l' augmentation FEM ◊ *an increase in traffic accidents* une augmentation des accidents de la route

to **increase** VERB

see also **increase** NOUN

augmenter

incredible ADJECTIVE
incroyable

indecisive ADJECTIVE
indécis (*person*)

independence NOUN
l' indépendance FEM

independent ADJECTIVE
indépendant
♦ **an independent school** une école privée

index NOUN
l' index MASC (*in book*)

index finger NOUN
l' index MASC

Indian summer NOUN
✱ l' été indien MASC

to **indicate** VERB
indiquer

indigestion NOUN
l' indigestion FEM
♦ **I have indigestion.** J'ai une indigestion.

individual ADJECTIVE

see also **individual** NOUN

individuel MASC
individuelle FEM

individual NOUN

see also **individual** ADJECTIVE

⒈ l' individu MASC ◊ *the rights of the individual* les droits de l'individu
⒉ la personne FEM ◊ *a rather strange individual* une personne un peu étrange
♦ **She's a real individual.** Elle est vraiment unique.

indoor ADJECTIVE
d'intérieur ◊ *indoor activities* les activités d'intérieur ◊ *indoor shoes* les chaussures d'intérieur ◊ *indoor sports* les sports d'intérieur
♦ **an indoor swimming pool** une piscine intérieure

indoors ADVERB
à l'intérieur ◊ *They're indoors.* Ils sont à l'intérieur.
♦ **to go indoors** rentrer ◊ *We'd better go indoors.* Nous ferions mieux de rentrer.

industrial ADJECTIVE

industriel MASC
industrielle FEM

industry NOUN
l' industrie FEM ◊ *the tourist industry* l'industrie du tourisme ◊ *the oil industry* l'industrie pétrolière ◊ *I'd like to work in industry.* J'aimerais travailler dans l'industrie.

inefficient ADJECTIVE
inefficace

inevitable ADJECTIVE
inévitable

inexpensive ADJECTIVE
bon marché MASC, FEM, PL ◊ *an inexpensive hotel* un hôtel bon marché ◊ *inexpensive holidays* des vacances bon marché

inexperienced ADJECTIVE
inexpérimenté

infection NOUN
l' infection FEM ◊ *an ear infection* une infection de l'oreille
♦ **a throat infection** un mal de gorge

infectious ADJECTIVE
contagieux MASC
contagieuse FEM ◊ *It's not infectious.* Ce n'est pas contagieux.

infinite ADJECTIVE
⒈ infini ◊ *an infinite variety* une variété infinie
⒉ illimité ◊ *The possibilities are infinite.* Les possibilités sont illimitées.

infinitive NOUN
l' infinitif MASC

inflatable ADJECTIVE
gonflable (*mattress, dinghy*)

inflation NOUN
l' inflation FEM

influence NOUN

see also **influence** VERB

l' influence FEM ◊ *He's a bad influence on her.* Il a mauvaise influence sur elle.

to **influence** VERB

see also **influence** NOUN

influencer

infomercial NOUN
l' infopublicité FEM

to **inform** VERB
informer
♦ **to inform somebody of something** informer quelqu'un de quelque chose ◊ *Nobody informed me of the new plan.* Personne ne m'a informé de ce nouveau projet.

informal ADJECTIVE

I

☞

1 décontracté (*person, party*)
◊ *"informal dress"* « tenue décontractée »
2 (*language*)
familier MASC
familière FEM ◊ *informal language* le langage familier
♦ **an informal visit from the principal** une visite non officielle du directeur

information NOUN
1 les renseignements MASC PL
◊ *important information* les renseignements importants
♦ **a piece of information** un renseignement
♦ **Could you give me some information about the Quebec Carnival?** Pourriez-vous me renseigner sur le Carnaval de Québec?
♦ **for your information** à titre de renseignement
2 l' information FEM ◊ *I found some information for my project on pollution.* J'ai trouvé de l'information pour mon projet sur la pollution.

information desk NOUN
le bureau de renseignements

infuriating ADJECTIVE
exaspérant

ingenious ADJECTIVE
ingénieux MASC
ingénieuse FEM

ingredient NOUN
l' ingrédient MASC

inhabitant NOUN
l' habitant MASC
l' habitante FEM

to **inherit** VERB
hériter de ◊ *She inherited her father's house.* Elle a hérité de la maison de son père.

initials PL NOUN
les initiales FEM PL ◊ *My initials are CDT.* Mes initiales sont CDT.

initiative NOUN
l' initiative FEM

to **inject** VERB
injecter (*drug*)

injection NOUN
la piqûre

to **injure** VERB
blesser

injury NOUN
la blessure

injustice NOUN
l' injustice FEM

ink NOUN
l' encre FEM

in-laws PL NOUN
les beaux-parents MASC PL

inn NOUN
l' auberge FEM

inner ADJECTIVE
intérieur
♦ **the inner city** les quartiers déshérités du centre ville

inner tube NOUN
la chambre à air

innocent ADJECTIVE
innocent

inquest NOUN
l' enquête FEM

to **inquire** VERB
♦ **to inquire about something** se renseigner sur quelque chose ◊ *I'm going to inquire about show times.* Je vais me renseigner sur les horaires de cinéma.

inquiry NOUN
♦ **to make inquiries about something** faire des demandes de renseignement ◊ *"inquiries"* « renseignements »

inquisitive ADJECTIVE
curieux MASC
curieuse FEM

insane ADJECTIVE
fou MASC
folle FEM

inscription NOUN
l' inscription FEM

insect NOUN
l' insecte MASC

insect repellent NOUN
l' antimoustiques MASC

insensitive ADJECTIVE
indélicat ◊ *That was a bit insensitive of you.* C'était un peu indélicat de ta part.

to **insert** NOUN
insérer ◊ *Insert the CD in the drive.* Insère le CD dans le lecteur. ◊ *You should insert a paragraph here, explaining your point.* Tu devrais insérer un paragraphe ici pour expliquer.

inside NOUN

> see also **inside** ADVERB

l' intérieur MASC

inside ADVERB, PREPOSITION

> see also **inside** NOUN

à l'intérieur ◊ *They're inside.* Ils sont à l'intérieur. ◊ *inside the house* à l'intérieur de la maison
♦ **to go inside** rentrer

♦ **Come inside!** Rentrez!

insincere ADJECTIVE
peu sincère

to **insist** VERB
insister ◊ *I didn't want to, but he insisted.* Je ne voulais pas, mais il a insisté.
♦ **to insist on doing something** insister pour faire quelque chose ◊ *She insisted on paying.* Elle a insisté pour payer.
♦ **He insisted he was innocent.** Il affirmait qu'il était innocent.

to **inspect** VERB
inspecter

inspector NOUN
l' inspecteur MASC
l' inspectrice FEM

to **install** VERB
installer ◊ *to install a piece of software* installer un logiciel ◊ *We've just installed new kitchen cupboards.* Nous venons d'installer de nouvelles armoires de cuisine.

instalment NOUN
1 le versement (*payment*) ◊ *to pay in instalments* payer en plusieurs versements
2 l' épisode MASC (*episode*)

instance NOUN
♦ **for instance** par exemple

instant ADJECTIVE
1 immédiat ◊ *It was an instant success.* Ça a été un succès immédiat.
2 instantané (*coffee, foods*) ◊ *instant pudding* le pouding instantané
♦ **instant messaging** la messagerie instantanée

instantly ADVERB
tout de suite

instead ADVERB
♦ **instead of (1)** (*followed by noun*) à la place de ◊ *He went instead of his brother.* Il y est allé à la place de son frère.
♦ **instead of (2)** (*followed by verb*) au lieu de ◊ *We played tennis instead of going swimming.* Nous avons joué au tennis au lieu d'aller nager.
♦ **The pool was closed, so we played tennis instead.** La piscine était fermée, alors nous avons joué au tennis.

instinct NOUN
l' instinct MASC

institute NOUN
l' institut MASC

institution NOUN
l' institution FEM

to **instruct** VERB
♦ **to instruct somebody to do something** donner l'ordre à quelqu'un de faire quelque chose ◊ *She instructed us to wait outside.* Elle nous a donné l'ordre d'attendre dehors.

instructions PL NOUN
1 les instructions FEM PL ◊ *Follow the instructions carefully.* Suivez soigneusement les instructions.
2 le mode d'emploi SING (*for product*) ◊ *Where are the instructions?* Où est le mode d'emploi?

instructor NOUN
le moniteur
la monitrice ◊ *a ski instructor* un moniteur de ski ◊ *a driving instructor* un moniteur d'auto-école

instrument NOUN
l' instrument MASC ◊ *Do you play an instrument?* Est-ce que tu joues d'un instrument?

insufficient ADJECTIVE
insuffisant

insulin NOUN
l' insuline FEM

insult NOUN
| *see also* **insult** VERB |
l' insulte FEM

to **insult** VERB
| *see also* **insult** NOUN |
insulter

insurance NOUN
l' assurance FEM ◊ *her car insurance* son assurance automobile
♦ **an insurance policy** une police d'assurance

intelligent ADJECTIVE
intelligent

to **intend** VERB
♦ **to intend to do something** avoir l'intention de faire quelque chose ◊ *I intend to do French at university.* J'ai l'intention d'étudier le français à l'université.

intense ADJECTIVE
intense

intensive ADJECTIVE
intensif MASC
intensive FEM

intention NOUN
l' intention FEM

intercom NOUN
l' interphone MASC

interest NOUN
| *see also* **interest** VERB |

☞

l' intérêt MASC ◊ *to show an interest in something* manifester de l'intérêt pour quelque chose
♦ **What interests do you have?** Quels sont tes centres d'intérêt?
♦ **My main interest is music.** Ce qui m'intéresse le plus c'est la musique.
♦ **an interest group** un groupe d'intérêt
♦ **interest rate** (*bank account*) le taux d'intérêt

to **interest** VERB

see also **interest** NOUN

intéresser ◊ *It doesn't interest me.* Ça ne m'intéresse pas.
♦ **to be interested in something** s'intéresser à quelque chose ◊ *I'm not interested in politics.* Je ne m'intéresse pas à la politique.

interesting ADJECTIVE
intéressant

to **interfere** VERB
♦ **Stop interfering in my social life.** Arrête de te mêler dans ma vie sociale.
♦ **The weather interfered with our plans.** Le mauvais temps a contrarié nos projets.

interior NOUN
l' intérieur MASC

interior designer NOUN
le décorateur d'intérieur
la décoratrice d'intérieur

intermediate ADJECTIVE
(*course, level*)
moyen MASC
moyenne FEM

intermission NOUN
l' entracte MASC

internal ADJECTIVE
interne

international ADJECTIVE
international
(MASC PL internationaux)

Internet NOUN
l' Internet MASC ◊ *on the Internet* sur Internet

Internet café NOUN
le cybercafé

Internet user NOUN
l' internaute MASC/FEM

to **interpret** VERB
⓵ servir d'interprète ◊ *He couldn't speak French, so his friend interpreted.* Comme il ne savait pas le français, son ami a servi d'interprète.
⓶ interpréter ◊ *I don't know how to interpret her response.* Je ne sais pas comment interpréter sa réaction.

interpreter NOUN
l' interprète MASC/FEM

to **interrupt** VERB
interrompre

interruption NOUN
l' interruption FEM

intersection NOUN
l' intersection FEM ◊ *What's the nearest intersection?* Quelle est l'intersection la plus proche? ◊ *Turn left at the next intersection.* Tourne à gauche à la prochaine intersection.

interview NOUN

see also **interview** VERB

⓵ l' interview FEM (*on TV, radio*)
⓶ l' entretien MASC (*for job*)

to **interview** VERB

see also **interview** NOUN

interviewer (*on TV, radio*) ◊ *I was interviewed on the radio.* J'ai été interviewé à la radio.

interviewer NOUN (*on TV, radio*)
l' interviewer MASC
l' intervieweuse FEM

intimate ADJECTIVE
intime

into PREPOSITION
⓵ dans ◊ *He got into the car.* Il est monté dans la voiture.
⓶ en ◊ *I'm going into town.* Je vais en ville. ◊ *Translate it into French.* Traduisez ça en français. ◊ *Divide into two groups.* Répartissez-vous en deux groupes.

intolerant ADJECTIVE
intolérant
♦ **She's lactose-intolerant.** Elle est intolérante au lactose.

intramurals PL NOUN
les activités intramurales FEM ◊ *Did you sign up for intramurals?* Tu t'es inscrit aux activités intramurales?

to **introduce** VERB
présenter ◊ *I'd like to introduce my grandmother.* Je vous présente ma grand-mère. ◊ *He introduced me to his parents.* Il m'a présentée à ses parents.

introduction NOUN
l' introduction FEM (*in book*)

intruder NOUN
l' intrus MASC
l' intruse FEM

intuition NOUN
l' intuition FEM

Inuit PL NOUN

see also **Inuit** ADJECTIVE

les Inuits MASC

Inuit ADJECTIVE

  see also **Inuit** NOUN

  inuit ◊ *traditional Inuit culture* la culture inuite traditionnelle

Inuk NOUN
  l' Inuit MASC
  l' Inuite FEM

to **invade** VERB
  envahir
  ♦ **to invade someone's privacy** s'ingérer dans la vie privée de quelqu'un

invasion NOUN
  l' envahissement MASC

to **invent** VERB
  inventer

invention NOUN
  l' invention FEM

inventor NOUN
  l' inventeur MASC
  l' inventrice FEM

investigation NOUN
  l' enquête FEM (*police*)

investment NOUN
  l' investissement MASC ◊ *Education is an investment in your future.* L'éducation, c'est un investissement dans ton avenir.

invincible ADJECTIVE
  invincible ◊ *He thinks he's invincible.* Il se croit invincible.

invisible ADJECTIVE
  invisible

invitation NOUN
  l' invitation FEM

to **invite** VERB
  inviter ◊ *You're all invited.* Vous êtes tous invités.
  ♦ **to invite somebody to a party** inviter quelqu'un à une fête

to **involve** VERB
  nécessiter ◊ *This job involves a lot of travelling.* Ce travail nécessite de nombreux déplacements.
  ♦ **to be involved in something** (*crime, drugs*) être impliqué dans quelque chose
  ♦ **to be involved with somebody** (*in relationship*) avoir une relation avec quelqu'un

IQ NOUN (= *intelligence quotient*)
  le Q.I. (= quotient intellectuel)

iron NOUN

  see also **iron** VERB

  ① le fer (*metal*)
  ② le fer à repasser (*for clothes*)

to **iron** VERB

  see also **iron** NOUN

  repasser

ironic ADJECTIVE
  ironique

ironing NOUN
  le repassage ◊ *to do the ironing* faire le repassage

ironing board NOUN
  la planche à repasser

irregular ADJECTIVE
  irrégulier MASC
  irrégulière FEM ◊ *an irregular verb* un verbe irrégulier

irrelevant ADJECTIVE
  hors de propos ◊ *That's irrelevant.* C'est hors de propos.

irresistible ADJECTIVE
  irrésistible ◊ *irresistible desserts* des desserts irrésistibles ◊ *an irresistible urge* une envie irrésistible

irresponsible ADJECTIVE (*person*)
  irresponsable ◊ *That was irresponsible of them.* C'était irresponsable de leur part.

irritating ADJECTIVE
  irritant

is VERB *see* **be**

Islamic ADJECTIVE
  islamique ◊ *Islamic law* la loi islamique

island NOUN
  l' île FEM

isolated ADJECTIVE
  isolé

ISP NOUN (= *Internet service provider*)
  le fournisseur de services Internet

issue NOUN

  see also **issue** VERB

  ① la question (*matter*) ◊ *a controversial issue* une question controversée
  ② le numéro (*of magazine*)

to **issue** VERB

  see also **issue** NOUN

  distribuer (*equipment, supplies*)

it PRONOUN

  Remember to check if **it** *stands for a masculine or feminine noun.*

  ① il ◊ *"Where's my book?" "It's on the table."* « Où est mon livre ? » « Il est sur la table. »
  elle ◊ *"When does the pool close?" "It closes at 8."* « La piscine ferme à quelle heure ? » « Elle ferme à vingt heures. »

☞

*Use **le** or **la** when **it** is the object of the sentence. **le** and **la** change to **l'** before a vowel and most words beginning with "h".*

2 le ◊ *There's a croissant left. Do you want it?* Il reste un croissant. Tu le veux?

l' ◊ *It's a good film. Did you see it?* C'est un bon film. L'as-tu vu?

la ◊ *I don't want this apple. Take it.* Je ne veux pas de cette pomme. Prends-la.

l' ◊ *"He's got a new car." "Yes, I saw it."* « Il a une nouvelle voiture. » « Oui, je l'ai vue. »

♦ **It's raining.** Il pleut.
♦ **It's 6 o'clock.** Il est six heures.
♦ **It's Friday tomorrow.** Demain, c'est vendredi.
♦ **"Who is it?" "It's me."** « Qui est-ce? » « C'est moi. »
♦ **It's expensive.** C'est cher.

italics NOUN
l' italique FEM ◊ *to put a word in italics* mettre un mot en italique

to **itch** VERB
♦ **It itches.** Ça me démange.
♦ **My head's itching.** J'ai des démangeaisons à la tête.

itchy ADJECTIVE
♦ **My arm is itchy.** J'ai le bras qui démange.

it'd = it had, it would

item NOUN
l' article MASC (*object*)

itinerary NOUN
l' itinéraire MASC

it'll = it will

its ADJECTIVE

*Remember to check if **its** refers to a masculine, feminine or plural noun.*

son MASC ◊ *What's its name?* Quel est son nom?
sa FEM ◊ *Every thing in its place.* Chaque chose à sa place.
ses PL ◊ *The dog is losing its hair.* Le chien perd ses poils.

it's = it is, it has

itself PRONOUN
se

*se changes to **s'** before a vowel and most words beginning with "h".*

◊ *The bear was trying to defend itself.* L'ours essayait de se défendre.

I've = I have

J

to **jab** VERB
  planter ◊ *He jabbed his fork into the potato.* Il a planté sa fourchette dans la pomme de terre.
  ♦ **She jabbed me with her elbow.** Elle m'a donné un coup de coude.

jack NOUN
  1 le cric (*for car*)
  2 le valet (*playing card*)

jacket NOUN
  le veston

jackknife NOUN
  le canif

jackpot NOUN
  le gros lot
  ♦ **to win the jackpot** gagner le gros lot

jail NOUN
  la prison
  ♦ **to go to jail** aller en prison
  ♦ **to put someone in jail** emprisonner quelqu'un

jam NOUN
  la confiture ◊ *strawberry jam* la confiture de fraises
  ♦ **a traffic jam** un embouteillage
  ♦ **to be in a jam** être dans le pétrin
  ♦ **to get somebody out of a jam** sortir quelqu'un du pétrin

jam jar NOUN
  le pot à confiture

jammed ADJECTIVE
  coincé ◊ *The window's jammed.* La fenêtre est coincée.

jam-packed ADJECTIVE
  bondé ◊ *The room was jam-packed.* La salle était bondée.

janitor NOUN
  le/la concierge ◊ *He's a janitor.* Il est concierge.

January NOUN
  janvier MASC
  ♦ **in January** en janvier

jar NOUN
  le bocal
  (PL les bocaux) ◊ *an empty jar* un bocal vide
  ♦ **a jar of honey** un pot de miel

javelin NOUN
  le javelot

jaw NOUN
  la mâchoire

jazz NOUN
  le jazz

jealous ADJECTIVE
  jaloux MASC
  jalouse FEM

jeans PL NOUN
  les jeans MASC

Jehovah's Witness NOUN
  le témoin de Jéhovah ◊ *She's a Jehovah's Witness.* Elle est témoin de Jéhovah.

Jello™ NOUN
  la gelée

jelly NOUN
  la gelée

jelly bean NOUN
  le bonbon haricot

jellyfish NOUN
  la méduse

jersey NOUN (*pullover*)
  le maillot

jet NOUN
  1 l' avion à réaction MASC (*plane*)
  2 le jet ◊ *a jet of water* un jet d'eau

jetlag NOUN
  ♦ **to be suffering from jetlag** subir les effets du décalage horaire

Jew NOUN
  le juif
  la juive

jewel NOUN
  le bijou
  (PL les bijoux)

jeweller NOUN
  le bijoutier
  la bijoutière ◊ *He's a jeweller.* Il est bijoutier.

jewellery NOUN
  les bijoux MASC PL

jewellery store NOUN
  la bijouterie

Jewish ADJECTIVE
  juif MASC
  juive FEM

jigsaw NOUN
  le puzzle

to **jingle** VERB
  1 tinter (*bells*)
  2 cliqueter (*coins*)

jinx NOUN
  le sort ◊ *to put a jinx on something* jeter un sort à quelque chose

job NOUN

☞

① l' emploi MASC ◊ *He lost his job.* Il a perdu son emploi.
♦ **I have a Saturday job.** Je travaille le samedi.
② (*chore, task*)
le travail
(PL les travaux) ◊ *That was a difficult job.* C'était un travail difficile.

job centre NOUN
le centre d'emploi

jobless ADJECTIVE
sans emploi

to **jog** VERB
faire du jogging

jogging NOUN
le jogging
♦ **to go jogging** faire du jogging

to **join** VERB
① s'inscrire à (*become member of*) ◊ *I'm going to join the ski club.* Je vais m'inscrire au club de ski.
② se joindre à ◊ *Do you mind if I join you?* Puis-je me joindre à vous?

joint NOUN
① l' articulation FEM (*in body*)
② le rôti (*of meat*)

joke NOUN

see also **joke** VERB

la plaisanterie
♦ **to tell a joke** raconter une plaisanterie
♦ **He can't take a joke.** Il prend mal la plaisanterie.
♦ **It's a joke.** (*waste of time*) C'est de la blague.
♦ **to play a joke on somebody** jouer un tour à quelqu'un

to **joke** VERB

see also **joke** NOUN

plaisanter ◊ *I'm only joking.* Je plaisante.

jolly ADJECTIVE
jovial
(MASC PL joviaux)

to **jot down** VERB
noter

journal NOUN
le journal ◊ *She keeps a journal of her experiences.* Elle note ses expériences dans un journal.

journalism NOUN
le journalisme

journalist NOUN
le/la journaliste ◊ *She's a journalist.* Elle est journaliste.

journey NOUN
① le voyage ◊ *I don't like long journeys.* Je n'aime pas les longs voyages.

♦ **to go on a journey** faire un voyage
② le trajet (*to school, work*) ◊ *The journey to school takes about half an hour.* Il y a une demi-heure de trajet pour aller à l'école.
♦ **a bus journey** un trajet en autobus

joy NOUN
la joie

joystick NOUN
la manette de jeu (*for computer game*)

judge NOUN

see also **judge** VERB

le/la juge ◊ *She's a judge.* Elle est juge.

to **judge** VERB

see also **judge** NOUN

juger

judo NOUN
le judo ◊ *My hobby is judo.* Je fais du judo.

jug NOUN
la cruche

juggler NOUN
le jongleur
la jongleuse

juice NOUN
le jus ◊ *orange juice* le jus d'orange

July NOUN
juillet MASC
♦ **in July** en juillet

jumble NOUN
le fouillis ◊ *a jumble of information* un fouillis de renseignements
♦ **a jumble of ideas** des pensées confuses
♦ **a jumble of papers** des papiers en vrac
♦ **Her thoughts were all in a jumble.** Ses pensées étaient toutes confuses.

to **jump** VERB
sauter
♦ **to jump over something** sauter par-dessus quelque chose
♦ **to jump out of the window** sauter par la fenêtre
♦ **to jump off the roof** sauter du toit
♦ **to jump to conclusions** sauter aux conclusions

jumper NOUN
la robe chasuble

June NOUN
juin MASC
♦ **in June** en juin

jungle NOUN
la jungle

junior ADJECTIVE

⓵ (*sports*)
<u>junior</u> MASC, FEM, PL ◊ *the junior leagues* les ligues junior
⓶ <u>subalterne</u> (*work*) ◊ *a junior employee* un employé subalterne
⓷ <u>fils</u> (*in names*) ◊ *Bill Smith, Jr.* Bill Smith, fils
♦ **in junior high school** à l'école secondaire de premier cycle
♦ **junior kindergarten** la prématernelle
♦ **She's three years my junior.** Elle a trois ans de moins que moi.

junk NOUN
⓵ le <u>bric-à-brac</u> NO PL (*old things*) ◊ *The attic's full of junk.* Le grenier est rempli de bric-à-brac.
⓶ la <u>camelote</u> (*worthless stuff*) ◊ *Don't read that, it's junk.* Ne lis pas ça, c'est de la camelote.
♦ **a junk shop** un magasin d'objets usagés
♦ **junk mail** la publicité-rebut
♦ **junk e-mail** le pourriel

junk food NOUN
⓵ la <u>malbouffe</u> (*in general*) ◊ *My parents are against junk food.* Mes parents sont contre la malbouffe.
◊ *Junk food is becoming a problem in our society.* La malbouffe est devenue un problème dans notre société.

⓶ l' <u>aliment vide</u> MASC (*specific food*)
◊ *Potato chips are junk food.* Les croustilles sont un aliment vide. ◊ *I ate junk food for lunch.* J'ai mangé des aliments vides pour le dîner.

jury NOUN
le <u>jury</u>

just ADVERB, ADJECTIVE
<u>juste</u> ◊ *just after Christmas* juste après Noël ◊ *We had just enough money.* Nous avions juste assez d'argent. ◊ *just in time* juste à temps ◊ *a just policy* une politique juste
♦ **They're just jealous.** Ils sont simplement jaloux.
♦ **I'm rather busy just now.** Je suis assez occupé en ce moment.
♦ **I did it just now.** Je viens de le faire.
♦ **He's just arrived.** Il vient d'arriver.
♦ **I'm just coming!** J'arrive!
♦ **It's just a suggestion.** Ce n'est qu'une suggestion.
♦ **just for you** spécialement pour toi
♦ **to be just about to do something** être sur le point de faire quelque chose

justice NOUN
la <u>justice</u>

to **justify** VERB
<u>justifier</u>

J

K

kangaroo NOUN
le kangourou

karaoke NOUN
le karaoké

karate NOUN
le karaté

kayak NOUN
le kayak

kebab NOUN
la brochette

keen ADJECTIVE
enthousiaste ◊ *He doesn't seem very keen.* Il n'a pas l'air très enthousiaste.
♦ **She's a keen student.** C'est une étudiante assidue.
♦ **to be keen on something** aimer quelque chose ◊ *I'm not very keen on that band.* Je n'aime pas trop cette bande.
♦ **to be keen on doing something** avoir très envie de faire quelque chose ◊ *I'm not very keen on going.* Je n'ai pas très envie d'y aller.

to **keep** VERB
① garder (*retain*) ◊ *You can keep it.* Tu peux le garder.
② rester (*remain*) ◊ *Keep still!* Reste tranquille!
♦ **Keep quiet!** Tais-toi!
♦ **I keep forgetting my keys.** J'oublie tout le temps mes clés.
♦ **to keep on doing something (1)** (*continue*) continuer à faire quelque chose ◊ *He kept on reading.* Il a continué à lire.
♦ **to keep on doing something (2)** (*repeatedly*) ne pas arrêter de faire quelque chose ◊ *The car keeps on breaking down.* La voiture n'arrête pas de tomber en panne.
♦ **"keep out"** « défense d'entrer »

to **keep up** VERB
suivre (*someone*) ◊ *She walks so fast I can't keep up.* Elle marche tellement vite que je n'arrive pas à la suivre. ◊ *I can't keep up with the rest of the class.* Je n'arrive pas à suivre le reste de la classe.
♦ **You should keep up your guitar lessons.** Tu devrais continuer tes cours de guitare.
♦ **Keep it up!** Continue!

kennel NOUN
la niche

kept VERB *see* **keep**

kerosene NOUN
le pétrole

ketchup NOUN
le ketchup

kettle NOUN
la bouilloire

key NOUN
① la clé
♦ **key word** le mot clé
♦ **key card** la carte magnétique
② la touche (*on keyboard*)
③ le ton (*music*) ◊ *to change key* changer de ton
♦ **in the key of C** en do
♦ **to sing off key** chanter faux
♦ **key signature** l'armature FEM

keyboard NOUN
le clavier ◊ *The musician on keyboards is...* Le musicien aux claviers est... ◊ *a computer keyboard* un clavier d'ordinateur

keychain NOUN
le porte-clés

to **key in** VERB
entrer ◊ *to key in data* entrer des données ◊ *Key in your password.* Entre ton mot de passe.

keypad NOUN
le pavé numérique

kick NOUN

| *see also* **kick** VERB |

le coup de pied

to **kick** VERB

| *see also* **kick** NOUN |

♦ **to kick somebody** donner un coup de pied à quelqu'un ◊ *He kicked me.* Il m'a donné un coup de pied. ◊ *She kicked the ball hard.* Elle a donné un bon coup de pied dans le ballon.
♦ **to kick off** (*football, soccer*) donner le coup d'envoi

kick-off NOUN
le coup d'envoi ◊ *The kick-off is at 10 o'clock.* Le coup d'envoi sera donné à dix heures.

kid NOUN

| *see also* **kid** VERB |

le/la jeune (*child*)

to **kid** VERB

| *see also* **kid** NOUN |

plaisanter ◊ *I'm just kidding.* Je plaisante.

♦ **You're kidding!** Sans blague!

to **kidnap** VERB
kidnapper

kidnapper NOUN
le kidnappeur
la kidnappeuse

kidnapping NOUN
l' enlèvement MASC

kidney NOUN
① le rein (*human*) ◊ *He's got kidney trouble.* Il a des problèmes de reins.
② le rognon (*to eat*) ◊ *I don't like kidneys.* Je n'aime pas les rognons.

to **kill** VERB
tuer ◊ *She was killed in a car accident.* Elle a été tuée dans un accident de voiture.
♦ **Luckily, nobody was killed.** Il n'y a heureusement pas eu de victimes.
♦ **Six people were killed in the accident.** L'accident a fait six morts.
♦ **to kill oneself** se suicider

killer NOUN
(*murderer*)
le meurtrier
la meurtrière
♦ **Meningitis can be a killer.** La méningite peut être mortelle.
♦ **That math test was a killer.** Ce test de maths était tuant.
♦ **killer whale** l'épaulard MASC

kiln NOUN
le four à céramique

kilo NOUN
le kilo ◊ *2 dollars a kilo* deux dollars le kilo

kilometre NOUN
le kilomètre

kilt NOUN
le kilt

kind ADJECTIVE

see also **kind** NOUN

gentil MASC
gentille FEM
♦ **to be kind to somebody** être gentil avec quelqu'un
♦ **Thank you for being so kind.** Merci pour votre gentillesse.

kind NOUN

see also **kind** ADJECTIVE

la sorte ◊ *It's a kind of sausage.* C'est une sorte de saucisse.

kindergarten NOUN
la maternelle

kindly ADVERB
gentiment ◊ *"Don't worry," she said kindly.* « Ne t'en fais pas », m'a-t-elle dit gentiment.

♦ **Kindly refrain from smoking.** Veuillez vous abstenir de fumer.

kindness NOUN
la gentillesse

king NOUN
le roi

kingdom NOUN
le royaume

kiosk NOUN
le kiosque

kipper NOUN
le hareng fumé

kiss NOUN

see also **kiss** VERB

le baiser ◊ *a passionate kiss* un baiser passionné

to **kiss** VERB

see also **kiss** NOUN

① embrasser ◊ *He kissed her passionately.* Il l'a embrassée passionnément.
② s'embrasser ◊ *They kissed.* Ils se sont embrassés.

kit NOUN
la trousse ◊ *a tool kit* une trousse à outils ◊ *a first aid kit* une trousse de secours ◊ *a tire repair kit* une trousse de réparations
♦ **a sewing kit** un nécessaire à couture

kitchen NOUN
la cuisine
♦ **a kitchen knife** un couteau de cuisine

kite NOUN
le cerf-volant
(PL les cerfs-volants)

kitten NOUN
le chaton

knapsack NOUN
le sac à dos

knee NOUN
le genou
(PL les genoux)
♦ **He was on his knees.** Il était à genoux.

to **kneel (down)** VERB
s'agenouiller

knew VERB see **know**

knife NOUN
le couteau
(PL les couteaux)
♦ **a kitchen knife** un couteau de cuisine
♦ **a hunting knife** un couteau de chasse

to **knit** VERB
tricoter

knitting NOUN
le tricot ◊ *I like knitting.* J'aime faire

K

☞

du tricot.

knives PL NOUN *see* **knife**

knob NOUN
le <u>bouton</u> (*on door, radio, TV, radiator*)

to **knock** VERB

> *see also* **knock** NOUN

<u>frapper</u> ◊ *Someone's knocking at the door.* Quelqu'un frappe à la porte.
♦ **to knock somebody down** renverser quelqu'un
♦ **to knock something over** renverser quelque chose ◊ *She knocked over a glass.* Elle a renversé un verre.
♦ **to knock somebody out** (*stun*) assommer ◊ *They knocked out the watchman.* Ils ont assommé le gardien.

knock NOUN

> *see also* **knock** VERB

le <u>coup</u>

knot NOUN
le <u>nœud</u>
♦ **to tie a knot in something** faire un nœud à quelque chose

to **know** VERB

> *Use* **savoir** *for knowing facts,* **connaître** *for knowing people and places.*

① <u>savoir</u> ◊ *"It's a long way." "Yes, I know."* « C'est loin. » « Oui, je sais. »
◊ *I don't know.* Je ne sais pas. ◊ *I don't know what to do.* Je ne sais pas quoi faire. ◊ *I don't know how to do it.* Je ne sais pas comment faire.
② <u>connaître</u> ◊ *I know her.* Je la connais. ◊ *I know Halifax well.* Je connais bien Halifax.
♦ **I don't know any German.** Je ne parle pas du tout allemand.
♦ **to know that...** savoir que... ◊ *I know*

that you like chocolate. Je sais que tu aimes le chocolat. ◊ *I didn't know that your dad was a policeman.* Je ne savais pas que ton père était policier.
♦ **to know about something (1)** (*be aware of*) être au courant de quelque chose ◊ *Do you know about the meeting this afternoon?* Tu es au courant de la réunion de cet après-midi?
♦ **to know about something (2)** (*be knowledgeable about*) s'y connaître en quelque chose ◊ *She knows a lot about cars.* Elle s'y connaît en voitures. ◊ *I don't know much about computers.* Je ne m'y connais pas bien en informatique.
♦ **to know how to do something** savoir faire quelque chose ◊ *He knows how to swim.* Il sait nager.
♦ **to get to know somebody** apprendre à connaître quelqu'un
♦ **I'll let you know tomorrow.** Je te le ferai savoir demain.
♦ **Let me know if you need any help.** Si tu as besoin d'aide, dis-le moi.
♦ **How should I know?** (*I don't know!*) Comment veux-tu que je le sache?
♦ **You never know!** On ne sait jamais!

know-how NOUN
le <u>savoir-faire</u>

know-it-all NOUN
le/la <u>je-sais-tout</u> ◊ *He's such a know-it-all!* C'est Monsieur je-sais-tout!

knowledge NOUN
la <u>connaissance</u>

knowledgeable ADJECTIVE
♦ **to be knowledgeable about something** s'y connaître en quelque chose ◊ *She's very knowledgeable about computers.* Elle s'y connaît bien en informatique.

known VERB *see* **know**

L

lab NOUN (= *laboratory*)
le labo
♦ **a lab technician** un laborantin

label NOUN
l' étiquette FEM

laboratory NOUN
le laboratoire

labour NOUN
♦ **to be in labour** être en train d'accoucher
♦ **the labour market** le marché du travail
♦ **a labour union** un syndicat

Labour Day NOUN
la fête du Travail

labourer NOUN
le/la manœuvre
♦ **a farm labourer** un ouvrier agricole

Labrador NOUN
le Labrador

lace NOUN
① le lacet (*of shoe*)
② la dentelle ◊ *a lace collar* un col en dentelle

lack NOUN
le manque ◊ *He got the job despite his lack of experience.* Il a obtenu le poste en dépit de son manque d'expérience.
♦ **There was no lack of volunteers.** Les volontaires ne manquaient pas.

lacquer NOUN
la laque

✹ **lacrosse** NOUN
la crosse ◊ *a lacrosse stick* une crosse

ladder NOUN
l' échelle FEM

lady NOUN
la dame
♦ **a young lady** une jeune fille
♦ **Ladies and gentlemen...** Mesdames, Messieurs...
♦ **the ladies' room** les toilettes pour dames FEM

ladybug NOUN
la coccinelle

to **lag behind** VERB
rester en arrière

laid VERB *see* **lay**

laid-back ADJECTIVE
relax ◊ *Ma mère est très relax.* My

mom is very laid-back.

lain VERB *see* **lie**

lake NOUN
le lac
♦ **Lake Superior** le lac Supérieur
♦ **Lake Erie** le lac Érié

lamb NOUN
l' agneau MASC
(PL les agneaux)
♦ **a lamb chop** une côtelette d'agneau

lame ADJECTIVE
♦ **to be lame** boîter ◊ *My pony is lame.* Mon poney boîte.
♦ **a lame excuse** une piètre excuse

lamp NOUN
la lampe

lampshade NOUN
l' abat-jour MASC
(PL les abat-jour)

land NOUN
see also **land** VERB
① la terre
♦ **a piece of land** un terrain
② le pays (*country*)

to **land** VERB
see also **land** NOUN
atterrir (*plane, passenger*)

landfill site NOUN
le site d'enfouissement

landing NOUN
① l' atterrissage MASC (*of plane*)
② le palier (*of staircase*)

landlady NOUN
la propriétaire

landlord NOUN
le propriétaire

landmark NOUN
le point de repère (*for finding your way*)
♦ **The CN Tower is one of Toronto's most famous landmarks.** La tour CN est l'un des sites les plus célèbres du paysage torontois.

landowner NOUN
le propriétaire terrien

landscape NOUN
le paysage

landslide NOUN
le glissement de terrain

lane NOUN
① l' entrée FEM (*leading to country*)

☞

house)

② la <u>voie</u> (*on highway*)

③ la <u>ruelle</u> (*small road in city*)

language NOUN

① la <u>langue</u> ◊ *French isn't a difficult language.* Le français n'est pas une langue difficile.

② le <u>langage</u> ◊ *the origin of language* l'origine du langage ◊ *Watch your language!* Surveille ton langage!
◊ *body language* le langage corporel

♦ **to use bad language** dire des grossièretés

lantern NOUN
la <u>lanterne</u>

lap NOUN

① le <u>tour de piste</u> (*sport*) ◊ *I ran 10 laps.* J'ai fait dix tours de piste en courant.

② la <u>longueur</u> (*pool*) ◊ *I swam 30 laps.* J'ai fait trente longueurs.

♦ **on my lap** sur mes genoux

laptop NOUN (*computer*)
le <u>portable</u>

large ADJECTIVE

① <u>grand</u> ◊ *a large house* une grande maison

② (*person, animal*)
<u>gros</u> MASC
<u>grosse</u> FEM ◊ *a large dog* un gros chien

largely ADVERB
<u>en grande partie</u> ◊ *It's largely the fault of the government.* C'est en grande partie la faute du gouvernement.

laryngitis NOUN
la <u>laryngite</u>

lasagna NOUN
la <u>lasagne</u>

laser NOUN
le <u>laser</u>

♦ **a laser printer** une imprimante laser

last ADJECTIVE, ADVERB

see also **last** VERB

① <u>dernier</u> MASC
<u>dernière</u> FEM ◊ *last Friday* vendredi dernier ◊ *last week* la semaine dernière ◊ *last summer* l'été dernier

② <u>en dernier</u> ◊ *She arrived last.* Elle est arrivée en dernier.

♦ **"I lost my wallet." "When did you see it last?"** « J'ai perdu mon portefeuille. » « Quand est-ce que tu l'as vu pour la dernière fois? »

♦ **When I last saw him, he was wearing a blue shirt.** La dernière fois que je l'ai vu, il portait une chemise bleue.

♦ **the last time** la dernière fois ◊ *the last time I saw her* la dernière fois que

je l'ai vue ◊ *That's the last time I take your advice!* C'est la dernière fois que je suis tes conseils!

♦ **last night (1)** (*evening*) hier soir ◊ *I got home at midnight last night.* Je suis rentré à minuit hier soir.

♦ **last night (2)** (*sleeping hours*) la nuit dernière ◊ *I couldn't sleep last night.* J'ai eu du mal à dormir la nuit dernière.

♦ **at last** enfin

to **last** VERB

see also **last** ADJECTIVE

<u>durer</u> ◊ *The concert lasts two hours.* Le concert dure deux heures.

lastly ADVERB
<u>finalement</u> ◊ *Lastly, what time do you arrive?* Finalement, à quelle heure arrives-tu?

late ADJECTIVE, ADVERB

① <u>en retard</u> ◊ *Hurry up or you'll be late!* Dépêche-toi, sinon tu vas être en retard! ◊ *I'm often late for school.* J'arrive souvent en retard à l'école.

♦ **to arrive late** arriver en retard ◊ *She arrived late.* Elle est arrivée en retard.

② <u>tard</u> ◊ *I went to bed late.* Je me suis couché tard.

♦ **in the late afternoon** en fin d'après-midi

♦ **in late May** fin mai

lately ADVERB
<u>ces derniers temps</u> ◊ *I haven't seen him lately.* Je ne l'ai pas vu ces derniers temps.

later ADVERB
<u>plus tard</u> ◊ *I'll do it later.* Je ferai ça plus tard.

♦ **See you later!** À tout à l'heure!

latest ADJECTIVE
<u>dernier</u> MASC
<u>dernière</u> FEM ◊ *their latest album* leur dernier album

♦ **at the latest** au plus tard ◊ *by 10 o'clock at the latest* à dix heures au plus tard

latter NOUN
le <u>second</u>
la <u>seconde</u>

♦ **the former..., the latter...** le premier..., le second... ◊ *The former lives in Saskatchewan, the latter in New Brunswick.* Le premier habite en Saskatchewan, le second au Nouveau-Brunswick.

♦ **The latter is the more expensive of the two systems.** Ce dernier système est le plus coûteux des deux.

laugh NOUN

see also **laugh** VERB

le <u>rire</u>
♦ **It was a good laugh.** (*it was funny*)
C'était bien amusant.

to **laugh** VERB

> *see also* **laugh** NOUN

<u>rire</u>
♦ **to laugh at something** (*make fun of*)
se moquer de quelque chose ◊ *They
laughed at her.* Ils se sont moqués
d'elle.

to **launch** VERB
<u>lancer</u> (*product, rocket, boat*)
◊ *They're going to launch a new
model.* Ils vont lancer un nouveau
modèle.

laundromat™ NOUN
le <u>lavoir</u>

laundry NOUN
1 le <u>linge</u> (*clothes*)
2 le <u>lavage</u> (*task*) ◊ *to do the laundry*
faire le lavage
3 le <u>lavoir</u> (*public, with machines*)
◊ *Does this campground have a
laundry?* Ce terrain de camping a un
lavoir?
♦ **laundry room**
la salle de lavage
♦ **coin laundry** le lavoir

Laurentians PL NOUN
les <u>Laurentides</u> FEM ◊ *We went
camping in the Laurentians.* Nous
avons fait du camping dans les
Laurentides.

law NOUN
1 la <u>loi</u> ◊ *The laws are very strict.* Les
lois sont très sévères.
♦ **It's against the law.** C'est illégal.
2 le <u>droit</u> (*subject*) ◊ *My brother
is studying law.* Mon frère fait des
études de droit.
♦ **law and order** l'ordre public MASC
♦ **law school** la faculté de droit

lawn NOUN
la <u>pelouse</u>

lawnmower NOUN
la <u>tondeuse à gazon</u>

lawyer NOUN
l' <u>avocat</u> MASC
l' <u>avocate</u> FEM ◊ *My mother's a
lawyer.* Ma mère est avocate.

to **lay** VERB

> **lay** *is also a form of* **lie** VERB.

<u>mettre</u> ◊ *He laid the baby in her crib.*
Il a mis le bébé dans son lit.

to **lay off** VERB
<u>mettre à pied</u> ◊ *My father has been
laid off.* Mon père a été mis à pied.

layer NOUN

la <u>couche</u> ◊ *the ozone layer* la couche
d'ozone

layout NOUN
1 la <u>mise en page</u> (*publishing*)
2 la <u>disposition</u> (*of house, buildings*)
◊ *It took me some time to get familiar
with the layout of the school.* J'ai mis
un certain temps à me familiariser
avec la disposition de l'école.

lazy ADJECTIVE
<u>paresseux</u> MASC
<u>paresseuse</u> FEM

lead NOUN

> *This word has two pronunciations.
> Make sure you choose the right
> translation.*

> *see also* **lead** VERB

le <u>plomb</u> (*metal*)
♦ **to be in the lead** être en tête ◊ *Our
team is in the lead.* Notre équipe est
en tête.
♦ **to have a two-point lead** avoir deux
points d'avance
♦ **to take the lead (1)** (*sports*) prendre
la tête
♦ **to take the lead (2)** (*act first*) prendre
l'initiative

to **lead** VERB

> *see also* **lead** NOUN

<u>mener</u> ◊ *the street that leads to the
arena* la rue qui mène à l'aréna
♦ **to lead the way** montrer le chemin
♦ **to lead somebody away** emmener
quelqu'un ◊ *The police led the man
away.* La police a emmené l'homme.

leader NOUN
1 le/la <u>chef</u> (*of expedition, gang,
political party*) ◊ *She's the party
leader.* C'est la chef du parti politique.
2 (*of organization, company*)
le <u>dirigeant</u>
la <u>dirigeante</u>

lead singer NOUN
le <u>chanteur principal</u>
la <u>chanteuse principale</u>

leaf NOUN
la <u>feuille</u>

leaflet NOUN
la <u>brochure</u>

league NOUN
la <u>ligue</u> ◊ *They are at the top of the
league.* Ils sont en tête de la ligue.
♦ **a minor league** une ligue mineure
♦ **a major league** une ligue majeure

leak NOUN

> *see also* **leak** VERB

la <u>fuite</u> ◊ *a gas leak* une fuite de gaz

L

to **leak** VERB

> see also **leak** NOUN

fuir (*pipe, water, gas*)

lean ADJECTIVE

> see also **lean** VERB

maigre ◊ *lean meat* la viande maigre

to **lean** VERB

> see also **lean** ADJECTIVE

1 s'appuyer (*support oneself*) ◊ *He leaned against the wall.* Il s'est appuyé contre le mur.
2 appuyer (*support an object*) ◊ *She leaned her bike against the railing.* Elle a appuyé son vélo contre la rampe.
♦ **The ladder was leaning against the wall.** L'échelle était appuyée contre le mur.
3 se pencher (*bend*) ◊ *Don't lean over too far.* Ne te penche pas trop. ◊ *She leaned out of the window.* Elle s'est penchée par la fenêtre. ◊ *to lean forward* se pencher en avant

to **leap** VERB

sauter ◊ *They leapt over the stream.* Ils ont sauté pour traverser la rivière.
♦ **He leapt out of his chair when his team scored.** Il s'est levé d'un bond lorsque son équipe a marqué.

leap year NOUN

l' année bissextile FEM

to **learn** VERB

apprendre ◊ *I'm learning to ski.* J'apprends à skier.

learner NOUN

♦ **She's a quick learner.** Elle apprend vite.
♦ **second language learners** ceux qui apprennent une langue seconde

learnt VERB *see* **learn**

leash NOUN

la laisse ◊ *Keep your dog on a leash.* Tenez votre chien en laisse.

least ADVERB, ADJECTIVE, PRONOUN

♦ **the least (1)** (*followed by noun*) le moins de ◊ *It takes the least time.* C'est ce qui prend le moins de temps.
♦ **the least (2)** (*after a verb*) le moins ◊ *Music is the subject I like the least.* La musique est la matière que j'aime le moins.

> *When **least** is followed by an adjective, the translation depends on whether the noun referred to is masculine, feminine or plural.*

♦ **the least... (1)** le moins... ◊ *the least expensive hotel* l'hôtel le moins cher
♦ **the least... (2)** la moins... ◊ *the least*

expensive seat la place la moins chère
♦ **the least... (3)** les moins... ◊ *the least expensive hotels* les hôtels les moins chers ◊ *the least expensive seats* les places les moins chères
♦ **It's the least I can do.** C'est le moins que je puisse faire.
♦ **at least (1)** au moins ◊ *It'll cost at least $200.* Ça va coûter au moins deux cents dollars.
♦ **at least (2)** du moins ◊ *...but at least nobody was hurt.* ...mais du moins personne n'a été blessé. ◊ *"It's totally unfair" "at least, that's my opinion."* « C'est vraiment injuste » « du moins c'est ce que je pense. »

leather NOUN

le cuir ◊ *a black leather jacket* un manteau de cuir noir

leave NOUN

> see also **leave** VERB

1 le congé (*from job*) ◊ *sick leave* le congé de maladie ◊ *maternity leave* le congé de maternité
2 la permission (*from army*) ◊ *My brother is on leave for a week.* Mon frère est en permission pendant une semaine.

to **leave** VERB

> see also **leave** NOUN

1 laisser (*deliberately*) ◊ *Don't leave your camera in the car.* Ne laisse pas ton appareil-photo dans la voiture.
2 oublier (*by mistake*) ◊ *I left my book at home.* J'ai oublié mon livre à la maison. ◊ *Make sure you haven't left anything behind.* Vérifiez bien que vous n'avez rien oublié.
3 partir (*go*) ◊ *The bus leaves at 8.* L'autobus part à huit heures. ◊ *She just left.* Elle vient de partir.
4 quitter (*go away from*) ◊ *We leave London at six o'clock.* Nous quittons London à six heures. ◊ *My sister left home last year.* Ma sœur a quitté la maison l'an dernier.
♦ **to leave somebody alone** laisser quelqu'un tranquille ◊ *Leave me alone!* Laisse-moi tranquille!

to **leave out** VERB

1 mettre à l'écart (*person*) ◊ *Not knowing the language, I felt really left out.* Comme je ne connaissais pas la langue, je me suis vraiment senti à l'écart.
2 omettre (*word, sentence*) ◊ *You left out a word there.* Tu as omis un mot là.

leaves PL NOUN *see* **leaf**

lecture NOUN

see also **lecture** VERB
[1] la conférence (*public*)
[2] (*at university*)
le cours magistral
(PL les cours magistraux)
[3] le sermon (*scolding*) ◊ *a lecture on table manners* un sermon sur les bonnes manières à table

*Be careful not to translate **lecture** by the French word **lecture**.*

to **lecture** VERB

see also **lecture** NOUN
[1] enseigner ◊ *He lectures at the technical college.* Il enseigne au collège technique.
[2] faire la morale ◊ *He's always lecturing us.* Il n'arrête pas de nous faire la morale.

led VERB *see* **lead**

leek NOUN
le poireau
(PL les poireaux)

left VERB *see* **leave**

left ADJECTIVE, ADVERB

see also **left** NOUN
[1] gauche ◊ *my left hand* ma main gauche ◊ *on the left side of the road* sur le côté gauche de la route
[2] à gauche ◊ *Turn left at the traffic lights.* Tournez à gauche aux prochains feux.
♦ **I have no money left.** Il ne me reste plus d'argent.

left NOUN

see also **left** ADJECTIVE
la gauche
♦ **on the left** à gauche ◊ *Our house is on the left.* Notre maison est à gauche.

left-hand ADJECTIVE
♦ **the left-hand side** la gauche ◊ *It's on the left-hand side.* C'est à gauche.

left-handed ADJECTIVE
gaucher MASC
gauchère FEM

leg NOUN
la jambe ◊ *She's broken her leg.* Elle s'est cassé la jambe.
♦ **a chicken leg** une cuisse de poulet
♦ **a leg of lamb** un gigot d'agneau

legal ADJECTIVE
[1] légal
(MASC PL légaux) ◊ *the legal driving age* l'âge légal pour conduire ◊ *Is it legal to copy this CD?* Est-il légal de faire une copie de ce CD?
[2] juridique ◊ *the legal system* le

système juridique ◊ *legal aid* l'aide juridique FEM ◊ *legal action* une poursuite juridique

legend NOUN
la légende

leggings NOUN
le collant SING

legible ADJECTIVE
lisible

❊ **Legislative Assembly** NOUN
l' Assemblée législative FEM

leisure NOUN
les loisirs MASC PL ◊ *What do you do in your leisure time?* Qu'est-ce que tu fais pendant tes loisirs?

leisure centre NOUN
le centre de loisirs

lemon NOUN
le citron

lemonade NOUN
la limonade

to **lend** VERB
prêter ◊ *I can lend you some money.* Je peux te prêter de l'argent.

length NOUN
la longueur
♦ **It's about a metre in length.** Ça fait environ un mètre de long.

lengthwise ADVERB
dans le sens de la longueur

lens NOUN
[1] la lentille cornéenne (*contact lens*)
[2] le verre (*of spectacles*)
[3] l' objectif MASC (*of camera*)

lent VERB *see* **lend**

lentil NOUN
la lentille

Leo NOUN
le Lion ◊ *I'm a Leo.* Je suis Lion.

leotard NOUN
le léotard

lesbian NOUN
la lesbienne

less PRONOUN, ADVERB, ADJECTIVE
[1] moins ◊ *He's less athletic than her.* Il est moins athlétique qu'elle. ◊ *A bit less, please.* Un peu moins, s'il vous plaît.
[2] moins de ◊ *I've got less time for hobbies now.* J'ai moins de temps pour les loisirs maintenant.
♦ **less than (1)** (*with amounts*) moins de ◊ *It's less than a kilometre from here.* C'est à moins d'un kilomètre d'ici. ◊ *It costs less than 100 dollars.* Ça coûte moins de cent dollars. ◊ *less than half* moins de la moitié

L

☞

less than (2) (*in comparisons*) moins que ◊ *He spent less than me.* Il a dépensé moins que moi. ◊ *I've got less than you.* J'en ai moins que toi. ◊ *It cost less than we thought.* Ça a coûté moins cher que nous ne le pensions.

lesson NOUN
1 la leçon ◊ *a French lesson* une leçon de français ◊ *"Lesson Sixteen"* (*in textbook*) "Leçon seize"
2 le cours ◊ *dancing lessons* des cours de danse ◊ *Each lesson lasts 40 minutes.* Chaque cours dure quarante minutes.

to **let** VERB
laisser (*allow*)
♦ **to let somebody do something** laisser quelqu'un faire quelque chose ◊ *Let me have a look.* Laisse-moi voir. ◊ *My parents won't let me stay out that late.* Mes parents ne me laissent pas sortir aussi tard.
♦ **to let somebody know** faire savoir à quelqu'un ◊ *I'll let you know as soon as possible.* Je vous le ferai savoir dès que possible.
♦ **to let down** décevoir ◊ *I won't let you down.* Je ne vous décevrai pas.
♦ **to let go** lâcher ◊ *Let me go!* Lâche-moi! ◊ *Let go of the rope.* Lâche la corde. ◊ *Let go!* Lâche prise!
♦ **to let in** laisser entrer ◊ *They wouldn't let me in because I was under 18.* Ils ne m'ont pas laissé entrer parce que j'avais moins de dix-huit ans.
♦ **to let out** laisser sortir ◊ *Don't let the cat out.* Ne laisse pas sortir le chat.
♦ **to let up** (*rain*) diminuer

*To make suggestions using **let's**, you can ask questions beginning with **si on**.*

◊ *Let's go to a movie!* Si on allait au cinéma?
♦ **Let's go!** Allons-y!

letter NOUN
la lettre

lettuce NOUN
la salade

leukemia NOUN
la leucémie

level ADJECTIVE

see also **level** NOUN

plan ◊ *A pool table must be perfectly level.* Une table de billard doit être parfaitement plane.

level NOUN

see also **level** ADJECTIVE

le niveau

(PL les niveaux) ◊ *The water level is rising.* Le niveau d'eau monte.

lever NOUN
le levier

liable ADJECTIVE
♦ **He's liable to lose his temper.** Il se met facilement en colère.
♦ **It's liable to snow tonight.** Il risque de neiger ce soir.

liar NOUN
le menteur
la menteuse

liberal ADJECTIVE
(*opinions*)
libéral
(MASC PL libéraux)

liberation NOUN
la libération

liberty NOUN
la liberté

Libra NOUN
la Balance ◊ *I'm a Libra.* Je suis Balance.

librarian NOUN
le/la bibliothécaire ◊ *She's a librarian.* Elle est bibliothécaire.

library NOUN
la bibliothèque

*Be careful not to translate **library** by librairie.*

licence NOUN
le permis
♦ **a driver's licence** un permis de conduire
♦ **fishing licence** le permis de pêche
♦ **licence plate** la plaque d'immatriculation
♦ **licence number** le numéro d'immatriculation

to **lick** VERB
lécher

licorice NOUN
la réglisse

lid NOUN
le couvercle

to **lie** VERB

see also **lie** NOUN

mentir (*not tell the truth*) ◊ *I know she's lying.* Je sais qu'elle ment.
♦ **to lie down** s'allonger
♦ **to be lying down** être allongé
♦ **He was lying on the sofa.** Il était allongé sur le sofa. ◊ *When I'm on holiday I lie on the beach all day.* Quand je suis en vacances, je reste allongé sur la plage toute la journée.

lie NOUN

see also **lie** VERB

le mensonge
♦ **to tell a lie** mentir
♦ **That's a lie!** Ce n'est pas vrai!

✵ **lieutenant-governor** NOUN
le lieutenant-gouverneur
la lieutenante-gouverneure

life NOUN
la vie

lifeboat NOUN
le canot de sauvetage

lifeguard NOUN
le sauveteur
la sauveteure

life jacket NOUN
le gilet de sauvetage

lifesaving NOUN
le sauvetage ◊ *I've done a course
in lifesaving.* J'ai pris des cours de
sauvetage.

lifestyle NOUN
le style de vie

to **lift** VERB

see also **lift** NOUN

soulever ◊ *It's too heavy. I can't lift
it.* C'est trop lourd. Je ne peux pas le
soulever.

lift NOUN

see also **lift** VERB

♦ **He gave me a lift to the movie theatre.**
Il m'a emmené au cinéma en voiture.
♦ **Would you like a lift?** Est-ce que je
peux vous déposer quelque part?

light ADJECTIVE

see also **light** NOUN, VERB

[1] (*not heavy*)
léger MASC
légère FEM ◊ *a light jacket* un veston
léger ◊ *a light meal* un repas léger
[2] clair (*colour*) ◊ *a light blue sweater*
un chandail bleu clair

light NOUN

see also **light** ADJECTIVE, VERB

[1] la lumière ◊ *to switch on the light*
allumer la lumière ◊ *to switch off the
light* éteindre la lumière
[2] la lampe ◊ *There's a light by my
bed.* Il y a une lampe près de mon lit.
♦ **the traffic lights** les feux MASC
♦ **Have you got a light?** (*match, lighter*)
Avez-vous du feu?

to **light** VERB

see also **light** ADJECTIVE, NOUN

allumer (*candle, fire*)

light bulb NOUN
l' ampoule FEM

lighter NOUN
le briquet

lighthouse NOUN
le phare

lightning NOUN
les éclairs MASC PL
♦ **a flash of lightning** un éclair

to **like** VERB

see also **like** PREPOSITION

[1] aimer ◊ *I don't like mustard.* Je
n'aime pas la moutarde. ◊ *I like
riding.* J'aime monter à cheval.

*Note that **aimer** also means to love,
so make sure you use **aimer bien** for
just liking somebody.*

[2] aimer bien ◊ *I like him, but I don't
want to go out with him.* Je l'aime
bien, mais je ne veux pas sortir avec
lui.
♦ **I'd like...** Je voudrais... ◊ *I'd like an
orange juice, please.* Je voudrais un
jus d'orange, s'il vous plaît. ◊ *Would
you like some coffee?* Voulez-vous du
café?
♦ **I'd like to...** J'aimerais... ◊ *I'd like to
go to Russia one day.* J'aimerais aller
en Russie un jour. ◊ *I'd like to wash
my hands.* J'aimerais me laver les
mains.
♦ **Would you like to go for a walk?** Tu
veux aller faire une promenade?
♦ **...if you like** ...si tu veux

like PREPOSITION

see also **like** VERB

comme ◊ *It's fine like that.* C'est bien
comme ça. ◊ *Do it like this.* Fais-le
comme ça. ◊ *a city like St. John's*
une ville comme St. John's ◊ *It's a bit
like salmon.* C'est un peu comme du
saumon.
♦ **What's the weather like?** Quel temps
fait-il?
♦ **to look like somebody** ressembler à
quelqu'un ◊ *You look like my brother.*
Tu ressembles à mon frère.

likely ADJECTIVE
probable ◊ *That's not very likely.*
C'est peu probable.
♦ **She's likely to come.** Elle viendra
probablement.
♦ **She's not likely to come.** Elle ne
viendra probablement pas.

lime NOUN
la lime (*fruit*)

limit NOUN
la limite ◊ *The speed limit is 100
km/h.* La vitesse limite est de cent
kilomètres à l'heure.

limousine NOUN

L

☞

la limousine

to **limp** VERB
boiter

line NOUN
1 la ligne ◊ *a straight line* une ligne droite ◊ *a bus line* une ligne d'autobus ◊ *There's static on the line.* Il y a de la friture sur la ligne.
2 le trait (*to divide, cancel*) ◊ *Draw a line under each answer.* Tirez un trait sous chaque réponse.
3 la queue (*lineup*) ◊ *We had to stand in line.* Nous avons dû faire la queue.
4 la rangée ◊ *a line of trees* une rangée d'arbres
♦ **Hold the line, please.** Ne quittez pas.
♦ **online** (*computing*) en ligne

linen NOUN
le lin ◊ *a linen jacket* un veston en lin

linguist NOUN
♦ **to be a good linguist** être doué pour les langues ◊ *She's a good linguist.* Elle est douée pour les langues.

lining NOUN
la doublure (*of jacket, skirt etc*)

link NOUN
see also **link** VERB
1 le rapport ◊ *the link between smoking and cancer* le rapport entre le tabagisme et le cancer
2 le lien (*computing*)

to **link** VERB
see also **link** NOUN
relier

linoleum NOUN
le linoléum

lion NOUN
le lion

lioness NOUN
la lionne

lip NOUN
la lèvre

to **lip-read** VERB
lire sur les lèvres

lip salve NOUN
la pommade pour les lèvres

lipstick NOUN
le rouge à lèvres

liquid ADJECTIVE
see also **liquid** NOUN
liquide

liquid NOUN
see also **liquid** ADJECTIVE
le liquide

list NOUN
see also **list** VERB
la liste

to **list** VERB
see also **list** NOUN
faire une liste de ◊ *List your hobbies.* Fais une liste de tes passe-temps.

to **listen** VERB
écouter ◊ *Listen to this!* Écoutez ceci! ◊ *Listen to me!* Écoutez-moi!

listener NOUN
l' auditeur MASC
l' auditrice FEM

lit VERB *see* **light**

literally ADVERB
vraiment (*completely*) ◊ *It was literally impossible to find a seat.* Il était vraiment impossible de trouver une place.
♦ **to translate literally** faire une traduction littérale

literature NOUN
la littérature ◊ *Canadian literature* la littérature canadienne

litre NOUN
le litre

litter NOUN
les ordures FEM PL

little ADJECTIVE
petit ◊ *a little boy* un petit garçon
♦ **a little** un peu ◊ *"How much would you like?" "Just a little."* « Combien en voulez-vous? » « Juste un peu. »
♦ **very little** très peu ◊ *We have very little time.* Nous avons très peu de temps.
♦ **little by little** petit à petit

live ADJECTIVE
see also **live** VERB
1 vivant (*animal*)
2 en direct (*broadcast*)
♦ **There's live music on Fridays.** Il y a des musiciens qui jouent le vendredi.

to **live** VERB
see also **live** ADJECTIVE
1 vivre ◊ *I live with my grandmother.* Je vis avec ma grand-mère.
♦ **to live on something** vivre de quelque chose ◊ *He lives on a small salary.* Il vit d'un modeste salaire.
2 habiter (*reside*) ◊ *Where do you live?* Où est-ce que tu habites? ◊ *I live in Moncton.* J'habite à Moncton.
♦ **to live together (1)** partager un appartement (*as roommates*) ◊ *She's living with two other students.* Elle partage un appartement avec deux autres étudiantes.
♦ **to live together (2)** vivre ensemble

◊ *My parents aren't living together any more.* Mes parents ne vivent plus ensemble.
♦ **They're not married, they're living together.** Ils ne sont pas mariés, ils vivent en union libre.

lively ADJECTIVE
animé ◊ *It was a lively party.* C'était une soirée animée.
♦ **He has a lively personality.** Il est plein de vitalité.

liver NOUN
le foie

lives PL NOUN
les vies FEM

livestock NOUN
les animaux d'élevage MASC

living NOUN
♦ **to make a living** gagner sa vie
♦ **What does she do for a living?** Qu'est-ce qu'elle fait dans la vie?

living room NOUN
la salle de séjour

lizard NOUN
le lézard

load NOUN

see also **load** VERB

♦ **loads of** un tas de ◊ *loads of money* un tas d'argent
♦ **That's a load of rubbish!** Tu ne dis que des niaiseries!

to **load** VERB

see also **load** NOUN

charger ◊ *a trolley loaded with luggage* un chariot chargé de bagages

loaf NOUN

see also **loaf** VERB

le pain
♦ **a loaf of bread** un pain

to **loaf** VERB

see also **loaf** NOUN

traîner ◊ *Are you going to loaf around all day?* Tu vas traîner toute la journée?

loan NOUN

see also **loan** VERB

le prêt ◊ *a bank loan* un prêt bancaire ◊ *to pay back a loan* payer un prêt

to **loan** VERB

see also **loan** NOUN

prêter

to **loathe** VERB
détester ◊ *I loathe country music.* Je déteste la musique country.

loaves PL NOUN *see* **loaf**

lobby NOUN
le hall ◊ *in the hotel lobby* dans le hall de l'hôtel

lobster NOUN
le homard

local ADJECTIVE
local
(MASC PL locaux) ◊ *the local paper* le journal local ◊ *a local call* un appel local

location NOUN
l' endroit MASC ◊ *a hotel set in a beautiful location* un hôtel situé dans un endroit magnifique

> Be careful not to translate **location** by the French word **location**.

lock NOUN

see also **lock** VERB

la serrure ◊ *The lock is broken.* La serrure est cassée.

to **lock** VERB

see also **lock** NOUN

fermer à clé ◊ *Make sure you lock your door.* N'oubliez pas de fermer votre porte à clé.

to **lock out** VERB
♦ **The door slammed and I was locked out.** La porte a claqué et je me suis retrouvé à la porte.

locker NOUN
le casier
♦ **the locker room** le vestiaire
♦ **storage lockers** (*airport, mall*) la consigne automatique

locket NOUN
le médaillon

loft NOUN
le grenier

log NOUN
la bûche (*of wood*)

to **log in** VERB
se connecter

to **log off** NOUN
se déconnecter

to **log on** VERB
se connecter

to **log out** VERB
se déconnecter

logical ADJECTIVE
logique

login NOUN
1 l' ouverture de session FEM (*action*)
2 le nom d'utilisateur (*ID*)

logo NOUN
le logo

L

lollipop NOUN
🐾 le suçon

loneliness NOUN
la solitude

lonely ADJECTIVE
seul
♦ **to feel lonely** se sentir seul ◊ *He feels a bit lonely.* Il se sent un peu seul.

lonesome ADJECTIVE
♦ **to feel lonesome** se sentir seul

long ADJECTIVE, ADVERB

see also **long** VERB

long MASC
longue FEM ◊ *She has long hair.* Elle a les cheveux longs. ◊ *The room is 6 metres long.* La pièce fait six mètres de long.
♦ **how long?** (*time*) combien de temps? ◊ *How long did you stay there?* Combien de temps êtes-vous resté là-bas? ◊ *How long have you been here?* Depuis combien de temps êtes-vous ici? ◊ *How long is the flight?* Combien de temps dure le vol?
♦ **I've been waiting a long time.** J'attends depuis longtemps.
♦ **It takes a long time.** Ça prend du temps.
♦ **as long as** si ◊ *I'll come as long as it's not too expensive.* Je viendrai si ce n'est pas trop cher.

to **long** VERB

see also **long** ADJECTIVE

♦ **to long to do something** attendre avec impatience de faire quelque chose
♦ **I'm longing to see my dad again.** J'attends avec impatience de revoir mon père.

long-distance ADJECTIVE
♦ **a long-distance call** un appel interurbain
♦ **to call long distance** faire un appel interurbain

longer ADVERB

see also **long** ADJECTIVE

♦ **They're no longer going out together.** Ils ne sortent plus ensemble.
♦ **I can't stand it any longer.** Je ne peux plus le supporter.

long jump NOUN
le saut en longueur

look NOUN

see also **look** VERB

♦ **to take a look** regarder ◊ *Take a look at this!* Regardez ceci!
♦ **I don't like the look of it.** Ça ne me dit rien qui vaille.

to **look** VERB

see also **look** NOUN

1 regarder ◊ *Look!* Regardez!
♦ **to look at something** regarder quelque chose ◊ *Look at this picture.* Regardez cette image.
2 avoir l'air (*seem*) ◊ *She looks surprised.* Elle a l'air surprise. ◊ *That cake looks delicious.* Ce gâteau a l'air délicieux. ◊ *It looks fine.* Ça a l'air bien.
♦ **to look like somebody** ressembler à quelqu'un ◊ *He looks like his brother.* Il ressemble à son frère.
♦ **What does he look like?** Comment est-il physiquement?
♦ **Look out!** Attention!
♦ **to look after** s'occuper de ◊ *I look after my little sister.* Je m'occupe de ma petite sœur.
♦ **to look for** chercher ◊ *I'm looking for my passport.* Je cherche mon passeport.
♦ **to look forward to something** attendre quelque chose avec impatience ◊ *I'm looking forward to the holidays.* J'attends les vacances avec impatience.
♦ **Looking forward to hearing from you...** J'espère avoir bientôt de tes nouvelles...
♦ **to look around (1)** (*look behind*) se retourner ◊ *I shouted and he looked around.* J'ai crié et il s'est retourné.
♦ **to look around (2)** (*have a look*) jeter un coup d'œil ◊ *I'm just looking around.* Je jette simplement un coup d'œil.
♦ **I like looking around the stores.** J'aime faire les magasins.
♦ **to look up** (*word, name*) chercher ◊ *If you don't know a word, look it up in the dictionary.* Si vous ne connaissez pas un mot, cherchez-le dans le dictionnaire.

lookout NOUN
le belvédère (*scenic*)

loon NOUN
le huard

🐾 **loonie** NOUN
le huard

loop NOUN
la boucle ◊ *Make a loop in the ribbon.* Fais une boucle au ruban.
♦ **to be in the loop** être au courant ◊ *Keep me in the loop.* Tiens-moi au courant.

loose ADJECTIVE
ample (*clothes*)
♦ **loose change** la petite monnaie
♦ **a loose sheet of paper** une feuille

volante
♦ **A tiger got loose.** Un tigre s'est
échappé.
♦ **This screw is loose.** Cette vis s'est
desserrée.

lopsided ADJECTIVE
de travers ◊ *Your sculpture looks a
bit lopsided.* Ta sculpture semble un
peu de travers.

to **lose** VERB
perdre ◊ *I lost my purse.* J'ai perdu
mon sac à main.
♦ **to get lost** se perdre ◊ *I was afraid
of getting lost.* J'avais peur de me
perdre.

loser NOUN
le perdant
la perdante
♦ **to be a bad loser** être mauvais
perdant

loss NOUN
la perte

lost VERB *see* **lose**

lost ADJECTIVE
perdu

lost-and-found NOUN
les objets perdus MASC

lot NOUN
♦ **a lot** beaucoup
♦ **a lot of** beaucoup de ◊ *a lot of work*
beaucoup de travail ◊ *We saw a lot
of interesting things.* Nous avons vu
beaucoup de choses intéressantes.
♦ **lots of** un tas de (*informal*) ◊ *She has
lots of money.* Elle a un tas d'argent.
◊ *He has lots of friends.* Il a un tas
d'amis.
♦ **"What did you do on the weekend?"
"Not a lot."** « Qu'as-tu fait en fin de
semaine ? » « Pas grand-chose. »
♦ **"Do you like baseball?" "Not a
lot."** « Tu aimes le baseball ? » « Pas
tellement. »
♦ **That's the lot.** C'est tout.

lottery NOUN
la loterie
♦ **to win the lottery** gagner à la loterie

loud ADJECTIVE
fort ◊ *The television is too loud.* La
télévision est trop forte.

loudly ADVERB
fort

lounge NOUN
le salon

lousy ADJECTIVE
infect ◊ *The food in the cafeteria is
lousy.* La nourriture de la cafétéria est
infecte.
♦ **I feel lousy.** Je ne me sens pas bien.

love NOUN
| *see also* **love** VERB |
l' amour MASC
♦ **to be in love** être amoureux ◊ *She's
in love with him.* Elle est amoureuse
de lui.
♦ **to make love** faire l'amour
♦ **Give your sister my love.** Embrasse ta
sœur pour moi.
♦ **Love, Rosemary.** Amitiés, Rosemary.

to **love** VERB
| *see also* **love** NOUN |
1 aimer (*be in love with*) ◊ *I love
you.* Je t'aime.
2 aimer beaucoup (*like a lot*)
◊ *Everybody loves her.* Tout le monde
l'aime beaucoup. ◊ *I'd love to come.*
J'aimerais beaucoup venir.
3 adorer (*things*) ◊ *I love chocolate.*
J'adore le chocolat. ◊ *I love skiing.*
J'adore le ski.

lovely ADJECTIVE
charmant ◊ *What a lovely surprise!*
Quelle charmante surprise ! ◊ *She's a
lovely person.* Elle est charmante.
♦ **It's a lovely day.** Il fait très beau
aujourd'hui.
♦ **a lovely meal** un repas délicieux
♦ **They've got a lovely house.** Ils ont
une très belle maison.
♦ **Have a lovely time!** Amusez-vous
bien !

lover NOUN
1 (*in relationship*)
l' amant MASC
la maîtresse
2 l' amateur MASC (*of hobby, wine*)
◊ *an art lover* un amateur d'art ◊ *He
is a lover of good food.* Il est amateur
de bonne cuisine.

low ADJECTIVE, ADVERB
(*price, level*)
bas MASC
basse FEM ◊ *That plane is flying very
low.* Cet avion vole très bas. ◊ *in the
low season* en basse saison

low-carb ADJECTIVE
faible en glucides ◊ *a low-carb snack*
une collation faible en glucides

lower ADJECTIVE
| *see also* **lower** VERB |
inférieur ◊ *on the lower floor* a
l'étage inférieur
♦ **Lower Canada** le Bas-Canada

to **lower** VERB
| *see also* **lower** ADJECTIVE |
baisser

low-fat ADJECTIVE
allégé ◊ *a low-fat yogurt* un yogourt

☞

L

allégé

loyal ADJECTIVE
loyal

✵ **Loyalist** NOUN
le/la Loyaliste

loyalty NOUN
la fidélité

lozenge NOUN
la pastille

luck NOUN
la chance ◊ *She hasn't had much luck.* Elle n'a pas eu beaucoup de chance.
♦ **Good luck!** Bonne chance!
♦ **Bad luck!** Pas de chance!

luckily ADVERB
heureusement

lucky ADJECTIVE
♦ **to be lucky (1)** (*be fortunate*) avoir de la chance ◊ *He's lucky. He has a job.* Il a de la chance. Il a un emploi. ◊ *"He wasn't hurt." "That was lucky!"* « Il n'a pas été blessé. » « C'est une chance! »
♦ **to be lucky (2)** (*bring luck*) porter bonheur ◊ *Four-leaf clovers are lucky.* Les trèfles à quatre feuilles portent bonheur.
♦ **a lucky charm** un porte-bonheur

luggage NOUN
les bagages MASC PL

lukewarm ADJECTIVE
tiède (*water, food*)
♦ **Their response was lukewarm.** Leur réaction a été peu enthousiaste.

lump NOUN
1 le morceau
(PL les morceaux) ◊ *a lump of butter* un morceau de beurre
2 la bosse (*swelling*) ◊ *He's got a lump on his forehead.* Il a une bosse sur le front.

lunatic NOUN
le cinglé
la cinglée ◊ *He's an absolute lunatic.* Il est complètement cinglé.

lunch NOUN
✵ le lunch
♦ **to have lunch**
✵ dîner ◊ *We have lunch at 12:30.* Nous dînons à midi et demie.

> ℹ *In Canada,* **le lunch** *is the noon meal. In France, it refers to a light meal consisting of a cold buffet.*

lung NOUN
le poumon
♦ **lung cancer** le cancer du poumon

to **lurk** VERB
1 rôder ◊ *The criminal is still lurking in the neighbourhood.* Le malfaiteur rôde encore dans le quartier.
2 badauder (*on Internet*) ◊ *She just lurks on that discussion group.* Elle ne fait que badauder dans ce groupe de discussion.

luscious ADJECTIVE
délicieux MASC
délicieuse FEM

lush ADJECTIVE
luxuriant

luxurious ADJECTIVE
luxueux MASC
luxueuse FEM

luxury NOUN
le luxe ◊ *It was luxury!* C'était un vrai luxe!
♦ **a luxury hotel** un hôtel de luxe

lying VERB *see* **lie**

lynx NOUN
le lynx

lyrics PL NOUN
les paroles FEM PL (*of song*)

M

macaroni NOUN
les macaronis MASC PL

machine NOUN
la machine

machinery NOUN
les machines FEM PL

mackerel NOUN
le maquereau
(PL les maquereaux)

mad ADJECTIVE
① (*angry*)
furieux MASC
furieuse FEM ◊ *She'll be mad when she finds out.* Elle sera furieuse quand elle va s'en apercevoir.
② (*insane*)
fou MASC
folle FEM ◊ *You're mad!* Tu es fou!
♦ **to get mad at somebody** se fâcher contre quelqu'un
♦ **like mad** comme un fou ◊ *I worked like mad.* J'ai travaillé comme un fou.
♦ **mad cow disease** la maladie de la vache folle

madam NOUN
madame FEM ◊ *Would you like to order, Madam?* Désirez-vous commander, Madame?

made VERB *see* **make**

madly ADVERB
♦ **They're madly in love.** Ils sont éperdument amoureux.

madness NOUN
la folie ◊ *It's absolute madness.* C'est de la pure folie.

magazine NOUN
le magazine

magic ADJECTIVE

see also **magic** NOUN

magique ◊ *a magic wand* une baguette magique
♦ **a magic trick** un tour de magie

magic NOUN

see also **magic** ADJECTIVE

la magie
♦ **My hobby is magic.** Je fais des tours de magie.

magician NOUN
(*conjurer*)
le prestidigitateur
la prestidigitatrice

magnet NOUN
l' aimant MASC

magnificent ADJECTIVE
magnifique ◊ *a magnificent view* une vue magnifique

magnifying glass NOUN
la loupe

maiden name NOUN
le nom de jeune fille

mail NOUN

see also **mail** VERB

le courrier ◊ *Here's your mail.* Voici ton courrier.
♦ **e-mail** (*electronic mail*) le courriel
♦ **by mail** par la poste

to **mail** VERB

see also **mail** NOUN

poster

mailbox NOUN
la boîte aux lettres

mailing list NOUN
la liste d'adresses

main ADJECTIVE
principal
(MASC PL principaux) ◊ *the main problem* le principal problème
♦ **main road** la grande route ◊ *I don't like biking on main roads.* Je n'aime pas faire du vélo sur les grandes routes.
♦ **the main thing is to...** l'essentiel est de...

mainland NOUN
le continent ◊ *A ferry travels between Newfoundland and the mainland.* Un traversier circule entre Terre-Neuve et le continent.
♦ **the Lower Mainland** la vallée du Bas-Fraser

mainly ADVERB
principalement

to **maintain** VERB
① entretenir (*machine, building*)
② maintenir (*insist*) ◊ *He maintains that he told the truth.* Il maintient qu'il a dit la vérité.

maintenance NOUN
l' entretien MASC (*of machine, building*)

majesty NOUN
la majesté
♦ **Your Majesty** Votre Majesté

major ADJECTIVE
majeur ◊ *a major problem* un problème majeur

☞

♦ **in C major** en do majeur

majority NOUN
la majorité

make NOUN

see also **make** VERB

la marque ◊ *What make is that car?* De quelle marque est cette voiture?

to **make** VERB

see also **make** NOUN

[1] faire ◊ *I'm going to make a cake.* Je vais faire un gâteau. ◊ *He made it himself.* Il l'a fait lui-même. ◊ *I make my bed every morning.* Je fais mon lit tous les matins. ◊ *2 and 2 make 4.* Deux et deux font quatre.
[2] fabriquer (*manufacture*) ◊ *made in Canada* fabriqué au Canada
[3] gagner (*earn*) ◊ *She makes a lot of money.* Elle gagne beaucoup d'argent.

♦ **to make somebody do something** obliger quelqu'un à faire quelque chose ◊ *My parents make me do my homework.* Mes parents m'obligent à faire mes devoirs.

♦ **to make lunch** préparer le repas ◊ *He's making supper.* Il prépare le souper.

♦ **to make a phone call** donner un coup de téléphone ◊ *I'd like to make a phone call.* J'aimerais donner un coup de téléphone.

♦ **to make fun of somebody** se moquer de quelqu'un ◊ *They made fun of me.* Ils se sont moqués de moi.

to **make it** VERB

[1] arriver ◊ *We finally made it to Calgary.* Nous sommes enfin arrivés à Calgary.

♦ **We made it to the finals.** Nous sommes allés en finale.

[2] venir ◊ *I'm sorry, I can't make it tonight.* Désolé, je ne peux pas venir ce soir.

[3] réussir ◊ *Way to go! You made it!* Bravo! Tu as réussi!

to **make out** VERB

[1] déchiffrer (*read*) ◊ *I can't make out the address on the label.* Je n'arrive pas à déchiffrer l'adresse sur l'étiquette.

[2] comprendre (*understand*) ◊ *I can't make out what she's trying to say.* Je n'arrive pas du tout à comprendre ce qu'elle veut dire.

[3] prétendre (*claim, pretend*) ◊ *They're making out it was my fault.* Ils prétendent que c'était ma faute.

♦ **to make a cheque out to somebody** libeller un chèque à l'ordre de quelqu'un

to **make up** VERB

[1] inventer (*invent*) ◊ *He made up the whole story.* Il a inventé cette histoire de toutes pièces.

[2] se réconcilier (*after argument*) ◊ *They had a quarrel, but soon made up.* Ils se sont disputés, mais se sont vite réconciliés.

maker NOUN
le fabricant ◊ *Europe's biggest car maker* le plus grand fabriquant de voitures d'Europe

make-up NOUN
le maquillage

male ADJECTIVE
[1] mâle (*animals, plants*) ◊ *a male ostrich* une autruche mâle

*When there are separate French words to refer to the female and male of an animal, **male** is often not translated.*

◊ *a male kitten* un chaton
[2] masculin (*person, on official forms*) ◊ *Sex: male.* Sexe : masculin.

♦ **Most football players are male.** La plupart des joueurs de football sont des hommes.

♦ **a male chauvinist** un macho
♦ **a male nurse** un infirmier

malicious ADJECTIVE
malveillant ◊ *a malicious rumour* une rumeur malveillante

*Be careful not to translate **malicious** by **malicieux**.*

mall NOUN
le centre commercial

mammoth NOUN

see also **mammoth** ADJECTIVE

le mammouth

mammoth ADJECTIVE

see also **mammoth** NOUN

monstre ◊ *a mammoth task* un travail monstre

man NOUN
l' homme MASC ◊ *an old man* un vieil homme

to **manage** VERB
[1] diriger (*be in charge of*) ◊ *She manages a big store.* Elle dirige un grand magasin. ◊ *Who manages your soccer team?* Qui dirige votre équipe de soccer?
[2] se débrouiller (*get by*) ◊ *We haven't got much money, but we manage.* Nous n'avons pas beaucoup d'argent, mais nous nous débrouillons. ◊ *It's okay, I can manage.* Ça va, je me débrouille.

♦ **Can you manage okay?** Tu y arrives?
♦ **to manage to do something** réussir
à faire quelque chose ◊ *Luckily I
managed to pass the exam.* J'ai
heureusement réussi à avoir mon
examen.
♦ **I can't manage all that.** (*food*) C'est
trop pour moi.

manageable ADJECTIVE
faisable (*task*)

management NOUN
① la gestion (*work of managing*)
◊ *He's responsible for the
management of the company.* Il
est responsable de la gestion de la
société.
② la direction (*people in charge*)
◊ *"under new management"*
« changement de direction »

manager NOUN
① (*of company*)
le directeur
la directrice
② (*of store, restaurant*)
le gérant
la gérante
③ (*of sports team*)
le gérant d'équipe
la gérante d'équipe
④ l' imprésario MASC (*of performer*)

mandarin NOUN
la mandarine (*fruit*)

mango NOUN
la mangue

mania NOUN
la manie

maniac NOUN
le fou
la folle ◊ *She drives like a maniac.*
Elle conduit comme une folle.

to **manipulate** VERB
manipuler

Manitoba NOUN
le Manitoba

manner NOUN
la façon
♦ **They were behaving in an odd
manner.** Ils se comportaient de façon
étrange.
♦ **He has a confident manner.** Il a de
l'assurance.

manners PL NOUN
les manières FEM PL ◊ *good manners*
les bonnes manières ◊ *Her manners
are appalling.* Elle a de très
mauvaises manières.
♦ **It's bad manners to speak with your
mouth full.** Ce n'est pas poli de parler
la bouche pleine.

to **manoeuvre** VERB
manœuvrer

mansion NOUN
le manoir

mantelpiece NOUN
la cheminée

manual NOUN
le manuel

manual ADJECTIVE
♦ **manual labour** la main-d'œuvre
♦ **manual controls** les commandes
manuelles FEM

to **manufacture** VERB
fabriquer

manufacturer NOUN
le fabricant

manure NOUN
le fumier

manuscript NOUN
le manuscrit

many ADJECTIVE, PRONOUN
beaucoup de ◊ *The film has many
special effects.* Le film a beaucoup
d'effets spéciaux. ◊ *He doesn't have
many friends.* Il n'a pas beaucoup
d'amis. ◊ *Were there many people
at the concert?* Est-ce qu'il y avait
beaucoup de gens au concert?
♦ **very many** beaucoup de ◊ *I don't
have very many CDs.* Je n'ai pas
beaucoup de CD.
♦ **Not many.** Pas beaucoup.
♦ **How many?** Combien? ◊ *How many
do you want?* Combien en veux-tu?
♦ **how many...?** combien de...? ◊ *How
many euros do you get for a dollar?*
Combien d'euros a-t-on pour un
dollar?
♦ **too many** trop ◊ *That's too many.*
C'est trop.
♦ **too many...** trop de... ◊ *She makes
too many mistakes.* Elle fait trop
d'erreurs.
♦ **so many** autant ◊ *I didn't know there
would be so many.* Je ne pensais pas
qu'il y en aurait autant.
♦ **so many...** autant de... ◊ *I've never
seen so many books.* Je n'ai jamais
vu autant de livres.

map NOUN
① la carte (*of country, area*)
② le plan (*of town*)

maple NOUN
l' érable MASC ◊ *maple syrup* le sirop
d'érable ◊ *a maple leaf* une feuille
d'érable

marathon NOUN
le marathon ◊ *the Terry Fox
Marathon of Hope* le marathon

M

☞

d'espoir de Terry Fox

marble NOUN
le marbre ◊ *a marble statue* une statue en marbre
♦ **to play marbles** jouer aux billes

March NOUN
mars MASC
♦ **in March** en mars
♦ **March Break** la semaine de relâche

march NOUN

see also **march** VERB

la manifestation (*demonstration*) ◊ *a peace march* une manifestation pour la paix

to **march** VERB

see also **march** NOUN

1 marcher au pas (*soldiers*)
2 défiler (*protesters*)

mare NOUN
la jument

margarine NOUN
la margarine

margin NOUN
la marge ◊ *Write notes in the margin.* Écrivez vos notes dans la marge.

marijuana NOUN
la marijuana

marina NOUN
la marina

maritime ADJECTIVE
maritime ◊ *the Maritime provinces* les provinces maritimes FEM
♦ **the Maritimes** les Maritimes

mark NOUN

see also **mark** VERB

1 la note (*in school*) ◊ *I get good marks in French.* J'ai de bonnes notes en français.
2 la tache (*stain*) ◊ *You've got a mark on your skirt.* Tu as une tache sur ta jupe.

to **mark** VERB

see also **mark** NOUN

corriger ◊ *The teacher hasn't marked my homework yet.* Le professeur n'a pas encore corrigé mon devoir.
♦ **to mark up the price of something** majorer le prix de quelque chose

marker NOUN
le marqueur (*pen*)

market NOUN
le marché

marketing NOUN
le marketing

marketplace NOUN
la place du marché

marmalade NOUN
la confiture d'oranges

maroon ADJECTIVE
bourgogne (*colour*)

marriage NOUN
le mariage

married ADJECTIVE
marié ◊ *They are not married.* Ils ne sont pas mariés. ◊ *They have been married for 15 years.* Ils sont mariés depuis quinze ans. ◊ *a married couple* un couple marié

marrow NOUN
♦ **bone marrow** la moelle

to **marry** VERB
épouser ◊ *He wants to marry her.* Il veut l'épouser.
♦ **to get married** se marier ◊ *My sister's getting married in June.* Ma sœur se marie en juin.

marsh NOUN
le marais

marshmallow NOUN
la guimauve ◊ *to roast marshmallows* rôtir des guimauves

martial ADJECTIVE
♦ **martial arts** les arts martiaux
♦ **martial law** la loi martiale

marvellous ADJECTIVE
1 excellent ◊ *He's a marvellous cook.* C'est un excellent cuisinier.
2 superbe ◊ *The weather was marvellous.* Il a fait un temps superbe.

Be careful not to translate marvellous as merveilleux.

marzipan NOUN
la pâte d'amandes

mascara NOUN
le mascara

mascot NOUN
la mascotte ◊ *The team's mascot is a wolverine.* La mascotte de l'équipe est le carcajou.

masculine ADJECTIVE
masculin

mashed potatoes PL NOUN
la purée de pommes de terre
◊ *sausages and mashed potatoes* des saucisses avec de la purée de pommes de terre

mask NOUN
le masque

masking tape
le ruban-cache

mass NOUN
1 la multitude ◊ *a mass of books*

and papers une multitude de livres et de papiers

2 la <u>masse</u> (*scientific*)

3 la <u>messe</u> (*in church*) ◊ *to go to mass* aller à la messe

♦ **the mass media** les médias

massage NOUN
le <u>massage</u>

massive ADJECTIVE
<u>énorme</u>

to **mass-produce** VERB
<u>fabriquer en série</u>

to **master** VERB
<u>maîtriser</u>

masterpiece NOUN
le <u>chef-d'œuvre</u>
(PL les chefs-d'œuvre)

mat NOUN
1 le <u>tapis</u> (*small rug*)
2 le <u>paillasson</u> (*doormat*)

♦ **a bath mat** un tapis de baignoire

♦ **an exercise mat** un tapis d'exercice

match NOUN

| see also **match** VERB |

1 l' <u>allumette</u> FEM ◊ *a box of matches* une boîte d'allumettes

2 (*sport*)
le <u>match</u>
(PL les matchs) ◊ *a tennis match* un match de tennis

♦ **He's no match for you.** Il n'est pas de taille à lutter contre toi.

♦ **They're a good match.** Ils sont bien assortis.

to **match** VERB

| see also **match** NOUN |

<u>être assorti à</u> ◊ *The jacket matches the pants.* La veste est assortie au pantalon.

♦ **These colours don't match.** Ces couleurs ne vont pas ensemble.

matching ADJECTIVE
<u>assorti</u> ◊ *My bedroom has matching wallpaper and curtains.* Ma chambre a du papier peint et des rideaux assortis.

material NOUN
1 le <u>tissu</u> (*cloth*)
2 la <u>documentation</u> (*information, data*) ◊ *I'm collecting material for my project.* Je rassemble une documentation pour mon dossier.

♦ **raw materials** les matières premières FEM

math NOUN
les <u>maths</u> FEM PL

mathematics NOUN
les <u>mathématiques</u> FEM PL

matter NOUN

| see also **matter** VERB |

la <u>question</u> ◊ *It's a matter of life and death.* C'est une question de vie ou de mort.

♦ **What's the matter?** Qu'est-ce qui ne va pas?

♦ **as a matter of fact** en fait

♦ **for that matter** d'ailleurs

♦ **no matter what** quelles que soient les circonstances

♦ **no matter what they say** quoi qu'ils disent

♦ **no matter where** où que ce soit

to **matter** VERB

| see also **matter** NOUN |

♦ **it doesn't matter (1)** (*I don't mind*) ça ne fait rien ◊ *"I can't give you the money today." "It doesn't matter."* « Je ne peux pas te donner l'argent aujourd'hui. » « Ça ne fait rien. »

♦ **it doesn't matter (2)** (*it makes no difference*) ça n'a pas d'importance ◊ *"Shall I phone today or tomorrow?" "Whenever, it doesn't matter."* « Est-ce que j'appelle aujourd'hui ou demain? » « Quand tu veux, ça n'a pas d'importance. »

♦ **It matters a lot to me.** C'est très important pour moi.

mattress NOUN
le <u>matelas</u>

mature ADJECTIVE
<u>mûr</u> ◊ *She's quite mature for her age.* Elle est très mûre pour son âge.

maximum NOUN

| see also **maximum** ADJECTIVE |

le <u>maximum</u>

maximum ADJECTIVE

| see also **maximum** NOUN |

<u>maximum</u> MASC, FEM, PL ◊ *The maximum speed is 100 km/h.* La vitesse maximum autorisée est de cent kilomètres à l'heure.

♦ **the maximum amount** le maximum

May NOUN
<u>mai</u> MASC

♦ **in May** en mai

may VERB

♦ **He may come.** Il va peut-être venir. ◊ *It may rain.* Il va peut-être pleuvoir.

♦ **"Are you going to the party?" "I don't know. I may."** « Est-ce que tu vas à la soirée? » « Je ne sais pas. Peut-être. »

♦ **May I come along?** Est-ce que je peux vous accompagner?

maybe ADVERB
<u>peut-être</u> ◊ *maybe not* peut-être pas ◊ *a bit boring, maybe* peut-être

M

☞

un peu ennuyeux ◊ *Maybe she's at home.* Elle est peut-être chez elle. ◊ *Maybe he'll change his mind.* Il va peut-être changer d'avis.

mayonnaise NOUN
la mayonnaise

mayor NOUN
le/la maire

maze NOUN
le labyrinthe

me PRONOUN

> *me becomes m' before a vowel sound.*

① me ◊ *Could you lend me your pen?* Est-ce que tu peux me prêter ton stylo?
m' ◊ *Can you tell me the way to the community centre?* Est-ce que vous pouvez m'indiquer le chemin du centre communautaire? ◊ *Can you help me?* Est-ce que tu peux m'aider? ◊ *They heard me.* Ils m'ont entendu.

> *moi is used in some exclamations and commands.*

② moi ◊ *Me too!* Moi aussi! ◊ *Excuse me!* Excusez-moi! ◊ *Look at me!* Regarde-moi! ◊ *Wait for me!* Attends-moi! ◊ *Come with me!* Suivez-moi!

> *moi is also used after prepositions and in comparisons.*

◊ *You're after me.* Tu es après moi.
◊ *Is it for me?* C'est pour moi?
◊ *She's older than me.* Elle est plus âgée que moi.

meal NOUN
le repas

mealtime NOUN
♦ **at mealtimes** aux heures de repas

to **mean** VERB

> *see also **mean** ADJECTIVE and **means** NOUN*

vouloir dire ◊ *What does "complet" mean?* Qu'est-ce que « complet » veut dire? ◊ *I don't know what it means.* Je ne sais pas ce que ça veut dire. ◊ *What do you mean?* Qu'est-ce que vous voulez dire? ◊ *That's not what I meant.* Ce n'est pas ce que je voulais dire.
♦ **Which one do you mean?** Duquel veux-tu parler?
♦ **Do you really mean it?** Tu es sérieux?
♦ **to mean to do something** avoir l'intention de faire quelque chose ◊ *I didn't mean to offend you.* Je n'avais pas l'intention de vous blesser.

mean ADJECTIVE

> *see also **mean** VERB and **means** NOUN*

méchant (*unkind*) ◊ *You're being mean to me.* Tu es méchant avec moi.
♦ **That's a really mean thing to say!** Ce n'est vraiment pas gentil de dire ça!

meaning NOUN
le sens

means NOUN

> *see also **mean** VERB and ADJECTIVE*

le moyen ◊ *She'll do it by any possible means.* Elle le fera par tous les moyens. ◊ *a means of transport* un moyen de transport
♦ **by means of** au moyen de ◊ *He got in by means of a stolen key.* Il est entré au moyen d'une clé volée.
♦ **by all means** bien sûr ◊ *"Can I come?" "By all means!"* « Est-ce que je peux venir? » « Bien sûr! »

meant VERB *see* **mean**

meanwhile ADVERB
pendant ce temps

measles NOUN
la rougeole

to **measure** VERB
① mesurer ◊ *I measured the desk.* J'ai mesuré le bureau.
② faire ◊ *The room measures 3 metres by 4.* La pièce fait trois mètres sur quatre.

measurements PL NOUN
① les dimensions FEM (*of object*)
◊ *What are the measurements of the room?* Quelles sont les dimensions de la pièce?
② les mensurations FEM (*of body*)
◊ *What are your measurements?* Quelles sont tes mensurations?
♦ **my waist measurement** mon tour de taille
♦ **What's your neck measurement?** Quel est votre tour de cou?

meat NOUN
la viande ◊ *I don't eat meat.* Je ne mange pas de viande.

mechanic NOUN
le mécanicien
la mécanicienne ◊ *He's a mechanic.* Il est mécanicien.

mechanical ADJECTIVE
mécanique

medal NOUN
la médaille
♦ **the gold medal** la médaille d'or

medallion NOUN
le médaillon

media PL NOUN
les médias MASC

median strip NOUN
le terre-plein central

medical ADJECTIVE

see also **medical** NOUN

médical
(MASC PL médicaux) ◊ *medical
treatment* les soins médicaux
♦ **medical insurance** l'assurance
maladie
♦ **a medical centre** un centre médical
♦ **to have medical problems** avoir des
problèmes de santé
♦ **She's a medical student.** Elle est
étudiante en médecine.

medical NOUN

see also **medical** ADJECTIVE

♦ **to have a medical** passer un examen
médical

medicine NOUN
① la médecine (*subject*) ◊ *I want to
study medicine.* Je veux étudier la
médecine.
♦ **alternative medicine** la médecine
douce
② le médicament (*medication*) ◊ *I
need some medicine.* J'ai besoin d'un
médicament.

medieval ADJECTIVE
① médiéval
(MASC PL médiévaux) ◊ *a medieval
town* une ville médiévale ◊ *in
medieval times* à l'époque médiévale
② du Moyen Âge (*person*) ◊ *a
medieval knight* un chevalier du
Moyen Âge

mediocre ADJECTIVE
médiocre ◊ *I think they're a mediocre
band.* À mon avis, c'est un groupe
musical médiocre.

medium ADJECTIVE
moyen MASC
moyenne FEM ◊ *a man of medium
height* un homme de taille moyenne

medium-sized ADJECTIVE
de taille moyenne ◊ *a medium-sized
town* une ville de taille moyenne

to **meet** VERB
① rencontrer (*by chance*) ◊ *I met
your sister in the street.* J'ai rencontré
ta sœur dans la rue. ◊ *Have you met
her before?* Tu l'as déjà rencontrée?
② se rencontrer ◊ *We met by chance
in the shopping centre.* Nous nous
sommes rencontrés par hasard au
centre commercial.
③ retrouver (*by arrangement*) ◊ *I'm
going to meet my friends.* Je vais
retrouver mes amis.
④ se retrouver ◊ *Let's meet in front
of the tourist office.* Retrouvons-nous

devant le bureau de tourisme.
♦ **I like meeting new people.** J'aime
faire de nouvelles connaissances.
⑤ aller chercher (*pick up*) ◊ *I'll meet
you at the airport.* J'irai te chercher à
l'aéroport.
♦ **to meet up** se retrouver ◊ *What time
shall we meet up?* On se retrouve à
quelle heure?

meeting NOUN
① la réunion (*gathering*) ◊ *a business
meeting* une réunion d'affaires
② la rencontre (*encounter*) ◊ *their
first meeting* leur première rencontre

mega ADJECTIVE
♦ **He's mega rich.** Il est hyper riche.
(*informal*)

megabyte NOUN
le mégaoctet

melody NOUN
la mélodie

melon NOUN
le melon

to **melt** VERB
fondre ◊ *The snow is melting.* La
neige est en train de fondre.

member NOUN
le membre ◊ *Are you a member of
the Student Council?* Es-tu membre
du Conseil des élèves?
♦ **We're all members of society.** Nous
faisons tous partie de la société.
♦ **a Member of Parliament** un député
❈ ♦ **a Member of the Legislative
Assembly** un député à l'Assemblée
législative
❈ ♦ **a Member of the National Assembly**
un député de l'Assemblée nationale
❈ ♦ **a Member of Provincial Parliament** un
député provincial

membership NOUN
l' adhésion FEM (*of party, union*) ◊ *to
apply for membership* faire une
demande d'adhésion

membership card NOUN
la carte de membre

memento NOUN
le souvenir

memorial NOUN
le monument ◊ *a war memorial* un
monument aux morts
♦ **a memorial service** un service
commémoratif

to **memorize** VERB
apprendre par cœur

memory NOUN
① la mémoire (*also for computer*)
◊ *I don't have a good memory.* Je
n'ai pas bonne mémoire. ◊ *Your*

☞

M

computer needs more memory.
Ton ordinateur a besoin de plus de
mémoire.

② le souvenir (*recollection*) ◊ *to
bring back memories* rappeler des
souvenirs

men PL NOUN *see* **man**
les hommes MASC

to **mend** VERB
réparer

meningitis NOUN
la méningite

mental ADJECTIVE
mental
(MASC PL mentaux) ◊ *a mental illness*
une maladie mentale
♦ **a mental hospital** un hôpital
psychiatrique

mentality NOUN
la mentalité

to **mention** VERB
mentionner
♦ **"Thank you!" "Don't mention it!"**
« Merci ! » « Il n'y a pas de quoi ! »

menu NOUN
le menu ◊ *Could I have the menu
please?* Est-ce que je pourrais avoir le
menu s'il vous plaît?

to **meow** VERB
miauler

mercy NOUN
la pitié

mere ADJECTIVE
♦ **a mere 5 percent** à peine cinq pour
cent
♦ **It's a mere formality.** C'est une simple
formalité.
♦ **the merest hint of criticism** la
moindre petite critique

meringue NOUN
la meringue

merry ADJECTIVE
♦ **Merry Christmas!** Joyeux Noël!

mess NOUN
① le fouillis ◊ *My bedroom's usually
a mess.* Il y a généralement du fouillis
dans ma chambre.
② le gâchis ◊ *We'd better clean up
this mess.* Nous devrions nettoyer ce
gâchis.
♦ **in a mess** en désordre

to **mess around** VERB
♦ **to mess around with something**
(*interfere with*) tripoter quelque
chose ◊ *Stop messing around with
my computer!* Arrête de tripoter mon
ordinateur!
♦ **Don't mess around with my things!**
Ne touche pas à mes affaires!

to **mess up** VERB
♦ **to mess something up** mettre la
pagaille dans quelque chose ◊ *My
little brother has messed up my CDs.*
Mon petit frère a mis la pagaille dans
mes CD.
♦ **I'm sorry, I really messed up.** Je
regrette, j'ai tout gâché.

message NOUN
le message

messenger NOUN
le messager
la messagère

messy ADJECTIVE
① salissant (*dirty*) ◊ *a messy job* un
travail salissant
② en désordre (*untidy*) ◊ *Your desk is
really messy.* Ton bureau est vraiment
en désordre.
③ désordonnée (*person*) ◊ *She's
so messy!* Elle est tellement
désordonnée!
♦ **My writing is terribly messy.** J'ai une
écriture de cochon.

met VERB *see* **meet**

metal NOUN
le métal
(PL les métaux)

meter NOUN
① le compteur (*for gas, hydro, taxi*)
② le parcomètre (*parking meter*)

method NOUN
la méthode

Métis NOUN

> *see also* **Métis** ADJECTIVE

le Métis
la Métisse

Métis ADJECTIVE

> *see also* **Métis** NOUN

métis MASC
métisse FEM

metre NOUN
le mètre

metric ADJECTIVE
métrique

mice PL NOUN *see* **mouse**

microchip NOUN
la puce

microphone NOUN
le microphone

microscope NOUN
le microscope

microwave oven NOUN
le four à micro-ondes

mid ADJECTIVE
♦ **in mid May** à la mi-mai

midday NOUN
le midi
♦ **at midday** à midi

middle NOUN
le milieu ◊ *in the middle of the road* au milieu de la route ◊ *in the middle of the night* au milieu de la nuit ◊ *the middle seat* la place du milieu
♦ **the Middle Ages** le Moyen Âge
♦ **the Middle East** le Moyen-Orient

middle-aged ADJECTIVE
d'âge moyen ◊ *a middle-aged man* un homme d'âge moyen
♦ **to be middle-aged** avoir la cinquantaine
♦ **She's middle-aged.** Elle a la cinquantaine.

middle-class ADJECTIVE
de la classe moyenne ◊ *a middle-class family* une famille de la classe moyenne

middle name NOUN
le deuxième prénom

midnight NOUN
minuit MASC
♦ **at midnight** à minuit

midwife NOUN
la sage-femme
(PL les sages-femmes) ◊ *She's a midwife.* Elle est sage-femme.

might VERB

*Use **peut-être** to express possibility.*

◊ *He might come later.* Il va peut-être venir plus tard. ◊ *We might go to the Yukon next year.* Nous irons peut-être au Yukon l'an prochain. ◊ *She might not have understood.* Elle n'a peut-être pas compris.

migraine NOUN
la migraine ◊ *I have a migraine.* J'ai la migraine.

mike NOUN
le micro

mild ADJECTIVE
doux MASC
douce FEM ◊ *The winters are quite mild.* Les hivers sont assez doux.

mile NOUN
le mille

ℹ️ *A **mile** is a nonmetric unit equal to about 1.6 km.*

◊ *It's five miles from here.* C'est à huit kilomètres d'ici.
♦ **We walked miles!** Nous avons marché plusieurs kilomètres!

military ADJECTIVE
militaire

milk NOUN

see also **milk** VERB

le lait ◊ *tea with milk* du thé au lait

to **milk** VERB

see also **milk** NOUN

traire

milk chocolate NOUN
le chocolat au lait

milkshake NOUN
le lait fouetté

mill NOUN
le moulin ◊ *a pepper mill* un moulin à poivre

millennium NOUN
le millénaire ◊ *the third millennium* le troisième millénaire
♦ **the millennium** le millénium

millimetre NOUN
le millimètre

million NOUN
le million

millionaire NOUN
le millionnaire

to **mimic** VERB
imiter

mincemeat pie NOUN
la tarte au mincemeat

to **mind** VERB

see also **mind** NOUN

♦ **Do you mind if I open the window?** Est-ce que ça vous dérange si j'ouvre la fenêtre?
♦ **I don't mind.** Ça ne me dérange pas. ◊ *I don't mind the noise.* Le bruit ne me dérange pas.
♦ **Never mind!** Ça ne fait rien!
♦ **Mind the step!** Attention à la marche!

mind NOUN

see also **mind** VERB

l' esprit ◊ *a logical mind* un esprit logique ◊ *Great minds think alike.* Les grands esprits se rencontrent. ◊ *to come to mind* venir à l'esprit
♦ **to make up one's mind** se décider ◊ *I haven't made up my mind yet.* Je ne me suis pas encore décidé.
♦ **to change one's mind** changer d'avis ◊ *He changed his mind.* Il a changé d'avis.
♦ **Are you out of your mind?** Tu as perdu la tête?
♦ **What's on your mind?** À quoi penses-tu?
♦ **to read somebody's mind** lire dans les pensées de quelqu'un
♦ **Put it out of your mind.** N'y pense plus.

M

mine PRONOUN

> see also **mine** NOUN

le mien + MASC NOUN ◊ *"Is this your coat?" "No, mine's black."* « C'est ton manteau? » « Non, le mien est noir. »
la mienne + FEM NOUN ◊ *"Is this your car?" "No, mine's green."* « C'est ta voiture? » « Non, la mienne est verte. »
les miens + MASC PL NOUN ◊ *her parents and mine* ses parents et les miens
les miennes + FEM PL NOUN ◊ *Your hands are dirty. Mine are clean.* Tes mains sont sales. Les miennes sont propres.
♦ **It's mine.** C'est à moi. ◊ *This book is mine.* Ce livre est à moi. ◊ *"Whose is this?" "It's mine."* « C'est à qui? » « À moi. »

mine NOUN

> see also **mine** PRONOUN

la mine ◊ *a diamond mine* une mine de diamants ◊ *a land mine* une mine terrestre

miner NOUN
le mineur
la mineuse

mineral NOUN
le minéral
(PL les minéraux)

mineral water NOUN
l' eau minérale FEM

miniature ADJECTIVE

> see also **miniature** NOUN

miniature ◊ *a miniature version* une version miniature

miniature NOUN

> see also **miniature** ADJECTIVE

la miniature

Minidisc™ NOUN
le minidisque

minimum NOUN

> see also **minimum** ADJECTIVE

le minimum

minimum ADJECTIVE

> see also **minimum** NOUN

minimum MASC, FEM, PL ◊ *the minimum wage* le salaire minimum ◊ *The minimum age for driving is 16.* L'âge minimum pour conduire est seize ans.
♦ **the minimum amount** le minimum

miniskirt NOUN
la minijupe

minister NOUN
1 le ministre (*in government*)
2 le pasteur (*of church*)

ministry NOUN
le ministère (*in government*) ◊ *the Ministry of the Environment* le ministère de l'Environnement

mink NOUN
le vison

minor ADJECTIVE
mineur ◊ *a minor problem* un problème mineur
♦ **in D minor** en ré mineur
♦ **a minor operation** une opération bénigne

minority NOUN
la minorité

mint NOUN
1 la menthe (*plant*) ◊ *mint ice cream* la crème glacée à la menthe
2 le bonbon à la menthe (*candy*)

minus PREPOSITION
moins ◊ *16 minus 3 is 13.* Seize moins trois égale treize. ◊ *It's minus two outside.* Il fait moins deux dehors. ◊ *I got a B minus.* J'ai eu un B moins.

minute NOUN

> see also **minute** ADJECTIVE

la minute ◊ *Wait a minute!* Attends une minute! ◊ *I'll do it right this minute.* Je le ferai tout de suite.

minute ADJECTIVE

> see also **minute** NOUN

minuscule ◊ *minute details* des détails minuscules

miracle NOUN
le miracle

mirror NOUN
1 le miroir (*on wall*)
2 le rétroviseur (*in car*)

to **misbehave** VERB
se conduire mal

miscellaneous ADJECTIVE
divers

mischief NOUN
les bêtises FEM PL ◊ *My little sister's always up to mischief.* Ma petite sœur fait constamment des bêtises.

mischievous ADJECTIVE
espiègle

miser NOUN
l' avare MASC/FEM

miserable ADJECTIVE
1 (*person*)
malheureux MASC MASC
malheureuse FEM ◊ *You look miserable.* Tu as l'air malheureux.
2 épouvantable (*weather*) ◊ *The weather was miserable.* Il faisait un

temps épouvantable.
♦ **to feel miserable** ne pas avoir le moral ◊ *I'm feeling miserable.* Je n'ai pas le moral.

misery NOUN
la tristesse (*unhappiness*) ◊ *All that money brought nothing but misery.* Tout cet argent n'a apporté que de la tristesse.

misfortune NOUN
le malheur

mishap NOUN
la mésaventure

to **misjudge** VERB
mal juger (*person*) ◊ *I've misjudged him.* Je l'ai mal jugé.
♦ **He misjudged the turn.** Il a mal pris le virage.

misleading ADJECTIVE
trompeur MASC
trompeuse FEM

to **misplace** VERB
égarer ◊ *I've misplaced my passport.* J'ai égaré mon passeport.

Miss NOUN
① Mademoiselle
(PL Mesdemoiselles)
② (*in address*)
Mlle
(PL Mlles)

> ❶ *Mademoiselle and Mlle are rarely used for single women any more, except in reference to a girl. It is better to use Madame (or the abbreviation Mme), the French equivalent of Ms, in person or in a letter.*

to **miss** VERB
① rater ◊ *Hurry or you'll miss the bus.* Dépêche-toi ou tu vas rater l'autobus. ◊ *He missed the target.* Il a raté la cible.
② manquer ◊ *to miss an opportunity* manquer une occasion
♦ **I miss you.** Tu me manques. ◊ *I'm missing my family.* Ma famille me manque.

missing ADJECTIVE
manquant ◊ *the missing piece* la pièce manquante
♦ **to be missing** avoir disparu ◊ *My backpack is missing.* Mon sac à dos a disparu. ◊ *Two members of the group are missing.* Deux membres du groupe ont disparu.

missionary NOUN
le/la missionnaire

mist NOUN

la brume

mistake NOUN

see also **mistake** VERB

① la faute (*slip*) ◊ *a spelling mistake* une faute d'orthographe
♦ **to make a mistake (1)** (*in writing, speaking*) faire une faute
♦ **to make a mistake (2)** (*be mistaken*) se tromper ◊ *I'm sorry, I made a mistake.* Je suis désolé, je me suis trompé.
② l' erreur FEM (*misjudgement*) ◊ *It was a mistake to buy those yellow shoes.* J'ai fait une erreur en achetant ces chaussures jaunes.
♦ **by mistake** par erreur ◊ *I took her bag by mistake.* J'ai pris son sac par erreur.

to **mistake** VERB

see also **mistake** NOUN

♦ **He mistook me for my sister.** Il m'a prise pour ma sœur.

mistaken ADJECTIVE
♦ **to be mistaken** se tromper ◊ *If you think I'm going to get up at six o'clock, you're mistaken.* Si tu penses que je vais me lever à six heures, tu te trompes.

mistook VERB see **mistake**

to **mistrust** VERB
se méfier de

misty ADJECTIVE
brumeux MASC
brumeuse FEM ◊ *a misty morning* un matin brumeux

to **misunderstand** VERB
mal comprendre ◊ *Sorry, I misunderstood you.* Je suis désolé, je t'avais mal compris.

misunderstanding NOUN
le malentendu

mitten NOUN
la mitaine

mix NOUN

see also **mix** VERB

le mélange ◊ *It's a mix of science fiction and comedy.* C'est un mélange de science-fiction et de comédie.
♦ **a cake mix** une préparation pour gâteau

to **mix** VERB

see also **mix** NOUN

① mélanger ◊ *Mix the flour with the sugar.* Mélangez la farine au sucre.
② combiner ◊ *He's mixing business with pleasure.* Il combine les affaires et le plaisir.
♦ **He doesn't mix with other people.** Il ☞

M

mixed → Monday   **English ~ French**

se tient à l'écart.
♦ **to mix up** (*people*) confondre ◊ *She always mixes me up with my brother.* Elle me confond toujours avec mon frère.
♦ **The travel agent mixed up the bookings.** L'agente de voyage s'est embrouillée dans les réservations.
♦ **I'm getting mixed up.** Je ne m'y retrouve plus.

mixed ADJECTIVE
♦ **a mixed salad** une salade composée
♦ **a mixed family** une famille mixte
♦ **a mixed grill** un assortiment de grillades

mixture NOUN
le mélange ◊ *a mixture of spices* un mélange d'épices

mix-up NOUN
la confusion

to **moan** VERB
gémir ◊ *He was moaning with pain.* Il gémissait de douleur.

mobile home NOUN
la maison mobile

mobile phone NOUN
le téléphone cellulaire

moccasin NOUN
le mocassin

to **mock** VERB

see also **mock** ADJECTIVE

ridiculiser

mock ADJECTIVE

see also **mock** VERB

♦ **a mock trial** une simulation de procès
♦ **a mock parliamentary debate** une simulation de débat parlementaire

model NOUN

see also **model** ADJECTIVE

[1] le modèle (*type*) ◊ *His car is the latest model.* Sa voiture est le tout dernier modèle.
[2] la maquette (*mock-up*) ◊ *a model of the castle* une maquette du château
[3] le mannequin (*fashion*) ◊ *She's a famous model.* C'est un mannequin célèbre.

model ADJECTIVE

see also **model** NOUN

♦ **a model plane** un modèle réduit d'avion
♦ **a model railway** un modèle réduit de voie ferrée
♦ **He's a model student.** C'est un élève modèle.

to **model** VERB

see also **model** NOUN

♦ **She was modelling an Alfred Sung outfit.** Elle présentait une tenue de la collection Alfred Sung.

modem NOUN
le modem

moderate ADJECTIVE
modéré ◊ *Her views are quite moderate.* Ses opinions sont assez modérées.
♦ **a moderate amount of** un peu de
♦ **a moderate price** un prix raisonnable

modern ADJECTIVE
moderne

to **modernize** VERB
moderniser

modest ADJECTIVE
modeste

to **modify** VERB
modifier

moist ADJECTIVE
humide (*skin, soil*) ◊ *Make sure the soil is moist.* Assurez-vous que la terre est humide.

moisture NOUN
l' humidité FEM

moisturizer NOUN
[1] la crème hydratante (*cream*)
[2] le lait hydratant (*lotion*)

mom NOUN

*You use **maman** only when you are talking to your mother or using it as her name; otherwise use **mère**.*

[1] la mère ◊ *my mom* ma mère ◊ *her mom* sa mère
[2] la maman ◊ *Mom!* Maman!
◊ *I'll ask Mom.* Je vais demander à maman.

moment NOUN
l' instant MASC ◊ *Could you wait a moment?* Pouvez-vous attendre un instant? ◊ *in a moment* dans un instant ◊ *Just a moment!* Un instant!
♦ **at the moment** en ce moment
♦ **any moment now** d'un moment à l'autre ◊ *They'll be arriving any moment now.* Ils vont arriver d'un moment à l'autre.

momentous ADJECTIVE
capital (*event*)

monarch NOUN
le monarque

monarchy NOUN
la monarchie

monastery NOUN
le monastère

Monday NOUN
le lundi ◊ *on Monday* lundi ◊ *on*

Mondays le lundi ◊ *every Monday*
tous les lundis ◊ *last Monday* lundi
dernier ◊ *next Monday* lundi prochain

money NOUN
l' argent MASC ◊ *I need to change
some money.* J'ai besoin de changer
de l'argent.
♦ **to make money** gagner de l'argent

monitor NOUN
le moniteur (*of computer*)

monk NOUN
le moine

monkey NOUN
le singe

to **monopolize** VERB
monopoliser ◊ *to monopolize
the conversation* monopoliser la
conversation ◊ *You're monopolizing
the phone!* Tu monopolises le
téléphone!

monotonous ADJECTIVE
monotone

monster NOUN
le monstre

month NOUN
le mois ◊ *this month* ce mois-ci
◊ *next month* le mois prochain ◊ *last
month* le mois dernier ◊ *every month*
tous les mois ◊ *at the end of the
month* à la fin du mois

monthly ADJECTIVE
mensuel MASC
mensuelle FEM

monument NOUN
le monument

mood NOUN
l' humeur FEM
♦ **to be in a bad mood** être de mauvaise
humeur
♦ **to be in a good mood** être de bonne
humeur

moody ADJECTIVE
① lunatique (*temperamental*)
② maussade (*in a bad mood*)

moon NOUN
la lune ◊ *There's a full moon tonight.*
Il y a pleine lune ce soir.
♦ **to be over the moon** (*happy*) être aux
anges

moonlight NOUN
le clair de lune ◊ *in the moonlight* au
clair de lune

to **moor** VERB
amarrer (*boat*)

moose NOUN
l' orignal MASC

✱ **mop** NOUN
la vadrouille (*for floor*)

moped NOUN
le cyclomoteur

moral ADJECTIVE

> see also **moral** NOUN

moral
(MASC PL moraux)

moral NOUN

> see also **moral** ADJECTIVE

la morale ◊ *the moral of the story* la
morale de l'histoire
♦ **morals** la moralité

morale NOUN
le moral ◊ *Their morale is very low.*
Leur moral est très bas.

more ADJECTIVE, PRONOUN, ADVERB

> *When comparing one amount with
> another, you usually use **plus**.*

① plus ◊ *Fruit is more expensive
in Britain.* Les fruits sont plus chers
en Grande-Bretagne. ◊ *Could you
speak more slowly?* Est-ce que vous
pourriez parler plus lentement? ◊ *a
bit more* un peu plus ◊ *There isn't
any more.* Il n'y en a plus.
♦ **more...than** plus...que ◊ *He's more
athletic than me.* Il est plus sportif que
moi. ◊ *She practises more than I do.*
Elle s'entraîne plus que moi. ◊ *More
boys play hockey than girls.* Il y a plus
de garçons que de filles qui jouent au
hockey.
② plus de (*followed by noun*) ◊ *There
are more girls in the class.* Il y a plus
de filles dans la classe. ◊ *I get more
homework than you do.* J'ai plus de
devoirs que toi. ◊ *I spent more than
500 dollars.* J'ai dépensé plus de cinq
cents dollars.

> *When referring to an additional
> amount, more than there is already,
> you usually use **encore**.*

③ encore ◊ *Is there any more?* Est-ce
qu'il y en a encore? ◊ *Would you like
some more?* Vous en voulez encore?
◊ *It'll take a few more days.* Ça
prendra encore quelques jours.
④ encore de (*followed by noun*)
◊ *Could I have some more fries?*
Est-ce que je pourrais avoir encore
des frites? ◊ *Do you want some more
tea?* Voulez-vous encore du thé?
♦ **more or less** plus ou moins
♦ **more than ever** plus que jamais

moreover ADVERB
en outre

morning NOUN
le matin ◊ *this morning* ce matin
◊ *tomorrow morning* demain matin
◊ *every morning* tous les matins

☞

♦ **in the morning** le matin ◊ *at 7 o'clock in the morning* à sept heures du matin
♦ **a morning paper** un journal du matin

mosque NOUN
la mosquée

mosquito NOUN
le moustique
♦ **a mosquito bite** une piqûre de moustique

most ADVERB, ADJECTIVE, PRONOUN

> *Use* **la plupart de** *when* **most (of)** *is followed by a plural noun and* **la majeure partie (de)** *when* **most (of)** *is followed by a singular noun.*

1 la plupart de ◊ *most of my friends* la plupart de mes amis ◊ *most people* la plupart des gens ◊ *Most cats are affectionate.* La plupart des chats sont affectueux.
♦ **most of them** la plupart d'entre eux
♦ **most of the time** la plupart du temps
2 la majeure partie de ◊ *most of the work* la majeure partie du travail ◊ *most of the class* la majeure partie de la classe ◊ *most of the night* la majeure partie de la nuit
♦ **the most** le plus ◊ *He's the one who talks the most.* C'est lui qui parle le plus.

> *When* **most** *is followed by adjective, the translation depends on whether the noun referred to is masculine, feminine or plural.*

♦ **the most... (1)** le plus... ◊ *the most expensive restaurant* le restaurant le plus cher
♦ **the most... (2)** la plus... ◊ *the most expensive seat* la place la plus chère
♦ **the most... (3)** les plus... ◊ *the most expensive restaurants* les restaurants les plus chers ◊ *the most expensive seats* les places les plus chères
♦ **for the most part** pour la plupart ◊ *The students seem to like French, for the most part.* Les élèves semblent aimer le français, pour la plupart.
♦ **to make the most of something** profiter au maximum de quelque chose
♦ **at the most** au maximum ◊ *Two hours at the most.* Deux heures au maximum.

mostly ADVERB
♦ **I went mostly because my friends were going.** (*mainly*) J'y suis allé surtout parce que mes amis y allaient.
♦ **The teachers are mostly quite nice.** La plupart des professeurs sont assez gentils.
♦ **We mostly do the shopping on Saturdays.** (*usually*) D'habitude, nous magasinons le samedi.

motel NOUN
le motel

moth NOUN
le papillon de nuit

mother NOUN
la mère ◊ *my mother* ma mère
♦ **mother tongue** la langue maternelle

mother-in-law NOUN
la belle-mère
(PL les belles-mères)

Mother's Day NOUN
la fête des Mères

motion NOUN
1 le mouvement ◊ *the motion of the train* le mouvement du train
2 le geste ◊ *He made a motion towards the door.* Il a fait un geste vers la porte.
♦ **in motion** en marche
♦ **motion sickness** le mal des transports
♦ **We were just going through the motions.** Nous le faisions tout à fait machinalement.

motionless ADJECTIVE
immobile

motivated ADJECTIVE
motivé ◊ *She is highly motivated.* Elle est très motivée.

motivation NOUN
la motivation

motive NOUN
le mobile ◊ *the motive for the crime* le mobile du crime

motor NOUN
le moteur ◊ *The boat has a motor.* Le bateau a un moteur.

motorbike NOUN
la moto

motorboat NOUN
le bateau à moteur

motorcycle NOUN
la motocyclette

motorcyclist NOUN
le motard
la motarde

motorist NOUN
l' automobiliste MASC/FEM

mouldy ADJECTIVE
moisi

to **mount** VERB
1 monter ◊ *He mounted his horse and rode off.* Il est monté à son cheval et est parti. ◊ *to mount a bicycle* monter sur un vélo ◊ *They're mounting a publicity campaign.* Ils

montent une campagne publicitaire.
2 augmenter ◊ *Tension is mounting.*
La tension augmente.

to **mount up** VERB
1 s'accumuler ◊ *The mail had mounted up during our holidays.* Les lettres s'étaient accumulées pendant nos vacances.
2 augmenter ◊ *My savings are mounting up gradually.* Mes économies augmentent progressivement.

mountain NOUN
la montagne
♦ **a mountain bike** un vélo de montagne
♦ **a mountain range** une chaîne de montagnes

mountainous ADJECTIVE
montagneux MASC
montagneuse FEM

✹ **Mountie** NOUN
l' agent de la GRC MASC
l' agente de la GRC FEM

mouse NOUN
la souris (*also for computer*) ◊ *white mice* des souris blanches

mouse pad NOUN
le tapis de souris

mousse NOUN
1 la mousse (*food*) ◊ *chocolate mousse* la mousse au chocolat
2 la mousse coiffante (*for hair*)

moustache NOUN
la moustache ◊ *He has a moustache.* Il a une moustache.
♦ **a man with a moustache** un moustachu

mouth NOUN
la bouche

mouthful NOUN
la bouchée

mouth organ NOUN
✹ la musique à bouche ◊ *I play the mouth organ.* Je joue de la musique à bouche.

mouthwash NOUN
le bain de bouche

move NOUN

  see also **move** VERB

1 le tour ◊ *It's your move.* C'est ton tour.
2 le déménagement ◊ *Our move from Edmundston to Pugwash...* Notre déménagement d'Edmundston à Pugwash...
♦ **to get a move on** se remuer ◊ *Get a move on!* Remue-toi!

to **move** VERB

  see also **move** NOUN

1 bouger ◊ *Don't move!* Ne bouge pas! ◊ *Could you move your stuff please?* Est-ce que tu peux bouger tes affaires s'il te plaît?
2 avancer ◊ *The car was moving very slowly.* La voiture avançait très lentement.
3 émouvoir ◊ *I was very moved by the film.* J'ai été très émue par ce film.
4 déménager ◊ *We're moving in July.* Nous allons déménager en juillet.
♦ **to move forward** avancer
♦ **to move in** emménager ◊ *They're moving in next week.* Ils emménagent la semaine prochaine.
♦ **to move over** se pousser ◊ *Could you move over a bit?* Est-ce que vous pouvez vous pousser un peu?

movement NOUN
le mouvement

movie NOUN
le film
♦ **the movies** le cinéma ◊ *Let's go to the movies!* Si on allait au cinéma?
♦ **a movie star** une vedette de cinéma

moving ADJECTIVE
1 en marche (*not stationary*) ◊ *a moving bus* un bus en marche
2 touchant (*touching*) ◊ *a moving story* une histoire touchante
♦ **a moving van** un camion de déménagement

to **mow** VERB
tondre
♦ **to mow the lawn** tondre le gazon

mower NOUN
la tondeuse à gazon

mown VERB *see* **mow**

MP NOUN
le député ◊ *She's an MP.* Elle est député.

MP3 ADJECTIVE
MP3 ◊ *an MP3 file* un fichier MP3
◊ *an MP3 player* un lecteur MP3

Mr NOUN
1 Monsieur
(PL Messieurs)
2 (*in address*)
M.
(PL MM.)

Mrs NOUN
1 Madame
(PL Mesdames)
2 (*in address*)
Mme
(PL Mmes)

M

MS NOUN (= *multiple sclerosis*)
la sclérose en plaques ◊ *He has MS.*
Il a la sclérose en plaques.

Ms NOUN
① Madame
(PL Mesdames)
② (*in address*)
Mme
(PL Mmes)

ⓘ *There isn't a direct equivalent of* **Ms** *in French. If you are writing to somebody and don't know whether she is married, use* **Madame**.

much ADJECTIVE, ADVERB, PRONOUN
① beaucoup (*with verb, adjective, adverb*) ◊ *Do you go out much?* Tu sors beaucoup? ◊ *I don't like sports much.* Je n'aime pas beaucoup le sport. ◊ *I feel much better now.* Je me sens beaucoup mieux maintenant.
② beaucoup de (*followed by noun*) ◊ *I haven't got much money.* Je n'ai pas beaucoup d'argent. ◊ *I don't want much rice.* Je ne veux pas beaucoup de riz.
♦ **very much** beaucoup ◊ *I enjoyed the film very much.* J'ai beaucoup apprécié le film. ◊ *Thank you very much.* Merci beaucoup. ◊ *I don't have very much money.* Je n'ai pas beaucoup d'argent.
♦ **not much (1)** pas beaucoup ◊ *"Do you have a lot of luggage?" "No, not much."* « As-tu beaucoup de bagages? » « Non, pas beaucoup. »
♦ **not much (2)** pas grand-chose ◊ *"What's on TV?" "Not much."* « Qu'est-ce qu'il y a à la télé? » « Pas grand-chose. » ◊ *"What did you think of it?" "Not much."* « Qu'est-ce que tu en as pensé? » « Pas grand-chose. »
♦ **How much?** Combien? ◊ *How much do you want?* Tu en veux combien? ◊ *How much time do you have?* Tu as combien de temps? ◊ *How much is it?* (*cost*) Combien est-ce que ça coûte?
♦ **too much** trop ◊ *That's too much!* C'est trop! ◊ *It costs too much.* Ça coûte trop cher. ◊ *They give us too much homework.* Ils nous donnent trop de devoirs.
♦ **so much** autant ◊ *I didn't think it would cost so much.* Je ne pensais pas que ça coûterait autant. ◊ *I've never seen so much traffic.* Je n'ai jamais vu autant de circulation.

mud NOUN
la boue

to **muddle up** VERB
confondre (*people*) ◊ *He muddles*

me up with my sister. Il me confond avec ma sœur.
♦ **to get muddled up** s'embrouiller ◊ *I'm getting muddled up.* Je m'embrouille.

muddy ADJECTIVE
boueux MASC
boueuse FEM

muesli NOUN
le muesli

muffin NOUN
le muffin

to **muffle** VERB
① étouffer (*voice*) ◊ *a muffled cry* un cri étouffé ◊ *in a muffled voice* d'une voix étouffée
② assourdir (*other sounds*) ◊ *to muffle the noise of traffic* assourdir le bruit de la circulation

muffler NOUN
le silencieux

mug NOUN

see also **mug** VERB

la grande tasse ◊ *Do you want a cup or a mug?* Est-ce que vous voulez une tasse normale ou une grande tasse?
♦ **mug shot** la photo d'identité judiciaire

to **mug** VERB

see also **mug** NOUN

agresser ◊ *He was mugged in the city centre.* Il s'est fait agresser au centre ville.

mugger NOUN
l' agresseur MASC ◊ *The mugger was a woman.* L'agresseur était une femme.

mugging NOUN
l' agression FEM

muggy ADJECTIVE
lourd ◊ *It's muggy out today.* Le temps est lourd aujourd'hui.

multicultural ADJECTIVE
multiculturel MASC
multiculturelle FEM

multimedia ADJECTIVE
multimédia ◊ *a multimedia presentation* une présentation multimédia

multiple choice test NOUN
le test à choix multiple

multiple sclerosis NOUN
la sclérose en plaques ◊ *She has multiple sclerosis.* Elle a la sclérose en plaques.

multiplication NOUN
la multiplication

to **multiply** VERB
    multiplier ◊ *to multiply 6 by 3*
    multiplier six par trois

multi-storey ADJECTIVE
    à plusieurs étages ◊ *a multi-storey parking garage*
✷ un stationnement à plusieurs étages

mummy NOUN
    la momie (*Egyptian*)

mumps NOUN
    les oreillons MASC PL

municipal ADJECTIVE
    municipal
    (MASC PL municipaux) ◊ *municipal government* le gouvernement municipal

mural NOUN
    la murale ◊ *The Grade 8s painted a mural in the gym.* Les élèves de huitième année ont peint une murale dans le gymnase.

murder NOUN

    see also **murder** VERB

    le meurtre MASC

to **murder** VERB

    see also **murder** NOUN

    assassiner

murderer NOUN
    l' assassin MASC
    l' assassine FEM

muscle NOUN
    le muscle

muscular ADJECTIVE
    musclé

museum NOUN
    le musée

mushroom NOUN
    le champignon ◊ *mushroom omelette* l'omelette aux champignons

music NOUN
    la musique

musical ADJECTIVE

    see also **musical** NOUN

    doué pour la musique ◊ *I'm not musical.* Je ne suis pas doué pour la musique.
♦ **a musical instrument** un instrument de musique

musical NOUN

    see also **musical** ADJECTIVE

    la comédie musicale

musician NOUN
    le musicien
    la musicienne

✷ **muskeg** NOUN
    le muskeg

Muslim NOUN
    le musulman
    la musulmane ◊ *He's a Muslim.* Il est musulman.

Muslim ADJECTIVE
    musulman

mussel NOUN
    la moule

must VERB

> When **must** means that you assume or suppose something is true, use **devoir**; when it means that someone has to do something, e.g., **I must buy some presents**, there are two choices. You can use **devoir**, or you can use **il faut que…**, which comes from the verb **falloir** and is followed by a verb in the subjunctive. The expression **il faut que** is more conversational.

1 devoir ◊ *You must be tired.* Tu dois être fatigué. ◊ *There must be some problem.* Il doit y avoir un problème. ◊ *I must clean up my room.* Je dois nettoyer ma chambre. ◊ *We must win this game.* Nous devons gagner ce match.
2 il faut que ◊ *I must buy some presents.* Il faut que j'achète des cadeaux. ◊ *I really must go now.* Il faut que j'y aille.

> When translating **must not**, you cannot use **devoir**.

♦ **You must not lie.** Il ne faut pas mentir.
♦ **Students must not operate this machine.** Les élèves n'ont pas le droit d'utiliser cet appareil.
♦ **You mustn't forget to send her a card.** N'oublie surtout pas de lui envoyer une carte.
♦ **You must come and see us.** (*invitation*) Venez donc nous voir.

mustard NOUN
    la moutarde

mustn't VERB = **must not**

mute ADJECTIVE
    muet MASC
    muette FEM

to **mutter** VERB
    marmonner

my ADJECTIVE
    mon MASC ◊ *my father* mon père
    ma FEM ◊ *my aunt* ma tante
    mes PL ◊ *my parents* mes parents

> **ma** becomes **mon** before a vowel sound.

♦ **my friend (1)** (*male*) mon ami
♦ **my friend (2)** (*female*) mon amie

M

☞

*Do not use **mon/ma/mes** with parts of the body.*

◊ *I want to wash my hair.* Je voudrais me laver les cheveux. ◊ *I'm going to brush my teeth.* Je vais me brosser les dents. ◊ *I've hurt my foot.* Je me suis fait mal au pied.

myself PRONOUN

① me ◊ *I've hurt myself.* Je me suis fait mal. ◊ *I really enjoyed myself.* Je me suis vraiment bien amusé. ◊ *... when I look at myself in the mirror.* ...quand je me regarde dans le miroir.
② moi ◊ *I don't like talking about myself.* Je n'aime pas parler de moi.
③ moi-même ◊ *I made it myself.* Je l'ai fait moi-même.

♦ **by myself** tout seul ◊ *I don't like travelling by myself.* Je n'aime pas voyager tout seul.

mysterious ADJECTIVE
mystérieux MASC
mystérieuse FEM

mystery NOUN
le mystère
♦ **a murder mystery** (*novel*) un roman policier

myth NOUN
① le mythe (*legend*) ◊ *a Greek myth* un mythe grec
② l' idée reçue FEM (*untrue idea*)
◊ *That's a myth.* C'est une idée reçue.

mythology NOUN
la mythologie

N

to **nag** VERB
harceler (*scold*) ◊ *They're always nagging me.* Ils me harcèlent constamment.

nail NOUN
① l' **ongle** MASC (*on finger, toe*)
◊ *Don't bite your nails!* Ne te ronge pas les ongles!
② le **clou** (*made of metal*)

nail brush NOUN
la **brosse à ongles**

nail clippers PL NOUN
le **coupe-ongles**
(PL les coupe-ongles)

nail file NOUN
la **lime à ongles**

nail polish NOUN
le **vernis à ongles**
♦ **nail polish remover** le dissolvant

naked ADJECTIVE
nu

name NOUN
see also **name** VERB
le **nom**
♦ **What's your name?** Comment vous appelez-vous?
♦ **to call somebody names** traiter quelqu'un de tous les noms

to **name** VERB
see also **name** NOUN
① **appeler** (*call*) ◊ *They named the baby Petra.* Ils ont appelé le bébé Petra.
♦ **I was named after my uncle.** J'ai reçu le nom de mon oncle.
② **nommer** ◊ *Name the provinces.* Nomme les provinces. ◊ *She was named Artist of the Year.* Elle a été nommée Artiste de l'année.

nanny NOUN
la **bonne d'enfants** ◊ *She's a nanny.* C'est une bonne d'enfants.

nap NOUN
le **petit somme**
♦ **to have a nap** faire un petit somme

napkin NOUN
la **serviette**

narrow ADJECTIVE
étroit

narrow-minded ADJECTIVE
borné

nasty ADJECTIVE
① **mauvais** (*bad*) ◊ *a nasty cold* un mauvais rhume ◊ *a nasty smell* une mauvaise odeur
② **méchant** (*unfriendly*) ◊ *He gave me a nasty look.* Il m'a regardé d'un air méchant.

nation NOUN
la **nation**

national ADJECTIVE
national
(MASC PL nationaux) ◊ *He's the national champion.* C'est le champion national.
✹ ♦ **the National Assembly** l'Assemblée nationale

national anthem NOUN
l' **hymne national** MASC ◊ *Our national anthem is "O Canada".* Notre hymne national est « Ô Canada ».

nationalism NOUN
le **nationalisme** ◊ *Québec nationalism* le nationalisme québécois

nationalist NOUN
le/la **nationaliste**

nationality NOUN
la **nationalité**

national park NOUN
le **parc national**
(PL les parcs nationaux)

native ADJECTIVE
natal ◊ *my native country* mon pays natal
♦ **native language** la langue maternelle ◊ *English is not their native language.* L'anglais n'est pas leur langue maternelle.
♦ **Native Peoples** les peuples autochtones MASC

natural ADJECTIVE
naturel MASC
naturelle FEM
♦ **natural resources** les ressources naturelles FEM

naturalist NOUN
le/la **naturaliste**

naturally ADVERB
naturellement ◊ *Naturally, we were very disappointed.* Nous avons naturellement été très déçus.

nature NOUN
la **nature**

naughty ADJECTIVE

☞

vilain usually goes before the noun.

vilain ◊ *Naughty dog!* Vilain chien!
◊ *Don't be naughty!* Ne fais pas le vilain!

nauseous ADJECTIVE
♦ **to feel nauseous** avoir la nausée
♦ **It made me nauseous.** Cela m'a donné la nausée.
♦ **a nauseous smell** une odeur écœurante

navel NOUN
le nombril

navy NOUN
la marine ◊ *He's in the navy.* Il est dans la marine.

navy blue ADJECTIVE
bleu marine MASC, FEM, PL ◊ *a navy blue skirt* une jupe bleu marine

Nazi NOUN
le nazi
la nazie ◊ *the Nazis* les nazis

near ADJECTIVE

see also **near** PREPOSITION

proche ◊ *It's fairly near.* C'est assez proche.
♦ **It's near enough to walk.** On peut facilement y aller à pied.
♦ **the nearest** le plus proche ◊ *Where's the nearest service station?* Où est la station-service la plus proche? ◊ *The nearest stores were three kilometres away.* Les magasins les plus proches étaient à trois kilomètres.

near PREPOSITION, ADVERB

see also **near** ADJECTIVE

près de ◊ *I live near Fredericton.* J'habite près de Fredericton. ◊ *near my house* près de chez moi
♦ **near here** près d'ici ◊ *Is there a bank near here?* Est-ce qu'il y a une banque près d'ici?

nearby ADVERB

see also **nearby** ADJECTIVE

à proximité ◊ *There's a supermarket nearby.* Il y a un supermarché à proximité.

nearby ADJECTIVE

see also **nearby** ADVERB

1 proche (*close*) ◊ *a nearby convenience store* un dépanneur proche
2 voisin (*neighbouring*) ◊ *We went to the nearby village of St. Jacob's.* Nous sommes allés à St. Jacob's, le village voisin.

nearly ADVERB
presque ◊ *Dinner's nearly ready.* Le dîner est presque prêt. ◊ *I'm nearly 15.* J'ai presque quinze ans.
♦ **I nearly missed the bus.** J'ai failli rater l'autobus.

neat ADJECTIVE
soigné ◊ *She has very neat writing.* Elle a une écriture très soignée.

neatly ADVERB
soigneusement ◊ *neatly folded* soigneusement plié
♦ **neatly dressed** impeccable

necessarily ADVERB
♦ **not necessarily** pas forcément

necessary ADJECTIVE
nécessaire

necessity NOUN
la nécessité ◊ *A car is a necessity, not a luxury.* Une voiture est une nécessité et non pas un luxe.

neck NOUN
1 le cou (*of body*)
♦ **a stiff neck** un torticolis
2 l' encolure FEM (*of garment*) ◊ *a V-neck sweater* un chandail avec une encolure en V

necklace NOUN
le collier

nectarine NOUN
la nectarine

to **need** VERB

see also **need** NOUN

avoir besoin de ◊ *I need a bigger size.* J'ai besoin d'une plus grande taille.
♦ **to need to do something** avoir besoin de faire quelque chose ◊ *I need to use the phone.* J'ai besoin d'utiliser le téléphone.

need NOUN

see also **need** VERB

♦ **There's no need to make reservations.** Il n'est pas nécessaire de réserver.

needle NOUN
l' aiguille FEM

negative NOUN

see also **negative** ADJECTIVE

le négatif (*photo*)

negative ADJECTIVE

see also **negative** NOUN

négatif MASC
négative FEM ◊ *He's got a very negative attitude.* Il a une attitude très négative.

neglected ADJECTIVE
mal tenu (*untidy*) ◊ *The garden is neglected.* Le jardin est mal tenu.

to **negotiate** VERB
négocier

negotiations PL NOUN
les négociations FEM

neighbour NOUN
le voisin
la voisine ◊ *the neighbours' garden*
le jardin des voisins

neighbourhood NOUN
le quartier

neither PRONOUN, CONJUNCTION, ADVERB
aucun des deux
aucune des deux ◊ *"Carrots or
peas?" "Neither, thanks."* « Des
carottes ou des petits pois? » « Aucun
des deux merci. » ◊ *Neither of them
is coming.* Aucun des deux ne vient.

♦ **neither...nor...** ni...ni... ◊ *Neither my
mom nor my dad is coming to the
school play.* Ni ma mère ni mon père
ne viennent à la pièce de l'école.

♦ **Neither do I.** Moi non plus. ◊ *"I don't
like him." "Neither do I!"* « Je ne
l'aime pas. » « Moi non plus! »

♦ **Neither have I.** Moi non plus.
◊ *"I've never been to the Northwest
Territories." "Neither have I."* « Je ne
suis jamais allé aux Territoires du
Nord-Ouest. » « Moi non plus. »

neon NOUN
le néon

♦ **a neon light** une lampe au néon

nephew NOUN
le neveu
(PL les neveux) ◊ *my nephew* mon
neveu

nerve NOUN
⒈ le nerf ◊ *She sometimes gets on
my nerves.* Elle me tape quelquefois
sur les nerfs.
⒉ le toupet (*boldness*) ◊ *He's got
some nerve!* Il a du toupet!

♦ **It's only nerves.** C'est de la nervosité.

♦ **to have an attack of nerves** avoir le
trac

nerve-racking ADJECTIVE
angoissant

nervous ADJECTIVE
(*tense*)
nerveux MASC
nerveuse FEM ◊ *I bite my nails when
I'm nervous.* Je me ronge les ongles
quand je suis nerveux.

♦ **to be nervous about something**
craindre quelque chose ◊ *I'm nervous
about my piano exam.* Je crains mon
examen de piano.

♦ **to be nervous about doing something**
craindre de faire quelque chose
◊ *I'm a bit nervous about flying to*

Newfoundland by myself. Je crains
un peu d'aller toute seule en avion à
Terre-Neuve.

nest NOUN
le nid

Net NOUN
Internet MASC ◊ *to surf the Net*
naviguer sur Internet

net NOUN
le filet ◊ *a volleyball net* un filet de
volleyball

network NOUN
le réseau
(PL les réseaux)

neurotic ADJECTIVE
névrosé

neutral ADJECTIVE
neutre ◊ *neutral colours* des couleurs
neutres ◊ *a neutral country* un pays
neutre ◊ *I don't want to take sides;
I'm staying neutral.* Je ne veux pas
prendre parti; je vais rester neutre.

never ADVERB
⒈ jamais ◊ *"Have you ever been to
the West Coast?" "No, never."* « Est-ce
que tu es déjà allé jusqu'à la côte
Ouest? » « Non, jamais. » ◊ *"When
are you going to phone him?"
"Never!"* « Quand est-ce que tu vas
l'appeler? » « Jamais! »

> *Add ne if the sentence contains a
> verb.*

⒉ ne...jamais ◊ *I never watch soap
operas.* Je ne regarde jamais les
téléromans. ◊ *I have never been
camping.* Je n'ai jamais fait de
camping. ◊ *Never leave valuables in
your car.* Ne laissez jamais d'objets de
valeur dans votre voiture.

♦ **Never again!** Plus jamais!
♦ **Never mind.** Ça ne fait rien.

new ADJECTIVE
⒈ nouveau MASC
nouvelle FEM
(MASC PL nouveaux) ◊ *her new bike* son
nouveau vélo ◊ *I need a new dress.*
J'ai besoin d'une nouvelle robe.

> ***nouveau** changes to **nouvel** before
> a vowel and most words beginning
> with "h".*

◊ *his new friend* son nouvel ami
♦ **New Age** le nouvel âge ◊ *New Age
music* la musique nouvel âge
⒉ (*brand new*)
neuf MASC
neuve FEM ◊ *They've got a new car.* Ils
ont une voiture neuve.

newborn NOUN
le nouveau-né

N

(PL les nouveau-nés)
la nouveau-née
(PL les nouveau-nées)
♦ **a newborn baby** un nouveau-né

New Brunswick NOUN
le Nouveau-Brunswick

newcomer NOUN
le nouveau venu
(PL les nouveaux venus)
la nouvelle venue

Newfoundland NOUN
Terre-Neuve

news NOUN
1 les nouvelles FEM PL ◊ *good news*
de bonnes nouvelles ◊ *I've had some
bad news.* J'ai reçu de mauvaises
nouvelles. ◊ *It was nice to get your
news.* J'ai été content d'avoir de tes
nouvelles.
2 la nouvelle (*single piece of news*)
◊ *That's wonderful news!* Quelle
bonne nouvelle!
3 le journal télévisé (*on TV*) ◊ *I watch
the news every evening.* Je regarde le
journal télévisé tous les soirs.
4 les informations FEM PL (*on radio*)
◊ *I listen to the news every morning.*
J'écoute les informations tous les
matins.

newspaper NOUN
le journal
(PL les journaux) ◊ *I deliver
newspapers.* Je distribue des
journaux.

newsstand NOUN
le kiosque à journaux

New Year's NOUN
le Nouvel An ◊ *to celebrate New
Year's* fêter le Nouvel An
♦ **Happy New Year!** Bonne Année!
♦ **New Year's Day**
🐾 le jour de l'An
♦ **New Year's Eve**
🐾 la veille du jour de l'An ◊ *a New Year's
Eve party* un réveillon du jour de l'An

next ADJECTIVE, ADVERB, PREPOSITION
1 prochain (*in time*) ◊ *next Saturday*
samedi prochain ◊ *next year* l'année
prochaine ◊ *next summer* l'été
prochain
2 suivant (*in sequence*) ◊ *the next
train* le train suivant ◊ *Next please!*
Au suivant!
3 ensuite (*afterwards*) ◊ *What
shall I do next?* Qu'est-ce que je fais
ensuite? ◊ *What happened next?*
Qu'est-ce qui s'est passé ensuite?
♦ **next to** à côté de ◊ *next to the bank* à
côté de la banque
♦ **the next day** le lendemain ◊ *The next
day we visited Windsor.* Le lendemain

nous avons visité Windsor.
♦ **the next time** la prochaine fois ◊ *the
next time you see her* la prochaine
fois que tu la verras
♦ **next door** à côté ◊ *They live next
door.* Ils habitent à côté. ◊ *the people
next door* les gens d'à côté
♦ **the next room** la pièce d'à côté

to **nibble** VERB
1 grignoter (*food*) ◊ *to nibble on a
cookie* grignoter un biscuit
2 mordiller ◊ *Don't nibble on your
pencil.* Ne mordille pas ton crayon.
♦ **nibble food** les amuse-gueules MASC

nice ADJECTIVE
1 (*kind*)
gentil MASC
gentille FEM ◊ *Your parents are very
nice.* Tes parents sont très gentils.
◊ *It was nice of you to remember my
birthday.* C'était gentil de ta part de te
souvenir de ma fête.
♦ **to be nice to somebody** être gentil
avec quelqu'un
2 joli (*pretty*) ◊ *That's a nice dress!*
Qu'est-ce qu'elle est jolie, cette robe!
◊ *Banff is a nice town.* Banff est une
jolie ville.
3 (*general term of approval*)
bon MASC
bonne FEM ◊ *a nice cup of coffee* une
bonne tasse de café
♦ **Have a nice time!** Amuse-toi bien!
♦ **nice weather** le beau temps
♦ **It's a nice day.** Il fait beau.

nickel NOUN
1 la pièce de cinq cents (*coin*)
2 le nickel (*mineral*)

nickname NOUN
le surnom

niece NOUN
la nièce ◊ *my niece* ma nièce

night NOUN
1 la nuit ◊ *I want a single room for
two nights.* Je veux une chambre
individuelle pour deux nuits.
♦ **My mother works nights.** Ma mère
travaille de nuit.
♦ **at night** la nuit
♦ **Good night!** Bonne nuit!
♦ **a night club** une boîte de nuit
2 le soir (*evening*) ◊ *tomorrow night*
demain soir
♦ **last night (1)** hier soir ◊ *We watched
a video last night.* Nous avons
regardé un vidéo hier soir.
♦ **last night (2)** la nuit dernière ◊ *Last
night I had a bad dream.* La nuit
dernière, j'ai fait un mauvais rêve.

nightgown NOUN
la chemise de nuit

nightmare NOUN
le <u>cauchemar</u> ◊ *It was a real nightmare!* Ça a été un vrai cauchemar!
♦ **to have a nightmare** faire un cauchemar

nightshirt NOUN
la <u>chemise de nuit</u>

nine NUMBER
<u>neuf</u> ◊ *He's nine.* Il a neuf ans.

nineteen NUMBER
<u>dix-neuf</u> ◊ *She's nineteen.* Elle a dix-neuf ans.

nineteenth ADJECTIVE
<u>dix-neuvième</u> ◊ *the nineteenth day of our holidays* la dix-neuvième journée de nos vacances ◊ *the nineteenth floor* le dix-neuvième étage
♦ **the nineteenth of August** le dix-neuf août

ninety NUMBER
<u>quatre-vingt-dix</u>

ninth ADJECTIVE
<u>neuvième</u> ◊ *the ninth floor* le neuvième étage
♦ **the ninth of August** le neuf août

no ADVERB, ADJECTIVE
1 <u>non</u> ◊ *"Are you coming?" "No."* « Est-ce que vous venez? » « Non. » ◊ *"Would you like some more?" "No thank you."* « Vous en voulez encore? » « Non merci. »
2 <u>pas de</u> (*not any*) ◊ *There's no hot water.* Il n'y a pas d'eau chaude. ◊ *There's no mail on Sundays.* Il n'y a pas de courrier le dimanche. ◊ *No problem.* Pas de problème.
♦ **I have no idea.** Je n'en ai aucune idée.
♦ **No way!** Pas question!
♦ **"no smoking"** « Défense de fumer »
♦ **No kidding!** Sans blague!

nobody PRONOUN
1 <u>personne</u> ◊ *"Who's going with you?" "Nobody."* « Qui t'accompagne? » « Personne. »

*Add **ne** if the sentence contains a verb.*

2 <u>ne...personne</u> ◊ *There was nobody in the office.* Il n'y avait personne au bureau.
♦ **Nobody likes this new rule.** Personne n'aime ce nouveau règlement.

to **nod** VERB
<u>acquiescer d'un signe de tête</u> (*in agreement*)
♦ **to nod at somebody** saluer quelqu'un d'un signe de tête (*as greeting*)

noise NOUN
le <u>bruit</u> ◊ *Please make less noise.* Faites moins de bruit, s'il vous plaît.

noisy ADJECTIVE
<u>bruyant</u>

to **nominate** VERB
<u>proposer</u> (*propose*) ◊ *I nominate Ian Alexander as president of the society.* Je propose Ian Alexander comme président de la société.
♦ **He was nominated for a Governor General's Award.** Il a été nominé pour un Prix du Gouverneur général.

none PRONOUN
1 <u>aucun</u>
<u>aucune</u> FEM ◊ *"How many sisters do you have?" "None."* « Tu as combien de sœurs? » « Aucune. » ◊ *"What sports do you play?" "None."* « Qu'est-ce que tu fais comme sport? » « Je n'en fais aucun. »

*Add **ne** if the sentence contains a verb.*

2 <u>aucun...ne</u> ◊ *None of my friends wanted to come.* Aucun de mes amis n'a voulu venir.
♦ **There's none left.** Il n'y en a plus.
♦ **There are none left.** Il n'y en a plus.

non-renewable ADJECTIVE
<u>non renouvelable</u> ◊ *non-renewable resources* les ressources non renouvelables

nonsense NOUN
les <u>niaiseries</u> FEM PL ◊ *She talks a lot of nonsense.* Elle dit beaucoup de niaiseries. ◊ *Nonsense!* Arrête tes niaiseries!

non-smoker NOUN
le <u>non-fumeur</u>
la <u>non-fumeuse</u> ◊ *I'm a non-smoker.* Je suis non-fumeur.

non-smoking ADJECTIVE
<u>non-fumeur</u> ◊ *a non-smoking section* une section non-fumeurs

non-stop ADJECTIVE, ADVERB
1 <u>direct</u> ◊ *a non-stop flight* un vol direct ◊ *We flew non-stop.* Nous avons pris un vol direct.
2 <u>sans arrêt</u> ◊ *He talks non-stop.* Il parle sans arrêt.

noodles PL NOUN
les <u>nouilles</u> FEM PL

noon NOUN
<u>midi</u> MASC ◊ *at noon* à midi ◊ *before noon* avant midi

no one PRONOUN
1 <u>personne</u> ◊ *"Who's going with you?" "No one."* « Qui t'accompagne? » « Personne. »

☞

Add ne if the sentence contains a verb.

② ne...personne ◊ *There was no one in the office.* Il n'y avait personne au bureau.
♦ **No one likes homework.** Personne n'aime les devoirs.

nor CONJUNCTION
♦ **neither...nor** ni...ni ◊ *neither the mall nor the pool* ni le centre commercial, ni la piscine
♦ **Nor do I.** Moi non plus. ◊ *"I didn't like the movie." "Nor did I."* « Je n'ai pas aimé le film. » « Moi non plus. »
♦ **Nor have I.** Moi non plus. ◊ *"I haven't seen her." "Nor have I."* « Je ne l'ai pas vue. » « Moi non plus. »

normal ADJECTIVE
① (*usual*)
habituel MASC
habituelle FEM ◊ *at the normal time* à l'heure habituelle
② (*standard*)
normal
(MASC PL normaux) ◊ *a normal car* une voiture normale

normally ADVERB
① généralement (*usually*) ◊ *I normally arrive at nine o'clock.* J'arrive généralement à neuf heures.
② normalement (*as normal*) ◊ *In spite of the strike, the airports are operating normally.* Malgré la grève, les aéroports fonctionnent normalement.

north ADJECTIVE, ADVERB

see also **north** NOUN

① nord MASC, FEM, PL ◊ *the north shore* la rive nord
♦ **a north wind** un vent du nord
② vers le nord ◊ *We were travelling north.* Nous allions vers le nord.
♦ **north of** au nord de ◊ *It's north of Cobourg.* C'est au nord de Cobourg.

north NOUN

see also **north** ADJECTIVE

le nord ◊ *in the north* dans le nord

North America NOUN
l' Amérique du Nord FEM

northbound ADJECTIVE ◊ *The truck was northbound on Hwy 400.* Le camion se trouvait sur l'autoroute 400 en direction du nord.
♦ **Northbound traffic is moving very slowly.** La circulation vers le nord avance très lentement.

northeast NOUN
le nord-est ◊ *in the northeast* au nord-est

northern ADJECTIVE
♦ **the northern part of the province** la partie nord de la province
♦ **Northern Québec** le Nord du Québec
♦ **the northern lights** l'aurore boréale FEM

North Pole NOUN
le pôle Nord

northwest NOUN
le nord-ouest ◊ *in the northwest* au nord-ouest

Northwest Territories NOUN
les Territoires du Nord-Ouest MASC

nose NOUN
le nez
(PL les nez)
♦ **to look down one's nose at someone** prendre quelqu'un de haut
♦ **to turn up one's nose at something** faire le dégoûté devant quelque chose
♦ **It was right under my nose.** C'était là juste sous mon nez.

nosebleed NOUN
♦ **to have a nosebleed** saigner du nez ◊ *I often get nosebleeds.* Je saigne souvent du nez.

nosy ADJECTIVE
fouineur MASC
fouineuse FEM

not ADVERB
① pas ◊ *Are you coming or not?* Est-ce que tu viens ou pas?
♦ **not really** pas vraiment
♦ **not at all** pas du tout
♦ **not yet** pas encore ◊ *"Are you finished?" "Not yet."* « As-tu fini? » « Pas encore. »

Add ne before a verb.

② ne...pas ◊ *I'm not sure.* Je ne suis pas sûr. ◊ *It's not raining.* Il ne pleut pas. ◊ *You shouldn't do that.* Tu ne devrais pas faire ça. ◊ *They haven't arrived yet.* Ils ne sont pas encore arrivés.
③ non ◊ *I hope not.* J'espère que non. ◊ *"Can you lend me $10?" "I'm afraid not."* « Est-ce que tu peux me prêter dix dollars? » « Non, désolé. »

note NOUN
① la note ◊ *to take notes* prendre des notes
② le mot (*letter*) ◊ *I'll write her a note.* Je vais lui écrire un mot.

notebook NOUN
① le carnet
② l' ordinateur bloc-notes MASC

to **note down** VERB
noter

notepad NOUN

le <u>bloc-notes</u>
(PL les blocs-notes)

nothing NOUN
① <u>rien</u> ◊ *"What's wrong?" "Nothing."*
« Qu'est-ce qui ne va pas ? » « Rien. »
◊ *nothing special* rien de particulier

> *Add **ne** if the sentence contains a verb.*

② <u>ne...rien</u> ◊ *He does nothing.* Il
ne fait rien. ◊ *He ate nothing for
breakfast.* Il n'a rien mangé au
déjeuner.
♦ **Nothing is open on Christmas Day.**
Rien n'est ouvert le jour de Noël.

notice NOUN

> *see also* **notice** VERB

(*sign*)
le <u>panneau</u>
(PL les panneaux)
♦ **to put up a notice** mettre un
panneau
♦ **a warning notice** un avertissement
♦ **Don't take any notice of her!** Ne fais
pas attention à elle !

to **notice** VERB

> *see also* **notice** NOUN

<u>remarquer</u>

notorious ADJECTIVE
<u>notoire</u> ◊ *a notorious criminal* un
criminel notoire ◊ *His pranks are
notorious.* Ses mauvais tours sont
notoires.

noun NOUN
le <u>nom</u>

Nova Scotia NOUN
la <u>Nouvelle-Écosse</u>

novel NOUN
le <u>roman</u>

novelist NOUN
le <u>romancier</u>
la <u>romancière</u>

November NOUN
<u>novembre</u> MASC
♦ **in November** en novembre

now ADVERB, CONJUNCTION
<u>maintenant</u> ◊ *What are you
doing now?* Qu'est-ce que tu fais
maintenant ?
♦ **just now** en ce moment ◊ *I'm rather
busy just now.* Je suis très occupé en
ce moment.
♦ **I did it just now.** Je viens de le faire.
♦ **He should be there by now.** Il doit
être arrivé à l'heure qu'il est.
♦ **It should be ready by now.** Ça devrait
être déjà prêt.
♦ **now and then** de temps en temps
♦ **now that you're here...** maintenant

que tu es là...

nowadays ADVERB
<u>de nos jours</u> ◊ *Nowadays we have
better medical care.* De nos jours, on
a de meilleurs soins de santé.

nowhere ADVERB
<u>nulle part</u> ◊ *nowhere else* nulle part
ailleurs

nuclear ADJECTIVE
<u>nucléaire</u> ◊ *nuclear power* l'énergie
nucléaire ◊ *a nuclear power station*
une centrale nucléaire ◊ *the nuclear
family* la famille nucléaire

nude ADJECTIVE
<u>nu</u>
♦ **to sunbathe nude** faire du bronzage
intégral

to **nudge** VERB
♦ **She nudged me when she saw him.**
Elle m'a donné un coup de coude
quand elle l'a vu.

nudist NOUN
le/la <u>nudiste</u>

nuisance NOUN
♦ **It's a nuisance.** C'est très embêtant.
♦ **Sorry to be a nuisance.** Désolé de
vous déranger.

numb ADJECTIVE
<u>engourdi</u> ◊ *My leg's gone numb.* J'ai
les jambes engourdies.
♦ **numb with cold** engourdi par le froid

number NOUN
① le <u>nombre</u> (*total amount*) ◊ *a large
number of people* un grand nombre
de gens
② le <u>numéro</u> (*of house, telephone,
bank account*) ◊ *They live at number
5.* Ils habitent au numéro cinq.
◊ *What's your phone number?* Quel
est votre numéro de téléphone ?
◊ *You've got the wrong number.* Vous
vous êtes trompé de numéro.
③ le <u>chiffre</u> (*figure, digit*) ◊ *I can't
read the second number.* Je n'arrive
pas à lire le deuxième chiffre.

nun NOUN
la <u>religieuse</u> ◊ *She's a nun.* Elle est
religieuse.

Nunavut NOUN
le <u>Nunavut</u>

nurse NOUN
l' <u>infirmier</u> MASC
l' <u>infirmière</u> FEM ◊ *She's a nurse.* Elle
est infirmière.

nursery NOUN
la <u>pépinière</u> (*for plants*)

nursery school NOUN
le <u>jardin d'enfants</u>

nut NOUN
① (*edible*)
la noix
(PL les noix)
② l' écrou MASC (*made of metal*)
♦ **You're a nut!** Tu es dingue!

nutmeg NOUN
la noix de muscade

nutrient NOUN
le nutriment

nutrition NOUN
la nutrition

nutritional ADJECTIVE
nutritif MASC

nutritive FEM ◊ *Junk food has almost no nutritional value.* La malbouffe n'a presque aucune valeur nutritive.

nutritionist NOUN
le/la nutritionniste

nutritious ADJECTIVE
nutritif MASC
nutritive FEM ◊ *a nutritious snack* une collation nutritive

nuts ADJECTIVE
♦ **He's nuts.** Il est dingue.

nylon NOUN
le nylon

O

oak NOUN
le <u>chêne</u> ◊ *an oak table* une table en chêne

oar NOUN
l' <u>aviron</u> MASC

oatmeal NOUN
le <u>gruau</u>

obedient ADJECTIVE
<u>obéissant</u>

to **obey** VERB
♦ **to obey the rules** respecter le règlement
♦ **to obey one's parents** obéir à ses parents

object NOUN
l' <u>objet</u> MASC ◊ *a familiar object* un objet familier

objection NOUN
l' <u>objection</u> FEM

objective NOUN
l' <u>objectif</u> MASC

oboe NOUN
le <u>hautbois</u> ◊ *I play the oboe.* Je joue du hautbois.

obscene ADJECTIVE
<u>obscène</u>

observant ADJECTIVE
<u>observateur</u> MASC
<u>observatrice</u> FEM

to **observe** VERB
<u>observer</u>

obsessed ADJECTIVE
<u>obsédé</u> ◊ *He's obsessed with trains.* Il est obsédé par les trains.

obsession NOUN
l' <u>obsession</u> FEM ◊ *It's getting to be an obsession with you.* Ça devient une obsession chez toi.
♦ **Hockey is an obsession of mine.** Le hockey est une de mes passions.

obsolete ADJECTIVE
<u>dépassé</u>

obstacle NOUN
l' <u>obstacle</u> MASC

to **obstruct** VERB
<u>bloquer</u> ◊ *A truck was obstructing the traffic.* Un camion bloquait la circulation.

to **obtain** VERB
<u>obtenir</u>

obvious ADJECTIVE
<u>évident</u>

obviously ADVERB
1 <u>évidemment</u> (*of course*) ◊ *"Do you want to pass the exam?" "Obviously!"* « Tu veux réussir à l'examen? » « Évidemment! »
♦ **Obviously not!** Bien sûr que non!
2 <u>manifestement</u> (*visibly*) ◊ *She was obviously exhausted.* Elle était manifestement épuisée.

occasion NOUN
l' <u>occasion</u> FEM ◊ *a special occasion* une occasion spéciale
♦ **on several occasions** à plusieurs reprises

occasionally ADVERB
<u>de temps en temps</u>

occupation NOUN
la <u>profession</u>

to **occupy** VERB
<u>occuper</u> ◊ *That seat is occupied.* Cette place est occupée.

to **occur** VERB
<u>avoir lieu</u> (*happen*) ◊ *The accident occurred yesterday.* L'accident a eu lieu hier.
♦ **It suddenly occurred to me that...** Il m'est soudain venu à l'esprit que...

ocean NOUN
l' <u>océan</u> MASC

o'clock ADVERB
♦ **at four o'clock** à quatre heures
♦ **It's five o'clock.** Il est cinq heures.

October NOUN
<u>octobre</u> MASC
♦ **in October** en octobre

octopus NOUN
la <u>pieuvre</u>

odd ADJECTIVE
1 <u>bizarre</u> ◊ *That's odd!* C'est bizarre!
2 <u>impair</u> ◊ *an odd number* un chiffre impair

of PREPOSITION
1 <u>de</u> ◊ *some photos of my holiday* des photos de mes vacances ◊ *a boy of ten* un garçon de dix ans

de changes to d' before a vowel and most words beginning with "h."

<u>d'</u> ◊ *a kilo of oranges* un kilo d'oranges

de + le changes to du, and de + les changes to des.

<u>du</u> ◊ *the end of the movie* la fin du

☞

film

des ◊ *the end of the holidays* la fin des vacances

2 en (*with quantity, amount*) ◊ *He has four sisters. I've met two of them.* Il a quatre sœurs. J'en ai rencontré deux. ◊ *Can I have half of that?* Je peux en avoir la moitié?

♦ **three of us** trois d'entre nous

♦ **a friend of mine** un de mes amis

♦ **the 14th of September** le quatorze septembre

♦ **That's very kind of you.** C'est très gentil de votre part.

♦ **It's made of wood.** C'est en bois.

off ADVERB, PREPOSITION, ADJECTIVE

> *For other expressions with* **off**, *see the verbs* **get, take, turn**, *etc.*

1 éteint (*heater, light, TV*) ◊ *All the lights are off.* Toutes les lumières sont éteintes.

2 fermé (*tap, gas*) ◊ *Are you sure the tap is off?* Tu es sûr que le robinet est fermé?

3 annulé (*cancelled*) ◊ *The game is off.* Le match est annulé.

♦ **to be off sick** être malade

♦ **a day off** un jour de congé ◊ *to take a day off work* prendre un jour de congé

♦ **She's off school today.** Elle n'est pas à l'école aujourd'hui.

♦ **I must be off now.** Je dois m'en aller maintenant.

♦ **I'm off.** Je m'en vais.

offence NOUN

le délit (*crime*)

♦ **No offence, but...** Sans vouloir t'offenser,...

♦ **to take offence at something** s'offenser de quelque chose

to **offend** VERB

offenser ◊ *Did my joke offend you?* Est-ce que ma plaisanterie t'a offensé?

♦ **to be offended by something** s'offenser de quelque chose

offensive ADJECTIVE

choquant

offer NOUN

> *see also* **offer** VERB

la proposition ◊ *a good offer* une proposition intéressante ◊ *Make me an offer.* Faites-moi une proposition.

♦ **$30 or best offer** 30 dollars ou offre la plus intéressante

to **offer** VERB

> *see also* **offer** NOUN

1 offrir ◊ *He offered me a cookie.* Il m'a offert un biscuit.

2 proposer ◊ *He offered to help me.* Il m'a proposé de m'aider. ◊ *I offered to go with them.* Je leur ai proposé de les accompagner.

office NOUN

le bureau

(PL les bureaux) ◊ *She works in an office.* Elle travaille dans un bureau.

officer NOUN

1 (*police*)

l' agent de police MASC

l' agente de police FEM

2 (*other*)

l' officier MASC

l' officière FEM

official ADJECTIVE

officiel MASC

officielle FEM

off-season NOUN

♦ **It's cheaper during the off-season.** C'est moins cher hors saison.

offside ADJECTIVE

hors jeu (*sports*)

often ADVERB

souvent ◊ *It often rains.* Il pleut souvent. ◊ *How often do you go to the movies?* Tu vas souvent au cinéma? ◊ *I'd like to go skiing more often.* J'aimerais aller skier plus souvent.

oil NOUN

> *see also* **oil** VERB

1 l' huile FEM (*for lubrication, cooking*)

♦ **an oil painting** une peinture à l'huile

2 le pétrole (*crude oil*) ◊ *oil from the Alberta tar sands* le pétrole des sables bitumineux de l'Alberta

to **oil** VERB

> *see also* **oil** NOUN

graisser

oil rig NOUN

la plateforme pétrolière ◊ *She works on an oil rig.* Elle travaille sur une plateforme pétrolière.

oil slick NOUN

la marée noire

oil well NOUN

le puits de pétrole

ointment NOUN

l' onguent MASC

okay EXCLAMATION, ADJECTIVE

d'accord (*agreed*) ◊ *"Could you call back later?" "Okay!"* « Tu peux rappeler plus tard? » « D'accord! » ◊ *I'll meet you at six o'clock, okay?* Je te retrouve à six heures, d'accord? ◊ *Is that okay?* C'est d'accord?

♦ **I'll do it tomorrow, if that's okay**

with you. Je le ferai demain, si tu es d'accord.
- **Are you okay?** Ça va?
- **"How was your holiday?" "It was okay."** « C'était comment tes vacances? » « Pas mal. »
- **"What's your teacher like?" "He's okay."** « Il est comment ton prof? » « Il est sympathique. » (*informal*)

old ADJECTIVE
1 <u>vieux</u> MASC
<u>vieille</u> FEM ◊ *an old dog* un vieux chien ◊ *an old house* une vieille maison

> *vieux changes to **vieil** before a vowel and most words beginning with "h".*

◊ *an old man* un vieil homme

> *When talking about people it is more polite to use **âgé** instead of **vieux**.*

<u>âgé</u> ◊ *old people* les personnes âgées
2 (*former*)
<u>ancien</u> MASC
<u>ancienne</u> FEM ◊ *my old school* mon ancienne école
- **How old are you?** Quel âge as-tu?
- **He's ten years old.** Il a dix ans.
- **my older brother** mon frère aîné ◊ *my older sister* ma sœur aînée
- **She's two years older than me.** Elle a deux ans de plus que moi.
- **I'm the oldest in the family.** Je suis l'aîné de la famille.

old-fashioned ADJECTIVE
1 <u>démodé</u> ◊ *She wears old-fashioned clothes.* Elle porte des vêtements démodés.
2 (*person*)
<u>vieux jeu</u> MASC, FEM, PL ◊ *My parents are rather old-fashioned.* Mes parents sont plutôt vieux jeu.

olive NOUN
l' <u>olive</u> FEM
- **olive oil** l'huile d'olive

Olympic ADJECTIVE
<u>olympique</u>
- **the Olympics** les Jeux olympiques MASC

omelette NOUN
l' <u>omelette</u> FEM

on PREPOSITION, ADVERB
see also **on** ADJECTIVE

> *There are several ways of translating **on**. Scan the examples to find one that is similar to what you want to say. For other expressions with **on**, see the verbs **go, put, turn**, etc.*

1 <u>sur</u> ◊ *on the table* sur la table ◊ *on an island* sur une île

2 <u>à</u> ◊ *on the left* à gauche ◊ *on the 2nd floor* au deuxième étage ◊ *I go to school on my bike.* Je vais à l'école à vélo.
- **on TV** à la télé ◊ *What's on TV?* Qu'est-ce qu'il y a à la télé?
- **on the radio** à la radio ◊ *I heard it on the radio.* Je l'ai entendu à la radio.
- **on the bus (1)** (*by bus*) en autobus ◊ *I go into town on the bus.* Je vais en ville en autobus.
- **on the bus (2)** (*inside*) dans l'autobus ◊ *There were no empty seats on the bus.* Il n'y avait pas de places libres dans l'autobus.
- **on holiday** en vacances ◊ *They're on holiday.* Ils sont en vacances.
- **on strike** en grève

> *With days and dates **on** is not translated.*

◊ *on Friday* vendredi ◊ *on Fridays* le vendredi ◊ *on Christmas Day* le jour de Noël ◊ *on June 20th* le vingt juin ◊ *on my birthday* le jour de mon anniversaire

on ADJECTIVE
see also **on** PREPOSITION

1 <u>allumé</u> (*heater, light, TV*) ◊ *I think I left the light on.* Je crois que j'ai laissé la lumière allumée.
2 <u>ouvert</u> (*tap, gas*) ◊ *You left the tap on.* Tu as laissé le robinet ouvert.
3 <u>en marche</u> (*machine*) ◊ *Is the dishwasher on?* Est-ce que le lave-vaisselle est en marche?
- **What's on at the movie theatre?** Qu'est-ce qui passe au cinéma?

once ADVERB
<u>une fois</u> ◊ *once a week* une fois par semaine ◊ *once more* encore une fois ◊ *I've been to Nunavut once before.* J'ai déjà été une fois à Nunavut.
- **Once upon a time...** Il était une fois...
- **at once** tout de suite
- **all at once** (*suddenly*) tout à coup
- **once in a while** de temps en temps

one NUMBER, PRONOUN

> *Use **un** for masculine nouns and **une** for feminine nouns.*

1 <u>un</u> ◊ *one day* un jour ◊ *"Do you need a stamp?" "No thanks, I've got one."* « Est-ce que tu as besoin d'un timbre? » « Non merci, j'en ai un. »
<u>une</u> ◊ *one minute* une minute ◊ *I have one brother and one sister.* J'ai un frère et une sœur.
2 <u>on</u> (*impersonal*) ◊ *One never knows.* On ne sait jamais.
- **one by one** un à un
- **one after the other** l'un après l'autre
- **this one (1)** celui-ci (*masculine*)

☞

O

◊ *"Which foot is hurting?" "This one."* « Quel pied te fait mal? » « Celui-ci. »
♦ **this one (2)** celle-ci (*feminine*)
◊ *"Which is the best photo?" "This one."* « Quelle est la meilleure photo? » « Celle-ci. »
♦ **that one (1)** celui-là (*masculine*)
◊ *"Which bag is yours?" "That one."* « Lequel est ton sac? » « Celui-là. »
♦ **that one (2)** celle-là (*feminine*)
◊ *"Which seat do you want?" "That one."* « Quelle place voulez-vous? » « Celle-là. »

oneself PRONOUN
① se ◊ *to hurt oneself* se faire mal
② soi-même ◊ *It's quicker to do it oneself.* C'est plus rapide de le faire soi-même.

one-way ADJECTIVE
♦ **a one-way street** une impasse

onion NOUN
l' oignon MASC ◊ *onion soup* la soupe à l'oignon

online ADJECTIVE
en ligne

only ADVERB, ADJECTIVE, CONJUNCTION
① seul ◊ *Monday is the only day I'm free.* Le lundi est le seul jour où je suis libre. ◊ *French is the only subject I like.* Le français est la seule matière que j'aime.
② seulement ◊ *"How much was it?" "Only $10."* « Combien c'était? » « Seulement dix dollars. » ◊ *Not only is she intelligent, she's also very nice.* Elle est non seulement intelligente, mais aussi très gentille.
③ ne...que ◊ *We only want to stay for one night.* Nous ne voulons rester qu'une nuit. ◊ *These cassettes are only $5.* Ces cassettes ne coûtent que cinq dollars.
④ mais ◊ *I'd like the same sweater, only in black.* Je voudrais le même chandail, mais en noir.
♦ **an only child** un enfant unique

Ontario NOUN
l'Ontario MASC

onwards ADVERB
à partir de ◊ *from July onwards* à partir de juillet

open ADJECTIVE

see also **open** VERB

① ouvert ◊ *The bakery is open on Sunday morning.* La boulangerie est ouverte le dimanche matin. ◊ *I'm open to suggestions.* Je suis ouvert aux suggestions.
② franc MASC

franche FEM ◊ *She was very open with me.* Elle a été tout à fait franche avec moi.
③ vacant ◊ *Is the position still open?* Est-ce que le poste est encore vacant?
♦ **in the open air** en plein air
♦ **to have an open mind** avoir l'esprit ouvert

to **open** VERB

see also **open** ADJECTIVE

① ouvrir ◊ *Can I open the window?* Est-ce que je peux ouvrir la fenêtre? ◊ *What time do the stores open?* Les magasins ouvrent à quelle heure?
② s'ouvrir ◊ *The door opens automatically.* La porte s'ouvre automatiquement. ◊ *The door opened and in came the teacher.* La porte s'est ouverte et la professeure est entrée.

opening NOUN
① l' ouverture FEM ◊ *the opening of Parliament* l'ouverture de la session parlementaire ◊ *an opening in the wall* une ouverture dans le mur
② l' entrée FEM (*to cave, tunnel*)
③ l' éclaircie FEM (*in clouds*)
④ le poste vacant (*for specific job*) ◊ *We have an opening for a receptionist.* Nous avons un poste vacant de réceptionniste.
⑤ le débouché (*potential job opportunity*) ◊ *There are a lot of openings in the computer industry.* Il y a beaucoup de débouchés dans l'informatique.

opera NOUN
l' opéra MASC

to **operate** VERB
① fonctionner ◊ *I don't know how the legal system operates in Québec.* Je ne sais pas comment fonctionne le système judiciaire au Québec.
② faire fonctionner ◊ *How do you operate the VCR?* Comment fait-on fonctionner le magnétoscope?
③ opérer (*medically*) ◊ *to operate on someone* opérer quelqu'un

operation NOUN
l' opération FEM ◊ *a major operation* une grave opération
♦ **to have an operation** se faire opérer ◊ *I have never had an operation.* Je ne me suis jamais fait opérer.

operator NOUN
le/la standardiste (*on telephone*)

opinion NOUN
l' avis MASC ◊ *in my opinion* à mon avis ◊ *He asked me my opinion.* Il m'a demandé mon avis.
♦ **What's your opinion?** Qu'est-ce que

vous en pensez?

opinion poll NOUN
le <u>sondage</u>

opponent NOUN
l' <u>adversaire</u> MASC/FEM

opportunity NOUN
l' <u>occasion</u> FEM
♦ **to have the opportunity to do something** avoir l'occasion de faire quelque chose ◊ *I've never had the opportunity to go to the Northwest Territories.* Je n'ai jamais eu l'occasion d'aller aux Territoires du Nord-Ouest.

opposed ADJECTIVE ◊ *I've always been opposed to violence.* J'ai toujours été contre la violence.
♦ **as opposed to** par opposition à

opposing ADJECTIVE
<u>opposé</u> (*team*)

opposite ADJECTIVE, PREPOSITION
① <u>opposé</u> ◊ *It's in the opposite direction.* C'est dans la direction opposée.
② <u>en face de</u> ◊ *the girl sitting opposite me* la fille assise en face de moi
♦ **the opposite sex** l'autre sexe

opposition NOUN
l' <u>opposition</u> FEM ◊ *the leader of the Opposition* le chef de l'opposition ◊ *We ran into a lot of opposition.* Nous avons rencontré beaucoup d'opposition.

optimist NOUN
l' <u>optimiste</u> MASC/FEM

optimistic ADJECTIVE
<u>optimiste</u>

option NOUN
le <u>choix</u> (*choice*) ◊ *Our only option is to take the bus.* Notre seul choix est de prendre l'autobus.

optional ADJECTIVE
<u>facultatif</u> MASC
<u>facultative</u> FEM

optometrist NOUN
l' <u>optométriste</u> MASC/FEM ◊ *I picked up my new glasses at the optometrist's.* J'ai passé prendre mes nouvelles lunettes chez l'optométriste.

or CONJUNCTION
① <u>ou</u> ◊ *Would you like tea or coffee?* Est-ce que tu veux du thé ou du café?

*Use **ni...ni** in negative sentences.*

◊ *I don't eat meat or fish.* Je ne mange ni viande ni poisson.
② <u>sinon</u> (*otherwise*) ◊ *Hurry up or you'll miss the bus.* Dépêche-toi,

sinon tu vas rater l'autobus.
♦ **Give me the money, or else!** Donne-moi l'argent, sinon tu vas le regretter!

oral ADJECTIVE
<u>oral</u>
(MASC PL oraux)
♦ **an oral presentation** une présentation orale

orange NOUN

| see also **orange** ADJECTIVE |

l' <u>orange</u> FEM
♦ **an orange juice** un jus d'orange

orange ADJECTIVE

| see also **orange** NOUN |

<u>orange</u> MASC, FEM, PL

orchard NOUN
le <u>verger</u>

orchestra NOUN
l' <u>orchestre</u> MASC ◊ *I play in the school orchestra.* Je joue dans l'orchestre de l'école.

order NOUN

| see also **order** VERB |

① l' <u>ordre</u> MASC (*sequence*) ◊ *in alphabetical order* en ordre alphabétique
② la <u>commande</u> (*instruction*) ◊ *The waiter took our order.* Le serveur a pris notre commande.
♦ **in order to** pour ◊ *She mows lawns in order to earn money.* Elle tond les gazons pour gagner de l'argent.
♦ **"out of order"** « en panne »

to **order** VERB

| see also **order** NOUN |

<u>commander</u> ◊ *I ordered a hamburger and fries.* J'ai commandé un hamburger et des frites. ◊ *Are you ready to order?* Vous êtes prêt à commander?
♦ **to order somebody around** donner des ordres à quelqu'un ◊ *She was fed up with being ordered around.* Elle en avait assez de toujours se faire donner des ordres.

ordinary ADJECTIVE
① <u>ordinaire</u> ◊ *an ordinary day* une journée ordinaire
② <u>comme les autres</u> (*people*) ◊ *an ordinary family* une famille comme les autres ◊ *He's just an ordinary guy.* C'est un type comme les autres.

organ NOUN
① l' <u>orgue</u> MASC (*instrument*) ◊ *I play the organ.* Je joue de l'orgue.
② l' <u>organe</u> MASC (*in body*)

organic ADJECTIVE
<u>biologique</u> (*vegetables, fruit*)

O

organization NOUN
l' **organisation** FEM

to **organize** VERB
organiser

origin NOUN
l' **origine** FEM

original ADJECTIVE
original
(MASC PL originaux) ◊ *It's a very original idea.* C'est une idée très originale.
♦ **Our original plan was to go camping.** Au départ, nous avions l'intention de faire du camping.

originally ADVERB
au départ

ornament NOUN
le **bibelot**

orphan NOUN
l' **orphelin** MASC
l' **orpheline** FEM

orthodontist NOUN
l' **orthodontiste** MASC/FEM ◊ *I have to go to the orthodontist this afternoon.* Il faut que j'aille chez l'orthodontiste cet après-midi.

ostrich NOUN
l' **autruche** FEM

other ADJECTIVE, PRONOUN
autre ◊ *Have you got these jeans in other colours?* Est-ce que vous avez ces jeans dans d'autres couleurs?
◊ *on the other side of the street* de l'autre côté de la rue ◊ *the other day* l'autre jour
♦ **the other one** l'autre ◊ *"This one?" "No, the other one."* « Celui-ci? » « Non, l'autre. »
♦ **the others** les autres ◊ *The others are going but I'm not.* Les autres y vont mais pas moi.
♦ **every other day** tous les deux jours
♦ **other than that** à part ça

otherwise ADVERB, CONJUNCTION
1 **sinon** (*if not*) ◊ *Write down the number, otherwise you'll forget it.* Note le numéro, sinon tu vas l'oublier. ◊ *Put some sunscreen on; you'll get burned otherwise.* Mets une crème solaire, sinon tu vas attraper des coups de soleil.
2 **à part ça** (*in other ways*) ◊ *I'm tired, but otherwise I'm fine.* Je suis fatigué, mais à part ça, ça va.

otter NOUN
la **loutre**

ought VERB

> To translate **ought to** use the conditional tense of **devoir**.

◊ *I ought to phone my parents.* Je devrais appeler mes parents. ◊ *He ought to win.* Il devrait gagner.

our ADJECTIVE
notre ◊ *Our house is quite big.* Notre maison est plutôt grande.
nos PL ◊ *Our neighbours are very nice.* Nos voisins sont très gentils.

ours PRONOUN
le nôtre + MASC NOUN ◊ *Your garden is very big. Ours is much smaller.* Votre jardin est très grand. Le nôtre est beaucoup plus petit.
la nôtre + FEM NOUN ◊ *Your school is very different from ours.* Votre école est très différente de la nôtre.
les nôtres + PL NOUN ◊ *"Our teachers are strict." "Ours are too."* « Nos professeurs sont sévères. » « Les nôtres aussi. »
♦ **Is this ours?** C'est à nous? ◊ *This car is ours.* Cette voiture est à nous. ◊ *"Whose is this?" "It's ours."* « C'est à qui? » « À nous. »

ourselves PRONOUN
1 **nous** ◊ *We really enjoyed ourselves.* Nous nous sommes vraiment bien amusés.
2 **nous-mêmes** ◊ *We built our garage ourselves.* Nous avons construit notre garage nous-mêmes.

out ADVERB

> There are several ways of translating **out**. Scan the examples to find one that is similar to what you want to say. For other expressions with **out**, see the verbs **go**, **put**, **turn**, etc.

1 **dehors** (*outside*) ◊ *It's cold out.* Il fait froid dehors.
2 **éteint** (*light, fire*) ◊ *All the lights are out.* Toutes les lumières sont éteintes.
♦ **She's out.** Elle est sortie.
♦ **He's out shopping.** Il est sorti faire des courses.
♦ **She's out for the afternoon.** Elle ne sera pas là de tout l'après-midi.
♦ **out there** dehors ◊ *It's cold out there.* Il fait froid dehors.
♦ **to go out** sortir ◊ *I'm going out tonight.* Je sors ce soir.
♦ **to go out with somebody** sortir avec quelqu'un ◊ *She's been going out with him for two months.* Elle sort avec lui depuis deux mois.
♦ **out of (1)** dans ◊ *to drink out of a glass* boire dans un verre
♦ **out of (2)** sur ◊ *in 9 cases out of 10* dans neuf cas sur dix
♦ **out of (3)** en dehors de ◊ *He lives out of town.* Il habite en dehors de la ville.

♦ **3 km out of town** à trois kilomètres de la ville
♦ **out of curiosity** par curiosité
♦ **out of date (1)** (*expired*) périmé
♦ **out of date (2)** (*outmoded*) démodé
♦ **out of work** sans emploi
♦ **That's out of the question.** C'est hors de question.
♦ **You're out!** (*in game*) Tu es éliminé!

outbreak NOUN
[1] l' <u>épidémie</u> FEM (*of disease*) ◊ *an outbreak of the flu* une épidémie de grippe
[2] le <u>début</u> ◊ *the outbreak of war* le début de la guerre

outcome NOUN
l' <u>issue</u> FEM ◊ *What was the outcome of the negotiations?* Quelle a été l'issue des négociations?

outdoor ADJECTIVE
<u>en plein air</u> ◊ *an outdoor swimming pool* une piscine en plein air
♦ **outdoor activities** les activités de plein air

outdoors ADVERB
<u>au grand air</u>

outer ADJECTIVE
<u>extérieur</u> ◊ *the outer surface* la surface extérieure ◊ *the outer door* la porte extérieure
♦ **outer space** l'espace MASC
♦ **outer clothing** les vêtements d'extérieur MASC

outfit NOUN
la <u>tenue</u> ◊ *She bought a new outfit for the wedding.* Elle a acheté une nouvelle tenue pour le mariage.
♦ **a cowboy outfit** un costume de cowboy

outgoing ADJECTIVE
<u>extraverti</u> ◊ *He's very outgoing.* Il est très extraverti.

outhouse NOUN
les <u>toilettes extérieures</u> FEM PL

outing NOUN
la <u>sortie</u> ◊ *to go on an outing* faire une sortie

outline NOUN
[1] les <u>grandes lignes</u> FEM (*summary*) ◊ *This is an outline of the plan.* Voici les grandes lignes du projet.
[2] les <u>contours</u> MASC PL (*shape*) ◊ *We could see the outline of the mountain in the mist.* Nous distinguions les contours de la montagne dans la brume.

outlook NOUN
[1] l' <u>attitude</u> FEM (*attitude*) ◊ *my outlook on life* mon attitude face à la vie

[2] les <u>perspectives</u> FEM PL (*prospects*) ◊ *the economic outlook* les perspectives économiques
♦ **The outlook is poor.** Les choses s'annoncent mal.

to **outnumber** VERB
♦ **We're outnumbered.** Ils sont plus nombreux que nous.
♦ **Girls outnumber boys three to one here.** Les filles sont trois fois plus nombreuses que les garçons ici.

outrageous ADJECTIVE
[1] (*behaviour*)
<u>scandaleux</u> MASC
<u>scandaleuse</u> FEM
[2] <u>exorbitant</u> (*price*)

outside NOUN

> see also **outside** ADJECTIVE

l' <u>extérieur</u> MASC

outside ADJECTIVE, ADVERB, PREPOSITION

> see also **outside** NOUN

[1] <u>extérieur</u> ◊ *the outside walls* les murs extérieurs
[2] <u>dehors</u> ◊ *It's very cold outside.* Il fait très froid dehors.
[3] <u>en dehors de</u> ◊ *outside the school* en dehors de l'école ◊ *outside school hours* en dehors des heures de cours

outskirts PL NOUN
la <u>banlieue</u> ◊ *on the outskirts of the town* dans les banlieues de la ville

outstanding ADJECTIVE
<u>remarquable</u>

oval ADJECTIVE
<u>ovale</u>

oven NOUN
le <u>four</u>

over PREPOSITION, ADVERB, ADJECTIVE

> *When there is movement over something, use **par-dessus**; when something is located above something, use **au-dessus de**.*

[1] <u>par-dessus</u> ◊ *The ball went over the wall.* Le ballon est passé par-dessus le mur.
[2] <u>au-dessus de</u> ◊ *There's a mirror over the washbasin.* Il y a un miroir au-dessus du lavabo.
[3] <u>plus de</u> (*more than*) ◊ *It's over twenty kilos.* Ça pèse plus de vingt kilos. ◊ *The temperature was over thirty degrees.* Il faisait une température de plus de trente degrés.
[4] <u>pendant</u> (*during*) ◊ *over the holidays* pendant les vacances ◊ *over Christmas* pendant les fêtes de Noël
[5] <u>terminé</u> (*finished*) ◊ *I'll be happy when the exams are over.* Je serai content quand les examens seront

O

☞

terminés.
♦ **over here** ici
♦ **over there** là-bas
♦ **all over the province** dans toute la province
♦ **I spilled coffee over my shirt.** J'ai renversé du café sur ma chemise.

overall ADVERB
dans l'ensemble (*generally*) ◊ *My marks were pretty good overall.* Mes notes étaient assez bonnes dans l'ensemble.

overalls PL NOUN
les vêtements de travail MASC PL

overcast ADJECTIVE
couvert ◊ *The sky was overcast.* Le ciel était couvert.

to **overcharge** VERB
♦ **He overcharged me.** Il m'a fait payer trop cher.
♦ **They overcharged us for the meal.** Ils nous ont fait payer trop cher pour le repas.

overcoat NOUN
le pardessus

overdone ADJECTIVE
trop cuit (*food*)

overdose NOUN
la surdose (*of drugs*) ◊ *He died of an overdose.* Il a succombé à une surdose.

overdue ADJECTIVE
♦ **This book is overdue.** Je suis en retard pour rendre ce livre.

to **overestimate** VERB
surestimer

to **overflow** VERB
déborder ◊ *to overflow with enthusiasm* déborder d'enthousiasme ◊ *The toilet is overflowing.* La toilette déborde. ◊ *The river has overflowed its banks.* La rivière a débordé de son lit.

overhead projector NOUN
le rétroprojecteur

to **overlap** VERB
se chevaucher ◊ *The boards overlap.* Les planches se chevauchent. ◊ *Your job overlaps with mine.* Ton travail et le mien se chevauchent.

to **overlook** VERB
① donner sur (*have view of*) ◊ *The hotel overlooks the beach.* L'hôtel donne sur la plage.
② négliger (*forget about*) ◊ *She had overlooked one important problem.* Elle avait négligé un problème important.

to **overreact** VERB

réagir de façon exagérée ◊ *I may have overreacted.* J'ai peut-être réagi de façon exagérée.
♦ **You're always overreacting.** Tu dramatises toujours tout.

overseas ADVERB
à l'étranger ◊ *I'd like to work overseas.* J'aimerais travailler à l'étranger.

oversight NOUN
l' oubli MASC

to **oversleep** VERB
se réveiller en retard ◊ *I overslept this morning.* Je me suis réveillé en retard ce matin.

overtime NOUN
① les heures supplémentaires FEM PL ◊ *to work overtime* faire des heures supplémentaires
② la prolongation (*sports*) ◊ *thirty minutes of overtime* trente minutes de prolongation ◊ *The game went into overtime.* Le match est allé en prolongation.

overweight ADJECTIVE
trop gros MASC
trop grosse FEM

to **overwhelm** VERB
① accabler ◊ *overwhelmed with work* accablé de travail ◊ *overwhelmed with sadness* accablé de tristesse
② inonder ◊ *We've been overwhelmed with offers of help.* Nous sommes inondés d'offres d'aide.
③ bouleverser ◊ *The experience overwhelmed me.* L'expérience m'a bouleversée.
♦ **overwhelming support** un soutien enthousiaste
♦ **Her kindness has been overwhelming.** Sa gentillesse m'a comblé.

to **owe** VERB
devoir
♦ **to owe somebody something** devoir quelque chose à quelqu'un ◊ *I owe you $50.* Je te dois cinquante dollars.

owl NOUN
le hibou
(PL les hiboux)

own ADJECTIVE

see also **own** VERB

propre ◊ *I have my own cell phone.* J'ai mon propre téléphone cellulaire.
♦ **I'd like a room of my own.** J'aimerais avoir une chambre à moi.
♦ **on his own** tout seul ◊ *on her own* toute seule ◊ *on our own* tout seuls

to **own** VERB

see also **own** ADJECTIVE
posséder

to **own up** VERB
<u>avouer</u>
♦ **to own up to something** admettre
quelque chose

owner NOUN
le/la <u>propriétaire</u>

oxygen NOUN
l' <u>oxygène</u> MASC

oyster NOUN
l' <u>huître</u> FEM

ozone NOUN
l' <u>ozone</u> FEM
♦ **the ozone layer** la couche d'ozone

O

P

PA NOUN
♦ **the PA system** (*public address*) les
haut-parleurs MASC PL

pace NOUN
l' allure FEM (*speed*) ◊ *He was walking
at a brisk pace.* Il marchait à vive
allure.

pacifier NOUN
la sucette

to **pack** VERB

see also **pack** NOUN

faire ses bagages ◊ *I'll help you
pack.* Je vais t'aider à faire tes
bagages.
♦ **I've already packed my suitcase.** J'ai
déjà fait ma valise.

pack NOUN

see also **pack** VERB

1 le paquet (*packet*) ◊ *a pack of gum*
un paquet de gomme à mâcher
2 le sac à dos (*backpack*) ◊ *Carry it
home in your pack.* Rapporte-le chez
toi dans ton sac à dos.
♦ **a pack of cards** un jeu de cartes

package NOUN
le paquet
♦ **a package holiday** un voyage
organisé

packed ADJECTIVE
plein (*crowded*) ◊ *The movie theatre
was packed.* Le cinéma était plein.

packet NOUN
le paquet ◊ *a packet of sunflower
seeds* un paquet de graines de
tournesol

pad NOUN
(*notepad*)
le bloc-notes
(PL les blocs-notes)

to **paddle** VERB

see also **paddle** NOUN

1 pagayer (*canoe*)
2 faire trempette (*play in water*)

paddle NOUN

see also **paddle** VERB

※ 1 l' aviron MASC (*canoe*)
2 la pagaie (*chiefly kayak*)

padlock NOUN
le cadenas

page NOUN

see also **page** VERB

1 la page (*of book*)
2 le/la page (*in Parliament*) ◊ *In
Grade 6 I was a parliamentary page
in Ottawa.* En sixième année, j'ai été
page parlementaire à Ottawa.

to **page** VERB

see also **page** NOUN

♦ **to page somebody** faire appeler
quelqu'un

pager NOUN
※ le téléavertisseur

paid VERB see **pay**

paid ADJECTIVE
1 rémunéré (*work*)
2 payé ◊ *3 weeks' paid holiday* trois
semaines de congés payés

pail NOUN
le seau
(PL les seaux)

pain NOUN
la douleur ◊ *a terrible pain* une
douleur insupportable
♦ **I have a pain in my stomach.** J'ai mal
à l'estomac.
♦ **to be in pain** souffrir ◊ *She's in a lot
of pain.* Elle souffre beaucoup.
♦ **He's a real pain.** Il est vraiment
pénible.

painful ADJECTIVE
douloureux MASC
douloureuse FEM ◊ *a painful injury*
une blessure douloureuse
♦ **a painful experience** une expérience
pénible
♦ **Is it painful?** Ça te fait mal?

painkiller NOUN
l' analgésique MASC

paint NOUN

see also **paint** VERB

la peinture

to **paint** VERB

see also **paint** NOUN

peindre ◊ *to paint something green*
peindre quelque chose en vert

paintbrush NOUN
le pinceau
(PL les pinceaux)

painter NOUN
le/la peintre

painting NOUN
1 la peinture ◊ *My hobby is painting.*
Je fais de la peinture.

2 (picture)
le tableau
(PL les tableaux) ◊ a painting by Jean Paul Lemieux un tableau de Jean Paul Lemieux

pair NOUN
la paire ◊ a pair of shoes une paire de chaussures ◊ a pair of scissors une paire de ciseaux
♦ **a pair of pants** un pantalon
♦ **a pair of jeans**
✻ une paire de jeans
♦ **a pair of underpants (1)** (briefs) une culotte
♦ **a pair of underpants (2)** (boxer shorts) un caleçon
♦ **in pairs** deux par deux ◊ We work in pairs. On travaille deux par deux.

pal NOUN
le copain
la copine

palace NOUN
le palais

pale ADJECTIVE
pâle ◊ a pale blue shirt une chemise bleu pâle

palm NOUN
la paume (of hand)
♦ **a palm tree** un palmier

pamphlet NOUN
la brochure

pan NOUN
1 la casserole (saucepan)
2 la poêle (frying pan)
3 le moule (baking) ◊ a cake pan un moule à gâteau

pancake NOUN
la crêpe

panic NOUN
| see also **panic** VERB |
la panique

to **panic** VERB
| see also **panic** NOUN |
s'affoler
♦ **Don't panic!** Pas de panique!

panther NOUN
la panthère

panties PL NOUN
la culotte SING

pantomime NOUN
la pantomime

pants PL NOUN
le pantalon SING ◊ a pair of pants un pantalon

pantyhose PL NOUN
✻ le bas-culotte SING
(PL les bas-culottes)

paper NOUN
1 le papier ◊ a piece of paper un morceau de papier ◊ a paper towel une serviette en papier
2 (newspaper)
le journal
(PL les journaux) ◊ I saw an ad in the paper. J'ai vu une annonce dans le journal.
♦ **an exam paper** un examen écrit

paperback NOUN
le livre de poche

paperboy NOUN
le livreur de journaux

paper clip NOUN
le trombone

papergirl NOUN
la livreuse de journaux

paper route NOUN
la tournée de distribution de journaux

paperwork NOUN
la paperasse ◊ She had a lot of paperwork to do. Elle avait beaucoup de paperasse à faire.

parachute NOUN
le parachute

parade NOUN
le défilé

paradise NOUN
le paradis ◊ a skiers' paradise un paradis pour les skieurs

paragraph NOUN
le paragraphe

parallel ADJECTIVE
parallèle

paralysed ADJECTIVE
paralysé

paramedic NOUN
l' ambulancier paramédical MASC
l' ambulancière paramédicale FEM

parcel NOUN
le colis

pardon NOUN
♦ **Pardon?** Pardon?

parent NOUN
1 le père (father)
2 la mère (mother)
♦ **my parents** mes parents MASC

park NOUN
| see also **park** VERB |
le parc
♦ **a national park** un parc national
♦ **a theme park** un parc d'attractions

to **park** VERB
| see also **park** NOUN |

P

✹ ⚀ stationner ◊ *Where can I park my car?* Où est-ce que je peux stationner ma voiture?

✹ ⚁ se garer ◊ *We couldn't find anywhere to park.* Nous avons eu du mal à nous garer.

parking NOUN
le stationnement ◊ *"no parking"* « stationnement interdit »

parking lot NOUN
✹ le stationnement

parking meter NOUN
le parcomètre

parking ticket NOUN
la contravention de stationnement

parliament NOUN
le parlement

parole NOUN
♦ **on parole** en liberté conditionnelle

parrot NOUN
le perroquet

parsley NOUN
le persil

part NOUN
⚀ la partie (*section*) ◊ *The first part of the movie was boring.* La première partie du film était ennuyeuse.
⚁ la pièce (*component*) ◊ *spare parts* les pièces de rechange
⚂ le rôle (*in play, film*)
♦ **for the most part** pour la plupart ◊ *They were co-operative for the most part.* Ils se sont montrés coopératifs pour la plupart.
♦ **to do one's part** fournir sa part ◊ *We each have to do our part.* Nous devons chacun fournir notre part.
♦ **to take part in something** participer à quelque chose ◊ *A lot of people took part in the demonstration.* Beaucoup de gens ont participé à la manifestation.

to part with VERB
♦ **to part with something** se défaire de quelque chose

to participate VERB
participer ◊ *The whole class participated in the discussion.* Toute la classe a participé à la discussion.

particular ADJECTIVE
particulier MASC
particulière FEM ◊ *Are you looking for anything particular?* Est-ce que vous voulez quelque chose de particulier?
♦ **nothing in particular** rien de particulier

particularly ADVERB
particulièrement

parting NOUN
la raie (*in hair*)

partly ADVERB
en partie

partner NOUN
⚀ le/la partenaire (*in game*)
⚁ (*in business*)
l' associé MASC
l' associée FEM
⚂ (*in dance*)
le cavalier
la cavalière
⚃ le compagnon (*boyfriend*)
la compagne (*girlfriend*)

part-time ADJECTIVE, ADVERB
à temps partiel ◊ *a part-time job* un travail à temps partiel ◊ *She works part-time.* Elle travaille à temps partiel.

party NOUN
⚀ la fête ◊ *a birthday party* une fête d'anniversaire ◊ *a New Year's party* une fête du Nouvel An
✹ ⚁ le party ◊ *a Halloween party* un party d'Halloween
⚂ la soirée (*more formal*) ◊ *I'm going to a party on Saturday.* Je vais à une soirée samedi.
⚃ le parti (*political*) ◊ *the Conservative Party* le Parti conservateur
⚄ le groupe (*group*) ◊ *reservations for a party of four* une réservation pour un groupe de quatre

pass NOUN

> see also **pass** VERB

⚀ le col (*in mountains*) ◊ *The pass was blocked with snow.* Le col était enneigé.
⚁ la passe (*in football*)
⚂ le laissez-passer ◊ *You can't get in without a pass.* Tu ne peux pas entrer sans laissez-passer.

to pass VERB

> see also **pass** NOUN

⚀ réussir (*exam*) ◊ *to pass an exam* réussir à un examen ◊ *I hope I pass the exam.* J'espère que je réussirai à l'examen. ◊ *Did you pass?* Tu as réussi?
⚁ passer ◊ *Could you pass me the salt, please?* Est-ce que vous pourriez me passer le sel, s'il vous plaît? ◊ *The time has passed quickly.* Le temps a passé rapidement.
⚂ passer devant ◊ *I pass his house on my way to school.* Je passe devant chez lui en allant à l'école.
⚃ adopter (*legislation*) ◊ *The bill was passed.* On a adopté le projet de loi.

Be careful not to translate to pass an exam by passer un examen.

♦ **to pass for** se faire passer pour ◊ *You could easily pass for 16.* Tu pourrais te faire passer pour un jeune de seize ans.

♦ **to pass up an opportunity** laisser passer une occasion

to **pass out** VERB
① s'évanouir (*faint*)
② distribuer (*hand out*) ◊ *Pass out the workbooks, please.* Distribue les cahiers, s'il te plaît.

passage NOUN
① le passage (*piece of writing*) ◊ *Read the passage carefully.* Lisez attentivement le passage.
② le couloir (*corridor*)

passenger NOUN
le passager
la passagère

passerby NOUN
le passant
la passante ◊ *We asked a passerby for the time.* Nous avons demandé l'heure à un passant.

passion NOUN
la passion

passive ADJECTIVE
passif MASC
passive FEM
♦ **passive smoking** le tabagisme passif

passport NOUN
le passeport ◊ *passport control* le contrôle des passeports

password NOUN
le mot de passe

past ADVERB, PREPOSITION

see also **past** NOUN

après (*beyond*) ◊ *It's on the right, just past the station.* C'est sur la droite, juste après la gare.
♦ **to go past (1)** passer ◊ *The bus went past without stopping.* Le bus est passé sans s'arrêter.
♦ **to go past (2)** passer devant ◊ *The bus goes past our house.* Le bus passe devant notre maison.
♦ **It's half past ten.** Il est dix heures et demie.
♦ **It's quarter past nine.** Il est neuf heures et quart.
♦ **It's ten past eight.** Il est huit heures dix.
♦ **It's past midnight.** Il est minuit passé.

past NOUN

see also **past** ADVERB

le passé ◊ *She lives in the past.* Elle

vit dans le passé.
♦ **He had a difficult past.** Il a eu un passé difficile.
♦ **in the past** (*previously*) autrefois ◊ *This was common in the past.* C'était courant autrefois.

pasta NOUN
les pâtes FEM PL ◊ *Pasta is easy to cook.* Les pâtes sont faciles à préparer.

paste NOUN
la colle (*glue*)

pastel NOUN
le crayon pastel
♦ **pastel colours** des tons pastels MASC

pastime NOUN
le passe-temps
(PL les passe-temps) ◊ *Her favourite pastime is biking.* Son passe-temps favori est le cyclisme.

pastry NOUN
① la pâte (*dough*) ◊ *pie pastry* la pâte à tarte
② la pâtisserie (*baked dessert*) ◊ *a plate of pastries* une assiette de pâtisseries

to **pat** VERB
♦ **She patted my cheek.** Elle m'a tapoté la joue.
♦ **to pat someone on the back (1)** (*literally*) donner une petite tape à quelqu'un dans le dos
♦ **to pat someone on the back (2)** (*compliment*) congratuler quelqu'un

patch NOUN
① la pièce ◊ *a patch of material* une pièce de tissu
② la rustine (*for flat tire*)
③ la tache (*colour*) ◊ *a patch of blue* une tache de bleu
♦ **a patch of ice** une plaque de glace
♦ **He's got a bald patch.** Il a le crâne dégarni.

patched ADJECTIVE
rapiécé ◊ *a pair of patched jeans* des jeans rapiécés

pâté NOUN
le pâté

path NOUN
① le chemin (*footpath*)
② l' allée FEM (*paved*)

pathetic ADJECTIVE
lamentable ◊ *Our team was pathetic.* Notre équipe a été lamentable.

patience NOUN
la patience ◊ *He doesn't have much patience.* Il n'a pas beaucoup de patience.

patient NOUN

P

☞

see also **patient** ADJECTIVE

le <u>patient</u>
la <u>patiente</u>

patient ADJECTIVE

see also **patient** NOUN

<u>patient</u>

patio NOUN
le <u>patio</u>

patriotic ADJECTIVE
<u>patriote</u>

patrol NOUN
la <u>patrouille</u>
♦ **patrol car** la voiture de police

pattern NOUN
le <u>motif</u> ◊ *a geometric pattern* un motif géométrique
♦ **a sewing pattern** un patron

pause NOUN
la <u>pause</u>

pavement NOUN
⒈ la <u>chaussée</u> (*roadway*)
⒉ l' <u>asphalte</u> MASC (*elsewhere*)

paw NOUN
la <u>patte</u>

pay NOUN

see also **pay** VERB

le <u>salaire</u>

to **pay** VERB

see also **pay** NOUN

⒈ <u>payer</u> ◊ *They pay her more on Sundays.* Elle est payée davantage le dimanche.
⒉ <u>régler</u> ◊ *to pay by cheque* régler par chèque ◊ *to pay by credit card* régler par carte de crédit
♦ **to pay for something** payer quelque chose ◊ *I paid for my ticket.* J'ai payé mon billet. ◊ *I paid 50 dollars for it.* Je l'ai payé cinquante dollars.
♦ **to pay extra for something** payer un supplément pour quelque chose ◊ *You have to pay extra for parking.* Il faut payer un supplément pour le stationnement.
♦ **to pay attention** faire attention ◊ *Don't pay any attention to him!* Ne fais pas attention à lui!
♦ **to pay somebody a visit** rendre visite à quelqu'un ◊ *They paid us a visit last night.* Ils nous ont rendu visite hier soir.
♦ **to pay somebody back** rembourser quelqu'un ◊ *I'll pay you back tomorrow.* Je te rembourserai demain.

payable ADJECTIVE
♦ **Make the cheque payable to "ABC Ltd".** Libellez le chèque à l'ordre de « ABC Ltd ».

payment NOUN
le <u>paiement</u>

pay phone NOUN
le <u>téléphone public</u>

PC NOUN (= *personal computer*)
le <u>PC</u> ◊ *She typed the report on her PC.* Elle a tapé le rapport sur son PC.

PE NOUN
l' <u>éducation physique</u> FEM ◊ *We have PE twice a week.* Nous avons l'éducation physique deux fois par semaine.

pea NOUN
le <u>petit pois</u>

peace NOUN
⒈ la <u>paix</u> (*after war*)
⒉ le <u>calme</u> (*quietness*)

peaceful ADJECTIVE
⒈ <u>paisible</u> (*calm*) ◊ *a peaceful afternoon* un après-midi paisible
⒉ <u>pacifique</u> (*not violent*) ◊ *a peaceful protest* une manifestation pacifique

peacekeeper NOUN
le <u>gardien de la paix</u>
la <u>gardienne de la paix</u>

peacekeeping NOUN
le <u>maintien de la paix</u>

peach NOUN
la <u>pêche</u>

peacock NOUN
le <u>paon</u>

peak NOUN

see also **peak** VERB

la <u>cime</u> (*of mountain*)
♦ **the peak rate** le plein tarif ◊ *You pay the peak rate for calls at this time of day.* On paie le plein tarif quand on appelle à cette heure-ci.
♦ **in peak season** en haute saison

to **peak** VERB

see also **peak** NOUN

♦ **The temperature peaked at 34 degrees.** La température a atteint trente-quatre degrés à son plus haut niveau.

peanut NOUN
l' <u>arachide</u> FEM ◊ *a packet of peanuts* un paquet d'arachides

peanut butter NOUN
le <u>beurre d'arachide</u> ◊ *a peanut-butter sandwich* un sandwich au beurre d'arachide

pear NOUN
la <u>poire</u>

pearl NOUN
la <u>perle</u>

pebble NOUN
le galet ◊ *a pebble beach* une plage de galets

pecan NOUN
la pacane ◊ *a pecan pie* une tarte aux pacanes

peculiar ADJECTIVE
bizarre ◊ *He's a bit peculiar.* Il est un peu bizarre.

pedal NOUN

> see also **pedal** VERB

la pédale

to **pedal** VERB

> see also **pedal** NOUN

pédaler

pedestrian NOUN
le piéton
la piétonne

pedestrian crossing NOUN
le passage à piétons

peek NOUN
♦ **to have a peek at something** jeter un coup d'œil à quelque chose
♦ **No peeking!** On ne regarde pas!

peel NOUN

> see also **peel** VERB

① l' écorce FEM (*orange*)
② la peau (*banana*)
③ l' épluchure FEM (*apple, potato*)

to **peel** VERB

> see also **peel** NOUN

① éplucher ◊ *Shall I peel the potatoes?* J'épluche les pommes de terre?
② peler ◊ *My nose is peeling.* Mon nez pèle.

peer pressure NOUN
la pression des pairs

peg NOUN
① (*for coats*)
le portemanteau
(PL les portemanteaux)
② la pince à linge (*clothes peg*)
③ le piquet (*tent peg*)

pellet NOUN
la boulette

✳ **pemmican** NOUN
le pemmican

pen NOUN
le stylo

to **penalize** VERB
pénaliser

penalty NOUN
① la peine (*punishment*)
♦ **the death penalty** la peine de mort
② la punition (*sports*) ◊ *a penalty*

for body-checking une punition pour mise en échec corporelle
♦ **a penalty shot** un lancer de pénalité
♦ **penalty box** le banc de punition
♦ **a penalty kick** un coup de pied de pénalité

pencil NOUN
le crayon
♦ **in pencil** au crayon
♦ **pencil crayons** les crayons de couleur

pencil case NOUN
la trousse

pencil sharpener NOUN
le taille-crayon

pendant NOUN
le pendentif

penguin NOUN
le pingouin

penicillin NOUN
la pénicilline

peninsula NOUN
la presqu'île

penis NOUN
le pénis

penknife NOUN
le canif

pennant NOUN
le fanion ◊ *Our school won the soccer pennant last year.* Notre école a gagné le fanion en soccer l'année dernière.

penny NOUN
le cent

penpal NOUN
le correspondant
la correspondante

pension NOUN
la retraite

pensioner NOUN
le retraité
la retraitée

pentathlon NOUN
le pentathlon

people PL NOUN
① les gens MASC ◊ *The people were nice.* Les gens étaient sympathiques.
② les personnes FEM (*individuals*) ◊ *six people* six personnes ◊ *several people* plusieurs personnes
③ le peuple (*nation*) ◊ *Canada's native peoples* les peuples autochtones du Canada ◊ *to give more power to the people* donner plus de pouvoir au peuple
♦ **How many people are there in your family?** Vous êtes combien dans votre famille?
♦ **French people** les Français

☞

P

♦ **black people** les Noirs
♦ **People say that...** On dit que...

pepper NOUN
⓵ le <u>poivre</u> (*spice*) ◊ *Pass the pepper, please.* Passez-moi le poivre, s'il vous plaît.
⓶ le <u>poivron</u> (*vegetable*) ◊ *a green pepper* un poivron vert
⓷ le <u>piment</u> (*chili*) ◊ *hot peppers* les piments piquants

peppermint NOUN
⓵ la <u>pastille de menthe</u> (*candy*)
⓶ la <u>menthe</u> (*flavour*) ◊ *I don't like chocolate and mint together.* Je n'aime pas le chocolat et la menthe ensemble.
♦ **peppermint chewing gum** la gomme à mâcher à la menthe

pepperoni NOUN
le <u>pepperoni</u>

per PREPOSITION
<u>par</u> ◊ *per day* par jour ◊ *per week* par semaine
♦ **30 miles per hour** trente miles à l'heure

percent ADVERB
<u>pour cent</u> ◊ *fifty percent* cinquante pour cent

percentage NOUN
le <u>pourcentage</u>

percussion NOUN
la <u>percussion</u> ◊ *I play percussion.* Je joue des percussions.

perfect ADJECTIVE
<u>parfait</u> ◊ *She speaks perfect English.* Elle parle un anglais parfait.

perfectly ADVERB
<u>parfaitement</u>

to **perform** VERB
<u>jouer</u> (*act, play*)

performance NOUN
⓵ le <u>spectacle</u> (*show*) ◊ *The performance lasts two hours.* Le spectacle dure deux heures.
⓶ l' <u>interprétation</u> FEM (*acting*) ◊ *his performance as Hamlet* son interprétation d'Hamlet
⓷ la <u>performance</u> (*results*) ◊ *the team's poor performance* la médiocre performance de l'équipe

performing arts PL NOUN
les <u>arts de la scène</u> MASC

perfume NOUN
le <u>parfum</u>

perhaps ADVERB
<u>peut-être</u> ◊ *a bit boring, perhaps* peut-être un peu ennuyeux ◊ *Perhaps he's sick.* Il est peut-être malade.
♦ **perhaps not** peut-être pas

period NOUN
⓵ la <u>période</u> ◊ *for a limited period* pour une période limitée
⓶ l' <u>époque</u> FEM (*in history*) ◊ *the Victorian period* l'époque victorienne
⓷ le <u>point</u> (*punctuation*) ◊ *You need a period at the end of a sentence.* Il faut un point à la fin de la phrase.
⓸ les <u>règles</u> FEM (*menstruation*) ◊ *I'm having my period.* J'ai mes règles.
⓹ le <u>cours</u> (*lesson time*) ◊ *Each period lasts forty minutes.* Chaque cours dure quarante minutes.

perm NOUN
la <u>permanente</u> ◊ *She has a perm.* Elle a une permanente.
♦ **to get a perm** se faire faire une permanente

🐾 **permafrost** NOUN
le <u>pergélisol</u>

permanent ADJECTIVE
<u>permanent</u>

permission NOUN
la <u>permission</u> ◊ *Could I have permission to leave early?* Pourrais-je avoir la permission de partir plus tôt?

permit NOUN
le <u>permis</u> ◊ *a fishing permit* un permis de pêche

to **persecute** VERB
<u>persécuter</u>

persistent ADJECTIVE
<u>tenace</u> (*person*)

person NOUN
la <u>personne</u> ◊ *She's a very nice person.* C'est une personne très sympathique.
♦ **in person** en personne

personal ADJECTIVE
<u>personnel</u> MASC
<u>personnelle</u> FEM
♦ **personals column** les annonces personnelles FEM PL

personality NOUN
la <u>personnalité</u>

personally ADVERB
<u>personnellement</u> ◊ *I don't know him personally.* Je ne le connais pas personnellement. ◊ *Personally I don't agree.* Personnellement, je ne suis pas d'accord.

personal stereo NOUN
le <u>baladeur</u>

personnel NOUN
le <u>personnel</u>

perspiration NOUN
la <u>transpiration</u>

to **persuade** VERB

persuader
♦ **to persuade somebody to do something** persuader quelqu'un de faire quelque chose ◊ *She persuaded me to go with her.* Elle m'a persuadé de l'accompagner.

pessimist NOUN
le/la <u>pessimiste</u> ◊ *I'm a pessimist.* Je suis pessimiste.

pessimistic ADJECTIVE
<u>pessimiste</u>

pest NOUN
l' <u>enquiquineur</u> MASC
l' <u>enquiquineuse</u> FEM

to **pester** VERB
<u>importuner</u>

pesticide NOUN
le <u>pesticide</u>

pet NOUN
l' <u>animal de compagnie</u> MASC ◊ *Have you got a pet?* Est-ce que tu as un animal de compagnie?
♦ **a pet shop** une animalerie

petition NOUN
la <u>pétition</u>

petrified ADJECTIVE
<u>pétrifié</u>

petroleum NOUN
le <u>pétrole</u>

phantom NOUN
le <u>fantôme</u>

pharmacy NOUN
la <u>pharmacie</u>

philosophy NOUN
la <u>philosophie</u>

phobia NOUN
la <u>phobie</u>

phone NOUN

see also **phone** VERB

le <u>téléphone</u> ◊ *Where's the phone?* Où est le téléphone? ◊ *Is there a phone here?* Est-ce qu'il y a un téléphone ici?
♦ **by phone** par téléphone
♦ **to be on the phone** être au téléphone ◊ *She's on the phone at the moment.* Elle est au téléphone en ce moment.
♦ **Can I use the phone, please?** Est-ce que je peux téléphoner, s'il vous plaît?

to **phone** VERB

see also **phone** NOUN

1 <u>appeler</u> ◊ *I'll phone the library.* Je vais appeler la bibliothèque.
2 <u>téléphoner</u> ◊ *Are you going to phone him, or send an e-mail?* Tu vas lui téléphoner, ou envoyer un

courriel?

phone bill NOUN
✱ le <u>compte de téléphone</u>

phone book NOUN
l' <u>annuaire</u> MASC

phone booth NOUN
la <u>cabine téléphonique</u>

phone call NOUN
l' <u>appel</u> MASC ◊ *There's a phone call for you.* Il y a un appel pour vous.
♦ **to make a phone call** téléphoner ◊ *Can I make a phone call?* Est-ce que je peux téléphoner?

phone card NOUN
la <u>carte téléphonique</u>

phone number NOUN
le <u>numéro de téléphone</u>

photo NOUN
la <u>photo</u>
♦ **to take a photo** prendre une photo
♦ **to take a photo of somebody** prendre quelqu'un en photo

photocopier NOUN
la <u>photocopieuse</u>

photocopy NOUN

see also **photocopy** VERB

la <u>photocopie</u>

to **photocopy** VERB

see also **photocopy** NOUN

<u>photocopier</u>

photograph NOUN

see also **photograph** VERB

la <u>photo</u>
♦ **to take a photograph** prendre une photo
♦ **to take a photograph of somebody** prendre quelqu'un en photo

to **photograph** VERB

see also **photograph** NOUN

<u>photographier</u>

photographer NOUN
le/la <u>photographe</u> ◊ *She's a photographer.* Elle est photographe.

photography NOUN
la <u>photo</u> ◊ *My hobby is photography.* Je fais de la photo.

phrase NOUN
l' <u>expression</u> FEM

phrase book NOUN
le <u>guide de conversation</u>

phys ed NOUN
l' <u>éducation physique</u> FEM

physical ADJECTIVE

see also **physical** NOUN

<u>physique</u>

P

physical NOUN

see also **physical** ADJECTIVE

l' examen médical MASC

physicist NOUN
le physicien
la physicienne ◊ *He's a physicist.* Il
est physicien.

physics NOUN
la physique ◊ *She teaches physics.*
Elle enseigne la physique.

physiotherapist NOUN
le/la physiothérapeute

physiotherapy NOUN
la physiothérapie

pianist NOUN
le/la pianiste

piano NOUN
le piano ◊ *I play the piano.* Je joue
du piano. ◊ *I take piano lessons.* Je
prends des leçons de piano.

pick NOUN

see also **pick** VERB

le médiator (*guitar*)
♦ **The youngest gets first pick.** Le plus
jeune choisit en premier.
♦ **Take your pick!** Faites votre choix!

to **pick** VERB

see also **pick** NOUN

1 choisir (*choose*) ◊ *I picked the
biggest piece.* J'ai choisi le plus gros
morceau.
2 sélectionner (*for team*) ◊ *I've
been picked for the team.* J'ai été
sélectionné pour faire partie de
l'équipe.
3 cueillir (*fruit, flowers*)
♦ **to pick on somebody** harceler
quelqu'un ◊ *He's always picking on
me.* Il me harcèle constamment.
♦ **to pick out (1)** choisir ◊ *"I like them
all - it's difficult to pick one out."* « Ils
me plaisent tous - c'est difficile d'en
choisir un. »
♦ **to pick out (2)** (*distinguish*) repérer
◊ *I can pick out her voice on the
recording.* Je peux repérer sa voix sur
l'enregistrement.
♦ **to pick out (3)** (*recognize*) reconnaître
◊ *Can you pick me out in this picture?*
Peux-tu me reconnaître sur cette
photo?
♦ **to pick up (1)** (*collect*) venir chercher
◊ *We'll come to the airport to pick
you up.* Nous irons vous chercher à
l'aéroport.
♦ **to pick up (2)** (*from floor*) ramasser
◊ *Could you help me pick up the
toys?* Tu peux m'aider à ramasser les
jouets?

♦ **to pick up (3)** (*learn*) apprendre ◊ *I
picked up some Spanish during my
holiday.* J'ai appris quelque mots
d'espagnol pendant mes vacances.

to **picket** VERB
piqueter ◊ *The workers picketed
the factory.* Les ouvriers ont piqueté
l'usine.
♦ **a picket line** une ligne de piquetage

pickle NOUN
le cornichon ◊ *dill pickles* les
cornichons à l'aneth

pickpocket NOUN
le voleur à la tire
la voleuse à la tire

pickup truck NOUN
la camionnette

picky ADJECTIVE
pointilleux MASC
pointilleuse FEM ◊ *Our teacher is
picky about grammar.* Notre prof est
pointilleux sur la grammaire.

picnic NOUN
le pique-nique
♦ **to have a picnic** pique-niquer ◊ *We
had a picnic on the beach.* Nous
avons pique-niqué sur la plage.

picture NOUN
1 l' illustration FEM ◊ *Children's
books have lots of pictures.* Il y a
beaucoup d'illustrations dans les
livres pour enfants.
2 la photo ◊ *My picture was in the
paper.* Ma photo était dans le journal.
3 (*painting*)
le tableau
(PL les tableaux) ◊ *a famous picture*
un tableau célèbre
♦ **to paint a picture of something**
peindre quelque chose
4 le dessin (*drawing*)
♦ **to draw a picture of something**
dessiner quelque chose

picturesque ADJECTIVE
pittoresque

pie NOUN
la tarte ◊ *an apple pie* une tarte aux
pommes
♦ **a pie chart** un graphique circulaire

piece NOUN
le morceau
(PL les morceaux) ◊ *A small piece,
please.* Un petit morceau, s'il vous
plaît.
♦ **a piece of furniture** un meuble
♦ **a piece of advice** un conseil

pier NOUN
la jetée

to **pierce** VERB

percer ◊ *She's going to get her ears pierced.* Elle va se faire percer les oreilles. ◊ *I have pierced ears.* J'ai les oreilles percées.

piercing ADJECTIVE
perçant ◊ *a piercing cry* un cri perçant

pig NOUN
le cochon

pigeon NOUN
le pigeon

piggyback NOUN
♦ **to give somebody a piggyback** ◊ *I can't give you a piggyback, you're too heavy.* Je ne peux pas te porter sur mon dos, tu es trop lourd.

pigtail NOUN
la couette

pike NOUN
le brochet ◊ *a northern pike* un grand brochet

pile NOUN

　see also **pile** VERB

① le tas (*untidy heap*)
② la pile (*tidy stack*)

to **pile** VERB

　see also **pile** NOUN

① empiler (*stack*) ◊ *I piled the books on the table.* J'ai empilé les livres sur la table.
② entasser (*heap*) ◊ *She piles her dirty clothes on the floor.* Elle entasse ses vêtements sales sur le plancher.
♦ **to pile up** s'accumuler ◊ *My homework is piling up.* Mes devoirs s'accumulent.

pile-up NOUN
le carambolage

pill NOUN
la pilule
♦ **to be on the Pill** prendre la pilule

pillar NOUN
le pilier

pillow NOUN
l' oreiller MASC

pilot NOUN
le/la pilote ◊ *She's a pilot.* Elle est pilote.

pimple NOUN
le bouton

pin NOUN
l' épingle FEM
♦ **I have pins and needles in my foot.** J'ai des fourmis dans le pied.
♦ **to be on pins and needles** être sur des charbons ardents

PIN NOUN (= *personal identification number*)
le NIP

pinball NOUN
🐾 la machine à boules ◊ *to play pinball* jouer à la machine à boules

to **pinch** VERB
pincer ◊ *He pinched me!* Il m'a pincé!

pine NOUN
le pin ◊ *a pine table* une table en pin
♦ **a pine cone** un cône de pin

pineapple NOUN
l' ananas MASC

pink ADJECTIVE
rose

pioneer NOUN
le pionnier
la pionnière

pipe NOUN
① (*for water, gas*)
le tuyau
(PL les tuyaux) ◊ *The pipes froze.* Les tuyaux d'eau ont gelé.
② la pipe (*for smoking*)
♦ **the pipes** (*bagpipes*) la cornemuse ◊ *He plays the pipes.* Il joue de la cornemuse.

pirate NOUN
le/la pirate

pirated ADJECTIVE
pirate ◊ *a pirated video* une vidéo pirate

Pisces NOUN
les Poissons MASC ◊ *I'm a Pisces.* Je suis Poissons.

pistol NOUN
le pistolet

pit NOUN
① la fosse (*deep hole*)
② le noyau (*in fruit*) ◊ *a peach pit* un noyau de pêche

pitch NOUN

　see also **pitch** VERB

① le lancer (*baseball*) ◊ *That was a fast pitch.* C'était un lancer rapide.
② la hauteur (*musical note*)
♦ **Excitement was at fever pitch.** L'excitation était à son comble.

to **pitch** VERB

　see also **pitch** NOUN

① planter (*tent*) ◊ *We pitched our tent near the beach.* Nous avons planté notre tente près de la plage.
② lancer (*baseball*) ◊ *Who's pitching?* Qui est-ce qui lance?

pitcher NOUN
① (*baseball*)
le lanceur

P

☞

la lanceuse
2 la cruche (*jug*) ◊ *a pitcher of lemonade* une cruche de limonade

pity NOUN

see also **pity** VERB

la pitié
♦ **What a pity!** Quel dommage!

to **pity** VERB

see also **pity** NOUN

plaindre

pizza NOUN
la pizza

place NOUN

see also **place** VERB

1 l' endroit MASC (*location*) ◊ *It's a quiet place.* C'est un endroit tranquille. ◊ *There are a lot of interesting places to visit.* Il y a beaucoup d'endroits intéressants à visiter.
2 la place (*space*) ◊ *a parking place* une place de stationnement ◊ *She was not in her usual place.* Elle n'était pas à sa place habituelle. ◊ *There were six places at the table.* Il y avait six places à la table.
♦ **to take someone's place** prendre la place de quelqu'un
♦ **to change places** changer de place ◊ *I'll change places with you.* Je changerai de place avec toi.
♦ **to take place** avoir lieu
♦ **at your place** chez toi ◊ *Shall we meet at your place?* On se retrouve chez toi?
♦ **to my place** chez moi ◊ *Do you want to come to my place?* Tu veux venir chez moi?
♦ **I feel out of place here.** Je ne me sens pas à ma place ici.

to **place** VERB

see also **place** NOUN

1 poser ◊ *He placed his hand on the keyboard.* Il a posé la main sur le clavier.
2 classer (*in competition, contest*)

placemat NOUN
le napperon

plagiarism NOUN
le plagiat

plaid ADJECTIVE
écossais ◊ *a plaid shirt* une chemise écossaise

plain NOUN

see also **plain** ADJECTIVE

la plaine

plain ADJECTIVE, ADVERB

see also **plain** NOUN

1 uni (*not patterned*) ◊ *a plain carpet* un tapis uni
2 simple (*not fancy*) ◊ *a plain white blouse* un chemisier blanc simple

plan NOUN

see also **plan** VERB

1 le projet ◊ *What are your plans for the holidays?* Quels sont tes projets pour les vacances? ◊ *to make plans* faire des projets
♦ **Everything went according to plan.** Tout s'est passé comme prévu.
2 le plan (*map*) ◊ *a floor plan of the new house* un plan à niveau de la nouvelle maison

to **plan** VERB

see also **plan** NOUN

1 préparer (*make plans for*) ◊ *We're planning a trip to Alberta.* Nous préparons un voyage en Alberta.
2 planifier (*make schedule for*) ◊ *Plan your day carefully.* Planifiez votre journée avec soin.
♦ **to plan to do something** avoir l'intention de faire quelque chose ◊ *I'm planning to go to university.* J'ai l'intention d'aller à l'université.

plane NOUN
l' avion MASC ◊ *by plane* en avion

planet NOUN
la planète

planning NOUN
la préparation ◊ *The trip needs careful planning.* Le voyage nécessite une préparation méticuleuse.
♦ **family planning** la planification familiale

plant NOUN

see also **plant** VERB

1 la plante ◊ *to water the plants* arroser les plantes
2 l' usine FEM (*factory*)

to **plant** VERB

see also **plant** NOUN

planter

plaque NOUN
1 la plaque (*on wall*)
2 la plaque dentaire (*on teeth*)

plaster NOUN
le plâtre
♦ **a plaster cast** un plâtre

plastic NOUN

see also **plastic** ADJECTIVE

le plastique ◊ *It's made of plastic.* C'est en plastique.

plastic ADJECTIVE

see also **plastic** NOUN

en plastique ◊ *a plastic bag* un sac
en plastique ◊ *a plastic raincoat* un
imperméable en plastique
♦ **plastic surgery** la chirurgie esthétique
♦ **plastic wrap** la pellicule de plastique

plate NOUN
l' assiette FEM (*for food*)

platform NOUN
① l' estrade FEM (*for performers*)
② le quai (*at station*) ◊ *on platform 7*
sur le quai numéro sept

play NOUN

see also **play** VERB

la pièce ◊ *a play by Rick Salutin* une
pièce de Rick Salutin
♦ **to put on a play** monter une pièce

to **play** VERB

see also **play** NOUN

① jouer ◊ *He's playing with his
friends.* Il joue avec ses amis. ◊ *What
sort of music do they play?* Quel
genre de musique jouent-ils?
② jouer contre (*against person,
team*) ◊ *Montreal will play Edmonton
tomorrow night.* Montréal jouera
contre Edmonton demain soir.
③ jouer à (*sport, game*) ◊ *I play
hockey.* Je joue au hockey. ◊ *Can you
play chess?* Tu sais jouer aux échecs?
④ jouer de (*instrument*) ◊ *I play the
guitar.* Je joue de la guitare.
⑤ écouter (*record, cassette, music*)
◊ *She's always playing that CD.* Elle
écoute tout le temps ce CD.

to **play down** VERB
dédramatiser ◊ *He tried to play
down his illness.* Il a essayé de
dédramatiser sa maladie.

player NOUN
(*of sport*)
le joueur
la joueuse ◊ *a hockey player* un
joueur de hockey
♦ **a piano player** un pianiste
♦ **a bass player** un bassiste

playful ADJECTIVE
espiègle

playground NOUN
① la cour de récréation (*at school*)
② l' aire de jeux FEM (*in park*)

playing card NOUN
la carte à jouer
(PI les cartes à jouer)

playing field NOUN
le terrain de sport

playoffs PL NOUN
les éliminatoires FEM

playtime NOUN
la récréation

playwright NOUN
le/la dramaturge

to **plead** VERB
♦ **to plead guilty** plaider coupable
♦ **I pleaded with them to stop.** Je les ai
suppliés d'arrêter.

pleasant ADJECTIVE
agréable

please EXCLAMATION
① s'il vous plaît (*polite form*) ◊ *Two
coffees, please.* Deux cafés, s'il vous
plaît.
② s'il te plaît (*familiar form*) ◊ *Please
write back soon.* Réponds vite, s'il te
plaît.

pleased ADJECTIVE
content ◊ *My mother's not going to
be very pleased.* Ma mère ne va pas
être contente du tout. ◊ *It's beautiful:
she'll be pleased with it.* C'est beau :
elle va être contente.
♦ **Pleased to meet you!** Enchanté!

pleasure NOUN
le plaisir ◊ *I read for pleasure.* Je lis
pour le plaisir.

plenty NOUN
largement assez ◊ *I've got plenty.*
J'en ai largement assez. ◊ *That's
plenty, thanks.* Ça suffit largement,
merci.
♦ **plenty of (1)** (*a lot*) beaucoup de ◊ *I
have plenty to do.* J'ai beaucoup de
choses à faire.
♦ **plenty of (2)** (*enough*) largement
assez de ◊ *I have plenty of money.*
J'ai largement assez d'argent.
◊ *We've got plenty of time.* Nous
avons largement le temps.

pliers PL NOUN
la pince SING
♦ **a pair of pliers** une pince

plot NOUN

see also **plot** VERB

① l' intrigue FEM (*of story, play*)
② la conspiration (*against
somebody*) ◊ *a plot against the
president* une conspiration contre le
président
③ le carré (*of land*) ◊ *a vegetable plot*
un carré de légumes

to **plot** VERB

see also **plot** NOUN

comploter ◊ *They were plotting to
kill him.* Ils complotaient de le tuer.

plough NOUN

see also **plough** VERB

P

la <u>charrue</u>

to **plough** VERB

> see also **plough** NOUN

<u>labourer</u>

plow NOUN

> see also **plow** VERB

la <u>déneigeuse</u> (snow)

to **plow** VERB

> see also **plow** NOUN

<u>déneiger</u> ◊ Have they plowed the roads yet? Est-ce qu'on a déjà déneigé les rues?

plug NOUN
    ① la <u>prise de courant</u> (electrical) ◊ The plug is faulty. La prise est défectueuse.
    ② le <u>bouchon</u> (for sink)

to **plug in** VERB
    <u>brancher</u> ◊ Is it plugged in? Est-ce que c'est branché?

plum NOUN
    la <u>prune</u> ◊ plum jam la confiture de prunes

plumber NOUN
    le <u>plombier</u>
    la <u>plombière</u> ◊ He's a plumber. Il est plombier.

plumbing NOUN
    la <u>plomberie</u> ◊ Our cottage doesn't have indoor plumbing. Notre chalet n'a pas de plomberie intérieure.

plump ADJECTIVE
    <u>dodu</u>

to **plunge** VERB
    <u>plonger</u>

plural NOUN
    le <u>pluriel</u> ◊ in the plural au pluriel

plus PREPOSITION, ADJECTIVE
    <u>plus</u> ◊ 4 plus 3 equals 7. Quatre plus trois égalent sept. ◊ three children plus a dog trois enfants plus un chien
    ♦ **I got a B plus.** J'ai eu un B plus.

p.m. ABBREVIATION
    ♦ **at 8 p.m.** à huit heures du soir

> **ℹ** In French, times are often given using the 24-hour clock.

    ♦ **at 2 p.m.** à quatorze heures

pneumonia NOUN
    la <u>pneumonie</u>

poached ADJECTIVE
    <u>poché</u> ◊ a poached egg un œuf poché

pocket NOUN
    la <u>poche</u>
    ♦ **pocket money** l'argent de poche MASC ◊ $10 a week pocket money dix dollars d'argent de poche par semaine

pocketknife NOUN
    le <u>canif</u>

poem NOUN
    le <u>poème</u>

poet NOUN
    le/la <u>poète</u>

poetry NOUN
    la <u>poésie</u>

point NOUN

> see also **point** VERB

    ① le <u>point</u> (spot, score) ◊ a point on the horizon un point à l'horizon ◊ They scored 5 points. Ils ont marqué cinq points.
    ② la <u>remarque</u> (comment) ◊ He made some interesting points. Il a fait quelque remarques intéressantes.
    ③ la <u>pointe</u> (tip) ◊ a pencil with a sharp point un crayon à la pointe aiguisée
    ④ le <u>moment</u> (in time) ◊ At that point, we decided to leave. À ce moment-là, nous avons décidé de partir.
    ♦ **a point of view** un point de vue
    ♦ **to get the point** comprendre ◊ Sorry, I don't get the point. Désolé, je ne comprends pas.
    ♦ **That's beside the point.** Cela n'a rien à voir.
    ♦ **to the point** précis ◊ His answer was short and to the point. Sa réponse était brève et précise.
    ♦ **That's a good point!** C'est vrai!
    ♦ **There's no point.** Cela ne sert à rien. ◊ There's no point in waiting. Cela ne sert à rien d'attendre.
    ♦ **What's the point?** À quoi bon? ◊ What's the point of leaving so early? À quoi bon partir si tôt?
    ♦ **Punctuality isn't my strong point.** La ponctualité n'est pas mon fort.
    ♦ **two point five (2.5)** deux virgule cinq (2,5)

to **point** VERB

> see also **point** NOUN

    <u>montrer du doigt</u> ◊ Don't point! Ne montre pas du doigt!
    ♦ **to point at somebody** montrer quelqu'un du doigt ◊ She pointed at her friend. Elle a montré son ami du doigt.
    ♦ **to point a gun at somebody** braquer un revolver sur quelqu'un
    ♦ **to point something out (1)** (show) montrer quelque chose ◊ The guide pointed out Sainte-Anne-de-Beaupré to us. Le guide nous a montré Sainte-Anne-de-Beaupré.

♦ **to point something out (2)** (*mention*)
signaler quelque chose ◊ *I should
point out that...* Je dois vous signaler
que...

pointless ADJECTIVE
inutile ◊ *It's pointless to argue.* Il est
inutile de discuter.

poison NOUN

see also **poison** VERB

le poison

to **poison** VERB

see also **poison** NOUN

empoisonner

poison ivy NOUN
✻ l' herbe à puce FEM

poisonous ADJECTIVE
[1] (*snake*)
venimeux MASC
venimeuse FEM
[2] (*plant, mushroom*)
vénéneux MASC
vénéneuse FEM
[3] toxique (*gas*)

to **poke** VERB
♦ **He poked the ground with his stick.** Il
tapotait le sol avec sa canne.
♦ **She poked me in the ribs.** Elle m'a
enfoncé le doigt dans les côtes.

poker NOUN
le poker ◊ *I play poker.* Je joue au
poker.

polar bear NOUN
l' ours blanc MASC

pole NOUN
le poteau
(PL les poteaux) ◊ *a telephone pole* un
poteau de téléphone
♦ **a tent pole** un montant de tente
♦ **a ski pole** un bâton de ski
♦ **the North Pole** le pôle Nord
♦ **the South Pole** le pôle Sud

pole vault NOUN
le saut à la perche

police PL NOUN
la police ◊ *We called the police.* Nous
avons appelé la police.
♦ **a police car** une voiture de police
♦ **a police dog** un chien policier
♦ **a police station** un commissariat de
police

police officer NOUN
le policier
la policière ◊ *She's a police officer.*
Elle est policière.

policy NOUN
la politique ◊ *the new immigration
policy* la nouvelle politique
d'immigration

polish NOUN

see also **polish** VERB

[1] le cirage (*for shoes*)
[2] la cire (*for furniture*)

to **polish** VERB

see also **polish** NOUN

[1] cirer (*shoes, furniture*)
[2] faire briller (*glass*)

polite ADJECTIVE
poli

politely ADVERB
poliment

politeness NOUN
la politesse

political ADJECTIVE
politique
♦ **political correctness** la rectitude
politique

politically ADVERB
♦ **politically correct** politiquement
correct

politician NOUN
le politicien
la politicienne

politics PL NOUN
la politique SING ◊ *I'm not interested
in politics.* La politique ne m'intéresse
pas.

polka dots PL NOUN
les pois MASC ◊ *a skirt with polka dots*
une jupe à pois

poll NOUN

see also **poll** VERB

[1] le sondage ◊ *A recent poll
revealed that...* Un sondage récent a
révélé que...
[2] le bureau de vote (*place to vote*)
◊ *The polls close at 9 p.m.* Les
bureaux de vote ferment à neuf
heures du soir.
♦ **to go to the polls** aller voter

to **poll** VERB

see also **poll** NOUN

♦ **We polled all the students to find
out which radio station was most
popular.** Nous avons sondé l'opinion
de tous les élèves pour savoir quelle
station de radio est la plus populaire.

pollen NOUN
le pollen

to **pollute** VERB
polluer ◊ *We have polluted the
rivers.* Nous avons pollué les rivières.

pollution NOUN
la pollution

polo shirt NOUN

P

le <u>polo</u>

pond NOUN
1. l' <u>étang</u> MASC (*big*)
2. la <u>mare</u> (*smaller*)
3. le <u>bassin</u> ◊ *We've got a pond in our garden.* Nous avons un bassin dans notre jardin.

pony NOUN
le <u>poney</u>

ponytail NOUN
la <u>queue de cheval</u> ◊ *He's got a ponytail.* Il a une queue de cheval.

poodle NOUN
le <u>caniche</u>

pool NOUN
1. la <u>piscine</u> (*for swimming*)
2. l' <u>étang</u> MASC (*pond*)
3. la <u>flaque</u> (*puddle*)
4. le <u>billard américain</u> (*game*) ◊ *Let's have a game of pool.* Jouons au billard américain.

poor ADJECTIVE
1. <u>pauvre</u> ◊ *a poor family* une famille pauvre ◊ *Your poor sister, she's very unlucky!* Ta pauvre sœur, elle n'a vraiment pas de chance!
♦ **the poor** les pauvres MASC
2. <u>médiocre</u> (*bad*) ◊ *a poor mark* une note médiocre

poorly ADVERB
<u>mal</u> ◊ *poorly designed* mal conçu

pop ADJECTIVE

> see also **pop** NOUN

<u>pop</u> ◊ *pop music* la musique pop ◊ *a pop star* une vedette pop ◊ *a pop group* un groupe pop ◊ *a pop song* une chanson pop

✳ **pop** NOUN

> see also **pop** ADJECTIVE

la <u>boisson gazeuse</u> ◊ *Do you want a can of pop?* Tu veux une canette de boisson gazeuse?

popcorn NOUN
1. le <u>maïs soufflé</u> (*popped*)
2. le <u>maïs à éclater</u> (*unpopped*)

pope NOUN
le <u>pape</u>

poppy NOUN
le <u>coquelicot</u>

Popsicle™ NOUN
la <u>sucette glacée</u>

popular ADJECTIVE
<u>populaire</u> ◊ *She's a very popular girl.* C'est une fille très populaire. ◊ *This is a very popular style.* C'est un style très populaire.

population NOUN

la <u>population</u>

pop-up ADJECTIVE
<u>contextuel</u> MASC
<u>contextuelle</u> FEM ◊ *a pop-up menu* un menu contextuel

porch NOUN
le <u>porche</u>

porcupine NOUN
le <u>porc-épic</u>
(PL les porcs-épics) ◊ *a porcupine quill* un piquant de porc-épic

pork NOUN
le <u>porc</u> ◊ *a pork chop* une côtelette de porc ◊ *I don't eat pork.* Je ne mange pas de porc.

pornographic ADJECTIVE
<u>pornographique</u> ◊ *a pornographic magazine* un magazine pornographique

pornography NOUN
la <u>pornographie</u>

porridge NOUN
le <u>gruau</u>

port NOUN
le <u>port</u> (*harbour*)

portable ADJECTIVE
<u>portable</u> ◊ *a portable TV* un téléviseur portable

portion NOUN
la <u>portion</u> ◊ *a large portion of fries* une grosse portion de frites

portrait NOUN
le <u>portrait</u>

posh ADJECTIVE
<u>chic</u> MASC, FEM, PL ◊ *a posh hotel* un hôtel chic

position NOUN
la <u>position</u> ◊ *an uncomfortable position* une position inconfortable

positive ADJECTIVE
1. (*good*)
<u>positif</u> MASC
<u>positive</u> FEM ◊ *a positive attitude* une attitude positive
2. <u>certain</u> (*sure*) ◊ *I'm positive.* J'en suis certain.

to **possess** VERB
<u>posséder</u>

possession NOUN
♦ **Have you got all your possessions?** Est-ce tu as toutes tes affaires?

possibility NOUN
♦ **It's a possibility.** C'est possible.

possible ADJECTIVE
<u>possible</u> ◊ *as soon as possible* aussitôt que possible

possibly ADVERB

peut-être (*perhaps*) ◊ *"Are you coming to the party?" "Possibly."* « Est-ce que tu viens à la soirée? » « Peut-être. »

♦ **...if you possibly can.** ...si cela vous est possible.

♦ **I can't possibly come.** Je ne peux vraiment pas venir.

post NOUN

> *see also* **post** VERB

① l' article de forum MASC (*on listserv*) ◊ *Did you read that last post?*Tu as lu ce dernier article de forum?
② (*pole*)
le poteau
(PL les poteaux) ◊ *The ball hit the post.* Le ballon a heurté le poteau.

to **post** VERB

> *see also* **post** NOUN

poster ◊ *I just posted a reply on the listserv.* Je viens de poster une réponse sur la liste de diffusion.

postage NOUN
l' affranchissement MASC

postal code NOUN
le code postal

postcard NOUN
la carte postale

poster NOUN
l' affiche FEM ◊ *I have posters on my bedroom walls.* J'ai des affiches sur les murs de ma chambre. ◊ *There are posters all over town.* Il y a des affiches dans toute la ville.

postmark NOUN
le cachet de la poste

post office NOUN
le bureau de poste ◊ *Where's the post office, please?* Où est le bureau de poste, s'il vous plaît? ◊ *She works for the post office.* Elle travaille au bureau de poste.

to **postpone** VERB
remettre à plus tard ◊ *The match has been postponed.* Le match a été remis à plus tard.

postscript NOUN
le post-scriptum

posture NOUN
la posture ◊ *Good posture is important when working at the computer.* La bonne posture est très importante quand on travaille à l'ordinateur.

♦ **to have poor posture** se tenir mal

pot NOUN
① la casserole (*for cooking*) ◊ *a pot of soup* une casserole de soupe

② la théière (*teapot*)
③ la cafetière (*coffeepot*)
♦ **the pots and pans** les casseroles

potato NOUN
la pomme de terre ◊ *potato salad* la salade de pommes de terre
♦ **mashed potatoes** la purée de pommes de terre
♦ **boiled potatoes** les pommes de terre bouillies
♦ **a baked potato** une pomme de terre en robe des champs

potential NOUN

> *see also* **potential** ADJECTIVE

♦ **He has great potential.** Il a de l'avenir.

potential ADJECTIVE

> *see also* **potential** NOUN

possible ◊ *a potential problem* un problème possible

pothole NOUN
le nid de poule (*in road*)

❈ **potlatch** NOUN
le potlatch

potted plant NOUN
la plante en pot

pottery NOUN
la poterie

pound NOUN

> *see also* **pound** VERB

la livre

> ❶ *A pound is a nonmetric unit of mass equal to 454 g.*

to **pound** VERB

> *see also* **pound** NOUN

battre ◊ *My heart was pounding.* J'avais le cœur qui battait.

to **pour** VERB
① verser (*liquid*) ◊ *She poured some water into the pan.* Elle a versé de l'eau dans la casserole.
♦ **He poured her a drink.** Il lui a servi à boire.
♦ **Shall I pour you a cup of tea?** Je vous sers une tasse de thé?
② pleuvoir à verse (*rain*) ◊ *It's pouring.* Il pleut à verse.
♦ **in the pouring rain** sous une pluie torrentielle

to **pout** VERB
faire la moue ◊ *Don't pout.* Ne fais pas la moue.

poverty NOUN
la pauvreté

powder NOUN
la poudre

P

☞

power NOUN
1 le courant (*electricity*) ◊ *The power's off.* Le courant est coupé.
♦ **a power cut** une coupure de courant
♦ **a power plant** une centrale électrique
2 l' énergie FEM (*energy*) ◊ *nuclear power* l'énergie nucléaire ◊ *solar power* l'énergie solaire
3 le pouvoir (*authority*) ◊ *to be in power* être au pouvoir
4 la puissance (*nation*) ◊ *the nuclear powers* les puissances nucléaires ◊ *a world power* une puissance mondiale

powerful ADJECTIVE
puissant

✹ **power play** NOUN
l' attaque à cinq FEM

practical ADJECTIVE
pratique ◊ *a practical suggestion* un conseil pratique
♦ **She's very practical.** Elle a l'esprit pratique.
♦ **a practical joke** une farce
♦ **a practical joker** un farceur ◊ *She's a real practical joker!* Elle est une vraie farceuse!

practically ADVERB
pratiquement ◊ *It's practically impossible.* C'est pratiquement impossible.

practice NOUN
l' entraînement MASC (*for sport*) ◊ *soccer practice* l'entraînement de soccer
♦ **It's common practice in our school.** C'est ce qui se fait dans notre école.
♦ **in practice** en pratique
♦ **a medical practice** un cabinet médical
♦ **out of practice** rouillé

to **practise** VERB
1 pratiquer ◊ *I practised my French when we were in Quebec.* J'ai pratiqué mon français quand nous étions au Québec. ◊ *I have to practise the piano.* Je dois pratiquer le piano.

> **pratiquer** can only be used with a following noun.

2 s'exercer ◊ *She loves basketball and practises dribbling every day.* Elle adore le basket-ball et s'exerce à dribbler tous les jours. ◊ *I should practise more.* Je devrais m'exercer d'avantage.
3 s'entraîner ◊ *The team practises on Thursdays.* L'équipe s'entraîne le jeudi.

prairie NOUN
la prairie ◊ *the Prairie provinces* les provinces des Prairies
✹ ♦ **a prairie dog** un chien-de-prairie

to **praise** VERB
faire l'éloge de ◊ *Everyone praises his cooking.* Tout le monde fait l'éloge de sa cuisine. ◊ *The teachers praised our work.* Les professeurs ont fait l'éloge de notre travail.

prank NOUN
la farce ◊ *to play a prank on somebody* faire une farce à quelqu'un

prawn NOUN
la crevette

to **pray** VERB
prier ◊ *to pray for something* prier pour quelque chose ◊ *to pray to God* prier Dieu

prayer NOUN
la prière

precaution NOUN
la précaution
♦ **to take precautions** prendre ses précautions

preceding ADJECTIVE
précédent

precious ADJECTIVE
précieux MASC
précieuse FEM

precise ADJECTIVE
précis ◊ *at that precise moment* à cet instant précis

precisely ADVERB
précisément ◊ *Precisely!* Précisément!
♦ **at 10 a.m. precisely** à dix heures précises

to **predict** VERB
prédire

predictable ADJECTIVE
prévisible ◊ *The movie had a very predictable plot.* Le film avait une intrigue très prévisible.
♦ **She's so predictable.** Ses réactions sont tellement prévisibles.

to **prefer** VERB
préférer ◊ *Which would you prefer?* Lequel préfères-tu? ◊ *I prefer French to phys ed.* Je préfère le français à l'éducation physique.

preferably ADVERB
de préférence ◊ *Save me a seat, preferably near the door.* Garde-moi une place, de préférence près de la porte.

preference NOUN
la préférence

pregnancy NOUN
la grossesse

pregnant ADJECTIVE
enceinte ◊ *She's six months*

pregnant. Elle est enceinte de six mois.

prehistoric ADJECTIVE
préhistorique

prejudice NOUN
1 le préjugé ◊ *That's just a prejudice.* C'est un préjugé.
2 les préjugés MASC PL ◊ *There's a lot of racial prejudice.* Il y a beaucoup de préjugés raciaux.

prejudiced ADJECTIVE
♦ **to be prejudiced against somebody** avoir des préjugés contre quelqu'un

premature ADJECTIVE
prématuré
♦ **a premature baby** un prématuré

✹ **premier** NOUN
le premier ministre
la première ministre ◊ *the premier of Manitoba* le premier ministre de Manitoba

premises PL NOUN
les lieux MASC ◊ *to vacate the premises* vider les lieux ◊ *Smoking is not allowed on the premises.* Il est interdit de fumer sur les lieux.

preoccupied ADJECTIVE
préoccupé

preparation NOUN
la préparation

to **prepare** VERB
préparer ◊ *to prepare a meal* préparer un repas ◊ *He has to prepare his valedictory address.* Il doit préparer son discours d'adieu.
♦ **to prepare for something** se préparer pour quelque chose ◊ *We're preparing for our skiing holiday.* Nous nous préparons pour nos vacances de ski.

prepared ADJECTIVE
♦ **to be prepared to do something** être prêt à faire quelque chose ◊ *I'm prepared to help you.* Je suis prêt à t'aider.

preschool NOUN
l' école maternelle FEM ◊ *My little brother goes to preschool.* Mon petit frère va à l'école maternelle.
♦ **a preschool child** un enfant d'âge préscolaire

to **prescribe** VERB
prescrire

prescription NOUN
l' ordonnance FEM ◊ *You can't get it without a prescription.* On ne peut pas se le procurer sans ordonnance.
♦ **a prescription drug** un médicament d'ordonnance

presence NOUN
la présence
♦ **presence of mind** présence d'esprit

present ADJECTIVE

  see also **present** NOUN, VERB

1 présent (*in attendance*) ◊ *He wasn't present at the meeting.* Il n'était pas présent à la réunion.
2 (*current*)
actuel MASC
actuelle FEM ◊ *the present situation* la situation actuelle
♦ **the present tense** le présent

present NOUN

  see also **present** ADJECTIVE, VERB

1 (*gift*)
le cadeau
(PL les cadeaux) ◊ *I'm going to buy presents.* Je vais acheter des cadeaux.
♦ **to give somebody a present** offrir un cadeau à quelqu'un
2 le présent (*time*) ◊ *up to the present* jusqu'à présent
♦ **for the present** pour l'instant
♦ **at present** en ce moment

to **present** VERB

  see also **present** ADJECTIVE, NOUN

1 donner (*play, concert*)
2 présenter (*information*)
♦ **to present somebody with something (1)** (*prize, medal*) remettre quelque chose à quelqu'un
♦ **to present somebody with something (2)** (*gift*) offrir quelque chose à quelqu'un
♦ **She presented herself very well.** Elle s'est très bien présentée.

presently ADVERB
actuellement (*at present*)
◊ *They're presently on tour.* Ils sont actuellement en tournée.

president NOUN
le président
la présidente

press NOUN

  see also **press** VERB

la presse
♦ **a press conference** une conférence de presse

to **press** VERB

  see also **press** NOUN

1 appuyer ◊ *Don't press too hard!* N'appuie pas trop fort!
2 appuyer sur ◊ *He pressed the button.* Il a appuyé sur le bouton.

pressed ADJECTIVE
♦ **We are pressed for time.** Le temps nous manque.

P

☞

pressure NOUN

> see also **pressure** VERB

la pression ◊ *She's under a lot of pressure at work.* Elle est sous pression au travail.
♦ **a pressure group** un groupe de pression

to **pressure** VERB

> see also **pressure** NOUN

faire pression sur ◊ *My parents are pressuring me.* Mes parents font pression sur moi.

to **pressurize** VERB
pressuriser ◊ *a pressurized spacesuit* une combinaison spatiale pressurisée

prestige NOUN
le prestige

prestigious ADJECTIVE
prestigieux MASC
prestigieuse FEM

presumably ADVERB
vraisemblablement

to **presume** VERB
supposer ◊ *I presume so.* Je suppose que oui.

to **pretend** VERB
♦ **to pretend to do something** faire semblant de faire quelque chose ◊ *He pretended to be asleep.* Il faisait semblant de dormir.

> *Be careful not to translate **to pretend** by **prétendre**.*

pretty ADJECTIVE, ADVERB
① joli ◊ *She's very pretty.* Elle est très jolie.
② plutôt (*rather*) ◊ *That film was pretty bad.* Ce film était plutôt mauvais.
♦ **The weather was pretty awful.** Il faisait très mauvais temps.
♦ **It's pretty much the same.** C'est pratiquement la même chose.

pretzel NOUN
le bretzel

to **prevent** VERB
① empêcher ◊ *They tried to prevent us from leaving.* Ils ont essayé de nous empêcher de partir.
② prévenir (*disease*) ◊ *in order to prevent AIDS* pour prévenir le sida
③ éviter (*accident, war, fire*)

preventive ADJECTIVE
préventif MASC
préventive FEM ◊ *preventive medicine* la médecine préventive
♦ **preventive measures** des mesures de prévention

preview NOUN

la bande-annonce (*of movie*)

previous ADJECTIVE
précédent

previously ADVERB
auparavant

prey NOUN
la proie ◊ *a bird of prey* un oiseau de proie

price NOUN
le prix ◊ *a high price* un prix élevé ◊ *the price list* la liste de prix

to **prick** VERB
piquer ◊ *I pricked my finger.* Je me suis piqué le doigt.

prickly ADJECTIVE
épineux MASC
épineuse FEM ◊ *a prickly plant* une plante épineuse

pride NOUN
① la fierté (*positive*) ◊ *She's her parents' pride and joy.* Elle est la fierté de ses parents.
♦ **to take pride in something** être fier de quelque chose
② l' orgueil MASC (*arrogance*) ◊ *Pride prevented him from apologizing.* L'orgueil l'a empêché de demander pardon.

priest NOUN
le prêtre ◊ *He's a priest.* Il est prêtre.

primarily ADVERB
principalement

primary ADJECTIVE
① (*main*)
principal
(MASC PL principaux) ◊ *our primary purpose* notre but principal
② primaire (*first*) ◊ *books for the primary grade level* des livres pour le niveau primaire

prime minister NOUN
le premier ministre
la première ministre

primitive ADJECTIVE
primitif MASC
primitive FEM

prince NOUN
le prince ◊ *the Prince of Wales* le prince de Galles

Prince Edward Island NOUN
l' Île-du-Prince-Édouard FEM

princess NOUN
la princesse ◊ *Princess Anne* la princesse Anne

principal NOUN
le directeur
la directrice

principle NOUN

le principe
♦ **on principle** par principe

print NOUN

| *see also* **print** VERB |

1 le tirage (*photo*) ◊ *colour prints*
des tirages en couleur
2 les caractères MASC (*letters*) ◊ *in small print* en petits caractères
3 l' empreinte digitale FEM (*fingerprint*)
4 la gravure FEM (*picture*) ◊ *a framed print* une gravure encadrée

to **print** VERB

| *see also* **print** NOUN |

imprimer (*print out, publish*) ◊ *Click on the icon to print the file.* Clique sur l'icône pour imprimer le fichier.

printer NOUN
l' imprimante FEM (*machine*)

printout NOUN
la sortie d'imprimante

priority NOUN
la priorité

prison NOUN
la prison
♦ **in prison** en prison

prisoner NOUN
le prisonnier
la prisonnière

prison guard NOUN
le gardien de prison
la gardienne de prison

privacy NOUN
l' intimité FEM

private ADJECTIVE
privé ◊ *a private school* une école privée
♦ **private property** la propriété privée
♦ **"private"** (*on envelope*) « personnel »
♦ **a private bathroom** une salle de bain individuelle
♦ **I take private lessons.** Je prends des cours particuliers.

to **privatize** VERB
privatiser

privilege NOUN
le privilège

prize NOUN
le prix ◊ *to win a prize* gagner un prix

prizewinner NOUN
le gagnant
la gagnante

prize-winning ADJECTIVE
primé ◊ *a prize-winning documentary* un film documentaire primé

pro NOUN
le/la pro (*athlete*)

♦ **You're a real pro at making crêpes!** Tu es une vraie pro de des crêpes!
♦ **the pros and cons** le pour et le contre ◊ *We weighed the pros and cons.* Nous avons pesé le pour et le contre.

probability NOUN
la probabilité

probable ADJECTIVE
probable

probably ADVERB
probablement ◊ *probably not* probablement pas

probation NOUN
♦ **on probation** en liberté surveillée

problem NOUN
le problème ◊ *No problem!* Pas de problème!

proceeds PL NOUN
les bénéfices MASC

process NOUN
le processus ◊ *the peace process* le processus de paix
♦ **to be in the process of doing something** être en train de faire quelque chose ◊ *We're in the process of painting the kitchen.* Nous sommes en train de peindre la cuisine.

procession NOUN
le défilé

to **procrastinate** VERB
♦ **I tend to procrastinate.** J'ai tendance à tout remettre au lendemain.

to **produce** VERB
1 produire (*create, manufacture*)
2 monter (*play, show*)

producer NOUN
1 (*of play, show*)
le metteur en scène
la metteuse en scène
2 (*business*)
le producteur
la productrice ◊ *Canada is the world's greatest producer of hydroelectric power.* Le Canada est le plus grand producteur d'hydro-électricité au monde.

product NOUN
le produit

production NOUN
1 la production ◊ *world coffee production* la production mondiale de café
2 la mise en scène (*play, show*) ◊ *a production of "Hamlet"* une mise en scène de « Hamlet »

profession NOUN
la profession

professional NOUN

P

---

see also **professional** ADJECTIVE

le professionnel
la professionnelle

professional ADJECTIVE

see also **professional** NOUN

(*player*)
professionnel MASC
professionnelle FEM ◊ *a professional musician* un musicien professionnel
♦ **a very professional piece of work** un vrai travail de professionnel

professor NOUN
le professeur d'université
la professeure d'université

profit NOUN
le bénéfice

profitable ADJECTIVE
rentable

program NOUN

see also **program** VERB

① le programme ◊ *a computer program* un programme informatique
② l' émission FEM (*on TV, radio*) ◊ *a TV program* une émission de télé
③ le programme (*of events*)

to **program** VERB

see also **program** NOUN

programmer (*computer*)

programmer NOUN
le programmeur
la programmeuse ◊ *She's a programmer.* Elle est programmeuse.

programming NOUN
la programmation

progress NOUN
le progrès ◊ *You're making progress!* Vous faites des progrès!

to **prohibit** VERB
interdire ◊ *Smoking is prohibited.* Il est interdit de fumer.

project NOUN
le projet ◊ *a development project* un projet de développement ◊ *I'm doing a project on the rain forest.* Je travaille à un projet de recherche sur la forêt pluviale.

projector NOUN
le projecteur

promise NOUN

see also **promise** VERB

la promesse ◊ *He made me a promise.* Il m'a fait une promesse.
♦ **That's a promise!** C'est promis!

to **promise** VERB

see also **promise** NOUN

promettre ◊ *He promised to write.* Il a promis d'écrire. ◊ *I'll write, I promise!* J'écrirai. C'est promis!

promising ADJECTIVE
prometteur MASC
prometteuse FEM ◊ *a promising player* un joueur prometteur

to **promote** VERB
promouvoir ◊ *Our school tries to promote recycling.* Notre école essaie de promouvoir le recyclage. ◊ *We made posters to promote the school play.* Nous avons fait des affiches pour promouvoir la pièce de théâtre de l'école.
♦ **to be promoted** être promu ◊ *She was promoted after six months.* Elle a été promue au bout de six mois.

promotion NOUN
la promotion

prompt ADJECTIVE, ADVERB
rapide ◊ *a prompt reply* une réponse rapide

promptly ADVERB
♦ **We left promptly at seven.** Nous sommes partis à sept heures précises.

pronoun NOUN
le pronom

to **pronounce** VERB
prononcer ◊ *How do you pronounce that word?* Comment est-ce qu'on prononce ce mot?

pronunciation NOUN
la prononciation

proof NOUN
la preuve

to **proofread** VERB
relire et corriger ◊ *Don't forget to proofread your book report.* N'oublie pas de relire et de corriger ton compte-rendu de livre.

prop NOUN
l' accessoire MASC (*for play*)

propaganda NOUN
la propagande

propane NOUN
le propane ◊ *a propane cylinder* (*for camping*) une bonbonne de propane ◊ *a propane stove* un réchaud au propane

proper ADJECTIVE
① vrai (*genuine*) ◊ *proper French bread* du vrai pain français ◊ *We didn't have a proper lunch, just sandwiches.* Nous n'avons pas pris de vrai lunch, juste des sandwichs.
♦ **It's difficult to get a proper job.** Il est difficile de trouver un travail correct.
② adéquat ◊ *You have to have*

the proper equipment. Il faut avoir l'équipement adéquat. ◊ *We need proper training.* Il nous faut une formation adéquate.
♦ **If you had come at the proper time...** Si tu étais venu à l'heure dite...

properly ADVERB
1 comme il faut (*correctly*) ◊ *You're not doing it properly.* Tu ne t'y prends pas comme il faut.
2 convenablement (*appropriately*) ◊ *Dress properly for your interview.* Habille-toi convenablement pour ton entrevue.

property NOUN
la propriété
♦ **"private property"** « propriété privée »
♦ **stolen property** les objets volés

proportional ADJECTIVE
proportionnel MASC
proportionnelle FEM ◊ *proportional representation* la représentation proportionnelle

proposal NOUN
la proposition (*suggestion*)

to **propose** VERB
proposer ◊ *I propose a new plan.* Je propose un changement de programme.
♦ **to propose to do something** avoir l'intention de faire quelque chose ◊ *What do you propose to do?* Qu'est-ce que tu as l'intention de faire?
♦ **to propose to somebody** (*for marriage*) demander quelqu'un en mariage ◊ *He proposed to her at the restaurant.* Il l'a demandée en mariage au restaurant.

to **prosecute** VERB
poursuivre en justice ◊ *They were prosecuted for murder.* Ils ont été poursuivis en justice pour meurtre.
♦ **"Trespassers will be prosecuted"** « Défense d'entrer sous peine de poursuites »

prospect NOUN
la perspective ◊ *It'll improve my career prospects.* Ça va améliorer mes perspectives d'avenir.

to **protect** VERB
protéger

protection NOUN
la protection

protein NOUN
la protéine

protest NOUN
see also **protest** VERB

la protestation ◊ *He ignored their protests.* Il a ignoré leurs protestations.
♦ **a protest march** une manifestation

to **protest** VERB
see also **protest** NOUN
protester

Protestant NOUN
see also **Protestant** ADJECTIVE
le protestant
la protestante

Protestant ADJECTIVE
see also **Protestant** NOUN
protestant ◊ *a Protestant church* une église protestante

protester NOUN
le manifestant
la manifestante

proud ADJECTIVE
fier MASC
fière FEM ◊ *Her parents are proud of her.* Ses parents sont fiers d'elle.

to **prove** VERB
prouver ◊ *The police couldn't prove it.* La police n'a pas pu le prouver.

proverb NOUN
le proverbe

to **provide** VERB
fournir
♦ **to provide somebody with something** fournir quelque chose à quelqu'un ◊ *They provided us with maps.* Ils nous ont fourni des cartes.

to **provide for** VERB
subvenir aux besoins de ◊ *She can now provide for her family.* Maintenant elle peut subvenir aux besoins de sa famille.

provided CONJUNCTION
à condition que

à condition que has to be followed by the subjunctive.

◊ *He'll play in the next game provided he comes to the practice.* Il jouera dans le prochain match, à condition qu'il vienne à l'entraînement.

province NOUN
la province

provincial ADJECTIVE
provincial
(MASC PL provinciaux) ◊ *the provincial capital* la capitale provinciale

prowler NOUN
le rôdeur
la rôdeuse

prune NOUN

P

le <u>pruneau</u>
(PL les pruneaux)

to **pry** VERB
 ♦ **to pry into other people's affairs** mettre son nez dans les affaires des autres

pseudonym NOUN
 le <u>pseudonyme</u>

psychiatrist NOUN
 le/la <u>psychiatre</u> ◊ *She's a psychiatrist.* Elle est psychiatre.

psychological ADJECTIVE
 <u>psychologique</u>

psychologist NOUN
 le/la <u>psychologue</u> ◊ *He's a psychologist.* Il est psychologue.

psychology NOUN
 la <u>psychologie</u>

public NOUN

 see also **public** ADJECTIVE

 le <u>public</u> ◊ *open to the public* ouvert au public
 ♦ **in public** en public

public ADJECTIVE

 see also **public** NOUN

 <u>public</u> MASC
 <u>publique</u> FEM
 ♦ **a public holiday** un jour férié
 ♦ **public opinion** l'opinion publique FEM
 ♦ **the public address system** les haut-parleurs
 ♦ **a public school** une école publique
 ♦ **public transport** les transports en commun MASC PL
 ♦ **public relations** les relations publiques FEM

publicity NOUN
 la <u>publicité</u>

to **publish** VERB
 <u>publier</u>

publisher NOUN
 la <u>maison d'édition</u> (*company*)

puck NOUN
 la <u>rondelle</u>

pudding NOUN
 le <u>pouding</u> ◊ *instant vanilla pudding* du pouding instantané à la vanille
 ♦ **rice pudding** le riz au lait

puddle NOUN
 la <u>flaque</u>

puffin NOUN
 le <u>macareux</u>

puff pastry NOUN
 la <u>pâte feuilletée</u>

to **pull** VERB
 ① <u>tirer</u> ◊ *Pull!* Tirez!
 ② <u>arracher</u> (*tooth, weed*)

 ♦ **to pull the trigger** appuyer sur la gâchette
 ♦ **to pull a muscle** se froisser un muscle ◊ *I pulled a muscle when I was training.* Je me suis froissé un muscle à l'entraînement.
 ♦ **You're pulling my leg!** Tu me fais marcher!
 ♦ **to pull off the road** arrêter la voiture sur le bord de la route
 ♦ **to pull out (1)** sortir (*from driveway, parking space*)
 ♦ **to pull out (2)** sortir de la file (*in traffic*) ◊ *The car pulled out to pass.* La voiture est sortie de la file pour doubler.
 ♦ **to pull out (3)** se retirer (*withdraw*) ◊ *He pulled out of the tournament.* Il s'est retiré du tournoi.
 ♦ **The police pulled us over.** La police nous a fait nous arrêter.
 ♦ **to pull through** s'en sortir ◊ *They think he'll pull through.* Ils pensent qu'il va s'en sortir.
 ♦ **to pull up** s'arrêter (*car*) ◊ *A black car pulled up beside me.* Une voiture noire s'est arrêtée à côté de moi.

pullover NOUN
 le <u>chandail</u>

pulse NOUN
 le <u>pouls</u> ◊ *The nurse felt my pulse.* L'infirmière a pris mon pouls.

pump NOUN

 see also **pump** VERB

 la <u>pompe</u> ◊ *a bicycle pump* une pompe à vélo ◊ *a gas pump* une pompe à essence

to **pump** VERB

 see also **pump** NOUN

 <u>pomper</u>
 ♦ **to pump up** gonfler (*tire*)

pumpkin NOUN
 la <u>citrouille</u>

punch NOUN

 see also **punch** VERB

 ① le <u>coup de poing</u> (*blow*)
 ② le <u>punch</u> (*drink*)
 ③ le <u>perforateur</u> (*tool*) ◊ *Use the three-hole punch on the teacher's desk.* Utilise le perforateur à trois trous sur le bureau de la prof.

to **punch** VERB

 see also **punch** NOUN

 ① <u>donner un coup de poing à</u> (*hit*) ◊ *She punched me!* Elle m'a donné un coup de poing!
 ② <u>perforer</u> (*papers*) ◊ *The pages are already punched.* Les feuilles sont déjà perforées.

③ poinçonner (*ticket*) ◊ *He forgot to punch my ticket.* Il a oublié de poinçonner mon billet.

punctual ADJECTIVE
ponctuel MASC
ponctuelle FEM

punctuation NOUN
la ponctuation

to **puncture** VERB
crever (*tire, balloon*)

to **punish** VERB
punir
♦ **to punish somebody for something** punir quelqu'un de quelque chose
♦ **to punish somebody for doing something** punir quelqu'un d'avoir fait quelque chose

punishment NOUN
la punition

punk NOUN
le/la punk (*person*)
♦ **a punk rock band** un groupe de punk rock

puppet NOUN
la marionnette

puppy NOUN
le chiot

to **purchase** VERB
acheter

pure ADJECTIVE
pur ◊ *pure orange juice* du pur jus d'orange ◊ *the pure sciences* les sciences pures

purple ADJECTIVE
violet MASC
violette FEM

purpose NOUN
le but ◊ *What is the purpose of these changes?* Quel est le but de ces changements? ◊ *his purpose in life* son but dans la vie
♦ **on purpose** exprès ◊ *She did it on purpose.* Elle l'a fait exprès.

to **purr** VERB
ronronner

purse NOUN
① le sac à main
(PL les sacs à main)
② (*for coins*)
le porte-monnaie
(PL les porte-monnaie)

to **pursue** VERB
poursuivre

pursuit NOUN
♦ **in pursuit of adventure** à la recherche de l'aventure
♦ **She escaped with her brother in hot pursuit.** Elle s'est échappée avec son

frère à ses trousses.

push NOUN
see also **push** VERB
♦ **to give somebody a push** pousser quelqu'un ◊ *He gave me a push.* Il m'a poussé.
♦ **a push for more affordable housing** une campagne pour des logements à loyer modéré

to **push** VERB
see also **push** NOUN
① pousser ◊ *Don't push!* Arrêtez de pousser!
② appuyer sur (*button*)
♦ **to push somebody to do something** pousser quelqu'un à faire quelque chose ◊ *My parents are pushing me to take piano.* Mes parents me poussent à prendre des cours de piano.
♦ **to push drugs** revendre de la drogue

to **push around** VERB
bousculer ◊ *Stop pushing people around.* Arrête de bousculer les gens.

to **push through** VERB
se frayer un passage ◊ *The paramedics pushed through the crowd.* Les ambulanciers se sont frayé un passage dans la foule.
♦ **I pushed my way through.** Je me suis frayé un passage.

pusher NOUN
(*of drugs*)
le revendeur
la revendeuse

push-up NOUN
la pompe
♦ **to do push-ups** faire des pompes

pussy willow NOUN
le saule à chatons

to **put** VERB
① mettre (*place*) ◊ *Where shall I put my things?* Où est-ce que je peux mettre mes affaires? ◊ *He's putting the baby to bed.* Il met le bébé au lit.
② écrire (*write*) ◊ *Don't forget to put your name on the paper.* N'oubliez pas d'écrire votre nom sur la feuille.

to **put aside** VERB
mettre de côté ◊ *Can you put this aside for me till tomorrow?* Est-ce que vous pouvez mettre ça de côté pour moi jusqu'à demain?

to **put away** VERB
ranger ◊ *Can you put away the dishes, please?* Tu peux ranger la vaisselle, s'il te plaît?

to **put back** VERB
remettre en place (*replace*) ◊ *Put*

☞

it back when you've finished with it.
Remets-le en place une fois que tu
auras fini.

to **put down** VERB
    ① poser ◊ *I'll put these bags down
for a minute.* Je vais poser ces sacs
une minute.
    ② noter (*in writing*) ◊ *I've put down a
few ideas.* J'ai noté quelques idées.
    ③ rabaisser (*belittle*) ◊ *I don't like
jokes that put other people down.*
Je n'aime pas les plaisanteries qui
rabaissent les autres. ◊ *Stop putting
yourself down.* Arrête de te rabaisser.
  ♦ **to have an animal put down** faire
piquer un animal ◊ *We had to have
our old dog put down.* Nous avons dû
faire piquer notre vieux chien.

to **put forward** VERB
    ① avancer (*clock*) ◊ *Next week it'll
be time to put the clocks forward an
hour.* La semaine prochaine, il sera
temps d'avancer les montres d'une
heure.
    ② proposer (*idea, argument*) ◊ *to put
forward a suggestion* proposer une
suggestion

to **put in** VERB
    installer (*install*) ◊ *We're going to get
new cupboards put in.* Nous allons
faire installer de nouvelles armoires.
  ♦ **She has put in a lot of work on this
project.** Elle a fourni beaucoup de
travail pour ce projet.

to **put off** VERB
    ① remettre à plus tard (*postpone*) ◊ *I
keep putting it off.* Je n'arrête pas de
remettre ça à plus tard.
    ② décourager (*discourage*) ◊ *He's
not easily put off.* Il ne se laisse pas
facilement décourager.

to **put on** VERB
    ① mettre (*clothes, lipstick, record*)
◊ *I'll put my coat on.* Je vais mettre
mon manteau.
    ② monter (*play, show*) ◊ *We're
putting on "Bon Voyage, Charlie
Brown".* Nous sommes en train
de monter « Bon voyage, Charlie
Brown ».
    ③ mettre à cuire ◊ *I'll put the
potatoes on.* Je vais mettre les
pommes de terre à cuire.
  ♦ **to put on weight** grossir ◊ *He's put
on a bit of weight.* Il a un peu grossi.

  ♦ **to put on two kilos** gagner deux
kilos

to **put out** VERB
    éteindre (*light, cigarette, fire*) ◊ *It
took them five hours to put out the
fire.* Ils ont mis cinq heures à éteindre
l'incendie.

to **put through** VERB
    ① passer ◊ *Can you put me through
to the manager?* Est-ce que vous
pouvez me passer le directeur?
  ♦ **I'm putting you through.** Je vous
passe la communication.
    ② soumettre ◊ *The new drug was
put through a series of tests.* On a
soumis le nouveau médicament à une
série d'épreuves.

to **put up** VERB
    ① mettre (*pin up*) ◊ *The poster's
great. I'll put it up on my wall.*
L'affiche est super. Je vais le mettre
au mur.
    ② monter (*tent*) ◊ *We put up our tent
in a field.* Nous avons monté la tente
dans un champ.
    ③ augmenter (*price*) ◊ *They've put
up the price.* Ils ont augmenté le prix.
    ④ héberger (*accommodate*) ◊ *My
friends will put me up for the night.*
Mes amis vont m'héberger pour la
nuit.
  ♦ **to put one's hand up** lever la main
◊ *If you have any questions, put up
your hand.* Si vous avez une question,
levez la main.
  ♦ **to put up with something** supporter
quelque chose ◊ *I'm not going to put
up with it any longer.* Je ne vais pas
supporter ça plus longtemps.

puzzle NOUN
  le puzzle (*jigsaw*)

puzzled ADJECTIVE
  perplexe ◊ *You look puzzled!* Tu as
l'air perplexe!

puzzling ADJECTIVE
  déconcertant

pyjamas PL NOUN
  le pyjama SING ◊ *my pyjamas* mon
pyjama
  ♦ **a pair of pyjamas** un pyjama
  ♦ **a pyjama top** un haut de pyjama

pyramid NOUN
  la pyramide

Q

quaint ADJECTIVE
pittoresque (*house, village*)

qualifications PL NOUN
les qualifications FEM ◊ *What are your qualifications?* Quelles sont vos qualifications professionnelles?

qualified ADJECTIVE
1 qualifié (*trained*) ◊ *a qualified driving instructor* un moniteur d'auto-école qualifié
2 diplômé (*nurse, teacher*) ◊ *a qualified nurse* une infirmière diplômée

to **qualify** VERB
se qualifier (*in competition*) ◊ *Our team didn't qualify.* Notre équipe ne s'est pas qualifiée.
♦ **to qualify for a job** avoir les compétences requises pour un poste
♦ **to qualify for unemployment benefits** avoir droit aux allocations d'assurance-emploi
♦ **That hardly qualifies as art.** Cela ne mérite guère le nom d'art.

quality NOUN
la qualité ◊ *good quality of life* une bonne qualité de vie ◊ *good quality ingredients* des ingrédients de bonne qualité ◊ *She has lots of good qualities.* Elle a beaucoup de qualités.

quantity NOUN
la quantité

quarantine NOUN
la quarantaine ◊ *in quarantine* en quarantaine

quarrel NOUN

| see also **quarrel** VERB |

la dispute

to **quarrel** VERB

| see also **quarrel** NOUN |

se disputer

quarry NOUN
la carrière (*for stone*)

quarter NOUN
le quart
♦ **three quarters** trois quarts
♦ **a quarter of an hour** un quart d'heure ◊ *three quarters of an hour* trois quarts d'heure
♦ **a quarter after ten** dix heures et quart
♦ **a quarter to eleven** onze heures moins le quart

quarterfinal NOUN

le quart de finale

quartet NOUN
le quatuor ◊ *a string quartet* un quatuor à cordes

queasy ADJECTIVE
♦ **to feel queasy** avoir mal au cœur ◊ *I'm feeling queasy.* J'ai mal au cœur.

Québec NOUN
le Québec

queen NOUN
1 la reine ◊ *Queen Elizabeth* la reine Élisabeth
2 la dame (*playing card*) ◊ *the queen of hearts* la dame de cœur
♦ **the Queen Mother** la reine mère
♦ **beauty queen** la reine de beauté
♦ **a queen-sized bed** un grand lit

query NOUN

| see also **query** VERB |

la question

to **query** VERB

| see also **query** NOUN |

mettre en question ◊ *No one queried my decision.* Personne n'a mis en question ma décision.

question NOUN

| see also **question** VERB |

la question ◊ *Can I ask a question?* Est-ce que je peux poser une question? ◊ *That's a difficult question.* C'est une question difficile.
♦ **It's out of the question.** C'est hors de question.
♦ **There's no question he's going to win.** Il est certain qu'il va gagner.
♦ **There's no question of you paying!** Il n'est pas question que tu payes!

to **question** VERB

| see also **question** NOUN |

interroger ◊ *He was questioned by the police.* Il a été interrogé par la police.

questionable ADJECTIVE
douteux MASC
douteuse FEM ◊ *questionable behaviour* une conduite douteuse

question mark NOUN
le point d'interrogation

questionnaire NOUN
le questionnaire

quick ADJECTIVE, ADVERB

rapide ◊ *a quick lunch* un déjeuner rapide ◊ *It's quicker by train.* C'est plus rapide en train.
- ◆ **Be quick!** Dépêche-toi!
- ◆ **She's a quick learner.** Elle apprend vite.
- ◆ **Quick, phone the police!** Téléphonez vite à la police!

quickly ADVERB
vite ◊ *It was all over very quickly.* Ça s'est passé très vite.

quicksand NOUN
le sable mouvant

quiet ADJECTIVE
[1] (*not talkative or noisy*)
silencieux MASC
silencieuse FEM ◊ *You're very quiet today.* Tu es bien silencieux aujourd'hui. ◊ *The engine is very quiet.* Le moteur est très silencieux.
[2] tranquille (*peaceful*) ◊ *a quiet little town* une petite ville tranquille ◊ *a quiet weekend* une fin de semaine tranquille
- ◆ **Be quiet!** Tais-toi!
- ◆ **Quiet!** Silence!

quietly ADVERB
[1] doucement (*speak*) ◊ *"She's very sick," he said quietly.* « Elle est très malade », déclara-t-il doucement.
[2] silencieusement (*move*) ◊ *He quietly opened the door.* Il a ouvert la porte sans faire de bruit.

quilt NOUN
[1] la courtepointe (*pieced, with special stitching*)
[2] la douillette (*comforter*)

to **quit** VERB quitter (*place, premises, job*)
◊ *She's decided to quit her job.* Elle a décidé de quitter son emploi.
- ◆ **I quit!** J'abandonne!

quite ADVERB
[1] assez (*rather*) ◊ *It's quite warm today.* Il fait assez chaud aujourd'hui.
[2] tout à fait (*entirely*) ◊ *I'm not quite sure.* Je n'en suis pas tout à fait sûr. ◊ *It's not quite the same.* Ce n'est pas tout à fait la même chose.
- ◆ **quite good** pas mal
- ◆ **I've been there quite a few times.** J'y suis allé pas mal de fois.
- ◆ **quite a lot of money** pas mal d'argent
- ◆ **It costs quite a lot to go to Europe.** Ça coûte assez cher d'aller en Europe.
- ◆ **It's quite a long way.** C'est assez loin.
- ◆ **It was quite a shock.** Ça a été tout un choc.
- ◆ **There were quite a few people there.** Il y avait pas mal de gens.

quiz NOUN
[1] l' interrogation FEM (*in school*)
[2] le questionnaire (*in magazine*)
- ◆ **a quiz show** un jeu-questionnaire

quota NOUN
le quota

quotation NOUN
la citation ◊ *a quotation from a book* une citation d'un livre

quote NOUN

> see also **quote** VERB

la citation ◊ *a quote from Pierre Trudeau* une citation de Pierre Trudeau
- ◆ **quotes** (*quotation marks*) les guillemets MASC ◊ *in quotes* entre guillemets

to **quote** VERB

> see also **quote** NOUN

citer ◊ *He's always quoting famous people.* Il n'arrête pas de citer des gens célèbres.

R

rabbi NOUN
le rabbin

rabbit NOUN
le lapin
♦ **a rabbit hutch** un clapier

rabies NOUN
la rage
♦ **a dog with rabies** un chien enragé

raccoon NOUN
le raton laveur

race NOUN

see also **race** VERB

1 la course (*sport*) ◊ *a bike race* une course cycliste
2 la race (*species*) ◊ *the human race* la race humaine
♦ **race relations** les relations interraciales FEM

to **race** VERB

see also **race** NOUN

1 faire la course (*have a race*)
♦ **I'll race you!** On fait la course!
2 courir ◊ *We raced to catch the bus.* Nous avons couru pour attraper l'autobus.

race car NOUN
la voiture de course

race car driver NOUN
le/la pilote de course

racecourse NOUN
le champ de courses

racehorse NOUN
le cheval de course
(PL les chevaux de course)

racer NOUN
le vélo de course (*bike*)

racetrack NOUN
la piste

racial ADJECTIVE
racial
(MASC PL raciaux) ◊ *racial discrimination* la discrimination raciale

racism NOUN
le racisme

racist ADJECTIVE

see also **racist** NOUN

raciste

racist NOUN

see also **racist** ADJECTIVE

le/la raciste

rack NOUN
1 (*for luggage*)
le porte-bagages
(PL les porte-bagages)
2 (*for coats*)
le portemanteau
(PL les portemanteaux)
3 l' égouttoir MASC (*for dishes*)

racket NOUN
le tapage (*noise*) ◊ *They're making a terrible racket.* Ils font un tapage de tous les diables. (*informal*)

racquet NOUN
la raquette

radar NOUN
le radar

radiation NOUN
la radiation

radiator NOUN
le radiateur

radio NOUN
la radio
♦ **on the radio** à la radio
♦ **a radio station** une station de radio

radioactive ADJECTIVE
radioactif MASC
radioactive FEM

radio-controlled ADJECTIVE
téléguidé (*model plane, car*)

radish NOUN
le radis

raffle NOUN
la tombola ◊ *a raffle ticket* un billet de tombola

raft NOUN
le radeau
(PL les radeaux)

rag NOUN
le chiffon
♦ **dressed in rags** en haillons

rage NOUN
la rage
♦ **to be in a rage** être furieux ◊ *She was in a rage.* Elle était furieuse.
♦ **It's all the rage.** Ça fait fureur.

raid NOUN

see also **raid** VERB

1 l' incursion FEM ◊ *a raid by enemy soldiers* une incursion de soldats ennemis
2 la descente ◊ *a police raid* une descente de police

to raid VERB

> *see also* **raid** NOUN

  ① faire une incursion dans (*military*)
  ② faire une descente dans (*police*)
  ◊ *The police raided the club.* La police a fait une descente dans le club.

rail NOUN
  le rail (*on railway line*)
  ♦ **by rail** en train

railing NOUN
  ① la rampe (*on stairs*)
  ② la balustrade (*on bridge, balcony*)
  ◊ *Don't lean over the railing!* Ne vous penchez pas sur la balustrade!

railway NOUN
  le chemin de fer ◊ *the privatization of the railways* la privatisation des chemins de fer
  ♦ **a railway crossing** une traverse
  ♦ **a railway line** une ligne de chemin de fer
  ♦ **a railway station** une gare

rain NOUN

> *see also* **rain** VERB

  la pluie ◊ *in the rain* sous la pluie

to rain VERB

> *see also* **rain** NOUN

  pleuvoir ◊ *It rains a lot here.* Il pleut beaucoup par ici.
  ♦ **It's raining.** Il pleut.

rainbow NOUN
  l' arc-en-ciel MASC
  (PL les arcs-en-ciel)

raincoat NOUN
  l' imperméable MASC

rainforest NOUN
  la forêt tropicale humide

rainy ADJECTIVE
  pluvieux MASC
  pluvieuse FEM

to raise VERB
  ① lever (*lift*) ◊ *He raised his hand.* Il a levé la main.
  ② élever (*children, animals*) ◊ *We raise pigs.* Nous élevons des porcs.
  ◊ *They've raised three children.* Ils ont élevé trois enfants.
  ③ améliorer (*improve*) ◊ *They want to raise standards in schools.* Ils veulent améliorer le niveau dans les écoles.
  ♦ **to raise money** collecter des fonds
  ◊ *The school is raising money for a new gym.* L'école collecte des fonds pour un nouveau gymnase.

raisin NOUN
  le raisin sec

rake NOUN

le râteau
(PL les râteaux)

rally NOUN
  ① le rassemblement (*of people*)
  ② le rallye (*sport*) ◊ *a rally driver* un pilote de rallye

ram NOUN

> *see also* **ram** VERB

  le bélier (*sheep*)

to ram VERB

> *see also* **ram** NOUN

  emboutir (*vehicle*) ◊ *The thieves rammed a police car.* Les voleurs ont embouti une voiture de police.

ramp NOUN
  ① la rampe d'accès (*for wheelchairs*)
  ② la bretelle (*on highway*)

ran VERB *see* **run**

ranch NOUN
  le ranch

random ADJECTIVE
  ♦ **a random selection** une sélection effectuée au hasard
  ♦ **at random** au hasard ◊ *We picked the number at random.* Nous avons choisi le numéro au hasard.

rang VERB *see* **ring**

range NOUN

> *see also* **range** VERB

  le choix ◊ *a wide range of colours* un grand choix de coloris
  ♦ **a range of subjects** diverses matières ◊ *We study a range of subjects.* Nous étudions diverses matières.
  ♦ **a mountain range** une chaîne de montagnes

to range VERB

> *see also* **range** NOUN

  ♦ **to range from...to** se situer entre... et ◊ *Temperatures in summer range from 18 to 33 degrees.* Les températures estivales se situent entre dix-huit et trente-trois degrés.
  ♦ **Tickets range from \$5 to \$40.** Les billets coûtent entre cinq et quarante dollars.

ranger NOUN
  le garde forestier
  la garde forestière

to rank VERB
  ♦ **She ranks third in Canada in speed skating.** Elle est classée troisième au Canada pour le patinage de vitesse.

ransom NOUN
  la rançon

rap NOUN
  le rap (*music*) ◊ *a rap singer* un

chanteur de rap

rapids PL NOUN
les <u>rapides</u> MASC PL

rare ADJECTIVE
1 <u>rare</u> (*unusual*) ◊ *a rare plant* une plante rare
2 <u>saignant</u> (*steak*)

rash NOUN
l' <u>éruption de boutons</u> FEM ◊ *I've got a rash on my chest.* J'ai une éruption de boutons sur la poitrine.

raspberry NOUN
la <u>framboise</u> ◊ *raspberry jam* la confiture de framboises

rat NOUN
le <u>rat</u>

rate NOUN
| see also **rate** VERB |

1 le <u>tarif</u> (*price*) ◊ *There are reduced rates for students.* Il y a des tarifs réduits pour les étudiants.
2 le <u>taux</u> (*level*) ◊ *the birth rate* le taux de naissances ◊ *a high rate of interest* un taux d'intérêt élevé

to **rate** VERB
| see also **rate** NOUN |

♦ **He is rated the best.** Il est considéré comme le meilleur.
♦ **How do you rate this film?** Qu'est-ce que vous pensez de ce film?
♦ **This rates a 9 out of 10.** Cela mérite un 9 sur 10.

rather ADVERB
<u>plutôt</u> ◊ *I was rather disappointed.* J'étais plutôt déçu.
♦ **rather than** plutôt que ◊ *We decided to camp rather than stay at a hotel.* Nous avons décidé de camper plutôt que d'aller à l'hôtel.
♦ **I'd rather...** J'aimerais mieux... ◊ *I'd rather stay in tonight.* J'aimerais mieux rester à la maison ce soir.
◊ *"Would you like a candy?" "I'd rather have an apple."* « Tu veux un bonbon? » « J'aimerais mieux une pomme. »

rattle NOUN
le <u>hochet</u> (*for baby*)

rattlesnake NOUN
le <u>serpent à sonnette</u>

to **rave** VERB
| see also **rave** NOUN |

<u>s'extasier</u> ◊ *They raved about the movie.* Ils se sont extasiés sur le film.

rave NOUN
| see also **rave** VERB |

✱ le <u>rave</u> (*party*)

♦ **rave music** la musique rave

ravenous ADJECTIVE
♦ **to be ravenous** avoir une faim de loup ◊ *I'm ravenous!* J'ai une faim de loup!

raw ADJECTIVE
<u>cru</u> (*food*)
♦ **raw materials** les matières premières FEM

razor NOUN
le <u>rasoir</u> ◊ *some disposable razors* des rasoirs jetables
♦ **a razor blade** une lame de rasoir

RCMP NOUN
la <u>GRC</u>

reach NOUN
| see also **reach** VERB |

♦ **out of reach** hors de portée ◊ *The light switch was out of reach.* L'interrupteur était hors de portée.
♦ **within easy reach of** à proximité de ◊ *The hotel is within easy reach of the town centre.* L'hôtel se trouve à proximité du centre-ville.

to **reach** VERB
| see also **reach** NOUN |

1 <u>arriver à</u> ◊ *We reached the hotel at 7 p.m.* Nous sommes arrivés à l'hôtel à sept heures du soir. ◊ *Have you reached a decision?* Tu es arrivé à une décision?
2 <u>parvenir à</u> (*decision*) ◊ *Eventually they reached a decision.* Ils sont finalement parvenus à une décision.
♦ **He reached for his flashlight.** Il a tendu la main pour prendre sa lampe de poche.

to **react** VERB
<u>réagir</u>

reaction NOUN
la <u>réaction</u>

reactor NOUN
le <u>réacteur</u> ◊ *a nuclear reactor* un réacteur nucléaire

to **read** VERB
<u>lire</u> ◊ *I don't read much.* Je ne lis pas beaucoup. ◊ *Have you read this book?* Est-ce que tu as lu ce livre? ◊ *Read the text out loud.* Lis le texte à haute voix.

reader NOUN
(*person*)
le <u>lecteur</u>
la <u>lectrice</u>

readily ADVERB
<u>volontiers</u> ◊ *She readily agreed.* Elle a accepté volontiers.

reading NOUN

R

☞

la <u>lecture</u> ◊ *Reading is one of my hobbies.* La lecture est l'une de mes activités favorites.

ready ADJECTIVE
<u>prêt</u> ◊ *She's nearly ready.* Elle est presque prête. ◊ *He's always ready to help.* Il est toujours prêt à rendre service.
♦ **to get ready** se préparer ◊ *She's getting ready to go out.* Elle est en train de se préparer pour sortir.
♦ **to get something ready** préparer quelque chose ◊ *He's getting dinner ready.* Il est en train de préparer le dîner.

ready-made ADJECTIVE
① <u>tout fait</u> ◊ *ready-made curtains* des rideaux tous faits ◊ *a ready-made solution* une solution toute faite
② <u>cuisiné</u> (*food*) ◊ *a ready-made meal* un plat cuisiné

real ADJECTIVE
① <u>vrai</u> ◊ *He wasn't a real policeman.* Ce n'était pas un vrai policier. ◊ *Her real name is Cordelia.* Son vrai nom est Cordelia.
② <u>véritable</u> ◊ *It's real leather.* C'est du cuir véritable. ◊ *It was a real nightmare.* C'était un véritable cauchemar.
♦ **in real life** dans la réalité

real estate NOUN
l' <u>immobilier</u> MASC ◊ *He works in real estate.* Il travaille dans l'immobilier.
♦ **a real estate agency** une agence immobilière
♦ **a real estate agent** un agent immobilier

realistic ADJECTIVE
<u>réaliste</u>

reality NOUN
la <u>réalité</u>

to **realize** VERB
♦ **to realize that...** se rendre compte que... ◊ *We realized that something was wrong.* Nous nous sommes rendu compte que quelque chose n'allait pas.

really ADVERB
<u>vraiment</u> ◊ *She's really nice.* Elle est vraiment sympathique. ◊ *"Do you want to go?" "Not really."* « Tu veux y aller ? » « Pas vraiment. »
♦ **"I'm learning to ride." "Really?"** « J'apprends à monter à cheval. » « Ah bon ? »
♦ **Do you really think so?** Tu es sûr?

rear ADJECTIVE
see also **rear** NOUN
<u>arrière</u> MASC, FEM, PL ◊ *a rear wheel* une roue arrière

rear NOUN
see also **rear** ADJECTIVE
l' <u>arrière</u> MASC ◊ *at the rear of the train* à l'arrière du train

reason NOUN
la <u>raison</u> ◊ *There's no reason to think that...* Il n'y a aucune raison de penser que...
♦ **for security reasons** pour des raisons de sécurité
♦ **That was the main reason I went.** C'est surtout pour ça que j'y suis allé.

reasonable ADJECTIVE
① <u>raisonnable</u> (*sensible*) ◊ *Be reasonable!* Sois raisonnable!
② <u>convenable</u> (*not bad*) ◊ *He wrote a reasonable essay.* Sa dissertation était convenable.

reasonably ADVERB
<u>raisonnablement</u> ◊ *The team played reasonably well.* L'équipe a joué raisonnablement bien.
♦ **reasonably priced accommodation** un logement à un prix raisonnable

to **reassure** VERB
<u>rassurer</u>

reassuring ADJECTIVE
<u>rassurant</u>

rebellious ADJECTIVE
<u>rebelle</u>

to **reboot** VERB
<u>redémarrer</u> ◊ *I rebooted the computer.* J'ai redémarré l'ordinateur.

receipt NOUN
le <u>reçu</u>

to **receive** VERB
<u>recevoir</u>

receiver NOUN
le <u>combiné</u> (*of phone*)
♦ **to pick up the receiver** décrocher

recent ADJECTIVE
<u>récent</u>

recently ADVERB
<u>ces derniers temps</u> ◊ *I've been doing a lot of biking recently.* J'ai fait beaucoup de cyclisme ces derniers temps.

reception NOUN
la <u>réception</u> ◊ *Please leave your key at reception.* Merci de laisser votre clé à la réception. ◊ *The reception will be at a big hotel.* La réception aura lieu dans un grand hôtel.

receptionist NOUN
le/la <u>réceptionniste</u>

recession NOUN

la <u>récession</u>

recipe NOUN
la <u>recette</u>

reclining ADJECTIVE
♦ **a reclining armchair** un fauteuil inclinable
♦ **a reclining seat** (*in plane, car*) un siège inclinable

recognizable ADJECTIVE
<u>reconnaissable</u>

to **recognize** VERB
<u>reconnaître</u> ◊ *You'll recognize me by my red hair.* Vous me reconnaîtrez à mes cheveux roux.

to **recommend** VERB
<u>recommander</u> ◊ *What do you recommend?* Qu'est-ce que vous me recommandez?

to **reconsider** VERB
<u>reconsidérer</u>

record NOUN

  see also **record** VERB

  ⓵ le <u>disque</u> (*recording*) ◊ *my favourite record* mon disque préféré
  ⓶ le <u>record</u> (*sport*) ◊ *the world record* le record du monde
♦ **in record time** en un temps record ◊ *She finished the job in record time.* Elle a terminé le travail en un temps record.
♦ **a criminal record** un casier judiciaire ◊ *She's got a criminal record.* Elle a un casier judiciaire.
♦ **records** (*of police, hospital*) les archives FEM ◊ *I'll check the records.* Je vais vérifier dans les archives.
♦ **There is no record of your booking.** Il n'y a aucune trace de votre réservation.

to **record** VERB

  see also **record** NOUN

<u>enregistrer</u> (*on film, tape*) ◊ *They've just recorded their new album.* Ils viennent d'enregistrer leur nouveau disque.

recorder NOUN
la <u>flûte à bec</u> (*instrument*) ◊ *She plays the recorder.* Elle joue de la flûte à bec.
♦ **a cassette recorder** un magnétophone à cassettes
♦ **a video recorder** un magnétoscope

recording NOUN
l' <u>enregistrement</u> MASC

record player NOUN
le <u>tourne-disque</u>

to **recover** VERB
<u>se remettre</u> ◊ *He's recovering from a knee injury.* Il se remet d'une blessure au genou.

recovery NOUN
le <u>rétablissement</u>
♦ **Best wishes for a speedy recovery!** Meilleurs vœux de prompt rétablissement!

recreational vehicle NOUN
la <u>caravane</u>

rec room NOUN
la <u>salle de jeux</u>

rectangle NOUN
le <u>rectangle</u>

rectangular ADJECTIVE
<u>rectangulaire</u>

to **recycle** VERB
<u>recycler</u>

recycling NOUN
le <u>recyclage</u>

red ADJECTIVE
  ⓵ <u>rouge</u> ◊ *a red rose* une rose rouge ◊ *red meat* la viande rouge
♦ **a red light** (*traffic light*) un feu rouge ◊ *to go through a red light* brûler un feu rouge
  ⓶ (*hair*)
  <u>roux</u> MASC
  <u>rousse</u> FEM ◊ *He's got red hair.* Il a les cheveux roux.

Red Crescent NOUN
le <u>Croissant-Rouge</u>

Red Cross NOUN
la <u>Croix-Rouge</u>

to **redecorate** VERB
<u>redécorer</u>

red-haired ADJECTIVE
<u>roux</u> MASC
<u>rousse</u> FEM

red-handed ADJECTIVE
♦ **to catch somebody red-handed** prendre quelqu'un la main dans le sac ◊ *We were caught red-handed.* Nous avons été pris la main dans le sac.

redhead NOUN
le <u>roux</u>
la <u>rousse</u>

to **redo** VERB
<u>refaire</u>

to **reduce** VERB
<u>réduire</u> ◊ *at a reduced price* à prix réduit
♦ **Reduce, reuse, recycle.** Réduire, réutiliser, recycler.

reduction NOUN
la <u>réduction</u> ◊ *a 5% reduction* une réduction de cinq pour cent

redwood NOUN

R

☞

la séquoia

reed NOUN
(*plant*)
le roseau
(PL les roseaux)

reel NOUN
le moulinet (*on fishing rod*)

to **reel in** VERB
ramener ◊ *I reeled in a huge trout.*
J'ai ramené une truite énorme.

to **refer** VERB
♦ **to refer to** faire allusion à ◊ *What are you referring to?* À quoi faites-vous allusion?

referee NOUN
l' arbitre MASC

reference NOUN
1 l' allusion FEM ◊ *He made no reference to the incident.* Il n'a fait aucune allusion à l'incident.
2 les références FEM (*for job application*) ◊ *Would you please give me a reference?* Pouvez-vous me fournir des références?
♦ **a reference book** un ouvrage de référence

to **refill** VERB
remplir à nouveau ◊ *She refilled my glass.* Elle a rempli mon verre à nouveau.

refinery NOUN
la raffinerie

to **reflect** VERB
refléter (*light, image*)

reflection NOUN
le reflet (*in mirror*)

reflex NOUN
le réflexe

reflexive ADJECTIVE
réfléchi ◊ *a reflexive verb* un verbe réfléchi

refresher course NOUN
le cours de recyclage

refreshing ADJECTIVE
rafraîchissant

refreshments PL NOUN
les rafraîchissements MASC PL

refrigerator NOUN
le réfrigérateur

to **refuel** VERB
se ravitailler en carburant ◊ *The plane stops in Montréal to refuel.*
L'avion s'arrête à Montréal pour se ravitailler en carburant.

refuge NOUN
le refuge

refugee NOUN

le réfugié
la réfugiée

refund NOUN
see also **refund** VERB
le remboursement

to **refund** VERB
see also **refund** NOUN
rembourser

refusal NOUN
le refus

to **refuse** VERB
refuser

to **regain** VERB
♦ **to regain consciousness** reprendre connaissance

regard NOUN
see also **regard** VERB
♦ **Give my regards to your mom.**
Transmettez mon bon souvenir à ta mère.
♦ **My parents send their regards.** Vous avez le bonjour de mes parents.
♦ **with regard to** quant à ◊ *with regard to the new rule...* quant au nouveau règlement...

to **regard** VERB
see also **regard** NOUN
♦ **to regard something as** considérer quelque chose comme
♦ **as regards...** concernant...

regarding PREPOSITION
relatif à MASC
relative à FEM ◊ *the laws regarding the export of animals* les lois relatives à l'exportation des animaux
♦ **Regarding your oral presentations,...**
Quant à vos présentations orales,...

regardless ADVERB
quand même (*nevertheless*) ◊ *We will go regardless.* Nous irons quand même.
♦ **regardless of the weather** peu importe le temps
♦ **regardless of the consequences** peu importent les conséquences

regiment NOUN
le régiment

region NOUN
la région

regional ADJECTIVE
régional
(PL régionaux)

to **register** VERB
s'inscrire (*sign up, enroll*)

registered ADJECTIVE
♦ **a registered letter** une lettre recommandée

registration NOUN
l' inscription FEM ◊ *The deadline for registration is March 6.* La date limite pour l'inscription est le 6 mars.

regret NOUN

see also **regret** VERB

le regret
♦ **I have no regrets.** Je ne regrette rien.

to **regret** VERB

see also **regret** NOUN

regretter ◊ *Give me the money or you'll regret it!* Donne-moi l'argent, sinon tu vas le regretter!
♦ **to regret doing something** regretter d'avoir fait quelque chose ◊ *I regret saying that.* Je regrette d'avoir dit ça.

regular ADJECTIVE
[1] régulier MASC
régulière FEM ◊ *at regular intervals* à intervalles réguliers ◊ *a regular verb* un verbe régulier
[2] (*standard*)
normal
(PL normaux) ◊ *a regular portion of fries* une portion de frites normale

regularly ADVERB
régulièrement ◊ *to exercise regularly* faire de l'exercice régulièrement

regulation NOUN
le règlement

rehearsal NOUN
la répétition

to **rehearse** VERB
répéter

rein NOUN
la rêne ◊ *the reins* les rênes

reindeer NOUN
le renne

to **reject** VERB
rejeter (*idea, suggestion*) ◊ *We rejected that idea right away.* Nous avons immédiatement rejeté cette idée.
♦ **I auditioned for the part but they rejected me.** J'ai auditionné pour le rôle, mais ils m'ont rejeté.

relapse NOUN
la rechute ◊ *to have a relapse* faire une rechute

related ADJECTIVE
apparenté (*people*) ◊ *We're related.* Nous sommes apparentés.
♦ **The two events were not related.** Il n'y avait aucun rapport entre les deux événements.

relation NOUN
[1] le rapport (*connection*) ◊ *It has no relation to reality.* Cela n'a aucun rapport avec la réalité.
♦ **in relation to** par rapport à
[2] (*person*)
le parent
la parente ◊ *He's a distant relation.* C'est un parent éloigné.

relationship NOUN
les relations FEM PL ◊ *We have a good relationship.* Nous avons de bonnes relations.
♦ **I'm not in a relationship at the moment.** Je ne sors avec personne en ce moment.

relative NOUN
le parent
la parente ◊ *my close relatives* mes proches parents
♦ **all her relatives** toute sa famille

relatively ADVERB
relativement

to **relax** VERB
se détendre ◊ *I listen to music to relax.* J'écoute de la musique pour me détendre.
♦ **Relax! Everything's fine.** Ne t'en fais pas! Tout va bien.

relaxation NOUN
la détente ◊ *I don't have much time for relaxation.* Je n'ai pas beaucoup de moments de détente.

relaxed ADJECTIVE
détendu

relaxing ADJECTIVE
reposant
♦ **I find cooking relaxing.** Cela me détend de faire la cuisine.

relay NOUN
♦ **a relay race** une course de relais

to **release** VERB

see also **release** NOUN

[1] libérer (*prisoner*)
[2] divulguer (*report, news*)
[3] sortir (*record, video*)

release NOUN

see also **release** VERB

la libération (*from prison*) ◊ *the release of the hostages* la libération des otages
♦ **the band's latest release** le dernier disque du groupe
♦ **a press release** un communiqué

relevant ADJECTIVE
approprié (*documents*)
♦ **That's not relevant.** Ça n'a aucun rapport.
♦ **to be relevant to something** être en rapport avec quelque chose ◊ *Education should be relevant to real life.* L'enseignement devrait être

R

☞

en rapport avec la réalité.

reliable ADJECTIVE
fiable ◊ *a reliable car* une voiture
fiable ◊ *He's not very reliable.* Il n'est
pas très fiable.

relief NOUN
le soulagement ◊ *That's a relief!*
Quel soulagement!

to **relieve** VERB
soulager ◊ *This injection will relieve
the pain.* Cette piqûre va soulager la
douleur. ◊ *I was relieved to hear...* J'ai
été soulagé d'apprendre...

religion NOUN
la religion

religious ADJECTIVE
1 religieux MASC
religieuse FEM ◊ *my religious beliefs*
mes croyances religieuses
2 croyant ◊ *Are you religious?* Tu es
croyant?

reluctant ADJECTIVE
♦ **to be reluctant to do something** être
peu disposé à faire quelque chose
◊ *They were reluctant to help us.* Ils
étaient peu disposés à nous aider.

reluctantly ADVERB
à contrecœur ◊ *She reluctantly
accepted.* Elle a accepté à contrecœur.

to **rely on** VERB
compter sur ◊ *I'm relying on you.* Je
compte sur toi.

to **remain** VERB
rester
♦ **to remain silent** garder le silence

remaining ADJECTIVE
♦ **the remaining ingredients** le reste des
ingrédients
♦ **my one remaining friend** le seul ami
qui me reste

remains PL NOUN
les restes MASC PL ◊ *the remains of
the picnic* les restes du pique-nique
◊ *human remains* des restes humains

remake NOUN
la nouvelle version (*of film*)

remark NOUN
la remarque

remarkable ADJECTIVE
remarquable

remarkably ADVERB
remarquablement

to **remarry** VERB
se remarier ◊ *She remarried three
years ago.* Elle s'est remariée il y a
trois ans.

rematch NOUN
♦ **There will be a rematch on Friday.** Le
match sera rejoué vendredi.

remedy NOUN
le remède ◊ *a good remedy for sore
throat* un bon remède contre le mal
de gorge

to **remember** VERB
se souvenir de ◊ *I can't remember
his name.* Je ne me souviens pas de
son nom. ◊ *I don't remember.* Je ne
m'en souviens pas.

> *In French you often say "don't forget"
> instead of **remember**.*

◊ *Remember your passport!* N'oublie
pas ton passeport! ◊ *Remember
to write your name on the form.*
N'oubliez pas d'écrire votre nom sur
le formulaire.

Remembrance Day NOUN
le jour du Souvenir MASC ◊ *on
Remembrance Day* le jour du
Souvenir

to **remind** VERB
rappeler ◊ *It reminds me of
Newfoundland.* Cela me rappelle
Terre-Neuve. ◊ *I'll remind you
tomorrow.* Je te le rappellerai
demain. ◊ *Remind me to speak to the
principal.* Rappelle-moi de parler au
directeur.

remorse NOUN
le remords ◊ *He showed no remorse.*
Il n'a manifesté aucun remords.

remote ADJECTIVE
isolé ◊ *a remote village* un village
isolé

remote control NOUN
la télécommande

remotely ADVERB
♦ **I'm not remotely interested.** Je ne
suis absolument pas intéressé.
♦ **Do you think it would be remotely
possible?** Pensez-vous que cela serait
éventuellement possible?

removable ADJECTIVE
amovible

to **remove** VERB
1 enlever ◊ *Please remove your bag
from my seat.* Est-ce que vous pouvez
enlever votre sac de mon siège?
◊ *She removed her coat.* Elle a enlevé
son manteau.
2 faire partir (*stain*) ◊ *Did you
remove the stain?* Est-ce que tu as fait
partir la tache?

rendezvous NOUN
le rendez-vous
(PL les rendez-vous)

to **renew** VERB
renouveler (*passport, licence*)

renewable ADJECTIVE
renouvelable (*energy, resource*)

to **renovate** VERB
rénover ◊ *The building's been renovated.* Le bâtiment a été rénové.

renowned ADJECTIVE
renommé

rent NOUN

see also **rent** VERB

le loyer

to **rent** VERB

see also **rent** NOUN

louer ◊ *We rented a car.* Nous avons loué une voiture.

rental NOUN
la location ◊ *Car rental is included in the price.* Le prix comprend la location d'une voiture.

rental car NOUN
la voiture de location

to **reorganize** VERB
réorganiser

rep NOUN (= *representative*)
le représentant
la représentante

repaid VERB *see* **repay**

to **repair** VERB

see also **repair** NOUN

réparer
♦ **to get something repaired** faire réparer quelque chose ◊ *We got the washing machine repaired.* Nous avons fait réparer la laveuse.

repair NOUN

see also **repair** VERB

la réparation

to **repay** VERB
rembourser (*money*)

repayment NOUN
le remboursement

to **repeat** VERB

see also **repeat** NOUN

répéter

repeat NOUN

see also **repeat** VERB

la répétition ◊ *This lesson was just a repeat of the last one.* Cette leçon n'était qu'une répétition de la précédente.

repeatedly ADVERB
à plusieurs reprises

repellent NOUN
♦ **insect repellent** l'insectifuge MASC
♦ **mosquito repellent** la lotion antimoustiques

repetitive ADJECTIVE
1 (*movement, work*)
répétitif MASC
répétitive FEM
2 plein de redites (*writing, speech*)

to **replace** VERB
remplacer

replay NOUN
la reproduction ◊ *an instant replay* une reproduction instantanée

replica NOUN
la réplique

reply NOUN

see also **reply** VERB

la réponse

to **reply** VERB

see also **reply** NOUN

répondre

report NOUN

see also **report** VERB

1 (*of event*)
le compte rendu
(PL les comptes rendus)
2 le reportage (*news report*) ◊ *a report in the paper* un reportage dans le journal
3 le bulletin scolaire (*at school*) ◊ *I got a good report this term.* J'ai un bon bulletin scolaire ce trimestre.
♦ **report card** le bulletin scolaire

to **report** VERB

see also **report** NOUN

1 signaler ◊ *I reported the theft to the police.* J'ai signalé le vol à la police.
2 se présenter ◊ *Report to reception when you arrive.* Présentez-vous à la réception à votre arrivée.
♦ **to report on something** rendre compte de quelque chose

reporter NOUN
le/la reporter ◊ *She is a reporter.* Elle est reporter.

to **represent** VERB
représenter

representative ADJECTIVE
représentatif MASC
représentative FEM

reproduction NOUN
la reproduction

reptile NOUN
le reptile

republic NOUN
la république

repulsive ADJECTIVE
repoussant

R

reputable ADJECTIVE
de bonne réputation

reputation NOUN
la réputation

request NOUN

see also **request** VERB

la demande

to **request** VERB

see also **request** NOUN

demander

to **require** VERB
exiger ◊ *The job requires a good knowledge of classical music.* Cet emploi exige une bonne connaissance de la musique classique.
♦ **a required course** une matière obligatoire

requirement NOUN
la condition requise ◊ *to meet the requirements* remplir les conditions requises
♦ **to meet somebody's requirements** (*please somebody*) satisfaire aux exigences de quelqu'un
♦ **entry requirements** (*for university*) les critères d'entrée

rerun NOUN
la rediffusion ◊ *There's nothing but reruns on TV tonight.* Il n'y a que des rediffusions à la télé ce soir.

to **rescue** VERB

see also **rescue** NOUN

sauver

rescue NOUN

see also **rescue** VERB

⊞ le sauvetage ◊ *a rescue operation* une opération de sauvetage ◊ *a rescue team* une équipe de sauvetage
⊡ le secours ◊ *rescue services* les services de secours
♦ **to come to somebody's rescue** venir au secours de quelqu'un ◊ *He came to my rescue.* Il est venu à mon secours.

research NOUN
⊞ la recherche (*experimental*) ◊ *He's doing research.* Il fait de la recherche.
⊡ les recherches FEM PL (*theoretical*) ◊ *She's doing some research in the library.* Elle fait des recherches à la bibliothèque.

resemblance NOUN
la ressemblance ◊ *a strong family resemblance* une grande ressemblance de famille

to **resent** VERB
être contrarié par ◊ *I really resented your criticism.* J'ai été vraiment contrarié par tes critiques.

resentful ADJECTIVE
plein de ressentiment
♦ **to feel resentful towards somebody** en vouloir à quelqu'un

reservation NOUN
la réservation (*booking*) ◊ *I'd like to make a reservation for this evening.* J'aimerais faire une réservation pour ce soir.

reserve NOUN

see also **reserve** VERB

la réserve ◊ *a First Nations reserve* une réserve indienne ◊ *a nature reserve* une réserve naturelle
♦ **oil reserves** des réserves de pétrole
♦ **to hold something in reserve** tenir quelque chose en réserve

to **reserve** VERB

see also **reserve** NOUN

réserver ◊ *I'd like to reserve a table for tomorrow evening.* J'aimerais réserver une table pour demain soir.

reserved ADJECTIVE
réservé ◊ *a reserved seat* une place réservée

reservoir NOUN
le réservoir

resident NOUN
le résident
la résidente

residential ADJECTIVE
résidentiel MASC
résidentielle FEM ◊ *a residential area* un quartier résidentiel

to **resign** VERB
donner sa démission

to **resist** VERB
résister à ◊ *to resist authority* résister à l'autorité
♦ **Sorry, I couldn't resist!** Pardon, je n'ai pas pu résister!
♦ **I couldn't resist having another cookie.** Je n'ai pas pu m'empêcher de prendre encore un biscuit.

resolution NOUN
la résolution
♦ **Have you made any New Year's resolutions?** Tu as pris de bonnes résolutions pour l'année nouvelle?

resort NOUN
le centre de villégiature
♦ **a ski resort** une station de ski
♦ **a seaside resort** une station balnéaire
♦ **as a last resort** en dernier recours

resource NOUN
la ressource

resourceful ADJECTIVE
débrouillard

respect NOUN

see also **respect** VERB

le respect

to **respect** VERB

see also **respect** NOUN

respecter

respectable ADJECTIVE
1 respectable
2 correct (standard, marks)

respectively ADVERB
respectivement

responsibility NOUN
la responsabilité

responsible ADJECTIVE
1 responsable ◊ He's responsible
for booking the tickets. Il est
responsable de la réservation des
billets. ◊ Humans are responsible for
the destruction of animal habitats.
Les humains sont responsables de la
destruction des habitats des animaux.
♦ to hold somebody responsible
for something tenir quelqu'un
responsable de quelque chose
♦ Who is responsible for this mess? Qui
a fait ce gâchis?
♦ She is responsible for our success.
Nous lui devons notre success.
♦ It's a responsible job. C'est un poste à
responsabilités.
2 (mature)
sérieux MASC
sérieuse FEM ◊ You should be more
responsible. Tu devrais être un peu
plus sérieux.

rest NOUN

see also **rest** VERB

1 le repos (relaxation) ◊ five
minutes' rest cinq minutes de repos
♦ to have a rest se reposer ◊ We
stopped to have a rest. Nous nous
sommes arrêtés pour nous reposer.
2 le reste (remainder) ◊ I'll do the
rest. Je ferai le reste. ◊ the rest of the
money le reste de l'argent
♦ the rest of them les autres ◊ The rest
of them went swimming. Les autres
sont allés nager.

to **rest** VERB

see also **rest** NOUN

1 se reposer (relax) ◊ She's resting
in her room. Elle se repose dans sa
chambre.
2 ménager (not overstrain) ◊ He has
to rest his knee. Il doit ménager son
genou.
3 appuyer (lean) ◊ I rested my bike

against the wall. J'ai appuyé mon
vélo contre le mur.

restaurant NOUN
le restaurant ◊ We don't often go
to restaurants. Nous n'allons pas
souvent au restaurant.
♦ a restaurant car (on train) un wagon-
restaurant

restful ADJECTIVE
reposant

restless ADJECTIVE
agité

restoration NOUN
la restauration

to **restore** VERB
restaurer (building, picture)

to **restrict** VERB
limiter

rest stop NOUN
1 la halte routière ◊ We ate our
sandwiches at the rest stop. Nous
avons mangé nos sandwichs à la
halte routière.
2 le restauroute (with restaurant, gas
station)

result NOUN

see also **result** VERB

le résultat ◊ my exam results mes
résultats d'examen ◊ "What was the
result?" "One-nothing." « Quel a été le
résultat? » « Un à zéro. »
♦ as a result of à la suite de

to **result** VERB

see also **result** NOUN

♦ to result in entraîner
♦ to result from résulter de

to **resume** VERB
reprendre ◊ They've resumed work.
Ils ont repris le travail.

Be careful not to translate **to resume**
by **résumer**.

résumé NOUN
le curriculum vitæ

to **retire** VERB
prendre sa retraite ◊ He retired last
year. Il a pris sa retraite l'an dernier.

retired ADJECTIVE
retraité ◊ She's retired. Elle est
retraitée.
♦ a retired teacher un professeur à la
retraite

retirement NOUN
la retraite

to **retrace** VERB
♦ to retrace one's steps revenir sur ses
pas ◊ I retraced my steps. Je suis

R

☞

revenu sur mes pas.

return NOUN

see also **return** VERB

le retour ◊ *after our return* à notre retour
♦ **the return trip** le voyage de retour
♦ **a return match** un match retour
♦ **a return ticket** un aller et retour ◊ *A return ticket to Winnipeg, please.* Un aller et retour pour Winnipeg, s'il vous plaît.
♦ **It costs $500 return.** L'aller et retour coûte cinq cent dollars.
♦ **in return** en échange ◊ *...and I help her in return* ...et je l'aide en échange
♦ **in return for** en échange de
♦ **Many happy returns!**
✹ Bonne fête!

to **return** VERB

see also **return** NOUN

① revenir (*come back*) ◊ *I've just returned from vacation.* Je viens de revenir de vacances.
♦ **to return home** rentrer à la maison
② retourner (*go back*) ◊ *He returned to Inuvik the following year.* Il est retourné à Inuvik l'année suivante.
③ rendre (*give back*) ◊ *She borrows my things and doesn't return them.* Elle m'emprunte mes affaires et ne me les rend pas.

reunion NOUN
la réunion

to **reuse** VERB
réutiliser

to **reveal** VERB
révéler

revenge NOUN
la vengeance ◊ *in revenge* par vengeance
♦ **to take revenge (1)** se venger ◊ *They planned to take revenge on him.* Ils voulaient se venger de lui.
♦ **to take revenge (2)** (*sports*) prendre sa revanche ◊ *The player who was defeated yesterday will be able to take revenge at tomorrow's game.* La joueuse battue hier pourra prendre sa revanche au match de demain.

to **reverse** VERB

see also **reverse** NOUN, ADJECTIVE

inverser ◊ *She reversed the two numbers by mistake.* Elle a inversé les deux chiffres par erreur.
♦ **to reverse the charges** (*telephone*) virer les frais
♦ **a call with charges reversed** un appel à frais virés

reverse NOUN

see also **reverse** VERB, ADJECTIVE

♦ **in reverse** dans l'ordre inverse ◊ *Now do the whole thing in reverse.* Maintenant fait tout dans l'ordre inverse.
♦ **This is the reverse of what happened yesterday.** C'est le contraire de ce qui est arrivé hier.

reverse ADJECTIVE

see also **reverse** VERB, NOUN

inverse ◊ *in reverse order* dans l'ordre inverse
♦ **in reverse gear** en marche arrière

review NOUN

see also **review** VERB

① la révision ◊ *We will have a thorough review before the test.* Nous ferons une révision complète avant l'épreuve.
② la critique (*of book, film, programme*) ◊ *The book had good reviews.* Ce livre a eu de bonnes critiques.

to **review** VERB

see also **review** NOUN

① réviser ◊ *The class reviewed the last chapter together.* La classe a révisé le dernier chapitre ensemble.
② faire la critique de ◊ *She reviewed the concert for the school newspaper.* Elle a fait la critique du concert pour le journal de l'école.

to **revise** VERB
réviser ◊ *They revise the dictionary every five years.* On révise le dictionnaire tous les cinq ans. ◊ *the revised edition* l'édition révisée
♦ **I've revised my opinion.** J'ai changé d'opinion.

to **revive** VERB
ranimer ◊ *The nurses tried to revive him.* Les infirmières ont essayé de le ranimer.

revolting ADJECTIVE
dégoûtant

revolution NOUN
la révolution
♦ **the Quiet Revolution** la révolution tranquille

revolutionary ADJECTIVE
révolutionnaire

to **revolve** VERB
tourner ◊ *The earth revolves around the sun.* La terre tourne autour du soleil.

reward NOUN
la récompense
♦ **a rewards card** (*at store*) une carte de

fidélité

rewarding ADJECTIVE
   gratifiant ◊ *a rewarding job* un travail gratifiant

to **rewind** VERB
   rembobiner ◊ *to rewind a cassette* rembobiner une cassette

rheumatism NOUN
   le rhumatisme

rhinoceros NOUN
   le rhinocéros

rhubarb NOUN
   la rhubarbe ◊ *a rhubarb pie* une tarte à la rhubarbe

to **rhyme** VERB
   rimer

rhythm NOUN
   le rythme

rib NOUN
   la côte

ribbon NOUN
   le ruban

rice NOUN
   le riz
   ♦ **rice pudding** le pudding au riz

rich ADJECTIVE
   riche
   ♦ **the rich** les riches MASC

to **rid** VERB
   ♦ **to get rid of** se débarrasser de ◊ *I want to get rid of some old clothes.* Je veux me débarrasser de vieux vêtements.

ridden VERB *see* **ride**

ride NOUN

   see also **ride** VERB

   ♦ **to go for a ride (1)** (*on horse*) monter à cheval
   ♦ **to go for a ride (2)** (*on bike*) faire un tour en vélo ◊ *We went for a bike ride.* Nous sommes allés faire un tour en vélo.
   ♦ **Can you give me a ride to the mall?** Tu peux m'emmener au centre commercial dans ta voiture?
   ♦ **It's a short bus ride to the town centre.** Ce n'est pas loin du centre-ville en autobus.
   ♦ **I had three rides on the roller coaster.** J'ai fait trois tours de montagnes russes.

to **ride** VERB

   see also **ride** NOUN

   monter à cheval (*on horse*) ◊ *I'm learning to ride.* J'apprends à monter à cheval.
   ♦ **to ride a bike** faire du vélo ◊ *Can you*

ride a bike? Est-ce que tu sais faire du vélo?
   ♦ **We rode into town on the bus.** Nous avons pris l'autobus pour aller en ville.

rider NOUN
   ① (*on horse*)
   le cavalier
   la cavalière ◊ *She's a good rider.* C'est une bonne cavalière.
   ② le/la cycliste (*on bike*)

ridiculous ADJECTIVE
   ridicule ◊ *Don't be ridiculous!* Ne sois pas ridicule!

riding NOUN
   ✹ ① la circonscription électorale (*for voting*)
   ② l' équitation FEM
   ♦ **to go riding** faire de l'équitation
   ♦ **a riding school** une école d'équitation

rifle NOUN
   le fusil ◊ *a hunting rifle* un fusil de chasse

to **rig** VERB
   truquer ◊ *The election was rigged.* L'élection a été truquée.

right ADJECTIVE, ADVERB

   see also **right** NOUN

   There are several ways of translating ***right***. *Scan the examples to find one that is similar to what you want to say.*

   ① (*factually correct, suitable*)
   bon MASC
   bonne FEM ◊ *the right answer* la bonne réponse ◊ *It isn't the right size.* Ce n'est pas la bonne taille. ◊ *We're on the right train.* Nous sommes dans le bon train.
   ♦ **Is this the right road for Peterborough?** Est-ce que c'est bien la route pour aller à Peterborough?
   ♦ **to be right (1)** (*person*) avoir raison ◊ *You were right!* Tu avais raison!
   ♦ **to be right (2)** (*statement, opinion*) être vrai ◊ *That's right!* C'est vrai!
   ② correctement (*correctly*) ◊ *Am I pronouncing it right?* Est-ce que je prononce ça correctement?
   ③ juste (*accurate*) ◊ *Do you have the right time?* Est-ce que vous avez l'heure juste?
   ④ bien (*morally correct*) ◊ *It's not right to behave like that.* Ce n'est pas bien d'agir comme ça.
   ♦ **I think you did the right thing.** Je pense que tu as bien fait.
   ⑤ droit (*not left*) ◊ *my right hand* ma main droite
   ⑥ à droite (*turn, look*) ◊ *Turn right at*

R

☞

the traffic lights. Tournez à droite aux prochains feux.
♦ **Right! Let's get started.** Bon! On commence.
♦ **right away** tout de suite ◊ *I'll do it right away.* Je vais le faire tout de suite.
♦ **right side out** à l'endroit ◊ *Put your T-shirt on again right side out.* Remets ton T-shirt à l'endroit.
♦ **right way up** à l'endroit ◊ *This picture is sideways. It must be put the right way up.* Ce tableau est de travers. Il faut le remettre à l'endroit.

right NOUN

see also **right** ADJECTIVE

⓵ le droit
♦ **You have no right to do that.** Vous n'avez pas le droit de faire ça.
⓶ la droite (*not left*)
♦ **on the right** à droite ◊ *Our house is on the right.* Notre maison est à droite.
♦ **right of way** la priorité ◊ *It was our right of way.* Nous avions la priorité.

right-hand ADJECTIVE
♦ **the right-hand side** la droite ◊ *It's on the right-hand side.* C'est à droite.
♦ **the right-hand drawer** le tiroir de droite

right-handed ADJECTIVE
droitier MASC
droitière FEM

rightly ADVERB
avec raison ◊ *He rightly decided not to go.* Il a décidé, avec raison, de ne pas y aller.
♦ **if I remember rightly** si je me souviens bien

rim NOUN
⓵ le bord (*edge*)
⓶ la monture ◊ *glasses with wire rims* des lunettes avec une monture métallique

ring NOUN

see also **ring** VERB

⓵ l' anneau MASC
(PL les anneaux) ◊ *a gold ring* un anneau en or
⓶ la bague (*with stones*) ◊ *a diamond ring* une bague de diamants
♦ **a wedding ring** une alliance
⓷ le cercle (*circle*) ◊ *to stand in a ring* se mettre en cercle
⓸ le coup de sonnette (*of bell*) ◊ *I was woken by a ring at the door.* J'ai été réveillé par un coup de sonnette.

to **ring** VERB

see also **ring** NOUN

sonner ◊ *The phone's ringing.* Le téléphone sonne.
♦ **to ring the bell** (*doorbell*) sonner à la porte ◊ *I rang the bell three times.* J'ai sonné trois fois à la porte.

rink NOUN
⓵ la patinoire (*for ice-skating*)
⓶ la piste (*for roller-skating*)

to **rinse** VERB
rincer

riot NOUN

see also **riot** VERB

l' émeute FEM

to **riot** VERB

see also **riot** NOUN

faire une émeute

to **rip** VERB
⓵ déchirer ◊ *I've ripped my jeans.* J'ai déchiré mes jeans.
⓶ se déchirer ◊ *My skirt ripped.* Ma jupe s'est déchirée.

to **rip off** VERB
⓵ escroquer (*cheat*) ◊ *The hotel ripped us off.* L'hôtel nous a escroqués.
⓶ copier ◊ *He ripped off that idea from a movie.* Il a copié cette idée d'un film.

to **rip up** VERB
déchirer ◊ *He read the note and then ripped it up.* Il a lu le mot, puis l'a déchiré.

ripe ADJECTIVE
mûr

rip-off NOUN
♦ **It's a rip-off!** C'est du vol! (*informal*)
♦ **Those shoes are just a rip-off of the other brand.** Ces souliers ne sont qu'une imitation de l'autre marque.

rise NOUN

see also **rise** VERB

la hausse (*in prices, temperature*)
◊ *a sudden rise in temperature* une hausse subite de température

to **rise** VERB

see also **rise** NOUN

⓵ augmenter (*increase*) ◊ *Prices are rising.* Les prix augmentent.
⓶ se lever ◊ *The sun rises early in June.* Le soleil se lève tôt en juin.

riser NOUN
♦ **to be an early riser** être matinal

risk NOUN

see also **risk** VERB

le risque
♦ **to take risks** prendre des risques
♦ **It's at your own risk.** C'est à vos risques et périls.

to **risk** VERB

> see also **risk** NOUN

risquer ◊ *You risk getting a fine.* Vous risquez de recevoir une amende.
♦ **I wouldn't risk it if I were you.** À votre place, je ne prendrais pas ce risque.

risky ADJECTIVE
risqué

rival NOUN

> see also **rival** ADJECTIVE

le rival
(PL les rivaux)
la rivale

rival ADJECTIVE

> see also **rival** NOUN

① rival ◊ *a rival gang* une bande rivale
② concurrent ◊ *a rival company* une société concurrente

rivalry NOUN
la rivalité (*between towns, schools*)

river NOUN
① la rivière ◊ *The river runs alongside the canal.* La rivière longe le canal.
② le fleuve (*major*) ◊ *the Fraser River* le fleuve Fraser

road NOUN
① la route ◊ *There's a lot of traffic on the roads.* Il y a beaucoup de circulation sur les routes.
② la rue (*street*) ◊ *They live across the road.* Ils habitent de l'autre côté de la rue.

road map NOUN
la carte routière

road rage NOUN
la rage au volant

road sign NOUN
le panneau de signalisation
(PL les panneaux de signalisation)

roast ADJECTIVE
rôti ◊ *roast chicken* le poulet rôti ◊ *roast potatoes* les pommes de terre rôties
♦ **roast pork** le rôti de porc
♦ **roast beef** le rôti de bœuf

to **rob** VERB
♦ **to rob somebody** voler quelqu'un ◊ *I've been robbed.* On m'a volé.
♦ **to rob somebody of something** voler quelque chose à quelqu'un ◊ *He was robbed of his wallet.* On lui a volé son portefeuille.
♦ **to rob a bank** dévaliser une banque

robber NOUN
le voleur
♦ **a bank robber** un cambrioleur de banques

robbery NOUN
le vol
♦ **a bank robbery** un cambriolage de banque
♦ **armed robbery** le vol à main armée

robin NOUN
le rouge-gorge

robot NOUN
le robot

rock NOUN

> see also **rock** VERB

① la roche (*substance*) ◊ *They tunnelled through the rock.* Ils ont creusé un tunnel dans la roche.
② le rocher (*boulder*) ◊ *I sat on a rock.* Je me suis assis sur un rocher.
③ la pierre (*stone*) ◊ *The crowd started to throw rocks.* La foule s'est mise à lancer des pierres.
④ le rock (*music*) ◊ *a rock concert* un concert de rock ◊ *She's a rock star.* C'est une vedette de rock.
♦ **rock and roll** le rock and roll

to **rock** VERB

> see also **rock** NOUN

① bercer ◊ *He rocked the baby in his arms.* Il berçait le bébé dans les bras. ◊ *The little boat was gently rocked by the waves.* Le petit bateau était doucement bercé par les vagues.
② ébranler (*shake*) ◊ *The explosion rocked the building.* L'explosion a ébranlé le bâtiment.

rocket NOUN
la fusée (*firework, spacecraft*)

rock garden NOUN
la rocaille

rocking chair NOUN
✳ la chaise berçante

rocky ADJECTIVE
rocheux MASC
rocheuse FEM
♦ **the Rocky Mountains** les montagnes Rocheuses

rod NOUN
la canne à pêche (*for fishing*)

rode VERB see **ride**

rodeo NOUN
le rodéo ◊ *The Calgary Stampede is a famous rodeo.* Le Stampede de Calgary est un rodéo célèbre.

role NOUN
le rôle

role play NOUN
le jeu de rôle
(PL les jeux de rôles) ◊ *to do a role play* faire un jeu de rôle

R

roll NOUN

see also **roll** VERB

[1] le rouleau
(PL les rouleaux) ◊ *a roll of tape* un rouleau de ruban adhésif ◊ *a roll of toilet paper* un rouleau de papier hygiénique
♦ **to be on a roll** avoir le vent en poupe
[2] le petit pain (*bread*)

to **roll** VERB

see also **roll** NOUN

rouler
♦ **to roll out pastry** abaisser la pâte

roller NOUN
le rouleau
(PL les rouleaux)

Rollerblade™ NOUN
le patin à roues alignées ◊ *a pair of Rollerblades* une paire de patins à roues alignées

roller coaster NOUN
les montagnes russes FEM PL

roller skates PL NOUN
les patins à roulettes MASC

roller skating NOUN
le patinage à roulettes
♦ **to go roller skating** faire du patinage à roulettes

rolling pin NOUN
le rouleau à pâtisserie

romance NOUN
[1] les romans d'amour MASC PL
(*novels*) ◊ *I read a lot of romance.* Je lis beaucoup de romans d'amour.
[2] le charme (*glamour*) ◊ *the romance of a walk in the moonlight* le charme d'une promenade au clair de la lune
♦ **a holiday romance** une idylle de vacances

romantic ADJECTIVE
romantique

roof NOUN
le toit

roof rack NOUN
le porte-bagages de toit

room NOUN
[1] la pièce ◊ *the biggest room in the house* la plus grande pièce de la maison
[2] la chambre (*bedroom*) ◊ *She's in her room.* Elle est dans sa chambre.
♦ **a single room** une chambre pour une personne
♦ **a double room** une chambre pour deux personnes
[3] la salle (*in school*) ◊ *the music room* la salle de musique

[4] la place (*space*) ◊ *There's no room for that box.* Il n'y a pas de place pour cette boîte.

roommate NOUN
[1] le/la colocataire (*in apartment*)
◊ *My sister gets along very well with her roommates.* Ma sœur s'entend à merveille avec ses colocataires.
[2] le/la camarade de chambre (*at boarding school*)

rooster NOUN
le coq

root NOUN
la racine

to **root out** VERB
traquer ◊ *They are determined to root out corruption.* Ils sont déterminés à traquer la corruption.

root beer NOUN
la bière d'épinette

rope NOUN
la corde

to **rope in** VERB
[1] enrôler ◊ *I was roped in to help with the refreshments.* J'ai été enrôlé pour servir les rafraîchissements.
[2] se faire embarquer ◊ *She was roped into another insane project.* Elle s'est encore fait embarquer dans un projet de fous.

rose VERB *see* **rise**

rose NOUN
la rose (*flower*)

to **rot** NOUN VERB
pourrir

rotten ADJECTIVE
pourri (*decayed*) ◊ *a rotten apple* une pomme pourrie
♦ **rotten weather** un temps pourri
♦ **That's a rotten thing to do.** Ce n'est vraiment pas gentil.
♦ **to feel rotten** filer un mauvais coton (*informal*)

rough ADJECTIVE
[1] (*surface*)
rugueux MASC
rugueuse FEM ◊ *My hands are rough.* J'ai les mains rugueuses.
[2] violent (*game*) ◊ *Hockey's a rough sport.* Le hockey est un sport violent.
[3] difficile (*area*) ◊ *It's a rough area.* C'est un quartier difficile.
[4] (*water*)
houleux MASC
houleuse FEM ◊ *The sea was rough.* La mer était houleuse.
[5] approximatif MASC
approximative FEM
♦ **I've got a rough idea.** J'en ai une idée

approximative.

roughly ADVERB
à peu près ◊ *It weighs roughly 20 kilos.* Ça pèse à peu près vingt kilos.

round ADJECTIVE

see also **round** NOUN

rond ◊ *a round table* une table ronde
♦ **all year round** toute l'année

round NOUN

see also **round** ADJECTIVE

① la manche (*of tournament*)
② le round (*of boxing match*)
♦ **a round of golf** une partie de golf

to **round off** VERB
① arrondir (*figure*) ◊ *Round each figure off to the nearest hundred.* Arrondissez chaque chiffre à la centaine près.
② terminer ◊ *They rounded off the meal with lemon sherbet.* Ils ont terminé le repas par du sorbet au citron.

to **round up** VERB
① rassembler (*sheep, cattle, suspects*)
② arrondir (*figure*)

round trip NOUN
l' aller et retour MASC
♦ **a round-trip ticket** un billet aller et retour

route NOUN
① l' itinéraire MASC ◊ *We're planning our route.* Nous établissons notre itinéraire.
② le parcours (*of bus*)

routine NOUN
♦ **my daily routine** ma routine quotidienne

row NOUN

see also **row** VERB

① la rangée ◊ *a row of houses* une rangée de maisons
② le rang (*of seats*) ◊ *Our seats are in the front row.* Nos places se trouvent au premier rang.
♦ **five times in a row** cinq fois d'affilée

to **row** VERB

see also **row** NOUN

① ramer ◊ *We took turns rowing.* Nous avons ramé à tour de rôle.
② faire de l'aviron (*as sport*)

rowboat NOUN
✻ la chaloupe

rowing NOUN
l' aviron MASC (*sport*) ◊ *My hobby is rowing.* Je fais de l'aviron.

royal ADJECTIVE

royal
(MASC PL royaux)
♦ **the royal family** la famille royale

Royal Canadian Mounted Police NOUN
la Gendarmerie royale du Canada

to **rub** VERB
① frotter (*stain*)
② se frotter (*part of body*) ◊ *Don't rub your eyes!* Ne te frotte pas les yeux!
♦ **to rub something out** effacer quelque chose

rubber NOUN
① le caoutchouc ◊ *rubber soles* des semelles en caoutchouc
② la gomme à effacer (*eraser*)
◊ *Can I borrow your rubber?* Je peux emprunter ta gomme à effacer?
♦ **a rubber band** un élastique

rubbish NOUN
① les ordures FEM PL (*refuse*) ◊ *When do they collect the rubbish?* Quand est-ce qu'ils ramassent les ordures?
✻ ② la niaiserie (*nonsense*) ◊ *Don't talk rubbish!* Ne dis pas de niaiseries!
♦ **That's a load of rubbish!** C'est vraiment n'importe quoi! (*informal*)

rude ADJECTIVE
① impoli (*impolite*) ◊ *It's rude to interrupt.* C'est impoli de couper la parole aux gens.
② (*offensive*)
grossier MASC
grossière FEM ◊ *a rude joke* une plaisanterie grossière ◊ *He was very rude to me.* Il a été très grossier avec moi.
♦ **a rude word** un gros mot

rug NOUN
le tapis ◊ *a Persian rug* un tapis persan

ruin NOUN

see also **ruin** VERB

la ruine ◊ *the ruins of the castle* les ruines du château
♦ **in ruins** en ruine

to **ruin** VERB

see also **ruin** NOUN

① abîmer ◊ *You'll ruin your shoes.* Tu vas abîmer tes chaussures.
② gâcher ◊ *It ruined our holiday.* Ça a gâché nos vacances.
③ ruiner (*financially*)

rule NOUN
① la règle ◊ *the rules of grammar* les règles de grammaire
♦ **as a rule** en règle générale
② le règlement (*regulation*) ◊ *It's against the rules.* C'est contre le règlement.

to **rule out** VERB

R

☞

écarter (*possibility*) ◊ *I'm not ruling anything out.* Je n'écarte aucune possibilité.

ruler NOUN
la règle ◊ *Can I borrow your ruler?* Je peux emprunter ta règle?

to **rummage** VERB
fouiller ◊ *She rummaged in her purse for some change.* Elle a fouillé dans son sac à main pour trouver de la monnaie.

rummage sale NOUN
la vente de charité

rumour NOUN
la rumeur ◊ *It's just a rumour.* Ce n'est qu'une rumeur.

run NOUN

> see also **run** VERB

① le coup de circuit (*baseball*) ◊ *to hit a home run* frapper un coup de circuit
② l' échelle FEM (*in nylons*)
♦ **to go for a run** courir ◊ *I go for a run every morning.* Je cours tous les matins.
♦ **I did a ten-kilometre run.** J'ai couru dix kilomètres.
♦ **on the run** en fuite ◊ *The criminals are still on the run.* Les criminels sont toujours en fuite.
♦ **in the long run** à long terme

to **run** VERB

> see also **run** NOUN

① courir ◊ *I ran five kilometres.* J'ai couru cinq kilomètres.
♦ **to run a marathon** participer à un marathon
② diriger (*manage*) ◊ *She runs a large company.* Elle dirige une grosse société.
③ organiser (*organize*) ◊ *They run music courses in the holidays.* Ils organisent des cours de musique pendant les vacances.
④ couler (*water*) ◊ *Don't leave the tap running.* Ne laisse pas couler le robinet.
♦ **to run a bath** faire couler un bain
⑤ conduire (*by car*) ◊ *I can run you to the station.* Je peux te conduire à la gare.
♦ **to run away** s'enfuir ◊ *They ran away before the police came.* Ils se sont enfuis avant l'arrivée de la police.
♦ **Time is running out.** Il ne reste plus beaucoup de temps.
♦ **to run out of something** se trouver à court de quelque chose ◊ *We ran out of money.* Nous nous sommes trouvés à court d'argent.
♦ **to run somebody over** écraser

quelqu'un
♦ **to get run over** se faire écraser ◊ *Be careful, or you'll get run over!* Fais attention, sinon tu vas te faire écraser!

rung VERB *see* **ring**

runner NOUN
le coureur
la coureuse

runner-up NOUN
le second
la seconde

running NOUN
la course ◊ *Running is my favourite sport.* La course est mon sport préféré.

running shoe NOUN
la chaussure de sport

runway NOUN
la piste

rural ADJECTIVE
rural
(MASC PL ruraux)

rush NOUN

> see also **rush** VERB

la hâte
♦ **in a rush** à la hâte

to **rush** VERB

> see also **rush** NOUN

① se précipiter (*run*) ◊ *Everyone rushed outside.* Tout le monde s'est précipité dehors.
② se dépêcher (*hurry*) ◊ *There's no need to rush.* Ce n'est pas la peine de se dépêcher.

rush hour NOUN
l' heure de pointe FEM ◊ *in the rush hour* à l'heure de pointe

rust NOUN

> see also **rust** VERB

la rouille

to **rust** VERB

> see also **rust** NOUN

rouiller ◊ *Your bike will rust if you leave it out in the rain.* Ton vélo va rouiller si tu le laisses sous la pluie.

rusty ADJECTIVE
rouillé ◊ *a rusty bike* un vélo rouillé ◊ *My French is very rusty.* Mon français est très rouillé.

ruthless ADJECTIVE
sans pitié

RV NOUN
la caravane

rye NOUN
le seigle
♦ **rye bread** le pain de seigle

S

sack NOUN

> see also **sack** VERB

le <u>sac</u>
♦ **to get the sack** être mis à la porte

to **sack** VERB

> see also **sack** NOUN

♦ **to sack somebody** mettre quelqu'un à la porte ◊ *She was sacked.* On l'a mise à la porte.

sacred ADJECTIVE
<u>sacré</u>

sacrifice NOUN
le <u>sacrifice</u>

sad ADJECTIVE
<u>triste</u>

saddle NOUN
la <u>selle</u>

saddlebag NOUN
la <u>sacoche</u>

sadly ADVERB
1 <u>tristement</u> ◊ *"She's gone," he said sadly.* « Elle est partie, » a-t-il dit tristement.
2 <u>malheureusement</u> (*unfortunately*) ◊ *Sadly, it was too late.* Malheureusement, il était trop tard.

safe NOUN

> see also **safe** ADJECTIVE

le <u>coffre-fort</u>
(PL les coffres-forts) ◊ *He put the money in the safe.* Il a mis l'argent dans le coffre-fort.

safe ADJECTIVE

> see also **safe** NOUN

1 <u>sans danger</u> ◊ *Don't worry, it's perfectly safe.* Ne vous inquiétez pas, c'est absolument sans danger.
♦ **Is it safe?** Ça n'est pas dangereux?
2 <u>sécuritaire</u> (*machine, ladder*) ◊ *This car isn't safe.* Cette voiture n'est pas sécuritaire.
3 <u>en sécurité</u> (*out of danger*) ◊ *You're safe now.* Vous êtes en sécurité maintenant.
♦ **to feel safe** se sentir en sécurité
♦ **safe sex** le sexe sans risques

safety NOUN
la <u>sécurité</u>
♦ **a safety belt** une ceinture de sécurité
♦ **a safety pin** une épingle de sûreté

Sagittarius NOUN
le/la <u>Sagittaire</u> ◊ *I'm a Sagittarius.* Je suis Sagittaire.

said VERB *see* **say**

sail NOUN

> see also **sail** VERB

la <u>voile</u>

to **sail** VERB

> see also **sail** NOUN

1 <u>faire de la voile</u> (*as skill, sport*) ◊ *Do you know how to sail?* Est-ce que tu sais faire de la voile?
2 <u>naviguer</u> (*travel*)
3 <u>prendre la mer</u> (*set off*) ◊ *The boat sails at eight o'clock.* Le bateau prend la mer à huit heures.

sailboat NOUN
le <u>voilier</u>

sailing NOUN
la <u>voile</u> ◊ *Her hobby is sailing.* Son passe-temps, c'est la voile.
♦ **to go sailing** faire de la voile
♦ **a sailing ship** un grand voilier

sailor NOUN
le/la <u>matelot</u> ◊ *He's a sailor.* Il est matelot.
♦ **I'm not much of a sailor.** Je n'ai pas le pied très marin.

saint NOUN
le <u>saint</u>
la <u>sainte</u>

sake NOUN
♦ **for the sake of** dans l'intérêt de

salad NOUN
la <u>salade</u> ◊ *a fruit salad* une salade de fruits ◊ *a Caesar salad* une salade César
♦ **salad dressing** la vinaigrette

salami NOUN
le <u>salami</u>

salary NOUN
le <u>salaire</u>

sale NOUN
les <u>soldes</u> MASC PL (*reductions*) ◊ *Spring sales will start soon.* Les soldes du printemps commenceront bientôt.
♦ **on sale** en vente
♦ **The factory's for sale.** L'usine est en vente.
♦ **"for sale"** « à vendre »

sales assistant NOUN
le <u>vendeur</u>
la <u>vendeuse</u> ◊ *She's a sales assistant.* Elle est vendeuse.

sales rep NOUN
le représentant
la représentante

salmon NOUN
le saumon

salon NOUN
le salon ◊ *a hair salon* un salon de coiffure ◊ *a beauty salon* un salon de beauté

salt NOUN
le sel

salty ADJECTIVE
salé

to **salute** VERB
saluer

same ADJECTIVE
même ◊ *the same model* le même modèle ◊ *at the same time* en même temps
♦ **They're exactly the same.** Ils sont exactement pareils.
♦ **It's not the same.** Ça n'est pas pareil.

sample NOUN
l' échantillon MASC

sand NOUN
le sable

sandal NOUN
la sandale ◊ *a pair of sandals* une paire de sandales

sand castle NOUN
le château de sable
(PL les châteaux de sable)

sandwich NOUN
le sandwich ◊ *a cheese sandwich* un sandwich au fromage

sang VERB *see* **sing**

sanitary napkin NOUN
la serviette hygiénique

sank VERB *see* **sink**

sarcastic ADJECTIVE
sarcastique

sardine NOUN
la sardine

SARS ABBREVIATION (= *Severe Acute Respiratory Syndrome*)
le SRAS (= syndrome respiratoire aigu sévère)

Saskatchewan NOUN
la Saskatchewan

sat VERB *see* **sit**

satellite NOUN
le satellite ◊ *satellite television* la télévision par satellite
♦ **a satellite dish** une antenne parabolique

satisfactory ADJECTIVE
satisfaisant

satisfied ADJECTIVE
satisfait

Saturday NOUN
le samedi ◊ *on Saturday* samedi ◊ *on Saturdays* le samedi ◊ *every Saturday* tous les samedis ◊ *last Saturday* samedi dernier ◊ *next Saturday* samedi prochain
♦ **I've got a Saturday job.** Je travaille le samedi.

sauce NOUN
la sauce

saucepan NOUN
la casserole

saucer NOUN
la soucoupe

sauna NOUN
le sauna

sausage NOUN
1 la saucisse
2 le saucisson (*sliced, served cold*)
♦ **a sausage roll** un friand

to **save** VERB
1 mettre de côté (*save up money*) ◊ *I've saved 50 dollars already.* J'ai déjà mis cinquante dollars de côté.
2 économiser (*spend less*) ◊ *I saved 20 dollars by waiting for the sale.* J'ai économisé vingt dollars en attendant les soldes.
♦ **to save time** gagner du temps ◊ *We took a taxi to save time.* Nous avons pris un taxi pour gagner du temps. ◊ *It saved us time.* Ça nous a fait gagner du temps.
3 sauver (*rescue*) ◊ *Luckily, all the passengers were saved.* Heureusement, tous les passagers ont été sauvés.
4 sauvegarder (*on computer*) ◊ *I saved the file onto a diskette.* J'ai sauvegardé le fichier sur disquette.
♦ **to save up** mettre de l'argent de côté ◊ *I'm saving up for a new bike.* Je mets de l'argent de côté pour un nouveau vélo.

savings PL NOUN
les économies FEM PL ◊ *She spent all her savings on a computer.* Elle a dépensé toutes ses économies en achetant un ordinateur.

saw VERB *see* **see**

saw NOUN
la scie

sax NOUN
le sax (*informal*) ◊ *I play the sax.* Je joue du sax.

saxophone NOUN

le <u>saxophone</u> ◊ *I play the saxophone.*
Je joue du saxophone.

to **say** VERB
<u>dire</u> ◊ *What did he say?* Qu'est-ce
qu'il a dit? ◊ *Did you hear what she
said?* Tu as entendu ce qu'elle a dit?
♦ **Could you say that again?** Pourriez-
vous répéter, s'il vous plaît?
♦ **That goes without saying.** Cela va
sans dire.

saying NOUN
le <u>dicton</u> ◊ *It's just a saying.* C'est
juste un dicton.

scale NOUN
① l' <u>échelle</u> FEM (*of map*) ◊ *a large-
scale map* une carte à grande échelle
② l' <u>ampleur</u> FEM (*size, extent*) ◊ *a
disaster on a massive scale* un
désastre d'une ampleur incroyable
③ la <u>gamme</u> (*in music*)

scales PL NOUN
la <u>balance</u> SING

scandal NOUN
① le <u>scandale</u> (*outrage*) ◊ *It caused a
scandal.* Ça a fait scandale.
② les <u>commérages</u> MASC PL (*gossip*)
◊ *It's just scandal.* Ce ne sont que des
commérages.

scar NOUN
la <u>cicatrice</u>

scarce ADJECTIVE
<u>limité</u> ◊ *scarce resources* des
ressources limitées
♦ **Jobs are scarce these days.** Il y a peu
de travail ces temps-ci.

scarcely ADVERB
<u>à peine</u> ◊ *I scarcely knew her.* Je la
connaissais à peine.

to **scare** VERB
♦ **to scare somebody** faire peur à
quelqu'un ◊ *He scares me.* Il me fait
peur.

scarecrow NOUN
l' <u>épouvantail</u> MASC

scared ADJECTIVE
♦ **to be scared** avoir peur ◊ *I was
scared stiff.* J'avais terriblement peur.
♦ **to be scared of** avoir peur de ◊ *Are
you scared of her?* Est-ce que tu as
peur d'elle?

scarf NOUN
le <u>foulard</u>

scary ADJECTIVE
<u>effrayant</u> ◊ *It was really scary.* C'était
vraiment effrayant.

scene NOUN
① les <u>lieux</u> MASC PL (*place*) ◊ *The police
were soon on the scene.* La police est
vite arrivée sur les lieux. ◊ *the scene*

of the crime les lieux du crime
② le <u>spectacle</u> (*event, sight*) ◊ *It
was an amazing scene.* C'était un
spectacle étonnant.
♦ **to make a scene** faire une scène

scenery NOUN
le <u>paysage</u> (*landscape*)

scent NOUN
le <u>parfum</u> (*perfume*)

schedule NOUN
le <u>programme</u> ◊ *a busy schedule* un
programme chargé
♦ **on schedule** comme prévu
♦ **to be behind schedule** avoir du retard

scheduled flight NOUN
le <u>vol régulier</u>

scheme NOUN
① le <u>truc</u> (*idea*) ◊ *a crazy scheme he
dreamed up* un truc farfelu qu'il a
inventé
② le <u>projet</u> (*project*) ◊ *the town's
road-widening scheme* le projet
municipal d'élargissement des routes

scholarship NOUN
la <u>bourse</u>

school NOUN
l' <u>école</u> FEM
♦ **to go to school** aller à l'école
♦ **a school of fish** un banc de poissons

schoolbag NOUN
le <u>sac d'école</u>

schoolbook NOUN
le <u>manuel scolaire</u>

school bus NOUN
l' <u>autobus scolaire</u> MASC

schoolyard NOUN
la <u>cour d'école</u>

science NOUN
la <u>science</u>

science fiction NOUN
la <u>science-fiction</u>

scientific ADJECTIVE
<u>scientifique</u>

scientist NOUN
① le/la <u>scientifique</u> (*academic*)
② (*doing research*)
le <u>chercheur</u>
la <u>chercheure</u>

scissors PL NOUN
les <u>ciseaux</u> MASC PL ◊ *a pair of scissors*
une paire de ciseaux

to **scoff** VERB
<u>se moquer</u> ◊ *They scoffed at my
idea.* Ils se sont moqués de mon idée.

scooter NOUN
la <u>trottinette</u>

scope NOUN

S

la dimension ◊ *the scope of the project* la dimension du projet

score NOUN

> *see also* **score** VERB

✹ le pointage ◊ *The score was three nothing.* Le pointage était trois à zéro.

to **score** VERB

> *see also* **score** NOUN

marquer (*goal, point*) ◊ *to score a goal* marquer un but
♦ **to score 6 out of 10** obtenir un pointage de six sur dix
♦ **He shoots, he scores!** Il lance et compte!

Scorpio NOUN

le Scorpion ◊ *I'm a Scorpio.* Je suis Scorpion.

scrambled eggs PL NOUN

les œufs brouillés MASC PL

scrap NOUN

> *see also* **scrap** VERB

① le bout ◊ *a scrap of paper* un bout de papier
♦ **They feed their dog scraps.** Ils nourrissent leur chien avec des restants.
② la bagarre (*fight*)
♦ **scrap iron** la ferraille

to **scrap** VERB

> *see also* **scrap** NOUN

abandonner (*plan*) ◊ *The idea was scrapped.* L'idée a été abandonnée.

scrapbook NOUN

l' album MASC

to **scratch** VERB

> *see also* **scratch** NOUN

① gratter ◊ *Can you scratch my back, please?* Peux-tu me gratter le dos, s'il te plaît? ◊ *Don't scratch your mosquito bites.* Ne gratte pas tes piqûres de maringouin.
② se gratter (*oneself*) ◊ *He scratched until it bled.* Il s'est gratté jusqu'au sang. ◊ *She scratched her head.* Elle s'est gratté la tête.
♦ **The cat scratched me.** Le chat m'a donné des coups de griffe.

scratch NOUN

> *see also* **scratch** VERB

l' égratignure FEM (*on skin*)
♦ **to start from scratch** partir de zéro

scream NOUN

> *see also* **scream** VERB

le hurlement

to **scream** VERB

> *see also* **scream** NOUN

hurler

screen NOUN

l' écran MASC

screen saver NOUN

l' économiseur d'écran MASC

screw NOUN

la vis

screwdriver NOUN

le tournevis

to **scribble** VERB

griffonner

to **scrub** VERB

récurer ◊ *to scrub a pan* récurer une casserole

sculpture NOUN

la sculpture

sea NOUN

la mer

seafood NOUN

les fruits de mer MASC PL ◊ *I don't like seafood.* Je n'aime pas les fruits de mer.

seagull NOUN

la mouette

seal NOUN

> *see also* **seal** VERB

le phoque (*animal*)

to **seal** VERB

> *see also* **seal** NOUN

coller (*letter*)

to **search** VERB

> *see also* **search** NOUN

fouiller ◊ *They searched the woods for her.* Ils ont fouillé les bois pour la trouver.
♦ **to search for something** chercher quelque chose ◊ *He searched for evidence.* Il cherchait des preuves.

search NOUN

> *see also* **search** VERB

la fouille

search engine NOUN

le moteur de recherche

search party NOUN

l' expédition de secours FEM

seashore NOUN

le bord de la mer ◊ *on the seashore* au bord de la mer

seasick ADJECTIVE

♦ **to be seasick** avoir le mal de mer

season NOUN

la saison ◊ *What's your favourite season?* Quelle est ta saison préférée?
♦ **in the off season** hors saison ◊ *It's cheaper to go there in the off season.*

C'est moins cher d'y aller hors saison.
♦ **during the holiday season** en période de vacances
♦ **out of season** hors saison ◊ *Cherries are out of season.* Les cerises sont hors saison.
♦ **a season ticket** un abonnement

seat NOUN
le siège

seat belt NOUN
la ceinture de sécurité

seaweed NOUN
les algues FEM PL

second ADJECTIVE

see also **second** NOUN

deuxième ◊ *on the second page* à la deuxième page
♦ **to come second** (*in race*) arriver deuxième
♦ **the second of March** le deux mars

second NOUN

see also **second** ADJECTIVE

la seconde ◊ *It'll only take a second.* Ça va prendre juste une seconde.

secondary school NOUN
l' école secondaire FEM

second-class ADJECTIVE
♦ **a second-class citizen** un citoyen de deuxième ordre

second-hand ADJECTIVE
usagé ◊ *a secondhand car* une voiture usagée

secondly ADVERB
deuxièmement
♦ **firstly...secondly...** premièrement... deuxièmement... ◊ *Firstly, it's too expensive. Secondly, it wouldn't work anyway.* Premièrement, c'est trop cher. Deuxièmement, ça ne marcherait quand même pas.

secret ADJECTIVE

see also **secret** NOUN

secret MASC
secrète FEM ◊ *a secret mission* une mission secrète

secret NOUN

see also **secret** ADJECTIVE

le secret ◊ *It's a secret.* C'est un secret. ◊ *Can you keep a secret?* Tu sais garder un secret?
♦ **in secret** en secret

secretary NOUN
le/la secrétaire ◊ *She's a secretary.* Elle est secrétaire.

secretly NOUN
secrètement

section NOUN

la section

security NOUN
① la sécurité ◊ *a feeling of security* un sentiment de sécurité ◊ *a campaign to improve airport security* une campagne visant à améliorer la sécurité dans les aéroports
♦ **job security** la sécurité de l'emploi
♦ **a security guard** un garde chargé de la sécurité (*on guard*)
② un convoyeur de fonds (*transporting money*)

security guard NOUN
① l' agent de sécurité MASC
l' agente de sécurité FEM
② le/la garde de voiture blindée (*with armoured car*)

to **see** VERB
voir ◊ *I can't see.* Je ne vois rien. ◊ *I saw him yesterday.* Je l'ai vu hier. ◊ *Have you seen him?* Est-ce que tu l'as vu?
♦ **See you!** Salut!
♦ **See you soon!** À bientôt!
♦ **to see to something** s'occuper de quelque chose ◊ *The window's stuck again. Can you see to it, please?* La fenêtre est encore coincée. Peux-tu t'en occuper, s'il te plaît?

seed NOUN
la graine ◊ *sunflower seeds* des graines de tournesol

to **seek** VERB
chercher
♦ **to seek help** chercher de l'aide

to **seem** VERB
avoir l'air ◊ *She seems tired.* Elle a l'air fatiguée. ◊ *The store seemed to be closed.* Le magasin avait l'air d'être fermé.
♦ **That seems like a good idea.** Ce n'est pas une mauvaise idée.
♦ **It seems that...** Il paraît que... ◊ *It seems they're getting married.* Il paraît qu'ils vont se marier.
♦ **There seems to be a problem.** Il semble y avoir un problème.

seen VERB *see* **see**

seesaw NOUN
la balançoire à bascule

see-through ADJECTIVE
transparent

seldom ADVERB
rarement

to **select** VERB
sélectionner

selection NOUN
la sélection

self-assured ADJECTIVE

S

☞

sûr de soi ◊ *She's very self-assured.* Elle est très sûre d'elle.

self-centred ADJECTIVE
égocentrique

self-confidence NOUN
la <u>confiance en soi</u> ◊ *He hasn't got much self-confidence.* Il n'a pas très confiance en lui.

self-conscious ADJECTIVE
♦ **to be self-conscious (1)**
(*embarrassed*) être mal à l'aise ◊ *She was really self-conscious at first.* Elle était vraiment mal à l'aise au début.
♦ **to be self-conscious (2)** (*shy*) manquer d'assurance ◊ *He's always been rather self-conscious.* Il a toujours manqué un peu d'assurance.

self-control NOUN
le <u>sang-froid</u>

self-defence NOUN
l' <u>autodéfense</u> FEM ◊ *self-defence classes* les cours d'autodéfense
♦ **She killed the dog in self-defence.** Elle a tué le chien en légitime défense.

self-discipline NOUN
l' <u>autodiscipline</u> FEM

self-disciplined ADJECTIVE
♦ **He is self-disciplined.** Il fait preuve d'autodiscipline.

self-employed ADJECTIVE
♦ **to be self-employed** travailler à son compte ◊ *He's self-employed.* Il travaille à son compte.
♦ **the self-employed** les travailleurs autonomes

selfish ADJECTIVE
<u>égoïste</u> ◊ *Don't be so selfish.* Ne sois pas si égoïste.

self-respect NOUN
l' <u>amour-propre</u> MASC

self-serve NOUN
le <u>libre-service</u> ◊ *This gas station is a self-serve.* Cette station-service est un libre-service.

to **sell** VERB
<u>vendre</u> ◊ *She sold it to me.* Elle me l'a vendu.
♦ **to sell off** liquider
♦ **The tickets are all sold out.** Il ne reste plus de billets.
♦ **The tickets sold out in three hours.** Tous les billets ont été vendus en trois heures.

to **sell out** VERB
① se vendre ◊ *The tickets sold out in three hours.* Les billets se sont tous vendus en trois heures.
② se prostituer (*compromise one's standards*) ◊ *The artist refused to sell*

out. L'artiste a refusé de se prostituer.

selling price NOUN
le <u>prix de vente</u>

semicircle NOUN
le <u>demi-cercle</u>

semicolon NOUN
le <u>point-virgule</u>

semi-detached house NOUN
la <u>maison jumelée</u> ◊ *We live in a semi-detached house.* Nous habitons dans une maison jumelée.

semi-final NOUN
la <u>demi-finale</u>

Senate NOUN
le <u>Sénat</u>

to **send** VERB
<u>envoyer</u> ◊ *She sent me a birthday card.* Elle m'a envoyé une carte de fête.
♦ **to send back** renvoyer
♦ **to send away for something** (*free*) se faire envoyer quelque chose ◊ *I've sent away for a brochure.* Je me suis fait envoyer une brochure.
♦ **to send out** envoyer ◊ *My mom sent me out to buy milk.* Ma mère m'a envoyé acheter du lait.

sender NOUN
l' <u>expéditeur</u> MASC
l' <u>expéditrice</u> FEM

senior ADJECTIVE
<u>principal</u> ◊ *senior accountant* la comptable principale ◊ *senior architect* l'architecte principal
♦ **senior citizen** la personne âgée
♦ **senior management** la haute direction
♦ **senior manager** le cadre supérieur

sensational ADJECTIVE
<u>sensationnel</u> MASC
<u>sensationnelle</u> FEM

sense NOUN

   see also **sense** VERB

① le <u>bon sens</u> (*wisdom*) ◊ *Use your common sense!* Un peu de bon sens, voyons!
♦ **It makes sense.** C'est logique.
♦ **It doesn't make sense.** Ça n'a pas de sens.
② le <u>sens</u> (*faculty*) ◊ *the five senses* les cinq sens
♦ **the sense of touch** le toucher
♦ **the sense of smell** l'odorat MASC
♦ **the sixth sense** le sixième sens
♦ **sense of humour** le sens de l'humour ◊ *He has no sense of humour.* Il n'a aucun sens de l'humour.

to **sense** VERB

see also **sense** NOUN

sentir ◊ *I sensed that she was afraid.*
J'ai senti qu'elle avait peur.

senseless ADJECTIVE
insensé

sensible ADJECTIVE
raisonnable ◊ *Be sensible!* Sois
raisonnable!

> Be careful not to translate **sensible**
> by the French word **sensible**.

sensitive ADJECTIVE
sensible ◊ *She's very sensitive.* Elle
est très sensible.

sensuous ADJECTIVE
sensuel MASC
sensuelle FEM

sent VERB *see* **send**

sentence NOUN

see also **sentence** VERB

1 la phrase ◊ *What does this
sentence mean?* Que veut dire cette
phrase?
2 la condamnation (*judgment*)
3 la peine (*punishment*) ◊ *the death
sentence* la peine de mort
♦ **He got a life sentence.** Il a été
condamné à la réclusion à perpétuité.

to **sentence** VERB

see also **sentence** NOUN

♦ **to sentence somebody to life
imprisonment** condamner quelqu'un
à la réclusion à perpétuité
♦ **to sentence somebody to death**
condamner quelqu'un à mort

sentimental ADJECTIVE
sentimental
(MASC PL sentimentaux)

separate ADJECTIVE

see also **separate** VERB

séparé ◊ *I wrote it on a separate
sheet.* Je l'ai écrit sur une feuille
séparée.
♦ **The children have separate rooms.**
Les enfants ont chacun leur chambre.
♦ **on separate occasions** à différentes
reprises

to **separate** VERB

see also **separate** ADJECTIVE

1 séparer
2 se séparer (*married couple*)

separately ADVERB
séparément

separation NOUN
la séparation

separatism NOUN
le séparatisme

separatist NOUN
le/la séparatiste

September NOUN
septembre MASC
♦ **in September** en septembre

sequel NOUN
la suite (*book, film*)

sequence NOUN
1 l' ordre MASC
♦ **in sequence** en ordre
♦ **a sequence of events** une succession
d'événements
2 la séquence (*in film*)

series NOUN
1 la série ◊ *a TV series* une série
télévisée
2 la suite (*of numbers, events*)

serious ADJECTIVE
1 sérieux MASC
sérieuse FEM ◊ *You look very serious.*
Tu as l'air sérieux.
♦ **Are you serious?** Sérieusement?
2 grave (*illness, mistake*)

seriously ADVERB
sérieusement ◊ *No, but seriously...*
Non, mais sérieusement...
♦ **to take somebody seriously** prendre
quelqu'un au sérieux
♦ **seriously injured** gravement blessé
♦ **Seriously?** Vraiment?

sermon NOUN
le sermon

to **serve** VERB

see also **serve** NOUN

1 servir ◊ *Dinner is served.* Le
souper est servi. ◊ *It's his turn to
serve.* C'est à son tour de servir.
2 purger (*prison sentence*)
♦ **to serve time** être en prison
♦ **It serves you right.** C'est bien fait
pour toi.

serve NOUN

see also **serve** VERB

le service (*tennis*)
♦ **It's your serve.** C'est à toi de servir.

server NOUN
le serveur (*computing*)

to **service** VERB

see also **service** NOUN

réviser (*car, washing machine*)

service NOUN

see also **service** VERB

1 le service ◊ *Service is included.* Le
service est compris.
2 la révision (*of car*)
♦ **a memorial service** un service
commémoratif

S

♦ a funeral service un service funèbre

service area NOUN
l' <u>aire de service</u> FEM

service charge NOUN
le <u>service</u> ◊ *There's no service charge.* Le service est compris.

service station NOUN
la <u>station-service</u>
(PL les stations-service)

serviette NOUN
la <u>serviette</u>

session NOUN
la <u>séance</u>

set NOUN

> see also **set** VERB

① le <u>jeu</u>
(PL les jeux) ◊ *a set of keys* un jeu de clés ◊ *a chess set* un jeu d'échecs
♦ a set of drums une batterie
♦ a train set un train électrique
② la <u>manche</u> (*in tennis*)

to **set** VERB

> see also **set** NOUN

① <u>mettre</u> ◊ *I set the alarm for 7 o'clock.* J'ai mis le réveil à sept heures. ◊ *Set the plants on the floor.* Mets les plantes sur le plancher.
② <u>établir</u> (*record*) ◊ *The world record was set last year.* Le record du monde a été établi l'année dernière.
③ <u>se coucher</u> (*sun*) ◊ *The sun was setting.* Le soleil se couchait.
♦ The film is set in Manitoba. L'action du film se déroule au Manitoba.
♦ to set off partir ◊ *We set off for Tadoussac at 9 o'clock.* Nous sommes partis pour Tadoussac à neuf heures.
♦ to set out partir ◊ *We set out for Saint John at 9 o'clock.* Nous sommes partis pour Saint John à neuf heures.
♦ to set sail prendre la mer
♦ to set the table
🞽 mettre la table

to **settle** VERB
① <u>résoudre</u> (*problem*)
② <u>régler</u> (*argument, account*)
♦ to settle down (*calm down*) se calmer
♦ Settle down! Du calme!
♦ to settle in s'installer
♦ to settle on something opter pour quelque chose

seven NUMBER
<u>sept</u> ◊ *She's seven.* Elle a sept ans.

seventeen NUMBER
<u>dix-sept</u> ◊ *He's seventeen.* Il a dix-sept ans.

seventeenth ADJECTIVE
<u>dix-septième</u> ◊ *his seventeenth birthday* son dix-septième anniversaire de naissance ◊ *the seventeenth floor* le dix-septième étage
♦ the seventeenth of August le dix-sept août

seventh ADJECTIVE
<u>septième</u> ◊ *the seventh floor* le septième étage
♦ the seventh of August le sept août

seventy NUMBER
<u>soixante-dix</u>

several ADJECTIVE, PRONOUN
<u>plusieurs</u> ◊ *several schools* plusieurs écoles
♦ several of them plusieurs ◊ *I've seen several of them.* J'en ai vu plusieurs.

to **sew** VERB
<u>coudre</u>
♦ to sew up (*tear*) recoudre

sewing NOUN
la <u>couture</u> ◊ *I like sewing.* J'aime faire de la couture.
♦ a sewing machine une machine à coudre

sewn VERB *see* **sew**

sex NOUN
le <u>sexe</u>
♦ to have sex with somebody coucher avec quelqu'un
♦ sex education l'éducation sexuelle FEM

sexism NOUN
le <u>sexisme</u>

sexist ADJECTIVE
<u>sexiste</u>

sexual ADJECTIVE
<u>sexuel</u> MASC
<u>sexuelle</u> FEM ◊ *sexual discrimination* la discrimination sexuelle ◊ *sexual harassment* le harcèlement sexuel

sexuality NOUN
la <u>sexualité</u>

sexy ADJECTIVE
<u>sexy</u> MASC, FEM, PL

shabby ADJECTIVE
<u>miteux</u> MASC
<u>miteuse</u> FEM

shade NOUN
① l' <u>ombre</u> FEM
♦ in the shade à l'ombre ◊ *It was 35 degrees in the shade.* Il faisait trente-cinq à l'ombre.
② la <u>nuance</u> (*colour*) ◊ *a shade of blue* une nuance de bleu

shadow NOUN
l' <u>ombre</u> FEM

to **shake** VERB
① <u>secouer</u> ◊ *She shook the rug.* Elle

a secoué le tapis.
2 trembler (*tremble*) ◊ *He was shaking with cold.* Il tremblait de froid.
♦ **to shake one's head** (*in refusal*) faire non de la tête
♦ **to shake hands with somebody** serrer la main à quelqu'un ◊ *They shook hands.* Ils se sont serré la main.

shaken ADJECTIVE
secoué ◊ *I was feeling a bit shaken.* J'étais un peu secoué.

shaky ADJECTIVE
tremblant (*hand, voice*)

shall VERB
♦ **Shall I shut the window?** Vous voulez que je ferme la fenêtre?
♦ **Shall we ask them to come with us?** Si on leur demandait de venir avec nous?

shallow ADJECTIVE
peu profond (*water, pool*)

shambles NOUN
la pagaille ◊ *It's a complete shambles.* C'est la pagaille complète.

shame NOUN
la honte ◊ *The shame of it!* Quelle honte!
♦ **What a shame!** Quel dommage!
♦ **It's a shame that...** c'est dommage que...

> *c'est dommage que* has to be followed by a verb in the subjunctive.

◊ *It's a shame he isn't here.* C'est dommage qu'il ne soit pas ici.

shampoo NOUN
le shampooing ◊ *a bottle of shampoo* une bouteille de shampooing

shape NOUN
la forme

share NOUN

> see also **share** VERB

1 la part ◊ *Everybody pays their share.* Tout le monde paie sa part.
2 l' action FEM (*in company*) ◊ *They have shares in several Canadian companies.* Ils ont des actions de plusieurs compagnies canadiennes.

to **share** VERB

> see also **share** NOUN

partager ◊ *to share a room with somebody* partager une chambre avec quelqu'un
♦ **to share out** distribuer ◊ *They shared the sweets out among the children.* Ils ont distribué les bonbons aux enfants.

shark NOUN
le requin

sharp ADJECTIVE
1 tranchant (*razor, knife*)
2 pointu (*spike, point*)
3 intelligent (*clever*) ◊ *She's very sharp.* Elle est très intelligente.
4 (*elegant*)
chic MASC
chic FEM ◊ *Those boots are really sharp!* Ces bottes sont vraiment chics!
♦ **at two o'clock sharp** à deux heures pile

to **shave** VERB
se raser (*oneself*)
♦ **to shave one's legs** se raser les jambes

shaver NOUN
♦ **an electric shaver** un rasoir électrique

shaving cream NOUN
la crème à raser

shaving foam NOUN
la mousse à raser

she PRONOUN
elle ◊ *She's very nice.* Elle est très gentille.

shed NOUN
la remise

she'd = she had, she would

sheep NOUN
le mouton

sheer ADJECTIVE
pur ◊ *It's sheer greed.* C'est de l'avidité pure.

sheet NOUN
le drap (*on bed*)
♦ **a sheet of paper** une feuille de papier

shelf NOUN
1 l' étagère FEM (*in house*)
2 le rayon (*in store*)

shell NOUN
1 le coquillage (*on beach*)
2 la coquille (*of egg, nut*)
3 l' obus MASC (*explosive*)

she'll = she will

shellfish NOUN
les fruits de mer MASC PL

shell suit NOUN
le survêtement

shelter NOUN
♦ **to take shelter** se mettre à l'abri
♦ **a bus shelter** un arrêt d'autobus

shelves PL NOUN *see* **shelf**

shepherd NOUN
le berger

S

sheriff NOUN
le shérif

she's = she is, she has

shield NOUN
le bouclier

shift NOUN

see also **shift** VERB

le poste ◊ *Her shift starts at 8 o'clock.*
Son poste commence à huit heures.
◊ *the night shift* le poste de nuit

to **shift** VERB

see also **shift** NOUN

1 changer ◊ *His position on the issue
continues to shift.* Sa position sur
cette question continue de changer.
◊ *The meaning of this word has
shifted.* Le sens de ce mot a changé.
2 tourner (*wind*) ◊ *The wind has
shifted a little.* Le vent a tourné un
peu.
3 détourner (*eyes, gaze*) ◊ *He shifted
his gaze so as not to embarrass her.*
Il a détourné son regard pour ne pas
l'embarrasser.
4 passer (*gears*) ◊ *She shifted into
reverse.* Elle a passé à la marche
arrière. ◊ *to shift into second* passer
en seconde
♦ **to shift gears** changer de vitesse

shifty ADJECTIVE
1 louche (*person*) ◊ *He looked shifty.*
Il avait l'air louche.
2 fuyant (*eyes*)

shin NOUN
le tibia

to **shine** VERB
briller ◊ *The sun was shining.* Le
soleil brillait.

shiny ADJECTIVE
brillant

ship NOUN
1 le bateau
(PL les bateaux)
2 le navire (*ocean-going*)

shipbuilding NOUN
la construction navale

shipwreck NOUN
le naufrage

shipwrecked ADJECTIVE
♦ **to be shipwrecked** faire naufrage

shipyard NOUN
le chantier naval

shirt NOUN
1 la chemise (*man's*)
2 le chemisier (*woman's*)

to **shiver** VERB
frissonner

shock NOUN

see also **shock** VERB

le choc
♦ **to get a shock (1)** (*surprise*) avoir un
choc
♦ **to get a shock (2)** (*electric*) recevoir
un choc électrique
♦ **an electric shock** un choc électrique

to **shock** VERB

see also **shock** NOUN

1 bouleverser (*upset*) ◊ *They were
shocked by the tragedy.* Ils ont été
bouleversés par la tragédie.
2 choquer (*scandalize*) ◊ *I was rather
shocked by her attitude.* J'ai été assez
choqué par son attitude.

shocking ADJECTIVE
1 choquant (*scandalous*) ◊ *It's
shocking!* C'est choquant!
2 bouleversant (*upsetting*) ◊ *That's
a shocking piece of news.* C'est une
nouvelle bouleversante.
3 épouvantable (*appalling*) ◊ *a
shocking waste* un gaspillage
épouvantable

shoe NOUN
1 le soulier
2 la chaussure

> In Canada, **le soulier** is used
> more frequently, while in other
> francophone countries **la chaussure**
> is most common.

shoelace NOUN
le lacet

shoe polish NOUN
le cirage

shoe store NOUN
le magasin de chaussures

shone VERB see **shine**

shook VERB see **shake**

to **shoot** VERB
1 abattre (*kill*) ◊ *He was shot by a
sniper.* Il a été abattu par un tireur
d'élite.
2 fusiller (*execute*) ◊ *He was shot at
dawn.* Il a été fusillé à l'aube.
3 tirer (*gun*) ◊ *Don't shoot!* Ne tirez
pas!
♦ **to shoot at somebody** tirer sur
quelqu'un
♦ **She was shot in the leg.** (*wounded*)
Elle a reçu une balle dans la jambe.
♦ **to shoot an arrow** envoyer une flèche
4 tourner (*film*) ◊ *The film was shot
in Toronto.* Le film a été tourné à
Toronto.

shooting NOUN
les coups de feu MASC PL ◊ *They heard*

shooting. Ils ont entendu des coups de feu.
♦ **a shooting** une fusillade
♦ **a drive-by shooting** un mitraillage à partir d'un véhicule

shop NOUN
⨞ la boutique ◊ *a gift shop* une boutique de cadeaux ◊ *a souvenir shop* une boutique de souvenirs

🛈 *In French, there are specific words for specific kinds of shop.*

♦ **a doughnut shop** une beignerie
② l' atelier MASC (*workshop*) ◊ *He has a shop in his basement.* Il a un atelier au sous-sol.
③ la menuiserie (*school subject*) ◊ *I made a bookshelf in shop class.* J'ai fait une étagère en menuiserie.

shoplifting NOUN
le vol à l'étalage

shopping NOUN
✱ ① les achats MASC PL (*purchases*) ◊ *Can you get the shopping from the car?* Tu peux aller chercher mes achats dans la voiture?
② le magasinage ◊ *I love shopping.* J'adore faire du magasinage.
♦ **to go shopping (1)** (*for food*) faire l'épicerie
♦ **to go shopping (2)** (*for pleasure*) faire du magasinage
♦ **a shopping bag** un sac à provisions
♦ **a shopping centre** un centre commercial

shore NOUN
le underline{rivage}
♦ **on shore** à terre

short ADJECTIVE
① court ◊ *a short skirt* une jupe courte ◊ *short hair* les cheveux courts
♦ **too short** trop court ◊ *It was a great holiday, but too short.* C'étaient des vacances super, mais trop courtes.
② petit (*person, period of time*) ◊ *She's quite short.* Elle est assez petite. ◊ *a short break* une petite pause ◊ *a short walk* une petite promenade
♦ **to be short of something** être à court de quelque chose ◊ *I'm short of money.* Je suis à court d'argent.
♦ **at short notice** au dernier moment
♦ **In short, the answer's no.** Bref, la réponse est non.

shortage NOUN
la pénurie ◊ *a water shortage* une pénurie d'eau

shortcut NOUN
le raccourci ◊ *I took a shortcut.* J'ai pris un raccourci.

shortly ADVERB
bientôt

shorts PL NOUN
le short SING
♦ **a pair of shorts** un short

short-sighted ADJECTIVE
myope

short story NOUN
la nouvelle

shot VERB *see* **shoot**

shot NOUN
① (*gunshot*)
le coup de feu
(PL les coups de feu)
② la photo (*photo*) ◊ *a shot of the Château Frontenac* une photo du château Frontenac
③ le vaccin (*vaccination*) ◊ *flu shot* le vaccin contre la grippe

should VERB
devoir ◊ *You should take more exercise.* Vous devriez faire plus d'exercice. ◊ *He should be there by now.* Il devrait être arrivé maintenant. ◊ *That shouldn't be too hard.* Ça ne devrait pas être trop difficile.
♦ **should have** avoir dû ◊ *I should have told you before.* J'aurais dû te le dire avant.
♦ **I should be so lucky!** Ça serait trop beau!

shoulder NOUN
l' épaule FEM
♦ **a shoulder bag** un sac à bandoulière

shouldn't = should not

to **shout** VERB

⌐ *see also* **shout** NOUN ⌐

crier ◊ *Don't shout!* Ne criez pas! ◊ *"Go away!" he shouted.* « Allez-vous-en! » a-t-il crié.

shout NOUN

⌐ *see also* **shout** VERB ⌐

le cri

shovel NOUN

⌐ *see also* **shovel** VERB ⌐

la pelle

to **shovel** VERB

⌐ *see also* **shovel** NOUN ⌐

pelleter ◊ *After the snowstorm I shovelled the driveway.* Après la tempête de neige, j'ai pelleté l'entrée. ◊ *We shovelled the dirt into the hole.* Nous avons pelleté la terre dans le trou.

show NOUN

⌐ *see also* **show** VERB ⌐

① le spectacle (*performance*)

S

☞

② l' émission FEM (TV)
③ le salon (exhibition)

to **show** VERB

see also **show** NOUN

① montrer
♦ **to show somebody something** montrer quelque chose à quelqu'un ◊ *Have I shown you my new DVD?* Est-ce que je t'ai montré mon nouveau DVD? ◊ *She showed me how to set up a blog.* Elle m'a montré comment monter un blogue.
② faire preuve de ◊ *She showed great courage.* Elle a fait preuve de beaucoup de courage.
③ projeter (movie) ◊ *What's showing at the movie theatre tonight?* Qu'est-ce qui est projeté au cinéma ce soir?
♦ **It shows.** Ça se voit. ◊ *"I've never been riding before." "It shows."* « Je n'ai jamais fait de cheval. » « Ça se voit. »
♦ **to show off** se vanter (informal)
♦ **to show up (1)** (arrive) se pointer ◊ *He showed up late as usual.* Il s'est pointé en retard comme d'habitude.
♦ **to show up (2)** (be noticeable) ◊ *The yellow font doesn't show up well on the screen.* Les caractères jaunes ne se voient pas sur l'écran.
♦ **to show somebody around** faire faire le tour à quelqu'un ◊ *She showed us around.* Elle nous a fait faire le tour.
♦ **Your slip is showing.** On voit ton jupon.

shower NOUN
① la douche
♦ **to have a shower** prendre une douche
② l' averse FEM (of rain)

showing NOUN
la projection (of film)

shown VERB *see* **show**

show-off NOUN
le vantard
la vantarde

shrank VERB *see* **shrink**

to **shriek** VERB
hurler

shrimp NOUN
la crevette ◊ *I like shrimp.* J'aime les crevettes.

to **shrink** VERB
rétrécir (clothes, fabric)

to **shrug** VERB
♦ **to shrug one's shoulders** hausser les épaules

shrunk VERB *see* **shrink**

to **shudder** VERB
frissonner

to **shuffle** VERB
♦ **to shuffle the cards** battre les cartes
♦ **I put the CD on shuffle mode.** J'ai mis le CD en lecture aléatoire.

to **shut** VERB
fermer ◊ *Shut the door.* Ferme la porte. ◊ *The door doesn't shut properly.* La porte ferme mal.
♦ **The door slammed shut.** La porte a claqué.
♦ **to shut down** fermer ◊ *The movie theatre shut down last year.* Le cinéma a fermé l'année dernière. ◊ *Did you shut down the computer?* As-tu fermé l'ordinateur?

shutters NOUN
les volets MASC PL

shuttle NOUN
la navette

shuttlecock NOUN
le volant (badminton)

shy ADJECTIVE
timide

sick ADJECTIVE
① malade (ill) ◊ *He was sick for four days.* Il a été malade pendant quatre jours.
② de mauvais goût (joke, humour) ◊ *That's really sick!* C'est vraiment de mauvais goût!
♦ **to be sick** (vomit) vomir ◊ *I feel sick.* J'ai envie de vomir.
♦ **to be sick of something** en avoir assez de quelque chose ◊ *I'm sick of your jokes.* J'en ai assez de tes plaisanteries.

sickening ADJECTIVE
écœurant

sickness NOUN
la maladie

sick note NOUN
① le mot d'absence (from parents)
② le certificat médical (from doctor)

side NOUN
① le côté (of object, building, car) ◊ *She was driving on the wrong side of the road.* Elle roulait du mauvais côté de la route. ◊ *She had the telephone by her side.* Le téléphone était à côté d'elle.
② le bord (of pool, river, road) ◊ *by the side of the lake* au bord du lac
③ le flanc (of hill)
♦ **He's on my side. (1)** (on my team) Il est dans mon équipe.
♦ **He's on my side. (2)** (supporting me) Il est de mon côté.
♦ **side by side** côte à côte
♦ **the side entrance** l'entrée latérale
♦ **to take sides** prendre parti ◊ *She*

always takes his side. Elle prend toujours son parti.

side-effect NOUN
l' effet secondaire MASC

side street NOUN
la petite rue transversale

sidewalk NOUN
le trottoir

sideways ADVERB
1 de côté (*look, be facing*)
2 de travers (*move*)

sieve NOUN
la passoire

sigh NOUN

see also **sigh** VERB

le soupir

to **sigh** VERB

see also **sigh** NOUN

soupirer

sight NOUN
1 la vue ◊ *Stay within sight of the group.* Restez à portée de vue du groupe. ◊ *At the sight of the police, he took off.* À la vue de la police, il s'est enfui.
♦ **to know somebody by sight** connaître quelqu'un de vue
2 le spectacle ◊ *It was an amazing sight.* C'était un spectacle époustouflant.
♦ **in sight** visible
♦ **out of sight** hors de vue
♦ **the sights** (*tourist spots*) les attractions touristiques
♦ **to see the sights of London** visiter Londres

sightseeing NOUN
le tourisme
♦ **to go sightseeing** faire du tourisme

sign NOUN

see also **sign** VERB

1 (*notice*)
le panneau
(PL les panneaux) ◊ *There was a big sign saying "private".* Il y avait un grand panneau indiquant « privé ».
♦ **a road sign** un panneau routier
2 le signe (*gesture, indication*)
◊ *There's no sign of improvement.* Il n'y a aucun signe d'amélioration.
♦ **What sign are you?** (*star sign*) Tu es de quel signe?

to **sign** VERB

see also **sign** NOUN

signer
♦ **to sign up** s'inscrire ◊ *She signed up for volleyball.* Elle s'est inscrite au volley-ball.

signal NOUN

see also **signal** VERB

le signal
(PL les signaux)

to **signal** VERB

see also **signal** NOUN

♦ **to signal to somebody** faire un signe à quelqu'un

signature NOUN
la signature

significance NOUN
l' importance FEM

significant ADJECTIVE
important

sign language NOUN
le langage des signes

signpost NOUN
le poteau indicateur

Sikh NOUN

see also **Sikh** ADJECTIVE

le sikh
la sikhe

Sikh ADJECTIVE

see also **Sikh** NOUN

sikh

silence NOUN
le silence

silent ADJECTIVE
silencieux MASC
silencieuse FEM

silk NOUN

see also **silk** ADJECTIVE

la soie

silk ADJECTIVE

see also **silk** NOUN

en soie ◊ *a silk scarf* un foulard en soie

silky ADJECTIVE
soyeux MASC
soyeuse FEM

silly ADJECTIVE
bête

silver NOUN
l' argent MASC ◊ *a silver medal* une médaille d'argent
♦ **a silver van** une fourgonnette de couleur argent

similar ADJECTIVE
semblable
♦ **similar to** semblable à

simple ADJECTIVE
simple ◊ *It's very simple.* C'est très simple.

simply ADVERB

S

☞

simplement ◊ *It's simply not possible.* Ça n'est tout simplement pas possible.

simultaneous ADJECTIVE
simultané

sin NOUN

see also **sin** VERB

le péché

to **sin** VERB

see also **sin** NOUN

pécher

since PREPOSITION, ADVERB, CONJUNCTION
[1] depuis ◊ *since yesterday* depuis hier ◊ *since then* depuis ce moment-là ◊ *I haven't seen him since.* Je ne l'ai pas vu depuis.
♦ **ever since** depuis ce moment-là
[2] depuis que ◊ *I haven't seen her since she left.* Je ne l'ai pas vue depuis qu'elle est partie.
[3] puisque (*because*) ◊ *Since you're tired, let's stay at home.* Puisque tu es fatigué, restons à la maison.

sincere ADJECTIVE
sincère

sincerely ADVERB
♦ **Yours sincerely... (1)** (*in business letter*) Veuillez agréer l'expression de mes sentiments les meilleurs...
♦ **Yours sincerely... (2)** (*in personal letter*) Cordialement...

to **sing** VERB
chanter ◊ *He sang out of tune.* Il chantait faux. ◊ *Have you ever sung this tune before?* Vous avez déjà chanté cet air-là?

singer NOUN
le chanteur
la chanteuse

singing NOUN
le chant ◊ *singing lessons* des cours de chant

single ADJECTIVE

see also **single** NOUN

célibataire (*unmarried*)
♦ **a single room** une chambre pour une personne
♦ **not a single thing** rien du tout

single NOUN

see also **single** ADJECTIVE

♦ **a CD single** un CD simple

single parent NOUN
♦ **She's a single parent.** Elle est parent unique.
♦ **a single-parent family** une famille monoparentale

singles PL NOUN

le simple SING (*in tennis*) ◊ *the women's singles* le simple dames

singular NOUN
le singulier ◊ *in the singular* au singulier

sinister ADJECTIVE
sinistre

sink NOUN

see also **sink** VERB

l'évier MASC

to **sink** VERB

see also **sink** NOUN

couler

sir NOUN
monsieur MASC
♦ **Yes, sir.** Oui, Monsieur.

siren NOUN
la sirène

sister NOUN
la sœur ◊ *my little sister* ma petite sœur

sister-in-law NOUN
la belle-sœur
(PL les belles-sœurs)

to **sit** VERB
s'asseoir ◊ *She sat on the chair.* Elle s'est assise sur la chaise.
♦ **to sit down** s'asseoir ◊ *Sit down, please.* Asseyez-vous, s'il vous plaît.
♦ **to be sitting** être assis

sitcom NOUN
la comédie de situation
(PL les comédies de situation)

site NOUN
[1] le site ◊ *an archaeological site* un site archéologique
♦ **the site of the accident** le lieu de l'accident
[2] l'emplacement de camping MASC (*campsite*)
♦ **a building site** un chantier de construction

sitting room NOUN
le salon

situated ADJECTIVE
♦ **to be situated** être situé ◊ *The village is situated on a hill.* Le village est situé sur une colline.

situation NOUN
la situation

six NUMBER
six ◊ *He's six.* Il a six ans.

sixteen NUMBER
seize ◊ *He's sixteen.* Il a seize ans.

sixteenth ADJECTIVE
seizième ◊ *the sixteenth floor* le seizième étage

♦ **the sixteenth of August** le seize août

sixth ADJECTIVE
sixième ◊ *the sixth floor* le sixième étage
♦ **the sixth of August** le six août

sixty NUMBER
soixante

size NOUN
1 la taille (*of object, clothing*) ◊ *What size do you take?* Quelle taille est-ce que vous portez?
♦ **I'm a size ten.** Je porte du dix ans.
2 la pointure (*of shoes*)
♦ **I take size six.** Je porte du six.

to **skate** VERB
1 faire du patin à glace (*ice-skate*)
2 faire du patin à roulettes (*roller-skate*)

skateboard NOUN
la planche à roulettes

skateboarder NOUN
le/la planchiste

skateboarding NOUN
la planche à roulettes ◊ *to go skateboarding* faire de la planche à roulettes ◊ *She's a skateboarding champ.* C'est une vraie championne de la planche à roulettes. ◊ *My brother loves skateboarding.* Mon frère adore la planche à roulettes.

skater NOUN
le patineur
la patineuse

skates PL NOUN
les patins MASC

skating NOUN
le patin à glace ◊ *to go skating* faire du patin à glace
♦ **a skating rink** une patinoire

skeleton NOUN
le squelette

sketch NOUN
see also **sketch** VERB
le croquis (*drawing*)

to **sketch** VERB
see also **sketch** NOUN
♦ **to sketch something** faire un croquis de quelque chose

ski NOUN
see also **ski** VERB
le ski
♦ **ski boots** les chaussures de ski FEM
♦ **a ski lift** un remonte-pente
♦ **ski pants** le pantalon de ski SING
♦ **a ski pole** un bâton de ski
♦ **a ski slope** une piste de ski
♦ **a ski suit** une combinaison de ski

to **ski** VERB
see also **ski** NOUN
skier ◊ *Can you ski?* Tu sais skier?

to **skid** VERB
déraper

skier NOUN
le skieur
la skieuse

skiing NOUN
le ski ◊ *to go skiing* faire du ski
♦ **to go on a skiing holiday** aller aux sports d'hiver

skilful ADJECTIVE
adroit

skill NOUN
le talent ◊ *He played with great skill.* Il a joué avec beaucoup de talent.

skilled ADJECTIVE
♦ **a skilled worker** un ouvrier spécialisé

skim milk NOUN
le lait écrémé

skimpy ADJECTIVE
1 minuscule (*clothes*)
2 maigre (*meal*)

skin NOUN
la peau
(PL les peaux)
♦ **skin cancer** le cancer de la peau

skinhead NOUN
le/la skinhead

skinny ADJECTIVE
maigre

skin-tight ADJECTIVE
collant

to **skip** VERB
sauter ◊ *to skip a meal* sauter un repas
♦ **to skip a class** sécher un cours

skirt NOUN
la jupe

skull NOUN
le crâne

sky NOUN
le ciel

skyscraper NOUN
le gratte-ciel
(PL les gratte-ciel)

slack ADJECTIVE
1 lâche (*rope*)
2 négligent (*person*)

to **slam** VERB
claquer ◊ *The door slammed.* La porte a claqué. ◊ *She slammed the door.* Elle a claqué la porte.

slang NOUN
l' argot MASC

S

slap NOUN

> see also **slap** VERB

la claque

to **slap** VERB

> see also **slap** NOUN

♦ **to slap somebody** donner une claque à quelqu'un

✹ **slapshot** NOUN
le lancer frappé

sled NOUN
✹ le traîneau

sledding NOUN
♦ **to go sledding**
✹ faire du traîneau

sleep NOUN

> see also **sleep** VERB

le sommeil
♦ **I need some sleep.** J'ai besoin de dormir.
♦ **to go to sleep** s'endormir

to **sleep** VERB

> see also **sleep** NOUN

dormir ◊ *I couldn't sleep last night.* J'ai mal dormi la nuit dernière.
♦ **to sleep with somebody** coucher avec quelqu'un
♦ **to sleep together** coucher ensemble

to **sleep in** VERB
① ne pas se réveiller (*accidentally*)
◊ *I'm sorry I'm late, I slept in.* Désolé d'être en retard : je ne me suis pas réveillé.
② faire la grasse matinée (*on purpose*)

sleeping bag NOUN
le sac de couchage
(PL les sacs de couchage)

sleeping pill NOUN
le somnifère

sleepy ADJECTIVE
♦ **to feel sleepy** avoir sommeil ◊ *I was feeling sleepy.* J'avais sommeil.
♦ **a sleepy little village** un petit village tranquille

sleet NOUN

> see also **sleet** VERB

✹ la neige fondante

to **sleet** VERB

> see also **sleet** NOUN

♦ **It's sleeting.**
✹ Il tombe de la neige fondante.

sleeve NOUN
① la manche ◊ *long sleeves* les manches longues ◊ *short sleeves* les manches courtes
② la pochette (*record sleeve*)

sleigh NOUN
le traîneau
(PL les traîneaux)

slept VERB *see* **sleep**

slice NOUN

> see also **slice** VERB

la tranche

to **slice** VERB

> see also **slice** NOUN

couper en tranches

slick NOUN
♦ **an oil slick** une marée noire

slide NOUN

> see also **slide** VERB

① la glissoire (*in playground*)
② la diapositive (*photo*)

to **slide** VERB

> see also **slide** NOUN

glisser

slight ADJECTIVE
léger MASC
légère FEM ◊ *a slight problem* un léger problème ◊ *a slight improvement* une légère amélioration

slightly ADVERB
légèrement

slim ADJECTIVE
mince

sling NOUN
l' écharpe FEM ◊ *She had her arm in a sling.* Elle avait le bras en écharpe.

slip NOUN

> see also **slip** VERB

① l' erreur FEM (*mistake*)
② le jupon (*underskirt*)
♦ **a slip of paper** un bout de papier
♦ **a slip of the tongue** un lapsus

to **slip** VERB

> see also **slip** NOUN

glisser ◊ *I slipped on the ice.* J'ai glissé sur le verglas.
♦ **to slip up** faire une erreur (*make a mistake*)

slipper NOUN
✹ la pantoufle
♦ **a pair of slippers** des pantoufles

slippery ADJECTIVE
glissant

slip-up NOUN
l' erreur FEM

slope NOUN
la pente

sloppy ADJECTIVE
① bâclé (*work*)
② négligé (*person, appearance*)

slot NOUN
la <u>fente</u>

slot machine NOUN
la <u>machine à sous</u> (*for gambling*)

✱ **slough** NOUN
le <u>bourbier</u>

slow ADJECTIVE, ADVERB
① <u>lent</u> ◊ *He's a bit slow.* Il est un peu lent.
② <u>lentement</u> ◊ *to go slow* (*person, car*) aller lentement ◊ *Drive slower!* Conduisez plus lentement!
♦ **My watch is slow.** Ma montre retarde.

to **slow down** VERB
<u>ralentir</u>

slowly ADVERB
<u>lentement</u>

slug NOUN
la <u>limace</u>

slum NOUN
le <u>quartier insalubre</u> (*area*)

slush NOUN
✱ la <u>neige fondante</u>

sly ADJECTIVE
<u>rusé</u> (*person*)
♦ **a sly smile** un sourire sournois

smack NOUN
see also **smack** VERB
la <u>tape</u>

to **smack** VERB
see also **smack** NOUN
♦ **to smack somebody** donner une tape à quelqu'un

small ADJECTIVE
<u>petit</u>
♦ **small change** la petite monnaie

smart ADJECTIVE
① <u>intelligent</u> (*clever*)
♦ **a smart idea** une idée astucieuse
② (*elegant*)
<u>chic</u> MASC
<u>chic</u> FEM

to **smash** VERB
① <u>casser</u> (*break*) ◊ *I've smashed my watch.* J'ai cassé ma montre.
② <u>se briser</u> (*get broken*) ◊ *The glass smashed into tiny pieces.* Le verre s'est brisé en mille morceaux.

smell NOUN
see also **smell** VERB
l' <u>odeur</u> FEM
♦ **the sense of smell** l'odorat MASC

to **smell** VERB
see also **smell** NOUN
① <u>sentir mauvais</u> ◊ *That old dog really smells!* Ce vieux chien sent

vraiment mauvais!
♦ **to smell like something** sentir quelque chose ◊ *It smells like gas.* Ça sent l'essence.
② <u>sentir</u> (*detect*) ◊ *I can't smell anything.* Je ne sens rien.

smelly ADJECTIVE
<u>qui sent mauvais</u> ◊ *He's got smelly feet.* Il a les pieds qui sentent mauvais.

smile NOUN
see also **smile** VERB
le <u>sourire</u>

to **smile** VERB
see also **smile** NOUN
<u>sourire</u>

smiley NOUN
la <u>binette</u>

smoke NOUN
see also **smoke** VERB
la <u>fumée</u>

to **smoke** VERB
see also **smoke** NOUN
<u>fumer</u> ◊ *I don't smoke.* Je ne fume pas.

✱ **smoked meat sandwich** NOUN
le <u>sandwich au smoked meat</u>

smoker NOUN
le <u>fumeur</u>
la <u>fumeuse</u>

smoking NOUN
♦ **to give up smoking** arrêter de fumer
♦ **Smoking is bad for you.** Le tabac, est mauvais pour la santé.
♦ **"no smoking"** « défense de fumer »

smooth ADJECTIVE
① <u>lisse</u> (*surface*)
② (*person*)
<u>mielleux</u> MASC
<u>mielleuse</u> FEM

smudge NOUN
la <u>bavure</u>

smug ADJECTIVE
<u>suffisant</u>

to **smuggle** VERB
① <u>passer en fraude</u> (*goods*) ◊ *to smuggle cigarettes into a country* faire passer des cigarettes en fraude dans un pays
② <u>faire passer clandestinement</u> (*people*)
♦ **They managed to smuggle her out of prison.** Ils ont réussi à la faire sortir de prison clandestinement.

smuggler NOUN
le <u>contrebandier</u>
la <u>contrebandière</u>

S

smuggling NOUN
la <u>contrebande</u>

snack NOUN
la <u>collation</u>
♦ **to have a snack** manger une collation

snack bar NOUN
🐾 le <u>casse-croûte</u>
(PL les casse-croûte)

snail NOUN
l' <u>escargot</u> MASC

snake NOUN
le <u>serpent</u>

to **snap** VERB
<u>casser net</u> (*break*) ◊ *The branch snapped.* La branche a cassé net.
♦ **to snap one's fingers** faire claquer ses doigts

snap fastener NOUN
le <u>bouton-pression</u>
(PL les boutons-pression)

snapshot NOUN
la <u>photo</u>

to **snarl** VERB
<u>gronder</u> (*animal*)

to **snatch** VERB
♦ **to snatch something from somebody** arracher quelque chose à quelqu'un ◊ *He snatched the keys from my hand.* Il m'a arraché les clés des mains.
♦ **My purse was snatched.** On m'a arraché mon sac à main.

to **sneak** VERB
♦ **to sneak in** entrer furtivement
♦ **to sneak out** sortir furtivement
♦ **to sneak up on somebody** s'approcher de quelqu'un sans faire de bruit

sneakers PL NOUN
les <u>chaussures de sport</u> FEM

to **sneeze** VERB
<u>éternuer</u>

to **sniff** VERB
① <u>renifler</u> ◊ *Stop sniffing!* Arrête de renifler!
② <u>flairer</u> ◊ *The dog sniffed my hand.* Le chien m'a flairé la main.

snob NOUN
le/la <u>snob</u>

snooker NOUN
le <u>billard</u> ◊ *to play snooker* jouer au billard

snooze NOUN
le <u>petit somme</u> ◊ *to have a snooze* faire un petit somme

to **snore** VERB
<u>ronfler</u>

snorkel NOUN
see also **snorkel** VERB
le <u>snorkel</u>

to **snorkel** VERB
see also **snorkel** NOUN
faire du snorkel ◊ *We went snorkelling.* Nous sommes allés faire du snorkel.

snow NOUN
see also **snow** VERB
la <u>neige</u> ◊ *snow sports* les sports d'hiver

to **snow** VERB
see also **snow** NOUN
<u>neiger</u> ◊ *It's snowing.* Il neige.

snowball NOUN
la <u>boule de neige</u>
(PL les boules de neige)

snowbank NOUN
🐾 le <u>banc de neige</u>
(PL les bancs de neige)

snow blindness NOUN
la <u>cécité des neiges</u>

snowblower NOUN
🐾 la <u>souffleuse</u> ◊ *My father used the snowblower to clear the driveway.* Mon père a passé la souffleuse pour déneiger l'entrée.

snowboard NOUN
la <u>planche à neige</u>

snowboarder NOUN
le/la <u>planchiste</u>

snowboarding NOUN
la <u>planche à neige</u> ◊ *to go snowboarding* faire de la planche à neige

snowflake NOUN
le <u>flocon de neige</u>
(PL les flocons de neige)

snowman NOUN
le <u>bonhomme de neige</u>
(PL les bonshommes de neige) ◊ *to build a snowman* faire un bonhomme de neige

snowmobile NOUN
🐾 la <u>motoneige</u>

snowmobiler NOUN
🐾 le/la <u>motoneigiste</u>

snowplow NOUN
🐾 la <u>déneigeuse</u>

snowstorm NOUN
la <u>tempête de neige</u>
(PL les tempêtes de neige)

snowy owl NOUN
le <u>harfang</u>

so CONJUNCTION, ADVERB
1 alors ◊ *The store was closed, so I went home.* Le magasin était fermé, alors je suis rentré chez moi. ◊ *So, have you always lived in Repentigny?* Alors, vous avez toujours vécu à Repentigny?
♦ **So what?** Et alors?
2 donc (*so that*) ◊ *It rained, so I got wet.* Il pleuvait, donc j'ai été mouillé.
3 tellement (*very*) ◊ *It was so heavy!* C'était tellement lourd! ◊ *She was talking so fast I couldn't understand.* Elle parlait tellement vite que je ne comprenais pas.
♦ **It's not so heavy!** Ça n'est pas si lourd que ça!
♦ **"How's your father?" "Not so good."** « Comment va ton père? » « Pas très bien. »
♦ **so much** (*a lot*) tellement ◊ *I love you so much.* Je t'aime tellement.
♦ **so much..., so many...** tellement de... ◊ *I have so much work.* J'ai tellement de travail. ◊ *I have so many things to do today.* J'ai tellement de choses à faire aujourd'hui.
4 aussi (*in comparisons*) ◊ *He's like his sister but not so outgoing.* Il est comme sa sœur mais pas aussi extraverti.
♦ **so do I** moi aussi ◊ *"I love horses." "So do I."* « J'aime les chevaux. » « Moi aussi. »
♦ **so have we** nous aussi ◊ *"I've been to Price Edward Island twice." "So have we."* « Je suis allé à l'Île-du-Prince-Édouard deux fois. » « Nous aussi. »
♦ **I think so.** Je crois.
♦ **I hope so.** J'espère bien.
♦ **That's not so.** Ça n'est pas le cas.
♦ **so far** jusqu'à présent ◊ *It's been easy so far.* Ça a été facile jusqu'à présent.
♦ **so far so good** jusqu'ici ça va
♦ **ten or so people** environ dix personnes
♦ **at five o'clock or so** à environ cinq heures

to **soak** VERB
tremper
♦ **soaking wet** trempé

soaked ADJECTIVE
trempé ◊ *By the time we got back we were soaked.* Nous sommes rentrés trempés.

soap NOUN
le savon

soap opera NOUN
le téléroman

to **sob** VERB
sangloter ◊ *She was sobbing.* Elle sanglotait.

sober ADJECTIVE
sobre

to **sober up** VERB
dessoûler

soccer NOUN
le soccer ◊ *We play soccer twice a week.* Nous jouons au soccer deux fois par semaine. ◊ *He's the best soccer player on the team.* C'est le meilleur joueur de soccer de l'équipe.

social ADJECTIVE
social
(MASC PL sociaux) ◊ *a social class* une classe sociale
♦ **I have a good social life.** Je vois beaucoup de monde.

social assistance NOUN
l' aide sociale FEM (*money*)
♦ **to be on social assistance** recevoir de l'aide sociale

socialism NOUN
le socialisme

socialist ADJECTIVE
⟦ see also **socialist** NOUN ⟧
socialiste

socialist NOUN
⟦ see also **socialist** ADJECTIVE ⟧
le/la socialiste

social worker NOUN
le travailleur social
(PL les travailleurs sociaux) ◊ *He's a social worker.* Il est travailleur social.
la travailleuse sociale ◊ *She's a social worker.* Elle est travailleuse sociale.

society NOUN
la société ◊ *We live in a multicultural society.* Nous vivons dans une société multiculturelle.

sociology NOUN
la sociologie

sock NOUN
la chaussette

socket NOUN
la prise de courant
(PL les prises de courant)

soda NOUN
le soda (*soda water*)

sofa NOUN
le divan
♦ **a sofa bed** un divan-lit

soft ADJECTIVE
1 (*fabric, texture*)
doux MASC
douce FEM
2 (*pillow, bed*)
mou MASC

S

☞

molle FEM
♦ **soft cheeses** les fromages à pâte molle
3 fin (*hair*)
♦ **to be soft on somebody** (*be kind to*) être indulgent avec quelqu'un
♦ **a soft drink** une boisson gazeuse

software NOUN
les logiciels MASC PL ◊ *Have you installed all the software?* As-tu installé tous les logiciels?
♦ **a piece of software** un logiciel ◊ *a piece of antivirus software* un logiciel antivirus

soggy ADJECTIVE
1 trempé (*soaked*) ◊ *a soggy tissue* un mouchoir de papier trempé
2 (*not crisp*)
mou MASC
molle FEM ◊ *soggy fries* des frites molles

soil NOUN
la terre

solar ADJECTIVE
solaire
♦ **solar panel** le panneau solaire

solar power NOUN
l' énergie solaire FEM

sold VERB *see* **sell**

soldier NOUN
le soldat
la soldate ◊ *She's a soldier.* Elle est soldate.

solid ADJECTIVE
1 (*not hollow*)
massif MASC
massive FEM ◊ *solid gold* l'or massif
2 solide ◊ *a solid wall* un mur solide
♦ **for three hours solid** pendant trois heures entières

solo NOUN
le solo ◊ *a guitar solo* un solo de guitare

solution NOUN
la solution

to **solve** VERB
résoudre

some ADJECTIVE, PRONOUN

> When **some** means "a certain amount of", use **du**, **de la** or **des** according to the gender of the French noun that follows it. **du** and **de la** become **de l'** when they are followed by a noun starting with a vowel.

1 du ◊ *Would you like some bread?* Voulez-vous du pain?
de la ◊ *Would you like some jam?* Voulez-vous de la confiture?

de l' ◊ *I would like some mineral water.* Je voudrais de l'eau minérale.
des ◊ *I have some detective novels.* J'ai des romans policiers.
♦ **Some people say that...** Il y a des gens qui disent que...
♦ **some day** un de ces jours
♦ **some day next week** un jour la semaine prochaine
2 certains (*some but not all*) ◊ *"Are these mushrooms poisonous?" "Only some."* « Est-ce que ces champignons sont vénéneux? » « Certains le sont. »
♦ **some of them** quelques-uns ◊ *I only sold some of them.* J'en ai seulement vendu quelques-uns.
♦ **I only took some of it.** J'en ai seulement pris un peu.
♦ **I'm going to buy some stamps. Do you want some too?** Je vais acheter des timbres. Est-ce que tu en veux aussi?
♦ **"Would you like some coffee?" "No thanks, I've got some."** « Tu veux du café? » « Non merci, j'en ai déjà. »

somebody PRONOUN
quelqu'un ◊ *Somebody stole my personal stereo.* Quelqu'un a volé mon baladeur.

somehow ADVERB
♦ **I'll do it somehow.** Je trouverai le moyen de le faire.
♦ **Somehow I don't think he believed me.** Quelque chose me dit qu'il ne m'a pas cru.

someone PRONOUN
quelqu'un ◊ *Someone stole my wallet.* Quelqu'un a volé mon porte-monnaie.

something PRONOUN
quelque chose ◊ *something special* quelque chose de spécial ◊ *Wear something warm.* Mets quelque chose de chaud. ◊ *That's really something!* C'est vraiment quelque chose! ◊ *It cost 100 dollars, or something like that.* Ça a coûté cent dollars, ou quelque chose comme ça.

sometime ADVERB
un de ces jours ◊ *You must come and see us sometime.* Passez donc nous voir un de ces jours.
♦ **sometime last month** dans le courant du mois dernier

sometimes ADVERB
quelquefois ◊ *Sometimes I think she hates me.* Quelquefois j'ai l'impression qu'elle me déteste.

somewhere ADVERB
quelque part ◊ *I left my keys somewhere.* J'ai laissé mes clés

quelque part. ◊ *I'd like to go somewhere sunny.* J'aimerais aller quelque part où il fait du soleil.

son NOUN
le <u>fils</u>

song NOUN
la <u>chanson</u>

son-in-law NOUN
le <u>gendre</u>

soon ADVERB
<u>bientôt</u> ◊ *very soon* très bientôt
♦ **soon afterwards** peu après
♦ **as soon as possible** aussitôt que possible

sooner ADVERB
<u>plus tôt</u> ◊ *Can't you come a bit sooner?* Tu ne peux pas venir un peu plus tôt?
♦ **sooner or later** tôt ou tard

soot NOUN
la <u>suie</u>

sorcerer NOUN
le <u>sorcier</u>

sore ADJECTIVE

see also **sore** NOUN

♦ **My feet are sore.** J'ai mal aux pieds.
♦ **It's sore.** Ça fait mal.
♦ **That's a sore point.** C'est un point sensible.

sore NOUN

see also **sore** ADJECTIVE

la <u>plaie</u>

sorry ADJECTIVE
<u>désolé</u> ◊ *I'm really sorry.* Je suis vraiment désolé. ◊ *I'm sorry, I don't have any change.* Je suis désolé, je n'ai pas de monnaie. ◊ *I'm sorry I'm late.* Je suis désolée d'être en retard.
♦ **sorry!** pardon!
♦ **sorry?** pardon?
♦ **I'm sorry about the noise.** Je m'excuse pour le bruit.
♦ **You'll be sorry!** Tu le regretteras!
♦ **to feel sorry for somebody** plaindre quelqu'un

sort NOUN
la <u>sorte</u> ◊ *What sort of bike do you have?* Quelle sorte de vélo as-tu?

to **sort out** VERB
① <u>ranger</u> (*objects*)
② <u>résoudre</u> (*problems*)

so-so ADVERB
<u>comme ci comme ça</u> ◊ *"How are you feeling?" "So-so."* « Comment est-ce que tu te sens? » « Comme ci comme ça. »

sought VERB *see* **to seek**

soul NOUN
① l' <u>âme</u> FEM (*spirit*)
② la <u>musique soul</u>

sound NOUN

see also **sound** VERB, ADJECTIVE

① le <u>bruit</u> (*noise*) ◊ *Don't make a sound!* Pas un bruit! ◊ *the sound of footsteps* des bruits de pas
② le <u>son</u> ◊ *Can I turn the sound down?* Je peux baisser le son?

to **sound** VERB

see also **sound** NOUN, ADJECTIVE

♦ **That sounds interesting.** Ça a l'air intéressant.
♦ **It sounds as if she's doing well at school.** Elle a l'air de bien travailler à l'école.
♦ **That sounds like a good idea.** C'est une bonne idée.

sound ADJECTIVE, ADVERB

see also **sound** NOUN, VERB

<u>bon</u> MASC
<u>bonne</u> FEM ◊ *That's sound advice.* C'est un bon conseil.
♦ **sound asleep** profondément endormi

sound effects PL NOUN
le <u>bruitage</u>
♦ **sound effect specialist** le bruiteur ◊ *She's a sound effect specialist.* Elle est bruiteuse.

soundtrack NOUN
la <u>bande sonore</u>

soup NOUN
la <u>soupe</u> ◊ *vegetable soup* la soupe aux légumes

sour ADJECTIVE
<u>aigre</u>

south ADJECTIVE, ADVERB

see also **south** NOUN

① <u>sud</u> MASC, FEM, PL ◊ *the south coast* la côte sud
② <u>vers le sud</u> ◊ *We were travelling south.* Nous allions vers le sud.
♦ **south of** au sud de ◊ *It's south of Hearst.* C'est au sud de Hearst.
♦ **South America** l'Amérique du Sud FEM

south NOUN

see also **south** ADJECTIVE, ADVERB

le <u>sud</u> ◊ *in the south* dans le sud ◊ *the south of Ontario* le sud de l'Ontario

southbound ADJECTIVE
♦ **Southbound traffic is moving very slowly.** La circulation en direction du sud est très ralentie.
♦ **The suspect vehicle was southbound on the 400.** Le véhicule suspect se trouvait sur l'autoroute 400 en

S

☞

direction du sud.

southeast NOUN
le sud-est ◊ *southeast Alberta* le sud-est de l'Alberta

southern ADJECTIVE
♦ **the southern part of the island** la partie sud de l'île
♦ **southern New Brunswick** le sud du Nouveau-Brunswick

South Pole NOUN
le pôle Sud

southwest NOUN
le sud-ouest ◊ *southwest Yukon* le sud-ouest du Yukon

souvenir NOUN
le souvenir
♦ **a souvenir shop** une boutique de souvenirs

sovereigntist NOUN
le/la souverainiste

sovereignty NOUN
la souveraineté ◊ *Are you in favour of Quebec sovereignty?* Êtes-vous en faveur de la souveraineté du Québec?

soya NOUN
le soya

soy sauce NOUN
la sauce soya

space NOUN
1 la place ◊ *There isn't enough space.* Il n'y a pas suffisamment de place.
♦ **a parking space** une place de stationnement
2 l' espace MASC (*universe, gap*)
◊ *Leave a space after your answer.* Laissez un espace après votre réponse.
♦ **a space shuttle** une navette spatiale

spacecraft NOUN
le vaisseau spatial

spade NOUN
la pelle
♦ **spades** (*in cards*) le pique SING ◊ *the ace of spades* l'as de pique

spam NOUN
1 le pollupostage (*practice of spamming*) ◊ *Spam has become a real problem.* Le pollupostage est devenu un vrai problème.
2 le polluriel (*message*) ◊ *I got some spam from that address.* J'ai reçu des polluriels de cette adresse.

spaniel NOUN
l' épagneul MASC

to **spank** VERB
♦ **to spank somebody** donner une fessée à quelqu'un

spare ADJECTIVE

see also **spare** VERB, NOUN

de rechange ◊ *spare batteries* des piles de rechange ◊ *a spare part* une pièce de rechange
♦ **a spare room** une chambre d'amis
♦ **spare time** le temps libre ◊ *What do you do in your spare time?* Qu'est-ce que tu fais pendant ton temps libre?
♦ **spare tire** un pneu de secours

to **spare** VERB

see also **spare** ADJECTIVE, NOUN

♦ **Can you spare a moment?** Vous pouvez m'accorder un instant?
♦ **I can't spare the time.** Je n'ai pas le temps.
♦ **There's no room to spare.** Il n'y a plus de place.
♦ **We arrived with time to spare.** Nous sommes arrivés en avance.

spare NOUN

see also **spare** ADJECTIVE, VERB

♦ **a spare** un autre ◊ *"I've lost my key." "Have you got a spare?"* « J'ai perdu ma clé. » « En as-tu une autre? »

sparkling ADJECTIVE
pétillant (*water*)

sparrow NOUN
le moineau
(PL les moineaux)

to **speak** VERB
parler ◊ *Do you speak English?* Est-ce que vous parlez anglais?
♦ **to speak to somebody** parler à quelqu'un ◊ *Have you spoken to him?* Tu lui as parlé? ◊ *She spoke to him about it.* Elle lui en a parlé.
♦ **spoken French** le français parlé

to **speak up** VERB
parler plus fort ◊ *Speak up, we can't hear you.* Parle plus fort, nous ne t'entendons pas.

speaker NOUN
1 (*loudspeaker*)
le haut-parleur
(PL les haut-parleurs)
2 (*in debate*)
l' intervenant MASC
l' intervenante FEM
3 (*at conference*)
le conférencier
la conférencière

special ADJECTIVE
spécial
(MASC PL spéciaux)

specialist NOUN
le/la spécialiste

to **specialize** VERB
se spécialiser ◊ *We specialize*

in skiing equipment. Nous nous spécialisons dans les articles de ski.

specially ADVERB
spécialement ◊ *It's specially designed for teenagers.* C'est spécialement conçu pour les adolescents.

specialty NOUN
la spécialité

species NOUN
l' espèce FEM

specific ADJECTIVE
⒈ (*particular*)
particulier MASC
particulière FEM ◊ *certain specific issues* certains problèmes particuliers
⒉ précis (*precise*) ◊ *Could you be more specific?* Est-ce que vous pourriez être plus précise?

specifically ADVERB
⒈ spécialement ◊ *It's specifically designed for teenagers.* C'est spécialement conçu pour les adolescents.
⒉ particulièrement ◊ *on the subject of snow sports, or more specifically snowboarding* au sujet des sports d'hiver, ou plus particulièrement de la planche à neige
♦ **I specifically said that...** J'ai clairement dit que...

spectacular ADJECTIVE
spectaculaire

spectator NOUN
le spectateur
la spectatrice

speech NOUN
le discours ◊ *to make a speech* faire un discours

speechless ADJECTIVE
muet MASC
muette FEM ◊ *speechless with admiration* muet d'admiration
♦ **I was speechless.** Je suis resté sans voix.

speed NOUN
la vitesse ◊ *a ten-speed bike* un vélo à dix vitesses ◊ *at top speed* à toute vitesse
♦ **speed limit** la limite de vitesse ◊ *The speed limit is 50 km/h here.* La limite de vitesse ici est de 50 kilomètres par heure. ◊ *to break the speed limit* faire un excès de vitesse

speedboat NOUN
le hord-bord
(PL les hors-bord)

speeding NOUN
l' excès de vitesse MASC ◊ *He was*

fined for speeding. Il a reçu une contravention pour excès de vitesse.

speedometer NOUN
l' indicateur de vitesse MASC

to **speed up** VERB
accélérer

to **spell** VERB
| *see also* **spell** NOUN |

⒈ écrire (*in writing*) ◊ *How do you spell that?* Comment est-ce que ça s'écrit?
⒉ épeler (*out loud*) ◊ *Can you spell that please?* Est-ce que vous pouvez épeler, s'il vous plaît?
♦ **I can't spell.** Je fais des fautes d'orthographe.

spell NOUN
| *see also* **spell** VERB |

♦ **to cast a spell on somebody** jeter un sort à quelqu'un
♦ **to be under somebody's spell** être sous le charme de quelqu'un

spelling NOUN
l' orthographe FEM ◊ *My spelling is terrible.* Je fais beaucoup de fautes d'orthographe.
♦ **a spelling mistake** une faute d'orthographe

to **spend** VERB
⒈ dépenser (*money*)
⒉ passer (*time*) ◊ *She spent a month in Quebec.* Elle a passé un mois au Québec.

spice NOUN
l' épice FEM

spicy ADJECTIVE
épicé

spider NOUN
l' araignée FEM

to **spill** VERB
⒈ renverser (*tip over*) ◊ *He spilled his coffee on his pants.* Il a renversé son café sur son pantalon.
⒉ se répandre (*get spilled*) ◊ *The soup spilled all over the table.* La soupe s'est répandue sur la table.

spinach NOUN
les épinards MASC PL

spine NOUN
la colonne vertébrale

spire NOUN
la flèche

spirit NOUN
⒈ l' esprit MASC ◊ *the human spirit* l'esprit humain
⒉ le courage (*courage*)
♦ **to be in good spirits** être de bonne humeur

S

③ l' **énergie** FEM (*energy*)

spiritual ADJECTIVE
spirituel MASC
spirituelle FEM ◊ *the spiritual leader of Tibet* le chef spirituel du Tibet ◊ *spiritual development* la croissance spirituelle

spit NOUN

> see also **spit** VERB

la **salive**

to **spit** VERB

> see also **spit** NOUN

cracher
♦ **to spit something out** cracher quelque chose

spite NOUN

> see also **spite** VERB

♦ **in spite of** malgré
♦ **out of spite** par méchanceté

to **spite** VERB

> see also **spite** NOUN

contrarier ◊ *She did it just to spite me.* Elle a fait ça juste pour me contrarier.

spiteful ADJECTIVE
① **méchant** (*action*)
② (*person*)
rancunier MASC
rancunière FEM

to **splash** VERB

> see also **splash** NOUN

éclabousser ◊ *Careful! Don't splash me!* Attention! Ne m'éclabousse pas!

splash NOUN

> see also **splash** VERB

le **plouf** ◊ *I heard a splash.* J'ai entendu un plouf.
♦ **a splash of colour** une touche de couleur

splendid ADJECTIVE
splendide

splint NOUN
l' **attelle** FEM

splinter NOUN
l' **écharde** FEM

to **split** VERB
① **fendre** (*break apart*) ◊ *He split the wood with an axe.* Il a fendu le bois avec une hache.
② **se fendre** ◊ *The ship hit a rock and split in two.* Le bateau a percuté un rocher et s'est fendu en deux.
③ **partager** (*divide up*) ◊ *They decided to split the profits.* Ils ont décidé de partager les bénéfices.
♦ **to split up (1)** (*couple*) rompre

♦ **to split up (2)** (*group*) se disperser

to **spoil** VERB
① **abîmer** (*object*)
② **gâcher** (*occasion, experience*)
③ **gâter** (*child*)
④ **se gâter** (*food*) ◊ *The fruit is beginning to spoil.* Les fruits commencent à se gâter.
♦ **If you leave the milk on the counter it'll spoil.** Si tu laisses le lait sur le comptoir, il va tourner.

spoiled ADJECTIVE
gâté ◊ *a spoiled child* une enfant gâtée

spoilsport NOUN
le/la **trouble-fête**

spoke VERB *see* **speak**

spoke NOUN
le **rayon** (*of wheel*)

spoken VERB *see* **speak**

spokesperson NOUN
le/la **porte-parole**
(PL les porte-parole)

sponge NOUN
l' **éponge** FEM

sponsor NOUN

> see also **sponsor** VERB

le/la **commanditaire**

to **sponsor** VERB

> see also **sponsor** NOUN

commanditer ◊ *The festival was sponsored by...* Le festival a été commandité par...

spontaneous ADJECTIVE
spontané

spooky ADJECTIVE
① **sinistre** (*eerie*)
♦ **a spooky story** une histoire qui fait froid dans le dos
② **étrange** (*strange*) ◊ *a spooky coincidence* une étrange coïncidence

spoon NOUN
la **cuillère**
♦ **a spoonful** une cuillerée

sport NOUN
le **sport** ◊ *What's your favourite sport?* Quel est ton sport préféré?
♦ **a sports bag** un sac de sport
♦ **a sports car** une voiture de sport
♦ **a sports jacket** une veste sport
♦ **Come on, be a sport!** Allez, sois sympa!

sportswear NOUN
les **vêtements de sport** MASC PL

sporty ADJECTIVE
sportif MASC
sportive FEM ◊ *I'm not very sporty.* Je

ne suis pas très sportif.

spot NOUN

see also **spot** VERB

① la <u>tache</u> (*mark*) ◊ *There's a spot on your shirt.* Il y a une tache sur ta chemise.
② le <u>coin</u> (*place*) ◊ *It's a lovely spot for a picnic.* C'est un coin agréable pour un pique-nique.
♦ **on the spot** (*immediately*) sur-le-champ ◊ *They gave her the job on the spot.* Ils lui ont offert le poste sur-le-champ.

to **spot** VERB

see also **spot** NOUN

<u>repérer</u> ◊ *I spotted a mistake.* J'ai repéré une faute.

spotless ADJECTIVE
<u>immaculé</u>

spotlight NOUN
le <u>projecteur</u>
♦ **The universities have been in the spotlight recently.** Les universités ont été sous le feu des projecteurs ces derniers temps.

spouse NOUN
l' <u>époux</u> MASC
l' <u>épouse</u> FEM

to **sprain** VERB

see also **sprain** NOUN

♦ **to sprain one's ankle** se faire une entorse à la cheville

sprain NOUN

see also **sprain** VERB

l' <u>entorse</u> FEM ◊ *It's just a sprain.* C'est juste une entorse.

spray NOUN

see also **spray** VERB

♦ **spray can** la bombe
♦ **spray bottle** l'atomiseur MASC
♦ **spray paint** la peinture en aérosol
♦ **perfume spray** le parfum en atomiseur ◊ *Do you have this perfume in spray form?* Vous avez ce parfum en atomiseur?

to **spray** VERB

see also **spray** NOUN

① <u>vaporiser</u> ◊ *to spray perfume on one's hand* se vaporiser du parfum sur la main
② <u>traiter</u> (*crops*) ◊ *They sprayed their crops with fertilizer.* Ils ont traité leurs champs à l'engrais.
③ <u>peindre avec une bombe</u> (*graffiti*) ◊ *Somebody had sprayed graffiti on the wall.* Quelqu'un avait peint des graffitis avec une bombe sur le mur.

spread NOUN

see also **spread** VERB

♦ **cheese spread** le fromage à tartiner
♦ **chocolate spread** le chocolat à tartiner

to **spread** VERB

see also **spread** NOUN

① <u>étaler</u> ◊ *to spread butter on a slice of bread* étaler du beurre sur une tranche de pain
② <u>se propager</u> (*disease, news*) ◊ *The news spread rapidly.* La nouvelle s'est propagée rapidement.
♦ **to spread out** (*people*) se disperser ◊ *The soldiers spread out across the field.* Les soldats se sont dispersés dans le champ.

spreadsheet NOUN
le <u>tableur</u> (*computer program*)

spring NOUN
① le <u>printemps</u> (*season*)
♦ **in spring** au printemps
② le <u>ressort</u> (*metal coil*)
③ la <u>source</u> (*water hole*)

spring cleaning NOUN
le <u>grand nettoyage du printemps</u>

sprinkler NOUN
l' <u>arroseur</u> MASC (*for lawn*)

sprint NOUN

see also **sprint** VERB

le <u>sprint</u>

to **sprint** VERB

see also **sprint** NOUN

<u>courir à toute vitesse</u> ◊ *He sprinted for the bus.* Il a couru à toute vitesse pour attraper le bus.

sprinter NOUN
le <u>sprinteur</u>
la <u>sprinteuse</u>

sprouts PL NOUN
♦ **Brussels sprouts** les choux de Bruxelles MASC PL
♦ **bean sprouts** les germes de soya MASC PL

spruce NOUN
l' <u>épinette</u> FEM

spy NOUN

see also **spy** VERB

l' <u>espion</u> MASC
l' <u>espionne</u> FEM

to **spy** VERB

see also **spy** NOUN

♦ **to spy on somebody** espionner quelqu'un

spying NOUN
l' <u>espionnage</u> MASC

to **squabble** VERB

S

☞

se chamailler ◊ *Stop squabbling!* Arrêtez de vous chamailler!

square NOUN

see also **square** ADJECTIVE

1 le carré ◊ *a square and a triangle* un carré et un triangle
2 la place ◊ *the town square* la place de l'hôtel de ville

square ADJECTIVE

see also **square** NOUN

carré ◊ *two square metres* deux mètres carrés
♦ **It's 2 metres square.** Ça fait deux mètres sur deux.

squash NOUN

see also **squash** VERB

le squash (*sport*) ◊ *I play squash.* Je joue au squash.
♦ **a squash court** un court de squash
♦ **a squash racquet** une raquette de squash

to **squash** VERB

see also **squash** NOUN

écraser ◊ *You're squashing me.* Tu m'écrases.

to **squeak** VERB

1 pousser un petit cri (*mouse, child*)
2 grincer (*creak*)

to **squeeze** VERB

1 presser (*fruit, toothpaste*)
2 serrer (*hand, arm*)
♦ **to squeeze into some tight jeans** rentrer tout juste dans des jeans serrés

to **squeeze in** VERB

1 trouver une petite place ◊ *It was a tiny car, but we managed to squeeze in.* La voiture était toute petite, mais nous avons réussi à trouver une petite place.
2 caser (*for appointment*) ◊ *I can squeeze you in at two o'clock.* Je peux vous caser demain à deux heures.

to **squint** VERB
loucher

squirrel NOUN
l' écureuil MASC

to **stab** VERB
poignarder

stable NOUN

see also **stable** ADJECTIVE

l' écurie FEM

stable ADJECTIVE

see also **stable** NOUN

stable ◊ *a stable relationship* une relation stable

stack NOUN
la pile ◊ *a stack of books* une pile de livres

stadium NOUN
le stade

staff NOUN

1 le personnel (*in company*)
2 les professeurs MASC PL (*in school*)

staffroom NOUN
le salon des professeurs

stage NOUN

1 la scène (*in plays*)
2 l' estrade FEM (*for speeches, lectures*)
♦ **at this stage (1)** à ce stade ◊ *at this stage in the negotiations* à ce stade des négociations
♦ **at this stage (2)** pour l'instant ◊ *At this stage, it's too early to comment.* Pour l'instant, il est trop tôt pour se prononcer.
♦ **to do something in stages** faire quelque chose étape par étape

Be careful not to translate **stage** by the French word **stage**.

to **stagger** VERB
chanceler

stain NOUN

see also **stain** VERB

la tache

to **stain** VERB

see also **stain** NOUN

tacher

stainless steel NOUN
l' acier inoxydable MASC

stain remover NOUN
le détachant

stair NOUN
la marche (*step*)

staircase NOUN
l' escalier MASC

stairs PL NOUN
l' escalier MASC SING

stale ADJECTIVE
rassis (*bread*)

stalemate NOUN

1 le pat (*in chess*)
2 l' impasse FEM ◊ *Negotiations have reached a stalemate.* Les négociations sont dans l'impasse.

stall NOUN

see also **stall** VERB

le stand MASC ◊ *She has a stall at the market.* Elle a un stand au marché.

to **stall** VERB

see also **stall** NOUN

caler (*car, engine*) ◊ *The school bus stalled.* L'autobus scolaire a calé.

stamina NOUN
l' endurance FEM

to **stammer** VERB
bégayer ◊ *She stammered a reply.* Elle a bégayé une réponse.

to **stamp** VERB

see also **stamp** NOUN

1 affranchir (*letter*)
2 tamponner ◊ *The customs agent stamped my passport.* Le douanier a tamponné mon passeport.
♦ **to stamp one's foot** taper du pied

stamp NOUN

see also **stamp** VERB

1 le timbre ◊ *a 50-cent stamp* un timbre de cinquante cents ◊ *My hobby is stamp collecting.* Je collectionne les timbres.
♦ **a stamp album** un album de timbres
♦ **a stamp collection** une collection de timbres
2 le timbre en caoutchouc (*rubber stamp*)

stamped ADJECTIVE
affranchi ◊ *The letter wasn't stamped.* La lettre n'était pas affranchie.
♦ **Enclose a stamped self-addressed envelope.** Joindre une enveloppe affranchie à vos nom et adresse.

to **stand** VERB

1 être debout (*be standing*) ◊ *He was standing by the door.* Il était debout à la porte.
2 se lever (*stand up*)
3 supporter (*tolerate, withstand*) ◊ *I can't stand all this noise.* Je ne supporte pas tout ce bruit.
♦ **to stand for (1)** (*be short for*) être l'abréviation de ◊ *"GST" stands for "Goods and Services Tax".* « TPS » est l'abréviation de « taxe sur les produits et services ».
♦ **to stand for (2)** (*tolerate*) supporter ◊ *I won't stand for it!* Je ne supporterai pas ça!
♦ **to stand in for somebody** remplacer quelqu'un
♦ **to stand one's ground** tenir bon ◊ *If they try to persuade you, stand your ground.* Si elles essaient de te persuader, tiens bon.
♦ **to stand out** se distinguer ◊ *All the contestants were good, but none of them stood out.* Tous les concurrents étaient bons, mais aucun ne se distinguait.

♦ **She really stands out in that orange coat.** Tout le monde la remarque avec ce manteau orange.
♦ **to stand up** (*get up*) se lever
♦ **to stand up for** défendre ◊ *Stand up for your rights!* Défendez vos droits!

standard ADJECTIVE

see also **standard** NOUN

1 courant ◊ *standard French* le français courant
2 ordinaire (*equipment*)
♦ **the standard procedure** la procédure normale
♦ **standard time** l'heure normale ◊ *We're back on standard time.* On est revenu à l'heure normale.

standard NOUN

see also **standard** ADJECTIVE

le niveau
(PL les niveaux) ◊ *The standard is very high.* Le niveau est très haut.
♦ **the standard of living** le niveau de vie
♦ **She has very high standards.** Elle est très exigeante.

standby ticket NOUN
le billet sans réservation

standpoint NOUN
le point de vue

stands PL NOUN
la tribune FEM SING (*at sports ground*)

stank VERB *see* **stink**

staple NOUN

see also **staple** VERB

1 l' agrafe FEM
2 l' aliment de base MASC (*food*) ◊ *Rice is an important staple.* Le riz est un aliment de base important.

to **staple** VERB

see also **staple** NOUN

agrafer

stapler NOUN
la brocheuse FEM

star NOUN

see also **star** VERB

1 l' étoile FEM (*in sky*)
2 la vedette (*celebrity*) ◊ *He's a TV star.* C'est une vedette de la télé.

to **star** VERB

see also **star** NOUN

être la vedette ◊ *to star in a film* être la vedette d'un film
♦ **The film stars Andrea Martin.** Le film a pour vedette Andrea Martin.
♦ **...starring Kiefer Sutherland** ...avec Kiefer Sutherland

to **stare** VERB

☞

stark → steering wheel

♦ **to stare at something** fixer quelque chose

stark ADVERB
♦ **stark naked** complètement nu

start NOUN

see also **start** VERB

① le début ◊ *It's not much, but it's a start.* Ce n'est pas grand chose, mais c'est un début.
♦ **Shall we make a start on the dishes?** On commence à faire la vaisselle?
② le départ (*of race*)

to **start** VERB

see also **start** NOUN

① commencer ◊ *What time does it start?* À quelle heure est-ce que ça commence?
♦ **to start doing something** commencer à faire quelque chose ◊ *I started learning French three years ago.* J'ai commencé à apprendre le français il y a trois ans.
② créer (*organization*) ◊ *He wants to start his own business.* Il veut créer sa propre entreprise.
③ organiser (*campaign*) ◊ *She started a campaign against drugs.* Elle a organisé une campagne contre la drogue.
④ démarrer (*car*) ◊ *He couldn't start the car.* Il n'a pas réussi à démarrer la voiture. ◊ *The car wouldn't start.* La voiture ne voulait pas démarrer.
♦ **to start off** (*leave*) partir ◊ *We started off first thing in the morning.* Nous sommes partis en début de matinée.

to **starve** VERB
mourir de faim ◊ *People were literally starving.* Les gens mouraient littéralement de faim.
♦ **I'm starving!** Je meurs de faim!

state NOUN

see also **state** VERB

l'état MASC
♦ **he was in a real state** il était dans tous ses états
♦ **the state** (*government*) l'État

to **state** VERB

see also **state** NOUN

① déclarer (*say*) ◊ *She stated her intention to resign.* Elle a déclaré son intention de démissionner.
② donner (*give*) ◊ *Please state your name and address.* Veuillez donner vos nom et adresse.

statement NOUN
la déclaration

station NOUN
la gare (*railway*)

♦ **the bus station**
✹ la gare d'autobus
♦ **a police station** un poste de police
♦ **a radio station** une station de radio

station wagon NOUN
✹ la familiale

statue NOUN
la statue

to **stay** VERB

see also **stay** NOUN

① rester (*remain*) ◊ *Stay here!* Reste ici!
♦ **to stay in** (*not go out*) rester à la maison
♦ **to stay up** rester debout ◊ *We stayed up till midnight.* Nous sommes restés debout jusqu'à minuit.
② loger (*spend the night*) ◊ *to stay with friends* loger chez des amis ◊ *Where are you staying?* Où est-ce que vous logez?
♦ **to stay the night** passer la nuit
♦ **We stayed in Nova Scotia for a few days.** Nous avons passé quelques jours en Nouvelle-Écosse.

stay NOUN

see also **stay** VERB

le séjour ◊ *my stay in the Gaspé* mon séjour en Gaspésie

steady ADJECTIVE
① régulier MASC
régulière FEM ◊ *steady progress* des progrès réguliers
② stable ◊ *a steady job* un emploi stable
③ ferme (*voice, hand*)
④ calme (*person*)
♦ **a steady boyfriend** un copain
♦ **a steady girlfriend** une copine
♦ **Steady!** Doucement!

steak NOUN (*beef*)
le steak ◊ *"How would you like your steak?" "Medium rare."* « Quelle cuisson, votre steak? » « À point. »

to **steal** VERB
voler

steam NOUN
la vapeur ◊ *a steam engine* une locomotive à vapeur

steel NOUN
l'acier MASC ◊ *a steel door* une porte en acier

steep ADJECTIVE
raide (*slope*)

steeple NOUN
le clocher

steering wheel NOUN
le volant

step NOUN

see also **step** VERB

[1] le pas (*pace*) ◊ *He took a step forward.* Il a fait un pas en avant.
[2] la marche (*stair*) ◊ *She tripped over the step.* Elle a trébuché sur la marche.

to **step** VERB

see also **step** NOUN

♦ to **step aside** faire un pas de côté
♦ to **step back** faire un pas en arrière

stepbrother NOUN
le demi-frère
(PL les demi-frères)

stepdaughter NOUN
la belle-fille
(PL les belles-filles)

stepfather NOUN
le beau-père
(PL les beaux-pères)

stepladder NOUN
l' escabeau MASC
(PL les escabeaux)

stepmother NOUN
la belle-mère
(PL les belles-mères)

stepsister NOUN
la demi-sœur
(PL les demi-sœurs)

stepson NOUN
le beau-fils
(PL les beaux-fils)

stereo NOUN
la chaîne stéréo
(PL les chaînes stéréo)

stew NOUN
le ragoût

stick NOUN

see also **stick** VERB

[1] le bâton
[2] la canne (*walking stick*)

to **stick** VERB

see also **stick** NOUN

coller (*with adhesive*) ◊ *Stick the stamps on the envelope.* Collez les timbres sur l'enveloppe.

to **stick out** VERB
sortir (*project*) ◊ *A pen was sticking out of his pocket.* Un stylo sortait de sa poche.
♦ to **stick out one's tongue** tirer la langue

sticker NOUN
l' autocollant MASC

sticky ADJECTIVE
[1] poisseux MASC

poisseuse FEM ◊ *to have sticky hands* avoir les mains poisseuses
[2] adhésif MASC
adhésive FEM ◊ *a sticky label* une étiquette adhésive

stiff ADJECTIVE, ADVERB
rigide (*rigid*)
♦ to **have a stiff back** avoir mal au dos
♦ to **feel stiff** avoir des courbatures
♦ to **be bored stiff** s'ennuyer à mourir
♦ to **be frozen stiff** être mort de froid
♦ to **be scared stiff** être mort de peur

still ADVERB

see also **still** ADJECTIVE

[1] encore ◊ *I still haven't finished.* Je n'ai pas encore fini. ◊ *Are you still in bed?* Tu es encore au lit?
♦ **better still** encore mieux
[2] quand même (*even so*) ◊ *She knows I don't like it, but she still does it.* Elle sait que je n'aime pas ça, mais elle le fait quand même.
[3] enfin (*after all*) ◊ *Still, it's the thought that counts.* Enfin, c'est l'intention qui compte.

still ADJECTIVE

see also **still** ADVERB

♦ **Keep still!** Ne bouge pas!
♦ **Sit still!** Reste tranquille!

sting NOUN

see also **sting** VERB

la piqûre ◊ *a bee sting* une piqûre d'abeille

to **sting** VERB

see also **sting** NOUN

piquer ◊ *I've been stung.* J'ai été piqué.

stingy ADJECTIVE
pingre

to **stink** VERB

see also **stink** NOUN

puer ◊ *It stinks!* Ça pue!

stink NOUN

see also **stink** VERB

la puanteur

to **stir** VERB
remuer

stir-fry NOUN

see also **stir-fry** VERB

le sauté ◊ *a vegetable stir-fry* un sauté de légumes

to **stir-fry** VERB

see also **stir-fry** NOUN

faire sauter ◊ *I stir-fried the vegetables.* J'ai fait sauter les légumes.

S

to **stitch** VERB
> see also **stitch** NOUN

coudre (*cloth*)

stitch NOUN
> see also **stitch** VERB

1. le point (*in sewing*)
2. le point de suture (*in wound*) ◊ *I had five stitches.* J'ai eu cinq points de suture.

stock NOUN
> see also **stock** VERB

1. la réserve (*supply*)
2. le stock (*in store*) ◊ *in stock* en stock
♦ **out of stock** épuisé
3. le bouillon ◊ *chicken stock* du bouillon de volaille

to **stock** VERB
> see also **stock** NOUN

avoir (*have in stock*) ◊ *Do you stock camping stoves?* Vous avez des réchauds de camping?
♦ **to stock up** s'approvisionner
◊ *to stock up on something* s'approvisionner en quelque chose

stole, stolen VERB *see* **steal**

stomach NOUN
l' estomac MASC

stomachache NOUN
♦ **to have a stomachache** avoir mal au ventre

stone NOUN
1. la pierre (*rock*) ◊ *a stone wall* un mur en pierre
2. (*in fruit*)
le noyau
(PL les noyaux) ◊ *a peach stone* un noyau de pêche

stood VERB *see* **stand**

stool NOUN
le tabouret

to **stop** VERB
> see also **stop** NOUN

1. arrêter ◊ *a campaign to stop whaling* une campagne pour arrêter la chasse à la baleine
2. s'arrêter ◊ *The bus doesn't stop there.* L'autobus ne s'arrête pas là. ◊ *I think the rain's going to stop.* Je pense qu'il va s'arrêter de pleuvoir.
♦ **to stop doing something** arrêter de faire quelque chose ◊ *to stop smoking* arrêter de fumer
♦ **to stop somebody from doing something** empêcher quelqu'un de faire quelque chose
♦ **Stop!** Stop!

stop NOUN
> see also **stop** VERB

l' arrêt MASC ◊ *a bus stop* un arrêt d'autobus
♦ **This is my stop.** Je descends ici.

stopwatch NOUN
le chronomètre

store NOUN
> see also **store** VERB

le magasin ◊ *a furniture store* un magasin de meubles

to **store** VERB
> see also **store** NOUN

1. garder ◊ *They store potatoes in the cellar.* Ils gardent des pommes de terre dans la cave.
2. enregistrer (*information*)

storey NOUN
l' étage MASC ◊ *a three-storey building* un immeuble à trois étages

storm NOUN
1. la tempête
2. l' orage MASC (*thunderstorm*)

stormy ADJECTIVE
orageux MASC
orageuse FEM

story NOUN
1. l' histoire FEM
2. le conte (*oral, traditional*) ◊ *stories from the Cree tradition* des contes cris ◊ *a book of classic children's stories* un livre de contes pour enfants

storyteller NOUN
le conteur
la conteuse

stove NOUN
1. la cuisinière (*in kitchen*)
2. le réchaud (*camping stove*)

straight ADJECTIVE, ADVERB
1. droit ◊ *a straight line* une ligne droite ◊ *He looked straight ahead.* Il a regardé droit devant lui. ◊ *Go straight ahead.* Allez tout droit.
2. raide ◊ *straight hair* les cheveux raides
3. hétéro (*heterosexual*)
4. directement ◊ *I went straight home.* Je suis rentré directement chez moi.

straightforward ADJECTIVE
simple

strain NOUN
> see also **strain** VERB

le stress
♦ **It was a strain.** C'était éprouvant.

to **strain** VERB

see also **strain** NOUN

se faire mal à ◊ *I strained my back.*
Je me suis fait mal au dos.
♦ **to strain a muscle** se froisser un
muscle

strained ADJECTIVE
froissé (*muscle*)

stranded ADJECTIVE
♦ **We were stranded.** Nous étions
coincés.

strange ADJECTIVE
bizarre ◊ *That's strange!* C'est
bizarre!

stranger NOUN
l' inconnu MASC
l' inconnue FEM ◊ *Don't talk to
strangers.* Ne parle pas aux inconnus.
♦ **I'm a stranger here.** Je ne suis pas
d'ici.

to **strangle** VERB
étrangler

strap NOUN
① la courroie (*of purse, camera,
suitcase*)
② la bretelle (*of bra, dress*)
③ la bride (*on shoe*)

straw NOUN
la paille
♦ **That's the last straw!** Ça, c'est le
comble!

strawberry NOUN
la fraise ◊ *strawberry jam* la confiture
de fraises ◊ *strawberry ice cream* la
crème glacée à la fraise

stray NOUN
♦ **a stray cat** un chat errant

stream NOUN
le ruisseau
(PL les ruisseaux)

street NOUN
la rue ◊ *in the street* dans la rue

streetcar NOUN
le tramway

streetlight NOUN
le réverbère

street musician NOUN
le musicien de rue
la musicienne de rue ◊ *There are a
lot of street musicians in Toronto.* Il
y a beaucoup de musiciens de rue à
Toronto.

street plan NOUN
le plan de la ville

streetwise ADJECTIVE
débrouillard

strength NOUN
la force

to **stress** VERB

see also **stress** NOUN

souligner ◊ *I would like to stress
that...* J'aimerais souligner que...

stress NOUN

see also **stress** VERB

le stress

to **stretch** VERB

see also **stretch** NOUN

① s'étirer (*person, animal*) ◊ *The dog
woke up and stretched.* Le chien s'est
réveillé et s'est étiré.
② étirer (*get bigger*) ◊ *My sweater
stretched when I washed it.* Mon
chandail a étiré au lavage.
③ tendre (*stretch out*) ◊ *They
stretched a rope between two trees.*
Ils ont tendu une corde entre deux
arbres.
♦ **to stretch out one's arms** tendre les
bras

stretcher NOUN
la civière

stretchy ADJECTIVE
élastique

strict ADJECTIVE
strict

strike NOUN

see also **strike** VERB

la grève
♦ **to be on strike** être en grève
♦ **to go on strike** se mettre en grève

to **strike** VERB

see also **strike** NOUN

① frapper (*hit*)
② sonner (*clock*) ◊ *The clock struck
three.* L'horloge a sonné trois heures.
③ se mettre en grève (*go on strike*)
♦ **to strike a match** frotter une allumette

striker NOUN
le/la gréviste (*person on strike*)

striking ADJECTIVE
① frappant (*noticeable*) ◊ *a striking
difference* une différence frappante
② en grève (*on strike*) ◊ *striking
miners* les mineurs en grève

string NOUN
① la ficelle ◊ *a piece of string* un bout
de ficelle
② la corde (*of violin, guitar*)

to **strip** VERB

see also **strip** NOUN

se déshabiller (*get undressed*)

strip NOUN

see also **strip** VERB

la bande
♦ **a comic strip** une bande dessinée

S

stripe NOUN
la rayure

striped ADJECTIVE
à rayures ◊ *a striped skirt* une jupe à rayures

to **stroke** VERB

see also **stroke** NOUN

caresser

stroke NOUN

see also **stroke** VERB

l' attaque FEM ◊ *to have a stroke* avoir une attaque

stroll NOUN
♦ **to go for a stroll** aller faire une petite promenade

stroller NOUN
le landau

strong ADJECTIVE
① fort ◊ *She's very strong.* Elle est très forte.
② résistant (*material*)

strongly ADVERB
fortement ◊ *We recommend strongly that...* Nous recommandons fortement que...
♦ **He smelt strongly of tobacco.** Il sentait fort le tabac.
♦ **strongly built** solidement bâti
♦ **I don't feel strongly about it.** Ça m'est égal.

struck VERB *see* **strike**

to **struggle** VERB

see also **struggle** NOUN

se débattre (*physically*) ◊ *She struggled, but she couldn't escape.* Elle s'est débattue, mais elle n'a pas pu s'échapper.
♦ **to struggle to do something (1)** (*fight*) se battre pour faire quelque chose ◊ *He struggled to get custody of his daughter.* Il s'est battu pour obtenir la garde de sa fille.
♦ **to struggle to do something (2)** (*have difficulty*) avoir du mal à faire quelque chose

struggle NOUN

see also **struggle** VERB

la lutte (*for independence, equality*)
♦ **It was a struggle.** Ça a été laborieux.

stub NOUN
le talon ◊ *Keep your ticket stub.* Garde le talon de ton billet.

to **stub** VERB
♦ **to stub one's toe** se cogner l'orteil ◊ *I stubbed my toe on a stone.* Je me suis cogné l'orteil contre une pierre.

stubborn ADJECTIVE
têtu

stuck VERB *see* **stick**

stuck ADJECTIVE
coincé (*jammed*) ◊ *It's stuck.* C'est coincé.
♦ **to get stuck** rester coincé ◊ *We got stuck in a traffic jam.* Nous sommes restés coincés dans un embouteillage.

stuck-up ADJECTIVE
coincé (*informal*)

stud NOUN
① la boucle d'oreille (*earring*)
② le clou (*on football boots*)

student NOUN
l' étudiant MASC
l' étudiante FEM

student driver NOUN
l' apprenti-conducteur MASC
l' apprentie-conductrice FEM
♦ **"Student Driver"** (*on car*) « Étudiant au volant »

studio NOUN
le studio ◊ *a TV studio* un studio de télévision
♦ **a studio apartment** un studio

to **study** VERB
① faire des études (*at university*) ◊ *I plan to study biology.* J'ai l'intention de faire des études en biologie.
② travailler (*do homework*) ◊ *I have to study tonight.* Je dois travailler ce soir.

stuff NOUN

see also **stuff** VERB

① la chose (*substance*) ◊ *I need some stuff for hay fever.* J'ai besoin de quelque chose contre le rhume des foins.
② les patentes FEM PL (*things*) ◊ *There's some stuff on the table for you.* Il y a des patentes sur la table pour toi. ◊ *I have a ton of stuff to do this weekend.* J'ai plein de patentes à faire en fin de semaine.
③ les affaires FEM PL (*possessions*) ◊ *Have you got all your stuff?* Est-ce que tu as toutes tes affaires?

to **stuff** VERB

see also **stuff** NOUN

① fourrer (*cram*) ◊ *He stuffed the notebook into his pack.* Il a fourré le cahier dans son sac à dos.
② farcir (*turkey*)

stuffed ADJECTIVE
♦ **stuffed animal (1)** (*toy*) l'animal en peluche
♦ **stuffed animal (2)** (*real*) l'animal empaillé
♦ **No thanks, I'm stuffed!** Non, merci,

j'ai l'estomac bien rempli!

stuffing NOUN
la <u>farce</u> (*in turkey*)

stuffy ADJECTIVE
<u>mal aéré</u> (*room*)
♦ **It's really stuffy in here.** On étouffe ici.

to **stumble** VERB
<u>trébucher</u>

stung VERB *see* **sting**

stunk VERB *see* **stink**

stunned ADJECTIVE
<u>sidéré</u> (*amazed*) ◊ *I was stunned.*
J'étais sidérée.

stunning ADJECTIVE
<u>superbe</u>

stunt NOUN
la <u>cascade</u> (*in film*)

stunt actor NOUN
le <u>cascadeur</u>
la <u>cascadeuse</u>

stupid ADJECTIVE
<u>stupide</u> ◊ *a stupid joke* une
plaisanterie stupide
♦ **Me, go jogging? Don't be stupid!**
Moi, faire du jogging? Ne dis pas de
niaiseries!

to **stutter** VERB
<u>bégayer</u>

style NOUN
le <u>style</u> ◊ *That's not his style.* Ça n'est
pas son style.

subject NOUN
⒈ le <u>sujet</u> ◊ *The subject of my project
was the Internet.* Le sujet de mon
projet était Internet.
⒉ la <u>matière</u> (*at school*) ◊ *What's
your favourite subject?* Quelle est ta
matière préférée?

subjunctive NOUN
le <u>subjonctif</u> ◊ *in the subjunctive* au
subjonctif

submarine NOUN
le <u>sous-marin</u>
♦ **submarine sandwich** le sous-marin

subscription NOUN
l' <u>abonnement</u> MASC (*to paper,
magazine*)
♦ **to take out a subscription to**
s'abonner à

to **subsidize** VERB
<u>subventionner</u>

substance NOUN
la <u>substance</u>
♦ **substance abuse** l'abus de
substances toxiques MASC

substitute NOUN

see also **substitute** VERB
(*person*)
le <u>remplaçant</u>
la <u>remplaçante</u>

to **substitute** VERB

see also **substitute** NOUN
<u>substituer</u> ◊ *to substitute A for B*
substituer A à B

subtitled ADJECTIVE
<u>sous-titré</u>

subtitles PL NOUN
les <u>sous-titres</u> MASC PL ◊ *a French film
with English subtitles* un film français
avec des sous-titres en anglais

subtle ADJECTIVE
<u>subtil</u>

to **subtract** VERB
<u>soustraire</u> ◊ *to subtract 3 from 5*
soustraire trois de cinq

suburb NOUN
la <u>banlieue</u> ◊ *a suburb of Vancouver*
une banlieue de Vancouver ◊ *They
live in the suburbs.* Ils habitent en
banlieue.

suburban ADJECTIVE
<u>de banlieue</u> ◊ *a suburban home* une
maison de banlieue

subway NOUN
le <u>métro</u> ◊ *a subway station* une
station de métro

to **succeed** VERB
<u>réussir</u> ◊ *to succeed in doing
something* réussir à faire quelque
chose

success NOUN
le <u>succès</u> ◊ *The play was a great
success.* La pièce a eu beaucoup de
succès.

successful ADJECTIVE
<u>réussi</u> ◊ *a successful attempt* une
tentative réussie
♦ **to be successful in doing something**
réussir à faire quelque chose
♦ **She's a successful entrepreneur.** Ses
affaires marchent bien.

successfully ADVERB
<u>avec succès</u>

successor NOUN
le <u>successeur</u>
la <u>successeure</u>

such ADJECTIVE, ADVERB
<u>si</u> ◊ *such nice people* des gens si
gentils ◊ *such a long journey* un
voyage si long
♦ **such a lot of** tellement de ◊ *such a lot
of work* tellement de travail
♦ **such as** (*like*) comme ◊ *spicy dishes,
such as Creole shrimp* les plats

S

☞

épicés, comme les crevettes à la créole
♦ **not as such** pas exactement ◊ *He's not an expert as such, but...* Ce n'est pas exactement un expert, mais...
♦ **There's no such thing.** Ça n'existe pas. ◊ *There's no such thing as the Sasquatch.* Le Sasquatch n'existe pas.

such-and-such ADJECTIVE
tel ou tel MASC
telle ou telle FEM ◊ *such-and-such a place* tel ou tel endroit

to **suck** VERB
sucer ◊ *to suck one's thumb* sucer son pouce

sudden ADJECTIVE
soudain ◊ *a sudden change* un changement soudain
♦ **all of a sudden** tout à coup

suddenly ADVERB
① brusquement (*stop, leave, change*)
② subitement (*die*)
③ soudain (*at beginning of sentence*) ◊ *Suddenly, the door opened.* Soudain, la porte s'est ouverte.

suede NOUN
le suède ◊ *a suede jacket* une veste en suède

to **suffer** VERB
souffrir ◊ *She was really suffering.* Elle souffrait beaucoup.
♦ **to suffer from a disease** avoir une maladie ◊ *I suffer from hay fever.* J'ai le rhume des foins.

to **suffocate** VERB
suffoquer

sugar NOUN
le sucre ◊ *Do you take sugar?* Est-ce que vous prenez du sucre?
♦ **a sugar bush** une érablière
♦ **a sugar shack** une cabane à sucre

★ sugaring off NOUN
le temps des sucres
♦ **a sugaring-off party** une partie de sucre

to **suggest** VERB
suggérer ◊ *I suggested they set off early.* Je leur ai suggéré de partir de bonne heure.

suggestion NOUN
la suggestion ◊ *to make a suggestion* faire une suggestion

suicide NOUN
le suicide
♦ **to commit suicide** se suicider

suit NOUN

see also **suit** VERB

① le costume (*man's*)

② le tailleur (*woman's*)

to **suit** VERB

see also **suit** NOUN

① convenir à (*be convenient for*) ◊ *What time would suit you?* Quelle heure vous conviendrait?
♦ **That suits me fine.** Ça m'arrange.
♦ **Suit yourself!** Comme tu veux!
② aller bien à (*look good on*) ◊ *That dress really suits you.* Cette robe te va vraiment bien.

suitable ADJECTIVE
① convenable ◊ *a suitable time* une heure convenable
② approprié (*clothes*) ◊ *suitable clothing* des vêtements appropriés

suitcase NOUN
la valise

suite NOUN
la suite (*of rooms*)
♦ **a bedroom suite** le mobilier de chambre à coucher

to **sulk** VERB
bouder

sulky ADJECTIVE
boudeur MASC
boudeuse FEM

sum NOUN
la somme (*amount*) ◊ *a sum of money* une somme d'argent

to **sum up** VERB
résumer

to **summarize** VERB
résumer

summary NOUN
le résumé

summer NOUN
l' été MASC
♦ **in summer** en été
♦ **summer clothes** les vêtements d'été
♦ **the summer holidays** les vacances d'été
♦ **a summer camp**
★ un camp de vacances

summit NOUN
le sommet

sun NOUN
le soleil ◊ *in the sun* au soleil

to **sunbathe** VERB
se bronzer

sunblock NOUN
l' écran solaire MASC

sunburn NOUN
le coup de soleil

sunburned ADJECTIVE
♦ **I got sunburned.** J'ai attrapé un coup de soleil.

Sunday NOUN
le <u>dimanche</u> ◊ *on Sunday* dimanche
◊ *on Sundays* le dimanche ◊ *every Sunday* tous les dimanches ◊ *last Sunday* dimanche dernier ◊ *next Sunday* dimanche prochain

sunflower NOUN
le <u>tournesol</u>

sung VERB *see* **sing**

sunglasses PL NOUN
les <u>lunettes de soleil</u> FEM PL

sunk VERB *see* **sink**

sunlight NOUN
le <u>soleil</u>
♦ **Avoid exposure to sunlight.** Évitez l'exposition au soleil.

sunny ADJECTIVE
<u>ensoleillé</u> ◊ *a sunny morning* une matinée ensoleillée
♦ **It's sunny.** Il fait du soleil.
♦ **a sunny day** une belle journée

sunrise NOUN
le <u>lever du soleil</u>

sunroof NOUN
le <u>toit ouvrant</u>

sunscreen NOUN
l' <u>écran solaire</u> MASC

sunset NOUN
le <u>coucher du soleil</u>

sunshine NOUN
le <u>soleil</u>

sunstroke NOUN
l' <u>insolation</u> FEM ◊ *to get sunstroke* attraper une insolation

suntan NOUN
le <u>bronzage</u>
♦ **suntan lotion** le lait solaire
♦ **suntan oil** l'huile solaire FEM

super ADJECTIVE
<u>formidable</u>

superb ADJECTIVE
<u>superbe</u>

supermarket NOUN
le <u>supermarché</u>

supernatural ADJECTIVE
<u>surnaturel</u> MASC
<u>surnaturelle</u> FEM

superstitious ADJECTIVE
<u>superstitieux</u> MASC
<u>superstitieuse</u> FEM

to **supervise** VERB
<u>surveiller</u>

supervisor NOUN
(*in factory*)
le <u>superviseur</u>
la <u>superviseure</u>

supper NOUN
✹ le <u>souper</u>

supplement NOUN
le <u>supplément</u> ◊ *a vitamin supplement* un supplément vitaminique

supplies PL NOUN
le <u>ravitaillement</u> SING

to **supply** VERB

> *see also* **supply** NOUN

<u>fournir</u> (*provide*)
♦ **to supply somebody with something** fournir quelque chose à quelqu'un ◊ *The centre supplied us with all the equipment.* Le centre nous a fourni tout l'équipement.

supply NOUN

> *see also* **supply** VERB

la <u>provision</u> ◊ *a supply of paper* une provision de papier
♦ **the water supply** (*to town*) l'approvisionnement en eau MASC

supply teacher NOUN
le <u>suppléant</u>
la <u>suppléante</u>

to **support** VERB

> *see also* **support** NOUN

① <u>soutenir</u> (*encourage*) ◊ *My mom has always supported me.* Ma mère m'a toujours soutenu.
② <u>être en faveur de</u> (*agree with*) ◊ *I support the new rule.* Je suis en faveur du nouveau règlement.
③ <u>subvenir aux besoins de</u> (*financially*) ◊ *She had to support five children on her own.* Elle a dû subvenir toute seule aux besoins de cinq enfants.

> Be careful not to translate **to support** by **supporter**.

support NOUN

> *see also* **support** VERB

le <u>soutien</u> (*backing*)

supporter NOUN
① le <u>sympathisant</u>
la <u>sympathisante</u> ◊ *a supporter of nuclear disarmament* un sympathisant du désarmement nucléaire
② (*donor*)
le <u>donateur</u>
la <u>donatrice</u>

to **suppose** VERB
<u>imaginer</u> ◊ *I suppose he's late.* J'imagine qu'il est en retard.
◊ *Suppose you won the lottery.* Imaginez que vous gagniez à la loterie.

S

☞

♦ **I suppose so.** J'imagine.
♦ **to be supposed to do something** être
censé faire quelque chose ◊ *You're
supposed to show your passport.* On
est censé montrer son passeport.

supposing CONJUNCTION
si ◊ *Supposing you won the lottery...*
Si tu gagnais à la loterie...

supreme ADJECTIVE
suprême ◊ *the Supreme Court* la
Cour suprême

surcharge NOUN
la surcharge

sure ADJECTIVE
sûr ◊ *Are you sure?* Tu es sûr?
♦ **Sure!** Bien sûr!
♦ **to make sure that...** vérifier que...
◊ *I'm going to make sure the door's
locked.* Je vais vérifier que la porte
est fermée à clé.

surf NOUN

see also **surf** VERB

le ressac

to **surf** VERB

see also **surf** NOUN

surfer
♦ **to go surfing** faire du surf
♦ **to surf the Net** surfer sur Internet

surface NOUN
la surface

surfboard NOUN
la planche de surf
(PL les planches de surf)

surfing NOUN
le surf ◊ *to go surfing* faire du surf

surgeon NOUN
le chirurgien
la chirurgienne ◊ *She's a surgeon.*
Elle est chirurgienne.

surgery NOUN
l' opération FEM ◊ *Surgery was
required.* Il a fallu faire une opération.
◊ *The surgery is scheduled for
Monday.* L'opération est prévue pour
lundi.
♦ **She underwent extensive surgery.**
Elle a subi une grave intervention
chirurgicale.

surname NOUN
le nom de famille
(PL les noms de famille)

surprise NOUN
la surprise

surprised ADJECTIVE
surpris ◊ *I was surprised to see him.*
J'ai été surprise de le voir.

surprising ADJECTIVE

surprenant

to **surrender** VERB
capituler

surrogate mother NOUN
la mère porteuse

to **surround** VERB
encercler ◊ *The police surrounded
the house.* La police a encerclé la
maison. ◊ *You're surrounded!* Vous
êtes encerclé!
♦ **surrounded by** entouré de ◊ *The
house is surrounded by trees.* La
maison est entourée d'arbres.

surroundings PL NOUN
le cadre SING ◊ *a hotel in beautiful
surroundings* un hôtel situé dans un
beau cadre

survey NOUN
l' enquête FEM (*research*)

survivor NOUN
le survivant
la survivante ◊ *There were
no survivors.* Il n'y a pas eu de
survivants.

to **suspect** VERB

see also **suspect** NOUN

soupçonner

suspect NOUN

see also **suspect** VERB

le suspect
la suspecte

to **suspend** VERB
① exclure (*from school, team*) ◊ *He's
been suspended.* Il s'est fait exclure.
② suspendre (*from job*)

suspenders PL NOUN
les bretelles FEM

suspense NOUN
① l' attente FEM (*waiting*) ◊ *The
suspense was terrible.* L'attente a été
terrible.
② le suspense (*in story*) ◊ *a film
with lots of suspense* un film avec
beaucoup de suspense

suspension NOUN
① l' exclusion FEM (*from school, team*)
② la suspension (*from job*)

suspicious ADJECTIVE
① méfiant ◊ *He was suspicious at
first.* Il était méfiant au début.
② louche (*suspicious-looking*) ◊ *a
suspicious person* un individu louche

to **swallow** VERB
avaler

swam VERB *see* **swim**

swan NOUN
le cygne

to **swap** VERB
échanger ◊ *Do you want to swap?*
Tu veux échanger? ◊ *to swap A for B*
échanger A contre B

to **swat** VERB
écraser

to **sway** VERB
osciller

to **swear** VERB
✹ sacrer (*make an oath, curse*)

swearword NOUN
✹ le sacre

sweat NOUN

> *see also* **sweat** VERB

la transpiration

to **sweat** VERB

> *see also* **sweat** NOUN

transpirer

sweater NOUN
le chandail

sweatshirt NOUN
le chandail en molleton

sweaty ADJECTIVE
1 en sueur (*person, face*) ◊ *I'm all sweaty.* Je suis en sueur.
2 moite (*hands*)

to **sweep** VERB
balayer
♦ **to sweep the floor** balayer

sweet ADJECTIVE
1 sucré (*taste*)
2 (*kind*)
gentil MASC
gentille FEM ◊ *That was really sweet of you.* C'était vraiment gentil de ta part.
3 (*cute*)
mignon MASC
mignonne FEM ◊ *Isn't she sweet?* Comme elle est mignonne!
♦ **sweet and sour pork** le porc à la sauce aigre-douce

sweets PL NOUN
les sucreries FEM

sweltering ADJECTIVE
♦ **It was sweltering.** Il faisait une chaleur étouffante.

swept VERB *see* **sweep**

to **swerve** VERB
faire une embardée ◊ *He swerved to avoid the cyclist.* Il a fait une embardée pour éviter la cycliste.

swim NOUN

> *see also* **swim** VERB

♦ **to go for a swim** aller se baigner

to **swim** VERB

> *see also* **swim** NOUN

nager ◊ *Can you swim?* Tu sais nager?
♦ **She swam across the river.** Elle a traversé la rivière à la nage.

swimmer NOUN
le nageur
la nageuse ◊ *She's a good swimmer.* C'est une bonne nageuse.

swimming NOUN
la natation ◊ *Do you like swimming?* Tu aimes la natation?
♦ **to go swimming** (*in a pool*) aller à la piscine
♦ **a swimming pool** une piscine
♦ **swimming trunks** le maillot de bain

swimsuit NOUN
le maillot de bain

swing NOUN

> *see also* **swing** VERB

la balançoire (*in playground, garden*)

to **swing** VERB

> *see also* **swing** NOUN

1 se balancer ◊ *A bunch of keys swung from his belt.* Un trousseau de clés se balançait à sa ceinture.
♦ **Sam was swinging an umbrella as he walked.** Sam balançait son parapluie en marchant.
2 virer ◊ *The canoe swung round sharply.* Le canot a viré brusquement.

switch NOUN

> *see also* **switch** VERB

l' interrupteur MASC (*for light, radio, etc.*)

to **switch** VERB

> *see also* **switch** NOUN

changer de ◊ *We switched partners.* Nous avons changé de partenaire.

to **switch off** VERB
1 éteindre (*electrical appliance*)
2 arrêter (*engine, machine*)

to **switch on** VERB
1 allumer (*electrical appliance*)
2 mettre en marche (*engine, machine*)

swollen ADJECTIVE
enflé (*arm, leg*)

sword NOUN
l' épée FEM

swore, sworn VERB *see* **swear**

swum VERB *see* **swim**

swung VERB *see* **swing**

symbol NOUN
le symbole

sympathetic ADJECTIVE

S

☞

compréhensif MASC
compréhensive FEM ◊ *The teacher was very sympathetic and allowed me to leave before the end of the class.* La professeure a été très compréhensive et m'a permis de partir avant la fin du cours.

> *Be careful not to translate* **sympathetic** *by* **sympathique**.

to **sympathize** VERB
  ♦ **to sympathize with somebody** comprendre quelqu'un

sympathy NOUN
  la compassion

symptom NOUN
  le symptôme

synagogue NOUN
  ① la synagogue

syndrome NOUN
  ② le syndrome
♦ **Down syndrome**
  le syndrome de Down
  ♦ **Severe Acute Respiratory Syndrome**
  le syndrome respiratoire aigu sévère
  ♦ **chronic fatigue syndrome** le syndrome de fatigue chronique

synthetic ADJECTIVE
  synthétique ◊ *synthetic fibres* des fibres synthétiques

syringe NOUN
  la seringue

system NOUN
  le système

T

table NOUN
la table ◊ to set the table mettre la table

tablecloth NOUN
la nappe

tablespoon NOUN
la cuillère à soupe
♦ **a tablespoon of sugar** une cuillerée à soupe de sucre

table tennis NOUN
le ping-pong ◊ to play table tennis jouer au ping-pong

tabloid NOUN
le tabloïd

tackle NOUN
see also **tackle** VERB
le tacle (in football)
♦ **fishing tackle** le matériel de pêche

to **tackle** VERB
see also **tackle** NOUN
① tacler (in football)
② plaquer (in rugby)
♦ **to tackle a problem** s'attaquer à un problème

tact NOUN
le tact

tactful ADJECTIVE
plein(e) de tact

tactics PL NOUN
la tactique SING

tactless ADJECTIVE
♦ **to be tactless** manquer de tact ◊ a tactless remark une remarque qui manque de tact

tadpole NOUN
le têtard

tag NOUN
l' étiquette FEM (label)

tail NOUN
la queue
♦ **Heads or tails?** Pile ou face?

tailor NOUN
le tailleur

to **take** VERB
① prendre ◊ Are you taking your new camera? Tu prends ton nouvel appareil photo? ◊ He took a plate from the cupboard. Il a pris une assiette dans l'armoire. ◊ It takes about an hour. Ça prend environ une heure.
② emmener (person) ◊ She goes to Toronto every week, but she never takes me. Elle va à Toronto toutes les semaines, mais elle ne m'emmène jamais.
♦ **to take something somewhere** emporter quelque chose quelque part ◊ Do you take your notebooks home? Vous emportez vos cahiers chez vous? ◊ Don't take anything valuable with you. N'emportez pas d'objets de valeur.
♦ **I'm going to take my coat to the cleaner's.** Je vais porter mon manteau chez le nettoyeur.
③ demander (effort, skill) ◊ that takes a lot of courage cela demande beaucoup de courage
♦ **It takes a lot of money to do that.** Il faut beaucoup d'argent pour faire ça.
④ supporter (tolerate) ◊ He can't take being criticized. Il ne supporte pas d'être critiqué.
⑤ passer (test) ◊ She's taking her driving test next week. Elle passe le test de conduire la semaine prochaine.
⑥ faire (subject) ◊ I decided to take French instead of music. J'ai décidé de faire du français au lieu de la musique.

to **take after** VERB
ressembler à ◊ She takes after her mother. Elle ressemble à sa mère.

to **take apart** VERB
♦ **to take something apart** démonter quelque chose

to **take away** VERB
① emporter (object)
② emmener (person)
♦ **to take something away** (confiscate) confisquer quelque chose

to **take back** VERB
rapporter ◊ I took it back to the store. Je l'ai rapporté au magasin.
♦ **I take it all back!** Je n'ai rien dit!

to **take down** VERB
① enlever (poster, sign)
② décrocher (painting, curtains)
③ démonter (tent, scaffolding)
④ prendre en note (make a note of) ◊ He took down the details in his notebook. Il a pris tous les détails en note dans son carnet.

to **take in** VERB
comprendre (understand) ◊ I didn't really take it in. Je n'ai pas bien

☞

take off → tart

compris.

to **take off** VERB

① décoller (*plane*) ◊ *The plane took off twenty minutes late.* L'avion a décollé avec vingt minutes de retard.
② enlever (*clothes*) ◊ *Take your coat off.* Enlevez votre manteau.

to **take out** VERB

sortir (*from container, pocket*)
♦ **They took us out to the movies.** Il nous ont emmenés au cinéma.
♦ **hot meals to take out** des plats chauds à emporter

to **take over** VERB

prendre la relève ◊ *I'll take over now.* Je vais prendre la relève.
♦ **to take over from somebody** remplacer quelqu'un

taken VERB *see* **take**

takeoff NOUN

le décollage (*of plane*)

takeout NOUN

① le plat à emporter (*meal*)
② le restaurant qui vend des plats à emporter ◊ *a Chinese takeout* un restaurant chinois qui vend des plats à emporter

tale NOUN

le conte FEM (*story*)

talent NOUN

le talent ◊ *He has lots of talent.* Il a beaucoup de talent.
♦ **to have a talent for something** être doué pour quelque chose ◊ *He has a real talent for languages.* Il est vraiment doué pour les langues.

talented ADJECTIVE

① talentueux MASC
② talentueuse FEM
♦ **She's a talented pianist.** C'est une pianiste talentueuse.

talk NOUN

see also **talk** VERB

① l' exposé MASC (*speech*) ◊ *She gave a talk on rock climbing.* Elle a fait un exposé sur l'escalade.
② la conversation (*conversation*) ◊ *I had a talk with my dad about it.* J'ai eu une petite conversation avec mon père à ce sujet.
③ les racontars MASC (*gossip*) ◊ *It's just talk.* Ce sont des racontars.

to **talk** VERB

see also **talk** NOUN

parler ◊ *to talk about something* parler de quelque chose
♦ **to talk something over with somebody** discuter de quelque chose avec quelqu'un

talkative ADJECTIVE

bavard

talk show NOUN

l' émission-débat FEM
(PL les émissions-débats)

tall ADJECTIVE

① grand (*person, tree*)
♦ **to be 2 metres tall** mesurer deux mètres
② haut (*building*)

tame ADJECTIVE

apprivoisé(e) (*animal*) ◊ *They have a tame ferret.* Ils ont un furet apprivoisé.

tampon NOUN

le tampon

tan NOUN

le bronzage ◊ *to have an amazing tan.* avoir un bronzage superbe.

tangerine NOUN

la mandarine

to **tangle up** VERB

emmêler ◊ *My hair is all tangled up.* Mes cheveux sont tout emmêlés.
♦ **to get tangled up** s'emmêler ◊ *His fishing line got tangled up with mine.* Sa ligne de pêche s'est emmêlée dans la mienne.

tank NOUN

① le réservoir (*for water, gasoline*)
② le char d'assaut (*military*)
♦ **a fish tank** un aquarium

tanker NOUN

① le pétrolier (*ship*)
♦ **an oil tanker** un pétrolier
② le camion-citerne (*truck*)

tap NOUN

① le robinet (*water tap*)
② la petite tape (*gentle touch*)

tap-dancing NOUN

la claquette FEM ◊ *I do tap-dancing.* Je danse la claquette.

to **tape** VERB

see also **tape** NOUN

enregistrer (*record*) ◊ *Did you tape that movie last night?* As-tu enregistré le film hier soir?

tape NOUN

see also **tape** VERB

① la cassette ◊ *a tape of Avril Lavigne* une cassette de Avril Lavigne
② le ruban adhésif (*adhesive tape*)

tape measure NOUN

le galon à mesurer

target NOUN

la cible

tart NOUN

la <u>tartelette</u> ◊ *a butter tart* une tartelette aux raisins secs

tartan ADJECTIVE
<u>écossais</u> ◊ *a tartan skirt* une jupe écossaise

task NOUN
la <u>tâche</u>

taste NOUN

> *see also* **taste** VERB

le <u>goût</u> ◊ *It has a really strange taste.* Ça a un goût vraiment bizarre. ◊ *a joke in bad taste* une plaisanterie de mauvais goût
♦ **Would you like a taste?** Tu veux goûter?

to **taste** VERB

> *see also* **taste** NOUN

<u>goûter</u> ◊ *Would you like to taste it?* Vous voulez y goûter?
♦ **to taste like something** avoir un goût de quelque chose ◊ *It tastes like fish.* Ça a un goût de poisson.
♦ **You can taste the garlic in it.** Ça a bien le goût d'ail.

tasteful ADJECTIVE
de bon <u>goût</u>

tasteless ADJECTIVE
1 <u>fade</u> (*food*)
2 de mauvais <u>goût</u> (*in bad taste*) ◊ *a tasteless remark* une remarque de mauvais goût

tasty ADJECTIVE
<u>savoureux</u> MASC
<u>savoureuse</u> FEM

tattoo NOUN
le <u>tatouage</u>

taught VERB *see* **teach**

Taurus NOUN
le <u>Taureau</u> ◊ *I'm a Taurus.* Je suis Taureau.

tax NOUN
1 les <u>impôts</u> MASC PL (*on income*)
2 la <u>taxe</u> (*on goods, alcohol*)

taxi NOUN
le <u>taxi</u>
♦ **a taxi driver** un chauffeur de taxi
♦ **a taxi stand** une station de taxi

TB NOUN
la <u>tuberculose</u>

tea NOUN
le <u>thé</u> ◊ *a cup of tea* une tasse de thé
♦ **a tea bag** un sachet de thé

to **teach** VERB
1 <u>apprendre</u> ◊ *My sister taught me to swim.* Ma sœur m'a appris à nager.
◊ *That'll teach you!* Ça t'apprendra!
2 <u>enseigner</u> (*in school*) ◊ *She teaches physics.* Elle enseigne la physique.

teacher NOUN
1 (*in secondary school*)
le <u>professeur</u>
la <u>professeure</u> ◊ *a math teacher* un professeur de maths ◊ *She's a teacher.* Elle est professeure.
2 (*in primary school*)
l' <u>enseignant</u> MASC
l' <u>enseignante</u> FEM ◊ *He's a primary school teacher.* Il est enseignant.

teacher's pet NOUN
le <u>chouchou</u>
la <u>chouchoute</u>

teaching assistant NOUN
l' <u>aide-enseignant</u> MASC
l' <u>aide-enseignante</u> FEM

team NOUN
l' <u>équipe</u> FEM ◊ *a football team* une équipe de football ◊ *She was on my team.* Elle était dans mon équipe.

teamwork NOUN
le <u>travail d'équipe</u> ◊ *That's teamwork!* C'est ça, le travail d'équipe! ◊ *Teamwork makes all the difference.* Travailler en équipe fait toute la différence.

teapot NOUN
la <u>théière</u>

tear NOUN

> *see also* **tear** VERB

la <u>larme</u> ◊ *The child was in tears.* L'enfant était en larmes.

to **tear** VERB

> *see also* **tear** NOUN

1 <u>déchirer</u> ◊ *Be careful or you'll tear the page.* Fais attention, tu vas déchirer la page.
2 se <u>déchirer</u> ◊ *It won't tear, it's very strong.* Ça ne se déchire pas, c'est très solide.
♦ **to tear up** déchirer ◊ *He tore up the letter.* Il a déchiré la lettre.

to **tease** VERB
1 <u>tourmenter</u> (*unkindly*) ◊ *Stop teasing that poor animal!* Arrête de tourmenter ce pauvre animal!
2 <u>taquiner</u> (*jokingly*) ◊ *He's teasing you.* Il te taquine.
♦ **I was only teasing.** Je plaisantais.

teaspoon NOUN
la <u>petite cuillère</u>
♦ **a teaspoon of sugar** une cuillerée à thé de sucre

tea towel NOUN
le <u>torchon</u>

technical ADJECTIVE
technique

technician NOUN
① le technicien
② la technicienne

technique NOUN
la technique

technological ADJECTIVE
technologique

technology NOUN
la technologie

teddy bear NOUN
le nounours

teenage ADJECTIVE
① pour les jeunes ◊ *a teenage magazine* un magazine pour les jeunes
② adolescent (*boys, girls*) ◊ *He has two teenage daughters.* Il a deux filles adolescentes.

teenager NOUN
l' adolescent MASC
l' adolescente FEM

teens PL NOUN
♦ **She's in her teens.** C'est une adolescente.

teeth PL NOUN
les dents FEM

to **teethe** VERB
faire ses dents

teetotal ADJECTIVE
♦ **I'm teetotal.** Je ne bois jamais d'alcool.

telecommunications PL NOUN
les télécommunications FEM

telephone NOUN

| *see also* **phone** NOUN and VERB |

le téléphone ◊ *on the telephone* au téléphone
♦ **a telephone booth** une cabine téléphonique
♦ **a telephone call** un coup de téléphone
♦ **the telephone directory** l'annuaire MASC
♦ **a telephone number** un numéro de téléphone

telescope NOUN
le télescope

television NOUN
la télévision
♦ **on television** à la télévision
♦ **a television program** une émission de télévision

television ad NOUN
la publicité télévisée

to **tell** VERB
dire
♦ **to tell somebody something** dire quelque chose à quelqu'un ◊ *Did you tell your mother?* Tu l'as dit à ta mère? ◊ *I told him that I was going on holiday.* Je lui ai dit que je partais en vacances.
♦ **to tell somebody to do something** dire à quelqu'un de faire quelque chose ◊ *He told me to wait a moment.* Il m'a dit d'attendre un moment.
♦ **to tell lies** dire des mensonges
♦ **to tell a story** raconter une histoire
♦ **I can't tell the difference between them.** Je n'arrive pas à les distinguer.

to **tell off** VERB
gronder

temper NOUN
le caractère ◊ *to have a bad temper.* avoir mauvais caractère.
♦ **to lose one's temper** se mettre en colère ◊ *I lost my temper.* Je me suis mis en colère.

temperature NOUN
la température (*of oven, water, person*)
♦ **The temperature was 30 degrees.** Il faisait trente degrés.
♦ **to have a temperature** avoir de la fièvre

temple NOUN
le temple

temporary ADJECTIVE
temporaire

to **tempt** VERB
tenter ◊ *I'm very tempted!* Je suis très tenté!
♦ **to tempt somebody to do something** persuader quelqu'un de faire quelque chose

temptation NOUN
la tentation

tempting ADJECTIVE
tentant

ten NUMBER
dix ◊ *She's ten.* Elle a dix ans.

tenant NOUN
le locataire
la locataire

to **tend** VERB
♦ **to tend to do something** avoir tendance à faire quelque chose ◊ *He tends to arrive late.* Il a tendance à arriver en retard.

tender ADJECTIVE
① tendre (*food*)
② sensible (*part of body*) ◊ *My feet are really tender.* J'ai les pieds très sensibles.

tennis NOUN
le tennis ◊ *Do you play tennis?* Vous jouez au tennis?
♦ **a tennis ball** une balle de tennis
♦ **a tennis court** un court de tennis
♦ **a tennis racquet** une raquette de tennis

tense ADJECTIVE

see also **tense** NOUN

tendu

tense NOUN

see also **tense** ADJECTIVE

♦ **the present tense** le présent
♦ **the future tense** le futur

tension NOUN
la tension

tent NOUN
la tente
♦ **a tent peg** un piquet de tente
♦ **a tent pole** un montant de tente

tenth ADJECTIVE
dixième ◊ *the tenth floor* le dixième étage
♦ **the tenth of August** le dix août

term NOUN
① le trimestre (*at school*)
② le terme ◊ *a short-term solution* une solution à court terme ◊ *a technical term* un terme technique
♦ **to come to terms with something** accepter quelque chose

terminal ADJECTIVE

see also **terminal** NOUN

incurable (*illness, patient*)

terminal NOUN

see also **terminal** ADJECTIVE

un terminal (*of computer*)
♦ **an airport terminal** une aérogare

terminally ADVERB
♦ **to be terminally ill** être condamné

terrace NOUN
la terrasse (*patio*)

terrible ADJECTIVE
épouvantable ◊ *He looks terrible.* Il a une mine épouvantable.

terribly ADVERB
① terriblement ◊ *He suffered terribly.* Il souffre terriblement.
② vraiment ◊ *I'm terribly sorry.* Je suis vraiment désolé.

terrier NOUN
le terrier

terrific ADJECTIVE
super (*wonderful*) ◊ *That's terrific!* C'est super!
♦ **You look terrific!** Tu es superbe!

terrified ADJECTIVE
terrifié ◊ *I was terrified!* J'étais terrifié!

❀ **Territorial Council** NOUN
le Conseil du territoire

territory NOUN
le territoire

terrorism NOUN
le terrorisme

terrorist NOUN
le/la terroriste
♦ **a terrorist attack** un attentat terroriste

test NOUN

see also **test** VERB

(*at school*)
① le test (*at school*) ◊ *I have a geography test today.* J'ai un test de géographie aujourd'hui.
② l' essai MASC (*trial, check*) ◊ *nuclear tests* les essais nucléaires
③ l' analyse FEM (*medical*) ◊ *a blood test* une analyse de sang ◊ *They're going to do some more tests.* Ils vont faire d'autres analyses.
♦ **driving test** l'examen du permis de conduire ◊ *She's taking her driving test tomorrow.* Elle subit son permis de conduire demain.

to **test** VERB

see also **test** NOUN

① essayer ◊ *to test something out* essayer quelque chose
② interroger (*class*) ◊ *My teacher tested us on the vocabulary.* Mon professeur nous a interrogés sur le vocabulaire.
♦ **She was tested for drugs.** On lui a fait subir un contrôle antidopage.

test tube NOUN
l' éprouvette FEM

tetanus NOUN
le tétanos ◊ *a tetanus injection* un vaccin contre le tétanos

text NOUN

see also **text** VERB

① le texte
② le minimessage (*mobile phone*)

to **text** VERB

see also **text** NOUN

♦ **to text someone** envoyer un minimessage à quelqu'un

textbook NOUN
le manuel ◊ *a French textbook* un manuel de français

than CONJUNCTION
que ◊ *She's taller than me.* Elle est plus grande que moi. ◊ *I have more* ☞

T

books than him. J'ai plus de livres que lui.
♦ **more than ten years** plus de dix ans
♦ **more than once** plus d'une fois

to **thank** VERB
remercier ◊ *Don't forget to write and thank them.* N'oublie pas de leur écrire pour les remercier.
♦ **thank you** merci
♦ **thank you very much** merci beaucoup

thanks EXCLAMATION
merci!
♦ **thanks to** grâce à ◊ *Thanks to her, everything went OK.* Grâce à elle, tout s'est bien passé.

that ADJECTIVE, PRONOUN, CONJUNCTION

> *Use ce when that is followed by a masculine noun, and cette when that is followed by a feminine noun. ce changes to cet before a vowel and before most words beginning with "h".*

① ce ◊ *that book* ce livre
cet ◊ *that man* cet homme
cette ◊ *that woman* cette femme
♦ **that road** cette route
♦ **THAT road** cette route-là
♦ **that one (1)** celui-là (*masculine*) ◊ *"This man?" "No, that one."* « Cet homme-ci ? » « Non, celui-là. »
♦ **that one (2)** celle-là (*feminine*) ◊ *"Do you like this photo?" "No, I prefer that one."* « Tu aimes cette photo ? » « Non, je préfère celle-là. »
② ça ◊ *You see that?* Tu vois ça?
♦ **What's that?** Qu'est-ce que c'est?
♦ **Who's that?** Qui est-ce?
♦ **Is that you?** C'est toi?
♦ **That's...** C'est... ◊ *That's my teacher.* C'est mon prof. ◊ *That's what she said.* C'est ce qu'elle a dit.

> *In relative phrases use qui when that refers to the subject of the sentence, and que when it refers to the object.*

③ qui ◊ *the man that saw us* l'homme qui nous a vus ◊ *the woman that spoke to us* la femme qui nous a parlé
④ que ◊ *the man that we saw* l'homme que nous avons vu

> *que changes to qu' before a vowel and before most words beginning with "h".*

◊ *the dog that she bought* le chien qu'elle a acheté ◊ *He thought that your brother was ill.* Il pensait que ton frère était malade. ◊ *I know that she likes chocolate.* Je sais qu'elle aime le chocolat.
♦ **the woman that we spoke to** la femme à qui nous avons parlé
♦ **It was that big.** Il était grand comme ça.
♦ **It's about that high.** C'est à peu près haut comme ça.
♦ **It's not that difficult.** Ça n'est pas si difficile que ça.

thatched ADJECTIVE
♦ **a thatched cottage** une chaumière

the ARTICLE

> *Use le with a masculine noun, and la with a feminine noun. Use l' before a vowel and most words beginning with "h". For plural nouns always use les.*

le ◊ *the boy* le garçon
l' ◊ *the man* l'homme MASC ◊ *the air* l'air MASC ◊ *the habit* l'habitude FEM
la ◊ *the girl* la fille
les ◊ *the children* les enfants

theatre NOUN (US **theater**)
le théâtre

theft NOUN
le vol

their ADJECTIVE
leur
(PL leurs) ◊ *their house* leur maison ◊ *their parents* leurs parents

theirs PRONOUN
le leur + MASC NOUN ◊ *It's not our garage, it's theirs.* Ce n'est pas notre garage, c'est le leur.
la leur + FEM NOUN ◊ *It's not our car, it's theirs.* Ce n'est pas notre voiture, c'est la leur.
les leurs + PL NOUN ◊ *They're not our ideas, they're theirs.* Ce ne sont pas nos idées, ce sont les leurs.
♦ **Is this theirs? (1)** C'est à eux? (*masculine owners*) ◊ *This car is theirs.* Cette voiture est à eux. ◊ *"Whose is this?" "It's theirs."* « C'est à qui ? » « À eux. »
♦ **Is this theirs? (2)** C'est à elles? (*feminine owners*)

them PRONOUN
① les ◊ *I didn't see them.* Je ne les ai pas vus.

> *Use leur when them means to them.*

② leur ◊ *I gave them some brochures.* Je leur ai donné des brochures. ◊ *I told them the truth.* Je leur ai dit la vérité.

> *Use eux or elles after a preposition.*

③ eux MASC ◊ *It's for them.* C'est pour eux.
elles FEM ◊ *My two sisters came, and my dad was with them.* Mes deux sœurs sont venues, et mon père était avec elles.

theme NOUN
le <u>thème</u>

theme park NOUN
le <u>parc d'attractions</u>

themselves PRONOUN
① <u>se</u> ◊ *Did they hurt themselves?* Est-ce qu'ils se sont fait mal?
② <u>eux-mêmes</u> MASC
<u>elles-mêmes</u> FEM ◊ *They did it themselves.* Ils l'ont fait eux-mêmes.

then ADVERB, CONJUNCTION
① <u>ensuite</u> (*next*) ◊ *I get dressed. Then I have breakfast.* Je m'habille. Ensuite je prends mon petit déjeuner.
② <u>alors</u> (*in that case*) ◊ *"My pen's run out." "Use a pencil then!"* « Il n'y a plus d'encre dans mon stylo. » « Alors utilise un crayon! »
③ <u>à l'époque</u> (*at that time*) ◊ *There was no electricity then.* Il n'y avait pas l'électricité à l'époque.
♦ **now and then** de temps en temps ◊ *"Do you play chess?" "Now and then."* « Vous jouez aux échecs? » « De temps en temps. »
♦ **By then it was too late.** Il était déjà trop tard.

therapy NOUN
la <u>thérapie</u>

there ADVERB
① <u>là</u> ◊ *Put it there, on the table.* Mets-le <u>là</u>, sur la table.
♦ **over there** là-bas
♦ **in there** là
♦ **on there** là
♦ **up there** là-haut
♦ **down there** là-bas
♦ **There he is!** Le voilà!
② <u>y</u> ◊ *She went there on Friday.* Elle y est allée vendredi. ◊ *Labrador? I've never been there.* Le Labrador? Je n'y suis jamais allé.
♦ **There is...** Il y a... ◊ *There's a factory near my house.* Il y a une usine près de chez moi.
♦ **There are...** Il y a... ◊ *There are five people in my family.* Il y a cinq personnes dans ma famille.
♦ **There has been an accident.** Il y a eu un accident.

therefore ADVERB
<u>donc</u>

there's = **there is, there has**

thermometer NOUN
le <u>thermomètre</u>

Thermos™ NOUN
le <u>thermos</u>

these ADJECTIVE, PRONOUN
① <u>ces</u> ◊ *these shoes* ces chaussures
♦ **THESE shoes** ces chaussures-là

② <u>ceux-ci</u> MASC ◊ *I want these!* Je veux ceux-ci!
<u>celles-ci</u> FEM ◊ *I'm looking for some sandals. Can I try these?* Je cherche des sandales. Je peux essayer celles-ci?

they PRONOUN

> *Check if **they** stands for a masculine or feminine noun.*

<u>ils</u> ◊ *"Are there any tickets left?" "No, they're all sold."* « Est-ce qu'il reste des billets? » « Non, ils sont tous vendus. »
<u>elles</u> ◊ *"Do you like those shoes?" "No, they're horrible."* « Tu aimes ces chaussures? » « Non, elles sont affreuses. »
♦ **They say that...** On dit que...

thick ADJECTIVE
(*not thin*)
<u>épais</u> MASC
<u>épaisse</u> FEM
♦ **The walls are one metre thick.** Les murs font un mètre d'épaisseur.

thief NOUN
le <u>voleur</u>
la <u>voleuse</u>
♦ **Stop thief!** Au voleur!

thigh NOUN
la <u>cuisse</u>

thin ADJECTIVE
① <u>mince</u> (*person, slice*)
② <u>maigre</u> (*skinny*)

thing NOUN
① la <u>chose</u> ◊ *beautiful things* de belles choses
※ ② la <u>patente</u> (*thingy*) ◊ *What's that thing called?* Comment s'appelle cette patente?
♦ **my things** (*belongings*) mes affaires FEM
♦ **You poor thing!** Mon pauvre!

to **think** VERB
① <u>penser</u> (*believe*) ◊ *I think you're wrong.* Je pense que vous avez tort. ◊ *What do you think about the war?* Que pensez-vous de la guerre?
② <u>réfléchir</u> (*spend time thinking*) ◊ *Think carefully before you reply.* Réfléchis bien avant de répondre. ◊ *I'll think about it.* Je vais y réfléchir.
♦ **What are you thinking about?** À quoi tu penses?
③ <u>imaginer</u> (*imagine*) ◊ *Think what life would be like without cars.* Imaginez la vie sans voitures.
♦ **I think so.** Oui, je crois.
♦ **I don't think so.** Je ne crois pas.
♦ **I'll think it over.** Je vais y réfléchir.

third ADJECTIVE

T

☞

see also **third** NOUN

troisième ◊ *the third day* le troisième jour ◊ *the third time* la troisième fois ◊ *I came third.* Je suis arrivé troisième.
♦ **the third of March** le trois mars

third NOUN

see also **third** ADJECTIVE

le <u>tiers</u> ◊ *a third of the population* un tiers de la population

thirdly ADVERB
<u>troisièmement</u>

thirst NOUN
la <u>soif</u>

thirsty ADJECTIVE
♦ **to be thirsty** avoir soif

thirteen NUMBER
<u>treize</u> ◊ *I'm thirteen.* J'ai treize ans.

thirteenth ADJECTIVE
<u>treizième</u> ◊ *her thirteenth birthday* son treizième anniversaire ◊ *the thirteenth floor* le treizième étage
♦ **the eighteenth of August** le treize août

thirty NUMBER
<u>trente</u>

this ADJECTIVE, PRONOUN

> *Use **ce** when **this** is followed by a masculine noun, and **cette** when **this** is followed by a feminine noun. **ce** changes to **cet** before a vowel and before most words beginning with "h".*

1 <u>ce</u> ◊ *this book* ce livre
<u>cet</u> ◊ *this man* cet homme
<u>cette</u> ◊ *this woman* cette femme
♦ **this road** cette route
♦ **THIS road** cette route-ci
♦ **this one (1)** celui-ci (*masculine*) ◊ *"Pass me that pen." "This one?"* « Passe-moi ce stylo. » « Celui-ci ? »
♦ **this one (2)** celle-ci (*feminine*) ◊ *Of the two photos, I prefer this one.* Des deux photos, c'est celle-ci que je préfère.
2 <u>ça</u> ◊ *You see this?* Tu vois ça?
♦ **What's this?** Qu'est-ce que c'est?
♦ **This is my father.** (*introduction*) Je te présente mon père.
♦ **This is Gavin speaking.** (*on the phone*) C'est Gavin à l'appareil.

thistle NOUN
le <u>chardon</u>

thorough ADJECTIVE
<u>minutieux</u> MASC
<u>minutieuse</u> FEM ◊ *She's very thorough.* Elle est très minutieuse.

thoroughly ADVERB

à fond (*examine*)

those ADJECTIVE, PRONOUN
1 <u>ces</u> ◊ *those shoes* ces chaussures
♦ **THOSE shoes** ces chaussures-là
2 <u>ceux-là</u> MASC ◊ *I want those!* Je veux ceux-là!
<u>celles-là</u> FEM ◊ *I'm looking for some sandals. Can I try those?* Je cherche des sandales. Je peux essayer celles-là?

though CONJUNCTION, ADVERB
<u>bien que</u>

> ***bien que** has to be followed by a verb in the subjunctive.*

◊ *Though it's raining...* Bien qu'il pleuve...
♦ **He's a nice person, though he's not very outgoing.** Il est sympathique, mais pas très extraverti.

thought VERB *see* **think**

thought NOUN
l' <u>idée</u> FEM (*idea*) ◊ *I've just had a thought.* Je viens d'avoir une idée.
♦ **It was a nice thought, thank you.** C'est gentil de ta part, merci.

thoughtful ADJECTIVE
1 (*deep in thought*)
<u>pensif</u> MASC
<u>pensive</u> FEM ◊ *You look thoughtful.* Tu as l'air pensif.
2 <u>prévenant</u> (*considerate*) ◊ *She's very thoughtful.* Elle est très prévenante.

thoughtless ADJECTIVE
♦ **He's completely thoughtless.** Il ne pense absolument pas aux autres.

thousand NUMBER
♦ **a thousand** mille ◊ *a thousand euros* mille euros
♦ **$2000** deux mille dollars
♦ **thousands of people** des milliers de personnes

thousandth ADJECTIVE, NOUN
le <u>millième</u>

thread NOUN
le <u>fil</u>

threat NOUN
la <u>menace</u>

to **threaten** VERB
<u>menacer</u> ◊ *to threaten to do something* menacer de faire quelque chose

three NUMBER
<u>trois</u> ◊ *She's three.* Elle a trois ans.

three-dimensional ADJECTIVE
<u>à trois dimensions</u>

threw VERB *see* **throw**

thrifty ADJECTIVE
économe

thrill NOUN
♦ **What a thrill!** Quelle émotion

thrilled ADJECTIVE
♦ **I was thrilled.** (*pleased*) J'étais absolument ravi.

thrilling ADJECTIVE
palpitant

throat NOUN
la gorge ◊ *to have a sore throat* avoir mal à la gorge

to **throb** VERB
♦ **a throbbing pain** un élancement
♦ **My arm's throbbing.** J'ai des élancements dans le bras.

throne NOUN
le trône

through PREPOSITION, ADJECTIVE, ADVERB
① par ◊ *through the window* par la fenêtre ◊ *I know her through my sister.* Je la connais par ma sœur. ◊ *to go through Winnipeg* passer par Winnipeg
♦ **to go through a tunnel** traverser un tunnel
② à travers ◊ *through the mist* à travers la brume ◊ *through the crowd* à travers la foule ◊ *The window was dirty and I couldn't see through.* La fenêtre était sale et je n'arrivais pas à voir à travers.
♦ **a through train** un train direct
♦ **"no through road"** « impasse »

throughout PREPOSITION
♦ **throughout Nova Scotia** dans toute la Nouvelle-Écosse
♦ **throughout the year** pendant toute l'année

to **throw** VERB
lancer ◊ *She threw the ball to me.* Elle m'a lancé le ballon.
♦ **to throw a party** organiser une soirée
♦ **That really threw him.** Ça l'a décontenancé.
♦ **to throw away (1)** (*garbage*) jeter
♦ **to throw away (2)** (*chance*) perdre
♦ **to throw out (1)** (*throw away*) jeter
♦ **to throw out (2)** (*person*) mettre à la porte ◊ *I threw him out.* Je l'ai mis à la porte.
♦ **to throw up** vomir

thug NOUN
le/la voyou

thumb NOUN
le pouce

thumbtack NOUN
la punaise

thunder NOUN
le tonnerre

thunderstorm NOUN
l' orage MASC

Thursday NOUN
le jeudi ◊ *on Thursday* jeudi ◊ *on Thursdays* le jeudi ◊ *every Thursday* tous les jeudis ◊ *last Thursday* jeudi dernier ◊ *next Thursday* jeudi prochain

thyme NOUN
le thym

tick NOUN

> see also **tick** VERB

le tic-tac (*of clock*)

to **tick** VERB

> see also **tick** NOUN

faire tic-tac (*clock*)

ticket NOUN

> *Be careful to choose correctly between le ticket and le billet.*

① le ticket (*for bus, subway, movie, museum*) ◊ *a subway ticket* un ticket de métro
② le billet (*for plane, train, theatre, concert*)
♦ **a parking ticket** une contravention (pour stationnement)
♦ **a speeding ticket** une contravention pour excès de vitesse

ticket office NOUN
le guichet

to **tickle** VERB
chatouiller

ticklish ADJECTIVE
chatouilleux MASC
chatouilleuse FEM ◊ *Are you ticklish?* Tu es chatouilleux?

to **tick off** VERB
♦ **to tick something off** cocher quelque chose
♦ **to tick somebody off** enguirlander quelqu'un

tide NOUN
la marée
♦ **high tide** la marée haute
♦ **low tide** la marée basse

tidy ADJECTIVE

> see also **tidy** VERB

① bien rangé (*room*) ◊ *Your room's very tidy.* Ta chambre est bien rangée.
② ordonné (*person*) ◊ *She's very tidy.* Elle est très ordonnée.

to **tidy** VERB

> see also **tidy** ADJECTIVE

ranger ◊ *Go and tidy your room.* Va ranger ta chambre.

T

☞

♦ **to tidy up** ranger ◊ *Don't forget to tidy up afterwards.* N'oubliez pas de ranger après.

tie NOUN

> see also **tie** VERB

la cravate (*necktie*)
♦ **It was a tie.** (*in sport*) Ils ont fait match nul.

to **tie** VERB

> see also **tie** NOUN

⏽ nouer (*ribbon, shoelaces*)
♦ **to tie a knot in something** faire un nœud à quelque chose
② faire match nul (*in sport*) ◊ *They tied three all.* Ils ont fait match nul, trois à trois.
♦ **to tie up (1)** (*parcel*) ficeler
♦ **to tie up (2)** (*dog, boat*) attacher
♦ **to tie up (3)** (*prisoner*) ligoter

tiger NOUN
le tigre

tight ADJECTIVE
⏽ moulant(e) (*tight-fitting*) ◊ *tight clothes* les vêtements moulants
② serré(e) (*too tight*) ◊ *These jeans are a bit tight.* Ces jeans sont un peu serrés.

to **tighten** VERB
⏽ tendre (*rope*)
② resserrer (*screw*)

tightly ADVERB
fort (*hold*)

tights PL NOUN
le collant SING

tile NOUN
(*on wall, floor*)
le carreau
(PL les carreaux)

tiled ADJECTIVE
carrelé (*wall, floor, room*)

till NOUN

> see also **till** PREPOSITION

la caisse

till PREPOSITION, CONJUNCTION

> see also **till** NOUN

⏽ jusqu'à ◊ *I waited till ten o'clock.* J'ai attendu jusqu'à dix heures.
♦ **till now** jusqu'à présent
♦ **till then** jusque-là

> Use **avant** if the sentence you want to translate contains a negative, such as "not" or "never".

② avant ◊ *It won't be ready till next week.* Ça ne sera pas prêt avant la semaine prochaine. ◊ *Till last year I'd never been to Gaspé.* Avant l'année dernière, je n'étais jamais allé en Gaspésie.

time NOUN
⏽ l' heure FEM (*on clock*) ◊ *What time is it?* Quelle heure est-il? ◊ *What time do you get up?* À quelle heure tu te lèves? ◊ *It was two o'clock, Vancouver time.* Il était deux heures, heure de Vancouver.
♦ **on time** à l'heure ◊ *She never arrives on time.* Elle n'arrive jamais à l'heure.
② le temps (*amount of time*) ◊ *I'm sorry, I don't have time.* Je suis désolé, je n'ai pas le temps.
♦ **from time to time** de temps en temps
♦ **in time** à temps ◊ *We arrived in time for lunch.* Nous sommes arrivés à temps pour le dîner.
♦ **just in time** juste à temps
♦ **in no time** en un rien de temps ◊ *It was ready in no time.* Ça a été prêt en un rien de temps.
♦ **It's time to go.** Il est temps de partir.
③ le moment (*moment*) ◊ *This isn't a good time to ask him.* Ce n'est pas le bon moment pour lui demander.
♦ **for the time being** pour le moment
④ la fois (*occasion*) ◊ *this time* cette fois-ci ◊ *next time* la prochaine fois ◊ *two at a time* deux à la fois
♦ **How many times?** Combien de fois?
♦ **at times** parfois
♦ **a long time** longtemps ◊ *Have you lived here for a long time?* Vous habitez ici depuis longtemps?
♦ **in a week's time** dans une semaine ◊ *I'll come back in a month's time.* Je reviendrai dans un mois.
♦ **Come and see us any time.** Venez nous voir quand vous voulez.
♦ **to have a good time** bien s'amuser ◊ *Did you have a good time?* Vous vous êtes bien amusés?
♦ **2 times 2 is 4** deux fois deux égalent quatre

time off NOUN
le temps libre

timer NOUN
la minuterie

time-share NOUN
la multipropriété ◊ *We have a time-share ski chalet in Whistler.* Nous avons un chalet de ski en multipropriété à Whistler.

timetable NOUN
l' horaire MASC (*for train, bus, school*)

time zone NOUN
le fuseau horaire ◊ *Canada has six time zones.* Le Canada a six fuseaux horaires.

tin NOUN
l' étain MASC (*type of metal*)

tinsel NOUN
les guirlandes FEM PL

tinted ADJECTIVE
teinté (*spectacles, glass*)

tiny ADJECTIVE
minuscule

tip NOUN

see also **tip** VERB

1 le pourboire (*money*) ◊ *Shall I give him a tip?* Je lui donne un pourboire?
2 le conseil (*advice*) ◊ *a useful tip* un bon conseil (*informal*)
3 le bout (*end*) ◊ *It's on the tip of my tongue.* Je l'ai sur le bout de la langue.

to **tip** VERB

see also **tip** NOUN

donner un pourboire à ◊ *Don't forget to tip the taxi driver.* N'oubliez pas de donner un pourboire a là chauffeuse de taxi.
♦ **to tip over** basculer ◊ *The vase tipped over.* Le vase a basculé.
♦ **to tip something over** faire basculer quelque chose ◊ *She tipped over the vase.* Elle a fait basculer le vase.

tiptoe NOUN
♦ **on tiptoe** sur la pointe des pieds

tire NOUN
le pneu
♦ **tire pressure** la pression des pneus

tired ADJECTIVE
fatigué ◊ *I'm tired.* Je suis fatigué.
♦ **to be tired of something** en avoir assez de quelque chose

tiring ADJECTIVE
fatigant

tissue NOUN
le mouchoir de papier ◊ *Have you got a tissue?* Tu as un mouchoir de papier?

title NOUN
le titre

title role NOUN
le rôle principal

to **to** PREPOSITION

à + le changes to *au. à + les* changes to *aux.*

1 à ◊ *to go to Toronto* aller à Toronto ◊ *to go to school* aller à l'école ◊ *a letter to his mother* une lettre à sa mère ◊ *the answer to the question* la réponse à la question
au ◊ *to go to the movies* aller au cinéma
aux ◊ *We said goodbye to the neighbours.* Nous avons dit au revoir aux voisins.
♦ **ready to go** prêt à partir
♦ **ready to eat** prêt à manger
♦ **It's easy to do.** C'est facile à faire.
♦ **something to drink** quelque chose à boire
♦ **I've got things to do.** J'ai des choses à faire.
♦ **from...to...** de...à... ◊ *from nine o'clock to half past three* de neuf heures à trois heures et demie
2 de ◊ *the train to London* le train de London ◊ *the road to Saskatoon* la route de Saskatoon ◊ *the key to the front door* la clé de la porte d'entrée
♦ **It's difficult to say.** C'est difficile à dire.
♦ **It's easy to criticize.** C'est facile de critiquer.

When referring to someone's house, store or office, use chez.

3 chez ◊ *to go to the doctor's* aller chez le docteur ◊ *Let's go to her house.* Si on allait chez elle?

When to refers to a country which is feminine, use en; when the country is masculine, use au.

4 en ◊ *to go to France* aller en France
au ◊ *to go to Portugal* aller au Portugal
5 jusqu'à (*up to*) ◊ *to count to ten* compter jusqu'à dix
6 pour (*in order to*) ◊ *I did it to help you.* Je l'ai fait pour vous aider. ◊ *He's too young to go to school.* Il est trop jeune pour aller à l'école.

toad NOUN
le crapaud

toadstool NOUN
le champignon vénéneux

toast NOUN
le toast ◊ *a piece of toast with peanut butter* un toast avec du beurre d'arachide

toaster NOUN
le grille-pain
(PL les grille-pain)

tobacco NOUN
le tabac

toboggan NOUN
la traîne sauvage

tobogganing NOUN
♦ **to go tobogganing**
faire de la traîne sauvage

today ADVERB
aujourd'hui ◊ *What did you do today?* Qu'est-ce tu as fait aujourd'hui?

toddler NOUN

T

le **bambin**
la **bambine**

toe NOUN
l' **orteil** MASC

toffee NOUN
le **caramel**

together ADVERB
1 **ensemble** ◊ *Are they still together?*
Ils sont toujours ensemble?
2 **en même temps** (*at the same time*) ◊ *Don't all speak together!* Ne
parlez pas tous en même temps!
♦ **together with** (*with person*) avec

toilet NOUN
la **toilette**

toilet paper NOUN
le **papier hygiénique**

toiletries PL NOUN
les **articles de toilette** MASC

told VERB *see* **tell**

tolerant ADJECTIVE
tolérant

toll booth NOUN
le **poste de péage** (*on bridge, highway*)

tomato NOUN
la **tomate** ◊ *tomato sauce* la sauce
tomate ◊ *tomato soup* la soupe aux
tomates

tomorrow ADVERB
demain ◊ *tomorrow morning* demain
matin ◊ *tomorrow night* demain soir
♦ **the day after tomorrow** après-demain

ton NOUN
♦ **a ton of homework** un tas de devoirs

tongue NOUN
la **langue**
♦ **to say something tongue in cheek**
dire quelque chose en plaisantant

tonic NOUN
le **soda tonique** (*tonic water*)

tonight ADVERB
1 **ce soir** (*this evening*) ◊ *Are you
going out tonight?* Tu sors ce soir?
2 **cette nuit** (*during the night*) ◊ *I'll
sleep well tonight.* Je dormirai bien
cette nuit.

tonne NOUN
la **tonne**

tonsillitis NOUN
l' **amygdalite** FEM

tonsils PL NOUN
les **amygdales** FEM

too ADVERB, ADJECTIVE
1 **aussi** (*as well*) ◊ *My sister came
too.* Ma sœur est venue aussi.
2 **trop** (*excessively*) ◊ *The water's*

too hot. L'eau est trop chaude. ◊ *We
arrived too late.* Nous sommes arrivés
trop tard.
♦ **too much (1)** (*with noun*) trop de
◊ *too much noise* trop de bruit
♦ **too much (2)** (*with verb*) trop ◊ *He
talks too much.* Il parle trop.
♦ **too much (3)** (*too expensive*) trop
cher ◊ *Fifty dollars? That's too much.*
Cinquante dollars? C'est trop cher.
♦ **too many** trop de ◊ *too many
hamburgers* trop de hamburgers
♦ **too bad!** tant pis!

took VERB *see* **take**

tool NOUN
l' **outil** MASC
♦ **a tool box** une boîte à outils

toolbar NOUN
la **barre d'outils**

✳ **toonie** NOUN
le **deux dollars**

tooth NOUN
la **dent**

toothache NOUN
le **mal de dents** ◊ *to have a
toothache* avoir mal aux dents

toothbrush NOUN
la **brosse à dents**

toothpaste NOUN
le **dentifrice**

top NOUN

see also **top** ADJECTIVE

1 le **haut** (*of page, ladder, garment*)
◊ *at the top of the page* en haut de
la page
♦ **a bikini top** un haut de bikini
2 le **sommet** (*of mountain*)
3 le **dessus** (*of table*)
♦ **on top of** (*on*) sur ◊ *on top of the
fridge* sur le frigo
♦ **to be on top of things** avoir la
situation bien en main
♦ **There's tax on top of that.** Il y a de la
taxe en plus.
♦ **from top to bottom** de fond en
comble ◊ *I searched the house from
top to bottom.* J'ai fouillé la maison
de fond en comble.
4 le **couvercle** (*of box, jar*)
5 le **bouchon** (*of bottle*)

top ADJECTIVE

see also **top** NOUN

grand (*first-class*) ◊ *a top surgeon*
une grande chirurgienne
♦ **a top model** un mannequin vedette
♦ **He always gets top marks in French.**
Il a toujours d'excellentes notes en
français.
♦ **the top floor** le dernier étage ◊ *on the*

top floor au dernier étage

topic NOUN
le <u>sujet</u> ◊ *The essay can be on any topic.* Cette dissertation peut être sur n'importe quel sujet.

topical ADJECTIVE
<u>d'actualité</u> ◊ *a topical issue* un sujet d'actualité

top-secret ADJECTIVE
<u>très secret</u> MASC
<u>très secrète</u> FEM ◊ *top-secret documents* des documents très secrets

tore, torn VERB *see* **tear**

tortoise NOUN
la <u>tortue</u>

torture NOUN

   see also **torture** VERB

la <u>torture</u> ◊ *It was pure torture.* C'était une vraie torture.

to **torture** VERB

   see also **torture** NOUN

<u>torturer</u> ◊ *Stop torturing that poor animal!* Arrête de torturer ce pauvre animal!

to **toss** VERB
<u>lancer</u>
♦ **to toss a salad** brasser une salade
♦ **Shall we toss for it?** On joue à pile ou face?
♦ **I tossed and turned all night.** Je n'ai pas arrêté de me tourner et de me retourner toute la nuit.

total ADJECTIVE

   see also **total** NOUN

<u>total</u>
(MASC PL totaux)
♦ **the total amount** le total

total NOUN

   see also **total** ADJECTIVE

le <u>total</u>
(PL les totaux)
♦ **the grand total** le total

totally ADVERB
<u>complètement</u> ◊ *This thing is totally useless.* Cette chose est complètement inutile.

touch NOUN

   see also **touch** VERB

♦ **to get in touch with somebody** prendre contact avec quelqu'un
♦ **to keep in touch with somebody** ne pas perdre contact avec quelqu'un
♦ **Keep in touch!** Donne-moi de tes nouvelles!
♦ **to lose touch** se perdre de vue
♦ **to lose touch with somebody** perdre

quelqu'un de vue

to **touch** VERB

   see also **touch** NOUN

<u>toucher</u>
♦ **Don't touch that!** N'y touche pas!

touchdown NOUN
l' <u>essai</u> MASC (*football*)

touched ADJECTIVE
<u>touché</u> ◊ *I was really touched.* Ça m'a beaucoup touché.

touching ADJECTIVE
<u>touchant</u>

touchpad NOUN
le <u>bloc à effleurement</u>

touchy ADJECTIVE
<u>susceptible</u> ◊ *She's a bit touchy.* Elle est susceptible.

tough ADJECTIVE
1 <u>dur</u> ◊ *It was tough, but I managed OK.* C'était dur, mais je m'en suis tiré. ◊ *It's a tough job.* C'est dur.
♦ **The meat's tough.** La viande est coriace.
2 <u>solide</u> (*strong*) ◊ *tough leather gloves* de solides gants en cuir ◊ *She's tough. She can take it.* Elle est solide. Elle tiendra le coup.
3 (*rough, violent*)
<u>dangereux</u> MASC
<u>dangereuse</u> FEM
♦ **He thinks he's a tough guy.** Il se prend pour un dur.
♦ **Tough luck!** C'est comme ça!

toupee NOUN
le <u>postiche</u>

tour NOUN

   see also **tour** VERB

1 le <u>tour</u> (*of town, museum*) ◊ *We went on a tour of the city.* Nous avons fait le tour de la ville.
♦ **a guided tour** une visite guidée
♦ **a package tour** un voyage organisé
2 la <u>tournée</u> (*by singer, group*) ◊ *on tour* en tournée
♦ **to go on tour** faire une tournée

to **tour** VERB

   see also **tour** NOUN

♦ **Ashley MacIsaac is touring Europe.** (*singer, artiste*) Ashley MacIsaac est en tournée en Europe.

tour guide NOUN
le/la <u>guide</u>

tourism NOUN
le <u>tourisme</u>

tourist NOUN
le/la <u>touriste</u>
♦ **tourist information office** le bureau d'information touristique

T

tournament NOUN
le tournoi

towards PREPOSITION
1 vers (*in the direction of*) ◊ *She came towards me.* Elle est venue vers moi.
2 envers (*of attitude*) ◊ *my feelings towards him* mes sentiments à son égard

towel NOUN
la serviette

tower NOUN
la tour

town NOUN
la ville ◊ *We went into town.* Nous sommes allés en ville.
♦ **the town centre** le centre-ville
♦ **the town hall** la mairie

tow truck NOUN
la dépanneuse

toy NOUN
le jouet ◊ *a toy store* un magasin de jouets
♦ **a toy car** une petite voiture

trace NOUN
see also **trace** VERB
la trace ◊ *There was no trace of the robbers.* Il n'y avait pas de trace des voleurs.

to **trace** VERB
see also **trace** NOUN
décalquer (*draw*)

tracing paper NOUN
le papier calque

track NOUN
1 le chemin (*dirt road*)
2 la voie ferrée (*railway line*)
3 la piste (*sports*) ◊ *two laps of the track* deux tours de piste
4 la chanson (*song*) ◊ *This is my favourite track on the CD.* C'est ma chanson préférée sur le CD.
5 les traces FEM PL (*trail*) ◊ *They followed the tracks for miles.* Ils ont suivi les traces pendant des kilomètres.

to **track down** VERB
♦ **to track somebody down** retrouver quelqu'un ◊ *The police never tracked down the killer.* La police n'a jamais retrouvé l'assassin.

track and field NOUN
l' athlétisme MASC

tracksuit NOUN
le survêtement

tractor NOUN
le tracteur

trade NOUN
see also **trade** VERB
1 le commerce ◊ *international trade* le commerce international
2 le métier (*skill, job*) ◊ *to learn a trade* apprendre un métier

to **trade** VERB
see also **trade** NOUN
1 échanger ◊ *Want to trade your apple for this orange?* Veux-tu échanger ta pomme contre cette orange?
2 faire du commerce ◊ *Canada trades with many countries.* Le Canada fait du commerce avec de nombreux pays.

tradition NOUN
la tradition

traditional ADJECTIVE
traditionnel MASC
traditionnelle FEM

traffic NOUN
la circulation ◊ *The traffic was terrible.* Il y avait une circulation épouvantable.

traffic jam NOUN
l' embouteillage MASC

traffic lights PL NOUN
les feux MASC

tragedy NOUN
la tragédie

tragic ADJECTIVE
tragique

trailer NOUN
1 la remorque (*vehicle*)
2 la bande-annonce (*for movie*)

train NOUN
see also **train** VERB
1 le train
2 la rame (*on subway*)

to **train** VERB
see also **train** NOUN
s'entraîner (*sports*) ◊ *to train for a race* s'entraîner pour une course
♦ **to train as a teacher** suivre une formation d'enseignant
♦ **to train an animal to do something** dresser un animal à faire quelque chose

trained ADJECTIVE
♦ **She's a trained nurse.** Elle est infirmière diplômée.

trainee NOUN
1 le/la stagiaire (*in profession*) ◊ *He's a trainee.* Il est stagiaire.
2 (*apprentice*)
l' apprenti MASC

l' apprentie FEM

trainer NOUN
  ① (*sports coach*)
  l' entraîneur MASC
  l' entraîneure FEM
  ② (*of animals*)
  le dompteur
  la dompteuse

training NOUN
  ① la formation ◊ *a training course* un stage de formation
  ② l' entraînement MASC (*sports*)

trampoline NOUN
  le trampoline

tranquillizer NOUN
  le tranquillisant ◊ *He's on tranquillizers.* Il prend des tranquillisants.

Trans-Canada highway NOUN
  la Transcanadienne

transfer NOUN
  ① le décalque (*sticker*)
  ② le transfert ◊ *a job transfer* un transfert d'emploi

transfusion NOUN
  la transfusion

transit NOUN
  le transit ◊ *in transit* en transit
  ♦ **public transit** les transports publics
  ♦ **the transit system** le système de transport

to **translate** VERB
  traduire ◊ *to translate something into English* traduire quelque chose en anglais

translation NOUN
  la traduction

translator NOUN
  le traducteur
  la traductrice ◊ *She's a translator.* Elle est traductrice.

transparency NOUN
  le transparent ◊ *Put the transparency on the overhead projector.* Mets le transparent dans le rétroprojecteur.

transparent ADJECTIVE
  transparent

transplant NOUN
  la greffe ◊ *a heart transplant* une greffe du cardiaque

transport NOUN
  see also **transport** VERB
  le transport ◊ *public transport* les transports publics

to **transport** VERB
  see also **transport** NOUN
  transporter

trap NOUN
  le piège

trapeze NOUN
  le trapèze
  ♦ **trapeze artist** le/la trapéziste

trash NOUN
  les ordures FEM PL
  ♦ **the trash can** la poubelle

traumatic ADJECTIVE
  traumatisant ◊ *It was a traumatic experience.* Ça a été une expérience traumatisante.

to **traumatize** VERB
  traumatiser

travel NOUN
  see also **travel** VERB
  les voyages MASC PL

to **travel** VERB
  see also **travel** NOUN
  voyager ◊ *I prefer to travel by plane.* Je préfère voyager en avion.
  ♦ **I'd like to travel around the world.** J'aimerais faire le tour du monde.
  ♦ **We travelled over 800 kilometres.** Nous avons fait plus de huit cents kilomètres.
  ♦ **News travels fast!** Les nouvelles circulent vite!

travel agency NOUN
  l' agence de voyages FEM

travel agent NOUN
  l' agent de voyages MASC
  l' agente de voyages FEM

traveller NOUN
  le voyageur
  la voyageuse

traveller's cheque NOUN
  le chèque de voyage

travelling NOUN
  ♦ **I love travelling.** J'adore les voyages.

travel sickness NOUN
  le mal des transports

tray NOUN
  le plateau
  (PL les plateaux)

treasure NOUN
  le trésor

treat NOUN
  see also **treat** VERB
  la gâterie (*food*)
  ♦ **to give somebody a treat** (*not food*) faire plaisir à quelqu'un

to **treat** VERB
  see also **treat** NOUN
  traiter (*well, badly*)
  ♦ **to treat somebody to something**

T

☞

offrir quelque chose à quelqu'un ◊ *He treated us to an ice cream.* Il nous a offert une crème glacée.

treatment NOUN
le <u>traitement</u>

treaty NOUN
le <u>traité</u>

tree NOUN
l' <u>arbre</u> MASC

to **tremble** VERB
<u>trembler</u>

tremendous ADJECTIVE
<u>énorme</u> ◊ *a tremendous success* un succès énorme

trend NOUN
la <u>mode</u> (*fashion*)

trendy ADJECTIVE
<u>branché</u>

trial NOUN
le <u>procès</u> (*in court*)

triangle NOUN
le <u>triangle</u>

trick NOUN

see also **trick** VERB

1 le <u>tour</u> ◊ *to play a trick on somebody* jouer un tour à quelqu'un
2 le <u>truc</u> FEM (*knack*) ◊ *It's not easy: there's a trick to it.* Ce n'est pas facile: il y a un truc.

to **trick** VERB

see also **trick** NOUN

♦ **to trick somebody** rouler quelqu'un

tricky ADJECTIVE
<u>délicat</u>

to **trim** VERB

see also **trim** NOUN

1 <u>égaliser</u> (*hair*)
2 <u>tondre</u> (*grass*)

trim NOUN

see also **trim** VERB

la <u>coupe d'entretien</u> (*haircut*) ◊ *to get a trim* se faire faire une coupe d'entretien

trip NOUN

see also **trip** VERB

le <u>voyage</u> ◊ *to go on a trip* faire un voyage ◊ *Have a good trip!* Bon voyage!
♦ **a day trip** une excursion d'une journée

to **trip** VERB

see also **trip** NOUN

<u>trébucher</u> (*stumble*)

triple ADJECTIVE

see also **triple** VERB

<u>triple</u>

to **triple** VERB

see also **triple** ADJECTIVE

<u>tripler</u>

triplets PL NOUN
les <u>triplés</u> MASC (*boys*)
les <u>triplées</u> FEM (*girls*)

trivial ADJECTIVE
<u>insignifiant</u>

trombone NOUN
le <u>trombone</u> ◊ *I play the trombone.* Je joue du trombone.

troops PL NOUN
les <u>troupes</u> FEM ◊ *Canadian troops* les troupes canadiennes

trophy NOUN
le <u>trophée</u> ◊ *to win a trophy* gagner un trophée

tropical ADJECTIVE
<u>tropical</u> ◊ *The weather was tropical.* Il faisait une chaleur tropicale.

tropics PL NOUN
les <u>tropiques</u> MASC ◊ *in the tropics* sous les tropiques

to **trot** VERB
<u>trotter</u>

trouble NOUN
le <u>problème</u> ◊ *The trouble is, it's too expensive.* Le problème, c'est que c'est trop cher.
♦ **to be in trouble** avoir des ennuis
♦ **What's the trouble?** Qu'est-ce qui ne va pas?
♦ **stomach trouble** troubles gastriques
♦ **to take a lot of trouble over something** se donner beaucoup de mal pour quelque chose
♦ **Don't worry, it's no trouble.** Mais non, ça ne me dérange pas du tout.

troublemaker NOUN
le <u>perturbateur</u>
la <u>perturbatrice</u>

trout NOUN
la <u>truite</u>

truck NOUN
le <u>camion</u>

trucker NOUN
le <u>camionneur</u>
la <u>camionneuse</u>

true ADJECTIVE
<u>vrai</u>
♦ **That's true.** C'est vrai.
♦ **to come true** se réaliser ◊ *I hope my dream will come true.* J'espère que mon rêve se réalisera.
♦ **true love** le grand amour

truly ADVERB
vraiment ◊ *It was a truly remarkable victory.* C'était vraiment une victoire remarquable.
♦ **Yours truly.** Je vous prie d'agréer mes salutations distinguées.

trumpet NOUN
la trompette ◊ *She plays the trumpet.* Elle joue de la trompette.

trunk NOUN
1 le tronc (*of tree*)
2 la trompe (*of elephant*)
3 le coffre (*of car*)

trust NOUN
see also **trust** VERB
la confiance ◊ *to have trust in somebody* avoir confiance en quelqu'un

to **trust** VERB
see also **trust** NOUN
♦ **to trust somebody** faire confiance à quelqu'un ◊ *Don't you trust me?* Tu ne me fais pas confiance? ◊ *Trust me!* Fais-moi confiance!

trusting ADJECTIVE
confiant

truth NOUN
la vérité

truthful ADJECTIVE
♦ **She's a very truthful person.** Elle dit toujours la vérité.

try NOUN
see also **try** VERB
l' essai MASC ◊ *his third try* son troisième essai
♦ **to have a try** essayer
♦ **It's worth a try.** Ça vaut la peine d'essayer.
♦ **to give something a try** essayer quelque chose

to **try** VERB
see also **try** NOUN
1 essayer (*attempt*) ◊ *to try to do something* essayer de faire quelque chose
♦ **to try again** refaire un essai
2 goûter (*taste*) ◊ *Would you like to try some?* Voulez-vous goûter?
♦ **to try on** essayer (*clothes*)
♦ **to try something out** essayer quelque chose

T-shirt NOUN
le T-shirt

tube NOUN
le tube

tuberculosis NOUN
la tuberculose

Tuesday NOUN
le mardi ◊ *on Tuesday* mardi ◊ *on Tuesdays* le mardi ◊ *every Tuesday* tous les mardis ◊ *last Tuesday* mardi dernier ◊ *next Tuesday* mardi prochain

tug-of-war NOUN
la lutte à la corde

tulip NOUN
la tulipe

tuna NOUN
le thon
♦ **tuna salad** la salade de thon

tundra NOUN
la toundra

tune NOUN
see also **tune** VERB
l' air MASC (*melody*)
♦ **to play in tune** jouer juste
♦ **to sing out of tune** chanter faux

to **tune** VERB
see also **tune** NOUN
1 accorder (*instrument*) ◊ *You need to tune your guitar.* Il faut que tu accordes ta guitare.
2 syntoniser (*radio*) ◊ *I tuned the radio to CBC.* J'ai syntonisé la radio sur Radio-Canada.

tunnel NOUN
le tunnel

tuque NOUN
la tuque

turkey NOUN
1 la dinde (*meat*)
2 le dindon (*live bird*)

turn NOUN
see also **turn** VERB
1 le tournant (*bend in road*)
♦ **"no left turn"** « défense de tourner à gauche »
2 le tour (*in game*) ◊ *It's my turn!* C'est à mon tour!

to **turn** VERB
see also **turn** NOUN
1 tourner ◊ *Turn right at the lights.* Tournez à droite aux feux.
2 devenir (*become*) ◊ *to turn red* devenir rouge
♦ **to turn into something** se transformer en quelque chose ◊ *The frog turned into a prince.* La grenouille s'est transformée en prince.

to **turn around** VERB
1 faire demi-tour (*car*)
2 se retourner (*person*)

to **turn back** VERB
faire demi-tour ◊ *We turned back.*

T

Nous avons fait demi-tour.

to **turn down** VERB
① refuser (*offer*)
② baisser (*radio, TV, heating*) ◊ *Shall I turn the heating down?* Je baisse le chauffage?

to **turn off** VERB
① éteindre (*light, radio*)
② fermer (*tap*)
③ arrêter (*engine*)

to **turn on** VERB
① allumer (*light, radio*)
② ouvrir (*tap*)
③ mettre en marche (*engine*)

to **turn out** VERB
♦ **It turned out to be a mistake.** Il s'est avéré que c'était une erreur.
♦ **It turned out that she was right.** Il s'est avéré qu'elle avait raison.

to **turn up** VERB
① arriver (*arrive*)
② monter (*increase*)
♦ **Could you turn up the radio?** Tu peux monter le son de la radio?

turnip NOUN
le navet

turquoise ADJECTIVE
(*colour*)
turquoise MASC, FEM, PL

turtle NOUN
la tortue

tutor NOUN
(*private teacher*)
le professeur particulier
la professeure particulière

TV NOUN
la télé

tweezers PL NOUN
la pince à épiler SING

twelfth ADJECTIVE
douzième ◊ *the twelfth floor* le douzième étage
♦ **the twelfth of August** le douze août

twelve NUMBER
douze ◊ *He's twelve.* Il a douze ans.
♦ **twelve o'clock (1)** (*midday*) midi
♦ **twelve o'clock (2)** (*midnight*) minuit

twentieth ADJECTIVE
vingtième ◊ *the twentieth time* la vingtième fois
♦ **the twentieth of May** le vingt mai

twenty NUMBER
vingt ◊ *He's twenty.* Il a vingt ans.

twice ADVERB
deux fois
♦ **twice as much** deux fois plus ◊ *He gets twice as much allowance as me.* Il a deux fois plus d'argent de poche que moi.

twin NOUN
le jumeau (*boy*)
la jumelle (*girl*)
(PL les jumeaux)
(FEM PL les jumelles)
♦ **my twin brother** mon frère jumeau
♦ **her twin sister** sa sœur jumelle
♦ **identical twins** les vrais jumeaux
♦ **a twin room** une chambre à deux lits

twinned ADJECTIVE
jumelé ◊ *Banff is twinned with Obama-cho.* Banff est jumelée avec Obama-cho.

to **twist** VERB
① tordre (*bend*)
② déformer (*distort*) ◊ *You're twisting my words.* Tu déformes ce que j'ai dit.

two NUMBER
deux ◊ *She's two.* Elle a deux ans.

type NOUN
see also **type** VERB
le type ◊ *What type of camera do you have?* Quel type d'appareil photo as-tu?

to **type** VERB
see also **type** NOUN
taper ◊ *Type your password.* Tape ton mot de passe.

typical ADJECTIVE
typique ◊ *That's just typical!* C'est typique!

tyrant NOUN
le tyran ◊ *He's a real tyrant.* C'est un vrai tyran.

U

UFO NOUN
l' <u>OVNI</u> MASC (= objet volant non identifié)

ugh EXCLAMATION
✻ <u>yark!</u>

ugly ADJECTIVE
<u>laid</u>

ulcer NOUN
l' <u>ulcère</u> MASC

ultimate ADJECTIVE
<u>suprême</u> ◊ *the ultimate challenge* le défi suprême
♦ **It was the ultimate adventure.** C'était la grande aventure.

ultimately ADVERB
<u>au bout du compte</u> ◊ *Ultimately, it's your decision.* Au bout du compte, c'est votre décision.

umbrella NOUN
① le <u>parapluie</u>
② le <u>parasol</u> (*for sun*)

umpire NOUN
l' <u>arbitre</u> MASC/FEM

UN NOUN
l' <u>ONU</u> FEM (= Organisation des Nations unies)

unable ADJECTIVE
♦ **to be unable to do something** ne pas pouvoir faire quelque chose ◊ *I was unable to come.* Je n'ai pas pu venir.

unacceptable ADJECTIVE
<u>inacceptable</u>

unanimous ADJECTIVE
<u>unanime</u> ◊ *a unanimous decision* une décision unanime

unattended ADJECTIVE
♦ **to leave something unattended** laisser quelque chose sans surveillance
<u>laissé sans surveillance</u> ◊ *Never leave pets unattended in your car.* Ne laisser jamais d'animaux domestiques sans surveillance dans votre voiture.

unavoidable ADJECTIVE
<u>inévitable</u>

unaware ADJECTIVE
♦ **to be unaware (1)** (*not know about*) ignorer ◊ *I was unaware of the rules.* J'ignorais le règlement.
♦ **to be unaware (2)** (*not notice*) ne pas se rendre compte ◊ *She was unaware that she was being filmed.* Elle ne s'était pas rendu compte qu'on la filmait.

unbearable ADJECTIVE
<u>insupportable</u>

unbeatable ADJECTIVE
<u>imbattable</u>

unbelievable ADJECTIVE
<u>incroyable</u>

unborn ADJECTIVE
♦ **the unborn child** le fœtus

unbreakable ADJECTIVE
<u>incassable</u>

uncanny ADJECTIVE
<u>étrange</u> ◊ *That's uncanny!* C'est étrange!
♦ **an uncanny resemblance** une ressemblance troublante

uncertain ADJECTIVE
<u>incertain</u> ◊ *The future is uncertain.* L'avenir est incertain.
♦ **to be uncertain about something** ne pas être sûr de quelque chose

uncivilized ADJECTIVE
<u>barbare</u>

uncle NOUN
l' <u>oncle</u> MASC ◊ *my uncle* mon oncle

uncomfortable ADJECTIVE
① <u>mal à l'aise</u> (*person*) ◊ *I feel uncomfortable at their house.* Je me sens mal à l'aise chez eux.
② <u>pas confortable</u> ◊ *The seats are rather uncomfortable.* Les sièges ne sont pas très confortables.

unconscious ADJECTIVE
<u>sans connaissance</u>

uncontrollable ADJECTIVE
<u>incontrôlable</u>

unconventional ADJECTIVE
<u>peu conventionnel</u> MASC
<u>peu conventionnelle</u> FEM

under PREPOSITION
① <u>sous</u> ◊ *The cat's under the table.* Le chat est sous la table. ◊ *The tunnel goes under the Fraser River.* Le tunnel passe sous le fleuve Fraser.
♦ **under there** là-dessous ◊ *What's under there?* Qu'est-ce qu'il y a là-dessous?
② <u>moins de</u> (*less than*) ◊ *under 20 people* moins de vingt personnes ◊ *children under 10* les enfants de moins de dix ans

undercover ADJECTIVE, ADVERB

☞

secret MASC
secrète FEM ◊ *an undercover agent*
🗱 un agent d'infiltration
♦ **He was working undercover.** Il travaillait sous une fausse identité.

to **underestimate** VERB
sous-estimer ◊ *I underestimated her.* Je l'ai sous-estimée.

to **undergo** VERB
subir (*operation, examination, change*)
♦ **to be undergoing repairs** être en réparation

underground ADJECTIVE, ADVERB
1 souterrain ◊ *an underground parking garage* un stationnement souterrain
2 sous terre ◊ *Moles live underground.* Les taupes vivent sous terre.

to **underline** VERB
souligner

underneath PREPOSITION, ADVERB
1 sous ◊ *underneath the carpet* sous le tapis
2 dessous ◊ *I got out of the car and looked underneath.* Je suis descendu de la voiture et j'ai regardé dessous.

underpaid ADJECTIVE
sous-payé ◊ *I'm underpaid.* Je suis sous-payé.

underpants PL NOUN
1 la culotte (*women's*)
2 le caleçon (*men's*)
🗱 3 les bobettes (*all kinds, informal*)

undershirt NOUN
🗱 la camisole

to **understand** VERB
comprendre ◊ *Do you understand?* Vous comprenez? ◊ *I don't understand this word.* Je ne comprends pas ce mot. ◊ *Is that understood?* C'est compris?

understanding ADJECTIVE
compréhensif MASC
compréhensive FEM ◊ *She's very understanding.* Elle est très compréhensive.

understood VERB *see* **understand**

undertaker NOUN
1 (*mortician*)
l' embaumeur MASC
l' embaumeuse FEM
🗱 2 (*funeral home director*)
le directeur de salon funéraire
la directrice de salon funéraire

underwater ADJECTIVE, ADVERB
sous l'eau ◊ *This sequence was filmed underwater.* Cette séquence a été filmée sous l'eau.
♦ **an underwater camera** un appareil photographique sous-marin
♦ **underwater photography** la photographie sous-marine

underwear NOUN
les sous-vêtements MASC PL

underwent VERB *see* **undergo**

to **undo** VERB
défaire (*buttons, knot*)

to **undress** VERB
se déshabiller (*get undressed*)
◊ *The doctor told me to undress.* Le médecin m'a dit de me déshabiller.

unemployed ADJECTIVE
au chômage ◊ *He's unemployed.* Il est au chômage. ◊ *I've been unemployed for a year.* Ça fait un an que je suis au chômage.
♦ **the unemployed** les chômeurs MASC

unemployment NOUN
le chômage

unexpected ADJECTIVE
inattendu ◊ *an unexpected visitor* un visiteur inattendu

unexpectedly ADVERB
à l'improviste ◊ *They arrived unexpectedly.* Ils sont arrivés à l'improviste.

unfair ADJECTIVE
injuste ◊ *It's unfair to everybody.* C'est injuste pour tout le monde.

unfamiliar ADJECTIVE
♦ **I heard an unfamiliar voice.** J'ai entendu une voix que je ne connaissais pas.

to **unfold** VERB
déplier ◊ *She unfolded the map.* Elle a déplié la carte.

unforgettable ADJECTIVE
inoubliable

unfortunately ADVERB
malheureusement ◊ *Unfortunately, I arrived late.* Malheureusement, je suis arrivé en retard.

unfriendly ADJECTIVE
pas aimable ◊ *The waiters are a bit unfriendly.* Les serveurs ne sont pas très aimables.

ungrateful ADJECTIVE
ingrat

unhappy ADJECTIVE
malheureux MASC
malheureuse FEM ◊ *He was very unhappy as a child.* Il était très malheureux quand il était petit.
♦ **to look unhappy** avoir l'air triste

unhealthy ADJECTIVE
1 (*person*)
maladif MASC
maladive FEM
2 malsain (*place, habit*)
3 pas sain (*food*)

uniform NOUN
l' uniforme MASC ◊ *the school uniform*
l'uniforme scolaire

unilingual ADJECTIVE
unilingue

uninhabited ADJECTIVE
inhabité

union NOUN
le syndicat (*trade union*)

unique ADJECTIVE
unique

unit NOUN
1 l' unité FEM ◊ *a unit of measurement* une unité de mesure
2 l' élément MASC (*piece of furniture*)
◊ *a kitchen unit* un élément de cuisine

United Nations NOUN
l' O.N.U. FEM (= Organisation des Nations Unies)

universe NOUN
l' univers MASC

university NOUN
l' université FEM ◊ *She's in university.*
Elle va à l'université. ◊ *Do you want to go to university?* Tu veux aller à l'université?

unleaded ADJECTIVE
sans plomb

unless CONJUNCTION
♦ **unless he leaves** à moins qu'il ne parte ◊ *I won't come unless you phone me.* Je ne viendrai pas à moins que tu ne me téléphones.

unlike PREPOSITION
contrairement à ◊ *Unlike him, I really enjoy flying.* Contrairement à lui, j'adore prendre l'avion.

unlikely ADJECTIVE
peu probable ◊ *It's possible, but unlikely.* C'est possible, mais peu probable.

unlisted ADJECTIVE
♦ **an unlisted number** un numéro confidentiel

to **unload** VERB
décharger ◊ *We unloaded the car.*
Nous avons déchargé la voiture.
◊ *The trucks go there to unload.* Les camions y vont pour être déchargés.

to **unlock** VERB
ouvrir ◊ *She unlocked the door of the car.* Elle a ouvert la portière de la voiture.

unlucky ADJECTIVE
♦ **to be unlucky (1)** (*number, object*)
porter malheur ◊ *They say thirteen is an unlucky number.* On dit que le nombre treize porte malheur.
♦ **to be unlucky (2)** (*person*) ne pas avoir de chance ◊ *"Did you win?"*
"No, I was unlucky." « Vous avez gagné? » « Non, je n'ai pas eu de chance. »

unmarried ADJECTIVE
célibataire (*person*) ◊ *an unmarried mother* une mère célibataire
♦ **an unmarried couple** un couple non marié

unnatural ADJECTIVE
pas naturel MASC
pas naturelle FEM

unnecessary ADJECTIVE
inutile

unofficial ADJECTIVE
(*meeting, leader*)
non officiel MASC
non officielle FEM

to **unpack** VERB
1 défaire ◊ *I unpacked my suitcase.*
J'ai défait ma valise.
2 déballer ses affaires ◊ *I went to my room to unpack.* Je suis allé dans ma chambre pour déballer mes affaires. ◊ *I haven't unpacked my clothes yet.* Je n'ai pas encore déballé mes vêtements.

unpleasant ADJECTIVE
désagréable

to **unplug** VERB
débrancher

unpopular ADJECTIVE
impopulaire

unpredictable ADJECTIVE
imprévisible

unreal ADJECTIVE
incroyable (*incredible*) ◊ *It was unreal!* C'était incroyable!

unrealistic ADJECTIVE
peu réaliste

unreasonable ADJECTIVE
pas raisonnable ◊ *Her attitude was completely unreasonable.*
Son attitude n'était pas du tout raisonnable.

unreliable ADJECTIVE
pas fiable (*car, machine*) ◊ *It's a nice car, but a bit unreliable.* C'est une belle voiture, mais elle n'est pas très fiable.
♦ **He's completely unreliable.** On ne peut pas du tout compter sur lui.

U

to **unroll** VERB
dérouler

unsatisfactory ADJECTIVE
insatisfaisant

to **unscrew** VERB
dévisser ◊ *She unscrewed the top of the bottle.* Elle a dévissé le bouchon de la bouteille.

unshaven ADJECTIVE
mal rasé

unstable ADJECTIVE
instable

unsteady ADJECTIVE
mal assuré (*walk, voice*)
♦ **He was unsteady on his feet.** Il marchait d'un pas mal assuré.

unsuccessful ADJECTIVE
vain (*attempt*)
♦ **to be unsuccessful in doing something** ne pas réussir à faire quelque chose ◊ *an unsuccessful artist* un artiste qui n'a pas réussi

unsuitable ADJECTIVE
inapproprié (*clothes, equipment*)

untidy ADJECTIVE
① en désordre ◊ *My bedroom's always untidy.* Ma chambre est toujours en désordre.
② débraillé (*appearance, person*) ◊ *He's always untidy.* Il est toujours débraillé.
③ désordonné (*in character*) ◊ *She's a very untidy person.* Elle est très désordonnée.

to **untie** VERB
① défaire (*knot, parcel*)
② détacher (*animal*)

until PREPOSITION, CONJUNCTION
① jusqu'à ◊ *I waited until ten o'clock.* J'ai attendu jusqu'à dix heures.
♦ **until now** jusqu'à présent ◊ *It's never been a problem until now.* Ça n'a jamais été un problème jusqu'à présent.
♦ **until then** jusque-là ◊ *Until then I'd never been to Quebec.* Jusque-là je n'étais jamais allé au Québec.

*Use **avant** if the sentence you want to translate contains a negative, such as "not" or "never".*

② avant ◊ *It won't be ready until next week.* Ça ne sera pas prêt avant la semaine prochaine. ◊ *Until last year I'd never been to New Brunswick.* Avant l'année dernière, je n'étais jamais allé au Nouveau-Brunswick.

unusual ADJECTIVE
① insolite ◊ *an unusual shape* une forme insolite

② rare ◊ *It's unusual to get snow at this time of year.* Il est rare qu'il neige à cette époque de l'année.

unwilling ADJECTIVE
♦ **to be unwilling to do something** ne pas être disposé à faire quelque chose ◊ *He was unwilling to help me.* Il n'était pas disposé à m'aider.

to **unwind** VERB
se détendre (*relax*)

unwise ADJECTIVE
imprudent (*person*) ◊ *That was rather unwise of you.* C'était plutôt imprudent de votre part.

unwound VERB *see* **unwind**

to **unwrap** VERB
déballer ◊ *After the meal we unwrapped the presents.* Après le repas, nous avons déballé les cadeaux.

up PREPOSITION, ADVERB

*For other expressions with **up**, see the verbs **go, come, put, turn** etc.*

en haut ◊ *up on the hill* en haut de la colline
♦ **up here** ici
♦ **up there** là-haut
♦ **up north** dans le nord
♦ **to be up** être debout (*out of bed*) ◊ *We were up at 6.* Nous étions debout à six heures. ◊ *He's not up yet.* Il n'est pas encore debout.
♦ **What's up?** Qu'est-ce qu'il y a? ◊ *What's up with him?* Qu'est-ce qu'il a?
♦ **to get up** (*in the morning*) se lever ◊ *What time do you get up?* À quelle heure est-ce que tu te lèves?
♦ **to go up** monter ◊ *The bus went up the hill.* L'autobus a monté la colline.
♦ **to go up to somebody** s'approcher de quelqu'un ◊ *She came up to me.* Elle s'est approchée de moi.
♦ **up to** (*as far as*) jusqu'à ◊ *to count up to fifty* compter jusqu'à cinquante ◊ *up to three hours* jusqu'à trois heures ◊ *up to now* jusqu'à présent
♦ **It's up to you.** C'est à vous de décider.

upbringing NOUN
l' éducation FEM

to **update** VERB
mettre à jour ◊ *I've updated the file.* J'ai mis à jour le fichier.

uphill ADVERB
♦ **to go uphill** monter

to **upload** VERB

see also **upload** NOUN

télécharger vers le serveur ◊ *I uploaded the file without any trouble.*

J'ai téléchargé le fichier vers le serveur sans difficulté.

upload NOUN

see also **upload** VERB

le téléchargement vers le serveur
◊ *The upload isn't finished yet.* Le téléchargement vers le serveur n'est pas encore terminé.

upper ADJECTIVE
supérieur ◊ *on the upper floor* à l'étage supérieur
♦ **Upper Canada** le Haut-Canada

upright ADJECTIVE
♦ **to stand upright** se tenir droit

upset NOUN

see also **upset** ADJECTIVE, VERB

♦ **a stomach upset** une indigestion

upset ADJECTIVE

see also **upset** NOUN, VERB

contrarié ◊ *She's still a bit upset.* Elle est encore un peu contrariée.
♦ **I had an upset stomach.** J'avais l'estomac dérangé.

to **upset** VERB

see also **upset** NOUN, ADJECTIVE

♦ **to upset somebody** contrarier quelqu'un

upside down ADVERB
à l'envers ◊ *That painting is upside down.* Ce tableau est à l'envers.

upstairs ADVERB
en haut ◊ *"Where's your coat?" "It's upstairs."* « Où est ton manteau? » « Il est en haut. »
♦ **to go upstairs** monter

uptight ADJECTIVE
tendu ◊ *She's really uptight.* Elle est très tendue.

up-to-date ADJECTIVE
1 moderne (*car, stereo*)
2 à jour (*information*) ◊ *an up-to-date timetable* un horaire à jour
♦ **to bring something up to date** moderniser quelque chose

urgent ADJECTIVE
urgent ◊ *Is it urgent?* C'est urgent?

urine NOUN
l' urine FEM

us PRONOUN
nous ◊ *They helped us.* Ils nous ont aidés. ◊ *They gave us a map.* Ils nous ont donné une carte.

use NOUN

see also **use** VERB

♦ **It's no use.** Ça ne sert à rien. ◊ *It's no use shouting, she's deaf.* Ça ne sert à

rien de crier, elle est sourde.
♦ **It's no use, I can't do it.** Il n'y a rien à faire, je n'y arrive pas.
♦ **to make use of something** utiliser quelque chose

to **use** VERB

see also **use** NOUN

utiliser ◊ *Can we use a dictionary on the exam?* Est-ce qu'on peut utiliser un dictionnaire durant l'examen?
♦ **Can I use your phone?** Je peux téléphoner?
♦ **to use the washroom** aller aux toilettes
♦ **to use up (1)** finir ◊ *We've used up all the paint.* Nous avons fini la peinture.
♦ **to use up (2)** (*money*) dépenser
♦ **I used to live in Timmins.** J'habitais à Timmins autrefois.
♦ **I used to dislike math, but now...** Avant, je n'aimais pas les maths, mais maintenant...
♦ **to be used to something** avoir l'habitude de quelque chose ◊ *He wasn't used to driving on the left.* Il n'avait pas l'habitude de conduire à gauche. ◊ *Don't worry, I'm used to it.* Ne t'inquiète pas, j'ai l'habitude.
♦ **a used car** une voiture usagée

useful ADJECTIVE
utile

useless ADJECTIVE
inutile ◊ *This map is just useless.* Cette carte est vraiment inutile.
♦ **It's useless!** Ça ne sert à rien!

user NOUN
l' utilisateur MASC
l' utilisatrice FEM

user-friendly ADJECTIVE
facile à utiliser

usual ADJECTIVE
habituel MASC
habituelle FEM
♦ **as usual** comme d'habitude

usually ADVERB
1 en général (*generally*) ◊ *I usually get to school at about half past eight.* En général, j'arrive à l'école vers huit heures et demie.
2 d'habitude (*when making a contrast*) ◊ *Usually I don't wear make-up, but today is a special occasion.* D'habitude je ne me maquille pas, mais aujourd'hui c'est spécial.

utility room NOUN
le local d'entretien (*in institution*)

U-turn NOUN
le demi-tour ◊ *to do a U-turn* faire demi-tour

U

V

vacancy NOUN
1 le poste vacant (*job*)
2 la chambre disponible (*room in hotel*)
♦ **"no vacancies"** (*on sign*) « complet »

vacant ADJECTIVE
libre

vacation NOUN
les vacances FEM PL ◊ *to be on vacation* être en vacances ◊ *to take a vacation* prendre des vacances

to **vaccinate** VERB
vacciner

to **vacuum** VERB
passer l'aspirateur ◊ *to vacuum the hall* passer l'aspirateur dans le couloir

vacuum cleaner NOUN
1 l' aspirateur MASC
✱ 2 la balayeuse

vagina NOUN le vagin

vague ADJECTIVE
vague

vain ADJECTIVE
vaniteux MASC
vaniteuse FEM ◊ *He's so vain!* Il est vraiment vaniteux!
♦ **in vain** en vain

valentine NOUN
1 (*person*)
le valentin
la valentine ◊ *Will you be my valentine?* Seras-tu ma valentine?
2 la carte de la Saint-Valentin ◊ *I sent her a valentine.* Je lui ai envoyé une carte de la Saint-Valentin. (*card*)

Valentine's Day NOUN
la Saint-Valentin

valid ADJECTIVE
valable ◊ *This ticket is valid for three months.* Ce billet est valable trois mois.

valley NOUN
la vallée

valuable ADJECTIVE
1 de valeur ◊ *a valuable picture* un tableau de valeur
2 précieux MASC
précieuse FEM ◊ *valuable help* une aide précieuse

valuables PL NOUN
les objets de valeur MASC PL ◊ *Don't take any valuables with you.* N'emportez pas d'objets de valeur.

value NOUN
la valeur

van NOUN
la camionnette
♦ **a moving van** un camion de déménagement

vandal NOUN
le/la vandale

vandalism NOUN
le vandalisme

to **vandalize** VERB
✱ vandaliser

vanilla NOUN
la vanille
♦ **vanilla ice cream** la crème glacée à la vanille

to **vanish** VERB
disparaître

variable ADJECTIVE
variable

varied ADJECTIVE
varié

variety NOUN
la variété

various ADJECTIVE
plusieurs ◊ *We visited various villages in the area.* Nous avons visité plusieurs villages de la région.

to **vary** VERB
varier

vase NOUN
le vase

VCR NOUN (= *video cassette recorder*)
le magnétoscope

veal NOUN
le veau

vegan NOUN
le végétalien
la végétalienne ◊ *I'm a vegan.* Je suis végétalien.

vegetable NOUN
le légume ◊ *vegetable soup* la soupe aux légumes

vegetarian ADJECTIVE

see also **vegetarian** NOUN

végétarien MASC
végétarienne FEM ◊ *I'm vegetarian.* Je suis végétarien. ◊ *vegetarian lasagna* une lasagne végétarienne

vegetarian NOUN

see also **vegetarian** ADJECTIVE

le <u>végétarien</u>
la <u>végétarienne</u> ◊ *I'm a vegetarian.*
Je suis végétarien.

vegetation NOUN
la <u>végétation</u>

vehicle NOUN
le <u>véhicule</u>

vein NOUN
la <u>veine</u>

velvet NOUN
le <u>velours</u>

vending machine NOUN
✹ la <u>distributrice automatique</u>

Venetian blind NOUN
le <u>store vénitien</u>

verb NOUN
le <u>verbe</u>

verdict NOUN
le <u>verdict</u>

vertical ADJECTIVE
<u>vertical</u>
(MASC PL verticaux)

very ADVERB
<u>très</u> ◊ *very tall* très grand ◊ *not very interesting* pas très intéressant
♦ **very much** beaucoup

vest NOUN
✹ la <u>veste</u>
♦ **a fleece vest** une veste en polaire

vet NOUN
le/la <u>vétérinaire</u> ◊ *She's a vet.* Elle est vétérinaire.

via PREPOSITION
<u>en passant par</u> ◊ *We went to Trois-Rivières via Québec City.* Nous sommes allés à Trois-Rivières en passant par Québec.

vice-president NOUN
le <u>vice-président</u>
la <u>vice-présidente</u>

vice-principal NOUN
le <u>directeur-adjoint</u>
la <u>directrice-adjointe</u>

vice versa ADVERB
<u>vice versa</u>

vicious ADJECTIVE
① <u>brutal</u>
(MASC PL brutaux) ◊ *a vicious attack* une agression brutale
② <u>méchant</u> (dog, person)
♦ **a vicious circle** un cercle vicieux

victim NOUN
la <u>victime</u> ◊ *He was the victim of a mugging.* Il a été victime d'une agression.

✹ **Victoria Day** NOUN
la <u>fête de la Reine</u>

❶ *In Québec,* **la fête de Dollard** *is the same day as Victoria Day. It commemorates the death of Adam Dollard des Ormeaux and his 16 companions in 1660 in a hopeless battle to avert an Iroquois siege of Ville Marie (now Montréal). In 2002, this holiday was officially replaced by* **la Journée nationale des patriotes.**

victory NOUN
la <u>victoire</u>

to **video** VERB
| see also **video** NOUN |
① <u>enregistrer</u> (from TV)
② <u>filmer</u> (with video camera)

video NOUN
| see also **video** VERB |
① la <u>vidéo</u> (movie) ◊ *to watch a video* regarder une vidéo ◊ *a video of my family on holiday* une vidéo de ma famille en vacances ◊ *It's out on video.* C'est sorti en vidéo.
② la <u>vidéocassette</u> (videocassette) ◊ *She lent me a video.* Elle m'a prêté une vidéocassette.
♦ **a video camera** une caméra vidéo
♦ **a videocassette** une vidéocassette
♦ **a video game** un jeu vidéo ◊ *She likes playing video games.* Elle aime les jeux vidéo.
♦ **a video recorder** un magnétoscope
♦ **a video rental store** un vidéoclub

videoconference NOUN
la <u>vidéoconférence</u>

view NOUN
① la <u>vue</u> ◊ *There's an amazing view when you get to the top.* Il y a une vue extraordinaire quand on arrive au sommet.
② l' <u>avis</u> MASC (opinion) ◊ *in my view* à mon avis

viewer NOUN
(television)
le <u>téléspectateur</u>
la <u>téléspectatrice</u>

viewpoint NOUN
le <u>point de vue</u>

vile ADJECTIVE
<u>dégoûtant</u> (smell, food)

village NOUN
le <u>village</u>

villain NOUN
① (criminal)
le <u>malfaiteur</u>
la <u>malfaitrice</u>
② (in movie)
le <u>méchant</u>
la <u>méchante</u>

vine NOUN
la vigne

vinegar NOUN
le vinaigre

vineyard NOUN
le vignoble

viola NOUN
l' alto MASC ◊ *I play the viola.* Je joue de l'alto.

violence NOUN
la violence

violent ADJECTIVE
violent

violin NOUN
le violon ◊ *I play the violin.* Je joue du violon.

violinist NOUN
le/la violoniste

virgin NOUN
la vierge ◊ *to be a virgin* être vierge

Virgo NOUN
la Vierge ◊ *I'm a Virgo.* Je suis Vierge.

virtual reality NOUN
la réalité virtuelle

virus NOUN
le virus (*also computing*)

visa NOUN
le visa

visible ADJECTIVE
visible

visit NOUN

> see also **visit** VERB

  ① la visite (*to museum*)
  ② le séjour (*to country*) ◊ *Did you enjoy your visit to Nova Scotia?* Ton séjour en Nouvelle-Écosse s'est bien passé?
♦ **my last visit to my grandmother** la dernière fois que je suis allé voir ma grand-mère

to **visit** VERB

> see also **visit** NOUN

  ① rendre visite à (*person*) ◊ *to visit somebody* rendre visite à quelqu'un
  ② visiter (*place*) ◊ *We'd like to visit the zoo.* Nous voudrions visiter le zoo.

visitor NOUN
  ① (*tourist*)
le visiteur
la visiteuse
  ② (*guest*)
l' invité MASC
l' invitée FEM
♦ **to have visitors** avoir de la visite

visual ADJECTIVE
visuel MASC
visuelle FEM

to **visualize** VERB
imaginer

vital ADJECTIVE
vital
(MASC PL vitaux)
♦ **vital signs** les signes vitaux

vitamin NOUN
la vitamine

vivid ADJECTIVE
(*colour*)
vif MASC
vive FEM
♦ **to have a vivid imagination** avoir une imagination débordante

vocabulary NOUN
le vocabulaire

vocational ADJECTIVE
professionnel MASC
professionnelle FEM
♦ **a vocational course** un stage de formation professionnelle

voice NOUN
la voix
(PL les voix)

voice mail NOUN
la messagerie vocale

volcano NOUN
le volcan

volleyball NOUN
le volley-ball ◊ *to play volleyball* jouer au volley-ball

volt NOUN
le volt

voltage NOUN
le voltage

voluntary ADJECTIVE
volontaire (*contribution, statement*)
♦ **to do voluntary work** travailler bénévolement

volunteer NOUN

> see also **volunteer** VERB

le/la volontaire

to **volunteer** VERB

> see also **volunteer** NOUN

♦ **to volunteer to do something** se porter volontaire pour faire quelque chose

to **vomit** VERB
vomir

to **vote** VERB
voter

voter NOUN
l' électeur MASC
l' électrice FEM

voucher NOUN
le bon ◊ *a gift voucher* un bon d'achat

vowel NOUN
la <u>voyelle</u>

vulgar ADJECTIVE
<u>vulgaire</u>

W

wage NOUN
le salaire ◊ *minimum wage* le salaire minimum

waist NOUN
la taille

to **wait** VERB
attendre
- ♦ **to wait for something** attendre quelque chose
- ♦ **to wait for somebody** attendre quelqu'un ◊ *I'll wait for you.* Je t'attendrai.
- ♦ **Wait for me!** Attends-moi!
- ♦ **Wait a minute!** Attends!
- ♦ **to keep somebody waiting** faire attendre quelqu'un ◊ *They kept us waiting for hours.* Ils nous ont fait attendre pendant des heures.
- ♦ **I can't wait for the holidays.** J'ai hâte d'être en vacances.
- ♦ **I can't wait to see him again.** J'ai hâte de le revoir.

to **wait up** VERB
attendre pour se coucher ◊ *My mom always waits up till I get in.* Ma mère attend toujours que je rentre pour se coucher.

waiter NOUN
le serveur

waiting list NOUN
la liste d'attente

waiting room NOUN
la salle d'attente

waitress NOUN
la serveuse

to **wake up** VERB
se réveiller ◊ *I woke up at six o'clock.* Je me suis réveillé à six heures.
- ♦ **to wake somebody up** réveiller quelqu'un ◊ *Please would you wake me up at seven o'clock?* Pourriez-vous me réveiller à sept heures?

to **walk** VERB

see also **walk** NOUN

1 marcher ◊ *She walks fast.* Elle marche vite.
2 aller à pied (*go on foot*) ◊ *Are you walking or going by bus?* Tu y vas à pied ou en autobus? ◊ *We walked 10 kilometres.* Nous avons fait dix kilomètres à pied.
- ♦ **to walk the dog** promener le chien

walk NOUN

see also **walk** VERB

la promenade ◊ *to go for a walk* faire une promenade
- ♦ **It's 10 minutes' walk from here.** C'est à dix minutes d'ici à pied.

walkie-talkie NOUN
l' émetteur-récepteur portatif MASC

walking NOUN
la randonnée ◊ *I did some walking in the Laurentians last summer.* J'ai fait de la randonnée dans les Laurentides l'été dernier.

walking stick NOUN
la canne

Walkman™ NOUN
le baladeur

wall NOUN
le mur

wallet NOUN
le portefeuille

walleye NOUN
le doré

wallpaper NOUN
la tapisserie

walnut NOUN
la noix
(PL les noix)

to **wander** VERB
- ♦ **to wander around** flâner ◊ *I just wandered around for a while.* J'ai flâné un peu.

to **want** VERB
vouloir ◊ *Do you want some cake?* Tu veux du gâteau?
- ♦ **to want to do something** vouloir faire quelque chose ◊ *I want to go to the movies.* Je veux aller au cinéma. ◊ *What do you want to do tomorrow?* Qu'est-ce que tu veux faire demain?

war NOUN
la guerre

ward NOUN
la salle (*room in hospital*)

wardrobe NOUN
1 la garde-robe (*clothes*) ◊ *She has an extensive wardrobe.* Elle a une garde-robe bien fournie.
2 l' armoire FEM (*piece of furniture*)

warehouse NOUN
l' entrepôt MASC

warm ADJECTIVE
1 chaud ◊ *warm water* l'eau chaude
- ♦ **It's warm in here.** Il fait chaud ici.

♦ **to be warm** (*person*) avoir chaud
◊ *I'm too warm.* J'ai trop chaud.
② chaleureux MASC
chaleureuse FEM ◊ *a warm welcome*
un accueil chaleureux

♦ **to warm up (1)** (*for sports*) s'échauffer
♦ **to warm up (2)** (*food*) réchauffer ◊ *I'll warm up some lasagna for you.* Je vais te réchauffer de la lasagne.

to **warn** VERB
prévenir ◊ *Well, I warned you!* Je t'avais prévenu!

♦ **to warn somebody to do something** conseiller à quelqu'un de faire quelque chose

warning NOUN
l' avertissement MASC

wart NOUN
la verrue

was VERB *see* **be**

to **wash** VERB
① laver ◊ *to wash something* laver quelque chose
② se laver (*get washed*) ◊ *Every morning I get up, wash and get dressed.* Tous les matins je me lève, je me lave et je m'habille.

♦ **to wash one's hands** se laver les mains
♦ **to wash one's hair** se laver les cheveux
♦ **to wash the dishes** faire la vaisselle

washbasin NOUN
le lavabo

washcloth NOUN
※ le débarbouillette

washing NOUN
le linge ◊ *dirty washing* du linge sale
♦ **Have you got any washing?** Tu as du linge à laver?
♦ **to do the washing**
※ faire le lavage

washing machine NOUN
※ la laveuse

wasn't = **was not**

wasp NOUN
la guêpe

waste NOUN

see also **waste** VERB

① le gaspillage ◊ *It's such a waste!* C'est vraiment du gaspillage!
♦ **It's a waste of time.** C'est une perte de temps.
② les déchets MASC (*garbage*)
◊ *nuclear waste* les déchets nucléaires

to **waste** VERB

see also **waste** NOUN

gaspiller ◊ *I don't like wasting money.* Je n'aime pas gaspiller de l'argent.
♦ **to waste time** perdre du temps
◊ *There's no time to waste.* Il n'y a pas de temps à perdre.

wastepaper basket NOUN
la poubelle

watch NOUN

see also **watch** VERB

la montre

to **watch** VERB

see also **watch** NOUN

① regarder ◊ *to watch television* regarder la télévision ◊ *Watch me!* Regarde-moi!
② surveiller (*keep a watch on*) ◊ *The police were watching the house.* La police surveillait la maison.
♦ **to watch out** faire attention
♦ **Watch out!** Attention!

water NOUN

see also **water** VERB

l' eau FEM

to **water** VERB

see also **water** NOUN

arroser ◊ *He was watering his tulips.* Il arrosait ses tulipes.

waterfall NOUN
la cascade

watering can NOUN
l' arrosoir MASC

watermelon NOUN
※ le melon d'eau

waterproof ADJECTIVE
imperméable ◊ *Is this coat waterproof?* Ce manteau est-il imperméable?
♦ **a waterproof watch** une montre étanche

water-skiing NOUN
le ski nautique ◊ *to go water-skiing* faire du ski nautique

wave NOUN

see also **wave** VERB

① la vague (*in water*)
② le signe (*of hand*) ◊ *We gave him a wave.* Nous lui avons fait signe.

to **wave** VERB

see also **wave** NOUN

faire un signe de la main ◊ *to wave at somebody* faire un signe de la main à quelqu'un
♦ **to wave goodbye** faire au revoir de la main ◊ *I waved goodbye to her.* Je lui ai fait au revoir de la main.

W

wavy ADJECTIVE
ondulé ◊ *wavy hair* les cheveux ondulés ◊ *a wavy line* une ligne ondulée

wax NOUN
la cire

way NOUN
1 la façon (*manner*) ◊ *She looked at me in a strange way.* Elle m'a regardé d'une façon étrange.
♦ **This book tells you the right way to do it.** Ce livre explique comment il faut faire.
♦ **You're doing it the wrong way.** Ce n'est pas comme ça qu'il faut faire.
♦ **in a way...** dans un sens...
♦ **a way of life** un mode de vie
2 le chemin (*route*) ◊ *I don't know the way.* Je ne connais pas le chemin.
♦ **on the way** en chemin ◊ *We stopped on the way.* Nous nous sommes arrêtés en chemin.
♦ **It's a long way.** C'est loin. ◊ *Kenora is a long way from Halifax.* Kenora est loin de Halifax.
♦ **Which way is it?** C'est par où?
♦ **The supermarket is this way.** Le supermarché est par ici.
♦ **Do you know the way to the mall?** Vous savez comment aller au centre commercial?
♦ **He's on his way.** Il arrive.
♦ **the way in** l'entrée FEM
♦ **the way out** la sortie
♦ **by the way...** en passant...

we PRONOUN
nous ◊ *We're staying here for a week.* Nous restons une semaine ici.

weak ADJECTIVE
faible

wealthy ADJECTIVE
riche

weapon NOUN
l' arme FEM

to **wear** VERB
porter (*clothes*) ◊ *He was wearing a hat.* Il portait un chapeau.
♦ **She was wearing black.** Elle était en noir.

weather NOUN
le temps ◊ *What was the weather like?* Quel temps a-t-il fait? ◊ *The weather was lovely.* Il a fait un temps magnifique.

weather forecast NOUN
la météo

Web NOUN
le Web

Web browser NOUN
le navigateur Web

webmaster NOUN
le/la webmestre

webography NOUN
la webographie

website NOUN
le site Web

webzine NOUN
le webzine

we'd = we had, we would

wedding NOUN
le mariage
♦ **wedding anniversary** l'anniversaire de mariage MASC
♦ **wedding dress** la robe de mariée

Wednesday NOUN
le mercredi ◊ *on Wednesday* mercredi ◊ *on Wednesdays* le mercredi ◊ *every Wednesday* tous les mercredis ◊ *last Wednesday* mercredi dernier ◊ *next Wednesday* mercredi prochain

weed NOUN
la mauvaise herbe ◊ *The garden's full of weeds.* Le jardin est plein de mauvaises herbes.

week NOUN
la semaine ◊ *last week* la semaine dernière ◊ *every week* toutes les semaines ◊ *next week* la semaine prochaine
♦ **a week from now** dans une semaine
♦ **a week from Friday** vendredi dans une semaine

weekday NOUN
♦ **on weekdays** en semaine

weekend NOUN
la fin de semaine ◊ *on weekends* la fin de semaine ◊ *last weekend* la fin de semaine dernière ◊ *next weekend* la fin de semaine prochaine

to **weigh** VERB
peser ◊ *How much do you weigh?* Combien est-ce que tu pèses? ◊ *They weighed my suitcase.* On a pesé ma valise.
♦ **to weigh oneself** se peser

weight NOUN
le poids
♦ **to lose weight** maigrir
♦ **to put on weight** grossir

weightlifter NOUN
l' haltérophile MASC/FEM

weightlifting NOUN
l' haltérophilie FEM

weird ADJECTIVE
bizarre

welcome NOUN

see also **welcome** VERB

l' <u>accueil</u> MASC ◊ *They gave her a warm welcome.* Ils lui ont fait un accueil chaleureux.
♦ **Welcome!** Bienvenue! ◊ *Welcome to Nunavut!* Bienvenue au Nunavut!

to **welcome** VERB

see also **welcome** NOUN

♦ **to welcome somebody** accueillir quelqu'un
♦ **"Thank you!" "You're welcome!"** « Merci! » « De rien! »

well ADJECTIVE, ADVERB

see also **well** NOUN

1 <u>bien</u> ◊ *You did that really well.* Tu as très bien fait ça.
♦ **to do well** réussir bien ◊ *He's doing really well at school.* Il réussit vraiment bien à l'école.
♦ **to be well** (*in good health*) aller bien ◊ *I'm not very well at the moment.* Je ne vais pas très bien en ce moment.
♦ **get well soon!** remets-toi vite!
♦ **well done!** bravo!
2 <u>enfin</u> ◊ *It's enormous! Well, quite big anyway.* C'est énorme! Enfin, c'est assez grand.
♦ **as well** aussi ◊ *We worked hard, but we had some fun as well.* Nous avons travaillé dur, mais nous nous sommes bien amusés aussi. ◊ *We went to Calgary as well as Edmonton.* Nous sommes allés à Edmonton et à Calgary aussi.

well NOUN

see also **well** ADJECTIVE

le <u>puits</u>
(PL les puits)

we'll = we will

well-behaved ADJECTIVE
<u>sage</u>

well-dressed ADJECTIVE
<u>bien habillé</u>

well-known ADJECTIVE
<u>célèbre</u> ◊ *a well-known movie star* une vedette de cinéma célèbre

well-off ADJECTIVE
<u>aisé</u>

went VERB *see* **go**

were VERB *see* **be**

we're = we are

weren't = were not

west NOUN

see also **west** ADJECTIVE

l' <u>ouest</u> MASC ◊ *in the west* dans l'ouest
♦ **the West** l'Occident MASC

west ADJECTIVE, ADVERB

see also **west** NOUN

1 <u>ouest</u> MASC, FEM, PL ◊ *the West Coast* la côte Ouest
♦ **west of** à l'ouest de ◊ *Toronto is west of Ottawa.* Toronto est à l'ouest d'Ottowa.
2 <u>vers l'ouest</u> ◊ *We were travelling west.* Nous allions vers l'ouest.

westbound ADJECTIVE
♦ **The truck was westbound on the highway.** Le camion roulait sur l'autoroute en direction de l'ouest.
♦ **Westbound traffic is moving very slowly.** La circulation en direction de l'ouest est très ralentie.

western NOUN

see also **western** ADJECTIVE

1 le <u>western</u> (*movie*)
2 le <u>sandwich western</u> (*sandwich*)

western ADJECTIVE

see also **western** NOUN

♦ **the western part of the island** la partie ouest de l'île
♦ **Western Europe** l'Europe de l'Ouest FEM
♦ **Western Canada** l'Ouest du Canada MASC

wet ADJECTIVE
<u>mouillé</u> ◊ *wet clothes* les vêtements mouillés
♦ **to get wet** se faire mouiller
♦ **dripping wet** trempé
♦ **wet weather** le temps pluvieux
♦ **It was wet all week.** Il a plu toute la semaine.

wetsuit NOUN
la <u>combinaison de plongée</u>
(PL les combinaisons de plongée)

we've = we have

whale NOUN
la <u>baleine</u>

what ADJECTIVE, PRONOUN
1 (*which*)
<u>quel</u> MASC
<u>quelle</u> FEM ◊ *What subjects are you taking?* Quelles matières est-ce que tu fais? ◊ *What colour is it?* C'est de quelle couleur? ◊ *What's the capital of Canada?* Quelle est la capitale du Canada? ◊ *What a mess!* Quel fouillis!
2 <u>qu'est-ce que</u> ◊ *What are you doing?* Qu'est-ce que vous faites? ◊ *What did you say?* Qu'est-ce que vous avez dit? ◊ *What is it?* Qu'est-ce que c'est? ◊ *What's the matter?* Qu'est-ce qu'il y a?
3 <u>qu'est-ce qui</u> ◊ *What happened?*

W

Qu'est-ce qui s'est passé? ◊ *What's bothering you?* Qu'est-ce qui te préoccupe?

*In relative phrases use **ce qui** or **ce que** depending on whether **what** refers to the subject or the object of the sentence.*

④ ce qui (*subject*) ◊ *I saw what happened.* J'ai vu ce qui est arrivé. ◊ *I know what's bothering you.* Je sais ce qui te préoccupe.

⑤ ce que (*object*) ◊ *Tell me what you did.* Dites-moi ce que vous avez fait. ◊ *I heard what he said.* J'ai entendu ce qu'il a dit.

♦ **What?** (*what did you say*) Comment?
♦ **What!** (*shocked*) Quoi!

wheat NOUN
le blé

wheel NOUN
la roue
♦ **the steering wheel** le volant

wheelchair NOUN
le fauteuil roulant

when ADVERB, CONJUNCTION
quand ◊ *When did he leave?* Quand est-ce qu'il est parti? ◊ *She was reading when I came in.* Elle lisait quand je suis entré.

where ADVERB, CONJUNCTION
où ◊ *Where's your sister today?* Où est ta sœur aujourd'hui? ◊ *Where do you live?* Où habites-tu? ◊ *Where are you going?* Où vas-tu? ◊ *a store where you can buy croissants* un magasin où l'on peut acheter des croissants

whether CONJUNCTION
si ◊ *I don't know whether to go or not.* Je ne sais pas si y aller ou non.

which ADJECTIVE, PRONOUN
① quel MASC
quelle FEM ◊ *Which flavour do you want?* Quel parfum est-ce que tu veux?

*When asking **which one** use **lequel** or **laquelle**, depending on whether the noun is masculine or feminine.*

♦ **"I know her brother." "Which one?"** « Je connais son frère. » « Lequel? »
♦ **"I know his sister." "Which one?"** « Je connais sa sœur. » « Laquelle? »
♦ **Which would you like?** Lequel est-ce que vous voulez?
♦ **Which of these are yours?** Lesquels sont à vous?

*In relative phrases use **qui** or **que** depending on whether **which** refers to the subject or the object of the sentence.*

② qui (*subject*) ◊ *the CD which is playing now* le CD qui passe maintenant
③ que (*object*) ◊ *the CD which I bought today* le CD que j'ai acheté hier

while CONJUNCTION

see also **while** NOUN

① pendant que ◊ *You hold the flashlight while I look inside.* Tiens la lampe de poche pendant que je regarde à l'intérieur.
② alors que ◊ *She is very dynamic, while he is more laid-back.* Elle est très dynamique, alors qu'il est plus relax.

while NOUN

see also **while** CONJUNCTION

le moment ◊ *after a while* au bout d'un moment
♦ **a while ago** il y a un moment ◊ *He was here a while ago.* Il était là il y a un moment.
♦ **for a while** pendant quelque temps ◊ *I lived in Thunder Bay for a while.* J'ai vécu à Thunder Bay pendant quelque temps.
♦ **quite a while** longtemps ◊ *quite a while ago* il y a longtemps ◊ *I haven't seen him for quite a while.* Ça fait longtemps que je ne l'ai pas vu.

whip NOUN

see also **whip** VERB

① le fouet
② le/la whip (*parliament*)

to **whip** VERB

see also **whip** NOUN

① fouetter (*person, animal*)
② battre (*eggs*)

whipped cream NOUN
la crème fouettée

whisk NOUN
le fouet

whiskers PL NOUN
les moustaches FEM

to **whisper** VERB
chuchoter

whistle NOUN

see also **whistle** VERB

le sifflet
♦ **The referee blew her whistle.** L'arbitre a sifflé.

to **whistle** VERB

see also **whistle** NOUN

siffler

white ADJECTIVE
blanc MASC
blanche FEM ◊ *He has white hair.* Il a les cheveux blancs.
♦ **white bread** le pain blanc
♦ **a white man** un Blanc
♦ **a white woman** une Blanche
♦ **white people** les Blancs

whiteout NOUN
le voile blanc

whiz NOUN
le/la virtuose

who PRONOUN
1 qui ◊ *Who said that?* Qui a dit ça? ◊ *Who is Adrienne Clarkson?* Qui est Adrienne Clarkson?

*In relative phrases use **qui** or **que** depending on whether **who** refers to the subject or the object of the verb.*

2 qui (*subject*) ◊ *the woman who saw us* la femme qui nous a vus ◊ *the woman who spoke to us* la femme qui nous a parlé
3 que (*object*) ◊ *the man who we saw* l'homme que nous avons vu ◊ *the man who she married* l'homme qu'elle a épousé

whole ADJECTIVE

see also **whole** NOUN

tout ◊ *the whole class* toute la classe ◊ *the whole afternoon* tout l'après-midi
♦ **a whole box of chocolates** toute une boîte de chocolats
♦ **the whole world** le monde entier
♦ **whole wheat** le blé entier ◊ *whole wheat pasta* des pâtes au blé entier
♦ **the whole works** le tout ◊ *I had a ton of assignments, but I finished the whole works in one evening.* J'avais un tas de devoirs, mais j'ai terminé le tout en une seule soirée.

whole NOUN

see also **whole** ADJECTIVE

♦ **The whole of Toronto was snowbound.** Toronto était complètement bloquée par la neige.
♦ **The whole of Montréal was talking about it.** On en parlait dans tout Montréal.
♦ **on the whole** dans l'ensemble

whom PRONOUN
qui ◊ *Whom did you see?* Qui avez-vous vu? ◊ *the man to whom I spoke* l'homme à qui j'ai parlé

whose PRONOUN, ADJECTIVE
1 à qui ◊ *Whose is this?* À qui est-ce? ◊ *I know whose it is.* Je sais à qui c'est. ◊ *Whose book is this?* À qui est ce livre?
2 dont (*after noun*) ◊ *the girl whose picture was in the paper* la jeune fille dont la photo était dans le journal

why ADVERB
pourquoi ◊ *Why did you do that?* Pourquoi avez-vous fait ça? ◊ *That's why he did it.* Voilà pourquoi il a fait ça. ◊ *Tell me why.* Dis-moi pourquoi.
♦ **"I've never been to Saskatchewan." "Why not?"** « Je ne suis jamais allé en Saskatchewan. » « Pourquoi? »
♦ **All right, why not?** D'accord, pourquoi pas?

wicked ADJECTIVE
1 méchant (*evil*)
2 (*really great*)
génial
(MASC PL géniaux)

wide ADJECTIVE, ADVERB
large ◊ *a wide road* une route large
♦ **wide open** grand ouvert ◊ *The door was wide open.* La porte était grande ouverte. ◊ *The windows were wide open.* Les fenêtres étaient grandes ouvertes.
♦ **wide awake** complètement réveillé

widow NOUN
la veuve ◊ *She's a widow.* Elle est veuve.

widower NOUN
le veuf ◊ *He's a widower.* Il est veuf.

width NOUN
la largeur

wife NOUN
la femme ◊ *She's his wife.* C'est sa femme.

wig NOUN
la perruque

wild ADJECTIVE
1 sauvage (*not tame*) ◊ *a wild animal* un animal sauvage
2 (*crazy*)
fou MASC
folle FEM

wilderness NOUN
la région sauvage
♦ **wilderness camping** le camping sauvage

wildlife NOUN
la nature ◊ *I'm interested in wildlife.* Je m'intéresse à la nature.

will NOUN

see also **will** VERB

le testament ◊ *She left me some money in her will.* Elle m'a laissé de l'argent dans son testament.

W

will VERB

see also **will** NOUN

♦ **I'll show you your room.** Je vais te montrer ta chambre.
♦ **I'll give you a hand.** Je vais t'aider.
Use the French future tense when referring to the more distant future.
♦ **I will finish it tomorrow.** Je le finirai demain.
♦ **It won't take long.** Ça ne prendra pas longtemps.
♦ **"Will you wash the dishes?" "No, I won't."** « Est-ce que tu peux faire la vaisselle? » « Non. »
♦ **Will you help me?** Est-ce que tu peux m'aider?
♦ **Will you be quiet!** Voulez-vous bien vous taire!
♦ **That will be the paperboy.** Ça doit être le livreur de journaux.

willing ADJECTIVE
♦ **to be willing to do something** être prêt à faire quelque chose

to **win** VERB

see also **win** NOUN

gagner ◊ *Did you win?* Est-ce que tu as gagné?
♦ **to win a prize** remporter un prix

win NOUN

see also **win** VERB

la victoire

to **wind** VERB

see also **wind** NOUN

1 enrouler (*rope, wool, wire*)
2 serpenter (*river, path*) ◊ *The road winds through the valley.* La route serpente à travers la vallée.

wind NOUN

see also **wind** VERB

le vent ◊ *There was a strong wind.* Il y avait beaucoup de vent.
♦ **a wind instrument** un instrument à vent
♦ **wind power** l'énergie éolienne FEM

🟊 **wind chill** NOUN
le refroidissement éolien ◊ *The wind chill factor is -10 today.* Le facteur de refroidissement éolien est de moins dix degrés aujourd'hui.

windmill NOUN
le moulin à vent
(PL les moulins à vent)

window NOUN
1 la fenêtre
2 la vitre (*in car, train*)
♦ **a store window** une vitrine

windshield NOUN
le pare-brise

(PL les pare-brise)

windshield wiper NOUN
l' essuie-glace MASC
(PL les essuie-glace)

windy ADJECTIVE
(*place*)
venteux MASC
venteuse FEM
♦ **It's windy.** Il y a du vent.

wing NOUN
l' aile FEM

to **wink** VERB
♦ **to wink at somebody** faire un clin d'œil à quelqu'un ◊ *He winked at me.* Il m'a fait un clin d'œil.

winner NOUN
le gagnant
la gagnante

winning ADJECTIVE
♦ **the winning team** l'équipe gagnante
♦ **the winning goal** le but décisif

winter NOUN
l' hiver MASC
♦ **in winter** en hiver

to **winterize** VERB
🟊 hivériser ◊ *We have to winterize our cottage.* Nous devons hivériser le chalet.

winter sports PL NOUN
les sports d'hiver MASC

to **wipe** VERB
essuyer
♦ **to wipe one's feet** s'essuyer les pieds ◊ *Wipe your feet!* Essuie-toi les pieds!
♦ **to wipe up** essuyer

wire NOUN
le fil

wireless ADJECTIVE
sans fil

wisdom tooth NOUN
la dent de sagesse
(PL les dents de sagesse)

wise ADJECTIVE
sage

to **wish** VERB

see also **wish** NOUN

♦ **to wish for something** souhaiter quelque chose ◊ *What more could you wish for?* Que pourrais-tu souhaiter de plus?
♦ **to wish to do something** désirer faire quelque chose ◊ *I wish to make a complaint.* Je désire porter plainte.
♦ **I wish you were here!** Si seulement tu étais ici!
♦ **I wish you'd told me!** Si seulement tu m'en avais parlé!

wish NOUN

| see also **wish** VERB |

le vœu
(PL les vœux) ◊ *to make a wish* faire un vœu
♦ **"best wishes"** (*on greeting card*) « meilleurs vœux »
♦ **"with best wishes, Kathy"** « bien amicalement, Kathy »

with PREPOSITION
1 avec ◊ *Come with me.* Venez avec moi. ◊ *He walks with a stick.* Il marche avec une canne.
♦ **a woman with blue eyes** une femme aux yeux bleus
2 chez (*at the home of*) ◊ *We stayed with friends.* Nous sommes restés chez des amis.
3 de ◊ *green with envy* vert de jalousie ◊ *to shake with fear* trembler de peur ◊ *Fill the jug with water.* Remplis la carafe d'eau.

within PREPOSITION
♦ **The stores are within easy reach.** Les magasins sont à proximité.
♦ **within a week** avant la fin d'une semaine

without PREPOSITION
sans ◊ *without a coat* sans manteau ◊ *without speaking* sans parler

witness NOUN
le/la témoin ◊ *There were no witnesses.* Il n'y a pas eu de témoins.

witty ADJECTIVE
spirituel MASC
spirituelle FEM

wives PL NOUN *see* **wife**

wizard NOUN
le magicien

wok NOUN
le wok

woke up, woken up VERB *see* **wake up**

wolf NOUN
le loup
♦ **a wolf cub** un louveteau

wolverine NOUN
le carcajou

woman NOUN
la femme ◊ *a woman doctor* une femme médecin

won VERB *see* **win**

to **wonder** VERB
se demander ◊ *I wonder why he said that.* Je me demande pourquoi il a dit ça. ◊ *I wonder what that means.* Je me demande ce que ça veut dire. ◊ *I wonder where my sister is.* Je me demande où est ma sœur.

wonderful ADJECTIVE
formidable

won't = will not

wood NOUN
le bois ◊ *It's made of wood.* C'est en bois.

wooden ADJECTIVE
en bois ◊ *a wooden chair* une chaise en bois

woods PL NOUN
le bois SING ◊ *We went for a walk in the woods.* Nous sommes allés nous promener dans le bois.

woodworking NOUN
la menuiserie ◊ *My hobby is woodworking.* Je fais de la menuiserie.

wool NOUN
la laine ◊ *a wool sweater* un chandail de laine

word NOUN
le mot ◊ *a difficult word* un mot difficile
♦ **What's the word for "store" in German?** Comment dit-on « magasin » en allemand?
♦ **in other words** en d'autres termes
♦ **to have a word with somebody** parler avec quelqu'un
♦ **the words** (*lyrics*) les paroles ◊ *I really like the words of this song.* J'adore les paroles de cette chanson.

word processing NOUN
le traitement de texte

wore VERB *see* **wear**

work NOUN

| see also **work** VERB |

le travail
(PL les travaux) ◊ *She's looking for work.* Elle cherche du travail. ◊ *He's at work at the moment.* Il est au travail en ce moment.
♦ **It's hard work.** C'est dur.
♦ **to be off work** (*sick*) être malade ◊ *He's been off work for a week.* Il est malade depuis une semaine.
♦ **He's out of work.** Il est sans emploi.

to **work** VERB

| see also **work** NOUN |

1 travailler (*person*) ◊ *She works in a store.* Elle travaille dans un magasin. ◊ *to work hard* travailler dur
2 marcher (*machine, plan*) ◊ *The heat isn't working.* Le chauffage ne marche pas. ◊ *My plan worked perfectly.* Mon plan a marché à merveille.
♦ **to work out (1)** (*exercise*) faire de l'exercice ◊ *I work out twice a week.* ☞

W

Je fais de l'exercice deux fois par semaine.
- ♦ **to work out (2)** (*turn out*) marcher ◊ *In the end it worked out really well.* Au bout du compte, ça a très bien marché.
- ♦ **to work out (3)** (*figure out*) arriver à comprendre ◊ *I just couldn't work it out.* Je n'arrivais pas du tout à comprendre.
- ♦ **It works out to $10 each.** Ça fait dix dollars chacun.

workaholic NOUN
le/la bourreau de travail

worker NOUN
① (*in factory*)
l' ouvrier MASC
l' ouvrière FEM
- ♦ **He's a factory worker.** Il est ouvrier.
② (*general*)
le travailleur
la travailleuse
- ♦ **She's a good worker.** Elle travaille bien.

workforce NOUN
la population active

workout NOUN
la séance d'entraînement

works NOUN
- ♦ **the whole works** le tout ◊ *I had a ton of assignments, but I finished the whole works in one evening.* J'avais un tas de devoirs, mais j'ai terminé le tout en une seule soirée.
- ♦ **a hamburger with the works** un hamburger tout garni

worksheet NOUN
la feuille d'exercices

workshop NOUN
l' atelier MASC ◊ *a drama workshop* un atelier de théâtre

workspace NOUN
l' espace de travail MASC (*computing*)

workstation NOUN
le poste de travail
(PL les postes de travail)

world NOUN
le monde
- ♦ **He's the world champion.** Il est champion du monde.

worm NOUN
le ver

worn VERB *see* **wear**

worn ADJECTIVE
usé ◊ *The carpet is a bit worn.* Le tapis est un peu usé.
- ♦ **worn out** (*tired*) épuisé

worried ADJECTIVE
inquiet MASC

inquiète FEM ◊ *She's very worried.* Elle est très inquiète.
- ♦ **to be worried about something** s'inquiéter pour quelque chose ◊ *I'm worried about the exams.* Je m'inquiète pour les examens.
- ♦ **to look worried** avoir l'air inquiet ◊ *She looks a bit worried.* Elle a l'air un peu inquiète.

to **worry** VERB
s'inquiéter
- ♦ **Don't worry!** Ne t'inquiète pas!

worse ADJECTIVE, ADVERB
① pire ◊ *It was even worse than that.* C'était encore pire que ça. ◊ *My marks were bad, but his were even worse.* Mes notes étaient mauvaises, mais les siennes étaient encore pires.
② plus mal ◊ *I'm feeling worse.* Je me sens plus mal.

to **worship** VERB
vénérer (*God*)
- ♦ **He really worships her.** Il est en adoration devant elle.

worst ADJECTIVE

   see also **worst** NOUN

- ♦ **the worst** le plus mauvais ◊ *the worst student in the class* le plus mauvais élève de la classe ◊ *She got the worst mark in the whole class.* Elle a eu la plus mauvaise note de toute la classe.
- ♦ **my worst enemy** mon pire ennemi
- ♦ **Math is my worst subject.** Les maths sont ma matière faible.

worst NOUN

   see also **worst** ADJECTIVE

le pire ◊ *The worst of it is that...* Le pire c'est que...
- ♦ **at worst** au pire
- ♦ **if worst comes to worst** au pire

worth ADJECTIVE
- ♦ **to be worth** valoir ◊ *It's worth a lot of money.* Ça vaut très cher. ◊ *How much is it worth?* Ça vaut combien?
- ♦ **It's worth it.** Ça vaut la peine. ◊ *Is it worth it?* Est-ce que ça vaut la peine? ◊ *It's not worth it.* Ça ne vaut pas la peine.

would VERB
- ♦ **Would you like a cookie?** Vous voulez un biscuit?
- ♦ **Would you like to go see a movie?** Est-ce que tu veux aller voir un film?
- ♦ **Would you close the door please?** Vous pouvez fermer la porte, s'il vous plaît?
- ♦ **I'd like...** J'aimerais... ◊ *I'd like to go to Labrador.* J'aimerais aller au Labrador. ◊ *"Shall we go see a*

movie?" "Yes, I'd like that." « Si on allait voir un film? » « Oui, j'aimerais bien. »
♦ **I said I would do it.** J'ai dit que je le ferais.
♦ **If you asked her, she'd do it.** Si vous le lui demandiez, elle le ferait.
♦ **If you had asked him he would have done it.** Si vous le lui aviez demandé, il l'aurait fait.

wouldn't = would not

wound NOUN

| see also **wound** VERB |

la <u>blessure</u>

to **wound** VERB

| see also **wound** NOUN |

<u>blesser</u> ◊ *He was wounded in the leg.* Il a été blessé à la jambe.

to **wrap** VERB
<u>emballer</u> ◊ *She's wrapping your birthday presents.* Elle est en train d'emballer tes cadeaux de fête.
♦ **Can you wrap it for me please?** (*in store*) Vous pouvez me faire un emballage cadeau, s'il vous plaît?
♦ **to wrap up** emballer

wrapping paper NOUN
le <u>papier emballage</u>

wreck NOUN

| see also **wreck** VERB |

① le <u>tas de ferraille</u> (*vehicle, machine*) ◊ *That car is a wreck!* Cette voiture est un tas de ferraille!
② la <u>loque</u> (*person*) ◊ *After the tournament I was a complete wreck.* Après le tournament, j'étais une véritable loque.

to **wreck** VERB

| see also **wreck** NOUN |

① <u>démolir</u> (*building, vehicle*) ◊ *The explosion wrecked the whole house.* L'explosion a démoli toute la maison.
② <u>ruiner</u> (*plan, holiday*) ◊ *The trip was wrecked by bad weather.* Le voyage a été ruiné par le mauvais temps.

wreckage NOUN
① les <u>débris</u> MASC PL (*of vehicle*)
② les <u>décombres</u> MASC PL (*of building*)

wrench NOUN
la <u>clé anglaise</u>

wrestler NOUN
le <u>lutteur</u>
la <u>lutteuse</u>

wrestling NOUN
la <u>lutte</u>

wrinkled ADJECTIVE
<u>ridé</u>

wrist NOUN
le <u>poignet</u>

to **write** VERB
<u>écrire</u> ◊ *to write a letter* écrire une lettre
♦ **to write to somebody** écrire à quelqu'un ◊ *I'm going to write to him in French.* Je vais lui écrire en français.
♦ **to write down** noter ◊ *I wrote down the address.* J'ai noté l'adresse.
♦ **Can you write it down for me, please?** Vous pouvez me l'écrire, s'il vous plaît?

writer NOUN
l' <u>écrivain</u> MASC
l' <u>écrivaine</u> FEM ◊ *She's a writer.* Elle est écrivaine.

writing NOUN
l' <u>écriture</u> FEM ◊ *I can't read your writing.* Je n'arrive pas à lire ton écriture.
♦ **in writing** par écrit

written VERB *see* **write**

wrong ADJECTIVE, ADVERB
① (*incorrect*)
<u>faux</u> MASC
<u>fausse</u> FEM ◊ *The information they gave us was wrong.* Les renseignements qu'ils nous ont donnés étaient faux.
♦ **the wrong answer** la mauvaise réponse
♦ **You've got the wrong number.** Vous vous êtes trompé de numéro.
② <u>mal</u> (*morally bad*) ◊ *Some people think hunting is wrong.* Certains pensent que c'est mal de chasser.
♦ **to be wrong** (*mistaken*) se tromper ◊ *You're wrong about that.* Tu te trompes.
♦ **to do something wrong** se tromper ◊ *You've done it wrong.* Tu t'es trompé.
♦ **to go wrong** (*plan*) mal tourner ◊ *The robbery went wrong and they got caught.* Le cambriolage a mal tourné et ils ont été pris.
♦ **What's wrong?** Qu'est-ce qu'il y a?
♦ **What's wrong with her?** Qu'est-ce qu'elle a?

wrote VERB *see* **write**

X

to **X-ray** VERB

> see also **X-ray** NOUN

♦ **to X-ray something** faire une radio de quelque chose ◊ *They X-rayed my arm.* Ils ont fait une radio de mon bras.

X-ray NOUN

> see also **X-ray** VERB

la radio ◊ *to have an X-ray* passer une radio

Y

yacht NOUN
1 le voilier (*sailing boat*)
2 le yacht (*luxury motorboat*)

yard NOUN
1 la cour (*of building*) ◊ *in the yard* dans la cour
2 le jardin (*of house*)

to **yawn** VERB
bâiller

year NOUN
1 l' an MASC ◊ *last year* l'an dernier
◊ *next year* l'an prochain
♦ **to be 15 years old** avoir quinze ans
♦ **an eight-year-old child** un enfant de huit ans
2 l' année FEM (*duration*) ◊ *Mom has been sick for several years.* Maman a été malade pendant plusieurs années.
◊ *throughout the year* à longueur d'année

to **yell** VERB
hurler

yellow ADJECTIVE
jaune

yes ADVERB
oui ◊ *"Do you like it?" "Yes."* « Tu aimes ça? » « Oui. » ◊ *"You don't like it?" "Yes I do!"* « Tu n'aimes pas ça? » « Mais oui, j'aime ça! »
♦ **"Would you like a cup of tea?" "Yes please."** « Voulez-vous une tasse de thé? » « Je veux bien. »

yesterday ADVERB
hier ◊ *yesterday morning* hier matin
◊ *yesterday afternoon* hier après-midi
◊ *yesterday evening* hier soir ◊ *all day yesterday.* toute la journée d'hier

yet ADVERB, CONJUNCTION
1 encore
♦ **not yet** pas encore ◊ *It's not finished yet.* Ce n'est pas encore fini.

♦ **not as yet** pas encore ◊ *There's no news as yet.* Nous n'avons pas encore de nouvelles.
♦ **Have you finished yet?** Vous avez fini?
2 pourtant (*nevertheless*) ◊ *It's nearly impossible, and yet it has to be done.* C'est presque impossible, et pourtant il faut le faire.

to **yield** VERB
céder le passage (*on road sign*)

yogurt NOUN
le yogourt

yolk NOUN
le jaune d'œuf
(PL les jaunes d'œuf)

you PRONOUN

> *Only use **tu** when speaking to one person of your own age or younger. If in doubt use **vous**.*

1 vous (*polite form or plural*) ◊ *Do you like basketball?* Est-ce que vous aimez le basket-ball? ◊ *Can I help you?* Est-ce que je peux vous aider?
◊ *It's for you.* C'est pour vous.
2 tu (*familiar singular*) ◊ *Do you like basketball?* Tu aimes le basket-ball?

> ***vous** never changes, but **tu** has different forms. When **you** is the object of the sentence use **te** not **tu**. **te** becomes **t'** before a vowel sound.*

3 te ◊ *I know you.* Je te connais. ◊ *I gave it to you.* Je te l'ai donné.
t' ◊ *I saw you.* Je t'ai vu. ◊ *I'll help you.* Je vais t'aider.

> ***toi** is used instead of **tu** after a preposition and in comparisons.*

4 toi ◊ *It's for you.* C'est pour toi.
◊ *I'll come with you.* Je viens avec toi. ◊ *She's younger than you.* Elle est

plus jeune que toi.

young ADJECTIVE
<u>jeune</u>
♦ **young people** les jeunes

younger ADJECTIVE
<u>plus jeune</u> ◊ *He's younger than me.* Il est plus jeune que moi.
♦ **my younger brother** mon frère cadet
♦ **my younger sister** ma sœur cadette

youngest ADJECTIVE
<u>le plus jeune</u>
<u>la plus jeune</u> ◊ *my youngest brother* mon plus jeune frère ◊ *She's the youngest.* C'est la plus jeune.

your ADJECTIVE

> *Only use **ton/ta/tes** when speaking to one person of your own age or younger. If in doubt use **votre/vos**.*

① <u>votre</u> ◊ *your house* votre maison
<u>vos</u> PL *(polite form or plural)* ◊ *your seats* vos places
② <u>ton</u> MASC ◊ *your brother* ton frère *(familiar singular)*
<u>ta</u> FEM ◊ *your sister* ta sœur
<u>tes</u> PL ◊ *your parents* tes parents

> ***ta** becomes **ton** before a vowel sound*

♦ **your friend (1)** *(male)* ton ami
♦ **your friend (2)** *(female)* ton amie

> *Do not use **votre/vos** or **ton/ta/tes** with parts of the body.*

◊ *Would you like to wash your hands?* Est-ce que vous voulez vous laver les mains? ◊ *Do you want to wash your hair?* Tu veux te laver les cheveux?

yours PRONOUN

> *Only use **le tien/la tienne/les tiens/les tiennes** when talking to one person of your own age or younger. If in doubt use **le vôtre/la vôtre/les vôtres**. The same applies to **à toi** and **à vous**.*

① <u>le vôtre</u> + MASC NOUN ◊ *I've lost my pen. Can I use yours?* J'ai perdu mon stylo. Je peux utiliser le vôtre?
<u>la vôtre</u> + FEM NOUN ◊ *I like that car. Is it yours?* J'aime cette voiture-là. C'est la vôtre?
<u>les vôtres</u> + PL NOUN ◊ *my parents and yours* mes parents et les vôtres
♦ **Is this yours?** C'est à vous? ◊ *This*

book is yours. Ce livre est à vous.
◊ *"Whose is this?" "It's yours."* « C'est à qui? » « À vous. »
♦ **Yours sincerely...** Veuillez agréer l'expression de mes sentiments les plus distingués...
② <u>le tien</u> + MASC NOUN ◊ *I've lost my pen. Can I use yours?* J'ai perdu mon stylo. Je peux utiliser le tien?
<u>la tienne</u> + FEM NOUN ◊ *I like that car. Is it yours?* J'aime cette voiture-là. C'est la tienne?
<u>les tiens</u> + MASC PL NOUN ◊ *my parents and yours* mes parents et les tiens
<u>les tiennes</u> + FEM PL NOUN ◊ *My hands are dirty, yours are clean.* Mes mains sont sales, les tiennes sont propres.
♦ **Is this yours?** C'est à toi? ◊ *This book is yours.* Ce livre est à toi. ◊ *"Whose is this?" "It's yours."* « C'est à qui? » « À toi. »

yourself PRONOUN

> *Only use **te** when talking to one person of your own age or younger; use **vous** to everyone else. If in doubt use **vous**.*

① <u>vous</u> *(polite form)* ◊ *Have you hurt yourself?* Est-ce que vous vous êtes fait mal? ◊ *Tell me about yourself!* Parlez-moi de vous!
② <u>te</u> *(familiar form)* ◊ *Have you hurt yourself?* Est-ce que tu t'es fait mal?

> *After a preposition, use **toi** instead of **te**.*

③ <u>toi</u> *(familiar form)* ◊ *Tell me about yourself!* Parle-moi de toi!
④ <u>toi-même</u> ◊ *Do it yourself!* Fais-le toi-même!
⑤ <u>vous-même</u> ◊ *Do it yourself!* Faites-le vous-même!

yourselves PRONOUN
① <u>vous</u> ◊ *Did you enjoy yourselves?* Vous vous êtes bien amusés?
② <u>vous-mêmes</u> ◊ *Did you make it yourselves?* Vous l'avez fait vous-mêmes?

youth club NOUN
le <u>centre de jeunes</u>

youth hostel NOUN
l' <u>auberge de jeunesse</u> FEM
(PL les auberges de jeunesse)

Yukon NOUN
le <u>Yukon</u>

Y

Z

Zamboni™ NOUN
la <u>surfaceuse</u>

zany ADJECTIVE
<u>loufoque</u>

zebra NOUN
le <u>zèbre</u>

zero NOUN
le <u>zéro</u>

zipper NOUN
la <u>fermeture éclair</u> MC
(PL les fermetures éclair)

to **zip up** VERB
<u>fermer</u> ◊ *Zip up your coat.* Ferme ton
manteau.
♦ **The dress zips up the back.** La robe
se ferme avec une fermeture éclair
au dos.

zit NOUN
le <u>bouton</u>

zodiac NOUN
le <u>zodiaque</u> ◊ *the signs of the zodiac*
les signes du zodiaque

zone NOUN
la <u>zone</u>

zoo NOUN
le <u>zoo</u>

zoom lens NOUN
le <u>zoom</u>

zucchini NOUN
la <u>courgette</u>